Design, Simulation and New Applications of Unmanned Aerial Vehicles—Volume I

Design, Simulation and New Applications of Unmanned Aerial Vehicles—Volume I

Editors

Andrzej Łukaszewicz
Wojciech Giernacki
Zbigniew Kulesza
Jaroslaw Alexander Pytka
Andriy Holovatyy

MDPI

Basel • Beijing • Wuhan • Barcelona • Belgrade • Novi Sad • Cluj • Manchester

Editors
Andrzej Łukaszewicz
Bialystok University of Technology
Bialystok
Poland

Wojciech Giernacki
Poznan University of Technology
Poznan
Poland

Zbigniew Kulesza
Bialystok University of Technology
Bialystok
Poland

Jaroslaw Alexander Pytka
Lublin University of Technology
Lublin
Poland

Andriy Holovatyy
Lviv Polytechnic National University
Lviv
Ukraine

Editorial Office
MDPI
St. Alban-Anlage 66
4052 Basel, Switzerland

This is a reprint of articles from the Topic published online in the open access journals *Applied Sciences* (ISSN 2076-3417), *Drones* (ISSN 2504-446X), *Energies* (ISSN 1996-1073), *Machines* (ISSN 2075-1702), *Materials* (ISSN 1996-1944), and *Sensors* (ISSN 1424-8220) (available at: https://www.mdpi.com/topics/UAV).

For citation purposes, cite each article independently as indicated on the article page online and as indicated below:

Lastname, A.A.; Lastname, B.B. Article Title. *Journal Name* **Year**, *Volume Number*, Page Range.

Volume I
ISBN 978-3-7258-0977-6 (Hbk)
ISBN 978-3-7258-0978-3 (PDF)
doi.org/10.3390/books978-3-7258-0978-3

Set
ISBN 978-3-7258-0975-2 (Hbk)
ISBN 978-3-7258-0976-9 (PDF)

Contents

About the Editors

Andrzej Łukaszewicz

Andrzej Łukaszewicz, Ph.D., has a position as an Assistant Professor at the Institute of Mechanical Engineering in the Faculty of Mechanical Engineering at Bialystok University of Technology, Poland (October 1997–present). He holds a Ph.D. degree in solid mechanics from the Warsaw University of Technology, Warsaw, Poland. He is interested in UAV design, CAx, CAD, topology optimization, lattice structures, the mechanics of materials, fracture mechanics, and material testing. His main research area is mechanical engineering. He has co-authored more than 170 publications in journals, conference proceedings, or book chapters and has reviewed more than 50 papers in 20 international journals. He is also a member of the Topical Advisory Panel of six international journals.

Wojciech Giernacki

Wojciech Giernacki, Ph.D., D.Sc. (Eng.), is an Associate Professor at the Institute of Robotics and Machine Intelligence of Poznan University of Technology. He received his Ph.D. degree in control engineering and robotics from the Poznan University of Technology in 2011 and his D.Sc. in 2019. He founded and heads the PUT AeroLab and Unmanned Aerial Vehicles Research Group, as well as the Division of Control and Optimization at the Institute of Robotics and Machine Intelligence. His scientific interests are focused on the issues of UAVs, especially robust and adaptive control, optimization techniques, and data fusion from sensors.

Zbigniew Kulesza

Zbigniew Kulesza, Ph.D., D.Sc., is an Associate Professor at the Faculty of Electrical Engineering, Bialystok University of Technology, Poland. His practical and theoretical results pertain to the area of control theory and robotics. His domain of interest includes control theory methods for rotor crack detection, damage detection filters, rotor dynamics, parametric and nonlinear vibrations, dynamics and control of robot manipulators and mobile robots, the design and programming of real-time control systems, the modeling and simulation of pneumatic drive systems, and the aerodynamics of micro aerial vehicles. Currently, he is involved in building an observation system for agricultural machines as well as in a robot manipulator fast path planning project.

Jaroslaw Alexander Pytka

Jaroslaw Alexander Pytka, D.Sc., Ph.D., M.S., Automotive Engineer, is working at the Department of Motor Vehicles, Lublin University of Technology, Poland, as a Researcher and Educator for undergraduate and graduate students of Automotive Technology. He has a position as an Associate Professor. He received his M.S. degree in Automotive Engineering in 1992 from the Lublin University of Technology. He earned his Ph.D. in Soil Physics from the Institute of Agrophysics, Lublin, Poland. His major research interest is wheel–soil interaction analysis with a focus on experimental studies.

Andriy Holovatyy

Andriy Holovatyy, Ph.D., is an Assistant Professor at the Department of Computer-Aided Design Systems at Lviv Polytechnic National University (Ukraine). He obtained his PhD degree with a specialisation in Computer-Aided Design Systems at Lviv Polytechnic National University (Ukraine) in 2010. He is the co-author of more than 60 publications in journals, conference proceedings, and book and monograph chapters. His domain of interest includes the simulation of complex heterogeneous systems using VHDL-AMS and Verilog-AMS, the automated design of microelectromechanical systems, the application of MEMS devices in intelligent systems, the development of microcontroller-based devices, software engineering, and hardware and software development for embedded systems. He is also interested in CAx systems for UAV design, FEA and CFD analysis in UAV design, MEMS application in UAS, embedded systems design for UAVs, and the development of algorithms and software for UAV/UAS. Currently, he is also a co-editor for the MDPI (Switzerland, Basel) Topic: "Innovation and Inventions in Aerospace and UAV Applications".

Preface

This collection is dedicated to presenting the current state of the art in UAV research. It explores the application of advanced methods, algorithms, and technologies, using, for example, artificial intelligence, neural networks, sensors, modern materials, and techniques.

This Topic reprint provides a platform for scientists and engineers to present the latest progresses, challenges, and opportunities in the field of multidisciplinary UAV system development.

The main goal is to emphasize the potential of integrating numerical simulations and design methods to achieve better autonomous unmanned flying platforms for a range of applications and to foster knowledge exchange and innovative research for effective UAV design, control, and exploitation.

Volume I contains 25 papers published in MDPI journals: *Drones* (15 papers), *Sensors* (5), *Energies* (3), *Applied Sciences* (2) in the period from 21.02.2022 to 13.10.2022.

Volume II contains 25 papers published in MDPI journals: *Drones* (16 papers), *Applied Sciences* (5), *Materials* (2), *Energies* (1), and *Machines* (1) in the period from 01.11.2022 to 31.10.2023.

The Editors would like to thank the authors of the 50 papers (Volume I and Volume II) featured in Topic "Design, Simulation and New Applications of Unmanned Aerial Vehicles" for their contributions to UAV advancement.

Andrzej Łukaszewicz, Wojciech Giernacki, Zbigniew Kulesza, Jaroslaw Alexander Pytka, and Andriy Holovatyy
Editors

sensors

MDPI

Article

Application of Filters to Improve Flight Stability of Rotary Unmanned Aerial Objects

Maciej Salwa and Izabela Krzysztofik *

Faculty of Mechatronics and Mechanical Engineering, Kielce University of Technology, Aleja Tysiąclecia Państwa Polskiego 7, 25-314 Kielce, Poland; maciejsalwa@tu.kielce.pl
* Correspondence: pssik@tu.kielce.pl

Abstract: The most common filters used to determine the angular position of quadrotors are the Kalman filter and the complementary filter. The problem of angular position estimation consist is a result of the absence of direct data. The most common sensors on board UAVs are micro electro mechanical system (MEMS) type sensors. The data acquired from the sensors are processed using digital filters. In the literature, the results of research conducted on the effectiveness of Kalman and complementary filters are known. A significant problem in evaluating the performance of the studied filters was the lack of an arbitrarily determined UAV position. The authors of this paper undertook the task of determining the best filter for a real object. The main objective of this research was to improve the stability of the physical quadrotor. For this purpose, we developed a research method using a laboratory station for testing quadrotor drones. Moreover, using the MATLAB environment, they determined the optimal parameters for the real filter applied using the PX4 software, which is new and has not been considered before in the available scientific literature. It should be mentioned that the authors of this work focused on the analysis of filters most commonly used for flight stabilization, without modifying the structure of these filters. By not modifying the filter structure, it is possible to optimize the existing flight controllers. The main contribution of this study lies in finding the most optimal filter, among those available in flight controllers, for angular position estimation. The special emphasis of our work was to develop a procedure for selecting the filter coefficients for a real object. The algorithm was designed so that other researchers could use it, provided they collected arbitrary data for their objects. Selected results of the research are presented in graphical form. The proposed procedure for improving the embedded filter can be used by other researchers on their subjects.

Keywords: extended Kalman filter; complementary filter; quadrotor; PX4; MATLAB; ROS

Citation: Salwa, M.; Krzysztofik, I. Application of Filters to Improve Flight Stability of Rotary Unmanned Aerial Objects. *Sensors* **2022**, *22*, 1677. https://doi.org/10.3390/s22041677

Academic Editors: Andrzej Łukaszewicz, Wojciech Giernacki, Zbigniew Kulesza, Jaroslaw Pytka and Andriy Holovatyy

Received: 12 January 2022
Accepted: 18 February 2022
Published: 21 February 2022

1. Introduction

The Kalman filter and the complementary filter are the most popular filters for determining the angular position of unmanned aerial vehicles (UAVs). The problem of angle estimation is the absence of direct data. The most common sensors on board UAVs are micro electro mechanical system (MEMS) sensors. Basic sensors are used, such as accelerometer, gyroscope, magnetometer sensors. The data acquired from the sensors are processed by using digital filters. The Kalman filter has been studied in [1–7]. Publications are available in which the authors have undertaken modifications to the structure of the Kalman filter. In 2015, Xiong, J.J., and Zheng, E.H. [8] developed an optimal Kalman filter (OKF) for quadrotor position estimation. In 2019, Alawsi, A.A.A., Jasim, B.H., and Raafat, S.M. [9] developed the unscented Kalman filter (UKF). In both these papers, the authors worked exclusively on simulation objects. Information about the complementary filter and its use in UAV navigation can be found in references [10–13]. The problem so far in evaluating the filter's performance has been the lack of an arbitrary UAV position. One of the first attempts to compare the two filters was made by Walter Higgins [14]. In his 1975 paper, he compared only the theoretical operation of the filters. The authors of reference [15] used a nine-degrees of freedom (DOF) sensor and analyzed the resulting angular position from the collected readings without reference to the actual value. A reference to the arbitrary value can be found in paper [16], in which the authors attempted to represent one arm of the drone by simulating it with two motors on a ramp. They read the true value using a potentiometer. The authors of this paper did not clearly answer which of the compared filters is better. They only conclude that for quadrotors for which the flight time is no more than 15 min, initial calibration bias is not a problem for stabilization purposes. Furthermore, the simplicity of the algorithm makes the complementary filter the best choice for embedded applications where there is not much computational power.

This conclusion inspired the authors of this paper to revisit the issue, albeit using a real drone. This is an innovative approach to the UAV flight stabilization problem and has not been explored in the scientific literature.

Similar work was carried out by Stanislaw Chudzik in 2021 [17]. He studied the behavior of the filters for angle estimation for a self-balancing robot. In his research he used the STM32 Discovery F303CTV6 development kit containing MEMS sensors. He used a rotary encoder to read the actual tilt value. He too did not provide an answer as to which filter is better for tilt angle estimation. In 2016, as an extension of their research on filters used for UAVs, Gabriel Schmitz, Tiago Alves, Renato Henriques, Edison Freitas, and Ebrahim El'Youssef [18] worked on a filter for the Pixhawk controller. However, this had not been undertaken by the time the following article was written.

The authors of this paper undertook the task of determining the best filter for a real object. For this purpose, they used an innovative method for comparing the performance of filters using a drone test-bench. As a goal, they set out to answer unequivocally which filter performs better on a real object using a physical radio-controlled quadrotor. They also decided to take up a theme left uninvestigated by the aforementioned researchers; they investigated a real Pixhawk controller to determine how the default filter implemented in the PX4 software works. During their research, they developed a way to improve the performance of an extended Kalman filter, which is embedded in the PX4 software. Details concerning its differences from a standalone Kalman filter were also described. The authors determined the optimal parameters for the filter using the MATLAB environment.

This paper is structured as follows. Section 2 presents an innovative test-bench for unmanned aerial vehicle, the method of data collection including the whole algorithm in a graphical form, and the drone on which the tests were carried out. Section 3 describes the filters including mathematical relationships. Section 4 presents how the archived data were processed. Section 5 presents the results of the conducted research. Section 6 contains a discussion of the obtained results and directions for further research. Section 7 is conclusion and describes concepts for improving the performance of physical flying objects using the methods described in the paper..

2. Measurement Method

A real drone was used to conduct experimental research. PX4 software was uploaded to the flight controller. It enabled the drone to connect to the computer, which is the central unit of the ROS (robot operating system). The Mavlink protocol data and parameters of the drone were transmitted using a 433 MHz radio module. The Mavros program supervised the exchange of information in real time. The raw data from the sensors were archived to a csv file along with the timestamp by ROS script (written in Python). The drone was controlled via radio by the operator during the research. In the next step, the archived data were processed and filtered. This made it possible to compare the two filters under the same conditions. The raw data were recorded for all degrees of freedom in which the sensors implemented in the flight controller operate. In parallel, through the same script, data were collected concerning the physical position of the frame on which the drone was mounted.

The information about the angular position of the frame was measured by 3 Baumer XX laser distance sensors. The sensors were spaced every 120 degrees (Figure 1). Each sensor collected data concerning the distance of the ring on which the laser beam fell. The output signal of the sensors is a voltage. The analog signals were processed using ADCs of the STM32 Nucleo-F429ZI development kit. The voltage values were divided by resistive voltage dividers to go from a 0–10 V sensor output range to a 0–3.3 V one, corresponding to the capabilities of the development board. The sensors were powered by an external 12 V power supply. Each voltage divider was made of three 470 Ohm precision resistors. The analog signals were read using a device memory access (DMA) mechanism. The microcontroller was clocked at a maximum frequency of 180 MHz. The analog readings were converted into distance values expressed in millimeters in the main program loop. The ring height was chosen to be within the sensor range of 100–600 mm. The width of the ring was chosen to be able to perform tilt and roll of the drone up to 10 degrees. This is a value consistent with the angular displacement that occurs in drones during flight, and the tests were conducted within this range.

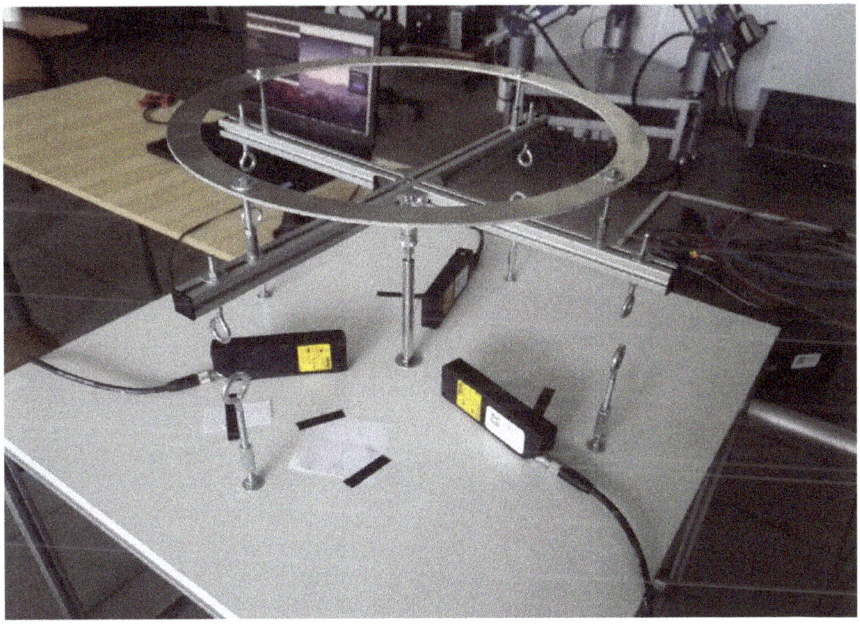

Figure 1. Test-bench for drones.

To convert the values from the three sensors to pitch and roll, the trigonometric relationships and the arcus tangent function were used. The pitch is calculated using the following formula:

$$\varphi = arctan\left(\frac{l_1 - \frac{(l_2+l_3)}{2}}{0.75d}\right) \tag{1}$$

where:

φ—pitch angle, rotation about the x axis,

l_1, l_2, l_3—the height determined by the particular sensors,

d—the diameter of the circle.

The difference in height between the reading of sensor no. 1 and the average of readings of sensors no. 2 and 3 is divided by the height of an equilateral triangle determined by the sensors. It is a triangle inscribed in a circle (Figure 2). The pitch angle is determined by relation (1).

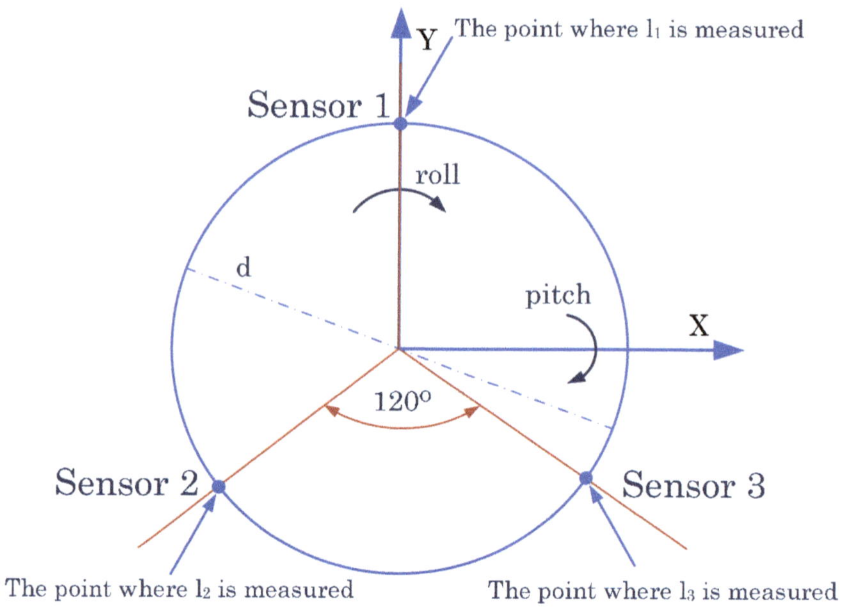

Figure 2. The position of the test-bench sensors in relation to the axis of the drone system.

The roll is determined from the following formula:

$$\theta = arctan\left(\frac{l_2 - l_3}{\frac{\sqrt{3}}{2} \cdot d}\right) \tag{2}$$

where:

θ—roll angle, rotation about the y axis.

The difference in height between sensor no. 2 and sensor no. 3 is divided by the side of the equilateral triangle defined by the sensors. The roll angle is determined by relation (2).

The described calculations were performed in the main loop of the program running in the STM32F429 microcontroller. The positions calculated from the arcus tangent function were compensated with a logical condition so that when the drone is in an angular position deviated from the zero value in a direction not consistent with the direction of the increment, a negative value is returned. The obtained values were sent to the ROS system node via ST-link. This is a built-in programmer along with a serial communication port. Libraries prepared by the Open Agriculture Foundation were used to send the data.

An ST-link programmer was connected via USB cable to the computer on which the roscore unit was running. The rosserial library was used to receive data from the nucleo development board. Data were data published to the topic from which the archiving script subscribed. The same script in parallel subscribed to the data published by the flight controller. The writing to the csv file was carried out line by line. Raw accelerometer and gyroscope data, angular position estimated by the default Kalman filter, arbitrary values from the test-bench collected by the development kit, and timestamp were written. Data recording occurred in real time. The flight controller published the data at 50 Hz. As soon as new data became available, the script archived it along with the corresponding data from the arbitrary test-bench.

The full algorithm of the conducted research is included below (Figure 3).

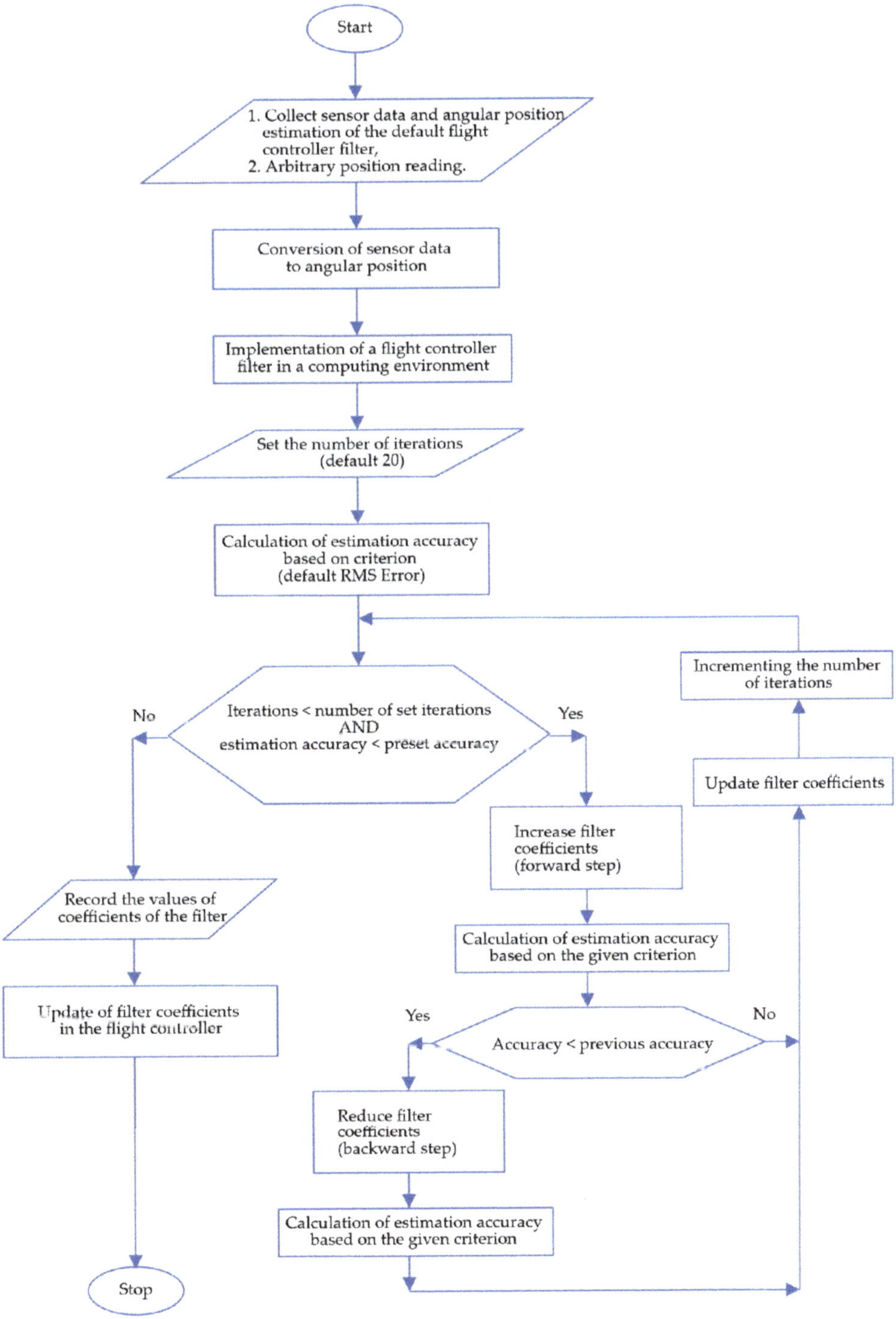

Figure 3. Block diagram of the filter optimization algorithm for a real flight controller.

The above diagram shows the filter coefficient optimization algorithm. The essence of this process is to collect the raw sensor data along with the arbitrary position. Then, optimization (which involves multiple iterations in the computational environment) is performed on the same data. Its effect is to obtain tuned filter coefficients, consistent in type with the filter built into the flight controller. In most flight controllers, the manufacturer's software allows the user to enter their own filter coefficients.

2.1. Parameters of Drone

The selected type of drone is a quadrotor. The flight controller used is Pixhawk 2.4.8 to which PX4 software v1.12.0 was uploaded. Communication with the operator is carried out via FrSky RC radio. The drone is powered by four DC brushless motors. The K_V constant of the motors, which is the motor speed constant measured in revolutions per minute (RPM) per volt, or radians per volt, is equal to 2300. The sensors are located on the board the flight controller. The drone was rigidly mounted to the aluminum profiles of the test stand (Figure 4). Roll and pitch are realized by the joint on which the profiles are supported. Rotational movement of the yaw does not take place.

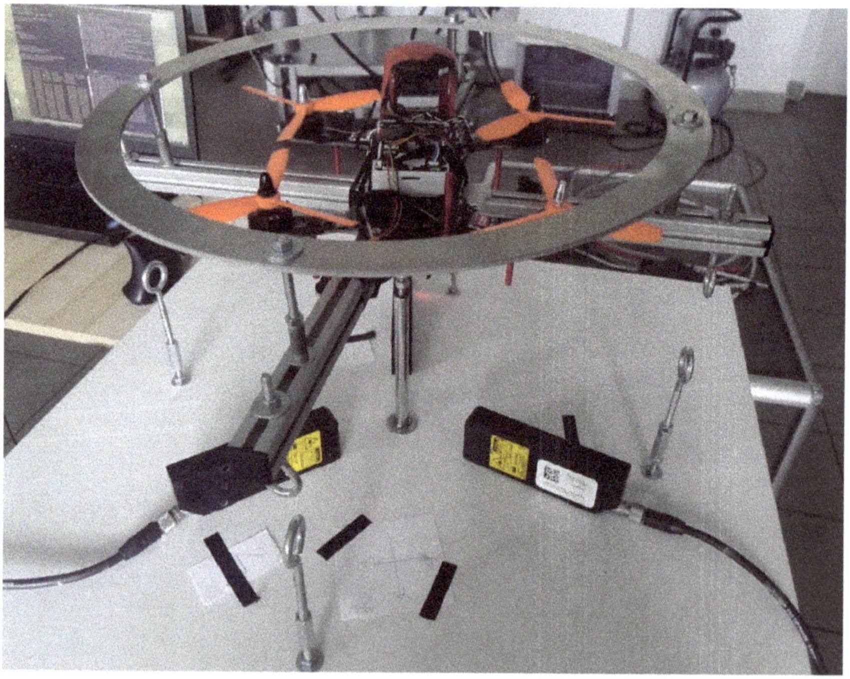

Figure 4. Drone mounted on the test-bench.

The position of the test-bench was leveled in the X and Y axes before the tests started. Then, through the QGroundControl software, the zero level was set for the default Kalman filter implemented in the PX4 software. Through the mavlink protocols, the flight controller communicated with the ROS version of Melodic Morenia installed inside the Ubuntu Mate 18.04 operating system.

2.2. Drone Sensors

Angular position information is required to stabilize the UAV. This can be provided indirectly from sensors measuring other values. Popular solutions include linear acceleration sensors (accelerometers) and angular velocity sensors (gyroscopes). To obtain the angular position from the accelerometer, the ground acceleration is used. Depending on the position of the accelerometer, it will be distributed across the axes. This requires establishing a base position where the object is parallel to the ground. The premise of the measurement is to detect roll or pitch by determining the deviation from the axis of gravity, which correlates with acceleration due to gravity. The disadvantage of this solution is the influence of other forces that generate linear acceleration. The noise caused is a high-frequency signal. To determine the angular position from the gyroscope, it is necessary to integrate the data obtained from this sensor. Before starting the integration, the angular position must be given as the initial condition for integration. During the process of computing, the data, accumulating small errors (resulting from integration) create a bias of the gyroscope. As a result, as time passes, the calculated outcome may deviate from the true value.

The following sensors are implemented on board the flight controller:

1. L3GD20;
2. MPU6000;
3. LSM303D;
4. MS5611.

L3GD20 [19] is a low power three-axis gyroscope. It is produced by ST microelectronics for navigation systems. The maximum sensitivity is 8.75 mdps (mili degrees per second)/digit.

MPU6000 [20] is used as main accelerometer and secondary gyroscope. Depending on the range of measured acceleration, the accuracy is from 2.048 to 16.384 lsb (least significant bit)/g (acceleration expressed in relation to the acceleration due to gravity). The gyroscope in this module is used secondarily. The measurements are used to verify the data from the master module and, in case of discrepancies, represent the reason for rejecting particular samples.

LSM303D [21] is three-dimension accelerometer, used as a secondary 3D magnetometer. A magnetometer is needed for calculation of the yaw angle.

MS5611 [22] is a barometric pressure sensor, the measurements of which are not relevant to the content of this paper.

3. Types of Filters

To obtain angular position, intermediate data are used by measuring other physical values. From the accelerometer readings, the deviation from the vertical position is determined by measuring the acceleration of the earth. From the trigonometric functions, the pitch and roll of the measurement system relative to the earth system are calculated. When other linear accelerations are involved, the ratio of the contribution of the ground acceleration to the individual accelerometer axes may be disturbed. This effect is called accelerometer noise. To obtain the angular position from the gyroscope readings, the collected data corresponding to the angular velocity in the respective axes must be integrated. The error that occurs in this case is called gyro drift. It is due to the integration process and imperfections in the system, which, with prolonged operation, begin to accumulate with the integration process. To compensate for these errors, digital filters are used (i.e., the complementary filter and the Kalman filter). The authors of this paper chose to consider these two mentioned filters due to their popularity in flight controllers.

3.1. Complementary Filter

The complementary filter is used when data come from different channels and sensors [10]. To obtain the final result, part of the data is added (Figure 5). For every single component, a specified filter (such as LPF (low-pass filter); HPF (high-pass filter)) is used.

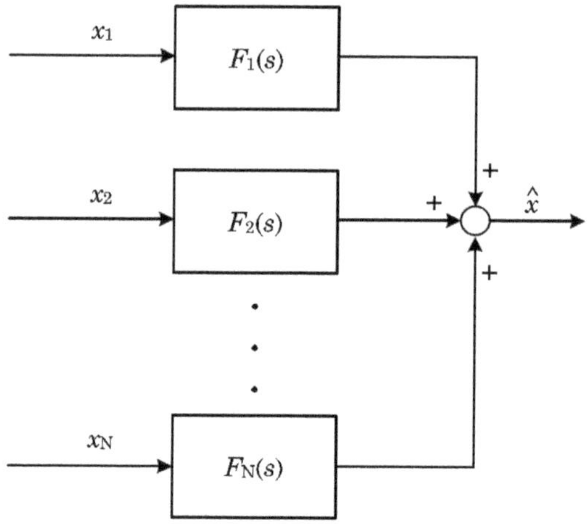

Figure 5. Summation of individual component signals.

The specificity of the filter can be described by the formula:

$$\sum_{i=1}^{N} F_i(s) = 1 \tag{3}$$

To obtain the angular position of the drone, the data from two independent channels are used (Figure 6). First, data comes from the gyroscope. The obtained value ω, which is the angular velocity, is integrated to the angular position. Then, it is passed through a high-pass filter. Secondly, data come from accelerometer and magnetometer. The pitch and roll are calculated from the acceleration values a (as described in Section 2.2), while the yaw is determined from the reading of the earth's magnetic field m [11]. The data are then passed through a low-pass filter.

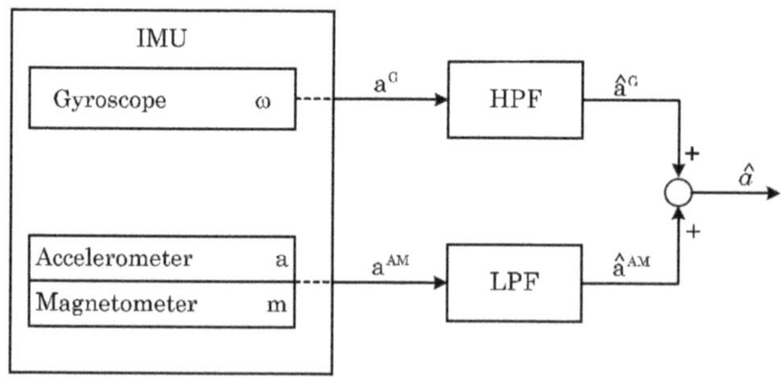

Figure 6. Processing of the IMU sensor data by the complementary filter.

The LPF transfer function can be represented as:

$$H_{LPF}(s) = \frac{1}{1 + T \cdot s} \tag{4}$$

where T is the time constant of inertial component and s is the complex variable. Analogously, according to the principle of the complementary filter, the HPF transfer function can be written as:

$$H_{HPF}(s) = 1 - H_{LPF}(s) = \frac{T \cdot s}{1 + T \cdot s} \tag{5}$$

The parameter for the complementary filter is f_0 which is defined as the cut-off frequency. It determines frequencies for both the low-pass filter and high-pass filter (Figure 7).

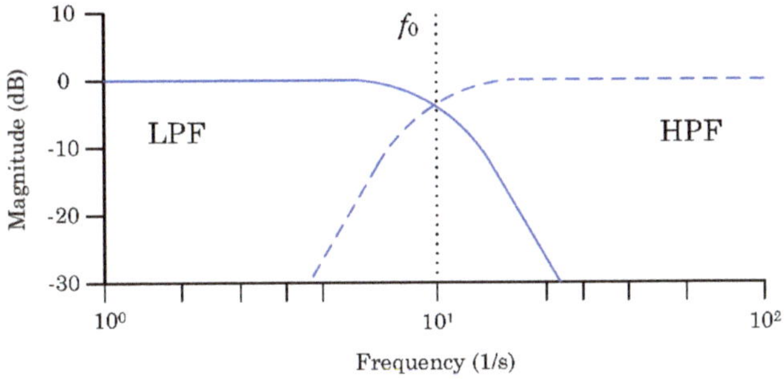

Figure 7. Cut-off frequency for complementary filter.

As may be noted in the figure above, by setting a boundary for one basic filter, it is necessary to apply it to the other as well. The optimization of the complementary filter comes down to determining this boundary.

3.2. Kalman Filter

The Kalman filter is an algorithm used for multiple measurements that contain inaccuracies, such as statistical noise observed over time. It produces estimates of unknown variable that are more accurate than results based on measurements from a single channel. From the time of its invention until now, the Kalman filter has been refined. There are now many versions of the Kalman filter that are the subject of scientific research [3].

The algorithm operates in a two-steps process. Considering the system as a discrete-time model in state space, the following equations can be written [5]:

$$x(t+1) = A \cdot x(t) + B \cdot u(t) + v(t) \tag{6}$$

$$y(t) = C \cdot x(t) + w(t) \tag{7}$$

where:

$x(t)$—state of the system at time t,
A—state matrix,
B—input matrix,
$v(t)$—process noise,
$y(t)$—system output,
C—output matrix,
$w(t)$—measurement noise.

The first step is called the time update and it consists in computing the single state prediction (i.e., the a priori estimate and its covariance).

$$\hat{x}(t+1) = A \cdot \hat{x}(t) + B \cdot u(t) \tag{8}$$

$$P(t+1) = A \cdot P(t) \cdot A^T + V \tag{9}$$

where:

$\hat{x}(t)$—a priori estimate,
$P(t)$—covariance matrix for $\hat{x}$,
V—covariance matrix for v.

In the next step, the time is increased by one and the algorithm goes on to update the measurement.

$$\varepsilon(t) = y(t) - C\cdot\hat{x}(t-1) \tag{10}$$

$$S(t) = C\cdot P(t-1)\cdot C^T + W \tag{11}$$

$$K(t) = P(t-1)\cdot C^T\cdot S^{-1}(t) \tag{12}$$

$$\hat{x}(t) = \hat{x}(t-1) + K(t)\cdot\varepsilon(t) \tag{13}$$

$$P(t) = P(t-1) - K(t)\cdot S(t)\cdot K^T(t) \tag{14}$$

where:

W—covariance matrix for w,

$\varepsilon(t)$—the difference between the most recent measurement and the value expected from state estimate,

S—covariance matrix for ε,

$K(t)$—Kalman gain.

Kalman gain decides what effect a new measurement has on the a posteriori estimate of the state versus the a priori estimate. The algorithm repeats its steps alternately. This is shown in Figure 8 [7].

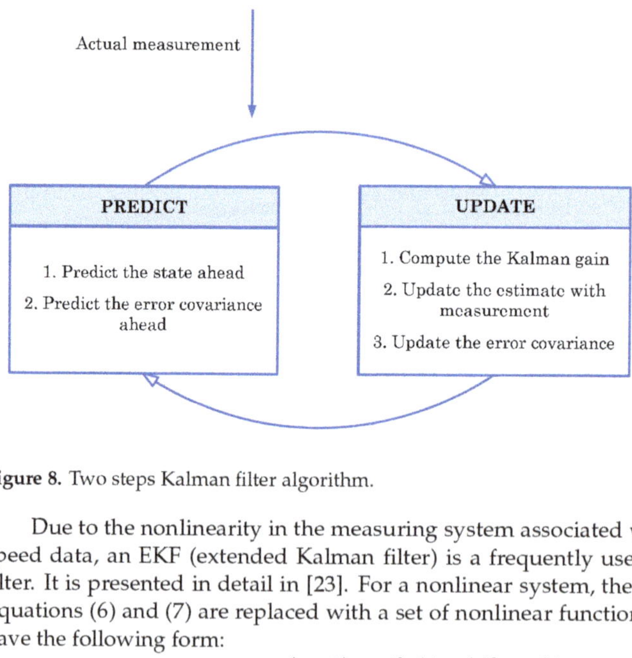

Figure 8. Two steps Kalman filter algorithm.

Due to the nonlinearity in the measuring system associated with the readout of the speed data, an EKF (extended Kalman filter) is a frequently used form of the Kalman filter. It is presented in detail in [23]. For a nonlinear system, the matrices appearing in Equations (6) and (7) are replaced with a set of nonlinear functions. The equations then have the following form:

$$x(t+1) = f[x(t), u(t)] + v(t) \tag{15}$$

$$y(t) = h[x(t), u(t)] + w(t) \tag{16}$$

where:

$u(t)$—input vector,

f, h—sets of nonlinear functions describing state and input dependencies.

In the case under consideration, the input vector is a measurement vector and can be represented as [6]:

$$z_k = \begin{pmatrix} {}^b a_t & {}^b w_t \end{pmatrix}^T \tag{17}$$

where:

${}^{b}a_t$—the measurements of the linear accelerations, obtained from a triaxial accelerometer,
${}^{b}w_t$—the three angular velocity measurements obtained from a triaxial rate-gyro.

Functions f, h must be differentiable after all parameters. This makes it possible to linearize the equations. In order to carry out this process, the above-mentioned functions should be developed into Taylor series. It is assumed that the obtained matrices A, B, C, D approximate the behavior of the studied nonlinear system in the neighborhood of the given operating point (x', u'). To obtain the desired matrices, it is necessary to determine the partial derivatives of the functions from the nonlinear model:

$$A = \left.\frac{\partial f}{\partial x}\right|_{x=x',u=u'} \tag{18}$$

$$B = \left.\frac{\partial f}{\partial u}\right|_{x=x',u=u'} \tag{19}$$

$$C = \left.\frac{\partial h}{\partial x}\right|_{x=x',u=u'} \tag{20}$$

$$D = \left.\frac{\partial h}{\partial u}\right|_{x=x',u=u'} \tag{21}$$

The EKF equations differ slightly from those of the linear Kalman filter and can be expressed as follows:

$$\hat{x}(t+1|t) = f[\hat{x}(t|t), u(t)] \tag{22}$$

$$P(t+1|t) = A(t|t)\cdot P(t|t)\cdot A^T(t|t) + V \tag{23}$$

Equations (10)–(14) corresponding to state updates can be reformulated as follows:

$$\varepsilon(t) = y(t) - h[\hat{x}(t|t-1), u(t)] \tag{24}$$

$$S(t) = C^T(t|t-1)\cdot P(t|t-1)\cdot C(t|t-1) + W \tag{25}$$

$$K(t) = P(t|t-1)\cdot C^T(t|t-1)\cdot S^{-1}(t) \tag{26}$$

$$\hat{x}(t|t) = \hat{x}(t|t-1) + K(t)\cdot\varepsilon(t) \tag{27}$$

$$P(t|t) = P(t|t-1) - K(t)\cdot S(t)\cdot K^T(t) \tag{28}$$

These equations are well known. Detailed considerations for the EKF can be found in the publications [4,23].

4. Data Processing

The MATLAB 2021a environment was used for data processing. Archived data were collected to 12 precision decimal places. Ready-made filters available from version 2019b were used to process the data. The arbitrary values are the data obtained from the measuring station.

The test procedure carried out in this paper to obtain the optimal filter and to improve the embedded filter included the following operations:

- Collection of position data along with arbitrary data;
- Obtaining position data from the readout of the sensors themselves;
- Data processing with complementary filter and EKF;
- Filter tuning;
- Comparison of the prepared results with the filter built in PX4 and arbitrary data;
- Update of the built-in filter (EKF coefficients);
- Repeating the experiment and collecting data;
- Comparison of the performance of the built-in filter after updating the coefficients.

4.1. Raw Data

Figures 9 and 10 show the angular position calculated from the data from the individual sensors. It can be noticed that the position obtained from the accelerometer looks much noisier in comparison to the position from the gyroscope. There are a lot of peaks in the figure, and the estimation run is very dynamically changed. It was assumed that the initial position of the gyroscope, necessary for the integration process, should be taken from the accelerometer.

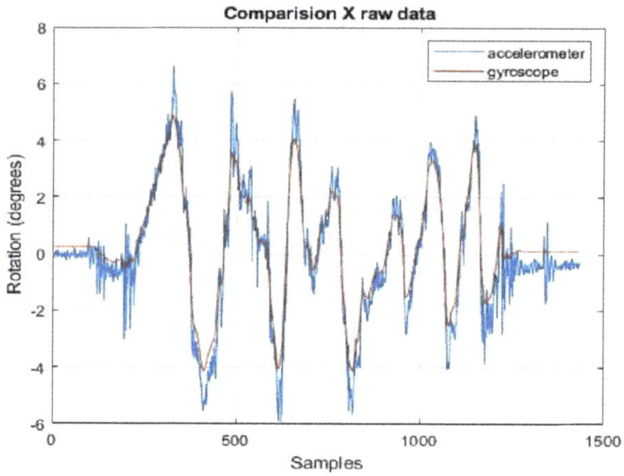

Figure 9. x-axis rotation readings from accelerometer and gyroscope.

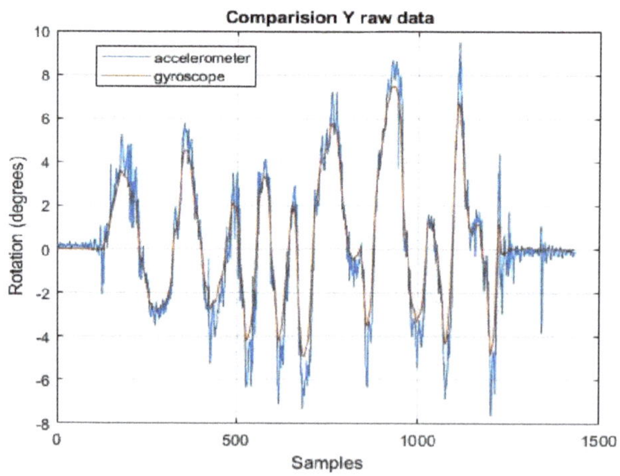

Figure 10. y-axis rotation readings from accelerometer and gyroscope.

Both figures above are taken from the raw data. They are provided to show how the angle estimation task is handled by the various sensors. In the next steps, the obtained estimates will be compared with the results obtained from the filters.

4.2. Complementary Filter

The complementary filter was designed using the ready-made 'complementaryFilter' object [24]. this corresponds to the theoretical considerations described in Section 3.1. The data obtained from the filter were converted to Euler angles and are presented in Figure 11.

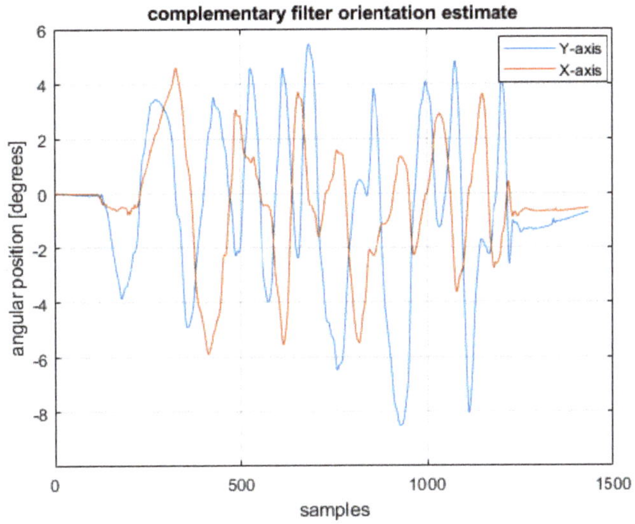

Figure 11. Position estimation using the complementary filter.

4.3. Extended Kalman Filter

The EKF was designed using the 'insfilterNonholonomic' object [25]. This object is a specialized version of the EKF, dedicated to work with data coming from IMU sensors. It has a 'tune' method allowing one to optimize the filter parameters referring to arbitrary data. The data obtained from this filter are shown in Figure 12.

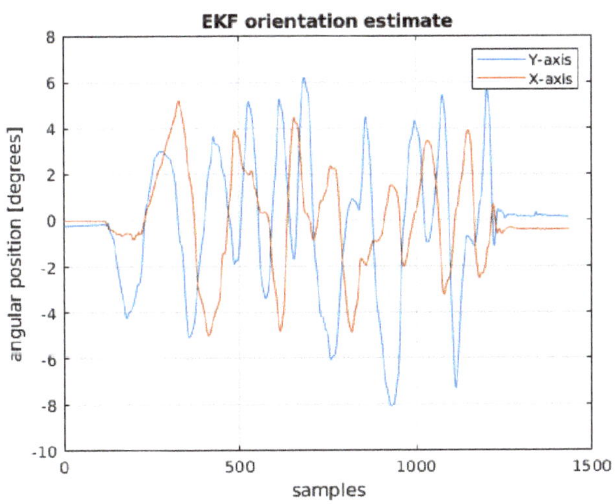

Figure 12. Position estimation using the EKF.

4.4. Comparison between Filters

To compare the filters, apart from those designed in MATLAB environment, a default filter implemented in PX4 software is presented. It is an extended Kalman filter. In Figures 13 and 14, a summary of these filters together with the arbitrary position obtained from the test-bench may be seen.

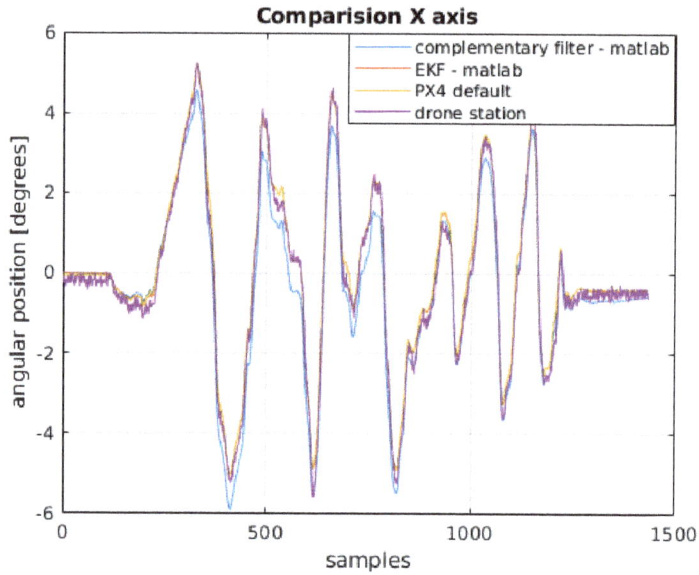

Figure 13. Comparison of the angular position obtained from the filters with the physical position for the x-axis.

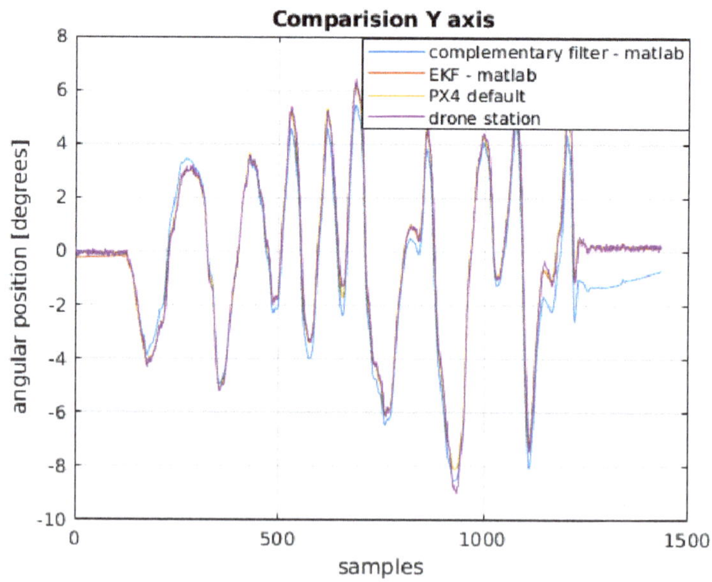

Figure 14. Comparison of the angular position obtained from the filters with the physical position for the y-axis.

5. Results

The criterion adopted to evaluate the filters is the integral absolute error (IAE). Estimations from raw data from both sensors, a complementary filter, an EKF implemented in MATLAB, and an EKF from PX4 software were evaluated. The results are presented in Table 1.

Table 1. Quality indicator.

	IAE for x Axis	IAE for y Axis
Gyroscope	704.6	628.9
Accelerometer	3897.8	4487.6
MATLAB complementary filter	489.4	472.5
MATLAB EKF	291.3	232.6
PX4 EKF	304.8	276.4

Definitely the worst in the comparison are the results estimated only on the basis of the reading from the accelerometer. This is due to the accelerometer noise. A significant improvement can be seen in the results obtained from integrating the gyroscope readings. It should be recalled that the initial condition for integration (i.e., the initial position of the drone) was assumed on the basis of the first reading from the accelerometer. Without this, obtaining the angular position would have been impossible, or it would have been necessary to assume that the drone always takes off from a specific position, which in reality is not very realistic. The best physical position was calculated by extended Kalman filters. The extended Kalman filter implemented in the PX4 firmware contains process and measurement noise covariance matrices that do not take into account the drone's physical parameters. These parameters can be changed in the configuration structure when uploading the software to the flight controller. This requires a change in the source code and a build for a specific controller model. A simpler method is to find and change the desired parameters in the QGroundControl software dedicated to the configuration of flight controllers running under PX4 control. During the research work, QGroundControl software version 4.1.1 was used. To compare the operation of filtering algorithms in the extended Kalman filter, parameters selected by the tune function from MATLAB [26] were uploaded to the flight controller. The bench test was carried out again. The results shown in Figures 15 and 16.

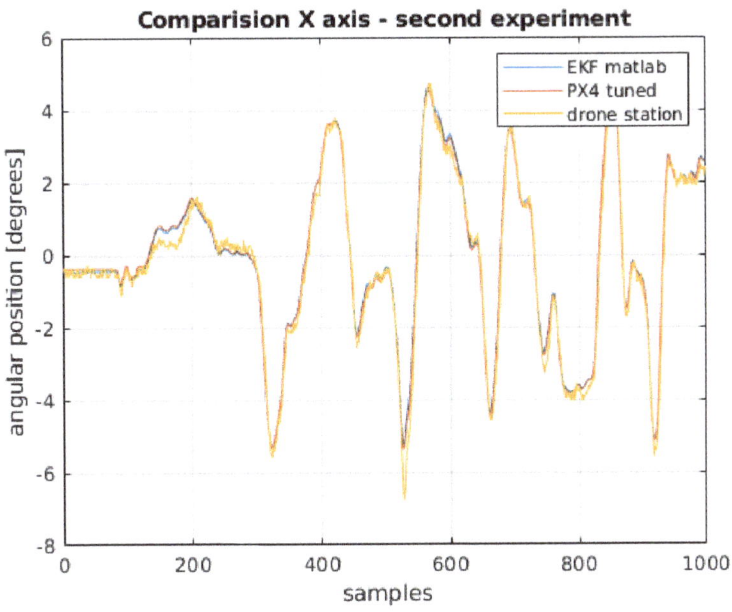

Figure 15. Comparison of angular position for x-axis.

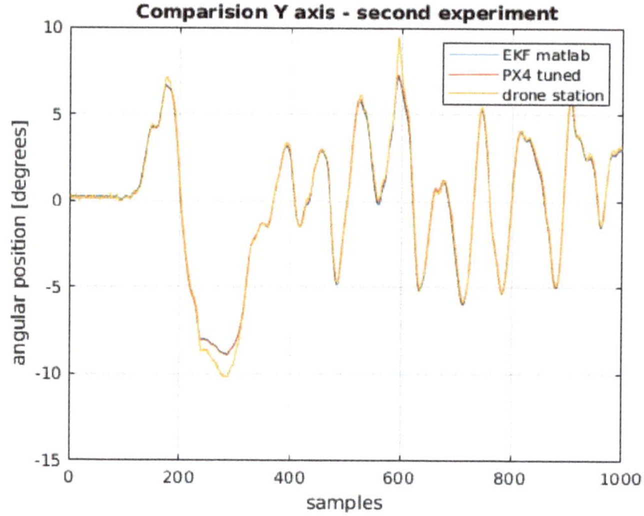

Figure 16. Comparison of angular position for *y*-axis.

After transferring the filter parameters from the MATLAB script to PX4 software, running the experiment on the test bench, re-archiving the data, processing the raw readings, and filtering with the previously designed EKF, there is no difference in the comparison of the estimation between the filter built in PX4 software and the filter designed in the MATLAB environment.

The integral absolute error values are close to being the same Table 2. The difference in values is less than 1% and can be considered negligible.

Table 2. Quality indicator.

	IAE for x Axis	IAE for y Axis
MATLAB EKF	238.3	311.0
PX4 EKF tuned	239.5	313.3

6. Discussion

The paper presents a comparison of available methods of filtering signals from the most popular sensors used in unmanned aerial vehicles. Its purpose was to develop and investigate an algorithm for improving angular position filtration in a real drone. The research was conducted on a drone that can be self-assembled from commonly available and affordable components. As can be seen from Table 1, using only one sensor is not sufficient to obtain reliable data. It is necessary to use filtering. The authors of this study showed that the extended Kalman filter is clearly preferable to the complementary filter. It reproduces the course of changes in the angular position of the real drone much better. Only during the biggest angular changes in peaks was the complementary filter closer to the real value. As can be seen from the data presented in Table 1, the EKF after tuning in MATLAB has the smallest IAE error. The development of embedded systems has made the extended Kalman filter, despite its greater computational complexity, a solution that does not overload the processing power of flight controllers.

Other researchers may use this work to practically improve the filter performance in their drones by reflecting drone station and our procedure presented at the beginning of Section 4. The authors recommend that anyone wishing to take advantage of the presented results perform the individual steps on their own object. Due to the physical specifications of the real quadrotor object, including sensors, it is not suitable to compare the results between different objects or between object and simulation. The MATLAB program was used to process the data collected from the real object. Then, based on multiple iterations of filtering processes on the same data, the best optimized filter was selected from those available in the flight controllers. A further research direction projected by the authors is to study the optimization of individual flying units and the effect of unit improvement on swarm behavior during a cooperative task of multiple UAVs.

7. Conclusions

This article shows how the filter embedded in the flight controller software can be improved. Popular flight controller software such as Ardupilot and PX4, have implemented filters whose parameters can be changed by the user. Based on arbitrary angular position data, a "tune" function was used to optimize the filter coefficients. Angular position estimation of the real drone has been improved, which was our goal.

Author Contributions: Conceptualization, I.K.; methodology, M.S. and I.K.; software, M.S.; validation, M.S. and I.K.; formal analysis, M.S. and I.K.; investigation, M.S.; resources, M.S. and I.K.; data curation, I.K. and M.S.; writing—original draft preparation, M.S.; writing—review and editing, I.K. and M.S.; visualization, M.S.; supervision, I.K. All authors have read and agreed to the published version of the manuscript.

Funding: This research received no external funding.

Institutional Review Board Statement: Not applicable.

Informed Consent Statement: Not applicable.

Data Availability Statement: The dataset used and analyzed in this study are available from the corresponding author upon reasonable request.

Conflicts of Interest: All authors declare no competing interest.

References

1. Mao, G.; Drake, S.; Anderson, B.D.O. Design of an Extended Kalman Filter for UAV Localization. In Proceedings of the Information, Decision and Control, Adelaide, Australia, 12–14 February 2007; pp. 224–229. [CrossRef]
2. Valade, A.; Acco, P.; Grabolosa, P.; Fourniol, J. A Study about Kalman Filters Applied to Embedded Sensors. *Sensors* **2017**, *17*, 2810. [CrossRef]
3. Kim, Y.; Bang, H. Introduction to Kalman Filter and its applications. In *Kalman Filter*; Kordic, V., Ed.; Intechopen: London, UK, 2018. [CrossRef]
4. Condomines, J.P. *Nonlinear Kalman Filter for Multi-Sensor Navigation of Unmanned Aerial Vehicles*; ISTE Press–Elsevier: London, UK, 2018. [CrossRef]
5. Grewal, M.; Andrews, A. *Kalman Filtering: Theory and Practice Using MATLAB*; John Wiley and Sons: New York, NY, USA, 2001.
6. Deibe, Á.; Antón Nacimiento, J.A.; Cardenal, J.; López Peña, F. A Kalman Filter for Nonlinear Attitude Estimation Using Time Variable Matrices and Quaternions. *Sensors* **2020**, *20*, 6731. [CrossRef]
7. Welch, G.; Bishop, G. *An Introduction to the Kalman Filter*; Department of Computer Science, University of North Carolina at Chapel Hill: Chapel Hill, NC, USA, 2006.
8. Xiong, J.J.; Zheng, E.H. Optimal Kalman filter for state estimation of a quadrotor UAV. *Optik* **2015**, *126*, 2862–2868. [CrossRef]
9. Alawsi, A.A.A.; Jasim, B.H.; Raafat, S.M. Nonlinear estimation of quadcopter states using unscented Kalman filter. *Period. Eng. Nat. Sci.* **2019**, *7*, 1626–1637. [CrossRef]
10. Cao, D.; Qu, Q.; Li, C.; He, C. Research of Attitude Estimation of UAV Based on Information Fusion of Complementary Filter. In Proceedings of the Fourth International Conference on Computer Sciences and Convergence Information Technology, Seoul, Korea, 24–26 November 2009; pp. 1290–1293. [CrossRef]
11. Euston, M.; Coote, P.; Mahony, R.; Kim, J.; Hamel, T. A Complementary Filter for Attitude Estimation of a Fixed-Wing UAV. In Proceedings of the IEEE/RSJ International Conference on Intelligent Robots and Systems, Nice, France, 22–26 September 2008; pp. 340–345. [CrossRef]
12. Mahony, R.; Hamel, T.; Pflimlin, J.-M. Complementary filter design on the special orthogonal group SO(3). In Proceedings of the 44th IEEE Conference on Decision and Control, Seville, Spain, 12–15 December 2005; pp. 1477–1484. [CrossRef]
13. Milic, L.D. Complementary Filter Pairs. In *Multirate Filtering for Digital Signal Processing: MATLAB Applications*; IGI Global: Hershey, PA, USA, 2009. [CrossRef]
14. Higgins, W.T.A. Comparison of Complementary and Kalman Filtering. *IEEE Trans. Aerosp. Electron. Syst.* **1975**, *AES-11*, 321–325. [CrossRef]

15. Haider, M.H.; Islam, T.; Islam, M.S.; Shajid-Ul-Mahmud, M. Comparison of Complementary and Kalman Filter Based Data Fusion for Attitude Heading Reference System. *AIP Conf. Proc.* **2017**, *1919*, 020002. [CrossRef]
16. Perez Paina, G.; Gaydou, D.; Redolfi, J.; Paz, C.; Canali, L. Experimental comparison of Kalman and complementary filter for attitude estimation. In Proceedings of the XII Argentine Symposium on Technology (AST 2011), Córdoba, Spain, 29 August–2 September 2011.
17. Chudzik, S. Intertial Sensors in the Stabilization System of the Balancing Vehicle. *Int. J. Electron. Telecommun.* **2021**, *67*, 241–246.
18. Schmitz, G.; Alves, T.; Henriques, R.; Pignaton de Freitas, E.; Elyoussef, E. A simplified approach to motion estimation in a UAV using two filters. *IFAC-PapersOnLine* **2016**, *49*, 325–330. [CrossRef]
19. Low Power 3-Axis Gyroscope, I2C/SPI Digital Output. Available online: https://www.st.com/en/mems-and-sensors/l3gd20.html (accessed on 6 August 2021).
20. MPU-6000 and MPU-6050 Product Specification. Available online: http://www.farnell.com/datasheets/1788002.pdf (accessed on 6 August 2021).
21. e-Compass: 3D Accelerometer, 3D Magnetometer, Ultra Compact, High Performance, I2C, SPI Interfaces. Available online: https://www.st.com/en/mems-and-sensors/lsm303d.html (accessed on 6 August 2021).
22. Barometric Pressure Sensor, with Stainless Steel Cap. Available online: https://www.te.com/commerce/DocumentDelivery/DDEController?Action=showdoc&DocId=Data+Sheet%7FMS5611-01BA03%7FB3%7Fpdf%7FEnglish%7FENG_DS_MS5611-01BA03_B3.pdf%7FCAT-BLPS0036 (accessed on 6 August 2021).
23. Ribeiro, M.I. *Kalman and Extended Kalman Filters: Concept, Derivation and Properties*; Institute for Systems and Robotics: Lisboa, Portugal, 2004.
24. Complementaryfilter. Available online: https://www.mathworks.com/help/nav/ref/complementaryfilter-system-object.html (accessed on 6 August 2021).
25. insfilterNonholonomic. Available online: https://www.mathworks.com/help/fusion/ref/insfilternonholonomic.html (accessed on 6 August 2021).
26. Tune. Available online: https://www.mathworks.com/help/fusion/ref/insfilternonholonomic.tune.html (accessed on 6 August 2021).

applied sciences

MDPI

Article

Robust Resource Allocation and Trajectory Planning of UAV-Aided Mobile Edge Computing in Post-Disaster Areas

Peng Cao [1,2], Yi Liu [1,3,*] and Chao Yang [1,3]

1 School of Automation, Guangdong University of Technology, Guangzhou 510006, China; lhcaopeng_2010@163.com (C.P.); chyang513@gdut.edu.cn (C.Y.)
2 Guangdong Key Laboratory of IoT Information Technology, Guangzhou 510006, China
3 Key Laboratory of Intelligent Detection and Internet of Manufacturing Things, Ministry of Education, Guangzhou 510006, China
* Correspondence: yi.liu@gdut.edu.cn

Abstract: When natural disasters strike, users in the disaster area may be isolated and unable to transmit disaster information to the outside due to the damage of communication facilities. Unmanned aerial vehicles can be exploited as mobile edge servers to provide emergency service for ground users due to its mobility and flexibility. In this paper, a robust UAV-aided wireless-powered mobile edge computing (MEC) system in post disaster areas is proposed, where the UAV provides charging and computing service for users in the disaster area. Considering the estimation error of users' locations, our target is to maximize the energy acquisition of each user by jointly optimizing the computing offloading process and the UAV trajectory. Due to the strongly coupled connectionbetween optimization variables and the non-convex nature for trajectory optimization, the problem is difficult to solve. Furthermore, the semi-infinity of the users' possible location makes the problem even more intractable. To tackle these difficulties, we ignore the estimation error of users' location firstly, and propose an iterative algorithm by using Lagrange dual method and successive convex approximation (SCA) technology. Then, we propose a cutting-set method to deal with the uncertainty of users' location. In this method, we degrade the influence of location uncertainty by alternating between optimization step and pessimization step. Finally, simulation results show that the proposed robust algorithm can effectively improve the user energy acquisition.

Keywords: unmanned aerial vehicle; mobile edge computing; wireless power transfer; trajectory planning; robust design

Citation: Cao, P.; Liu, Y.; Yang, C. Robust Resource Allocation and Trajectory Planning of UAV-Aided Mobile Edge Computing in Post-Disaster Areas. *Appl. Sci.* **2022**, *12*, 2226. https://doi.org/10.3390/app12042226

Academic Editors: Andrzej Łukaszewicz and Yosoon Choi

Received: 24 January 2022
Accepted: 15 February 2022
Published: 21 February 2022

1. Introduction

Natural disasters, such as earthquake, flood, and typhoon, often cause huge and unpredictable losses to human lives and properties [1–3]. Most of these disasters will result in unavailability of, or severe damage to, traditional terrestrial wireless infrastructures, as well as disruption to regional communication, which brings challenges to post-disaster response and relief [4–6]. By virtue of the advantages of dynamic mobility, flexibility, and on-demand deployment, unmanned aerial vehicles (UAVs) have been deemed as a promising technique in post-disaster area communication recovery [7–9]. In particular, the existence of line-of-sight (LoS) links between UAV and ground users has aroused a fast-growing interest in utilizing UAVs as aerial wireless platforms [10–13], while the limited power supply in disaster areas restricts the users' survival time and equipment performance, which also puts forward higher requirements for UAV-aided post-disaster services.

To tackle the above mentioned challenge, the combination of mobile edge computing (MEC) and wireless power transfer (WPT) seems to be an effective approach [14–16]. On one hand, by offloading computation tasks to UAVs, users can significantly improve their data processing capabilities [17–20]. On the other hand, with the aid of WPT technology, users can harvest radio-frequency (RF) signals from UAVs to prolong their survival time [21–23].

Unfortunately, the severe propagation loss of the wireless signals over long distances will degrade the performance of wireless information transfer (WIT) and WPT [24–26]. To improve the efficiency of WIT and WPT, UAVs should know the exact location of users in advance. However, in post-disaster areas, the exact location of users is difficult to obtain. The incomplete location information profoundly affects the trajectory planning of UAV and reduces the energy acquisition efficiency of users and the service quality of UAV [27–30]. Therefore, the robust design of trajectory and resource allocation of UAVs in post-disaster areas is of paramount importance.

Motivated by the requirements of a UAV-enabled wireless platform in a post-disaster area, we consider a robust UAV-enabled wireless-powered MEC system in this paper. In this system, a UAV equipped with MEC device and RF transmitter flies to the post-disaster area to provide computing and charging services for ground users. In this paper, we assume that terrestrial communications were destroyed in the disaster. Affected by this, the UAV only knows the rough areas where the users are, but the exact locations of the users are unknown. In order to ensure that users have enough power to maintain until the arrival of ground rescue, our target is to maximize the energy acquisition of each user while meeting the computation needs of users.

The considered problem is a non-convex semi-infinite optimization problem, which is intractable and hard to solve. In order to solve this intractability, we transform the original problem into a solvable form by ignoring the uncertainty of location first. Considering the coupling between computation offloading optimization and trajectory planning, an iterative optimization method is proposed by using Lagrange dual method and successive convex approximation (SCA) technology, respectively. Then, a cutting-set method is proposed to continuously decrease the impact of worst-case location of users on optimization. Due to the worst-case location of users changing with the optimization of UAV trajectory, the cutting-set method is achieved by alternating optimization, i.e., optimizing the UAV trajectory for given subsets of worst-case users' locations in the optimization step, and updating the subsets of worst-case users' locations according to UAV trajectory in the pessimization step.

To summarize, the difference between our work and those in [13,18] is mainly twofold. First, the proposed system considers the imperfect location information of users, which is more suitable for practical applications. Second, the proposed robust algorithm can effectively degrade the influence of location uncertainty on user energy acquisition. To our best knowledge, there are few studies that address the robust design for a UAV-enabled wireless-powered MEC system. In summary, the main contributions of this paper are as follows:

- We propose a UAV-enabled wireless-powered MEC system in a post-disaster area, while the imperfect location of users is considered. To ensure users have enough power in the post-disaster area, UAV provides charging and computing services for users.
- We propose a joint resource allocation and trajectory planning algorithm under known users' location to solve the strong coupling between optimization variables.
- We propose a robust cutting-set method to degrade the influence of worst-case location of users on optimization.

The rest of this paper is organized as follows. We describe the system model and formulate the optimization problem in Section 2. Then, we give a joint resource allocation and trajectory planning algorithm under known users' location in Section. In Section 4, we propose a robust cutting-set method. After this, the numerical results are presented in Section 5. Finally, we draw conclusions of our work in Section 6.

2. System Model and Problem Formulation

In this work, we propose a UAV-enabled wireless-powered MEC system in a post-disaster area, as shown in Figure 1. The terrestrial wireless infrastructures were damaged in the disaster. In order to get the situation of the disaster area and prepare for further rescue, a UAV, which is equipped with an RF transmitter and an MEC device, provides charging and computing services for a set $\mathcal{N} \triangleq \{1, \ldots, N\}$ of ground users, which has certain computation tasks R_n to complete, trapped in the disaster area.

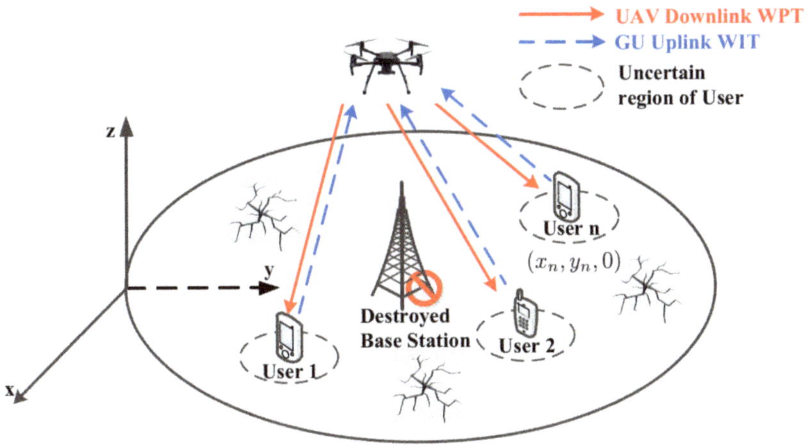

Figure 1. The UAV-enabled wireless-powered MEC system in post-disaster area.

Without loss of generality, we adopt a three-dimensional Euclidean coordinate system to represent the locations, and measure all dimensions in meters. Affected by the destruction of terrestrial wireless infrastructures, the UAV only knows the approximate location of nth users, denoted by $\mathbf{q}_n = (x_n, y_n, 0)$, with limited location information, while the exact location of nth users is $\bar{\mathbf{q}}_n = (\bar{x}_n, \bar{y}_n, 0)$, with a estimation error $\Delta\mathbf{q}_n$. The relation between the exact and approximate location of nth users is given by

$$\begin{gathered} \bar{\mathbf{q}}_n = \mathbf{q}_n + \Delta\mathbf{q}_n, \\ \Delta\mathbf{q}_n \in \Omega_n \triangleq \{\|\Delta\mathbf{q}_n\| \leq \varepsilon_n\}, \end{gathered} \tag{1}$$

where Ω_n is a continuous set of possible location estimation errors for the nth users, and ε_n denotes the radius of the uncertainly region Ω_n.

We assume that the UAV takes off and lands at a safe location $\mathbf{q}_s = (x_s, y_s, 0)$ within finite flight duration $\mathcal{T}$. The flight duration $\mathcal{T}$ is discretized into T sufficiently small time slots with equal length $\delta = \mathcal{T}/T$. Thus, the UAV can be seen as fixed in a certain position in each time slot, and its horizontal plane coordinate at tth slot is $\mathbf{q}_u[t] = (x_t, y_t)$. Similar to [29], we assume that the UAV flies at a constant altitude H to avoid the flight energy consumption caused by frequent ascend or descend. Correspondingly, the distance between UAV and user n is

$$d_n[t] = \sqrt{H^2 + \| \mathbf{q}_u[t] - \mathbf{q}_n \|^2}, \tag{2}$$

where $\|\cdot\|$ denotes the Euclidean norm. Similar to [18], we assume the wireless channel between the UAV and users is LoS link. Then, the channel power gain between UAV and users is

$$g_n[t] = \beta_0 d_n[t]^{-2}, \tag{3}$$

where β_0 is the channel power gain at $d_0 = 1$ m.

In downlink WPT mode, we consider that the UAV uses constant transmission power P_u for wireless power transmission. The energy harvested by nth user is given as

$$E_h[t] = \eta g_n[t] P_u \delta, \tag{4}$$

where $0 < \eta \leq 1$ denotes the energy conversion efficiency of each user, while in uplink WIT mode, for given offloading power $P_{o,n}[t]$, the offloading rate $r_{tr,n}[t]$ of nth user in the tth slot is given as

$$r_{tr,n}[t] = Blog_2(1 + \frac{P_{o,n}[t]g_n[t]}{\sigma^2}), \tag{5}$$

where B is the communication bandwidth, and σ^2 is the variance of additive white Gaussian noise with zero mean.

To utilize the energy in an efficient way, we assume that both UAV and users can adaptively adjust the CPU frequency [29]. The computation task amounts $R_{c,n}$ and the computation energy consumption $E_{c,n}$ of nth user in the tth slot are given as

$$\begin{aligned} R_{c,n} &= \frac{f_n[t]\delta}{C_n}, \\ E_{c,n} &= \theta_n f_n[t]^3\delta, \end{aligned} \tag{6}$$

where $f_n[t]$ represents the CPU frequency of users, C_n denotes the number of CPU cycles to complete the computation, and θ_n is the effective capacitance coefficient of the CPU. The expressions of computation amounts $R_{c,u}$ and computation energy consumption $E_{c,u}$ of UAV are consistent with users, which are not listed here.

For given UAV trajectory, we can obtain the flight speed of UAV on the horizontal plane:

$$v_u(t) = \frac{\|\mathbf{q}_{u,t+1} - \mathbf{q}_{u,t}\|}{\delta}. \tag{7}$$

For safety consideration, the maximum flight speed of UAV is v_{max}. In order to focus on designing the robust algorithm of trajectory planning and computation offloading optimization, we adopt a simplified flight energy consumption model in this work, while many factors will affect the flight energy consumption of UAV in reality. The flight energy consumption of UAV can be expressed as

$$E_{fly}[t] = 0.5m_u\delta v_u[t]^2, \tag{8}$$

where m_u is the mass of UAV.

Considering the inconvenience of obtaining energy in post-disaster areas, it is necessary for users to obtain charging and computing services from UAVs as much as possible to ensure that users gain more energy. The energy gain of the nth user is given as

$$E_{gain,n} = \sum_{t=1}^{T}(\eta g_n[t]P_u - \theta_n f_n[t]^3) - \sum_{t=1}^{T-1} P_{o,n}[t]. \tag{9}$$

In this work, our target is to maximize the minimum energy gain among users while guaranteeing the completion of computation task; the UAV trajectory and offloading optimization variables are jointly optimized under the estimation error of users' location. Then, the optimization problem can be formulated as

$$\begin{aligned}
\mathbf{P1}: \quad & \max_{\Theta} \min_{n\in\mathcal{N}} \max_{\Delta\mathbf{q}_n\in\Omega_n} E_{gain,n}, && \text{(10a)}\\
s.t. \quad & C1: \sum_{t=1}^{T}(E_{fly}[t]+P_u) + \sum_{t=2}^{T}\theta_u f_u[t]^3 \leq E_{bat}, && \text{(10b)}\\
& C2: \sum_{t=1}^{T}\frac{f_n[t]}{C_n} + \sum_{t=1}^{T-1} r_{tr,n}[t] \geq R_n, \forall n\in\mathcal{N}, && \text{(10c)}\\
& C3: \sum_{t=2}^{T}\frac{f_u[t]}{C_u} \geq \sum_{n=1}^{N}\sum_{t=1}^{T-1} r_{tr,n}[t], \forall t\in\mathcal{T}, && \text{(10d)}\\
& C4: f_u[t]\geq 0, f_n[t]\geq 0, \forall n\in\mathcal{N}, && \text{(10e)}\\
& C5: \mathbf{q}_u[1] = \mathbf{q}_u[T+1] = \mathbf{q}_s, && \text{(10f)}\\
& C6: v_u[t] \leq v_{max}, \forall t\in\mathcal{T}. && \text{(10g)}
\end{aligned}$$

where $\Theta = \{\mathbf{q}_u[t], f_u[t], f_n[t], P_{o,n}[t]\}$ is the optimal variable set, and $\mathcal{T}_{-T}$ represents the set $\mathcal{T}$ except the Tth time slot. C1 is the UAV battery constraint; C2 represents all computation tasks for each user need to be processed; C3 denotes that all computation task from users should to be handled by UAV in time; C4 are the CPU frequency constraints of user and UAV; C5 indicates that the UAV takes off and lands at the same safe position; C6 gives the maximum flight speed constraint of UAV.

3. Joint Resource Allocation and Trajectory Planning under Known Users' Location

In this section, we propose a joint resource allocation and trajectory planning algorithm to solve problem **P1** under known users' location. For the known users' location, we can ignore the estimation error ε_n of users, i.e., let $\hat{\mathbf{q}}_n := \mathbf{q}_n, \forall n \in \mathcal{N}$. Then, the original optimization problem **P1** can be transformed to

$$\begin{aligned}
\mathbf{P2}: \quad & \max_{\Theta} \min_{n\in\mathcal{N}} \hat{E}_{gain,n}, && \text{(11a)}\\
s.t. \quad & C1 - C6. && \text{(11b)}
\end{aligned}$$

Due to the coupling among the optimization variables, **P2** is still difficult to solve. Thus, we divide the optimization problem into two parts, i.e., computation offloading optimization and trajectory planning, and optimize them alternately. Firstly, we optimize the computation offloading resources by Lagrangian duality method under given UAV trajectory. Then, the SCA method is adopted to optimize the UAV trajectory for given computation offloading resources.

3.1. Computation Offloading Optimization

For given UAV trajectory, we can obtain the computation offloading variables optimization problem **P3:**

$$\begin{aligned}
\mathbf{P3}: \quad & \min_{P_{o,n}, f_u, f_n} \sum_{t=1}^{T}\theta_n f_n[t]^3 + \sum_{t=1}^{T-1} P_{o,n}[t], \\
s.t. \quad & C2, C4.
\end{aligned} \qquad (12)$$

Obviously, **P3** is a convex problem, which can be easily solved by Lagrange duality method. Then, we can obtain Theorem 1 by solving the Lagrangian function.

Theorem 1. *For given UAV trajectory* $\mathbf{q}_u(t)$*, the optimal offloading power and CPU frequencies of usern can be respectively expressed as*

$$P_{o,n}^{opt}[t] = \left[\frac{\lambda B}{ln2} - \frac{\sigma^2}{g_n[t]}\right]^+, \tag{13}$$

$$f_n^{opt}[t] = \sqrt{\frac{\lambda}{3\theta_n C_n}}, \tag{14}$$

where $\lambda \geq 0$ *denotes the dual variable associated with the constraint C2.*

Proof. See the Appendix A. □

Then, we adopt the subgradient method to obtain the value of dual variables.

$$\lambda(i+1) = [\lambda(i) - \theta(i)\Delta\lambda(i)]^+, \tag{15}$$

where i represents the iteration index, $\theta(i)$ denotes the iterative step, and the corresponding subgradient $\Delta\lambda(i)$ can be obtained by

$$\Delta\lambda(i) = \sum_{t=1}^{T} \frac{f_n^{i,opt}[t]}{C_n} + \sum_{t=1}^{T-1} Blog_2(1 + \frac{P_{o,n}^{i,opt}[t]g_n[t]}{\sigma^2}) - R_n, \tag{16}$$

where $f_n^{i,opt}[n]$, $P_{o,n}^{i,opt}[t]$ represent the optimal solutions at the ith iteration.

Then, according to optimal offloading power $P_{o,n}^{i,opt}[t]$ and constraint C3, we can obtain the optimal CPU frequencies of UAV

$$f_u^{i,opt}[t] = \frac{B}{\delta} \sum_{n=1}^{N} log_2(1 + \frac{P_{o,n}^{i,opt}[t]g_n[t]}{\sigma^2}), \tag{17}$$

since the lowest computation energy consumption can be obtained only when the computation frequency is a constant.

3.2. UAV's Trajectory Planning

For given computation offloading variables, the UAV's trajectory optimization problem **P4** can be expressed as

$$\begin{aligned} \mathbf{P4}: \quad & \max_{\mathbf{q}_u[t]} \min_{n\in\mathcal{N}} \sum_{t=1}^{T} \eta g_n[t] P_u \\ \text{s.t.} \quad & C1, C2, C5, C6. \end{aligned} \tag{18}$$

Due to the objective function of **P4** being non-concave and the constraint $C2$ being non-convex with respect to $\mathbf{q}_u[t]$, the problem **P4** is non-convex. For this problem, we choose the SCA method to solve.

By adopting the SCA method, we can obtain

$$\begin{aligned} r_{tr,n}[t] \geq r_{tr,n}^{low} = B\log_2\left(1 + \frac{P_{o,n}[t]\beta_0}{\sigma^2(H^2 + l_n^j[t]^2)}\right) \\ - \frac{P_{o,n}[t]\beta_0 log_2 e(l_n[t]^2 - l_n^j[t]^2)}{(H^2 + l_n^j[t]^2)(\sigma^2 H^2 + \sigma^2 l_n^j[t]^2 + P_{o,n}[t]\beta_0)}, \end{aligned} \tag{19}$$

where $l_n[t] = \| \mathbf{q}_u[t] - \mathbf{q}_n \|$, the r_k^{low} is the lower bound of $r_n[t]$, and the equality holds when $l_n[t] = l_n^j[t]$.

Similarly, we can obtain the lower bound g_n^{low} of $g_n[t]$:

$$g_n[t] \geq g_n^{low} = \frac{\beta_0(H^2 + 2l_n^j[t]^2 - l_n[t]^2)}{(H^2 + l_n^j[t]^2)^2}. \tag{20}$$

According to Formulas (19) and (20), we can transform the problem **P4** to

$$\mathbf{P4.1}: \quad \max_{\mathbf{q}_u[t]} \sum_{t=1}^{N} \eta g_n^{low} P_u \tag{21a}$$

$$s.t. \quad C2.1: \sum_{t=1}^{T} \frac{f_n[t]}{C_n} + \sum_{t=1}^{T-1} r_{tr,n}^{low} \geq R_n, \forall n \in N, \tag{21b}$$

$$C1, C5, C6. \tag{21c}$$

In problem **P4.1**, we can find that the objective function and the constraint C2.1 are both convex with respect to $\mathbf{q}_u[t]$. Thus, the problem **P4.1** is a convex problem. We can use CVX to solve this problem.

3.3. Alternative Algorithm for Solving P2

Based on the Lagranginan duality method and SCA method, we propose a joint resource allocation and trajectory planning (JRATP) algorithm under known users' location in this subsection. The detailed JRATP algorithm is shown in Algorithm 1.

Algorithm 1 Joint Resource Allocation and Trajectory Planning Algorithm under known users' location

Input: Initialize $P_{o,n}^1[t]$, $f_n^1[t]$, $f_u^1[t]$, $\mathbf{q}_u^1[t]$ with feasible solution.
Initialization: Set the radio environment parameters B, β_0, σ^2, the operation parameters P_u, η, C_n, C_u, θ_n, θ_u, and the tolerance error ε_1, ε_2
For each iteration i
  Calculate $P_{o,n}^{i,opt}[t]$, $f_n^{i,opt}[t]$ by Theorem 1 and calculate $f_u^{i,opt}[t]$ according to (17);
  Update $\Delta\mu(i)$, and $\mu(i+1)$ by subgradient formula;
  $P_{o,n}^{i+1}[t] = P_{o,n}^{i,opt}[t]$, $f_n^{i+1}[t] = f_n^{i,opt}[t]$, $f_u^{i+1}[t] = f_u^{i,opt}[t]$, $q_u^j[t] = q_u^i[t]$.
For each iteration j
  Using CVX to solve **P4.1** for given $P_{o,n}^{opt,j}[t]$, $f_n^{opt,j}[t]$, $f_u^{opt,j}[t]$ and obtain $\mathbf{q}_u^{opt,i}[t]$;
  If $\sum_{t=1}^{N} \| \mathbf{q}_u^{j+1}[t] - \mathbf{q}_u^j[t] \| \leq \varepsilon_2$, $\mathbf{q}_u^i[t] = \mathbf{q}_u^j[t]$, break
  End If
  update $j = j+1$;
End For
  If $|| \sum_{t=1}^{T}(R_{c,n}^i[t] - R_{c,n}^{i-1}[t]) + \sum_{t=1}^{T-1}(R_{o,n}^i[t] - R_{o,n}^{i-1}[t])|| \leq \varepsilon_1$, break
  End If
  update $i = i+1$;
End For
Output $P_{o,n}^{opt}[t]$, $f_n^{opt}[t]$, $f_u^{opt}[t]$, $\mathbf{q}_u^{opt}[t]$.

The complexity of Algorithm 1 comes from three aspects: (1) the computation of offloading power and CPU frequencies, (2) the computation of the dual variables, and (3) the application of CVX for computing UAV trajectory. Let L_1 and L_2 denote the number of iterations required for the outer loop and the inner loop of Algorithm 1. Let ϕ denote the tolerance error for the subgradient method. Then, we can obtain the total complexity of Algorithm 1 as $\mathcal{O}[L_1(2NT + 1/\phi^2 + L_2T^3)]$, where $\mathcal{O}(\cdot)$ is the big-O notation.

By solving each subproblem alternately, Algorithm 1 can guarantee convergence, while, due to the usage of SCA method and alternating optimization, the global optimum of problem **P2** cannot be strictly guaranteed.

4. Robust Design Based on Cutting-Set Method

In this section, we give a cutting-set method to degrade the influence from the uncertainty of the users' locations. The robust design is achieved by alternating between optimization steps and pessimization steps. In the optimization step, joint resource allocation and trajectory planning are optimized under a given finite subset of worst-case users' locations by Algorithm 1. Then, in the pessimization step, the subset of worst-case users' locations is updated according to the UAV trajectory obtained in the optimization step.

4.1. Optimization Step under Finite Subsets of Users' Location

Note that the worst-case locations of users are changed with the change of UAV trajectory in the optimization process. To simplify the problem, we assume that the worst-case locations of users are included in a finite subset of potential locations. Let $\mathcal{S}_n$ denote the potential worst-case locations of the nth user. Then, we can express the finite subset of the nth user in the kth optimization as $\mathcal{S}_n^k \subset \mathcal{S}_n$. For a given finite subset, we can transform the original problem to

$$\begin{aligned} \mathbf{P5}: \quad & \max_{\Theta} \min_{n \in \mathcal{N}} \max_{\mathbf{q}_n \in \mathcal{S}_n^k} E_{gain,n} \\ s.t. \quad & C1 - C6, \end{aligned} \tag{22}$$

while the problem **P5** can be solved by Algorithm 1.

4.2. Pessimization Step under Given UAV Trajectory

For a given UAV trajectory obtained from the optimization step, the worst-case users' location is updated in this step. Considering that the distances $d_n[t]$ between the UAV and users are larger than the estimation error $\Delta \mathbf{q}_n$, in the optimization process, we discretize the potential locations of the nth user into equal spacing grids-based worst-case locations with the resolution of π.

For the UAV, the worst-case locations under different trajectories is also different. Thus, the worst-case users' location needs to be updated after each trajectory planning, while, for the users, the location with the least energy harvest and the most transmission energy consumption corresponds to the worst-case location. Thus, the worst-case location $\mathbf{q}_n^{w,k}$ of nth user after kth optimization is obtained as

$$\|\mathbf{q}_u - \mathbf{q}_n^{w,k}\| = \|\mathbf{q}_n - \mathbf{q}_n^{w,k}\| + \varepsilon_n. \tag{23}$$

Then, the obtained worst-case locations $\mathbf{q}_n^{w,k}$ of the nth user is added into the infinite subset $\mathcal{S}_n^k$ for the next turn of optimization.

4.3. Total Algorithm of Robust Resource Allocation and Trajectory Planning

Based on the cutting-set method, we propose a robust resource allocation and trajectory planning algorithm to solve the uncertainty of users' location in this subsection. The detailed robust algorithm is shown in Algorithm 2.

As shown in Algorithm 2, the finite subset of potential users' locations are firstly initialized. Firstly, for a given finite subset of users' locations, the optimal computation offloading variables $P_{o,n}^k[t]$, $f_n^k[t]$, $f_u^k[t]$ and UAV trajectory $\mathbf{q}_u^k[t]$ are obtained by solving **P5** with Algorithm 1. Then, based on the UAV trajectory from the previous step, we can obtain the worst-case users' location and add it into $\mathcal{S}_n^k$ for the next turn of optimization. The robust algorithm processes alternately until the improvement reaches the stable point or reaches the maximum number k of iterations.

Algorithm 2 Robust Offloading Trajectory and Computation Offloading Algorithm with uncertainty of users' location

Initialization: Set the iterative number $k = 1$.
Input: Initialize finite subset $\mathcal{S}_n^k$.
repeat
  calculate $P_{o,n}^k[t]$, $f_n^k[t]$, $f_u^k[t]$ and $\mathbf{q}_u^k[t]$ by Algorithm 1;
  compute $\mathbf{q}_n^{w,k}$ for given $\mathbf{q}_u^k[t]$;
  update finite subset $\mathcal{S}_n^{k+1} = \{\mathcal{S}_n^k, \mathbf{q}_n^{w,k}\}$;
  update $k = k + 1$;
until reach the stable point or the maximum iterative number k
Output $P_{o,n}^k[t]$, $f_n^k[t]$, $f_u^k[t]$, $\mathbf{q}_u^k[t]$.

5. Numerical Results

In this section, simulation results are presented to validate the performance of the proposed robust joint resource allocation and trajectory planning algorithm, and are compared with three benchmark schemes. (1) Non-robust: In this scheme, we ignore the estimation error and optimize the problem under the estimated locations. (2) No-resource-allocation-optimization: In this scheme, we offload all computation tasks to UAV with fixed offloading power $P_{o,n} = P_{o,max}$. (3) No-trajectory-planning: In this scheme, we set the UAV trajectory as a circle around users with a radius 200 m.

According to the parameters adopted in [21,30], we consider a 500 × 500 m^2 post-disaster area which includes five ground users. The location estimation errors of the users are $\varepsilon_n = 20$ m. The flight altitude of UAV is $H = 50$ m, and the maximum flight speed of UAV is set as $V_{max} = 25$ m/s. The detailed environment settings are given in Table 1.

Table 1. Simulation parameters.

B	5 MHz	The channel bandwidth.
β_0	−50 dB	The channel power gain at distance $d_0 = 1$ m.
σ^2	10^{-9} W	The receiver noise power.
$P_{o,n}^{max}$	0.5 W	The maximum WIT transmit power of user.
P_u	50 W	The WPT transmit power of UAV.
η	0.15	The energy conversion efficiency of user.
C_n, C_u	10^3 cycles/bit	The number of CPU cycles.
θ_n, θ_u	10^{-28}	The effective switched capacitance.
$f_{n,max}, f_{u,max}$	10 GHz	The maximum frequency of CPU.

In Figure 2, we present the optimized UAV trajectories of the proposed robust joint resource allocation and trajectory planning algorithm and non-robust scheme under different battery capacity. From Figure 2, we can find that with the increase of battery capacity, the UAV can approach each user to provide services. The reason is that on the premise of completing the computation task, the larger the UAV battery capacity, the closer it can be to the users to provide efficient charging services. Note that under the same battery capacity, the proposed robust algorithm is much closer to users than the non-robust scheme. This is because in order to eliminate the impact of the worst-case location error on the users' power supply, the UAV should be close to the user greatly affected by the location error.

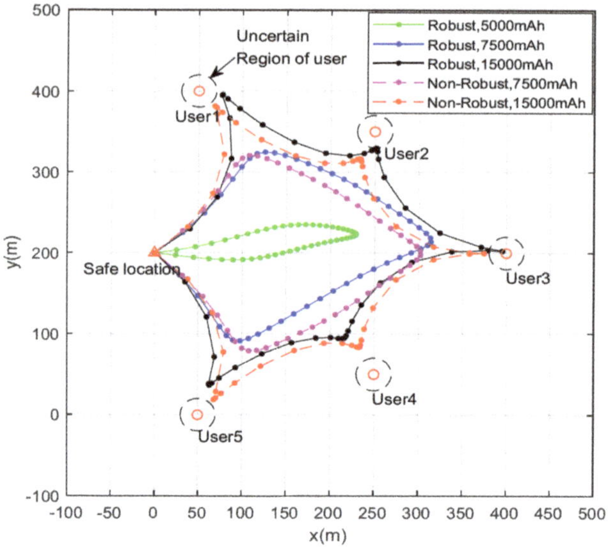

Figure 2. The optimized UAV trajectories under different schemes and battery capacity.

Figure 3 shows the minimum energy gain of users of the proposed robust algorithm with the other three benchmark schemes with different battery capacity of UAV. According to Figure 3, we can find that the proposed robust algorithm obtains the highest energy gain compared with other schemes. The reason is that the proposed robust algorithm can maximize the minimum energy gain of users by jointly optimizing UAV's trajectory and offloading process, and decreasing the influence of estimation location errors, while the other three schemes only optimize two of the three variables. We can also observe that with the increase of battery capacity, the energy gain of users increases rapidly, and then slows down gradually. That is, a larger UAV battery capacity can ensure UAV approach to users to provide much more efficient charging services.As the distance between UAV and users decreases, the impact of distance on energy supply decreases gradually, which leads to the slowing down of energy gain. In addition, the energy gain of the no-trajectory-planning scheme is a constant when battery capacity is bigger than 11,000 mAh. The reason is that when the battery capacity can ensure that the UAV flies according to the fixed trajectory, the distance between UAV and user is a constant. Then, the increase of battery capacity will not affect the energy gain of users.

In Figure 4, we compare the minimum energy gain of users of the proposed robust algorithm with the other three benchmark schemes with different estimation errors of users. From Figure 4, we can find that with the increase of the estimation errors, the minimum energy gain is decreased, while the reduction of the proposed robust algorithm is less than the non-robust scheme and the no-trajectory-planning scheme. This is because with the increase of the estimation errors, the worst-case location error will greatly increase the distance between UAV and user. Furthermore, compared with the no-trajectory-planning scheme flying as a circle, the non-robust scheme has less time to approach the user, which also leads to the fastest decline among all the schemes. Therefore, for the environment with location errors, it is necessary to introduce robust design into trajectory optimization.

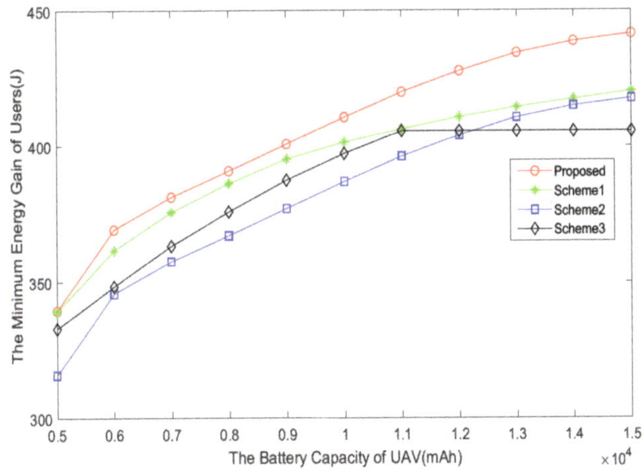

Figure 3. Energy gain of users under different schemes and battery capacity of UAV.

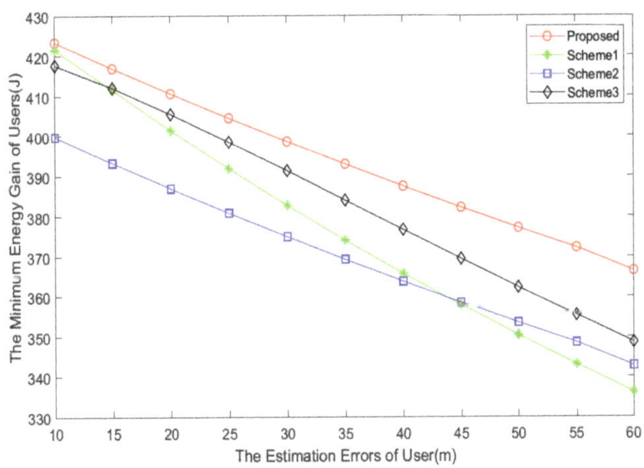

Figure 4. Energy gain of users under different schemes and estimation errors of users.

The distance between UAV and user is affected by horizontal distance and flight altitude. Thus, we present the minimum energy gain of users of the proposed robust algorithm with the other three benchmark schemes with different flight altitude of UAV in Figure 5. It can be seen that with the increase of flight altitude, the decrease of user energy gradually speeds up. The reason is that when the flight altitude is greater than the horizontal distance $d_n[t]$, the distance between the UAV and users is mainly affected by the flight altitude, and vice versa. Thus, in order to ensure that users receive more energy, the UAV can appropriately reduce the flight altitude when the estimation error is small.

Figure 6 also compares the minimum energy gain of users of the proposed robust algorithm with the other three benchmark schemes with different WPT transmit power of UAV. We can find that the energy gain achieved by the proposed robust algorithm is the highest among the schemes, while the increase of energy is proportional to the transmission power. That is, the user's energy gain is only affected by the transmitting power of the UAV when the computation task is processed.

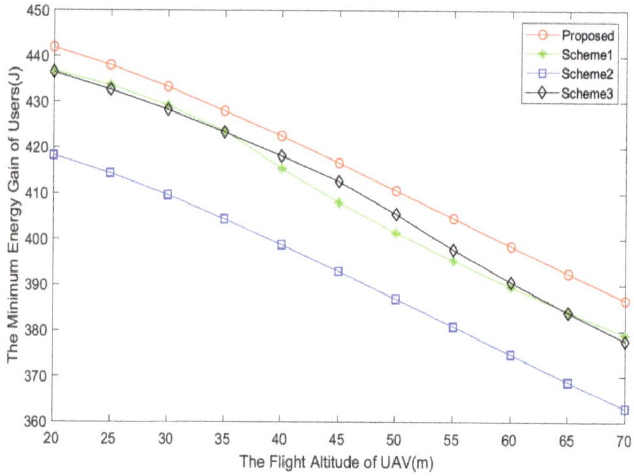

Figure 5. Energy gain of users under different schemes and flight altitude of UAV.

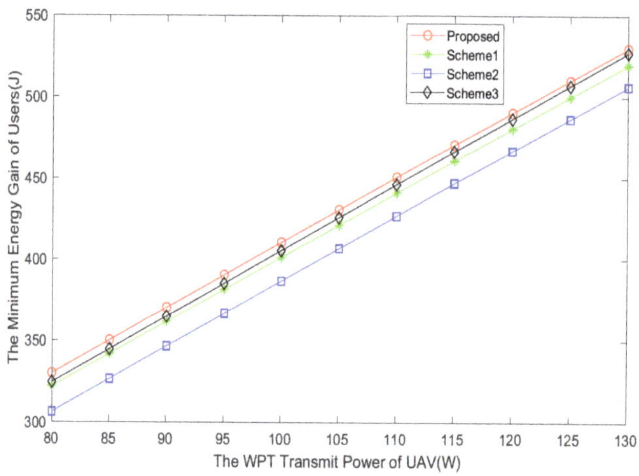

Figure 6. Energy gain of users under different schemes and WPT transmit power of UAV.

6. Conclusions

In this paper, we proposed a robust UAV-aided wireless-powered MEC system in a post-disaster area, where the UAV provides charging and computing services for ground users to ensure that users have enough power. To maximize the energy acquisition of each user, we jointly optimized the computing offloading and UAV trajectory. Particularly due to the destruction of terrestrial communications, the UAV only has an imperfect location of the users. Considering the strongly coupled connectionbetween optimization variables and the influence of user location estimation error, the robust resource allocation and trajectory planning was carefully addressed. Firstly, we proposed a joint resource allocation and trajectory planning algorithm under known users' location. Then, the robust cutting-set method was proposed to reduce the impact of worst-case location of users on optimization. Finally, we conducted extensive simulations to verify the effectiveness of the proposed robust algorithm.

Author Contributions: Conceptualization, P.C. and Y.L.; methodology, P.C. and Y.L.; software, P.C. and Y.L.; validation, Y.L. and C.Y.; formal analysis, P.C.; investigation, P.C.; resources, P.C.; data curation, P.C. and C.Y.; writing—original draft preparation, P.C. and C.Y.; writing—review and editing, Y.L. and C.Y.; visualization, C.Y.; supervision, Y.L. and C.Y.; project administration, Y.L.; funding acquisition, Y.L. All authors have read and agreed to the published version of the manuscript.

Funding: This work was supported in part by the National National Key R&D Program of China under Grants 2020YFB1807805, 2020YFB1807800; in part by the Guangdong Basic and Applied Basic Research foundation under Grant 2019A151501114.

Institutional Review Board Statement: Not applicable.

Informed Consent Statement: Not applicable.

Data Availability Statement: Not applicable.

Conflicts of Interest: Not applicable.

Abbreviations

The following abbreviations are used in this manuscript:

UAV	Unmanned aerial vehicle
MEC	Mobile edge computing
WPT	Wireless power transfer
WIT	Wireless information transfer
RF	Radio frequency
SCA	Successive convex approximation

Appendix A

Proof of Theorem 1. Let $\lambda \geq 0$ denotes the dual variable associated with the constraint C2. Then, for each user, we can get the Lagrangian function of $\mathbf{P}_{4-1}$ as

$$\mathcal{L}(\Theta) = \sum_{t=1}^{T}(\eta g_n[t]P_u - \theta_n f_n[t]^3) - \sum_{t=1}^{T-1} P_{o,n}[t] + \lambda\{\sum_{t=1}^{T}\frac{f_n[t]}{C_n} + \sum_{t=1}^{T-1} r_{tr,n}[t] - R_n\}.$$

Taking the derivative of the Lagrangian function $\mathcal{L}$ w.r.t CPU frequency $f[n]$ and offloading power $P_{o,n}[t]$ yields

$$\frac{\partial \mathcal{L}(\Theta)}{\partial P_{o,n}[t]} = \lambda \frac{B}{ln2} \frac{\widetilde{g}_n[t]}{\sigma^2 + P_{o,n}[t]\widetilde{g}_n[t]} - 1,$$
$$\frac{\partial \mathcal{L}(\Theta)}{\partial f_n[t]} = -3\theta_n f_n[t]^2 + \frac{\lambda}{C_n}.$$

Let $\frac{\partial \mathcal{L}}{\partial P_{o,n}[t]} = 0$ and $\frac{\partial \mathcal{L}}{\partial f_n[t]} = 0$, the optimal $P_{o,n}^{opt}[t]$ and $f_n^{opt}[t]$ can be obtained. The proof of Theorem 1 is finished. □

References

1. Erdelj, M.; Natalizio, E.; Chowdhury, K.R.; Akyildiz, I.F. Help from the Sky: Leveraging UAVs for Disaster Management. *IEEE Pervasive Comput.* **2017**, *16*, 24–32. [CrossRef]
2. Yao, Z.; Cheng, W.; Zhang, W.; Zhang, H. Resource Allocation for 5G-UAV-Based Emergency Wireless Communications. *IEEE J. Sel. Areas Commun.* **2021**, *39*, 3395–3410. [CrossRef]
3. Chen, W.; Su, Z.; Xu, Q.; Luan, T.H.; Li, R. VFC-Based Cooperative UAV Computation Task Offloading for Post-disaster Rescue. In Proceedings of the IEEE INFOCOM 2020-IEEE Conference on Computer Communications, Toronto, ON, Canada, 6–9 July 2020; pp. 228–236.
4. Zhang, S.; Liu, J. Analysis and Optimization of Multiple Unmanned Aerial Vehicle-Assisted Communications in Post-Disaster Areas. *IEEE Trans. Veh. Technol.* **2018**, *67*, 12049–12060. [CrossRef]
5. Gao, M.; Zhang, B.; Wang, L. A Dynamic Priority Packet Scheduling Scheme for Post-disaster UAV-assisted Mobile Ad Hoc network. In Proceedings of the 2021 IEEE Wireless Communications and Networking Conference (WCNC), Nanjing, China, 29 March–1 April 2021; pp. 1–6. [CrossRef]

6. Saif, A.; Dimyati, K.; Noordin, K.A.; Shah, N.S.M.; Abdullah, Q.; Mukhlif, F. Unmanned Aerial Vehicles for Post-Disaster Communication Networks. In Proceedings of the 2020 IEEE 10th International Conference on System Engineering and Technology (ICSET), Shah Alam, Malaysia, 9 November 2020 ; pp. 273–277. [CrossRef]
7. Tang, H.; Wu, Q.; Xu, J.; Chen, W.; Li, B. A Novel Alternative Optimization Method for Joint Power and Trajectory Design in UAV-Enabled Wireless Network. *IEEE Trans. Veh. Technol.* **2019**, *68*, 11358–11362. [CrossRef]
8. Ouyang, T.; Zhou, Z.; Chen, X. Follow Me at the Edge: Mobility-Aware Dynamic Service Placement for Mobile Edge Computing. *IEEE J. Sel. Areas Commun.* **2018**, *36*, 2333–2345. [CrossRef]
9. Cao, P.; Liu, Y.; Yang, C.; Xie, S.; Xie, K. MEC-Driven UAV-Enabled Routine Inspection Scheme in Wind Farm Under Wind Influence. *IEEE Access* **2019**, *7*, 179252–179265. [CrossRef]
10. Yang, C.; Lou, W.; Liu, Y.; Xie, S. Resource Allocation for Edge Computing-Based Vehicle Platoon on Freeway: A Contract-Optimization Approach. *IEEE Trans. Veh. Technol.* **2020**, *69*, 15988–16000. [CrossRef]
11. Wu, Z.; Yang, Z.; Yang, C.; Lin, J.; Liu, Y.; Chen, X. Joint deployment and trajectory optimization in UAV-assisted vehicular edge computing networks. *J. Commun. Netw.* **2021** , 1–12. [CrossRef]
12. Li, P.; Xu, J. Fundamental Rate Limits of UAV-Enabled Multiple Access Channel With Trajectory Optimization. *IEEE Trans. Wirel. Commun.* **2020**, *19*, 458–474. [CrossRef]
13. Xie, L.; Xu, J.; Zhang, R. Throughput Maximization for UAV-Enabled Wireless Powered Communication Networks. *IEEE Internet Things J.* **2019**, *6*, 1690–1703. [CrossRef]
14. Liu, Y.; Yang, C.; Jiang, L.; Xie, S.; Zhang, Y. Intelligent Edge Computing for IoT-Based Energy Management in Smart Cities. *IEEE Netw.* **2019**, *33*, 111–117. [CrossRef]
15. Lv, B.; Yang, C.; Chen, X.; Yao, Z.; Yang, J. Task Offloading and Serving Handover of Vehicular Edge Computing Networks Based on Trajectory Prediction. *IEEE Access* **2021**, *9*, 130793–130804. [CrossRef]
16. Zhang, X.; Zhong, Y.; Liu, P.; Zhou, F.; Wang, Y. Resource Allocation for a UAV-Enabled Mobile-Edge Computing System: Computation Efficiency Maximization. *IEEE Access* **2019**, *7*, 113345–113354. [CrossRef]
17. Liu, Y.; Xie, S.; Zhang, Y. Cooperative Offloading and Resource Management for UAV-Enabled Mobile Edge Computing in Power IoT System. *IEEE Trans. Veh. Technol.* **2020**, *69*, 12229–12239. [CrossRef]
18. Zhou, F.; Wu, Y.; Hu, R.Q.; Qian, Y. Computation Rate Maximization in UAV-Enabled Wireless Powered Mobile-Edge Computing Systems. *IEEE J. Sel. Areas Commun.* **2018**, *36*, 1927–1941. [CrossRef]
19. Liu, Y.; Xie, S.; Yang, Q.; Zhang, Y. Joint Computation Offloading and Demand Response Management in Mobile Edge Network With Renewable Energy Sources. *IEEE Trans. Veh. Technol.* **2020**, *69*, 15720–15730. [CrossRef]
20. Liu, Y.; Xiong, K.; Ni, Q.; Fan, P.; Letaief, K.B. UAV-Assisted Wireless Powered Cooperative Mobile Edge Computing: Joint Offloading, CPU Control, and Trajectory Optimization. *IEEE Internet Things J.* **2020**, *7*, 2777–2790. [CrossRef]
21. Liu, Y.; Qiu, M.; Hu, J.; Yu, H. Incentive UAV-Enabled Mobile Edge Computing Based on Microwave Power Transmission. *IEEE Access* **2020**, *8*, 28584–28593. [CrossRef]
22. Xie, L.; Xu, J.; Zeng, Y. Common Throughput Maximization for UAV-Enabled Interference Channel With Wireless Powered Communications. *IEEE Trans. Commun.* **2020**, *68*, 3197–3212. [CrossRef]
23. Zhang, S.; Zhang, H.; Di, B.; Song, L. Cellular UAV-to-X Communications: Design and Optimization for Multi-UAV Networks. *IEEE Trans. Wirel. Commun.* **2019**, *18*, 1346–1359. [CrossRef]
24. Zhong, W.; Xie, K.; Liu, Y.; Yang, C.; Xie, S.; Zhang, Y. Multi-Resource Allocation of Shared Energy Storage: A Distributed Combinatorial Auction Approach. *IEEE Trans. Smart Grid* **2020**, *11*, 4105–4115. [CrossRef]
25. Zhong, W.; Xie, K.; Liu, Y.; Xie, S.; Xie, L. Chance Constrained Scheduling and Pricing for Multi-Service Battery Energy Storage. *IEEE Trans. Smart Grid* **2021**, *12*, 5030–5042. [CrossRef]
26. Zhong, W.; Xie, S.; Xie, K.; Yang, Q.; Xie, L. Cooperative P2P Energy Trading in Active Distribution Networks: An MILP-Based Nash Bargaining Solution. *IEEE Trans. Smart Grid* **2021**, *12*, 1264–1276. [CrossRef]
27. Gao, Y.; Tang, H.; Li, B.; Yuan, X. Robust Trajectory and Power Control for Cognitive UAV Secrecy Communication. *IEEE Access* **2020**, *8*, 49338–49352. [CrossRef]
28. Cui, M.; Zhang, G.; Wu, Q.; Ng, D.W.K. Robust Trajectory and Transmit Power Design for Secure UAV Communications. *IEEE Trans. Veh. Technol.* **2018**, *67*, 9042–9046. [CrossRef]
29. Zhou, Y.; Zhou, F.; Zhou, H.; Ng, D.W.K.; Hu, R.Q. Robust Trajectory and Transmit Power Optimization for Secure UAV-Enabled Cognitive Radio Networks. *IEEE Trans. Commun.* **2020**, *68*, 4022–4034. [CrossRef]
30. Yang, T.; Taghizadeh, O.; Hu, Y.; Xu, H.; Caire, G. Robust Secure UAV Communication Systems with Full-Duplex Jamming. In Proceedings of the 2021 IEEE Wireless Communications and Networking Conference (WCNC), Nanjing, China, 29 March–1 April 2021; pp. 1–6. [CrossRef]

drones

Review

A Review of Counter-UAS Technologies for Cooperative Defensive Teams of Drones

Vittorio Ugo Castrillo *, Angelo Manco, Domenico Pascarella and Gabriella Gigante

CIRA—Italian Aerospace Research Centre, Via Maiorise, 81043 Capua, Italy; a.manco@cira.it (A.M.); d.pascarella@cira.it (D.P.); g.gigante@cira.it (G.G.)
* Correspondence: v.castrillo@cira.it

Abstract: In recent years, the drone market has had a significant expansion, with applications in various fields (surveillance, rescue operations, intelligent logistics, environmental monitoring, precision agriculture, inspection and measuring in the construction industry). Given their increasing use, the issues related to safety, security and privacy must be taken into consideration. Accordingly, the development of new concepts for countermeasures systems, able to identify and neutralize a single (or multiples) malicious drone(s) (i.e., classified as a threat), has become of primary importance. For this purpose, the paper evaluates the concept of a multiplatform counter-UAS system (CUS), based mainly on a team of mini drones acting as a cooperative defensive system. In order to provide the basis for implementing such a system, we present a review of the available technologies for sensing, mitigation and command and control systems that generally comprise a CUS, focusing on their applicability and suitability in the case of mini drones.

Keywords: counter-UAS systems; sensing; neutralization; command and control; drones; cooperative systems

Citation: Castrillo, V.U.; Manco, A.; Pascarella, D.; Gigante, G. A Review of Counter-UAS Technologies for Cooperative Defensive Teams of Drones. *Drones* **2022**, *6*, 65. https://doi.org/10.3390/drones6030065

Academic Editors: Andrzej Łukaszewicz, Wojciech Giernacki, Zbigniew Kulesza, Jaroslaw Pytka and Andriy Holovatyy

Received: 24 January 2022
Accepted: 24 February 2022
Published: 1 March 2022

1. Introduction

In recent years, the drone market has had a significant expansion, especially in the consumer sector. Drones destined for this market are easily accessible thanks to their relatively low cost. In addition, the characteristics of weight, size, and the ability to carry a payload, such as a camera, allow them to be used in various fields, from the recreational to the professional sector. In addition, from a research point of view, the use of these flying platforms helps the development of technologies whose applications have a positive impact on the community, such as search and rescue operations, intelligent logistics, environmental monitoring or precision agriculture.

Given the increasing use of these technologies, the issues related to safety, security and privacy must be taken into consideration. Their use could cause damage to the community due to failures and improper or criminal use. A significant increase has been observed in the number of accidents involving drones or unmanned aerial systems (UAS) [1]. For example, improper use in the vicinity of an airport can represent a serious threat to public safety and a source of discomfort, as evidenced by the hundreds of flights canceled at London Gatwick airport in a few months of 2018 [2].

For this reason, the development of technologies for the detection, identification and mitigation of malicious drones has become of primary importance. A countermeasure system, also called a counter-UAS (C-UAS) or counter-UAS system (CUS), can identify and neutralize an intruder drone classified as a threat.

From an architectural point of view, an anti-drone system generally consists of the following fundamental sub-systems:

- Sensing system;
- Mitigation system;
- Command and control (C2) system.

The sensing system consists of one or more sensors capable of collecting information from the surrounding environment. The mitigation system consists of one or more mitigating elements capable of disabling, destroying or taking control of the drone identified as a threat. The C2 system collects data from sensors and executes detection algorithms, based on which it establishes the presence of a threat, identifies it (i.e., classifies its entity) and decides the most appropriate tracking and mitigation mode.

There are several C-UAS systems on the market. There are integrated systems that implement both the detection part and the mitigation part on the same platform, but the most adopted solution is to separate the mitigation part from the sensing one, distributing it on different platforms, giving rise to distinct commercial products. For example, most of the available solutions are ground-based, especially for the sensing part, while the sky-based part is typically relegated to mitigation. Thus, a single platform may implement only some of the sub-systems of the CUS (or part of them) and a network architecture is required to implement the interactions between the platforms.

In this paper, a multiplatform CUS, based mainly on a team of mini drones acting as a cooperative defensive system, has been used as a reference. Indeed, mini drones represent an effective solution for the implementation of a CUS, being the ideal platforms for the proximal sensing and tracking of moving targets (e.g., intruder drones) in high-mobility scenarios. Moreover, a team of mini drones may be arranged as a mobile sensor network: on the one hand, the single drones may act as mobile sensor nodes to keep the closeness with moving targets; on the other hand, a cooperative behavior may be established by means of the network of drones and a suitable coordination protocol. Such cooperative behavior may ensure the simultaneous perception and tracking of different moving targets, and may provide efficient coverage by balancing the load of the sensing and tracking tasks amongst the sensor nodes. In the end, defensive drones may also be equipped to implement proper neutralization actions with respect to intruder drones.

In order to provide the basis for the future implementation activities of a cooperative drone-based CUS, this work presents a review of the available technologies for sensing, mitigation and C2 systems by means of mini drones. In addition, the paper discusses some challenges about the key technological enablers for the effective implementation of these systems. This paper does not provide a review of the available technologies for the communication network and for the cooperation algorithms, which are exhaustively described in other works.

The remainder of this article is organized as follows. Section 2 presents the definitions and the basic concepts for cooperative drone-based CUSs. In Section 3, the sensing system is introduced, with a literature review and a comparison on the sensing techniques that could be used aboard drones. In Section 4, different neutralization techniques are discussed and neutralizers using mini drones are highlighted. A detailed description of the C2 system is provided in Section 5. Section 6 presents some of the technological challenges. Section 7 discusses the main results of the work, while the last section is about the conclusions.

2. Definitions and Basic Concepts for Cooperative Drone-Based Counter-UAS Systems

This section provides the main definitions and the basic concepts about cooperative drone-based CUSs.

2.1. Drones

A drone or unmanned aerial vehicle (UAV) is an aircraft with no human pilot on-board. It is the central element of a UAS, which is the set comprised of the aircraft and all the other elements supporting the service of a drone. In detail, a UAS is made up of the main following components:

- Airframe, which is the mechanical part of the vehicle, including the propulsion system;
- Navigation and motion sensors that collect the information about the drone position and its flight trajectory;

- Flight control system (FCS), which controls the propulsion system and the servos in order to apply a flight trajectory;
- Payload, which is the specific equipment to accomplish a given mission;
- Ground control station (GCS), which is a computer system or a network of computer systems on the ground, which monitor and control UAS operation;
- Communication infrastructure, which is the set of data links and related equipment for the communication between the vehicle and the GCS (or other external elements).

There are different classifications of drones according to several parameters, such as weight, altitude, endurance, degree of autonomy, etc. Reference [3] provides a survey of the main classification of drones. For example, the military domain includes a NATO UAS classification system, which is shown in Figure 1. It sets three classes, based on the weight. The classes are further divided according to other parameters, such as the employment, the operating altitude and the mission radius. According to such a classification system, mini drones are Class I drones with a weight less than 15 kg, whereas microdrones are Class I drones with a maximum energy state less than 66 J.

UAS CLASSIFICATION

Class	Category	Normal Employment	Normal Operating Altitude	Normal Mission Radius	Primary Supported Commander	Example Platform
Class III (> 600 kg)	Strike/ Combat *	Strategic/National	Up to 65,000 ft	Unlimited (BLOS)	Theatre	Reaper
	HALE	Strategic/National	Up to 65,000 ft	Unlimited (BLOS)	Theatre	Global Hawk
	MALE	Operational/Theatre	Up to 45,000 ft MSL	Unlimited (BLOS)	JTF	Heron
Class II (150 kg - 600 kg)	Tactical	Tactical Formation	Up to 18,000 ft AGL	200 km (LOS)	Brigade	Hermes 450
Class I (< 150 kg)	Small (>15 kg)	Tactical Unit	Up to 5,000 ft AGL	50 km (LOS)	Battalion, Regiment	Scan Eagle
	Mini (<15 kg)	Tactical Sub -unit (manual or hand launch)	Up to 3,000 ft AGL	Up to 25 km (LOS)	Company, Platoon, Squad	Skylark
	Micro ** (<66 J)	Tactical Sub -unit (manual or hand launch)	Up to 200 ft AGL	Up to 5 km (LOS)	Platoon, Squad	Black Widow

* Note: in the event the UAS is armed, the operator should comply with the applicable joint mission qualifications in AP-3.3.7 (STANAG 4670) and the system will need to comply with applicable airworthiness standards, regulations, policy, and legal considerations.
** Note: UAS that have a maximum energy state less than 66 Joules are not likely to cause significant damage to life or property, and do not need to be classified or regulated for airworthiness, training, etc. purposes unless they have the ability to handle hazardous payloads (explosive, toxins, chemical/biological agents, etc.).

Figure 1. NATO's UAS classification system [4].

A slightly different classification for micro-, mini and small UAVs (sUAS, NATO Class I) is described in [5] and shown in Table 1. The latter also reports endurance and payload capabilities, as well as weight, altitude, range and same example platforms available on the market.

Table 1. Micro-, mini and small UAV classifications based on weight, altitude, range and payload.

Category	Weight (in kg)	Normal Operating Altitude (in m)	Mission Radius, Range (in km)	Typical Endurance (in h)	Payload (in kg)	Available UAV Models in Market
Micro	<2	<140	5	<1	<1	DJI Spark, DJI Mavic, Parrot Bebop2
Mini	2–25	<1000	25	2–8	<10	DJI Matrice600, DJI Inspire2, Airborne Vanguard
Small	25–150	<1700	50	4–12	<50	AAI Shadow 200, Scorpion 3 Hoverbike

2.2. Multi-Drone Missions

Without the need for an on-board pilot, drones were usually designed to accomplish the D-cube (dull, dangerous and dirty) envelope [6], which is the set of the following mission classes: dull, i.e., monotonous or requiring high endurance for human occupants; dirty, i.e., that could pose a health risk to a human crew; dangerous, i.e., that could result in the loss of life for the on-board pilot. However, if the region of interest of a mission is large and/or the mission objectives are several, the execution of a single-drone mission may solicit a considerable amount of time and may entail poor performance in terms of mission effectiveness.

Multi-drone missions may overcome this issue. They are essentially missions that engage two or more drones with some common objectives. Thus, a multi-drone mission aims at increasing the effectiveness with respect to the equivalent single-drone mission and requires a sort of collaboration amongst the involved drones.

There is no common agreement about the definitions for this multi-drone collaboration and the classification of the different levels of collaboration. For the purposes of this work, the definitions in [7] are adopted and the following levels of collaborations in a multi-drone setting are considered:

- Isolated individual—in this case, a drone independently acts. It may be piloted, or it may exhibit a given degree of autonomy for the execution of its mission on its own.
- Group—a group of drones comprised of several isolated individuals, each with their own mission without coordination, i.e., collaboration is not present.
- Team—a team of drones is a networked set of drones with a common mission, in which all members are assigned specialized and different tasks to accomplish the global mission.
- Swarm—a swarm of drones is a uniform mass of undifferentiated drones. Thus, a swarm is typically composed of a large number of homogeneous drones, which perform a single task.

According to the above classification, only drone teams and swarms envisage a significant collaboration level, which entails a cooperation within the overall system. Such cooperation should allow the achievement of more complex missions and/or effective results with respect to isolated individuals and groups of drones. Cooperation is mediated by coordination (or coordination protocol), which represents the mechanism ensuring that the activities of the single vehicles keep the desired relationships and that the collective behavior (intended as the set of individual behaviors in the system) achieve the objectives for the global system. The members of a swarm usually coordinate each other only through simple and local interactions, whereas the coordination of a team requires diverse mechanisms for the allocation of several, possibly heterogeneous, tasks. In regard to the coordination of a swarm, the emergency concept is usually adopted to indicate the ability of the swarm to achieve a collective behavior for a complex operation by exploiting limited interactions of the single vehicles, which individually accomplish simple behaviors and tasks.

Other definitions and classifications are possible for the collaborative sets of drones. Indeed, such sets may be also managed as an interoperable system of systems (SoS) in order to apply the interoperability concepts, as in reference [8]. In any case, the joint performance of a networked set of drones (teams or swarms) for a common mission is expected to exceed the sum of the performances achievable in the equivalent single-drone mission. In more detail, the following general advantages are expected for a typical multi-drone mission with teams or swarms of drones:

- Multiple simultaneous interventions—the system may simultaneously collect data from multiple locations.
- Efficiency—the system may split up in order to efficiently cover a large area, optimizing available resources.
- Complementarity—the system may perform different tasks with growing accuracy. Clearly, this feature holds for drone teams.
- Reliability—the system assures fault-tolerant missions by providing redundancy and capability of reconfiguration in the case of a failure of individual vehicles.
- Safety—the team or swarm may usually apply the smallest vehicles for a mission with respect to the equivalent single-drone mission. For a permit to fly, the usage of smaller drones is safer than a single great and heavy drone.
- Cost efficiency—a single vehicle to execute some tasks may be an expensive solution when compared with several low-cost vehicles.

2.3. Counter-UAS Systems

In the literature, it is possible to find numerous surveys that have explored the characteristics of anti-drone systems (see for example [5,9–13]). In this regard, the taxonomy presented in [9] is of particular interest, in which CUS are grouped into two categories: ground-based and sky-based, depending on their deployment, respectively, on the ground or in the air using drones or other flying platforms (for example, stratospheric platforms). Ground-based systems can be of the static type, if installed, even temporarily, in a fixed manner within the perimeter to be defended, or of the mobile type if installed on-board land vehicles or transported by hand by humans (human-handled). Sky-based systems are implemented on board drones, UAS, balloons or stratospheric platforms, and deployed as needed. They differ in high altitudes and low altitudes, depending on the operating altitude.

The two types of CUSs oppose each other with respect to the level of operational mobility and the characteristics of weight, size and energy required for operation (size, weight and power, SWaP). Ground systems have the clear advantage of being able to count on weak SWaP requirements (increasingly from static systems to human-handled ones), but have little flexibility in terms of adapting to the unpredictable behavior of malicious drones. On the other hand, sky-based systems have greater adaptability thanks to the inherent maneuverability and flexibility that are afforded with the much more stringent SWaP requirements due to the limited power of the batteries and the low payload capacity for the lighter flying platforms. In choosing the platform to be adopted, it is important to consider its advantages and disadvantages and the operational scenario in which the solution is used.

It is also possible to create a hybrid CUS as a heterogeneous and cooperative network of different platforms (both ground-based and sky-based) to balance the limits that each solution would have if used individually. Indeed, although a CUS can consist of a single platform, it is difficult for such a solution to deal with the threats represented by a malicious drone or even by several malicious drones, so solutions that offer greater reliability and spatial coverage are represented by CUSs comprised of multiple platforms. In this case, the platforms are networked to cooperate, maximizing the effectiveness.

2.4. Cooperative Drone-Based Counter-UAS Systems

This paper is focused on cooperative drone-based CUSs. These represent an instance of hybrid CUS (as defined in Section 2.3), including a cooperative set of drones. Thus, according to the definitions reported in Section 2.2, such a cooperative set represents a team or swarm of drones.

For the purposes of this work, teams of mini drones (based on the NATO's UAS classification system, as shown in Figure 1, or on the classification reported in [5] and shown in Table 1) are considered as a reference subsystem of the hybrid CUS. This choice is due to the following expected advantages, which are added to the advantages of a generic multi-drone mission (described in Section 2.2):

Mobility—mini drones show extreme mobility; it is possible to bring them closer to the malicious drones and the sensing operations could be done in the proximity of the target. So, mini drones offer a mobile proximal sensing solution for a CUS, which can improve the detection and identification phases by lowering the probability of a false alarm.

Coverage expansion—it is possible to increase the coverage of the protected area. In fact, drones can be easily moved in order to circumvent obstacles and/or monitor areas that are not covered or not effectively covered by ground platforms. In other words, it is easy to extend the area protected by the CUS without increasing the number of used platforms. Nevertheless, proper bases allocation, jointly with re-charging issues, must be guaranteed. Coverage expansion can also be obtained using a single high-altitude platform, but supposedly with higher costs.

Deployment flexibility—compared to other flying platforms, they are simpler and faster to use, allowing lower response times to any threat.

Cooperative sensor network—the defensive team may be arranged as a cooperative sensor network, i.e., as a set of mobile sensor nodes, which may cooperatively perceive, identify and track one or more threats from different "perspectives". This is even more necessary for mobile proximal sensing to keep the closeness with different moving targets. Thus, a cooperative sensor network may be implemented for a distribution of the sensing tasks and a load balancing amongst the sensor nodes. Such network is expected to be reconfigurable for maintaining optimal performance. Clearly, the same concept may be applied also for mitigation purposes if the drones are equipped with the proper neutralization payloads.

Team coordination—as described in Section 2.2, a swarm requires a large mass of homogeneous vehicles and the coordination of a swarm occurs by means of the emergency concept. These features are not deemed suitable for a cooperative drone-based CUS. Indeed, the homogeneity of vehicles may be incompatible with the heterogeneous tasks in a CUS. Moreover, the large mass of vehicles and the emergency of a swarm imply a non-deterministic behavior and the absence of a specific organizational structure since they are based on individuals' reactions [7]. Thus, it may be difficult to estimate the probability of success of a mission, which is generally unacceptable for a CUS. To the contrary, a drone team usually exhibits an explicit organizational structure by means of a deliberated coordination. A team may also satisfy the requirement about the heterogeneous tasks for the cooperative drone-based CUS.

Automated decision-making—given the speeds involved in the operating environment for CUS systems, an automated decision-making capability is essential to aid an operator in the selection of the most proper actions to manage the given threat scenario or attack scenario and to enable the fastest possible reactions on the part of the defense system. Mini drones, with their well-known aptitudes for autonomous behaviors (also as a team), represent an ideal platform to support such capability.

Neutralization—if the intruder drone(s) did not immediately manifest the malicious intentions, the defensive team would act in proximity by physically chasing it and would be ready for mitigation when the threat has manifested [14], thus allowing a higher probability of success for the neutralization phase. In the literature, there have been several recent studies on the use of a drone team as a defensive tool (e.g., [15,16]). Indeed, the features for mobile proximal sensing may be adapted also for mitigation purposes, and some defensive drones may be equipped with specific electronic or kinetic-mechanical neutralization systems in order to perform preliminary mitigation actions and to take advantage of the closeness to the moving targets.

Scalability—Traditional CUSs lack scalability and are not usually able to face intrusions of drone teams or swarms. To the contrary, a defensive team of drones inherently represents a scalable solution. Indeed, the coordination mechanisms usually exhibit a scalable computational complexity with respect to the cardinality of the team, especially when decentralized approaches (i.e., without central decision points) are applied. These approaches ensure self-configuration and robustness of the team in front of individual off-nominal events (i.e., failures, communication losses, etc.) or threats (i.e., attacks to the individual defensive drones). Moreover, with the proper sizing and payload configuration, a defensive team may detect and track a team or swarm of rogue drones.

The suitability of drone teams for CUS solutions has also been confirmed by state-of-the-art research works in the fields of autonomous multi-agent systems and cooperative robotics, which have proposed several applications with some similarities with CUSs' required capabilities. Indeed, examples of these applications are those related to multi-robot systems for the observation of multiple moving targets, for which different control approaches already exist, such as cooperative multi-robot observation of multiple moving targets (CMOMMT), cooperative search–acquisition–track (CSAT), multi-robot pursuit evasion (MPE) [17]. In addition, multi-drone systems have been analyzed in terms of distributed multi-agent systems for multi-target tracking problems [18]. In the end, the environmental domain presents some advanced multi-drone solutions for environmental monitoring of dynamic natural threats, such as the ones for tracking the dispersion of contaminant clouds [19]. Additionally, some current international projects are developing cooperative drone-based solutions for surveillance and situational awareness applications, such as the following European projects: ResponDrone [20], which aims at developing a multi-UAS platform for first responders to enhance their situation awareness in support assessment missions, search and rescue operations, forest fire fighting, etc.; ROBORDER [21], which aims at developing and demonstrating an autonomous border surveillance system with unmanned mobile robots, including aerial, water surface, underwater and ground vehicles, which will incorporate multimodal sensors as part of an interoperable network; LABYRINTH [22], which proposes a road traffic surveillance by means of a multi-drone system; 5D-AeroSafe [23], which aims at developing multi-drone solutions for the monitoring of airport and waterway daily operations; Drones4Safety [24], which aims at developing a system of autonomous, self-charging and collaborative drones that can inspect a big portion of transportation infrastructures in a continuous operation; RAPID [25], which aims at delivering a fully automated and drone-based maintenance inspection service for bridges, ship hull surveys and more. All these technologies and solutions represent a sound starting point for the future cooperative drone-based solutions in the counter-UAS domain.

Besides, some recent works have already analyzed multi-agent systems for CUS, although they were focused on the single phases of the counter-UAS process, i.e., sensing or mitigation separately. For example, reference [14] proposed a network of defense drones, which is capable of self-organizing its formation to intercept malicious drones. However, this work specifically focused on formation management algorithms to realize intercept and capture formations for the mitigation of drone intrusions, without considering neutralization aspects. Instead, reference [26] proposed a multi-drone framework for the autonomous detection of rogue drones in a defined airspace and detailed the preliminary development of a hardware and software testbed, based on commercial systems.

Other ongoing research activities are developing a cooperative drone-based CUS covering all the phases of the counter-UAS process. For example, the SWADAR (Swarm Advanced Detection And Tracking) project [27] has been awarded the Defense Innovation Prize 2020 (https://www.edrmagazine.eu/defence-innovation-prize, last accessed on 13 February 2022) (20.RTI.PRZ.080, "Innovative Solutions/Technologies for the Countering of Swarms of UAVs, specifically on the Protection of Static and Dynamic Land Facilities and Platforms"), assigned by the European Defense Agency (EDA). SWADAR builds an intelligent drone-based network for mobile proximal sensing, tracking and neutralization of intruder swarms, as shown in Figure 2. Based on sensing and tracking data, SWADAR autonomously assesses the behavior of the rogue swarm by evaluating instantaneous and variational swarming metrics (i.e., cohesion, segregation, etc.) that can help in identifying the attack scenario and predicting the course of action of the swarm attack. Such information supports the selection of optimal neutralization actions to suppress the enemy swarming behavior. Moreover, SWADAR relies on on-board sensors, like LiDAR (light detection and ranging), optical and infrared sensors, etc., which are typically available on the market.

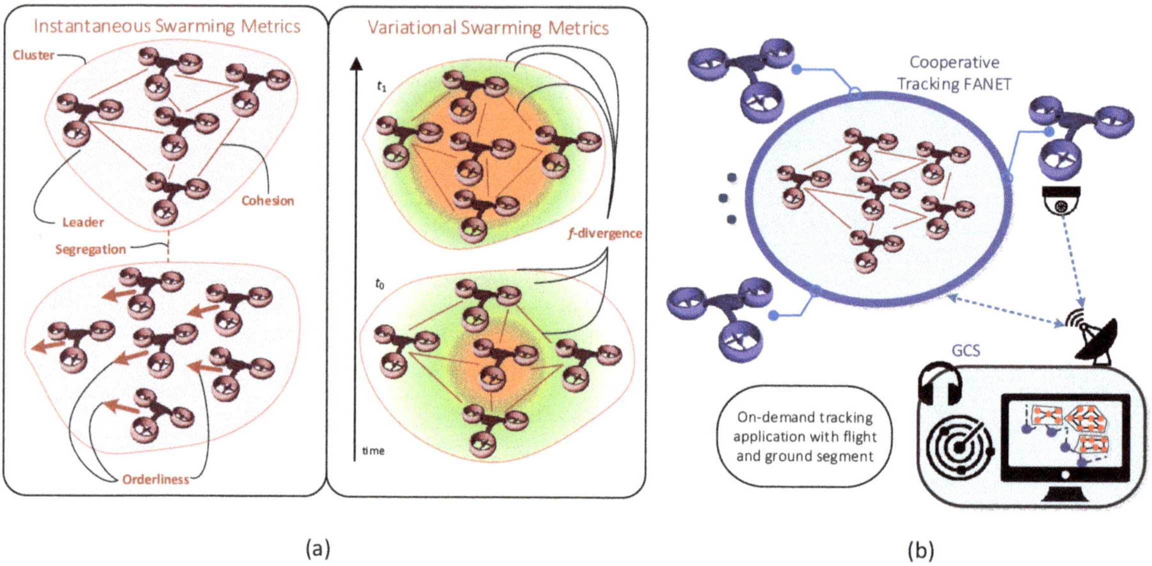

Figure 2. SWADAR concept for assessing swarming metrics (**a**) and for multi-UAV cooperative tracking (**b**) [27]. The left part shows some examples of useful metrics to measure the swarm behavior of intruder drones. Some of these metrics are: the cohesion, the segregation, the presence of hierarchical structures and clusters and the f-divergence (i.e., the temporal variation of the spatial distributions of the swarm).

In the US, the DARPA is funding the Aerial Dragnet program that seeks to perform persistent wide-area surveillance of multiple small drones in urban terrain on a city-wide scale. This innovative sensor array should be mounted on tethered drones, enabling a non-line-of-sight (NLOS) tracking and identification of a wide range of slow, low-flying threats [28].

Worthy of note is also the European project JEY-CUAS (Joint European System for Countering Unmanned Aerial Systems) [29], which will pave the way for the development of a joint European counter-UAS capability by developing a new-generation C-UAS system based on a modular and flexible plug'n'play architecture to include the emerging challenge of mini drones, increasingly used for defense purposes. The solution will contribute to an improvement of the situational awareness and reaction engagement by reducing the minimum reaction time.

However, not everything can be achieved through the use of mini drones. In some cases, ground systems are required—if we consider the case of early detection, it would be inefficient to keep drones in flight permanently to check for the presence of malicious drones in the area to be protected. Furthermore, with mini drones, we should consider SWaP constraints, and consequently, not all of the operations necessary to fight the threat could be performed via these platforms. For example, it is not possible to use strong neutralizers (like high-power electromagnetics or high-power laser), which cannot be integrated on mini drones due to obvious SWaP constraints. However, mini drones can be a suitable solution, especially in civil contexts where protection is mainly required towards small drones.

3. Sensing System

The perception of a threat makes use of the sensing system, consisting of one or more sensors capable of collecting the information extrapolated from the electromagnetic or acoustic spectrum, depending on the technology and the signal processing involved. In general, the perception operation can be divided into the following phases:

- Detection: The finding of one or more object within the airspace to be monitored. In this first phase, the system is not yet able to distinguish whether the detected object is actually a drone. This phase can be characterized through the two indicators "Detection Rate" and "False Alarm Rate", which express the probability, respectively, of correct detection and false alarm.
- Classification: Once the detection event has occurred, it is necessary to verify that the detected object is actually present and that it is a drone. It could happen, for example, that the target detected in the previous phase is a bird, which has electromagnetic characteristics that can be similar to those of a drone (the radar cross section or the size and geometric shape that is possible recognize visually). This verification is also called "recognition" or "identification". Subsequently, the system extrapolates some salient attributes (features) of the drone, such as the type (size, type of propulsion, number of rotors, model), the possible location of a remote pilot, the presence of a payload and its typology. This phase may be found in the literature under the term "identification".
- Localization/Tracking: The target is located by estimating its position in terms of angle and distance. Triangulation techniques can be used to increase accuracy. Once the target has been locked in, it must be tracked throughout its flight. Flight trajectory could also be predicted.

The level of reliability of this information must be as high as possible so that the C2 system can perform the threat analysis and select and adopt the most appropriate mitigation measures in the shortest time interval. Detection, recognition and identification (or classification) could be performed by a single type of sensor if the technology and associated processing are compatible with the required output. Where this is not the case, it is possible to adopt a heterogeneous sensing system consisting of sensors with different technologies, which can contribute, thanks to data/sensor fusion techniques, to obtain a reliable level of identification and to improve performance in terms of range, detection time of the anti-drone system, detection rate and reduction of false alarms.

Clearly, to face an attack by a team or swarm of drones, the sensing system should be enriched with functionalities for the perception and the processing of information about the features that are strictly related to the teaming or swarming behavior of the attacker.

In more detail, one of the most complex scenarios that an anti-drone system can face is that relating to the attack of a drone swarm, e.g., for saturation attacks and to overwhelm the counter-capability of the target's defense. As for a hostile team, this scenario requires that the detection capabilities are also used for the extraction of "global" features that characterize the swarm and not only for the "local" features related to the drones that compose it. Moreover, specific information should be collected to quantify swarming metrics (e.g., consistency, cohesion, etc.) related to the swarming behavior. For this purpose, it may be useful to acquire both local information (e.g., flight configuration, geometry characteristics and speed) and global information (e.g., number of vehicles, relative distances, geometry of the swarm, etc.) [30]. Such information will be essential to infer the mitigation decisions, since they may support the identification of the drones that represent the "focal points" within the hostile swarm.

3.1. Sensing Technologies

An anti-drone system, to fulfill its purpose, must be equipped with a sensing system consisting of one or more sensors, including those of different technologies. There are, in fact, different types of sensors, which are characterized by the observed phenomenon, electromagnetic or acoustic, and by the spectrum band they use. For example, image sensors operate in the electromagnetic spectrum, in all visible frequencies, while a radar can operate at microwave frequencies.

The first technological distinction to which we can refer for the classification of sensors is between active and passive sensing. The substantial difference between the two types is based on the use of energy to "feel" the objects present in space. For active sensors, an electromagnetic or acoustic radiation is emitted, with which it is possible to directly measure the distance of objects in space through, for example, the measurement of the delay between the radiation emitted by the sensor itself and that received by the back-scattered reflections of the objects. Radars and LiDAR sensors belong to this category. On the other hand, passive sensors receive energy from the environment and from the object to be detected, which can be used to reconstruct useful information. Most of the passive sensors used are optical and infrared cameras.

There are many reviews on the current state-of-the art technology in this wide variety of sensors, both commercial and academic ones (for example: [31]). Instead, in the following subsections, we are focusing on the literature with drone-based-only use cases. So, it is possible to assume that all the following sensing technologies are suitable for use aboard mini and micro-drones.

3.1.1. Acoustic Sensors

The engine and propellers of the drones generate acoustic waves in the frequency range between 20 Hz and 20 kHz, which give rise to the acoustic signature of the vehicle. A single microphone can acquire this information and thanks to the comparison with a library of acoustic signatures, it can distinguish a drone from other objects and carry out the identification phase of the aircraft by obtaining information on the model. If the number of microphones is increased, it is possible to adopt spatial diversity techniques or use beamforming techniques by arranging the installation of an array of microphones onboard the drone. In this way, it is possible to estimate the azimuth and elevation of one or more targets through the direction of arrival (DoA), perform multiple target tracking and mitigate the ego-noise effects, i.e., the noises of the electric motors and the moving propellers of the drone itself.

This type of sensor is particularly economical, but is sensitive to environmental noise and climatic conditions related to wind or temperature and typically has a detection range that depends also on the microphone array size. This technology is typically used for ground-based counter-UAS platforms, but no airborne commercial products have been found. However, as the following articles demonstrate, the dimensions of a microphone array are compatible with the installation onboard a drone. For example, in [32] and in [33], some small-sized drones were set up with an array of microphones to locate a generic noise source. The ability to perform localization and tracking in terms of DoA and to identify noise sources were analyzed in [34], in which a circular array (ground-based) was used and, thanks to sound signal processing and array signal processing, an identification success rate of 80% was shown under the test conditions described in the article.

The detection range depends on the quality of the microphones, the characteristics of the array and the type of processing performed. In fact, the results that can be found in the literature vary in a fairly wide range, from 5 m of [35] up to 600 m of [36]. In [37], a ground-based system of two arrays of four microphones (spaced by 1 m) each was used for the location of a drone through the calculation of the DoA. Comparable results were obtained with GPS accuracy and a detection range of 100 m. In [36], a ground-based configuration was used with the arrangement of the array of tetrahedron microphones. In this case, a detection range of up to 600 m with a success rate of 99.5% was highlighted, at the same time, however, the tracking capabilities were poor. In [38], on the other hand, an array of 120 elements arranged on a spherical structure allowed the detection and identification of various commercial drones up to about 290 m. It should be noted that the classification range may be lower than the detection range, as shown by the test campaigns carried out for the system described in [39].

Finally, an array of eight microphones was used in a scenario that is very similar to the one considered in this study ([35]), involving a tracker drone and an intruder drone. In this case, machine learning was used, and signal processing is done in real-time onboard the aircraft. The detection range was extremely small, equal to about 5 m, but there were excellent tracking capabilities.

3.1.2. Radio Frequency Sensors

Radio frequency (RF) sensors capture the electromagnetic signals radiated by a malicious drone or by the remote pilot's radio control, if present. It is, therefore, a passive method that does not require the transmission of electromagnetic waves and, therefore, has no restrictions on use (e.g., in an urban environment). Most commercial drones use an uplink radio channel for remote control commands and a downlink channel for telemetry and video signal. In the case of autonomous drones, there may be only direct downlink transmission to the ground control station (GCS) or communication between the nodes of the network in a swarm. The detection systems based on this technology make use of a RF receiver between 400 MHz and 6 GHz and an array of antennas for the possible exploitation of MIMO techniques. The receiver can be implemented through software-defined radio (SDR) due to the reconfigurability and flexibility characteristics of the radio frequency front-end and associated baseband processing. RF detection can be performed with techniques based on a known protocol or recognition of the spectral pattern. In this case, we refer to drones that communicate with the remote pilot through communication standards such as IEEE 802.11 (Wi-Fi), a case that covers a large part of commercial drones. In this way, it is possible to retrieve the MAC address of the device and trace the specific drone model.

In addition to the recognition of the spectrum and the communication protocol, it is possible to recognize the RF fingerprint of the radio controller and then carry out the classification of the drone through machine learning techniques, as described in [40]. These techniques are not very effective if a known pattern is not used, if the communication scheme has been customized or if the MAC address database is not updated ([41]).

For this reason, techniques based on the localization of the RF signal have been developed. So, the DoA estimation is carried out in two different ways: based on received signal strength (RSS) or spectral analysis. In the first case, the results are less accurate than in the second. For example, in [42], an architecture based on an array of four antennas and an SDR platform for processing was proposed, in which an angular precision between 1.9° and 6° was achieved over a coverage range between −60° and 60°. In [43], an experiment was presented in which, thanks to the use of commercial SDR platforms (FPGA-based), it was possible to localize small drones with a maximum range of 75 m. Although previous publications have been ground-based, they described techniques that could also be used on-board. In [15], a UAV-based system was described, in which a tracker drone can track an intruder drone by measuring RSS. The coordinated use of multiple drones for locating the RF source was also considered in [44,45]. In the latter, the air-to-air communication channel was simulated and compared with the ground-to-air one in an urban context. The research aimed to analyze the differences in terms of location accuracy vs. SNR. The results showed a clear advantage for the air-to-air solution.

3.1.3. Optical Sensors

Optical sensors detect electromagnetic waves in the range of frequencies from infrared (300 GHz) to ultraviolet (790 THz). It is a passive technology, therefore with low energy consumption, which can provide two-dimensional images of the surrounding environment. Optical sensors can be divided into two main categories, depending on the frequency band in which they work: visible (VIS) or non-visible. For example, the first category includes optical cameras, which can detect electromagnetic radiation in the 430–790 THz frequency range, while the second category includes thermal cameras, which convert infrared radiation (300–430 THz) into images.

Thanks to image processing techniques based on computer vision (CV), it is possible to detect, classify and track drones that fall within the field of view (FoV) of the optical sensor. The aforementioned operations are similar to object detection and tracking, which is a much-studied problem in the CV field. An object can be detected thanks to features such as geometric shape or outline and features related to movement between consecutive frames. In the event that the sensing system is mounted on-board a drone, the dynamism of the scene must be considered, which introduces problems of variation in lighting conditions and background characteristics. The sensors that operate in the visible frequency band show their limits in the case of adverse weather conditions (rain and fog) and the case of low ambient light such as at night.

Infrared (IR) sensors allow us to overcome these limits ([46,47]) and offer greater robustness against rapid changes in illumination [48]. Two types of existing approaches in the literature are essential [49]: direct or feature-based techniques and machine learning methods. The first category includes algorithms that try to identify a specific region of interest in the image by looking at the best similarity with a reference representation of the target. In direct techniques, information on the local gradient is used in each pixel of the image, while in feature-based techniques, features are used that are followed in a sequence of frames through specific descriptors. The detection and tracking capabilities are good, as highlighted in [50], where the processing is based on techniques of background subtraction and optical flow calculation.

Machine learning techniques are very popular among the scientific community. The training of a neural network for target detection and classification is one of the most studied fields of CV. In fact, given the great accessibility of standard optical cameras, this research area has reached a fairly mature stage. Thanks to the large availability of public image datasets, UAV detection challenges are often organized at international conference workshops, such as Advanced Video and Signal-based Surveillance (AVSS) conference and International Conference on Computer Vision Systems (ICCVS).

Image classification with the deep learning paradigm is one of the most active fields of research. Most of the works that employ deep neural networks (DNNs) for drone classification problems utilize a generic object detection architecture, with a powerful DNN as a classification model targeted for drones. The most used architectures are:

- Single-shot multi-box detectors (SSD)
- Faster R-CNN

A particular SSD architecture is the You Only Look Once (YOLO) model, which has gained great popularity thanks to a particular computational efficiency that allows its use also on embedded systems in real time.

The adoption of different CNN architectures (e.g., Zeiler–Fergus (ZF), visual geometry group (VGG16)) for drone detection has been investigated in [51]. To overcome the limited amount of data available for training the deep networks, authors exploited transfer learning from ImageNet and performed a pre-training to fine-tune the models. The experimental results revealed that VGG16 with faster region-based convolutional neural network (R-CNN) achieved the best performance among all the considered architectures.

The authors of "Drone Detection in Long-Range Surveillance" [52] worked on a previous iteration of the same dataset, with quite good results in the detection of small objects. They applied a Faster R-CNN network with various backbones and showed that ResNet-101 had the best results.

In [53], a deep-learning-based detection method was adopted, termed YOLOv2, whose training is performed using an artificial dataset obtained by mixing images of real birds and drones, each with a different background. The obtained results demonstrated that the diversity and the scale of the dataset have a positive impact on the detection and tracking processes.

The size, weight, required power and cost of the cameras is such that their use on drones does not find particular impediments and certainly makes it possible to use them as a sensing system for C-UAS for all operations of detection, identification and tracking.

3.1.4. LiDAR Sensors

LiDAR uses electromagnetic radiation at the optical and infrared wavelengths. It is an active sensor that emits electromagnetic waves and receives reflected waves, similarly to the operation of the radar, only at much higher frequencies, between 200 THz and 400 THz. Thanks to the calculation of the time difference between the emitted and received ray (time of flight), it is possible to process a 3D map of the surrounding environment and, thus, obtain the position, direction and speed of the objects in the scene. The speed can also be calculated from the doppler shift due to moving objects. These sensors are widely used in the automotive sector for safety systems related to autonomous driving (adaptive cruise control, lane-keeping, emergency braking). They can be used for simultaneous localization and mapping (SLAM), which allows robots to orient themselves in an unknown space and GPS-denied environment. The compact size allows it to be used on-board UAVs, both as a payload, for example for aerial mapping applications, and as avionics for collision avoidance systems.

There are different types of LiDAR sensors: those that measure only the range, called 1D, to those that measure the angle of arrival in the azimuth and elevation, as in an optical camera, and in addition, they obtain information on the range. It should be noted that the maximum operating range depends on the reflectivity value of the material and the color of the object hit by the light radiation. Given the wavelengths, the LiDAR (especially in the 1D case) can have a reduced operation in conditions of fog, clouds or rain, but offers the advantage of being able to be used also in conditions of low ambient light (at night, for example). The processing of the data acquired by this type of sensor requires a relatively low–medium processing effort compared to other types of sensors.

Most publications in the context of counter-UAS systems are ground-based. In [54], a LADAR (laser detection and ranging) is described, based on LASER, with a peak power of 700 kW, which allows for the increase of the operating range up to 2 km. In [55], an interesting experimental test campaign was carried out with a 3D LiDAR system mounted on a land vehicle to determine the probability of detection for mini drones. The results showed how, with sensors with a maximum operating range of 100 m, it is possible to have a high detection success rate for targets within 30 m. In [56], sensor fusion techniques were applied between a 3D LiDAR sensor and an RGB camera for detection, localization and tracking applications, with a maximum range of 50 m.

In addition to the CUS systems, publications in the field of collision avoidance systems (CAS) for UAVs that use sensing techniques based on LiDAR were also considered. The problem of obstacle detection is very similar to that of the detection/identification and localization of malicious UAVs. In [57], machine learning and data fusion techniques were used for the combined use of 3D LiDAR and optical cameras, obtaining an obstacle detection range of about 30 m. In [58], a 2D LiDAR sensor was used, obtaining a detection range of about 8 m compared to the sensor's maximum range of 25 m. The analysis of the state of the art shows how LiDAR-based technology is widely used for the detection of targets concerning CUS systems and obstacles concerning CAS. The ability to separate objects from the background and range measurement are interesting features for this category of sensors and can be used, for example, in the extrapolation of geometric features related to a possible scenario involving a hostile swarm.

3.1.5. Radar Sensors

A radar is an active sensor, consisting of a transmitting segment that radiates electromagnetic waves in the frequency range from 3 MHz to 300 GHz, depending on the application. The waves are reflected by the target objects and are received by the receiving segment of the radar. By properly processing the received signal, it is possible, for example, to calculate the time of arrival and the frequency shift due to the Doppler effect to obtain information on the distance and speed of the target. The power of the received signal is directly proportional to the radar cross section (RCS), a parameter that measures how easily an object is detectable and which depends on the size, material, distance and angle of the incident and reflected wave. The RCS of mini-sized drones and their speed have lower values than that of larger drones and aircrafts for which classic radar systems are designed. To increase the detection possibilities of drones, the micro movements of vibrating and rotating structures, such as motors and propellers, can be taken into consideration. In fact, such structures have a characterizing micro-Doppler signature (mDS) [59]), thanks to which, they can be recognized. There is a category of radars, called passive, which are not equipped with a transmitter but use the electromagnetic radiation emitted by external sources, such as those of the towers for broadcasting the DVB-T television signal, normally already present in the communication channel. This category will not be taken into consideration because it requires a priori knowledge of these sources and a static installation of the passive radar.

The main advantages of the radar are related to the robustness against environmental conditions: the operation is independent of the light conditions and atmospheric conditions. The disadvantage is that to obtain a high detection range, it is necessary to increase the transmission power, the limit of which will depend on the power available on-board the drone. For this reason, it is not possible to use a classic surveillance radar, and the use of the FMCW type (frequency-modulated continuous wave) is preferred, which has, among other things, a more affordable cost. Signal processing can be done on software-defined radio platforms equipped with FPGA technology and RF front-end. The most popular radars in this area are mmWave and UWB radars, with one millimeter and ultra-wideband respectively.

The literature analysis ([60–62]) showed that the detection range is typically around 100 m for millimeter-wave radars. In [63], a pair of UWB radars were used to locate a drone up to about 80 m. The classification skills are very good ([64–67]), thanks to machine learning techniques. In particular, in [67], the authors were able to discern the weight of the payload of a commercial drone through the analysis of the mDS. Using a radar system operating at the 2.4 GHz frequency, the classification allowed recognition of the cases that belonged to the set {no payload, 200 g payload, 500 g payload} with 90% success and a maximum detection distance of 100 m. In addition to the analysis of the scientific literature relating to CUS systems, it is also possible to investigate that relating to the applications of radar for collision avoidance, as the detection problem is common to the two systems. In this regard, by deepening the survey proposed in [68], it is possible to confirm the feasibility of installing these systems on-board small drones, despite the stringent SWaP constraints.

3.2. Sensing Technologies Comparison

As seen, the proximal sensing capability of a team of mini drones is the main clear advantage over a static, ground-based CUS. For example, the optical occlusion problem could have a minor impact on a drone-based video sensing system thanks to the possibility to change the perspective, taking advantage of the mobility of the drone itself. On the other hand, there is the need for an accurate video stabilization to mitigate the blur effect due to the drone movement. In Table 2, some pros and cons of using sensing technologies integrated in mini-drone-based platforms with respect to the static ground case are summed up.

Table 2. Pros and cons of using sensing technologies on-board a drone.

Sensing Technique	Pros	Cons
Acoustic	Possibility to move close to the target and improve the identification task.	Need for proper ego-noise cancellation due to the propellers noise.
Optical	Possibility to change the perspective and to operate close to the target with a higher resolution and better identification capabilities.	Limited computational power; need for efficient video stabilization.
RF	Better conditions of the air-to-air channel with respect to the ground-to-air one.	
LiDAR	Possibility to move close to the target and improve the detection phase.	Limited on-board power.
Radar	Thanks to the proximal sensing, less power of the active sensor is required.	Limited on-board power.

Each technology has a different detection range, classification capacity and energy requirement. For example, the optical sensors in the visible work very well only in line of sight (LOS) conditions, while the RF sensors can work in non-line of sight (NLOS) conditions. It is, therefore, impossible to reach a satisfactory situational awareness level with the adoption of a single technology and, in this regard, the simultaneous adoption of different sensing techniques is the winning way, as previously addressed in the concept of the defensive team and the related cooperative sensor network. Using sensor or data fusion algorithms allows for better results than those that would be obtained individually. For example, in [69], test campaigns were carried out on a detection system that showed how the use of the data fusion technique increased the detection rate. These improvements were achieved at the expense of system complexity and computational effort. The identification of the technologies that best complement each other is a useful activity in order to optimize the level of situational awareness with respect to the complexity and cost of the system.

The following tables have been constructed to better highlight the characteristics of each technology. Table 3 contains a rough estimate of the performance in terms of "detection", "classification" and "global features characterization". It is not easy to establish the performance of each technology in absolute terms, which is why "low" to "high" range values have been indicated and express a qualitative judgment based on the literature reported in the previous paragraphs. It should be noted that the distances detected in the experimental setups can be numerically very different from the datasheet of the CUS products that can be found on the market. The explanation of this deviation could depend on the different level of optimization that an engineering product has in front of the experimental setup and the different requirements of ground- and sky-based devices. However, the relationship between the different technologies should be respected beyond the absolute numerical values.

Table 3. Sensing techniques' relative performances.

Sensing Technique	Detection Range	Classification Capability	Global Feature Characterization
RF Scanner	Higher than 150 m	High	Low
RF RSS	Higher than 150 m	Low	Low
Acoustic	Higher than 150 m	Medium	Low
Lidar	Between 50 m and 150 m	Low	Low
Radar	Higher than 150 m	Medium	Medium
VIS	Higher than 150 m	High	High
IR	Lower than 150 m	Low	Low

Table 4 is populated with the characteristics of localization/tracking and robustness against adverse environmental and meteorological conditions.

Table 4. Sensing techniques' tracking properties and robustness against environmental and meteorological conditions.

Sensing Technique	Localization	Multi-Tracking	Meteorological Conditions	Environmental Conditions
RF Scanner	DoA	Possible	-	RF Spectrum congestion
RF RSS	DoA	Possible	-	RF Spectrum congestion
Acoustic	DoA	Yes	Wind	Noise
Lidar	DoA/Range	Possible	Fog, rain	Direct Light
Radar	DoA/Range/Speed	Yes	-	-
Optical VIS	DoA	Yes	Fog, rain	Night
Optical IR	DoA	Yes	Fog, rain	Background temperature

The RF, acoustic, radar and optical VIS sensors have a wide detection range, in particular, the first two are able to work also in NLOS mode. Optical sensors, however, are not a good choice in the presence of adverse weather conditions, and, in particular, VIS sensors are unable to work in the absence of light.

As far as the classification process is concerned, optical systems are best expressed in conditions of proximal sensing. RF and acoustic sensors use machine learning-based pattern recognition techniques for the identification of remotely piloted amateur drones. RF systems also allow for the estimation of the position of the pilot in addition to the specific model of drone used. Radars have good classification capabilities based on the micro-Doppler signature.

Radar allows the direct estimation of the distance and speed of one or more drones; for this reason, it can be considered as an adequate technology for the extraction of the global features of a drone swarm, and for their localization and for operation of tracking. The use of optical sensors flanked by the ranging capability of the LiDAR allows, in this case, for the extraction of visual features that allow the determination of the geometric characteristics of the swarm, such as the occupied area and the flight configuration. Furthermore, tracking is a task that is typically dealt with via computer vision with a good level of reliability.

Table 5 proposes a subdivision into "main" and "complementary" technologies on the basis of the information developed so far.

Table 5. Main and complementary technologies.

Task	Main	Complementary
Detection	Radar, Acoustic, RF	Optical
Classification	Optical, RF, Acoustic	Radar
Global Feature	Optical, Radar	Lidar
Localization	Radar, Lidar	RF, Acoustic
Tracking	Radar, Optical, Acoustic	Lidar, RF

For each phase of the sensing, "main" technologies are indicated, which have a high probability of completing the task successfully. The "complementary" technologies were considered those that can improve the result obtained by the "main" ones.

4. Neutralization Systems

Neutralization systems are activated by the command-and-control system to respond to the threat posed by the detected malicious drone(s). Multiple neutralization systems can be activated simultaneously in order to cooperate to improve the effectiveness of the neutralization. Furthermore, these systems can be located on one or more distinct platforms according to the CUS physical architecture.

According to the classification reported in [9], neutralization systems can carry out the following actions: warning, control, interruption, disabling and destruction. These actions are implemented through neutralization techniques, more simply indicated as neutralizers (or mitigators). Neutralizers have been classified in different ways in the literature. In [9], neutralizers were divided into physical and non-physical based on whether there was physical damage to the m-drone. Moreover, in the case of non-physical neutralizers, there is no contact between the neutralizer and the m-drone, but some of them can actually cause damage to the m-drone. A similar subdivision was also shown in [10], even if some neutralizers fell into different classes. However, in [5], the subdivision was made between electronic neutralizers, based substantially on electromagnetic waves that do not cause direct damage to the m-drone (for example jamming), and kinetics neutralizers, which intercept the drone with physical means (for example nets), but the latter ones also include high power lasers and microwaves. Given that each definition described gives rise to some ambiguity, the following classification will be adopted:

- Electronic neutralizers, based on the use of electromagnetic waves capable of interrupting (operations), disabling or even destroying (at least partially) a drone;
- Kinetic-mechanical neutralizers, based on the use of mechanical means, which involve contact between the neutralizer (or a part of it) and the malicious drone.

4.1. Electronic Neutralizers

Electronic neutralizers allow instant actions, can easily aim at the target and are not affected by environmental agents (for example wind and gravity). They can be implemented with different techniques, such as cyber-attacks, high-powered electromagnetics and lasers. Cyber-attacks include jamming and spoofing techniques, which constitute the vast majority of neutralizers used in the context of UAVs, protocol-based attacks (for example, de-authentication and address resolution protocol (ARP) cache poisoning in the case of Wi-Fi networks) and replay attacks. Below a survey is reported.

4.1.1. Radio Frequency Jamming

Radio frequency (RF) jamming techniques allow users to disturb, lower the quality of or interrupt communications between the malicious drone and the respective remote-control station. They consist of generating an interfering signal in order to lower the SINR (signal-to-interference-plus-noise ratio) input into the receiver of the m-drone in order to make it difficult, if not impossible, to receive the information sent by remote control. Obviously, it is also possible to jam on the remote control in order to disturb any feedback data sent by the m-drone. A jammed drone can have different reactions depending on how it is designed [5]: it can make a landing in its current position, it can perform a return-to-home procedure, it can fall to the ground without control or it can fly in a random direction with no control.

RF jamming can be applied to other signals in addition to the remote control one. For example, in [70], jamming was applied to a video link used for the first-person view (FPV) function, showing the possibility of disabling this function and preventing the operator from maneuvering the drone in the absence of LOS conditions. Jamming can also be used to improve the robustness of a wireless communication in the presence of an eavesdropper. This is the case of cooperative jamming, in which a relay node transmits a jamming signal at the same time as the legitimate source transmits its message in order to disturb any eavesdropper [71]. By reversing the perspective, jamming can also be used to increase the probability of interception of a communication. In [72], for example, a legitimate drone, used to follow the flight of two suspicious UAVs in order to prevent any threats, transmits jamming signals to the receiving UAV in order to force the decrease of the exchanged data rate and increase the likelihood of interception of information exchanged between suspicious drones.

There are several radio frequency jamming techniques. In this paper, we refer to the simplified taxonomy used in [10], but a more detailed one is available in [73]. The first technique, the noise jamming (also known as barrage jamming), is the simplest to implement and consists of applying a noisy signal to a portion or to the entire spectral band occupied by the signal which has to be jammed in order to reduce the channel capacity and increase the number of errors in the received data. Noise jamming can also be used in the presence of m-drones equipped with a synthetic aperture radar (SAR) able to offer autonomy thanks to SLAM techniques. In this case, the interference generated by the jamming signal may be sufficient to mask the echoes related to the SAR, making the latter unusable, as highlighted in [74]. The second technique is the tone jamming: in this case, one or more tones (i.e., narrow band signals) are employed for the purpose of generating interference. The effectiveness depends on the positioning of the tones and the transmitted power. The third technique, named sweep jamming, consists of transmitting a narrow band signal that sweeps the spectrum of frequencies of interest over time. At each instant of time, only a portion of the spectrum is covered, but in a certain period (the amount of time necessary to make a complete sweep) the whole band of interest is affected. The fourth, and final, technique is smart jamming, also known as protocol-aware jamming. It is applicable when the characteristics of the target signal are known a priori. For example, if the communication system under jamming uses frequency hopping spread spectrum (FHSS) and the hopping pattern is known, then the neutralizer can perform the same frequency hops as the target and reduce the bandwidth required by the interfering signal. Similarly, if the target communication system uses direct sequence spread spectrum (DSSS), the spreading properties of the signal to be attacked can be used to transmit a jamming signal possessing a high correlation with respect to the original one in order to increase the bit error rate of the communication to neutralize. Therefore, smart jamming is both effective, as it is calibrated precisely on the target signal to be disturbed, and efficient in power, as it operates only in correspondence with the target signal (in time and frequency). In any case, if no prior knowledge of the communication system to be neutralized is known, an analysis of the relevant signal must be carried out in order to identify its characteristics and weak points. Consequently, SDR technologies are well suited to the implementation of smart jamming; thanks to their flexibility, they allow for both the analysis of the target signal and the reproduction of an ad hoc signal to be used as an interfering signal ([75,76]).

The performance of the above jamming techniques can be assessed with respect to most available communications on commercial drones, i.e., the communications based on spread spectrum, like the transmission systems ACCST (Advanced Continuous Channel Shifting Technology), based on FHSS, and FASST (Futuba Advanced Spread Spectrum Technology), based on FHSS with the addition of Gaussian filtering and DSSS applied on the data. Furthermore, in order to consider even drones equipped with Wi-Fi connection, the IEEE 802.11b standard, based on DSSS, and the 802.11g standard, based on orthogonal frequency division multiplexing (OFDM), can be assessed. The listed systems cannot complete the panorama of implementable communications, but offer an early coverage of the transmission protocols (with reference to the physical layer) typically used by drones. The experimental evaluation of tone, sweep and smart jamming with respect to ACCST and FASST is shown in [75]. The results showed that smart jamming is significantly more efficient than tone and sweep jamming—the tone jammer can successfully jam a single channel of the link but is not sufficient to terminate the remote control link, and the sweep jammer requires relatively high jammer-to-signal ratios (JSRs) to completely prevent the communication, whereas smart achieves successful jamming at relatively low JSRs but requires significant knowledge about the targeted system. In the same work, noise jamming was also evaluated (with respect to an FHSS/DSSS hybrid system by means of simulations), resulting in the techniques which require a higher JSR to prevent the communication. When considering the impact that the jamming signals have on WLAN devices, a comparison between noise and tone jamming is shown in [77]. If the jamming signal is stronger than the desired signal, the 802.11g system cannot operate in any mode unlike the 802.11b system, which uses lower rate DSSS modes, however, at the certain packet error ratio (PER) the 802.11g system can offer higher data rates than the 802.1lb system under wideband jamming. When tone jamming is used, the performance of the 802.11g system depends highly on the jamming frequency. In DSSS systems, the jamming frequency is not as important a factor as in OFDM, but higher JSRs are required to increase the PER with respect to the noise jamming. An experimental comparison between sweep and smart jamming for the WLAN case is shown again in [75]; in the most extreme cases, the sweep jammer halted the WLAN communication, while the protocol-aware jammer solely limited its maximum throughput.

Neutralizers based on RF jamming techniques, also known as jammers, can be integrated on static, mobile and/or portable ground platforms (examples are illustrated in [78–80]). It is also possible to integrate them on aerial platforms, like mini drones. Finally, they can be active, i.e., they continuously transmit interfering RF signals or randomly to save energy, or are reactive, i.e., they transmit interfering signals only after having determined that the monitored frequency spectrum is occupied by unknown signals (see [81]).

4.1.2. GNSS Jamming

GNSS (Global Navigation Satellite System) jamming is not a different technique from RF jamming, but simply refers to the jamming of GNSS signals. It is treated separately because of its relevance considering that GNSS signals are typically those most subject to neutralization. Signals received from satellites are characterized by low power value and, thus, are vulnerable to interfering signals; therefore, the technique under consideration can be effective. In fact, as reported in the study in [82], jamming the GPS receiver of a commercial drone can result in drifting and control difficulties, as well as preventing the return to home (RTH) procedure from working properly.

To implement GNSS jamming, the same radio frequency techniques illustrated in the preceding paragraph can be used. These techniques have been analyzed and evaluated in relation to GPS signals in [83], together with successive pulses jamming, which involves transmitting a sequence of pulses over time with a small duty cycle to the central frequency of interest and can be seen as a particular implementation of noise jamming. Best results are obtained with smart jamming and sweep jamming—the first technique is the most effective when compared to its purpose (making the GPS signal to the receiver unusable), while the strength of the second one is the simplicity of implementation, although it should be noted that the obtained efficiency depends on the speed used to sweep the frequency band.

GNSS jamming can be ineffective when malicious drones are equipped with IMU sensors. In this case, if the drone is equipped with a remote control link, RF jamming can also be useful. Similarly, GNSS jamming is highly important with m-drones not equipped with a remote control (i.e., RF jamming is not applicable), which follow a pre-programmed route with the aid of GNSS. Consequently, intrinsic weaknesses shown by RF and GNSS jamming can be compensated for by their simultaneous deployment in order to improve neutralization effectiveness.

Finally, considering the strategic importance of GNSS services, it should be noted that much research has been done in order to prevent and/or mitigate GNSS jamming; some methods, including those ones based on antenna arrays, are illustrated in the study reported in [5]. Therefore, a CUS shall pay attention to the effects obtained by means of such a neutralization.

4.1.3. Spoofing

Spoofing consists of generating a plausible fake signal with enough strength to trick the malicious drone receiver into believing it is the legitimate signal. The signals under spoofing can be related to some different applications or devices: remote control communications, payload data communications, GNSS, sensors. In order to perform spoofing, it is necessary to know the communication protocol stacks used (not only the physical layer) so that they can be reproduced. If the stacks are known it is possible to analyze them a priori, otherwise first it is necessary to determine them in some way. Therefore, spoofing is a complicated method and not always a successful one. In any case, at least in theory, by using spoofing techniques, it could be possible to take control of the malicious drone and make it move away from a protected area. Some examples are shown in [84,85].

As mentioned above, a typical class of signals often involved in spoofing is represented by GNSS signals. In this specific case, it is possible to make the m-drone land, engage the autopilot, remain hovering or follow a desired path. Studies presenting methods for hijacking or disabling a drone using GNSS spoofing are reported in [86–88]. An interesting study is reported in [89], where the authors determined the necessary conditions for capturing a drone through GPS spoofing and examined a possible post-capture control system. Furthermore, two different strategies are depicted: overt spoofing and covert spoofing. In the first case, the spoofer (i.e., the spoofing-based neutralizer) does not hide its attempt to "subjugate" the target system and, therefore, does not align the forged signals with the legitimate ones. In particular, after a first phase in which it jams on the GPS receiver in order to force it to lose the lock and reacquire all the signals, it can take control, as long as the counterfeited signals have a power that satisfies two conditions: exceeding the receiver acquisition threshold and forcing the authentic GPS signals below the aforementioned threshold exploiting the receiver AGC (automatic gain controller) function. Experimental trials have shown that when the ratio between the counterfeit signal power (Pc) and the legitimate signal (Pl) is equal to 10 dB, the previous conditions are satisfied (as confirmed also in [90]). Instead, in the case of covert spoofing, the spoofer assumes that the GPS receiver and the navigation system are equipped with spoofing detection techniques, which must be evaded using appropriate counterfeit signals. Experimentally, it has been verified that if the spoofer can estimate the speed and position of the target drone with errors under certain thresholds (respectively below 10 m/s and 50 m), then it can reliably and covertly take control of the tracking loops of commercial receivers using small Pc over Pl ratio (of the order of units of dB). Notice that covert spoofing can be generalized and applied to any type of communication, especially if it has been assumed that the malicious drone receiver is equipped with anti-spoofing technology. In these cases, the counterfeit signal should be correlated to the legitimate signal as much as possible and with a similar power level trend over time, so that it can be confused with the legitimate one.

Rather than generating compatible counterfeit signals, GNNS spoofing can also be accomplished by meaconing ([10,90]), a technique consisting in interception and retransmission (at higher power) of the original signal to the malicious drone's receiver. Whereas the GPS signal is encrypted, a technique similar to meaconing, called security code estimation and replay (SCER) ([10,90]), can be used. It provides for the estimation of each symbol of the used coding by observing the signal received in the corresponding symbol period. The symbol estimation is continuously updated and is used simultaneously in the spoofing signal, trying to replicate the encoding as closely as possible.

Finally, spoofing applied to on-board sensors also deserve some attention. In this case, the spoofing source sends false signals to sensors, which can lead to the destabilization of the malicious drone control system. For example, as indicated in [91] and in references reported there, gyroscopes and accelerometers are sensitive to ultrasound at their resonant frequency and this vulnerability can be attacked. In [92], the authors spoofed the gyroscope of a drone, causing it to land. However, these attacks require powerful speakers and are limited in range due to the degradation of the sound wave with distance. Furthermore, a reference for a possible solution to an acoustic attack is always present in [91]. Other sensors that can be spoofed are those of the optical flow type. Their vulnerability was demonstrated in [93], where a method was presented to hijack a drone by spoofing the camera (thus affecting the stabilization algorithm) by means of a laser and a projector aimed at the drone's surface. Again, in [91], there was evidence of the fact that the presence of a magnetic field in the vicinity of a drone, in this case the DJI Phantom, always requires the recalibration of the relative magnetometer before take-off.

4.1.4. Neutralizers Exploiting Protocol-Based Attacks and Replay Attacks

Some cyber-attacks try to exploit the vulnerabilities present in the protocols used in communication networks to perpetrate malicious actions. These attacks include denial-of-service (DoS) attacks, which consist in disabling a machine (or network), making it inaccessible to intended users. Wi-Fi de-authentication, which consists of disconnecting a user from the relative access point (WAP), and flooding, which consists of sending a large amount of traffic to the target in order to make it unable to process legitimate messages, belong to the above family. These attacks can also be aimed at drones. For example, as documented in [91], some commercial drones based on Wi-Fi communications that do not require authentication for network access have proved to be vulnerable to de-authentication and flooding towards the drone network interface controller (NIC). In particular, with de-authentication, it was possible to disconnect the commercial drone from its remote pilot in order to activate a security procedure and take advantage of the disconnection window to take control of it. Another cyber-attack used to disconnect a commercial drone from its controller is the address resolution protocol (ARP) cache poisoning attack, as shown in [94]. Many of these attacks can be prevented using a network access with authentication, but the basic idea can be used to implement a neutralizer to exploit this kind of attack. In other words, as in the spoofing case, it is possible analyze the protocols used by drones to determine some weaknesses, at one or more layers of the communication stack, to be used to carry out neutralization operations. It follows that this kind of neutralizer can be applicable and effective for commercial drones whose protocols are known. They are definitively not a robust solution if the above exploited weaknesses can be patched up by the users, however they could be applicable as a first neutralization technique for commercial drones used improperly but without illegal purpose.

Other techniques useful to implement as neutralizers are replay attacks. According to the classification reported in [91], they can be included within the family of protocol-based attacks. They are based on the interception of a data transmission and its subsequent retransmission with a certain delay and can be used to hijack and disorient a drone. Examples are reported in [95,96]. In the first case, a drone used by the police was hijacked by exploiting a replay of the control commands sent to the drone by the ground control station using the XBee 868LP protocol. In the second case, it was possible to hijack amateur drones using the MAVLink protocol with replay attack. Therefore, even these kinds of attacks can be taken in account, but because they are very simple, eventual countermeasures adopted by the malicious drone(s) should be considered. For instance, the study reported in [97] showed a detection mechanism applicable to replay attacks based on the authentication of the pilot who controls the drone manually. The mechanism uses a classifier capable of recognizing the pilot's distinctive control style by exploiting data from on-board motion sensors.

4.1.5. High-Power Electromagnetics and Lasers

High-power electromagnetics can be used to create beams of electromagnetic energy over a broad spectrum of frequencies, in a narrow- or a wideband way, causing a range of temporary or permanent effects on electronics of targeted drones. According to the classification shown in [9] they can be categorized in two classes: narrowband electromagnetics (also referred as high-power microwaves, HPM), which include high power on a nearly single-tone frequency, and wideband electromagnetics, which have short pulses in the time domain and the energy distributed over a wide band. HMP requires very high power on a single frequency. Consequently, the determination of the effective frequency, which causes malfunctions in the drone to be attacked, is a key factor.

High-power electromagnetics must be directed precisely towards the target to be effective, otherwise lethality is significantly reduced and some devices may still function after their use. Hence, the assessment of the neutralization effectiveness after a shot is also an issue. An HPM-type device manufactured by Raytheon is illustrated in [98].

Lasers used as mitigators are capable of disabling or destroying an m-drone. As described in [9], an electrolaser ionizes the path to the drone and emits an electric current down the conductive track of the ionized plasma. Lasers can be categorized into low-power or high-power lasers [9]: low-power ones can be used to neutralize some sensitive sensors of the drone (for example, electro-optical sensors); high-power ones (operating at megawatts) can be a real weapon, able to burn part of the drone and destroy it. For both categories, accurate aiming is required, which implies sufficient time to track the target. Laser weaknesses are represented by the need for high technological development for their implementation (for the high-power lasers), sensitivity to weather conditions, accurate pointing and tracking time. A laser-based neutralizer manufactured by Boeing is illustrated in [99].

Both high-power electromagnetics and high-power lasers are a strong interdiction measure, typically used in a military context. In a civil environment, they cannot be a viable option, especially in crowded areas, due the risk of the uncontrolled drone crashing or of triggering the deployment of dangerous payloads. Nor are they suitable for airports and the surrounding space, due to the collateral hazard to aviation operations [5].

Finally, based on limited information available on the market about high-power electromagnetics and high-power lasers, we can easily deduce that they always show large size and weight and require a high power supply. Therefore, they can be mainly integrated into terrestrial platforms (typically they are mounted on tracks) and are not suitable for low-altitude platforms like mini drones.

4.2. *Kinetic-Mechanical Neutralizers*

Kinetic-mechanical neutralizers are able to physically block or even destroying m-drones. Aiming and/or tracking of malicious drones is required in order to effectively neutralize; in fact, these neutralizers must act as closely as possible to the drone under attack. Let us briefly examine the various types of the available kinetic-mechanical neutralizers, mainly using the data of the survey reported in [9].

For the sake of completeness, note that there is also a simple and economical method of neutralization, classifiable as kinetic-mechanical, not linked to technology and based on appropriately trained birds. This method, used for example by the Scottish and Dutch police (see [9] and relative bibliography), is limited to slow and small drones (with respect to speed and size and of the birds) and is not appropriate to mitigate multiple drones simultaneously [9]. For obvious reasons, we do not consider it as a possible part of a CUS system based on mini drones.

4.2.1. Neutralizers Based on Projectiles

These neutralizers are real weapons using projectiles capable of destroying m-drones. They include machine guns, munitions, guided missiles, artillery, mortars and rockets. Some of them (guided missiles) may require a guidance and tracking system in order to track and hit the drone target, while others can be equipped with an optical sensor for object detection and tracking. They are an expensive solution (the cost per shot is high) and typically used in military contexts. Finally, they are also capable of causing collateral effects, as the hit drone can fall to the ground causing damage to people and/or infrastructures.

4.2.2. Collision UAVs

In this case, a dedicated UAV (drone), equipped with detection and tracking capabilities, follows the malicious drone in order to collide and destroy it. The neutralizer drone requires high speeds to chase the malicious drone and, typically, it is effective for small drones located in protected areas. Collision UAVs can employ detection methods based on computer vision techniques and can carry explosives to maximize damage during impact with the m-drone. They can cause collateral damage, as in the case of projectiles, and compared to the latter they are characterized by a higher neutralization delay. In conclusion, these neutralizers are disposable systems, acting as a hybrid system halfway between a drone and a missile. An example of a collision UAV is shown in [100].

4.2.3. Nets

Nets are used to trap and immobilize m-drones. They can be projected by a net cannon (an example is shown in [101]) or can be carried by other drones (an example is shown in [102]). Nets are useful for neutralizing small drones, which are difficult to intercept by guns or guided missiles (see bibliography in [9]). They can then be equipped with parachutes to assure a safe descent for the drone/net assembly and to prevent collateral damages to other facilities or for forensic analysis. In any case, the effective neutralization range is short.

4.3. Neutralizers Using Mini Drones

Aerial platforms, like mini drones, show some interesting characteristics, such as high maneuverability, flexibility and deployment speed, but have limitations in terms of SWaP constraints. Therefore, as already stated in the previous paragraphs, it is not feasible to integrate neutralizers like high-power electromagnetics and high-power lasers in these platforms. In addition, neutralizers based on projectiles are not applicable to mini drones, both for SWaP constraints and because they are typically designed to be used with the surface-to-air launcher installed in terrestrial platforms. Small projectiles could be installed on mini drones, but they can be assimilated to nets. All other shown neutralizers, electronic and kinetic-mechanical, can be used with mini drones, even if the use of low-power lasers requires accurate pointing, which could represent a critical issue to solve. In particular, in the case of collision UAVs, the platform is itself a neutralizer.

The use of mini drones can help to maximize the effectiveness or efficiency of some neutralization techniques. An example is RF jamming: by exploiting the mobility of a drone equipped with a jammer, it is possible to approach the m-drone in order to reduce the power necessary to disturb the signal under attack. Let us assume, for example, that in the case of a jammer installed on a ground platform, the minimum distance between jammer and malicious drone is 100 m, and that in the case of a jammer installed on a mini drone, the aforementioned distance is 10 m. The signal produced by the jammer installed on the mini drone consequently undergoes an attenuation lower than 20 dB compared to the signal emitted by the ground platform jammer. This advantage could be partially or totally compensated considering that in the ground platform, a directive antenna can be used to amplify the power transmitted in a certain direction, but, as shown in the work reported in [103], an antenna system capable of offering some directivity can be installed also on mini drones. Furthermore, multiples drones, which simultaneously transmit a jamming signal, could be used in a cooperative way to increase the power of the resulting interfering signal. An example is shown [104], where the authors investigated the problem of simultaneous tracking and jamming of a rogue drone in a 3D space with a team of cooperative drones.

Finally, a drone team can be used directly as a neutralization technique. In the work reported in [16], a drone-based system was proposed for the purpose of intercepting and escorting an m-drone outside a restricted flight zone. The system consists of a defensive swarm, which is capable of self-organizing its defense formation in the event of intruder detection and chasing the malicious drone as a networked swarm. The neutralization approach is as follows: the swarm forms a three-dimensional cluster around the m-drone in such a way that the m-drone has a minimum set of movement possibilities. Assuming that the m-drone is going to avoid collisions with the drones of the swarm to maintain its functioning, by moving the defensive drones in a cooperative way, it is possible to escort the m-done outside the restricted flight zone.

4.4. Comparison of the Neutralizers

A comparison of the neutralizers considered in this paper is shown in Table 6. For each neutralizer, both features and limitations are shown together with the pros and cons of using them as integrated in mini-drone-based platforms.

Table 6. Comparison of the neutralization techniques and their suitability with mini drones.

Neutralizers	Features	Limitations	Pros and Cons with Drones
RF Jamming	• Interfering RF signals are used to lower the SINR (signal to interference plus noise ratio) to the receiver of the malicious drone • Can be used with land platforms (static, mobile, portable) or even aerial platforms (included mini drones) • Can interrupt or lower the quality of the command-and-control link of the receiver drone • Directional antennas can be used to minimize unwanted interference • Allows users to increase the interception capacity of a UAV communication • Can increase the security level of a communication (cooperative jamming) • If the receiver of the malicious drone gets saturated, there are not countermeasures	• Ineffective with autonomous malicious drones (i.e., without command-and-control links) • The range of use depends on the power delivered by the jammer and the distance between the jammer and the malicious drone • Can create unwanted interference, disturbing other communications (even critical ones) • Regulatory restrictions can limit its use • Can cause uncontrolled flights or crashes of the malicious drones with possible collateral damage • Anti-jamming techniques can undermine its effectiveness	• Mini drones can provide limited power for the RF jamming • Needed power for RF jamming can be decreased approaching the defensive drone to the malicious one • A lower jamming power decreases unwanted interference • Needed RF power per drone can be further decreased using more drones simultaneously • A defensive drone can be used as a relay node, transmitting a jamming signal in order to disturb an eavesdropper • Using more drones simultaneously surrounding a malicious drone could allow users to counter some anti-jamming techniques (e.g., those ones based on the angle of arrival)
GNSS Jamming	• Can interrupt the GPS connection of the malicious drone • Makes it more difficult to control the malicious drone • GNSS signals are weak and vulnerable (if not encrypted), therefore this technique can be simple to apply • In some cases, it can prevent the return-to-home function • Can be used with land platforms (static, mobile, portable) or even aerial platforms (including mini drones)	• Ineffective with malicious drones equipped with IMU sensors • Dangerous if used near areas where satellite navigation is required • It can cause uncontrolled flights or crashes of the malicious drones with possible collateral damage • Regulatory restrictions can limit its use • Anti-jamming techniques can undermine its effectiveness	• Same pros and cons as for the RF jamming technique

Table 6. *Cont.*

Neutralizers	Features	Limitations	Pros and Cons with Drones
Spoofing	• Can be used to replace the C2 link or the GNSS service, allowing users to control the malicious drone • Can be applied to on-board sensors to destabilize the malicious drone control system • Can be used with land platforms (static, mobile, portable) or even aerial platforms (included mini drones)	• Information on the systems that are integrated in the malicious drone (sensors, link C2) must be available • An accurate analysis of the communication link or of the sensors to be attacked must be carried out • The technique is often complex and could not be successful (e.g., it is not ineffective for encrypted GPS) • Regulatory restrictions can limit its use • Anti-spoofing techniques can undermine its effectiveness	• No substantial advantages compared to static platforms other than the possibility of exploiting the mobility of drones to increase the operative range • Sensor spoofing could be not suitable with mini drones (e.g., pointing accuracy of the sensor to be spoofed could be an issue)
Protocol-Based and Replay Attacks	• Exploit vulnerabilities in drone communications protocols • Are often easy to implement • Allow to hijack a malicious drone, destabilize its flight or cause return-to-home procedures	• If the vulnerabilities of the communications have been corrected, they are ineffective • Can be mitigated with the help of machine learning (e.g., in the case of replay attacks)	• No substantial advantages compared to static platforms other than the possibility of exploiting the mobility of drones to increase the operative range
High-Power Electromagnetics	• Can damage the electronic systems of the malicious drone • Can be of two different categories: narrowband (high power over a narrow frequency spectrum) and wideband (short pulses in the time domain) • Aggressive countermeasure characterized by an extended range of action	• Accurate pointing towards the malicious drone is required • Lethality for the malicious drone could be low • It is difficult to assess the effectiveness obtained with this mitigation • Can cause uncontrolled flights or crashes of the malicious drones with possible collateral damage	• Not suitable for mini drones because they require large size and weight and a high power supply
Projectiles	• Traditional neutralizer (ammunition, guided missiles, etc.) • Fast response times	• Require accurate pointing • Wind and gravity also need to be considered (depending on the type of the projectiles) • Can cause crashes of the malicious drone with possible collateral damage • High cost per shot in the case of missiles equipped with a tracking and detection system	• Small projectiles could be installed on mini drones, but they can be assimilated to the nets case

Table 6. *Cont.*

Neutralizers	Features	Limitations	Pros and Cons with Drones
Collision UAVs	• Require detection and tracking capabilities of the malicious drone to be impacted • Are a hybrid system between a projectile and a small UAV • Effective for small drones	• Require capabilities of tracking and approach to the malicious drone to be impacted • Low-speed pursuit can result in delays in neutralization • The crash following the impact can cause collateral damage	• The drone itself is a neutralizer
Nets	• Can be projected from cannons or from flying platforms (included mini drones) • Nets equipped with parachutes allow a safe landing of the malicious drone • After the capture of the malicious drone, information can be extracted from its hardware	• Not appropriate at airports as they can cause side effects to other aircrafts • They need small distances from the malicious drone to have an effective neutralization • Accuracy can depend on the surrounding environmental conditions • Variable reaction times depending on the behavior of the malicious drone • Effectiveness also depends on the behavior of the malicious drone	• Small distance from the malicious drone to neutralize can be obtained thanks to the mobility of mini drones • The defensive drone must track and pursue the malicious one • Another approach is based on a team of drones forming a three-dimensional cluster around the malicious drone in order to limit or force its movement possibilities. The team of drones can be seen as a "net".

5. Command and Control Systems

The command-and-control system (C2) is one of the sub-systems of a CUS and it is an essential part for the implementation of the automated decision-making feature, which has been addressed in Section 2. Indeed, it is in charge of (possibly automated) high-level decision-making operations, such as:

- Providing a classification of the attack scenario to assess its threat level, based on the feedbacks coming from the sensing system;
- Granting permission to fly over a specific protected area (for non-malicious drones);
- Selecting the proper mitigation techniques to be used based on the attack scenario and its threat level;
- Planning CUS operations and monitoring their execution.

By means of the previous capabilities, the C2 system may aid the operator in facilitating the automated decision-making for mitigation actions. It can also perform the supervision and the management of the other sub-systems in a CUS. However, it may be convenient to distribute these functions by deploying them in dedicated systems, especially in the case of a cooperative drone-based CUS. In other words, the C2 system may be implemented not as a single centralized decision-making entity, but as a coordinated set of distributed decision-making entities. The rationale behind this assumption is as follows: a single management system could not be feasible in a complex application, such as a CUS with a higher number of platforms, in which some of the operations to be performed require a high degree of autonomy. A single decision-making entity would not be able to provide complete control of all the platforms, but it would have, at most, partial control over the operations performed by the individual platforms, despite having an overview of the threat represented by the malicious drone(s). A centralized decision-making system would be extremely complex, both for the required computational capacity and for the communication network to be used to connect the various platforms. The latter, in fact, should be able to convey all the raw data collected by the platforms to the C2 system and to spread all the commands given by this latter system to the platforms of the CUS.

Clearly, one of the most critical design aspects of the C2 system is related to its planning capability, which has to guarantee an automated execution and has to affect the defensive team as a whole. Indeed, this capability represents the key enabler for the automated decision-making feature of the system. Generally speaking, planning is the reasoning side of acting and is an abstract and explicit deliberation process that chooses and organizes actions by assessing the current environment's situation (i.e., through automated situational awareness) and by anticipating the expected outcomes of the planned actions. This deliberation aims to achieve some predefined objectives as best as possible. It has to be implemented according to the principles of automated planning, which is an area of artificial intelligence (AI) that studies this deliberation process from a computational point of view [105].

The addressed planning problem includes aspects of different planning cases, such as activity planning (which is concerned with the allocation of activities or targets to a given entity), route planning (which is concerned with the synthesis of routes from a starting position to a set of targets a in a given area of interest), perception planning (which is concerned with the planning around sensing actions for gathering information), communication planning (which is concerned with the planning of communication actions for the cooperation between different entities, both human and artificial), etc. All these planning cases may be combined in the mission planning case, which is related to the planning of actions or tasks by projecting the results of those actions according to a model of the involved entities and by evaluating the desirability of those results. In the specific case of an unmanned system (UMS) and of a network of unmanned systems (NUMS), mission planning is defined as the process for the synthesis of a sequence of tasks in terms of tactical objectives, a route (general or specific), timing and coordination actions [106]. According to these definitions, mission planning mainly refers to a strategic horizon, since it represents a decision-making process to set objectives and tasks and to compute high-level steps (e.g., routes, sensing actions, communication actions, etc.) to satisfy the assigned objectives and tasks. Thus, it usually covers a wide temporal and spatial range with respect to the missions. The outcomes of the mission planning process have to be provided to tactical planners (e.g., the autopilots of the single vehicles), which have to compute short-term and short-range actions (e.g., the real trajectories) to satisfy the assigned tasks.

In the reference CUS, the C2 system has to optimize the operations carried out by the CUS and solve the mission planning process by:

- Computing the set of tasks to be carried out to counter the identified threat;
- Processing the optimal schedule (i.e., assignment and ordering) of the tasks, e.g., the allocation and the sequencing of the target areas to be protected and of the vehicle counter activities (in terms of detection, identification, classification, tracking and neutralization) to be executed;
- Operating over the entire time horizon and space horizon of the threat resolution.

Thus, it is a strategic planning level that sets the general objectives (the threat resolution strategy) and articulates the high-level steps to achieve them. Moreover, the reference mission planning is a dynamic (i.e., online) mission planning to face the dynamic threat scenario of the drone attack. Generally speaking, it is possible to carry out, where necessary or convenient, the following hierarchical decomposition for the C2 system: a module of the system may be explicitly in charge of the coordination of the team by means of a defensive team planning. Such a module is fed by the mission goals and the data of the team and deliberates the defensive tasks for all the vehicles by evaluating their effectiveness from the point of view of the team's mission and by considering the team's relationships and possible conflicts. It could be integrated in all the drones in order to obtain a decentralized architecture, in a single drone (working as team leader) or a in ground platform in the case of a centralized architecture. Instead, lower-level planners, integrated in all the drones are in charge of the planning logic for the single vehicle and are fed by the team plan that is deliberated at the higher level. The functional architecture of this planning logic is illustrated in Figure 3.

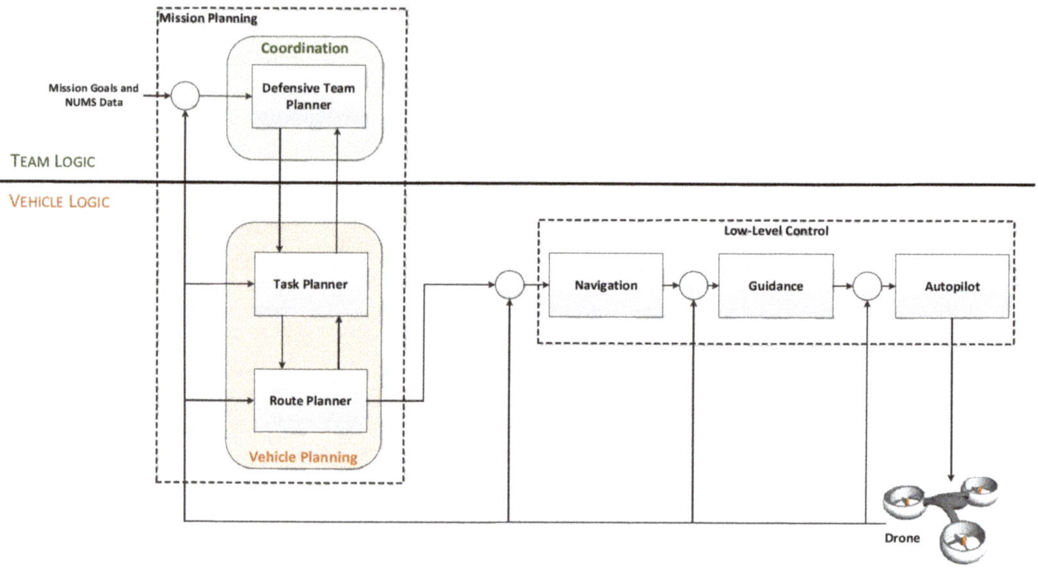

Figure 3. Functional architecture of the planning logic for the C2 system. Such logic is divided into team logic and vehicle logic. The former contributes to the planning of the actions of the overall team. Starting from the team plan, the latter performs the planning and the execution for the single vehicle.

The functional architecture in Figure 3 is compliant with the multilevel optimization principle [107] in order to ensure that the CUS-wide objectives and constraints are respectively optimized and satisfied along the hierarchy. In particular, the global planning problem is broken into simpler problems, which are independently solved. Moreover, the upper levels coordinate the solutions of the decoupled problems of lower levels by means of management functions.

The above hierarchical decomposition can also be used for operations provided by the other systems that comprise the CUS. Detection carried out through the simultaneous use of multiple drones is an example. In this case, based on the number of drones making up the detection system, a model based on "cooperative autonomous systems" can be applied, characterized by a collection of distinct decision-making entities (one per drone) or by a centralized control implemented into a drone hired as the team leader. In both the solutions, similarly to the previous case, the detection activity associated with drones could be subdivided into detection planning (the mission planning), aimed at coordinating the steps to complete the specific detection operation, and trajectory/flight planning (the vehicle planning), consisting of the generation of the trajectories of the individual drones between specific navigation points (scheduled by the detection planning).

Regardless of the shown hierarchical decomposition, it is clear that the use of mini drones could inherently require decentralization of C2 operations in order to simplify the overall CUS architecture.

6. Technological Challenges

A CUS based on mini drones can exploit some peculiarities of these platforms that give added value compared to CUS based on other types of platforms. The fundamental aspect concerns the use of teams, which allows operators to rework some of the techniques of detection, classification, tracking and mitigation systems in order to maximize performance and effectiveness. However, in order to use drone teams, it is necessary to investigate and develop still-challenging technologies. These technologies are listed below.

6.1. Team Coordination

The coordination mechanism (i.e., the underlying mechanism to achieve a cooperative behavior) may concern: the imposition of an artificial interaction structure as a control or communication structure, aspects of the task specification, interaction dynamics of agent behaviors, etc. This may be seen as the "society design" or "macro design" of a multi-agent system, that is, the synthesis of a logical and physical protocol to ensure that the single agents interact to successfully achieve the global tasks and to avoid pursuing conflicting strategies or plans [108]. Coordination may be also defined as the "process by which an agent reasons about its local actions and the (anticipated) actions of others to try and ensure the community acts in a coherent manner" [109]. These definitions highlight that an effective coordination requires that each agent has to consider the actions of the other agents and that the main achievement is related to coherency, i.e., the goodness of the joint behavior according to the performance of interest for the given problem.

In regard to the design of the coordination mechanism of a team for a given application, one critical point concerns the decision-making architecture, centralized or decentralized. Note that, for the distinction between a centralized and decentralized coordination from an algorithmic perspective, stricter criteria should be adopted, which establish that a coordination of a planning problem is centralized if [110]:

- A single agent solves the overall problem; or
- All the agents solve the same overall problem; or
- The agents employ a wide number of communications (or a wide communication band) to plan their coordinated actions; or
- The agents exchange full plans.

To the contrary, a coordination is decentralized if the agents make their decisions independently and if they employ limited communications (i.e., to exchange positions, maps, etc.). This algorithmic classification introduces a degree of decentralization and influences the theoretical and technical challenges to deal with for the coordination of teams of unmanned vehicles. Indeed, the maximization of the degree of decentralization represents a crucial aspect, looking also at the most recent works. However, such maximization should also consider additional issues, often overlooked in the modelling, including the following realistic scenarios: failures and cyberattacks, sensing noise and modelling uncertainties, intermittent or limited communication, etc.

6.2. Team Communication Network

Considering the mobility characteristics of the drones belonging to a team, the communication network will be a FANET with certain requirements of throughput, latency, transmission robustness, multiple access, flexibility and with constraints of available energy in relation to the mobile nodes (i.e., drones). A review on the communications perspectives of FANETs, with key enabling wireless technologies, applications, challenges and open research topics, is shown in [111]. In particular, the following key elements must be taken care of.

- Routing—the algorithms used must be able to support a routing table capable of rapidly adapting to the continuous topological variations of the network due to the mobility of drones. A survey of routing techniques in FANETs is shown in [112].
- Reliability and security—the network must ensure availability and integrity (and, depending on the application, confidentiality) of the communication between the nodes, characteristics that can be obtained both by operating at a physical level and at some higher levels.

- Scalability—some network drones competing in the execution of a task may need to be replaced for technical reasons or due to the exhaustion of their energy resources, so it is necessary to add other drones to the team to efficiently complete the assigned task.
- Quality of service—different performances must be guaranteed according to the type of information transmitted and the level of criticality.
- Placement—the drones may need to be appropriately arranged in the 3D space in order to maximize the amount of information exchanged and minimize the time required for the exchange, so as to satisfy any energy constraints characterizing the nodes themselves. Clearly, this aspect also falls within the problem of coordination.

6.3. Team Simulation Framework

As previously mentioned, a CUS is a complex system that integrates multiple platforms and different technologies, and the use of a team of drones further emphasizes its complexity. Therefore, having a framework available to simulate the behavior of the CUS and its systems, in particular, those based on teams, would allow users: to carry out a sizing of the aforementioned systems, so that they can be "calibrated" based on the area to be protected and on the possible threat (consisting of one or more m-drones), to simulate scenarios in which teams are used and evaluate the performances by the CUS and to develop and verify the procedures to be adopted for managing the threats.

Simulation can be used in different phases of the CUS development. The functional allocations could be supported by a modelling framework of the systems, where different architectural choices can be modelled, and by simulation and stressing or failure scenarios, through which it is possible to assess the architecture according to different aspects. Accordingly, looking also at the engineering guidelines on architectural assessment, CUS system architecture metrics could be identified and assessed by means of simulation. The architecture can be assessed with respect to its safety (for example to avoid bottle necks, or single points of failures), its efficiency and in terms of the coverage of the extension area or the coverage of different adversarial conditions.

The simulation can be used to build scenarios of attacks to verify the effectiveness of the CUS and also to assure its evolutive behavior. Attack-building can leverage on different techniques. The goal-based strategies aim to maximize the damages induced by the attacking drones to the critical infrastructure. In this way, the assessment from the CUS system of the threat scenarios can be verified and can be improved, assuring its continuous learning. Going deeper in the simulation chain, the attacking drones can be set up by using the generative adversarial networks (GAN), very promising techniques for image synthesis, in order to ensure proper data for the training of the employed artificial intelligence techniques

Finally, simulation can allow for the understanding of the proper human–machine balancing and the level of automation of the CUS system.

7. Discussion

For the purposes of this work, teams of mini drones have been considered as a reference subsystem of the hybrid CUS. This choice was due to several advantages in terms of mobility, coverage expansion, deployment flexibility, team coordination, automated decision-making, neutralization and scalability. The suitability of drone teams for CUS solutions was also confirmed by the analysis of the state-of-the-art research works in the fields of autonomous multi-agent systems and cooperative robotics. Moreover, some current international projects are developing both cooperative drone-based solutions for surveillance and situational awareness applications, as well as cooperative drone-based CUS.

In regard to the sensing phase, this work argues that the proximal sensing capability of a team of mini drones is the main clear advantage over a static ground-based CUS. Drone-based video sensing systems are less affected by the optical occlusion problem, but there is the need for an accurate video stabilization to mitigate the blur effect due to the drone movement. Moreover, drone teams represent an ideal solution to balance the pros and cons of the different sensing technologies by means of a hybrid configuration of the team and data fusion techniques. The selection of the technologies that best complement each other is a useful activity in order to optimize the level of situational awareness with respect to the complexity and cost of the system, considering the specific requirements (i.e., range, accuracy, etc.) of the application.

In regard to the neutralization phase, the use of mini drones can help in maximizing the effectiveness or efficiency of some neutralization techniques. For example, RF jamming may exploit the mobility of a single drone to reduce the power necessary to disturb the signal under attack, or the mobility of multiples drones, which can be used in a cooperative way to increase the power of the resulting jamming signal. Moreover, a drone team can be used directly as a neutralization technique, or small projectiles could be installed on mini drones, offering a similar solution to the nets case. In any case, for some techniques, it must be taken into account that the target pointing required by the neutralization integrated in the defensive drones can be a challenging issue.

In regard to C2 systems, teams of drones are prone to automated decision-making capabilities according to the multilevel optimization principle. Based on the number of drones, a model based on "cooperative autonomous systems" can be applied, which is usually characterized by a collection of distinct decision-making entities for the decentralization of C2 operations.

In the end, the implementation of a cooperative drone-based CUS raises several technological challenges, in terms of team coordination, team communication network and team simulation framework. All these challenges are also related to the reworking of some of the techniques of detection, classification, tracking and mitigation systems, in order to maximize performance and effectiveness by exploiting the underlying coordination network of the team.

8. Conclusions

This paper focused on the concept of a multiplatform CUS, which consists of a team of mini drones acting as an autonomous and cooperative system. In order to evaluate the feasibility of this concept, the paper provided a systematic review of the main technological pillars: sensing, mitigation and command and control. The analysis has confirmed the effectiveness of the proposed system, while also highlighting the need for decentralization of command-and-control operations. Moreover, the paper discussed some key challenges in terms of team coordination, communication network and simulation framework.

Future work will regard the detailed design, the sizing and configuration of the cooperative drone-based architecture for a specific scenario (e.g., intrusion in critical infrastructures such airports) and preliminary implementation and testing of basic capabilities (coordinated detection of intrusions, cooperative tracking, etc.).

Author Contributions: Conceptualization, V.U.C., A.M., D.P. and G.G.; investigation, V.U.C. and A.M.; writing—original draft preparation, V.U.C. and A.M.; writing—review and editing, D.P. and G.G.; visualization, V.U.C., A.M., D.P. and G.G.; supervision, V.U.C. All authors have read and agreed to the published version of the manuscript.

Funding: This research was funded by the national project MATIM (Maturazione Tecnologie Innovative Mini e Micro Droni), with grant PRORA (Programma Nazionale di Ricerche Aerospaziali) DM662.

Institutional Review Board Statement: Not applicable.

Informed Consent Statement: Not applicable.

Conflicts of Interest: The authors declare no conflict of interest.

References

1. Federal Aviation Administration. Available online: https://www.faa.gov/uas/resources/uas-sightings-report/ (accessed on 10 October 2021).
2. CBNC. Available online: https://www.cnbc.com/2018/12/20/drone-sightings-shut-down-britains-gatwick-airport.html (accessed on 10 October 2021).
3. Hassanalian, M.; Abdelkefi, A. Classifications, applications, and design challenges of drones: A review. *Prog. Aerosp. Sci.* **2017**, *91* 99–131. [CrossRef]
4. Nato Standardization Office (NSO). NATO Standard AJP-3.3. Allied Joint Doctrine for Air and Space Operations. Edition B Version 1. April 2016. Available online: https://www.japcc.org/wp-content/uploads/AJP-3.3-EDB-V1-E.pdf (accessed on 14 February 2022).
5. Lykou, G.; Moustakas, D.; Gritzalis, D. Defending Airports from UAS: A Survey on Cyber-Attacks and Counter-Drone Sensing Technologies. *Sensors* **2020**, *20*, 3537. [CrossRef] [PubMed]
6. Lopez, J.; Royo, P.; Barrado, C.; Pastor, E. Modular avionics for seamless reconfigurable UAS missions. In Proceedings of the 2008 IEEE/AIAA 27th Digital Avionics Systems Conference, St. Paul, MN, USA, 26–30 October 2008; pp. 1.A.3-1–1.A.3-10. [CrossRef]
7. Beaudoin, L.; Gademer, A.; Avanthey, L.; Germain, V.; Vittori, V. Potential Threats of UAS Swarms and the Countermeasure's Need. In Proceedings of the European Conference on Information Warfare and Security (ECIW), Tallinn, Estonia, 7–8 July 2011, pp. 24–30.
8. Gigante, G.; Pascarella, D.; Luongo, S.; Di Benedetto, C.; Vozella, A.; Persechino, G. Game-theoretic approach for the optimal configuration computing of an interoperable fleet of unmanned vehicles. *Expert Syst.* **2018**, *35*, e12293. [CrossRef]
9. Kang, H.; Joung, J.; Kim, J.; Kang, J.; Cho, Y.S. Protect Your Sky: A Survey of Counter Unmanned Aerial Vehicle Systems. *IEEE Access* **2020**, *8*, 168671–168710. [CrossRef]
10. Chamola, V.; Kotesh, P.; Agarwal, A.; Gupta, N.; Guizani, M. A Comprehensive Review of Unmanned Aerial Vehicle Attacks and Neutralization Techniques. *Ad Hoc Netw.* **2020**, *111*, 102324. [CrossRef] [PubMed]
11. Samaras, S.; Diamantidou, E.; Ataloglou, D.; Sakellariou, N.; Vafeiadis, A.; Magoulianitis, V.; Lalas, A.; Dimou, A.; Zarpalas, D.; Votis, K.; et al. Deep Learning on Multi Sensor Data for Counter UAV Applications—A Systematic Review. *Sensors* **2019**, *19*, 4837. [CrossRef]
12. Wang, J.; Liu, Y.; Song, H. Counter-Unmanned Aircraft System(s) (C-UAS): State of the Art, Challenges, and Future Trends. *IEEE Aerosp. Electron. Syst. Mag.* **2021**, *36*, 4–29. [CrossRef]
13. Seongjoon, P.; Hyeong, T.K.; Sanagmin, L.; Hyeontae, J.; Hwangnam, K. Survey on Anti-Drone Systems: Components, Designs, and Challenges. *IEEE Access* **2021**, *9*, 42635–42659.
14. Brust, M.R.; Danoy, G.; Stolfi, D.H.; Bouvry, P. Swarm-Based Counter UAV Defense System. *Discov. Internet Things* **2021**, *1*, 2. [CrossRef]
15. Dressel, L.; Kochenderfer, M.J. Hunting Drones with Other Drones: Tracking a Moving Radio Target. In Proceedings of the 2019 International Conference on Robotics and Automation (ICRA), Montreal, QC, Canada, 20–24 May 2019.
16. Brust, M.R.; Danoy, G.; Bouvry, P.; Gashi, D.; Pathak, H.; Goncalves, M.P. Defending against Intrusion of Malicious UAVs with Networked UAV Defense Swarms. In Proceedings of the 2017 IEEE 42nd Conference on Local Computer Networks Workshops (LCN Workshops), Singapore, 9 October 2017.
17. Khan, A.; Rinner, B.; Cavallaro, A. Cooperative robots to observe moving targets. *IEEE Trans. Cybern.* **2016**, *48*, 187–198. [CrossRef]
18. Zhao, Y.; Wang, X.; Wang, C.; Cong, Y.; Shen, L. Systemic design of distributed multi-UAV cooperative decision-making for multi-target tracking. *Auton. Agents Multi-Agent Syst.* **2019**, *33*, 132–158. [CrossRef]
19. Sinha, A.; Tsourdos, A.; White, B. Multi UAV Coordination for Tracking the Dispersion of a Contaminant Cloud in an Urban Region. *Eur. J. Control* **2009**, *15*, 441–448. [CrossRef]
20. ResponDrone, Situational Awareness System for First Responders. Available online: https://respondroneproject.com/ (accessed on 13 February 2022).
21. ROBORDER. Available online: https://roborder.eu/ (accessed on 13 February 2022).
22. Labyrinth, Ensuring Drone Traffic Control and Safety. Available online: https://labyrinth2020.eu/ (accessed on 13 February 2022).
23. 5D-AeroSafe. Available online: https://5d-aerosafe.eu/ (accessed on 13 February 2022).
24. DRONES4SAFETY, Building a Cooperative, Autonomous, Operating Drone System to Enhance Transport Safety. Available online: https://drones4safety.eu/ (accessed on 13 February 2022).
25. RAPID, Risk-Aware Autonomous Port Inspection Drones. Available online: https://rapid2020.eu/ (accessed on 13 February 2022).
26. Pozniak, M.; Ranganathan, P. Counter UAS Solutions through UAV Swarm Environments. In Proceedings of the 2019 IEEE International Conference on Electro Information Technology (EIT), Brookings, SD, USA, 20–22 May 2019; pp. 351–356. [CrossRef]
27. Pascarella, D.; Gigante, G.; Persechino, G.; Vozella, A. SWADAR (SWarm Advanced Detection and Tracking) Factsheet. 2020. Available online: https://www.edrmagazine.eu/wp-content/uploads/2020/12/EDA2020-Prize_SWADAR.pdf (accessed on 14 February 2022).
28. Keeping a Watchful Eye on Low-Flying Unmanned Aerial Systems in Cities. Available online: https://www.darpa.mil/news-events/2016-09-13 (accessed on 13 February 2022).
29. JEY-CUAS, Joint European System for Countering Unmanned Aerial Systems. Available online: https://ec.europa.eu/defence-industry-space/system/files/2021-06/EDIDP2020_factsheet_CUAS_JEY-CUAS.pdf (accessed on 13 February 2022).

30. Liu, Q.; He, M.; Xu, D.; Ding, N.; Wang, Y. A Mechanism for Recognizing and Suppressing the Emergent Behavior of UAV Swarm. *Math. Probl. Eng.* **2018**, *2018*, 6734923. [CrossRef]
31. Besada, J.A.; Campaña, I.; Carramiñana, D.; Bergesio, L.; de Miguel, G. Review and Simulation of Counter-UAS Sensors for Unmanned Traffic Management. *Sensors* **2022**, *22*, 189. [CrossRef]
32. Hoshiba, K.; Washizaki, K.; Wakabayashi, M.; Ishiki, T.; Kumon, M.; Bando, Y.; Gabriel, D.; Nakadai, K.; Okuno, H.G. Design of UAV-Embedded Microphone Array System for Sound Source Localization in Outdoor Environments. *Sensors* **2017**, *17*, 2535. [CrossRef]
33. Salvati, D.; Drioli, C.; Ferrin, G.; Foresti, G.L. Acoustic Source Localization from Multirotor UAVs. *IEEE Trans. Ind. Electron.* **2020**, *67*, 8618–8628. [CrossRef]
34. Guo, J.; Ahmad, I.; Chang, K. Classification, positioning, and tracking of drones by HMM using acoustic circular microphone array beamforming. *J. Wirel. Commun. Netw.* **2020**, *2020*, 9. [CrossRef]
35. Cabrera-Ponce, A.A.; Martinez-Carranza, J.; Rascon, C. Detection of Nearby UAVs Using a Multi-Microphone Array on Board a UAV. *Int. J. Micro Air Veh.* **2020**, *12*, 1756829320925748. [CrossRef]
36. Benyamin, M.; Goldman, G.H. *Acoustic Detection and Tracking of a Class I UAS with a Small Tetrahedral Microphone Array*; US Army Research Laboratory: Adelphi, MD, USA, 2014.
37. Chang, X.; Yang, C.; Wu, J.; Shi, X.; Shi, Z. A Surveillance System for Drone Localization and Tracking Using Acoustic Arrays. In Proceedings of the 2018 IEEE 10th Sensor Array and Multichannel Signal Processing Workshop (SAM), Sheffield, UK, 8–11 July 2018.
38. Busset, J.; Perrodin, F.; Wellig, P.; Ott, B.; Heutschi, K.; Rühl, T.; Nussbaumer, T. Detection and Tracking of Drones Using Advanced Acoustic Cameras. In *Unmanned/Unattended Sensors and Sensor Networks XI; and Advanced Free-Space Optical Communication Techniques and Applications*; SPIE: Bellingham, WA, USA, 2015; Volume 9647.
39. Sedunov, A.; Haddad, D.; Salloum, H.; Sutin, A.; Sedunov, N.; Yakubovskiy, A. Stevens Drone Detection Acoustic System and Experiments in Acoustics UAV Tracking. In Proceedings of the 2019 IEEE International Symposium on Technologies for Homeland Security (HST), Woburn, MA, USA, 5–6 November 2019.
40. Ezuma, M.; Erden, F.; Anjinappa, C.K.; Ozdemir, O.; Guvenc, I. Micro-UAV Detection and Classification from RF Fingerprints Using Machine Learning Techniques. In Proceedings of the 2019 IEEE Aerospace Conference, Big Sky, MT, USA, 2–9 March 2019.
41. Fu, H.; Abeywickrama, S.; Zhang, L.; Yuen, C. Low-Complexity Portable Passive Drone Surveillance via SDR-Based Signal Processing. *IEEE Commun. Mag.* **2018**, *56*, 112–118. [CrossRef]
42. Oliveira, M.T.; Miranda, R.K.; da Costa, J.P.C.L.; de Almeida, A.L.F.; de Sousa, R.T. Low Cost Antenna Array Based Drone Tracking Device for Outdoor Environments. *Wirel. Commun. Mob. Comput.* **2019**, *2019*, 5437908. [CrossRef]
43. Mototolea, D.; Stolk, C. Detection and Localization of Small Drones Using Commercial off-the Shelf Fpga Based Software Defined Radio Systems. In Proceedings of the 2018 International Conference on Communications (COMM), Bucharest, Romania, 14–16 June 2018; pp. 465–470.
44. Koohifar, F.; Guvenc, I.; Sichitiu, M.L. Autonomous Tracking of Intermittent RF Source Using a UAV Swarm. *IEEE Access* **2018**, *6*, 15884–15897. [CrossRef]
45. Azari, M.M.; Sallouha, H.; Chiumento, A.; Rajendran, S.; Vinogradov, E.; Pollin, S. Key Technologies and System Trade-Offs for Detection and Localization of Amateur Drones. *IEEE Commun. Mag.* **2018**, *56*, 51–57. [CrossRef]
46. Andraši, P.; Radišić, T.; Muštra, M.; Ivošević, J. Night-Time Detection of UAVs Using Thermal Infrared Camera. *Transp. Res. Procedia* **2017**, *28*, 183–190. [CrossRef]
47. Birch, G.C.; Woo, B.L. *Counter Unmanned Aerial Systems Testing: Evaluation of VIS SWIR MWIR and LWIR Passive Imagers*; Sandia National Lab. (SNL-NM): Albuquerque, NM, USA, 2017.
48. Goecks, V.G.; Woods, G.; Valasek, J. Combining Visible and Infrared Spectrum Imagery Using Machine Learning for Small Unmanned Aerial System Detection. In *Automatic Target Recognition XXX*; Overman, T.L., Hammoud, R.I., Mahalanobis, A., Eds.; SPIE: Bellingham, WA, USA, 2020.
49. Opromolla, R.; Fasano, G.; Accardo, D. A Vision-Based Approach to UAV Detection and Tracking in Cooperative Applications. *Sensors* **2018**, *18*, 3391. [CrossRef]
50. Li, J.; Ye, D.H.; Chung, T.; Kolsch, M.; Wachs, J.; Bouman, C. Multi-Target Detection and Tracking from a Single Camera in Unmanned Aerial Vehicles (UAVs). In Proceedings of the 2016 IEEE/RSJ International Conference on Intelligent Robots and Systems (IROS), Daejeon, Korea, 9–14 October 2016.
51. Saqib, M.; Daud Khan, S.; Sharma, N.; Blumenstein, M. A study on detecting drones using deep convolutional neural networks. In Proceedings of the 2017 14th IEEE International Conference on Advanced Video and Signal Based Surveillance (AVSS), Lecce, Italy, 29 August–1 September 2017; pp. 1–5.
52. Nalamati, M.; Kapoor, A.; Saqib, M.; Sharma, N.; Blumenstein, M. Drone Detection in Long-Range Surveillance Videos. In Proceedings of the 2019 16th IEEE International Conference on Advanced Video and Signal Based Surveillance (AVSS), Taipei, Taiwan, 18–21 September 2019; pp. 1–6.
53. Aker, C.; Kalkan, S. Using deep networks for drone detection. In Proceedings of the 2017 14th IEEE International Conference on Advanced Video and Signal Based Surveillance (AVSS), Lecce, Italy, 29 August–1 September 2017; pp. 1–6.
54. Kim, B.H.; Khan, D.; Bohak, C.; Choi, W.; Lee, H.J.; Kim, M.Y. V-RBNN Based Small Drone Detection in Augmented Datasets for 3D LADAR System. *Sensors* **2018**, *18*, 3825. [CrossRef]

55. Hammer, M.; Hebel, M.; Borgmann, B.; Laurenzis, M.; Arens, M. Potential of Lidar Sensors for the Detection of UAVs. In *Laser Radar Technology and Applications XXIII*; Turner, M.D., Kamerman, G.W., Eds.; SPIE: Bellingham, WA, USA, 2018.
56. Hammer, M.; Borgmann, B.; Hebel, M.; Arens, M. UAV Detection, Tracking, and Classification by Sensor Fusion of a 360° Lidar System and an Alignable Classification Sensor. In *Laser Radar Technology and Applications XXIV*; Turner, M.D., Kamerman, G.W., Eds.; SPIE: Bellingham, WA, USA, 2019.
57. Wei, P.; Cagle, L.; Reza, T.; Ball, J.; Gafford, J. LiDAR and Camera Detection Fusion in a Real-Time Industrial Multi-Sensor Collision Avoidance System. *Electronics* **2018**, *7*, 84. [CrossRef]
58. Zheng, L.; Zhang, P.; Tan, J.; Li, F. The Obstacle Detection Method of UAV Based on 2D Lidar. *IEEE Access* **2019**, *7*, 163437–163448. [CrossRef]
59. Chen, V.C.; Li, F.; Ho, S.S.; Wechsler, H. Analysis of Micro-Doppler Signatures. *IEE Proc.-Radar Sonar Navigat.* **2003**, *150*, 271–276. [CrossRef]
60. Drozdowicz, J.; Wielgo, M.; Samczynski, P.; Kulpa, K.; Krzonkalla, J.; Mordzonek, M.; Bryl, M.; Jakielaszek, Z. 35 GHz FMCW Drone Detection System. In Proceedings of the 2016 17th International Radar Symposium (IRS), Krakow, Poland, 10–12 May 2016.
61. Caris, M.; Johannes, W.; Stanko, S.; Pohl, N. Millimeter Wave Radar for Perimeter Surveillance and Detection of MAVs (Micro Aerial Vehicles). In Proceedings of the 2015 16th International Radar Symposium (IRS), Dresden, Germany, 24–26 June 2015.
62. Guvenc, I.; Ozdemir, O.; Yapici, Y.; Mehrpouyan, H.; Matolak, D. Detection, Localization, and Tracking of Unauthorized UAS and Jammers. In Proceedings of the 2017 IEEE/AIAA 36th Digital Avionics Systems Conference (DASC), St. Petersburg, FL, USA, 17–21 September 2017.
63. Lazzari, F.; Buffi, A.; Nepa, P.; Lazzari, S. Numerical Investigation of an UWB Localization Technique for Unmanned Aerial Vehicles in Outdoor Scenarios. *IEEE Sens. J.* **2017**, *17*, 2896–2903. [CrossRef]
64. Oh, B.-S.; Guo, X.; Lin, Z. A UAV Classification System Based on FMCW Radar Micro-Doppler Signature Analysis. *Expert Syst. Appl.* **2019**, *132*, 239–255. [CrossRef]
65. Coluccia, A.; Parisi, G.; Fascista, A. Detection and Classification of Multirotor Drones in Radar Sensor Networks: A Review. *Sensors* **2020**, *20*, 4172. [CrossRef]
66. Molchanov, P.; Egiazarian, K.; Astola, J.; Harmanny, R.I.A.; Wit, J.J.M. Classification of Small UAVs and Birds by Mi-Cro-Doppler Signatures. In Proceedings of the 2013 European Radar Conference, Nuremberg, Germany, 9–11 October 2013; pp. 172–175.
67. Fioranelli, F.; Ritchie, M.; Griffiths, H.; Borrion, H. Classification of Loaded/Unloaded Micro-drones Using Multistatic Radar. *Electron. Lett.* **2015**, *51*, 1813–1815. [CrossRef]
68. Yasin, J.N.; Mohamed, S.A.S.; Haghbayan, M.-H.; Heikkonen, J.; Tenhunen, H.; Plosila, J. Unmanned Aerial Vehicles (UAVs): Collision Avoidance Systems and Approaches. *IEEE Access* **2020**, *8*, 105139–105155. [CrossRef]
69. Shi, X.; Yang, C.; Xie, W.; Liang, C.; Shi, Z.; Chen, J. Anti-Drone System with Multiple Surveillance Technologies: Architecture, Implementation, and Challenges. *IEEE Commun. Mag.* **2018**, *56*, 68–74. [CrossRef]
70. Luo, A. Drones Hijacking—Multi-Dimensional Attack Vectors and Countermeasures. In Proceedings of the DEFCON 24 Conference, Las Vegas, NV, USA, 4–7 August 2016; Available online: https://www.youtube.com/watch?v=R6RZ5KqSVcg (accessed on 28 February 2022).
71. Dong, L.; Han, Z.; Petropulu, A.P.; Poor, H.V. Cooperative jamming for wireless physical layer security. In Proceedings of the 2009 IEEE/SP 15th Workshop on Statistical Signal Processing, Cardiff, UK, 31 August–3 September 2009.
72. Li, K.; Voicu, R.C.; Kanhere, S.S.; Ni, W.; Tovar, E. Energy efficient legitimate wireless surveillance of UAV communications. *IEEE Trans. Veh. Technol.* **2019**, *68*, 2283–2293. [CrossRef]
73. Lichtman, M.; Poston, J.D.; Amuru, S.; Shahriar, C.; Clancy, T.C.; Buehrer, R.M.; Reed, J.H. A communications jamming taxonomy. *IEEE Secur. Priv.* **2016**, *14*, 47–54. [CrossRef]
74. Junfei, Y.; Jingwen, L.; Bing, S.; Yuming, J. Barrage jamming detection and classification based on convolutional neural network for synthetic aperture radar. In Proceedings of the IGARSS 2018—2018 IEEE International Geoscience and Remote Sensing Symposium, Valencia, Spain, 22–27 July 2018; pp. 4583–4586.
75. Parlin, K.; Alam, M.M.; Le Moullec, Y. Jamming of UAV Remote Control Systems Using Software Defined Radio. In Proceedings of the 2018 International Conference on Military Communications and Information Systems (ICMCIS), Warsaw, Poland, 22–23 May 2018.
76. Nguyen, D.; Sahin, C.; Shishkin, B.; Kandasamy, N.; Dandekar, K.R. A real-time and protocol-aware reactive jamming framework built on software-defined radios. In Proceedings of the 2014 ACM Workshop on Software Radio Implementation Forum, Chicago, IL, USA, 18 August 2014; pp. 15–22.
77. Karhima, T.; Silvennoinen, A.; Hall, M.; Haggman, S.-G. IEEE 802.11 b/g WLAN tolerance to jamming. In Proceedings of the Military Communications Conference, IEEE MILCOM 2004, Monterey, CA, USA, 31 October–3 November 2004; Volume 3, pp. 1364–1370.
78. DroneShield, DroneGun Tactical. Available online: https://www.droneshield.com/dronegun-tactical (accessed on 4 June 2021).
79. Blighter, AUDS Anti-UAV Defence System. Available online: https://www.blighter.com/products/auds-anti-uav-defence-system/ (accessed on 4 June 2021).
80. MCTECH, MC-HORIZON D360 v3 Battle Proven Reactive Anti-Drone/Quadcopter/Small UAV Jamming System. Available online: https://mctech-jammers.com/products/mc-horizon/mc-horizon-d360.html (accessed on 4 June 2021).

81. Mpitziopoulos, A.; Gavalas, D.; Konstantopoulos, C.; Pantziou, G. A Survey on Jamming Attacks and Countermeasures in WSNs. *IEEE Commun. Surv. Tutor.* **2009**, *11*, 42–56. [CrossRef]
82. Robinson, M. Knocking My Neighbors Kids Cruddy Drone Offline. DEF CON 23. Available online: https://academic.csuohio.edu/yuc/mobile/GPS-Knocking-My-Neighbors-Kid-Drone-compressed.pdf (accessed on 4 June 2021).
83. Ferreira, R.; Gaspar, J.; Sebstiao, P.; Souto, N. Effective GPS Jamming Techiniques for UAVs using Low Cost SDR Platforms. *Wirel. Pers. Commun.* **2020**, *115*, 2705–2727. [CrossRef]
84. Summers, N. Icarus Machine Can Commandeer a Drone Mid-Flight. October 2016. Available online: https://www.engadget.com/2016-10-28-icarus-hijack-dmsx-drones.html?guccounter=1 (accessed on 4 June 2021).
85. Moskvitch, K. Are Drones the Next Target for Hackers? 2014. Available online: https://www.bbc.com/future/article/20140206-candrones-be-hacked (accessed on 4 June 2021).
86. Noh, J.; Kwon, Y.; Son, Y.; Shin, H.; Kim, D.; Choi, J.; Kim, Y. Tractor beam: Safe-hijacking of consumer drones with adaptive GPS spoofing. *ACM Trans. Priv. Secur.* **2019**, *22*, 12:1–12:26. [CrossRef]
87. He, D.; Qiao, Y.; Chen, S.; Du, X.; Chen, W.; Zhu, S.; Guizani, M. A friendly and low-cost technique for capturing non-cooperative civilian unmanned aerial vehicles. *IEEE Netw.* **2018**, *33*, 146–151. [CrossRef]
88. Vervisch-Picois, A.; Samama, N.; Taillandier-Loize, T. Influence of GNSS spoofing on drone in automatic flight mode. In Proceedings of the ITSNT 2017: 4th International Symposium of Navigation and Timing, Toulouse, France, 14–17 November 2017; pp. 1–9.
89. Kerns, A.J.; Shepard, D.P.; Bhatti, J.A.; Humphreys, T.E. Unmanned aircraft capture and control via GPS spoofing. *J. Field Robot.* **2014**, *31*, 617–636. [CrossRef]
90. Humphreys, T.E. Detection Strategy for Cryptographic GNSS Anti-Spoofing. *IEEE Trans. Aerosp. Electron. Syst.* **2013**, *49*, 1073–1090. [CrossRef]
91. Nassi, B.; Shabtai, A.; Masuoka, R.; Elovici, Y. SoK—Security and Privacy in the Age of Drones: Threats, Challenges, Solution Mechanisms, and Scientific Gaps. *arXiv* **2019**, arXiv:1903.05155.
92. Son, Y.; Shin, H.; Kim, D.; Park, Y.-S.; Noh, J.; Choi, K.; Choi, J.; Kim, Y. Rocking drones with intentional sound noise on gyroscopic sensors. In Proceedings of the 24th USENIX Security Symposium, Washington, DC, USA, 12–14 August 2015; pp. 881–896.
93. Davidson, D.; Wu, H.; Jellinek, R.; Singh, V.; Ristenpart, T. Controlling UAVs with sensor input spoofing attacks. In Proceedings of the WOOT 10th USENIX Conference on Offensive Technologies, Austin, TX, USA, 8–9 August 2016; pp. 221–231.
94. Hooper, M.; Tian, Y.; Zhou, R.; Cao, B.; Lauf, A.P.; Watkins, L.; Robinson, W.H. Securing commercial WiFi-based UAVs from common security attacks. In Proceedings of the MILCOM 2016—2016 IEEE Military Communications Conference, Baltimore, MD, USA, 1–3 November 2016.
95. Rodday, N. Hacking a professional drone. In Proceedings of the Black Hat ASIA 2016, Singapore, 29 March–1 April 2016.
96. Highnam, K.; Angstadt, K.; Leach, K.; Weimer, W.; Paulos, A.; Hurley, P. An uncrewed aerial vehicle attack scenario and trustworthy repair architecture. In Proceedings of the 46th Annual IEEE/IFIP, International Conference on Dependable Systems and Networks Workshop (DSN-W), Toulouse, France, 28 June–1 July 2016; pp. 222–225.
97. Shoufan, A. Continuous authentication of UAV flight command data using behaviometrics. In Proceedings of the 2017 IFIP/IEEE International Conference on Very Large Scale Integration (VLSI-SoC), Abu Dhabi, United Arab Emirates, 23–25 October 2017; pp. 1–6.
98. Raytheon, Phaser High-Power Microwave System. Available online: https://www.raytheonmissilesanddefense.com/capabilities/products/phaser-high-power-microwave (accessed on 4 June 2021).
99. Boeing, Laser-Focused Battlefield Defense. Available online: https://www.boeing.com/defense/missile-defense/directed-energy/index.page (accessed on 4 June 2021).
100. CDET, RAM UAV Combat Unmanned Aerial System. Available online: https://ramuav.com/ (accessed on 4 June 2021).
101. Drone Defence, NetGun X1—Short Range Drone Protection. Available online: https://www.dronedefence.co.uk/netgun-x1/ (accessed on 4 June 2021).
102. Delft Dynamics, Dronecatcher. Available online: https://dronecatcher.nl/ (accessed on 4 June 2021).
103. Lee, C.U.; Noh, G.; Ahn, B.; Yu, J.; Lee, H.L. Tilted-Beam Switched Array Antenna for UAV Mounted Radar Applications with 360° Coverage. *Electronics* **2019**, *8*, 1240. [CrossRef]
104. Papaioannou, S.; Kolios, P.; Panayiotou, C.G.; Polycarpou, M.M. Cooperative Simultaneous Tracking and Jamming for Disabling a Rogue Drone. In Proceedings of the 2020 IEEE/RSJ International Conference on Intelligent Robots and Systems (IROS), Las Vegas, NV, USA, 24 October–24 January 2021.
105. Ghallab, M.; Nau, D.; Traverso, P. *Automated Planning—Theory and Practice*; Morgan Kaufmann Publishers: San Francisco, CA, USA, 2004.
106. National Institute of Standards and Technology. *Autonomy Levels for Unmanned Systems (ALFUS) Framework*; NIST Special Publication 1011-I-2.0; Terminology Version 2.0; NIST: Gaithersburg, MD, USA, 2008; Volume I.
107. Kolitz, S.E.; Beaton, R.M. Overall System Concepts in Mission Planning. In *New Advances in Mission Planning and Rehearsal Systems*; AGARD Lecture Series; AGARD: Neuilly Sur Seine, France, 1993; Volume 192.
108. Wooldridge, M.J. *An Introduction to MultiAgent Systems*, 2nd ed.; John Wiley & Sons Ltd.: Chichester, UK, 2009.
109. Jennings, N.R. Coordination Techniques for Distributed Artificial Intelligence. In *Foundations of Distributed Artificial Intelligence*; O'Hare, G.M.P., Jennings, N.R., Eds.; John Wiley & Sons Ltd.: New York, NY, USA, 2000; pp. 187–210.

110. Nigam, N. The multiple unmanned air vehicle persistent surveillance problem: A review. *Machines* **2014**, *2*, 13–72. [CrossRef]
111. Noor, F.; Khan, M.A.; Al-Zahrani, A.; Ullah, I.; Al-Dhlan, K.A. A Review on Communications Perspective of Flying Ad-Hoc Networks: Key Enabling Wireless Technologies, Applications, Challenges and Open Research Topics. *Drones* **2020**, *4*, 65. [CrossRef]
112. Oubbati, O.S.; Atiquzzaman, M.; Lorenz, P.; Tareque, H.; Hossain, S. Routing in Flying Ad Hoc Networks: Survey, Constraints and Future Challenge Perspectives. *IEEE Access* **2017**, *7*, 81057–81105. [CrossRef]

drones

MDPI

Review

Ice Accretion on Fixed-Wing Unmanned Aerial Vehicle—A Review Study

Manaf Muhammed * and Muhammad Shakeel Virk

Arctic Technology & Icing Research Group, UiT—The Arctic University of Norway, 8514 Narvik, Norway; muhammad.s.virk@uit.no
* Correspondence: manaf.muhammed@uit.no; Tel.: +47-98863857

Abstract: Ice accretion on commercial aircraft operating at high Reynolds numbers has been extensively studied in the literature, but a direct transformation of these results to an Unmanned Aerial Vehicle (UAV) operating at low Reynolds numbers is not straightforward. Changes in Reynolds number have a significant impact on the ice accretion physics. Previously, only a few researchers worked in this area, but it is now gaining more attention due to the increasing applications of UAVs in the modern world. As a result, an attempt is made to review existing scientific knowledge and identify the knowledge gaps in this field of research. Ice accretion can deteriorate the aerodynamic performance, structural integrity, and aircraft stability, necessitating optimal ice mitigation techniques. This paper provides a comprehensive review of ice accretion on fixed-wing UAVs. It includes various methodologies for studying and comprehending the physics of ice accretion on UAVs. The impact of various environmental and geometric factors on ice accretion physics is reviewed, and knowledge gaps are identified. The pros and cons of various ice detection and mitigation techniques developed for UAVs are also discussed.

Keywords: atmospheric icing; UAV; LWC; MVD; Reynolds number; aerodynamic penalties; IPS; modal analysis

Citation: Muhammed, M.; Virk, M.S. Ice Accretion on Fixed-Wing Unmanned Aerial Vehicle—A Review Study. *Drones* **2022**, *6*, 86. https://doi.org/10.3390/drones6040086

Academic Editors: Andrzej Łukaszewicz, Wojciech Giernacki, Zbigniew Kulesza, Jaroslaw Pytka and Andriy Holovatyy

Received: 28 February 2022
Accepted: 20 March 2022
Published: 28 March 2022

1. Introduction

UAV is an aircraft without an onboard human pilot. The main components of a UAV are the aircraft structure, ground control center (remote), payload (camera), and a data link for the communication between aircraft and ground control center [1]. According to their structure, UAVs are classified into four broad categories: *fixed-wing UAVs, rotary-wing UAVs, flapping-wing UAVs, and blimps* [2]. The smallest UAVs operate at less than 1200 feet above ground level, while the largest can fly up to 60,000 feet. The size and cost of UAVs vary according to application, ranging from pocket-sized micro-UAVs to large UAVs comparable in size to passenger aircraft. Even though crew safety is not a primary concern for UAVs due to their unmanned nature, but due diligence must be exercised in the design and manufacture of UAVs to avoid any financial losses. Historically, UAVs were used exclusively for military and defense purposes. However, over the last decade, UAVs have demonstrated their potential for use in various civil and public safety applications, including mapping, surveying, and photography. In 2021, a German marketing consultancy reported that UAVs have been used in 237 different applications [3]. As per the Unmanned Aircraft System Roadmap 2005–2030 [4], currently, more than 250 models of UAVs are manufactured globally by 32 nations.

With an increase in human activity in ice-prone high north regions, the use of UAVs has increased as well, with potential applications including ice reconnaissance, determining sea-ice thickness, surface roughness, and surface temperature over ice, water, and land, retrieving the spectral albedo of land surfaces, and monitoring coastal erosion [5]. UAVs also play a critical role in emergency and catastrophe scenarios in cold regions [6]. In addition,

UAVs can help ships to navigate safely by detecting icebergs. Arctic regions can serve as a showcase for UAVs to demonstrate their capabilities in light of the global climate change scenario. However, for optimal and safe UAV operation in ice-prone regions, ice accumulation on its structure is a significant safety problem. Icing is considered as one of the predominant causes of aircraft loss of control [7]. Three General Atomics MQ-1 Predator UAVs of the US military were crashed in Afghanistan in 2001 and 2002 due to icing hazards. The US military's Northrop Grumman Global Hawk UAV crashed due to icing during the Enduring Freedom operation in Afghanistan [8]. Military UAV missions have frequently been aborted due to inclement weather, which significantly impacts the mission's success [9]. For example, icing prevents Hunter UAV flights from October to April in Kosovo [10]. As a result, there is a growing need for a thorough understanding of ice accretion physics and the development of ice mitigation measures to ensure the safe operation of UAVs in icing conditions.

The operation of UAVs in high north regions is prone to three main challenges: low temperature, high wind speeds, and atmospheric icing. Some materials can become brittle at low temperatures and develop cracks due to expansion and contraction. Additionally, batteries lose their capacities in low temperatures and thus reduce the range and endurance limits of a UAV flight. The lithium-ion battery used in UAVs is more sensitive to low temperatures [11]. UAVs have a lower flight speed, lighter takeoff weight, smaller size, and lower flight altitude than manned aircraft, so these factors make UAVs more susceptible to wind disturbance compared to manned aircraft [12]. High wind speeds challenge the stability of small UAVs operating at a velocity less than 20 m/s. It can lead to loss of control and trajectory excursions resulting in a crash. Atmospheric icing can be considered the most dangerous hazard for UAVs operating in high north regions (See Figure 1). The ice accretion along a UAV structure causes deterioration of aerodynamic performance and structural characteristics leading to catastrophic failures. Atmospheric icing occurs when the super cooled water droplets freeze into ice upon impingement on a surface. In-cloud icing on structures are mainly classified into rime, glaze, and mixed ice. Glaze ice can result in the formation of complex ice structures like horns, large feathers, and "lobster tail like structures", and are therefore considered as the most dangerous icing condition.

Figure 1. Ice accretion on fixed-wing UAV [13,14].

UAVs are more prone to icing than conventional manned aircraft for the following reasons: (1) The presence of supercooled water droplets is pervasive in the lower 10 km of the atmosphere. Above 10 km, the concentration of supercooled water droplets decreases due to the extremely low temperature (>−45 °C) and low liquid water content [15]. As most UAVs fly in the lower atmosphere, they are more susceptible to ice accumulation than manned aircraft [16]. The high-altitude UAVs flying above 10 km must still pass through the icing layers during takeoff and landing and are also prone to icing effects. (2) UAVs operating at lower velocities than conventional aircraft have prolonged exposure to icing environments. (3) Manned aircraft operate with ice mitigation systems, but most UAVs operate without any ice protection systems because of their weight and power constraints.

(4) Composite materials used in the manufacturing of UAVs have lower thermal conductivity than the conventional metal-based airframes used for manned aircraft. Thus, the rate of heat transfer and dissipation of latent heat of fusion released during solidification is much slower for composite materials. It results in severe water runback and the formation of complex rivulet-like ice structures on the surface of UAVs [17]. (5) Low Reynolds number airfoils are so sensitive that even small changes on the surface of the main lifting element could significantly impact its performance. Thus, ice accretion on unmanned aerial vehicles (UAVs) must be studied separately from that on manned aircraft to understand the icing characteristics better and propose appropriate ice detection and mitigation measures.

Ice accretion can deteriorate the aerodynamic performance, structural integrity, and aircraft stability. Several studies can be found in the literature investigating the aerodynamic performance of aircraft under icing conditions [18]. In the last couple of decades, similar studies were also done for UAVs. Ice accretion on the UAV can alter its weight, which in turn changes its center of gravity and thus causes a deterioration of the performance and stability of aircraft [19]. Thus, proper ice mitigation techniques need to be implemented to avoid performance losses due to ice accretion.

2. Methods of Studying Ice Accretion on a UAV

Atmospheric icing research was mainly focused on the ice accretion problems in large Reynolds number applications like manned aircraft and the icing on structures like wind turbines, power networks, and so on [18–23]. The study of ice accretion on UAVs has gained interest only from the beginning of the 21st century and only a few researchers have worked in this field of science. One of the earlier works for icing on UAVs was published by Siquig in 1990 [16]. This can be considered a first reported work that discusses the ice accretion characteristics and related aerodynamic consequences of UAVs explicitly. The operational challenges of different UAVs under icing conditions and the need for better forecasting techniques are discussed. Ice accretion on a UAV can be studied using four different methodologies: (1) Analytical methods (2) Field measurements (3) Lab experiments (4) Numerical simulation.

2.1. *Analytical Modelling*

An analytical expression for studying the ice accretion on structures was formulated by Finstad et al. in 1986 [24]. Even though this analytical model is used to study aircraft icing, it is based on her works about ice accretion on the cylinder and therefore cannot be used directly for the icing on UAVs. Another analytical model suitable for the ice accretion on UAVs was derived by Szilder et al. in 2011 [25]. This model was based on the conservation of mass and energy for the impinging, flowing, and freezing droplets on the surface of the airfoil, and it relates the atmospheric temperature (T_∞) and Liquid Water Content (LWC) for a specified Reynolds number (Re), Median Volume Diameter (MVD) and runback limit.

2.2. *Field Measurements*

Field measurements based on actual flight tests are the most accurate way to study the ice accretion process. But these tests are costly and need constant monitoring and waiting for the desired operating conditions. Only a few such studies are available in the open literature for fixed-wing UAV icing. Avery [26] in 2013 performed flight testing of a small UAV to characterize the atmospheric icing environments. In 2016, Williams et al. [27] tested the Kahu-Hawk UAV's aerodynamics and flight stability. Before the flight, prefabricated ice shapes were glued to the wing's leading edge. Similar studies were done by Matiychyk et al. [28] in 2019 on a UAV M-10-2 "Oko". In contrast to the previous study, ice was naturally allowed to accrete on the UAV. Ice deposits were observed along the wing's full length leading edge, the tail unit's leading-edge, on the front surfaces of the pitot-static tube and video antennas. An ice thickness of 1.5 mm was observed on the wing leading edge. The performance parameters were obtained with the help of a Mode of Flight Recorder (MFR), and it was observed that the drag force increased about 40% due to icing.

The increase in the drag force increased the power requirement by 10%, and thus, the average index of the battery rose from 25.5 A to 35 A. In 2021, Siddique [29] performed inflight testing of a Sonicmodell Skyhunter fixed-wing UAV at three different flight conditions of calm, windy, and icing conditions at the Iowa State University's Bio Century Research Farm (BCRF). The T_{∞} value observed during the icing condition test was −1.5 °C and it leads to glaze ice formation on all leading edges and propellers. Water runback rivulets were visible on the top surface of the wing downstream of the leading edge. The propellers were heavily iced, leading to the formation of horns and ridges on pressure and suction sides. A dramatic increase in power requirement of 240% was observed during the ice accretion compared to calm weather conditions, leading to more battery power consumption.

2.3. Lab Experiments

Two major lab-based experimental techniques are employed to study the ice accretion phenomenon: Icing wind tunnels and cold room experiments. Icing wind tunnels are like standard wind tunnels with an additional cooling system to maintain the low temperatures and a spray system to inject water droplets into the airflow prior to entering the tunnel test section. The use of such icing wind tunnels allows for the prediction of ice shapes along with the measurement of aerodynamic loads and forces [30]. In 1944, NASA built the Icing Research Tunnel (IRT) at the Lewis Flight Propulsion Laboratory in Cleveland, Ohio. Several icing experiments were then conducted to understand the effect of ice accretion on the aerodynamic performance of aircraft [31,32]. However, most icing wind tunnels operate without a force balance measure system and therefore can only be used to trace ice shapes, but the ability to provide performance data is limited. NASA IRT [33], Boeing ice wind tunnel [34], altitude icing wind tunnel research facility in Canada [35], Braunschweig icing wind tunnel [36], Cranfield University icing wind tunnel [37], and CIRA ice wind tunnel in Italy [38] are some typical ice wind tunnels around the world. Cold room experiments are carried out in refrigerated cold rooms or outdoors in cold climates. A spray system located in front of the test vehicle creates the icing cloud. The major drawback of these rooms is their low operating velocity and they are often quite large in size [39]. Experiments on lab facilities did not offer the necessary precision and accuracy in simulating the icing conditions expected to be found in nature. A detailed discussion about the similarity parameters and scaling laws considered during lab based icing studies can be found in [40].

2.4. Numerical Simulation

Numerical icing simulations have four major modules: (1) Aerodynamic simulations for air flow field determination, (2) Determination of water droplet trajectories using a droplet impingement solver, (3) Ice growth process using a thermodynamic model, and (4) Remeshing module. Potential flow or Navier-Stokes stokes-based solvers are used for flow field determination and the Eulerian or Lagrangian approach is used to determine droplet trajectories. The thermodynamic solvers of most existing ice growth solvers are based on the Messinger model [41]. A detailed description of the physics involved in these processes can be found in [18]. Atmospheric parameters like wind speed, ambient temperature, Liquid Water Content (LWC), Median Volume Diameter (MVD), or droplet size distribution and duration of the icing event need to be supplied as an input to the numerical solver. The typical ice accretion modeling tools include LEWICE based on a 2D panel method developed by NASA Lewis Research Center [42], ONERA 2D/3D governed by Euler equations developed by ONERA in France [43,44], IMPIN3D developed by CIRA, Italy [45], CANICE based on the panel method developed by Bombardier Aerospace and Ecole Polytechnique de Montreal, Canada [46], MORPHICE based on the morphogenetic ice accretion model [47], and the second-generation 3D icing simulation system FENSAP-ICE based on Reynolds-Averaged Navier-Stokes developed by Newmerical Technologies International, Canada [48,49].

Icing tunnel experimental results are only available for the high Reynolds number applications in the past. The paucity of low Reynolds number investigations hinders the validation of numerical ice accretion prediction codes for low Reynolds number applications like ice accretion on UAVs. Therefore, such validations were performed in the past by comparing the numerical predictions with the available lowest Reynolds number test results. Szilder et al. in 2011 performed the validation of his numerical icing code based on the morphogenetic ice growth model (MORPHICE) at low Reynolds number by comparing its predictions with the results of icing tunnel test studies done on NACA 0012 airfoil at $Re = O(10^6)$ [50,51]. Following Szilder's work, Hann et al. [52] in 2018 also used the same experimental results to validate FENSAP ICE and LEWICE codes as a part of his ice accretion studies on UAVs. The ice shapes predicted by icing tunnel tests and numerical simulations vary greatly. The numerical codes underpredicted ice thickness, and the icing extents are more than experimental predictions. Thus, the validation of the existing numerical codes at low Re remains as a knowledge gap in the scientific literature.

To cover this gap, Williams et al. in 2017 [27] performed experimental studies on RG-15 airfoil at the NRC Altitude Icing Wind Tunnel (AIWT), Canada. The icing test was performed for a continuous maximum and an intermittent maximum icing condition as per FAR 25 Appendix C atmospheric icing envelope [53]. Glaze ice was observed for $T_\infty = -5$ °C and rime ice characteristics were observed at $T_\infty = -20$ °C. Later Richard Hann of the Norwegian University of Science and Technology (NTNU), Norway conducted three major experimental campaigns to generate the ice shapes data for UAV airfoils at low Reynolds number. In spring 2019, Hann [54] performed experiments on RG-15 and NREL S826 airfoil at the Cranfield icing wind tunnel. Ice conditions were chosen to generate three different icing morphologies of glaze, mixed, and rime for Reynolds number in the order of 10^5. The studies implemented and discussed two novel methods to capture the ice shapes in experiments: 3D scanning and photogrammetry. Numerical icing simulations were performed using FENSAP-ICE and LEWICE to validate the results, but there was a significant difference in the prediction of ice shapes. In fall 2019, Hann et al. [55,56] again performed icing studies on RG15 airfoil at the icing wind tunnel of the Technical Research Centre of Finland (VTT). The experiments were done for the glaze and mixed ice conditions to obtain the ice shapes as shown in Figure 2. In 2020, he [57] extended his experimental studies to NREL S826 airfoil for three different icing conditions of glaze, mixed, and rime ice respectively as shown in Figure 3.

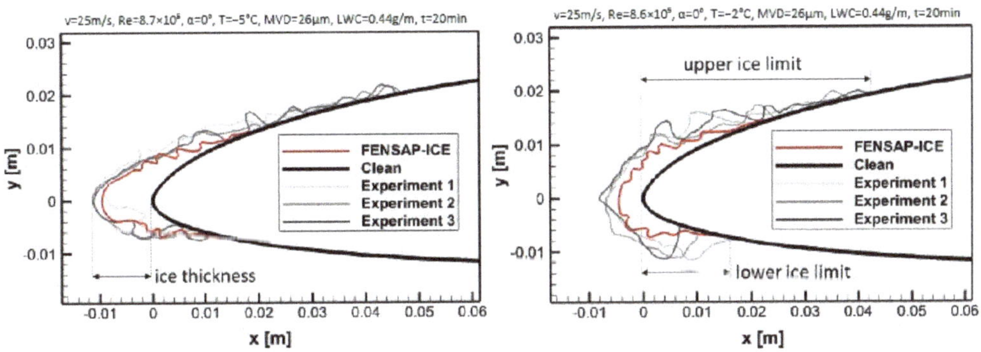

Figure 2. Experimental ice shapes on RG-15 airfoil [56].

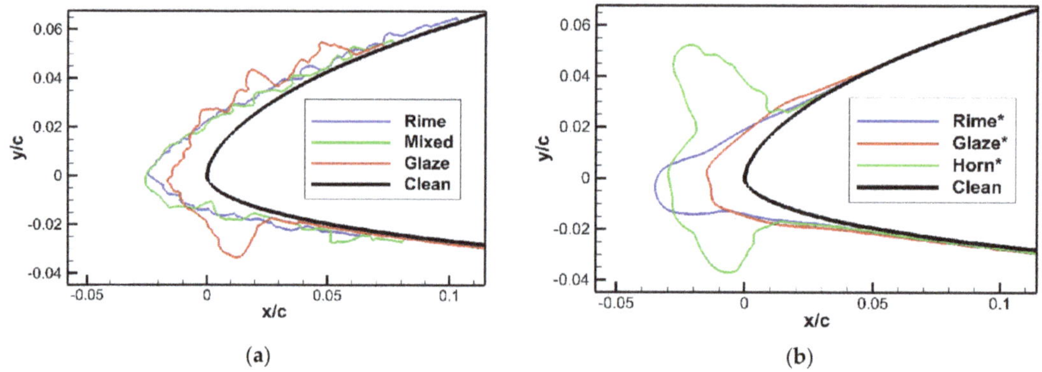

Figure 3. Ice shape predicted by (**a**) experiments and (**b**) numerical codes on NREL S826 airfoil [57]. These simulated ice shapes are marked with an asterisk to distinguish them from the experimental shapes.

Numerical ice accretion studies on UAVs have been performed by researchers primarily using three major icing codes: MORPHICE, LEWICE, and Ansys FENSAP-ICE. The validation of MORPHICE at low Reynolds number ($<O(10^5)$) is not reported in open literature at the time of writing this review paper. Hann et al. validated the LEWICE and FENSAP-ICE ice codes by comparing their predictions with the results of his icing tunnel tests [56]. Additionally, Hann compared the performance of these codes in predicting the ice accretion on NACA 0012 and NREL S826 airfoil [52]. Overall, the predictions for the rime ice conditions are better than the glaze ice, and the FENSAP ICE predictions were closer to the experimental results. However, the numerical codes underpredict the ice thickness and the ice limits, especially on the suction side. The ice shape predicted by LEWICE is smooth, in contrast with the rugged ice surface in experimental results. For glaze ice, the predictions of the FENSAP ICE validate with the experiments better than the LEWICE predictions. This may be because of the limitations of the panel method in predicting the complex flow behaviors, but on the other hand, FENSAP ICE based on the Navier stokes equation showed higher accuracy.

These validation studies indicate the capability of existing numerical icing codes to predict the ice shapes for different meteorological conditions. Overall, the numerical codes can reliably predict the rime ice accretions but fall short of accurately predicting glaze ice due to the intricate physics involved. Kind et al. [40] also made a similar observation for ice accretion studies on manned aircraft. The difference in the ice shape predicted by numerical codes and experiments can be attributed to the numerical model's limitations or experimental uncertainties. Experimental uncertainties mainly include the limitation of existing techniques and the possibility of errors and some of them are listed here. (1) Ice accretion is a dynamic process, and the shape of the accreted ice keeps on changing with time. Therefore, the ice shapes obtained by manual tracing correspond to the ice shape at a particular instant of time. So advanced ice shape tracing techniques need to be developed to get the ice shape at various time instants. (2) Proper calibration of LWC and MVD with accurate droplet distribution is necessary to obtain more realistic experimental conditions. (3) The ice density variability during tunnel simulations is another challenge for experiments [54]. (4) The ice accretion is usually obtained for a fixed value of angle of attack, but the angle of attack keeps on changing during the actual flight trajectory. (5) The assumption of the infinite wing concept in most studies also limits the accuracy by restricting the flow dimensions to 2D. (6) The spatial and temporal variability of the ice accretion test results is another phenomenon that questions the accuracy of icing tunnel tests [51]. (7) When tests are conducted on a sub-scale model, dynamic similarity parameters for the airflow, droplet trajectories, and thermodynamic freezing process must be satisfied, but it is difficult to achieve in practice. Numerical models are usually built based on various simplifications and assumptions, and there is always a question of the validity of the numerical models used. Unlike the fluid flow simulation, ice accretion modeling includes coupling of a fluid flow solver, droplet trajectory module, and heat transfer module. Thus, there are approximations at all three stages, which can considerably affect the accuracy of the results. In addition, the accurate modeling of the boundary layer, roughness effects, and the turbulent flow characteristics need to be considered. Additionally, the existing numerical techniques and associated models are developed for ice accretion at a high Reynolds number. Thus, it is necessary to validate these models at low Reynolds numbers or develop approaches and models specifically for low Re situations. Surface roughness has a considerable impact on the heat transfer process [58,59] and heat transfer (especially convective heat transfer) is one of the significant mechanisms that control the ice accretion process [60]. Roughness also has a major influence on the fluid flow and droplet impingement module of the ice accretion modeling [61,62]. Therefore, the final ice shape is very sensitive to the evolution of local surface roughness at the start and during the ice accretion process and this demands efficient roughness models. Accurate experimental results are mandatory to enhance the existing numerical models and develop new models. The lack of proper experimental results for ice accretion at low Reynolds number still remains a gap in this area.

3. Effect of Environmental, Geometrical, and Material Conditions on Ice Accretion

By the beginning of the 21st century, more researchers started working on icing-related issues of UAVs. Most of them were concentrated on studying the sensitivity of nature and the shapes of accreted ice to environmental and geometric conditions. The nature of the ice forms depends primarily on free stream velocity (V_∞), atmospheric temperature (T_∞), Liquid Water Content (LWC), the droplet Median Volume Diameter (MVD), angle of attack (α), Reynolds number (Re), and the geometry of the structure (airfoil, chord, mean effective camber and material). In this section, an attempt is made to review the studies by various researchers to understand the influence of these parameters on the ice accretion behavior of UAVs at low Reynolds number values. The results presented in this section are mainly based on numerical studies using various ice accretion simulation codes.

3.1. *Effect of Atmospheric Temperature* (T_∞)

The effect of atmospheric temperature (T_∞) on ice accretion of a UAV was studied by Koenig et al. in 2001 [63] and Szilder in 2011 [25,64]. The nature of the ice changed from glaze to rime with a mixed ice behavior in between with a decrease in T_∞. In both these studies, the influence of T_∞ is studied independently by keeping the MVD and LWC value constant. However, the parameters are no longer independent when the studies are based on the FAR 25 Appendix C icing envelope. Such studies were done by Szilder in 2015 [65], 2017 [66], Krøgenes and Hann in 2017 [57,67], and Fajt in 2019 [68] on different airfoil geometries. The observations were qualitatively similar to Szilder's initial studies that the low temperatures favor rime ice formation and glaze formed at a temperature near the freezing point with mixed ice formed in between. For temperatures very close to the freezing point like $T_\infty = -2$ °C the heat transfer process is not high enough to freeze all the droplets upon impingement, therefore a part of the impinging droplets runback along the airfoil surface leading to the glaze ice formation. Whereas at very low temperatures of $T_\infty = -10$ °C and above, most droplets freeze upon impingement leading to rime ice formation. Additionally, it was observed that the rime ice formed at lower temperatures (−30 °C) is just a scaled-up version of the same at higher temperatures (−10 °C), this is due to the low value of the LWC at higher negative temperatures as defined in the FAR 25 Appendix C icing envelope. Fajt also pointed out that the ice mass increases with temperature.

3.2. Effect of LWC and MVD

The combined effect of LWC and MVD on ice accretion of UAV was studied by Koenig et al. [63] in 2002. The ice shape changes from smooth rime ice with no oblique protrusion or horns to glaze ice with two enormous horns when the LWC and MVD values increase. Additionally, a considerable rise in the amount of ice deposited is observed. In 2011, Szilder studied the influence of LWC independently on the ice accretion behavior by keeping the MVD or LWC and T_∞ constant [25,64]. For temperature greater than −8 °C the ice shape changes from rime to mixed (glaze ice formed at the stagnation leading edge and rime ice formed in the downstream region) and then to glaze ice with water run back along the surface with an increase in LWC. Szilder [64] also pointed out that an increase in the size of the droplet tends to diminish the parametric space for rime but increases the space for the glaze. When the investigations are done based on FAR 25 Appendix C icing envelope [55,64–67], the ice accreted is a function of T_∞, MVD and LWC values. Smaller MVD values correspond to large LWC values and favored glaze ice formation. When the LWC is large, the latent heat that must be removed in order for the impinging droplets to completely freeze is also large, thus favoring glaze ice. However, T_∞ also plays an important role here as the potential to remove the latent heat increases at lower temperatures. Fajt [68] observed that when the LWC is less than 0.2 g/m^3, the ice formed is always streamline shaped (rime) irrespective of MVD and T_∞. When Li [69] studied the effect of LWC and MVD based on the FAR 25 icing envelope in 2020, it was observed that as the value of MVD increases, the size of the ice horns decreases because of the reduction in the LWC. With further increase in MVD, the presence of a horn has completely vanished, and ice accreted in a streamlined fashion, increasing the effective camber and enhancing the aerodynamic performance. From the analysis of droplet trajectories, Szilder inferred that the larger droplets have higher inertia and have a slower response to the spatial variations in the flow. It increases the collision efficiency and leads to a greater impingement extent. At temperatures close to freezing point, the heat transfer rate is not high enough to freeze all the water droplets leading to a glaze ice formation with water runback. Additionally, the smallest droplets result in the greatest local maximum ice thickness (especially at the leading edge) due to the large value of LWC as per the Appendix C icing envelope. Similar observations were also made by Avery [26]. However, a contradicting observation is made by Cistriani in 2007 [70] as a part of his studies on the design of Low *Re* airfoil for the Falco UAV. The formation of the worst ice shape at Continuous Maximum (CM) conditions with a low value of LWC compared to Intermittent Maximum (IM) conditions with higher LWC values is mentioned. Since this study was not dedicated to icing issues, much information regarding the software used and ice shapes formed at the remaining conditions is unavailable. Koenig [10] in 2003 pointed out that the clustering of the LWC value also has an effect on the ice accretion based on his icing tunnel test with constant and variable rate LWC.

3.3. Effect of Reynolds Number (Re)

The ice accretion behavior at high *Re* has been widely studied in the literature but a direct transformation of these results to low *Re* is not possible due to the problems discussed in Section 1. Therefore, Szilder in 2011 [64] studied the effect of *Re* on the ice accretion behavior by conducting numerical icing studies at two different *Re* of 5×10^6 and 5×10^4 [25,64]. The Reynolds number is varied by changing the values of V_∞ and *C*. The nature of the ice changes from rime to mixed and then to glaze with an increase in LWC for low *Re*. Whereas the nature of the ice remains glaze for all the values of LWC at high *Re* with only the extent of ice increasing with LWC. Further the thickness of the ice is considerably smaller when compared to the low Re number cases. The reduction in the thickness and decrease in the rate of icing can be attributed to the high values of aerodynamic heating at higher velocities. Low Reynolds favors the formation of rime ice which results in less aerodynamic penalties, but at the same time increases the relative ice thickness making the total ice mass high.

3.4. Effect of Free Stream Air Velocity (V_∞)

Bottyan et al. in 2013 [71,72] observed that the increase in true airspeed from 10 m/s to 130 m/s changes the ice behavior from less dangerous dry ice to more dangerous wet ice with horns at $T_\infty = -4.2$ °C. Further, an increase in the rate of icing with velocity is also observed. Ice thickness at the stagnation region decreases, and it completely vanishes at higher velocities leading to the formation of horns at an oblique angle with the surface. The horns also got thicker and thicker with velocity. The decrease in the leading-edge ice thickness can be because of the increase in the aerodynamic heating at higher velocities. In 2021, Hann et al. [55] concluded that the free stream velocity significantly affects the ice accretion behavior of the glaze and mixed ice more than rime ice. As the velocity increases, the streamwise thickness of glaze ice decreases, whereas the spanwise extension increases. At a very high velocity of 100 m/s, no ice was formed for the glaze icing conditions due to increased surface temperature beyond the freezing point because of aerodynamic heating. For mixed ice conditions, a large value of velocity is chosen by Krøgenes and Hann [57,67] to obtain artificial ice shapes with distinct horn shape formation. It is in line with the observation of Bottyan et al. [71] that an increase in the velocity leads to the formation of significant horns near the leading edge.

3.5. Effect of Angle of Attack (α)

In 2015, Szilder et al. compared the UAV ice accretion behavior at cruise conditions with $\alpha = 3°$ to the same at landing flight conditions with $\alpha = 9°$ [65]. During landing, the large value of angle of attack increases the vertical component of drop velocity than cruise conditions and the droplet impingement (and therefore the extent of ice formation) is more on the lower surface of the airfoil. For the ice shapes obtained for landing conditions, the stagnation region is shifted due to the large angle of attack, and a corresponding shift in the icing location is observed. A similar shift is observed during the icing tunnel studies of Williams on RG-15 airfoil [27].

3.6. Effect of Geometric Parameters

Various geometric parameters such as airfoil chord length, mean camber, thickness, aspect ratio, and leading-edge cylinder diameter can affect ice accretion by influencing flow behavior, droplet trajectories, and rate of heat transfer. Hann et al. in 2021 [55] studied the effect of change in chord length on the ice accretion behavior and observed that the extent of icing and its thickness increases with a decrease in chord length. In 2017, Szilder et al. performed ice accretion studies on various UAV airfoils [66] and concluded that the ice mass accumulated is small on a thinner airfoil. The ice thickness at the stagnation point is very similar, but differences in the ice extends are observed. This could be due to variations in the vertical component of drop velocity near an airfoil.

Most existing literature on numerical studies of UAV icing is limited to 2D airfoils. An ice accretion simulation on a 3D swept wing was performed by Szilder et al. in 2017 [66]. The ice mass increased towards the wing root section because of growing wing thickness near the root. The ice thickness decreases as we move along the leading edge from tip to root because of the decrease in convective heat transfer coefficient in that direction due to the reduction in velocity. Additionally, the extent of ice accretion is greater towards the root section due to the water runback caused by less efficient freezing of water and a large impingement mass. The changes in the ice accretion behavior along the spanwise direction were also observed due to the difference in local chord length and wing shape. Yirtici in 2020 [73] performed numerical icing simulations on a rectangular wing with NREL S826 airfoil at three different aspect ratios and it was observed that the loss in C_L/C_D decreases with the increase in wing aspect ratio.

3.7. Effect of Material Properties

In 2018, Li investigated the effect of thermal conductivity on ice accretion on the airframe surface [17]. The ice accretion process on aluminum (representing the manned aircraft) and thermoplastic material (representing UAV) were investigated during the studies. Under the same operating conditions, the thermoplastic material with a lower thermal conductivity value causes a much slower dissipation of the released latent heat of fusion associated with the solidification of the supercooled water droplets impinging on the surface. Thus, resulting in water runback and the formation of more complex ice structures like rivulets when compared to the aluminum surface with higher thermal conductivity.

Discussion: The investigations revealed the influence of various environmental geometric and material properties on ice accretion. Reynolds number, free stream velocity, and chord length can significantly influence the ice accretion behavior. These parameters distinguish the operating conditions of manned aircraft from that of UAVs. Therefore, the ice accretion phenomenon on a UAV needs to be studied separately from that of manned aircraft. Siquig [16] reported the most vulnerable icing conditions as T_∞ between 0 to $-$ 10 °C, LWC more than 0.1 g/m^3, and droplet diameter between 30 and 400 microns. Rime ice formation is favored at low temperatures, whereas glaze is formed at a temperature near the freezing point with mixed ice formed in between. All the other factors discussed above can influence the icing extend, thickness, horns, ice lobes, and feather-like structures. Szilder [65] concluded that the extent of ice formation increases with drop size, but LWC mostly governs ice thickness. Fajt [68] observed the highest ice mass at MVD of 20 µm and $T_\infty = -2$ °C even though the LWC value at MVD of 20 µm is 20% less than the same at MVD of 15 µm, this can be because of the larger droplet size. Thus, the nature and shape of ice formed can be considered as a function of the complex interplay of various environmental and geometric parameters. Most studies are concentrated on the temperatures of $T_\infty = -2$ °C, -5 °C and $-$ 10 °C with the corresponding LWC and MVD values proposed by Appendix C of FAR 25. It is observed from various studies that glaze ice conditions can lead to more complex ice shapes, with a special case of mixed icing conditions at $T_\infty \geq -4$ °C. Thus, the ice accretion studies need to be refined to more temperature conditions between -2 °C and $-$ 10 °C. Additionally, the detrimental effect of Supercooled Large Droplets (SLD) is discussed in the literature, but the same is not studied from the scope of low Reynolds number problems or UAVs. Since ice accretion is a dynamic process and is highly sensitive to atmospheric and geometric conditions, the nature and shape of the ice formed can differ from the expectations. Therefore, a correlation between various geometric and environmental conditions and the ice formed cannot be easily made. However, such attempts can be made from a research point of view so that future researchers can correlate their predictions with these benchmarks and the variations can be reported.

4. Aerodynamic Performance Penalties

Aerodynamic performance penalties can be considered as a significant consequence of ice accretion on airfoil structures. So, it is essential to understand how icing affects the aerodynamic performance of an airfoil. To study iced airfoil aerodynamic penalties, one can use an icing wind tunnel like the NASA IRT, where the aerodynamic forces are recorded simultaneously with the ice accretion process. This can be considered as the precise method of measuring the aerodynamic forces and moments of the iced airfoil as the process is fully transient. To the author's knowledge, no such experiments have been reported for a fixed-wing UAV in the open literature to date. Another option is to 3D print the iced profile obtained from an icing tunnel test or numerical simulation and attach it to the airfoil's leading edge. It is then tested in a wind tunnel to determine the aerodynamic forces and moments. Most researchers employ this approach because conventional wind tunnels are more readily available than icing wind tunnels. However, the accuracy of the measurements is compromised in this method because the ice shapes and aerodynamic forces are measured only for a particular instant of time and are no longer transient. In addition, the ice shape generated for a specific angle of attack (at which the numerical simulation or icing tunnel experiment is carried out) is used to study aerodynamic performance as a function of the angle of attack. In a way, this can lead to misleading results as the shape, location, and nature of the ice accreted changes with the angle of attack and affects aerodynamic forces and moments. Both approaches can also be used in numerical studies to predict the aerodynamic coefficients of an iced airfoil.

Cistriani et al. in 2007 [70] studied the aerodynamic performance of an iced UAV airfoil in the wind tunnel. Icing reduced the maximum lift by 30% compared to the clean airfoil. Szilder et al. performed the aerodynamic simulation of iced UAV airfoils SD7037 [65], HQ309, and SD7032 [66] with the ice shapes obtained from MORPHICE simulations. The turbulence model employed is the $\gamma - Re_{\theta t}$ transition model [74]. In glaze ice conditions at −2 °C the SD7037 airfoil lost 16% lift, tripled drag (300%) and stalled prematurely at 9° (clean airfoil stalls at 11°) along with a 12% decrease in pitching moment. The aerodynamic penalties for rime ice are relatively smaller as it covers only a smaller portion of the airfoil. It is worth noting that for large values of angle of attack, the aerodynamic performance improved for the glaze ice more than rime ice. The author attributes this to the increase in the effective camber due to the drooped leading edge, which delays the flow separation. Overall, HQ309 with less thickness has better aerodynamic performance than SD707 at a low value of α, and is reversed at higher α values. SD7032 revealed the best aerodynamic performance at rime ice condition. The observations were based on numerical results and no experimental validation is performed at low Reynolds number.

Hann et al. conducted wind tunnel studies on iced NREL S826 airfoil with the ice shape obtained from the LEWICE simulations [67] and the icing tunnel experiments [57]. Surface roughness effects were superimposed on the models using half-spheres arranged in a staggered pattern. The diameter of the sphere is the equivalent sand grain roughness (k_s) calculated using an empirical relation proposed by Shin et al. [31]. Former studies show severe performance penalties for the mixed ice with 30% reduction in lift and 340% increase in drag due to flow separation induced by the presence of horn structures. In contrast, the icing tunnel predicts more complex ice shapes for glaze conditions, and no prominent horns were observed for mixed ice conditions. Therefore, glaze ice had the largest aerodynamic penalties. Low Reynolds number indicates severe performance penalties, as does the increased surface roughness, especially for rime ice. In 2018, Hann [52] compared the aerodynamic performance of the ice shapes predicted by FENSAP ICE and LEWICE codes using the fluid flow solver FENSAP employing the SA turbulence model. The significant difference in the ice shape predicted by both codes was also reflected in the aerodynamic behavior. Overall, mixed ice showed severe performance degradation followed by glaze and rime. Further, numerical simulations were done with a forcibly tripped boundary layer and compared with the fully turbulent simulations. The tripped cases showed slightly higher performance penalties comparatively [57]. Severe aerodynamic penalties of RG-15 airfoil at glaze ice conditions with an increase in drag coefficient up to 160% were also reported by Fajt [68] based on his numerical studies using FENSAP and by Oswald [75] based on his experiments at wind tunnel facility. Fajt [68] also presented an index visualization of the aerodynamic coefficients to understand the intensity of performance degradation for different icing conditions, as shown in Figure 4. In 2021, Hann [55] reported that the increase in flow velocity has a detrimental effect on the aerodynamic performance of an RG15 airfoil, whereas an increase in chord length is favorable.

The numerical and experimental research forecast aerodynamic coefficients differently [57]. Viscous boundary layer effects overwhelm the inertia effects at low Reynolds numbers, favoring laminar flow. Existing turbulence models presume fully turbulent flows and hence cannot accurately resolve these issues. Flow transition from laminar to turbulent is another challenge; the initial laminar flow is so sensitive that even a mild pressure gradient can separate the flow. The separated flow re-attaches under certain flow conditions and forms a Laminar Separation Bubble (LSB) while transitioning from laminar to a turbulent state. LSB is a function of airfoil geometry and flow velocity and can be observed in the Reynolds number regime of 5×10^4 to 3×10^6 [76]. The flow separation induced by ice formation on the airfoil's leading edge is called an Ice Induced Separation Bubble (ISB) [77]. The ISB formed immediately downstream of the accreted ice at the leading edge, increasing its size with α. In contrast, an LSB formed downstream from the leading edge and moved upstream with increasing α. The formation of ISB or LSB changes the behavior of the boundary layer from laminar before separation to turbulent after reattachment. Additionally, the size of the LSB is contracted with the increase in *Re* [78], leading to complex flow behavior at low Reynolds numbers.

Oo et al. performed studies on clean and iced RG-15 airfoil to understand the behavior of LSB and ISB (Figure 5). The ice shapes were adopted from the icing tunnel studies of Williams [27]. In 2018 [79], unsteady numerical simulations were done by employing the Scale-Adaptive Simulation-Shear-Stress Transport (SAS-SST) model for turbulence [80]. LSB is not observed, and the flow is fully turbulent for the angle of attack considered. He extended the studies by performing transient Large Eddy Simulations (LES) at a different angle of attack (0°, 3° and 6°) in the successive years [81,82]. LSB is not observed on a clean airfoil at $\alpha = 0°$, but separation near the trailing edge is observed. With an increase in value of α, LSB is formed downstream of leading edge, and it moves upstream with further increase of α. ISBs are observed for the iced airfoil and the extend of separation bubble increased from 10 to 13% of the chord with increase in angle of attack, but the origin of separation remains the same. High frequency oscillations were observed in the transitional regions of ISB and LSB [83]. The frequency of these oscillations can sometimes be higher than the vortex shedding frequency of an airfoil [84]. The author also concluded that the characteristics of ISB and LSB are pretty similar, which agrees with the previous observation made by Bragg [85]. Oo [83] further extended the studies to a lower Reynolds number of 5×10^4. One of the key observations is that the flow reattachment is delayed for low Reynolds numbers and the extent of separation increases. The formation of a secondary separation bubble for $\alpha = 2°$ and 3° at a low Reynolds number is also observed. Similar observations on the behavior of LSB on RG-15 airfoil are also made by Oswald [75,86]. In contrary to all previous observations on aerodynamic behavior, Oo observed an increase in the lift coefficient from 0.11 to 0.22 and a decrease in drag for iced airfoils compared to clean airfoil (RG-15). The author suggested that the lift increment can be due to the boundary layer tripping, and the drag reduction can be due to the larger laminar separation bubble on clean airfoil relative to the ice induced separation bubble.

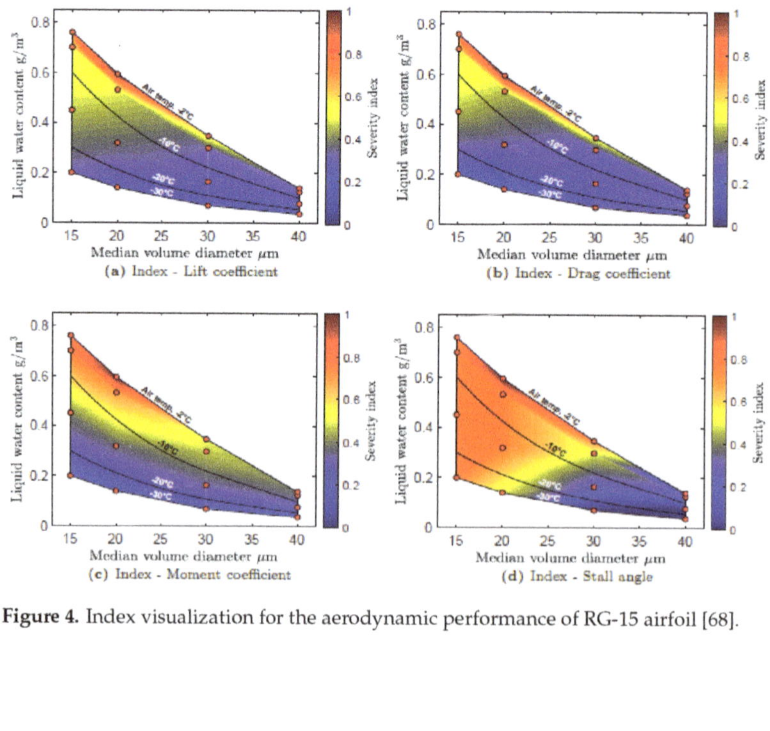

Figure 4. Index visualization for the aerodynamic performance of RG-15 airfoil [68].

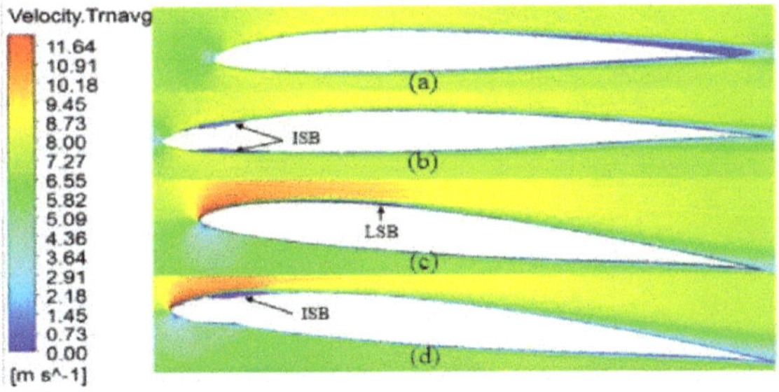

Figure 5. Formation of Laminar Separation Bubble (LSB) and Induced Separation Bubble (ISB): (**a**) 0° clean, (**b**) 0° iced, (**c**) 6° clean, (**d**) 6° iced [81].

A transitional three-equation turbulence model with a separated shear layer fix called the SPF $k - v^2 - \omega$ model [87] was used by Li in 2020 [69] to investigate the aerodynamic performance of an iced NREL S826 airfoil. It is observed that the pre-stall and near-stall characteristics predicted by the turbulence model match well with the experimental results compared to SST and SA turbulence models, which usually fail in the region close to the stall. The maximum loss in lift coefficient is 24.3% and the stall angle decreases by 6 degrees. One of the major attractions of this paper is the optimization of the airfoil design under icing conditions. The optimized airfoil design improves the lift coefficient by 18% by modifying the ice shape.

Discussion: It can be concluded from the reviewed work that icing can lead to severe aerodynamic penalties like loss of lift, an increase of drag, and premature stalling. A maximum reduction in the lift of up to 35% and an increase in drag of up to 340% is observed in UAVs due to ice accretion. Premature stalling also occurs at an angle of attack as low as 7°. The reduction in the maximum lift value affects the stability of the UAV and the increase in the drag coefficient leads to more power consumption. This can potentially limit the range and endurance of the UAV and thus affect the successful completion of its mission. Koenig [63] pointed out that glaze ice has a more significant impact on aerodynamic characteristics due to the greater surface roughness and larger extend. Further, glaze ice can lead to the formation of horns at an oblique angle with the surface, which in turn can lead to flow separation. The magnitude of the aerodynamic penalties depends on the shape, location, and extend of the ice accreted. The accumulated ice also adds weight to the structure of the UAV, which also has an indirect effect on its performance. The magnitude of the performance degradation is a function of ice shape, location, and extent. Fajt [68] highlights that one of the important uncertainties in the icing simulation is the assumption of fully turbulent flow. This can be valid for high values of angle of attack, due to the earlier flow separation but, for a small angle of attack, the flow can still be laminar at the leading edge. Thus, the assumption of fully turbulent flow induces artificial viscosity affects the delay of any possible flow separation. This can lead to overprediction of the lift coefficient and stall angle while underpredicting the drag coefficient. Additionally, the turbulent flow may increase the evaporation rate and thus reduce the liquid content leading to the wrong prediction of ice shapes as emphasized by Hann [88]. Thus, proper transition turbulence models must be implemented to model the laminar-turbulent transition phenomenon. Most studies are limited to the use of the SA and K-ω SST turbulence model, but they failed to predict the stall angle and maximum lift coefficient of the iced airfoil. Most existing studies used the profile of ice accreted at an 0° angle of attack to study aerodynamic performance as a function of the angle of attack. However, the position of ice changes with the angle of attack and leads to a considerable difference in the value of aerodynamic coefficients. Therefore, representative ice shapes at different angles of attack must be used to obtain more reliable aerodynamic coefficients. A database for various studies related to icing on fixed wing UAVs is given in Table 1.

Table 1. Database of existing studies on ice accretion on Unmanned Aerial Vehicle (UAV).

Reference	Year	Re $\times 10^5$	Airfoil	C (m)	Aerodynamic Data	Comments
Siquig [16]	1990	-	-	-	×	The impact of icing on two different UAVs is compared.
Koenig [63]	2000	-	UAV airfoil	-	×	Influence of T_∞, LWC, and MVD on ice accretion.
Koenig [10]	2003	-	NACA 0012	-	×	Influence of LWC clustering on ice accretion.
Avery [26]	2003	-	-	-	×	Influence of T_∞ and LWC on ice accretion.
Cistriani [70]	2007	10	flap slotted airfoil	0.6	✓	Ice accretion at CM and IM conditions.
Szilder [64]	2011	0.5, 1, 5, 1, 50	NACA 0012	0.0625 to 0.625	×	Influence of Re, T_∞, LWC and MVD on ice accretion.
Szilder [25]	2012					
Bottyan [71]	2013	4	Roncz Low Drag airfoil	0.3	×	Influence of V_∞ on ice accretion.
		40	NASA NLF 1015	1.6		
Szilder [65]	2015	9	SD7037	0.47	✓	Influence of T_∞, α, LWC, and MVD on ice accretion.
Szilder [66]	2017	9	HQ309, SD7032SD7037	0.47	✓	Effect of airfoil geometry on ice accretion.
Williams [27]	2017	2	RG15	0.21	✓	Icing tunnel experiments for 4 different cases.
Hann [89]	2017	15	NREL S826	0.3	✓	Aerodynamic performance studies based on flight simulation.
Hann [52]	2018	4	NREL S826	0.45	✓	Comparison of LEWICE and FENSAP-ICE.
Oo [79]	2018	2	RG-15	0.21	✓	Flow separation behavior is studied using the SAS-SST turbulence model.
Oo [81]	2018	1	RG-15	0.21	×	Flow separation behavior is studied using LES.
Fajt [68]	2019	8.6–10	RG-15	0.45	✓	Influence of T_∞, LWC, and MVD on ice accretion.
Hann [54]	2019	8.7	NREL S826, RG-15	0.45	×	Icing Tunnel studies, Two new ice shape acquisition techniques are discussed.
Hann [57]	2020	4	NREL S826	0.45	✓	Aerodynamic data is generated for three different Re of 2×10^5, 4×10^5, 6×10^5.
Oo [82]	2020	1.07	RG-15	0.21	×	Flow separation behavior is studied using LES.
Oo [83]	2020	0.5, 1	RG-15	0.21	×	Flow separation behavior is studied using LES.
Yirtici [73]	2020	4	NREL S826	0.45	✓	Influence of aspect ratio on ice accretion.
Oswald [75,86]	2021	8.7	RG-15	0.45	✓	Aerodynamic data is generated for three different Re of 2×10^5, 4×10^5, 7.5×10^5.
Hann [55]	2021	8.7	RG-15	0.45	✓	Effect of velocity and chord length on ice accretion.
Li [69]	2021	20	NREL S826	0.45	✓	A three-equation turbulence model is used, Design optimization of airfoils.

5. Effect of Icing on the Structural Integrity of UAVs

Ice accretion is a dynamic process, and the distribution of ice on the surface of a UAV wing or propeller blade is not uniform. Most ice accreted on the stagnation regions like the leading edge of wings or propellers, with the amount of ice accretion increasing from root to tip of the propeller blade. Further, the melting and ice shedding effects also contribute to uneven mass distribution. This mass imbalance can cause excessive vibrations. The ice accretion on the leading edge of the airfoil also shifts the center of gravity towards the elastic axis (increasing the critical flutter speed), increases the mass and inertia properties, increases the effective chord length, increases the aerodynamic drag and pitching moment loads, and decreases the lift [90]. These changes in the aerodynamic and structural behavior due to ice accretion can change the wing's modal properties (natural frequencies and damping ratio). They may lead to resonance and excess vibrations, affecting the aeroelastic behavior [91] and fatigue life of the structure [92]. These fatigue loads considerably reduce the lifetime of the UAV structure. Lighter systems like UAVs are more susceptible to aeroelastic instabilities like flutter. Studies related to the understanding of the effect of ice accretion on UAVs' structural behavior are not developed and need to be addressed to avoid potential structural damages. Similar studies were done on wind turbine applications and other structures. A detailed review of such works is not intended here, but a few of them are addressed here as a motivation for similar studies on UAVs. Etemaddar [92] pointed out that "*The aerodynamic properties are affected from the early stage of icing due to change in roughness and geometry of the leading edge of the blade, whereas the change in structural properties needs longer time and more ice accretion*". Additionally, he pointed out that the effect of icing on fatigue life is negligible due to the short duration of operation under icing conditions compared to the total lifetime.

In 2016, Gantasala et al. [91] studied the influence of ice accretion on the modal behavior of wind turbines. The natural frequency and damping factor of the blade decrease with ice accumulation. The ice mass distributed along the blade length determines the rate of reduction in frequencies. The damping factor is a function of aerodynamic coefficients; therefore, it depends mainly on the ice shape. It is also observed that the damping factor has a more considerable reduction due to icing than the natural frequencies. The variation of natural frequencies of the iced blade with wind velocities is negligible. Reducing the damping factor to even negative values is observed at higher velocities, leading to unstable vibrations. In 2017 [90], he conducted studies to understand the effect of aerodynamic and structural responses on flutter instability. As the ice mass increases, the center of gravity moves towards the elastic axis, and the flutter wind velocity increases. The flutter velocities also tend to decrease when considering the chord length increase. This can be due to increased pitching moment loads with the chord length. When aerodynamic behavior is also considered, the flutter velocity increases for ice shapes with lower aerodynamic loads and vice versa. Thus, the changes in the aerodynamic performance due to icing can be considered a critical parameter that alters the flutter instability. Thus, the accumulation of ice mass on the wing reduces its natural frequency and damping factor, decreasing the flutter wind velocity, and increasing the risk of aeroelastic instability. If resonance occurs, it can lead to excess vibration leading to failure and near-resonant vibrations can reduce the fatigue life of the wings.

6. Ice Detection and Ice Mitigation Techniques

Anti-icing and de-icing systems are the two types of Ice Protection Systems (IPS). The anti-icing mode heats the structure surface continually to prevent ice formation and can be done in two ways: *fully evaporative or running wet*. There can be no water run back in the first mode because the heat supplied entirely evaporates the droplet at the impingement location. However, it requires considerable heat flux and results in high surface temperatures. In the latter option, the heat is only used to keep the water from freezing. This mode requires less heat flux and lower surface temperature, but the surface must be heated extensively to prevent droplet freezing during water runback. In de-icing, ice is allowed to accumulate on the surface, and heat is used to melt it. The ice-surface interface can be melted or shed by aerodynamic forces. Dei-icing uses less power, but the accumulated ice might cause drag and structural damage during ice shedding. The problem of ice accretion on manned aircraft is extensively investigated, and suitable ice mitigation techniques are developed [19,93]. Traditional aircraft anti-icing methods use heat from engine bleed air, electro-thermal systems, or freezing point depressant chemicals to prevent ice buildup. Electromechanical systems like pneumatic de-icing boots, electro-expulsive systems, and electro-impulsive systems are typically used as de-icing systems. These systems are sophisticated, power-hungry, and require regular maintenance, limiting their use in smaller aircraft or UAVs.

Proper ice detection techniques need to be developed for the successful operation of an IPS. A brief overview of such systems designed for UAVs is done here before going to the review of an IPS. Botura [94] developed an Ice/No-Ice Sensor System (INISS) based on impedance measurement technique for in-flight ice detection on UAVs in 2003. The sensors are capable of detecting even thin coatings of ice. Cristofarao et al. (2015) proposed a Multiple Model Adaptive Estimation (MMAE)-based ice detection system for UAVs [95]. Unknown Input Observer (UIO) methods detect and estimate ice using changes in equilibrium caused by ice accumulation. A UIO-based ice detection method for UAVs with linearized longitudinal motion is proposed by Cristofaro et al. in 2015 [96]. This method is extended to the longitudinal nonlinear aircraft dynamics using Linear Parameter Varying (LPV) methods by Rotondo in 2015 [97]. Seron in 2015 [98] coupled the UIO and MMAE methods to develop an ice detection system with prespecified accuracy. An icing detection method based on the diagnosis of lift and drag changes on a UAV wing was proposed by Sørensen et al. in 2015 [99] and was modified by Wenz et al. in 2016 [100]. Rotondo developed an icing detection system that provides information about the icing location in 2017 [101]. The author published an extension of this work in 2019 [102]. A Fault Detection and Isolation (FDI) framework that uses model-based estimators of the various faults, implemented with multiple Kalman and Bayes filters, was proposed by Haaland et al. in 2021 [103].

Electromechanical de-icing systems shed the ice by applying impulse force on the wing surface with the help of some actuators. In 1988, Leonard Haslim invented the Electro Expulsive Separation System (EESS) consisting of two conductors embedded in a flexible material glued to the wing's leading edge. The magnetic fields of the conductors repel each other when current flows through them and provide enough impact to melt the ice [104]. Bhakta proposed a magnetostrictive de-icing method for UAVs in 2005 [105]. When the magnetostrictive materials are magnetized, they exhibit a change in length and create an impulse action. The ability of piezoelectric crystals to strain under an applied electric field is called the piezoelectric effect. The waves, generated through piezoelectric patches bonded onto the inner surface of the wing skin, cause a shear action at the ice/skin interface [106]. The magnitude of this shear action is amplified at specific excitation frequencies (Lamb waves), corresponding to wave lengths commensurable with the skin thickness. In 2014, Ameduri et al. [107] investigated the use of lamb waves as dei-icing systems for UAVs. The ultrasonic sound waves propagating at low frequency into a material can cause vibrations and debonding [108]. Shape Memory Alloy (SMA) on heating can change shape and create force through a martensitic phase shift [109].

Carbon Nano Tubes (CNT) have excellent electrical and thermal conductivity, making them ideal for de-icing UAVs using the Joule heating property of conductors [110–115]. Buschhorn et al. [110] in 2013 developed a CNT-based IPS, which can prevent icing with a power supply of only 1 kw/m^2 during less harsh icing conditions. In 2015, Sørensen et al. developed an electrically conductive paint based on graphene and carbon black nanoparticles that heat up when electricity passes through it [116]. A disadvantage of this system is the power consumption and increase in the weight of the UAV because of the coating, battery, and other components. Thermodynamic analysis [117] and flight testing [118] of the IPS are performed in successive years. The icing conditions at the high airspeed and low ambient temperature necessitate significant power consumption. In 2020, Idris et al. [115] used extrusion printing to fabricate electrical contacts on carbon fibers. The carbon fiber composites are then integrated into UAV wings to create a self-heating de-icing mechanism.

The carbon-based materials can shield the radio frequency signals, so an RF transmitting heat was proposed by Hwang et al. in 2020 [119].

Hann et al. [88] evaluated LEWICE with FENSAP ICE for simulating and estimating anti-icing loads in 2019. A sudden increase in the heat flux is observed at the transition region as the rate of convective heat transfer increases due to higher turbulence. The studies reveal the necessity of proper transition modeling for the icing studies at low Reynolds numbers. Hann [120] then tested Sørensen's IPS mounted on a wing with RG-15 airfoil for ice detection, anti-icing, and completely autonomous capabilities. The stagnation point at the leading edge has the highest power requirements. The author also concluded that the average heat flux numbers might not be a fair estimate of overall necessary heat loads, but the peak values around the leading edge are more significant. Hann et al. [120] tested the anti-icing, de-icing, and Parting Strip (PS) approach for ice mitigation on the same IPS in 2021. In the PS method, the stagnation zone at the leading edge is continuously heated to avoid ice formation, separating the ice on the upper and lower part of the airfoil. The ice split increases the aerodynamic force on the ice and allows for better shedding, as shown in Figure 6. The parting strip model requires substantially less shedding time and heat flux than conventional techniques. Thus, the author considers the parting strip mode as the most energy-efficient ice mitigation mode.

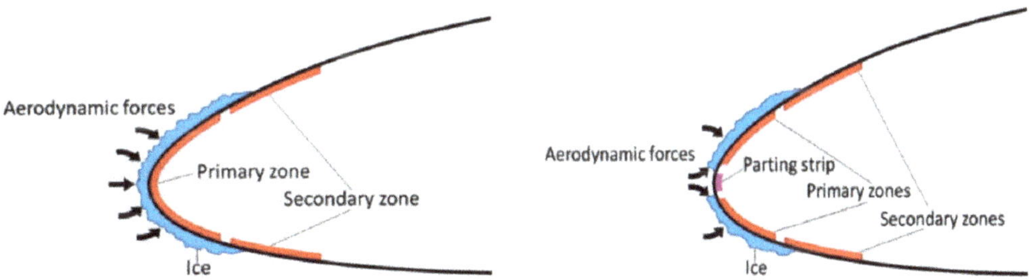

(**a**) (**b**)

Figure 6. Conventional (**a**) and Parting Strip (**b**) de-icing methods [120].

Superhydrophobic coatings can reduce the surface free energy and can generate hierarchical micro/nano-structured roughness. This can reduce the ice adhesion strength on the surface and thus prevent ice accumulation. Numerous studies related to different superhydrophobic coatings and the applicability of the same as an aircraft anti-icing material are done by Bhushan et al. [121–124] and Farzaneh et al. [23,125–129]. Ice accretion behavior of three different aluminum surfaces (hydrophilic, hydrophobic, and superhydrophobic) were compared by Wang in 2010 [130]. The research focuses on transmission line anti-icing; however, the findings can also be used for UAV ice mitigation. Initially, just a few portions of the superhydrophobic sample were coated with water droplets, whereas the hydrophobic was partially and the hydrophilic was entirely covered. Water droplets turned into the ice with increasing spraying time; however, no new ice crystals developed on superhydrophobic surfaces. Ice covered more of the hydrophobic surface and the whole of the hydrophilic surface with time. Thus, super hydrophobicity reduces surface wettability by increasing the average water contact angle to over 150°. The same for hydrophobic surfaces of more than 90° and for hydrophilic surfaces, it is less than 70°. Piscitelli [131] in 2020 proposed a superhydrophobic coating for small aircraft that can reduce the surface free energy by 99% with respect to the reference considered in the study. Additionally, the proposed coating was effective at temperatures as low as −27 °C.

Discussion: The following are the primary requirements for an efficient IPS: (1) lightweight, (2) low power consumption, (3) low maintenance and cost, and (4) reliable operation and short response time. (5) Minimal/no change in aerodynamic design. The main disadvantage of electromechanical and electrical heating systems is their weight. Continuous use of electromechanical systems can cause structural damage, while electric heating requires more power, and superhydrophobic coatings degrade over time. As a result, an optimal ice protection system for UAVs that meets all requirements has yet to be developed.

7. Conclusions

The existing scientific knowledge about the ice accretion phenomenon on fixed-wing UAVs has been reviewed and the significant limitations in the current understanding of the same are identified. Icing tunnel experiments and numerical icing simulations are the most prominent methods used to study ice accretion. Icing tunnel experiments have the limitation of being unable to precisely generate the icing conditions found in nature, whereas numerical codes are lagging due to a lack of proper validation data. The capability of existing numerical icing codes in predicting the ice accretion for glaze ice conditions is limited due to the complex physics involved in its formation. Therefore, improved understanding and modeling of such physics are required. The shape, size, and nature of the ice formed are governed by the complex interplay of various environmental, geometrical, and material properties. The accretion of ice on the surface of an airfoil can deteriorate the aerodynamic shape of the airfoil as well as alter the surface characteristics like roughness, mean camber, and effective chord length. The variation of these parameters can alter the aerodynamic behavior by inducing flow transition (laminar to turbulent), flow separation, and it can also affect the distribution of pressure and shear force on the surface of the airfoil. Icing causes severe aerodynamic penalties like a decrease in the lift, increase in drag, and premature stalling. Therefore, the development of low-cost, lightweight, and energy-efficient ice mitigation systems is necessary to ensure the all-weather operation of UAVs.

Author Contributions: Conceptualization, M.M. and M.S.V.; methodology, M.M.; investigation, M.M.; data curation, M.M.; writing—original draft preparation, M.M.; writing—review and editing, M.M.; supervision, M.S.V. All authors have read and agreed to the published version of the manuscript.

Funding: The work reported in this paper is supported by the UiT- The Arctic University of Norway (Project no-7400-72104) & nICE project of UiT & Research Council of Norway (Project no-324156).

Institutional Review Board Statement: Not applicable.

Informed Consent Statement: Not applicable.

Data Availability Statement: The data presented in this study are available on request from the corresponding author.

Conflicts of Interest: The authors declare no conflict of interest.

References

1. Singhal, G.; Bansod, B.S.; Mathew, L. Unmanned Aerial Vehicle Classification, Applications and Challenges: A Review. *Preprints* **2018**, 2018110601. [CrossRef]
2. Gupta, S.; Ghonge, M.; Jawandhiya, P. Review of Unmanned Aircraft System (UAS). *Int. J. Adv. Res. Comput. Eng. Technol.* **2013**, *2*, 1646–1657. [CrossRef]
3. Alvarado, E. Drone Application Report 2021. 2021. Available online: https://droneii.com/237-ways-drone-applications-revolutionize-business (accessed on 15 January 2022).
4. Weatherington, D.; Deputy, U. *Unmanned Aircraft Systems Roadmap, 2005–2030*; U.S. Department of Defense: Washington, DC, USA, 2005.
5. Curry, J.; Maslanik, J.; Holland, G.; Pinto, J. Applications of Aerosondes in the Arctic. *Bull. Am. Meteorol. Soc.-Bull. Am. Meteorol. Soc.* **2004**, *85*, 1855–1861. [CrossRef]
6. Clark, D.G.; Ford, J.D.; Tabish, T. What Role Can Unmanned Aerial Vehicles Play in Emergency Response in the Arctic: A Case Study from Canada. *PLoS ONE* **2018**, *13*, e0205299. [CrossRef] [PubMed]
7. CAA. CAP 1036: Global Fatal Accident Review 2002 to 2011. In *Civil Aviation Authority 1036*; CAA: Los Angeles, CA, USA, 2013; pp. 1–134.
8. Haulman, D.L. *US Unmanned Aerical Vehicles in Combat 1991–2003*; Air Force Historical Research Agency: Montgomery, AL, USA, 2003.

9. Peck, L.; Ryerson, C.C. *Army Aircraft Icing*; Technical Report ERDC/CRREL TR-02-13; US Army Corps of Engineers: Washington, DC, USA, 2002.
10. Koenig, G.; Ryerson, C.; Larsson, J.; Reehorst, A. Effect of Variable LWC on Ice Shape in the NASA-GRC IRT. In Proceedings of the 41st Aerospace Sciences Meeting and Exhibit, Reno, NV, USA, 6–9 January 2003.
11. Li, N.; Liu, X.; Yu, B.; Li, L.; Xu, J.; Tan, Q. Study on the environmental adaptability of lithium-ion battery powered UAV under extreme temperature conditions. *Energy* **2021**, *219*, 119481. [CrossRef]
12. Wang, B.H.; Wang, D.B.; Ali, Z.A.; Ting Ting, B.; Wang, H. An overview of various kinds of wind effects on unmanned aerial vehicle. *Meas. Control* **2019**, *52*, 731–739. [CrossRef]
13. How Is an UAV Affected by In-Flight Icing and Can We Simulate It Accurately? Available online: https://uavicinglab.com/2021/05/28/how-is-an-uav-affected-by-in-flight-icing-and-can-we-simulate-it-accurately/ (accessed on 15 January 2022).
14. Avery, A.S. *Ice Accretion on Small Unmanned Aircraft*; Oklahoma State University: Stillwater, OK, USA, 2019.
15. Hacker, P.T.; Dorsch, R.G. *A Summary of Meteorological Conditions Associated with Aircraft Icing and a Proposed Method of Selecting Design Criterions for Ice-Protection Equipment*; National Advisory Committee for Aeronautics: Washington, DC, USA, 1951.
16. Siquig, R.A. *Impact of Icing on Unmanned Aerial Vehicle (UAV) Operations*; Naval Environmental Prediction Research Facility: Monterey, CA, USA, 1990.
17. Li, L.; Liu, Y.; Zhang, Z.; Hu, H. Effects of thermal conductivity of airframe substrate on the dynamic ice accretion process pertinent to UAS inflight icing phenomena. *Int. J. Heat Mass Transf.* **2019**, *131*, 1184–1195. [CrossRef]
18. Lynch, F.; Khodadoust, A. Effects of ice accretions on aircraft aerodynamics. *Prog. Aerosp. Sci.* **2001**, *37*, 669–767. [CrossRef]
19. Bragg, M.B.; Broeren, A.P.; Blumenthal, L.A. Iced-airfoil aerodynamics. *Prog. Aerosp. Sci.* **2005**, *41*, 323–362. [CrossRef]
20. Makkonen, L.E. *Ice and Construction*, 1st ed.; CRC Press: Boca Raton, FL, USA, 1994.
21. Makkonen, L. Modeling of Ice Accretion on Wires. *J. Appl. Meteorol. Climatol.* **1984**, *23*, 929–939. [CrossRef]
22. Makkonen, L.; Laakso, T.; Marjaniemi, M.; Finstad, K. Modelling and Prevention of Ice Accretion on Wind Turbines. *Wind. Eng.* **2001**, *25*, 3–21. [CrossRef]
23. Farzaneh, M. *Atmospheric Icing of Power Networks*; Springer: Dordrecht, The Netherlands, 2008.
24. Finstad, K.J. *Numerical and Experimental Studies of Rime Ice Accretion on Cylinders and Airfoils*; University of Alberta: Edmonton, AB, Canada, 1986.
25. Szilder, K.; McIlwain, S. In-flight icing of UAVs—The influence of flight speed coupled with chord size. *Can. Aeronaut. Space J.* **2012**, *58*, 83–94. [CrossRef]
26. Avery, A.S.; Jacob, J.D. Evaluation of Low Altitude Icing Conditions for Small Unmanned Aircraft. In Proceedings of the 9th AIAA Atmospheric and Space Environments Conference, Denver, CO, USA, 5–9 June 2017; p. 3929.
27. Williams, N.B.A.; Brian, G.; Ol, M. The effect of icing on small unmanned aircraft low Reynolds number airfoils. In Proceedings of the 17th Australian International Aerospace Congress (AIAC), Melbourne, Australia, 26–28 February 2017.
28. Matiychyk, L.; Suvorova, N.; Tereshchenko, D.; Plakhotniuk, I.; Trachuk, K.; Komarova, K. Influence of Icing on Aircraft Performance of Unmanned Aerial Vehicle M-10-2 "Oko". *Proc. Natl. Aviat. Univ.* **2017**, *4*, 52–59. [CrossRef]
29. Siddique, M.A. An Experimental Study on the Effects of Adverse Weathers on the Flight Performance of an Unmanned-Aerial-System (UAS). Ph.D. Thesis, Iowa State University, Ames, Iowa, 2021. [CrossRef]
30. Gray, V.H. *Aerodynamic Effects Caused by Icing of an Unswept NACA 65A004 Airfoil*; National Advisory Commitee for Aeronautics, Lewis Flight Propulsion Laboratory: Cleveland, OH, USA, 1958.
31. Shin, J.; Bond, T.H. Experimental and computational ice shapes and resulting drag increase for a NACA 0012 airfoil. In Proceedings of the Fifth Symposium on Numerical and Physical Aspects of Aerodynamic Flows, Long Beach, CA, USA, 13–15 January 1992.
32. Shin, J.; BOND, T. Results of an icing test on a NACA 0012 airfoil in the NASA Lewis icing research tunnel. In Proceedings of the 30th Aerospace Sciences Meeting and Exhibit, Reno, NV, USA, 6–9 January 1992; p. 647.
33. Potapczuk, M.C. Aircraft Icing Research at NASA Glenn Research Center. *J. Aerosp. Eng.* **2013**, *26*, 260–276. [CrossRef]
34. Cain, G.E.; Yurczyk, R.F.; Belter, D.L.; Chintamani, S.H. *Boeing Research Aerodynamic/Icing Tunnel Capabilities and Calibration*; SAE Technical Paper; SAE International: Warrendale, PA, USA, 1994. [CrossRef]
35. Oleskiw, M.; Hyde, F.; Penna, P. In-flight icing simulation capabilities of NRC's altitude icing wind tunnel. In Proceedings of the 39th Aerospace Sciences Meeting and Exhibit, Reno, NV, USA, 8–11 January 2001.
36. Bansmer, S.E.; Baumert, A.; Sattler, S.; Knop, I.; Leroy, D.; Schwarzenboeck, A.; Jurkat-Witschas, T.; Voigt, C.; Pervier, H.; Esposito, B. Design, construction and commissioning of the Braunschweig Icing Wind Tunnel. *Atmos. Meas. Tech.* **2018**, *11*, 3221–3249. [CrossRef]
37. Hammond, D. Cranfield University Icing Wind Tunnel. In Proceedings of the 41st Aerospace Sciences Meeting and Exhibit, Reno, NV, USA, 6–9 January 2003; p. 901.
38. Vecchione, L.; De Matteis, P. An Overview of the CIRA Icing Wind Tunnel. In Proceedings of the 41st Aerospace Sciences Meeting and Exhibit, Reno, NV, USA, 6–9 January 2003; p. 900.
39. Fengler, M. *Study of Propeller Icing Hazard in Mini-UAV Aviation*; Meteomatics GmbH Technical Report; Meteomatics GmbH: Berlin, Germany, 2017.
40. Kind, R.; Potapczuk, M.; Feo, A.; Golia, C.; Shah, A. Experimental and computational simulation of in-flight icing phenomena. *Prog. Aerosp. Sci.* **1998**, *34*, 257–345. [CrossRef]

41. Messinger, B.L. Equilibrium Temperature of an Unheated Icing Surface as a Function of Air Speed. *J. Aeronaut. Sci.* **1953**, *20*, 29–42 [CrossRef]
42. Wright, W. *User's Manual for LEWICE Version 3.2*; NTRS—NASA Technical Reports Server (NASA/CR—2008-214255 November 2008); NASA Technical Reports Server (NTRS): Cleveland, OH, USA, 2008.
43. Hedde, T.; Guffond, D. ONERA three-dimensional icing model. *AIAA J.* **1995**, *33*, 1038–1045. [CrossRef]
44. Trontin, P.; Kontogiannis, A.; Blanchard, G.; Villedieu, P. Description and assessment of the new ONERA 2D icing suite IGLOO2D. In Proceedings of the 9th AIAA Atmospheric and Space Environments Conference, Denver, CO, USA, 5–9 June 2017. [CrossRef]
45. Mingione, G.; Brandi, V.; Saporiti, A. A 3D ice accretion simulation code. In Proceedings of the 37th Aerospace Sciences Meeting and Exhibit, Reno, NV, USA, 11–14 January 1999; p. 247.
46. Paraschivoiu, I.; Saeed, F. Ice accretion simulation code canice. In Proceedings of the International Areospace Symposium Bucharest, Romania, 19–20 October 2001; pp. 81–86.
47. Szilder, K.; Lozowski, E.P. Simulation of airfoil icing with a novel morphogenetic model. *J. Aerosp. Eng.* **2005**, *18*, 102–110. [CrossRef]
48. Morency, F.; Beaugendre, H.; Baruzzi, G.; Habashi, W. FENSAP-ICE-A comprehensive 3D simulation system for in-flight icing. In Proceedings of the 15th AIAA Computational Fluid Dynamics Conference, Anaheim, CA, USA, 11–14 June 2001; p. 2566.
49. Tran, P.; Barruzi, G.; Tremblay, F.; Habashi, W.; Petersen, P.; Ligget, M.; Vos, J.; Benquet, P.; Fiorucci, S. FENSAP-ICE applications to unmanned aerial vehicles (UAV). In Proceedings of the 42nd AIAA Aerospace Sciences Meeting and Exhibit, Reno, NV, USA 5–8 January 2004.
50. Kind, R.J. *Ice Accretion Simulation Evaluation Test (Essai d'evaluation de la simulation de l'accumulation de glace)*; North Atlantic Treaty Organization RTO Technical Rept. TR-038; Nato Research and Technology Organization: Neuilly-Sur-Seine, France, 2001; p. 32.
51. AC-9C Aircraft Icing Technology Committee. *Icing Wind Tunnel Interfacility Comparison Tests*; Aerospace Information Report, AIR5666, SAE Aerospace; SAE International: Warrendale, PA, USA, 2012. [CrossRef]
52. Hann, R. UAV Icing: Comparison of LEWICE and FENSAP-ICE for Ice Accretion and Performance Degradation. In Proceedings of the 2018 Atmospheric and Space Environments Conference, Atlanta, Georgia, 25–29 June 2018.
53. Jeck, R.K. *Icing Design Envelopes (14 CFR Parts 25 and 29, Appendix C) Converted to a Distance-Based*; Federal Aviation Administration, U.S. Department of Transportation: Washington, DC, USA, 2002.
54. Hann, R. UAV Icing: Ice Accretion Experiments and Validation In Proceedings of the International Conference on Icing of Aircraft, Engines, and Structures, Minneapolis, MN, USA, 17–21 June 2019.
55. Hann, R.; Johansen, T.A. UAV icing: The influence of airspeed and chord length on performance degradation. *Aircr. Eng. Aerosp Technol.* **2021**, *93*, 832–841. [CrossRef]
56. Hann, R. Atmospheric Ice Accretions, Aerodynamic Icing Penalties, and Ice Protection Systems on Unmanned Aerial Vehicles. Ph.D. Thesis, Norwegian University of Science and Technology, Trondheim, Norway, 2020.
57. Hann, R.; Hearst, R.J.; Sætran, L.; Bracchi, T. Experimental and Numerical Icing Penalties of an S826 Airfoil at Low Reynolds Numbers. *Aerospace* **2020**, *7*, 46. [CrossRef]
58. Tummers, M.J.; Steunebrink, M. Effect of surface roughness on heat transfer in Rayleigh-Bénard convection. *Int. J. Heat Mass Transf.* **2019**, *139*, 1056–1064. [CrossRef]
59. Zhang, Y.-Z.; Sun, C.; Bao, Y.; Zhou, Q. How surface roughness reduces heat transport for small roughness heights in turbulent Rayleigh–Bénard convection. *J. Fluid Mech.* **2018**, *836*, R2. [CrossRef]
60. Myers, T.G. Extension to the Messinger Model for Aircraft Icing. *AIAA J.* **2001**, *39*, 211–218. [CrossRef]
61. Dukhan, N.; Va, G., Jr.; Masiulaniec, K.; DeWitt, K. Convective heat transfer coefficients from various types of ice roughened surfaces in parallel and accelerating flow. In Proceedings of the 34th Aerospace Sciences Meeting and Exhibit, Reno, NV, USA, 15–18 January 1996.
62. Henry, R.C.; Guffond, D.; Garnier, F.; Bouveret, A. Heat Transfer Coefficient Measurement on Iced Airfoil in Small Icing Wind Tunnel. *J. Thermophys. Heat Transf.* **2000**, *14*, 348–354. [CrossRef]
63. Koenig, G.; Ryerson, C.; Kmiec, R. UAV icing flight simulation. In Proceedings of the 40th AIAA Aerospace Sciences Meeting & Exhibit, Reno, NV, USA, 14–17 January 2002.
64. Szilder, K.; McIlwain, S. *In-Flight Icing of UAVs—The Influence of Reynolds Number on the Ice Accretion Process*; SAE Technical Paper 2011-01-2572; SAE International: Warrendale, PA, USA, 2011. [CrossRef]
65. Szilder, K.; Yuan, W. The Influence of Ice Accretion on the Aerodynamic Performance of a UAS Airfoil. In Proceedings of the 53rd AIAA Aerospace Sciences Meeting, Kissimmee, FL, USA, 5–9 January 2015. [CrossRef]
66. Szilder, K.; Yuan, W. In-flight icing on unmanned aerial vehicle and its aerodynamic penalties. *Prog. Flight Phys.* **2017**, *9*, 173–188. [CrossRef]
67. Krøgenes, J.; Brandrud, L.; Hann, R.; Bartl, J.; Bracchi, T.; Sætran, L. Aerodynamic Performance of the NREL S826 Airfoil in Icing Conditions. *Wind. Energ. Sci. Discuss.* **2017**, *2017*, 1–17. [CrossRef]
68. Fajt, N.; Hann, R.; Lutz, T. The Influence of Meteorological Conditions on the Icing Performance Penalties on a UAV Airfoil. In Proceedings of the 8th European Conference for Aeronautics and Space Sciences (EUCASS), Madrid, Spain; 2019.
69. Li, H.; Zhang, Y.; Chen, H. Optimization design of airfoils under atmospheric icing conditions for UAV. *Chin. J. Aeronaut.* **2021**, *35*, 118–133. [CrossRef]

70. Cistriani, L. Falco UAV Low Reynolds Airfoil Design and Testing at Galileo Avionica. In *UAV Design Processes/Design Criteria for Structures*; Galileo Avionica Ronchi Dei Legionari (Italy) Simulators and Uav Business Unit; RTO: Neuilly-sur-Seine, France, 2007.
71. Bottyán, Z. In-flight icing characteristics of unmanned aerial vehicles during special atmospheric condition over the Carpathian-basin. *Landsc. Environ.* **2013**, *7*, 74–80.
72. Bottyán, Z. Estimation of in-flight icing characteristics of UAVs during different meteorological conditions. In Proceedings of the 8th International Conference on Intelligent Unmanned Systems (ICIUS 2012), Singapore, 22 October 2012; pp. 418–422.
73. Körpe, D.S.; Yırtıcı, Ö.; Özgen, S. Aerodynamic Performance Losses due to Ice Formation on the UAV's Wings. *J. Aeronaut. Space Technol.* **2020**, *13*, 207–215.
74. Langtry, R.B.; Menter, F. Correlation-Based Transition Modeling for Unstructured Parallelized Computational Fluid Dynamics Codes. *AIAA J.* **2009**, *47*, 2894–2906. [CrossRef]
75. Oswald, J.W.; Enache, A.; Hann, R.; Glabeke, G.; Lutz, T. UAV Icing: Experimental and Numerical Study of Glaze Ice Performance Penalties on an RG-15 Airfoil. In Proceedings of the AIAA Scitech 2022 Forum, San Diego, CA, USA, 3–7 January 2022.
76. Hain, R.; Kähler, C.; Radespiel, R. Dynamics of laminar separation bubbles at low-Reynolds-number aerofoils. *J. Fluid Mech.* **2009**, *630*, 129–153. [CrossRef]
77. Gurbacki, H. Ice-Induced Unsteady Flowfield Effects on Airfoil Performance. Ph.D. Thesis, University of Illinois at Urbana-Champaign, Champaign, IL, USA, 2003.
78. O'Meara, M.M.; Mueller, T.J. Laminar separation bubble characteristics on an airfoil at low Reynolds numbers. *AIAA J.* **1987**, *25*, 1033–1041. [CrossRef]
79. Oo, N.L.; Kay, N.J.; Brenkley, A.J.; Sharma, R.N. Investigation into the behaviour of an iced low Reynolds number aerofoil. In Proceedings of the 10th International Micro-Air Vehicles Conference, Melbourne, Australia, 22–23 November 2018.
80. Garbaruk, A.; Shur, M.; Strelets, M. NACA0021 at 60 deg. incidence. *Notes Numer. Fluid Mech. Multidisiplinary Des.* **2009**, *103*, 127–139.
81. Oo, N.L.; Richards, P.J.; Sharma, R.N. Numerical investigation of clean and ice-accreted aerofoils at low Reynolds number and low angle of attack. In Proceedings of the 21st Australasian Fluid Mechanics Conference, Adelaide, Australia, 10–13 December 2018.
82. Oo, N.L.; Richards, P.J.; Sharma, R.N. Ice-Induced Separation Bubble on RG-15 Airfoil at Low Reynolds Number. *AIAA J.* **2020**, *58*, 5156–5167. [CrossRef]
83. Oo, N.L.; Richards, P.; Sharma, R. Influence of an ice-induced separation bubble on the laminar separation bubble on an RG-15 airfoil at low Reynolds numbers. In Proceedings of the AIAA AVIATION 2020 FORUM, Virtual, 15–19 June 2020. [CrossRef]
84. Huang, R.F.; Lin, C.L. Vortex shedding and shear-layer instability of wing at low-Reynolds numbers. *AIAA J.* **1995**, *33*, 1398–1403. [CrossRef]
85. Bragg, M.B.; Khodadoust, A.; Spring, S.A. Measurements in a leading-edge separation bubble due to a simulated airfoil ice accretion. *AIAA J.* **1992**, *30*, 1462–1467. [CrossRef]
86. Oswald, J.W. UAV Icing: Numerical and Experimental Study of Performance Penalties on an RG-15 Airfoil. Master's Thesis, University of Stuttgart, Stuttgart, Germany, 2021.
87. Li, H.; Zhang, Y.; Chen, H. Aerodynamic Prediction of Iced Airfoils Based on Modified Three-Equation Turbulence Model. *AIAA J.* **2020**, *58*, 3863–3876. [CrossRef]
88. Hann, R. UAV Icing: Comparison of LEWICE and FENSAP-ICE for Anti-Icing Loads. In Proceedings of the AIAA Scitech 2019 Forum, San Diego, CA, USA, 7–11 January 2019.
89. Hann, R.; Wenz, A.; Gryte, K.; Johansen, T. Impact of Atmospheric Icing on UAV Aerodynamic Performance. In Proceedings of the 2017 Workshop on Research, Education and Development of Unmanned Aerial Systems (RED-UAS), Linköping, Sweden, 3–5 October 2017.
90. Gantasala, S. *Flutter Analysis of an Aerofoil Section with Different Ice Shapes at the Leading Edge*; Luleå University of Technology: Luleå, Sweden, 2017.
91. Gantasala, S.; Luneno, J.-C.; Aidanpää, J.-O. Influence of Icing on the Modal Behavior of Wind Turbine Blades. *Energies* **2016**, *9*, 862. [CrossRef]
92. Etemaddar, M.; Hansen, M.; Moan, T. Wind turbine aerodynamic response under atmospheric icing conditions. *Wind. Energy* **2014**, *17*, 241–265. [CrossRef]
93. Thomas, S.K.; Cassoni, R.P.; MacArthur, C.D. Aircraft anti-icing and de-icing techniques and modeling. *J. Aircr.* **1996**, *33*, 841–854. [CrossRef]
94. Botura, G.; Fahrner, A. Icing Detection System—Conception, Development, Testing and Applicability to UAVs. In Proceedings of the 2nd AIAA Unmanned Unlimited Conference and Workshop & Exhibit, San Diego, CA, USA, 15–18 September 2003.
95. Cristofaro, A.; Johansen, T.A.; Aguiar, A.P. Icing detection and identification for unmanned aerial vehicles: Multiple model adaptive estimation. In Proceedings of the 2015 European Control Conference (ECC), Linz, Austria, 15–17 July 2015; pp. 1651–1656.
96. Cristofaro, A.; Johansen, T.A. An unknown input observer approach to icing detection for unmanned aerial vehicles with linearized longitudinal motion. In Proceedings of the 2015 American Control Conference (ACC), Chicago, IL, USA, 1–3 July 2015; pp. 207–213.

97. Rotondo, D.; Cristofaro, A.; Johansen, T.A.; Nejjari, F.; Puig, V. Icing detection in unmanned aerial vehicles with longitudinal motion using an LPV unknown input observer. In Proceedings of the 2015 IEEE Conference on Control Applications (CCA), Sydney, Australia, 21–23 September 2015; pp. 984–989.
98. Seron, M.M.; Johansen, T.A.; Doná, J.A.D.; Cristofaro, A. Detection and estimation of icing in unmanned aerial vehicles using a bank of unknown input observers. In Proceedings of the 2015 5th Australian Control Conference (AUCC), Gold Coast, Australia, 5–6 November 2015; pp. 87–92.
99. Sorensen, K.L.; Blanke, M.; Johansen, T.A. Diagnosis of Wing Icing Through Lift and Drag Coefficient Change Detection for Small. *IFAC-PapersOnLine* **2015**, *48*, 541–546. [CrossRef]
100. Wenz, A.; Johansen, T.A. Icing detection for small fixed wing UAVs using inflight aerodynamic coefficient estimation. In Proceedings of the 2016 IEEE Conference on Control Applications (CCA), Buenos Aires, Argentina, 19–22 September 2016; pp. 230–236.
101. Rotondo, D.; Cristofaro, A.; Hassani, V.; Johansen, T.A. Icing diagnosis in unmanned aerial vehicles using an LPV multiple model estimator. *IFAC-PapersOnLine* **2017**, *50*, 5238–5243. [CrossRef]
102. Wenz, A.; Johansen, T.A. Icing Detection for Small Fixed Wing UAVs using Inflight Aerodynamic Coefficient Estimation. In Proceedings of the 2019 IEEE Aerospace Conference, Big Sky, MT, USA, 2–9 March 2019; pp. 1–9.
103. Haaland, O.M.; Wenz, A.W.; Gryte, K.; Hann, R.; Johansen, T.A. Detection and Isolation of Propeller Icing and Electric Propulsion System Faults in Fixed-Wing UAVs. In Proceedings of the 2021 International Conference on Unmanned Aircraft Systems (ICUAS), Athens, Greece, 15–18 June 2021; pp. 377–386.
104. Energy-Efficient Systems Eliminate Icing Danger for UAVs. Available online: https://spinoff.nasa.gov/Spinoff2010/ps_2.html (accessed on 15 January 2022).
105. Bhakta, B. Novel Ice Protection System Suitable for Unmanned Aerial Vehcile Wing. Ph.D. Thesis, Cranfield University, Cranfield, UK, 2005.
106. Venna, S.V.; Lin, Y.-J.; Botura, G. Piezoelectric Transducer Actuated Leading Edge De-Icing with Simultaneous Shear and Impulse Forces. *J. Aircr.* **2007**, *44*, 509–515. [CrossRef]
107. Ameduri, S.; Guida, D. Investigations on the use of Lamb waves for de-icing purposes. In Proceedings of the ICAST2014: 25nd International Conference on Adaptive Structures and Technologies, The Hague, The Netherlands, 6–8 October 2014.
108. Palacios, J.; Smith, E.; Gao, H.; Rose, J. Ultrasonic Shear Wave Anti-Icing System for Helicopter Rotor Blades. In Proceedings of the American Helicopter Society 62nd Annual Forum, Phoenix, AZ, USA, 9–11 May 2006.
109. Myose, R.Y.; Horn, W.J.; Hwang, Y.; Herrero, J.; Huynh, C.; Boudraa, T. *Application of Shape Memory Alloys for Leading Edge Deicing*; SAE Technical Paper; SAE: Warrendale, PA, USA, 1999. [CrossRef]
110. Buschhorn, S.T.; Kessler, S.S.; Lachmann, N.; Gavin, J.; Thomas, G.; Wardle, B.L. Electrothermal Icing protection of Aerosurfaces Using Conductive Polymer Nanocomposites. In Proceedings of the 54th AIAA/ASME/ASCE/AHS/ASC Structures, Structural Dynamics, and Materials Conference, Boston, MA, USA, 8–11 April 2013.
111. Farcas, C.; Galao, O.; Vertuccio, L.; Guadagno, L.; Romero-Sánchez, M.D.; Rodríguez-Pastor, I.; Garcés, P. Ice-Prevention and De-Icing Capacity of Epoxy Resin Filled with Hybrid Carbon-Nanostructured Forms: Self-Heating by Joule Effect. *Nanomaterials* **2021**, *11*, 2427. [CrossRef]
112. Redondo, O.; Prolongo, S.G.; Campo, M.; Sbarufatti, C.; Giglio, M. Anti-icing and de-icing coatings based Joule's heating of graphene nanoplatelets. *Compos. Sci. Technol.* **2018**, *164*, 65–73. [CrossRef]
113. Guadagno, L.; Foglia, F.; Pantani, R.; Romero-Sanchez, M.D.; Calderón, B.; Vertuccio, L. Low-Voltage Icing Protection Film for Automotive and Aeronautical Industries. *Nanomaterials* **2020**, *10*, 1343. [CrossRef]
114. Vertuccio, L.; Foglia, F.; Pantani, R.; Romero-Sánchez, M.D.; Calderón, B.; Guadagno, L. Carbon nanotubes and expanded graphite based bulk nanocomposites for de-icing applications. *Compos. Part B Eng.* **2021**, *207*, 108583. [CrossRef]
115. Idris, M.K.; Qiu, J.; Melenka, G.W.; Grau, G. Printing electronics directly onto carbon fiber composites: Unmanned aerial vehicle (UAV) wings with integrated heater for de-icing. *Eng. Res. Express* **2020**, *2*, 025022. [CrossRef]
116. Sorensen, K.; Helland, A.; Johansen, T. Carbon nanomaterial-based wing temperature control system for in-flight anti-icing and de-icing of unmanned aerial vehicles. In Proceedings of the IEEE Aerospace Conference Proceedings, Big Sky, MT, USA, 7–14 March 2015. [CrossRef]
117. KimLynge Sørensen, T.A.J. Thermodynamics of a Carbon Nano-Materials Based Icing Protection System for Unmanned Aerial Vehicle. In Proceedings of the IEEE Aerospace Conference, Big Sky, MT, USA, 5–12 March 2016.
118. S⊘rensen, K.L.; Johansen, T.A. Flight test results for autonomous icing protection solution for small unmanned aircraft. In Proceedings of the 2017 International Conference on Unmanned Aircraft Systems (ICUAS), Miami, FL, USA, 13–16 June 2017; pp. 971–980.
119. Hwang, H.; Ma, K.Y.; Kim, J.W.; Yuk, D.; Hong, J.; Jung, J.H.; Yong, S.-M.; Choi, J.; Kim, J.Y.; Shin, H.S. Radio-frequency-transmitting hexagonal boron nitride-based anti- and de-icing heating system. *Nanoscale* **2020**, *12*, 21895–21900. [CrossRef]
120. Hann, R.; Enache, A.; Nielsen, M.C.; Stovner, B.N.; van Beeck, J.; Johansen, T.A.; Borup, K.T. Experimental Heat Loads for Electrothermal Anti-Icing and De-Icing on UAVs. *Aerospace* **2021**, *8*, 83. [CrossRef]
121. Bhushan, B.; Chae Jung, Y. Wetting study of patterned surfaces for superhydrophobicity. *Ultramicroscopy* **2007**, *107*, 1033–1041. [CrossRef] [PubMed]

22. Michael, N.; Bhushan, B. Hierarchical roughness makes superhydrophobic states stable. *Microelectron. Eng.* **2007**, *84*, 382–386. [CrossRef]
23. Nosonovsky, M.; Bhushan, B. Roughness-induced superhydrophobicity: A way to design non-adhesive surfaces. *J. Phys. Condens. Matter* **2008**, *20*, 225009. [CrossRef]
24. Nosonovsky, M.; Bhushan, B. Patterned Nonadhesive Surfaces: Superhydrophobicity and Wetting Regime Transitions. *Langmuir* **2008**, *24*, 1525–1533. [CrossRef]
25. Farhadi, S.; Farzaneh, M.; Kulinich, S.A. Anti-icing performance of superhydrophobic surfaces. *Appl. Surf. Sci.* **2011**, *257*, 6264–6269. [CrossRef]
26. Farzaneh, M.; Ryerson, C. Anti-icing and deicing techniques. *Cold Reg. Sci. Technol.* **2011**, *65*, 88–96. [CrossRef]
27. Kulinich, S.; Farzaneh, M. How Wetting Hysteresis Influences Ice Adhesion Strength on Superhydrophobic Surfaces. *Langmuir ACS J. Surf. Colloids* **2009**, *25*, 8854–8856. [CrossRef]
28. Kulinich, S.A.; Farzaneh, M. Ice adhesion on super-hydrophobic surfaces. *Appl. Surf. Sci.* **2009**, *255*, 8153–8157. [CrossRef]
29. Kulinich, S.A.; Farzaneh, M. Effect of contact angle hysteresis on water droplet evaporation from super-hydrophobic surfaces. *Appl. Surf. Sci.* **2009**, *255*, 4056–4060. [CrossRef]
30. Wang, F.; Li, C.; Lv, Y.; Lv, F.; Du, Y. Ice accretion on superhydrophobic aluminum surfaces under low-temperature conditions. *Cold Reg. Sci. Technol.* **2010**, *62*, 29–33. [CrossRef]
31. Piscitelli, F.; Chiariello, A.; Dabkowski, D.; Corraro, G.; Marra, F.; Di Palma, L. Superhydrophobic Coatings as Anti-Icing Systems for Small Aircraft. *Aerospace* **2020**, *7*, 2. [CrossRef]

applied sciences

MDPI

Article

Automatic Air-to-Ground Recognition of Outdoor Injured Human Targets Based on UAV Bimodal Information: The Explore Study

Fugui Qi [1,†], Mingming Zhu [1,2,†], Zhao Li [1], Tao Lei [1], Juanjuan Xia [1], Linyuan Zhang [1], Yili Yan [1], Jianqi Wang [1] and Guohua Lu [1,*]

1 Department of Military Biomedical Engineering, Air Force Military Medical University, Xi'an 710032, China; qifgbme@outlook.com (F.Q.); 15928198580@163.com (M.Z.); lizhaofmmu@fmmu.edu.cn (Z.L.); pan-ds@live.com (T.L.); magnolxia@163.com (J.X.); zly2947@163.com (L.Z.); richard1207@163.com (Y.Y.); wangjq@fmmu.edu.cn (J.W.)

2 Drug and Instrument Supervisory & Test Station of Xining Joint Service Support Center, PLA, Lanzhou 730050, China

* Correspondence: lugh1976@fmmu.edu.cn; Tel.: +86-29-84711471

† These authors contributed equally to this work.

Abstract: The rapid air-to-ground search of injured people in the outdoor environment has been a hot spot and a great challenge for public safety and emergency rescue medicine. Its crucial difficulties lie in the fact that small-scale human targets possess a low target-background contrast to the complex outdoor environment background and the human attribute of the target is hard to verify. Therefore an automatic recognition method based on UAV bimodal information is proposed in this paper. First, suspected targets were accurately detected and separated from the background based on multispectral feature information only. Immediately after, the bio-radar module would be released and would try to detect their corresponding physiological information for accurate re-identification of the human target property. Both the suspected human target detection experiments and human target property re-identification experiments show that our proposed method could effectively realize accurate identification of ground injured in outdoor environments, which is meaningful for the research of rapid search and rescue of injured people in the outdoor environment.

Keywords: air-to-ground search; human target; multispectral imagery; bio-radar

Citation: Qi, F.; Zhu, M.; Li, Z.; Lei, T.; Xia, J.; Zhang, L.; Yan, Y.; Wang, J.; Lu, G. Automatic Air-to-Ground Recognition of Outdoor Injured Human Targets Based on UAV Bimodal Information: The Explore Study. *Appl. Sci.* **2022**, *12*, 3457. https://doi.org/10.3390/app12073457

Academic Editors: Andrzej Łukaszewicz, Wojciech Giernacki, Zbigniew Kulesza, Jaroslaw Pytka and Andriy Holovatyy

Received: 4 March 2022
Accepted: 26 March 2022
Published: 29 March 2022

1. Introduction

The search for injured people in outdoor environments has always been a hot topic in the field of social public safety and emergency rescue medicine, and mainly include two types [1]. The first search scenario is about the trapped survivors under ruins in an abnormal post-disaster environment, such as natural or sudden disasters (earthquakes, building collapses, landslides, etc.). The detection challenge under this scenario is how to penetrate the ruins to reliably detect weak physiological movements of surviving human beings in the post-disaster site with relatively limited area. To address this problem, a new *bio-radar* detection technology, which is a combination of biomedical engineering technology and radar technology, was firstly proposed by our group in the academic field. Bio-radar emits electromagnetic waves to detect survivors' physiological activities (breathing and heartbeat) through the ruins and corresponding vital signs would be acquired by demodulating the radar echo. Leveraging the bio-radar and various signal processing technologies [2–4], a series of bio-radar equipment was developed, and corresponding functions are gradually enriched so that we can not only detect the vital signs [5–8] but also localized information. Specifically, with our proposed equipment and algorithms, we can even detect multiple (Max. 3) survivors simultaneously [9,10]. Currently, our latest technologies are aiming to distinguish between human and animals (non-human targets) under ruins [11,12], and even recognize human activities [13,14]. In practical applications, typical equipment we have developed was also successfully used in many search-and-rescue operations (such as "SJ-3000" and "SJ-6000" search-and-rescue UWB bio-radar used in the Wenchuan earthquake in 2008, Yushu earthquake in 2010, Ludian earthquake in 2014, and so on in China) and made a great contribution.

Another widespread and frequently occurring search scenario is about the injured person in a normal outdoor environment, namely a natural environment, such as the lost donkeys, crashed parachute jumpers, and wilderness travelers almost submerged in the vast and diverse natural environment. For example, during a distressing disaster at a sporting event, a large number of athletes suffered a safety accident due to the sudden change of weather in the 2021 4th Yellow River Shilin Mountain Marathon 100 km cross-country race in China [15]. Many athletes experienced the severe hypothermia phenomenon and were trapped in the mountains, making it urgent but difficult to locate and detect them quickly. However, due to the lack of air-to-ground rapid search and location technology, the information of the trapped people in the outdoor environment was not sent to the rear security center in time, resulting in a number of deaths that could not be treated in time.

In general, human target search technology in an outdoor natural environment can be divided into constrained and unconstrained modes. For constrained methods, humans need pre-wear auxiliary positioning devices, such as portable radio stations, wearable GPS personal terminals, or wireless search devices with vital signs monitoring functions. Nevertheless, these methods suffer from some inevitable deficiencies including increasing body load, inconvenient operation, and high costs [16–18]. Moreover, in the above scenario, our searching targets are often located in some extreme mountain forest environments or carry-on devices might have been seriously damaged, making it hard or even incapable to receive the information. Instead of wearing the auxiliary device, the unconstrained search technology based on unmanned detection technology could effectively avoid the above problems [19].

Currently, there is indeed some unconstrainedly unmanned aerial vehicle (UAV)-based air-to-ground detection technologies for human target search in ideal background environments. Different carried payloads mean different detection principles and detection capabilities, and current technologies mainly include RGB high-definition camera [20,21] and thermal imaging camera [22] on UAV for low altitude search. But the RGB camera still appears to have insufficient resolution and low SNR when the detection distance is long or the object is similar in color with the environment, and even appears underexposure or overexposure when the ambient light changes [23]. Similarly, the thermal signal of the human body would be covered by the halos when the ambient temperature is higher than 30 °C.

As an optimized form of hyperspectral technology, multispectral could relatively streamline data volume and realize real-time imaging processing by rationally selecting 4~10 characteristic spectrum bands for data processing [24], which could ensure sufficient information volume. By analyzing the differences of spectral characteristic curves between target and circumstances, specific features in different bands can be exploited to identify the target. At present, UAV-based multispectral detection technology is widely used in agricultural, forestry, and environmental monitoring under low altitude cruise conditions. Based on this technology, researchers have successfully achieved some detection performance, such as the damage assessment to rapeseed crop after winter [25], decision support system design for variable rate irrigation [26], fast Xylella symptoms detection in olive trees [27] and inferring the spatial distribution of chlorophyll concentration and turbidity in surface waters to monitor the nearshore–offshore water quality [25] and so on.

However, for the rapid detection and identification of injured human subjects in an outdoor environment, the detection scenario is remarkably different from the above scenarios, showing more severe detection difficulties and challenges. Unfortunately, there is still a lack of corresponding effective technology. Fundamentally, the key difficulties lie in: (1) the injured human subject in an outdoor environment is always in a still state without remarkable motion, such as lying on the ground, making it difficult to be detected; (2) the injured human target is just a small target with a much smaller area compared with the surrounding environment under an airborne high-altitude view; (3) the difference between the clothing of injured people and the surrounding environment is weak, showing low target-background contrast; (4) additionally, all these methods cannot acquire unique physiological characteristics to identify the human attribute of the suspected target.

In this paper, we propose an automatic recognition method for injured human targets in an outdoor natural environment based on UAV bimodal information. It can not only efficiently detect the suspected human subjects based on multispectral features under low target-background contrast but also acquire the vital signals for re-identification through autonomously scanning large areas using a quad-rotor UAV equipped with a multispectral imaging sensor and bio-radar.

This paper will be organized as follows: The materials and methods will be introduced in Section 2, including multispectral image acquisition, multispectral image pre-processing, and target identification. Section 3 presents the results of each step mentioned above. Section 4 discusses the experiment results and conclusion.

2. Bimodal Information Collection System

In order to obtain bimodal information of ground targets, this study builds a bimodal information collection system based on a UAV carrying dual sensors (shown in Figure 1), with the main function of obtaining spectral feature information and vital sign information. It is mainly composed of three components. Their relationship and system operation principle is illustrated by Figures 2 and 3, respectively: (1) the optimal multispectral sensing module acquires spectral information for the preliminary detection of suspected human targets; (2) miniature bio-radar module acquires vital sign information for human subject reconfirmation; (3) UAV carrying system and ground workstation are mainly responsible for carrying out flight and information transmission control tasks. In the following, we will give a detailed description of the 3 main components of the whole system and the coordination between them.

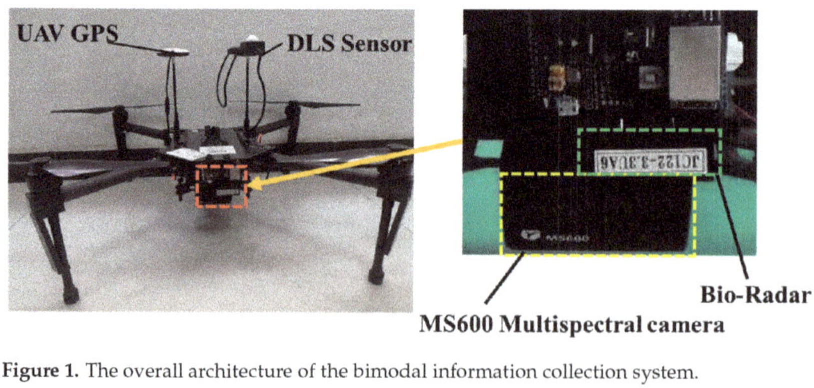

Figure 1. The overall architecture of the bimodal information collection system.

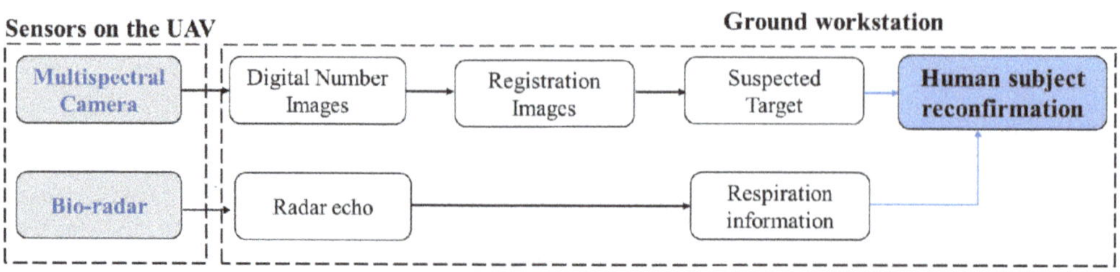

Figure 2. The diagram of the bimodal information collection system.

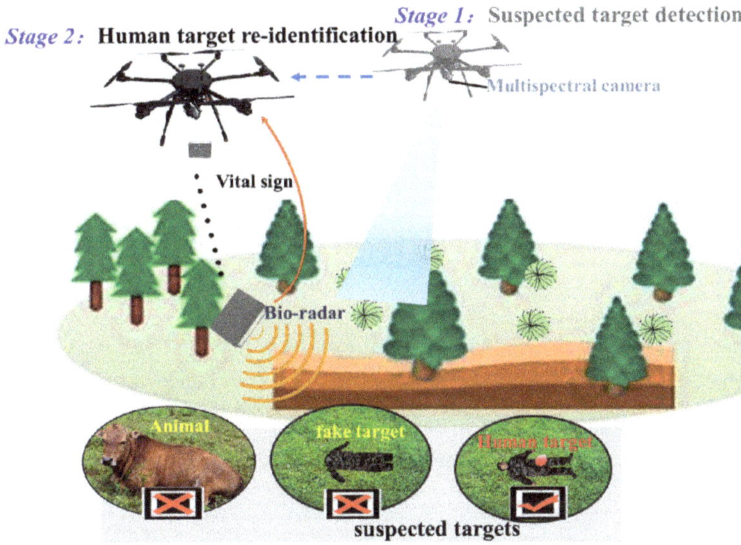

Figure 3. Suspected target detection and human nature re-identification based on UAV bio-modal information from multispectral camera and bio-radar.

2.1. The Optimized Multispectral Sensing Module

The multispectral sensing (MSS) module on a cruising UAV at high altitude is used to acquire some specific spectral features of the target background for suspected human targets detection, which is referred to in *stage 1* in Figure 3 during the entire search process. In our study, a few multispectral bans are specifically selected by observing and analyzing the sensitivity of different spectral bands to the environment and background. Consequently, some optimal bands would be picked out from numerous hyperspectral bands, which has the greatest ability to distinguish suspected human targets from the natural environment with complex background situations.

Since the relative reflectivity was defined as follows:

$$R_{relative} = \frac{L_{subject}}{L_{board}} \cdot R_{board} \quad (1)$$

where $R_{relative}$ and R_{board} are the reflectivity of subject and reference board, $L_{subject}$ and L_{board} are the spectral radiance of subject and reference board. According to the spectral curve, we could pick out corresponding characteristic points which are promising to distinguish green clothes from grassland.

In our study, a large number of preliminary measurement experiments were carried out to obtain the wavelength-relative reflectivity curve for green vegetation (to simulate background) and green camouflage (to simulate suspected injured human target outdoors) using a spectrometer. Here, the ATP9100 portable object spectrometer was used to measure the current spectral parameters of ground objects (wavelength range of 300~1100 nm, 2048-pixel CCD detector, spectral resolution of 1.4 nm, wavelength accuracy of 0.5 nm, and signal-to-noise ratio > 800) [28]. The instrument parameters are set as follows: automatic integral time, multiple detections, and followed with dark-current correction. Specifically, we measured three times the ground objects in one validation experiment. The measurement duration is 1–10 s and they will be integrated optimally. Then, the average spectral parameters of ground objects could be acquired by averaging. Finally, the spectral reflectance curve of green clothes and green vegetation can be acquired as shown in Figure 4.

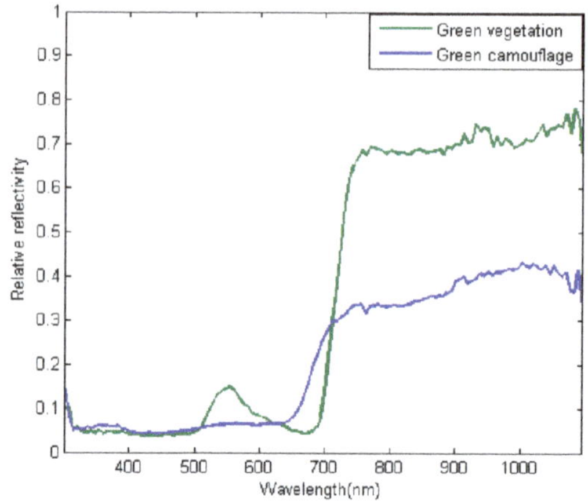

Figure 4. The spectral relative reflectivity of green vegetation and green camouflage.

Target recognition based on single-band features is vulnerable and unstable. Therefore by constructing sensitive spectral indexes through inter-band operations, background-target differences could be enhanced, which would facilitate the target extraction. By observing the wavelength-relative reflectivity curve in Figure 4, there are six bands showing significant differences between background and the target; thus, they are promising for later target identification: (1) in the 400~500 nm band, the spectral curves of camouflage clothing and green vegetation follow the same trend, and the reflectance is low and difficult to distinguish, so the band of 450 nm can be used as the reference point for the inter-band calculation; (2) there is a reflection peak caused by vegetation chlorophyll in the spectrum curve of green vegetation in 550~560 nm band, which is much higher than that of green camouflage. So, the band of 555 nm is selected; (3) in the 660~690 nm band, there is an absorption peak that corresponds to the reflectance of green vegetation, which is much lower than the reflectance of camouflage clothing, so the band of 660 nm is selected; (4) nearby 710 nm, the reflectance of green vegetation rose sharply and reached the peak rapidly, thus the band of 710 nm is adopted as the first high-reflectivity band; (5) the high-reflectivity-platform continues until 1000 nm. This band of camouflage clothing has high contrast with green vegetation, and the characteristics are obvious. Therefore, the band of 840 nm and 940 nm are reasonably selected for feature recognition. Within a certain band number range, more spectra contain richer information. Through extracting features from these selected specific bands in the blue band, green band, red band, red edge band, near-infrared band, the ability to specifically characterize the target will be strengthened, which would greatly facilitate the target identification.

Based on the analysis above and market research, a multispectral sensor that meets our requirements above, the MS600 camera, was adopted in our study. It is composed of six single-band cameras. Each camera has its own optical path and photocarrier that records the data of the corresponding imaging band. Six spectral bands (shown in Table 1) could be acquired to form MS600 multispectral camera. Band selection should meet the requirements of large amounts of information and small correlation between bands. The camera was equipped with 1/3-inch sensor size, 1280 × 960 pixels, global shutter, 1.5 s maximum capture rate, 7.5 cm ground pixel resolution at 120 m altitude, size 77 × 72 × 47 mm, weight 170 g, DLS (downwelling light sensor) and GPS module, each image can record GPS information in real-time. The image data collected by MS600 multispectral sensor were sets of DN values (remote sensing image pixel brightness value) of six bands, which were used to record the gray value of ground objects.

Table 1. The selected spectral bands.

Band Number	Band Name	Centre Wavelength (nm)	Bandwidth (nm)
1	blue	450 ± 3 nm	22 ± 5 nm
2	green	555 ± 3 nm	22 ± 5 nm
3	red	660 ± 3 nm	22 ± 5 nm
4	red edge	710 ± 3 nm	32 ± 5 nm
5	near-infrared	840 ± 3 nm	32 ± 5 nm
6		940 ± 3 nm	32 ± 5 nm

2.2. Micro-Bio-Radar Module

After the suspected targets are detected by multispectral technology, the bio-radar module will play another critical role in re-identifying the human nature of these suspected targets, which is referred to *stage 2* in Figure 3 during the entire search process. Just as the working principle illustrated by Figure 3, after the suspected human target is detected, the bio-radar module will be triggered and accurately released around the target. Based on the radar Doppler principle [4], the physiological activity information of the suspected target can be obtained. Our group has successfully realized the detection of human respiration and body movement in the field environment [29]. So, taking physiological motion features (respiration rate or heartbeat rate) as a reference, accurate re-identification of surviving human targets will be possible.

The bio-radars, which were thrown out to remote sensing the respiratory in our study is JC122-3.3UA6 module. It is a 24 GHz continuous wave (CW) micro-radar and its effective detection range is 10 m. The hardware of this system mainly includes a radar sensor for human chest breathing detection [4], STM32 single-chip microcomputer, and LoRa module for initial data A/D convert and data sending.

2.3. UAV Carrying System and Ground Workstation

The overall architecture of the bimodal information collection system is shown in Figure 1. The M100 Quad-rotor UAV system [30], which could vertical take-off and land with a payload of 1245 g, is adopted here to carry the multispectral camera and the bio-radar module. The ground workstation is responsible for information transmission, target identification, and system control. The coordination between the system mainly includes four parts: (1) the MSS module on the cruising UAV first detect the suspected targets; (2) ground workstation sends commands to the UAV, which automatically triggers an airborne dropper to drop the bio-radar to a location around the target; (3) the bio-radar sensor can transmit asymmetric wide beam signal and obtain the microwave echo reflected by human chest moving. After being filtered and amplified, the respiratory signal is converted into digital signals through STM32 A/D and sent to the ground -workstation receiver by LoRa module; (4) by further analysis and judgment based on embedded algorithms, both respiration rate detection and human target property re-identification could be realized.

3. Bimodal-Information-Based Human Targets Recognition Method

Based on the ground target information collected by the above system, a bimodal-information-based human target recognition method, namely a scheme, is proposed for accurate injured human subject identification in an outdoor environment. The flowchart of this method is shown in Figure 5 and is consist of two main parts: (1): suspected target detection based on multispectral feature information, including multispectral images pre-processing spectral feature extraction, and decision tree (DT) construction for suspected target detection; (2) human subject reconfirmation based on respiration information detected by bio-radar.

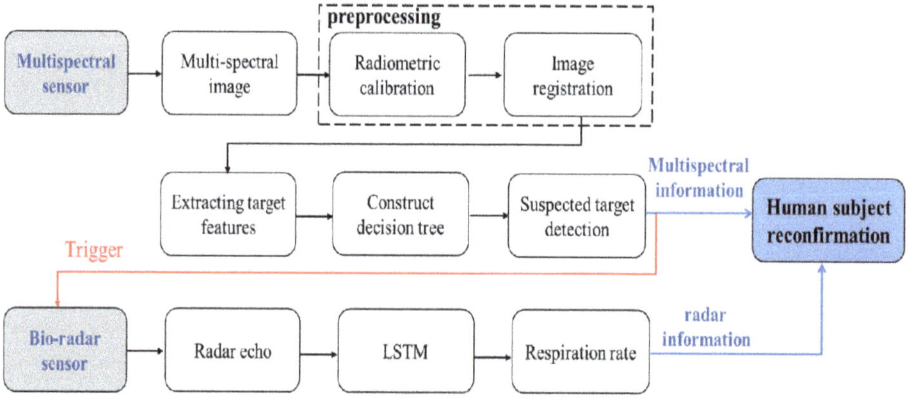

Figure 5. The flowchart of bimodal-information-based human targets recognition method.

3.1. Suspected Target Detection Based on Multispectral Feature Information

(1) Multispectral image preprocessing

Before further analyzing and processing the multispectral images, it is necessary to preprocess them to remove multifactor interference effects. The preprocessing process is shown in Figure 6.

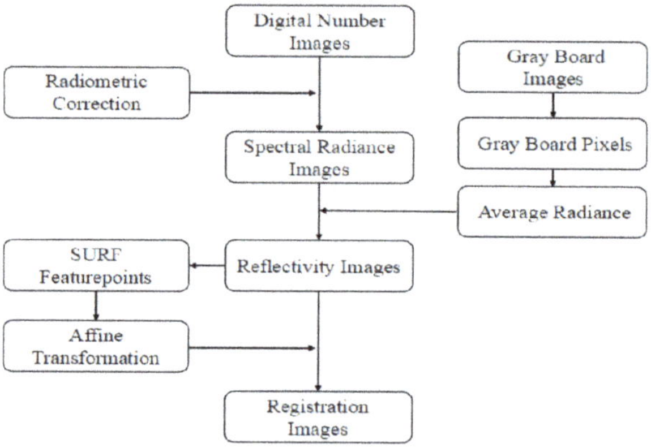

Figure 6. Flow chart of multispectral imagery preprocessing.

1st step: Radiometric calibration. Radiometric calibration consists of radiometric correction and reflectance calculation. Radiometric correction mainly converts the DN value into spectral radiance value and corrects radiation distortion caused by lens transmission and sensor response [31]. The calculated reflectivity can reflect the real spectral characteristics of ground objects. We should identify and calculate the average radiance of the gray board pixels from gray board images, which were obtained by MS600 before the flight. At the first step, identify the gray board area in the images by selecting the largest nonzero connected region after running the function of binarization and image closure. Then, locate the center of the gray board using the average values of row coordinates and column coordinates. Make a square mask centered on the center coordinate point. The DN value of the gray board area can be extracted by dot multiplication of mask and gray board image. Finally, we can calculate the radiance of each pixel. With the above steps, the DN value of the multispectral images was converted into the reflectivity value, and the vignetting effect was corrected.

2nd step: Image registration. Each exposure of the MS600 camera can generate six single-band images. Although this kind of sensor has the advantages of simple design and low cost, the limitation of the structure will lead to a dislocation between imaging bands. Image registration must be done before further processing. In this stage, the main task is to synthesize these six single-band images into one data file in TIFF format. Firstly, the SURF (Speeded Up Robust Features) algorithm is used to detect the feature points in every image, which is a robust local feature point detection and description algorithm [32]. The Hessian matrix is constructed to generate all interest points, build scale space, locate feature points, and generate feature point descriptors. Then, after matching the feature points between every two images, the RANSAC (random sample consensus) algorithm is used to eliminate mismatching points [33]. Finally, abnormal matching points would be eliminated by computing the affine transformation matrix between each image and the registration will be completed through the affine transform.

(2) Multispectral feature extraction

The regions of interest (ROI) can be extracted manually according to the low altitude high-definition images, which can show the distribution of experimental subjects (3 typical objects are selected, including human subjects, vegetation, and soil). The reflectivity feature is the top preferred feature. Here, a statistic experiment on the reflectivity feature distribution of different targets is carried out based on numerous collected data. The statistical result of the reflectivity of 3 ground objects in the image analyzed by ENVI software is shown in Figure 7a. It is obvious reflectivity features of six bands could be exploited to distinguish between target and background to some extent but cannot solve the problem entirely.

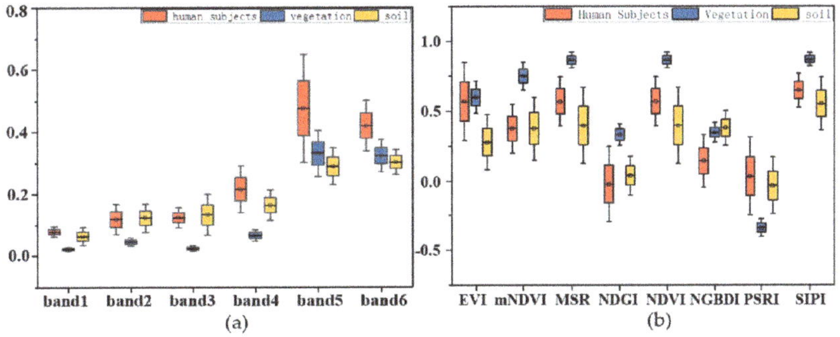

Figure 7. Two kinds of features for 3 typical subjects. (**a**) Reflectivity of six bands, (**b**) Spectral indexes.

The spectral index can be another kind of feature to enhance target difference and quantify it by band math. According to the spectral curves captured from the green camouflage, vegetation, and bare soil, the following 8 spectral indexes were taken into consideration, and they are calculated as shown in Table 2. Where *NDVI* stands for Normalized Difference Vegetation Index, *NDGI* (Normalized Difference Green Index), *NGBDI* (Normalized Green-Blue Difference Index), *PSRI* (Plant Senescence Reflectance Index), SIPI (Structure Insensitive Pigment Index), *mNDVI* (modified red edge Normalized Difference Vegetation Index), *MSR* (Modified Simple Ratio Index), *EVI* (Enhanced Vegetation Index), *R* means reflectivity, R_{blue} (band1), R_{green} (band2), R_{red} (band3), R_{710} (band4), R_{nir} and R_{840} (band5).

The statistical results of the 6 spectral indices over 3 ground objects based on numerous data are shown in Figure 7b. It can be noticed that *NDVI*, *mNDVI*, *MDR*, *PSRI*, and *SIPI* could separate vegetation from the ground subjects effectively. We chose *NDVI* to set the upper bound and *PSRI* to set the lower bound that could achieve the best effect of separating vegetation. Then, bare soil should be separated from the remaining area, *EVI* and *NGBDI* were chosen to set a reasonable threshold to exclude the bare soil area. Band 6 was selected to filter the human subjects according to the band reflectivity figure and combined with the size of the target area that noise spot could be excluded out.

Table 2. Calculation formula of 8 spectral indexes.

Number	Calculation Formula	Number	Calculation Formula
1	$NDVI = \frac{R_{nir}-R_{red}}{R_{nir}+R_{red}}$	5	$SIPI = \frac{R_{nir}-R_{blue}}{R_{nir}+R_{red}}$
2	$NDGI = \frac{R_{red}-R_{green}}{R_{red}+R_{green}}$	6	$mNDVI = \frac{R_{nir}-R_{redge}}{R_{nir}+R_{redge}-2*R_{blue}}$
3	$NGBDI = \frac{R_{green}-R_{blue}}{R_{green}+R_{blue}}$	7	$MSR = \frac{R_{nir}/R_{red}-1}{R_{nir}/R_{red}+1}$
4	$PSRI = \frac{R_{red}-R_{green}}{R_{nir}}$	8	$EVI = \frac{2.5*(R_{nir}-R_{red})}{R_{nir}+6*R_{red}-7.5*R_{blue}+1}$

(3) Decision tree construction for suspected target detection

The DT is exploited as the target classification and identification model for automatic recognition and positioning in this study. As a method of extracting species information DT classification has the characteristics of convenience and high efficiency, which is widely used in the classification of below three species [34]. Vegetation index and band reflectivity were selected as spectral variables to classify by threshold method. Based on the spectral index, band reflectance, and target area, we constructed a DT and set reasonable thresholds to complete target identification as shown in Figure 8. Specifically, the NDVI threshold of 0.75 comes from the maximization of interclass variance (Otsu) and statistical experience based on a large number of measured experiments.

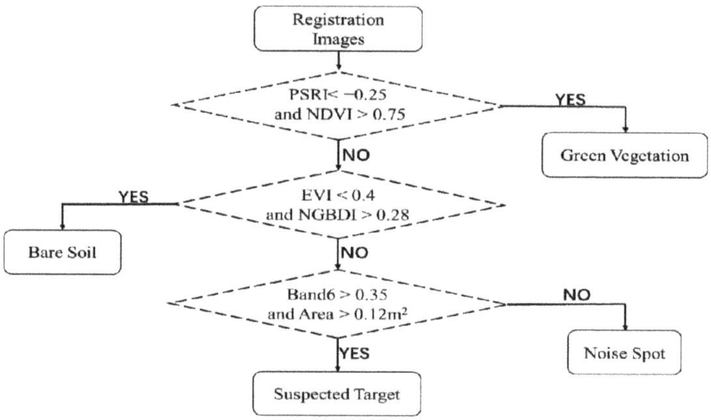

Figure 8. The DT for identification of suspected target.

3.2. Human Subject Reconfirmation Based on Respiration Information Detected by Bio-Radar

After detecting the suspected human target based on the spectral features above, the bio-radar module will be triggered and released near ground targets. It aims to detect the physiological features of the suspected target for the reconfirmation of human attributes. The CW bio-radar will transmit electromagnetic waves to illuminate the human target around and the echo is modulated by micromotions of the body surface, such as breathing. By demodulating the echo and obtaining the phase information, we can obtain the respiration-related features. However, the outdoor environment is full of noise and clutter, resulting in serious interference with radar echo, making it difficult to obtain a stable and effective breathing signal. Therefore, finding a way to filter out the clutter and noise interference from the radar is highly important.

Based on the characteristics analysis of the noise and breathing signals, the adaptive line enhancer (ALE) is adopted for noise cancellation. The ALE is a deformation of the adaptive pair eliminator, and we can use various adaptive filtering algorithms to process the signal when the main and reference inputs are determined. Here the Normalized Last

Mean Squares (NLMS) error algorithm is adopted for many reasons such as robustness, timeliness, and convergence speed. The flow of the algorithm is as follows (Figure 9).

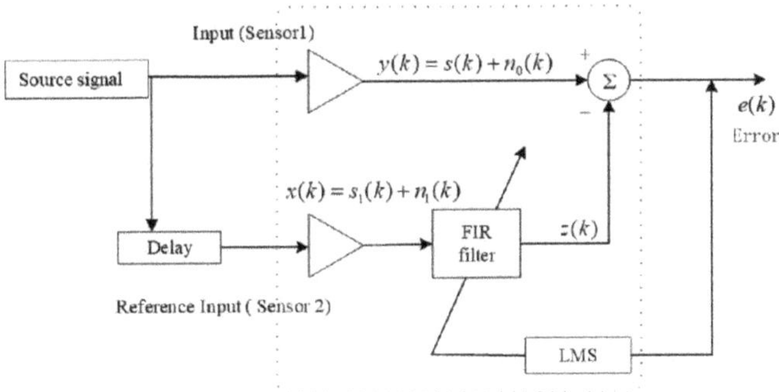

Figure 9. Block diagram of ALE.

$s(k)$ is the useful respiration signal, $n_0(k)$ is noise signal, namely wideband signal. $s_1(k)$ is the delayed respiration signal of $s(k)$; thus, they have a strong correlation after the delay, so the correlation between them is weak. According to the principle of self-use pair eliminator, during the process of $e(k)$ minimizing through $z(k)$ and $y(k)$ gradually becoming close, the only way is to make the $s_1(k)$ and $s(k)$ closest through FIR filter with adjustable coefficients. Consequently, respiration signals with high SNR could be acquired from $z(k)$.

After the noise and clutter cancellation, the respiration rate could be acquired by performing some frequency domain analysis on the preprocessed signal, which would be the most direct and specific feature for human attributions reconfirmation.

4. Experiment and Results

4.1. Experimental Setup

The setup of the bimodal information collection system is shown in Figure 1. The MS600 multispectral module containing those six specific bands and bio-radar module are carried by the M100 Quad-rotor UAV system for target detection and recognition. The flight mission was carried out in a wheat field in Hu County, Xi'an City, Shaanxi Province on 24 March 2021. The weather is sunny, cloudless with downwards third-class winds, which is suitable for the UAV flight. The flight remained at an altitude of 120 m, 5.3 m/s, 5 routes with 80% course overlap rate and 75% side overlap rate.

Two kinds of typical experiments were carried out in this study, namely the suspected target detection experiment based on multispectral feature information only and the human subject reconfirmation experiment with auxiliary human vital sign information. More specifically, the first kind of experiment was also conducted in two typical scenarios illustrated by Figure 10. *Scenario 1* holds a relatively homogeneous environmental background with a few kinds of components (green grassland and, a small piece of land). Twelve sets of green camouflage clothes were laid on the field randomly to disguise as human subjects. *Scenario 2* is purposely selected as an outdoor bush environment in autumn, which is more complex and closer to practical applications as shrubs, green lawns, trees, dark yellow, and other vegetation randomly scattered. Here, three colors of camouflage (11 pieces of camouflage and one real person in desert camouflage) were placed in different vegetation areas of similar colors. Further, in the complex *Scenario 2* described above, the subsequent human subject reconfirmation experiment aims to distinguish between fake targets and true human targets from multiple suspected targets with additional respiration information detected by bio-radar.

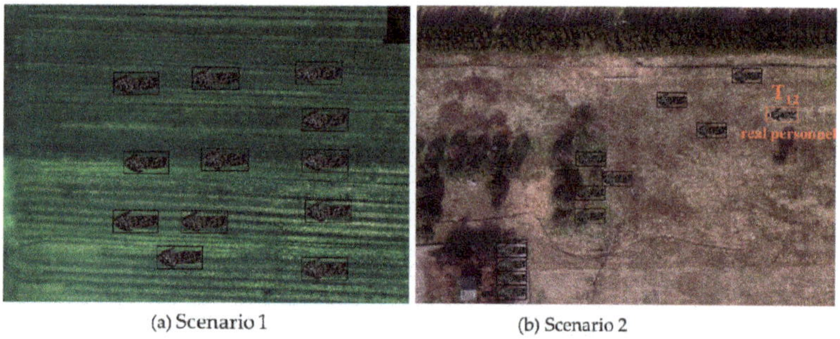

Figure 10. Illustration of experimental settings for two scenarios. (**a**) *Scenario 1*: 12 sets of green camouflage clothes in a homogeneous grassland background, (**b**) 11 sets of green camouflage clothes, and one real personnel in green camouflage clothing in a complex background.

4.2. Preliminary Detection of Suspected Human Targets

(1) Suspected human target detection in *Scenario 1*

Based on the multispectral sensor module, each exposure would acquire six bands of remote sensing images (a certain area under the field of view for one exposure) as shown in Figure 11. We can notice that the DN value of each band image is different because different subjects have different spectral reflectance for different bands. In addition, we can clearly observe the vignetting effect in the band six image that we must correct to achieve accurate results.

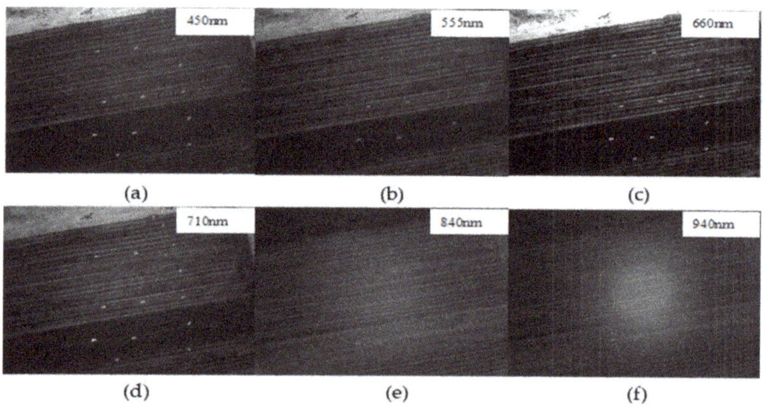

Figure 11. Local multispectral remote sensing images in *Scenario 1* acquired by MS600 (one exposure): (**a**) 450 nm; (**b**) 555 nm; (**c**) 660 nm; (**d**) 710 nm; (**e**) 840 nm; (**f**) 940 nm.

To facilitate data analysis, it is necessary to preprocess the original multispectral images. After the preprocessing on multiple sets of images from multiple exposures, including image registration and radiometric calibration, and so on, a complete reflectance panorama is formed as shown in Figure 12. Although we can visually find some suspected target points, they need to be identified automatically and reasonably. Especially, when the search range is large, it is impossible to find and locate the target quickly and accurately rely on the human eye. Additionally, human subjectivity and visual fatigue have a great impact on the results.

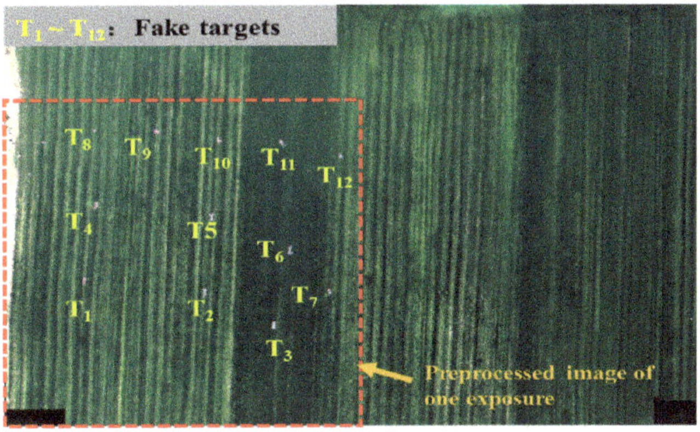

Figure 12. The complete reflectance panorama in *Scenario 1*.

Next, the selected multispectral indexes and features in this study were fed to the decision mechanism and applied to preliminarily identify and extract suspected human targets automatically by setting a reasonable threshold. As the suspected target recognition result shown in Figure 13, the red targets mean suspected targets. Obviously, 13 remarkable suspected targets (corresponding to 13 red parts) were detected, including one undesired recognition mistake and 12 non-human fake targets (camouflage). Results show that this detection method based on multispectral feature information can effectively detect suspected targets in this outdoor environment with a relatively single background.

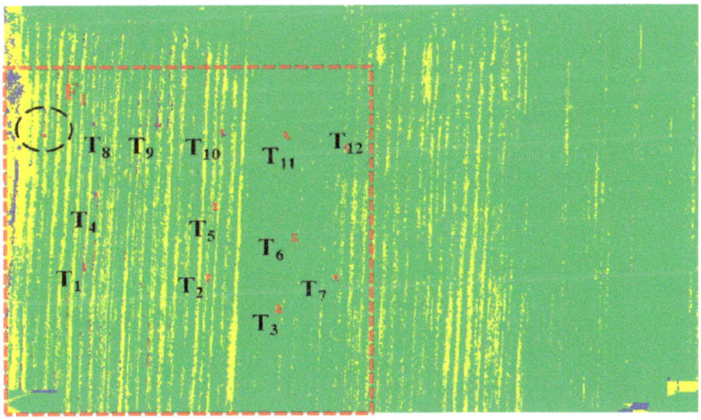

Figure 13. Suspected target recognition result in *Scenario 1* (*green for vegetation*, *yellow for soil*, *red for suspected target*, *blue for noise spot*).

Moreover, we also compared the classification or recognition performance of the DT with the state-of-art machine learning algorithms including Back Propagation neural network (BP), Random Forest (RF), and Support Vector Machine (SVM) with a radial basis kernel function. All these four classifiers are trained based on the same training dataset, and the preprocessed image of one exposure marked in the red dashed box in Figure 12 is taken as the test data. The classification results are as shown in Table 3. Obviously, based on the same training data and test data, the recognition performance of different classifiers does not differ greatly. It means that spectral features are the main factor affecting the recognition results to some extent.

Table 3. Recognition performance comparison of the state-of-art machine learning algorithms.

ML Algorithms	Accuracy	F_1 Score
DT	99.76%	98.08%
BP	99.58%	99.62%
RF	99.37%	99.41%
SVM	99.65%	99.67%

(2) Suspected human target detection in *Scenario 2*

Scenario 2 is comprehensive and more representative for practical applications. The background consists of many components with different colors (shrubs, green lawns, trees, dark yellow, and other vegetation). The detection targets (eleven pieces of camouflage and one real person in desert camouflage to disguise the human subject) contain three types of color attributes and they were placed in different vegetation areas of similar colors. Since the above analysis has demonstrated that the impact of different classifiers is not significant here we just chose DT as the representative classification algorithm in the subsequent study.

After the same preprocessing on multiple sets of images from multiple exposures, a complete reflectance panorama is formed in *Scenario 2* as shown in Figure 14. Obviously, it is visually difficult to observe the ground suspected target in this complex scenario Especially for the target T_9–T_{12}, it is almost impossible to find them, due to their color characteristics being similar to the background. Then, the proposed method based on multispectral information only is applied to preliminarily detect suspected human targets automatically as shown in Figure 15. It is clear that all the 12 suspected human targets were still successfully detected in such a complex environment.

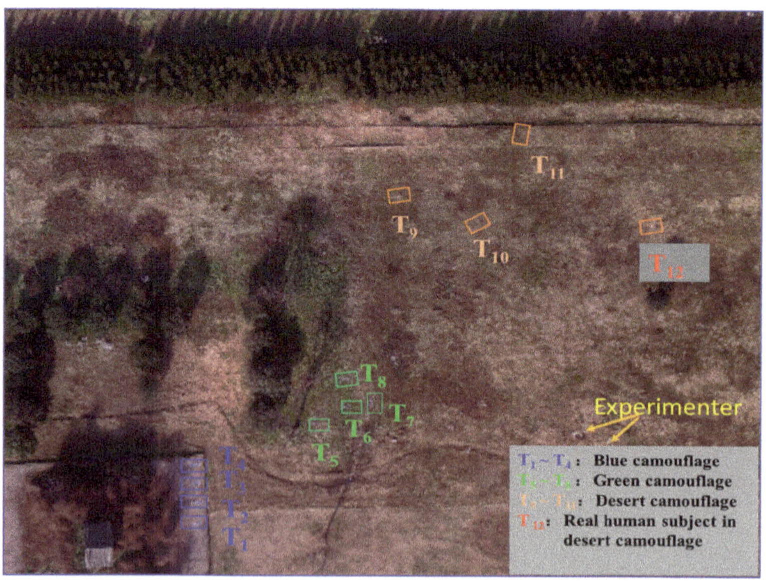

Figure 14. The complete reflectance panorama in *Scenario 2*.

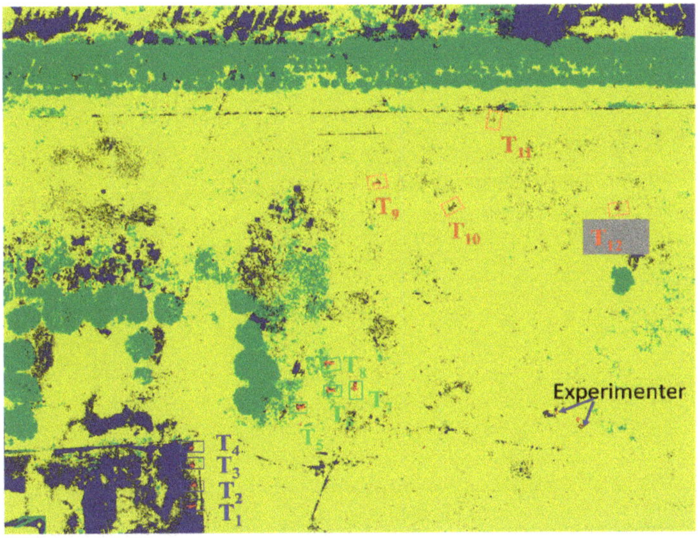

Figure 15. Suspected target recognition result in *Scenario 2* (*green for vegetation, yellow for soil, red for suspected target, blue for noise spot*).

However, we need to note that only suspected target T_{12} is a real human target. In other words, just based on the multispectral information alone, we cannot distinguish clothes and true human targets just relying on multispectral images. Therefore, this complex *Scenario 2* is taken as a typical example to test the effectiveness of the human subject property re-identification method based on vital sign information proposed in this paper.

4.3. Accurate Re-Identification of Surviving Human Targets Using Bio-Radar

Based on the multispectral technology above, we can only detect the suspected human targets in *Scenario 2* but cannot make an accurate identification of surviving human targets. Therefore, when suspected human subjects were found by aerial multispectral imaging, the bio-radar will be released around the suspected target (within 8 m) to non-contact detect respiratory signal (the detection direction of radar can be adjusted by the included control components).

Just as shown in Figure 16a, since the human subjects are distributed in the outdoor environment, we can find that the radar echo contains a lot of interference and noise, which drowns out the breathing signal severely. Consequently, although the respiratory frequency of the subject can be detected as 0.24 Hz in the normalized frequency spectrum, it still contains a large amount of noise and interference components. When the environmental interference is more intense, respiration detection would be more difficult. The noise cancellation result of this signal using our proposed NLMS-ALE method is shown in Figure 16b. Obviously, noise and interference are effectively removed from radar echo, and significant respiration frequency can be acquired in the normalized frequency spectrum. This means that even when the outdoor environment interference is strong, we are still able to detect the breathing characteristics of the target using bio-radar. Then, this respiration information would be transmitted wirelessly. Consequently, we can make accurate identification of surviving human target (T_{12}) as shown in Figure 16c and eliminate fake targets.

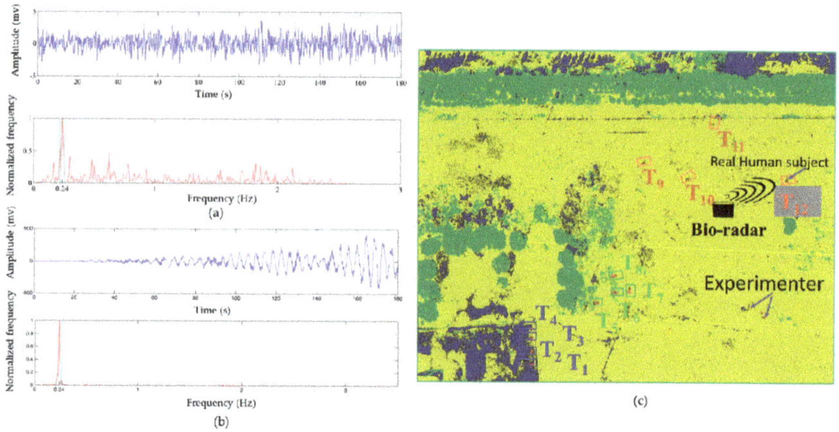

Figure 16. Radar echo of human target T_{12} from 8 m and corresponding frequency analysis, (**a**) original signal and normalized frequency spectrum, (**b**) noise cancellation signal and normalized frequency spectrum, (**c**) human target reconfirmation result.

5. Discussion

Based on suspected target detection experiments under two typical *Scenarios*, experimental results above clearly show that all suspected targets could be accurately detected and separated from the background based on multispectral feature information only (with only an additional detection mistake), even under a complex outdoor bush environment. However, the study also amply demonstrates that the human attributes of the suspected target cannot be confirmed and verified based on unimodal information alone. Furthermore, combined with auxiliary physiological information from the bio-radar, only the true human target in *Scenario 2* was accurately identified. Therefore, the bimodal-information-based human target recognition method proposed is initially proven to be effective for ground injured human subject search in an outdoor environment. For this challenging identification task, the recognition is satisfactory to some extent. However, this method also has a few limitations for practical application in the future.

With respect to the initial suspected target detection, the recognition algorithm adopted in this experiment is the decision tree in supervised learning. Objects are classified by different properties thresholds, which is conducive to real-time processing. Meanwhile, it also leads to the problem that the robustness of the classification method is weak because we cannot conclude spectral of all the clothes and find appropriate thresholds. Therefore, our future research work will focus on superior target features with higher stability and more intelligent and excellent recognition algorithms, such as deep learning recognition algorithms. In addition, reducing the time complexity of the model and more robust target recognition-based multimodal optoelectronic information fusion are also our future research directions.

On the other hand, just as what we tried in this paper, the bio-radar is applied to acquire the vital signals, which can help us to make the judgment whether the subject is human or not and to infer the state of life. However, the detection environment and condition are totally different and even more challenging than that of our previous indoor vital sign detection in the medical field [35], and survivors detection under the ruins in the post-disaster search-rescue field [7]. (1) Firstly, the effective detection range of the micro-bio-radar is only 10 m, so finding a way to throw the bio-radar from the UAV platform to a proper location around the suspected target to acquire vital signals is still a challenging job. Secondly, the problem of "differentiation between human and non-human (animal) live targets" and "respiration rate varies in different physiological conditions" are inevitable issues to consider in the outdoor detection environment. Fortunately, our past studies have tried some very similar exploring experiments [12,36,37]. These studies confirmed that some differences can be observed between human body respiration and that of other animals (cats, dogs, pigs, etc.) in the time domain, but they are not significant. Nevertheless, the human and other non-human (animal) live targets can be accurately differentiated based on multi-domain features (time domain, time-frequency domain) combined with some machine learning method. Therefore, we will try to embed these algorithms into the UAV bio-modal system and improve it by carrying out some test experiments in our future work. And for the problem of "the same subject's respiration varies in different conditions", it can be solved by similar ideas.

6. Conclusions

In response to the challenging task of rapid search of ground injured human targets in outdoor environments, a UVA-based detection and recognition technology combined with bimodal sensors is developed. Considering that the key difficulties of the identification task arise from the characteristics of the target and the detection environment, such as small-scale target property compared to the ground background, low target-background contrast, and weak physiological sign, an automatic recognition method based on bimodal information is proposed. First, suspected targets were accurately detected and separated from the background based on multispectral feature information only. Immediately after, a bio-radar module would be released to detect the physiological information for accurate re-identification of human target property. Both the suspected human target detection experiments and human target property re-identification experiments show that our proposed method could effectively realize accurate identification of ground injured in outdoor environments, which is important for the research of rapid search and rescue of injured people in the outdoor environment. Meanwhile, the robustness and convenience of this technology in a practical application need to be further improved.

Our future work will focus on extracting superior target features with higher stability and trying a more intelligent integration approach of feature extraction and recognition, aiming to improve the recognition accuracy and application robustness. In this experiment, there are few kinds of ground objects, and the complexity of the experimental environment is not enough. In the follow-up research, the complexity of the field condition will be gradually increased, thus the reliability of the identification model would be further improved. Moreover, if the state of the target's physical signs detected by bio-radar can be quickly assessed based on vital signs and transmitted to the rear command timely, it is of great significance for the search and rescue of injured people in the outdoor environment.

Author Contributions: Conceptualization, G.L. and J.W.; methodology, M.Z.; software, T.L.; formal analysis, J.X.; investigation, Y.Y. and L.Z.; data curation, Z.L.; writing—original draft preparation, M.Z.; writing—review and editing, F.Q.; visualization, M.Z.; supervision, G.L.; funding acquisition, G.L. All authors have read and agreed to the published version of the manuscript.

Funding: This research was funded by Key Research and Development Program of Shaanxi (2021ZDLGY09-07 and 2022SF-482). And the APC was funded by (2021ZDLGY09-07).

Institutional Review Board Statement: Not applicable.

Informed Consent Statement: Not applicable.

Conflicts of Interest: The authors declare no conflict of interest.

References

1. Brüggemann, B.; Wildermuth, D.; Schneider, F.E. Search and Retrieval of Human Casualties in Outdoor Environments with Unmanned Ground Systems—System Overview and Lessons Learned from ELROB 2014. In *Field and Service Robotics*; Springer: Berlin/Heidelberg, Germany, 2016; pp. 533–546. [CrossRef]
2. Jianqi, W.; Chongxun, Z.; Guohua, L.; Xijing, J. A New Method for Identifying the Life Parameters via Radar. *EURASIP J. Adv. Signal Process.* **2007**, *2007*, 031415. [CrossRef]
3. Guohua, L.; Jianqi, W.; Yu, Y.; Xijing, J. Study of the Ballistocardiogram signal in life detection system based on radar. In Proceedings of the 2007 29th Annual International Conference of the IEEE Engineering in Medicine and Biology Society, Lyon, France, 22–26 August 2007; pp. 2191–2194.

4. Zhang, Y.; Qi, F.; Lv, H.; Liang, F.; Wang, J. Bioradar Technology: Recent Research and Advancements. *IEEE Microw. Mag.* **2019**, *20*, 58–73. [CrossRef]
5. Li, Z.; Li, W.; Lv, H.; Zhang, Y.; Jing, X.; Wang, J. A Novel Method for Respiration-Like Clutter Cancellation in Life Detection by Dual-Frequency IR-UWB Radar. *IEEE Trans. Microw. Theory Tech.* **2013**, *61*, 2086–2092. [CrossRef]
6. Lv, H.; Jiao, T.; Zhang, Y.; An, Q.; Liu, M.; Fulai, L.; Jing, X.; Wang, J. An Adaptive-MSSA-Based Algorithm for Detection of Trapped Victims Using UWB Radar. *IEEE Geosci. Remote Sens. Lett.* **2015**, *12*, 1808–1812. [CrossRef]
7. Lv, H.; Li, W.; Li, Z.; Zhang, Y.; Jiao, T.; Xue, H.; Liu, M.; Jing, X.; Wang, J. Characterization and Identification of IR-UWB Respiratory-Motion Response of Trapped Victims. *IEEE Trans. Geosci. Remote Sens.* **2014**, *52*, 7195–7204. [CrossRef]
8. Ren, W.; Qi, F.; Foroughian, F.; Kvelashvili, T.; Liu, Q.; Kilic, O.; Long, T.; Fathy, A.E. Vital Sign Detection in Any Orientation Using a Distributed Radar Network via Modified Independent Component Analysis. *IEEE Trans. Microw. Theory Tech.* **2021**, *69*, 4774–4790. [CrossRef]
9. Lv, H.; Liu, M.; Jiao, T.; Zhang, Y.; Yu, X.; Li, S.; Jing, X.; Wang, J. Multi-target human sensing via UWB bio-radar based on multiple antennas. In Proceedings of the 2013 IEEE International Conference of IEEE Region 10 (TENCON 2013), Xi'an, China, 22–25 October 2013; pp. 1–4. [CrossRef]
10. Zhang, Y.; Ma, Y.; Yu, X.; Wang, P.; Lv, H.; Liang, F.; Li, Z.; Wang, J. A coarse-to-fine detection and localization method for multiple human subjects under through-wall condition using a new telescopic SIMO UWB radar. *Sens. Actuators A Phys.* **2021**, *332*, 113064. [CrossRef]
11. Zhao, L.; Yangyang, M.; Yang, Z.; Fulai, L.; Xiao, Y.; Fugui, Q.; Hao, L.; Guohua, L.; Jianqi, W. UWB Radar Features for Distinguishing Humans From Animals in an Actual Post-Disaster Trapped Scenario. *IEEE Access* **2021**, *9*, 154347–154354. [CrossRef]
12. Ma, Y.; Liang, F.; Wang, P.; Lv, H.; Yu, X.; Zhang, Y. An Accurate Method to Distinguish Between Stationary Human and Dog targets Under Through-Wall Condition Using UWB Radar. *Remote Sens.* **2019**, *11*, 2571. [CrossRef]
13. Qi, F.; Li, Z.; Ma, Y.; Liang, F.; Lv, H.; Wang, J.; Fathy, A.E. Generalization of Channel Micro-Doppler Capacity Evaluation for Improved Finer-Grained Human Activity Classification Using MIMO UWB Radar. *IEEE Trans. Microw. Theory Tech.* **2021**, *69*, 4748–4761. [CrossRef]
14. Qi, F.; Lv, H.; Wang, J.; Fathy, A.E. Quantitative Evaluation of Channel Micro-Doppler Capacity for MIMO UWB Radar Human Activity Signals Based on Time–Frequency Signatures. *IEEE Trans. Geosci. Remote Sens.* **2020**, *58*, 6138–6151. [CrossRef]
15. Xia, H. 16 Dead During Mountain Marathon in China's Gansu. Available online: http://www.xinhuanet.com/english/2021-05/23/c_139963997_2.htm (accessed on 23 May 2021).
16. Takagi, Y.; Yamada, K.; Goto, A.; Yamada, M.; Naka, T.; Miyazaki, S. Life Search—A Smartphone Application for Disaster Education and Rescue. In Proceedings of the 2017 Nicograph International (NicoInt), Kyoto, Japan, 2–3 June 2017; p. 94. [CrossRef]
17. Maciel-Pearson, B.G.; Akcay, S.; Atapour-Abarghouei, A.; Holder, C.; Breckon, T.P. Multi-Task Regression-Based Learning for Autonomous Unmanned Aerial Vehicle Flight Control Within Unstructured Outdoor Environments. *IEEE Robot. Autom. Lett.* **2019**, *4*, 4116–4123. [CrossRef]
18. Hou, X.; Bergmann, J. Pedestrian Dead Reckoning With Wearable Sensors: A Systematic Review. *IEEE Sens. J.* **2020**, *21*, 143–152. [CrossRef]
19. Rosser, J.C.; Vignesh, V.; Terwilliger, B.A.; Parker, B.C. Surgical and Medical Applications of Drones: A Comprehensive Review. *J. Soc. Laparoendosc. Surg.* **2018**, *22*, e2018.00018. [CrossRef] [PubMed]
20. Sun, J.; Song, J.; Chen, H.; Huang, X.; Liu, Y. Autonomous State Estimation and Mapping in Unknown Environments with Onboard Stereo Camera for MAVs. *IEEE Trans. Ind. Inform.* **2019**, *16*, 5746–5756. [CrossRef]
21. Bency, A.J.; Karthikeyan, S.; De Leo, C.; Sunderrajan, S.; Manjunath, B.S. Search Tracker: Human-Derived Object Tracking in the Wild Through Large-Scale Search and Retrieval. *IEEE Trans. Circuits Syst. Video Technol.* **2016**, *27*, 1803–1814. [CrossRef]
22. Chen, Y.; Song, B.; Du, X.; Guizani, M. Infrared Small Target Detection Through Multiple Feature Analysis Based on Visual Saliency. *IEEE Access* **2019**, *7*, 38996–39004. [CrossRef]
23. Lygouras, E.; Santavas, N.; Taitzoglou, A.; Tarchanidis, K.; Mitropoulos, A.; Gasteratos, A. Unsupervised Human Detection with an Embedded Vision System on a Fully Autonomous UAV for Search and Rescue Operations. *Sensors* **2019**, *19*, 3542. [CrossRef] [PubMed]
24. Jiang, J.; Zheng, H.; Ji, X.; Cheng, T.; Tian, Y.; Zhu, Y.; Cao, W.; Ehsani, R.; Yao, X. Analysis and Evaluation of the Image Preprocessing Process of a Six-Band Multispectral Camera Mounted on an Unmanned Aerial Vehicle for Winter Wheat Monitoring. *Sensors* **2019**, *19*, 747. [CrossRef] [PubMed]
25. Jeowicki, Ł.; Sosnowicz, K.; Ostrowski, W.; Osińska-Skotak, K.; Bakuła, K. Evaluation of Rapeseed Winter Crop Damage Using UAV-Based Multispectral Imagery. *Remote Sens.* **2020**, *12*, 2618. [CrossRef]
26. Shi, X.; Han, W.; Zhao, T.; Tang, J. Decision Support System for Variable Rate Irrigation Based on UAV Multispectral Remote Sensing. *Sensors* **2019**, *19*, 2880. [CrossRef] [PubMed]
27. Nisio, A.D.; Adamo, F.; Acciani, G.; Attivissimo, F. Fast Detection of Olive Trees Affected by Xylella Fastidiosa from UAVs Using Multispectral Imaging. *Sensors* **2020**, *20*, 4915. [CrossRef] [PubMed]
28. OPTOSKY. ATP9100 Portable Object Spectrometer. Available online: https://www.optosky.com/ (accessed on 11 February 2022).

29. Li, C.; Chen, F.; Qi, F.; Liu, M.; Li, Z.; Liang, F.; Jing, X.; Lü, G.; Wang, J. Searching for Survivors through Random Human-Body Movement Outdoors by Continuous-Wave Radar Array. *PLoS ONE* **2016**, *11*, e0152201. [CrossRef] [PubMed]
30. DJI. M100 Quad-Rotor UAV System. Available online: https://www.dji.com/cn/matrice100 (accessed on 12 February 2022).
31. Imai, M.; Kurihara, J.; Kouyama, T.; Kuwahara, T.; Fujita, S.; Sakamoto, Y.; Sato, Y.; Saitoh, S.-I.; Hirata, T.; Yamamoto, H.; et al. Radiometric Calibration for a Multispectral Sensor Onboard RISESAT Microsatellite Based on Lunar Observations. *Sensors* **2021**, *21*, 2429. [CrossRef]
32. Bansal, M.; Kumar, M.; Kumar, M. 2D object recognition: A comparative analysis of SIFT, SURF and ORB feature descriptors. *Multimed. Tools Appl.* **2021**, *80*, 18839–18857. [CrossRef]
33. Wang, G.; Sun, X.; Shang, Y.; Wang, Z.; Shi, Z.; Yu, Q. Two-View Geometry Estimation Using RANSAC With Locality Preserving Constraint. *IEEE Access* **2020**, *8*, 7267–7279. [CrossRef]
34. Berhane, T.M.; Lane, C.R.; Wu, Q.; Autrey, B.C.; Anenkhonov, O.A.; Chepinoga, V.V.; Liu, H. Decision-Tree, Rule-Based, and Random Forest Classification of High-Resolution Multispectral Imagery for Wetland Mapping and Inventory. *Remote Sens.* **2018**, *10*, 580. [CrossRef] [PubMed]
35. Qi, F.; Li, C.; Wang, S.; Zhang, H.; Wang, J.; Lu, G. Contact-Free Detection of Obstructive Sleep Apnea Based on Wavelet Information Entropy Spectrum Using Bio-Radar. *Entropy* **2016**, *18*, 306. [CrossRef]
36. Ma, Y.; Wang, P.; Huang, W.; Qi, F.; Liang, F.; Lv, H.; Yu, X.; Wang, J.; Zhang, Y. A robust multi-feature based method for distinguishing between humans and pets to ensure signal source in vital signs monitoring using UWB radar. *EURASIP J. Adv. Signal Process.* **2021**, *2021*, 27. [CrossRef]
37. Wang, P.; Zhang, Y.; Ma, Y.; Liang, F.; An, Q.; Xue, H.; Yu, X.; Lv, H.; Wang, J. Method for distinguishing humans and animals in vital signs monitoring using IR-UWB radar. *Int. J. Environ. Res. Public Health* **2019**, *16*, 4462. [CrossRef] [PubMed]

drones

Article

Investigation of Rotor Efficiency with Varying Rotor Pitch Angle for a Coaxial Drone

Knut Erik Teigen Giljarhus [1,*], Alessandro Porcarelli [2] and Jørgen Apeland [3]

1 Department of Mechanical and Structural Engineering and Materials Science, University of Stavanger, PB 8600, 4036 Stavanger, Norway
2 Neptech AB, Enskededalen, 121 34 Stockholm, Sweden; alessandro@neptech.se
3 Nordic Unmanned AS, Rådhusgata 3, 4306 Sandnes, Norway; ja@nordicunmanned.com
* Correspondence: knut.e.giljarhus@uis.no

Abstract: Coaxial rotor systems are appealing for multirotor drones, as they increase thrust without increasing the vehicle's footprint. However, the thrust of a coaxial rotor system is reduced compared to having the rotors in line. It is of interest to increase the efficiency of coaxial systems, both to extend mission time and to enable new mission capabilities. While some parameters of a coaxial system have been explored, such as the rotor-to-rotor distance, the influence of rotor pitch is less understood. This work investigates how adjusting the pitch of the lower rotor relative to that of the upper one impacts the overall efficiency of the system. A methodology based on blade element momentum theory is extended to coaxial rotor systems, and in addition blade-resolved simulations using computational fluid dynamics are performed. A coaxial rotor system for a medium-sized drone with a rotor diameter of 71.12 cm is used for the study. Experiments are performed using a thrust stand to validate the methods. The results show that there exists a peak in total rotor efficiency (thrust-to-power ratio), and that the efficiency can be increased by 2% to 5% by increasing the pitch of the lower rotor. The work contributes to furthering our understanding of coaxial rotor systems, and the results can potentially lead to more efficient drones with increased mission time.

Keywords: computational fluid dynamics; blade element momentum theory; coaxial rotor; aerodynamics

Citation: Giljarhus, K.E.T.; Porcarelli, A.; Apeland, J. Investigation of Rotor Efficiency with Varying Rotor Pitch Angle for a Coaxial Drone. *Drones* **2022**, *6*, 91. https://doi.org/10.3390/drones6040091

Academic Editors: Andrzej Łukaszewicz, Wojciech Giernacki, Zbigniew Kulesza, Jaroslaw Pytka and Andriy Holovatyy

Received: 28 February 2022
Accepted: 30 March 2022
Published: 4 April 2022

1. Introduction

Several designs for unmanned aerial vehicles exist today, with varying compromises in terms of size, fuel system and speed [1]. Multirotor drones have the advantage of small footprint, non-restrictive take-off/landing area requirements, high maneuverability and high hovering capability. Multirotor drone designs can be found in sizes ranging from light vehicles below 50 g [2,3] to larger vehicles designed for human transport [4,5].

The power unit on a multirotor drone is important, as it determines the type of operations a drone can perform. The most common power source on multirotor drones is batteries, although some designs exist that employ, e.g., hydrogen [6,7]. Increasing the efficiency of the drones is important as it can extend the flight time, thereby extending mission time or even enabling new types of mission capabilities.

The projected area of a drone can be a critical factor, as it determines how the drone can be transported and the type of areas it can fly in. In a coaxial rotor system, one rotor is put above the other instead of placing them side by side. Compared to larger aircrafts, coaxial multirotor drones typically use fixed-pitch rotors to avoid complex mechanical design [8]. The coaxial layout increases the thrust without increasing the projected area, making this an attractive option for multirotor drones.

However, a disadvantage of a coaxial rotor system is that there is a loss of efficiency, since the lower rotors operate in the wake of the upper rotors. Some attempts have been made to increase the efficiency by adjusting the distance between the rotors [9–11].

There are also some commercial designs using a different pitch for the lower rotor (e.g., CarbonCore Cortex X8 and Himax CR2816), and this has been proposed as a way to increase the efficiency [12]. Although several studies on coaxial rotors exist in the scientific literature, the influence of pitch has not been thoroughly explored. Most studies have also been performed on larger rotors with systems for dynamically changing the collective pitch of the blades, while in recent years, smaller drones with fixed pitches are becoming increasingly relevant.

Yoon et al. [13] investigated changing the collective pitch of the lower rotor in a coaxial system using detailed computational fluid dynamics (CFD) simulations. The study used the XV-15 rotor with a diameter of 3.8 m. The emphasis was on balancing torque by adjusting the pitch and the impact on thrust-to-power efficiency was not investigated. Jinghui et al. [14] performed both wind tunnel tests and CFD simulations of a coaxial rotor system with large blades of 4 m in diameter. This study also found that the thrust on the lower rotor was lower than the upper since the effective angle of attack is lower, but did not investigate the effect on efficiency of modifying the pitch of the lower rotor. Kim et al. [15] used CFD simulations to study the efficiency of a coaxial rotor setup for a conceptual personal air vehicle. They found that the optimal pitch for the upper rotor was different than that of the lower rotor, but they did not perform simulations specifically with different pitches for the two rotors. Leishman and Ananthan [16] looked specifically at the influence of pitch angle in a coaxial rotor system. They performed simulations using blade element momentum theory (BEMT) of a 7.6 m Harrington helicopter rotor in a coaxial configuration. They found an optimal design where the pitch of the lower rotor is higher than the upper rotor for the downwash region, with a slightly lower pitch than the upper rotor for the outer part of the rotor.

This work uses a combination of simplified analysis with blade element momentum theory and detailed blade-resolved CFD simulations to investigate the influence of changing the pitch of the lower rotor in a coaxial system for a medium-sized drone. Experiments in single-rotor and coaxial rotor setups are performed to validate the computational models. The main contributions of the paper are to demonstrate that a simplified BEMT model can give reasonable results for coaxial rotors with varying pitch angles, and also to provide insight into the impact of using different pitch angles for the upper and lower rotor.

2. Computational Methods

2.1. Blade Element Momentum Theory

Blade element momentum theory (BEMT) combines two theories; momentum theory and blade element theory. In momentum theory the rotor acts as a disk injecting momentum into the flow, while in blade element theory, the rotor is divided into small, independent elements and aerodynamic forces are calculated using tabulated values for lift and drag for the airfoil. The methodology has been extensively used for both rotor systems and wind turbines, and detailed derivations can be found elsewhere [17–19]. Hence, only a brief explanation of the method applied in this study is given here. Figure 1 gives an overview of both the momentum theory control volume and the blade element theory approach.

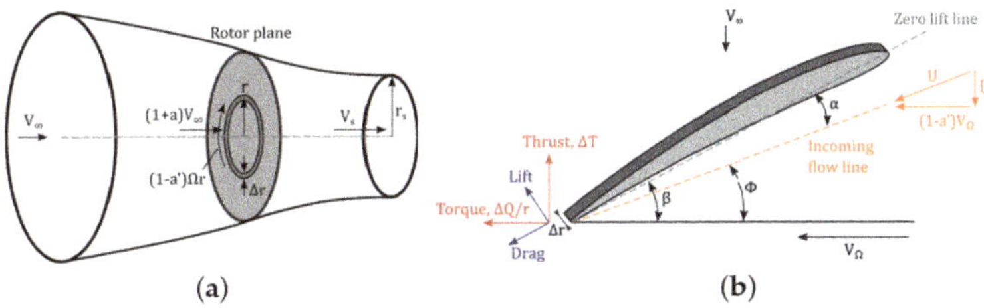

Figure 1. Illustration of parameters and forces for blade element momentum theory. (**a**) Momentum theory control volume. (**b**) Blade element.

For a propeller, power is applied to the rotor to generate thrust along the rotation axis. The incoming velocity that a blade element is subjected to is not a simple addition of the flow velocity in the axial direction and the angular velocity of the rotor in the tangential direction. The axial velocity is accelerated due to the presence of the rotor and the tangential velocity is reduced due to swirl. This can be accounted for by introducing axial and tangential induction factors,

$$v = (1+a)V_\infty, \tag{1}$$
$$v' = (1-a')V_\Omega = (1-a')\Omega r, \tag{2}$$
$$U = \sqrt{v^2 + v'^2}, \tag{3}$$

where v and v' are axial and tangential velocities, and a and a' are the axial and tangential induction factors, respectively. U is the incoming velocity seen from the blade element.

In blade element theory, the force on a single blade element can be expressed by

$$\Delta T = \sigma\pi\rho U^2 C_T r \Delta r, \tag{4}$$
$$\Delta Q = \sigma\pi\rho U^2 C_Q r^2 \Delta r, \tag{5}$$

where T is the thrust, i.e., force in axial direction, and Q is the torque, i.e., the moment around the axial direction. $\sigma = Bc/(2\pi R)$ is the blade solidity, where B is the number of blades and c is the chord length. The thrust and torque coefficients in the above expressions are calculated as

$$C_T = C_L \cos\phi - C_D \sin\phi, \tag{6}$$
$$C_Q = C_L \sin\phi + C_D \cos\phi. \tag{7}$$

The drag and lift coefficients, C_D and C_L, respectively, are extracted from tabulated values for the airfoil using the local angle of attack for the airfoil,

$$\alpha = \beta - \phi. \tag{8}$$

Similar expressions as in Equations (4) and (5) for the incremental forces can also be found from momentum theory,

$$\Delta T = 4\pi\rho r V_\infty^2 (1+a)a\Delta r, \tag{9}$$
$$\Delta Q = 4\pi\rho r^3 V_\infty \Omega (1+a)a'\Delta r. \tag{10}$$

Combining these equations, the induction factors can be expressed directly as

$$a = \frac{1}{\kappa - 1}, \tag{11}$$
$$a' = \frac{1}{\kappa' + 1}, \tag{12}$$
$$\kappa = \frac{4\sin^2\phi}{\sigma C_T}, \tag{13}$$
$$\kappa' = \frac{4\sin\phi\cos\phi}{\sigma C_Q}. \tag{14}$$

From the rotor force diagram for a blade element, Figure 1, the local inflow angle ϕ can be expressed from the local velocities as

$$\tan\phi = \frac{(1+a)\Omega R}{(1-a')V_\infty}. \tag{15}$$

Once a solution for the inflow angle is found, the forces are calculated from the blade element equations and integrated along the rotor to find the total forces. A well-known issue with BEMT methods is the overprediction of forces near the tip, since vortex shedding from the tip is not accounted for in the induced velocities. This is typically alleviated by the use of tip-loss correction methods. In this work, the classic Prandtl tip-loss method is used [20], where a correction factor, F, is multiplied into the expressions for thrust and torque for each element, Equations (9) and (10). This expression factor is given as

$$F = \frac{2}{\pi}\cos^{-1} e^{-f}, \tag{16}$$

$$f = \frac{B}{2}\frac{R-r}{r\sin\phi}. \tag{17}$$

The above method is implemented in the open source software pyBEMT [21], developed by one of the authors. Equation (15) is solved for ϕ using root-finding functions from the `SciPy` library [22].

Note that for the hover situation considered in this work, Equation (15) is not defined since the axial inflow velocity is zero. To circumvent this, this velocity is instead set to a low value, $V_\infty = 1 \times 10^{-6}$.

The modelling of the coaxial rotor is based on momentum theory [17,23]. The lower rotor will be in the slipstream created by the upper rotor. Some authors have been considering the varying slipstream contraction [24], but here a fully developed slipstream will be considered. Additionally, it is assumed that the rotors are hovering, i.e., there is a zero velocity inflow to the upper rotor, and that the lower rotor is a sufficient distance below the upper rotor so that the slipstream is fully developed. For this case, the continuity equation gives

$$V_i \pi R^2 = V_s \pi R_s^2, \tag{18}$$

where V_i is the induced velocity just below the rotor and V_s is the slipstream velocity in the fully developed wake. R_s is the radius of the slipstream region. For the momentum, the thrust generated from the upper rotor is equal to the change in momentum from the static region to the slipstream,

$$T = \rho V_i A V_s. \tag{19}$$

Finally, the work done by the upper rotor is equal to the kinetic energy in the slipstream

$$TV_i = \frac{1}{2}\rho V_i A V_s^2. \tag{20}$$

From these equations, the following expressions for the slipstream properties are found:

$$R_s = \frac{R}{\sqrt{2}} \tag{21}$$

$$v_s = C_s\sqrt{\frac{2T}{\rho A}} \tag{22}$$

Here, C_s is a model constant, accounting for the fact that for smaller UAV rotors, the hub is a large part of the rotor, and there is not a sharp transition from the hub of the rotor to the rotor, or from the slipstream to the outer part of the lower rotor. In this work, this constant is set to $C_s = 0.8$. Additionally, the model assumes that the velocity tapers linearly off from the slipstream to the outer part. The end of this taper region is set to the middle of the slipstream radius and the radius of the rotor.

For the pitch adjustment of the lower rotor in the coaxial setup, it is desirable to maintain the same thrust when the pitch is modified. This is achieved by adjusting the angular velocity of the lower rotor to obtain the same total thrust. In the BEMT solver, the root-finding functions of the `SciPy` library are used for this purpose.

2.2. Computational Fluid Dynamics

Several detailed simulation methods for rotor systems based on CFD methodology exist today. These include blade-resolved methods where the blade is explicitly modelled [13,25–28] and methods where the blade is modelled using embedded BEMT methods or similar techniques and then represented as a volume force in the CFD simulation [29–31].

In this work, the blade-resolved method is used. The CFD simulations are performed by solving the transient, incompressible Reynolds-averaged Navier–Stokes equations, together with the k-omega shear stress transport (SST) turbulence model [32]. In Yoon et al. [26], it was found that an eddy-resolved method performed better than the Reynolds-averaged approach for rotor flows. However, this was because the eddy viscosity grows in the far-field due to how the turbulent length scale is modelled in the Spalart–Allmaras (SA) turbulence model. The turbulence length scale in the SA model is dependent on the distance from the wall, thereby growing larger than typical eddy sizes in the far-field. In the k-omega SST model, the turbulence length scale is $l_t \sim \sqrt{k}/\omega$, thereby circumventing this issue.

The simulations are performed using the open source software OpenFOAM [33,34] v7, which is based on the finite volume method. The PIMPLE algorithm is used for the pressure–velocity coupling and the time marching. This algorithm allows a larger time step to be taken while maintaining numerical stability, combining outer pressure-momentum corrections with inner pressure corrections. Here, the rotor is allowed to rotate 1° per time step. Up to 50 outer correctors are used, reducing the sub-iteration residual by three orders of magnitude at each time step. The implicit Euler scheme is used for temporal discretization. For the spatial discretization, second-order schemes are used for all terms, and in particular, the upwind-weighted `linearUpwind` scheme is used for the convective terms.

Rotation of the rotors is handled using Arbitrary Mesh Interface (AMI). A cylindrical domain around the rotor is meshed separately and allowed to rotate at a constant angular velocity. This region is then coupled to the surrounding static mesh using the `cyclicAMI` boundary condition. At each time step, each face at the AMI boundary identifies overlapping faces from the neighboring patch and the contribution from these faces is weighted according to the intersecting area [35].

As for the BEMT solver, when a case is solved with a modified pitch for the coaxial rotor setup, the angular velocity should be modified to maintain the same total thrust. This is achieved by writing a custom version of the solid body motion solver in OpenFOAM, where the angular velocity is adjusted during the simulation using a binary search algorithm until the desired total thrust is found.

The simulations are run in parallel on a cluster using Intel Xeon E5-2695 v4 processors. With the case decomposed over 108 cores, a single simulation of 10 full rotor revolutions has an execution time of approximately 40 h.

3. Numerical Setup

3.1. Rotor Geometry

The main parameters of the rotor geometry are listed in Table 1. The geometry is based on the commercial T-MOTOR G28x9.2 carbon fiber rotor, which has diameter $D = 28'' = 71.12\,\text{cm}$ and pitch $P = 9.2'' = 23.368\,\text{cm}$. This rotor size is chosen as it is used in several commercial designs [36,37] and in research [11,38], due to giving sufficient thrust for industrial payloads while maintaining a reasonable footprint for transportation and storage.

Table 1. Description of rotor geometry.

Quantity	Unit	Value
Rotor diameter, D	cm	71.12
Number of blades	-	2
Hub diameter	cm	5.4
Pitch at $0.75R$	in	9.2
Chord at $0.75R$	cm	4.4

The chord length is kept fixed for all blades, based on measurements of the T-MOTOR rotor. The twist angle of the blade is varied according to the following formula,

$$\beta(r) = \arctan\left(\frac{P}{2\pi r}\right), \tag{23}$$

where P is the pitch at $0.75R$ given in metres, except close to the hub of the blade where the twist is gradually reduced to yield a geometry suitable for manufacturing. The twist angles considered in this work along with the chord length along the blade span are shown in Figure 2.

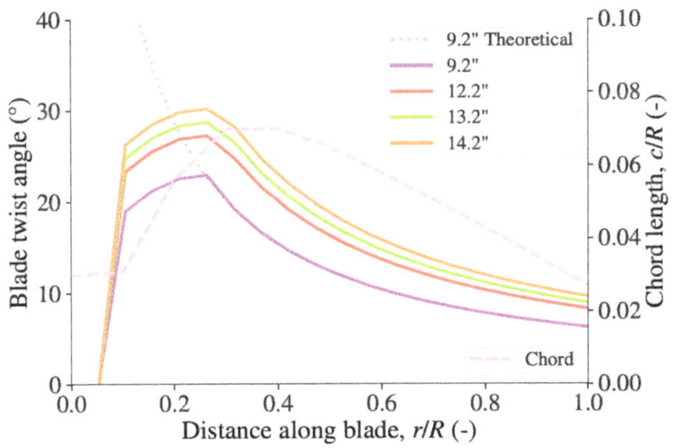

Figure 2. Twist angle and chord length of the rotor blade.

For consistency, the rotor geometry is constructed using a single airfoil instead of using the actual airfoil shape from the commercial rotor. The chosen airfoil is the Archer A18 airfoil, originally built for free-flight airplanes [39]. The coordinates for the airfoil are taken from the UIUC Airfoil Coordinates Database [40]. A comparison of the A18 airfoil against measurements of the commercial rotor is shown in Figure 3. Although there are some discrepancies, especially towards the trailing edge where a thin edge is challenging to manufacture for small rotors, the overall agreement is good. The tip of the rotor is also simplified compared to the commercial airfoil, with a simple cut-off at the tip of the blade. Figure 4 shows the 3D geometry used in the CFD simulations.

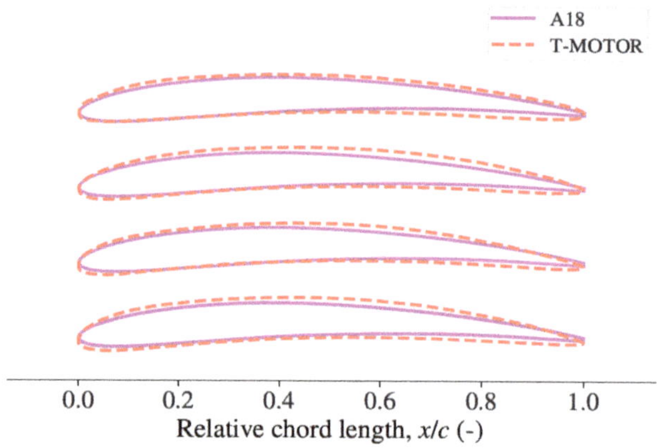

Figure 3. Comparison of A18 airfoil against airfoils along the commercial T-MOTOR G28x9.2″ blade at four radial stations. From the bottom: $0.3R$, $0.5R$, $0.7R$, $0.9R$.

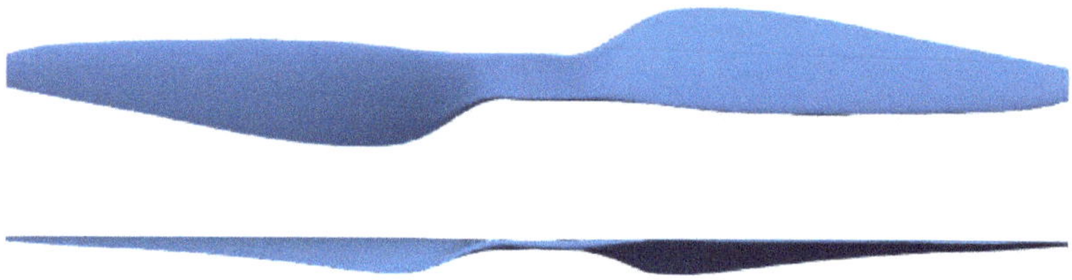

Figure 4. Top view (**top**) and front view (**bottom**) of the computational 3D rotor geometry for a pitch of 9.2″.

The aerodynamic drag and lift coefficients for the airfoil, to be used in the BEMT solver, are obtained by performing XFOIL simulations through the QBlade interface [41,42]. For the sake of simplicity, a constant Reynolds number of Re = 175,000 is used, which is approximately the Reynolds number at $r = 0.75R$ at a rotational speed of 2000 RPM. The resulting drag and lift coefficients, along with the aerodynamic efficiency (drag-to-lift ratio), are shown in Figure 5. The airfoil reaches a peak in aerodynamic efficiency of $C_L/C_D = 80$ at angle of attack $\alpha = 5°$.

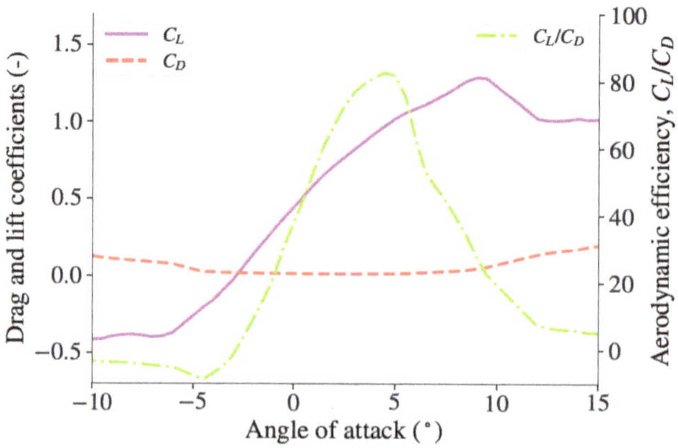

Figure 5. Aerodynamic drag and lift coefficients for the A18 airfoil, calculated using XFOIL at Re = 175,000.

3.2. Mesh

The numerical simulations are performed over a mixed-element unstructured grid developed at neptech AB using Pointwise® (Cadence Design Systems, San Jose, CA, USA) [43], a mesh-generation software specifically developed for CFD applications. Particular attention is paid to the rotor surface mesh, which is shown in Figure 6a. Stretched anisotropic quadrilaterals have been extruded from the leading edge and the trailing edge using the 2D T-Rex algorithm. T-Rex allows us to grow layers of rectangular cells given the first cell thickness and a growth factor, and the inflation is stopped once a smooth dimensional transition with the rest of the surface mesh is achieved. The rest of the upper and lower surface domains consist of triangles and quads generated by the "advancing front ortho" algorithm, and are automatically shaped to comply with high-quality criteria, whilst fulfilling a specified maximum cell dimension. The grid at the blunt trailing edge and at the wingtip has been designed to transition smoothly to the T-Rex-extruded upper and lower surface cells using a structured-dominant approach.

Once a reasonably fine and high-quality 2D grid is obtained, the 3D T-Rex algorithm is employed to inflate layers of high-aspect-ratio hexahedra and prisms in the near-wall region to effectively capture viscous effects. The remaining AMI block is filled with isotropic tetrahedra. As shown in Figure 6b, T-Rex ensures a smooth dimensional transition between the last extruded prism or hexahedron and the outer tetrahedra through one layer of high-quality pyramids. The remainder of the far-field domain surrounding the AMI blocks is cylindrical and fully consists of isotropic tetrahedra with increased characteristic dimension (Figure 6c). In order to achieve a more detailed solution in the far-field for the wake immediately downstream of the rotor, a cylindrical source has been shaped enclosing this region to introduce a local grid refinement.

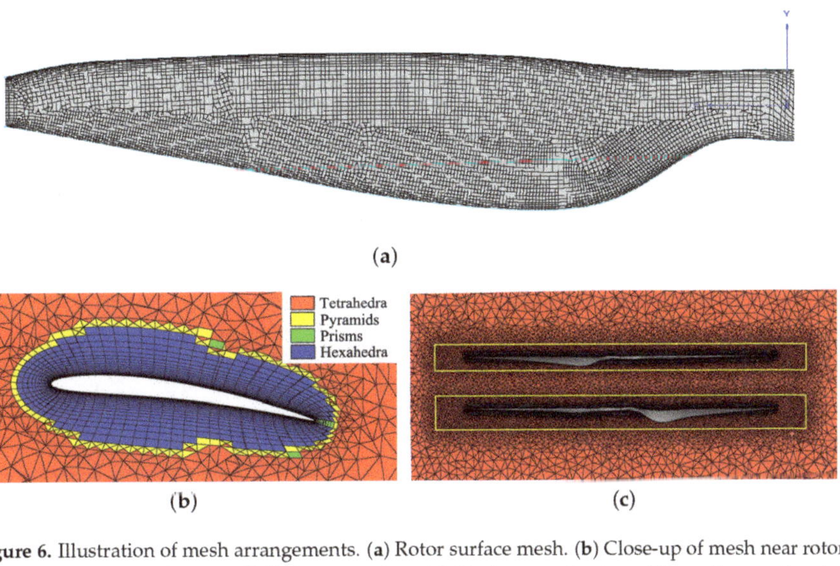

Figure 6. Illustration of mesh arrangements. (**a**) Rotor surface mesh. (**b**) Close-up of mesh near rotor with layers generated using 3D T-Rex extrusion. (**c**) Mesh around rotors. The yellow rectangles indicate the AMI blocks.

The geometric dimensions of the cylindrical source and mesh blocks are reported in Table 2. The lower AMI block height has been adjusted to fit with the increased pitch of the lower rotors. The values of the most relevant grid setup parameters are summarised in Table 3.

Pointwise's mesh quality-check tool can effectively cope with the strict constraints of OpenFOAM. For instance, the solver is particularly sensitive to cells showing a high non-orthogonality, which can potentially lead to simulation divergence. A reasonable trade-off between cost efficiency and cell quality has been found, with the number of severely non-orthogonal cells (>70) reduced to less than 600 per AMI block and grouped in non-critical flow regions. Preliminary simulations provided a reasonably stable solution. Figure 7 shows the y^+ values over the blades at $r = 0.75R$. The y^+ value is lower than one over the majority of the rotor surface, except in a small region at the leading edge. It is overall lower than two across the entire blade, thus indicating a satisfactory resolution for the viscous effects.

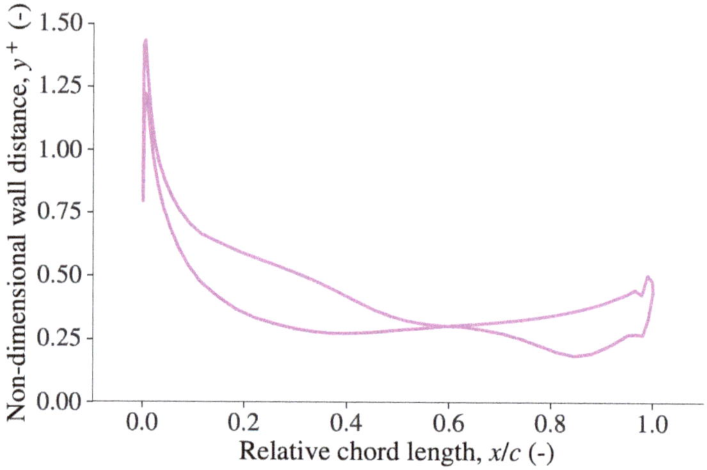

Figure 7. Non-dimensional wall distance along rotor surface at radius $r = 0.7R$ for RPM = 2200.

Table 2. Mesh size parameters for the cylindrical blocks and source.

Object	Base Diameter	Height	Ratio to D
Upper AMI block	84.0 cm	5.50 cm	
Lower AMI block	84.0 cm	6.95 cm	
Cylindrical source	1.00 m	3.00 m	∼4 D
Far-field block	10.0 m	10.0 m	∼14 D

Table 3. Main mesh setup parameters.

Quantity	Unit	Value	Ratio to D
Rotor surface maximum cell size	mm	2.00	$\sim D/350$
3D T-Rex 1st layer thickness	m	1×10^{-5}	
3D T-Rex inflation growth factor	-	1.2	
AMI block maximum cell size	mm	5.00	$\sim D/140$
Source delimited region max. cell size	cm	2.00	$\sim D/35$
Far-field block maximum cell size	cm	20.0	$\sim D/4$
Total number of cells	-	14.1×10^6	

4. Experimental Setup

The experiments are performed on a RCbenchmark Series 1780 dynamometer and thrust stand. The experimental setup is shown in Figure 8. The rotors used are T-MOTOR G28x9.2 rotors, driven by T-MOTOR U8II KV100 brushless motors with power supplied by 1500 W power supplies. For the coaxial setup, the rotors are mounted facing each other and rotating in opposite directions.

The angular speed is measured by an optical tachometer, and the thrust and torque are measured by a load cell with a given experimental tolerance of ±0.5%.

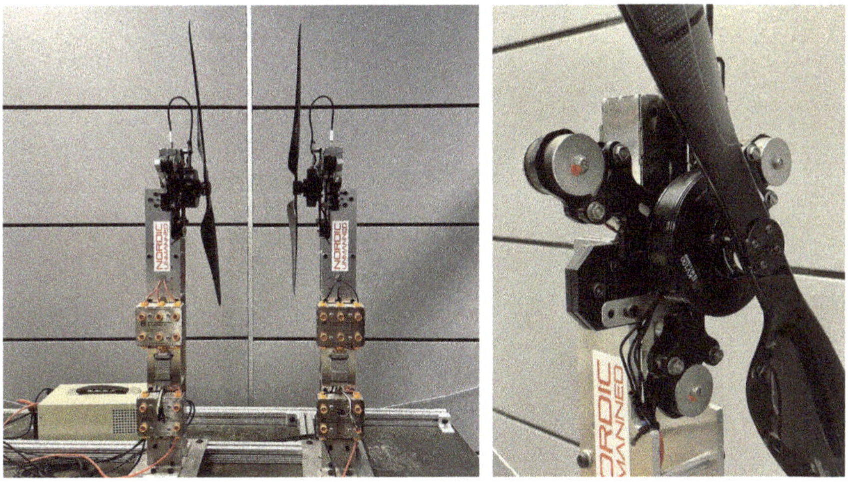

(a) (b)

Figure 8. Picture of experimental setup showing the thrust stand in coaxial configuration and a close-up view of the load cell and motor. (**a**) Thrust stand. (**b**) Load cell and motor.

5. Validation

5.1. Mesh Sensitivity Study

The reliability of the mesh was tested through a mesh sensitivity study for a single rotor. When designing a refined and coarser mesh setup, it was found that changes in the cell dimension over the rotor surface grid resulted in poorer quality 3D blocks, with an increased number of severely non-orthogonal cells. This phenomenon can affect the solution stability and thus lead to a non-reliable mesh sensitivity study. Therefore, in order to provide setups with overall similar quality, the characteristic maximum dimension of the tetrahedra of the AMI block was varied. This parameter was increased to 10.0 mm for the coarser setup and decreased to 3.75 mm in the finer setup. Table 4 shows the total number of cells of the three configurations along with their simulation results. The coarse setup solution highlights a reasonable but non-negligible change in thrust and efficiency compared to the chosen medium setup. In contrast, the fine setup shows only minor differences, hence the medium mesh is chosen for the remainder of the simulations in this work.

Table 4. Mesh sensitivity study.

Number of Cells ($\times 10^6$)	Thrust (N)	Efficiency (N W^{-1})
5.50	25.5	0.124
8.78	25.9	0.127
13.2	26.0	0.127

5.2. Single-Rotor Validation

Figure 9a shows a comparison of the computed thrust with BEMT and CFD against the experimental values for varying angular velocities. Included also are data from the vendor for the T-MOTOR G28x9.2 rotor [44]. The vendor data are in good agreement with the performed experiments, acting as validation of the experimental setup. The CFD simulations match the trend of the experiments, but predict thrust values to be approximately 15% lower. It should be noted that since the simulated rotor geometry does not exactly match the commercial rotor design, an exact match can not be expected. In particular, the tip design of the commercial rotor is expected to be more efficient than the simulated design. The BEMT results are also in good agreement with the experiments, but with increasing underprediction at higher angular velocities.

Figure 9b shows a comparison of the computed efficiency with BEMT and CFD against the experimental values for varying angular velocities. The efficiency is defined as the thrust-to-power ratio, where the power is calculated as the torque multiplied by the rotational velocity. Similar trends as for the thrust are observed here. The CFD simulations are close to the experiments, with an underprediction of approximately 2% to 5%. The BEMT simulations also follow the same trend as the experiments but with an overprediction ranging from around 15% at low rotational speeds to 5% at high rotational speeds.

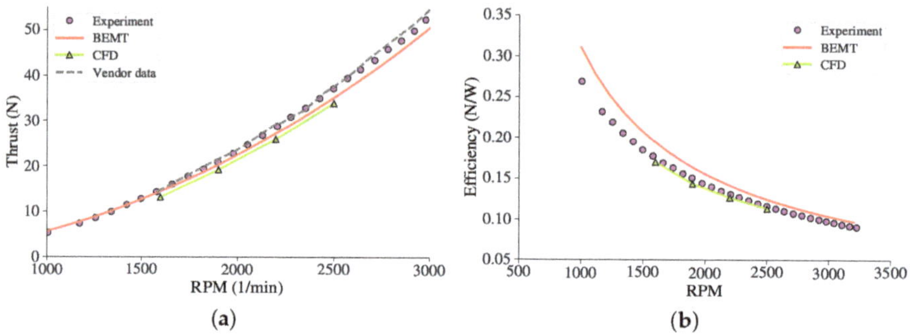

Figure 9. Comparison between experiments, BEMT simulations and CFD simulations for a single rotor. (**a**) Thrust. (**b**) Efficiency.

Further details of the flow pattern are given in Figure 10, which shows the averaged velocity magnitude from the CFD simulations in a vertical slice at the four simulated angular speeds. The flow pattern is the same for all angular speeds, but with an increase in the velocity magnitude for higher angular speeds. Flow is accelerated from the static air above the rotor, resulting in a high-velocity wake below the rotor. There is a low-velocity region just underneath the rotor hub where there is no pitched airfoil to accelerate the flow. The wake clearly contracts into a vena contracta, with a close-to-uniform velocity in the center of the blade and a sharp fall-off to zero at the sides. Although the wakes become closer towards the center at a distance from the rotor, a lower-velocity core remains at the center.

Figure 11 shows the vertical velocity component as a function of radial distance, at a distance of 0.115 m below the rotor. This is the distance where the lower rotor is placed for the coaxial simulations. The predicted inflow velocity from the coaxial BEMT model is shown as dashed lines. There appears to be good agreement between the velocity simulated from CFD and the velocity predicted from the BEMT model. This indicates that the BEMT model is also applicable to coaxial systems.

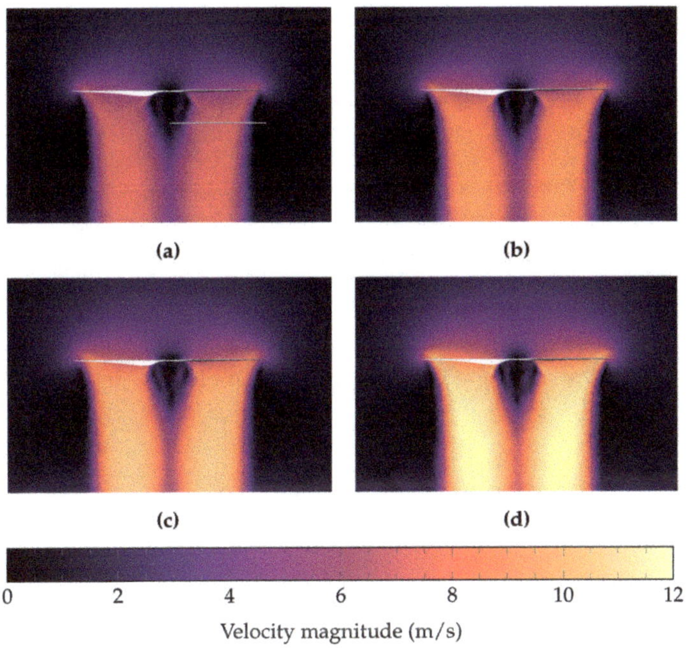

Figure 10. Magnitude of velocity vector for single-rotor setup at varying RPM. The grey line indicated in (**a**) shows the position of the second rotor for the coaxial setup. (**a**) RPM = 1600. (**b**) RPM = 1900. (**c**) RPM = 2200. (**d**) RPM = 2500.

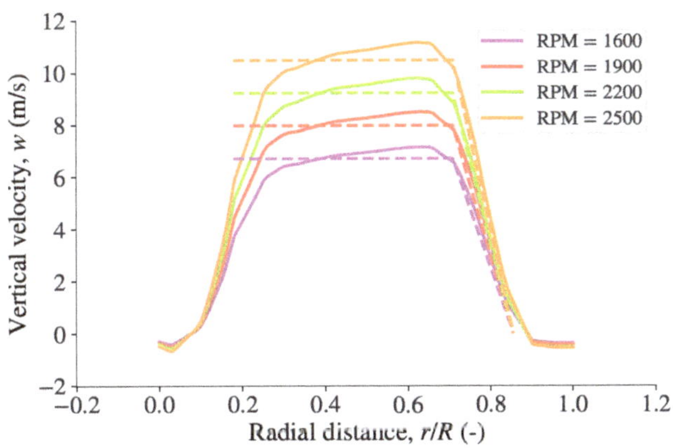

Figure 11. Vertical velocity at a vertical distance 0.115 m from the rotor (indicated by the grey line in Figure 10), estimating inflow velocity for the lower rotor in the coaxial setup. The dashed lines are the values predicted from the coaxial BEMT model.

5.3. *Coaxial Rotor Validation*

The same validation was performed for a coaxial setup, using two T-MOTOR G28x9.2 rotors. The rotors are placed at a distance of 0.115 m apart, rotating in opposite directions at the same angular velocity. Figure 12a shows a comparison of the computed thrust with BEMT and CFD against the experimental values for varying angular velocities. The experimental results and CFD results for the upper rotor are almost identical to the isolated rotor results, indicating that the upper rotor is not significantly affected by the lower rotor. Note that for the CFD results, the thrust values presented here are averaged results. In the coaxial setup, the thrust will oscillate based on the angular position of the rotor relative to the lower rotor. The lower rotor, as expected, shows lower thrust than the upper rotor. For the experiments, the thrust values are 60% to 65% of the upper rotor. The CFD results are again close to the experimental results. For the lower rotor there is a maximum of 6.5% discrepancy in the results. The coaxial BEMT model gives an underprediction of the thrust from 10% at lower angular speeds to 20% at higher angular speeds.

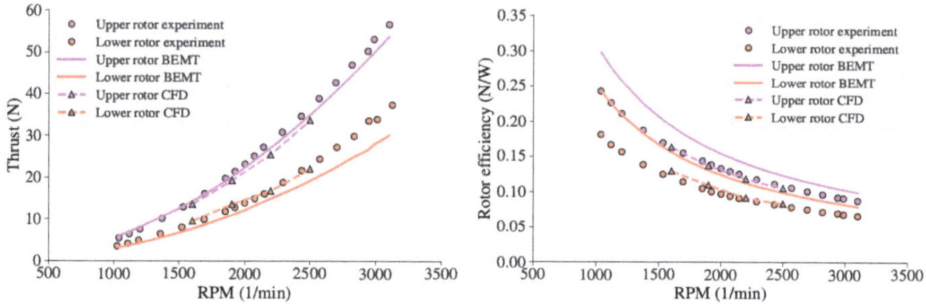

Figure 12. Comparison between experiments, BEMT simulations and CFD simulations for the coaxial rotor setup. (**a**) Thrust. (**b**) Efficiency.

Figure 12b shows a comparison of the computed efficiency with BEMT and CFD against the experimental values for varying angular velocities. The efficiency for the CFD simulations again follow the trend of the experiments and have values in good agreement with the experimental values. The BEMT method also follows the same trends, but significantly overpredicts the efficiency for the lower rotor with values 20% to 35% higher than the experimental values. This is an indication that there are interactions between the rotors not captured by the simple coaxial model used in this work. Still, as both the CFD method and the BEMT method predict the same trends as the experiments, both in terms of thrust and efficiency, they should provide valuable insight on the effect of changing the pitch of the lower rotor.

The CFD method has the additional benefit of capturing more flow details and rotor interactions than the BEMT method. Figure 13 shows the averaged velocity magnitude from the CFD simulations in a vertical slice at the four simulated angular speeds. The velocities are larger than in the corresponding Figure 10 for the single-rotor setup, due to the additional thrust from the lower rotor. It is also clear that the outer region of the lower rotor operates outside the wake of the upper rotor. The total wake from both rotors is also wider than for the single rotor, with a higher velocity core from the combined wake of the two rotors and a lower velocity outer rim from the wake generated by the outer region of the lower rotor. These observations are similar to previous simulations performed on a larger coaxial rotor system by Jinghui et al. [14].

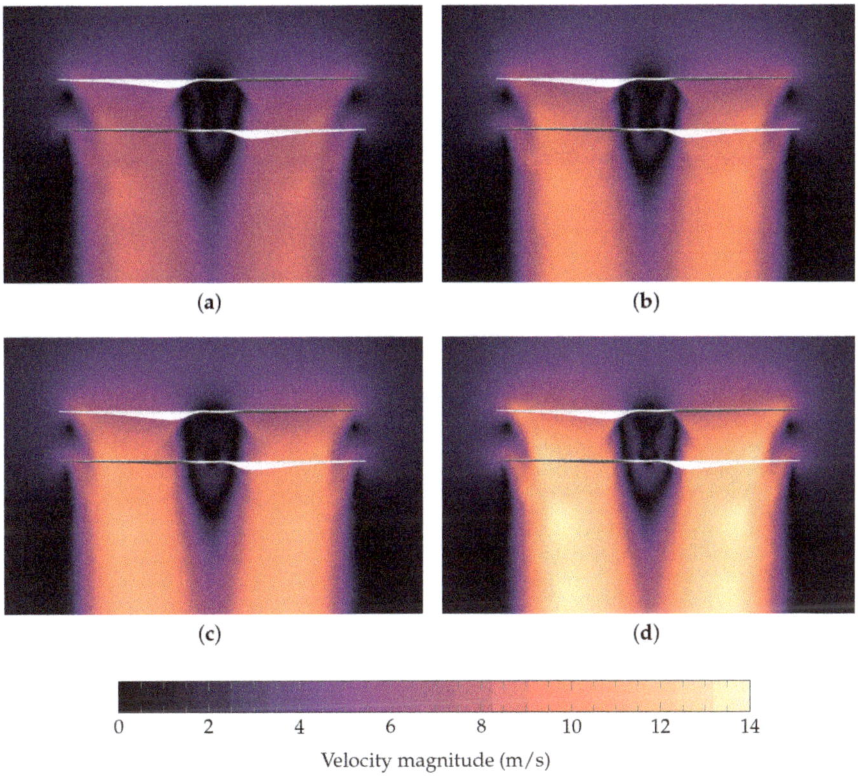

Figure 13. Magnitude of velocity vector for coaxial rotor setup at varying RPM. (**a**) RPM = 1600. (**b**) RPM = 1900. (**c**) RPM = 2200. (**d**) RPM = 2500.

6. Results

In this section, the impact of the lower rotor pitch on efficiency is investigated. First, the BEMT method is used to sweep over a range of pitches for the lower rotor. The case of RPM = 2200 and a pitch of 9.2″ for both rotors is used as a reference case. The pitch of the lower rotor is varied from 8.2″ to 16.2″ and the RPM of the lower rotor is adjusted to give the same total thrust for each case. Using the CFD method, three pitches of 12.2″, 13.2″ and 14.2″ are simulated, while also adjusting the RPM of the lower rotor until the same total thrust as the reference case is obtained.

The resulting efficiencies are plotted in Figure 14. The BEMT results indicate a clear peak in efficiency at a pitch of 14″, with an improvement in efficiency of 2.3%. For the CFD method, the peak is found at a pitch of 13.2″, and with a higher improvement in efficiency of 5.0%. Both methods predict a peak in the efficiency, and the location of the peak is also found at a similar pitch, but the CFD method predicts a higher efficiency value. To compare the two solutions, Figure 15 shows the thrust along the rotor for the two methods for a pitch of 14.2″. For the middle part of the rotor, the methods have similar thrust, which indicates that the coaxial model in the BEMT method works well. The transition from the part of the rotor that is inside the slipstream to the outer part of the rotor is sharper in the BEMT solution than in the CFD solution. Although the coaxial model has a linear transition in incoming velocity, as seen in Figure 11, there should be an additional smoothing to match the CFD solution. Additionally, the tip correction appears to be too high, as the thrust tapers off towards the tip of the rotor faster than in the CFD solution. Despite these differences, the BEMT method captures the overall behavior of the lower rotor.

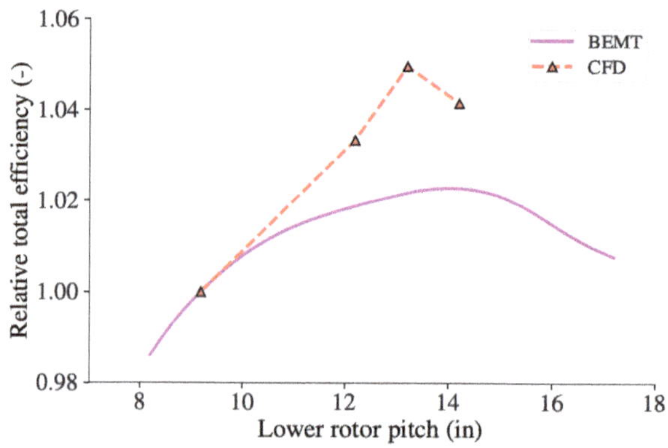

Figure 14. Total efficiency relative to total efficiency at pitch 9.2″ for the coaxial rotor system as a function of lower rotor pitch.

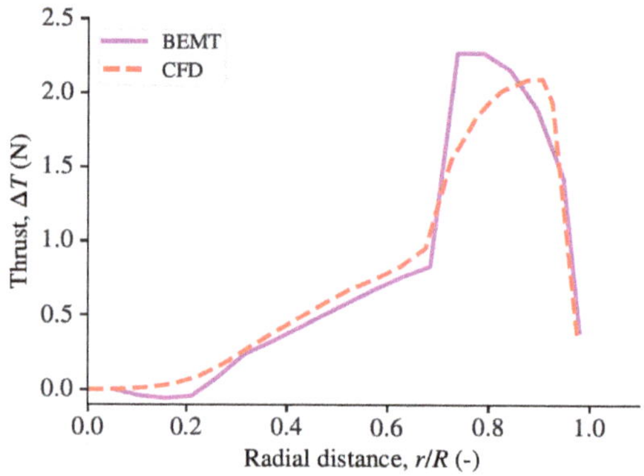

Figure 15. Comparison of BETM and CFD for thrust along blade for pitch 14.2″.

Figure 16a shows the thrust along the blade from the BEMT method for three different pitches. It is clear that the majority of the thrust is produced at the outer region, outside of the wake from the upper rotor. As the pitch is increased from 9.2″ to 14.2″, the amount of thrust generated from the inner region is increased while the amount of thrust from the outer region is decreased. The reduction in thrust from the outer region is due to the reduction in angular velocity to maintain the same total thrust. The angular velocity is reduced from RPM = 2200 to RPM = 1714 for the lower rotor. This also leads to an overall improvement in aerodynamic efficiency, as shown in Figure 16b. This means that at the original angular velocity of RPM = 2200 and at the original pitch of 9.2″, the airfoil is not operating at its optimal point. Increasing the pitch to 14.2″ brings it close to the peak efficiency in the outer region, as evident in Figure 16b. When the pitch is further increased to 17.2″, the airfoil is still below its stall point, hence lift is still increased and the angular velocity is further reduced to RPM = 1554 to maintain the same total thrust. However, at this pitch, the outer region has an angle of attack higher than the optimal point, thus drastically reducing the aerodynamic efficiency by almost half compared to a pitch of 14.2″. Hence, even though the efficiency is improved for the inner region, the total efficiency is still reduced.

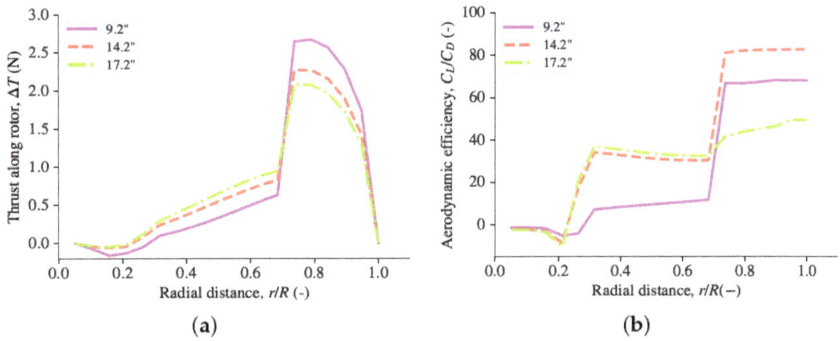

Figure 16. BEMT results along the blade for the lower rotor for three different pitches. (**a**) Thrust along blade. (**b**) Aerodynamic efficiency along blade.

Next, some results from the corresponding CFD simulations are shown, to give further details of the influence of changing the lower rotor pitch. Figure 17b shows contour plots of the pressure coefficient at a radial distance of $r = 0.3R$, i.e., in the inner region of the blade. The plot also shows the flow pattern as seen by the blade (the velocity subtracted by the angular velocity), visualized using the line integral convolution technique [45]. For the pitch of 9.2″, the incoming flow comes in at a negative angle of attack, leading to a region of low pressure near the leading edge at the beginning of the pressure side of the airfoil. At the pitch of 14.2″, the incoming flow operates at an angle of attack close to zero, hence leading to a pressure profile that is more optimal, with lower pressure on the suction side and higher pressure on the pressure side compared to the original pitch.

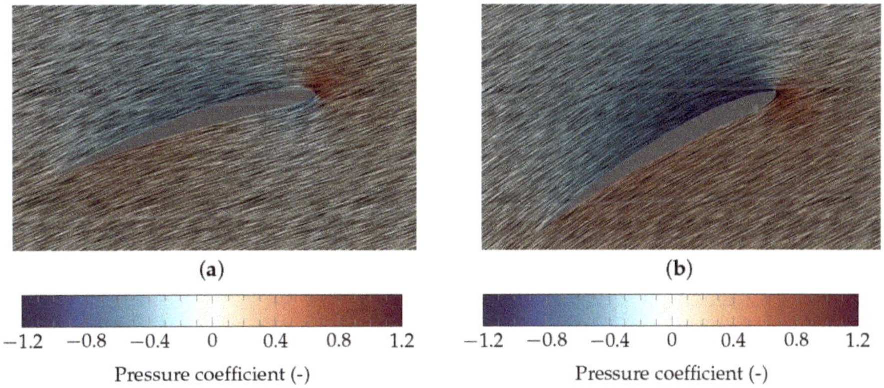

Figure 17. Pressure coefficient and flow pattern (as seen from the rotor) for the lower rotor at radius $r = 0.3R$ for two different pitches. (**a**) Pitch 9.2″. (**b**) Pitch 14.2″.

The pressure coefficient over the blade for the two cases is also plotted in Figure 18. Here, the drop in pressure at the leading edge for pitch 9.2″ is clearly seen. It is also apparent that for pitch 14.2″, the pressure is lower on the suction side and higher on the pressure side over the entirety of the airfoil compared to the original pitch of 9.2″.

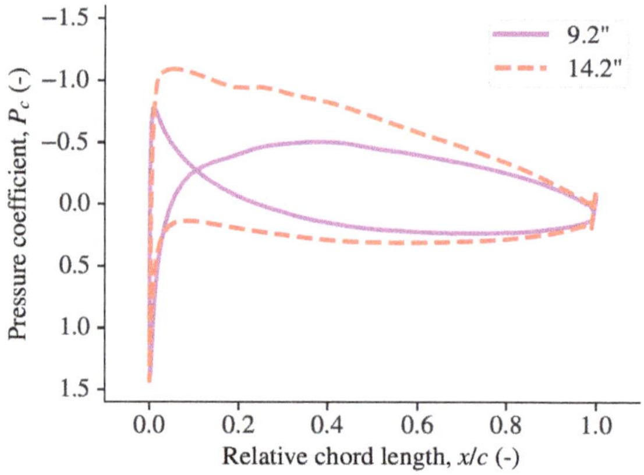

Figure 18. Pressure coefficient over the lower rotor blade at radius $r = 0.3R$ for two different pitches.

7. Conclusions

A computational study was performed investigating the influence of varying pitch on the rotor efficiency in a coaxial rotor setup. An efficient blade element momentum theory method for a coaxial rotor system was developed, and detailed computational fluid dynamics simulations were performed. The chosen rotor has a diameter of 71.12 cm, corresponding to a typical rotor size used in medium-sized multirotor drones.

The two methodologies were validated by comparing against experiments on a single-rotor system and a coaxial rotor system. The CFD methodology showed good agreement on both systems. The BEMT methodology reproduced the experimental trends, but over-predicted the efficiency of the coaxial rotor system.

The results showed that an optimum value for the pitch of the lower rotor could be obtained with both methods, where the total efficiency of the coaxial system was increased by 2% to 5% compared to using the same pitch for the upper and lower rotors. This was found to be due to increasing the efficiency of both the inner region of the rotor, acting in the wake of the upper rotor, and the outer region of the rotor.

Future work will focus on further optimizing the rotor setup. As the current work only used a single pitch for the entire rotor, further increases in the efficiency could be obtained by tailoring the rotor pitch fully to a coaxial setup with pitches designed to be optimal over the entire rotor. This could also include using different airfoils for different parts of the rotor to better match the induced angles of attack. Currently, commercial rotor designs are not available for the high pitches proposed in this work. Future work will also aim to manufacture optimized rotor designs to test experimentally. The current work also only considered the situation of a hovering rotor, and having a system in forward flight should also be investigated. Finally, a more detailed study of the rotor dynamics and wake interactions should be performed, as well as investigating full drone setups with rotor–body interactions.

Author Contributions: Conceptualization, K.E.T.G. and J.A.; methodology, K.E.T.G., A.P. and J.A.; software, K.E.T.G.; validation, K.E.T.G., A.P. and J.A.; investigation, K.E.T.G.; resources, K.E.T.G., A.P. and J.A.; data curation, K.E.T.G. and A.P.; writing—original draft preparation, K.E.T.G. and A.P.; writing—review and editing, K.E.T.G. and A.P.; visualization, K.E.T.G.; project administration, K.E.T.G. and J.A. All authors have read and agreed to the published version of the manuscript.

Funding: This research received no external funding.

Data Availability Statement: The data that support the findings of this study are available from the corresponding author upon reasonable request.

Acknowledgments: The authors wish to acknowledge the following students at the University of Stavanger for their assistance with the experimental and numerical setups: Stian Runestad Hidle,

Vetle Byremo Ingebretsen, Sondre Andersen Gysland, Kjell Vistnes Randeberg, Adrian Otter Falch Günther and Abuzar Ghaffari. We also thank the anonymous reviewers for their constructive comments, which helped improve the manuscript.

Conflicts of Interest: The authors declare no conflicts of interest.

References

1. Hassanalian, M.; Abdelkefi, A. Classifications, applications, and design challenges of drones: A review. *Prog. Aerosp. Sci.* **2017**, *91*, 99–131. [CrossRef]
2. Miiller, H.; Palossi, D.; Mach, S.; Conti, F.; Benini, L. F²unfiiber-Drone: A Modular Open-Platform 18-grams Autonomous Nano-Drone. In Proceedings of the Design, Automation & Test in Europe Conference & Exhibition, Virtual, 1–5 February 2021; pp. 1610–1615.
3. Giernacki, W.; Skwierczyński, M.; Witwicki, W.; Wroński, P.; Kozierski, P. Crazyflie 2.0 quadrotor as a platform for research and education in robotics and control engineering. In Proceedings of the 22nd International Conference on Methods and Models in Automation and Robotics (MMAR), Miedzyzdroje, Poland, 28–31 August 2017; pp. 37–42.
4. Shamiyeh, M.; Rothfeld, R.; Hornung, M. A performance benchmark of recent personal air vehicle concepts for urban air mobility. In Proceedings of the 31st Congress of the International Council of the Aeronautical Sciences, Belo Horizonte, Brazil, 9–14 September 2018; Volume 14.
5. Moore, M.D. *Personal Air Vehicle Exploration (PAVE)*; NASA Langley Research Center: Hampton, VI, USA, 2002; pp. 1–48.
6. Bradley, T.H.; Moffitt, B.A.; Fuller, T.F.; Mavris, D.N.; Parekh, D.E. Comparison of design methods for fuel-cell-powered unmanned aerial vehicles. *J. Aircraft* **2009**, *46*, 1945–1956. [CrossRef]
7. Apeland, J. Use of Fuel Cells to Extend Multirotor Drone Endurance. Ph.D. Thesis, University of Stavanger, Stavanger, Norway, 2021.
8. Prior, S.D. Reviewing and investigating the use of Co-Axial rotor systems in small UAVs. *Int. J. Micro Air Veh.* **2010**, *2*, 1–16. [CrossRef]
9. Lei, Y.; Ji, Y.; Wang, C. Optimization of aerodynamic performance for co-axial rotors with different rotor spacings. *Int. J. Micro Air Veh.* **2018**, *10*, 362–369. [CrossRef]
10. Brazinskas, M.; Prior, S.D.; Scanlan, J.P. An empirical study of overlapping rotor interference for a small unmanned aircraft propulsion system. *Aerospace* **2016**, *3*, 32. [CrossRef]
11. Weishäupl, A.B.; Prior, S.D. Influence of Propeller Overlap on Large-Scale Tandem UAV Performance. *Unmanned Sys.* **2019**, *7*, 245–260. [CrossRef]
12. Prior, S.D. *Optimizing Small Multi-Rotor Unmanned Aircraft: A Practical Design Guide*; CRC Press: Boca Raton, FL, USA, 2018.
13. Yoon, S.; Chan, W.M.; Pulliam, T.H. Computations of torque-balanced coaxial rotor flows. In Proceedings of the 55th AIAA Aerospace Sciences Meeting, Grapevine, TX, USA, 9–13 January 2017; p. 52.
14. Jinghui, D.; Feng, F.; Huang, S.; Yongfeng, L. Aerodynamic characteristics of rigid coaxial rotor by wind tunnel test and numerical calculation. *Chin. J. Aeronaut.* **2019**, *32*, 568–576.
15. Kim, Y.T.; Park, C.H.; Kim, H.Y. Three-Dimensional CFD Investigation of Performance and Interference Effect of Coaxial Propellers. In Proceedings of the IEEE 10th International Conference on Mechanical and Aerospace Engineering (ICMAE), Brussels, Belgium, 22–25 July 2019; pp. 376–383.
16. Leishman, J.G.; Ananthan, S. An optimum coaxial rotor system for axial flight. *J. Am. Helicopter Soc.* **2008**, *53*, 366–381. [CrossRef]
17. Leishman, G.J. *Principles of Helicopter Aerodynamics*; Cambridge University Press: Cambridge, UK, 2006.
18. Manwell, J.F.; McCowan, J.; Rogers, A.L. Wind energy explained: Theory, design and application. *Wind Eng.* **2006**, *30*, 169.
19. Schmitz, S. *Aerodynamics of Wind Turbines: A Physical Basis for Analysis and Design*; John Wiley & Sons: Hoboken, NJ, USA, 2020.
20. Glauert, H. Airplane propellers. In *Aerodynamic Theory*; Springer: Berlin/Heidelberg, Germany, 1935; pp. 169–360.
21. Giljarhus, K.E.T. pyBEMT: An implementation of the Blade Element Momentum Theory in Python. *J. Open Source Softw.* **2020**, *5*, 2480. [CrossRef]
22. Virtanen, P.; Gommers, R.; Oliphant, T.E.; Haberland, M.; Reddy, T.; Cournapeau, D.; Burovski, E.; Peterson, P.; Weckesser, W.; Bright, J.; et al. SciPy 1.0: Fundamental Algorithms for Scientific Computing in Python. *Nat. Methods* **2020**, *17*, 261–272. [CrossRef] [PubMed]
23. Leishman, J.G.; Syal, M. Figure of merit definition for coaxial rotors. *J. Am. Helicopter Soc.* **2008**, *53*, 290–300. [CrossRef]
24. Lee, S.; Dassonville, M. Iterative Blade Element Momentum Theory for Predicting Coaxial Rotor Performance in Hover. *J. Am. Helicopter Soc.* **2020**, *65*, 1–12. [CrossRef]
25. Lakshminarayan, V.K.; Baeder, J.D. Computational investigation of microscale coaxial-rotor aerodynamics in hover. *J. Aircr.* **2010**, *47*, 940–955. [CrossRef]
26. Yoon, S.; Chaderjian, N.; Pulliam, T.H.; Holst, T. Effect of turbulence modeling on hovering rotor flows. In Proceedings of the 45th AIAA Fluid Dynamics Conference, Dallas, TX, USA, 22–26 June 2015; p. 2766.
27. Lopez, O.D.; Escobar, J.A.; Pérez, A.M. Computational study of the wake of a quadcopter propeller in hover. In Proceedings of the 23rd AIAA Computational Fluid Dynamics Conference, Denver, CO, USA, 5–9 June 2017; p. 3961.

28. Loureiro, E.V.; Oliveira, N.L.; Hallak, P.H.; de Souza Bastos, F.; Rocha, L.M.; Delmonte, R.G.P.; de Castro Lemonge, A.C. Evaluation of low fidelity and CFD methods for the aerodynamic performance of a small propeller. *Aerosp. Sci. Tech.* **2021**, *108*, 106402. [CrossRef]
29. Barbely, N.L.; Komerath, N.M.; Novak, L.A. A Study of Coaxial Rotor Performance and Flow Field Characteristics. In Proceedings of the 2016 AHS Technical Meeting on Aeromechanics Design for Vertical Lift, San Francisco, CA, USA, 20–22 January 2016.
30. Cornelius, J.K.; Schmitz, S.; Kinzel, M.P. Efficient computational fluid dynamics approach for coaxial rotor simulations in hover. *J. Aircraft* **2020**, *58*, 197–203. [CrossRef]
31. Panjwani, B.; Quinsard, C.; Przemysław, D.G.; Furseth, J. Virtual Modelling and Testing of the Single and Contra-Rotating Co-Axial Propeller. *Drones* **2020**, *4*, 42. [CrossRef]
32. Menter, F.R. Two-equation eddy-viscosity turbulence models for engineering applications. *AIAA J.* **1994**, *32*, 1598–1605. [CrossRef]
33. Weller, H.G.; Tabor, G.; Jasak, H.; Fureby, C. A tensorial approach to computational continuum mechanics using object-oriented techniques. *Comput. Phys.* **1998**, *12*, 620–631. [CrossRef]
34. Jasak, H.; Jemcov, A.; Tukovic, Z. *OpenFOAM: A C++ Library for Complex Physics Simulations*; CMND. IUC: Dubrovnik, Croatia, 2007; Volume 1000.
35. Farrell, P.; Maddison, J. Conservative interpolation between volume meshes by local Galerkin projection. *Comput. Method Appl. Mech. Eng.* **2011**, *200*, 89–100. [CrossRef]
36. Nordic Unmanned. Staaker BG-200. Available online: https://nordicunmanned.com/drones/staaker-bg200/ (accessed on 10 March 2022).
37. PRODRONE. PD6B-Type2. Available online: https://www.prodrone.com/products/pd6b-type2/ (accessed on 10 March 2022).
38. Czerhoniak, M.S. Scaling up the Propulsion System of an Aerial and Submersible Multirotor Vehicle. Ph.D. Thesis, Rutgers University-School of Graduate Studies, Piscataway, NJ, USA, 2018.
39. Selig, M.S. *Summary of Low Speed Airfoil Data*; SOARTECH Publications: Virginia Beach, VI, USA, 1995.
40. Selig, M.S. UIUC Airfoil Data Site. 1996. Available online: https://m-selig.ae.illinois.edu/ads.html (accessed on 10 March 2022).
41. Drela, M. XFOIL: An analysis and design system for low reynolds number airfoils. In *Low Reynolds number Aerodynamics*; Springer: Berlin/Heidelberg, Germany, 1989; pp. 1–12.
42. Marten, D.; Wendler, J.; Pechlivanoglou, G.; Nayeri, C.N.; Paschereit, C.O. QBLADE: an open source tool for design and simulation of horizontal and vertical axis wind turbines. *Int. J. Emer. Tech. Adv. Eng.* **2013**, *3*, 264–269.
43. Cadence Design Systems. Pointwise® V18.4R4. Available online: https://www.pointwise.com (accessed on 25 December 2021).
44. T-MOTOR. T-MOTOR U8II. Available online: https://store.tmotor.com/goods.php?id=476 (accessed on 8 Febraury 2019).
45. Cabral, B.; Leedom, L.C. Imaging vector fields using line integral convolution. In Proceedings of the 20th annual conference on Computer graphics and interactive techniques, Anaheim, CA, USA, 2–6 August 1993; pp. 263–270.

sensors

MDPI

Article

Research on UAV Robust Adaptive Positioning Algorithm Based on IMU/GNSS/VO in Complex Scenes

Jun Dai [1,2], Xiangyang Hao [1,*], Songlin Liu [1] and Zongbin Ren [1]

1 Institute of Geospatial Information, Information Engineering University, Zhengzhou 450001, China; daijun502@163.com (J.D.); lsl759514@126.com (S.L.); rzb13017600350@163.com (Z.R.)
2 School of Aerospace Engineering, Zhengzhou University of Aeronautics, Zhengzhou 450001, China
* Correspondence: xiangyanghao2004@163.com; Tel.: +86-135-9804-9970

Abstract: As an important component of autonomous intelligent systems, the research on autonomous positioning algorithms used by UAVs is of great significance. In order to resolve the problem whereby the GNSS signal is interrupted, and the visual sensor lacks sufficient feature points in complex scenes, which leads to difficulties in autonomous positioning, this paper proposes a new robust adaptive positioning algorithm that ensures the robustness and accuracy of autonomous navigation and positioning in UAVs. On the basis of the combined navigation model of vision/inertial navigation and satellite/inertial navigation, based on ESKF, a multi-source fusion model based on a federated Kalman filter is here established. Furthermore, a robust adaptive localization algorithm is proposed, which uses robust equivalent weights to estimate the sub-filters, and then uses the sub-filter state covariance to adaptively assign information sharing coefficients. After simulation experiments and dataset verification, the results show that the robust adaptive algorithm can effectively limit the impact of gross errors in observations and mathematical model deviations and can automatically update the information sharing coefficient online according to the sub-filter equivalent state covariance. Compared with the classical federated Kalman algorithm and the adaptive federated Kalman algorithm, our algorithm can meet the real-time requirements of navigation, and the accuracy of position, velocity, and attitude measurement is improved by 2–3 times. The robust adaptive localization algorithm proposed in this paper can effectively improve the reliability and accuracy of autonomous navigation systems in complex scenes. Moreover, the algorithm is general—it is not intended for a specific scene or a specific sensor combination– and is applicable to individual scenes with varied sensor combinations.

Keywords: UAV; robust adaptation filter; multi-source fusion; error state Kalman filter (ESKF); information sharing coefficient

Citation: Dai, J.; Hao, X.; Liu, S.; Ren, Z. Research on UAV Robust Adaptive Positioning Algorithm Based on IMU/GNSS/VO in Complex Scenes. *Sensors* **2022**, *22*, 2832. https://doi.org/10.3390/s22082832

Academic Editors: Jaroslaw Pytka, Andrzej Łukaszewicz, Zbigniew Kulesza, Wojciech Giernacki and Andriy Holovatyy

Received: 8 March 2022
Accepted: 4 April 2022
Published: 7 April 2022

1. Introduction

With the rapid development of research on autonomous and intelligent unmanned systems, UAVs can now operate in high-risk and complex environments, thus expanding the scope for human activities by virtue of their flexibility, low cost, and strong adaptability. Therefore, research on their application is of great significance to the military and civilian fields [1–3].

At present, sensors that can be used for autonomous navigation and positioning include inertial sensors, visual sensors, satellite navigation sensors, and so on [4]. As the heart and eyes of autonomous navigation systems, these sensors are intrinsic to the realization of autonomous and intelligent drones. However, satellite signals are interrupted by urban canyons and complex environments; in fog, heavy snow, and disaster scenarios, visual sensors lack sufficient feature points; inertial sensors face problems such as long-term error accumulation. Therefore, a single type of sensor alone cannot meet the autonomous navigation requirements of UAVs used in complex scenarios; multi-source sensors need to be used for fusion navigation. The multi-source fusion method can make up for the shortcomings of using a single type of sensor and establish complementary advantages and information supplementation between different sensors [5,6]. In this way, optimal estimations are obtained, and the reliability and real-time performance of an autonomous navigation system can be guaranteed.

Multi-source fusion localization algorithms include sequential filtering, decentralized filtering, centralized Kalman filtering, etc., [7,8]. As a distributed multi-source fusion filtering method, the federated Kalman method can facilitate plug-and-play in a multi-source fusion mode, thereby ensuring the navigational integrity and accuracy of the system. A. Carlson [9] proposed a two-stage distributed filtering federated Kalman filter algorithm, which includes N sub-filters, all of which are evenly distributed with information distribution coefficients.

However, in practical applications, the performance and estimation accuracy of a local system constantly change with the complex navigation environment, and the traditional Kalman filter information sharing coefficient is fixed, which means the different requirements of the navigation system cannot be met in complex scenarios. In order to improve the performance of the federated filter, Shen et al. [10] proposed a new adaptive federated Kalman filter with time-varying information sharing coefficients based on an observability analysis of the integrated navigation of unmanned ground vehicles. Xiong et al. [11] designed a novel dynamic vector-form information-sharing method based on an analysis of the error covariance matrix and the observation matrix of federated filters in highly dynamic environments. Zhang et al. [12] proposed a multi-source information fusion localization algorithm based on the federated Kalman filter, which has verified that the algorithm proposed in this paper displays fault tolerance and reduces the amount of required computation by comparing the centralized Kalman filter. Yue et al. [13] proposed an adaptive federated filtering algorithm that can calculate the information distribution coefficient using previous information and adjust the information distribution coefficient in real time. Lyu et al. [14] proposed an adaptive joint interactive multi-model (IMM) filter for complex underwater environments, which combines adaptive joint filtering with the IMM algorithm. Focusing on the problem of the variable accuracy of each navigation sensor, Guo et al. [15] designed an adaptive allocation algorithm of information factors based on prediction residuals. However, most of these studies focus on specific scenarios and the failure of a single sensor and lack discussions of different scenarios and different types of sensor failures. In this paper, we consider general adaptability. The proposed robust adaptive algorithm is not aimed at a single specific scene with a specific combination of sensors but is suitable for similar scenes with variable sensor combinations.

Focusing on the problems of GNSS signal interruption and the lack of sufficient feature points for visual sensors in complex scenes, this paper proposes a new robust adaptive positioning algorithm for UAV based on IMU/GNSS/VO, which can achieve the autonomous navigation and positioning of UAVs. Based on the ESKF, this paper establishes an integrated navigation model of IMU/GNSS and IMU/VO, incorporating system error model, measurement model and so on. Then, a robust adaptive localization algorithm is proposed based on a federated Kalman filter as the algorithmic framework, combined with robust equivalent weights and sub-filter adaptive shared coefficients. Finally, the time and accuracy of the three schemes are compared and analyzed through mathematical simulation experiments; the 'OutBuilding' scene data are selected, and the reliability and robustness of the proposed algorithm are verified through dataset tests.

This paper is organized as follows: A multi-source fusion model based on ESKF and federated Kalman filtering is established in Section 2, on the basis of the IMU/GNSS and IMU/VO integrated navigation model. In Section 3, an equivalent weight adaptive filtering algorithm is proposed based on robust equivalent weights and sub-filter adaptive shared coefficients. In Section 4, the accuracy and real-time performance of the three schemes are discussed and analyzed through mathematical simulation experiments. In Section 5, the effectiveness of the proposed algorithm is proven through dataset validation. Finally, the conclusions are drawn in Section 6.

2. Multi-Source Fusion Model

2.1. ESKF (Error State Kalman Filter)

Compared with the classical Kalman filter, the ESKF can constrain the error state to run at a position close to the origin, thereby avoiding the possible parameter singularity and gimbal lock problems and ensuring parameter linearization. In this paper, a loose combination of vision/inertial navigation and satellite/inertial navigation is modeled based on the ESKF. Similar to the classic Kalman approach, the ESKF performs prediction and measurement updates. The prediction model is kinematically updated based on the IMU (Inertial Measurement Unit) model, and the measurement is updated based on VO (Visual Odometry—the position and attitude data are obtained by solving camera image poses) and GNSS (Global Navigation Satellite Systems) measurement data.

2.1.1. Predictive Model

This paper adopts the local navigation coordinate system, and the system state quantity is $[q, v, p, a_b, \omega_b]^{\mathrm{T}}$, where q represents UAV attitude quaternion, v represents UAV speed, p represents UAV position, a_b represents the accelerometer bias, and ω_b represents the angular velocity bias. The UAV kinematics equation is as follows:

$$\begin{cases} \dot{q} = \frac{1}{2} q \otimes (\omega_m - \omega_b) \\ \dot{v} = C_b^n (a_m - a_b) \\ \dot{p} = \delta v \\ \dot{a}_b = 0 \\ \dot{\omega}_b = 0 \end{cases} \tag{1}$$

Considering that the actual measurement contains errors, here, the state quantity is set to the error state $x(t) = [\delta\theta, \delta v, \delta p, \delta a_b, \delta\omega_b]^{\mathrm{T}}$. The UAV error state equation is as follows:

$$\begin{cases} \delta\dot{\theta} = [\omega_m - \omega_b]_\times \delta\theta - \delta a_b - w_\omega \\ \delta\dot{v} = -C_b^n [a_m - a_b]_\times \delta\theta - C_b^n \delta\omega_b - C_b^n w_a \\ \delta\dot{p} = \delta v \\ \delta\dot{a}_b = w_{a_b} \\ \delta\dot{\omega}_b = w_{\omega_b} \end{cases} \tag{2}$$

where $\delta\theta$ is the attitude angle error state that satisfies $\delta q = e^{\delta\theta/2}$, δv is the velocity error state, δp is the position error state, δa_b is the accelerometer bias error state, and $\delta\omega_b$ is the angular velocity bias error state. ω_m is the measurement value of the gyroscope, w_ω is the measurement noise of the gyroscope, and w_{ω_b} is the noise of the gyroscope bias. a_m is the measurement value of the accelerometer, w_a is the measurement noise of the accelerometer, and w_{a_b} is the noise of the accelerometer bias.

With reference to Equation (2), the equation for state is:

$$\dot{x}(t) = F(t)x(t) + G(t)w(t)$$

$$F(t) = \begin{bmatrix} [\omega_m - \omega_b]_\times & 0_{3\times3} & 0_{3\times3} & -I_{3\times3} & 0_{3\times3} \\ -C_b^n[a_m - a_b]_\times & 0_{3\times3} & 0_{3\times3} & 0_{3\times3} & -C_b^n \\ 0_{3\times3} & 0_{3\times3} & I_{3\times3} & 0_{3\times3} & 0_{3\times3} \\ 0_{3\times3} & 0_{3\times3} & 0_{3\times3} & 0_{3\times3} & 0_{3\times3} \\ 0_{3\times3} & 0_{3\times3} & 0_{3\times3} & 0_{3\times3} & 0_{3\times3} \end{bmatrix} \quad (3)$$

$$G(t) = \begin{bmatrix} -I_{3\times3} & 0_{3\times3} & 0_{3\times3} & 0_{3\times3} \\ 0_{3\times3} & -C_b^n & 0_{3\times3} & 0_{3\times3} \\ 0_{3\times3} & 0_{3\times3} & 0_{3\times3} & 0_{3\times3} \\ 0_{3\times3} & 0_{3\times3} & I_{3\times3} & 0_{3\times3} \\ 0_{3\times3} & 0_{3\times3} & 0_{3\times3} & I_{3\times3} \end{bmatrix} w(t) = \begin{bmatrix} w_a \\ w_\omega \\ w_{a_b} \\ w_{\omega_b} \end{bmatrix}$$

Using Taylor expansion, the formula is discretized, and the following formula is thus obtained:

$$\begin{aligned} x_{k+1} &= (I + F\Delta T)x_k + G\Delta T w_k \\ &= \Phi_k x_k + \Gamma_k w_k \end{aligned} \quad (4)$$

where ΔT is the sampling time.

2.1.2. Measurement Update

The UAV measurement update equation is as follows:

$$z_k = H_k x_k + v_k \quad (5)$$

The GNSS measurement data are converted into the local navigation coordinate system of this paper, and the measurement matrix is obtained as follows:

$$\begin{gathered} H_k^{GNSS} = [\ I_{3\times3} \quad I_{3\times3} \quad 0_{3\times3} \quad 0_{3\times3} \quad 0_{3\times3}\ ] \\ v_k = [\ n_v^{GNSS} \quad n_p^{GNSS}\ ]^{\mathrm{T}}, n_v^{GNSS} \sim N(0, \sigma^2_{n_v^{GNSS}}), n_p^{GNSS} \sim N(0, \sigma^2_{n_p^{GNSS}}) \end{gathered} \quad (6)$$

where n_v^{GNSS} is the velocity measurement white noise, and n_p^{GNSS} is the white noise produced by position measurement.

Similarly, the VO measurement data are the position and attitude values obtained from the original image through pose calculation, and the measurement matrix is as follows:

$$\begin{gathered} H_k^{VO} = [\ I_{3\times3} \quad 0_{3\times3} \quad I_{3\times3} \quad 0_{3\times3} \quad 0_{3\times3}\ ] \\ v_k = [\ n_\theta^{VO} \quad n_p^{VO}\ ]^{\mathrm{T}}, n_\theta^{VO} \sim N(0, \sigma^2_{n_\theta^{VO}}), n_p^{VO} \sim N(0, \sigma^2_{n_p^{VO}}) \end{gathered} \quad (7)$$

where n_θ^{VO} is the attitude measurement white noise, and n_p^{VO} is the position measurement white noise.

2.2. *Fusion Model*

The UAV measurement data are derived from two types of sensors, GNSS and VO, so the multi-source fusion method is used for state estimation. Considering the need to ensure the fault tolerance and reliability of the navigation system, the distributed filtering method is adopted in this paper. Figure 1 shows the classic fusion feedback mode of federated

Kalman [16]. Two sub-filters are established using GNSS/IMU and VO/IMU, respectively, and finally the UAV navigation state is estimated by fusing the data of the two sub-filters.

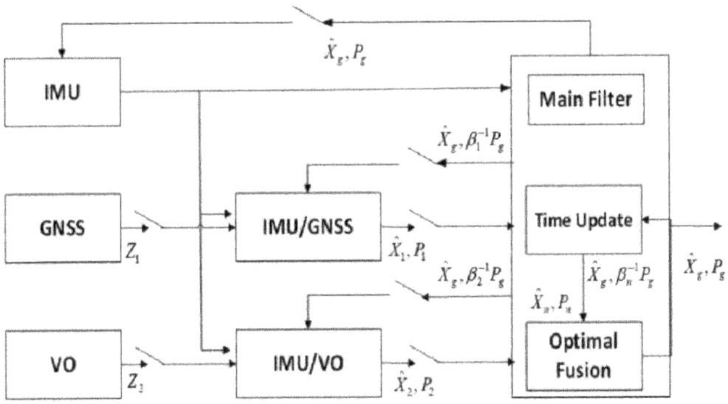

Figure 1. Federated Kalman filter.

2.2.1. Time Update

The measurement update equation is as follows:

$$\begin{cases} X_{k+1/k}^{i} = \Phi_{k+1/k}^{i} X_{k}^{i}, i = 1 \cdots N, m \\ P_{k+1/k}^{i} = \Phi_{k+1/k}^{i} P_{k}^{i} {\Phi_{k+1/k}^{i}}^{\mathrm{T}} + \Gamma_{k}^{i} Q_{k}^{i} (\Gamma_{k}^{i})^{\mathrm{T}} \end{cases} \tag{8}$$

where X_k^i is the state quantity of the i-th ($i = 1 \cdots N$) filter at time k, X_k^m is the state quantity of the main filter at time k, $X_{k+1/k}^i$ is the one-step predicted state, Q_k^i is the system state covariance, $\Phi_{k+1/k}^i$ is the state transition matrix of the i-th filter, and $P_{k+1/k}^i$ is the one-step predicted state covariance of the i-th filter.

2.2.2. Measurement Update

The measurement update equation is as follows:

$$\begin{cases} K_{k+1}^{i} = P_{k+1/k}^{i} (H_{k+1}^{i})^{T} \left(H_{k+1}^{i} P_{k+1/k}^{i} (H_{k+1}^{i})^{T} + R_{k+1}^{i}\right)^{-1} \\ X_{k+1}^{i} = X_{k+1/k}^{i} + K_{k+1}^{i} (Z_{k+1}^{i} - H_{k+1}^{i} X_{k+1/k}^{i}) \\ P_{k+1}^{i} = (I - K_{k+1}^{i} H_{k+1}^{i}) P_{k+1/k}^{i}, i = 1 \cdots N \end{cases} \tag{9}$$

where K_{k+1}^i is the gain matrix, H_{k+1}^i is the measurement matrix, R_{K+1}^i is the measurement state covariance, X_{k+1}^i is the predicted state, and P_{k+1}^i is the predicted state covariance.

2.2.3. Information Fusion

The state quantity and state covariance of the main filter are obtained by fusing the sub-filters. The fusion equation is as follows:

$$\begin{cases} P_{k+1}^{g} = \left[\sum\limits_{i=1}^{N} (P_{k}^{i})^{-1}\right]^{-1}, i = 1 \cdots N, m \\ X_{k+1}^{g} = P_{k+1}^{g} \left[\sum\limits_{i=1}^{N} (P_{k}^{i})^{-1} X_{k+1}^{i}\right] \end{cases} \tag{10}$$

where P_{k+1}^g is the state covariance after the main filter fusion, and X_{k+1}^g is the state quantity after the fusion of the main filter.

2.2.4. Information Sharing and Feedback

The information sharing and feedback factor model is as follows:

$$\begin{cases} Q_k^i = \beta_i{}^{-1} Q_k^g \\ P_k^i = \beta_i{}^{-1} P_k^g \\ \sum_{i=1}^{N} \beta_i = 1 \\ X_k^i = X_k^g, i = 1 \cdots N, m \end{cases} \tag{11}$$

where β_i is the sub-filter sharing factor, and β_m is the main filter sharing factor.

3. Robust Adaptive Filtering

In a complex environment, considering that errors, or even gross errors, arise in the measurement values of random dynamic systems, the statistical characteristics of noise will change, which will reduce the accuracy of Kalman filtering, and even cause divergence [15,17]. In this case, the availability of sub-filter data is reduced or even completely eliminated. One should consider performing residual testing and robustness processing on the sub-filters before the data fusion of the main filter in order to reduce the availability of observations. Unusable observations are isolated from the main filter so as not to contaminate the entire filtering process, thus improving the accuracy and fault tolerance of the entire system.

3.1. Robust Equivalent Weight Filtering

The system state residual is determined by both the model error and the observation error. When the model error is small, the residual can be used to represent the observation error, and the robustness equivalent weight factor can be used to alter the observation availability gain [18–21].

The state residual is $s_k^i = (z_k^i - H_k^i x_{k/k-1}^i)$, and its covariance matrix is $w_k^i = H_k^i P_{k/k-1}^i H_k^{iT} + R_k^i$.

Here, s_k^i represents the residual of the *i*-th filter at time k in distributed filtering.

The residual of the *i*-th subfilter is normalized as follows:

$$v_i = (s_i)^T (w_i)^{-1} s_i \tag{12}$$

Here, the IGG3 [22] weight function is introduced for robust processing, and the residual gain matrix is adaptively adjusted using the system's normalized residual.

$$\mu_i = \begin{cases} 1 & |v_i| \le k_0 \\ (k_0/|v_i|) d_i^2 & k_0 < |v_i| \le k_1 \\ 0 & |v_i| > k_1 \end{cases} \quad d_i = \frac{k_1 - |v_i|}{k_1 - k_0} \tag{13}$$

In the absence of gross errors in observations, the normalized residuals v_i obey the standard state distribution: $v_i \sim N(0,1)$. Robust processing is performed on observations that exceed the 95% confidence level, where k_0 is set to 1 and k_1 is set to 2. After the observation robustness is processed, the measurement update is performed as follows:

$$\begin{cases} X_{k+1}^i = X_{k+1/k}^i + \mu_i K_{k+1}^i (Z_{k+1}^i - H_{k+1}^i X_{k+1/k}^i) \\ \overline{P}_{k+1}^i = (I - \mu_i K_{k+1}^i H_{k+1}^i) P_{k+1,k}^i, i = 1 \cdots N \end{cases} \tag{14}$$

3.2. Adaptive Information Sharing Coefficient

In the classical federated Kalman, the sub-filters equally distribute the information sharing coefficient, i.e., $\beta_1 = \ldots = \beta_n = 1/n$ [17,23].

In practice, considering that the filtering accuracy of different sub-filters is inconsistent, it is necessary to adjust the proportion of information in each of the sub-filters according to the filtering accuracy. The information sharing coefficient determines the role of each sub-filter in the information fusion process. Specifically, the larger the information sharing coefficient, the larger the proportion of the state estimates dealt with by the local sub-filters [24].

In filtering, the state covariance P_i positively reflects the filtering quality of the filter. The smaller the value of P_i, the more accurate the filter, and vice versa. Here, the accuracy of the sub-filter $\lambda_i(k)$ and the state covariance P_i are defined by Equation (15), as follows.

$$\lambda_i(k) = \sqrt{tr(P_i(k) \cdot P_i(k)^{\mathrm{T}})} \tag{15}$$

As discussed in the previous section, the normalized residuals v_i reflect the availability of filter observations, so we can combine v_i and P_i to comprehensively consider the accuracy of the sub-filters. Here, the IGG3 weight function is introduced to constrain the availability of observations. Considering Equations (13) and (15), the accuracy of the sub-filter can be determined as follows:

$$\lambda_i(k) = \mu_i(k) \cdot \sqrt{tr(\overline{P}_i(k) \cdot \overline{P}_i(k)^{\mathrm{T}})} \tag{16}$$

given that in the federated Kalman filter, the information sharing coefficient satisfies [25–28]:

$$\sum_{i=1}^{N} \beta_i(k) = 1, 0 \leq \beta_i(k) \leq 1 \tag{17}$$

where $\beta_i(k)$ is the information sharing coefficient of the i-th filter at step k.

Here, the main filter does not distribute information, so the adaptive information sharing coefficient and sub-filter precision $\lambda_i(k)$ are expressed as follows:

$$\beta_i(k) = \frac{1/\lambda_i(k)}{1/\lambda_1(k) + 1/\lambda_2(k) + \cdots + 1/\lambda_N(k)}, i = 1, 2, \cdots, N \tag{18}$$

3.3. Robust Adaptive Multi-Source Model

As shown in Figure 2, based on the federated Kalman filter, this study uses IMU/GNSS/VO to build a multi-source fusion navigation system. Robust filtering is performed on IMU/GNSS and IMU/VO, respectively, and the information sharing coefficients are adaptively adjusted by robust equivalent weights.

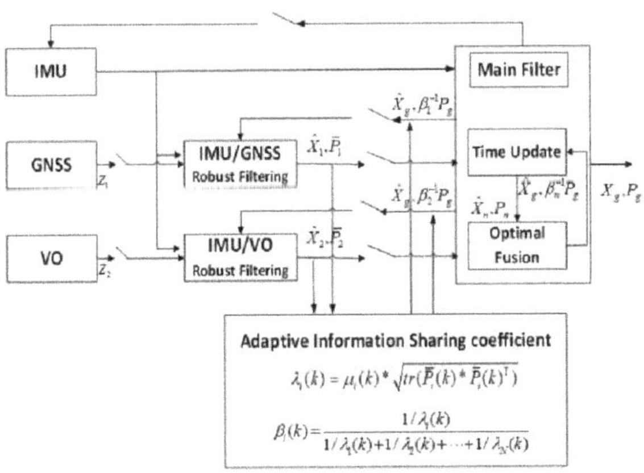

Figure 2. Robust adaptive multi-source model.

4. Simulation Experiment

In order to verify the effectiveness and robustness of the algorithm proposed in this paper, the parameters are set in alignment with the real characteristics of different sensors, and the scene is set with consideration for the complexity of the real environment Simulation experiments are carried out to compare and analyze different schemes in different scenarios. We here highlight that the following simulation experiments have been developed and realized on the basis of the PSINS toolbox, completed by Prof. Yan Gongmin of Northwestern Polytechnical University.

4.1. Simulation Settings

4.1.1. Track Settings

The simulation is set up with the initial position (local coordinates) as [0 m; 0 m; 0 m], the initial attitude (pitch, roll, yaw) as [0°; 0°; 0°], and the initial velocity (local coordinates) as [0 m/s; 0 m/s; 0 m/s]. The trajectory of the drone in the air is simulated, including acceleration, climbing, turning, descending, decelerating, and landing.

4.1.2. Scene Settings

In consideration of the real urban environment, the challenging scenarios faced by UAV flight are here simulated. The following two periods are prone to measurement errors and have been designed considering the limitations of the motion model, and the complexity of the terrain and the environment.

Period 1: 100 s~200 s, when the UAV is flying between buildings; because there are few feature points, 20 times the R_{VO} gross error is added to the VO positioning measurement. R_{VO} is the measurement error value, including position error and attitude error, as shown in Table 1.

Table 1. Sensor parameter settings.

Sensor Type	Parameter	Value
IMU	Gyro bias error	0.1°/h
	Gyro random walk error	$0.08^{\circ}/\sqrt{\text{h}}$
	Accelerometer bias error	200 μg
	Accelerometer random walk error	$50\ \mu\text{g}/\sqrt{\text{h}}$
	Frequency	100 Hz
GNSS	Position error	[1 m; 1 m; 3 m]
	Speed error	[0.1 m/s; 0.1 m/s; 0.1 m/s]
	Frequency	1 Hz
VO	Position error	[0.5 m; 0.5 m; 0.5 m]
	Attitude error	[0.5°; 0.5°; 0.5°]
	Frequency	2 Hz

Period 2: 270 s~370 s, when the UAV flying height drops; here, the urban canyon environment is simulated, and 20 times R_{GNSS} gross error is added to the GNSS positioning measurement. R_{GNSS} is the measurement error value, including position error and speed error, as shown in Table 1.

4.1.3. Sensor Parameter Settings

Table 1 shows the measurement error parameters and update frequency settings of each sensor (IMU, GNSS, VO).

4.1.4. Simulation Scheme

In this paper, three schemes are designed to simulate the trajectory of the UAV in the above simulation.

Scheme 1: Traditional federated Kalman filtering. Information sharing coefficients are distributed equally.

Scheme 2: Adaptive federated Kalman filtering. The sub-filter remains unchanged, and the main filter adaptively adjusts the information sharing coefficient according to the accuracy of the sub-filter.

Scheme 3: Robust adaptive federated Kalman filtering. The sub-filter performs robust filtering, and the main filter adaptively adjusts the information sharing coefficient according to the accuracy of the sub-filter.

4.2. Experimental Results and Discussions

4.2.1. Information Sharing Coefficient Simulation

The capacity of the information sharing coefficient for online adaptation can improve the accuracy and fault tolerance of the whole system in the case of partial sensor failure. The following shows a comparative analysis of the information sharing coefficients of the three schemes.

Figure 3 shows the distribution of information sharing coefficients for the three schemes proposed in this paper. In Scheme 1, the sub-filter information sharing coefficients are evenly distributed. In Scheme 2, since the sub-filter observation error holds a fixed value, the mean square error shows a stable change trend, and the final factor weight of sub-filter information allocation is not changed. In Scheme 3, the information sharing coefficient shows a changing trend in periods 1 and 2. This is due to the presence of gross measurement or model errors, and the sub-filters worsen. The adaptive algorithm proposed in this paper can automatically reduce its corresponding information sharing coefficient and increase the sharing factors of the other two sub-filters. This is in line with expectations. Therefore, the algorithm can guarantee the fault tolerance of the whole system in a complex environment.

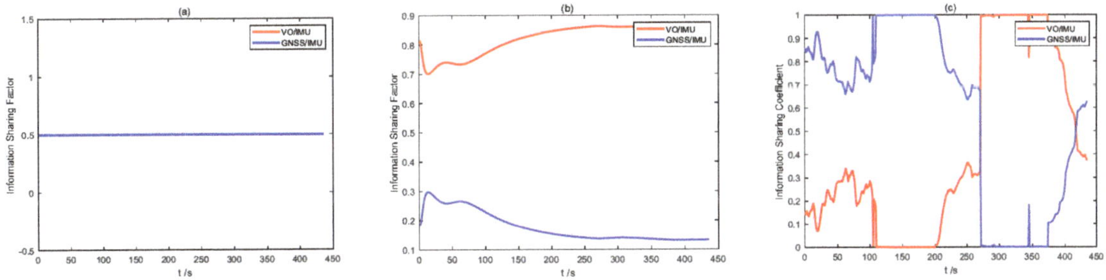

Figure 3. Comparison of information sharing coefficients of three schemes: (**a**) Scheme 1; (**b**) Scheme 2; and (**c**) Scheme 3.

4.2.2. Comparison of State Estimation of Different Combined Systems

In Figure 4, the black line represents the real trajectory, the red line represents the VO/IMU estimated trajectory, the green line represents the GNSS/IMU estimated trajectory, and the blue line represents the VO/GNSS/IMU estimated trajectory. If the three sub-filters are used for independent navigation, the state estimation accuracy will decrease due to the presence of gross errors in the observation values in different time periods (1, 2), which will cause a deviation from the true trajectory and mean the accuracy requirements of the entire navigation system are unmet. As expected, the performance of the VO/GNSS/IMU's global optimal fusion is not seriously affected by abnormal signals given by local sensors and can achieve high accuracy.

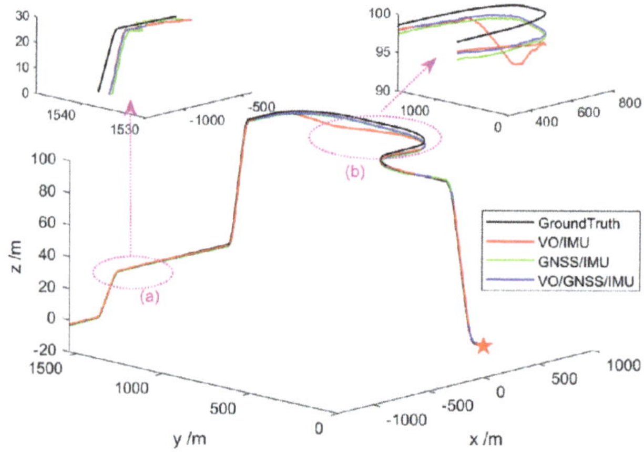

Figure 4. Comparison of state estimation of different combined systems. Asterisk indicates the starting position, the dotted line indicates the position of the enlarged area, and the arrow indicates the specific enlarged area (**a**,**b**).

4.2.3. Comparison of the Results of Different Schemes

In Figure 5, the black line represents the true trajectory. The red line represents Scheme 1, which is the estimated trajectory of the federated Kalman filter. The green line represents Scheme 2, which is the estimated trajectory of the adaptive federal Kalman filter. The blue line represents Scheme 3, which is the estimated trajectory of the robust adaptive federal filtering proposed in this paper. It can be seen from Figure 5 that all three filtering methods can be used for VO/GNSS/GNSS system navigation. However, on the whole, and especially during the 100~200 s and 270~370 s periods, compared to the estimated trajectories of adaptive federated Kalman filtering and federated Kalman filtering, the estimated trajectories of the robust adaptive federal filter are the closest to the true values. This is because the robust adaptive federated Kalman can perform robust and adaptive adjustments on the sub-filter estimates, and the main filter performs adaptive information sharing coefficient allocation according to the estimated weights of the sub-filters. As expected, the performance of the main globally optimal fusion filter is not severely affected by local sensor anomalies and can achieve high accuracy.

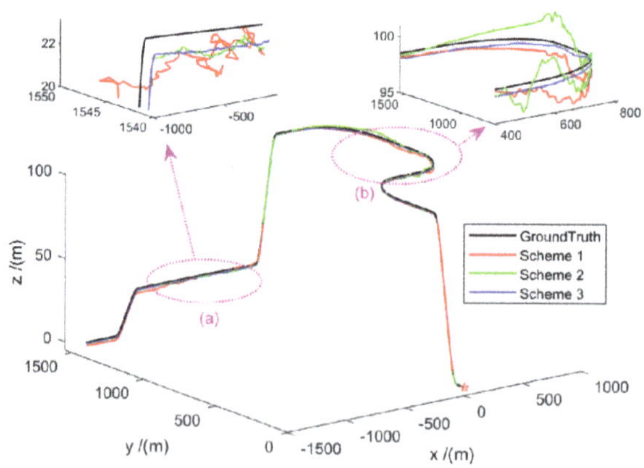

Figure 5. Comparison of trajectories of different schemes. Asterisk indicates the starting position, the dotted line indicates the position of the enlarged area, and the arrow indicates the specific enlarged area (**a**,**b**).

The attitude error estimation curve is shown in Figure 6. The attitude angle estimates obtained by the three filtering methods can all track the change in the true attitude angle, but their estimation accuracies are different. The error in the pitch angle and roll angle is within 100 arc seconds, and the error in the yaw angle is within 30 arc minutes. Compared with the actual data, the error here is small, which has a strong impact on the accuracy of the initial value and initial state covariance set by the simulation. At the same time, it can be seen that the accuracy of Scheme 3 is greatly improved compared with the other two schemes.

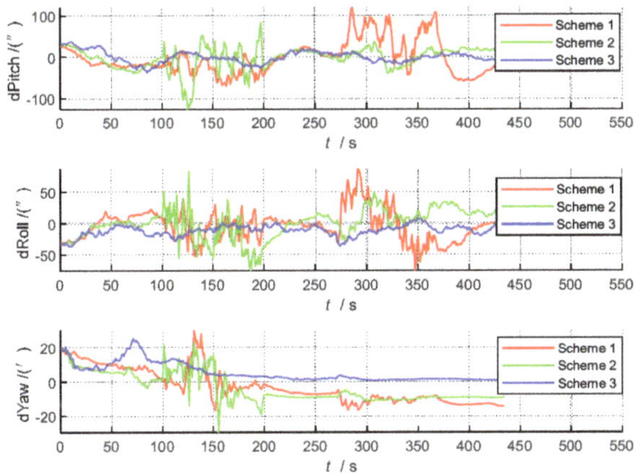

Figure 6. Comparison of attitude errors.

Figures 7 and 8 show the comparison charts of speed and position error. According to the error estimation curve, it can be seen that the overall error of Scheme 3 is relatively stable, with a slight oscillation around the zero value. In the two time periods set in this paper, even when the local sensors are interfered with or fail entirely, the whole system can still maintain sufficiently high precision for navigation. This is because Scheme 3 can switch between different systems in time to reassign weights when local sensors are affected by external disturbances. Therefore, the robust adaptive filter can use the current adaptive state of each local system and can effectively utilize sub-filters with higher state accuracy, thereby reducing the estimated value of the error.

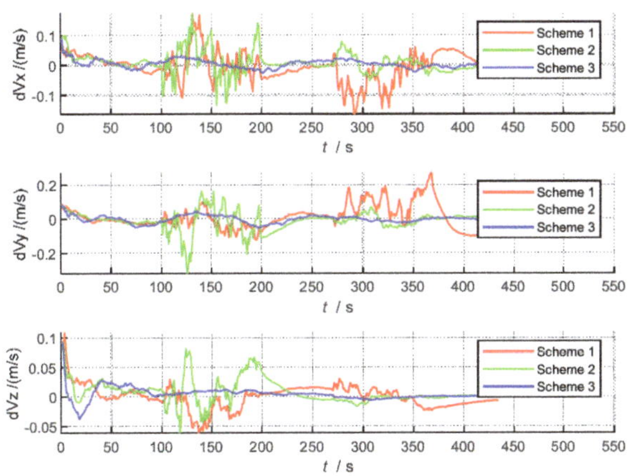

Figure 7. Speed error comparison chart.

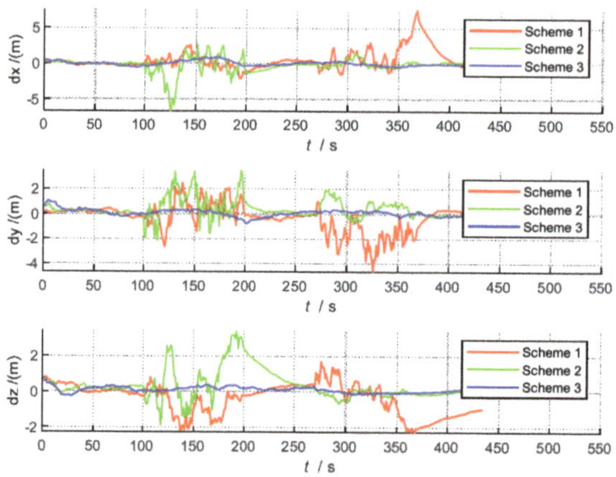

Figure 8. Comparison of position errors.

In order to further compare the three schemes used for information fusion, we carried out 20 Monte Carlo simulations analogous to the real environment. The noise, trajectory and speed of each setting are different. The mean absolute errors (MAEs) of the position errors for the 20 experiment groups are listed in Table 2, and the average error precision is shown in Figure 9.

Table 2. The MAEs of position errors (m) in the 20 experiment group.

Number	Scheme 1	Scheme 2	Scheme 3
1	0.4818	0.1813	0.1470
2	0.3065	0.1891	0.0755
3	0.3805	0.2339	0.1125
4	0.3480	0.1894	0.0616
5	0.3754	0.1758	0.0641
6	0.4136	0.1953	0.0983
7	0.4064	0.2052	0.0929
8	0.3724	0.2280	0.0258
9	0.4319	0.1735	0.0093
10	0.4257	0.2243	0.0267
11	0.4267	0.2148	0.0140
12	0.3838	0.2646	0.0730
13	0.4428	0.2031	0.0542
14	0.4273	0.2063	0.0559
15	0.5012	0.1648	0.0162
16	0.4434	0.1562	0.1018
17	0.4471	0.2241	0.0882
18	0.4030	0.2017	0.0671
19	0.3493	0.2318	0.1115
20	0.3860	0.1759	0.0357

As shown in Figure 9 and Table 2, the accuracy of Scheme 3 (robust adaptive Federated Kalman filtering) is significantly better than those of the other two schemes. The average position error accuracies of the 20 experiment groups were calculated separately, and the errors of the three schemes were obtained as follows: 0.4009 m, 0.2117 m, and 0.0719 m. Compared with Scheme 2, the accuracy of Scheme 3 increased by 66%, and compared with Scheme 1, it increased by 82%. The discussion and analysis of the above results further prove that the robust adaptive federated Kalman filtering algorithm proposed in this paper achieves high accuracy and good robustness, and the algorithm can be applied to complex environments.

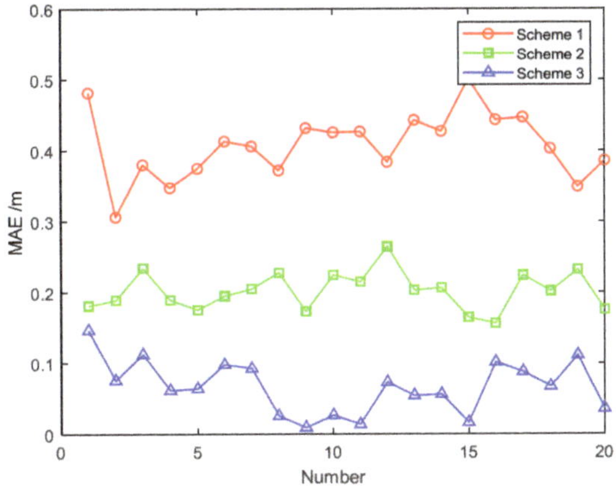

Figure 9. The MAEs of position errors (m) in the 20 experiment groups.

The calculation times of the three algorithms have been tested. The test environment was Windows C++, and the test platform was configured at 1.99 GHz, with Intel(R) Core (TM) i7-8550U CPU. The times required for the single-step execution of the three schemes are shown in Table 3. The time required for the single-step execution of the robust adaptive federated Kalman filter algorithm was 2.12×10^{-2}, which meets the real-time requirements of practical applications.

Table 3. The time required for the single-step execution of the three schemes.

	Scheme 1	Scheme 2	Scheme 3
Time (s)	7.56×10^{-3}	9.01×10^{-3}	2.12×10^{-2}

5. Dataset Validation

On the basis of the simulation verification preformed in the previous section, the dataset collected by the Shanghai Beidou Navigation and Location Services Key Laboratory (UAV configuration sensors and related parameters are shown in Figure 10 and Table 4) are used for verification. This dataset includes four scenarios: 5 × 5 × 2.5 m testing room with Vicon, "Room"; 8 × 12 × 5 m hall of office with Vicon, "Hall"; 20 × 20 m outdoor square, "OutSquare"; 50 m^2 outdoor area near the building, "OutBuilding". Among the four scenarios, "OutBuilding" ("OutBuilding" is shown in Figure 10) is the most representative, and offers the conditions of short-term errors in or interruptions of GNSS and VO measurement due to signal occlusion or single features. In order to test the applicability of the algorithm in this paper in a complex environment, the SE_OutBuilding_06.bag data are here used to artificially add errors in different time periods. By comparing the final results of the three different schemes, the effectiveness of the algorithm in this paper is verified.

First, based on the ESKF model, the state estimation results of the VO/IMU, GNSS/IMU, and VO/GNSS/IMU integrated navigation systems are obtained, as shown in Figure 11. It can be seen that these integrated navigation systems meet the needs of navigation and positioning, without model or measurement errors. The positioning accuracy is determined by the accuracy and combination of the sensors themselves. The VO/GNSS/IMU combination shows the highest accuracy, followed by the VO/IMU combination, and finally GNSS/IMU.

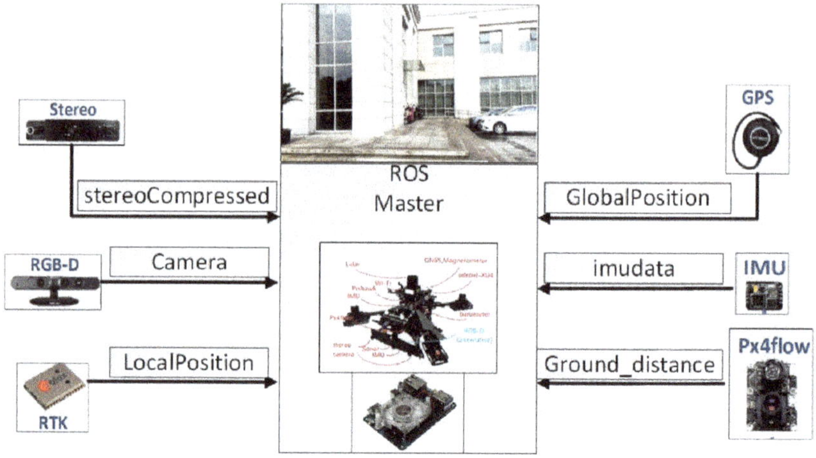

Figure 10. UAV sensor configuration (different sensors and mounting locations for UAV) and "OutBuilding".

Table 4. Sensors and related parameters.

Sensor	Product Model	Collection Frequency (Hz)
Optical flow	Px4flow v1.3.1	20
Stereo camera	640 × 480 × 2 OV7725	30
IMU	MPU9250	40
RGB-D Camera	ASUS Xtion Pro Live	40
Vicon	Vero 360	100
RTK GNSS receiver	Ublox M8P	10

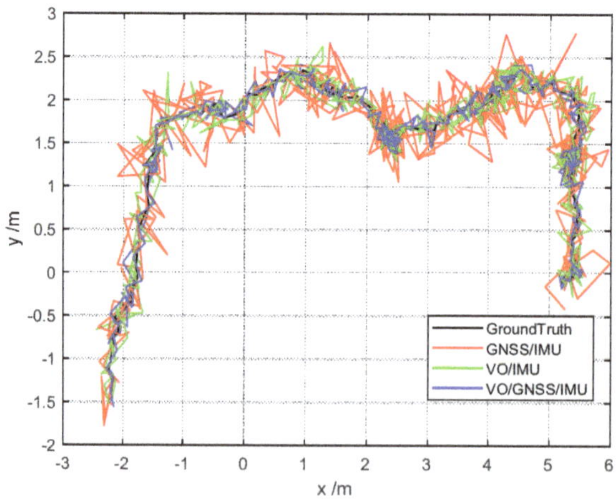

Figure 11. Location estimation for different scenarios.

In consideration of the real properties of the sensor and the complex external environment, the following two time periods are set. These two periods contain model and measurement errors, which can enable us to more effectively verify the algorithm proposed in this paper.

Period 1: 10~40 s; non-Gaussian noise is added to RGB-D Camera measurement, which obeys the following distribution:

$$g(\omega) = \frac{1-\varepsilon}{\sigma_1\sqrt{2\pi}}\exp(-\frac{\omega^2}{2\sigma_1^2}) + \frac{\varepsilon}{\sigma_2\sqrt{2\pi}}\exp(-\frac{\omega^2}{2\sigma_2^2})$$

where $\sigma_1 = 2500$ μrad, $\sigma_2 = 4\sigma_1$ and $\varepsilon = 0.5$.

Period 2: 60~90 s; 20R random error is added to RTK GNSS receiver positioning measurement.

As shown in Figure 12, the information sharing coefficients of different schemes show different trends, as consistent with the simulation results in Section 4.2. Since the measurement accuracy of the vision sensor is higher than that of GNSS, when the information sharing coefficient in Scheme 2 stabilizes, the ratio of VO/IMU will be higher. At the same time, the information sharing coefficient of Scheme 3 shows a change trend, which indicates that the information sharing coefficient of the robust adaptive equivalent Kalman filter algorithm can be adjusted online when the environment changes, thereby improving the accuracy of the entire system.

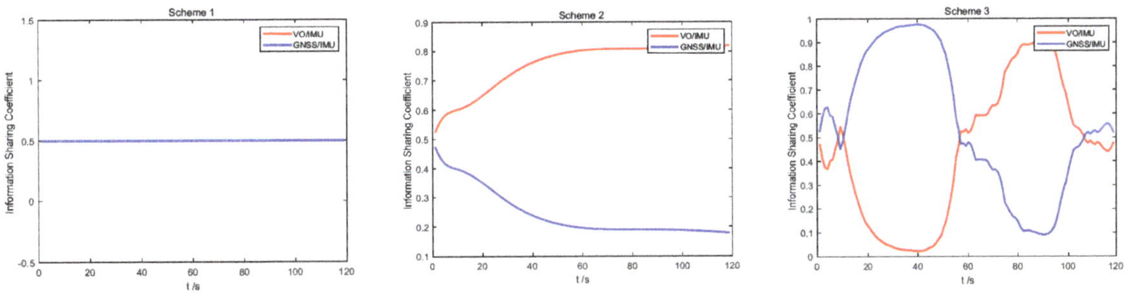

Figure 12. Information sharing coefficient of different schemes (Scheme 1, Scheme 2, Scheme 3).

Using the three schemes set in Section 4.1, a position estimate is obtained as shown in Figure 13. Here, the black line represents the true trajectory; the red line (Scheme 1) represents the estimated trajectory of the federated Kalman filter; the green line (Scheme 2) represents the estimated trajectory of the adaptive information sharing coefficient of the main filter; the blue line (scenario 3) represents the estimated trajectory of the robust adaptive federated filter proposed in this paper. As can be seen, the robust adaptive federated Kalman filter proposed in this paper can effectively track the ground truth.

Figure 14 shows a comparison of the position, velocity, and attitude errors of the three schemes. Compared with Scheme 1 and Scheme 2, Scheme 3 has a higher overall accuracy, which is consistent with the simulation results shown in Section 4.2. For the next 20 analyses, the mean absolute errors (MAEs) and standard deviations (STDs) of the state estimation errors of the three schemes are obtained individually, as shown in Table 5.

As can be seen from Table 5, compared with Scheme 1 and Scheme 2, the average value of the pitch angle and roll angle in Scheme 3 is increased by 1 degree, and the average value of the yaw angle is increased by 2 degrees. The average speed is increased by 0.2 m/s, and the average position is increased by about 0.2 m. These experimental results further demonstrate that the robust adaptive Kalman filter algorithm proposed in this paper can effectively improve the accuracy and robustness of the multi-source fusion navigation system. Scheme 3 is significantly better than the other two schemes, with an overall accuracy improvement of 2–3-fold.

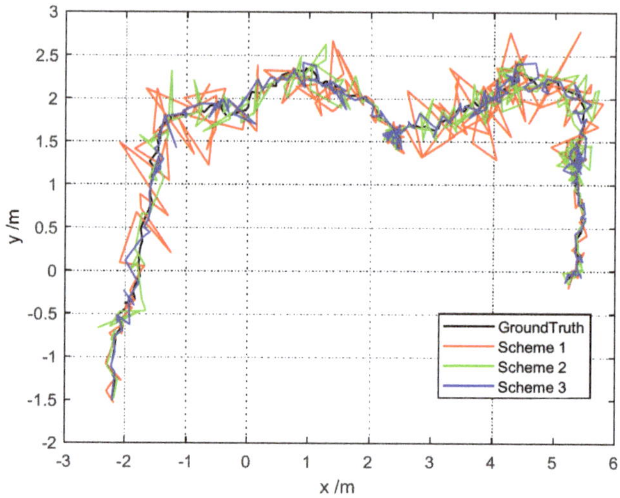

Figure 13. Position estimation for different scenarios.

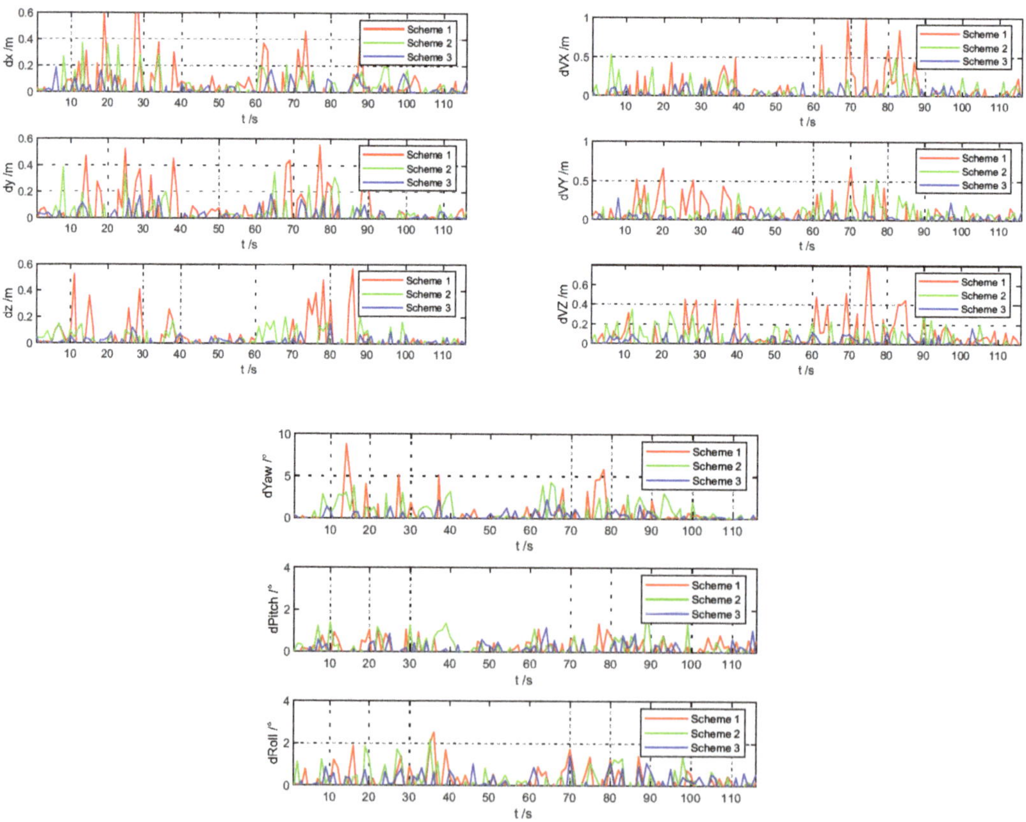

Figure 14. Comparison of position, speed, and attitude errors of different schemes.

Table 5. Accuracy statistics of different schemes (the mean absolute errors (MAEs) and standard deviations (STDs) of the state estimation errors of the three schemes).

Error		Pitch (°)	Roll (°)	Yaw (°)	VX (m/s)	VY (m/s)	VZ (m/s)	X (m)	Y (m)	Z (m)
Scheme 1	MAE	1.56	1.62	3.01	0.30	0.25	0.22	0.26	0.24	0.19
	STD	0.95	0.97	1.97	0.23	0.22	0.19	0.50	0.55	0.64
Scheme 2	MAE	1.08	1.12	1.78	0.15	0.14	0.12	0.13	0.12	0.11
	STD	0.81	0.85	1.25	0.15	0.11	0.09	0.32	0.45	0.84
Scheme 3	MAE	0.62	0.55	0.95	0.07	0.07	0.06	0.06	0.07	0.06
	STD	0.41	0.23	0.52	0.10	0.08	0.07	0.15	0.18	0.14

6. Conclusions

With the intention of improving the reliability and robustness of UAV autonomous navigation and positioning in complex scenarios, we have here designed an autonomous positioning fusion algorithm. The main innovation is that the algorithm can not only independently evaluate the working performance of the sub-filters online, but it can also dynamically adjust the information sharing coefficient. In order to verify the effectiveness and robustness of the algorithm proposed in this paper, an urban canyon scene has been simulated. Through comparative analysis of the two scenarios and three schemes set up, Scheme 3 displayed the highest accuracy of robust adaptive federal kalman filtering, followed by Scheme 2 (adaptive federal Kalman filtering), and finally Scheme 1 (federal Kalman filtering). In addition, by testing the time taken for the single-step debugging of the robust adaptive federal Kalman filter, it has been proven that the algorithm can meet the requirements of actual real-time measurements. Further, this paper used the Beidou Navigation and Location Services Key Laboratory dataset for verification. Using the "Out-Building" data, the artificially simulated model errors and measurement gross errors have been added, and the final results show that the overall accuracy of the algorithm proposed in this paper is improved 2–3-fold. In summary, the algorithm can significantly improve the accuracy and tolerance of the navigation system in complex environments and can be applied to UAV autonomous navigation in urban canyons and GNSS loss-of-lock scenarios. Moreover, the algorithm is general, and can be applied in similar complex scenes and other sensor combinations. Therefore, using the robust adaptive fusion algorithm proposed in this paper, reliable, adaptive, robust and high-precision positioning information can be obtained. Next, we will focus on the actual application of UAVs in complex environments to verify the effectiveness of the algorithm proposed in this paper.

Author Contributions: J.D., X.H., S.L. and Z.R. conceived and designed this study; J.D. and X.H. performed the experiments; J.D. wrote the paper; S.L. and Z.R. reviewed and edited the manuscript. All authors have read and agreed to the published version of the manuscript.

Funding: The research was supported by the Science and Technology Department of Henan Province through the project on Research on Key Technologies for Fully Autonomous Operation of Multi-rotor Agricultural Plant Protection UAVs (NO.222102110029), the project on Research on Collaborative Assembly Technology of Aviation Complex Parts Based on Multi-Agent Reinforcement Learning (NO.222102220095) and the project on intelligent plant protection drones (NO.162102216237).

Institutional Review Board Statement: Not applicable.

Informed Consent Statement: Not applicable.

Data Availability Statement: Not applicable.

Conflicts of Interest: The authors declare no conflict of interest.

References

1. Sun, Y.; Song, L.; Wang, G. Overview of the development of foreign ground unmanned autonomous systems in 2019. *Aerodyn. Missile J.* **2020**, 30–34.
2. Cao, F.; Zhuang, Y.; Yan, F. Long-term Autonomous Environment Adaptation of Mobile Robots: State-of-the-art Methods and Prospects. *Acta Autom. Sin.* **2020**, *46*, 205–221.
3. Zhang, T.; Li, Q.; Zhang, C.S.; Liang, H.W.; Li, P.; Wang, T.M.; Li, S.; Zhu, Y.L.; Wu, C. Current Trends in the Development of Intelligent Unmanned Autonomous Systems. *Unmanned Syst. Technol.* **2018**, 11–22. [CrossRef]
4. Jiang, W.; Li, Y.; Rizos, C. A Multi-sensor Navigation System Based on an Adaptive Fault-Tolerant GOF Algorithm. *IEEE Trans. Intell. Transp. Syst.* **2016**, *18*, 103–113. [CrossRef]
5. Groves, D.P. Principles of GNSS, inertial, and multi-sensor integrated navigation systems. *Ind. Robot.* **2013**, *67*, 191–192.
6. Guo, C. Key Technical Research of Information Fusion for Multiple Source Integrated Navigation System. Ph.D. Thesis, University of Electronic Science and Technology of China, Chengdu, China, 2018.
7. Gao, B.; Hu, G.; Zhong, Y.; Zhu, X. Cubature rule-based distributed optimal fusion with identification and prediction of kinematic model error for integrated UAV navigation. *Aerosp. Sci. Technol.* **2020**, *109*, 106447. [CrossRef]
8. Wang, D.; Lu, Y.; Zhang, L.; Jiang, G. Intelligent Positioning for a Commercial Mobile Platform in Seamless Indoor/Outdoor Scenes based on Multi-sensor Fusion. *Sensors* **2019**, *19*, 1696. [CrossRef]
9. Carlson, N.A. Federated Square Root Filter for Decentralized Parallel Processes. *IEEE Trans. Aerosp. Electron. Syst.* **1990**, *26*, 517–525. [CrossRef]
10. Shen, K.; Wang, M.; Fu, M.; Yang, Y.; Yin, Z. Observability Analysis and Adaptive Information Fusion for Integrated Navigation of Unmanned Ground Vehicles. *IEEE Trans. Ind. Electron.* **2019**, *67*, 7659–7668. [CrossRef]
11. Xiong, Z.; Chen, J.H.; Wang, R.; Liu, J.Y. A new dynamic vector formed information sharing algorithm in federated filter. *Aerosp. Sci. Technol.* **2013**, *29*, 37–46. [CrossRef]
12. Zhang, J.; Chen, H.; Chen, Y. A Multi-sensor Fusion Positioning Algorithm Based on Federated Kalman Filter. *Missiles Space Veh.* **2018**, 90–98.
13. Yue, Z.; Lian, B.; Tang, C.; Tong, K. A novel adaptive federated filter for GNSS/INS/VO integrated navigation system. *Meas. Sci. Technol.* **2020**, *31*, 085102. [CrossRef]
14. Lyu, W.; Cheng, X.; Wang, J. Adaptive Federated IMM Filter for AUV Integrated Navigation Systems. *Sensors* **2020**, *20*, 6806. [CrossRef] [PubMed]
15. Guo, T.; Chen, S.; Tan, J. Research on Multi-source Fusion Integrated Navigation Algorithm of SINS/GNSS/OD/Altimeter Based on Federated Filtering. *Navig. Position. Timing* **2021**, *8*, 20–26.
16. Tang, L.; Tang, X.; Li, B.; Liu, X. A Survey of Fusion Algorithms for Multi-source Fusion Navigation Systems. *GNSS Word China* **2018**, *43*, 39–44.
17. Yan, G.; Deng, Y. Review on practical Kalman filtering techniques in traditional integrated navigation system. *Navig. Position. Timing* **2020**, *7*, 50–64.
18. Xu, X.; Pang, F.; Ran, Y.; Bai, Y.; Zhang, L.; Tan, Z.; Wei, C.; Luo, M. An Indoor Mobile Robot Positioning Algorithm Based on Adaptive Federated Kalman Filter. *IEEE Sens. J.* **2021**, *21*, 23098–23107. [CrossRef]
19. Yang, Y.X. The principle of equivalent weight-robust least squares solution of parametric adjustment model. *Bull. Surv. Mapp.* **1994**, *4*, 33–35.
20. Yang, Y.X. *Robust Estimation Theory and Its Application*; Bayi Press: Beijing, China, 1993; p. 77.
21. Yang, Y.X. *Adaptive Dynamic Navigation and Positioning*; Surveying and Mapping Press: Beijing, China, 2006; pp. 191–192.
22. Hu, G.; Wang, W.; Zhong, Y.; Gao, B.; Gu, C. A new direct filtering approach to INS/GNSS integration. *Aerosp. Sci. Technol.* **2018**, *77*, 755–764. [CrossRef]
23. Li, H.; Tang, S.; Huang, J. A discussion on the selection of constants for several selection iterative methods in robust estimation. *Surv. Mapp. Sci.* **2006**, 70–71.
24. Wang, Y.; Zhao, B.; Zhang, W.; Li, K. Simulation Experiment and Analysis of GNSS/INS/LEO/5G Integrated Navigation Based on Federated Filtering Algorithm. *Sensors* **2022**, *22*, 550. [CrossRef] [PubMed]
25. Qi-Tai, G.U.; Wang, S. Optimized Algorithm for Information-sharing Coefficients of Federated Filter. *J. Chin. Inert. Technol.* **2003**, *11*, 1–6.
26. Wang, Q.; Cui, X.; Li, Y.; Ye, F. Performance Enhancement of a USV INS/CNS/DVL Integration Navigation System Based on an Adaptive Information Sharing Factor Federated Filter. *Sensors* **2017**, *17*, 239. [CrossRef] [PubMed]
27. Hu, G.; Gao, S.; Zhong, Y.; Gao, B.; Subic, A. Modified federated Kalman filter for INS/GNSS/CNS integration. *Proc. Inst. Mech. Eng. Part G J. Aerosp. Eng.* **2016**, *230*, 30–44. [CrossRef]
28. Xu, J.; Xiong, Z.; Liu, J.; Wang, R. A Dynamic Vector-Formed Information Sharing Algorithm Based on Two-State Chi Square Detection in an Adaptive Federated Filter. *J. Navig.* **2019**, *72*, 101–120. [CrossRef]

drones

MDPI

Article

Autonomous Unmanned Heterogeneous Vehicles for Persistent Monitoring

Vaios Lappas [1,*], Hyo-Sang Shin [2], Antonios Tsourdos [2], David Lindgren [3], Sylvain Bertrand [4], Julien Marzat [4], Hélène Piet-Lahanier [4], Yiannis Daramouskas [5] and Vasilis Kostopoulos [5]

1 Department of Aerospace Science & Technology, National & Kapodistrian University of Athens, 34400 Athens, Greece
2 Centre for Cyberphysical and Autonomous Systems, School of Aerospace, Transport and Management, Cranfield University, Cranfield MK43 0AL, UK; h.shin@cranfield.ac.uk (H.-S.S.); a.tsourdos@cranfield.ac.uk (A.T.)
3 Swedish Defence Research Agency FOI, 90621 Umea, Sweden; david.lindgren@foi.se
4 Traitement de l'Information et Systèmes, ONERA, Université Paris Saclay, 91190 Palaiseau, France; sylvain.bertrand@onera.fr (S.B.); julien.marzat@onera.fr (J.M.); helene.piet-lahanier@onera.fr (H.P.-L.)
5 Applied Mechanics Lab, Department of Mechanical Engineering and Aeronautics, University of Patras, 26504 Patras, Greece; daramousk@ceid.upatras.gr (Y.D.); kostopoulos@upatras.gr (V.K.)
* Correspondence: valappas@aerospace.uoa.gr

Abstract: Swarms of unmanned vehicles (air and ground) can increase the efficiency and effectiveness of military and law enforcement operations by enhancing situational awareness and allowing the persistent monitoring of multiple hostile targets. The key focus in the development of the enabling technologies for swarm systems is the minimisation of uncertainties in situational awareness information for surveillance operations supported by 'system of systems' composed of static and mobile heterogeneous sensors. The identified critical enabling techniques and technologies for adaptive, informative and reconfigurable operations of unmanned swarm systems are robust static sensor network design, mobile sensor tasking (including re-allocation), sensor fusion and information fusion, including behaviour monitoring. The work presented in this paper describes one of the first attempts to integrate all swarm-related technologies into a prototype, demonstrating the benefits of swarms of heterogeneous vehicles for defence applications used for the persistent monitoring of high-value assets, such as military installations and camps. The key enabling swarm system technologies are analysed here, and novel algorithms are presented that can be implemented in available COTS-based unmanned vehicles. The algorithms have been designed and optimised to require small computational power, be flexible, be reconfigurable and be implemented in a large range of commercially available unmanned vehicles (air and ground).

Keywords: unmanned systems; persistent monitoring; autonomy

Citation: Lappas, V.; Shin, H.-S.; Tsourdos, A.; Lindgren, D.; Bertrand, S.; Marzat, J.; Piet-Lahanier, H.; Daramouskas, Y.; Kostopoulos, V. Autonomous Unmanned Heterogeneous Vehicles for Persistent Monitoring. *Drones* **2022**, *6*, 94. https://doi.org/10.3390/drones6040094

Academic Editors: Andrzej Łukaszewicz, Wojciech Giernacki, Zbigniew Kulesza, Jaroslaw Pytka and Andriy Holovatyy

Received: 10 February 2022
Accepted: 18 March 2022
Published: 10 April 2022

1. Introduction

Advances in microelectronics, UAV development, autonomous systems and guidance, navigation and control systems have enabled the development of unmanned vehicles to perform complex missions, such as surveillance and persistent monitoring tasks. These autonomous systems, mostly operated in small groups, are able to deliver significant amounts of data in real time; however, they are constrained by the levels of autonomy available and the difficulties of integrating multiple vehicles in swarms. Multiple unmanned vehicles can add not only strength in numbers, but unique capabilities in redundancy, mission flexibility and target tracking/monitoring which can enhance mission capabilities for defence and law enforcement needs. Asymmetrical warfare and the need to simultaneously detect unidentified targets with multiple behaviours are challenging current autonomous systems, as a single, yet capable UAV is not necessarily able to detect, track and persistently monitor multiple targets. Furthermore, large conventional unmanned vehicles, or UAVs, do not have advanced levels of autonomy to date, but rather use human-in-the-loop decision making and control protocols and resources to perform surveillance and monitoring tasks which might become fully automated. Our paper presents the results of a recently completed research project in which a pilot scaled autonomous swarm of unmanned vehicles performed a persistent monitoring mission to protect a mock high-value asset, such as a military installation. A fully integrated, autonomous swarm-based framework was developed and simulated, in which sensor fusion, behaviour monitoring, target and resource allocation and guidance/control algorithms facilitate efficiently tracking hostile targets. A scaled outdoor demonstration using 7–10 UAVs and UGVs has shown the feasibility, challenges and benefits of using a swarm of unmanned vehicles for defence missions. The paper presents an overview of the mission scenario addressed and the swarm system architecture developed. Section 3 details the swarm tracking and control strategy developed. Section 4 details the situational awareness and sensor fusion algorithms developed for implementation in unmanned aerial and ground vehicles which have limited computational power. Section 5 describes the guidance laws developed for the swarm, and Section 6 presents the fully integrated swarm system that was successfully implemented on multiple unmanned vehicles in an outdoor environment (Cranfield Airport) and used to provide persistent monitoring of a high-value asset.

2. Swarm System Architecture

The work presented in this paper was focused on testing and demonstrating that efficient and effective operation of unmanned swarm systems can bring a profound impact to the military arena. The key focus in the development of the enabling technologies was the minimization of uncertainties in situational awareness information for surveillance operations supported by a swarm system of systems composed by static and mobile heterogeneous sensors. The functionalities and features of the main enabling technologies developed can be summarized as follows: (i) an optimal sensor network—static sensors to sense the environment and potential targets; (ii) mobile tasking, including decision making, assigning mobile sensing platforms to the set of tasks, completing the situational awareness information gap on the sensor network and improving the searching and monitoring capabilities; (iii) sensor fusion, target detection and identification, improving the accuracy of the target tracking performance; (iv) information fusion, behaviour monitoring and target assessment (obtaining the threat levels of the targets), to improve the decision making of the mobile sensing platforms; (v) cooperative guidance, path planning and following mobile sensing platforms. Research on all building blocks of a swarm system is extensive [1–15] (task allocation, trajectory planning, etc.), and various new techniques can be applied to swarm scenarios, such as for nonlinear trajectory estimation [15].

Swarm Mission Scenario, Functionalities and Requirements

A mission scenario is used in the work in which a specific area of high interest requires persistent monitoring/surveillance. It is assumed that the scenario takes place near a battlefield in a conflict with a well-armed and competent opponent. The high-value asset (HVA), a military camp, is located in a rough and partly hilly terrain, and a sophisticated sensor system to support perimeter surveillance is available. As the terrain limits the visibility in the protected area, centralized sensors are ineffective. Instead, ground sensors are distributed in a large area around the camp that facilitate early indications of enemy reconnaissance or approaching formations. The ground sensors are sensitive to the presence of humans, vehicles and animals and give prompt alarms if potential targets are in the vicinity. The ground sensors do little to assess the nature and severity of the threats but are on the other hand robust and persistent. They enable coverage of a large area for their price and maintenance requirements. To support alarm verification, the network of ground sensors is completed with drones (air and ground) that operate autonomously in the sensor system. The drones are only activated for special tasks and missions. For instance, on a ground sensor alarm, the drones do a verification that may give the guard high fidelity video and other sensor data from the target or target area in real time. The drones are autonomous and can collaborate in pairs, groups or swarms to meet the high demands on service quality and persistence toward hostile means of deception and attacks.

The key top level functional requirements in the HVA mission scenario are presented in Table 1.

Table 1. Key top level functional requirements in the HVA mission scenario.

Num.	Functional Requirement	Vehicles	Time (min)	Performance Metrics
1	Swarm performs persistent monitoring in an indoor environment 20 × 5 × 3 m with 2 targets	1 UGV 2 UAV	~20′	Position accuracy, speed, situational awareness, path planning accuracy, target position accuracy, speed, time to track, loss of data, link robustness, resilience, bandwidth
2	Swarm performs persistent monitoring of a 500 × 500 × 100 m area with multiple targets	2 UGV 5 UAV	~20–30′	

3. Swarm Sensor Tasking and Control

The task allocation problem is assigning each agent (mobile platform and/or onboard sensor) to a task or a bundle of tasks. The strength of autonomous swarm systems of aerospace vehicles hinges on the distributed nature of the resources available, making the successful assignment of these resources key to maximize its operational advantages and thus minimizing uncertainties.

Efficient cooperation of a swarm of autonomous systems, termed as task allocation, is a vital part for mission success. Task allocation problems are defined as reward function maximization problems. The main objective of task allocation algorithm is to find out the agent and task combinations which maximize the reward function. For the problems with small numbers of agents and tasks, it is possible to calculate the reward function values of all the possible agents and tasks combinations and select the combination with the maximum reward function value. However, since task allocation problem is combinatorial and NP hard, as the numbers of agents and tasks enlarge, computation loads dramatically increase. In this report, approximate algorithms are applied for task allocation problems. One advantage of approximate algorithms is that the computation load is mathematically calculated. This implies that the required computation load for the given task allocation problem and optimization algorithm. The other one is that, although approximate algorithms cannot guarantee the actual optimal solution, they provide solutions with mathematically guaranteed certain levels of optimality.

It is evident that the key enabler of the task allocation is allocation with near real time, so that the agents in the swarm system should be immediately allocated to appropriate task(s). To this end, this project will develop an approximation. Remind that approximation algorithms balance between the optimality and the computational time. Moreover, their quality of the solution and polynomial time convergence could be theoretically guaranteed as long as the objective function satisfies certain conditions, e.g., submodularity. The first focus will be to design a new task allocation model in a manner guaranteeing the submodularity. Note that the objective function of the task allocation problem in the project will be the situational awareness information. It is well-known that the information generally holds the submodularity. Hence, it will be possible to design the problem to hold the submodularity condition. Once the submodularity of the new task allocation model is proven, then implementation of such an approximate algorithm will enable resolution of the task allocation problem in an almost optimal manner in real time. A novel task allocation algorithm based on the greedily excluding technique was developed and validated for EuroSWARM which was shown to be more computationally efficient than current algorithms and can enable the use of existing, low power COTS processing technology available in the UAV and microelectronics markets.

Recently, there have been scientifically interesting developments in approximation algorithms for submodular maximization subject to abstract matroid constraints. In this section a novel decentralized task allocation algorithm has been developed for swarms which consist of for Multi Robot Systems (MRS) using approximation guarantees for general positive-valued submodular utility functions. Two approximate algorithms are investigated and enhanced for swarm control. The well-known greedy algorithm was analysed and enhanced as a greedily excluding algorithm. In the newly developed algorithm, in contrast with other submodular maximization algorithms, at the beginning, all the tasks are assigned to each agent. In each step, the new algorithm reward function reduces, by 'excluding' all subtasks of each task (which are calculated), and then the task with the smallest reward function reduction is then excluded. These procedures are repeated until each of all of the tasks is assigned to a single agent. The main purpose of introducing greedily excluding algorithm is to relieve the computation load of the task allocation algorithm. The two major criteria of performance validation on task allocation algorithms are the level of guaranteed optimality and computation load, as mentioned above. The task allocation algorithms are required to be operated in real time for rapidly changing environments, such as those encountered in battlefield scenarios. However, in cases with large numbers of tasks, the computation loads dramatically increase. This implies that low computation load is a major requirement for the application of task allocation algorithms to rapidly changing problems with many tasks. In the proposed task allocation algorithm, the computation load is reduced using a greedily excluding algorithm. This computation load reduction capability is mathematically calculated, and it is shown that the reduction grows as the number of tasks enlarges. The optimality of the greedily excluding algorithm is tested and compared with the greedy and exhaustive algorithms through simulation.

The Greedy algorithm (Figures 1 and 2) is one of the most well-known submodular maximization algorithms. The element which provides the largest marginal gain is selected and added to the solution set. The selected element is excluded from the ground set. The same procedures are repeatedly conducted while predefined constraints are satisfied. The greedy algorithm under cardinality constraint could be expressed as below (Algorithm 1).

Algorithm 1 Greedy Algorithm with Cardinality Constraint

1: $A \leftarrow \varphi$
2: while $|A| < k$ do
3: $\quad e^* \leftarrow \text{argmax}_{e \in G} f_A(e)$
4: $\quad A \leftarrow A \cup \{e^*\}$
5: $\quad G \leftarrow G \backslash \{e^*\}$
6: end
7: return A

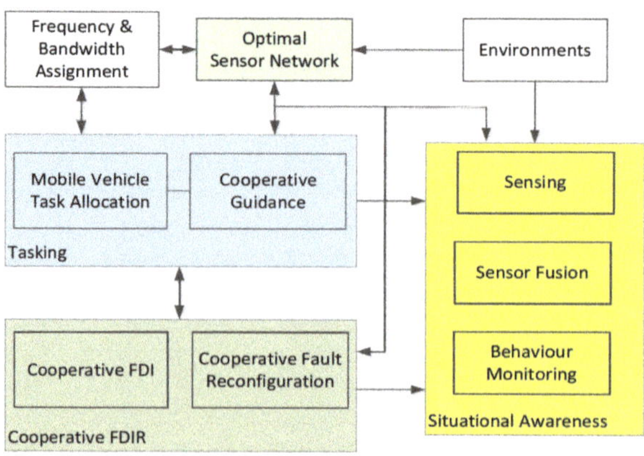

Figure 1. An overview of the autonomous swarm framework building blocks.

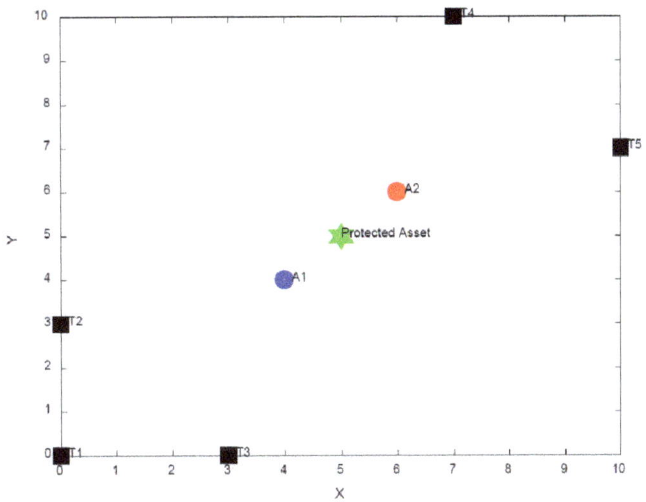

Figure 2. Swarm task allocation with multiple UAV agents and targets.

A is the solution set and G is the ground set, k is the cardinality limit of the solution set and $f(\cdot)$ is the reward function. As shown in the above figure, the algorithm terminates when the number of elements of the solution set reaches the cardinality limit. The task allocation algorithm proposed in this section is based on the basic greedy algorithm. In each step, the marginal reward function values for all the possible agent and task combinations. The agent and task combination with the largest marginal gain is selected and this task is assigned to the solution set of that agent. The assigned task is excluded from the ground set of tasks. This algorithm is described in Algorithm 2.

Algorithm 2 Task Allocation Algorithm using Greedy Algorithm

$A_1, \ldots, A_N \leftarrow \varphi$
while $|T| > 0$ do
  $e^*, i^* \leftarrow \text{argmax}_{e \in T,\, i \in [1, N]} f_{Ai}(e)$
  $A_{i^*} \leftarrow A_{i^*} \cup \{e^*\}$
  $T \leftarrow T \setminus \{e^*\}$
end
return $A_1, \ldots, A_N$

Where Ai is the solution set of agent i and N is the number of agents, T is the ground set of tasks. As described in the above figure, this algorithm assigns one task at each step. After all the tasks are assigned, the algorithm terminates.

The Greedily excluding algorithm is introduced and used as the swarm task allocation algorithm and builds on the previously presented algorithms shown in Figures 1 and 2. In this algorithm, all the elements of the ground set are assigned to the solution set. In each step, the element whose exclusion results in the smallest reward function value reduction, is excluded, from the solution set. This procedure is repeated until a certain constraint is satisfied. Here, the cardinality constraint is implemented as shown in Algorithm 3.

Algorithm 3 Greedily Excluding Algorithm with Cardinality Constraint

```
1: A ← G
2: while |A| > k do
3:     e* ← argmin_{e∈A'} [f(A) − f(A − {e})]
4:     A ← A\{e*}
5: end
6: return A
```

The proposed task allocation approach using the Greedily excluding algorithm is shown in Algorithm 4.

Algorithm 4 Task Allocation Algorithm using Greedy Excluding Algorithm

```
1: A_1, ..., A_N ← T
2: A*_1, ..., A*_1 ← T
3: while each of the tasks is assigned to a single event, do
4:    e*_i ← argmin_{e∈A*'} [f(A) − f(A − {e})] for i∈[1, N]
5:    A_i ← A\{e*_i}
6:    A*_i ← A*_i\{e*_i}
7:    for all the tasks
8:      if a task e' is not assigned to any agent,
9:          k* ← argmax_k[f(A_k + {e'}) − f(A_k)] where k ∈ {}i | e*_i = e' }
10:         A_{k*} ← A_{k*} + {e*}
11:     end
12: end
13: end
14: return A_1, ..., A_N
```

The reward function consists of two parts. The first part is the function which shows whether the targets are matched with the proper sensors. In this reward function, the visibility of the j-th target, λ_j, is assumed to be defined as a simple Gaussian distribution with mean and variance.

$$\lambda_j = N\left(\mu_j, \sigma_j^2\right) \tag{1}$$

The sensing characteristics of i-th sensor, are also defined as a simple Gaussian distribution:

$$\nu_i \sim N\left(\mu_i, \sigma_i^2\right) \tag{2}$$

Bhattacharyya distance between the probability distribution functions of i-th agent and j-th target is defined as:

$$\Delta(\lambda_i, \nu_i) = \frac{1}{8}(\mu_j - \mu_i)^T \left(\frac{\sigma_j^2 + \sigma_i^2}{2}\right)(\mu_j - \mu_i) + \frac{1}{2} ln\left(\frac{\left(\sigma_j^2 + \sigma_i^2\right)/2}{\sqrt{\sigma_j^2 \sigma_i^2}}\right) \tag{3}$$

Using Bhattacharyya distance, the relevancy between i-th agent and j-th target ω_{ij} is obtained:

$$\omega_{ij} = e^{-\frac{\Delta^2(\lambda_j, \nu_i)}{2\sigma^2}} \tag{4}$$

where σ is a design parameter. In order to limit the relevancy between agent and task set, the reward function on sensor suitability, f^1, is developed as shown below:

$$f^1(A_i) = min\{M_i(A_i), \delta M_i(T)\} \tag{5}$$

where $\delta \in [0, 1]$ is a design parameter and T is the ground set of tasks. The second part of the reward function is to prevent assigning excessively many tasks to a single or small part of agents. This reward function, f^2, for i-th agent is defined as follows:

$$f^2(A_i) = \sum_{j=1}^{|A_i|} \mathrm{I} - \frac{j}{|T|} \tag{6}$$

where A_i is the set of tasks assigned to i-th agent and T is the ground set of tasks. Note that the sum of f^2 for all agents diminishes as the tasks are concentrated on a single agent. The total reward function, f^{TOT}, for i-th agent is defined as the weighted sum of those two partial reward functions, f^1 and f^2:

$$f^{TOT}(A_i) = a_1 f^1(A_i) + a_2 f^2(A_i) \tag{7}$$

where α_1 and α_2 are the weights on each part, and they are defined by the users according to the problem cases. The total reward function for the task allocation result is defined as the sum of f^{TOT} for all the agents.

$$f(A_1, \ldots, A_N) = \sum_{i=1}^{N} f^{TOT}(A_i) \tag{8}$$

Swarm Task Allocation Numerical Simulation

In order to demonstrate the performance of the proposed task allocation algorithm, a simulation of a swarm system of aerial and ground unmanned vehicles is constructed, which consists of 3 enemy soldiers and 2 enemy vehicles which approach a protected high-value asset (camp), and the positions and visibility of the targets defined in Table 2 and Figure 1. 2 UAVs detect the targets in this case. One UAV is equipped with an infrared sensor, and the other UAV has an optical sensor.

Table 2. Swarm task allocation simulation parameters.

	j	(X_{Ti}, Y_{Ti})	μ_j	σ_j^2
Soldiers	1	(0, 0)	1	1^2
	2	(0, 3)	1	1^2
	3	(3, 0)	1	1^2
Vehicles	4	(7, 10)	10	5^2
	5	(10, 7)	10	5^2
	i	(X_{Ai}, Y_{Ai})	μ_i	σ_j^2
Infrared Camera	1	(4, 4)	1	1^2
Optical Camera	2	(6, 6)	10	5^2

The design parameters for the reward function selected are (σ, $\alpha1$, $\alpha2$) = (1, 0.5, 0.5). In the simulation mission scenario, moving targets are approaching a protected asset, and the agents with sensors are operated to track and observe the targets. The initial positions of the targets are assumed to be known from external sensors, and the task allocation is autonomously. The main objective of the task allocation, as shown in Figure 2, is to assign targets to the agents equipped with IR/optical sensor which fits the characteristics of them most. Additionally, the tasks should not be assigned excessively on a certain agent; they should be assigned as evenly as possible to the agents. Two sorts of moving targets are considered in this simulation study. The first group is the enemy soldiers, which emit a heat signature. The second group is the enemy ground vehicles, whose purpose differs from their equipment. Two types of UAVs are considered to detect mobile targets. Some of the UAVs are equipped with an infrared sensor (IR), which is suitable for sensing heat emitted from human bodies. The other UAVs are equipped with optical sensors.

The task allocation results for the swarm simulation are obtained using the task allocation formulation of Equations (1)–(7).

The task allocation in results, Table 3, show that the computation loads of the newly developed task allocation approximate algorithms are significantly less than exhaustive search case while achieving the same level of optimality. The computation load of the newly developed greedily excluding algorithm is smaller than that of greedy algorithm by 40% (number of f^{TOT} calculations). Despite the differences in computation effort, all three of the task allocation algorithms compared show the same task allocation performance output, having assigned all the soldiers to the infrared camera-equipped UAV and all the vehicles to the optical camera.

Table 3. Swarm task allocation simulation results.

Algorithm	Task Allocation Result	# of f^{TOT} Calculation	$f(A_1,\ldots,A_N)$	Optimality (%)
Greedy	$A_1 = \{1,2,3\}$ $A_2 = \{4,5\}$	60	4.1	100
Greedy Excluding	$A_1 = \{1,2,3\}$ $A_2 = \{4,5\}$	36	4.1	100
Exhaustive (Optimal)	$A_1 = \{1,2,3\}$ $A_2 = \{4,5\}$	3^5 (=243)	4.1	100

The task allocation algorithms using approximate submodular maximization and compared for swarm type of scenarios have been selected due to their ability to handle multiple agents. In order to decrease the computation load of the well-known greedy algorithm, a greedily excluding algorithm was developed. Through simulation and using different mission scenarios (number of agents/targets), it is shown that the computation load of the newly developed greedily excluding algorithm is smaller than that of greedy algorithm, and the difference increases as the number of tasks becomes larger. The task allocation problem for target detection was set up and simulated using the greedy and greedily excluding algorithms. The results are compared with the actual optimal solution, which requires much larger computation load. The simulation results show that the computation loads are smaller in the greedily excluding algorithm, but the task allocation results are the same with the optimal solution. The proposed task allocation algorithm will thus enable the use of existing, low power COTS processing technology available in the UAV and microelectronics markets for use on swarm scenarios for defence applications which use multiple unmanned vehicles and targets.

4. Situational Awareness

Compared to traditional traffic surveillance sensors such as loop detectors and video cameras positioned at fixed locations, UAV aerial sensing can provide better coverage with the capability to survey large areas at a high speed without being confined to prescribed ground navigation routes. Therefore, this airborne monitoring capability enables suspicious or unusual behaviour in road traffic or on the battlefield to be identified and investigated promptly so that operator's situational awareness is increased in support of border patrol, law enforcement and protecting infrastructure. Typical behaviour monitoring or abnormal detection approach requires domain experts to analyse the obtained data to detect the potentially suspicious behaviours. This approach is cumbersome and unsustainable under a deluge of data and information which could result from complex scenes. Therefore, there is a strong need to develop high-level analysis algorithms to process target information and detect anomalous behaviours, to reduce the human operator's workload. Behaviour monitoring, or more generally detecting anomalous behaviours, usually can be classified into two routes: the first approach codifies the behaviours using experience and domain knowledge of experts and the behaviours are learned from data in the second approach. A general framework for autonomous behaviour has been developed for the monitoring of ground vehicles/targets using airborne surveillance to notify the human commander about the potentially dangerous vehicles.

4.1. Mathematical Model of Target Monitoring

The proposed approach consists of a trajectory analysis tool and an abnormal driving mode classifier based on Refs. [16,17]. The trajectory analysis tool extracts the driving (target) modes, defined by specific alpha-numeric strings, from the filtered target trajectories using speed and curvature analysis. The driving mode classifier provides potential threat alerts by means of a learning-based string-matching approach. With reference to the pattern matching process, a neural-network based regular expression dictionary (RD) algorithm is introduced to match commonly observed target behaviours. The advantage of utilizing the RD, instead of simple string matching, lies in its flexibility and generality in handling the minor differences between two patterns that perform almost the same behaviours of interest. Simulation results are performed to demonstrate the effectiveness of the proposed framework.

The proposed monitoring method utilises a regular expression dictionary (RD) to match commonly observed target behaviours. The RD contains several bins with each bin representing a set of regular expressions of behaviours that have same regularity level. The advantage of utilising the regular expression, instead of simple string matching, lies in its flexibility and generality in handling the minor differences between two patterns that perform almost the same behaviours of interest. Compared to typical learning-based approaches, especially neural network, the proposed RD approach can be easily adapted to different scenarios without significant changes. This can be carried out by simply moving one string from one bin to another bin or simply adding one specific string to one bin, depending on the application scenarios. Another promising advantage of the proposed RD approach is that it can significantly reduce the computational time by a top-to-down search, compared with purely neural network assessment. The behind reason of this aspect is that most targets are normal and therefore, their corresponding behaviours can be readily matched by the top bins.

The simplest and most intuitive way to implement the pattern matching for abnormal detection is to define a reference RD pattern and match the extracted driving modes with the reference patterns to find particular threat. The advantage of this approach is that it can precisely identify particular behaviours of interest. However, it is clear that this approach requires domain experts to define the reference patterns for specific scenarios and therefore, is case-by-case solution, which is not in a cost-effective manner. To tackle this issue and provide the possibility to detect general unexpected target behaviours that significantly differ from the regular manoeuvres exhibited by the vehicles. In this section, a new learning-based pattern matching approach is used for behaviour monitoring by a swarm of agents/unmanned vehicles.

The proposed approach defines a driving mode m_k at each time instant k. The driving mode characterises the moving behaviour of the monitored target vehicle during the considered time-window. These modes can then be leveraged for defining classes of complex behaviours that could draw the attention on the monitored target. This is achieved by comparing the driving modes, extracted from the filtered vehicle trajectories, with particular pre-defined behaviour strings by the means of pattern/string matching. Considering, for example, the case where the monitoring UAV is interested in detecting a 'deceleration + stop/slowly moving' manoeuvre performed by a vehicle near a protected military base. An example of pattern to look for could be '444,000', meaning that the vehicle decelerates for achieving a velocity that is close to zero or keeping stationary to monitor the military base. Obviously, lots of similar strings could be recognised as this peculiar behaviour, e.g., '944,000', and '994,400'. Therefore, using simple exact string matching might be an excessively strict policy to pattern recognition and cannot account for minor differences in the compared strings. This means that the exact string matching might consider a potentially threat as a normal vehicle. Although one can use thresholding to account for the minor difference between the referenced patterns and extracted driving mode strings, the tuning of the threshold is often a complex process, requiring deep insight into the considered scenario. These observations motivate the investigation of a new and flexible approach to define the reference patterns. In order to overcome the shortcomings of simple string matching, this report suggests a more flexible way to define the reference patterns by the means of RD. This allows defining a fixed binding structure for the behavioural patterns of interest, specifying mandatory and optional terms.

The objects of the proposed learning process are patterns of driving modes, which are sequences of alphanumerical characters with no ordinal meaning. Given this characterisation, the most suitable learning approach appears to be the use of a neural network. This tool, if properly trained, can accept a sequence of driving modes of fixed length as input and produce a single value denoting to what extent the pattern can be assumed as normal or abnormal. After properly training the neural network, it can be utilised to assess the vehicle trajectories. However, the issues here are the assessment tends to suffer from a high computational burden for real-time applications when considering complex scenarios and the neural network needs to be re-trained when adding some 'assumed normal/abnormal' behaviours to the neural network for some specific scenarios. For example, the 'deceleration + stop/slowly moving' pattern is a normal behaviour when we consider public traffic monitoring but is becomes abnormal when a vehicle is loitering a high-value asset such as a military base. In order to accommodate these issues, a RD dictionary algorithm is created by summarising the observed manoeuvre patterns provided by the neural network. This can be carried out by providing a new dataset, called RD-training set, as an input dataset to the neural network and follows the same procedure used for the NN-training set. Since the output of the neural network lies in [0, 1], the RD-training driving patterns can be divided into several bins based on their associated neural network output as:

$$\begin{cases} net(p_i) > \gamma \\ net(p_i) \in \left[1 - \frac{(1-\gamma)(j-1)}{N_b}, 1 - \frac{(1-\gamma)j}{N_b}\right] \end{cases} => p_i \in b_j \tag{9}$$

where $net\ (\cdot)$ denotes the neural network operator; p_i is i-th pattern of the RD-training set; γ is the threshold on the neural network output for the pattern to be considered; N_b represents the number of bins of the RD dictionary; and b_j stands for the j-th bin. After splitting the RD-training patterns into different bins, a set of regular expressions is then generated for each bin to represent the level of regularity. As we stated earlier, by utilising the regular expressions, one can accommodate the minor difference between two different but almost same patterns. Given a RD dictionary, the assessment can then be performed by searching the dictionary from the top to find the regular expression that matches with the input pattern. Note that most of the driving patterns in a real-world scenario are normal. Therefore, searching from the top bin can save the computational power. Assume that the querying result of a generic input pattern is q, then, the normal level of this pattern is given by:

$$1 - \frac{(1-\gamma)(q-1)}{N_b} \tag{10}$$

As stated earlier, the advantage of the RD dictionary, compared with the neural network, is that it can be easily updated in a real time. This can be carried out by adding a new pattern into one bin or moving one pattern from one bin to another bin. For example, '44,000' is a normal behaviour pattern when applying to public traffic/driving behaviour monitoring of targets, but it might be a suspicious pattern when considering a high-value asset/military base monitoring scenario. Therefore, when the scenario changes to a military base monitoring, one needs to move the regular expression that represents '44,000' pattern to a bin with the output close to 0. By doing so, the proposed approach can quickly adapt to different scenarios without changing the assessment architecture and thus reducing complexity and computational effort.

4.2. Numerical Simulation of Target Monitoring Algorithm

This section validates the proposed approach through numerical simulations. In order to train the neural network, the dataset with positive labels are manually created by the means Markov Chain. By means of the Markov Chain, plausible patterns are generated as the positive data to train the neural network. As for the negative dataset, the pattern is generated as a random sequence of driving modes where a sub-sequence is added that represent a known abnormal behaviour. The following datasets have been produced when applying the proposed algorithm: (i) NN-training set: 20,000 patterns, including 75% positive and 25% negative data, used to train the neural network; (ii) RD-training set: 20,000 patterns, including 75% positive and 25% negative data, used to query the trained network and create the RD dictionary. A simplified military scenario using the high-value asset (military base) baseline shown in Figure 3 is used, to showcase the performance benefits of the proposed behaviour recognition algorithm as shown in Figures 4 and 5. In the considered scenario, there are six different roads, as shown in Figure 4, and the routes or roads of interests are 2, 3, 4, 5 as they are around the military base.

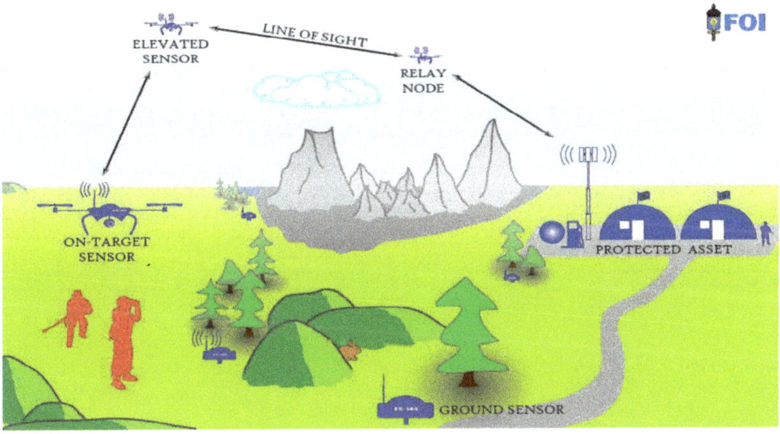

Figure 3. Surveillance of a high-value military asset, where a swarm of air/ground drones serve multiple purposes, such as acquisition of completing camera angles and establishing relay chains for effective and secure communication (source FOI).

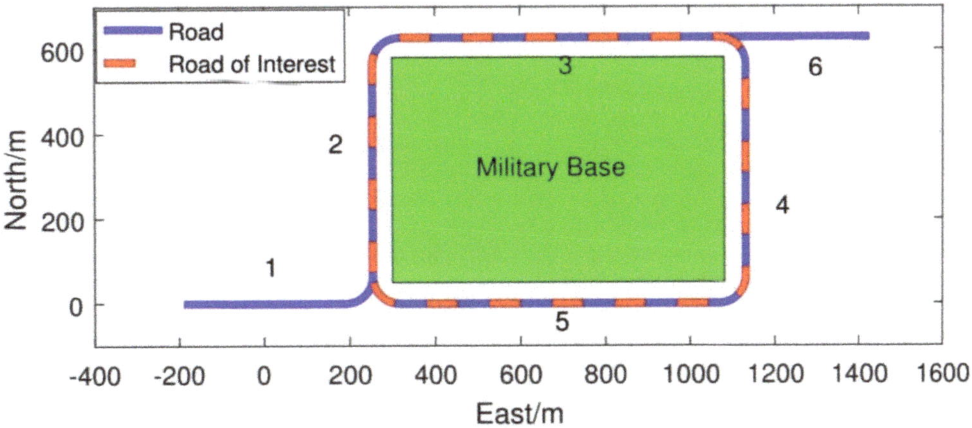

Figure 4. Simulation scenario for monitoring a high value asset (military base).

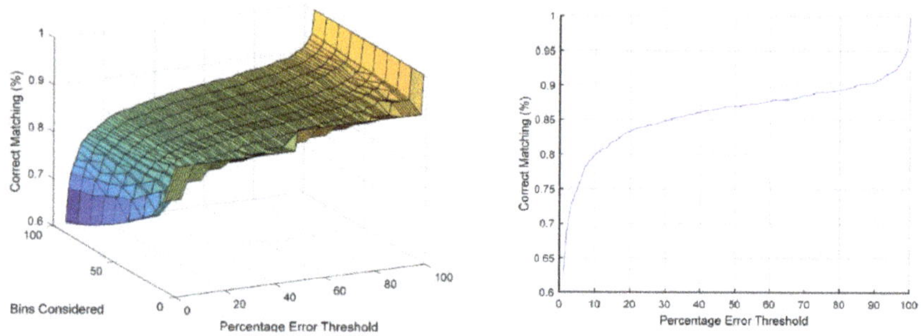

(**a**) (**b**)

Figure 5. (**a**) Results for the RD dictionary using the neural network. (**b**) Results for the RD dictionary using the neural network with 100 bins.

With regard to the accuracy of the generated RD dictionary, as it is generated by the trained neural network, it is reasonable to see to what extent the RD dictionary query output matches with that of the neural network for various test patterns. To assess the accuracy of the algorithm, a test set with 2000 randomly generate patterns is used, for this comparison. The simulation results are shown in Figure 6a,b. The correct matching in the results means that the difference of the outcomes of these two methods lies within a given error threshold. The numeric results indicate that the proposed dictionary query approach has been able to reproduce the NN outputs for a fair portion of the test patterns accounting for approximately 85% of correct matching assuming an error threshold of 20%.

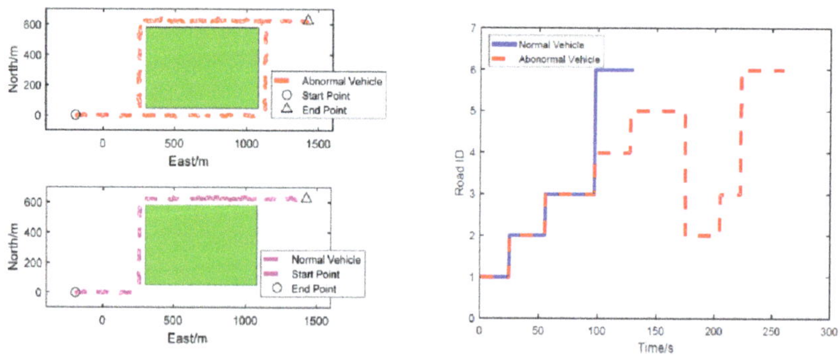

(**a**) (**b**)

Figure 6. (**a**) Assessment for the normal vehicle. (**b**) Assessment for the abnormal vehicle.

Two vehicles, normal and abnormal, with different trajectories are considered. For the abnormal vehicle, it starts from Road 1, loitering the military base through Roads 2, 3, 4, 5, and performs a 'deceleration + stop/slowly moving' manoeuvre at time 145 s at Road 5. For the normal vehicle, it starts from Road 1, regularly pass the military base through Roads 2, 3, and ends at Road 6. The trajectories of these two vehicles are presented in Figure 6a and the road histories are shown in Figure 6b. The assessment results, using neural network and RD dictionary query, of these two vehicles are provided in Figure 7a,b, where Figure 7a is for the normal vehicle and Figure 7b is for the abnormal one. It is clear that the regularity level, provided by both neural network and RD dictionary, of the normal vehicle is very close to 1. This means that the proposed approach considers this car behaves regularly. From Figure 7b, it can be observed that the proposed assessment method successfully identifies the potential threat at around 145 s which is indicated by the output regularity level is close to 0. The recorded running time shows that the RD dictionary query saves approximate 50% time than that of the neural network method. This clearly verifies the proposed new RD method can reduce the computational time.

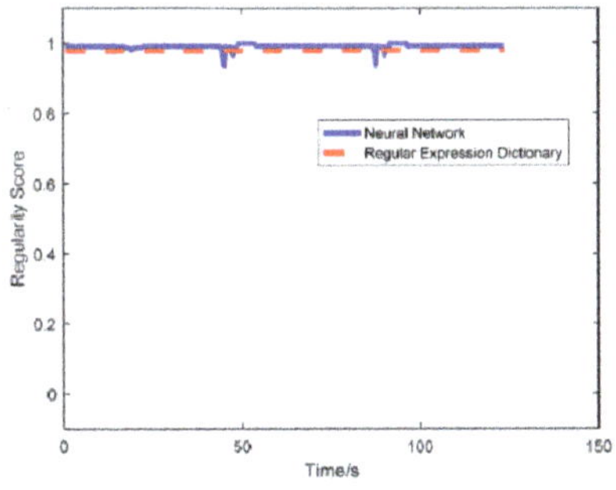

(a)

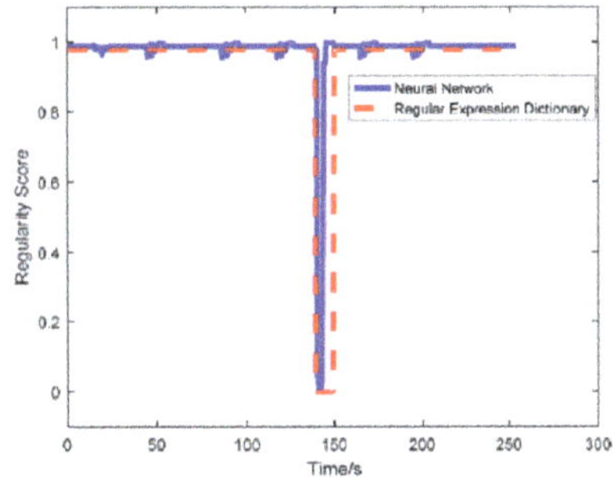

(b)

Figure 7. (**a**) Assessment for the normal vehicle. (**b**) Assessment for the abnormal vehicle.

For improved situational awareness of swarms of unmanned aerospace vehicles, a novel behaviour recognition algorithm was developed based on regular dictionary techniques (RD) to detect target behaviours. Simulations using multiple agents in a swarm have shown that the novel RD dictionary algorithm saves approximate 50% time than that of neural network methods when used in a swarm to detect multiple targets thus reduce the computational time needed.

5. Sensor Fusion

Sensor fusion is synonymous with technology to support the commander's situational awareness. Automatic target detection and tracking are fundamental sensor fusion tasks upon which both situational awareness and other support functions such as anomaly detection rely. An efficient system will detect targets early and produce reliable target coordinates, regardless environmental factors and hostile attempts to mislead or disrupt the system. Target tracking is not only concerned with the progress of target coordinates, but also the coordinates of mobile or UAV borne sensors that provide target input. A challenge in systems that rely on sensors swarms is indeed to and a (cost) effective solution that produce the sensor positions and orientation, collectively termed their pose. To that end, tracking also relies on sensor calibration, that is, the sensor data need to be interpreted in accurate real-world geometrical terms. Techniques for sensor positioning include satellite positioning systems (GNSS), inertial measurement units, ultra-wideband transceivers, simultaneous localization and mapping, and so on. These techniques will however, not be reviewed here. Instead, the focus will be on the relation between pose error and tracking feasibility and accuracy in scenarios relevant for the swarm mission scenario shown in Figure 1. The algorithm developed for tracking follows a decentralized architecture such as the one depicted in Figure 8. In contrast to distributed variants, detections are collected at a possibly local fusion node, where exclusively the target state in terms of real-world coordinates is estimated. To be mentioned, today's research and development, however, strive toward distributed tracking algorithms with an aim to increase fault tolerance while simultaneously meeting bandwidth restrictions.

The sensor fusion algorithm used for the swarm mission analysed in this work is broken down in the four steps. First an abstract idea on how the targets and sensors shall move is formulated using concrete matrices with sampled object coordinates and sensor detections. A motion planning program uses a script that indicates the object speed along the associated spline, and between station points. For each station point, the script determines the speed, or maximum speed, to be aimed for to the next station point, and if the object shall pause, or if there is a rendezvous with another object, and so on (Figure 9). The motion planning program samples the object coordinates at desired sampling frequency, for instance 10 Hz, and also generates soft transitions by imposing continuity requirements on the acceleration. A six-state tracking filter is used to track all agents and targets. Figure 9a shows the targets and sensor allocations from the airborne UAV-sensor field of view, while Figure 9b shows the full view of three UAVs flying over a single ground target and performing the required monitoring task with sensor fusion from three UAV sensors.

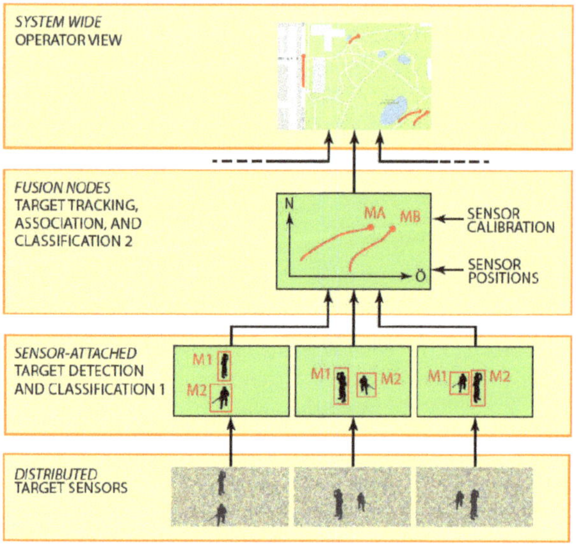

Figure 8. Breakdown of the target tracking components. Sensors were used with sensor-attached detectors that propagated target detections in terms of coordinates to a local fusion node.

(a) (b)

Figure 9. (**a**) Screenshot of simulated targets and sensor motions, where the sensor is a UAV-borne camera trained for the (red) person in the centre (**b**) full view.

The evaluation of the sensor fusion algorithm is based on Monte-Carlo simulations given a scenario with three UAV-born sensors over a single ground target, as shown in Figure 10. To evaluate the robustness against navigation errors, the true sensor position and orientation are perturbed by band limited Gaussian processes. The bandwidth of the perturbation is selected to 1/100 Hz. Regarding the orientation, the major perturbation is on the yaw angle, while the pitch and yaw receive only a tenth of the variation. This reflects the assumption, that the yaw is more difficult to determine than the vertical axis, which can be given by a rather simple inclinometer or g-sensor. An ordinary magnetic compass, on the other hand, would be susceptible for spurious magnetic fields from power lines and iron masses and would also depend on local magnetic declination. Regarding the position, the perturbations for the east, north, and up components are independent and equally distributed. In the simulation, the ground target is moving at different speeds 3–8 km/h and is occasionally standing still at the station points. Three air borne sensors are trained at the ground target, of which two exhibit an (almost) perpendicular linear motion, and the third a circular motion. The sensor levels are 25–30 m above ground. The sensors continuously travel back and forth along their preferred trajectories with speed up to 10 km/h. No occlusion occurs in this scenario. However, the knowledge (certainty) of sensor positions and/or orientations is assumed to be limited. The simulation time is 185 s and the sampling frequency is 10 Hz. The primary evaluation criterion is the tracking root mean square error distance, RMSE.

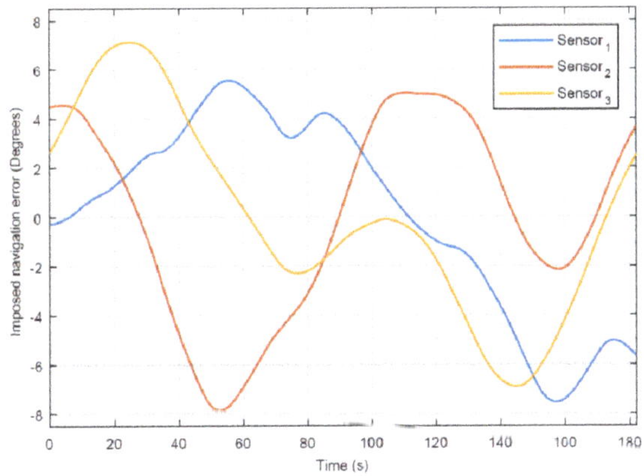

Figure 10. Simulated swarm navigation errors from UAV sensors.

Figures 11–14 show a single realization with and without collaborative positioning. Here, only the sensor orientation is perturbed with the realization illustrated in Figure 11, that is, σ_{yaw} = 4° (standard deviation). The target tracking simulation outcome is presented in Figure 12 (without collaborative positioning) and in Figure 13 (with collaborative positioning.) Without collaborative positioning, to start with, the tracking error is on average RMSE-j = 1.2 m, but can apparently exceed 5 m, occasionally. Indeed, with collaborative positioning the error is significantly reduced, RMSE-j = 0.5 m, and the estimate follows the ground truth curve. For clarity it should be mentioned, that the RMSE is computed in three dimensions, while the vertical error is transparent in Figures 13 and 14. Collaborative positioning with yaw compensation allows larger orientation errors, but it has not always positive effect in the presence of position errors. Target tracking from a swarm of UAVs and UGVs requires that the platforms are fitted with suitable and well-calibrated sensors and that they have navigation ability to determine the position and orientation of the sensors with some accuracy. The tracking performance deteriorates quickly with increased navigation error. In the example scenario with three UAVs and a single ground target, the average yaw error must not exceed 4.5° and the average position error must fall below 0.4 m to meet an example requirement on tracking RMSE < 1 m. If the navigation units carry inertial measurement units, it can be assumed that the navigation error varies slowly, compared with platform and target movements. Then, techniques for collaborative positioning can be used to mitigate the effects of navigation errors, which in turn can reduce overall cost and weight on navigation solutions. In the example scenario it was demonstrated that collaborative positioning in the form of yaw error compensation reduced the susceptibility for orientation error by almost 50%. It was also observed that yaw compensation alone can increase the sensitivity for position error, so future investigations of combined yaw and position error compensation are indeed warranted. In the swarm demonstration phase, practical test results with real time swarm-based tracking, based on the algorithm presented in this section will be presented, using real data from a swarm of unmanned aerial and ground vehicles.

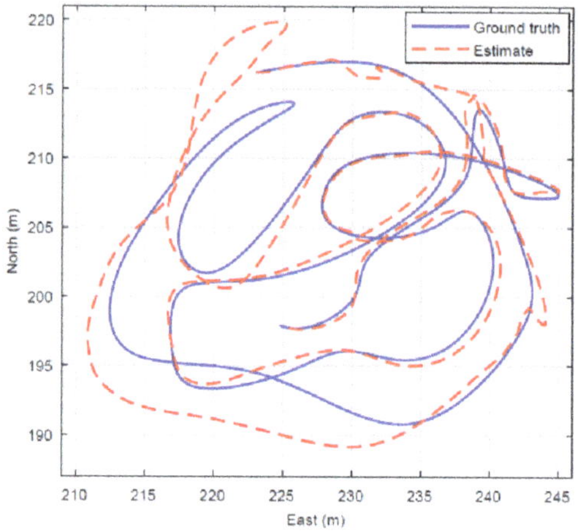

Figure 11. Simulation of target tracking. The continuous curve (blue) is the true track, and the dashed curve (red) is the EKF estimate. The corresponding tracking RMSE is 1.2 m.

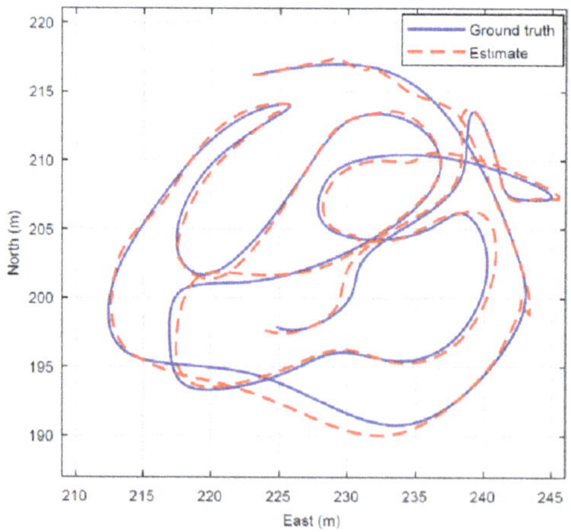

Figure 12. Simulation as in Figure 15 but with implementation of the collaborative positioning algorithm. The corresponding tracking is significantly reduced to <0.5 m.

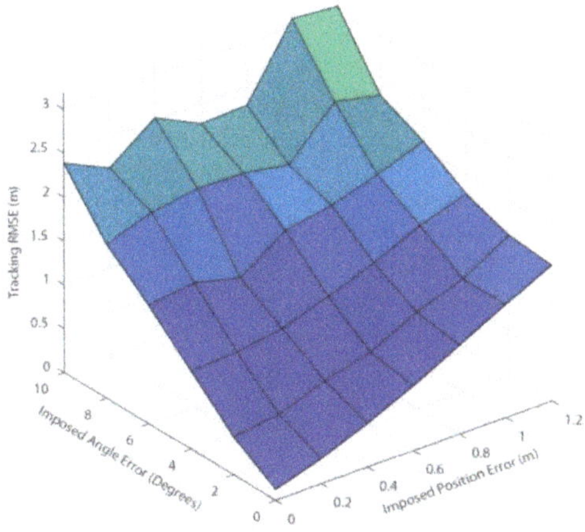

Figure 13. Tracking RMSE resulting from the Monte Carlo simulation.

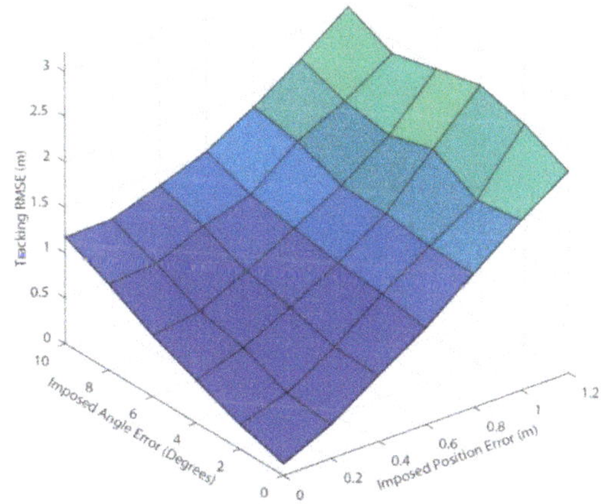

Figure 14. Tracking RMSE using a collaborative positioning algorithm. The corresponding tracking is significantly reduced by up to 50%.

6. Guidance for Swarm System Control

The mission of interest is the persistent monitoring mission described in Section 1. A static network of N_g sensor is assumed to be deployed on the ground and provide information regarding to possible intruders inside an area of interest around a protected asset. In addition to the ground static sensors, N mobile vehicles equipped with onboard sensors are assumed to be available. They may consist in ground mobile robots and/or aerial vehicles (UAVs). To define the objectives of the cooperative guidance and reconfiguration algorithms to be designed the following requirements are introduced and will be used:

- R1: enabling cooperation among the vehicles of the swarm to safely perform the monitoring task
- R2: ensuring complementarity between mobile vehicles of the swarm and the ground static sensor network
- R3: compensating by mobile vehicles for possible faults in the static sensor network.

From the mobile vehicles' point of view, the mission consists of reaching assigned targets while contributing to improve the monitoring of the area of interest along the performed trajectories. The targets are assumed to be assigned by the "Mobile Vehicle Task Allocation" building block (see Figure 5) and defined as way points. They can correspond for example to locations of intruders detected by the ground sensors, to locations of areas over which complementary information is required to improve situational awareness or to locations of faulty ground sensors. It is assumed that a target is assigned to each vehicle of the swarm, with the possibility to assign multiple vehicles at the same location. In this section a reactive and distributed cooperative guidance law is designed as in Ref. [4] for the mobile vehicles involved in the analysed monitoring mission. A common criterion reflecting the mission and safety objectives is defined and evaluated according to each vehicle action and result, taking also into account the interaction between vehicles. Interactions between the vehicles and the static sensor network can also be handled by this criterion to ensure complementarity and reconfiguration in the monitoring mission. Guidance laws can be thus derived by optimization of this criterion, relying on approaches such as model predictive control (MPC).

6.1. UAV Swarm Guidance Algorithm

MPC has been widely used for the guidance of UAVs in various contexts, for example UAV flocking and formation flight have been discussed in [1]. In distributed MPC [5–7], each vehicle computes its control inputs at each timestep as a solution of an optimization problem over the future predicted trajectory. For tractability reasons, finite prediction and control horizon lengths, respectively, denoted as H_p and H_c are used. The future control inputs and the resulting state trajectories of a vehicle i are written as:

$$\begin{aligned} U_i &= \{u_i(t), u_i(t+1), \ldots, u_i(t+H_c-1)\} \\ X_i &= \{\xi(t+1), \xi_i(t+2), \ldots, \xi_i(t+H_p)\} \end{aligned} \tag{11}$$

If $H_c < H_p$, the control input is set to 0 after H_c steps. Once the optimal input sequence U_i^* has been computed, each vehicle communicates its predicted trajectory to the rest of the fleet and applies the first sample of the computed optimal control sequence $u_i^*(t)$. The optimization problems at time t takes the following form:

$$\begin{aligned} &\text{minimize } J_i(U_i, X_i) \\ &\text{over } U_i \in U_i^{H_c} \\ &\text{subject to } \forall k \in [t+1; t+H_p], \xi_i(k) \in X_i \end{aligned} \tag{12}$$

where J_i is the cost function associated with vehicle i. The constraints coupling the dynamics of the vehicles, such as collision avoidance, are taken into account by means of a penalty factor in the cost function. At the next timestep, each vehicle searches for its solution of the optimization problem. The cost function J_i is composed of a weighted sum of terms reflecting the objectives of the mission. These terms are detailed in the following sections. Each cost function or its subcomponents are defined such that their norm is less or equal to 1 and weighted with a coefficient $w_\bullet$ to give priority to some of the objectives with respect to the others. Each vehicle defines its own trajectory online to achieve the mission objectives and constraints: (i) Head towards its assigned waypoint (ii) Maximize the cumulated area covered, in cooperation with the ground static sensors and the other mobile vehicles (iii) Avoid collisions between vehicles (iv) Minimize energy consumption to increase the monitoring capability. The associated global cost function is given as:

$$J_i = J_i^{nav} + J_i^{cov} + J_i^{safe} + J_i^u \tag{13}$$

The instant of time at which all these computations are carried out is t. The cost J_i^{nav} to guide the vehicle i towards its assigned waypoint p_i^p has the following expression:

$$J_i^{nav} = \frac{1}{2H_p v_{max}} \sum_{n=t}^{t+H_p} w_p \| p_i(n) - \hat{p}_i(n) \| + w_f D\left(p_i(t+H_p) - B_i^{t+H_p}\right) \tag{14}$$

The first part penalises the distance of the predicted trajectory p_i over the horizon H_p to a virtual best-case trajectory $\hat{p}_i$ which is a straight line towards the waypoint p_i^p at nominal speed v_{nom}. The second part encourages the vehicle to reach closer to the waypoint at the end of the predicted trajectory by penalising the distance to a reference ball B_i around the waypoint as illustrated in Figure 15.

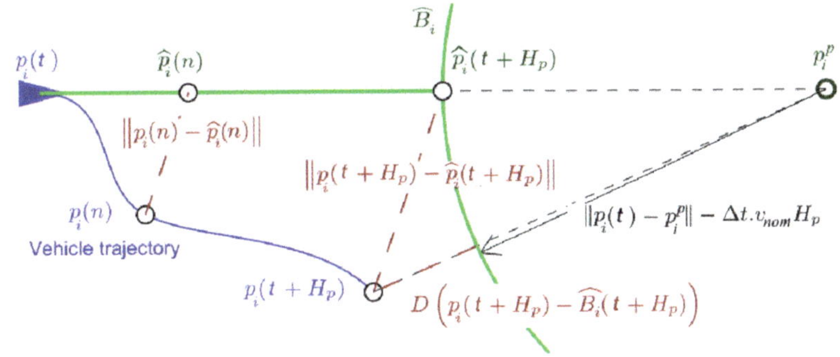

Figure 15. Definition of virtual trajectory and ball for navigation cost.

The cost J_i^{safe} to avoid collisions between the vehicles is defined as:

$$J_i^{safe} = w_{safe} \cdot \frac{2}{H_p} \sum_{n=t+1}^{t+H_p} \sum_{\substack{j=1 \\ j \neq i}}^{N} \frac{1}{2}\left[1 + \tanh\left((d_{ij}(n) - \beta).\alpha\right)\right] \tag{15}$$

where $d_{ij}(n) = \|p_i(n) - p_j(n)\|$ denotes the distance between vehicles i and j, and $p_i = [x_i, y_i]^T$.

The coefficients α and β, respectively, parameterize the width of the interval of fast variation of the hyperbolic tangent and its inflexion point. Two distances are defined: d_{des} is the activation distance of the collision avoidance mechanism and d_{safe} is the mandatory safety distance between vehicles. They are related to α and β by $\alpha = \frac{6}{(d_{des} - d_{safe})}$ and $\beta = \frac{1}{2}\left(d_{des} + d_{safe}\right)$.

With this choice, the cost variation is less than 5% of its maximal value in the range $[d_{des}, +\infty]$. For implementation, the penalty function is set to 0 for $d_{ij} > d_{des}$, i.e., the vehicles do not consider each other above this distance. The cost J_i^u to limit the energy spent by the vehicles is:

$$J_i^u = \frac{1}{H_p} \sum_{n=t}^{t+H_p} \frac{w_v}{v_{max}} (v_i(n) - v_{nom})^2 + \frac{w_\omega}{\omega_{max}} \omega_i^2(n) \tag{16}$$

It penalizes the difference between the actual speed and the desired speed v_{nom} and favours straight lines over curved trajectories. The cost function J_i^{cov} should reflect the gain in terms of map coverage for a potential trajectory. Each vehicle is assumed to have an attached sensor (of range r_{sensor}), described by a function f_{cov} of the relative position between the observed point and the vehicle. The cooperatively covered area at time t is:

$$\Omega = \bigcup_{\substack{n=1,\dots,t \\ i=1,\dots,N+N_g}} D_i^n \tag{17}$$

where D_i^n is the sensing footprint of vehicle i at timestep n. Since this representation is impractical, the mission field is approximated as a grid of resolution d_{grid}. A matrix G stores the level of exploration of each cell of the grid. Each element $G_{l,m}$ (where (l, m) are the integer coordinates of the cell of the grid) ranges between 0 when no vehicle has covered this location on a reference period and 1 when it has been entirely observed. Each vehicle stores a copy of this exploration map and updates it with the information from the rest of the fleet and the ground sensors (if their status is healthy). The precision of the representation only depends on the parameter d_{grid}. When a vehicle comes at a distance d from the centre of cell (l,m), the exploration level is updated:

$$G_{l,m}^{+} = \max(G_{l,m}, f_{cov}(d)) \tag{18}$$

The exploration index is increased only if the vehicle is close enough. The function f_{cov} is chosen to be continuous and identically 0 for $d > r_{sensor}$ as:

$$f_{cov}(d) = \begin{cases} 0 \ if \ d \geq r_{sensor} \\ \frac{1}{2}\left(1 + \cos\left(\frac{\pi d}{r_{sensor}}\right)\right) \ if \ d < r_{sensor} \end{cases} \tag{19}$$

The coverage matrix also takes into account the information from the ground sensor: the sensor footprint of each ground sensor whose status is known to be healthy is incorporated in G, hence ensuring complementarity between static and mobile sensors. In case of failure detection in a static sensor, the corresponding footprint is changed back to "not covered" in the map. This allows the mobile vehicles to take into account this new information in the computation of their next control input and naturally reconfigure the coverage mission of the swarm. The coverage cost function is thus defined to reward trajectories that cooperatively increase the global level of exploration of the map. Note that it takes negative values since the overall cost function is minimized, while the objective is to maximize the coverage.

$$J_i^{cov} = -w_{cov} \sum_{l,m} G_{l,m}(t + H_p) - G_{l,m}(t) = -w_{cov}\mathbf{1}^T (G(t + H_p) - G(t))\mathbf{1} \tag{20}$$

where $G(t + H_p)$ is the predicted exploration map associated with the vehicle trajectory and $\mathbf{1}$ is the vector of appropriate dimension whose components are all $\mathbf{1}$. This cost function represents the total increase in the global coverage level resulting from a predicted trajectory. Since the vehicles share information, flying in already covered zones (by mobile or static sensors) is therefore, penalized and this also allows covering the area leaved free by a faulty sensor.

6.2. MPC Optimization and Cost Function Online Computation

The MPC optimization problem is a constrained nonlinear program, the solution of which cannot be found analytically. Numerical optimization must hence be used to approximate the solution. Global optimization procedures based, for example, on interval analysis [9] or genetic algorithms [10] can be used but may in practice be computationally prohibitive for real-time implementation. Numerical optimization methods, such as Sequential Quadratic Programming (SQP), Active Set or Interior Point methods are thus generally preferred [11]. Other methods suitable for MPC problems have also been developed [12,13]. Nevertheless, a global solution can be hard to find because of potential local minima. The computational time required for a MPC approach strongly depends on the parameterization of the control sequence. Low dimensional parameterizations have, for example, enabled successful applications to control systems with fast dynamics. Another solution consists of considering a finite set of predefined feasible control sequences, from which the one minimizing the cost function will be. This last solution is used in this paper for implementation of the MPC strategy, based on [8]. This systematic search strategy has several main advantages over a traditional optimization procedure. Firstly, the computation load necessary to find a control sequence is constant in all situations leading to a constant computation delay. The second advantage is that the systematic search strategy can be less sensitive to local minima problems since the entire control space is explored. Finally, the systematic search requires no initialization of the optimization procedure. The studied search procedure consists of defining, prior to the mission, a set S of candidate control sequences that satisfy control constraints. At each timestep, the control problem is solved using the proposed search procedure, as follows:

1. Using a model of the vehicle dynamics, predict the effect of each control sequence of the set of candidates S on the state of the vehicle;
2. Remove from S all of the candidate control sequences that lead to a violation of constraints on the state of the vehicle;
3. Compute the cost J_i corresponding to each remaining candidate control sequence;
4. Select the control sequence that entails the smallest cost.

Since all of the feasible candidates in the set S will be evaluated, the computation load of associated predictions should be as limited as possible. A simple parameterization of the control sequence is therefore, adopted, by considering a control input constant over the control horizon H_c and then null over the remainder of the prediction horizon H_p. In addition, the distribution of the candidate control sequences is chosen so as to limit their number, while providing a good coverage of the control space.

The following three rules have been chosen:

- The set S of candidates includes the extreme control inputs, to exploit the full potential of the vehicles;
- The set S of candidates includes the null control input, to allow the same angular and linear accelerations to be continued with;
- Candidates are distributed over the entire control space, with an increased density around the null control input.

6.3. Swarm Guidance Algorithm Numerical Simulation

This section presents the evaluation and performance analysis of the proposed swarm guidance algorithm. Different simulation scenarios are considered to illustrate the compliance with the three requirements listed in Section 6.1 and influence of simulation parameters. The parameters of the swarm simulation scenarios performed are shown in Table 4.

Table 4. Swarm guidance simulation parameters.

Parameter	Value
$(v_{min} v_{max} v_{nom})$	(0.3, 1, 0.7) ms^{-1}
$(w_{min} w_{max} \Delta w_{max})$	(−0.2, 0.2, 0.05) $rads^{-1}$
(Δv_{max})	0.1 ms^{-1}
$\left(d_{des} d_{safe} d_{grid}\right)$	(9, 3, 2.5) m
$(w_p w_v w_{cov})$	1, 0.5. 2
$w_f w_\omega w_{safe}$	4, 0.5, 10
r_{sensor}	5 m
$(H_p H_c)$	21, 3

Five mobile vehicles represented by arrows are considered in Figure 16. The circle around each vehicle represents its sensor footprint. Five mobile vehicles are available. Two targets are assigned to two groups of two vehicles. A fifth target is assigned to the remaining vehicle. A fifth target is assigned to the remaining vehicle. A target way point (coloured dot) is assigned to each vehicle. The area covered by the sensor footprint of each vehicle during the mission is represented in grey levels corresponding to the exploration value (Equation (18)). Footprints of ground static sensors are represented by blue circles inside which the area is assumed to be covered. All vehicles successfully reach the assigned targets, starting from randomly chosen initial conditions in terms of position, orientation and velocities. While arriving close to their targets, the vehicles start to perform trajectories to improve monitoring while staying as close as possible to the targets. This results in a quasi-circular trajectory for the green vehicle and local cooperative trajectories ensuring collision avoidance and complementarity in the monitoring for the three others. The ground static sensor network is assumed to be composed of:

- Four high range sensors ($r^g{}_{sensor}$ = 10 m) located at the centre of the area and with overlapping footprints (e.g., sensors monitoring a protected asset),
- Four middle range sensors ($r^g{}_{sensor}$ = 5 m) and 12 low range sensors ($r^g{}_{sensor}$ = 1.5 m) located all around the centre of the area as an "early warning frontier".

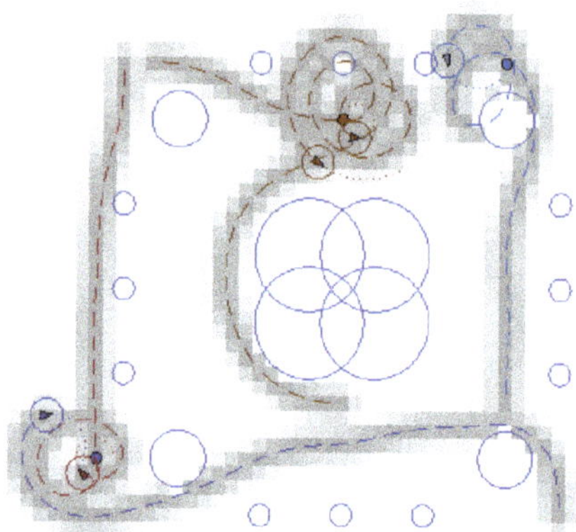

Figure 16. Monitoring mission—nominal scenario.

Illustration of fulfilment of the reconfiguration requirement (R3) is addressed through three simulation scenarios:

- a "nominal scenario" with no failure among the static sensors,
- a "reconfiguration scenario 1" with failure of two high range and one low range sensors during the execution of the mission,
- a "reconfiguration scenario 2" with failure of one middle range sensor and one low range sensor during the execution of the mission.

Faulty sensors are represented by red circles.

In the nominal scenario shown in Figure 16, cooperation between the vehicles enables to improve monitoring in a cooperative way to the static sensor network while minimizing overlaps as much as possible. As already mentioned, when the vehicles become close to their assigned targets, they keep moving close to the targets and improving coverage in this area. In the faulty scenario 1 presented in Figure 17, the trajectory of one of the vehicles is modified online to cope with failure of two high-range sensors. Some information is therefore, collected by opportunity over the areas not covered anymore by the static sensors. A failure has also been simulated for a small range sensor located on the top part of the area. Vehicles close to this sensor also start to modify their trajectories, because of the event. Online reconfiguration is also performed in the faulty scenario 2 shown in Figure 18, where trajectories of the vehicles are adapted online to compensate for missing information from the faulty sensors. Note that if one would wish to "permanently" compensate for faulty sensors by ensuring a full or persistent coverage of the area not monitored anymore, a new target should be assigned to some vehicle(s) in this/these location(s). Hence, the vehicle(s) would perform "circular"-like motions over the area(s) compensating for the faulty sensor(s).

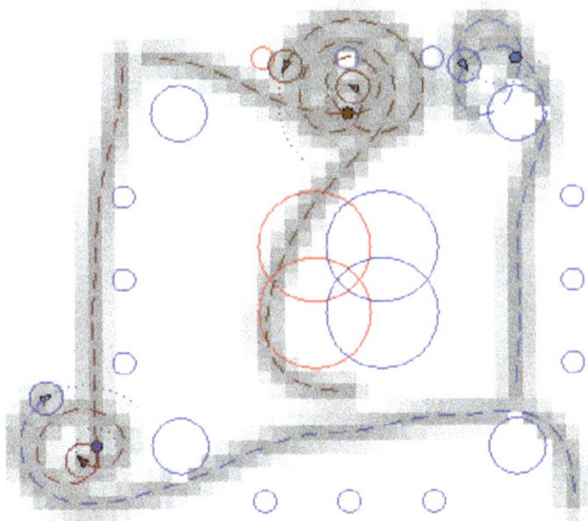

Figure 17. Monitoring mission—faulty scenario 1 (faulty sensors in red).

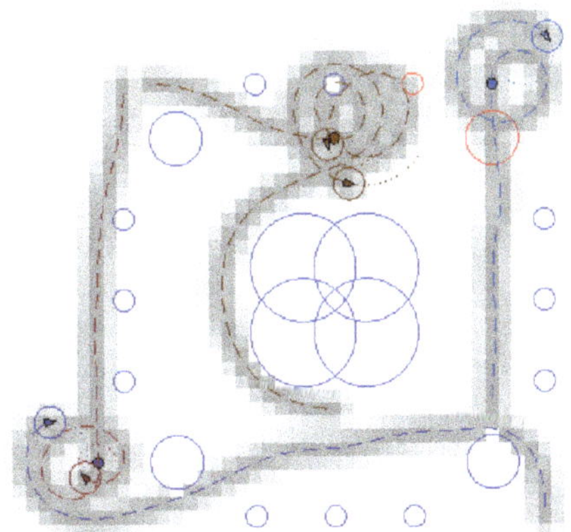

Figure 18. Monitoring mission—faulty scenario 2 (faulty sensors in red).

In summary, a reactive and distributed cooperative FDIR/guidance algorithm has been designed for mobile vehicles enabling cooperation and reconfiguration has been proposed for a persistent monitoring mission. The algorithm is based on Model Predictive Control and is designed in a distributed way, enabling each vehicle to compute its own control input, resulting in more robustness with respect to failure of one of the mobile vehicles. The algorithm enables to ensure monitoring complementarity among the vehicles in combination with a ground static sensor network. It also addresses safety issues by avoiding collisions between the vehicles in case of conflicting trajectories. The algorithm is validated via simulation and online reconfiguration is shown to cope with possible failures among the ground sensors.

7. Practical Swarm Demonstration

All swarm technologies presented in earlier sections are combined, simulated and then validated via a practical demonstration in a scaled outdoor environment. Due to the time and budget constraints the testing areas was limited in size and the unmanned platforms used to form a swarm of robots were based on COTS systems available in the market. The main objectives of the practical demonstration were to set up the demonstration environment, communications network and test the swarm functionalities for a persistent monitoring scenario as shown in Figure 7. For the outdoor demonstration 8 air and ground unmanned vehicles/agents were used in combination with static and mobile (ground) targets. All agents are targets and are connected to a WIFI network or used radio telemetry. The navigation information of each agent and targets are shared via ROS based protocols. The task allocation system also is connected to ROS and the results of task allocation are also shared in ROS. Each agent is using the allocated mission information which is shared by the task allocation algorithm. Multiple combinations of agents, type of vehicles and number of targets where implemented, thus assessing homogeneous (same type of vehicle/sensors) and heterogeneous vehicles (optical/IR sensors, fixed wing/quadrotor UAVs). The unmanned systems used, and their physical Specifications of agents are summarized in Table 5.

Table 5. Physical specification of agents.

Parameter	Parrot Bebop 2	Parrot Disco	Erle Copter	Erle Hexacopter	Erle-Rover

Width	330 mm	1150 mm	360 mm	590 mm	325 mm
Length	330 mm	580 mm	360 mm	515 mm	465 mm
Height	89 mm	120 mm	95 mm	95 mm	145 mm
Weight	500 g	750 g	1300 g	1700 g	2100 g
Endurance			~30 min		
Max Speed	40 km/h	40 km/h	30 km/h	30 km/h	5 km/h

The targets consist of two types: static targets (Type 1) and moving vehicles (Type 2), both using the Erle-Rover UGV. The outdoor demonstration took place at the Cranfield University Airport on 8 February 2018. Considering the proposed mission scenario, resource availability, project time limitations and costs/vehicle compatibility, the following demonstration parameters are used: 4 quadrotors, 1 fixed wing micro drone and 3 unmanned ground vehicle (UGV), operating in a 100 × 100 × 30 m volume using GPS-optical guidance/navigation as shown in Table 6.

Table 6. Unmanned vehicles for swarm outdoor demonstration.

	Model	Type	Units
Agent	Bebop	UAV	3
Agent	Erle-copter	UAV	1
Agent	Rover	UGV	1
Agent	Disco	Fixed wing UAV	1
Target	Rover	UGV	2
Target	Stationary target	Stationary target	5
GCS	PC	GCS	1

Figure 19a shows the guidance, navigation and control structure for the first outdoor demonstration. An Erle-copter and a rover are integrated as agents newly and they are operated with own navigation and control system in on-board system. The navigation systems are based on the GNSS and INS integrated navigation system. A fixed wing UAV (Disco) is operated as a top-layer observer.

Figure 19b shows the network structure for the swarm outdoor demonstration. All agents are targets are connected to ROS through WIFI network. The results of the target behaviour monitoring algorithm, target detection algorithm, and sensor fusion algorithm are shared in ROS. The target information which is acquired from these algorithms also can be utilized in task allocation algorithm through ROS. An example of one of the outdoor demonstration/trials is presented in Figure 20a, which took place at Cranfield University Airport on 9 February 2018. The swarm system consisted with four agents and three moving targets with the mission trajectory shown in Figure 20a, where the dotted lines represent moving target's trajectories, the square markers are the stationary targets, and the solid lines are trajectories of each UAV. Figure 20b shows the target detection probability which indicates the probability of detection of all the targets. If the probability becomes 1, it means all the targets are detected. The results show that the maximum probabilities of detection converge to 1 in the heterogeneous swarm case.

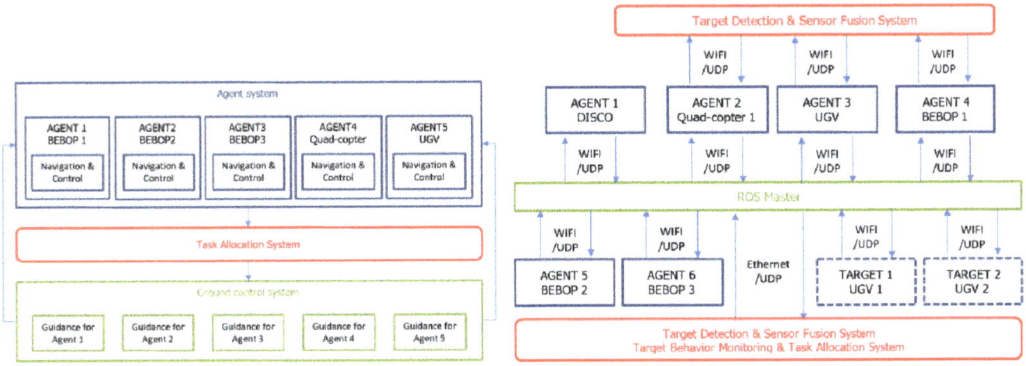

(a) (b)

Figure 19. Swarm structure for (**a**) guidance, navigation and control system; (**b**) network.

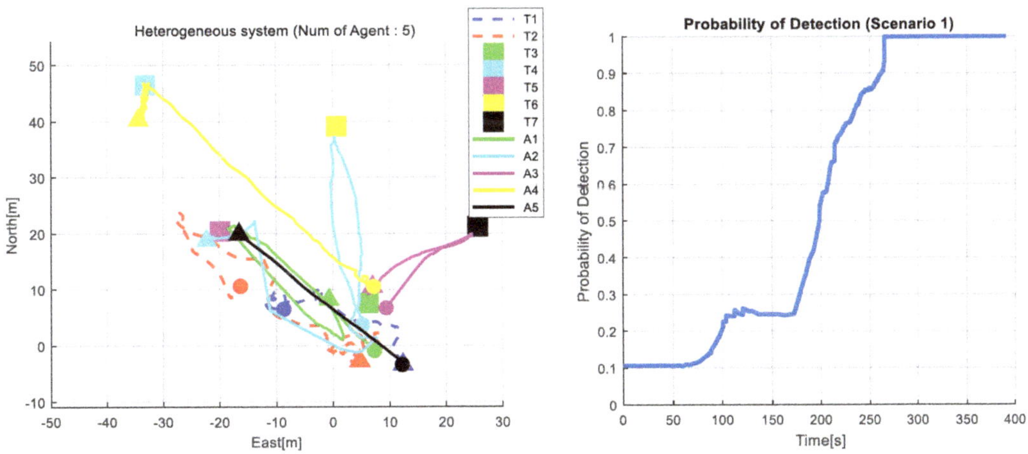

(a) (b)

Figure 20. (**a**) Mission trajectory for the EuroSWARM outdoor experiment. (**b**) Time history of target detection probability.

8. Conclusions

A swarm of unmanned vehicles, mostly composed of micro-UAVs has been studied for use in the defence sector, for the protection of high-value assets such as military bases or installations. By testing and demonstrating an autonomous swarm of heterogenous vehicles, it has been shown that efficient and effective operation of unmanned swarm systems can bring a profound impact to the military arena. The key focus in the development of the enabling technologies has been the minimisation of uncertainties in situational awareness information for surveillance operations supported by a swarm 'system of systems' composed by static and mobile heterogeneous sensors. Critical enabling techniques and technologies for adaptive, informative and reconfigurable operations of unmanned swarm systems were developed in the work presented via the use of computationally efficient algorithms for, mobile sensor tasking (including re-allocation), sensor fusion, information fusion including behaviour monitoring. Simulation and practical results, described in the paper, from a demonstration using a swarm of 10 micro-UAVs and UGVs has demonstrated the benefits of swarms of heterogeneous vehicles for defence applications such as for the persistent monitoring of high-value assets. Novel guidance, sensor fusion and task allocation algorithms which form the basic technologies for swarm systems have been matured in this work, through the development of algorithms which can be implemented in COTS based unmanned vehicles available today. The described algorithms have been integrated in a fully autonomous swarm system of a small scale and were designed and optimised to require small computational power, be flexible, reconfigurable and with the ability to be implemented in a large range of commercially available unmanned vehicles (air and ground). A realistic, persistent surveillance and monitoring scenario was implemented showing that efficient and effective operation of unmanned swarm systems can allow the swarm system end user in the battlefield to obtain real-time, relevant situational awareness information and help commanders make time efficient and effective decisions, while reducing risk/mission costs and human exposure to threats.

Author Contributions: Conceptualization, V.L. and A.T.; Formal analysis, D.L.; methodology, H.-S.S.; validation, S.B., J.M. and H.P.-L.; investigation, Y.D.; writing—review and editing, V.L. and H.-S.S.; project administration, V.K.; funding acquisition, V.L. All authors have read and agreed to the published version of the manuscript.

Funding: The work described in this paper was funded by the European Defence Agency through grant 'PP-15-INR-01—EuroSWARM: Unmanned Heterogeneous Swarm of Sensor Platforms'.

Conflicts of Interest: The authors declare no conflict of interest.

References

1. Dunbar, W.; Murray, R. Distributed receding horizon control for multi-vehicle formation stabilization. *Automatica* **2006**, *42*, 549–558. [CrossRef]
2. Olfati-Saber, R.; Dunbar, W.; Murray, R. Cooperative control of multi-vehicle systems using cost graphs and optimization. In Proceedings of the American Control Conference, Denver, CO, USA, 4–6 June 2003; IEEE: Piscataway, NJ, USA, 2003; Volume 3, pp. 2217–2222.
3. Dunbar, W.; Murray, R. Receding Horizon Control of Multi-Vehicle Formations: A Distributed Implementation. In Proceedings of the 43rd IEEE Conference on Decision and Control, Paradise Island, Bahamas, 14–17 December 2004; IEEE: Piscataway, NJ, USA, 2004; Volume 2, pp. 1995–2002.
4. Gorecki, T.; Piet-Lahanier, H.; Marzat, J.; Balesdent, M. Cooperative guidance of UAVs for area exploration with final target allocation. In Proceedings of the 19th IFAC Symposium on Automatic Control in Aerospace, Würzburg, Germany, 2–6 September 2013; Elsevier: Amsterdam, The Netherlands, 2013.
5. Scattolini, R. Architectures for distributed and hierarchical model predictive control–A review. *J. Process Control* **2009**, *19*, 723–731. [CrossRef]
6. Bertrand, S.; Marzat, J.; Piet-Lahanier, H.; Kahn, A.; Rochefort, Y. MPC strategies for cooperative guidance of autonomous vehicles. *Aerosp. Lab. J.* **2014**, *8*, 1–18.
7. Richards, A.; How, J.P. Robust distributed model predictive control. *Int. J. Control* **2007**, *80*, 1517–1531. [CrossRef]
8. Rochefort, Y.; Piet-Lahanier, H.; Bertrand, S.; Beauvois, D.; Dumur, D. Model predictive control of cooperative vehicles using systematic search approach. *Control Eng. Pract.* **2014**, *32*, 204–217. [CrossRef]
9. Hansen, E. *Global Optimization Using Interval Analysis*; CRC Press: Boca Raton, FL, USA, 2004.
10. Potocnik, P.; Grabec, I. Nonlinear model predictive control of a cutting process. *Neurocomputing* **2002**, *43*, 107–126. [CrossRef]
11. Martinsen, F.; Biegler, L.T.; Foss, B.A. A new optimization algorithm with application to nonlinear MPC. *J. Process Control* **2004**, *14*, 853–865. [CrossRef]
12. Diehl, M.; Bock, H.G.; Schloder, J.P.; Findeisen, R.; Nagy, Z.; Allgower, F. Real-time optimization and nonlinear model predictive control of processes governed by differential-algebraic equations. *J. Process Control* **2002**, *12*, 577–585. [CrossRef]
13. Alamir, M.; Murilo, A. Swing-up and stabilization of a twin-pendulum under state and control constraints by fast NMPC scheme. *Automatica* **2008**, *44*, 1319–1324. [CrossRef]
14. Frew, E.W. Receding horizon control using random search for UAV navigation with passive, non-cooperative sensing. In Proceedings of the AIAA Guidance, Navigation and Control Conference and Exhibit, San Francisco, CA, USA, 15–18 August 2005.
15. Jin, X.-B.; Gong, W.-T.; Kong, J.-L.; Bai, Y.-T.; Su, T.-L. PFVAE: A Planar Flow-Based Variational Auto-Encoder Prediction Model for Time Series Data. *Mathematics* **2022**, *10*, 610. [CrossRef]

16. Shin, H.-S.; Turchi, D.; He, S.; Tsourdos, A. Behavior Monitoring Using Learning Techniques and Regular-Expressions-Based Pattern Matching. *IEEE Trans. Intell. Transp. Syst.* **2018**, *20*, 1–14. [CrossRef]
17. Oh, H.; Kim, S.; Shin, H.-S.; Tsourdos, A.; White, B. Coordinated standoff tracking of moving target groups using multiple UAVs. *IEEE Trans. Aerosp. Electron. Syst.* **2013**, *51*, 969–977. [CrossRef]

drones

MDPI

Article

Novel Drone Design Using an Optimization Software with 3D Model, Simulation, and Fabrication in Drone Systems Research

Ahmed. O. MohamedZain [1,*], Huangshen Chua [2], Kianmeng Yap [1,*], Pavithren Uthayasurian [3] and Teoh Jiehan [3]

[1] Research Centre for Human-Machine Collaboration, Department of Computing and Information Sys-tems, School of Engineering and Technology, Sunway University, Bandar Sunway, Petaling Jaya 47500, Malaysia
[2] Department of Mechatronics Engineering, School of Engineering, UOW Malaysia KDU Penang Univer-sity College, Jalan Anson, George Town 10400, Malaysia; hs.chua@kdu.edu.my
[3] School of Electrical and Electronics Engineering, University of Wollongong Ma-laysia KDU, Glenmarie Campus, Shah Alam 40150, Malaysia; 0128252@kdu-online.com (P.U.); 0122320@kdu-online.com (T.J.)
* Correspondence: 19102003@imail.sunway.edu.my (A.O.M.); kmyap@sunway.edu.my (K.Y.)

Abstract: This paper presents the design of a small size Unmanned Aerial Vehicle (UAV) using the 3DEXPERIENCE software. The process of designing the frame parts involves many methods to ensure the parts can meet the requirements while conforming to safety and industry standards. The design steps start with the selection of materials that can be used for the drone, which are polylactic acid (PLA), acrylonitrile styrene acrylate (ASA), and acrylonitrile butadiene styrene (ABS). The drone frame consists of four main parts, which are the center top cover (50 g), the side top cover (10 g), the middle cover (30 g), and the drone's arm (80 g). A simulation was carried out to determine the stress, displacement, and weight of the drone's parts. Additionally, a trade-off study was conducted to finalize the shapes of the parts and the various inputs based on their priorities. The outcome of this new design can be represented in design concepts, which involve the use of the snap hook function to assemble two body parts together, namely the middle cover and the center top cover, without the need of an additional fastener.

Keywords: UAV; polylactic acid; acrylonitrile styrene acrylate; acrylonitrile butadiene styrene; trade-off study

Citation: MohamedZain, A.O.; Chua, H.; Yap, K.; Uthayasurian, P.; Jiehan, T. Novel Drone Design Using an Optimization Software with 3D Model, Simulation, and Fabrication in Drone Systems Research. *Drones* **2022**, *6*, 97. https://doi.org/10.3390/drones6040097

Academic Editors: Andrzej Łukaszewicz, Wojciech Giernacki, Zbigniew Kulesza, Jaroslaw Pytka and Andriy Holovatyy

Received: 12 February 2022
Accepted: 11 March 2022
Published: 14 April 2022

1. Introduction

A drone is an aircraft without a human pilot inside and it is also known as an Unmanned Aerial Vehicle. It has many functions and applications such as for medical transport [1], health care service [2], high-rise firefighting [3], drone monitoring application for marine megafauna [4], and many other usages in our current modern society. This research presents a new design concept and creative 3D design idea of a drone that was designed with the 3DEXPERIENCE software. The main reason for using 3DExperience software for this project is that it is a software that emphasizes having a collaborative environment. Since this project has included a few people, and each with a different role, it has been convenient to use the software for project sharing and discussion all within the platform, especially during the current COVID-19 pandemic situation. The platform itself has a variety of applications within it, which include software for 3D modelling (CATIA and SOLIDWORKS), simulation (SIMULIA), social and collaborative (ENOVIA) as well as information intelligence (NETVIBES) [5]. Therefore, each user can have roles such as project manager, simulation engineer, and 3D designer and use the applications according to their roles. With that, the tasks can be distributed easily based on different roles, the project models and files can be seen and shared by everyone in the group, and the project timeline can be managed within the platform, which allows easy tracking of the project. All these can be done within the same software, which makes the software a good choice for a group project that requires much collaboration. Three dimensional designing through simulation rather than creating a prototype can reduce the cost for a designer. Since it is a 3D design, engineers can come up with more advanced engineering knowledge and technology. This process is necessary to ensure the parts are able to meet the requirements while conforming to safety and industry standards. While using 3DModelling, the applications used are Part Design and Assembly Design. This research concentrates on the design phase of the drone. The various designing steps included in this phase are discussed. The objectives of this research are to simulate a drone frame to optimize the bottom cover, to study and compare concept shapes of the top cover, arm, leg bracket, and bottom cover of a drone using a trade-off study, and to analyze the force that is generated by the motors in order to determine how much the drone can handle.

Researchers have a lot of interest in designing the parts of a drone and the design is dependent on the application of the drone, where there are many factors to be considered such as speed-motor selection and airframe selection [6]. In this research project, the design of the drone has been made for parcel delivery purposes, which consists of four DC motors. The single motor has a thrust of 5227 Ibs/g. The researchers in [7] studied and analyzed the efficiency of a small quadrotor using air-foils. In this work, the modelling and control design were demonstrated through a series of repeated flights. The researchers in [8] analyzed the aerodynamic interaction between rotors of a micro-quadcopter. Equation (1) was used to calculate the Reynolds number [8], where Re represents the Reynolds number, ρ represents the density of air, Ω represents the rotor angular velocity, and μ represents the dynamic viscosity of air.

$$Re = \frac{\rho \Omega Rc}{\mu} \tag{1}$$

Figure 1 depicts the different designs of drone available for development, which are X-design, H-design, and hybrid H-design. Each design has its own advantages and disadvantages. X-design has the advantage of being light and is usually used for racing purposes [9]; however, it requires long landing gear. H-design has the disadvantage of being heavy [10]. Part Design is an integrated application in 3DEXPERIENCE that includes design, weight calculation, and 3D structure. The application's aim is to give a better view of the design when the design is constructed. The Assembly Design application in 3DEXPERIENCE helps to fix the parts that have been designed and shows the constraint between the parts. This can optimize the design and can solve the issue of overlapping. As shown in Table 1, the drone design has a total of six different parts, and they are classified into two main groups. The upper part of the drone is the drone frame and the lower part of the drone is the drone carriage, which is used to carry the payload. The details of the parts included in each of the categories and the number of parts contributing to the overall drone are presented in Table 1. Figure 2 shows the novel design of the drone using 3DEXPERIENCE. Three Dimensional printing, also known as additive manufacturing, is used in this project for the fabrication of the drone frame. With the use of a CAD software, which in this case is 3DEXPERIENCE, the designed models can be sent to a 3D printer and the parts can be printed within a few hours [11–13]. A 3D printer is a device used for computer-aided manufacturing, whereby it creates 3D objects through "printing" and solidifying of materials [11,14], which range from polymers (thermoplastic) to metal and even food [15]. Thermoplastics are the most widely adopted 3D printing material and they come in various forms such as the most used extrusion (also known as filament), resin, and powder [16].

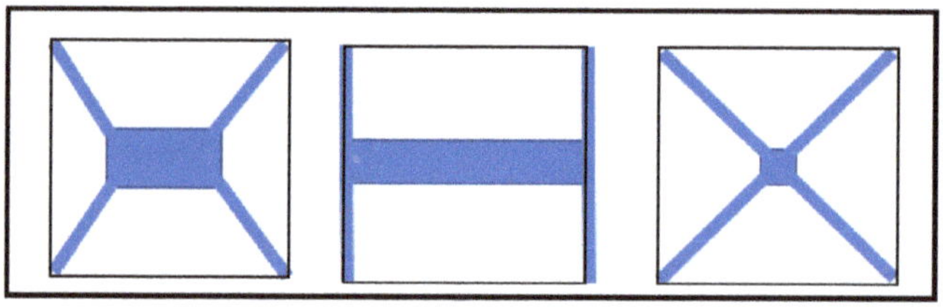

Figure 1. Drone hybrid H-design, H-design, and X-design Available for Development [8].

Table 1. Drone's Parts.

Category		Part Name	Numbers of Parts
Upper drone	Drone Frame	Centre Top Cover	1
		Side Top Cover	2
		Drone Arm	4
Lower drone	Carriage (Payload)	Middle Cover	1
		Leg Bracket	4
		Bottom Cover	1

Figure 2. Original Design of the Drone using 3DEXPERIENCE.

The technique used for the 3D printing of the thermoplastic is known as the Fused Filament Fabrication (FFF) [17] where the working principle of the desktop FFF 3D printer is originated from the Fused Deposition Modelling technology [18]. The FFF technique works on the principle of fabricating parts layer by layer. The thermoplastic material, which is in the form of a filament roll, is firstly heated and melted then extruded through a nozzle. The nozzle extrudes the melted filament to a platform in layers based on the predefined pattern of the model [19,20]. The figure below shows an example of a desktop FFF 3D printer.

Using the technology of 3D printing, a wide range of applications can be performed, which range from manufacturing UAV parts with different functionalities and specifications [21–24] to fabricating medical devices [25], and even the field of musical instrument research [26]. This shows that 3D printing has a high potential in diverse applications.

2. Materials and Methods

In this section, a simulation model of the drone is presented by using 3Dexperience software, where an overview of the drone frame and the originality of the design is provided. The type of chassis of the frame used in this design is X-Chassis. Choosing this chassis rather than the (+) chassis or H chassis ensures that the drone can be stable. This chassis can hover longer compared to other chassis and it is easy to control and maneuver. The suitable location for the center of gravity is in the middle of the drone, which will make controlling the drone easier and will make the drone more stable. Therefore, the components' weight will be distributed on the drone based on the most suitable position for the center of gravity. The momentum theory represents the basic understanding of the drone motion, where the thrust is calculated based on this theory [26].

The general forces considered for all parts are the gravity, the landing force, and the lifting force as shown in Table 2. The gravity will usually be at the center of the part with a standard value of 9.8 m/s or 9.8 N/kg. These slight forces may have an effect; thus, they have been included in the consideration for the design of the parts. In normal conditions, when the drone lands, the force acting on it is the weight of the whole drone with the payload or without the payload if it is a return journey. Thus, the landing force can also be considered as the weight of the drone. On the other hand, the lifting force occurs when the motors turn the propellers and lift the drone. Each of the motors will produce a lifting force of 5 N, hence, giving a total lifting force of 20 N. Equation (2) [27] represents the thrust in terms of mathematical samples, where T is the thrust measured in Newton (N), A is the area of the propeller rotor in meter square (m^2), ρ is the density of the air in kilogram per cubic meter (kg/m^3), v is the velocity of the air at the propeller in meter per second (m/s), and Δv is the velocity of the air accelerated by the propeller in meter per second.

$$T = A \times \rho \times v \times \Delta v \quad (2)$$

Table 2. Landing and Lifting Forces.

Landing Force	
1 part	1600 g/15.6906 N
2 parts	800 g/7.8453 N
4 parts	400 g/3.9227 N
Lifting Force	
1 part	20 N
2 parts	10 N
4 parts	5 N

2.1. Drone Frame and Originality in Design

The drone frame consists of parts that will be used to place the controller, the battery, the motor, etc. Figure 3 illustrates the design of the drone arm, center top cover, side cover, and middle cover. The outcome of this new design can be represented in design concepts through the use of the snap hook function to assemble 2 body parts together, namely the middle cover and the center top cover, without the need of an additional fastener. Figure 3c shows the cantilever snap fit design. This design will help to reduce extra cost and the weight of the drone. It will also reduce the time needed when performing maintenance. Furthermore, snap fit allows the process of assembly and disassembly of the parts to be carried out easily. The body of the drone was designed referring to honeycomb design. Honeycomb sandwich structures are frequently used to attain these aims in the aerospace, automotive, housing, packaging, and sports equipment sectors, among others [28]. A honeycomb construction is created by sandwiching an array of hollow tubes or cells between two solid walls. The advantage of the design is also reducing weight and it increases the structure impact resistance. It also increases the cooling of the electrical components and increases the lifespan of the components. The honeycomb design can carry weight as well as being a light structure. The hexagonal shape of the honeycomb design is usually the strongest shape. This design will be more rigid and also lightweight, where it is a new concept in drone designs. Other than that, it also increases the air flow in the middle cover where the components are placed. This can cool down the electronic components and can reduce overheating.

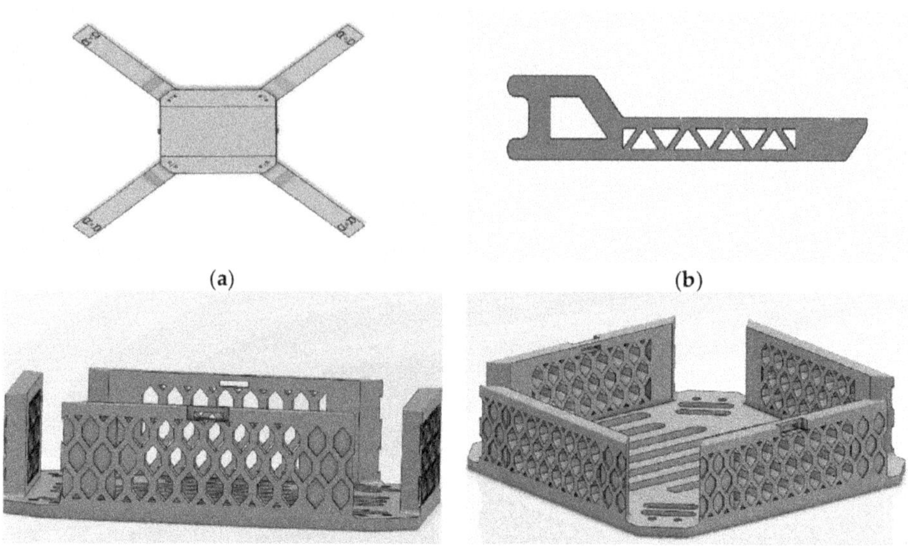

Figure 3. Drone's Frame Design. (**a**) Top View of Drone. (**b**) Drone's Arm. (**c**) Cantilever Snap Fit Design for Side Cover. (**d**) Cantilever Snap Fit Design for Middle Cover.

2.2. Material Selection

The focus of the project is to design a lightweight quadcopter drone for parcel delivery purposes. From the material specifications, both ASA and ABS have a similar density value. However, ABS material has a higher Young's Modulus, which indicates that the material is stiffer as compared to ASA [29]. On top of that, the maximum stress that ABS can take before breaking is also higher than ASA, which makes it good for parts such as the drone arm that requires some flexibility since it is attached to the motors that will provide lifting force.

Although the weather and thermal resistant properties of ASA are higher than ABS [30,31], there are a few drawbacks of using ASA. ASA is more expensive, and it has a lower market availability as compared to ABS [32]. On top of that, ASA can be difficult to print as it requires a higher extruder temperature during the printing process; hence, it is harder to facilitate. Since the electronics components used will not produce too much heat, ABS is chosen to be used as it can fulfil the requirements and budget constraints. According to [33], the glass transition temperature (Tg) of PLA is between 55 °C and 80 °C depending on the different types of molecular weight and stereochemistry, while the melting point ranges between 130 °C and 180 °C. Thus, these temperature ranges should be sufficient for the average temperature in Malaysia, which falls within 21 °C and 32 °C [34]. The materials used for the drone are PLA, ASA, and ABS. The materials were defined in 3DEXPERIENCE using the Material Definition App according to the values given in Table 3. However, PLA and ABS material are chosen to be used in the final design of the drone. PLA is used for most parts that need to be denser, stiffer, and stronger, as it can protect the inner part of the drone, while ABS material is chosen to be used for some parts to reduce the overall weight of the drone since it is light but is still much stiffer and can withstand a greater stress before breaking as compared to ASA material. Only the core material is defined because the covering material does not have much effect during the simulation. Figures 4–6 show the materials chosen to be used from 3DEXPERIENCE and their stress–strain curves, which show the maximum stress that can be withstood before breaking. On top of that, the maximum stress suggested that the deflection of a part should be less than 4.7 mm, as shown in the setting of the materials using the Material Definition App and their respective stress–strain curves.

Table 3. Material Specifications.

Material	PLA	ASA	ABS	PETG
Density (kg/m^3)	1240	1070	1050	1270
Young's Modulus (MPa)	1.98×10^9	1.35×10^9	1.70×10^9	1.38×10^9
Poisson Ratio			0.33	
Maximum Stress before breaking (MPa)	47	28	35	-

The drone is to be manufactured using 3D printing. In general, there are 4 types of material that can be used while performing FDM/FFF Thermoplastics 3D printing and they are PLA, ASA, ABS, and PETG. Each of them provides a different performance based on the nature of the material. Since the objective of this project is to build a drone that is lightweight but strong enough to fly at a certain height for the longest period of time, the main characteristics that need to be assessed are the density and the Young's Modulus of the materials.

For the center top cover, the material selected to be used as the core material is ABS material. Since this part implements the snap hook system, it has to be slightly flexible; moreover, ABS material is not too stiff as compared to PLA material. For the side top cover and the middle cover, the material selected to be used is PLA material. This is because PLA is stiffer and stronger than the other materials as mentioned earlier. Thus, it can "protect" the inner accessories of the drone as the battery, controller, ESC, etc., that are utilized for controlling the drone will be inside these parts. For the drone arm, the material selected to be used as the core material is ABS material. This is because ABS is stiffer as compared to ASA material, but it is lighter as compared to PLA material. Thus, it can bend slightly without breaking since it is not too stiff, as the drone arm will be directly connected to the motor.

2.3. Sketch Constraint and Design for Manufacturability

Constraints are ideal for creating practical 3D printing objects. It is important to pick the sketch objects that are desired to be limited in order to apply a constraint and click the corresponding constraint in the menu. The order in which the objects are picked will also influence how the constraint is implemented. The costs of manufacturing a drone can be reduced by designing a part or assembly for manufacturability. Manufacturability refers to the situation where a product can be quickly assembled from fewer parts. For example, the whole drone design is made up of six parts, which are shown in Table 1. Thus, this product is easier to be assembled and built in a shorter period of time. The parts of the drone are designed with standard sizes and they are easier to fabricate. This helps to optimize the parts of the drone such that it can be created more easily and at a cheaper cost. Reducing the cost and increasing the quality will make sure the product is sustainable in the market. The labor cost is also reduced, thanks to the fewer parts.

2.4. Carriage (Payload) and DOF

The most important factor when flying a drone is the degree of freedom (DOF). This factor has a large impact when it comes to the stability of the drone in maneuvering and travelling over a distance. The six main parts' DOFs should be followed to ensure more smooth and stable movements. Referring to the drone designed, it can move longitudinally, vertically, and laterally. This will also ensure the drone can make roll, pitch, and yaw movements on each axis.

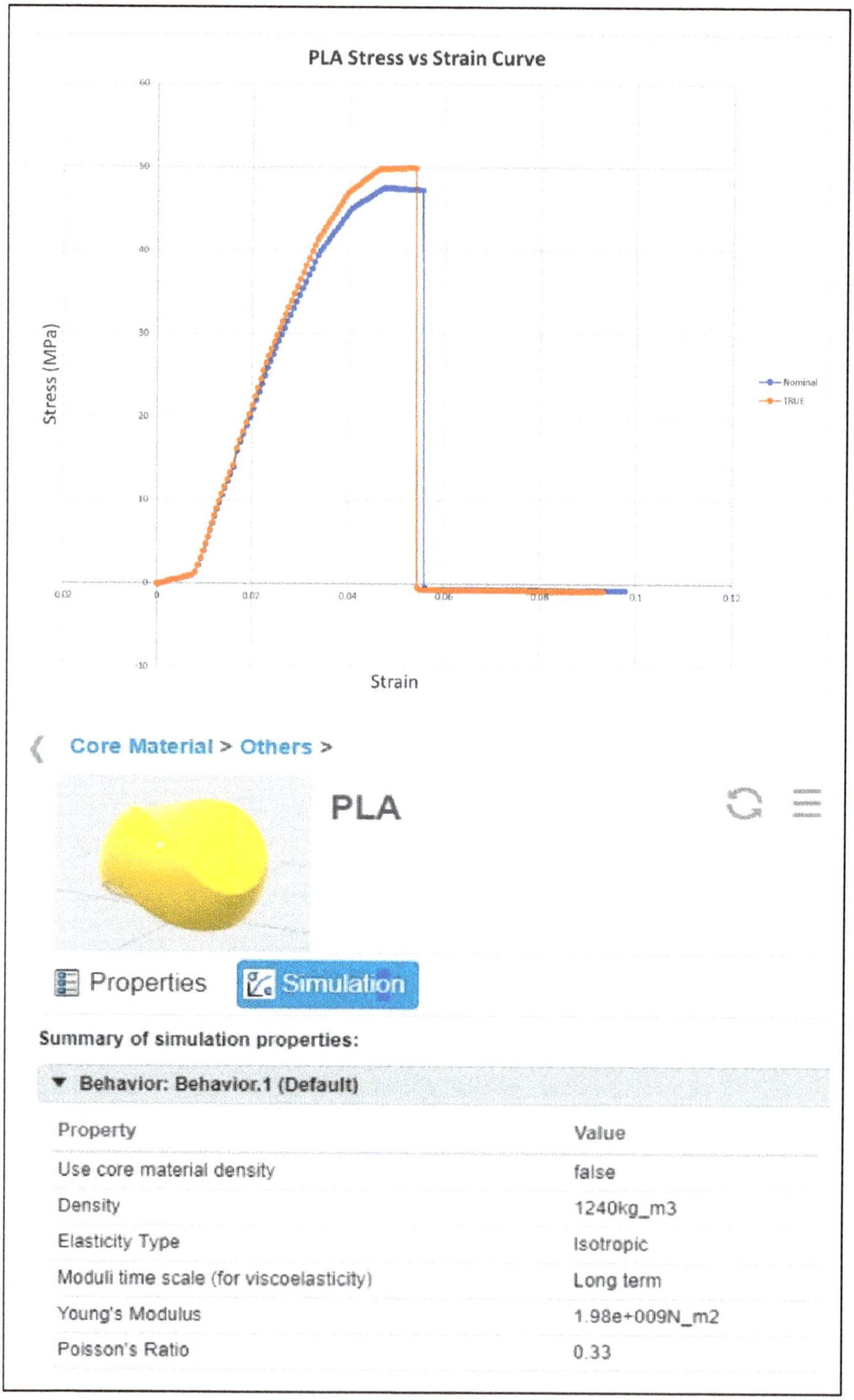

Property	Value
Use core material density	false
Density	1240kg_m3
Elasticity Type	Isotropic
Moduli time scale (for viscoelasticity)	Long term
Young's Modulus	1.98e+009N_m2
Poisson's Ratio	0.33

Figure 4. PLA Stress Curve.

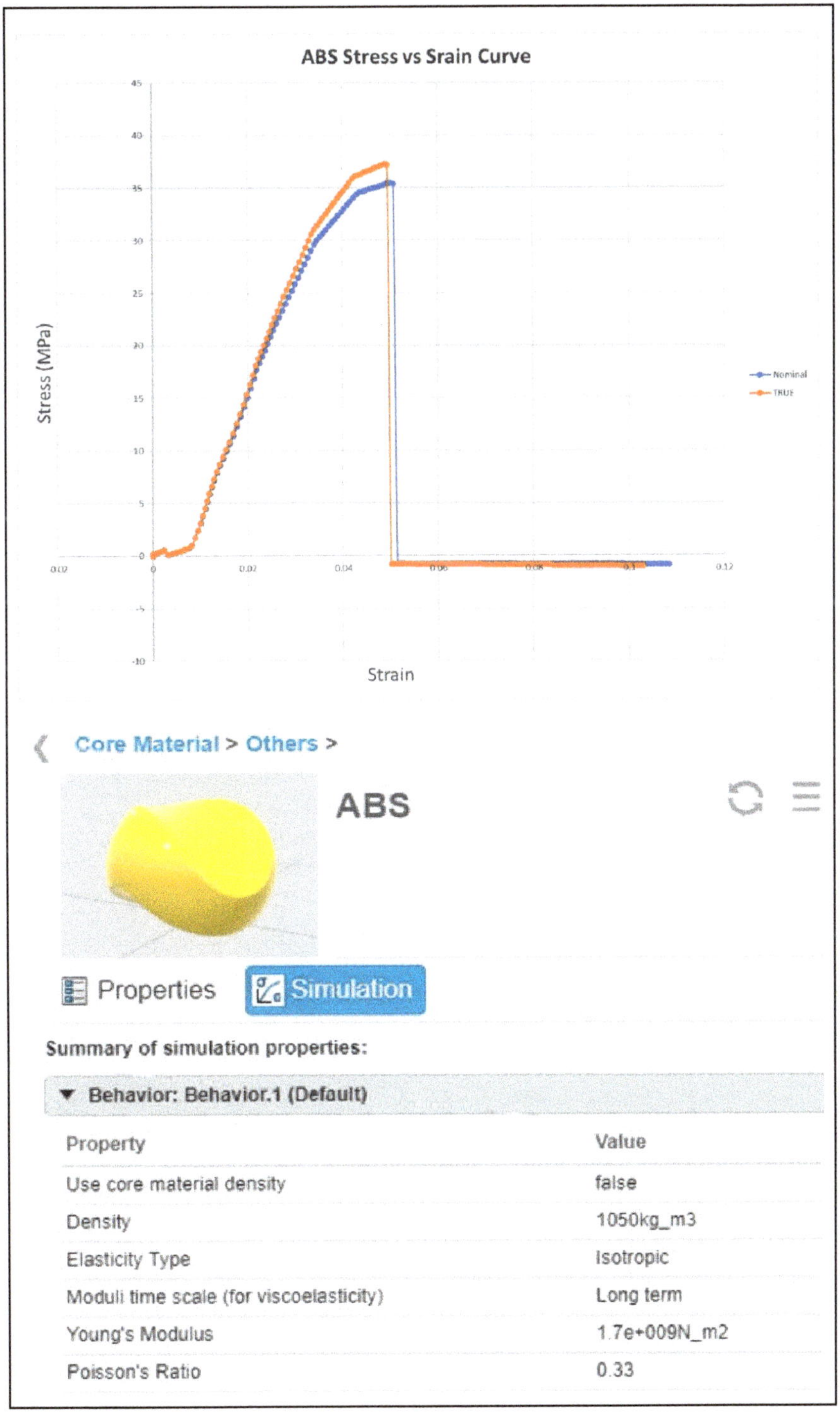

Figure 5. ABS Stress Curve.

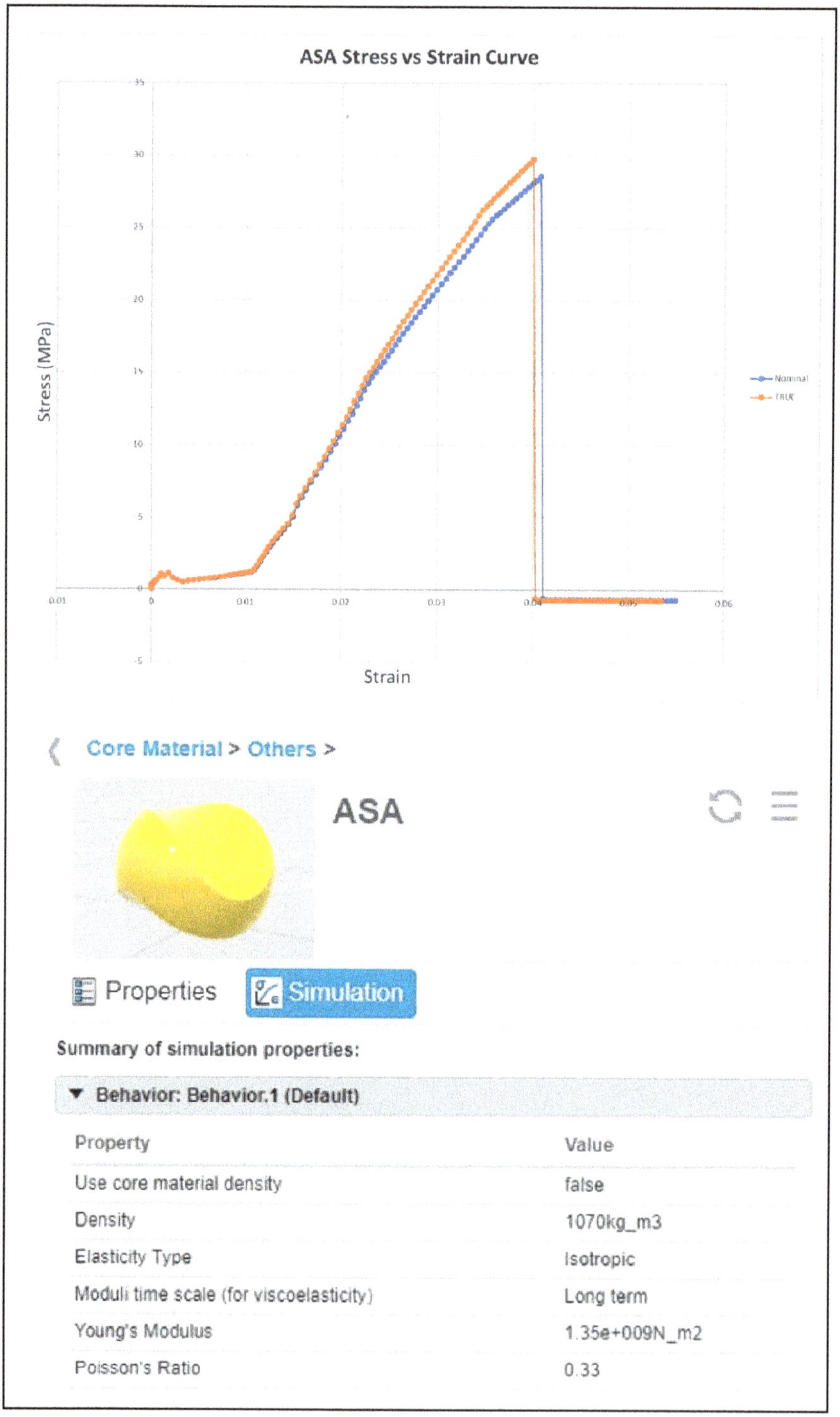

Figure 6. ASA Stress Curve.

3. System Simulation

Due to their wide range of applications, the attention towards drones has been constantly growing for the past decade. With the help of CAD software, many studies have been conducted to continue optimizing the performances of current drones in recent years while adapting the use of 3D printing technologies because they will play an integral part in the fourth industrial revolution [35]. Table 4 represents several examples of drone designs. Three Dimensional printing, which is a type of rapid prototyping, allows the low cost of drone fabrication [36,37], while CAD software enable the simulation such as the finite element analysis (FEA) to be carried out [38]. The main application used to simulate the design of the drone is the Functional Generative Design (FGD) application. Generative design is a revolutionizing product design and development technique of exploring multiple permutations of a solution to obtain the best design option. This application aims to optimize manufacturability and create a lightweight design; hence, saving material usage during manufacturing of the product. By applying different inputs based on the requirement and target, multiple variations can be generated in the system, which allows the user to perform a trade-off study to compare and analyze the options available. Finally, a detailed design can be constructed based on the chosen design for additive manufacturing.

Table 4. Several examples of drone designs.

Drone Type	Designs of Drones	Material Used
PoliDrone UAV [36]		Customizable multirotor drone frame
Iris + drone [39]		Drone frame can be printed using the Fused Filament Fabrication (FFF)
Skeleton X-14 Quadcopter [40]		FFF-printable with a single-piece body

As well as the FGD application, another element that is used is the Linear Structural Validation (LSV) application. This application is used to provide a simple insight into the design; hence, informed design decisions can be made easily. It is based on a powerful finite element solver that allows complex simulations. The four types of methods available for LSV are static stress, buckling, frequency, and thermal. This is usually used at the end of the design process to validate the final model used. Static stress analysis is used in this project, which includes evaluation of the stress, strain, and displacement of the model.

Restrain/Connection

For the center top cover, restraining is performed using a "clamp" at both inner sides of the part as shown in Figure 7a. The two sides will be attached to the middle cover using a snap hook system; therefore, it should be fixed throughout the flight. For the side top cover, restraining is performed using a "clamp" where the four holes at the sides are clamped as shown in Figure 7b. The four holes will be bolted to the middle cover; hence, the degree of freedom should be fixed as it is undesired for the part to move. For the middle cover, restraining is performed using a "clamp" at the eight holes, which are at each of the corners as well as at the side of the middle part that will be connected to the top cover using the snap hook system as shown in Figure 7c. The eight holes will be bolted to the leg bracket and the drone arm as well as the side top cover; thus, the degree of freedom should be fixed as it is undesired for the part to move. As well as that, the sides where the snap hook system is applied are clamped as well because they will be connected to the center top cover.

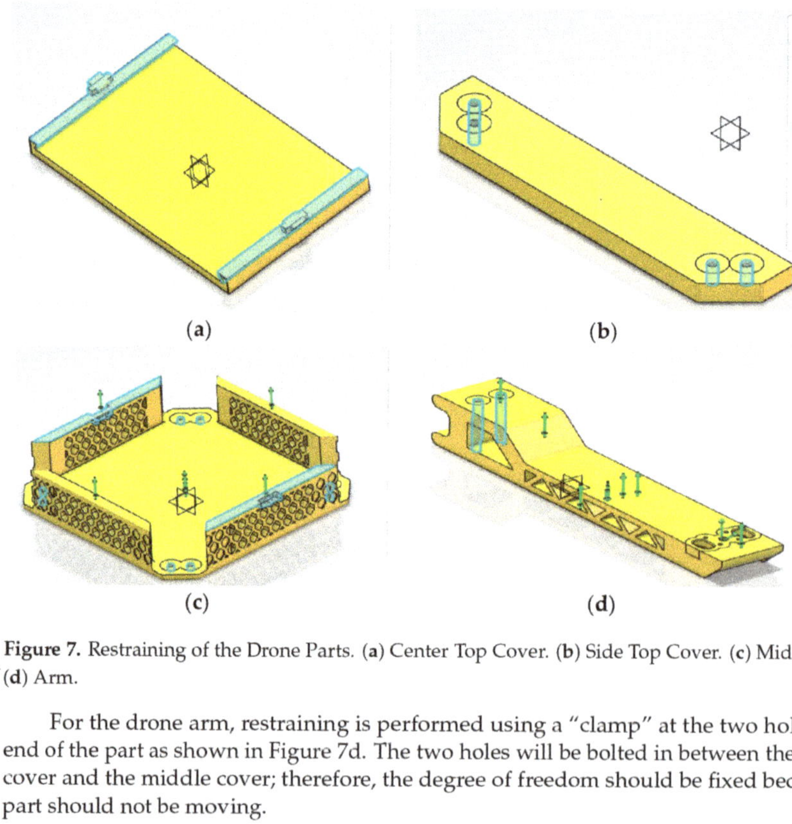

Figure 7. Restraining of the Drone Parts. (**a**) Center Top Cover. (**b**) Side Top Cover. (**c**) Middle Cover. (**d**) Arm.

For the drone arm, restraining is performed using a "clamp" at the two holes at the end of the part as shown in Figure 7d. The two holes will be bolted in between the side top cover and the middle cover; therefore, the degree of freedom should be fixed because the part should not be moving.

4. Results and Discussion

4.1. Drone's Parts' Stress and Displacement

Figure 8 shows the simulation results of the drone frame, which includes the center top cover, the middle cover, the side top cover, and the drone arm. From the results obtained, it is safe to conclude that the drone frame will not fail when it needs to sustain the maximum possible lift force from the motor as well as during the landing process. This is because the Setup Validation showed that the stress and the displacement of the parts were within the accepted range. Furthermore, for the parts that looked bent after going through the simulation, the values were actually very small and insignificant. Figure 9 illustrates the simulation results of the drone carriage that is used to carry the payload, and it includes the leg bracket and the bottom cover. Similar to the rest of the parts in the drone frame, the deformation value was actually very small. For future enhancements, a slight optimization of the center top cover and side top cover can be performed because the parts have a very plain surface, where some unnecessary edges can be removed to reduce the weight of the parts. However, the optimization conducted will just be minimal because these parts will be used to cover up the components inside the drone; hence, it should not have too many holes or else the components may drop out during the flight. Similar to the center top cover and the side top cover, the middle cover can also be optimized, but not by much since this is the part where the components will be placed and it is undesired for the parts to drop off during the flight. As for the drone arm, the part is still very bulky even though a more optimized design is used to start off with. Hence, the optimization process can also be performed for this part to reduce its unnecessary weight.

4.2. Trade-Off Study

For the center top cover, the top four concept shapes generated were compared by performing a trade-off study. The variants that were assessed were the mass, the displacement, and the stress of the part. The mass was given the highest priority; hence, it was set to have a key performance indicator (KPI) of 5. The target of the mass was also set. As well as that, the stress and displacement were given a KPI of 3 as they were less important for this part as it is connected at both ends. As shown in Figure 10, based on the variants and their respective KPIs, the first design scored the highest with a score of 60.3502. However, since this part is supposed to cover up the components inside, it is not suitable for it to have a big hole at the middle of the part. Thus, Centre Top Cover Sim 1 Shape Validation 5, which scored the second highest, was chosen to be the final design since the other variants were still in the acceptable range. For the side top cover, only two concept shapes generated were compared by performing a trade-off study since not much optimization can be conducted for this part.

The variants assessed were the mass, the displacement, and the stress of the part. The mass was given the highest priority; hence, it was set to have a KPI of 5. As well as that, the stress and displacement were given a KPI of 3 as they were not that important for this part as it is connected at both ends. As shown in Figure 11, based on the variants and their respective KPIs, the first design scored higher as compared to the second design with a score of 100. Thus, Side Top Cover Sim 1 Shape Validation 2 was chosen to be the final design since the other variants were still in the acceptable range. For the middle cover, the top three concept shapes generated were compared by performing a trade-off study. Similarly, the variants assessed were the mass, the displacement, and the stress of the part. The mass was given the highest priority; hence, it was set to have a KPI of 5. As well as that, the stress and displacement were given a KPI of 3 as they were not that important for this part as it is connected at all corners.

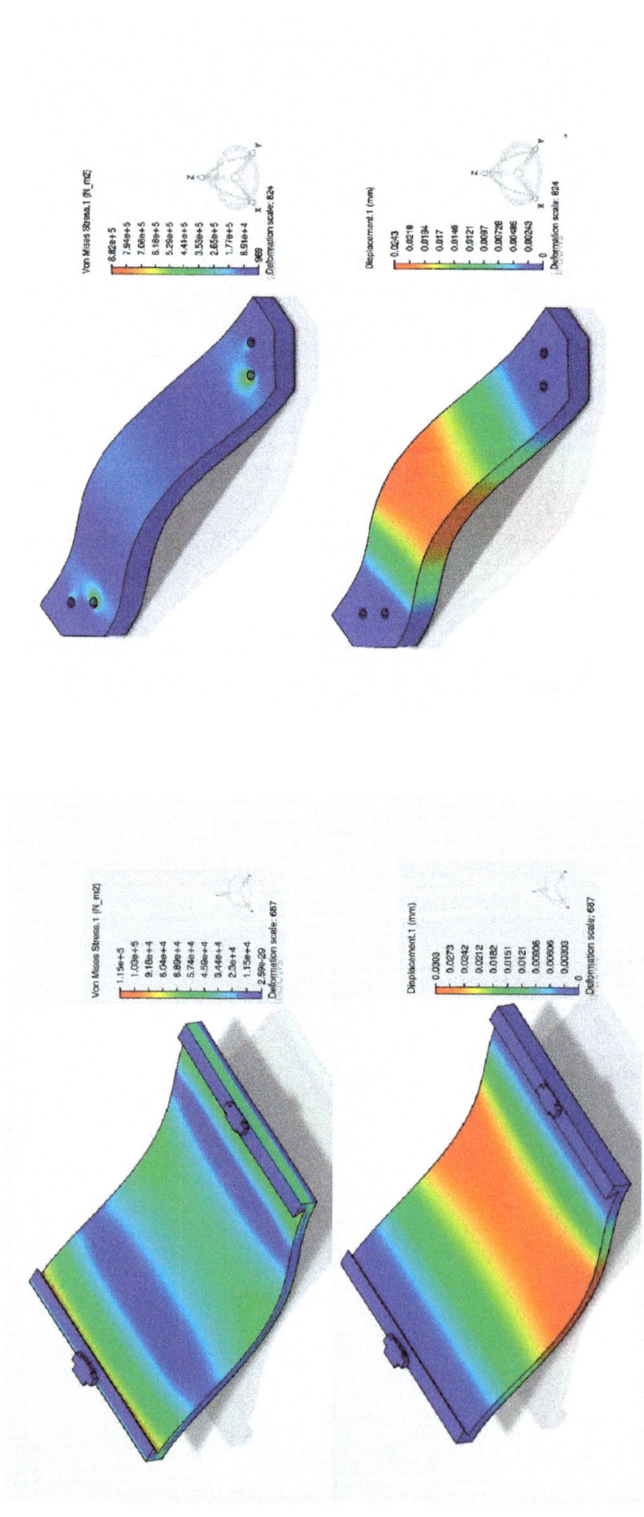

Figure 8. *Cont.*

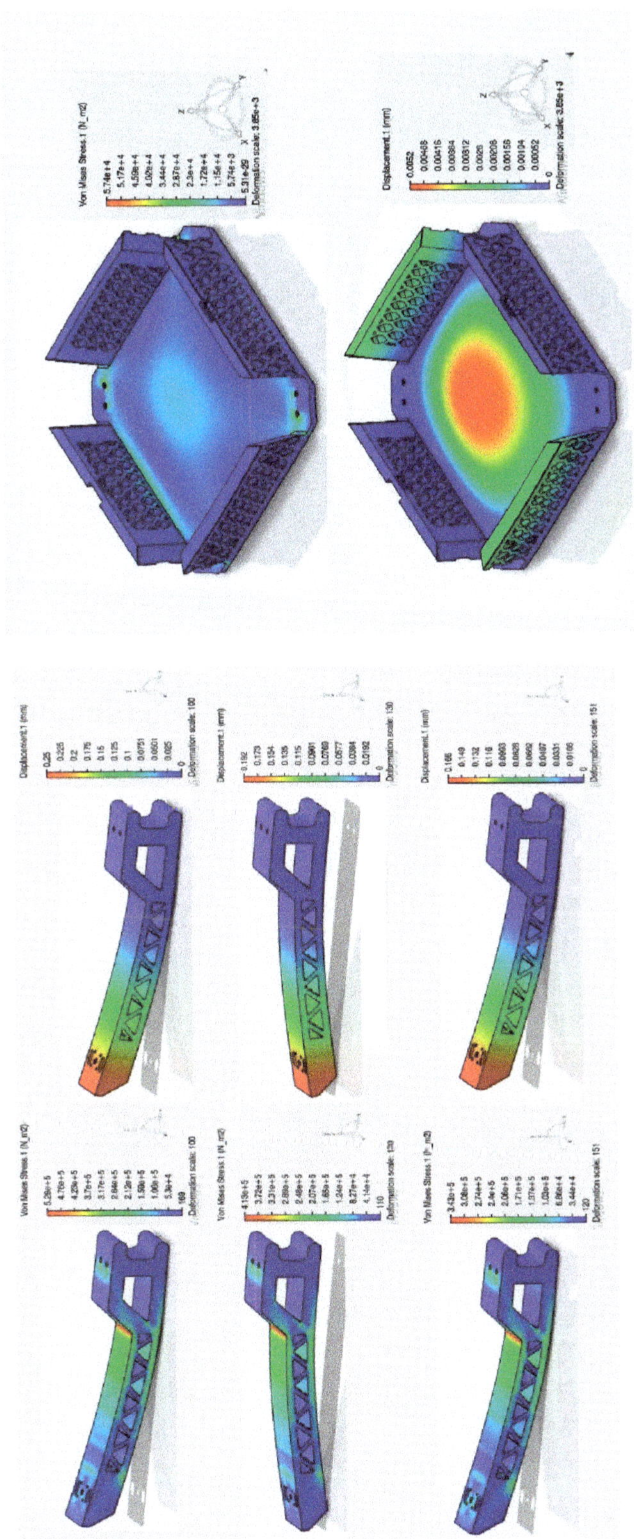

Figure 8. Stress and Displacement of the Drone's Parts. (**a**) Centre Top Cover. (**b**) Side Top Cover. (**c**) Drone's Arm. (**d**) Middle Cover.

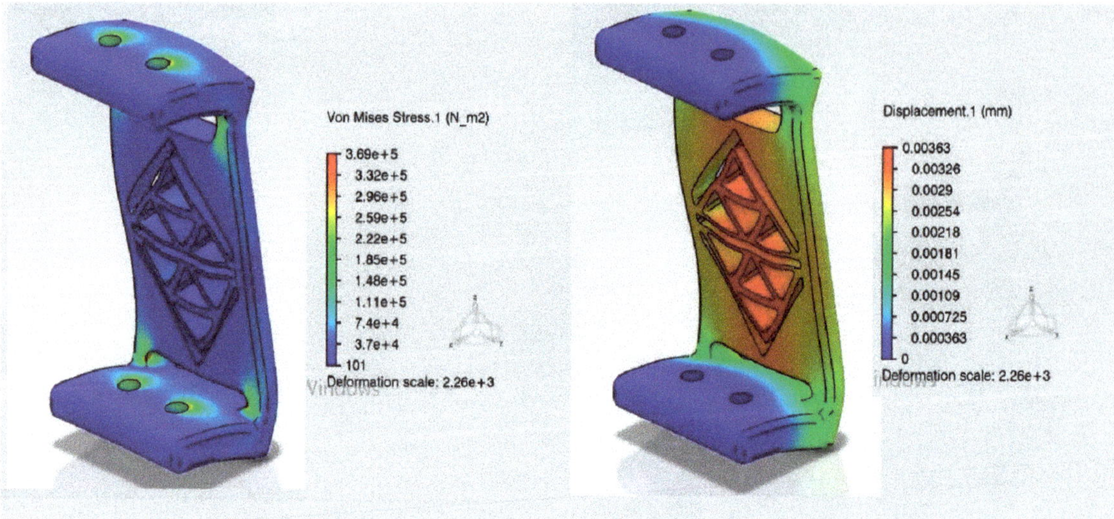

(a)

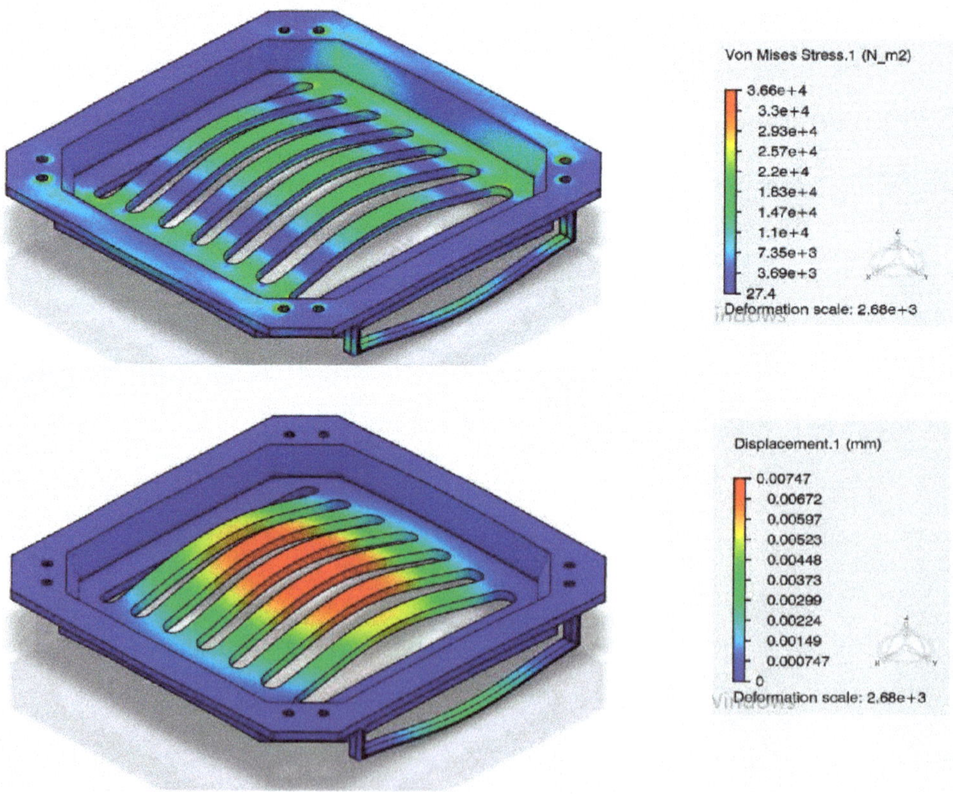

(b)

Figure 9. Drone's Carriage Stress and Displacement. (**a**) Leg Bereket. (**b**) Bottom Cover.

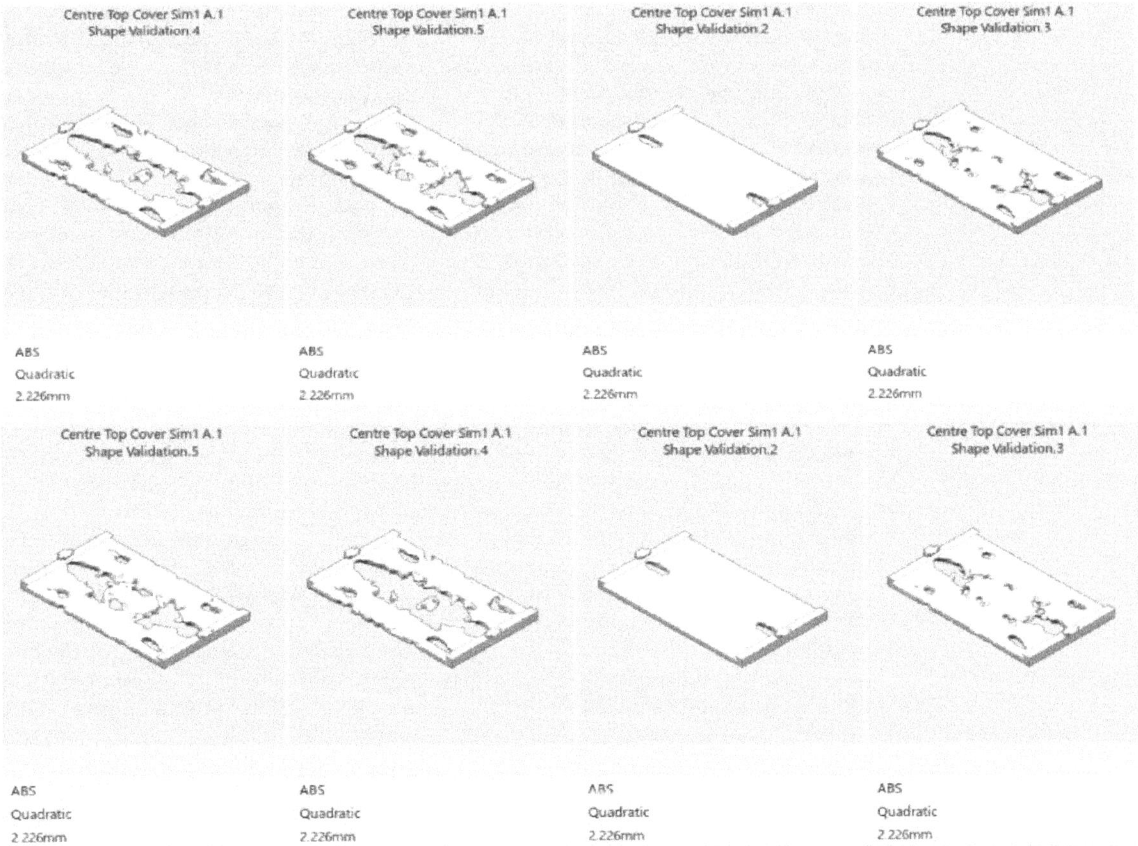

Figure 10. KPI of Centre Top Cover.

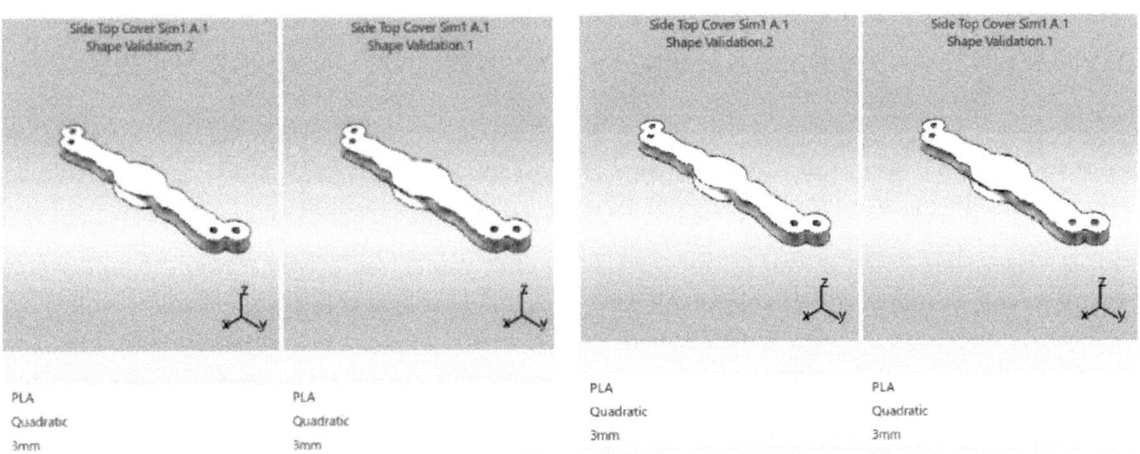

Figure 11. KPI of Side Top Cover.

As shown in Figure 12, based on the variants and their respective KPIs, the first design scored the highest with a score of 87.8811. Thus, Middle Cover Sim 2 Shape Validation 2 was chosen to be the final design as all the other variants were in the acceptable range as well. A trade-off study was conducted for the drone arm, where the top four concept shapes generated were compared. The variants assessed were the mass, the displacement, and the stress of the part. The mass was given the highest priority; hence, it was set to have a KPI of 5. As well as that, the stress and displacement were given a KPI of 4 as they were slightly more important as compared to the previous parts because one end of this part is not be clamped to the other parts. As shown in Figure 13, based on the variants and their respective KPIs, the fourth design scored the highest with a score of 90.2502. Thus, Drone Arm Sim 2 Shape Validation 6 was chosen to be the final design as all the other variants of the parts were in the acceptable range as well. For the leg bracket, the top three concept shapes generated were compared by performing a trade-off study. The variants assessed were the mass, the displacement, and the stress of the part. The mass was given the highest priority; hence, it was set to have a KPI of 5. The targeted mass was also inserted. On the other hand, the stress and displacement were given a KPI of 3 as they were not that important for this part since it is connected to both the top and bottom. As shown in Figure 14, based on the variants and their respective KPIs, the third design scored the highest with a score of 54.5. However, the mass of that part differed quite a lot from the targeted mass. Hence, Leg Bracket Sim 3 Shape Validation 2 that scored slightly lower but had a mass that was closer to the targeted mass was chosen to be the final design since the other variants were still in the acceptable range. For the bottom cover, the top three concept shapes generated were compared by performing a trade-off study. The variants assessed were the mass, the displacement, and the stress of the part. The mass was given the highest priority; hence, it was set to have a KPI of 5. The targeted mass was also inserted. On the other hand, the stress and displacement were given a KPI of 4 since they were equally important after the mass.

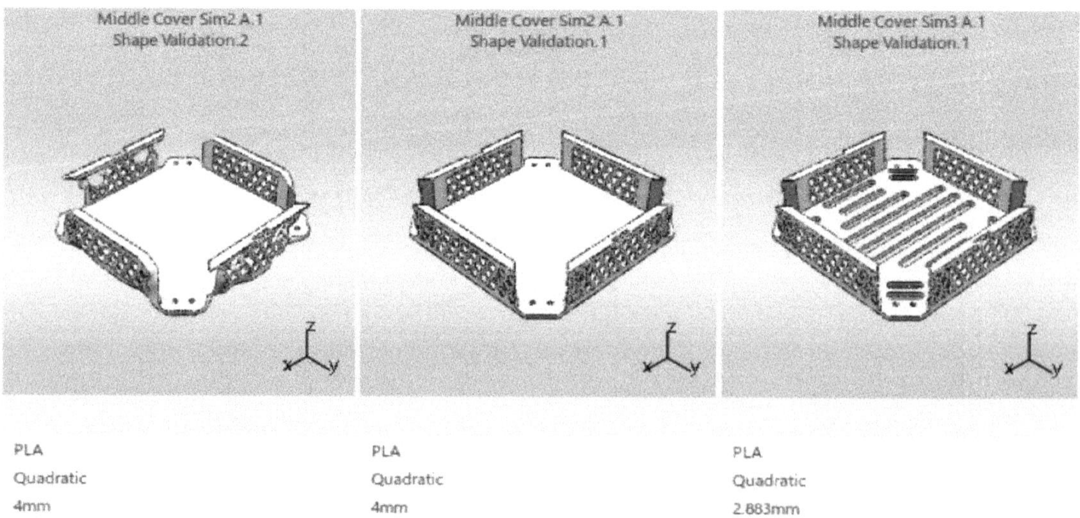

Figure 12. *Cont.*

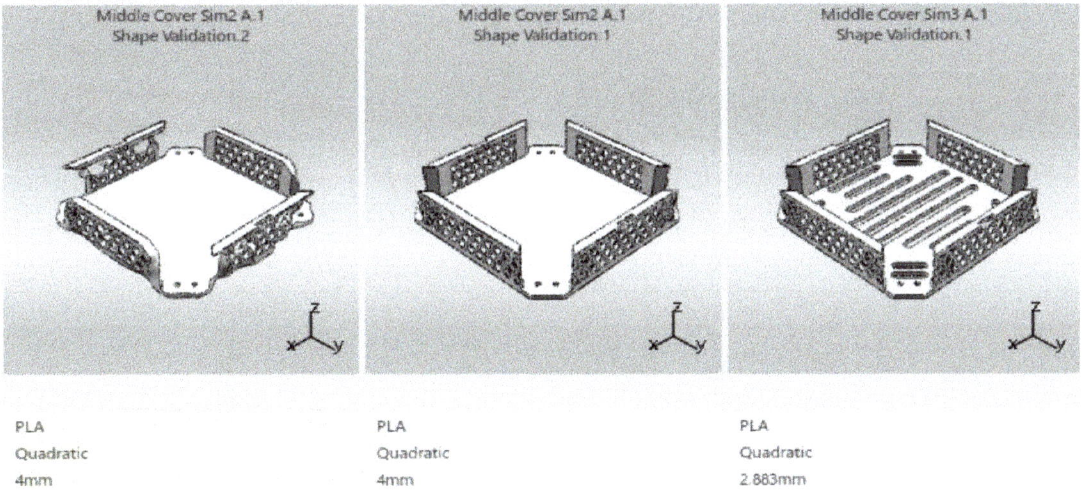

Figure 12. KPI of Middle Cover.

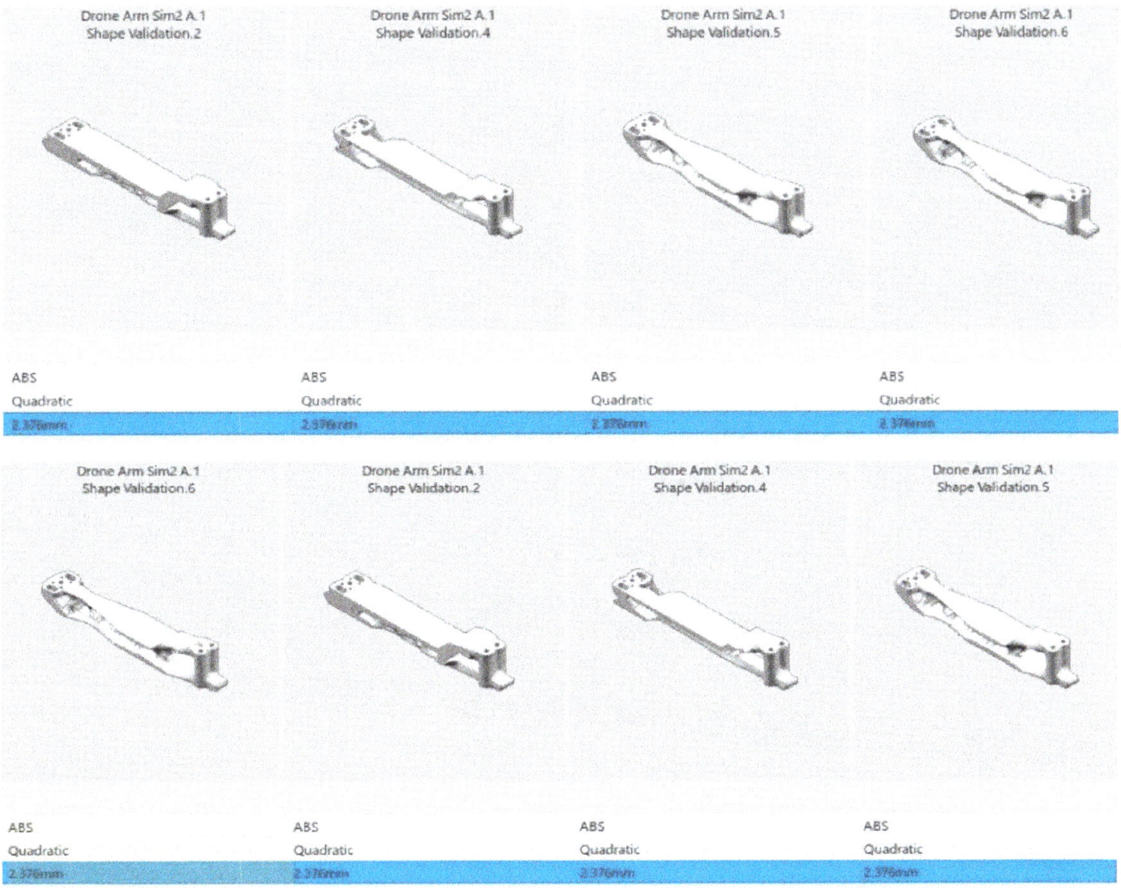

Figure 13. KPI of Arm.

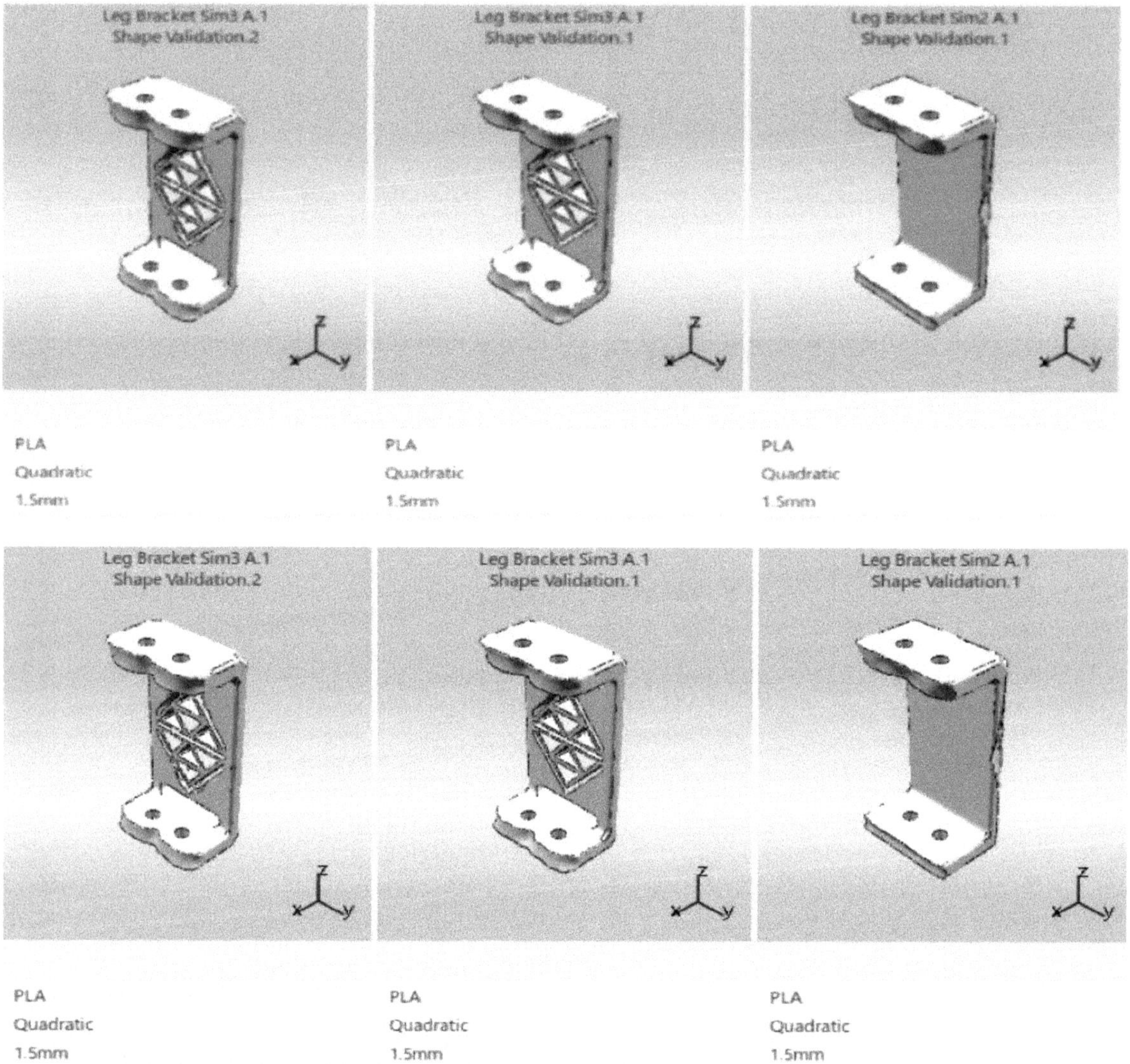

Figure 14. KPI of Leg Bracket.

As shown in Figure 15, based on the variants and their respective KPIs, the third design scored the highest with a score of 84.4588. The stress and the displacement were within the acceptable range as well. Furthermore, it was not the lightest design, the stress was lower as compared to the first design, and it had the smallest displacement. Therefore, Bottom Cover Sim 1 Shape Validation 1 scored the highest among the three designs and it was chosen to be used as the final design.

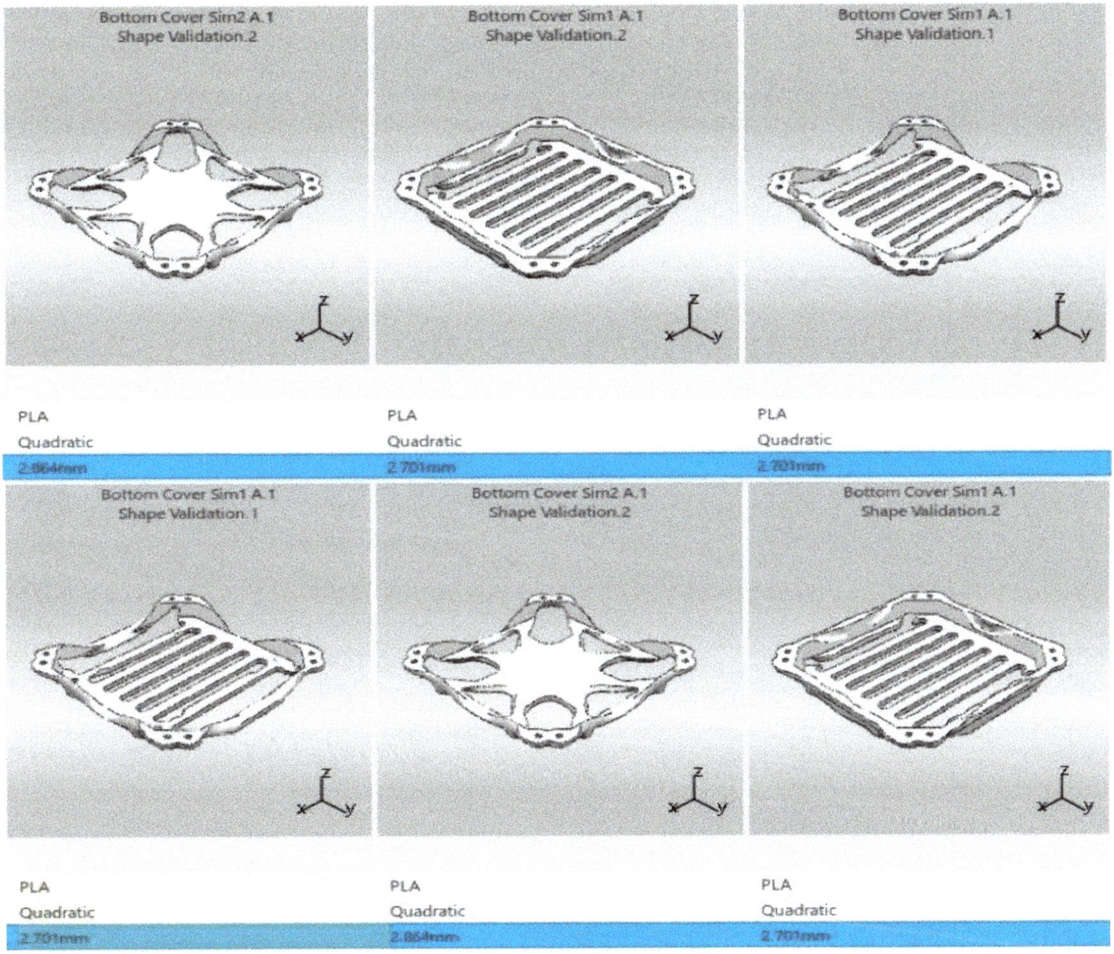

Figure 15. KPI of Bottom Cover.

4.3. Simulation Results of Drone's Weight

The Centre top cover was set to have a weight of 0.050 kg as shown in Figure 16a. It was set based on the initial assumption, where this part's targeted weight was at 50 g. The simulation was set to run for 150 cycles to produce the maximum stiffness for a given mass and it was shown that the target weight was reached at the end of the simulation. The side top cover was set to have a weight of 0.015 kg as shown in Figure 16b. This is based on the initial assumed weight, where this part's targeted weight was at 15 g each. The simulation was set to run for 50 cycles to produce the maximum stiffness for a given mass, where the simulation results show that the weight was suitable for this part and the target weight was reached at the end of the simulation. The execution stopped at the 46th cycle when all the constraints had been met. The middle cover was set to have a weight of 0.1 kg as shown in Figure 16c. The value of the weight was determined based on the initial assumed weight, where this part's targeted weight was at 100 g. The simulation was set to run for 80 cycles to produce the maximum stiffness for a given mass, where the simulation results show that the weight was suitable for this part and the target weight was reached at the end of the simulation. The execution stopped at the 68th cycle when all the constraints had been met. The drone arm was set to have a mass of 0.8 kg as shown in Figure 16d. Although the initial assumed weight showed that the targeted mass of this part was 30 g, the preserved faces already had a mass of 30 g. Therefore, the system would have to remove everything to reach the target, which is not possible. With that, the target mass was increased slightly to 80 g. The simulation was set to run for 80 cycles to produce the maximum stiffness for a given mass, where the simulation results show that the weight was suitable for this part and the target weight was reached at the end of the simulation. The execution stopped at the 76th cycle when all the constraints had been met.

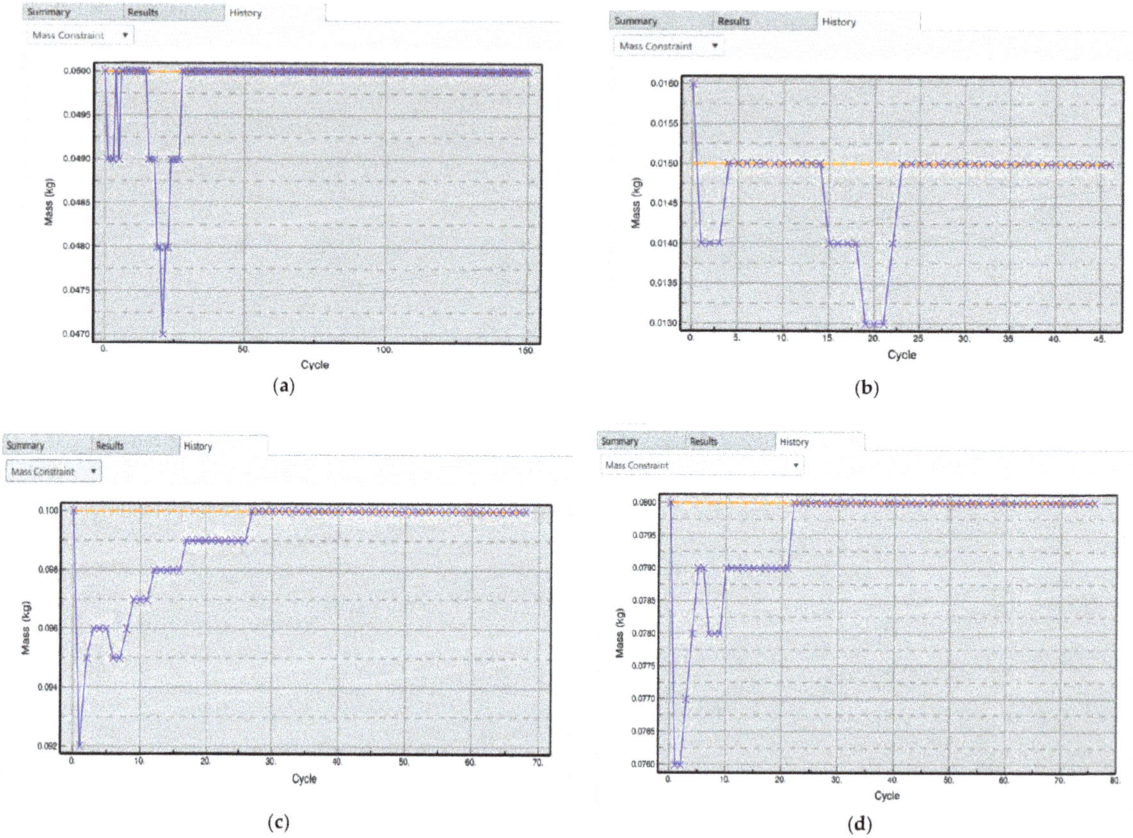

Figure 16. Output Weight of the Drone's Parts. (**a**) Center Top Cover. (**b**) Side Top Cover. (**c**) Middle Cover. (**d**) Drone's Arm.

4.4. Final Hardware Design

As shown in Figure 17, the final design of the drone consists of four main parts referred to in the Supplementary Material. The first part is the middle cover, which has the advantages of being lightweight and having good heat dissipation. The second part is the top cover, which is for electronic components' protection. The third part is the brackets, where there are four brackets to support the landing force. The brackets are locked between the frame and the carriage. The fourth part is the hook cover mechanism, which is used to close the upper side of the casing.

Figure 17. Hardware of the Drone Design.

4.5. Three Dimensional Printing Process

The drone was printed using the ANYCUBIC I3 MEGA. The Cura software was used to convert stl file format into G-code format to print the drone parts. The infill was set to 100% to increase the design structure strength. The types of filament used were PLA; 195 degree Celsius is the standard to print PLA material. The retraction speed was adjusted to 40 mm/s. The retraction distance was adjusted to 4.5 mm, the layer height adjusted to 0.2 mm, and the bed temperature was set to 60 degree Celsius. It takes an average of 6 h to print a part. The steps listed below were followed:

1. Download and install Cura.
2. Slice the 3D model into smaller pieces.
3. Three Dimensional model saved to an SD card as G-Code.
4. SD card is inserted into the 3D printer.
5. Load filament into the 3D printer.
6. Activate the printing application.

5. Conclusions

Modelling for a drone's parts has been presented in this project. Simulation of the parts was conducted using the 3DEXPERIENCE software, which provides modelling, simulation, and optimization functions, to obtain the best design option and to make sure that the final design of the parts was aesthetically novel with no un-smooth edges or uneven shapes. Simulation of the drone's stress and displacement was carried out, where the results show that the drone frame will not fail when it needs to sustain the maximum possible lift force from the motor as well as during the landing process. In addition, the concept shapes that were generated were compared by performing a trade-off study. The variants assessed were the mass, the displacement, and the stress of the parts. Simulation of the drone's weight was carried out for the center top cover (50 g), side top cover (10 g), middle cover (30 g), and drone's arm (80 g). The simulation of the parts was performed by using 3D Designer; hence, more details can be obtained through the trade-off study and the simulation of the drone's weight.

Supplementary Materials: The following supporting information can be downloaded at: https://www.mdpi.com/article/10.3390/drones6040097/s1, Figure S1: Dimention of drone Leg breaket; Figure S2: Dimention of drone side top cover. Figure S3: Dimention of drone arm, Figure S4: Dimention of drone midell cover, Figure S5: 3D printer model, Figure S6: Side top cover, meddle cover and center top cover of the drone, Figure S7: Description of 3D printed parts.

Author Contributions: Methodology, A.O.M. and H.C.; software, P.U.; validation, K.Y. and H.C.; formal analysis, T.J.; investigation, T.J.; writing—original draft preparation, A.O.M., H.C., P.U. and T.J.; writing—review and editing, A.O.M. and K.Y.; supervision, K.Y. and H.C.; funding acquisition, K.Y. and H.C. All authors have read and agreed to the published version of the manuscript.

Funding: This research was funded by [Sunway University postgraduate studentship and School of Engineering UOW Malaysia KDU Penang University Colleg e, Postgraduate & Research Centre (PGRC)]. And the APC was funded by [Sunway University postgraduate studentship and School of Engineering UOW Malaysia KDU Penang University College, Postgraduate & Research Centre (PGRC)].

Institutional Review Board Statement: Not applicable.

Informed Consent Statement: Not applicable.

Acknowledgments: We would like to acknowledge the support of Sunway University postgraduate studentship and School of Engineering UOW Malaysia KDU Penang University College , Postgraduate & Research Centre (PGRC). Additionally, we would like to acknowledge the help in 3D printing and fabrication by: Lee Wei Hou, Chan Lap Foong, Seerla Kanagarajoo, Betharajoo, and Simon Anandaraj Doss.

Conflicts of Interest: The authors declare no conflict of interest.

References

1. Oakey, A.; Waters, T.; Zhu, W.; Royall, P.; Cherrett, T.; Courtney, P.; Majoe, D.; Jelev, N. Quantifying the Effects of Vibration on Medicines in Transit Caused by Fixed-Wing and Multi-Copter Drones. *Drones* **2021**, *5*, 22. [CrossRef]
2. Hiebert, B.; Nouvet, E.; Jeyabalan, V.; Donelle, L. The Application of Drones in Healthcare and Health-Related Services in North America: A Scoping Review. *Drones* **2020**, *4*, 30. [CrossRef]
3. Akhloufi, M.; Couturier, A.; Castro, N. Unmanned Aerial Vehicles for Wildland Fires: Sensing, Perception, Cooperation and Assistance. *Drones* **2021**, *5*, 15. [CrossRef]
4. Barreto, J.; Cajaíba, L.; Teixeira, J.; Nascimento, L.; Giacomo, A.; Barcelos, N.; Fettermann, T.; Martins, A. Drone-Monitoring: Improving the Detectability of Threatened Marine Megafauna. *Drones* **2021**, *5*, 14. [CrossRef]
5. A Game Changer for Business and Innovation. Available online: https://www.3ds.com/3dexperience (accessed on 28 February 2022).
6. Royo, P.; Pastor, E.; Barrado, C.; Cuadrado, R.; Barrao, F.; Garcia, A. Hardware Design of a Small UAS Helicopter for Remote Sensing Operations. *Drones* **2017**, *1*, 3. [CrossRef]
7. Dawkins, J.; Devries, L. Modeling, Trim Analysis, and Trajectory Control of a Micro-Quadrotor with Wings. *Drones* **2018**, *2*, 21. [CrossRef]
8. Shukla, D.; Komerath, N. Multirotor Drone Aerodynamic Interaction Investigation. *Drones* **2018**, *2*, 43. [CrossRef]
9. Castiblanco, J.M.; Garcia-Nieto, S.; Simarro, R.; Salcedo, J. Experimental study on the dynamic behaviour of drones designed for racing competitions. *Int. J. Micro Air Veh.* **2021**, *13*, 17568293211005757. [CrossRef]
10. Basson, C.; Hansraj, S.; Stopforth, R.; Mooney, P.; Phillips, R.; Van Niekerk, T.; Du Preez, K. A Review of Collaborated Educational Drone Development and Design at the BRICS 2018 Future Skills Challenge. In Proceedings of the 2019 Southern African Universities Power Engineering Conference/Robotics and Mechatronics/Pattern Recognition Association of South Africa (SAUPEC/RobMech/PRASA), Bloemfontein, South Africa, 28–30 January 2019; pp. 17–22. [CrossRef]
11. Jo, B.W.; Song, C.S. Thermoplastics and Photopolymer Desktop 3D Printing System Selection Criteria Based on Technical Specifications and Performances for Instructional Applications. *Technologies* **2021**, *9*, 91. [CrossRef]
12. Horvath, J.; Cameron, R. The Desktop 3D Printer. In *3D Print with MatterControl*; Springer: Berkeley, CA, USA, 2015; pp. 3–13. [CrossRef]
13. Kacmarcik, J.; Spahic, D.; Varda, K.; Porca, E.; Zaimovic-Uzunovic, N. An investigation of geometrical accuracy of desktop 3D printers using CMM. *IOP Conf. Series: Mater. Sci. Eng.* **2018**, *393*, 012085. [CrossRef]
14. 3D Printing Third Edition. Available online: https://lib.hpu.edu.vn/handle/123456789/31244 (accessed on 27 February 2022).
15. Shahrubudin, N.; Lee, T.; Ramlan, R. An Overview on 3D Printing Technology: Technological, Materials, and Applications. *Procedia Manuf.* **2019**, *35*, 1286–1296. [CrossRef]
16. Arefin, A.; Khatri, N.; Kulkarni, N.; Egan, P. Polymer 3D Printing Review: Materials, Process, and Design Strategies for Medical Applications. *Polymers* **2021**, *13*, 1499. [CrossRef]

17. Antreas, K.; Piromalis, D. Employing a Low-Cost Desktop 3D Printer: Challenges, and How to Overcome Them by Tuning Key Process Parameters. *Int. J. Mech. Appl.* **2021**, *10*, 11–19. [CrossRef]
18. Haryńska, A.; Carayon, I.; Kosmela, P.; Szeliski, K.; Łapiński, M.; Pokrywczyńska, M.; Kucińska-Lipka, J.; Janik, H. A comprehensive evaluation of flexible FDM/FFF 3D printing filament as a potential material in medical application. *Eur. Polym. J.* **2020**, *138*, 109958. [CrossRef]
19. Krishnanand; Soni, S.; Taufik, M. Design and assembly of fused filament fabrication (FFF) 3D printers. *Mater. Today Proc.* **2020**, *46*, 5233–5241. [CrossRef]
20. Vasudevarao, B.; Natarajan, D.P.; Henderson, M. Sensitivity of Rp Surface Finish to Process. In Proceedings of the 2000 International Solid Freeform Fabrication Symposium, Austin, TX, USA, 25–27 July 2000; pp. 251–258.
21. Galatas, A.; Hassanin, H.; Zweiri, Y.; Seneviratne, L. Additive Manufactured Sandwich Composite/ABS Parts for Unmanned Aerial Vehicle Applications. *Polymers* **2018**, *10*, 1262. [CrossRef]
22. Bishay, P.L.; Burg, E.; Akinwunmi, A.; Phan, R.; Sepulveda, K. Development of a New Span-Morphing Wing Core Design. *Designs* **2019**, *3*, 12. [CrossRef]
23. Sharma, V. Advances in Drone Communications, State-of-the-Art and Architectures. *Drones* **2019**, *3*, 21. [CrossRef]
24. Muralidharan, N.; Pratheep, V.; Shanmugam, A.; Hariram, A.; Dinesh, P.; Visnu, B. Structural analysis of mini drone developed using 3D printing technique. *Mater. Today Proc.* **2021**, *46*, 8748–8752. [CrossRef]
25. Negrelli, V. "From earth to heaven": How professional 3D Printing and Windform® GT material helped in the construction of drone and medical devices. *Reinf. Plast.* **2017**, *61*, 179–183. [CrossRef]
26. Kantaros, A.; Diegel, O. 3D printing technology in musical instrument research: Reviewing the potential. *Rapid Prototyp. J.* **2018**, *24*, 1511–1523. [CrossRef]
27. Shen, C.H.; Albert, F.Y.C.; Ang, C.K.; Teck, D.J.; Chan, K.P. Theoretical development and study of takeoff constraint thrust equation for a drone. In Proceedings of the 2017 IEEE 15th Student Conference on Research and Development (SCOReD), Wilayah Persekutuan Putrajaya, Malaysia, 13–14 December 2017; pp. 18–22. [CrossRef]
28. Research and Development in Modern Materials. Available online: https://blogs.deakin.edu.au/remstep/materials-activities/honeycomb-structures/ (accessed on 1 January 2022).
29. Amza, C.G.; Zapciu, A.; Eyþórsdóttir, A.; Björnsdóttir, A.; Borg, J. Mechanical properties of 3D printed composites with ABS/ASA substrate and glass fiber inserts. In Proceedings of the MATEC Web of Conferences, Kursk, Russia, 1 November 2019; Volume 290, p. 04002. [CrossRef]
30. Afshar, A.; Wood, R. Development of Weather-Resistant 3D Printed Structures by Multi-Material Additive Manufacturing. *J. Compos. Sci.* **2020**, *4*, 94. [CrossRef]
31. Butt, J.; Bhaskar, R. Investigating the effects of annealing on the mechanical properties of FFF-printed thermoplastics. *J. Manuf. Mater. Process.* **2020**, *4*, 94. [CrossRef]
32. Comparing 3D Printing Filament Features: ABS vs. ASA Filament. Available online: https://www.makeshap-er.com/2020/01/24/3d-printing-filament-features-abs-vs-asa-filament/ (accessed on 28 February 2022).
33. Iannace, S.; Sorrentino, L.; Di Maio, E. *Biodegradable Biomedical Foam Scaffolds*; Woodhead Publishing Limited: Federico II, Italy, 2014; pp. 163–187. [CrossRef]
34. Malaysian Information Climate. Available online: https://www.malaysia.gov.my/portal/content/144 (accessed on 28 February 2022).
35. Rayna, T.; Striukova, L. From rapid prototyping to home fabrication: How 3D printing is changing business model innovation. *Technol. Forecast. Soc. Chang.* **2016**, *102*, 214–224. [CrossRef]
36. Brischetto, S.; Torre, R. Preliminary Finite Element Analysis and Flight Simulations of a Modular Drone Built through Fused Filament Fabrication. *J. Compos. Sci.* **2021**, *5*, 293. [CrossRef]
37. Kantaros, A.; Piromalis, D.; Tsaramirsis, G.; Papageorgas, P.; Tamimi, H. 3D Printing and Implementation of Digital Twins: Current Trends and Limitations. *Appl. Syst. Innov.* **2022**, *5*, 7. [CrossRef]
38. Kantaros, A.; Karalekas, D. FBG Based In Situ Characterization of Residual Strains in FDM Process. *Conf. Proc. Soc. Exp. Mech. Ser.* **2014**, *8*, 333–337. [CrossRef]
39. 3D Robotics IRIS + RTF Kit (433). Available online: https://www.megapixel.cz/3d-robotics-iris-433 (accessed on 2 March 2022).
40. Skeleton X-14 Quadcopter. Available online: https://cults3d.com/en/3d-model/gadget/skeleton-x-14-quadcopter (accessed on 2 March 2022).

drones

MDPI

Article

Flight Test of Autonomous Formation Management for Multiple Fixed-Wing UAVs Based on Missile Parallel Method

Guang Zhan [1,*], Zheng Gong [2], Quanhui Lv [2], Zan Zhou [2], Zian Wang [2], Zhen Yang [1] and Deyun Zhou [1]

1 School of Electronics and Information, Northwestern Polytechnical University, Xi'an 710072, China; nwpuyz@mail.nwpu.edu.cn (Z.Y.); dyzhou@nwpu.edu.cn (D.Z.)
2 Department of Aerospace Engineering, College of Aerospace Engineering, Nanjing University of Aeronautics and Astronautics, Nanjing 210095, China; matthewzhenggong@nuaa.edu.cn (Z.G.); quanhui.lv@nuaa.edu.cn (Q.L.); zhouzan@nuaa.edu.cn (Z.Z.); wangzian@nuaa.edu.cn (Z.W.)
* Correspondence: zhanguang@mail.nwpu.edu.cn

Abstract: This paper reports on the formation and transformation of multiple fixed-wing unmanned aerial vehicles (UAVs) in three-dimensional space. A cooperative guidance law based on the classic missile-type parallel-approach method is designed for the multi-UAV formation control problem. Additionally, formation transformation strategies for multi-UAV autonomous assembly, disbandment, and special circumstances are formed, effective for managing and controlling the formation. When formulating the management strategy for formation establishment, its process is divided into three steps: (i) selecting and allocating target points, (ii) forming loose formations, and (iii) forming short-range formations. The management of disbanding the formation is formulated through reverse thinking: the assembly process is split and recombined in reverse, and a formation disbanding strategy that can achieve a smooth transition from close to lose formation is proposed. Additionally, a strategy is given for adjusting the formation transformation in special cases, and the formation adjustment is completed using the adjacency matrix. Finally, a hardware-in-the-loop simulation and measured flight verification using a simulator show the practicality of the guidance law in meeting the control requirements of UAV formation flight for specific flight tasks.

Keywords: formation management; missile parallel method; flight test

Citation: Zhan, G.; Gong, Z.; Lv, Q.; Zhou, Z.; Wang, Z.; Yang, Z.; Zhou, D. Flight Test of Autonomous Formation Management for Multiple Fixed-Wing UAVs Based on Missile Parallel Method. *Drones* **2022**, *6*, 99. https://doi.org/10.3390/drones6050099

Academic Editors: Andrzej Łukaszewicz, Andriy Holovatyy, Wojciech Giernacki, Jarosław Pytka and Zbigniew Kulesza

Received: 14 March 2022
Accepted: 13 April 2022
Published: 19 April 2022

1. Introduction

Form formation management is an important research topic for multiple unmanned aerial vehicles (UAVs) flying in cooperative formation [1,2]. Because of the limited control of fixed-wing UAVs, their formation management is very different from that of quadrotor UAVs. By contrast, static and fixed-wing UAVs cannot wait for other UAVs during formation [3], which makes stable and reliable formation challenging.

In recent decades, many scholars have researched the formation of fixed-wing UAVs. Zhang [4] proposed a proportional integral–derivative (PID) integrated control method based on robust control; this comprehensive control method improves the hit rate and flight stability of UAV formation, reduces the dynamic response of the steady-state error, and shortens the convergence time, but the influence of the coupling effect of the integrated controller on the entire control system was not considered in the corresponding experiment. Kada [5] proposed (i) a smooth distributed cooperative control method for multiple aircraft (such as UAVs) based on multi-agent system (MAS) consistency and (ii) a smooth distributed consistency algorithm, as well as designing a formation control model for three-dimensional (3D) geometry tracking; however, the disadvantage of this approach is that it fails to consider (i) formation tracking in the case of external interference and (ii) obstacle avoidance among flying agents. Wang [6] analyzed the optimality of formation configuration, provided an optimal formation design strategy for multi-UAV patrol tasks, and developed a model prediction trajectory replanning algorithm. However, the disadvantages of this approach are that it (i) considers only the mission and motion planning level and (ii) does not involve low-level flight-control problems. Reference [7] proposed a robust decentralized tracking control scheme for a large-scale UAV-formation network control system and verified it in such a system.

Research on formation maintenance and transformation remains sparse. Proposed herein is a formation management method based on cooperative waypoint following. Additionally, formation reconfiguration strategy is designed considering how some typical unexpected situations influence cooperative formations. Combining the guidance law of the parallel-approach method [8,9] and the calculation method of virtual dynamic tracking points, a method is proposed for cooperative path-point following in formation control [10–12] to realize multi-machine formation flight of fixed-wing UAVs. It has the advantages of fast tracking response in the low-altitude formation flight, and rapid formation reconstruction in unexpected situations. Finally, the stability and agility of the guidance law in formation cooperative control are verified by hardware-in-the-loop [13–15] simulation and flight-test measurements.

Based on the flight control of a single fixed-wing aircraft [13–15], this paper designs a layered control framework, as shown in Figure 1. The control framework includes four submodules: the intermachine communication module, the cooperative waypoint-following control module, the cooperative formation module, and the stabilization loop control module. After receiving the instruction to start the formation, the cooperative formation module generates the desired waypoints for the UAVs. Compared with trajectory tracking, waypoint tracking is more widely used in aviation, and a series of static waypoints often represent common single-plane flight tasks. Waypoint tracking is used more widely in aviation, and a series of static waypoints often represent common single-plane flight tasks.

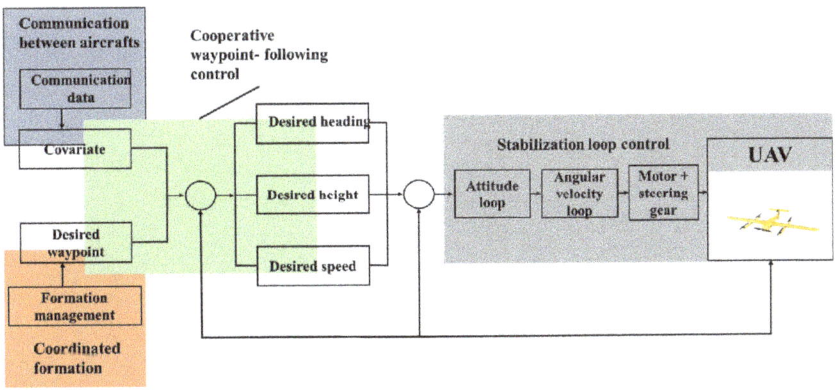

Figure 1. Formation control framework based on cooperative waypoint-following.

2. Design of Guidance Law and Verification by Simulation

2.1. Design of Guidance Law

The required lateral movement is determined by calculating virtual dynamic tracking points according to the formation relative distance of the formation, and the virtual dynamic tracking points are those of the wingmen.

Assuming that the UAVs are all mass points when flying in formation, as shown in Figure 2, in the case of two UAVs, let point A be where the leader is located, let point B be where the virtual dynamic tracking point is located, and let point C be where the wingman is located. Define the coordinate formation system $O_fX_fY_fZ_f$ fixed to the lead plane L:O_fX_f is parallel to the direction of the speed vector of the lead plane and points forward; the axis O_fY_f is perpendicular to O_fX_f and points to the right of the flight direction; the axis O_fZ_f is perpendicular to $O_fX_fY_f$ and points downward. Points A and B are on concentric circular arcs whose lengths are Δx and *arc*, respectively, and the concentric circular arcs are on $O_f X_f Y_f$; Δy is the length of the straight line of the leader aircraft to the arc, R_L is the flight radius of the lead aircraft, R is the radius of the concentric circular arcs, and φ is the included angle of point A and B. In this coordinate system, point B is relative to point A and its positional differences are Δx_{err} and Δy_{err}, whose lengths can be obtained geometrically.

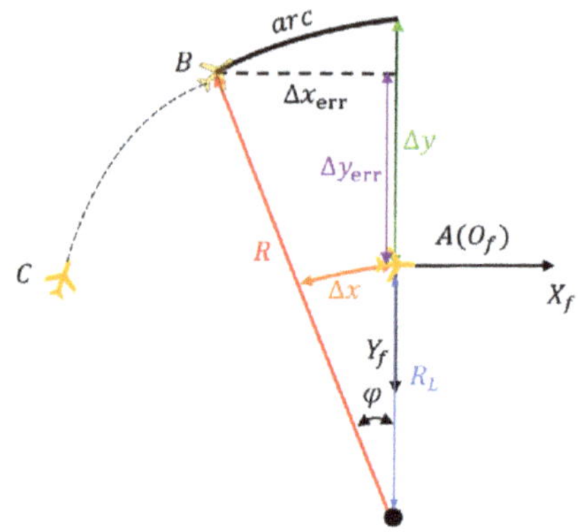

Figure 2. Schematic for calculating the virtual dynamic tracking point.

When φ is small, we have

$$\begin{cases} \Delta x_{err} = arc \\ \Delta y_{err} = \Delta y \end{cases} \tag{1}$$

When φ is larger, we have

$$\begin{cases} \Delta x_{err} = \frac{arc}{\varphi} \sin \varphi \\ \Delta y_{err} = \Delta y - \frac{arc}{\varphi}(1 - \cos \varphi) \end{cases} \tag{2}$$

where *arc* is calculated as

$$arc = R\varphi \tag{3}$$

Therefore, the distance difference $[x_{err} \quad y_{err}]^T$ between the virtual dynamic tracking point B and the leader A can be obtained through the distance $[\Delta x \quad \Delta y]^T$ set for the formation.

The transformation matrix for converting from the formation coordinate system $x_f O_f y_f$ to the ground coordinate system $x_g O_g y_g$ is

$$L_{gf} = \begin{bmatrix} \cos \psi_L & \sin \psi_L \\ -\sin \psi_L & \cos \psi_L \end{bmatrix} \tag{4}$$

where ψ_L is the angle between the two vector axes Ox_f and Ox_g.

Then, the coordinate difference between points A and B in the ground coordinate system is

$$\begin{bmatrix} x'_{err} \\ y'_{err} \end{bmatrix} = L_{gf} \begin{bmatrix} x_{err} \\ y_{err} \end{bmatrix} \tag{5}$$

As can be seen, the coordinates of point B are

$$\begin{bmatrix} x'_L \\ y'_L \end{bmatrix} = \begin{bmatrix} x_L - x'_{err} \\ y_L - y'_{err} \end{bmatrix} \tag{6}$$

Letting the distance difference between points B and C be $[P_x \quad P_y]^T$, we obtain

$$\begin{bmatrix} p_x \\ p_y \end{bmatrix} = \begin{bmatrix} x_F - x'_L \\ y_F - y'_L \end{bmatrix} \tag{7}$$

The key to designing the guidance law for the wingmen in the formation is to convert the relative distances between the UAVs and the target tracking points, the velocity vector deviations, the heading deviations, and other information into guidance commands. The algorithm for the guidance law can be designed using either geometric methods or control-theory methods. The former use the geometric relationship between UAV and target point to design the guidance law, characterized by convenient analysis and simulation; geometric methods are the ones used most commonly in engineering practice.

The geometric parallel-approach method is used as the guidance law for cooperative formation. The parallel-approach method was designed originally for missile interception and attacking targets, and the resulting trajectories are relatively straight. The specific implementation of the parallel-approach method herein is to keep the line of sight from UAV to target point unchanged during flight, and the line-of-sight angle forms a set of parallel lines in space, as shown in Figure 3.

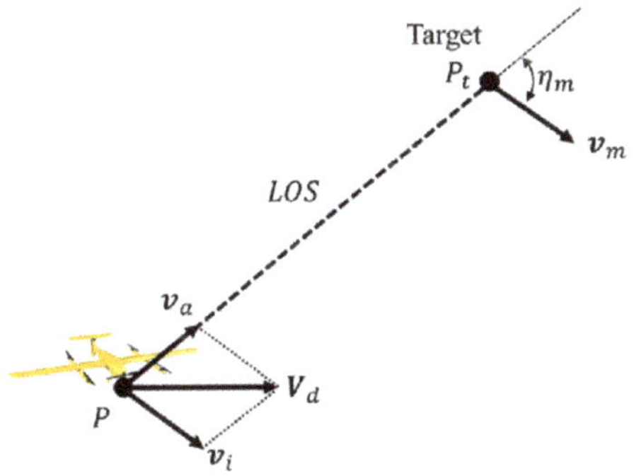

Figure 3. Schematic of guidance by parallel-approach method.

In Figure 3, v_m is the velocity vector of the UAV tracking the target point whose azimuth angle is η_m. The velocity vector V_d of the UAV has components v_i that are equal to v_m, i.e.,

$$v_i = v_m \tag{8}$$

In the formation of the lead-aircraft–wingman control mode selected herein, the lead aircraft sends real-time status information through an airborne data link, and the wingmen in the formation obtain v_m and η_m of the lead aircraft through calculation.

The realization of the parallel-approach method in this paper is to keep the line-of-sight angle q between the wingman and the dynamic tracking point unchanged during the flight. In the ground coordinate system, the line-of-sight angle between the wingman and the dynamic tracking point is ψ_e, and the angle between the velocity vector and the line-of-sight direction is defined as the lead angle, as shown in Figure 4. Then, the flight speed of the wingman is V_F, the speed azimuth is ψ_F, and the lead angle is η_F; the flight speed of the dynamic tracking point is $V_L{}'$, the speed azimuth is $\psi_F{}'$, and the lead angle is $\eta_F{}'$. The horizontal straight-line distance between the wingman and the dynamic tracking point is d_{horiz}.

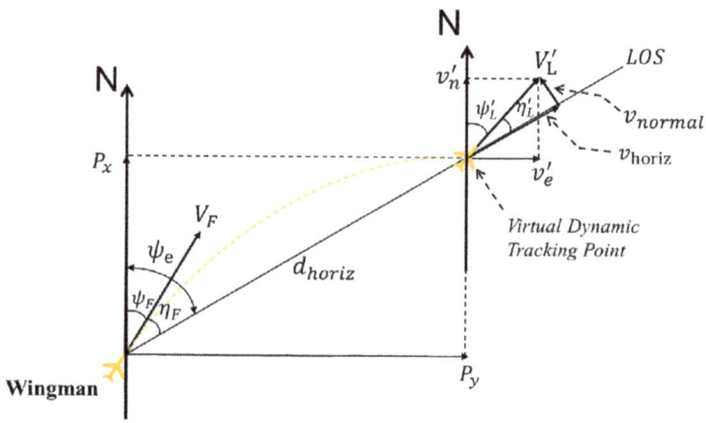

Figure 4. Relationship between wingman and dynamic tracking point.

The following geometric relationships exist between the lead angle, velocity azimuth angle, and line-of-sight angle of the wingman and the dynamic tracking point:

$$\begin{cases} \eta_F = \psi_e - \psi_F \\ \eta_L' = \psi_e - \psi_L' \end{cases} \tag{9}$$

The relative motion speed $\dot{d}_{horiz}$ of the wingman and the dynamic tracking point is

$$\dot{d}_{horiz} = V_F \cos\eta_F - V_L' \cos\eta_L' \tag{10}$$

The change law of the line-of-sight angle between the wingman and the dynamic tracking point is

$$\dot{\psi}_e = \frac{1}{d_{horiz}}(V_L' \sin\eta_L' - V_F \sin\eta_F) \tag{11}$$

These two formulas are the guiding equations of the parallel-approach method.
The constraints of the equation are:

$$\varepsilon = \dot{\psi}_e = 0 \tag{12}$$

In the formula, ψ_e can be calculated from the position of the wingman and the position of the dynamic tracking point. As shown in Figure 2, the coordinate difference between points B and C is $[P_x \quad P_y]^T$, and the positional relationship is shown in Figure 4, then the calculation of ψ_e is

$$\psi_e = \arctan\frac{P_y}{P_x} \tag{13}$$

$V_L' \sin\eta_L'$ is the projection of the velocity of the dynamic tracking point in the normal direction of the line of sight, v_{normal}, shown in Figure 4, using the calculation method of vector dot product. Let the position difference vector $P = [P_x \quad P_y]^T$ between the wingman and the virtual dynamic point, the speed vector of the virtual dynamic point is $v = [v_n{}' \quad v_e{}']^T$, then $Pv = |P||v|\cos\eta_L{}'$, where $|v|\cos\eta_L{}'$ is the speed of the dynamic virtual point $V_L{}'$ on the vector P Tangential projection of v_{horiz}.

$$v_{horiz} = |v|\cos\eta_L' = \frac{(P_x v_n' + P_y v_e')}{|P|} \tag{14}$$

The vector of velocity v_{horiz} is expressed as

$$v_{horiz} = \begin{bmatrix} \frac{P_x v_{horiz}}{|P|} & \frac{P_y v_{horiz}}{|P|} \end{bmatrix}^T \tag{15}$$

The normal projection velocity vector of the velocity V_L' of the dynamic virtual point on the vector $\vec{P}$ is denoted as $v_{normal} = v - v_{horiz}$. The modulus of v_{normal} is recorded as $|v_{normal}|$, which is the numerical value of $|v_{normal}|$, and the expected heading control command of the wingman can be obtained as

$$\psi_{Fc} = \psi_e - \arcsin\frac{|v_{normal}|}{V_F} \tag{16}$$

2.2. *Simulation Verification of Guidance Law*

Here, we introduce the method of using software modeling and simulation to simulate the built formation model, which is an effective way to test the algorithm's robustness and provide data support for the subsequent actual flight. The specific method is to model the stand-alone control models of the lead plane and the wingmen under MATLAB/Simulink and perform modular encapsulation processing to facilitate the subsequent expansion of the formation scale. At the same time, the guidance-law part is also modeled to simulate the control of the aircraft by the guidance law and the control law during actual flight. Finally, the aircraft's control, trajectory, and attitude parameters are output for subsequent data analysis and visual trajectory analysis.

2.2.1. Construction of Simulation Model

The guidance-law simulation is mainly to verify the performance of the guidance-law module. Here, we establish a particle model of a sample UAV. The channel dynamics of the leader and wingman control models are simulated using transfer functions, and their response is the same as the current design control. The law remains the same. Each control channel of the UAV in the particle model can respond to the command signal given by the guidance law in time and at the same time directly output basic information such as altitude, speed, and attitude angle. The output form is convenient for subsequent analysis of the simulated flight trajectory.

The lateral-heading control channel's modeling involves the roll-angle-rate control loop as a first-order inertial link because bank-to-turn is used in control herein to control the heading channel. Therefore, the modeling of the heading channel can be realized based on the roll channel and on the complex number field; the physical relationship is

$$\psi(s) = \frac{g \tan\phi}{v_g}\frac{1}{s} \tag{17}$$

where ψ is the heading angle, ϕ is the roll angle, v_g is the target speed, and g is the acceleration of gravity.

As shown in Figure 5, the model input is the roll-angle command ϕ_c of the formation guidance-law module, and the outputs are the UAV model's roll angle and heading angle. The intermediate variable of the control channel is the control of the angular roll rate, and we use a first-order transfer function with a bandwidth of $\omega_n = 6$ to simulate the dynamics of the angular-rate channel.

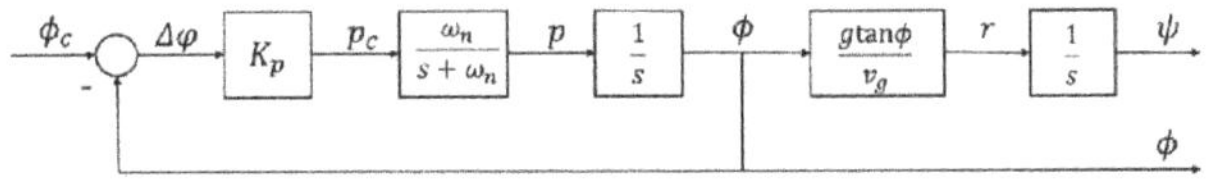

Figure 5. Attitude control modeling of lateral-heading channel.

The modeling of the longitudinal pitch control channel involves regarding the pitch-angle-rate control loop as a first-order inertial link, as shown in Figure 6. The input is the pitch-angle command θ_c of the formation guidance-law module, and the output is the pitch angle of the UAV model. The intermediate variable of the control channel is the pitch rate, and the modeling uses a first-order transfer function with a bandwidth of $\omega_n = 7$ to simulate the dynamics of the angular-rate channel.

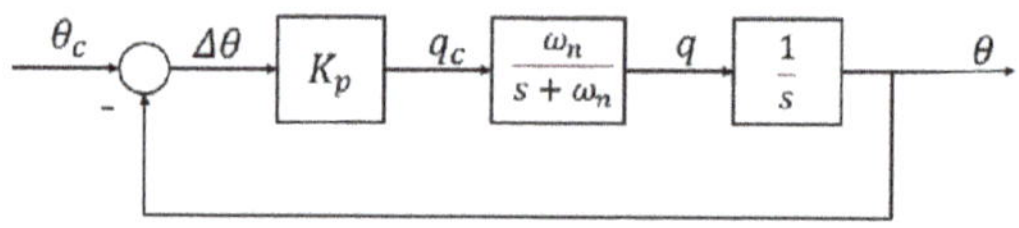

Figure 6. Attitude control modeling of pitch channel.

The longitudinal velocity control channel is modeled by considering acceleration as a first-order inertial link, as shown in Figure 7. The input is the target-speed command v_{gc} of the formation guidance-law module, and the output is the indicated airspeed of the UAV model currently flying. The acceleration is modeled using a first-order transfer function with a bandwidth of $\omega_n = 3$ to simulate its dynamics.

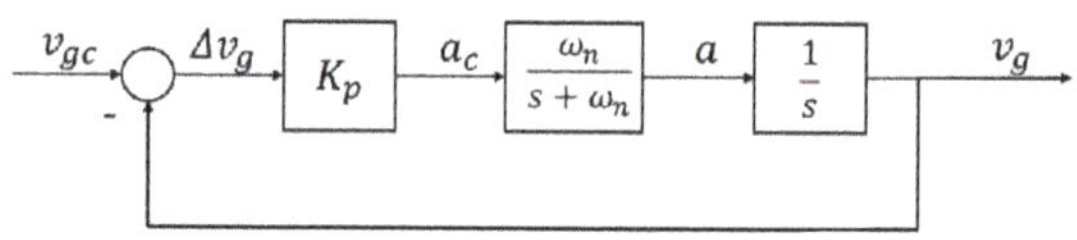

Figure 7. Control modeling of velocity channel.

2.2.2. Results of Simulation of Guidance Law

The formation guidance law can be simulated by building the leader–follower formation simulation model. The intermediate variables of the flight trajectory and guidance law are stored temporarily in the MATLAB workspace, and various output data can be visualized and analyzed by graph-drawing scripts.

The core index of the guidance law of the parallel-approach method is the tracking effect of the heading channel. Figure 8 shows the dynamic change in the heading angles and velocities of the leader and the three wingmen with time. When the heading of the leader changes rapidly, the heading channels of the three wingmen respond and track it in time. When the lead plane's heading becomes stable, the wingmen follow it smoothly after a small amount of overshoot in time.

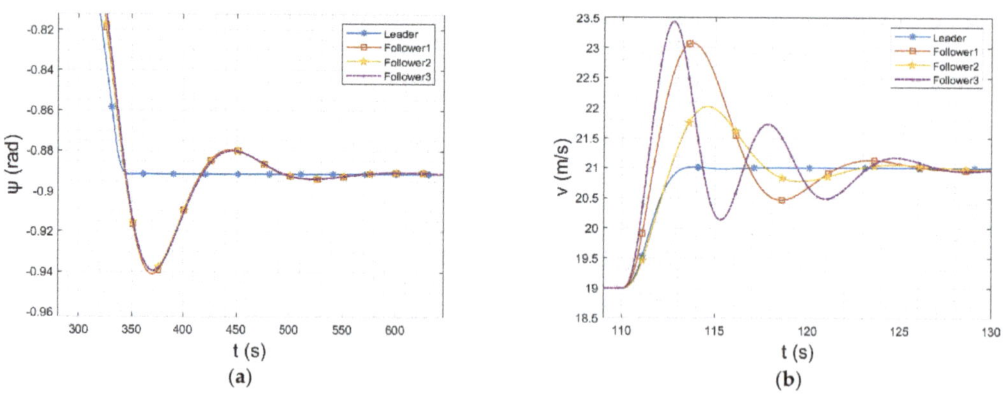

Figure 8. Tracking effect of wingman: (**a**) time histories of the heading angle; (**b**) time histories of the velocities.

In summary, the guidance law designed herein leads to a good formation and meets the requirements of fast response and stable tracking. Therefore, it can be used in the subsequent semiphysical simulation and actual flight.

3. Formation Management and Control

The flight mission of the leader in the cooperative formation [16–18] is described by a set of waypoints known as a waypoint list. After switching to fixed-wing mode, the lead pilot executes a mission route consisting of waypoints, flying to each waypoint in the list in turn. Before the wingmen enter formation mode, there are also waypoints to maintain normal fixed-wing flight. The waypoints in the lead waypoint list are represented using the position vector

$$p_i = (x_i, y_i, z_i)^T, \tag{18}$$

and those of the wingman is represented by the position vector

$$p_{fi} = (x_i, y_i, z_i + d_z i)^T, \tag{19}$$

where d_z is the cross-track error of the wingman waypoint relative to the leader in the vertical direction, thereby allowing calculation of the list of waypoints that each wingman flies before entering formation mode.

The cooperative formation-management method [19–22] herein involves the lead plane flying in formation with the wingmen in the link by managing a set of cooperative waypoints. The lead plane coordinates and moves the set of waypoints when formation changes are required. As shown in Figure 9, a group of parallel cooperative path points is generated by the wingmen following the leader, and a straight formation is formed.

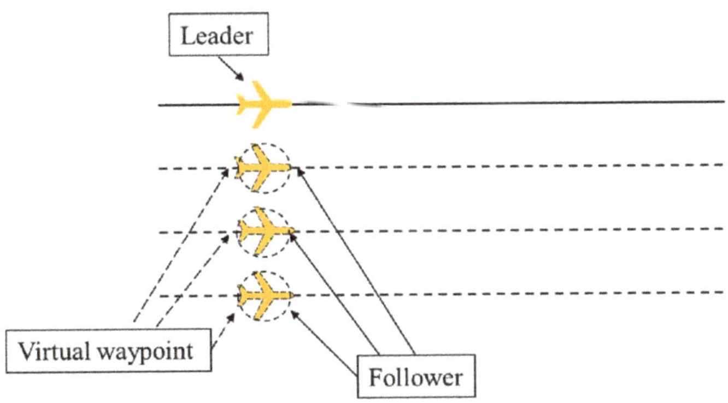

Figure 9. Schematic of linear formation for collaborative waypoint management.

3.1. Formation Keeping Based on Coordinated Waypoints

The formation maintenance of cooperative formations is studied in the formation coordinate system. As the coordinator, the lead aircraft generates a list of cooperating waypoints by adjusting their positions, and it sends it to the corresponding wingmen in the link through the intermachine communication module. The wingmen then extract the corresponding waypoints from the list of cooperative waypoints assigned by the lead plane according to its own, thereby realizing coordinated formation flight. Based on this method, we design the following three types of formation.

1. Linear formation. In the formation coordinate system, the position coordinates of the lead aircraft are (0, 0), those of the first cooperative path point are (0, x_{offset}), and those of the other i cooperative path points are (0, $x_{offset} \times i$). We then construct the list of cooperative waypoints for a straight-line formation. Figure 10 shows the relationship of coordinated waypoints in straight horizontal formation.

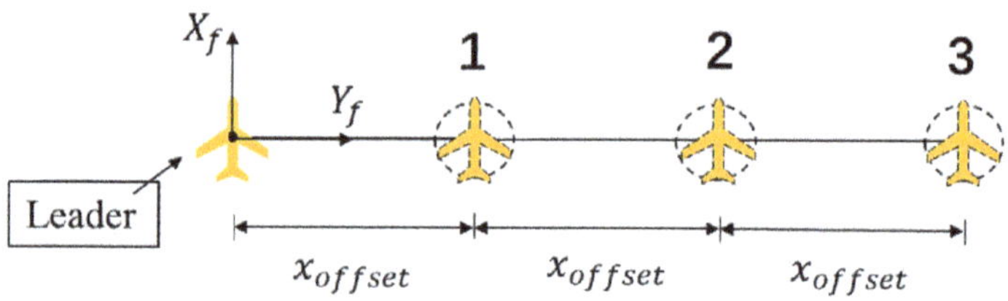

Figure 10. Relationship of coordinated waypoints in straight horizontal formation.

2. Triangular formation. In the formation coordinate system, the position coordinates of the lead aircraft are (0, 0), and there are at most $(2n-1)$ cooperative waypoints in n lines, i.e., one line has one cooperative waypoint, and two lines have three cooperative waypoints. The y-axis coordinate interval between every two rows of collaborative path points is y_{offset}, and the x-axis coordinate interval between every two columns of collaborative path points is x_{offset}. A list of cooperating waypoints for a triangular formation can be constructed from this. Figure 11 shows the relationships of cooperating waypoints in horizontal triangular formations.

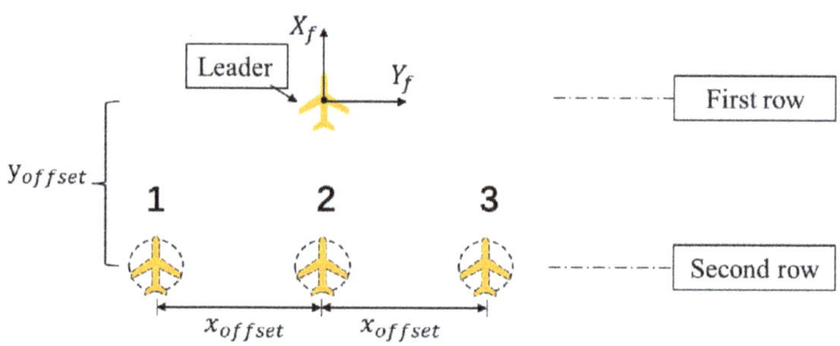

Figure 11. Relationship of cooperating waypoints in horizontal triangular formation.

3. Stepped formation. A stepped formation is 3D, and in the formation coordinate system, the position coordinates of the leader are (0, 0) and each line has only one collaborative path point. As shown in the plan view of the stepped formation in Figure 12, the y-axis coordinate interval between every two rows of cooperative waypoints in the horizontal direction is y_{offset}, and the x-axis coordinate interval between every two columns of cooperative waypoints is x_{offset}. The side view of the stepped formation in Figure 13 shows that in the vertical direction, the z-axis coordinate interval between every two rows of cooperative path points is z_{offset}, and the z-axis coordinate interval between every two columns of cooperative path points is x_{offset}. A list of cooperating waypoints for the stepped formation can be constructed from this.

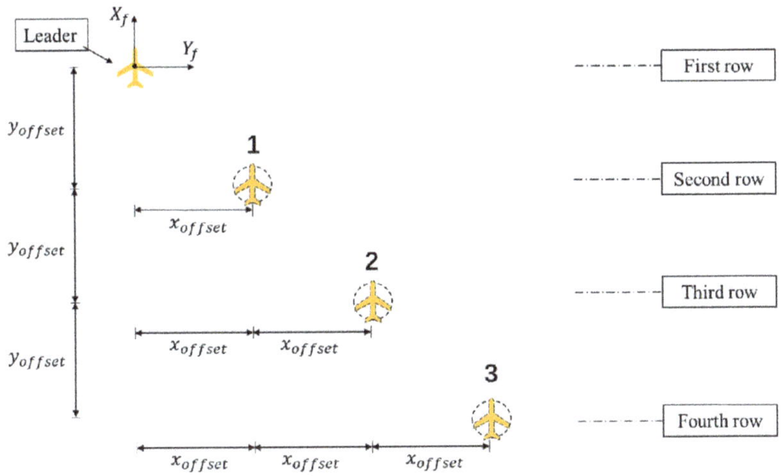

Figure 12. Plan view of relationship among coordination waypoints for stepped formation.

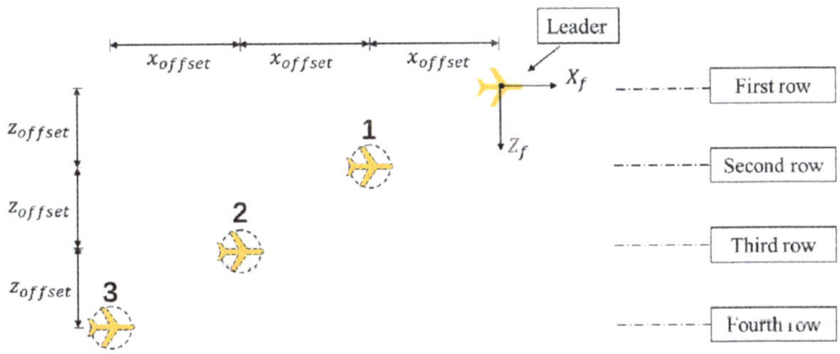

Figure 13. Side view of relationship among coordination waypoints for stepped formation.

The formations mentioned above are three common ones in which the target tracking position can be determined by moving several waypoints on the spatial geometric position. Each wingman invokes the guidance-law algorithm according to its position and the positional relationship with the reference cooperative waypoint, and it controls the speed and attitude of its UAV to reach the desired position and form a specific formation.

3.2. Research on Formation Transformation Method of Cooperative Formation

In many mission scenarios, UAVs must form different formations to adapt to changes in the mission, which requires research on changes of collaborative formations. After creating a coordinated formation, the UAVs will continue to fly in the existing formation until a new mission requirement arises. Herein, a command from the ground-station software initiates a change in formation. For the coordinated formation of fixed-wing UAVs, the under-actuation and control limitations of the fixed-wing make it impossible to form trajectories from all initial positions to the desired formation; the only possible trajectories involve movement that maintains normal airspeed while approaching the desired location. Additionally, the intermediate transition process of cooperative formation change is very important [23–26], and it is necessary to consider possible collisions in the process of short-range formation change. According to the control strategy of formation keeping, we design a method for changing formation while also preventing collisions.

Before discussing the formation transformation method, we define the standard for forming a close-range formation. The current position of the center of mass of each wingman is p_i, which includes the 3D position information, i.e.,

$$p_i = (x_{fi}, y_{fi}, z_{fi})^T \tag{20}$$

The location of each collaborative waypoint is

$$w_i = (x_{wi}, y_{wi}, z_{wi})^T \tag{21}$$

and the position error distance d_{err} of a wingman and a cooperative waypoint in the horizontal direction determines whether the formation forms a tight formation on the $X_f O_f Y_f$ surface, where

$$d_{err} = \sqrt{(x_{fi} - x_{wi})^2 + (y_{fi} - y_{wi})^2} \tag{22}$$

We define the variable k to indicate whether the cooperative formation has formed a tight formation; $k = 0$ means that a wingman has not reached the cooperative target waypoint in the horizontal direction, whereas $k = 1$ implies that the wingman has reached the cooperative target waypoint in the horizontal direction and is now partnered with the leader. The value of k is judged by the relay method, with the judgment condition depending on the position error distance d_{err} between the wingman position and the cooperative path point; we have

$$k = \begin{cases} 0, if(d_{err} > r_{\max}) \\ 1, if(d_{err} \le r_{\max}) \end{cases} \tag{23}$$

where r_{max} is the distance difference between judging whether the wingman reaches the cooperative path point, which is related to the UAV's wingspan and formation spacing; for the actual flight, we use $r_{\max} = 2m$.

The formation transformation method [27–30] for cooperative formation proposed herein involves performing formation transformation in the horizontal direction first and then in the vertical direction when the wingmen in the horizontal direction reach the constraint condition of close formation. The specific method is when it means that the wingman has not yet reached the cooperative target waypoint in the horizontal direction, and the control of the altitude channel is the height of the wingman waypoint, which means that the formation has completed the close formation in the horizontal direction. At this time, the wingmen set the control target of the altitude channel. To correspond to the heights of the cooperative waypoints, the transformation process is as shown in Figure 14.

As an example to illustrate the process of formation transformation, we take the transformation from a linear formation to a stepped formation. As shown in Figure 15, the formation keeps flying in a straight formation until time t_1, and it begins to adjust the flight altitude of each wingman to the corresponding waypoint altitude. At time t_2, the lead plane starts to redistribute the list information of the cooperative waypoints, transforming from a linear formation to a stepped one. At time t_3, the positions of the cooperative waypoints are reassigned, and the wingmen begin to track the new cooperative waypoints. At time t_4, the horizontal direction satisfies the constraints for a tight formation. After that, the vertical formation height control is carried out to meet the corresponding vertical spacing requirements of the stepped formation. After this, the formation has completed a transformation. The advantage of this method is that in the formation transformation process, it effectively reduces the probability of collision between the UAVs in short-range formation.

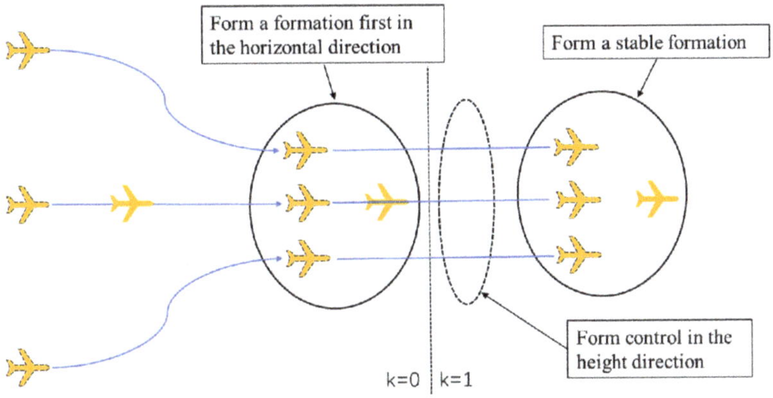

Figure 14. Schematic of formation transformation process.

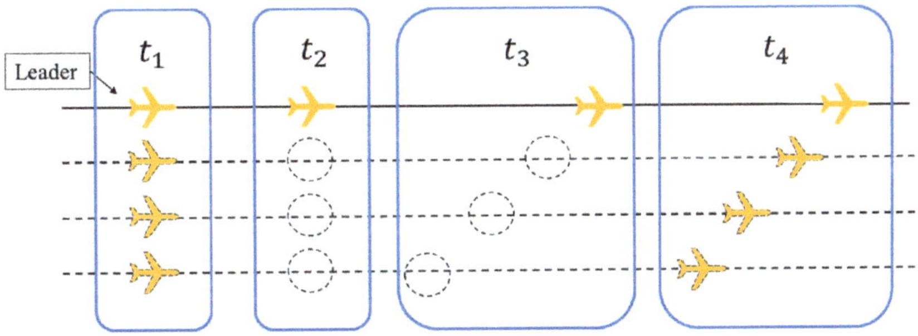

Figure 15. Example of formation change process.

4. Formation Reconfiguration Strategy

The coordinated formation of UAVs involves some complex flight environments; there is a certain probability that some UAVs will suffer structural damage or power failure during the flight mission. Some complex electromagnetic environments may also cause the loss of communication links. These contingencies must be incorporated into the formation control strategy to complete the established formation flight mission.

To this end, we design a formation reconstruction strategy for some typical unexpected situations, which we divide into two types: (i) data-link topology damage and (ii) UAV self-failure. The data links use the mesh networking mode with antidestruction characteristics for this topic. In cases where there is no direct path between the transmitting node and the target node, automatic path searching can be enabled to find and provide path information to ensure that data are delivered to the destination node. By discovering unknown paths automatically and using the best one to transfer the data to the expected destination effectively, the redundancy of the data channel can be maintained when the data-link topology is damaged. As shown in Figure 16, there are multiple redundant channels for the communication between each UAV and the others. Taking the communication connection from vehicle A to vehicle C as an example, there are three paths in the link that can reach vehicle C, i.e., ABC, AFC, and AEDC; therefore, if the communication of a node is damaged, it will not affect the data transmission from vehicle A to vehicle C.

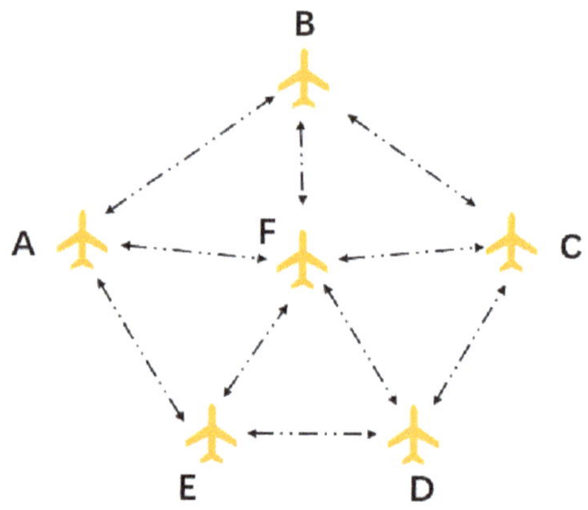

Figure 16. Data-link survivable network architecture.

Failure of a UAV itself is divided into (i) lead-aircraft failure and (ii) wingman failure. In the coordinated formation of leader–follower mode, all the wingmen receive the position information of the leader in real-time. When more than λ communication cycles, the wingman still does not receive the leader's data, and the leader is considered to be damaged. The follower with the minimum ID number in the link then acts as the leader; the other wingmen begin to receive the control information from the new leader, who also begins to output the list of cooperative waypoints.

In coordinated formation flight in leader–wingman mode, the wingmen far outnumber the leader, so the probability of a wingman being damaged is higher. When flying in a coordinated formation, the lead plane maintains a status table of whether each wingman is online. This status table is calculated based on the heartbeat packets sent by the wingmen to the lead plane. The specific logic is as follows: if the lead plane continues to receive a wingman's heartbeat packet for time T_{min}, then add this wingman to the online status table; if the lead plane does not receive a wingman's heartbeat packet for time T_{max}, then remove this wingman from the online status table. Here, T_{min} is the shortest time for the lead plane and a wingman to establish a stable connection, and T_{max} is the longest waiting time for the lead plane and a wingman to lose the connection; these two times are set according to the specific indicators of the data links. Therefore, when a wingman loses connection, the leader must remove it from the online status table, and the formation's coordinated waypoint list is also adjusted accordingly. As shown in Figure 17, if vehicle 2 is damaged, then vehicle 3 moves to take its place.

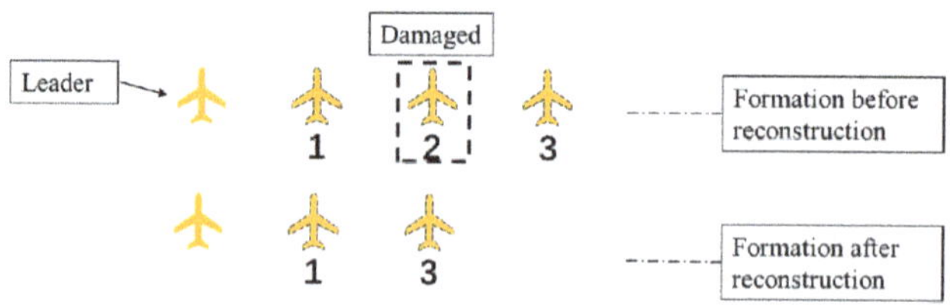

Figure 17. Schematic of formation reconstruction.

5. Hardware-In-The-Loop Simulation

5.1. System Composition

The semiphysical simulation system consisted of a simulation machine, a flight-control system, ground-station telemetry software, trajectory display software, and data-link communication equipment. The relationship among the different approaches is shown in Figure 18. The nonlinear six-degrees-of-freedom dynamic model of the UAV ran in the simulator, and the flight-control computer received the model data of the simulator for calculation. The command signal was output to the simulator to control the model. The data links were responsible for the communication between the flight-control computers and the ground-station software. The latter was divided into a display area and a command area: the display area displayed status information about the UAV flight, while the command area contained common remote-control commands to control the UAV formation. Finally, the Tacview trajectory-display software can display the flight trajectories of all the UAVs in the formation, thereby showing the formation more intuitively.

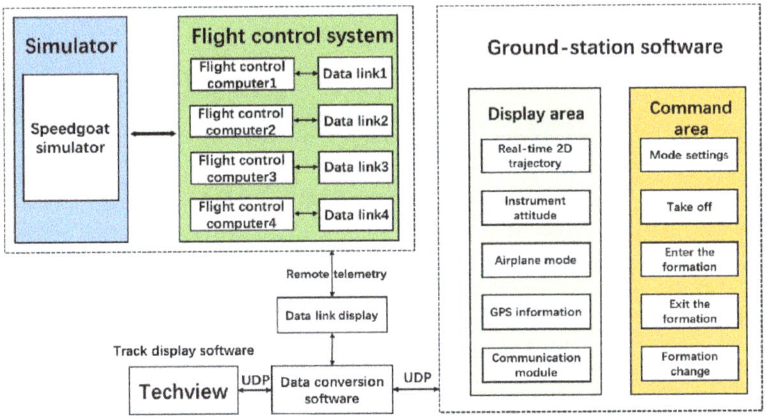

Figure 18. Relationship among all systems in hardware-in-the-loop simulation.

The equipment connection relationship of the constructed semiphysical simulation system is shown in Figure 19. The simulation machine used the Speedgoat real-time simulation platform. The ground-station computer was responsible for starting the simulator, running the ground-station software, and establishing communication with the simulator through network protocols. The ground-station computer was connected to a communication node of the data communication link to establish wireless communication with all flight-control computers participating in the simulation; communication between the simulator and the flight-control computers was carried out through an RS422 serial port.

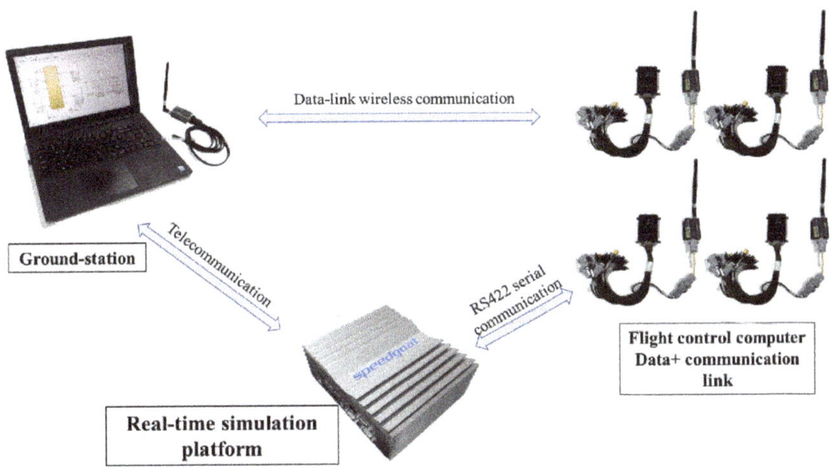

Figure 19. Device connection diagram for hardware-in-the-loop simulation.

The Speedgoat real-time simulation system is the official hardware platform of MATLAB/Simulink, and its operating system and software were developed by MathWorks and integrates MATLAB/Simulink seamlessly. The simulation system used an Intel processor and had powerful computing ability. All the logic was written in Simulink, and there was no need to write much code; the model could also be converted directly into real-time code for execution. This project used the Baseline-S basic-version simulator from Speedgoat, which is small and easy to move, weighing only 2.56 kg. It has two RS232 ports and three USB ports, which can be connected to multiple UAVs simultaneously.

The flight-control computer and the data communication links constituted the flight-control system. We used four sets of flight-control systems to simulate the formation of four aircraft. Each control system was connected to the Speedgoat real-time simulation system, receiving simulation data and controlling the dynamic model running in the simulator. The data communication links click the four sets of flight-control computers with the ground-station computers for networking communication.

5.2. Semiphysical Simulation Process

The flight-control system had to be started first to perform semiphysical simulation. After establishing a connection with the ground-station software, we set the flight-control system to the hardware-in-the-loop simulation mode, we then started the Speedgoat simulator, whereupon the UAV model in the simulator started to run and output data to the flight-control computer. After the ground-station software had checked that the flight-control computer system was in a normal state, each UAV model took off in sequence, and then a formation start command was sent in fixed-wing mode to enter the formation simulation verification.

The semiphysical simulation was a desktop simulation verification link before the actual flight test in the field, and it was necessary to test the scenes used in the flight accordingly. Herein, we report the semiphysical simulation of the following scenarios.

- Case 1: Simulation of formation-mode flight

This simulation was aimed at multiple UAVs flying in cooperative formation, with a two-aircraft formation and a four-aircraft formation used as the research objects to conduct semiphysical simulations. The specific operation was for each UAV to takeoff according to the process and enter the fixed. Start the coordinated formation flight mode after the wings are in the state. Figure 20 shows the simulation results from the perspectives of the ground station (Figure 20a) and the Tacview trajectory-display software (Figure 20b) in cooperative formation mode. As can be seen, each wingman maintained a fixed distance from the leader to fly cooperatively.

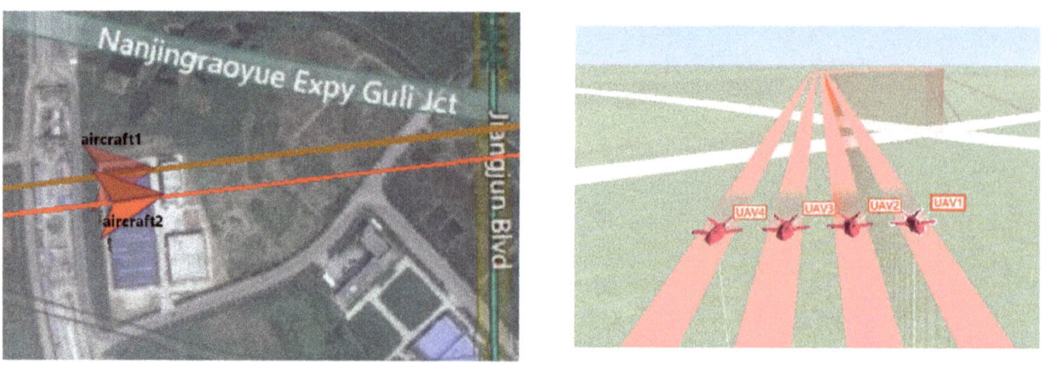

(a) (b)

Figure 20. Hardware-in-the-loop simulation: (**a**) ground-station perspective; (**b**) Tacview software perspective.

- Case 2: Simulation of formation change

The simulation of formation transformation verified the proposed method for transforming the cooperative formation. First, the UAVs were operated to form a stable formation, whereupon the ground-station software issued the command for formation transformation. The transformation of the four-machine formation from the triangular formation to the stepped formation as the research object shows the transformation results in Figure 21.

(a) (b) (c)

Figure 21. Three-dimensional view of hardware-in-the-loop simulation of formation transformation: (**a**) triangular formation; (**b**) formation in the middle of changing; (**c**) stepped formation.

The position changes in the formation transformation simulation are related to the formation before and after the transformation, as shown in Figure 22, where the ordinate is the position difference between wingman and leader during formation flight. During triangular formation flight, the three wingmen were distributed behind the leader: follower 2 was the closest to the leader and was located directly behind it, and followers 1 and 3 were on either side of follower 2. After the formation had changed to the stepped formation, the three followers were distributed evenly on one side of the leader plane in turn and flew at fixed distances; follower 3 was on the outermost side of the formation and farthest from the lead plane. Figure 22 shows that the trajectories of position movement during the formation transformation were relatively stable with no rapid jumps.

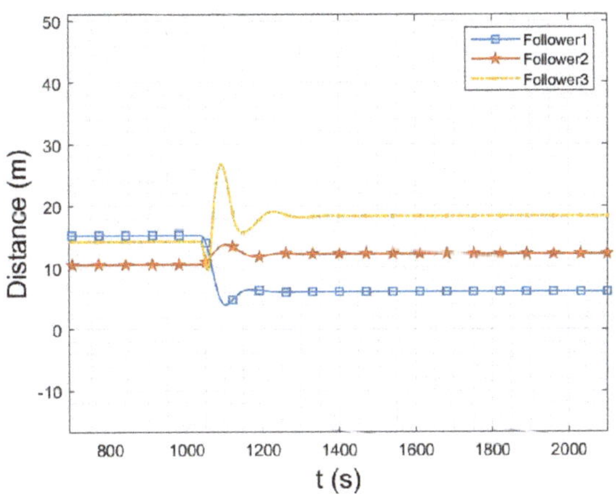

Figure 22. Changes of positions of wingmen relative to leader in formation change.

The formation transformation simulation also verifies the guidance law's response characteristics to changes regarding the guidance target. The most important parameter to change is the heading angle. In this semiphysical simulation, the lead plane and the wingmen kept the same heading and flew parallel in the triangular formation. The formation management module generated a new path tracking point after receiving the formation change command, and the wingman guidance law guided the UAVs to the unique path tracking point, which mainly produced changes in the heading angle. Having completed the formation change, the lead plane and the wingmen flew in the new stepped formation and kept the same heading while flying in parallel. Figure 23 shows the evolution of heading angle in the formation change. As can be seen, the wingman heading angle changed rapidly after the command to change the formation, and the wingman heading converged quickly upon completion of the formation change.

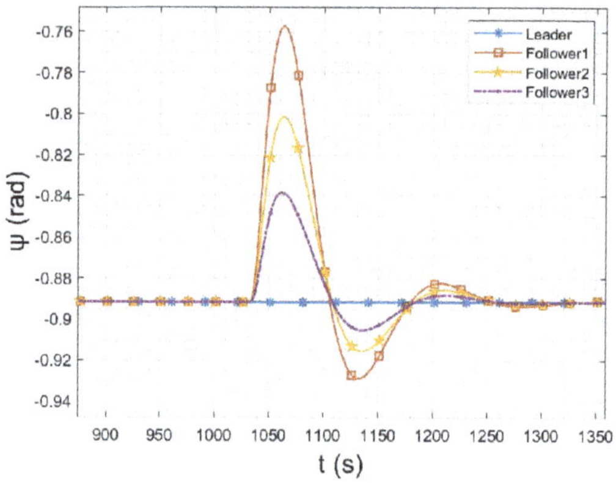

Figure 23. Change in heading angle during formation transformation.

6. Actual Flight Verification

6.1. Flight Platform and Ground Measurement and Control System

The UAVs used in the test are electric vertical takeoff and landing aircraft (eVTOL). The aircraft in this layout can takeoff and land vertically with the rotor, thereby extending the total flight time, which can fly in the air for a long time to verify the control method proposed in this paper. As shown in Figure 24, it adopts the layout of large wingspan and high flat tail. The wingspan is 2.2 m and the takeoff weight is 6 kg. The main parameters of the UAV are shown in Table 1.

Figure 24. Electric vertical takeoff and landing aircraft.

Table 1. The main parameters of the UAV.

Item	Parameter
Mass (kg)	6.0
Reference area (m^2)	0.46
Reference span (m)	2.2
Cruising speed (m/s)	20
Maximum airspeed (m/s)	23
Minimum airspeed (m/s)	17

As the best way to show the practicality of the designed control method, the actual flight test in the field was the final verification link of the fixed-wing UAV cooperative formation control method intended herein. The main equipment involved in the real flight test was the UAV flight platform and the ground measurement and control system, described separately below.

The UAV flight platform comprised two categories of equipment: (i) the flight-control system comprising the flight-control computer and the data-link radio and (ii) the actuating equipment, such as motors, electric speed controllers, and steering gears. The complete equipment of the flight platform is shown in Figure 25.

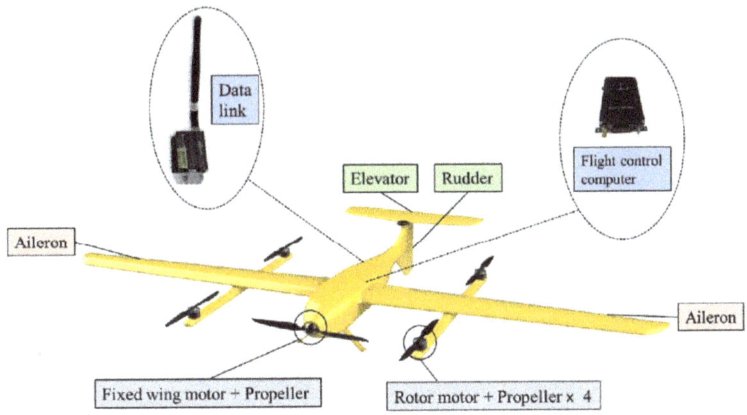

Figure 25. UAV flight platform equipment.

The main parts of the ground measurement and control system were the ground-station computer, the real-time kinematic (RTK) base station, and the data-link desktop terminal, as shown in Figure 26. Among these, the ground-station computer was the main equipment for remote control and telemetry between the ground station and the UAVs; it was responsible for checking the real-time status of the UAVs and sending control instructions. The RTK base station generated differential positioning data; coordinated formation flight requires high positioning accuracy. The differential data generated by the base station were transmitted to the flight-control computer through the data link to enable the drones to enter positioning mode with centimeter-level accuracy. The desktop end of the data link was a node of the data link, and this node was connected to the ground-station computer, securing the ground-station software to the entire communication link.

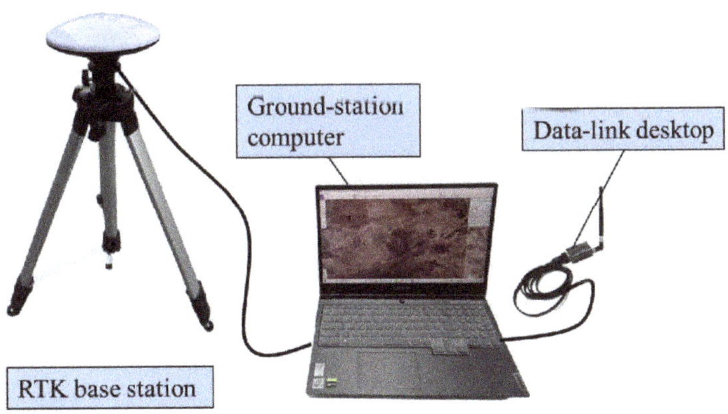

Figure 26. Connections of ground measurement and control system.

The UAV flight platform and the ground measurement and control system were the core equipment of the formation flight test. Figure 27 shows the equipment connection for the four-machine formation flight test, where a dotted line is a wireless connection between data links. The ground-station system monitored the status of each UAV flight platform in real-time during flight and also initiated some control commands, such as opening, changing, and closing the formation.

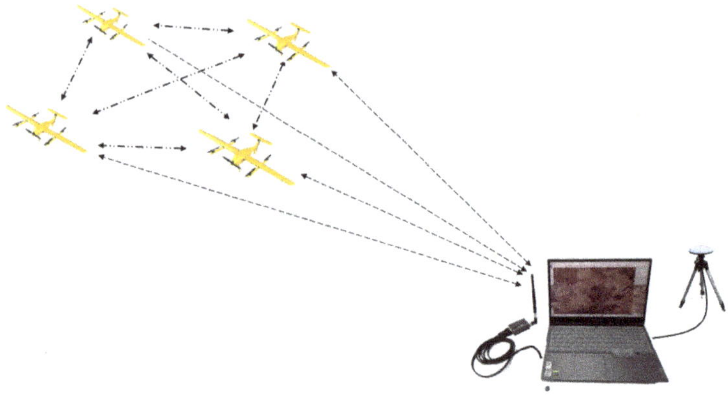

Figure 27. Connections of formation test equipment.

6.2. *Formation Flight Test*

The outdoor flight test reported herein involved a four-aircraft formation. Figure 28 shows a photograph of the UAVs before takeoff.

Figure 28. Photograph of four-plane coordinated formation before takeoff.

First, each UAV was placed at a fixed takeoff point and a power-on operation was performed. After the flight-control computer system was initialized, the ground station began to detect the states of the UAVs. If any of the drones did not meet the takeoff status, the status of all the drones was rechecked until the takeoff conditions were met. Send the takeoff command, then all drones enter the fixed-wing mode, when all drones are flying to the right place. The station sends the "open formation" command, and the drones enter the cooperative formation flight mode. At this time, the command was sent to change the cooperative formation, and the flight modes of the wingmen in the tight formation were changed according to the flight requirements. After the formation test was completed, the ground station sent a "close formation" command, whereupon the leader and wingmen exited the coordinated formation mode, flew along their respective routes, and finally returned to their takeoff points for recovery (Figure 29).

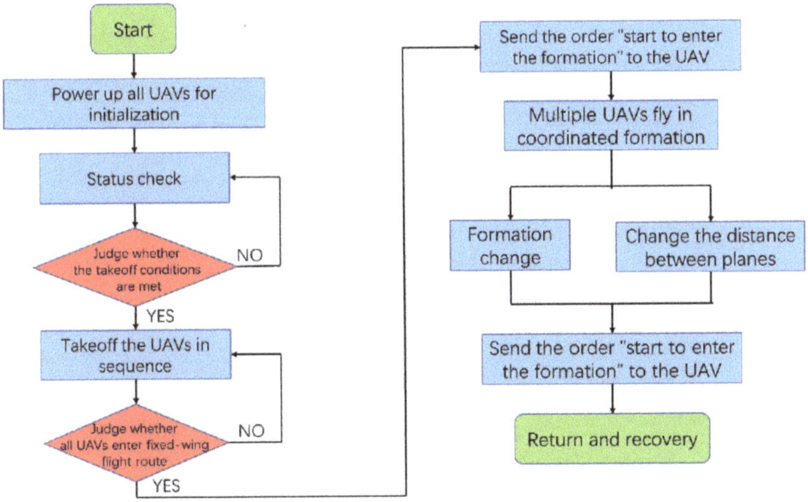

Figure 29. Flow chart of formation flight test.

The ground-station software was connected to the communication links of the UAVs through the ground data-link node, and it was responsible for real-time communication with all the UAVs in the formation to (i) monitor their status during the flight, (ii) send the takeoff and landing instructions to each aircraft, and (iii) send the mission instructions, among other duties. The flight-control interface of the ground-station software is shown in Figure 30.

Figure 30. Flight interface of ground-station software.

In the figure, the corresponding commands can be sent to the drone through the control panel. The status of the current drone can be seen in the attitude instrument and flight parameter information in the upper-right corner.

The command panel of the ground-station software was the main functional area for controlling the flight of the UAVs, including the command areas related to (i) single-aircraft takeoff and landing and (ii) formation. The instructions for single-aircraft takeoff and landing are to complete the takeoff and landing of a single UAV, including unlocking, locking, takeoff, and landing. The formation commands control the opening and closing of the formation mode and set the formation parameters after the UAVs entered the fixed-wing flight state; they included instructions such as turning the formation mode on and off and setting the formation shape and spacing parameters.

In this test, two types of coordinated formation flight were carried out, i.e., the stepped formation and the straight-line formation. The two formation arrangements were relatively simple but could also verify the control method of formation maintenance and change proposed herein. This outdoor flight began with a coordinated flight in a straight formation, and then the ground-station software issued the "set stepped formation" command, and the formation changed to a stepped formation and continued to fly. Figure 31 shows the actual outdoor flight conditions of the linear collaborative formation (Figure 31a) and the stepped collaborative formation (Figure 31b).

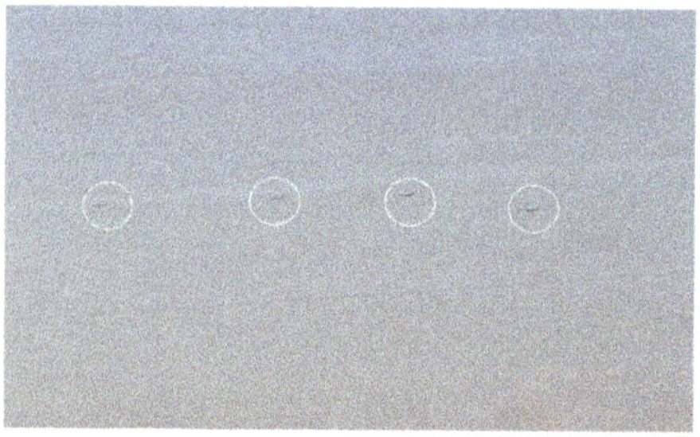
(a)

(b)

Figure 31. Photographs of actual flight of four-machine coordinated formation: (**a**) ground view of straight formation; (**b**) aerial view of stepped formation.

When it was necessary for the UAVs to return, the ground station sent the command to dissolve the formation, and all the UAVs participating in the formation exited the formation mode and automatically returned to the mission route of single-machine flight (Figure 32). Finally, the ground station sent the software command to return to the takeoff points and complete the return landing and recovery one by one.

Figure 32. UAV returning after leaving formation.

6.3. Flight Data Analysis

Analyzing the flight outcome provides direct and effective data to support the results of the outdoor flight. After the outdoor flight test was completed, the track file recorded in the flight-control computer was imported for data analysis. The data were processed in different drawing and visualization software to analyze the flight results from other dimensions.

The direct indicator of the guidance-law effect in the data is the wingman heading angle's tracking development after the guidance target change. Figure 33 shows the change curve of the heading angle of each UAV in the formation for times between 634 and 654 s in the track record file. As can be seen, when the heading angle of the leader changed, those of the wingmen responded and tracked it in time. Therefore, the response characteristics of the guidance law used herein are verified, and it is shown that the guidance-law algorithm can meet practical needs.

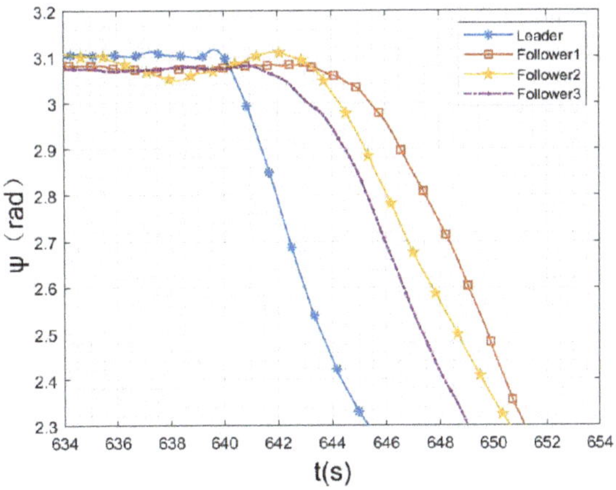

Figure 33. Control effect of actual flight-heading channels of four aircraft in cooperative formation.

Furthermore, the flight trajectory of each UAV in the formation reflects intuitively the effect of cooperative formation from the data. Figure 34a shows the 3D trajectories of the actual flight route as plotted from the data for a stable formation section. The trajectories comprise the three geographical coordinates of longitude, latitude, and altitude; the horizontal coordinates are longitude and latitude, and the vertical coordinate is altitude. As can be seen, each UAV kept a fixed distance within the allowable error range, and the UAVs flew together. Figure 34b shows the entire formation trajectory, which intuitively reflects the flying effect of the trajectory in the real scene.

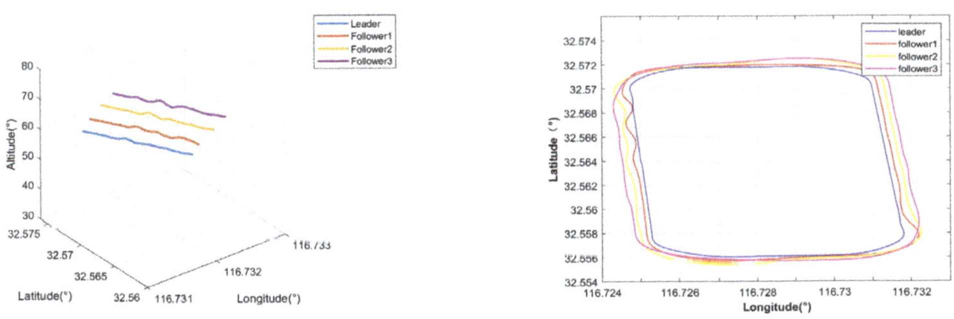

Figure 34. Three-dimensional maps of actual flight route of four-plane cooperative formation: (**a**) trajectory diagram from plotting software; (**b**) flight trajectory.

Within a certain allowable range of control error, this paper reports research on a cooperative formation control method for fixed-wing UAVs. The effect of the actual flight of the formation meets the design requirements and the requirements of formation control for some specific tasks.

7. Conclusions

The management of UAVs entering and departing from formation is an indispensable part of intelligent and information-based UAV operations. Aimed at the problem of maintaining a multi-UAV formation, reported herein was the design of a collaborative guidance law based on the classic missile-type parallel-approach method. According to (i) the flight mission characteristics of a lead aircraft following a route and wingmen following the lead aircraft and (ii) the general characteristics of the route, a guidance law was designed for three guidance modes: straight line, turning, and circling. The design of the entry and departure management of the formation led to strategies for the access and departure management of multi-machine independent assembly, dissolution, and special cases, thereby allowing effective management and control of the formation. An entry and departure adjustment strategy for special circumstances was given. The hardware-in-the-loop simulation and measured flight verification showed that the guidance law is practical in meeting UAV formation flight-control requirements for specific flight missions. Although it was tested on low-speed UAV platforms, it is still applicable to high-speed UAV platforms. Future work will focus the algorithm on high-speed platform validation.

Author Contributions: Conceptualization, G.Z. and Z.G.; methodology, G.Z.; software, G.Z. and Z.G.; validation, G.Z., Z.G. and Q.L.; formal analysis, Z.Z.; investigation, Z.Y.; resources, G.Z.; data curation, Z.W.; writing—original draft preparation, G.Z. and Z.Z.; writing—review and editing, Z.W. and Q.L.; visualization, D.Z.; supervision, Z.Y.; project administration, G.Z. All authors have read and agreed to the published version of the manuscript.

Funding: This research received no external funding.

Institutional Review Board Statement: Not applicable.

Informed Consent Statement: Not applicable.

Data Availability Statement: Data available on request due to restrictions eg privacy or ethical. The data presented in this study are available on request from the corresponding author. The data are not publicly available due to commercial use.

Conflicts of Interest: The authors declare no conflict of interest.

References

1. Bian, L.; Sun, W.; Sun, T. Trajectory Following and Improved Differential Evolution Solution for Rapid Forming of UAV Formation. *IEEE Access* **2019**, *7*, 169599–169613. [CrossRef]
2. Wang, G.; Luo, H.; Xiaohuan, H.; Huaiwei, M. A Survey on Coordinated UAV Formation Management. *Electron. Opt. Control.* **2013**, *20*, 48–53.
3. Anderson, B.; Fidan, B.; Yu, C.; Walle, D. UAV Formation Control: Theory and Application. *Lect. Notes Control. Inf. Sci.* **2008**, *371*, 15–33.
4. Zhang, J.; Yan, J. A Novel Control Approach for Flight-Stability of Fixed-Wing UAV Formation With Wind Field. *IEEE Syst. J.* **2020**, *15*, 2098–2108. [CrossRef]
5. Kada, B.; Khalid, M.; Shaikh, M.S. Distributed cooperative control of autonomous multi-agent UAV systems using smooth control. *J. Syst. Eng. Electron.* **2020**, *31*, 1297–1307. [CrossRef]
6. Wang, Y.; Yue, Y.; Shan, M.; He, L.; Wang, D. Formation Reconstruction and Trajectory Replanning for Multi-UAV Patrol. *IEEE/ASME Trans. Mechatron.* **2021**, *26*, 719–729. [CrossRef]
7. Lee, M.-Y.; Chen, B.-S.; Tsai, C.-Y.; Hwang, C.-L. Stochastic H∞ Robust Decentralized Tracking Control of Large-Scale Team Formation UAV Network System With Time-Varying Delay and Packet Dropout Under Interconnected Couplings and Wiener Fluctuations. *IEEE Access* **2021**, *9*, 41976–41997. [CrossRef]
8. Kebo, I.L.; Chen, L.; Bai, X.Z. Differential geometric modeling of guidance problem for interceptors. *Sci. China Technol. Sci.* **2011**, *54*, 13.
9. Sun, S.; Zhou, D.; Hou, W.T. A guidance law with finite time convergence accounting for autopilot lag. *Aerosp. Sci. Technol.* **2013**, *25*, 132–137. [CrossRef]
10. Wang, Y.; Shan, M.; Wang, D. Motion Capability Analysis for Multiple Fixed-Wing UAV Formations With Speed and Heading Rate Constraints. *IEEE Trans. Control. Netw. Syst.* **2019**, *7*, 977–989. [CrossRef]
11. Zhang, J.; Yan, J.; Zhang, P. Multi-UAV Formation Control Based on a Novel Back-Stepping Approach. *IEEE Trans. Veh. Technol.* **2020**, *69*, 2437–2448. [CrossRef]

12. Dong, X.; Yu, B.; Shi, Z.; Zhong, Y. Time-Varying Formation Control for Unmanned Aerial Vehicles: Theories and Applications. *IEEE Trans. Control. Syst. Technol.* **2014**, *23*, 340–348. [CrossRef]
13. Yang, J.; Wang, X.; Baldi, S.; Singh, S.; Fari, S. A software-in-the-loop implementation of adaptive formation control for fixed-wing UAVs. *IEEE/CAA J. Autom. Sin.* **2019**, *6*, 1230–1239. [CrossRef]
14. Gomez, M.B.; Gomez, B.M. Hardware-in-the-Loop Simulation. *Transp. Res. Part C Emerg. Technol.* **2001**, *12*, 73–89.
15. Ren, W.; Steurer, M.; Baldwin, T.L. Improve the Stability and the Accuracy of Power Hardware-in-the-Loop Simulation by Selecting Appropriate Interface Algorithms. In Proceedings of the Industrial & Commercial Power Systems Technical Conference IEEE, Edmonton, AB, Canada, 6–11 May 2007.
16. Duan, H.; Qiu, H. Unmanned Aerial Vehicle Distributed Formation Rotation Control Inspired by Leader-Follower Reciprocation of Migrant Birds. *IEEE Access* **2018**, *6*, 23431–23443. [CrossRef]
17. Chang, L.B.; Ng, Q.S. A flexible virtual structure formation keeping control for fixed-wing UAVs. In Proceedings of the IEEE International Conference on Control & Automation IEEE, Santiago, Chile, 19–21 December 2011.
18. Li, N.H.; Liu, H.H. Formation UAV flight control using virtual structure and motion synchronization. In Proceedings of the American Control Conference IEEE, Seattle, WA, USA, 11–13 June 2008.
19. Tanner, G.H.; Pappas, G.J.; Kumar, V. Leader-to-Formation Stability. *IEEE Trans. Robot. Autom.* **2004**, *20*, 443–455. [CrossRef]
20. Stipanovic, D.M.; Inalhan, G.; Teo, R.; Tomlin, C.J. Decentralized overlapping control of a formation of unmanned aerial vehicles. In Proceedings of the IEEE Conference on Decision & Control IEEE, Maui, HI, USA,, 9–12 December 2003.
21. Vignoni, A.; Garrelli, F.; García-Nieto, S.; Picó, J. UAV Reference Conditioning for Formation Control Via Set Invariance and Sliding Modes. *IFAC Proceeding Vol.* **2012**, *45*, 317–322. [CrossRef]
22. Liao, F.; Teo, R.; Wang, J.L.; Dong, X.; Lin, F.; Peng, K. Distributed Formation and Reconfiguration Control of VTOL UAVs. *IEEE Trans. Control. Syst. Technol.* **2017**, *25*, 270–277. [CrossRef]
23. Wei, L. Distributed UAV formation control using differential game approach. *Aerosp. Technol.* **2014**, *35*, 54–62.
24. Liu, C. Multiple UAV formation control based on consensus control structure. *J. Huazhong Univ. Sci. Technol.* **2015**, *43*, 481–485.
25. Gosiewski, Z.; Ambroziak, L. UAV Autonomous Formation Flight Experiment with Virtual Leader Control Structure. *Solid State Phenom.* **2013**, *198*, 254–259. [CrossRef]
26. Shen, D.B.; Sun, Z.; Sun, W. Leader-follower formation control without leader's velocity information. *Sci. China Inform. Sci.* **2014**, *57*, 1–12. [CrossRef]
27. Shi-Cai, L.I.U.; Da-Long, T.A.N.; Guang-Jun, L.I.U. Robust Leader-follower Formation Control of Mobile Robots Based on a Second Order Kinematics Model. *Acta Autom. Sin.* **2007**, *33*, 947–955.
28. Guo, D.; Wang, H.; Weidong, C. Image-based Leader-Follower Formation Control of Mobile Robots with Uncalibrated On-board Camera. In Proceedings of the IEEE International Conference on Robotics and Automation, Seattle, DC, USA, 26–30 May 2015.
29. Ajorlou, A.; Moezzi, K.; Aghdam, A.G., Nersesov, S.G. Two-stage time-optimal formation reconfiguration strategy. *Automatica* **2013**, *62*, 496–502. [CrossRef]
30. Wang, J.; Zhang, J.; Cao, X.; Wang, F. Optimal satellite formation reconfiguration strategy based on relative orbital elements. *Acta Astronaut.* **2012**, *76*, 99–114. [CrossRef]

drones

MDPI

Article

User Preferences in Drone Design and Operation

Kyungdoh Kim

Department of Industrial & Data Engineering, Hongik University, Seoul 04066, Korea;
kyungdoh.kim@hongik.ac.kr; Tel.: +82-2-320-1627

Abstract: Drones, which were first used in military applications, are now widely used by civilians for various purposes such as for deliveries and as cameras. There has been a lack of research into what drone users expect in terms of drone design and operation from a user perspective. In order to figure out what users want from drones, it is necessary to investigate the perception and design preferences of users with regard to drones. Surveys were conducted to collect data on preferences for various aspects of the design and operation of drone technology. Features relevant to the design and operation of drones were considered. We have identified the underlying factor structures of drone design and operation: outdoor mission type, user interface, military mission type, usefulness, risk, special mission type, and concern. The most important factors that contribute to all the dependent variables are the user interface and usefulness. The fact that drones will be increasingly used in the future is clear; however, the purpose of this study was to find out the areas on which to focus and pay further attention.

Keywords: drones; design; operation; user preference; user interface; usefulness

Citation: Kim, K. User Preferences in Drone Design and Operation. *Drones* **2022**, *6*, 133. https://doi.org/10.3390/drones6050133

Academic Editors: Andrzej Łukaszewicz, Wojciech Giernacki, Zbigniew Kulesza, Jaroslaw Pytka and Andriy Holovatyy

Received: 22 April 2022
Accepted: 21 May 2022
Published: 23 May 2022

1. Introduction

Drones, which were first used in military applications, are now widely used by civilians for various purposes such as for deliveries and as cameras. They have endless possibilities for scientific investigations, emergency response, traffic control, and aerial photography [1]. The drone market has grown steadily and it is predicted that in the future, they will become an indispensable product in our daily lives similar to smartphones [2]. However, despite these prospects, drones are not widely used in our society due to concerns about safety [3,4]. In addition, user-controlled accidents account for a high proportion of drone accidents [5].

Drone-piloting experience using a joystick controller has some problems. The current experience of piloting a drone using a joystick is not intuitive, so it is not well-understood how the drone is operated [6]. In addition, the experience of piloting a drone requires a high mental workload, which can lead to accidents [7]. This could be a big problem in the civilian drone market for users with poor drone-piloting skills. Therefore, it is important to design safe and intuitive ways to interact with aerial systems [8].

Most of the control interfaces for short-range drones utilize radio controller (RC)-based joysticks [9]. However, a lot of skill is required to control the drone using the RC-based control interface [10]. There has been a study that proposed using speech, body position, hand gestures, and visual marker interactions to directly send commands to a drone [8]. Interfaces utilizing a user's natural behavior are more intuitive and easier to learn than interfaces created utilizing communication through machines [11]. In addition, these interfaces are known to require a low mental workload [12]. Therefore, utilizing a more natural interface could solve the problems of the existing drone-piloting experience, such as a lack of intuition, a difficult learning curve, and a high cognitive load.

There has been a lack of research into what drone users expect in terms of drone design and operation from a user perspective. In order to figure out what users want from drones, it is necessary to investigate the perceptions and design preferences of users with regard to drones. Therefore, a survey was conducted on the perception, design, and operation of drones from the perspective of drone users. Surveys were conducted to collect data on preferences for various aspects of the design and operation of drone technology. Features relevant to the design and operation of drones were considered. Our findings will be able to help make drone use more convenient and reduce drone accidents caused by users. Through this, our research is expected to contribute to the popularization and activation of drones.

2. Background

A drone is a flying robot that can be remotely controlled or fly autonomously using software-controlled flight plans; therefore, a drone is considered an unmanned air vehicle (UAV) [13,14]. Drones range in size from vast fixed-wing unmanned air vehicles to smart dust (SD) that consist of many tiny micro-electro-mechanical systems including sensors or robots [15].

Drones are used in a variety of environments. Drone classifications are based on the type of mission (military/civil), the type of flight zone (outdoor/indoor), and the type of environment (underwater/on the water/ground/air/space). A wide variety of drones have been used for military and civilian purposes [15]. Although drones are considered a vital part of military missions, they are also being increasingly used for performing environmental actions, such as managing national parks and agricultural lands, tracking wildlife in different areas, observing the effects of climate change, and monitoring the biodiversity of different ecosystems from rainforests to oceans [16]. Drones can be used for the recognition and investigation of natural disasters including forest fires, avalanches, etc. [17]. Drones can perform both outdoor and indoor missions in very challenging environments [18]. Drones can be equipped with various sensors and cameras for intelligence, surveillance, and reconnaissance missions.

Drones are used for a variety of purposes. Drones can be used for search and rescue missions, environmental protection, mailing and delivery, performing missions in oceans or other planets, and other miscellaneous applications [19]. Drones have been used for military surveillance, planetary exploration, and search-and-rescue in the past few years [20]. One of the environments in which drones can be used is space and the exploration of other planets. Drones can be applied in marine environments to study marine organisms, identify the location of oil spills, and for other military or civilian applications [21–23]. Drones' miscellaneous applications include anti-drones, runway drones, drones that scare birds away from airport runways, window-cleaning drones, gutter-cleaning drones, solar panel-cleaning drones, and hobby drones.

Drones can provide a rapid overview of a target area without any danger. Drones equipped with infrared cameras can provide images even in darkness [24]. Drones can be put into action immediately without any loss of time. Modular drones provide operational benefits in terms of readiness and size. They also have advantages in terms of delivery time and energy consumption compared to non-modular drones [25].

Recently, drone delivery services have become an interesting topic for different companies around the world. Many companies are now using drones to deliver packages to customers. For delivery, the designed drones land and take off vertically and are programmed with the customer's address for delivery of the cargo. Recently, there was a study about consumer preference for drone delivery [26]. Australian people preferred a traditional delivery service over drone delivery, but drone delivery services could become competitive if they are considered faster and cheaper than traditional delivery services.

Human factors should be addressed to improve drone design [27]. A number of options, features, and confusing choices need to be improved [27]. A standardized set of core functions using common terminology is required for drone interfaces [27]. Providing the main functions only for the drone interface makes the operator faithful to the mission [27]. For controlling the drone camera, an uncluttered and efficient user interface (UI) is preferred [28].

Drone-related problems were investigated for drone users [29]. According to their flight experience, there were many problems with user interactions. Controlling drones is seen as difficult. Leisure drones provide a camera function by default. However, with the addition of camera capabilities in drones, users have faced increasing difficulties. They have had to learn to master the drone operation as well as use the camera function [30]. In order to improve the camera function, research on a gimbal system that can reduce vibrations has been conducted [31].

It was found that users experience a significant cognitive load just by controlling RC-based drones. An even higher cognitive load is experienced by users with a drone that includes a camera. This could be a factor that hinders the user experience. An egocentric drone-control interface was proposed to lower the user's cognitive load and as a result, the egocentric drone-control interface outperformed the traditional drone-centric control interface by removing the cognitive load of mental rotation [32]. It is possible to consider a multimodal drone display to provide the pilot with information about the drone's surroundings [33]. Haptic information delivered to the joystick improved situation awareness. Multimodal displays may reduce the cognitive and perceptual workload levels [33].

The guidance, navigation, and control (GNC) of drones are traditionally carried out using three methods, namely radio control, video base, and autopilot [34]. One of the most common ways to control and navigate drones is using a radio-control system. The best way to guide, navigate, and control a drone is an autopilot system. Google glass was applied to control a quadrotor drone using head movements. By using a brain–computer interface (BCI), they made the quadrotor turn, rise, dip, and even fly through a ring [35]. To control and navigate the movement of small drones, smartphones have also been utilized.

Camera drones are receiving increased attention and delivery drones and drone-racing for leisure sports are also gaining interest [36]. In order to popularize drones, relevant regulations or laws need to be revised. However, there are still concerns about the negative side of the spread of drones [29]. Australians were relatively neutral about drones [37]. They did not consider drone technology to be overly unsafe, dangerous, beneficial, or threatening [37]. A lack of knowledge about drones was identified as the biggest concern. Also, privacy, safety, and security were significant public concerns. Nguyen, Manley, and Saidi investigated how drones are being used in public safety operations [38]. They found out that the use of drones in some public safety operations needs to increase.

Therefore, it is necessary to investigate the perception and design preferences of the users of drones. Previously, there were no user-centered studies related to user expectations of drone technology. Therefore, this study will perform a survey related to user preferences of drone design and operation.

3. Study Method

The current study investigates what potential users expect with regard to drone design and operation since user-centered insights have not been well-established. We created questionnaire items related to various issues in drone-related areas from the literature [15,37,39]. The questionnaire consists of two parts (Appendix A). The first part asks about the extent to which the participants have experienced drone technology. The second part contains questions about drone design and operations. A 7-point Likert-type scale was used for the response categories.

Then, surveys were conducted to collect data on preferences for various aspects of the design and operation of drone interfaces. The participants were invited by email or were personal contacts. The voluntary nature of the survey was explained during the process of invitation and no compensation was paid for participation. The participants were given the web page address of the questionnaire and completed it at their own convenience. Features relevant to the design and operation of drones were considered. Various issues in drone-related areas were perceptions of drone technology, applications, interface, and control.

Through factor analysis, the issues related to drone design and operation will be grouped into several categories and multiple regression analyses will be performed to identify the factors necessary for the further popularization of drones.

4. Results

A total of 173 people participated in the survey from May to July 2019. Data from one participant was removed because the participant rated the same score for all items. Of the remaining 172 participants, 129 were male and 43 were female. With regard to their level of education, 52 participants were undergraduate students, 59 held a bachelor's degree, 24 held a master's degree, and 37 held a Ph.D. The average age of the participants was 31.2 years, with a standard deviation of 8.73 (Min = 19, Max = 49). A total of 131 participants were from the College of Engineering and 22 were from Management. The other 19 participants were recruited from science and liberal arts areas (science 8, liberal arts 6, design 4, and no major, 1).

The level of early adopter was neutral (M = 4.2, SD = 1.38). The level of hearing-drone technology was high (M = 5.5, SD = 1.63). The level of knowing how to control a drone and the level of experiencing drone technology were rather low, respectively (M = 3.3, SD = 1.98; M = 3.2, SD = 2.03). Since our focus was to investigate what people expect from drone technology, we did not exclude potential drone users without drone experience from the survey. To sum up, many participants have heard about drone technology but have not had much experience with it.

The internal consistency of the survey responses was assessed by measuring the intercorrelation among the two-paired questionnaire items. The values of Cronbach's alpha for the two-paired features of compatibility and delivery functions were 0.75 and 0.84, indicating that the participants were answering the questions consistently.

The mean and standard deviation for each rating are shown in Appendix B. Since there were so many items, we checked whether dimension reduction could be made by performing principal component analysis (PCA) with the correlation matrix. We obtained seven eigenvalues above the point where the curve starts to level off in a scree plot, which explained 61.20% of the variance. Therefore, the individual items can be grouped into seven factors.

To establish a factor structure and derive important design and operational factors among the many drone technology aspects, exploratory factor analysis was performed. The results of this analysis are shown in Table 1. The seven factors derived were labeled as outdoor mission type, user interface, military mission type, usefulness, risks, special mission type, and concerns.

Factor 1 is a dominating factor that explained 31.4% of the total variance of the data. The first factor, outdoor mission type, includes survey items about people's general perceptions of various outdoor missions that drones can offer. As drones can be used in a variety of outdoor environments, the outdoor mission type was a dominating factor. Factor 2, user interface, contains the survey items asking people's opinions about the drone user interface. Factor 3 consists of the military mission type questions or statements. Factor 4, usefulness, includes survey question items about people's thoughts on drone usefulness. Factor 5 is about the risk issues related to drones. Lastly, Factors 6 and 7 consist of survey items about special mission types and people's concerns about drones, respectively.

The means, standard deviations, and Cronbach's alphas of the factors are listed in Table 2. It shows that all factor items were well-grouped. All factors except for risk have above-neutral (>4) levels, with their means ranging from 4.5 to 5.6. People believe that drone technology can conduct many outdoor missions, military missions, and special missions. The current user interface and usefulness levels are mediocre. People believe that drone technology is not that risky but they still have some concerns.

Table 1. Factor analysis results.

Item Number	Rotated Factor Pattern						
	Factor1	Factor2	Factor3	Factor4	Factor5	Factor6	Factor7
18	**0.58051**	0.14129	0.29829	0.18243	0.01440	0.03895	0.29160
19	**0.66074**	0.16379	0.37771	0.09782	0.07361	0.09898	0.10496
21	**0.50973**	0.17347	0.22055	0.17077	−0.04194	0.12588	0.38103
28	**0.60638**	0.22438	0.38708	0.18359	−0.01064	0.17462	−0.01864
29	**0.59450**	0.24390	0.27694	0.09267	−0.11973	0.23810	0.26732
30	**0.67305**	0.09209	0.23379	0.30475	−0.02514	0.10006	0.14565
31	**0.82253**	0.15125	0.08977	0.05967	0.04294	0.17182	0.13171
32	**0.76550**	0.16515	0.16819	0.07912	−0.02949	0.24092	0.10310
33	**0.85618**	0.13096	0.17729	0.07390	0.09309	0.18043	0.04625
34	**0.78426**	0.13917	0.07050	0.00594	0.10209	0.22370	−0.01851
36	**0.82153**	0.19672	−0.01443	0.06616	0.10209	0.08474	0.06911
37	**0.80788**	0.19884	−0.09086	−0.00566	0.10099	0.10235	0.02001
38	**0.74703**	0.21540	0.10520	0.10684	0.14839	0.26398	0.03754
45	0.22011	**0.65910**	0.18134	0.14012	0.02192	0.20998	−0.00899
46	0.20637	**0.63776**	0.32202	0.13286	0.06021	0.07088	−0.13414
47	0.25218	**0.72321**	0.31873	0.05612	−0.07713	0.13403	−0.04737
48	0.14274	**0.74136**	0.20577	0.23047	−0.09223	−0.03693	0.17310
49	0.18651	**0.73657**	0.25018	0.13506	−0.09388	−0.02096	0.12309
50	0.15125	**0.79333**	0.05167	0.13027	0.03061	0.14112	0.09679
51	0.14559	**0.65839**	0.05978	0.14050	−0.12534	0.15677	−0.25837
52	0.17287	**0.60020**	−0.00647	0.19214	−0.16439	0.22088	−0.13612
16	0.09169	0.01141	**0.65635**	0.09617	0.05607	−0.00270	0.05269
24	0.15814	0.37096	**0.69304**	0.06606	0.04537	0.19877	0.00784
25	0.19694	0.27910	**0.67789**	0.09292	0.13633	0.21797	−0.15718
26	0.25988	0.30174	**0.68803**	0.16714	0.00681	0.06445	−0.07147
3	0.16631	0.24537	0.12328	**0.63438**	0.02998	0.19190	−0.22658
4	0.19443	0.01340	0.18146	**0.62420**	−0.09167	0.02573	0.11905
8	0.00236	0.20293	0.01055	**0.65065**	0.06637	0.05216	−0.18265
9	−0.03478	0.23252	0.03868	**0.75011**	−0.07970	0.16718	−0.03579
10	0.14145	0.25148	0.29347	**0.58828**	0.13929	0.09074	0.05975
1	−0.02479	0.14085	−0.20787	0.37868	**−0.60480**	−0.04155	−0.09430
2	0.14450	−0.08022	0.18095	−0.08256	**0.63714**	0.01547	0.24078
5	0.01081	0.03857	−0.14457	0.16055	**0.75389**	−0.08031	−0.06839
6	0.01211	−0.05507	−0.27106	0.21590	**0.66892**	−0.18336	0.10796
14	0.24827	−0.16538	0.03950	−0.04306	**0.61840**	0.02059	0.32013
15	0.06304	−0.04685	0.12704	−0.10211	**0.67330**	0.11834	0.09963
39	0.42414	0.01166	0.12089	0.25289	0.06540	**0.51730**	0.02259
40	0.36496	0.33513	0.21849	0.01976	0.10000	**0.51511**	−0.11413
41	0.30574	0.07305	0.13604	0.28482	−0.07393	**0.66121**	0.16045
42	0.32674	0.18405	0.03951	0.13254	−0.06027	**0.73790**	0.04610
43	0.32936	0.26914	0.09471	0.13159	0.00958	**0.75548**	0.07646
11	0.04818	−0.19738	−0.07369	−0.22532	0.32765	−0.02774	**0.53197**
12	0.22976	0.10359	0.02802	−0.03289	0.20016	0.05106	**0.75466**
13	0.24622	−0.04545	−0.03079	0.04905	0.22699	0.16188	**0.76377**

For each factor, bold font indicates the significant component factors.

Table 2. Mean and standard deviation of each factor for drone design and operation.

Factors	Mean	SD	Cronbach's Alpha
Outdoor mission type	5.6	1.11	0.95
User interface	4.8	1.12	0.90
Military mission type	5.2	1.32	0.84
Usefulness	4.5	1.09	0.79
Risk	3.8	1.09	0.79
Special mission type	5.1	1.21	0.85
Concern	4.7	1.32	0.74

To determine which of the seven factors strongly influence the various dependent variables, multiple regression analyses were performed using SAS 9.4. The data we used are the average scores for each factor since each factor contains several items. The seven dependent variables we selected are the intention of buying drones, interest in drone functions, self-vision about using drone technology in 5 years' time, the intention of using drones, the increase in satisfaction in daily life, saving time in daily life, and saving energy in daily life. Table 3 shows the multiple regression results for various dependent variables.

Table 3. Multiple regression results.

Factors	Partial R-Square	Model R-Square	F Value	Pr > F
Prediction for intention of buying drones				
F2	0.3589	0.3589	95.16	<0.0001
F4	0.0383	0.3972	10.74	0.0013
F5	0.0128	0.41	3.65	0.0578
F1	0.0175	0.4275	5.1	0.0252
Prediction for interest in drone functions				
F2	0.371	0.371	100.25	<0.0001
F4	0.0653	0.4363	19.59	<0.0001
F6	0.0314	0.4677	9.92	0.0019
F5	0.017	0.4847	5.51	0.0201
F1	0.0069	0.4916	2.25	0.1354
Prediction for self-vision about using drone technology in 5 years' time				
F2	0.2723	0.2723	63.62	<0.0001
F4	0.0916	0.364	24.35	<0.0001
F6	0.0201	0.3841	5.48	0.0204
F5	0.0145	0.3986	4.04	0.0461
Prediction for intention of use with drone technology				
F2	0.3828	0.3828	105.42	<0.0001
F4	0.0748	0.4576	23.3	<0.0001
F5	0.0177	0.4752	5.66	0.0185
F6	0.0152	0.4904	4.97	0.0271
Prediction for increase in satisfaction in daily life				
F4	0.3829	0.3829	105.48	<0.0001
F2	0.1308	0.5137	45.45	<0.0001
F6	0.0118	0.5255	4.17	0.0426
F5	0.0143	0.5397	5.17	0.0242
Prediction for saving time in daily life				
F4	0.3473	0.3473	90.47	<0.0001
F2	0.0636	0.4109	18.23	<0.0001
F5	0.0143	0.4252	4.17	0.0427
F6	0.0133	0.4384	3.94	0.0487
Prediction for saving energy in daily life				
F4	0.3728	0.3728	101.06	<0.0001
F2	0.0779	0.4508	23.98	<0.0001
F5	0.0165	0.4673	5.21	0.0237
F6	0.0107	0.478	3.41	0.0666

Using the intention of buying drones as the dependent variable and the seven factors as the independent variables, we performed a stepwise regression analysis to select the relevant independent variables. The results of the regression indicated a significant difference for the intention of buying drones regarding four variables ($F(4, 167) = 31.18$, $p < 0.0001$).

R^2 was 0.4275. The four variables that were selected are user interface, usefulness, risks, and outdoor mission type. Obviously, risks were affected negatively.

Using the interest in drone functions as the dependent variable, the results of the regression indicated a significant difference for the interest in drone functions regarding five variables ($F(5, 166) = 32.11$, $p < 0.0001$). R^2 was 0.4916. The five variables that were selected are user interface, usefulness, special mission type, risks, and outdoor mission type.

Using self-vision about using drone technology in 5 years' time as the dependent variable, the results of the stepwise regression analysis indicated a significant difference for self-vision about using drone technology in 5 years' time regarding four variables ($F(4, 167) = 27.67$, $p < 0.0001$). R^2 was 0.3986. The four variables that were selected are user interface, usefulness, special mission type, and risks.

Using the intention of using drones as the dependent variable, the results of the regression indicated a significant difference for the intention of using drones regarding four variables ($F(4, 167)= 40.17$, $p < 0.0001$). R^2 was 0.4904. The four variables that were selected are user interface, usefulness, risks, and special mission type.

Using the increase in satisfaction in daily life as the dependent variable, the results of the regression indicated a significant difference for the increase in satisfaction in daily life regarding four variables ($F(4, 167) = 48.96$, $p < 0.0001$). R^2 was 0.5397. The four variables that were selected are usefulness, user interface, special mission type, and risks.

Using saving time in daily life as the dependent variable, the results of the regression indicated a significant difference for saving time in daily life regarding four variables ($F(4, 167) = 32.59$, $p < 0.0001$). R^2 was 0.4384. The four variables that were selected are usefulness, user interface, risks, and special mission type.

Using saving energy in daily life as the dependent variable, the results of the regression indicated a significant difference for saving energy in daily life regarding four variables ($F(4, 167) = 38.23$, $p < 0.0001$). R^2 was 0.4780. The four variables that were selected are usefulness, user interface, risks, and special mission type.

The variable that had the greatest influence on drone purchase and the intention to use drone technology was the user interface. Therefore, we can increase the intention to purchase and use drones through the improvement of the user interface. Also, the variable that most affects the daily use of drones was usefulness. It was found that the usefulness needs to be increased in order to use drones in daily life more. In addition, risks and special mission type were also influential factors. If the risks of using drones are reduced and the special mission types of drones are provided, greater utilization will occur in daily life.

5. Discussion & Conclusions

One-hundred and seventy-two subjects participated in the preference survey to investigate what potential users expect with regard to drone design and operation. We have identified the underlying factor structures of drone design and operation: outdoor mission type, user interface, military mission type, usefulness, risk, special mission type, and concern. From multiple regression analyses, four main factors for drone-buying intention were derived. They are user interface, usefulness, risk, and outdoor mission type, which explained 42.75% of the variance that accounts for users' drone-purchasing intentions. The most important factors are user interface and usefulness, which account for 39.72% of the total variance contributing to drone-purchasing intention. By identifying these, we are able to provide drone designers and manufacturers with the advice that the user interface and usefulness factors should receive the most attention for achieving drone technology success.

From regression analyses, five main factors for interest in drone functions were derived. They are user interface, usefulness, special mission, risk, and outdoor mission type, which explained 49.16% of the variance that accounts for users' interest in drones. Again, the most important factors are user interface and usefulness, which account for 43.63% of the total variance contributing to interest in drones.

From regression analyses, four main factors for self-vision about using drone technology in 5 years' time, drone use intention, increase in satisfaction in daily life, saving time in daily life, and saving energy in daily life, were derived. They are user interface, usefulness, risk, and special mission type, which explained 39.86%, 49.04%, 53.97%, 43.84%, and 47.80% of the variance. The most important factors are user interface and usefulness, which account for 36.40%, 45.76%, 51.37%, 41.09%, and 45.08% of the total variance.

The most important factors are user interface and usefulness, which contribute to all the dependent variables. They should be improved and garner more attention to achieve the popularization and success of drones. The most important factor in the intention to buy drones, interest in drone functions, self-vision about using drone technology in 5 years' time, and intention of using drones is user interface, whereas the most important factor in the increase in satisfaction in daily life, saving time in daily life, and saving energy in daily life is usefulness. User interface must be improved to allow users to buy and use drones, and the usefulness of drones must also be enhanced to heighten user satisfaction. As in the study of Merkert et al. [26], the more useful drones are, the more competitive they become.

People believe that drone technology can conduct many outdoor missions, military missions, and special missions. The similarity of our findings to those of Nguyen et al. [38] with regard to public safety operations suggests that drone technology can play a significant role in various missions. The current user interface and usefulness levels are not very high. People believe that drone technology is not that risky but they still have some concerns. People know that drone technology can be used for various purposes but they still feel that the UI or usefulness levels are not high. It is important to help people understand that drones are highly useful through practical experience. In addition, we need to improve the UI for better control and utilization of drones. Although we do not feel it is very dangerous, there are still concerns about drone technology so it seems necessary to promote it in order to address these concerns as well as to increase people's experience and utilization of drones.

We were able to develop a questionnaire for drone technology to ask about user preferences in the perception, design, and operation of drones. The questionnaire consisted of two parts. The first part asks about the extent to which the participants have experienced drone technology. The second part contains questions about drone design and operation. The questionnaire can provide a drone design and operation checklist for drone designers and manufacturers. The current study investigated what potential users expect with regard to drone design and operation since user-centered guidelines have not been well-established.

A limitation of this research is as follows. It was difficult to derive specific design guidelines and only the overall preference for the operation was investigated. If we had performed an experimental study, we could have established detailed drone design guidelines. Also, we recruited the survey participants from the Korean population, but we did not consider other populations such as the United States, China, etc. If we had performed the survey with other populations, we might have been able to provide different implications. Nevertheless, this research makes several contributions to drone design and operation by identifying the underlying factor structures of drone technology and several important dimensions that influence the popularization and success of drones. The fact that drones will be increasingly used in the future is clear but for now, this study has discovered the areas on which to focus and pay further attention.

Funding: This research was partially supported by the Basic Science Research Program through the National Research Foundation of Korea (NRF) and was funded by the Ministry of Education (No. 2020R1F1A1049180).

Informed Consent Statement: Informed consent was obtained from all subjects involved in the study.

Data Availability Statement: https://docs.google.com/forms/d/1gJ5odAj0slHBFNgjL9olJCJPZcA5QixJKmpnx7QWGRc/edit#responses, accessed on 20 May 2022.

Conflicts of Interest: The author declares no conflict of interest.

Appendix A Drone Survey Questionnaire

Evaluating Preferences for Drone design and operation

Welcome to the drone survey!

The purpose of this survey is to see what you expect with regard to drone design and operation. Drones are flying robots that include unmanned air vehicles (UAVs) that fly thousands of kilometers and small drones that fly in confined spaces. In answering, please consider the following.

Read each statement. Decide how much you agree or disagree or how much you like or dislike and mark the appropriate response.

The survey consists of two parts. The first part is about your demographic information. Part I comprises eight questions. The second part will ask you about what you expect with regard to drone technology. There are 60 questions related to preferences about drone design and operation in Part II.

It takes about 10 min in total to complete the whole survey.

I. Part I

Please fill out every question in the following questionnaire.

1. What is your gender?

☐ Male ☐ Female

2. The year of birth (e.g., 1976): ______________________

3. What is your highest degree?

☐ High school (undergraduate student)
☐ Bachelor's degree
☐ Master's degree
☐ Doctorate degree
☐ Other ______________

4. What is your major/area of study? ______________________

Decide how much you agree or disagree or like or dislike and mark the appropriate response.

1 Strongly disagree	2	3	4	5	6	7 Strongly agree

5. I am an early adopter.

1	2	3	4	5	6	7

6. I have heard about drone technology.

1	2	3	4	5	6	7

7. I know how to control a drone.

1	2	3	4	5	6	7

8. I have experienced drone technology.

1	2	3	4	5	6	7

II. Part I

1. Drone technology is safe.

1	2	3	4	5	6	7

2. Drone technology is risky.

1	2	3	4	5	6	7

3. Drone technology is beneficial to my family and me.

1	2	3	4	5	6	7

4. Drone technology is beneficial to society.

1	2	3	4	5	6	7

5. Drone technology is threatening to my family and me.

1	2	3	4	5	6	7

6. Drone technology is threatening to society.

1	2	3	4	5	6	7

7. Drone technology is as safe or safer than other technologies that perform the same task.

1	2	3	4	5	6	7

8. Using drone technology will be compatible with all aspects of my work.

1	2	3	4	5	6	7

9. Using drone technology will fit into my lifestyle.

1	2	3	4	5	6	7

10. Basically, I find drone technology useful.

1	2	3	4	5	6	7

11. I want no drones over my property.

1	2	3	4	5	6	7

12. What bothers me is that there is no way to identify whether the drone is filming.

1	2	3	4	5	6	7

13. What bothers me is that I cannot infer the purpose of use from the appearance of drones.

1	2	3	4	5	6	7

14. I fear injuries from an accident with a drone.

1	2	3	4	5	6	7

15. Drones scare me.

1	2	3	4	5	6	7

16. How much do you like the idea that a drone can be used for military missions?

1 Very much dislike	2	3	4	5	6	7 Very much like

17. How much do you like the idea that a drone can be used for civil missions?

1	2	3	4	5	6	7

18. How much do you like the idea that a drone can be used for planetary exploration?

1	2	3	4	5	6	7

19. How much do you like the idea that a drone can be used for search-and-rescue?

1	2	3	4	5	6	7

20. How much do you like the idea that a drone can be used for mailing and delivery?

1	2	3	4	5	6	7

21. Drones should perform outdoor missions in very challenging environments.

1 Strongly disagree	2	3	4	5	6	7 Strongly agree

22. Drones should perform indoor missions in very challenging environments.

1	2	3	4	5	6	7

23. Drones with various sensors and cameras should perform intelligence missions.

1	2	3	4	5	6	7

24. Drones with various sensors and cameras should perform reconnaissance missions.

1	2	3	4	5	6	7

25. Drones with various sensors and cameras should perform surveillance missions.

1	2	3	4	5	6	7

26. How much do you like the idea that drones equipped with infrared cameras can give images even in darkness?

1 Very much dislike	2	3	4	5	6	7 Very much like

27. How much do you like the idea that drones can provide a rapid overview around the target area without any danger?

1	2	3	4	5	6	7

28. How much do you like the idea that drones can be put into action immediately without any loss of time?

1	2	3	4	5	6	7

29. How much do you like the idea that drones can manage national parks and agricultural lands?

1	2	3	4	5	6	7

30. How much do you like the idea that drones can track wildlife in different areas?

1	2	3	4	5	6	7

31. How much do you like the idea that drones can observe the effects of climate change?

1	2	3	4	5	6	7

32. How much do you like the idea that drones can monitor the biodiversity of different ecosystems?

1	2	3	4	5	6	7

33. How much do you like the idea that drones can be used for the recognition and investigation of natural disasters?

1	2	3	4	5	6	7

34. How much do you like the idea that a drone can be used for environmental protection?

1	2	3	4	5	6	7

35. How much do you like the idea that drones can be used for delivering packages to customers?

1	2	3	4	5	6	7

36. How much do you like the idea that drones can be applied in marine environments?

1	2	3	4	5	6	7

37. How much do you like the idea that drones can be used for studying marine organisms?

1	2	3	4	5	6	7

38. How much do you like the idea that drones can be used for identifying the location of oil spills?

1	2	3	4	5	6	7

39. Anti-drones that are used to take down offensive drones are needed.

1 Strongly disagree	2	3	4	5	6	7 Strongly agree

40. Runway drones that can be used as a runway for another drone are needed.

1	2	3	4	5	6	7

41. Drones that scare birds away from airport runways are needed.

1	2	3	4	5	6	7

42. Window-cleaning drones are needed.

1	2	3	4	5	6	7

43. Solar panel-cleaning drones are needed.

1	2	3	4	5	6	7

44. Hobby drones are needed.

1	2	3	4	5	6	7

45. How much do you like the idea that drones are controlled and navigated using a radio-control system?

1 Very much dislike	2	3	4	5	6	7 Very much like

46. How much do you like the idea that drones are controlled and navigated using a camera installed on the drone?

1	2	3	4	5	6	7

47. How much do you like the idea that drones are controlled and navigated using an autopilot system?

1	2	3	4	5	6	7

48. How much do you like the idea that drones are controlled and navigated using smartphones?

1	2	3	4	5	6	7

49. How much do you like the idea that drones are controlled and navigated using a brain–computer interface (BCI)?

1	2	3	4	5	6	7

50. How much do you like the idea that drones are controlled and navigated using a smart glass?

1	2	3	4	5	6	7

51. I believe that my interaction with a drone will be clear and understandable.

1 Strongly disagree	2	3	4	5	6	7 Strongly agree

52. I believe that it is easy for drone technology to do what I want it to do.

1	2	3	4	5	6	7

53. Overall, I believe that a drone is easy to use.

1	2	3	4	5	6	7

54. If cost is not an issue, I would consider buying drone technology.

1	2	3	4	5	6	7

55. I am really interested in the sort of functions a drone could offer.

1	2	3	4	5	6	7

56. I could see myself utilizing drone technology in 5 years' time.

1	2	3	4	5	6	7

57. I would like to utilize drone technology.

1	2	3	4	5	6	7

58. A drone will increase satisfaction in my daily life.

1	2	3	4	5	6	7

59. A drone will be able to save time that I spend in my daily life.

1	2	3	4	5	6	7

60. A drone will be able to save efforts that I spend in my daily life.

1	2	3	4	5	6	7

Appendix B

Table A1. Mean and standard deviation of ratings for each item (n = 172).

Variables	Mean	SD	Variables	Mean	SD
a1	4.2	1.38	b29	5.7	1.35
a2	5.5	1.63	b30	5.6	1.32
a3	3.3	1.98	b31	5.6	1.51
a4	3.2	2.03	b32	5.5	1.41
b1	3.9	1.41	b33	5.8	1.34
b2	4.3	1.50	b34	5.5	1.55
b3	4.4	1.60	b35	5.1	1.50
b4	5.3	1.31	b36	5.4	1.53
b5	3.1	1.45	b37	5.3	1.56
b6	3.5	1.52	b38	5.5	1.41
b7	4.2	1.38	b39	5.1	1.55
b8	3.9	1.60	b40	4.8	1.36
b9	4.1	1.47	b41	5.2	1.55
b10	5.0	1.36	b42	5.1	1.60
b11	4.1	1.82	b43	5.2	1.52
b12	5.1	1.49	b44	4.8	1.60
b13	4.9	1.57	b45	4.8	1.39
b14	4.5	1.74	b46	5.0	1.43
b15	3.4	1.69	b47	5.0	1.47
b16	5.2	1.68	b48	5.1	1.54
b17	5.2	1.49	b49	4.9	1.47
b18	5.9	1.30	b50	4.7	1.43
b19	6.1	1.34	b51	4.7	1.44
b20	5.4	1.54	b52	4.6	1.43
b21	5.8	1.40	b53	4.4	1.47
b22	4.7	1.78	c1	5.0	1.75

Table A1. *Cont.*

Variables	Mean	SD	Variables	Mean	SD
b23	5.4	1.39	c2	5.0	1.59
b24	5.2	1.51	c3	4.5	1.58
b25	5.0	1.69	c4	4.9	1.54
b26	5.1	1.54	c5	4.5	1.51
b27	5.3	1.45	c6	4.5	1.70
b28	5.3	1.36	c7	4.5	1.61

References

1. Valavanis, K.P.; Vachtsevanos, G.J. *Handbook of Unmanned Aerial Vehicles-5 Volume Set*; Springer: New York, NY, USA, 2014.
2. Giones, F.; Brem, A. From toys to tools: The co-evolution of technological and entrepreneurial developments in the drone industry. *Bus. Horiz.* **2017**, *60*, 875–884. [CrossRef]
3. Wild, G.; Murray, J.; Baxter, G. Exploring Civil Drone Accidents and Incidents to Help Prevent Potential Air Disasters. *Aerospace* **2016**, *3*, 22. [CrossRef]
4. Chamata, J. Factors Delaying the Adoption of Civil Drones: A Primitive Framework. *Int. Technol. Manag. Rev.* **2017**, *6*, 125–132. [CrossRef]
5. Williams, K.W. *A Summary of Unmanned Aircraft Accident/Incident Data: Human Factors Implications*; Federal Aviation Administration: Oklahoma City, OK, USA, 2004.
6. Cha, M.; Kim, B.; Lee, J.; Ji, Y. Usability evaluation for user interface of a drone remote controller. In Proceedings of the ESK Conference, Washington, DC, USA, 31 March–2 April 2016.
7. De la Torre, G.G.; Ramallo, M.A.; Cervantes, E. Workload perception in drone flight training simulators. *Comput. Hum. Behav.* **2016**, *64*, 449–454. [CrossRef]
8. Fernández, R.A.S.; Sanchez-Lopez, J.L.; Sampedro, C.; Bavle, H.; Molina, M.; Campoy, P. Natural user interfaces for human-drone multi-modal interaction. In Proceedings of the 2016 International Conference on Unmanned Aircraft Systems (ICUAS), Arlington, VA, USA, 7–10 June 2016.
9. Graff, C. Drone Piloting Study. Bachelor's Thesis, University of Italian Switzerland, Lugano, Switzerland, 2016.
10. Self, B.; Ercoline, W.; Olson, W.; Tvaryanas, A. 10. Spatial Disorientation in Uninhabited Aerial Vehicles. In *Human Factors of Remotely Operated Vehicles*; Emerald Group Publishing Limited: Bingley, UK, 2006; Volume 7, pp. 133–146. [CrossRef]
11. Yu, J.; Paik, W. Efficiency and Learnability Comparison of the Gesture-based and the Mouse-based Telerobotic Systems. *Stud. Inform. Control* **2019**, *28*. [CrossRef]
12. Oviatt, S. Human-centered design meets cognitive load theory: Designing interfaces that help people think. In Proceedings of the 14th ACM International Conference on Multimedia, Santa Barbara, CA, USA, 23–27 October 2006.
13. Earls, A.R. Drone (UAV). IoT Agenda 2019. Available online: https://www.techtarget.com/iotagenda/definition/drone (accessed on 25 August 2021).
14. Cavoukian, A. *Privacy and Drones: Unmanned Aerial Vehicles*; Information and Privacy Commissioner of Ontario: Toronto, ON, Canada, 2012.
15. Hassanalian, M.; Abdelkefi, A. Classifications, applications, and design challenges of drones: A review. *Prog. Aerosp. Sci.* **2017**, *91*, 99–131. [CrossRef]
16. Gallagher, K. The Sky's the Limit with Drone-Assisted Mapping. The Simulyze Blog 2016. Available online: https://www.simulyze.com/blog/drone-assisted-mapping-applications (accessed on 4 February 2022).
17. Restas, A. Drone applications for supporting disaster management. *World J. Eng. Technol.* **2015**, *3*, 316. [CrossRef]
18. Rodríguez, R.M.; Alarcón, F.; Rubio, D.S.; Ollero, A. Autonomous management of an UAV Airfield. In Proceedings of the 3rd International Conference on Application and Theory of Automation in Command and Control Systems, Naples, Italy, 28–30 May 2013.
19. Yan, R.-J.; Pang, S.; Sun, H.-B.; Pang, Y.-J. Development and missions of unmanned surface vehicle. *J. Mar. Sci. Appl.* **2010**, *9*, 451–457. [CrossRef]
20. Hassanalian, M.; Abdelkefi, A.; Wei, M.; Ziaei-Rad, S. A novel methodology for wing sizing of bio-inspired flapping wing micro air vehicles: Theory and prototype. *Acta Mech.* **2016**, *228*, 1097–1113. [CrossRef]
21. Koski, W.R.; Allen, T.; Ireland, D.; Buck, G.; Smith, P.R.; Macrander, A.M.; Halick, M.A.; Rushing, C.; Sliwa, D.J.; McDonald, T.L. Evaluation of an Unmanned Airborne System for Monitoring Marine Mammals. *Aquat. Mamm.* **2009**, *35*, 347–357. [CrossRef]
22. Koh, L.P.; Wich, S.A. Dawn of Drone Ecology: Low-Cost Autonomous Aerial Vehicles for Conservation. *Trop. Conserv. Sci.* **2012**, *5*, 121–132. [CrossRef]
23. Fingas, M.; Brown, C. Review of oil spill remote sensing. *Mar. Pollut. Bull.* **2014**, *83*, 9–23. [CrossRef] [PubMed]
24. Stuchlík, R.; Stachoň, Z.; Láska, K.; Kubíček, P. Unmanned Aerial Vehicle—Efficient mapping tool available for recent research in polar regions. *Czech Polar Rep.* **2015**, *5*, 210–221. [CrossRef]
25. Lee, J. Optimization of a modular drone delivery system. In Proceedings of the 2017 Annual IEEE International Systems Conference (SysCon), Montreal, QC, Canada, 24–27 April 2017.

26. Merkert, R.; Bliemer, M.C.; Fayyaz, M. Consumer preferences for innovative and traditional last-mile parcel delivery. *Int. J. Phys. Distrib. Logist. Manag.* **2022**, *52*, 261–284. [CrossRef]
27. Mouloua, M.; Gilson, R.; Daskarolis-Kring, E.; Kring, J.; Hancock, P. Ergonomics of UAV/UCAV mission success: Considerations for data link, control, and display issues. In *Proceedings of the Human Factors and Ergonomics Society Annual Meeting*; SAGE Publications: Los Angeles, CA, USA, 2001.
28. Ellwanger, A.; Hoesl, A.; Butz, A. Axis-plus Content-based Control for Camera Drones: Design and Evaluation of User Interface Concepts. In Proceedings of the 4th ACM Workshop on Micro Aerial Vehicle Networks, Systems, and Applications, Munich, Germany, 10–15 June 2018.
29. Ha, K.; Pan, Y. A study on interaction ux for drone for individual use. In Proceedings of the KSDS Conference, Gwangju, Korea, 17–23 October 2015; pp. 102–103.
30. Kim, G.-D.; Yu, S.-M. Aerial photography training using drones. *Broadcast. Media Mag.* **2017**, *22*, 85–94.
31. Song, M.; Jeon, S.; Roh, J.; Jin, W.; Chung, M. Development of Gimbal System for Aviation Photograph using Smartphone. In Proceedings of the Korean Society for Precision Engineering Autumn Conference, Changwon, Korea, 29–31 October 2014.
32. Cho, K.; Cho, M.; Jeon, J. Fly a Drone Safely: Evaluation of an Embodied Egocentric Drone Controller Interface. *Interact. Comput.* **2017**, *29*, 345–354. [CrossRef]
33. McCarley, J.S.; Wickens, C.D. *Human Factors Concerns in UAV Flight*; Institute of Aviation, Aviation Human Factors Division, University of Illinois at Urbana-Champaign: Champaign, IL, USA, 2004; pp. 1–5.
34. Hassanalian, M.; Radmanesh, M.; Ziaei-Rad, S. Sending instructions and receiving the data from MAVs using telecommunication networks. In Proceedings of the International Micro Air Vehicle Conference (IMAV2012), Braunschweig, Germany, 3–6 July 2012.
35. Mailonline, V.W.F. Would You Fly on a Mind-Controlled Plane? Scientist Pilots a Drone Using Just His Thoughts—And the Technology Could One Day Be Used on Commercial Aircraft. Mail Online 2015. Available online: https://www.dailymail.co.uk/sciencetech/article-2970073/Would-fly-mind-controlled-plane-Scientist-pilots-drone-using-just-thoughts-technology-one-day-used-commercial-aircraft.html (accessed on 4 February 2022).
36. Choi, S. Drone's Leisure Sports Industry Status and Prospect. *Monthly KOTI Magazine on Transport*, April 2017; Volume 230, pp. 10–13.
37. Clothier, R.A.; Greer, D.; Greer, D.G.; Mehta, A.M. Risk Perception and the Public Acceptance of Drones. *Risk Anal.* **2015**, *35*, 1167–1183. [CrossRef] [PubMed]
38. Nguyen, H.V.; Manley, T.W.; Saidi, K.S. *Survey of Drone Usage in Public Safety Agencies*; U.S. Department of Commerce, National Institute of Standards and Technology: Gaithersburg, MD, USA, 2020. [CrossRef]
39. Yoo, W.; Yu, E.; Jung, J. Drone delivery: Factors affecting the public's attitude and intention to adopt. *Telemat. Inform.* **2018**, *35*, 1687–1700. [CrossRef]

energies

MDPI

Article

An Acoustic Fault Detection and Isolation System for Multirotor UAV

Adam Bondyra *, Marek Kołodziejczak, Radosław Kulikowski and Wojciech Giernacki

Faculty of Automatic Control, Robotics and Electrical Engineering, Institute of Robotics and Machine Intelligence, Poznan University of Technology, ul. Piotrowo 3a, 60-965 Poznan, Poland; marek.s.kolodziejczak@student.put.poznan.pl (M.K.); radoslaw.kulikowski@student.put.poznan.pl (R.K.); wojciech.giernacki@put.poznan.pl (W.G.)

* Correspondence: adam.bondyra@put.poznan.pl

Abstract: With the rising popularity of unmanned aerial vehicles (UAVs) and increasing variety of their applications, the task of providing reliable and robust control systems becomes significant. An active fault-tolerant control (FTC) scheme requires an effective fault detection and isolation (FDI) algorithm to provide information about the fault's occurrence and its location. This work aims to present a prototype of a diagnostic system intended to recognize and identify broken blades of rotary wing UAVs. The solution is based on an analysis of acoustic emission recorded with an onboard microphone array paired with a lightweight yet powerful single-board computer. The standalone hardware of the FDI system was utilized to collect a wide and publicly available dataset of recordings in real-world experiments. The detection algorithm itself is a data-driven approach that makes use of an artificial neural network to classify characteristic features of acoustic signals. Fault signature is based on Mel Frequency Spectrum Coefficients. Furthermore, in the paper an extensive evaluation of the model's parameters was performed. As a result, a highly accurate fault classifier was developed. The best models allow not only a detection of fault occurrence, but thanks to multichannel data provided with a microphone array, the location of the impaired rotor is reported, as well.

Keywords: UAV; fault detection; rotor; data-driven; acoustic

Citation: Bondyra, A.; Kołodziejczak, M.; Kulikowski, R.; Giernacki, W. An Acoustic Fault Detection and Isolation System for Multirotor UAV. *Energies* **2022**, *15*, 3955. https://doi.org/10.3390/en15113955

Academic Editor: Francisco Manzano Agugliaro

Received: 6 May 2022
Accepted: 24 May 2022
Published: 27 May 2022

1. Introduction

1.1. Background

The increasing number and variety of applications of unmanned aerial vehicles raise the question of operational safety and reliability [1,2]. Few recent studies have pointed out the key causes of drone accidents in flight, with actuator faults being one of the major issues, both in military and commercial UAVs [3,4]. This challenge is often addressed with fault-tolerant control systems, which provide minimal performance for the aerial vehicle in the occurrence of faults [5]. FTC strategies are typically divided into two categories. Passive approaches aim to provide robustness of control algorithms and utilize hardware redundancy. On the other hand, active systems are based on the fault detection algorithm and real-time adjustment of the control laws [6]. The fault diagnosis stage itself is frequently divided into the basic detection of the fault followed by its isolation, which is defined as the determination of the exact location of the faulty component [7]. It is believed that precise fault detection and isolation systems, as crucial components of FTC control schemes, will significantly increase the safety of operating UAVs and, as a result, accelerate their introduction to practical applications [8].

1.2. Research Motivation

In this article, a new approach to the problem addressed in a couple of our previous works [9,10] is presented. The main focus was placed on the problem of efficient fault detection and isolation of damaged propellers of multirotor UAV. The initial approaches were based on the analysis of airframe vibrations thanks to data obtained with microelectromechanical (MEMS) accelerometers. These methods have proven to be efficient, with classification accuracy exceeding 96%. First, there is still room for improvement in terms of detection accuracy itself. Additionally, our solutions lacked precision in locating faulty rotors, especially in a situation where more than one blade was damaged. Finally, the method based on a sensory network required quite serious interference with the structure and equipment of the drone. Conducting experiments with vibration data led to the observation of clearly audible differences in the sound of healthy and damaged rotors. It leads to the concept of utilizing acoustic emission as a source of information about the propellers' condition.

1.3. Literature Review

The topic of FDI schemes designed to detect UAV actuator faults is covered in quite a few recent papers. The first category of approaches to this diagnostic problem utilizes model-based fault diagnosis with sophisticated methods to evaluate model residuals and conclude on the fault's occurrence. Notable examples are articles published by Cen et al. that comprise a series of developments, from initial proof of concept to practical implementation [11–13]. Their method is based on a nonlinear observer which was later boosted with adaptive mechanisms and implemented in real-time application on multirotor UAV. However, the study addresses only the consequence of the rotor's impairment, since the analyzed type of fault is a simulated loss of effectiveness (LoE) in thrust generation. Some other papers follow the same approach with various methods of model-based fault estimation algorithms and following control strategies [14,15]. It is worth mentioning that the literature considers other types of UAV actuator faults, including stuck control signal [16] or multiple fault class scenarios. An example is an article describing the method that enabled the detection of wear of rotor shaft bearings, LoE and increases in winding resistance at the same time [17].

The problem of detecting physical damage to drone rotors is frequently solved thanks to data-driven FDI methods. They are based on statistical modeling and classification algorithms with sensory data used as a source of information. Some solutions are based on analysis of system states, such as attitude, angular rate and values of control signals. A notable example [18] that allows detection of a significantly damaged rotor is based on an artificial recurrent neural network (RNN) with long short-term memory architecture (LSTM) and provides a fault detection accuracy of approximately 92%. However, the majority of papers focus on two types of raw sensor signals: vibrations and acoustic emission. Among the first category, a few articles present methods based on characteristic features of vibration signals obtained with on-board inertial measurement units (IMUs). The work of Pourpanah et al. shows that such an approach, boosted with motor current measurements, can improve the accuracy of fault detection by more than 94% [19]. In another example, the success rate of fault classification is even higher at the cost of long (over 10 s in most cases) analysis time. It is worth mentioning that our previous works fall into this category as well.

Only a couple of papers describe FDI systems based on the analysis of acoustic emission. A notable example is the work of Gino et al. [20], with outstanding fault detection accuracy that exceeds 98%. However, the experiments were performed with a stationary, ground-fixed drone and an external high-class microphone. In addition, the detected fault was an imbalance of the rotor, which, as the authors assumed, was comparable to an actual partial loss of the blade. The results show a high potential for acoustic waves as a source of information on the occurrence of faults. In another article, a similar neural-based algorithm with physically impaired rotors and data collected in a real flight scenario resulted in only 92% of fault detection accuracy [21]. A paper written by Altinors et al. [22] considers even a wider set of fault conditions, including broken rotor blade, bearing failure and eccentric shaft faults. The algorithm presented was based on one-second-long sound samples collected with external recording equipment placed in the vicinity of faulty motors. Several different classification algorithms have proven to be very accurate in classifying fault signatures based on statistical features of audio signals. This is yet another work showing the potential of using acoustic emission in data-driven FDI systems for UAV actuators.

1.4. Main Contribution

We consider that acoustic-based FDI for UAV rotors proves to be a very promising field, both in terms of improving accuracy and the possibility of practical implementation. However, to the best of our knowledge, no method has been developed that would include the isolation of a faulty rotor. In addition, all of the existing works were carried out with external audio recording systems and very limited coverage of different flight scenarios. We consider that the acoustic emission of the hovering drone is significantly different from that of intensive maneuvers during which the rotors' angular velocity varies more significantly. A number of papers show great potential in audio signals as a source of information on the fault occurrence and its properties. However, no experiments were performed using the signals recorded on board in close proximity to the rotors. The accuracy of data-driven FDI based on such data remains unclear. Therefore, we share an extensive dataset of audio recordings collected in different flight phases with multiple fault classes related to the location of a broken propeller. The data were collected with our custom-built onboard microphone array subsystem. Finally, the algorithm presented in this article shows the practical application of a highly accurate FDI system based on the mentioned dataset with an onboard acoustic data acquisition and processing system.

1.5. Study Outline

The following parts of this paper are composed as follows: the next section describes some major technical details of our work. It includes specific aspects of the *Falcon V5* UAV used in experiments and the custom hardware setup for the acquisition and processing of audio signals. In addition, some initial observations and conclusions about the effects of operating broken UAV rotors are also presented. The third section provides a broad description of our fault detection and isolation algorithm, with consecutive steps of signal processing and feature classification explained. The fourth part of the article presents an acoustic dataset with multiple fault types and shows the results of the experimental evaluation. The final section summarizes the paper with some conclusions and future improvement plans.

2. Analyzed Uav System

2.1. Rotor Impairments

Partial destruction of the rotor leads to a series of consequences. At first, there are some practical implications of operating the UAV with such a fault. To show these negative effects, a short series of experiments was carried out using a stationary propulsion test stand [23]. The rig allows measuring thrust, power consumption and angular velocity of various motor–rotor setups. Three exemplary types of rotors were used, one in brand new condition and two that were diversely damaged. Figure 1 shows the blades used in stationary tests, with (H) a healthy rotor, one with a damaged edge (E) and several ones with fractured tips (F), as well as the general structure of the test stand.

A BrushLess Direct Current (BLDC) motor, rotor and Electronic Speed Controller (ESC) used in the experiments were identical to those mounted on our *Falcon V5* UAV, which was later used for validation experiments. Multiple series of test runs were carried out with a full range of control signal applied and the results were averaged for every rotor. The performance graphs are shown in Figure 2. The measured values were the total thrust F_T generated by the rotor and the power efficiency η, expressed as the amount of thrust in relation to a single watt of electrical power.

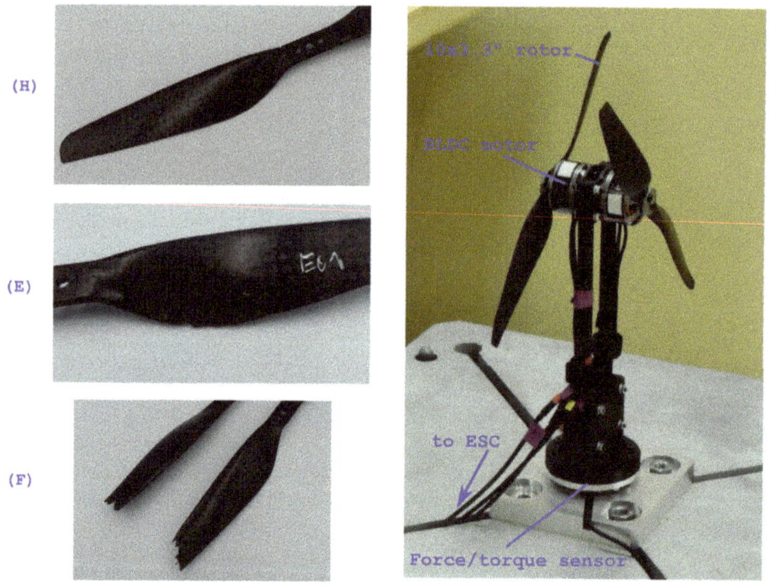

Figure 1. Samples of rotors used in fault detection experiments and overview of the propulsion test rig.

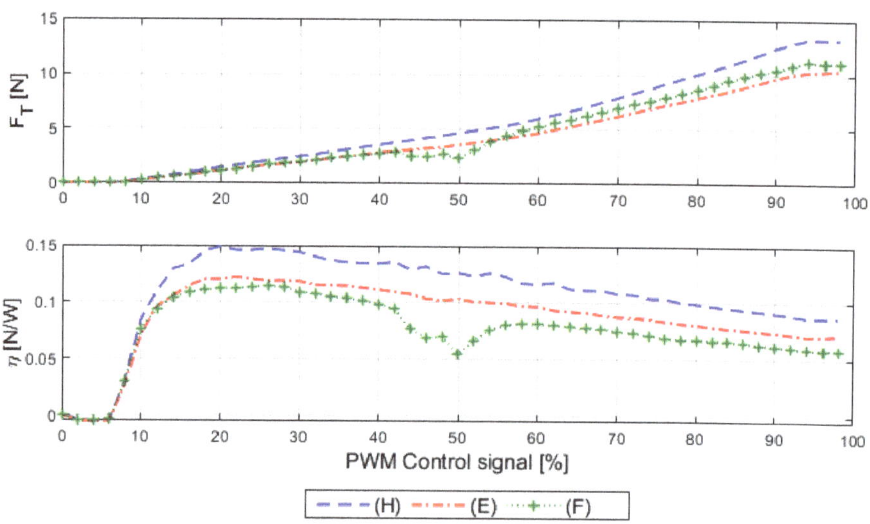

Figure 2. Performance comparison of faulty and undamaged rotors: thrust of a single motor–rotor unit (**top**) and achieved power efficiency (**bottom**).

Stationary analysis of faulty propulsion shows that even slight damage to the rotor blades results in an observable loss in the thrust produced. The power efficiency drops significantly as well, therefore reducing flight time and payload capabilities of the UAV. In addition, during those test runs that utilized faulty units, a vibration resonance was observed. It confirms state-of-the-art knowledge on the effects of the broken and, as a result, the imbalanbced rotor [24,25]. In the case of undamaged blades, the mass distribution is symmetric around the motor shaft, which is the pivot point. After the fracture, it becomes irregular and the centrifugal forces induced by rotating blades no longer compensate. The resultant force leads to observable vibrations. In our previous works, this phenomenon was measured directly with MEMS accelerometers and used as a basis for fault diagnosis. In the presented solution, we utilize sound waves as derivatives of vibrations themselves. We consider several possible advantages of this new data source. Initially, some additional audio signal features that come from the aerodynamic effects of the broken rotor blade may increase the accuracy of the FDI system. Furthermore, microphones provide a much wider frequency coverage compared to inertial data.

2.2. Falcon V5 Uav

The *Falcon V5* UAV was used to collect the acoustic recording dataset. It is a custom-built aerial research platform based on the so-called X8 quadrotor configuration and our custom-built avionics system. The vehicle provides high lift capabilities, a flight time of about 8 min and numerous data and power interfaces for attaching additional equipment used in experiments. An overview of the drone is presented in Figure 3.

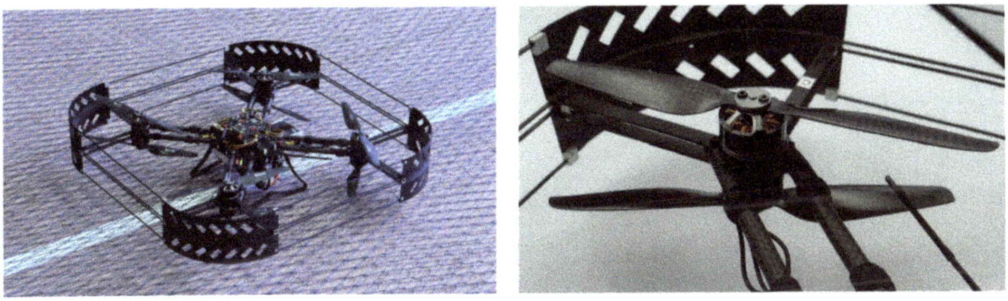

Figure 3. The *Falcon V5* UAV used for FDI experiments and a detailed view of the coaxial propulsion unit.

The main chassis of the UAV is designed as a four-arm cross with coaxial propulsion units at each end. The span of opposite rotors is equal to 450 mm with a vehicle mass of 2300 g. Eight *MN3110* electric BLDC motors allow up to 65 N of total thrust to be produced within compact external dimensions of the UAV, as small as 610 × 610 mm. Each propulsion unit consists of two vertically aligned motors with 10 × 3.3″ rotors. This design has been shown to be redundant in hardware and safer to operate in the event of partial or complete rotor loss [26], which greatly benefited us during numerous flight tests in faulty scenarios.

2.3. Acoustic Diagnostic System

In order to capture in-flight acoustic signals, a prototype of a data acquisition and processing system was developed. The aim was to utilize easily available off-the-shelf components to shorten preparations for experiments and provide a proof-of-concept solution that precedes the development of a dedicated embedded subsystem. Our setup is based on a single-board computer (SBC) *Raspberry Pi 3B+* and a dedicated microphone array module. The latter component is *Respeaker 4-mic Array* (https://respeaker.io/4_mic_array/, accessed on 28 April 2022), a printed circuit initially designed for IoT (Internet of Things) solutions and dedicated to create voice-enabled applications in particular. The stack of *RaspberryPi* SBC and *ReSpeaker* "hat" is shown in Figure 4.

The key components of the *ReSpeaker* microphone array are four *MSM321A3729H9BP* top-port miniature microphones manufactured in MEMS technology. They are located in every corner of the rectangular printed circuit board, which in our intention will allow one to locate the faulty rotor. Since these components are equipped with an analog output, the *ReSpeaker* module consists of a dedicated *AC108* analog-to-digital converter (ADC). The ADC provides four independent channels of acquisition, a programmable gain block and a I^2S output bus. The maximum sampling rate for all four microphones reaches up to

48 kSps. Some important parameters of the *MSM321A3729H9BP* microphone are presented in Table 1.

Figure 4. The stack of *Raspberry Pi 3B+* SBC and microphone array module.

Table 1. Selected properties of the MSM321A3729H9BP microphone.

Parameter	Value	Unit
Frequency band	100∼10 k	[Hz], range of ±3 dB
THD	0.1	[%]
AOP	123	[dB SPL]
SNR	65	[dB]
Sensitivity	−32 dB	[dB] for 1 kHz in relation to 1 V/Pa

It is worth mentioning that although the performance of the array is quite mediocre in comparison to high-end components of this class and significantly lower in comparison to full-scale regular microphones, such a low-cost system provided us with satisfactory results. However, one of the key parameters in our consideration was the acoustic overload point (AOP) of the microphones, which is commonly defined as a level of sound pressure at which the total harmonic distortion (THD) factor exceeds 10%. The importance of AOP is crucial since the array is located in the direct vicinity of loud rotors. Some of the other MEMS microphone-based devices tested did not satisfy our needs, as the recorded sound was distorted beyond the level that would enable accurate fault detection.

The ready-to-flight experimental setup consisting of *Falcon* drone, SBC and microphone array is depicted in Figure 5. Custom 3D-printed brackets were prepared to fix the *ReSpeaker* module above the main avionics of the UAV.

Custom software was developed for a Linux-based *Rapsberry Pi* computer. The set of *Python* programming language scripts was written based on the official driver for the *ReSpeaker* microphone array. Combined with built-in *Wi-Fi* connectivity and remote access mechanism such as SSH, the data acquisition system allows convenient experiments in flight. In addition, the quite considerable computing power of SBC enables the implementation of not only data acquisition, but also further signal processing and fault classification algorithms.

Figure 5. Experimental setup to acquire acoustic data.

3. Proposed Method

Our approach to the stated FDI problem utilizes data-driven fault detection that takes advantage of a machine learning-based fault classifier with multichannel acoustic signal features as the model input. The following section describes the processing pipeline in a sequential manner, from raw acoustic data to the FDI system output indicating detected fault class.

3.1. Signal Processing

An algorithm is based on short chunks of the acoustic signal acquired with the UAV onboard microphone array. The length of the signal acquisition period is a factor that affects the classification performance, since longer chunks contain more information and provide the classifier with better-quality data.

At first, the raw acoustic signal is multiplied by a window function. The process is applied to all four channels of the audio file concurrently since the fault classifier is processing the data from all of the microphones combined. A Kaiser windowing function was used in presented analysis.

Afterward, the Mel Frequency Cepstrum Coefficients (MFCCs) are extracted independently for every audio channel. MFCC-based signal features are applied primarily and quite broadly in speech recognition systems [27]. However, they have also been used in numerous applications in the field of condition monitoring and fault detection as well [28,29]. The main idea behind the MFCC technique is first to convert every signal frame into a magnitude spectrum by applying a Fast Fourier Transform (FFT). Afterward, the obtained spectrum is passed through a set of triangle-shaped band-pass filters known as the Mel filter bank. The number of filters in the bank, annotated as n_f, is an adjustable variable. The name "mel" corresponds to a unit of measure with variable spacing that is more natural to the frequency perceived by the human ear. In the next step, the logarithm is applied to filter bank outputs and finally, the discrete cosine transform of the resultant signal is taken to obtain MFCCs. In our algorithm, 104 cepstral coefficients are extracted from each channel. As a result, the fault classifier is provided with a 425-element input vector, consisting of MFCCs from 4 microphones and 9 labels of considered fault classes. The process of pre-processing acoustic signals in the FDI system is summarized in Figure 6.

3.2. Fault Classification

Several models were developed for the fault classification task and two of them were chosen for further evaluation as the most promising ones. The first classifier is based on the LSTM artificial neural network (ANN) architecture. This kind of ANN falls into the category of recurrent neural networks with the great advantage of being able to overcome a vanishing gradient problem. LSTM-based models are commonly used in a variety of tasks that involve speech and acoustic recognition algorithms [30]. Such networks have been shown to be very efficient in time series prediction and keeping track of long-term dependencies [31]. In recent years, they have received widespread attention in the fields of fault diagnosis and condition monitoring, with a particularly high number of applications in the data-driven diagnosis of rotating machinery [32,33].

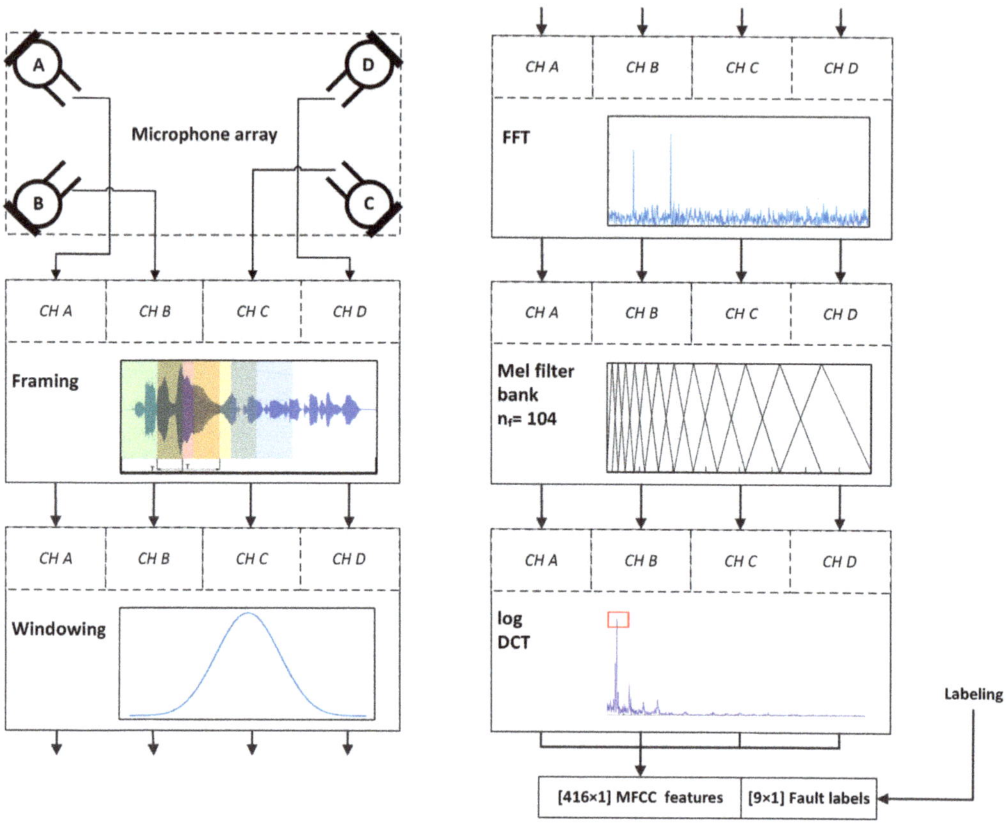

Figure 6. Summary of the pretraining signal processing steps.

The LSTM-based network is more computationally demanding than the regular RNN because of the more complicated structure of a single cell of the LSTM network. An LSTM unit consists of a cell, an input gate, an output gate and a forget gate. The cell stores values over some arbitrary time intervals and the gates control the flow of data from subsequent iterations. This ensures that the output is affected by data from any range without gradient fading. Our model consists of one LSTM layer and two fully connected layers. The latter serves as an output layer to return the probability of the occurrence of a predefined fault type. The network outputs 9 such values, of which the first 8 are meant for combinations of two fault types at four different rotor locations (please refer to Table 2 for details about considered fault classes). The last output reports whether all the rotors are in healthy condition. The structure of the described ANN is shown in Figure 7.

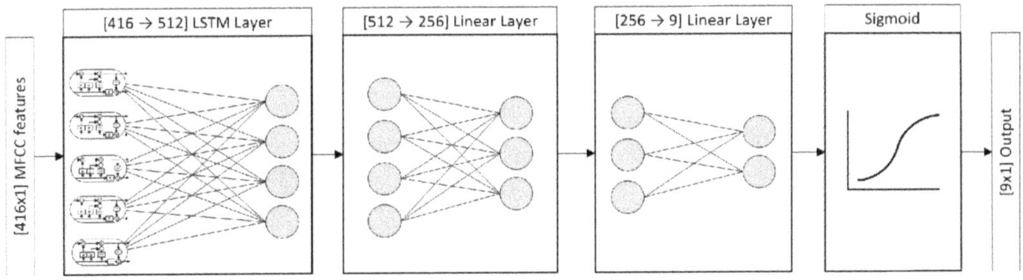

Figure 7. Structure of the LSTM-based fault classifier.

Table 2. Summary of flight experiments conducted and the quantities of data for every fault class considered.

Flight Scenario			**No. Flights**	**Audio Data Length [s]**
Nominal (healthy) condition		10	2400	
Single damaged blade		12	2400	
Two damaged rotors	Adjacent locations		9	1800
	Opposite locations		5	1000

Fault Class	**Broken Blade Location**				**Fault Type**	**No. Flights**	**Audio Data Length [s]**
	A	**B**	**C**	**D**			
H	–	–	–	–	none	10	2400
AF	+	–	–	–	fractured tip	5	1000
BF	–	+	–	–		5	1000
CF	–	–	+	–		5	1000
DF	–	–	–	+		4	800
AE	+	–	–	–	edge distortion	4	800
BE	–	+	–	–		5	1000
CE	–	–	+	–		3	600
DE	–	–	–	+		6	1200

The second classifier developed in our solution is based on convolutional ANN (CNN). Applications of this architecture proliferated mainly in the field of image processing. However, many successful attempts at machine diagnosis have been made [34,35]. A distinguishing feature of CNNs is that in the process of training, the parameters of neuron-shared filters are affected, instead of training weights that connect each neuron of one layer with each neuron of the next layer. This approach significantly reduces the memory size of the network. In each layer, a certain number of kernels move every stride along the input vector, creating representations that serve as inputs to subsequent layers.

A model consisting of six convolutional layers and one fully connected output layer was used to solve the rotor fault detection problem. The first convolutional layer has four channels, which corresponds to the data from the four-channel microphone array collected during the study. A *ReLu* activation function is used along with batch normalization to regularize inputs and prevent overfitting. The second layer has 64 channels, and each subsequent layer doubles the number of channels. The last convolutional layer reduces the number of channels down to 1 in order to link it to a fully connected output layer, whose input size depends on the number of convolutional layers and the size of the kernel. In our case, it has 9 outputs that serve as fault indicators in a manner similar to the previously presented LSTM-based classifier. Figure 8 shows a graphical representation of the structure of the CNN fault classifier.

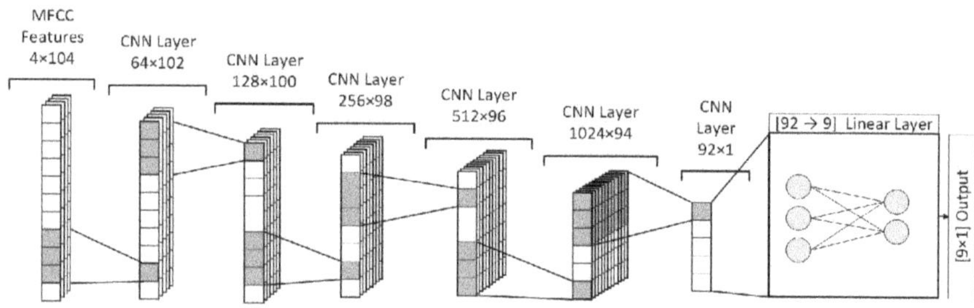

Figure 8. Structure of CNN-based fault classifier.

4. Experimental Evaluation

4.1. Acoustic Dataset

In order to train and validate the presented fault classifiers, a series of flight experiments was carried out. The idea behind them was to collect acoustic data in flight in different scenarios with variable locations and types of faulty rotors. There were 36 flights in total and during each one of them, 200 to 240 s of 4-channel audio data were recorded. The rotors were switched in between the experiments, with variable location, type and number of damaged blades placed in the system. The sampling rate of sound signals is equal to 44,100 Hz. Recordings made during flights with damaged rotors were shorter due to the increased power consumption of the propulsion system. The methodology of the conducted experiments is shown in Figure 9.

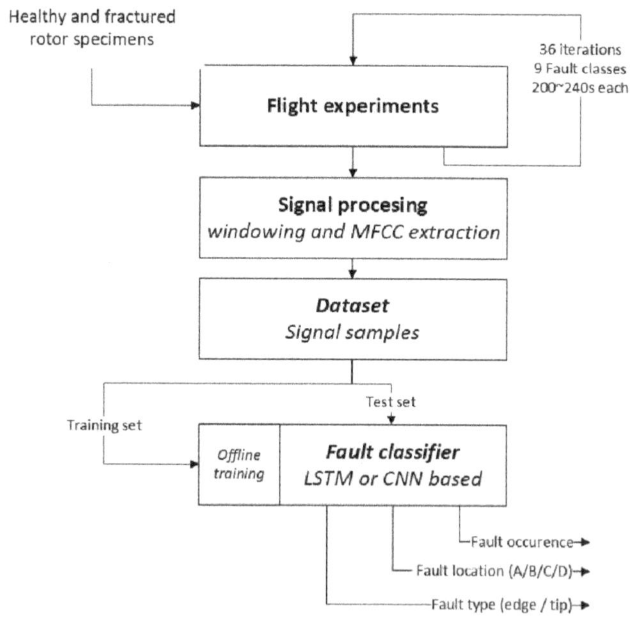

Figure 9. Process of gathering samples of acoustic dataset and evaluating FDI method.

During every experiment, the UAV trajectory included a mix of hovering, ascending, descending and translational motions. The tests were carried out indoors inside the sports hall with dimensions of about 20 × 10 × 5 m. Three main categories of experiment scenarios were considered: flights with all-healthy rotors, the occurrence of a single damaged propeller and UAV equipped with two impaired rotors at the same time. In the latter variant, some of the tests were performed with two adjacent rotors damaged and the others with faults in opposite actuators. Figure 10 shows the flight variants performed.

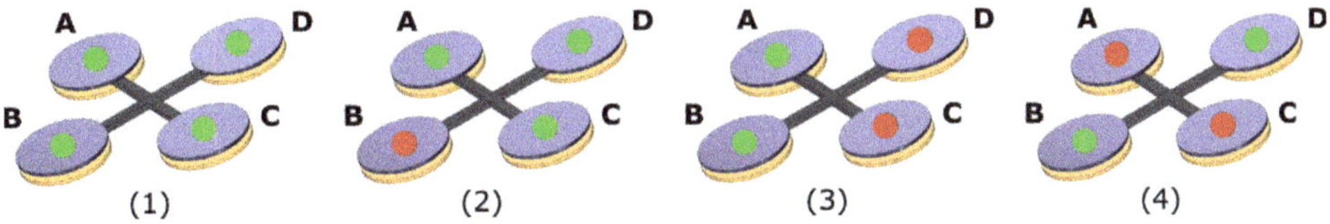

Figure 10. Types of fault scenarios considered in experiments: (**1**) no faults, (**2**) single damaged rotor, (**3**) dual fault, adjacent, (**4**) dual fault, opposite actuators.

Multiple specimens of damaged rotors were used and healthy–damaged combinations were chosen in a way that provides all fault classes with a similar and sufficient amount of data for training the intelligent classifier. In the analysis, two types of blade impairment are considered: the fractured rotor tip and distorted edge, just as the initial examples analyzed with the stationary test stand. The structure and fault classes included in the dataset are summarized in Table 2.

The signal frames used in processing were extracted from audio files using variable window length and overlap, thus boosting the number of samples to several thousand for every model training process. In Figure 11, some selected samples of raw audio signals are shown. They are taken from the recordings of all-healthy flight (a) and the scenario with a single damaged propeller present in the system (b,c). Sample (b) was recorded with the microphone located opposite to the fault location, while frame (c) was acquired with the sensor located in the closest vicinity of the faulty rotor. Next to the raw signals, a power spectral density estimate is plotted to show differences in the frequency content of the recorded sounds.

In further analysis, the dataset was split into training, validation and testing sets. Signals from different flights were used in each of the three subsets to avoid overfitting the models. It is worth mentioning that to reduce data bias, the whole dataset was not always used for training and validation. However, since we aim to share the data publicly, all of the recordings are included, since some approaches may utilize different parts of the dataset. Refer to the Data Availability section at the end of the article for more details on access to the dataset.

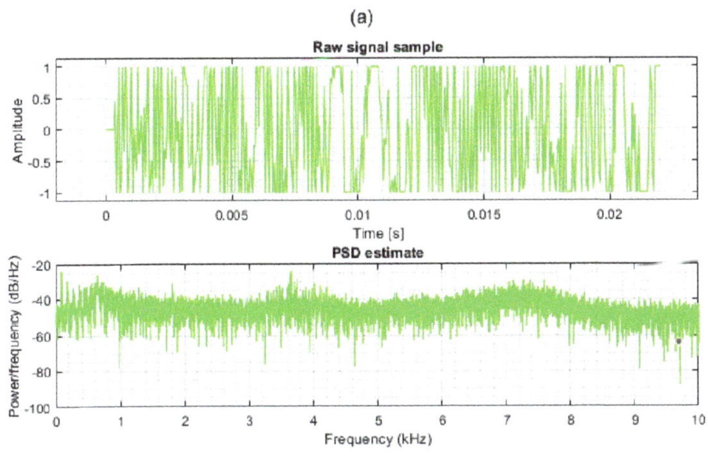

Figure 11. *Cont.*

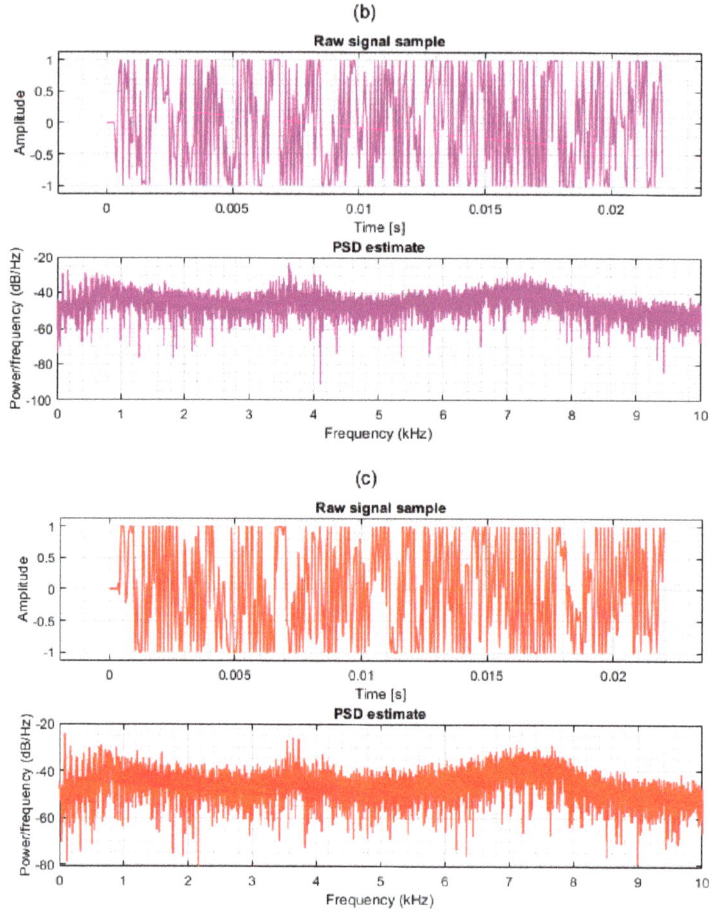

Figure 11. Samples of recorded audio signals along with their PSD estimates: (**a**) all rotors healthy, (**b**) single damaged rotor, opposite microphone, (**c**) single damaged rotor, closest microphone.

4.2. Classification Results

The developed fault classifiers were put through the evaluation process to determine the impact of certain parameters of the signal processing and classification pipeline on the final efficiency. A set of conventional performance metrics was used to compare different models with accuracy, precision, recall and F-score among them. The two best classifiers mentioned in the previous section were considered as a reference point and several of their parameters were evaluated to show the capabilities of the proposed FDI scheme.

4.2.1. LSTM-Based Fault Classifier

At first, the lightweight LSTM model was evaluated with regard to the impact of layer sizes. The smallest ANN considered used 64 LSTM cells and 32 neurons in a linear layer. From this point on, the size of the network doubled at every step, to the point where no substantial improvement in performance metrics was observed. Table 3 summarizes the change in classifier efficiency due to the increase in the size of the layers.

The fourth model was selected for further analysis since no further performance improvement was observed. It is noticeable that even the smallest network provided satisfactory results. However, a low precision score meant that a higher proportion of false positives was reported. Therefore, models based on smaller ANNs provided a higher rate of false alarms. The hyperparameters of the selected classifier are summarized in Table 4.

Table 3. Evaluation of the LSTM-based fault classifier.

Id	LSTM Layer Size	Linear Layer Size	F-Score	Precision	Recall	Accuracy
1	64	32	0.910	0.858	0.969	0.967
2	128	64	0.936	0.900	0.975	0.977
3	256	128	0.982	0.987	0.978	0.994
4	512	256	0.985	0.989	0.980	0.995

Table 4. Parameters of the selected LSTM-based fault classifier.

Parameter	Value
Number of input layer neurons	512
Number of hidden layer neurons	256
Number of output layer neurons	9
Batch size	640
Loss function	*CrossEntropyLoss*
Output layer activation function	*Sigmoid*
Optimizer	*Adam*
Compiler metric	*accuracy*
Checkpoint monitor	*validation loss*
Number of epochs	866
Training loss	2.19
Training accuracy	1
Validation loss	2.36
Validation accuracy	0.998
Test accuracy	0.994

For the selected model, a final classification test was performed with a 7900-element subset of data derived from separate sound recordings. The confusion matrices for every fault class considered are shown in Table 5.

Table 5. Confusion matrices for the LSTM-based fault classifier.

AF	Prediction		AE	Prediction		BF	Prediction	
True Label	0	1	True Label	0	1	True Label	0	1
0	6727	0	0	6270	66	0	6335	1
1	39	1134	1	52	1512	1	10	1554
BE	Prediction		**CF**	Prediction		**CE**	Prediction	
True Label	0	1	True Label	0	1	True Label	0	1
0	6317	19	0	6321	15	0	6726	1
1	29	1535	1	95	1469	1	2	1171
DF	Prediction		**DE**	Prediction		**H**	Prediction	
True Label	0	1	True Label	0	1	True Label	0	1
0	6336	0	0	6331	5	0	7404	25
1	0	1564	1	11	1553	1	1	470

The results of the classification test show that although some fault classes are predicted with more false negatives and positives, the differences are relatively small in comparison with the correct predictions. Both types of faults are clearly distinguishable from each other.

4.2.2. CNN-Based Model

The second fault classifier was evaluated first on the basis of the internal parameters of the network. Different counts of convolutional layers, two kernel sizes and a variable number of filters were considered. The results are summarized in Table 6.

Table 6. Evaluation of CNN-based fault classifier.

Kernel Size	No. Kernels	No. Filters	F-Score	Precision	Recall	Accuracy
3	4	2	0.789	0.707	0.893	0.918
		4	0.876	0.839	0.918	0.956
		8	0.889	0.850	0.932	0.960
		16	0.884	0.817	0.962	0.957
		32	0.963	0.968	0.957	0.987
		64	0.964	0.973	0.956	0.988
	5	2	0.804	0.736	0.885	0.926
		4	0.910	0.881	0.940	0.968
		8	0.939	0.930	0.948	0.979
		16	0.963	0.971	0.955	0.987
		32	0.965	0.972	0.958	0.988
		64	0.969	0.978	0.961	0.990
	6	2	0.811	0.748	0.886	0.929
		4	0.910	0.907	0.912	0.969
		8	0.957	0.973	0.942	0.986
		16	0.967	0.977	0.957	0.989
		32	0.963	0.976	0.949	0.987
		64	0.980	0.986	0.975	0.993
5	4	2	0.844	0.789	0.908	0.942
		4	0.896	0.862	0.934	0.963
		8	0.949	0.943	0.956	0.983
		16	0.957	0.960	0.954	0.985
		32	0.971	0.978	0.964	0.990
		64	0.973	0.983	0.964	0.991
	5	2	0.862	0.801	0.933	0.949
		4	0.937	0.926	0.947	0.978
		8	0.948	0.941	0.955	0.982
		16	0.966	0.974	0.959	0.989
		32	0.965	0.975	0.956	0.988
		64	0.970	0.978	0.961	0.990
	6	2	0.909	0.898	0.921	0.969
		4	0.931	0.938	0.924	0.976
		8	0.940	0.958	0.924	0.980
		16	0.965	0.974	0.956	0.988
		32	0.964	0.974	0.954	0.988
		64	0.971	0.975	0.967	0.990

Performance metrics increase along with the number of convolutional layers and filters. Enlarging the kernel size increases accuracy with a small number of filters. However, it is the latter parameter that affects the memory footprint of the model most significantly. The best results were obtained with the highlighted model and therefore it was the subject of final testing. The global parameters of the selected classifier are summarized in Table 7.

Table 7. Parameters of the best developed CNN-based fault classifier.

Parameter	Value
Batch size	640
Loss function	*CrossEntropyLoss*
Output layer activation function	*Sigmoid*
Between layer activation function	*ReLU*
Optimizer	*Adam*
Compiler metric	*accuracy*
Checkpoint monitor	*validation loss*
Number of epochs	38
Training loss	2.27
Training accuracy	1
Validation loss	2.38
Validation accuracy	0.997
Test accuracy	0.993

Detailed confusion matrices of the best CNN model are presented in Table 8.

Table 8. Confusion matrices for CNN-based fault classifier.

AF	Prediction		**AE**	Prediction		**BF**	Prediction	
True Label	0	1	True Label	0	1	True Label	0	1
0	6725	2	0	6269	67	0	6334	2
1	34	1139	1	43	1521	1	19	1545
BE	Prediction		**CF**	Prediction		**CE**	Prediction	
True Label	0	1	True Label	0	1	True Label	0	1
0	6310	26	0	6318	18	0	6725	2
1	63	1501	1	106	1458	1	23	1150
DF	Prediction		**DE**	Prediction		**H**	Prediction	
True Label	0	1	True Label	0	1	True Label	0	1
0	6330	6	0	6326	10	0	7394	35
1	0	1564	1	6	1558	1	21	450

Both fault detectors yield satisfactory results, with the main performance metrics scoring more than 97%. In either case, accuracy was the highest value, since it was a main metric used in the training process. Slightly better results were achieved with the LSTM-based model with regard to precision and recall. However, the differences are small enough to consider both approaches equally successful. On the other hand, the convolutional network is much more complicated with a larger number of layers and individual neurons. Therefore, some additional validation steps were performed.

4.2.3. Computation Time

Both models were tested for computational demands. The code was run using a PC workstation equipped with AMD Ryzen 9 3950X CPU, 128 GB DDR3 RAM and supported with an Nvidia RTX 2070 graphics card. Execution time of the signal processing stage, model training and single sample classification were gathered. The results are summarized in Table 9.

Table 9. Execution time for feature extraction, training and classification steps.

		LSTM	CNN
MFCC extraction	Avg. per frame [ms]	2.860	
	Std dev. [ms]	0.032	
Model training	Total [min]	24	7
Fault classification	Avg. per frame [ms]	0.037	0.630
	Std dev. [ms]	0.003	0.011

As suspected, the time of fault signature classification for a single signal frame with four channels and 204 cepstral coefficients each is significantly higher in the case of a more sophisticated CNN-based model. Training of the latter classifier has a shorter duration. However, it is not a problematic issue since our plans for further development assume deploying an already pretrained classifier to an onboard embedded system. Another noteworthy fact is the relation of processing time in consecutive steps of the processing pipeline. The classification stage that consumes a fraction of a millisecond contributes to a small extent to the time elapsed from a fault's occurrence to detection, since MFCC extraction consumes around 3 ms and the time of signal acquisition for considered models equals half of a second. However, we expect that the target implementation of signal processing on a low-power SBC will result in considerably longer computation. Therefore, substantial effort was put into optimizing the fault classifier.

4.2.4. Signal Frame Length

Since signal acquisition time contributes to the highest degree to a full FDI process, additional validation of the LSTM model was performed with shorter bursts of audio data. The main aim was to investigate how far the signal frame can be reduced with satisfactory performance metrics maintained. The results of the analysis are summarized in Table 10.

Table 10. Effects of the length of the signal frame on the performance of the LSTM-based fault classifier.

Frame Length [ms]	F-Score	Precision	Recall	Accuracy
600	0.980	0.986	0.975	0.993
500	0.985	0.989	0.980	0.995
400	0.975	0.980	0.969	0.991
300	0.964	0.972	0.955	0.988
200	0.947	0.956	0.938	0.982
100	0.907	0.896	0.919	0.968
75	0.868	0.842	0.896	0.953

It is clearly seen that buffer lengths below 200 ms result in a significant drop in performance, with precision and recall falling rapidly in the first place. Acquisition time is directly related to the spectral resolution of FFT as a part of the MFCC extraction process. With a constant sampling frequency, frame length becomes the only factor that affects the process. Therefore, with longer data frames, it is possible to observe and extract more detailed patterns. The results are consistent with our previous works [9,10], where similar lengths of vibration signals proved to be sufficient.

4.2.5. Number of Cepstral Coefficients

The last step of validation was to analyze the performance of the selected LSTM-based fault classifier due to the size of an input vector. Several quantities of MFCCs extracted for every channel were selected and performance metrics were computed. Table 11 shows the results with a similar outcome to the frame length validation. Since the number of mel filters controls how many frequencies are clustered into one cepstrum, a smaller number of MFCCs results in less detailed signal features. Some key fault frequencies might contribute to a smaller number of more generalized values and, as a result, be ignored by the model. However, the performance of fault classification decreases with the number of coefficients doubled in relation to the reference model. We suspect that such a phenomenon occurs due to the size of the ANN layers being insufficient for the 4 × 208 input vector.

Table 11. Performance of the LSTM fault classifier with different numbers of cepstral coefficients extracted for every audio channel.

No. MFCC	F-Score	Precision	Recall	Accuracy
208	0.971	0.980	0.962	0.990
104	0.985	0.989	0.980	0.995
52	0.960	0.959	0.962	0.986
26	0.915	0.891	0.940	0.970
13	0.885	0.836	0.939	0.958

5. Conclusions

In the article, the development of a comprehensive, data-driven FDI method for multirotor UAV rotor faults is presented. An algorithm is aimed towards early detection of damaged rotor faults, which lead to degraded flight stabilization, decrease safety of the UAV operation and increase power consumption of the power train. An intelligent fault classification algorithm is based on the MFCC-based features extracted from the four-channel audio signal. The data were recorded in real-life flight experiments using a custom-built onboard microphone array subsystem. Various rotor impairments and their locations were considered with flights that included single- and double-damaged rotors in different combinations. The dataset was split into individual audio frames and MFCCs were extracted as input for the ANN-based fault classifiers. Two main approaches were tested, with convolutional and LSTM-based neural networks validated. Both variants provided satisfactory results, with the prediction accuracy and the F1 metric exceeding 98%. However, the LSTM-based model is more lightweight and consumes less computing time. Therefore, it was selected for further evaluation with the goal of decreasing fault detection and isolation time. The final analysis has shown that the longest step of the process, signal acquisition, can be further shortened with a slight drop in performance. As a result, the presented FDI algorithm based on 200 ms long signal samples achieved an accuracy exceeding 98%. The proposed method is able to accurately detect broken rotor blade faults with an additional ability to precisely predict which propulsion unit is damaged. Furthermore, both evaluated classification methods correctly distinguished between two types of impairment—fractured tip and damaged edge of the blade.

Our further development plans include real-time implementation of the fault classification algorithm on the low-power onboard SBC. Therefore, the method was tested with a decreased number of cepstral coefficients since the MFCC extraction step introduces the largest amount of computational load. Furthermore, many possible improvements to the FDI system are considered, such as training the classifier to recognize different actuator-related faults. Some initial analysis of the audio data suggests that the statistical and spectral features of the signals may allow the proposed FDI system to recognize motor-related bearing faults. Other possible improvements include extending the dataset with experiments carried out using different UAVs and combining features of vibration and acoustic signals to boost the FDI capabilities.

Author Contributions: Conceptualization, A.B. and W.G.; methodology, A.B., R.K. and M.K.; software, R.K. and M.K.; validation, A.B., M.K. and R.K.; resources, A.B., M.K. and R.K.; data curation,

M.K. and R.K.; writing—original draft preparation, A.B; writing—review and editing, W.G. and A.B.; supervision, W.G. All authors have read and agreed to the published version of the manuscript.

Funding: This research was funded by Poznan University of Technology grant number 0214/S-BAD/0237.

Institutional Review Board Statement: Not applicable.

Informed Consent Statement: Not applicable.

Data Availability Statement: The datasets gathered and analyzed during the current study are available at https://chmura.put.poznan.pl/s/tu52v0Dlx4hfmfO (accessed on 23 May 2022). The data are shared under CC-BY-NC 4.0 license.

Conflicts of Interest: The authors declare no conflict of interest.

Abbreviations

The following abbreviations are used in this manuscript:

ADC	Analog-to-Digital Converter
ANN	Artificial Neural Network
AOP	Acoustic Overload Point
BLDC	Brushless Direct Current
CNN	Convolutional Neural Network
ESC	Electronic Speed Controller
FDI	Fault Detection and Isolation
FFT	Fast Fourier Transform
FTC	Fault-Tolerant Control
I^2S	Inter-IC Sound
IMU	Inertial Measurement Unit
LoE	Loss of Effectiveness
LSTM	Long Short-Term Memory
MEMS	Micro-electro-mechanical Systems
MFCC	Mel Frequency Cepstral Coefficients
RNN	Recurrent Neural Network
SBC	Single-Board Computer
SNR	Signal-to-Noise Ratio
SSH	Secure Shell
THD	Total Harmonic Distortion
UAV	Unmanned Aerial Vehicle

References

1. Stöcker, C.; Bennett, R.; Nex, F.; Gerke, M.; Zevenbergen, J. Review of the Current State of UAV Regulations. *Remote. Sens.* **2017**, *9*, 459. [CrossRef]
2. Zhai, Q.; Ye, Z.S. How reliable should military UAVs be? *IISE Trans.* **2020**, *52*, 1234–1245. [CrossRef]
3. Wild, G.; Murray, J.; Baxter, G. Exploring Civil Drone Accidents and Incidents to Help Prevent Potential Air Disasters. *Aerospace* **2016**, *3*, 22. [CrossRef]
4. Susini, A. A Technocritical Review of Drones Crash Risk Probabilistic Consequences and its Societal Acceptance. In Proceedings of the RIMMA 2014 Berlin, Risk Information Management, Risk Models and Applications Conference, Berlin, Germany, 28–30 October 2015.
5. Witczak, M.; Pazera, M. Fault tolerant-control: Solutions and challenges. *Pomiary Autom. Robot.* **2016**, *20*, 5–16. [CrossRef]
6. Simani, S.; Fantuzzi, C.; Patton, R.J. Model-based fault diagnosis techniques. In *Model-Based Fault Diagnosis in Dynamic Systems Using Identification Techniques*; Springer: London, UK, 2003; pp. 19–60.
7. Fekih, A. Fault diagnosis and Fault Tolerant Control design for aerospace systems: A bibliographical review. In Proceedings of the 2014 American Control Conference, Portland, OR, USA, 4–6 June 2014; pp. 1286–1291.
8. Fourlas, G.K.; Karras, G.C. A Survey on Fault Diagnosis and Fault-Tolerant Control Methods for Unmanned Aerial Vehicles. *Machines* **2021**, *9*, 197. [CrossRef]
9. Bondyra, A.; Gasior, P.; Gardecki, S.; Kasiński, A. Fault diagnosis and condition monitoring of UAV rotor using signal processing. In Proceedings of the 2017 Signal Processing: Algorithms, Architectures, Arrangements, and Applications (SPA), Poznan, Poland, 22–24 September 2017; pp. 233–238.

10. Bondyra, A.; Gasior, P.; Gardecki, S.; Kasinski, A.J. Development of the Sensory Network for the Vibration-based Fault Detection and Isolation in the Multirotor UAV Propulsion System. In Proceedings of the 15th International Conference on Informatics in Control, Automation and Robotics, ICINCO, Porto, Portugal, 29–31 July 2018; pp. 112–119.
11. Cen, Z.; Noura, H.; Younes, Y.A. Robust Fault Estimation on a real quadrotor UAV using optimized Adaptive Thau Observer. In Proceedings of the 2013 International Conference on Unmanned Aircraft Systems (ICUAS), Atlanta, Georgia, 28–31 May 2013; pp. 550–556.
12. Cen, Z.; Noura, H. An Adaptive Thau Observer for estimating the time-varying LOE fault of quadrotor actuators. In Proceedings of the 2013 Conference on Control and Fault-Tolerant Systems (SysTol), Nice, France, 9–11 October 2013; pp. 468–473.
13. Cen, Z.; Noura, H.; Susilo, T.B.; Younes, Y.A. Engineering implementation on fault diagnosis for quadrotors based on nonlinear observer. In Proceedings of the 2013 25th Chinese Control and Decision Conference (CCDC), Guiyang, China, 25–27 May 2013; pp. 2971–2975.
14. Sharifi, F.; Mirzaei, M.; Gordon, B.W.; Zhang, Y. Fault tolerant control of a quadrotor UAV using sliding mode control. In Proceedings of the 2010 Conference on Control and Fault-Tolerant Systems (SysTol), Nice, France, 6–8 October 2010; pp. 239–244.
15. Moghadam, M.; Caliskan, F. Actuator and sensor fault detection and diagnosis of quadrotor based on Two-Stage Kalman Filter. In Proceedings of the 2015 5th Australian Control Conference (AUCC), Gold Coast, Australia, 5–6 November 2015; pp. 182–187.
16. Freddi, A.; Longhi, S.; Monteriù, A. Actuator fault detection system for a mini-quadrotor. In Proceedings of the 2010 IEEE International Symposium on Industrial Electronics, Bari, Italy, 4–7 July 2010; pp. 2055–2060.
17. Cândido, A.S.; Harrop Galvão, R.K.; Yoneyama, T. Actuator fault diagnosis and control of a quadrotor. In Proceedings of the 2014 12th IEEE International Conference on Industrial Informatics (INDIN), Porto Alegre, Brazil, 27–30 July 2014; pp. 310–315.
18. Fu, J.; Sun, C.; Yu, Z.; Liu, L. A hybrid CNN-LSTM model based actuator fault diagnosis for six-rotor UAVs. In Proceedings of the 2019 Chinese Control And Decision Conference (CCDC), Nanchang, China, 3–5 June 2019; IEEE: Piscataway, NJ, USA, 2019; pp. 410–414.
19. Pourpanah, F.; Zhang, B.; Ma, R.; Hao, Q. Anomaly Detection and Condition Monitoring of UAV Motors and Propellers. In Proceedings of the 2018 IEEE SENSORS, Seoul, Korea, 12–14 March 2018; pp. 1–4.
20. Iannace, G.; Ciaburro, G.; Trematerra, A. Fault Diagnosis for UAV Blades Using Artificial Neural Network. *Robotics* **2019**, *8*, 59. [CrossRef]
21. Liu, W.; Chen, Z.; Zheng, M. An Audio-Based Fault Diagnosis Method for Quadrotors Using Convolutional Neural Network and Transfer Learning. In Proceedings of the 2020 American Control Conference (ACC), New Orleans, LA, USA, 1–3 July 2020; pp. 1367–1372.
22. Altinors, A.; Yol, F.; Yaman, O. A sound based method for fault detection with statistical feature extraction in UAV motors. *Appl. Acoust.* **2021**, *183*, 108325. [CrossRef]
23. Aszkowski, P.; Błoszyk, K.; Bondyra, A.; Gąsior, P.; Giernacki, W. UAV propulsion analysis system with reconfigurable controller feature. *Meas. Autom. Monit.* **2017**, *63*, 171–173.
24. Ou, L.; Li, D.; Li, J. Shaft center orbit diagnoses technology of broken-blade propeller induced shaft vibration fault. In Proceedings of the 2013 International Conference on Quality, Reliability, Risk, Maintenance, and Safety Engineering (QR2MSE), Chengdu, China, 15–18 July 2013; pp. 1777–1780.
25. Fries, J. *The Effect of Helicopter Main Rotor Blade Damage on the Rotor Disk (Whole Rotor) Motion*; Technical Report; U.S. Army Research Lab: Aberdeen, MD, USA, 2000.
26. Peng, C.; Bai, Y.; Gong, X.; Gao, Q.; Zhao, C.; Tian, Y. Modeling and robust backstepping sliding mode control with Adaptive RBFNN for a novel coaxial eight-rotor UAV. *IEEE/CAA J. Autom. Sin.* **2015**, *2*, 56–64.
27. Gupta, D.; Bansal, P.; Choudhary, K. The state of the art of feature extraction techniques in speech recognition. *Speech Lang. Process. Hum.-Mach. Commun.* **2018**, *664*, 195–207.
28. Marwala, T. Data processing techniques for condition monitoring. *Cond. Monit. Using Comput. Intell. Methods* **2012**, 27–51.
29. Shaikh, K.B.T.; Jawarkar, N.P.; Ahmed, V. Machine diagnosis using acoustic analysis: A review. In Proceedings of the 2021 IEEE Conference on Norbert Wiener in the 21st Century (21CW), Melbourne, Australia, 13–16 July 2021; pp. 1–6.
30. Yu, Y.; Si, X.; Hu, C.; Zhang, J. A Review of Recurrent Neural Networks: LSTM Cells and Network Architectures. *Neural Comput.* **2019**, *31*, 1235–1270. [CrossRef] [PubMed]
31. Smagulova, K.; James, A.P. A survey on LSTM memristive neural network architectures and applications. *Eur. Phys. J. Spec. Top.* **2019**, *228*, 2313–2324. [CrossRef]
32. Lindemann, B.; Maschler, B.; Sahlab, N.; Weyrich, M. A survey on anomaly detection for technical systems using LSTM networks. *Comput. Ind.* **2021**, *131*, 103498. [CrossRef]
33. Jalayer, M.; Orsenigo, C.; Vercellis, C. Fault detection and diagnosis for rotating machinery: A model based on convolutional LSTM, Fast Fourier and continuous wavelet transforms. *Comput. Ind.* **2021**, *125*, 103378. [CrossRef]
34. Zhang, T.; Dai, J. Mechanical Fault Diagnosis Methods Based on Convolutional Neural Network: A Review. *J. Phys. Conf. Ser.* **2021**, *1750*, 012048. [CrossRef]
35. Neupane, D.; Seok, J. Bearing fault detection and diagnosis using case western reserve university dataset with deep learning approaches: A review. *IEEE Access* **2020**, *8*, 93155–93178. [CrossRef]

drones

Article

Mission Chain Driven Unmanned Aerial Vehicle Swarms Cooperation for the Search and Rescue of Outdoor Injured Human Targets

Yusen Cao [1,2,†], Fugui Qi [1,2,†], Yu Jing [1,2], Mingming Zhu [1,3], Tao Lei [1,2], Zhao Li [1,2], Juanjuan Xia [1,2], Jianqi Wang [1,2] and Guohua Lu [1,2,*]

1 Department of Military Biomedical Engineering, Air Force Military Medical University, Xi'an 710032, China; higher1212@fmmu.edu.cn (Y.C.); qifg1992@fmmu.edu.cn (F.Q.); jingyu1998@fmmu.edu.cn (Y.J.); bme19005@fmmu.edu.cn (M.Z.); leitaoxman@fmmu.edu.cn (T.L.); lizhaofmmu@fmmu.edu.cn (Z.L.); magnolxia@fmmu.edu.cn (J.X.); wangjq@fmmu.edu.cn (J.W.)
2 Shaanxi Provincial Key Laboratory of Bioelectromagnetic Detection and Intelligent Perception, Xi'an 710032, China
3 Drug and Instrument Supervisory & Test Station of PLA Xining Joint Logistics Support Center, Lanzhou 730050, China
* Correspondence: lugh1976@fmmu.edu.cn; Tel.: +86-29-84711471
† These authors contributed equally to this work.

Citation: Cao, Y.; Qi, F.; Jing, Y.; Zhu, M.; Lei, T.; Li, Z.; Xia, J.; Wang, J.; Lu, G. Mission Chain Driven Unmanned Aerial Vehicle Swarms Cooperation for the Search and Rescue of Outdoor Injured Human Targets. *Drones* **2022**, 6, 138. https://doi.org/10.3390/drones6060138

Academic Editors: Andrzej Łukaszewicz, Wojciech Giernacki, Zbigniew Kulesza, Jaroslaw Pytka and Andriy Holovatyy

Received: 4 May 2022
Accepted: 26 May 2022
Published: 28 May 2022

Abstract: A novel cooperative strategy for distributed unmanned aerial vehicle (UAV) swarms with different functions, namely the mission chain-driven unmanned aerial vehicle swarms cooperation method, is proposed to allow the fast search and timely rescue of injured human targets in a wide-area outdoor environment. First, a UAV-camera unit is exploited to detect the suspected human target combined with improved deep learning technology. Then, the target location information is transferred to a self-organizing network. Then, the special bio-radar-UAV unit was released to recheck the survivals through a respiratory characteristic detection algorithm. Finally, driven by the location and vital sign status of the injured, a nearby emergency-UAV unit will perform corresponding medical emergency missions, such as dropping emergency supplies. Experimental results show that this strategy can identify the human targets autonomously from the outdoor environment effectively, and the target detection, target sensing, and medical emergency mission chain is completed successfully relying on the cooperative working mode, which is meaningful for the future search-rescue mission of outdoor injured human targets.

Keywords: cooperative strategy; UAV swarms; deep learning; self-organizing network; bio-radar

1. Introduction

After natural disasters, wars, and other public safety events, complex environments put forward severe tests for the search for the wounded. A wide range of areas in distress makes the search for the wounded inefficient, thus missing the best rescue time for the wounded. In addition, if rescuers can obtain the location information and life status of the injured in a timely manner, it is crucial to improve the rescue effect. At this stage, the wounded search equipment includes mainly individual search equipment and wounded search unmanned aerial vehicles. Common single-soldier search equipment includes chest bands, wristbands, and handheld search devices, and the main vital signs monitored include breathing, heart rate, and blood oxygen [1]. This kind of equipment has the following deficiencies: first, the equipment needs to be distributed in advance, and it is easy to cause inconvenience in the movement of the user personnel; second, when this equipment is damaged by impact, fire, etc., the accuracy of the collection of life information of the injured will be reduced. To solve the limitations of wearable technology, researchers can effectively improve the search efficiency of outdoor injured people by using an unmanned aerial vehicle (UAV) equipped with a variety of sensors to detect injured people in large areas of distress [2].

Multirotor UAVs have strong manoeuvrability, hovering stability, and flexibility and are not affected by terrain and landforms. Multirotor UAVs with sensors are widely used in power line inspection, remote sensing, and disaster rescue. The image obtained by the visible light camera of the UAV is processed by methods such as semantic segmentation to extract the power lines in the image. Compared with traditional human power line inspection, it is more efficient [3]. Through the UAV-based multispectral camera system, all the ground targets would be screened, and specific features of the spectral image would be extracted for target recognition [4]. Therefore, the UAV-based searching system is adopted in various search-rescue environments, such as maritime distress and post-earthquakes, effectively reducing task risk and improving rescue efficiency [5–7].

However, a single UAV is limited by its endurance and communication distance, and it is difficult to complete some large-scale tasks. The technology of UAV swarms will make the working mode of the above scenes better expanded and deepened [8,9]. Affected by the limited power of the UAV and irregular distribution of the wounded, the search and rescue capability of a single UAV is very weak in a rescue mission. If an information-sharing network is established among multiple UAVs to coordinate the work of UAVs with different functions, rescue efficiency will be improved. Therefore, it is necessary to establish a sharing network in advance to realize the combination of searching and sensing the wounded by UAV swarms [10].

In the existing UAV networking solutions, centralized and distributed approaches occupy the mainstream [11–13]. The centralized networking solution adopts a one-to-many communication module that will return the status of the UAVs to the ground workstation processing and then the ground workstation coordination. The distributed network solution mainly adopts each UAV carrying onboard edge device real-time processing of UAV images or external sensor data, directly controlling the status of the UAV to realize the coordination of the cluster. Both have their own advantages and disadvantages in different application scenarios. The former does not require an additional load, but the higher bandwidth of transferring the data to the ground station causes a delay in the system response. The latter improves the response speed, but the computing power is lower than the computing power of the ground station equipment.

The construction of shared networks makes collaboration between different functional UAVs possible. Besides, the real-time search for injured outdoor human targets in the jungle requires a high-performance object-detection algorithm. A large number of object-detection algorithms have been proposed based on deep convolutional neural networks (CNNs) to extract target features and improve detection accuracy. Such algorithms mainly include two categories, and one is the regression-based single-stage, which directly uses CNN to extract features to predict object classification and location. The other is the two-stage algorithm, which generates preselected boxes (region proposals) that may contain the objects to be inspected in advance and then uses the CNN to classify each box. The two-stage includes R-CNN and Faster R-CNN [14]. Typical single-stage detection algorithms include single-shot detection (SSD) [15] and You Only Look Once (YOLO) [16]. Although single-stage networks expose a deficiency of lower accuracy than two-stage networks, it outperforms two-stage networks in terms of processing speed. Thanks to this, single-stage networks deployed on Nvidia edge devices are optimized through TensorRT to meet real-time and accuracy requirements [17], which greatly improves the inference speed for vehicle recognition. For this reason, the TensorRT-based optimized YOLO is suitable and thus adopted in our searching task for outdoor injured human targets.

Subsequently, after the UAV cluster obtains the target detection results of the injured outdoor personnel, it is necessary to judge the survival status of the target in time to provide detailed data support for the rescue plan. To realize this, acquiring vital signs of the target is a convincing and direct way and serves as a trigger for the emergency UAV to throw corresponding medical emergency supplies.

In this paper, a novel mission chain-driven unmanned aerial vehicle swarms cooperation method is proposed to improve the performance of UAV swarms during the search-rescue task for injured outdoor human targets and solve the problems of low endurance and low efficiency of individual UAVs. It combines long-range radio (LoRa) self-organizing network, machine vision, bio-radar, and medical emergency together. Thus, the human targets would be screened twice via different modal sensors, providing effective rescue guidance for ground search and rescue personnel.

2. System Design

The UAV swarm collaboration system, shown in Figure 1, consists of the LoRa self-organizing network, human target detection, and remote sensing of breath signals. In one mission execution, the system will first use the LoRa self-organizing network to establish information sharing between UAVs. Secondly, the onboard edge device (Nvidia jetson Nano) will use an object-detection algorithm to process the images captured by the camera in real-time. Finally, the UAV equipped with a bio-radar will further perceive the breath signals of the remote sense target. UAVs carrying emergency relief supplies will deliver medical supplies to the targets. A schematic diagram of the collaboration between UAVs with different functions is shown in Figure 2.

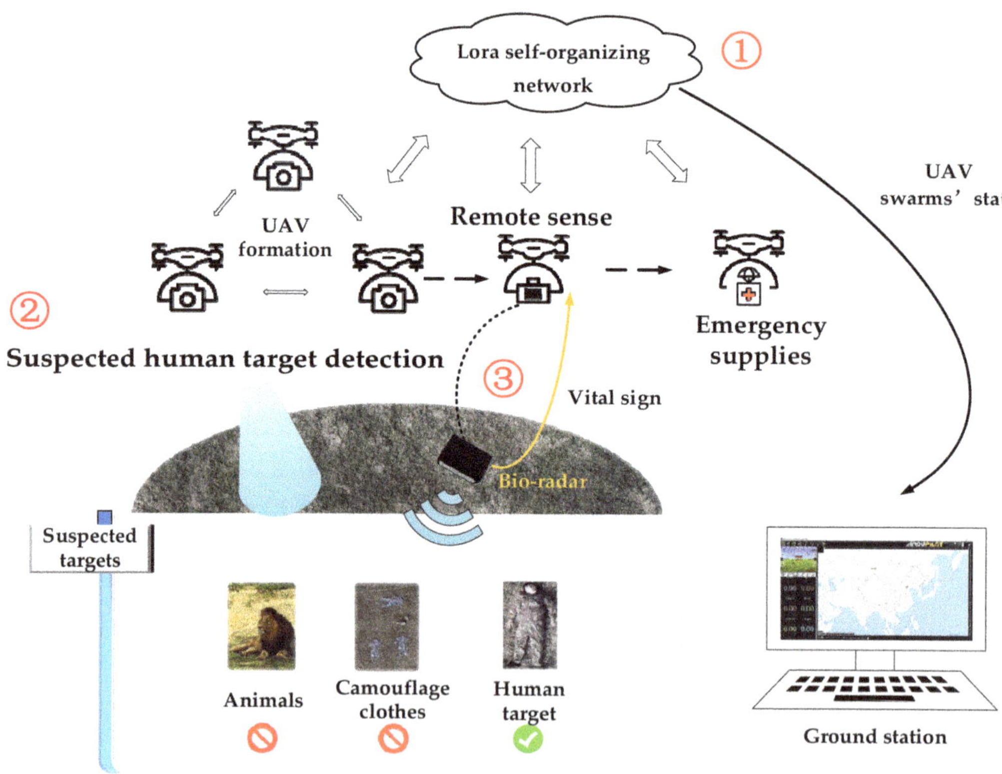

Figure 1. UAV swarm's collaboration system.

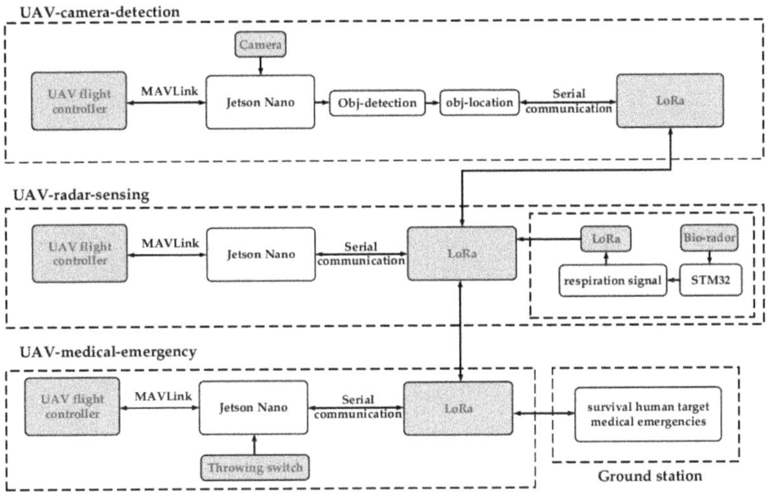

Figure 2. Collaboration between UAVs with different functions.

2.1. Main Hardware of the System

2.1.1. UAV Swarms

For UAV swarms that collaborate on missions outdoors, excellent manoeuvrability, flexibility, and hover stability are essential. To adapt to better communication and control, we chose a quadcopter UAV as a delivery platform, which can cooperate with Jetson Nano to fly autonomously and combine external modules such as communication modules and cameras to form a multifunctional intelligent unmanned aerial vehicle system. The camera has 12.4 million pixels and can provide an effective target detection image at a height of 70 metres. This program-based development control design greatly improves the intelligent control performance of the UAV cluster and reduces manpower expenditure in the search and rescue mission. Figure 3 shows the appearance of these UAV swarms.

Figure 3. UAV swarms for carrying real-time target detection and sensing systems.

2.1.2. Bio-Radar Module and First Aid Kit

The bio-radar sensor (model: JC122-3.3UA6) was custom-developed. When a normal person breathes with minute displacement, the thoracic cavity will reflect the microwave emitted by the radar sensor to generate an echo signal. According to the Doppler effect [18,19], there will be a phase difference between the original radar beams and the echo beams. The relationship between the phase variation and the chest displacement can be expressed as below:

$$\Delta\theta(t) = \frac{4\pi}{\lambda}\Delta x(t) \quad (1)$$

where $\Delta x(t)$ is the chest displacement, λ is the wavelength of the bioradar, and $\Delta\theta(t)$ is the phase change introduced by the breathing activity of the human subject.

After analogue amplification and filtering, the respirational waveform can be obtained. Observing this waveform can be used to judge the physiological condition of a person. The bioradar operated with a wavelength of 1.25 cm and provided continuous linear waves with a maximum transmission power of 1 mW. Taking advantage of the wide sensing range of the bio-radar (horizontal angle: $\pm 60°$, vertical angle: $\pm 16°$), the respiration signal of the tested target is detected by throwing multiple bio-radars at different angles and distances.

The appearance of the outdoor first aid kit is shown in Figure 4. The first aid kit is equipped with commonly used medicines and equipment, including scissors, fixing belts, tourniquets, cotton wool, various dressings, haemostatic drugs (powder), quick-acting rescue pills, hypertension drugs, nitroglycerine, Star intestine medicine, malaria medicine, cold medicine, cough medicine, etc.

Figure 4. Main configuration of the outdoor first-aid kit.

2.1.3. Control and Information Processing Center

Jetson Nano is a powerful embedded device produced by Nvidia. The device contains a 128-core Maxwell architecture graphics processing unit (GPU), which achieves balanced processing in terms of power consumption, volume, and price. The official test frame rate of Tiny YOLO running on Jetson Nano after TensorRT acceleration is FPS = 38. Combining the advantages of small size and excellent computing power, Jetson Nano can meet the needs of onboard suspected target detection.

The model of the LoRa chip we used for networking is ATK-LoRa-SX1278. Based on spread spectrum technology, the LoRa chip can perform ultralong-distance wireless transmission and has the characteristics of low power consumption and many networking nodes. Jetson Nano will configure the LoRa channel, baud rate, and other parameters to build a communication network between UAVs.

This shared network could further achieve the function of the secondary screening of suspected targets through UAV-based radar. Based on the open-source Python-dronekit control library, we have developed programs for autonomous flight of UAVs based on shared point locations. The UAV that performs the detection of life forms will throw the perception module equipped with bio-radar near the target to obtain the target's respiration signal.

2.2. Mission Chain Driven UAV Swarms Cooperation Algorithm

Based on the above platform, for the real-time search and rescue of injured human targets in a wide-area environment, we propose a cooperative process based on the functional differences driven by the mission chain. The collaboration process of the UAV swarm refers to the three function types of UAVs: detect, sense, and supply. The schematic diagrams of the three are shown in Figure 5.

(1) UAV-camera-based suspected human target detection. After the UAVs receive the Take-off command, they will automatically form a formation to go to the mission point and automatically perform the search task according to the "zigzag" pattern.
(2) UAV-radar-based human target reconfirmation. We wrote a Python script to obtain the location of the UAV when the target was detected and share the location information of the injured to the sensing UAV through the self-organizing network. The sensing UAV will autonomously fly near the injured person and throw a sensing module to further obtain the breath signal of the target.
(3) Medical emergencies through the emergency UAV. Finally, after the target survival is determined, the UAVs that deliver emergency rescue will provide the necessary support to keep the wounded alive.

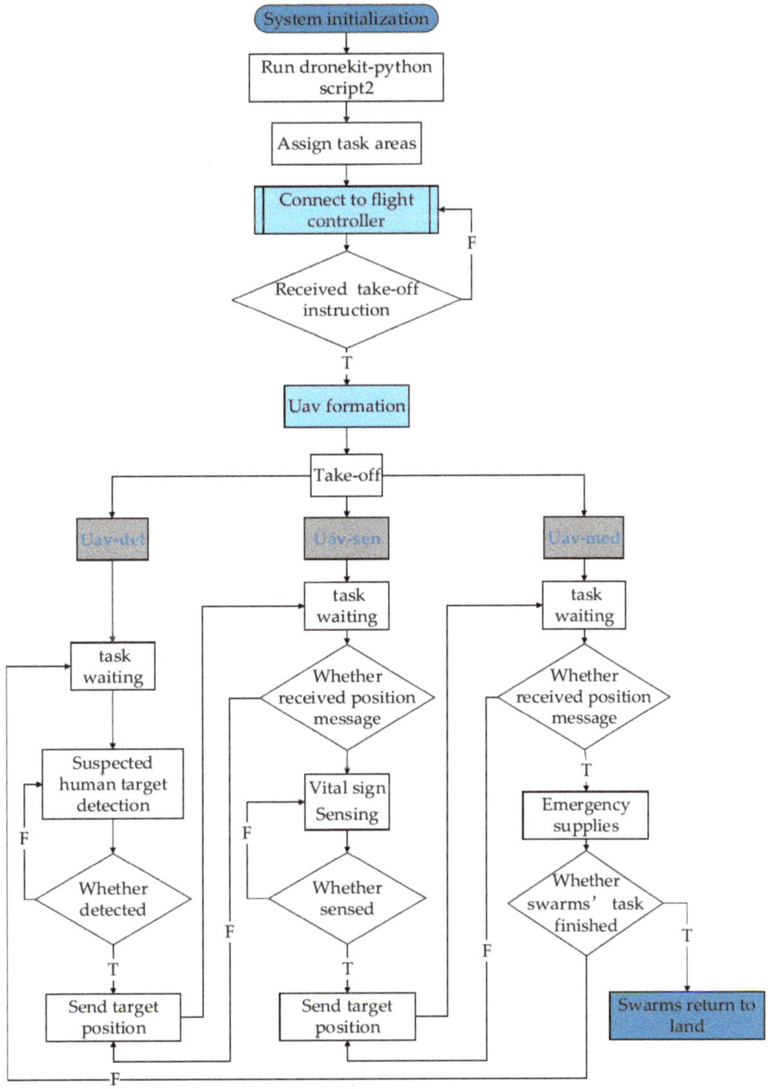

Figure 5. Schematic diagram of UAV Swarms.

2.2.1. UAV-Camera-Based Suspected Human Target Detection

(1) Tiny Yolov4

To meet the real-time and accuracy requirements of target recognition detection algorithms on airborne edge devices, we tried the recognition and detection effects of the YOLO series of algorithms on low-contrast targets in the grass, including yolov3, yolov4, and yolov4-tiny. The Yolov4-tiny structure is a simplified version of Yolov4, a lightweight model. The overall network structure has a total of 38 layers. Using three residual units, the activation function uses LeakyReLU, the classification and regression of the target are changed to use two feature layers, and the feature pyramid network (FPN) is used when merging the effective feature layers.The feature structure of Yolov4 tiny is shown in Figure 6.

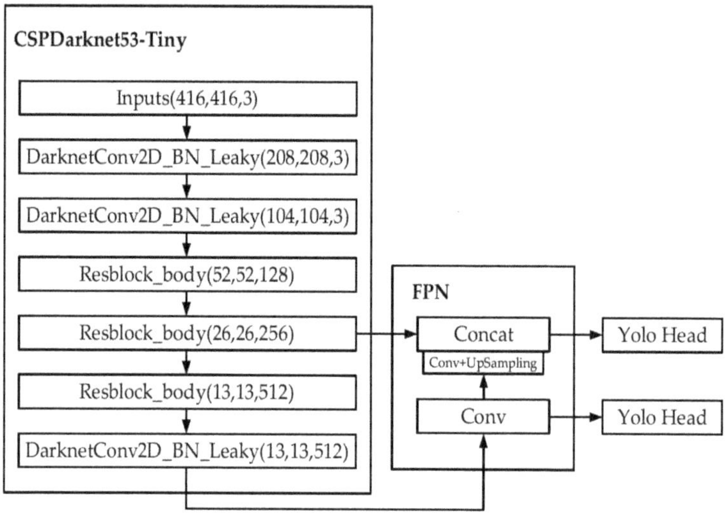

Figure 6. Yolov4-tiny feature structure diagram.

(2) K-means clustering methods

In object recognition detection, the network model learns the target category based on multiple features and needs to learn the position and size of the target in the graph. Therefore, algorithms such as Faster regional-based convolutional neural network (RCNN), SSD, and YOLO preset a set of reference boxes of different sizes and aspect ratios on the image in advance before recognition and detection. These cover almost all positions of the picture to match the width and height of the target in the datasets to calculate the target box faster and better. It is called the anchor point in the Faster RCNN, and the SSD is called the previous bounding box. Starting with YOLOv2, the detection mechanism of the YOLO series uses an anthropology mechanism. The difference is that in Faster-RCNN, anchor points are set manually; however, for different datasets, one needs to preset the appropriate anchors based on the target size. In YOLO, the k-means clustering algorithm is used to cluster the bounding boxes in the training set. Finding the appropriate size of the anchor solves this problem very well.

(3) TensorRT Acceleration

In the actual deep learning model deployment link, the efficiency of using the original network framework is relatively inefficient, so Nvidia has developed a TensorRT inference library for its own GPU. TensorRT is a C++ inference framework that can run on Nvidia's various GPU hardware platforms. We use PyTorch, TF, or other frameworks to train the model, which can be converted to TensorRT format, and then use the TensorRT inference engine to run our model, thereby improving the speed of this model running on Nvidia GPUs.

2.2.2. UAV-Radar-Based Human Target Reconfirmation

After receiving the location information of the suspected target, the UAV equipped with bio-radar will fly near the target, collect the breath signal of the suspected target by throwing the sense device, determine whether the target is still alive, and transmit this information to the lower layer. There are two important problems to be solved in the process of life information perception of the wounded: the acquisition of the wounded information and the long-distance transmission of the information. Therefore, the design of the system adopts modularization, which is composed of three modules: a life sensing device, an air communication device, and a ground station processing terminal, as shown in Figure 7.

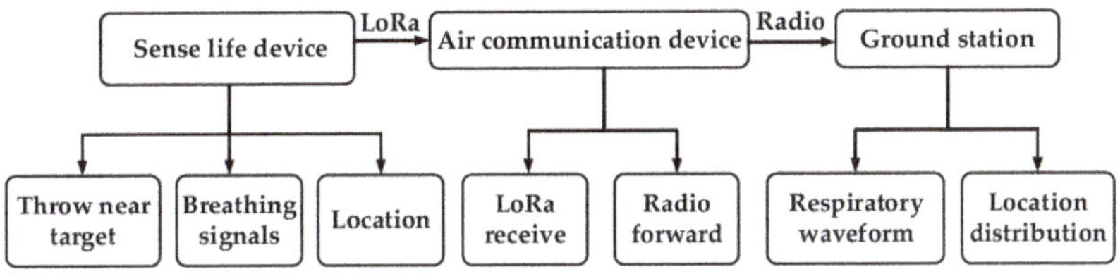

Figure 7. Schematic diagram of sensing life.

The life-sensing device uses bio-radar to collect the respiration signal of the casualty noncontact. It throws multiple life-sensing devices integrating the positioning module, bio-radar, and communication modules at the target point (Figure 8) to collect the position and respiration signal of the casualty. The information is processed by the Stm32 controller and sent to the air communication device in the form of data packets through LoRa. The ground network and air communication transfer are used to expand the perception range of the wounded. The ground station processing terminal is responsible for the visualization of the life information and location information of the wounded, big data analysis, injury level assessment, and other operations, providing effective information for searchers.

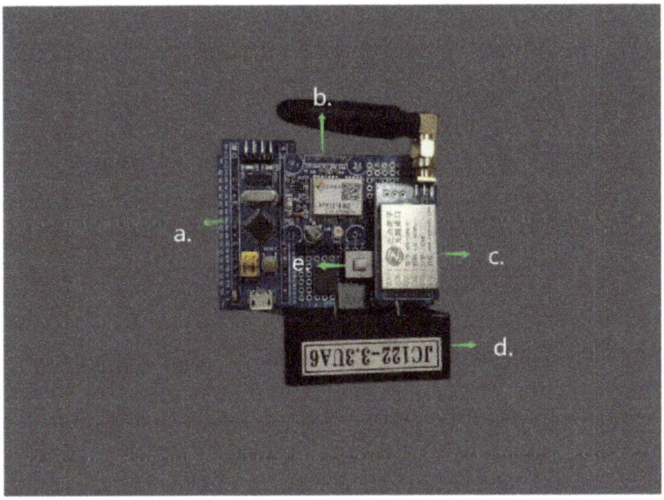

Figure 8. Design of the life sensing device; (**a**) Stm32F103; (**b**) Positioning module; (**c**) LoRa; (**d**) Bio-radar; (**e**) System power switch.

The air communication device is carried on the UAV. It is responsible for connecting the life sense device and the ground station processing terminal up and down, using LoRa and radio to transmit data. First, the life sensing device autonomously alarms after detecting a life signal. It simultaneously transmits the life information of the wounded to the unmanned air communication terminal, and then the wireless transmitter transmits the information to the ground workstation processing terminal. A physical diagram of the air communication device is shown in Figure 9.

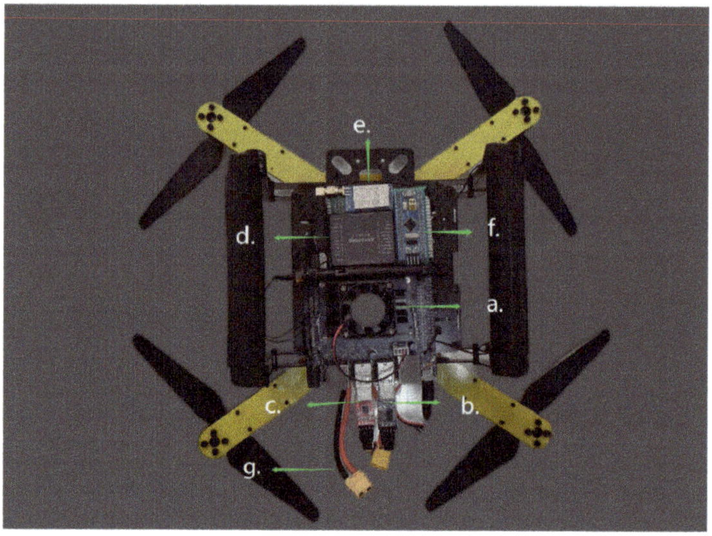

Figure 9. Design of the air communication device on the UAV; (**a**) Nvidia Jetson Nano; (**b**) Usb-ttl; (**c**) Usb-ttl; (**d**) Radio module; (**e**) LoRa; (**f**) Stm32F103; (**g**) Battery.

3. Experiments and Discussion

To verify the actual performance of the UAV swarm, the experiment was divided into three parts for testing:

(1) Multi-UAV cooperation: The communication distance of the ad hoc network and the task coordination based on functional differences are mainly tested.
(2) Human target detection: The YOLOv4-Tiny algorithm was tested to match the accuracy and speed of object recognition detection.
(3) Human Target reconfirmation: The accuracy of the sensing device on the respiration signal acquisition of human targets was tested and analysed.
(4) Medical emergencies through the emergency UAV

3.1. Multi-UAV Cooperation

First, we tested the communication distance of the LoRa ad hoc network: the maximum communication distance of a single node was tested in a relatively open offsite environment. Change the distance between the LoRa acquisition and receiver ends. Test signal strength and packet loss were tested at 1000 m, 1500 m, and 1600 m, and the communication was stable at 1500 m without data loss. The packet loss rate was 5% at 1500 m and more than 50% at 1600 m.

Second, the communication distance between the air communication device and the ground station was tested in the same way, and the communication quality between them was stable at 1500 m. By combining two communication modules, the communication range is effectively expanded, and the communication quality is stable. In the subsequent testing process, the communication protocol will be improved to enhance the anti-jamming performance of the system wireless communication in different environments.

Multi-UAV cooperation includes two parts: four-UAV formations and three-UAV cooperation. We conducted a formation test of four UAVs outdoors to verify whether multiple UAVs could respond to ground workstation commands in real-time. As shown in Figure 10a, after receiving the take-off command from the ground workstation, the four

UAVs fly to the vicinity of the target area according to the "one-line" formation and the search mission. The test results show that the formation effect is ideal, the action feedback is accurate and timely, and the planned mission area can be covered.

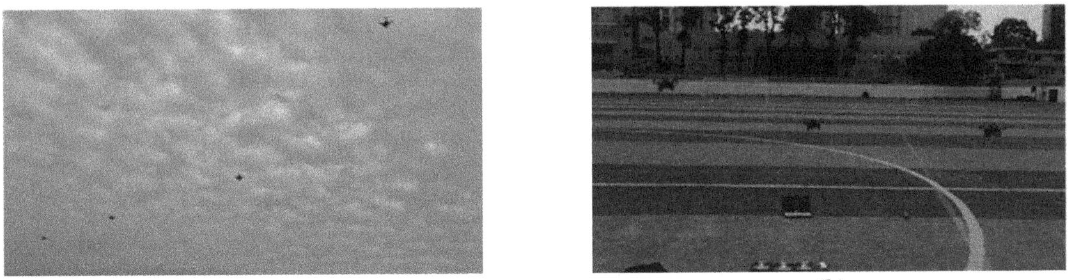

(a) (b)

Figure 10. (**a**) Real-time formation test of four UAVs, (**b**) Target detection experiment based on UAV swarms with different functions.

Then, we carried out a simulated searching experiment of outdoor injured people in the playground and designed a working group of two search UAVs and a sensing UAV. The two UAVs responsible for the search sent the simulated position of the wounded to the perception UAV in the coverage search mission. After receiving the position, the perception UAV quickly went to the point to throw the respiration signal perception module. As shown in Figure 10b, the cooperation of three UAVs can be initially realized, and the information transmission and receiving in communication (like the target's position information) among them could reach 65%. To solve this problem, we analysed the reason for the external interference to affect the stability of the communication. In the future, we will propose a method to improve the stability of communication protocol, and we will continue to improve the accuracy.

3.2. Human Target Detection

3.2.1. Experimental Design and Configuration

This experiment mainly simulates the identification and detection of wounds in an outdoor low-contrast environment. It builds a training platform for an in-depth learning model and a platform for UAV target identification and detection. Among these operating modes, the former trains the data with better computing power, thus providing good training and testing standards for the airborne system of the latter.

The main experiment process includes making datasets, model training, and algorithm deployment. First, 2130 images of targets at different heights and positions were collected, and the wounded targets in these images were labelled. The data were divided into a training set and a test set at a ratio of 7:3. The algorithm is trained by a neural network, and the precision and recall rate of the test set are calculated. The parameters of the deep learning platform we use for training data are mainly shown in Table 1.

Table 1. Key Parameters of the System Setup.

Parameter	Configuration
CPU	Inter i7-1180H
GPU	Nvidia RTX 3050
System	Windows10/Ubuntu20.04
Accelerate environment	CUDA11.4 cuDNN8.2
Training framework	Darknet

3.2.2. Results and Analysis

Based on the above dataset and experimental configuration, the dataset was preprocessed by operations such as labeling and normalization. The initial learning rate (0.001) and decay parameter (0.0005) have the best training effect. Using mean average precision (mAP^{50}) (IOU = 50) and frames per second (FPS) detection speed as evaluation indicators, we compared the detection effects of the original Yolov4-tiny, clustered yolov4-tiny, Yolov4-tiny after clustering, and TensorRT acceleration.

As shown in Table 2, compared to the original Yolov4-tiny, the detection accuracy of Yolov4-tiny after clustering the anchor box by the K-means clustering algorithm increased by 23.69%. The detection speed remained unchanged. The clustered Yolov4-tiny refers to the size of the anchor box clustered in advance when predicting the target, which improves the detection effect. The detection accuracy of the TensorRT acceleration of the clustered Yolov4-tiny decreased by 3.86% and the detection speed increased by 171% compared to the clustered Yolov4-tiny. Compared with the original Yolov4-tiny, the detection speed was improved on the premise of ensuring a higher detection accuracy. The results show that the algorithm has a good detection effect on low-contrast targets with a height of less than 70 m. As shown in Figure 11, it can accurately detect the wounded in trenches and weed coverage, and can meet the needs of UAV target detection.

Table 2. Comparison of experimental results.

Model	mAP^{50}	FPS
Yolov4-tiny	67.38%	14
clustered yolov4-tiny	91.07%	14
Yolov4-tiny after clustering and TensorRT acceleration	87.21%	38

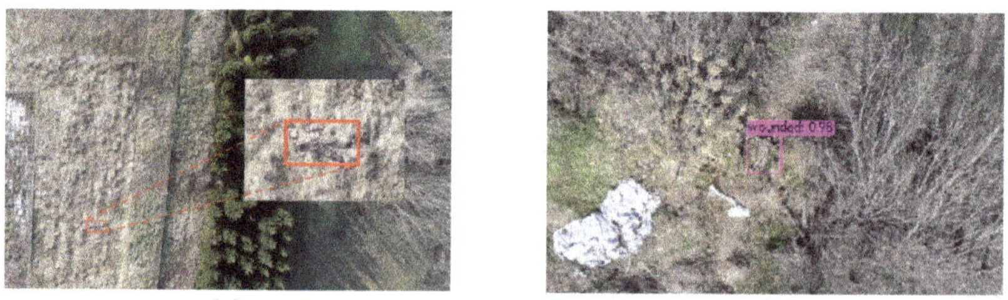

(a) (b)

Figure 11. Human target detection. (**a**) Human target in the weed cover. (**b**) Human target in the gully.

3.3. Human Target Reconfirmation

After a suspected human target has been detected based on a UAV camera, the following necessary mission is to confirm further whether it is a surviving human body and to sense the corresponding physiological state.

Therefore, once the video detects a suspected target, the drone will be triggered, and the bio-radar module will be precisely dropped around the human target. Since the electromagnetic waves emitted by bio-radar can detect regular chest wall movement caused by human respiratory movement, the respiratory characteristic analysis of radar echoes can determine whether the suspected target is a human body. In addition, a previous research group showed that after human injury (blood loss, temperature loss), human respiratory radar echoes would have morphologically specific characteristics, which can be used to assess the physiological state of survivors. The physical state of the survivor is good or bad, or even terrible (being dying), which could directly represent the urgency of the need of the survivor to be treated in time.

To test the effectiveness of detecting human respiration signals by throwing bio-radar, we tested the detection distance and angle of the bio-radar separately. Ideally, it is assumed that the radar can be accurately thrown to the position of 0.5 m in front of the human chest. The experiment of the effective detection distance of the respiration signal was carried out by increasing the distance by 0.5 m successively. Then, with the human body target as the centre, the detection effect of different angles (the view angle to the human chest wall) (0 degrees, 45 degrees, 90 degrees, 135 degrees, 180 degrees) at 0.5 m were tested with 0 degrees in the direction of the chest cavity. Finally, the detection effect of different angles corresponding to different distances was tested.

Like the respiratory detection results of a typical example (0 degrees, 2 m) shown in Figure 12, a strong and regular respiratory signal was clearly acquired. There was only weak and chaotic noise when the human target left, demonstrating that the respiration feature acquired by bio-radar could convincingly confirm the human attribution. Moreover, the statistical results of different detection positions (angle and position) show that almost all human respiration can be detected from most view angles within a distance. Even the detection failure at 90 degrees can be solved by throwing over two radar modules or using our proposed omnidirectional bio-radar integrated module [20].

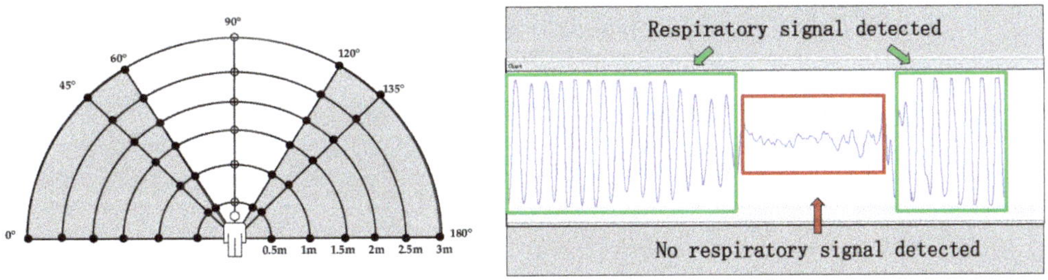

(a) (b)

Figure 12. Respiration signal detection. (**a**) Different distances and angles. (**b**) Respiration signal waveform.

However, our previous studies have effectively verified that the injured human body will go through four typical physiological stages, including normal, transitioning, and agonal stages. Fortunately, the bio-radar could effectively detect and judge these stages based on some signal features combined with machine learning methods [21]. Consequently, it could help determine the most appropriate rescue strategy of emergency UAV swarms for rescuers and finally help save more lives.

3.4. Medical Emergencies through the Emergency UAV

The degree of urgency and priority of medical treatment depends mainly on the degree of injury and physiological state. Therefore, these medical emergency UAVs will perform reasonable treatment missions according to the physiological state evaluation based on the detected respiratory radar signal. As shown in Figure 13, this type of UAV is equipped with a throwing switch and an outdoor first-aid kit for autonomously throwing medical supplies. Bandages and haemostatic drugs can provide the injured person with timely treatment for trauma. In addition, quick-acting rescue pills, cold medicine, and nitroglycerin can relieve some sudden acute symptoms and effectively obtain more rescue time for those in distress.

Figure 13. Emergency UAV for emergency supply.

4. Conclusions

Targeting the challenging mission chain, including searching, sensing, and emergency treatment of injured human targets under a wide-area outdoor jungle environment, a novel cooperative strategy for distributed UAV swarms is proposed. In this way, the multi-UAV network will work collaboratively to perform a quick search, accurate sensing, and timely medical treatment. This provides a strong basis for the planning of rescue programs, reducing the difficulty of searching for the wounded and effectively improving the efficiency of searching for and rescuing the wounded. The combination of casualty search and technology such as drones, machine vision, and bio-radar will subvert traditional search and rescue methods. Generally, however, the collaborative search and rescue of the outdoor injured based on the distributed drone swarms could also be continuously improved, such as the accuracy of physiological state evaluation. However, it is promising to lay a foundation for the intelligent search and rescue of the injured in the new era.

Author Contributions: Conceptualization, G.L. and J.W.; methodology, M.Z.; software, T.L.; investigation, Y.J. and J.X.; data curation, Z.L.; writing—original draft preparation, Y.C.; writing—review and editing, F.Q.; visualization, Y.C.; supervision, G.L; funding acquisition, G.L. All authors have read and agreed to the published version of the manuscript.

Funding: This research was funded by the Key Research and Development Program of Shaanxi (2021ZDLGY09-07 and 2022SF-482). The APC was funded by 2021ZDLGY09-07.

Institutional Review Board Statement: Not applicable.

Informed Consent Statement: Not applicable.

Data Availability Statement: Not applicable.

Conflicts of Interest: The authors declare no conflict of interest.

Abbreviations

Definition	Acronyms
Unmanned Aerial Vehicle	UAV
Deep Learning	DL
Convolutional Neural Networks	CNN
You Only Look Once	YOLO
Region-CNN	RCNN
Long-range Radio	LoRa
Graphics Processing Unit	GPU

Leaky Rectified Linear Unit	LeakyReLU
Feature Pyramid Network	FPN
Single Shot MultiBox Detector	SSD
Mean average precision	mAP
Frames per second	FPS

References

1. Jayasekera, S.; Hensel, E.; Robinson, R. Feasibility Assessment of Wearable Respiratory Monitors for Ambulatory Inhalation Topography. *Int. J. Environ. Res. Public Health* **2021**, *18*, 2990. [CrossRef] [PubMed]
2. Yeom, S. Moving People Tracking and False Track Removing with Infrared Thermal Imaging by a Multirotor. *Drones* **2021**, *5*, 65. [CrossRef]
3. Zhao, W.; Dong, Q.; Zuo, Z. A Method Combining Line Detection and Semantic Segmentation for Power Line Extraction from Unmanned Aerial Vehicle Images. *Remote Sens.* **2022**, *14*, 1367. [CrossRef]
4. Qi, F.; Zhu, M.; Li, Z.; Lei, T.; Xia, J.; Zhang, L.; Yan, Y.; Wang, J.; Lu, G. Automatic Air-to-Ground Recognition of Outdoor Injured Human Targets Based on UAV Bimodal Information: The Explore Study. *Appl. Sci.* **2022**, *12*, 3457. [CrossRef]
5. Wang, S.; Han, Y.; Chen, J.; Zhang, Z.; Du, N. A deep-learning-based sea search and rescue algorithm by UA V remote sensing. In Proceedings of the 2018 IEEE CSAA Guidance, Navigation and Control Conference (GNCC), Xiamen, China, 10–12 August 2018; pp. 1–5.
6. Ding, J.; Zhang, J.; Zhan, Z.; Tang, X.; Wang, X. A Precision Efficient Method for Collapsed Building Detection in Post-Earthquake UAV Images Based on the Improved NMS Algorithm and Faster R-CNN. *Remote Sens.* **2022**, *14*, 663. [CrossRef]
7. Pedersen, C.B.; Nielsen, K.G.; Rosenkrands, K.; Vasegaard, A.E.; Nielsen, P.; El Yafrani, M. A GRASP-Based Approach for Planning UAV-Assisted Search and Rescue Missions. *Sensors* **2022**, *22*, 275. [CrossRef] [PubMed]
8. Liu, H.; Ge, J.; Wang, Y.; Li, J.; Ding, K.; Zhang, Z.; Guo, Z.; Li, W.; Lan, J. Multi-UAV Optimal Mission Assignment and Path Planning for Disaster Rescue Using Adaptive Genetic Algorithm and Improved Artificial Bee Colony Method. *Actuators* **2021**, *11*, 4. [CrossRef]
9. Qin, B.; Zhang, D.; Tang, S.; Wang, M. Distributed Grouping Cooperative Dynamic Task Assignment Method of UAV Swarm. *Appl. Sci.* **2022**, *12*, 2865. [CrossRef]
10. Hildmann, H.; Kovacs, E.; Saffre, F.; Isakovic, A.F. Nature-Inspired Drone Swarming for Real-Time Aerial Data-Collection Under Dynamic Operational Constraints. *Drones* **2019**, *3*, 71. [CrossRef]
11. Camarillo-Escobedo, R.; Flores, J.L.; Marin-Montoya, P.; García-Torales, G.; Camarillo-Escobedo, J.M. Smart Multi-Sensor System for Remote Air Quality Monitoring Using Unmanned Aerial Vehicle and LoRaWAN. *Sensors* **2022**, *22*, 1706. [CrossRef] [PubMed]
12. Davoli, L.; Pagliari, E.; Ferrari, G. Hybrid LoRa-IEEE 802.11s Opportunistic Mesh Networking for Flexible UAV Swarming. *Drones* **2021**, *5*, 26. [CrossRef]
13. Okulski, M.; Ławryńczuk, M. How Much Energy Do We Need to Fly with Greater Agility? Energy Consumption and Performance of an Attitude Stabilization Controller in a Quadcopter Drone: A Modified MPC vs. PID. *Energies* **2022**, *15*, 1380. [CrossRef]
14. Ren, S.; He, K.; Girshick, R.; Sun, J. Faster R-CNN: Towards real-time object detection with region proposal networks. *IEEE Trans. Pattern Anal. Mach. Intell.* **2017**, *39*, 1137–1149. [CrossRef] [PubMed]
15. Liu, W.; Anguelov, D.; Erhan, D.; Szegedy, C.; Reed, S.; Fu, C.Y.; Berg, A.C. SSD: Single shot multibox detector. In Proceedings of the European Conference on Computer Vision, Amsterdam, The Netherlands, 8–16 October 2016; pp. 21–37.
16. Redmon, J.; Divvala, S.; Girshick, R.; Farhadi, A. You only look once: Unified, real-time object detection. In Proceedings of the IEEE Conference on Computer Vision and Pattern Recognition, Las Vegas, NV, USA, 26 June–1 July 2016; pp. 779–788.
17. Li, X.; He, B.; Ding, K.; Guo, W.; Huang, B.; Wu, L. Wide-Area and Real-Time Object Search System of UAV. *Remote Sens.* **2022**, *14*, 1234. [CrossRef]
18. Kathuria, N.; Seet, B.-C. 24 GHz Flexible Antenna for Doppler Radar-Based Human Vital Signs Monitoring. *Sensors* **2021**, *21*, 3737. [CrossRef] [PubMed]
19. Gouveia, C.; Vieira, J.; Pinho, P. A Review on Methods for Random Motion Detection and Compensation in Bio-Radar Systems. *Sensors* **2019**, *19*, 604. [CrossRef] [PubMed]
20. Li, C.; Chen, F.; Qi, F.; Liu, M.; Li, Z.; Liang, F.; Jing, X.; Lu, G.; Wang, J. Searching for survivors through random human-body movement outdoors by continuous-wave radar array. *PLoS ONE* **2016**, *11*, e0152201. [CrossRef] [PubMed]
21. Ma, Y.; Wang, P.; Xue, H.; Liang, F.; Qi, F.; Lev, H.; Yu, X.; Wang, J.; Zhang, Y. Non-contact vital states identification of trapped living bodies using ultra-wideband bio-radar. *IEEE Access* **2020**, *9*, 6550–6559. [CrossRef]

sensors

MDPI

Article

Enhanced Single Shot Small Object Detector for Aerial Imagery Using Super-Resolution, Feature Fusion and Deconvolution

Mahdi Maktab Dar Oghaz [1,*,†], Manzoor Razaak [2,†] and Paolo Remagnino [3,†]

1 Faculty of Science and Engineering, Anglia Ruskin University, Cambridge CB1 1PT, UK
2 The Robot Vision Team, Kingston University London, London KT1 2EE, UK; manzoor.razak@kingston.ac.uk
3 Department of Computer Science, Durham University, Upper MountJoy, Durham DH1 3LE, UK; paolo.remagnino@gmail.com
* Correspondence: mahdi.maktabdar@aru.ac.uk
† These authors contributed equally to this work.

Citation: Maktab Dar Oghaz, M.; Razaak, M.; Remagnino, P. Enhanced Single Shot Small Object Detector for Aerial Imagery Using Super-Resolution, Feature Fusion and Deconvolution. *Sensors* **2022**, *22*, 4339. https://doi.org/10.3390/s22124339

Academic Editors: Jaroslaw Pytka, Andrzej Łukaszewicz, Zbigniew Kulesza, Wojciech Giernacki, Andriy Holovatyy and Petros Daras

Received: 21 March 2022
Accepted: 27 May 2022
Published: 8 June 2022

Abstract: One common issue of object detection in aerial imagery is the small size of objects in proportion to the overall image size. This is mainly caused by high camera altitude and wide-angle lenses that are commonly used in drones aimed to maximize the coverage. State-of-the-art general purpose object detector tend to under-perform and struggle with small object detection due to loss of spatial features and weak feature representation of the small objects and sheer imbalance between objects and the background. This paper aims to address small object detection in aerial imagery by offering a Convolutional Neural Network (CNN) model that utilizes the Single Shot multi-box Detector (SSD) as the baseline network and extends its small object detection performance with feature enhancement modules including super-resolution, deconvolution and feature fusion. These modules are collectively aimed at improving the feature representation of small objects at the prediction layer. The performance of the proposed model is evaluated using three datasets including two aerial images datasets that mainly consist of small objects. The proposed model is compared with the state-of-the-art small object detectors. Experiment results demonstrate improvements in the mean Absolute Precision (mAP) and Recall values in comparison to the state-of-the-art small object detectors that investigated in this study.

Keywords: deconvolution; feature fusion; small object detection; SSD; super-resolution

1. Introduction

Object detection is one of the core research areas in computer vision. Recent breakthroughs in Convolutional Neural Network (CNN) and object detection unlocked new horizons and possibilities in various domains ranging from security and surveillance applications, such as face detection, crowd analysis and activity recognition to medical image analysis and self-driving vehicles research [1–4].

Despite the contextual similarities of these domains, they utilize different image acquisition techniques that often require significant adaptation and alteration of the state-of-the-art general purpose object detectors to achieve desirable results. A prominent example of such a domain is Unmanned Aerial Vehicles (UAV) imagery. The UAV imagery is getting more popular than ever before with a variety of applications including smart farming [5], search and rescue [6], disaster management [7], archaeological structure modeling [8], security and surveillance [9] and many others. In UAV imagery, due to the flight altitude, the top-down camera perspective and wide-angle lenses, object shapes and appearances are relatively unconventional and they usually take up a small fraction of the image area, as illustrated in Figure 1. General purpose object detectors are trained and tuned on datasets, such as ImageNet and COCO, which mainly offer ground-level medium-sized images. These detectors fail to provide good detection accuracy when it comes to out-of-ordinary small objects captured by UAVs. A reliable small object detection demands mechanisms that preserve and enhance small object feature representation in the detection layer [10].

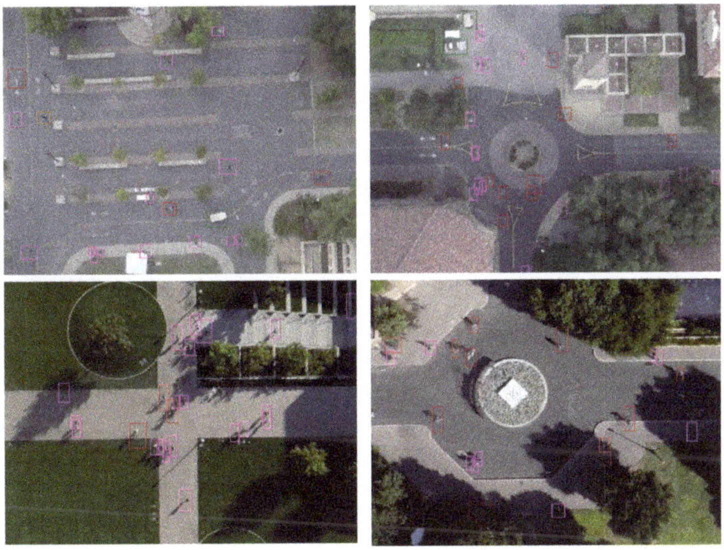

Figure 1. Objects in UAV images are usually small in size (proportional to total image size) and general purpose object detectors are not designed to cope with it [11].

Pre-deep learning object detection techniques, such as boosted cascade [12], Histograms of Oriented Gradients (HOG) [13] and Deformable Part Models (DPM) [14] were relatively inaccurate and unreliable for real-world applications; however, availability of GPU computing and abundant of labeled training data (ImageNet) fast-tracked the rise of CNN-based object detection. The CNN-based object detectors have become the preferred choice for many researchers due to their unprecedented accuracy and availability of ample training data and processing power. These approaches can be categorized into one-stage and two-stage object detectors.

The *one-stage* object detectors require only a single pass through the neural network to detect and localize the objects. These methods treat object detection as a simple regression problem by taking an input image and learning the class probabilities and bounding box coordinates. For instance, *You Only Look Once* (YOLO), which is one of the notable *one-stage* object detectors, splits the input image into a grid of $S \times S$ cells [15]. If a bounding box center falls into a cell, that cell is "responsible" for detecting the existence of that object. More precisely, each cell is in charge of predicting the exact coordinates of bounding boxes, a confidence score indicates the likelihood that the cell contains an object, and a probability of object class conditioned on the existence of an object in the bounding box. The YOLO utilize a fairly standard CNN (similar to GoogLeNet) that receives the input image, extracts spatial features, and at the end outputs an encoded vector designed to predict bounding boxes, confidence for those boxes, and class probabilities.

When it comes to the small objects, the efficiency and reliability of this and similar approaches degrade. To successfully detect small objects, a considerably finer $S \times S$ grid is required to reliably predict the coordinates of the bounding boxes and maintain the significance of the confidence scores. This exponentially increases the computational complexity of the detector for an insignificant accuracy boost in return. Overall, the *one-stage* object detectors are simpler and faster, although they can sometimes struggle with localization and detection accuracy. The most prominent examples of one-stage object detectors are YOLO and *Single Shot multi-box Detector* (SSD) [16].

On the other hand, *two-stage* object detectors first attempt to extract candidate regions of objects (region proposal), which significantly reduces the number of locations that are likely to contain the objects and then they employ a combination of ConvNets and other techniques to classify and refine the extracted region proposals. For instance, the *Region-based Convolutional Neural Network* (R-CNN) [17], which is one of the earliest *two-stage* object detectors, uses selective search to extract 2000 region proposals. This method employs a graph-based segmentation algorithm [18] to generate an over-segmented segmentation map and then iteratively and hierarchically merges these segments into larger region proposals based on their color, texture, size, and shape similarity.

In the second stage, pre-trained AlexNet is used to extract the feature vector of the cropped/reshaped region proposals. Then, *Support Vector Machines* (SVMs) are used to generate a confidence score classify these regions into different classes. A greedy non-maximum suppression algorithm only retains overlapping regions with a higher confidence scores. Finally, a linear regression model is used to further refine the bounding boxes for each identified object. Two-stage detectors have higher localization and object recognition accuracy; however, these techniques tend to be significantly slower than their *one-stage* counterparts. These methods are fairly slow to begin with and it can be argued that they require a significantly higher number of region proposals to deal with small objects. Moreover, we have realized that the segment merging process is less effective when it comes to small-sized objects. Popular *two-stage* detectors are the R-CNN detectors and the various extensions of it [17,19,20].

In recent years, novel techniques, including Detection Transformer (DETR) [21], Saliency detection [22], Swin Transformer [23], and Hybrid Task Cascade (HTC) [24], have been conceived to improve object detection and segmentation accuracy; while these techniques managed to successfully improve object detection accuracy, their primary focus is on general and reasonably sized objects on datasets such as COCO and not small objects in aerial images.

Most object detection algorithms perform well when the objects are represented with reasonable size, proportion, and resolution; however, when it comes to small-sized objects, they under-perform severely. This is mainly caused by weak feature representation of the small-sized objects in deeper layers of CNN and a significant imbalance between the background and target objects proportion. Though there is no standard definition of the scale of an object to be qualified as a *small object*, the (D)etection, (O)bservation, (R)ecognition and (I)dentification (DORI) criteria conceived by [25] states that 10% of the image height is required for the object observation and detection. In Figure 1 in [11], it can be observed that the objects are considerably small/insignificant proportional to the total image size and can be categorized as small objects. Figure 2 illustrates how a typical CNN fails to properly resolve and represent small objects features. At each layer of the network, features of the small object down-sampled through pooling or stride >1 (typically, with half the resolution size of the previous layer) results in a progressive reduction and sometimes disappearance of small object feature representation at the prediction layer, which deteriorates the learning and detection process.

The majority of the image and video acquisition applications, such as surveillance, autonomous driving, and satellite and aerial imagery, can only capture distant objects in small sizes, mainly due to technological and physical constraints and limitations. Current general purpose object detectors, including SSD, YOLO, R-CNN, CenterNet++, and their variants, under-perform when it comes to the detection of small objects [26]. For instance, although the SSD utilizes a multi-scale feature representation that supposedly provides a relatively better detection accuracy for small objects, it uses a fairly deep CNN (VGG16) in its back-end, which degrades the spatial resolution of the small objects and makes detection of these objects difficult [27–29]. CenterNet++ [30], a state-of-the-art object detector that benefits local perception swin transformer in its backbone is capable of generating accurately positioned bonding boxes and achieve outstanding mAP, but it relatively under-performs when it comes to datasets that mainly exhibit small objects.

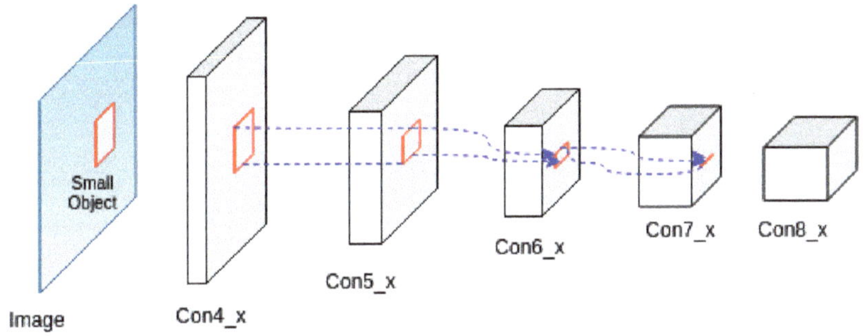

Figure 2. Poor feature representation of small objects at deeper layers of typical Convolutional Neural Networks, which are usually caused by multiple pooling and stride >1 processes.

Therefore, innovative measures are required to develop object detectors, capable to demonstrate high accuracy in detecting small objects. Small object detection is a relevant research problem and is gaining research attention. One approach that is particularly explored for small object detection is the multi-scale feature representations structure in the network architectures. Object detectors such as SSD and Deconvolutional Single Shot Detector (DSSD) [31] use multi-scale representations in their network for predictions. Features from different layers in the network are explored and combined for better representation of object features and to improve the detection of smaller objects. Table 1 provides an overview of some of the recent works related to CNN-based small object detection and summarizes their approaches.

Table 1. A summary of selected works on CNN-object detection for small objects in images.

Strategy	Authors	Model Features	Data	Results
Two-stage detectors	[32]	Feature extraction CNN combined with the R-CNN framework	Mobile Mapping Systems (MMS) images	mAP of up to 85%. Comparatively, 12% higher accuracy than ResNet-152
	[33]	R-CNN network combined with Tiny-Net, global attention block followed by a final classification block	Remote sensing images	Higher detection accuracy than R-CNN variants
	[34]	A R-CNN network combined with a deconvolution layer	Remote sensing images	Higher accuracy than Faster R-CNN is reported
	[35]	A region proposal network combined with fusion network that concatenates spatial and semantic information	Remote sensing	Improved detection accuracy compared to state-of-the-art
	[27]	Multi-block SSD consists of three stages, including patching, detection, and stitching	Railway scene dataset	Improved detection rate of small objects by 23.2% in comparison with the baseline object detectors

Table 1. *Cont.*

Strategy	Authors	Model Features	Data	Results
Single stage detectors	[36]	Various configurations of SSD architecture, including stride elimination at different parts of the network	MS COCO dataset	Better detection accuracy for small objects in the COCO dataset when compared to baseline SSD
	[25]	Tiling-based approach for training and inference on an SSD network	Micro aerial vehicle imagery	Improved the detection performance on small objects when compared with full frame approaches
	[37]	Modification of YOLOv3 model for multi-scale feature representation	UAV imagery	Improvement in small object detection when compared to base YOLOv3 model
	[38]	YOLO model with multi-scale feature fusion	Traffic imagery for car accident detection	Able to detect car accidents in 0.04 seconds with 90% accuracy
	[39]	Feature fusion and feature dilation combined with YOLO model	Vehicle imagery	Improved accuracy in the range of 80% and 88% on different datasets
	[40]	YOLOv3 Residual blocks optimized by concatenating two ResNet units that have the same width and height	UAV imagery	Improved IoU to over 70% to 80% across different datasets compared with the baseline models
	[41]	Region Context Network attention mechanism shortlists most promising regions, while discarding the rest of the input image to keep high resolution feature maps in deeper layers.	USC-GRAD-STD and MS COCO dataset	Improvement in average precision from 50.8% in baseline models to 57.4%
	[42]	Feature fusion and spatial attention-based Multi-block SSD	LAKE-BOAT dataset	79.3% mean average precision
Super-resolution	[43]	Patch-based and pixel-based CNN architectures for image segmentation to identify small objects	Remote sensing images	Classification accuracy of 87% reported
	[26]	A super-resolution-based generator network for up-sampling small objects	COCO dataset	Improved detection performance on small objects when compared with R-CNN models
	[44]	Super-resolution method for feature enhancement to improve small object detection accuracy	Several RGB image datasets	Better detection accuracy compared to other super-resolution-based methods
	[45]	A super-resolution-based Generative Adversarial Network (GAN) for small object detection	Several RGB image datasets	Achieved higher detection accuracy in comparison to R-CNN variants

Table 1. *Cont.*

Strategy	Authors	Model Features	Data	Results
Feature Pyramids	[46]	Extended feature pyramid network which employs large-scale super-resolution features with rich regional details to decouple small and medium object detection	Small traffic-sign Tsinghua-Tencent and MS COCO dataset	Better accuracy across both datasets compared to the state-of-the-art methods
	[47]	A two-stage detector (similar to the Faster-RCNN) which first adopts the feature pyramid architecture with lateral connections, then utilizes specialized anchors to detect the small objects from large resolution image	Small traffic-sign Tsinghua-Tencent dataset	Significant accuracy improvement compared with state-of-art methods
	[48]	A parallel feature pyramid network constructed by widening the network width instead of increasing the network depth. Spatial pyramid pooling adopted to generate a pool of feature	MS-COCO dataset	7.8% better average precision over latest variant of SSD
	[49]	Multi-branch parallel feature pyramid network (MPFPN) used to boost feature extraction of the small objects. The parallel branch is designed to recover the features that missed in the deeper layers and a supervised spatial attention module used to suppress background interference	VisDrone-DET dataset	Competitive performance compared with other state-of-the-art memthods
	[50]	Feture fusion and scaling-based SSD network with spatial context analysis	UAV imagery	Achieved 65.84% accuracy on PASCAL Visual Object Classes dataset. High accuracy on small objects in UAV images

This study attempts to address the small object detection problem using a multi-scale feature representation CNN model. The proposed model design includes the SSD network as the baseline network and extends it with an additional deconvolution module, super-resolution module and a shallow layer feature-fusion module. These three additions result in better preservation of small object features at deeper CNN layers that subsequently improved small objects detection accuracy compared to the base SSD model.

The main contributions of this study are as follows:

- A novel deep model capable of improving feature representation of small objects at the prediction layer that leads to overall better small objects detection accuracy;
- A deconvolution module that up-scales small objects' feature resolution and provides more details to the prediction layer;
- A super-resolution module that applies residual and up-sampling blocks to shallow layers and improves scale invariancy and enhances resolution of the small objects at the prediction layer;
- A shallow layer feature fusion module that combines features from multiple stages of the network and improves scale invariancy and feature representation.

These contributions are collectively aiming to improve feature representation of small objects at the prediction layer that eventually leads to overall better small object detection accuracy. The rest of the paper is organized as follows: the proposed network is described in detail in Section 2, followed by Section 3, which discusses its implementation, evaluation, and results. A discussion on the proposed model is provided in Section 4 followed by the conclusion.

2. System Overview

The proposed small object detection model consists of SSD as the baseline paired with three other modules: a *Shallow Layer Feature Fusion* module, a *Deconvolutional Module*, and a *Super-resolution* module. This model is partially inspired by the Deconvolutional Single Shot Detector (DSSD) [31], Deep CNN with Skip Connection and Network in Network (DCSCN) [51], and Super-Resolution Generative Adversarial Network (SRGAN) [52], and incorporates some variant of these techniques to improve small object detection accuracy. Figure 3 shows the architecture of the proposed small object detector model. In this figure, the super-resolution module along with the feature fusion module are illustrated in green and with a '+' symbol, respectively. The SSD layers are illustrated in blue followed by a series of a deconvolution layers (red) that end with a prediction layer.

Figure 4 shows a schematic comparison of the proposed approaches against various other object detectors. Figure 4a represents the approach used by single stage detectors (e.g., YOLO) that solely relies on the final feature representation for detection. These approaches work with relatively limited features that negatively impact small object detection; however, they demonstrate high detection speeds. Figure 4b shows the multi-level presentation of the features at the detection layer that are used by models such as the SSD. They usually perform better for small objects but have relatively lower detection speeds. The shallow layer feature fusion approach shown in Figure 4c and used in models such as the FSSD and the FFSSD improves on the SSD by concatenating additional features from lower layers to enhance small object detection performance. The DSSD approach extends the SSD model by combining the SSD layers with additional deconvolutional layers for better representation of features at the prediction layer, as shown in Figure 4d. Figure 4e shows the structure of our proposed network. The presented approach combines deconvolution and feature fusion methods to provide richer, multi-scale feature maps at the prediction layer. The overall goal of this architecture is to provide a mechanism to collate features from multiple layers across the network and present them at the prediction layer. The multi-scale features at the prediction layer provide enhanced feature representations for small objects and improve their detection accuracy.

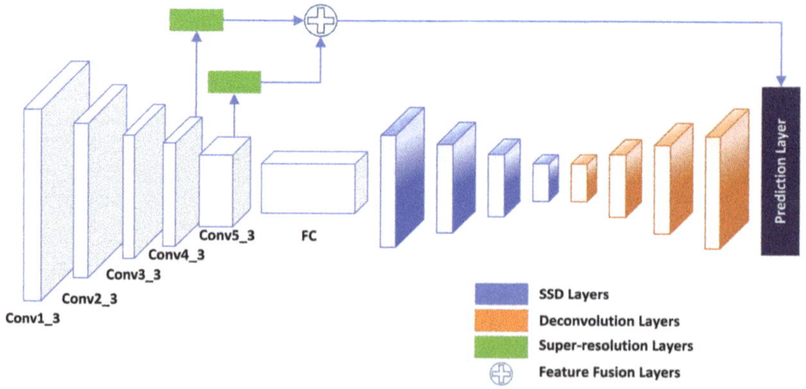

Figure 3. Network architecture of the proposed object detection model. The SSD model is used as the baseline network and extended to include deconvolution module (orange), super-resolution module (green), and shallow layer feature fusion module (+).

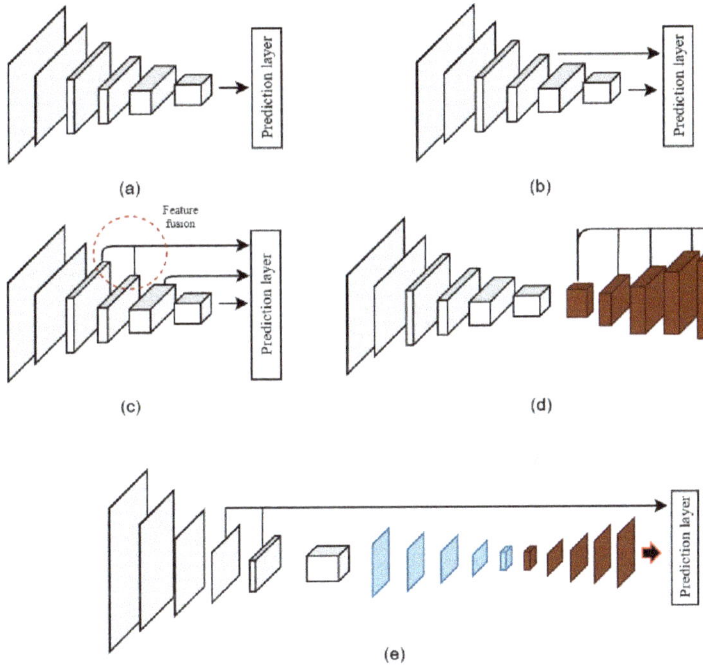

Figure 4. Schematic comparison of approaches used by different types of object detectors. (**a**) Single stage detectors (e.g., YOLO). (**b**) Multi-level features used at prediction layer (e.g., SSD). (**c**) Approach of supplying shallow layer features for prediction (e.g., FSSD). (**d**) Deconvolutional layers for improved feature representation (e.g., DSSD). (**e**) Network schema of our proposed approach.

2.1. Single Shot Multibox Detector (SSD)

The SSD is used as the baseline network in our model due to its high speed and accuracy in object detection. The SSD detector itself is composed of a base network (VGG16) followed by six extra convolutional layers and a Non-Maximum Suppression (NMS) layer for final detection [53]. The base VGG16 network (without its final classification layers) is purely used for feature extraction. The additional six convolutional layers that are attached to the end of the VGG network (apart from the first one) will be used for prediction of the bounding boxes and confidence score for different objects. These layers progressively decrease in their size to accommodate detection of objects at multiple scales; however, due to structural limitation of SSD, small object detection accuracy remains undesirable [27,29].

The SSD's performance relies heavily on default boxes, specifically their scale and aspect ratios. Each feature map corresponds to a specific scale of default box along with a list of five aspect ratios for each scale. The minimum and maximum scales are set to 0.2 and 0.9, respectively, while aspect ratios are 1, 2, 3, 1/2, and 1/3. The prediction layers receive several feature maps from *"Extra feature layers"*, representing multiple scales/aspect ratios and determining classification scores and bounding box coordinates [16]. The pyramidal feature hierarchy in *"Extra feature layers"* enables SSD detect objects of various sizes in the images; however, its performance for small objects is sub-optimal [27–29].

In our proposed model, we extend the multi-scale feature representation concept for enhanced feature representation at the prediction layer by applying the feature fusion, deconvolutional. and super-resolution modules.

2.2. Deconvolution Module

In the SSD model after the VGG16 network, the feature maps are scaled down considerably and lack fine details of the objects. The large objects might be sufficiently represented and detected; however, the feature resolution might be insufficient for small objects, leading to poor detection. A deconvolution operation up-scaling the feature resolution [54] and provides more details to the prediction layer. In our proposed network, after the SSD layers, a series of deconvolution layers are added. This structure inspired by [31] partially addresses the inefficiency of feature resolution for small object detection.

The deconvolution module includes a series of five consecutive deconvolution layer that successively increases the feature maps supplied to the prediction layer. This module includes a 2 × 2 deconvolutional layer with a stride of 2, followed by a convolutional layer activated by the ReLU activation layer and a batch normalization. Figure 5 shows the deconvolution module used in our network. Furthermore, every deconvolution layer is fused with a corresponding SSD of the same resolution size. The fusion is done using an element-wise sum operation followed by a ReLU activation.

A deconvolutional layer is added for each SSD convolutional layer, effectively up-scaling all the feature layers to be used by the prediction layer. The feature maps of the SSD convolutional layer and deconvolutional layer are combined through an element-wise sum operation. Each SSD layer undergoes two sets of two convolutional operations followed by batch normalization and a ReLU activation layer before combining with the deconvolution feature maps. The element-wise sum operation allows point to point combination of the feature maps at different levels into equivalent weights, as shown in Figure 6.

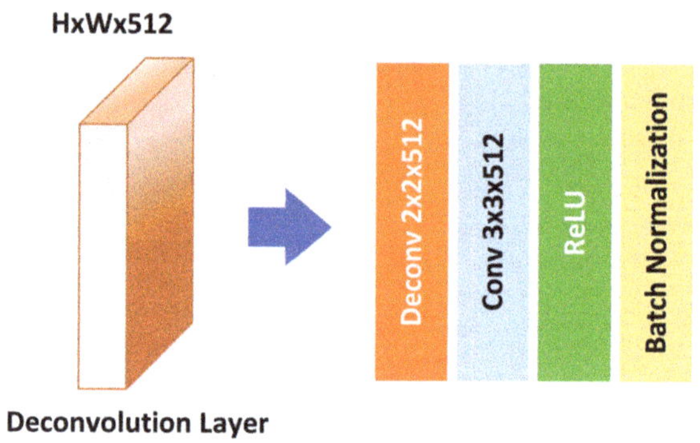

Figure 5. A deconvolutional module unit used after the SSD layers.

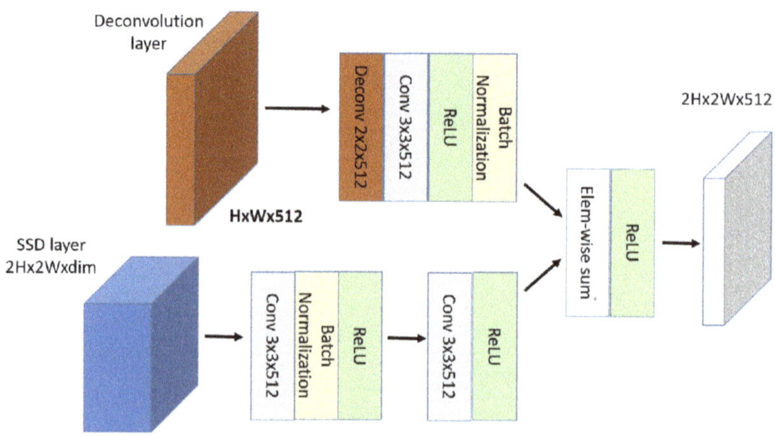

Figure 6. A deconvolutional module unit merged with an SSD layer using element-wise sum operation.

2.3. Super-Resolution Module

The super-resolution (SR) method enables deriving high resolution (HR) features from low resolution (LR) feature maps [55]. SR is a well-explored topic and is applied in various areas, including remote sensing [56] and video SR [57]. In our proposed model, the two shallow layers *Conv4_3* and *Conv5_3* are considered as LR feature maps. The SR method is applied to derive a HR version of the two shallow layers. Inspired by the techniques proposed by [58,59], we apply an SR technique on the *Conv4_3* and *Conv5_3* layers to obtain HR feature maps.

The SR module in our network is based on *residual* and *up-sampling* blocks, as illustrated in Figure 7. Two residual blocks are applied to both of the shallow layers. Furthermore, each residual block consists of two sub-block units of a 3 × 3 convolutional layer, a batch normalization layer and a ReLU activation layer. As with residual blocks, skip connections are achieved using an elementwise sum operation. The two residual blocks are followed by an elementwise sum operation, concatenating the shallow layer output with the residual layer outputs. The residual blocks enable to obtain multi-scaled features of both shallow layers. The concatenation operation is followed by two up-sampling blocks. The up-sampling blocks help in achieving SR in our model. For the up-sampling purpose, the Pixelshuffle [58] layer, which is used in several SR approaches including [52,59], was employed in this study.

PixelShuffle is an operation used in SR models to increase the spatial resolution of the feature maps. This technique utilizes sub-pixel convolutions with a fractional stride of $1/r$ (up-sampling ratio) in the LR space. PixelShuffle specifically rearranges elements in a tensor of shape $(*, C \times r^2, H, W)$ to a tensor of shape $(*, C, H \times r, W \times r)$, where r is the up-sampling ratio and C is the color channels; essentially, it trades layer depth with higher spatial resolution [58]. The up-sampling block in our proposed architecture consists of a 3 × 3 convolutional layer, a pixelshuffle layer, and a ReLU activation layer.

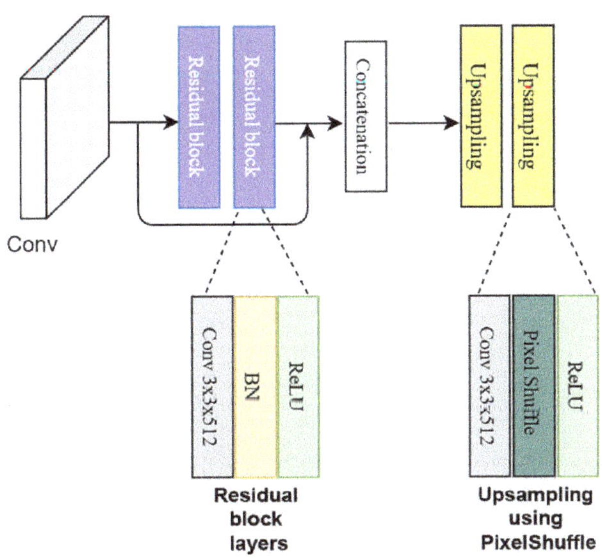

Figure 7. The super-resolution module.

2.4. Shallow Layer Feature Fusion Module

Multi-scale feature representation works by combining features from multiple stages of the network to provide an enhanced feature map at the prediction layer and improve small object detection accuracy. Such approach has been used in Feature fusion Single

Shot multi-box Detector (FSSD) [60], Deconvolutional SSD (DSSD) [31], Feature-Fused SSD (FF-SSD) [61], and Feature fusion and Scaling-based SSD (FS-SSD) [50].

The feature fusion approach used in our implementation mitigates loss of small object features. The feature maps from the *Conv*4_3 and *Conv*5_3 are fused and supplied to the prediction layer. There are two different ways to fuse features from shallow layers: *concatenation* and *element-wise summation*. The concatenation approach requires inputs with matching shapes except for the concatenation axis. However, element-wise summation works with tensors with similar batch sizes and follows arrays broadcasting rules [62]. In the shallow layer feature fusion module, a 1×1 convolution layer is applied after the concatenation, which leads to better learning and enhancement of small objects' features over the background. The concatenation operation is illustrated in Figure 8.

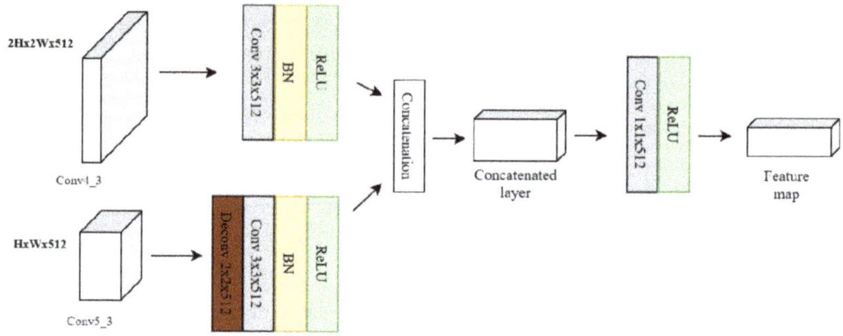

Figure 8. Concatenation of the *Conv*4_3 and *Conv*5_3 feature layers.

The *Conv*5_3 layer feature resolution differs from the resolution of the *Conv*4_3 feature layer. For fusion of both the layers, the *Conv*5_3 layer is up-sampled to the same size of the *Conv*4_3 layer. The up-sampling is achieved through a deconvolution operation at the *Conv*5_3 layer. Next, both the feature layers undergo a 3×3 convolution operation, batch normalization, and ReLu activation function. The output feature map of the feature fusion module is supplied to the prediction layer. In comparison to the standard SSD network, the prediction layer of our model receives more feature maps with potentially better representation of the small objects.

3. Experiments

The proposed model is evaluated for its object detection accuracy with an emphasis on small object detection. The details of multiple experiments conducted with the proposed model are presented in the following sections.

3.1. Datasets

The model was evaluated on three datasets: a custom UAV image dataset of livestock captured as part of the 5G rural integrated test-bed (5GRIT) project [63], the Stanford Drone Dataset (SDD) [11], and a crowd monitoring dataset acquired as part of the European Union (EU) project, MONICA [64]. The custom livestock dataset consists of aerial images of livestock captured over farms across the UK. The dataset includes only one labeled class of livestock (sheep). The images were captured from a UAV flown at 50 m altitude. In total, 425 RGB images with a very high resolution of 5400×3600 pixels were acquired. Figure 9 shows some example images of the dataset.

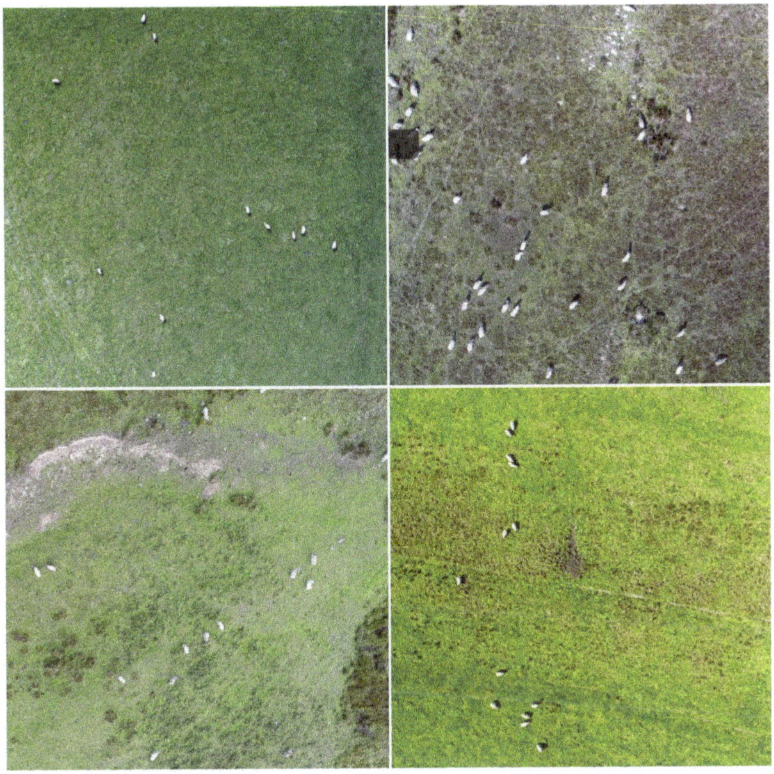

Figure 9. Example images of the livestock dataset. In the images, sheep are small targets for the object detectors.

As can be seen in Figure 9, the livestock dataset exhibits aerial images of livestock (sheep) with considerably small spatial size proportional to the total image size. This poses a challenge to the existing state-of-the-art object detectors, which make this dataset a suitable test-bed and use case to evaluate our small object detector performance. Since images in the livestock dataset have very high resolution, it is not possible to use them directly for the training of a neural network model. Hence, each image was split (cropped) into multiple images of 300 × 300 resolution. As a result of this operation, a total of 3900 images were available for training based on the livestock dataset.

The SDD dataset consists of 400 aerial images of people captured using a UAV at an original resolution of 6000 × 4000 pixels. The *Pedestrian* category images were used for training and evaluation in our study. Since images in the SDD dataset are of very high resolution, each image was split into multiple images of 600 × 400 for training. We used different cropping factors in livestock (300 × 300) and the SDD dataset (600 × 400) mainly to equalize the average scale of small objects across both datasets. Livestock dataset objects (sheep) are considerably smaller than benchmark SDD objects (Pedestrian). This helped to improve the consistency of our experiments and results across both datasets. Figure 1 shows some example images of this dataset. After training and evaluation using the SDD dataset on *Pedestrian* category, the MONICA dataset, which consists of images of the crowd, is used for further evaluation of our proposed model.

3.2. Implementation

The proposed model is based on the SSD object detector. For our experiments, the Keras implementation of SSD with VGG16 used in [65] is employed as our baseline architecture network. For training purposes, parameters from the original SSD implementation is used in our studies. The anchor box ratios, scaling factors, and other parameters were kept unchanged from the original recommendation. To improve the volume of the training dataset, the data augmentation process recommended in the original SSD implementation is adopted to increase the training dataset image count. The data augmentation process includes randomly sampling an entire original input image such that it has a minimum Jaccard index with objects of around 0.1, 0.3, 0.5, 0.7, or 0.9, and then randomly sampling a patch. The batch size was set to 32 for training and the learning rate ranged from 0.001 for the first 60 k steps, 0.0001 for up to 80 k and 0.00001 for 100 k steps. The maximum iteration was set to 100 k steps.

3.3. Comparison on the Livestock Dataset

The performance of our model is compared with several popular CNN-based object detectors including Faster R-CNN [20], variants of SSD including SSD300 and SSD512 [16], YOLOv3 [66], and CenterNet++ [30]. Moreover, the proposed model has been compared with several state-of-the-art small object detectors including Deconvolutional SSD (DSSD) [31], FS-SSD [50], FF-SSD [61], MPFPN [49], and EFPN [46].

The mean Average Precision (mAP) of all the detectors are shown in Table 2. The mAP is adopted as the primary criterion (Figure of merit) for detection accuracy, which is an indicator related to the Intersection over Union (IoU) threshold. We take the most used threshold IoU = 0.5 in our experiments.

All the target objects in the Livestock dataset have been checked for fulfillment of DORI's small object criterion [25]. Bear in mind that, objects in the Livestock dataset are considerably small (significantly smaller than what DORI outlines as small object) and general purpose object detectors in this comparison such as YOLOv3, SSD, CenterNet++, and Faster R-CNN are not purely made to deal with such small scale of objects. The enclosure of general purpose object detectors in this comparison is mainly to demonstrate how purposely made small object detectors can positively contribute to the small object detection performance in aerial imagery.

For the livestock dataset, our proposed model achieves the highest accuracy with a mAP of 79.12%. The YOLOv3 and Faster R-CNN show the lowest mAP and Recall compared to other detectors considered in the experiment. Among general purpose object detectors, CenterNet++ with a respective mAP and Recall of 76.18 and 92.44 ourperformed other general purpose object detector; however, it came short when compared to small object detectors. In terms of Recall, once again the proposed model, with 94.10%, outperformed all other detectors in this comparison. The FS-SSD, with a mAP and Recall of 77.14% and 93.91%, respectively, was the second-best detector in this comparison; however, with 17.35 Frames per Second (FPS), FS-SSD outperformed our model in this respect.

Small object detection is important in UAV and satellite imagery as the object sizes are usually small relative to the total image size. The livestock dataset consists of considerably small top-down images of livestock (sheep) and our proposed model performs well in detecting these objects compared to other methods in this comparison. Figure 10 shows a qualitative comparison of the original SSD300 object detector, FS-SSD, and our proposed model. Images in Figure 10 have been chosen randomly to retain the fairness of our qualitative comparison. It can be observed that the SSD misses several instances of livestock across the images; however, FS-SSD's performance and accuracy is very comparable to our proposed model. It is worth mentioning that due to extremely small object sizes, all models in this comparison fail to detect sheep in a few instances. Keep in mind that the majority of the models in this comparison are very close in terms of mAP and Recall values (around 2% mAP difference between our model and the second best model in this study based on livestock dataset results) and qualitative comparison of these models using a few random sample images might not be a good indication of their overall performance.

Figure 10. Comparison of small object detection between the proposed network (**bottom row**), the SSD network (**middle row**) and the FS-SSD network (**top row**) on the custom livestock dataset.

Furthermore, a qualitative evaluation of the proposed model detection performance is shown in Figure 11. The ground truth and the predicted bounding boxes are shown in blue and red, respectively. It can be observed that the prediction bounding boxes are reasonably aligned with the ground truth and the object in the image.

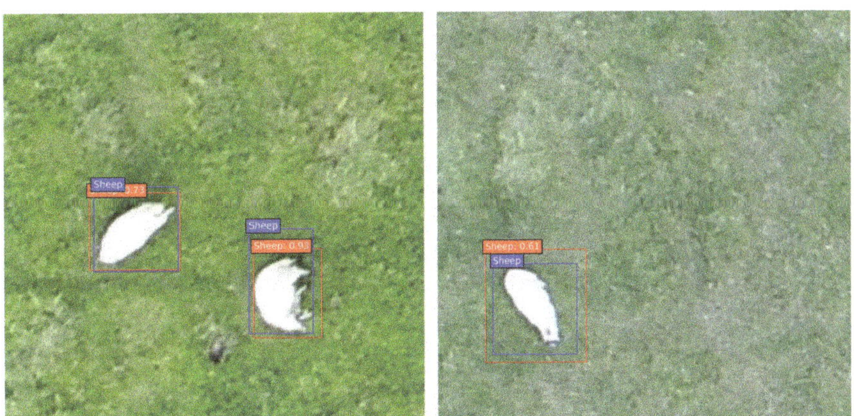

Figure 11. Qualitative evaluation of bounding box predictions by the proposed network on custom livestock dataset. Blue boxes correspond to the ground truth label and red boxes are the predicted bounding boxes.

Table 2. The mAP, Recall, and FPS comparison of the proposed model with the state-of-the-art small object detectors on our custom livestock dataset. Some of the general purpose object detectors have been included in this comparison.

Model	FPS	Recall (%)	mAP (%)
SSD300	36.50	88.20	74.80
SSD512	19.25	91.32	75.20
CenterNet++	4.70	92.44	76.18
YOLOv3	**48.95**	78.23	69.40
Faster R-CNN	7.40	83.60	71.20
DSSD	10.30	93.15	76.40
FS-SSD	17.35	93.91	77.14
FF-SSD	41.36	91.01	75.93
MPFPN	2.04	86.18	72.94
EFPN	4.14	90.23	74.81
Proposed	8.75	**94.10**	**79.12**

3.4. Comparison with the Stanford Drone Dataset (SDD)

One major use case for small object detection is person detection and localization from aerial images. Hence, we attempted to evaluate and compare our model performance in this area. For this experiment, the *Pedestrian* category images from the Stanford Drone Dataset (SDD) is considered [11]. This dataset has been used by many other researchers for small object detection in aerial imagery. Contenders of this comparison are the same as our previous comparison on the Livestock dataset.

The quantitative results of this comparison are shown in Table 3. In terms of *Pedestrian* detection, our proposed model achieves the highest mAP of 68.71%, followed closely by DSSD and FS-SSD with a mAP of 66.20% and 66.02% respectively. Again, general purpose object detectors including YOLOv3 and Faster R-CNN show the lowest mAP when compared to other detectors in the experiment. Among general purpose object detectors only, once again, CenterNet++, with respective a mAP and Recall of 66.01 and 83.91, performed the best; however, it came short when compared to small object detectors such as the proposed, DSSD, and FS-SSD. In terms of Recall, DSSD with 87.26% outperformed any other models in this comparison including our proposed model, with a Recall rate of 85.95%. In terms of inference speed, our proposed model with an average FPS of 8.75 meets the requirements of real-time detection. However, for applications such as oncoming traffic analysis, where detection speed is critical, FF-SSD with 42.51 FPS might be the preferred option.

Figure 12 shows a qualitative comparison of the proposed model against SSD300 using sample images from the SDD dataset. It can be observed that the SSD300 misses several instances of Pedestrian across the sample images. However, as the models in this comparison are competing closely in terms of mAP and Recall values, qualitative comparison using a few random sample images might not be a good indication of their overall performance.

To identify how our model performs in other similar datasets, the trained model on the SDD dataset has been tested qualitatively for person detection on images obtained from the MONICA project dataset [64]. Images in the MONICA dataset were captured from surveillance cameras at various public outdoor events. Due to an insufficient number of labeled samples in this dataset, we have only reported the qualitative comparison results mainly to demonstrate how these models perform under different conditions and they can be adopted to different scenarios and circumstances. The qualitative results for person detection using the MONICA dataset are shown in Figure 13, while both models exhibit inferior results in terms of Recall compared to what we saw in the previous experiments, the proposed model seems to have a slight edge over the SSD in this comparison. A drop in both models' performance was predictable, as these models were trained on a different dataset (SDD) with a relatively different nature, camera perspective, object scale, and lighting condition. Although this might be less than ideal, it shows the adaptability of the proposed model to similar real-world scenarios such as surveillance. Due to a limited number of labeled images in the MONICA dataset, we are unable to provide statistically reliable quantitative comparison results. Furthermore, on some occasions, the proposed model mistakenly combines the bounding boxes of the nearby objects. We believe this is mainly caused by the difference in the objects' scale in training (SDD) and testing (MONICA) datasets and can be mitigated by readjusting the raw input image slicing-factor (cropping) to equalize the average size of objects in the training dataset (SDD) and testing datasets (MONICA).

Figure 12. Comparison of small object detection of our proposed network (bottom row) with the SSD network (top row) onthe *Pedestrian* category from the Stanford drone dataset.

Table 3. The mAP, Recall, and FPS comparison of the proposed model with state-of-the-art small object detectors on a subset of SDD dataset containing aerial images. Some of the general purpose object detectors have been included in this comparison.

Model	FPS	Recall (%)	mAP (%)
SSD300	36.40	81.45	64.31
SSD512	19.35	83.58	65.24
CenterNet++	4.72	83.91	66.01
YOLOv3	**49.20**	78.64	57.42
Faster R-CNN	7.40	80.75	59.60
DSSD	10.30	**87.26**	66.20
FS-SSD	18.05	85.88	66.02
FF-SSD	42.51	83.66	65.36
MPFPN	2.35	79.32	61.79
EFPN	4.33	82.11	63.94
Proposed	8.75	85.95	**68.71**

Figure 13. Comparison of small object detection of our proposed network (**bottom row**) with SSD network (**top row**) on a custom dataset acquired under MONICA project data.

3.5. Ablation Studies of the Proposed Network

Ablation studies allow us to identify the impact of different modules on our model performance and speed. These experiments were conducted incrementally in isolation to identify how feature fusion, super-resolution, and deconvolution modules individually and collectively improve baseline SDD300 model performance and how they impact its inference speed in term of FPS in small object detection. The ablation study is conducted on the livestock dataset. The results of the ablation study are shown in Table 4. In the ablation study, SSD300 in the void of other modules is considered as the baseline network of our proposed model and achieved mAP 74.80%. The first study is to evaluate the shallow layer feature fusion model, wherein both the *element-wise sum* and the *concatenation* operations are evaluated. The *element-wise sum* method improved the accuracy of SSD300 from 74.80% to 75.70%. However, the *concatenation* method of feature fusion showed a slightly better performance of 76.10%. Hence, for the remaining ablation studies of the *deconvolutional* and the *super-resolution* modules, the *concatenation* feature fusion approach used as the preferred option. In terms of FPS, there is no significant difference between the *element-wise sum* and the *concatenation* operations and both of these techniques drop the FPS from 36.50 in the baseline SSD300 to around 22 FPS. Next, we attempted to identify how the shallow layer feature fusion (concatenation) performs along with the super-resolution module. The result shows improved performance of 77.20% was achieved as a result of this combination. In terms of FPS, inclusion of super-resolution module dropped the FPS from 22.42 to 17.64. The ablation study on the combination of deconvolutional and the shallow layer feature fusion (concatenation) further improved the mAP to 77.90%, but it dropped the inference FPS down to 14.52 only. Finally, the complete proposed model, including the super-resolution, the shallow layer feature fusion (concatenation), and the deconvolutional module, attained the best mAP performance of 79.12%; however, it slowed down the baseline SSD300 from 36.50 to 8.75 FPS.

Table 4. Ablation study of the proposed network on the livestock dataset. Different combinations of the feature fusion methods, super-resolution, and deconvolution were evaluated based on mAP and FPS.

Feature Fusion	Deconvolution	SuperResolution	mAP	FPS
NA	NA	NA	74.80	36.50
Element-wise sum	NA	NA	75.70	22.86
Concatenation	NA	NA	76.10	22.42
Concatenation	NA	YES	77.20	17.64
Concatenation	YES	NA	77.90	14.52
Concatenation	YES	YES	79.12	8.75

4. Discussion

UAV imagery is getting more popular than ever before with a variety of applications, including urban planning, smart farming, search and rescue, and security and surveillance. Due to many intrinsic characteristics of UAV imagery, such as high flight altitude, top-down camera perspective, and wide-angle lenses, objects in aerial imagery appear to have a distinctive shape and spatial properties and they usually take up a small fraction of the entire frame, which may pose a challenge to conventional object detectors.

Many researchers have attempted to address small object detection by introducing additional feature enhancement modules to conventional object detectors. Likewise, the proposed model in this research utilizes the SSD as the baseline network and improves its small object detection performance by incorporating deconvolution, super-resolution, and feature fusion modules. These modifications allow better feature representation of small objects at the prediction layer, which improves the baseline model's mAP (IoU = 0.5) in small object detection while retaining the requirements for the majority of real-time applications. Figure 14 shows the speed and accuracy comparison of the proposed model against the state-of-the-art models on the livestock dataset.

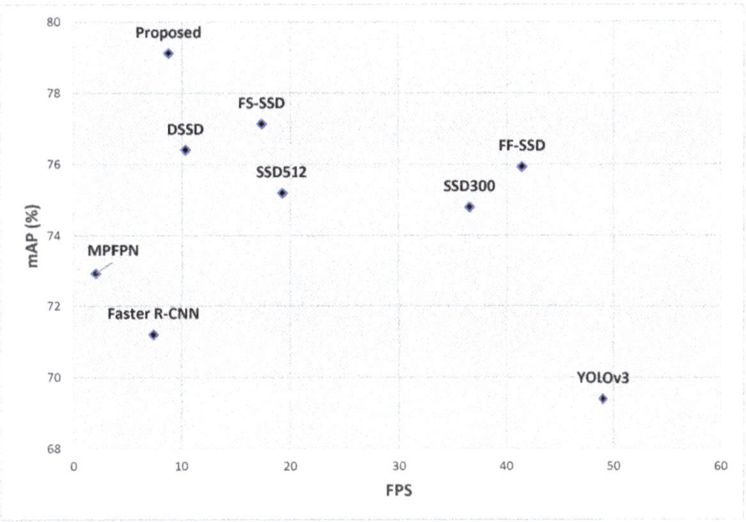

Figure 14. Speed and accuracy comparison of the proposed method with the state-of-the-art methods on the livestock dataset. It can be observed that the proposed model supersedes other approaches in terms of mAP, which makes it suitable for applications where accuracy is critically important.

As can be observed in Figure 14, the proposed model trumped other models in this comparison in terms of mAP. Other models, such as FS-SSD and FF-SSD, also managed to deliver reasonably good accuracy; however, their superior performance in terms of FPS makes them a more desirable option for applications such as oncoming traffic analysis where detection speed is critical. The proposed model can be used in applications such as precision farming, search and rescue, and disaster management, where accuracy is critically important. The majority of the images in the livestock dataset exhibit a low-contrast scenery of greenery with distinct foreground objects (livestock), which might skew the detection results. Hence, besides the livestock dataset, we have tested our model performance on the Stanford Drone Dataset (SDD). The SDD is a popular benchmark dataset used by many researchers [11,50,67,68] for (small) object detection in aerial imagery. Again, our comparative results showed the superiority of the proposed model over methods in the comparison. Although the focus of our comparison was mainly on the *Pedestrian* category of the SDD dataset, further investigations showed that our model performs equally well in some other object categories, including *Bicyclist* and *Car* on the SDD dataset. Figure 15 illustrates this comparison.

Beside the mean average precision (mAP) with an IoU of 0.5, we have attempted to investigate how the proposed model performs and compares with other detectors using a challenging IoU of 0.75. As expected, we observed a significant drop in mAP across all models involved in the comparison. Although our model is not the best performer in this experiment, it performs comparably with other detectors in this study and is better than the baseline model. Figure 16 illustrates comparison of mAP with IoU of 0.5 and 0.75 on *Pedestrian* category of SDD dataset across selected models in this study. Such an abrupt drop in accuracy indicates models in this comparison are having a hard time aligning the bounding boxes with the ground-truth labels in the regression process. Due to the smaller size of the objects, a slight misalignment significantly degrades the area of overlap and increases the area of union, which negatively impacts mAP.

The results of our experiments and ablation studies imply deconvolution, super-resolution, and feature fusion modules enhanced feature representation of small objects at the prediction layer, which results in better accuracy in small object detection. Our proposed model not only improved the overall accuracy of the baseline SSD300 model but also competes with some of the state-of-the-art small object detectors.

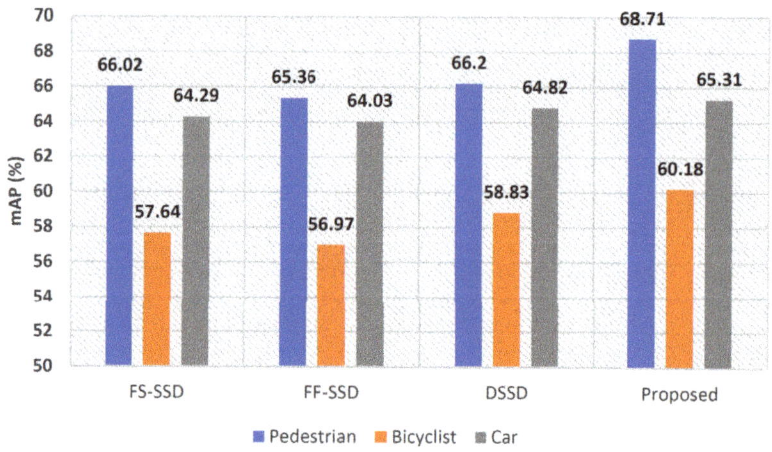

Figure 15. Comparison between the proposed model mAP with some other object detectors on the SDD dataset. Car, Bicyclist, and Pedestrian categories were considered in this comparison.

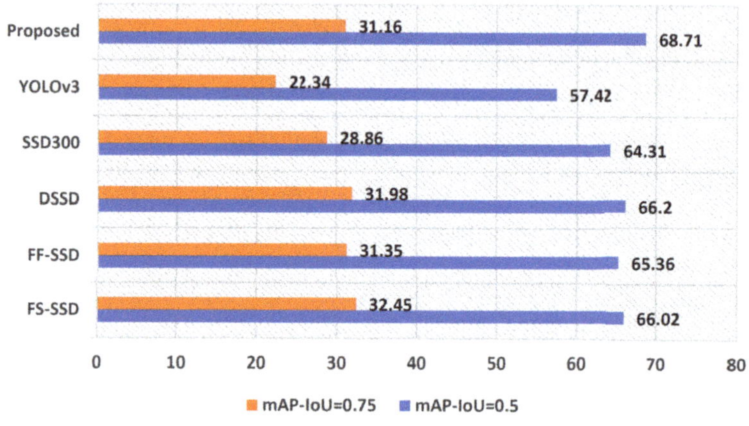

Figure 16. Comparison of mAP with IoU of 0.5 and 0.75 on the *Pedestrian* category of the SDD dataset.

5. Conclusions

In this paper, an object detection model with the goal of improving small object detection in aerial images is presented. The proposed model extends the SSD using the methods of deconvolution, super-resolution, and shallow layer feature fusion. The proposed extension enhances the feature representation of the objects at the prediction layer and leads to improved object detection accuracy. This approach is particularly beneficial for small object detection because with many state-of-the-art object detectors, the features of small objects are not represented sufficiently at the prediction layer for a reliable detection. The proposed model was trained and evaluated on two datasets: a custom UAV dataset of livestock, and the Stanford drone dataset. The results of the experiments showed that the proposed model performs mostly better than other object detectors considered in the comparative study. The proposed model can be used in applications such as precision farming, search and rescue, and disaster management, where accuracy is critically important.

Author Contributions: Writing, Review and Editing, M.M.D.O.; Writing—Original Draft and Methodology, M.R.; Supervision and Project Administration, P.R. All authors have read and agreed to the published version of the manuscript.

Funding: This research received no external funding.

Data Availability Statement: Data and source code can be made available upon request from the corresponding author.

Conflicts of Interest: The authors declare no conflict of interest.

References

1. Qin, H.; Yan, J.; Li, X.; Hu, X. Joint training of cascaded CNN for face detection. In Proceedings of the IEEE Conference on Computer Vision and Pattern Recognition, Las Vegas, NV, USA, 27–30 June 2016; pp. 3456–3465.
2. Subetha, T.; Chitrakala, S. A survey on human activity recognition from videos. In Proceedings of the 2016 International Conference on Information Communication and Embedded Systems (ICICES), Chennai, India, 25–26 February 2016; pp. 1–7.
3. Ukil, A.; Bandyoapdhyay, S.; Puri, C.; Pal, A. IoT healthcare analytics: The importance of anomaly detection. In Proceedings of the 2016 IEEE 30th International Conference on Advanced Information Networking and Applications (AINA), Crans-Montana, Switzerland, 23–25 May 2016; pp. 994–997.
4. Feng, D.; Rosenbaum, L.; Dietmayer, K. Towards safe autonomous driving: Capture uncertainty in the deep neural network for LIDAR 3D vehicle detection. In Proceedings of the 2018 21st International Conference on Intelligent Transportation Systems (ITSC), Maui, HI, USA, 4–7 November 2018; pp. 3266–3273.
5. Lottes, P.; Khanna, R.; Pfeifer, J.; Siegwart, R.; Stachniss, C. UAV-based crop and weed classification for smart farming. In Proceedings of the 2017 IEEE International Conference on Robotics and Automation (ICRA), Marina Bay Sands, Singapore, 29 May–3 June 2017; pp. 3024–3031.
6. Niedzielski, T.; Jurecka, M.; Miziński, B.; Remisz, J.; Ślopek, J.; Spallek, W.; Witek-Kasprzak, M.; Kasprzak, Ł.; Chlaściak, M. A real-time field experiment on search and rescue operations assisted by unmanned aerial vehicles. *J. Field Robot.* **2018**, *35*, 906–920. [CrossRef]
7. Giordan, D.; Manconi, A.; Remondino, F.; Nex, F. *Use of Unmanned Aerial Vehicles in Monitoring Application and Management of Natural Hazards*; Taylor & Francis: Oxfordshire, UK, 2017.
8. Mesas-Carrascosa, F.; Garcia, M.N.; Larriva, J.; Garcia-Ferrer, A. An analysis of the influence of flight parameters in the generation of unmanned aerial vehicle (UAV) orthomosaics to survey archaeological areas. *Sensors* **2016**, *16*, 1838. [CrossRef] [PubMed]
9. Saska, M.; Vonásek, V.; Chudoba, J.; Thomas, J.; Loianno, G.; Kumar, V. Swarm distribution and deployment for cooperative surveillance by micro-aerial vehicles. *J. Int. Robot. Syst.* **2016**, *84*, 469–492. [CrossRef]
10. Li, Y.; Wang, S.; Tian, Q.; Ding, X. Feature representation for statistical-learning-based object detection: A review. *Pattern Recognit.* **2015**, *48*, 3542–3559. [CrossRef]
11. Robicquet, A.; Sadeghian, A.; Alahi, A.; Savarese, S. Learning social etiquette: Human trajectory understanding in crowded scenes. In Proceedings of the European Conference on Computer Vision, Amsterdam, The Netherlands, 11–14 October 2016; pp. 549–565.
12. Viola, P.; Jones, M. Rapid object detection using a boosted cascade of simple features. In Proceedings of the 2001 IEEE Computer Society Conference on Computer Vision Furthermore, Pattern Recognition, CVPR, Kauai, HI, USA, 8–14 December 2001; Volume 1.
13. Dalal, N.; Triggs, B. Histograms of oriented gradients for human detection. In Proceedings of the 2005 IEEE Computer Society Conference on Computer Vision and Pattern Recognition (CVPR'05), San Diego, CA, USA, 20–25 June 2005; Volume 1, pp. 886–893.
14. Felzenszwalb, P.; Girshick, R.; McAllester, D. Cascade object detection with deformable part models. In Proceedings of the 2010 IEEE Computer Society Conference on Computer Vision and Pattern Recognition, San Francisco, CA, USA, 13–18 June 2010; pp. 2241–2248.
15. Redmon, J.; Divvala, S.; Girshick, R.; Farhadi, A. You only look once: Unified, real-time object detection. In Proceedings of the IEEE Conference on Computer Vision and Pattern Recognition, Las Vegas, NV, USA, 27–30 June 2016; pp. 779–788.
16. Liu, W.; Anguelov, D.; Erhan, D.; Szegedy, C.; Reed, S.; Fu, C.; Berg, A. SSD: Single shot multibox detector. In Proceedings of the European Conference on Computer Vision, Amsterdam, The Netherlands, 11–14 October 2016; pp. 21–37.
17. Girshick, R.; Donahue, J.; Darrell, T.; Malik, J. Rich feature hierarchies for accurate object detection and semantic segmentation. In Proceedings of the IEEE Conference on Computer Vision and Pattern Recognition, Columbus, OH, USA, 23–28 June 2014; pp. 580–587.
18. Felzenszwalb, P.; Huttenlocher, D. Efficient graph-based image segmentation. *Int. J. Comput. Vis.* **2004**, *59*, 167–181. [CrossRef]
19. Girshick, R. Fast R-CNN. In Proceedings of the IEEE International Conference on Compuer Vision, Columbus, OH, USA, 23–28 June 2015; pp. 1440–1448.
20. Ren, S.; He, K.; Girshick, R.; Sun, J. Faster R-CNN: Towards real-time object detection with region proposal networks. *Adv. Neural Inf. Process. Syst.* **2015**, *28*, 91–99. [CrossRef]
21. Carion, N.; Massa, F.; Synnaeve, G.; Usunier, N.; Kirillov, A.; Zagoruyko, S. End-to-end object detection with transformers. In Proceedings of the European Conference on Computer Vision, Glasgow, UK, 23–28 August 2020; pp. 213–229.
22. Jian, M.; Zhang, W.; Yu, H.; Cui, C.; Nie, X.; Zhang, H.; Yin, Y. Saliency detection based on directional patches extraction and principal local color contrast. *J. Vis. Commun. Image Represent.* **2018**, *57*, 1–11. [CrossRef]
23. Liu, Z.; Lin, Y.; Cao, Y.; Hu, H.; Wei, Y.; Zhang, Z.; Lin, S.; Guo, B. Swin transformer: Hierarchical vision transformer using shifted windows. In Proceedings of the IEEE/CVF International Conference on Computer Vision, Nashville, TN, USA, 20–25 June 2021; pp. 10012–10022.

24. Chen, K.; Pang, J.; Wang, J.; Xiong, Y.; Li, X.; Sun, S.; Feng, W.; Liu, Z.; Shi, J.; Ouyang, W. Others Hybrid task cascade for instance segmentation. In Proceedings of the IEEE/CVF Conference on Computer Vision and Pattern Recognition, Long Beach, CA, USA, 15–20 June 2019; pp. 4974–4983.
25. Unel, F.; Ozkalayci, B.; Cigla, C. The power of tiling for small object detection. In Proceedings of the IEEE/CVF Conference on Computer Vision and Pattern Recognition Workshops, Long Beach, CA, USA, 15–20 June 2019.
26. Bai, Y.; Zhang, Y.; Ding, M.; Ghanem, B. SOD-MTGAN: Small object detection via multi-task generative adversarial network. In Proceedings of the European Conference on Computer Vision (ECCV), Munich, Germany, 8–14 September 2018; pp. 206-221.
27. Yundong, L.; Han, D.; Hongguang, L.; Zhang, X.; Zhang, B.; Zhifeng, X. Multi-block SSD based on small object detection for UAV railway scene surveillance. *Chin. J. Aeronaut.* **2020**, *33*, 1747–1755.
28. Sun, C.; Ai, Y.; Wang, S.; Zhang, W. Mask-guided SSD for small-object detection. *Appl. Intell.* **2021**, *51*, 3311–3322. [CrossRef]
29. Li, H.; Lin, K.; Bai, J.; Li, A.; Yu, J. Small object detection algorithm based on feature pyramid-enhanced fusion SSD. *Complexity* **2019**, *2019*, 7297960. [CrossRef]
30. Duan, K.; Bai, S.; Xie, L.; Qi, H.; Huang, Q.; Tian, Q. CenterNet++ for Object Detection. *arXiv* **2022**, arXiv:2204.08394.
31. Fu, C.; Liu, W.; Ranga, A.; Tyagi, A.; Berg, A. DSSD: Deconvolutional single shot detector. *arXiv* **2017**, arXiv:1701.06659.
32. Yang, Z.; Liu, Y.; Liu, L.; Tang, X.; Xie, J.; Gao, X. Detecting Small Objects in Urban Settings Using SlimNet Model. *IEEE Trans. Geo Remote Sens.* **2019**, *57*, 8445–8457. [CrossRef]
33. Ye, Q.; Huo, H.; Zhu, T.; Fang, T. Harbor detection in large-scale remote sensing images using both deep-learned and topological structure features. In Proceedings of the 2017 10th International Symposium on Computational Intelligence and Design (ISCID), Hangzhou, China, 9–10 December 2017; Volume 1, pp. 218–222.
34. Zhang, W.; Wang, S.; Thachan, S.; Chen, J.; Qian, Y. Deconv R-CNN for Small Object Detection on Remote Sensing Images. In Proceedings of the IGARSS 2018-2018 IEEE International Geoscience and Remote Sensing Symposium, Valencia, Spain, 22–27 July 2018; pp. 2483–2486.
35. Liu, J.; Yang, S.; Tian, L.; Guo, W.; Zhou, B.; Jia, J.; Ling, H. Multi-component fusion network for small object detection in remote sensing images. *IEEE Access* **2019**, *7*, 128339–128352. [CrossRef]
36. Mudassar, B.; Mukhopadhyay, S. *Rethinking Convolutional Feature Extraction for Small Object Detection*; BMVC: Cardiff, UK, 2019; Volume 1, p. 234.
37. Hu, Y.; Wu, X.; Zheng, G.; Liu, X. Object detection of UAV for anti-UAV based on improved YOLO v3. In Proceedings of the 2019 Chinese Control Conference (CCC), Guangzhou, China, 27–30 July 2019; pp. 8386–8390.
38. Tian, D.; Zhang, C.; Duan, X.; Wang, X. An Automatic Car Accident Detection Method Based on Cooperative Vehicle Infrastructure Systems. *IEEE Access* **2019**, *7*, 127453–127463. [CrossRef]
39. Ju, M.; Luo, J.; Zhang, P.; He, M.; Luo, H. A simple and efficient network for small target detection. *IEEE Access* **2019**, *7*, 85771–85781. [CrossRef]
40. Liu, M.; Wang, X.; Zhou, A.; Fu, X.; Ma, Y.; Piao, C. UAV-YOLO: Small object detection on unmanned aerial vehicle perspective. *Sensors* **2020**, *20*, 2238. [CrossRef]
41. Bosquet, B.; Mucientes, M.; Brea, V. STDnet: Exploiting high resolution feature maps for small object detection. *Eng. Appl. Artif. Intell.* **2020**, *91*, 103615. [CrossRef]
42. Jiang, D.; Sun, B.; Su, S.; Zuo, Z.; Wu, P.; Tan, X. FASSD: A feature fusion and spatial attention-based single shot detector for small object detection. *Electronics* **2020**, *9*, 1536. [CrossRef]
43. Kampffmeyer, M.; Salberg, A.; Jenssen, R. Semantic segmentation of small objects and modeling of uncertainty in urban remote sensing images using deep convolutional neural networks. In Proceedings of the IEEE Conference on Computer Vision and Pattern Recognition Workshops, Las Vegas, NV, USA, 27–30 June 2016; pp. 1–9.
44. Noh, J.; Bae, W.; Lee, W.; Seo, J.; Kim, G. Better to follow, follow to be better: Towards precise supervision of feature super-resolution for small object detection. In Proceedings of the IEEE/CVF International Conference on Computer Vision, Seoul, Korea, 27–28 October 2019; pp. 9725–9734.
45. Li, J.; Liang, X.; Wei, Y.; Xu, T.; Feng, J.; Yan, S. Perceptual generative adversarial networks for small object detection. In Proceedings of the IEEE Conference on Computer Vision and Pattern Recognition, Honolulu, HI, USA, 21–26 July 2017; pp. 1222–1230.
46. Deng, C., Wang, M., Liu, L., Liu, Y. & Jiang, Y. Extended Feature Pyramid Network for Small Object Detection. *IEEE Trans. Multimedia* **2021**, *24*, 1968–1979.
47. Liang, Z.; Shao, J.; Zhang, D.; Gao, L. Small object detection using deep feature pyramid networks. In Proceedings of the Pacific Rim Conference on Multimedia, Hefei, China, 21–22 September 2018; pp. 554–564.
48. Kim, S.; Kook, H.; Sun, J.; Kang, M.; Ko, S. Parallel feature pyramid network for object detection. In Proceedings of the European Conference on Computer Vision (ECCV), Munich, Germany, 8–14 September 2018; pp. 234–250.
49. Liu, Y.; Yang, F.; Hu, P. Small-object detection in UAV-captured images via multi-branch parallel feature pyramid networks. *IEEE Access* **2020**, *8*, 145740–145750. [CrossRef]
50. Liang, X.; Zhang, J.; Zhuo, L.; Li, Y.; Tian, Q. Small object detection in unmanned aerial vehicle images using feature fusion and scaling-based single shot detector with spatial context analysis. *IEEE Trans. Circuits Syst. Video Technol.* **2019**, *30*, 1758–1770. [CrossRef]

51. Yamanaka, J.; Kuwashima, S.; Kurita, T. Fast and accurate image super resolution by deep CNN with skip connection and network in network. In Proceedings of the International Conference on Neural Information Processing System, Long Beach, CA, USA, 4–9 December 2017; pp. 217–225.
52. Ledig, C.; Theis, L.; Huszár, F.; Caballero, J.; Cunningham, A.; Acosta, A.; Aitken, A.; Tejani, A.; Totz, J.; Wang, Z. Photo-realistic single image super-resolution using a generative adversarial network. In Proceedings of the IEEE Conference on Computer Vision and Pattern Recognition, Honolulu, HI, USA, 21–26 June 2017; pp. 4681–4690.
53. Simonyan, K.; Zisserman, A. Very deep convolutional networks for large-scale image recognition. *arXiv* **2014**, arXiv:1409.1556.
54. Xu, L.; Ren, J.; Liu, C.; Jia, J. Deep convolutional neural network for image deconvolution. *Adv. Neural Inf. Process. Sys.* **2014**, *27*, 1790–1798.
55. Yang, J.; Wright, J.; Huang, T.; Ma, Y. Image super-resolution via sparse representation. *IEEE Trans. Image Process.* **2010**, *19*, 2861–2873. [CrossRef]
56. Shao, Z.; Wang, L.; Wang, Z.; Deng, J. Remote Sensing Image Super-Resolution Using Sparse Representation and Coupled Sparse Autoencoder. *IEEE J. Sel. Top. Appl. Earth Obs. Remote Sens.* **2019**, *12*, 2663–2674. [CrossRef]
57. Yi, P.; Wang, Z.; Jiang, K.; Shao, Z.; Ma, J. Multi-temporal ultra dense memory network for video super-resolution. *IEEE Trans. Circuits Syst. Video Technol.* **2019**, *30*, 2503–2516. [CrossRef]
58. Shi, W.; Caballero, J.; Huszár, F.; Totz, J.; Aitken, A.; Bishop, R.; Rueckert, D.; Wang, Z. Real-time single image and video super-resolution using an efficient sub-pixel convolutional neural network. In Proceedings of the IEEE Conference on Computer Vision and Pattern Recognition, Las Vegas, NV, USA, 27–30 June 2016; pp. 1874–1883.
59. Li, J.; Fang, F.; Mei, K.; Zhang, G. Multi-scale residual network for image super-resolution. In Proceedings of the European Conference on Computer Vision (ECCV), Munich, Germany, 8–14 September 2018; pp. 517–532.
60. Li, Z. & Zhou, F. FSSD: Feature fusion single shot multibox detector. *arXiv* **2017**, arXiv:1712.00960.
61. Cao, G.; Xie, X.; Yang, W.; Liao, Q.; Shi, G.; Wu, J. Feature-fused SSD: Fast detection for small objects. In Proceedings of the Ninth International Conference on Graphic and Image Processing, Qingdao, China, 14–16 October 2017.
62. Van Der Walt, S.; Colbert, S.; Varoquaux, G. The NumPy array: A structure for efficient numerical computation. *Comput. Sci. Eng.* **2011**, *13*, 22–30. [CrossRef]
63. 5G Rural Integrated Testbed. 2018. Available online: http://www.5grit.co.uk/ (accessed on 1 July 2019).
64. MONICA Project. 2018. Available online: https://www.Monica-project.eu/MONICA (accessed on 5 January 2020).
65. A Keras Port of Single Shot MultiBox Detector. 2017. Available online: https://github.com/rykov8/ssd_keras (accessed on 5 January 2020).
66. Redmon, J.; Farhadi, A. Yolov3: An incremental improvement. *arXiv* **2018**, arXiv:1804.02767.
67. Tang, T.; Deng, Z.; Zhou, S.; Lei, L.; Zou, H. Fast vehicle detection in UAV images. In Proceedings of the 2017 International Workshop On Remote Sensing With Intelligent Processing (RSIP), Shanghai, China, 19–21 May 2017; pp. 1–5.
68. Wang, X.; Cheng, P.; Liu, X.; Uzochukwu, B. Fast and accurate, convolutional neural network based approach for object detection from UAV. In Proceedings of the IECON 2018-44th Annual Conference Of The IEEE Industrial Electronics Society, Washington, DC, USA, 21–23 October 2018; pp. 3171–3175.

energies

MDPI

Article

Hybrid Quasi-Optimal PID-SDRE Quadrotor Control

Wojciech Giernacki [1,*], Sławomir Stępień [2], Marcin Chodnicki [3] and Agnieszka Wróblewska [4]

[1] Institute of Robotics and Machine Intelligence, Faculty of Automatic Control, Robotics and Electrical Engineering, Poznan University of Technology, Piotrowo 3a, 60-965 Poznan, Poland
[2] Institute of Automatic Control and Robotics, Faculty of Automatic Control, Robotics and Electrical Engineering, Poznan University of Technology, Piotrowo 3a, 60-965 Poznan, Poland; slawomir.stepien@put.poznan.pl
[3] Aircraft Composite Structures Division, Air Force Institute of Technology, 6 Ksiecia Boleslawa St., 01-494 Warsaw, Poland; marcin.chodnicki@itwl.pl
[4] Institute of Heat Energy, Faculty of Environmental and Power Engineering, Poznan University of Technology, Piotrowo 5, 61-138 Poznan, Poland; agnieszka.wroblewska@put.poznan.pl
* Correspondence: wojciech.giernacki@put.poznan.pl; Tel.: +48-61-665-2377

Abstract: In the paper, a new cascade control system for an autonomous flight of an unmanned aerial vehicle (UAV) based on Proportional–Integral–Derivative (PID) and finite-time State-Dependent Riccati Equation (SDRE) control is proposed. The PID and SDRE controllers are used in a hybrid control system for precise control and stabilization, which is necessary to increase the drone's flight stability and maneuver precision. The hybrid PID-SDRE control system proposed for the quadrotor model is quasi-optimal, since the suboptimal control algorithm for the UAV stabilization is used. The combination of the advantages of PID and SDRE control gives a significant improvement in the quality of control while maintaining the simplicity of the control system. Furthermore, the use of the suboptimal control technique provides the UAV attitude tracking in finite time. These remarks are drawn from a series of simulation tests conducted for the drone model.

Keywords: state-dependent riccati equation technique; SDRE control; PID control; attitude control; UAV; quadrotor

Citation: Giernacki, W.; Stępień, S.; Chodnicki, M.; Wróblewska, A. Hybrid Quasi-Optimal PID-SDRE Quadrotor Control. *Energies* **2022**, *15*, 4312. https://doi.org/10.3390/en15124312

Academic Editor: Adel Merabet

Received: 12 May 2022
Accepted: 10 June 2022
Published: 13 June 2022

1. Introduction

In recent years, there has been a strong trend in the development of control and estimation techniques for unmanned aerial vehicles (UAVs) [1]. This is mainly due to their wide availability, which, in combination with photo- and video-recording devices, greatly extends the scope of their applicability. To operate safely and precisely in an environment close to humans [2], drones need appropriate hardware and sensory tools as well as efficient control algorithms.

Currently, a cascade closed-loop control system is widely used [3]. The speed and precision of control is there based on the outer and inner loops for adjusting the orientation and position of the drone in 3D space. It usually uses well-known, simple, fixed-value controllers in the P, PD or PID structure. For an underactuated plant such as a drone, using four inputs expressing the expected/reference position of the drone and its orientation around the Z axis (yaw angle) in the observer (Earth) coordinate system, already roughly selected controller gains allow for a stable, controllable, autonomous flight, which in terms of image recording from a camera equipped with a stabilizer is more than enough.

The situation is quite different in the cases that require greater precision. Here, more advanced solutions are sought to ensure fast stabilization in flights with variable mass [4], mobile manipulation [5], or military missions [6]. Often in military tasks, the vector correlated with the front of the drone marks the target, and it is necessary not only to move the drone from point to point but also to orientate and stabilize it in the 3D space by tracking predefined angles that express the orientation of the drone (roll, pitch, yaw angles). This paper is devoted to this application problem, which is still recognized and classified as one of the key areas of research in the UAV community. In the following article, the proposed hybrid quasi-optimal PID-SDRE quadrotor control method will serve to achieve this goal.

The potential of the SDRE control strategy being considered and extended here has already been validated with the success by the UAV community over the last two decades. For the first time in the world scientific literature, a non-linear UAV control system based on state-dependent Riccati equations (SDRE) was proposed in [7], where its aim is to stabilize a desired velocity vector and the attitude of a multirotor UAV model. In [8], an INS/GPS sensor fusion scheme was introduced as an alternative to the extended Kalman filter (EKF). There, the state-dependent Riccati equation navigation filter was tested in the flight scenario. The aim was to minimize the influence of linearization errors on the tracking performance of the reference signals. In the paper, one may also find the stability proof of the SDRE non-linear filter and comparison with the classical EKF filter. Furthermore, in [9], through the integration process of the differential SDRE filter algorithm and the finite-horizon SDRE technique, the authors created an efficient online technique to control the missile guidance system.

The latest research trends in the use of the SDRE method in UAVs are, respectively:

- Development of a flight controller for quad tilt-wing UAV that during its transition flight (with the change of wing angle) will be able to deal with high nonlinearity in this situation and provide drone stability [10];
- Development of a suboptimal integral sliding mode trajectory tracking anti-interference controller based on the state-dependent Riccati equation [11];
- Development of non-linear controllers for cargo UAVs to obtain precise robot flight and efficient reduction of load oscillations by exploiting the natural coupling between horizontal UAV movement and payload oscillation [12].

Last but not least (to summarize the state-of-the-art of SDRE methods for UAVs) are the papers of Nekoo, Acosta and Ollero [13–15]. They are devoted to aerial–acrobatic maneuvers and collision avoidance of the SDRE controller using the artificial potential field method.

Except for the SDRE control method, state-of-the-art analysis for UAV control provides a wide spectrum of approaches, both model-free and model-based [16–18]. In this paper and research, using the advantages of both, we proposed a hybrid method, in which the model-free PID control is used to control the UAV's position, while the model-based finite-time SDRE method will increase the precision level in tracking the UAV orientation (via attitude control in inner loop).

The novelty and added value of our work is the development of an original cascade hybrid finite-time quasi-optimal PID-SDRE quadrotor control system as well as comparative simulation tests for the problem of stabilization of the set orientation of the drone in a predefined time horizon.

The new contribution of this work is described as follows:

- Optimal attitude stabilization and control with finite time;
- An increasing precise attitude control method;
- Elimination of the PID stabilizer and the tuning problem.

The paper is organized as follows: In Section 2, the dynamical model of the quadrotor is presented. Section 3 contains a description of the control system design with the new PID-SDRE attitude controller, the P-PID attitude controller, and the finite-time SDRE stabilizer, respectively. The UAV used in simulation experiments, as well as their comprehensive report and analysis, can be found in Section 4. Finally, the conclusion is drawn in Section 5.

2. Quadrotor Model

In most mathematical models of UAVs, its dynamics is considered for the structure treated as a rigid body with the mass of the UAV placed in the center of gravity and the mass of each of four propulsion units placed symmetrically in the cross-type frame. Therefore, the rigid body equations of motion are the differential equations that describe the evolution of the basic states of the quadrotor.

Furthermore, regarding the shape of the drone (Figure 1), and its natural X-type layout configuration, the North-East-Down (NED) axes convention with regard to the observer's coordinate system (the so-called Earth frame—$\{\mathcal{EF}\}$) is used. In this convention, the x axis of the UAV's local coordinate system (body frame—$\{\mathcal{BF}\}$) follows the camera direction, the y axis is perpendicular to the right, and the z axis is looking down according to the right-hand rule, respectively.

Figure 1. AtraxASF UAV used for drone modeling and simulation experiments.

The dynamics of the quadrotor is generally defined using Newton's force and moment equations [3]. The force equation is the following

$$\boldsymbol{F} = m(\dot{\boldsymbol{v}} + \boldsymbol{\omega} \times \boldsymbol{v}), \tag{1}$$

where $\boldsymbol{v}$ is a quadrotor linear velocity, $\boldsymbol{\omega}$ is the angular velocity, m is the mass of the aircraft and $\boldsymbol{F}$ denotes the force vector. For completeness, the moment equation should also be considered. The equation describes all the moments that act on the aircraft, which are equal to the rate of change in angular momentum.

$$\boldsymbol{M} = \boldsymbol{I}\dot{\boldsymbol{\omega}} + \boldsymbol{\omega} \times \boldsymbol{I}\boldsymbol{\omega}, \tag{2}$$

where $\boldsymbol{I}$ is an aircraft inertia matrix and $\boldsymbol{M}$ denotes the moment vector. When considering the vector $\boldsymbol{v}$ defined for all components in the direction x, y and z and $\boldsymbol{\omega}$ for roll ϕ, pitch θ and angle of yaw ψ

$$\boldsymbol{v} = \begin{bmatrix} u & v & w \end{bmatrix}^T \tag{3}$$

and

$$\boldsymbol{\omega} = \begin{bmatrix} p & q & r \end{bmatrix}^T \tag{4}$$

then equations of aircraft aerodynamics can be defined for linear and angular speeds. In addition, because of symmetry, in the inertia matrix, only the diagonal elements become nonzero

$$\boldsymbol{I} = \begin{bmatrix} I_x & 0 & 0 \\ 0 & I_y & 0 \\ 0 & 0 & I_z \end{bmatrix}. \tag{5}$$

The system of non-linear equations that describes the flight dynamics of aircraft, considering gravity force g and force due to thrust F_T, is the following

$$\begin{bmatrix} \dot{u} \\ \dot{v} \\ \dot{w} \end{bmatrix} = \begin{bmatrix} rv - qw + \frac{1}{m}F_x \\ pw - ru + \frac{1}{m}F_y \\ qu - pv + \frac{1}{m}F_z \end{bmatrix}, \tag{6}$$

$$\begin{bmatrix} \dot{p} \\ \dot{q} \\ \dot{r} \end{bmatrix} = \begin{bmatrix} \frac{I_z - I_y}{I_x} rq + \frac{1}{I_x} M_x \\ \frac{I_x - I_z}{I_y} pr + \frac{1}{I_y} M_y \\ \frac{I_y - I_x}{I_z} pq + \frac{1}{I_z} M_z \end{bmatrix}, \tag{7}$$

where $F_x = k_1\dot{x}$, $F_y = k_2\dot{y}$, $F_z = k_3\dot{z}$, $M_x = k_4\dot{\varphi}^2$, $M_y = k_5\dot{\theta}^2$, $M_z = k_6\dot{\psi}^2$, and k_1, k_2, k_3 are translational air drag coefficients, while k_4, k_5, k_6 are aerodynamic friction coefficients.

Equations (6) and (7) are non-linear functions of states, and they have to be easily formed as the state-dependent coefficient (SDC) form. Therefore, the separation of (6) and (7) is not complicated because, in general, the variables in the state are in the form of products.

To describe the aircraft orientation, the kinetic equations should be considered as functions that transform its angular position from the Earth frame to the body frame

$$\begin{bmatrix} \dot{\phi} \\ \dot{\theta} \\ \dot{\psi} \end{bmatrix} = \begin{bmatrix} p + (qsin\phi + rcos\phi)tan\theta \\ qcos\phi - rsin\phi \\ (qsin\phi + rcos\phi)sec\theta \end{bmatrix}, \tag{8}$$

where $sec\theta = 1/cos\theta$.

To convert between the body frame (BF) and the Earth frame (EF), the following rotation matrix from BF to EF is used:

$$\boldsymbol{R_{BE}} = \begin{bmatrix} cos\theta cos\psi & sin\varphi\theta cos\psi - cos\varphi sin\psi & cos\psi sin\theta cos\varphi + cos\psi sin\varphi \\ cos\theta sin\psi & sin\psi sin\theta sin\varphi + cos\varphi cos\psi & sin\psi sin\theta cos\varphi - cos\psi sin\varphi \\ -sin\theta & cos\theta sin\varphi & cos\theta cos\varphi \end{bmatrix}, \tag{9}$$

where $R_X(\varphi)$, $R_Y(\theta)$, and $R_Z(\psi)$, are matrices of Euler angles: roll (φ), pitch (θ) and yaw (ψ), defined as

$$R_X(\varphi) = \begin{bmatrix} 1 & 0 & 0 \\ 0 & cos\varphi & -sin\varphi \\ 0 & sin\varphi & cos\varphi \end{bmatrix}, \tag{10}$$

$$R_Y(\theta) = \begin{bmatrix} cos\theta & 0 & sin\theta \\ 0 & 1 & 0 \\ -sin\theta & 0 & cos\theta \end{bmatrix}, \tag{11}$$

$$R_Z(\psi) = \begin{bmatrix} cos\psi & -sin\psi & 0 \\ sin\psi & cos\psi & 0 \\ 0 & 0 & 1 \end{bmatrix}. \tag{12}$$

3. Control System Design

3.1. PID-SDRE Attitude Controller

The quadrotor is an unstable plant. Therefore, a UAV control system should contain a stabilization subsystem in design to make attitude control fast in response and free from overshoots. Then, from the point of view of practical implementation and drone usefulness, both the angular and linear speeds should stabilize. This is a reason why two blocks of controllers are proposed: one to control the orientation in space by the angular position and the other to stabilize the angular quadrotor speeds. These requirements can be achieved by using a PID attitude controller coupled to PID stabilizers. However, the use of PID-type controllers has affected efforts to tune and achieve optimal performance for the control system. Thus, a better idea is to use the PID-SDRE coupled solution or full integrated SDRE controller, which does not need to be optimized because it is optimal for control purposes.

Taking into account the above, this paper deals with the hybrid PID-SDRE controller dedicated to attitude control and finite-time stabilization. The control system schema is presented in Figure 2.

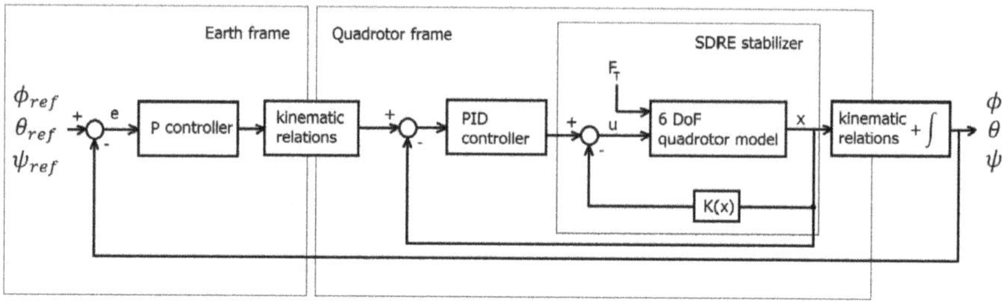

Figure 2. PID-SDRE control schema of the 6 DoF quadcopter model.

As shown, the controller consists of three control units. The attitude control system is implemented in outer closed-loop systems using the P controller, but the speed stabilization problem is performed by the inner closed-loop subunit with the PID controller and the feedback compensator employing the finite-time SDRE control technique. The stabilization problem can also be realized by the following:

- PID controller without SDRE stabilizer;
- SDRE feedback compensator neglecting PID stabilizer.

This means that the PID speed controller or SDRE speed compensator is redundant and the system can work as a two-unit and two-closed-loop control system. In this case, a thrust force F_T is set as constant and allows one to obtain the desired altitude. The other variables contained in Figure 2 denote: $\boldsymbol{x} = \begin{bmatrix} v & \omega \end{bmatrix}^T = \begin{bmatrix} u & v & w & p & q & r \end{bmatrix}^T$—state vector of the 6 DoF model, $\boldsymbol{u} = \begin{bmatrix} M_x & M_y & M_z \end{bmatrix}^T$—attitude control vector and error vector of the attitude angles $\boldsymbol{e} = \begin{bmatrix} \phi_{ref} - \phi & \theta_{ref} - \theta & \psi_{ref} - \psi \end{bmatrix}^T$.

3.2. P-PID Attitude Controller

The control system presented in Figure 2 includes two PID-based controllers: situated in the main loop P controller for attitude control and located in the inner loop PID controller for angular speed control (stabilization). The main P controller operates in the Earth frame and performs the UAV space orientation task, controlling the attitude angles: roll ϕ, pitch θ, and yaw ψ to the reference values. The inner-loop PID controller is used to stabilize the attitude speeds to zero. The PID-based control system works when fine and optimal tuning of P and PID controllers is achieved; however, sometimes it is problematic and not easy.

Considering the kinematic relations from Earth to the quadrotor frame, the control law for the main P controller is as follows

$$\boldsymbol{u}_p = \begin{bmatrix} p_p \\ q_p \\ r_p \end{bmatrix} = \begin{bmatrix} (e_\phi - e_\psi sin\theta)k_{p\phi} \\ (e_\theta cos\phi - e_\psi sin\phi cos\theta)k_{p\theta} \\ (e_\psi cos\phi cos\theta - e_\theta sin\phi)k_{p\psi} \end{bmatrix}, \tag{13}$$

where

$$\boldsymbol{e} = \begin{bmatrix} e_\phi \\ e_\theta \\ e_\psi \end{bmatrix} = \begin{bmatrix} \phi_{ref} - \phi \\ \theta_{theta} - \phi \\ \psi_{ref} - \psi \end{bmatrix} \tag{14}$$

is the error signal $\boldsymbol{e}$, which is a vector of three elements fed to the P controller. The PID controller used to stabilize the quadrotor space consists of three independent controllers for the rolling speed p, the pitching speed q, and the yawing speed r. The output of a PID controller $\boldsymbol{u_{PID}} = \begin{bmatrix} M_{xPID} & M_{yPID} & M_{zPID} \end{bmatrix}^T$ is calculated in the time domain from the feedback speed error as follows:

$$\boldsymbol{u_{PID}} = \boldsymbol{k_P}\omega + \boldsymbol{k_I}\int \omega dt + \boldsymbol{k_D}\frac{d\omega}{dt}. \tag{15}$$

The speed error signal is equal to ω, because the reference angular speed is equal to zero. Then, a three-element vector fed to the PID controller is computed that performs the proportional, derivative, and integral functions of this signal with respect to time. $\boldsymbol{k_P}$, $\boldsymbol{k_I}$, and $\boldsymbol{k_D}$ are proportional, integral, and derivative gain matrices:

$$\begin{aligned} \boldsymbol{k_P} &= diag\left(k_{P_p}, k_{P_q}, k_{P_r}\right), \\ \boldsymbol{k_I} &= diag\left(k_{I_p}, k_{I_q}, k_{I_r}\right), \\ \boldsymbol{k_D} &= diag\left(k_{D_p}, k_{D_q}, k_{D_r}\right). \end{aligned} \tag{16}$$

The integral matrix gain $\boldsymbol{k_I}$ times the integral of the error vector plus the derivative matrix gain $\boldsymbol{k_D}$ times the derivative of the error vector are calculated using its approximation and creating the digital form of the PID. This is a standard formulation of digital PID that uses the bilinear transformation of the continuous integral and derivative action [1].

3.3. Finite-Time SDRE Stabilizer

The state-dependent Riccati equation (SDRE) optimal control method is a promising and rapidly emerging tool for the control of non-linear systems. The technique with further improvement and a modified approach is widely described in recent literature [19–23]. Scientists can follow the state-dependent Riccati equation (SDRE) approach in the context of the non-linear control problem with a quadratic objective function [24–27]. The formulation based on a quadratic objective function is commonly used in practical solutions because the objective function defines energy, i.e., energy lost and delivered to the system, which is compatible with practical applications.

The finite-time control problem consists of finding an optimal control law that minimizes the following objective function defined for control time t_f [28]

$$J(\boldsymbol{u}) = 1/2\boldsymbol{x}^T(t_f)\boldsymbol{S}(\boldsymbol{x}(\boldsymbol{t_f}))\boldsymbol{x}(t_f) + 1/2\int_0^{t_f}\left(\boldsymbol{x}^T\boldsymbol{Q}(\boldsymbol{x})\boldsymbol{x} + \boldsymbol{u}^T\boldsymbol{R}(\boldsymbol{x})\boldsymbol{u}\right)dt \tag{17}$$

subject to non-linear dynamics for affine systems

$$\dot{\boldsymbol{x}} = \boldsymbol{F}(\boldsymbol{x}) + \boldsymbol{B}(\boldsymbol{x})\boldsymbol{u}. \tag{18}$$

Non-linear dynamics (18) can be written using the state-dependent coefficient (SDC) form [29]

$$\dot{\boldsymbol{x}} = \boldsymbol{A}(\boldsymbol{x})\boldsymbol{x} + \boldsymbol{B}(\boldsymbol{x})\boldsymbol{u}, \tag{19}$$

where $\boldsymbol{S}(\boldsymbol{x})$ and $\boldsymbol{Q}(\boldsymbol{x})$ are symmetric, positive semi-definite weighting matrices for states, and $\boldsymbol{R}(\boldsymbol{x})$ is the symmetric, positive definite weighting matrix for control inputs. Equation (18) includes the vector $\boldsymbol{F}(\boldsymbol{x})$, which is piecewise continuous in time and smooth with respect to its arguments, and that satisfies the Lipschitz condition.

Taking into account the SDC approximation (19), if the pair $\boldsymbol{A}(\boldsymbol{x}), \boldsymbol{B}(\boldsymbol{x})$ is a stabilizable parameterization of the system, then to check the controllability of the affine system, this pair in the linear sense should be controllable. On the other hand, checking the controllability of that pair does not require state or control input information [19,21,27]. It can be simply checked by the matrix

$$\boldsymbol{M}(\boldsymbol{x}) = \begin{bmatrix} \boldsymbol{B}(\boldsymbol{x}) & \boldsymbol{A}(\boldsymbol{x})\boldsymbol{B}(\boldsymbol{x}) & \ldots & \boldsymbol{A}^{n-1}\boldsymbol{B}(\boldsymbol{x}) \end{bmatrix} \tag{20}$$

often called the controllability matrix. Then, the system (18) or (19) is controllable if the controllability matrix (20) has full rank.

Employing Hamiltonian theory, the optimal control law is as follows

$$u = -R(x)^{-1}B(x)^T K(x)x, \tag{21}$$

where $K(x)$ is a state-dependent feedback compensator that can be obtained from the solution of a state-dependent differential Riccati equation (SDDRE)

$$\dot{K}(x) + K(x)A(x) + A(x)^T K(x) - K(x)B(x)R(x)^{-1}B(x)^T K(x) + Q(x) = 0. \tag{22}$$

Equation (22) is in the form of a differential SDRE for affine systems and must be solved many times for each x throughout the control process with the final condition $K(x(t_f)) = S(x(t_f))$. The solution of the equation exactly results in suboptimal control because it neglects the so-called 'SDRE necessary condition for optimality', which tends to zero [19,23,27]. Equation (22) known as differential SDRE or shortly SDDRE (State-Dependent Differential Riccati Equation); it can be solved numerically employing different algorithms. In the literature, there are many efficient algorithms dedicated to finding a solution of the SDDRE. The most popular are: backward iteration, state transition matrix approach, Lyapunov-based method, Riccati root method, etc. [30].

4. Experimental Results

4.1. UAV Used in Simulation Experiments

In the conducted experiments with the use of MATLAB/Simulink environment, a dynamical model of a military AtraxASF drone (shown in Figure 1) was used. AtraxASF is a quadrotor specially designed to perform precise test flights to inspect wild animals, especially in terms of detecting wild boars suffering from ASF (African swine fever). It was built as part of the research and development project financed by the National Center for Research and Development (Poland) and constructed by the Air Force Institute of Technology (ITWL, Warsaw, Poland). The UAV is equipped with a high-resolution thermal imaging sensor and has the following parameters:

- Take-off mass: 13 kg,
- Max. flight time: 40 min,
- Flight range: 4.5 kg,
- Optimal flight speed: 30 km/h,
- Max. flight speed: 60 km/h.

This military UAV was chosen to be modeled, as the authors of this article have all the UAV data (some can be provided on request) and its hardware and software characteristics gathered and verified during laboratory, test stand, and flight tests with AtraxASF.

4.2. Simulation Experiments

The non-linear UAV model is applied to check the PID-SDRE control for attitude and stabilization when it tries to find the desired angular position during flight or take-off. Using the governing equations that describe the UAV aerodynamics in SDC form (19), the control problem consists of finding the ϕ, θ, and ψ moments with trust generated by UAV rotors. As defined in (6) and shown in Figure 2, the thrust acts positively along the positive body axis z. To perform the attitude control, to adjust its ψ angle, or to make it turn left or right, the vehicle applies more thrust to one set of motors generating ψ moment. ϕ and θ are adjusted by applying more thrust to one rotor and less to the other opposing rotor, generating ϕ and θ moments. In this simple way, rolling, pitching, or yawing moments are generated. According to the control schema proposed in Figure 2, the control applied to the UAV is a sum of the PID control and the SDRE stabilizator control, where the controller outputs are ϕ, θ, and ψ moments. Z-axis force related to altitude is assumed to be constant, and the forces on the x and y axes generated by the controller are neglected. Therefore, the output of an SDRE subcontroller $\boldsymbol{u_{SDRE}} = \begin{bmatrix} M_{xSDRE} & M_{ySDRE} & M_{zSDRE} \end{bmatrix}^T$ is calculated from (21). Using the described UAV model, the PID-SDRE control technique is applied to control the UAV attitude considering finite-time horizon SDRE feedback compensation for stabilization. To be exact, as shown in Figure 2, the attitude is controlled by the P controller (13), but the PID stabilization works, zeroing angular speeds (15). An additional SDRE feedback compensator additionally stabilizes the UAV angular position and makes it possible not only in finite time but also for rapid attitude changes. Briefly, the PID-SDRE method makes possible rapid response for user commands and moreover enables rapid stabilization of the path of flight when unexpected external forces try to change its position and orientation during flying action. Taking into account the above, the control problem consists of finding the state dynamics of the UAV and the PID-SDRE controls for the prescribed attitude for $\phi_{ref} = 30$ deg, $\theta_{ref} = 45$ deg, $\psi_{ref} = 15$ deg with and reference angular speed $p_{ref} = 0$ deg/s, $q_{ref} = 0$ deg/s, $r_{ref} = 0$ deg/s.

In association with (13), the gains of the P attitude controller are: $kp_{\phi} = 10$, $kp_{\theta} = 20$, $kp_{\psi} = 100$. PID stabilizer gains (15) are chosen as: $\boldsymbol{k_P} = 0,3\boldsymbol{I_{3\times3}}$, $\boldsymbol{k_I} = 0,1\boldsymbol{I_{3\times3}}$, $\boldsymbol{k_D} = diag(0.01, 0.01, 0.0)$ and finally, the quadratic functional cost weighting matrices defined in (22) are as follows: $\boldsymbol{S} = 2\boldsymbol{I_{6\times6}}$, $\boldsymbol{Q} = 0,5\boldsymbol{I_{6\times6}}$ and $\boldsymbol{R} = 0,1\boldsymbol{I_{6\times6}}$.

The dynamics of the state of the UAV, in other words, the speed response, including its orientation to the desired angle position, is shown in Figures 3 and 4. The UAV attitude control has been activated at time $t = 1$ s; then, the UAV angulary has been moved from the "zero" attitude to the reference angular position. First, simulations are performed for the UAV controlled by the P and PID stabilizer only, neglecting the SDRE stabilizer.

Looking at the above figures (Figures 3 and 4), the angular position and speed responses are quick due to the large gains in the P-controller. However, the presented P-PID technique controls the attitude with overshoots and oscillations. Generally, the control works and is easy to implement; however, the system fails in precision operation in airspace. In this type of control, stabilization and improvement of accuracy seems to be necessary.

Next, simulations are performed for the complete PID-SDRE controller to show how the UAV can stabilize in a finite time t_f in the context of angular speeds. To verify precision and rapidity and to compare the proposed technique considering the SDRE based method with the commonly used PID technique, a numerical experiment is performed three final times: $t_f = 4$ s, $t_f = 2$ s, and $t_f = 1$ s with the same reference attitude. The simulation results are presented in Figures 5–10 with the impact of the successively reduced control time t_f from 4 to 1 s.

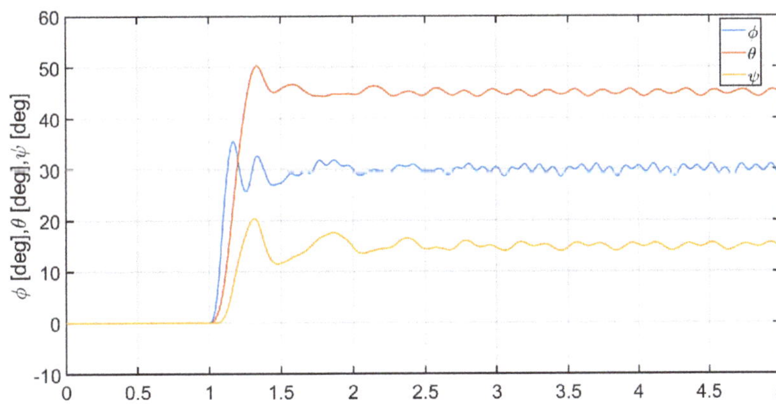

Figure 3. UAV angular response—PID control mode.

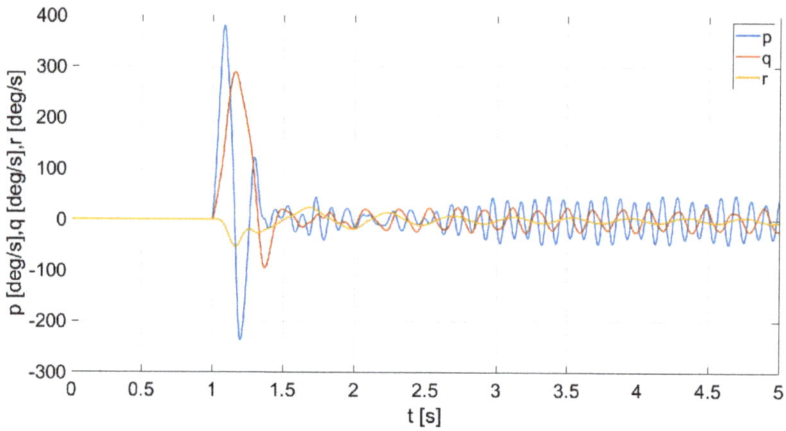

Figure 4. UAV angular speed response—PID control mode.

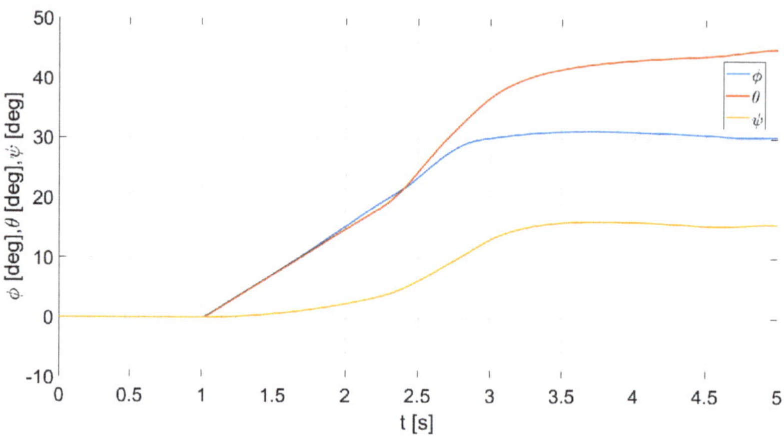

Figure 5. Angular response of UAV—PID-SDRE control mode, $t_f = 4$ s.

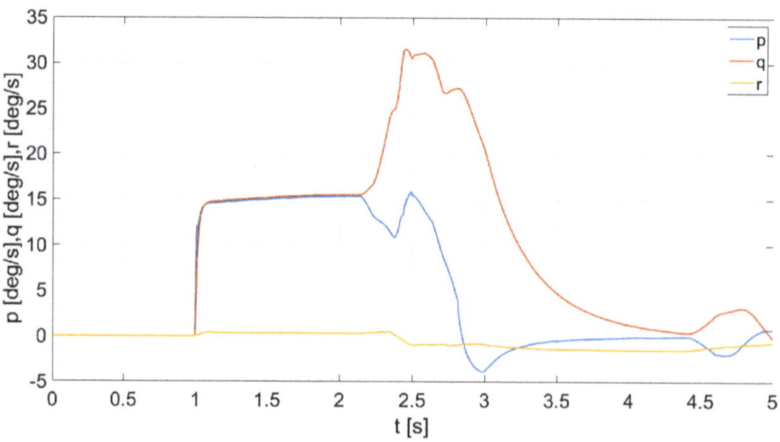

Figure 6. UAV angular speed response—PID-SDRE control mode, $t_f = 4$ s.

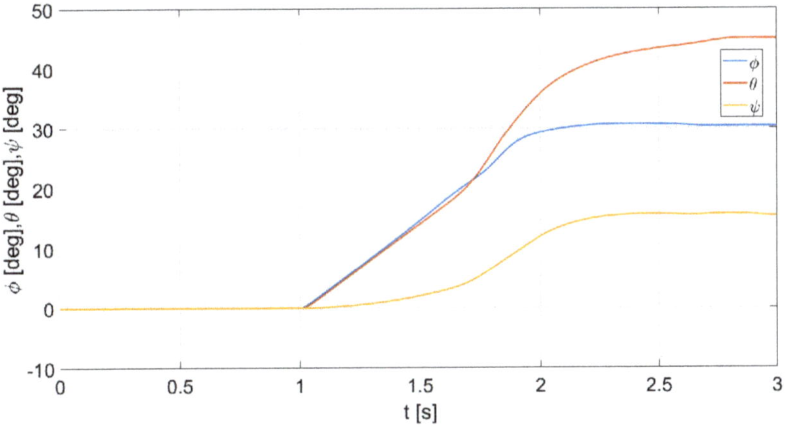

Figure 7. Angular response of UAV—PID-SDRE control mode, $t_f = 2$ s.

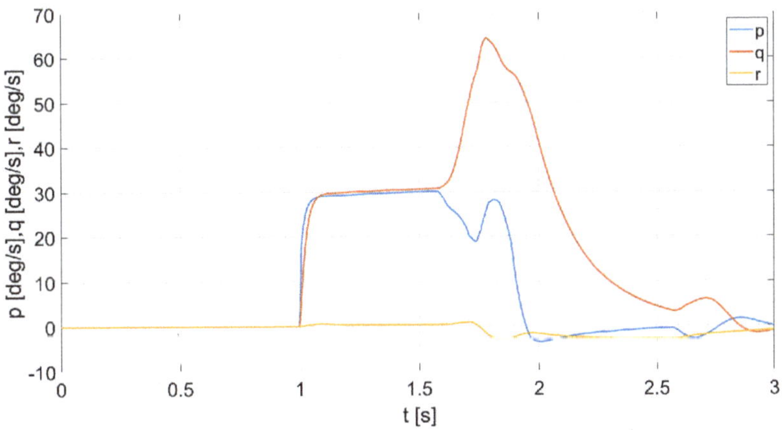

Figure 8. UAV angular speed response—PID-SDRE control mode, $t_f = 2$ s.

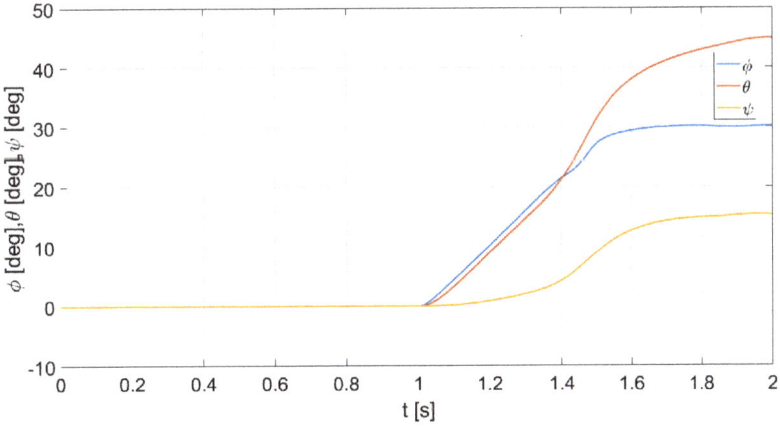

Figure 9. Angular response of the UAV—PID-SDRE control mode, $t_f = 1$ s.

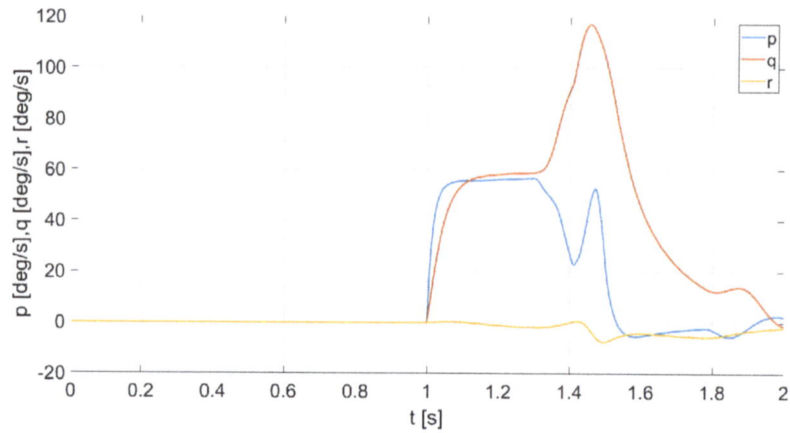

Figure 10. UAV angular speed response—PID-SDRE control mode, $t_f = 1$ s.

When looking at and analyzing Figures 5 and 6, the proposed PID-SDRE control shows that the quadrotor can be successfully controlled to referenced angles, zeroing angular speed, and reducing or eliminating overshoots. As expected, the referenced attitude is reached at the control time $t_f = 4$ s. When considering the following Figures 7–10, the same results are obtained for different control times $t_f = 2$ s and $t_f = 1$ s. Therefore, the insertion and use of the SDRE optimal stabilizer in the standard PID control system increases the complexity of the controller, making a hybrid PID-SDRE controller appropriate, because it allows for avoiding oscillations and allows the possibility of operating in airspace with high precision and adjustable control time t_f. The results presented as an effect of performed numerical experiments prove the usefulness and correctness of the proposed technique; moreover, they allow us to verify its behavior.

5. Conclusions

The hybrid PID-SDRE finite-time control technique is formulated and solved for the UAV-quadrotor attitude control problem. The UAV non-linear 6 DoF state-dependent parametrized model is proposed. The P-PID fine-tuned control methodology with an optimal non-linear SDRE feedback speed stabilizer, performing attitude control and stabilization task, is analyzed. The effectiveness of the presented technique is demonstrated in a numerical example in which a UAV response is found using a finite-time SDRE-based technique. The presented results show that the proposed technique can be successively applied to UAV flight control systems when it must operate precisely in airspace. The next step of the analysis and research performed is preparation for application in a real UAV control system.

Author Contributions: Methodology, W.G. and S.S.; software, M.C.; validation, W.G. and S.S.; writing—original draft preparation, W.G. and M.C.; writing—review and editing, W.G., M.C. and S.S.; supervision, A.W. All authors have read and agreed to the published version of the manuscript.

Funding: This research was financially supported as a statutory work of the Poznan University of Technology (No. 0214/SBAD/0237).

Institutional Review Board Statement: Not applicable.

Informed Consent Statement: Not applicable.

Data Availability Statement: Not applicable.

Conflicts of Interest: The authors declare no conflict of interest.

Abbreviations

The following abbreviations are used in this manuscript:

BF	Body Frame
EF	Earth Frame
EKF	Extended Kalman Filter
GPS	Global Positioning System
INS	Inertial Navigation System
NED	North-East-Down
PID	Proportional–Integral–Derivative Controller
QTW UAV	Quad Tilt-Wing Unmanned Aerial Vehicle
SDC	State-Dependent Coefficient
SDRE	State-Dependent Riccati Equation
UAV	Unmanned Aerial Vehicle

References

1. Kim, J.; Gadsden, S.A.; Wilkerson, S.A. A Comprehensive Survey of Control Strategies for Autonomous Quadrotors. *Can. J. Electr. Comput. Eng.* **2020**, *43*, 3–16. [CrossRef]
2. Kornatowski, P.M.; Bhaskaran, A.; Heitz, G.M.; Mintchev, S.; Floreano, D. Last-Centimeter Personal Drone Delivery: Field Deployment and User Interaction. *IEEE Robot. Autom. Lett.* **2018**, *43*, 3813–3820. [CrossRef]
3. Rao, J.; Li, B.; Zhang, Z.; Chen, D.; Giernacki, W. Position Control of Quadrotor UAV Based on Cascade Fuzzy Neural Network. *Energies* **2022**, *15*, 1763. [CrossRef]
4. Lungu, M. Auto-landing of UAVs with variable centre of mass using the backstepping and dynamic inversion control. *Aerosp. Sci. Technol.* **2020**, *103*, 105912. [CrossRef]
5. Orsag, M.; Korpela, C.; Oh, P. Modeling and Control of MM-UAV: Mobile Manipulating Unmanned Aerial Vehicle. *J. Intell. Robot. Syst. Vol.* **2013**, *69*, 227–240. [CrossRef]
6. Huang, H.; Zhao, X.; Zhang, X. Intelligent Guidance and Control Methods for Missile Swarm. *Comput. Intell. Neurosci.* **2022**, *2022*, 8235148. [CrossRef]
7. Voos, H. Nonlinear state-dependent Riccati equation control of a quadrotor UAV. In Proceedings of the 2006 IEEE Conference on Computer Aided Control System Design, 2006 IEEE International Conference on Control Applications, 2006 IEEE International Symposium on Intelligent Control, Munich, Germany, 4–6 October 2006; pp. 2547–2552. [CrossRef]
8. Nemra, A.; Aouf, N. Robust INS/GPS Sensor Fusion for UAV Localization Using SDRE Nonlinear Filtering. *IEEE Sens. J.* **2010**, *10*, 789–798. [CrossRef]
9. Khamis, A. Nonlinear Finite-Horizon Regulation and Tracking for Systems with Incomplete State Information Using Differential State Dependent Riccati Equation. *Int. J. Aerosp. Eng.* **2014**, *78628*, 178628. [CrossRef]
10. Takayama, T.; Uchiyama, K.; Masuda, K. Controller Design Using SDRE Method for Tilt-Wing UAV. In Proceedings of the 2020 11th International Conference on Mechanical and Aerospace Engineering (ICMAE), Athens, Greece, 14–17 July 2020; pp. 102–106. [CrossRef]
11. Hua, Z. Suboptimal Integral Sliding Mode Trajectory Tracking Control of a UAV Based on SDRE Method. In *Advances in Guidance, Navigation and Control, Proceedings of the 2020 International Conference on Guidance, Navigation and Control, ICGNC 2020, Tianjin, China, 23–25 October 2020*; Part of the Lecture Notes in Electrical Engineering Book Series (LNEE); Springer: Singapore, 2021; Volume 644, pp. 67–77. [CrossRef]
12. Guerrero-Sanchez, M.E.; Lozano, R.; Castillo, P.; Hernandez-Gonzalez, O.; Garcia-Beltran, C.D.; Valencia-Palomo, G. Nonlinear control strategies for a UAV carrying a load with swing attenuation. *Appl. Math. Model.* **2021**, *91*, 709–722. [CrossRef]
13. Nekoo, S.R.; Acosta, J.A.; Ollero, A. Quaternion-based state-dependent differential Riccati equation for quadrotor drones: Regulation control problem in aerobatic flight. *Robotica* **2022**, *40*, 1–16. [CrossRef]
14. Nekoo, S.R.; Acosta, J.A.; Ollero, A. Geometric control using the state-dependent Riccati equation: application to aerial-acrobatic maneuvers. *Int. J. Control.* **2021**, 1–16. [CrossRef]
15. Nekoo, S.R.; Acosta, J.A.; Ollero, A. Collision Avoidance of SDRE Controller using Artificial Potential Field Method: Application to Aerial Robotics. In Proceedings of the 2020 International Conference on Unmanned Aircraft Systems (ICUAS), Athens, Greece, 1–4 September 2020. [CrossRef]
16. Monti, C. *Model-Free Control of an Unmanned Aircraft Quadcopter Type System*; Rochester Institute of Technology: Rochester, NY, USA, 2020.
17. Bold, S.; Sosorbaram, B.; Chuluunjav, S. Mathematical Model Based PID Control of the Raspi Drone. *Lect. Notes Electr. Eng.* **2021**, *712*, 29–39. [CrossRef]
18. Karahan, M.; Kasnakoglu, C. Modeling and Simulation of Quadrotor UAV Using PID Controller. In Proceedings of the 2019 11th International Conference on Electronics, Computers and Artificial Intelligence (ECAI), Pitesti, Romania, 27–29 June 2019.
19. Banks, H.T.; Lewis, B.M.; Tran, H.T. Nonlinear feedback controllers and compensators: A state-dependent Riccati equation approach. *Comput. Optim. Appl.* **2018**, *37*, 177–218. [CrossRef]

20. Çimen, T.; Banks, S.P. Global optimal feedback control for general nonlinear systems with non-quadratic performance criteria. *Syst. Control Lett.* **2004**, *53*, 327–346. [CrossRef]
21. Çimen, T. Systematic and effective design of nonlinear feedback controllers via the state-dependent Riccati equation (SDRE) method. *Annu. Rev. Control.* **2010**, *34*, 32–51. [CrossRef]
22. Cloutier, J.R.; D'Souza, C.N.; Mracek, C.P. Nonlinear regulation and nonlinear $H\infty$ control via the state-dependent Riccati equation technique: Part 1, Theory; Part 2, Examples. In Proceedings of the First International Conference on Nonlinear Problems in Aviation and Aerospace, Daytona Beach, FL, USA, 9–11 May 1996; pp. 117–141.
23. Shamma, J.S.; Cloutier, J.R. Existence of SDRE stabilizing feedback. *IEEE Trans. Autom. Control.* **2003**, *48*, 513–517. [CrossRef]
24. Erdem, E.B.; Alleyne, A.G. Design of a class of nonlinear controllers via state dependent Riccati equations. *IEEE Trans. Control. Syst. Technol.* **2004**, *12*, 133–137. [CrossRef]
25. Hammett, K.D.; Hall, C.D.; Ridgely, D.B. Controllability issues in nonlinear state-dependent Riccati equation control. *J. Guid. Control. Dyn.* **1998**, *21*, 767–773. [CrossRef]
26. Heydari, A.; Balakrishnan, S.N. Closed-form solution to finite-horizon suboptimal control of nonlinear systems. *Int. J. Robust Nonlinear Control* **2015**, *25*, 2687–2704. [CrossRef]
27. Mracek, C.; Cloutier, J. Control designs for the nonlinear benchmark problem via the state-dependent Riccati equation method. *Int. J. Robust Nonlinear Control.* **1998**, *8*, 401–433. [CrossRef]
28. Wernli, A.; Cook, G. Suboptimal control for the nonlinear quadratic regulator problem. *Automatica* **1975**, *11*, 75–84. [CrossRef]
29. Liang, Y.; Lin, L. Analysis of SDC matrices for successfully implementing the SDRE scheme. *Automatica* **2013**, *49*, 3120–3124. [CrossRef]
30. Korayem, M.; Nekoo, S. Finite-time state-dependent Riccati equation for time-varying nonaffine systems: Rigid and flexible joint manipulator control. *ISA Trans.* **2015**, *54*, 125–144. [CrossRef] [PubMed]

drones

Article

An Autonomous Control Framework of Unmanned Helicopter Operations for Low-Altitude Flight in Mountainous Terrains

Zibo Jin [1], Lu Nie [2], Daochun Li [1], Zhan Tu [1,3,*] and Jinwu Xiang [1]

1 School of Aeronautic Science and Engineering, Beihang University, Beijing 100191, China; jinzibo@buaa.edu.cn (Z.J.); lidc@buaa.edu.cn (D.L.); xiangjw@buaa.edu.cn (J.X.)
2 Beijing Institute of Space Long March Vehicle, Beijing 100076, China; nielu@buaa.edu.cn
3 Institute of Unmanned System, Beihang University, Beijing 100191, China
* Correspondence: zhantu@buaa.edu.cn; Tel.: +86-(010)-82338079

Abstract: Low-altitude flight in mountainous terrains is a difficult flight task applied in both military and civilian fields. The helicopter has to maintain low altitude to realize search and rescue, reconnaissance, penetration, and strike operations. It contains complex environment perception, multilevel decision making, and multi-objective flight control; thus, flight is currently mainly conducted by human pilots. In this work, a control framework is implemented to realize autonomous flight for unmanned helicopter operations in an unknown mountainous environment. The identification of targets and threats is introduced using a deep neural network. A 3D vector field histogram method is adopted for local terrain avoidance based on airborne Lidar sensors. In particular, we propose an intuitive direct-viewing method to judge and change the visibilities of the helicopter. On this basis, a finite state machine is built for decision making of the autonomous flight. A highly realistic simulation environment is established to verify the proposed control framework. The simulation results demonstrate that the helicopter can autonomously complete flight missions including a fast approach, threat avoidance, cover concealment, and circuitous flight operations similar to human pilots. The proposed control framework provides an effective solution for complex flight tasks and expands the flight control technologies for high-level unmanned helicopter operations.

Keywords: autonomous flight control; unmanned helicopter operation; terrain avoidance; visual servo control; threat avoidance

Citation: Jin, Z.; Nie, L.; Li, D.; Tu, Z.; Xiang, J. An Autonomous Control Framework of Unmanned Helicopter Operations for Low-Altitude Flight in Mountainous Terrains. *Drones* **2022**, *6*, 150. https://doi.org/10.3390/drones6060150

Academic Editors: Andrzej Łukaszewicz, Wojciech Giernacki, Zbigniew Kulesza, Jaroslaw Pytka and Andriy Holovatyy

Received: 1 June 2022
Accepted: 14 June 2022
Published: 17 June 2022

1. Introduction

Unmanned aerial vehicles (UAVs) have received substantial interest from the research community and the general public alike in recent years [1,2], especially small UAVs and multi-rotors, whose low cost and convenient use provide ideal testbeds and development impetus for innovative technologies of control approaches [3,4], advanced intelligent perception [5], and complete autonomy [6–9]. Small and medium UAVs can hardly meet the demands of high payloads and long flight distances. Therefore, more and more large-scale UAVs are being developed to provide long-endurance flights and perform various missions like manned aircraft. There are also related research projects developing independent autonomous equipment [10,11] or executing modifications [12] to convert manned aircraft to UAVs. There is a great need to investigate autonomy flight technologies for application scenarios of large-scale UAVs, manned aircraft, and helicopters for unmanned operations.

Helicopters demonstrate unique characteristics of maneuverability and low-speed performance, significantly extending their application in both military and civil fields [13]. With the development of advanced sensing devices and technologies, various sensor systems including cameras, radar, laser/light detection and ranging (Lidar), electro-optical (EO) system, acoustic system, and infrared (IR) sensors are deployed on helicopters to realize a higher level of perception and automation [14,15]. Researchers have been motivated to investigate autopilot technologies based on multi-source information perception to complete typical helicopter missions, such as target tracking [16–18], autonomous landing [16,19,20], and obstacle avoidance [21–24]. There have also been some studies of unmanned helicopter operations focused on specific flight scenes and missions. Gimenez [25,26] presented a transportation system for carrying a suspension payload through two helicopters considering collision avoidance, wind disturbance, and reasonable distribution of load weight. A ship–helicopter cooperative system was extensively investigated to allow helicopters to automatically approach and land on vessel decks [27–30]. Many studies demonstrated the landing performance of helicopter recovery on the vessels under visual guidance [31,32]. Chen [33] presented an efficient algorithm for the path-planning problem of multiple-helicopter formations in a realistic environment. Different solutions and control frameworks for formation flight and formation reconfiguration can be found in [34–36]. Recently, some new control frameworks including deep reinforcement learning framework [37,38] and genetic fuzzy trees [39] were applied and achieved good results. Chamberlain [40] presented an autonomy package allowing a full-scale unmanned helicopter to automatically fly through unmapped, obstacle-laden terrain, find a landing zone, and perform a safe landing near a casualty, all with no human control or input. Nikolayevich [41] proposed a new method based on enhanced 3D motion primitives for 3D path planning close to the flight dynamics limits of helicopters, enhancing their assistance and autonomy in missions. Schopferer [42] studied onboard and online flight path planning for small-scale unmanned rotorcraft to plan safe, dynamically feasible, and time-efficient flight paths using cubic splines. To summarize, the existing studies of unmanned helicopter operations mainly focused on basic tasks such as path planning, target tracking, and obstacle avoidance. Due to the lack of a higher level of autonomy and integrated control frameworks, few adequate solutions of complex tasks with diversified flight missions have been proposed.

Low-altitude flight in complex mountainous terrains is a difficult flight task applied in many fields. Especially for military applications, a low-altitude penetration flight is a typical example making use of the ultralow-altitude maneuvering of helicopters, so as to effectively use the terrain to avoid the detection and threat of the defense system, as well as improve flight survivability. Low-altitude flight is also widely used in civil fields for low-level reconnaissance, remote site material delivery, search and rescue, and casualty evacuation. Matthew [43] studied the low-altitude flight of a full-scale helicopter in complex terrains and demonstrated a tight integration of terrain avoidance, control, and autonomous landing. During the low-altitude flight, increasing levels of concealment are achieved by adopting different tactics such as terrain following, terrain avoidance, and threat avoidance [44]. For low-altitude flight, obstacle avoidance and terrain avoidance are the core flight tasks [45]. Zheng [46] designed a real-time flight control algorithm combining the fuzzy obstacle avoidance algorithm with the L1 control algorithm for helicopter low-altitude flight in complex environment. Chandrasekaran [47] reviewed helicopter wire strike protection and prevention devices for low-altitude flight, and carried out a multicriteria decision-making analysis to rank different wire strike prevention methods. Merz [48] introduced a system enabling robotic helicopters to fly safely without user interaction at low altitude over unknown terrain with static obstacles. Wang [49] proposed a collision avoidance strategy method and the corresponding calculation approach of optimal collision avoidance for small unmanned helicopters in low-altitude applications. There have also been many studies focusing on UAV obstacle avoidance in dynamic building environments [50,51]. Low-altitude flight also involves threat/target identification, visibility judgement, multilevel decision making, and multi-objective flight control. It poses a challenge to the implementation of unmanned operations. To automatically realize unmanned low-altitude flight like human pilots. It is necessary to establish an integrated control framework, which was rarely studied systematically in previous research.

In this research, the unmanned helicopter operations of low-altitude flight in complex mountainous terrains are investigated in detail. The flight scenes and mission requirements of low-altitude flight are discussed considering target/threat recognition and decision making on the basis of the recognition result. Low-altitude flight is divided into several basic tasks: target/threat recognition, target tracking, threat avoidance, and terrain following. We developed the control methods of the basic tasks according to the application scenarios of the mountainous terrains. A new method for judging target visibilities is proposed, which is inspired by the human perceptual method and is especially suitable for a complex and unknown environment. Then, we combined the basic tasks and established a coupled control method to realize flight missions including active approaching, threat avoidance, and circuitous flight operations. The control methods presented in this research were verified through high-realistic flight simulations.

The remainder of the paper is organized as follows: we briefly describe the mission requirements of low-altitude flight in mountainous terrains and present the modeling method of the simulation environment in Section 2; the implementation of target recognition, visual servo control, and terrain avoidance is investigated in Section 3, which also contains simulation verification and performance evaluation; Section 4 details the visibility judgment method and proposes the overall control framework based on a finite state machine; Section 5 presents the simulation validation of the proposed control framework; lastly, the conclusions are summarized in Section 6.

The main contributions and innovations of this research are listed as follows:

- We extend the low-altitude penetration flight by introducing target recognition and threat determination into the existing tactics [52–54], providing a wide perspective for the complicated flight tasks and various flight scenes of helicopter low-altitude flight.
- The helicopter visibility with respect to ground threats or specific facilities is investigated in this research, which was rarely studied in previous studies about threat avoidance or survivability assessment [55,56]. We also propose a direct viewing method to judge and change the visibility quickly and robustly.
- On the basis of the visibility judgement, an integrated control framework is established using the finite state machine. Compared with many existing studies [13,19,40,47,57], this framework focuses on solving complex multi-objective flight tasks and realizing unmanned helicopter operations of cover concealment and circuitous flight similar to human pilots.

2. Problem Formulation

2.1. *Low-Altitude Flight in Complex Mountainous Terrains*

Low-altitude flight is generally applied for mountainous or undulating terrains, where helicopters can make full use of the terrain to block detection and give full play to the advantages of mobility. Here, the low-altitude penetration flight used in military fields provides a great example which covers massive flight scenes of the low-altitude flight. We intend to state the basic tasks of the penetration flight and extend them to develop a more comprehensive control framework for the low-altitude flight. The main feature of penetration flight is maintaining a low flight altitude to avoid radar detection, and flying covertly to avoid ground defense and various detectors. To increase the level of concealment, TF/TA^2 tactics [58] have been developed and adopted as typical flight tasks of the penetration flight. The tactics are described as follows:

- Terrain following: flight maneuvering with the terrain contour in the vertical plane according to the predetermined minimum ground clearance. This penetration method can use terrain cover and reach the destination in a short time.
- Terrain avoidance: flight maneuvering in the azimuth plane, flying around mountains and other tall obstacles. This penetration method can make full use of the terrain as cover and facilitate hiding, but increases the likelihood of colliding with terrain obstacles.

- Threat avoidance: flight maneuvering in the azimuth plane, avoiding detection and weapon attacks, fully approaching the target, realizing sudden attacks, and reducing enemy interference.

The above tactics constitute the basic needs of the penetration flight, but there is still a lack of an integrated decision-making framework or specific maneuvering methods when facing various flight missions. Therefore, we extend the above tactics, and put forward broader flight tasks as follows:

- Target/threat recognition: identifying the target/threat facilities during the flight and determining the threat degrees; making maneuvering decisions on the basis of the recognition result.
- Target approaching: identifying the target using airborne cameras, tracking and approaching the target through visual servo control, avoiding terrain obstacles, and maintaining the ability to approach the target when it is blocked or temporarily lost.
- Cover concealment: when a threat is detected, finding cover through the terrains and moving to the terrain cover to escape the threat; discriminating and changing the helicopter's visibility through flight maneuvers.
- Circuitous flight: comprehensive flight maneuvering around the terrain, avoiding the threat, and following the terrain contour near the predetermined heading, so as to finally reach the destination safely.

In this work, we focus on the implementations of the unmanned helicopter operations of these flight tasks. Furthermore, we build a decision-making framework which can autonomously deal with different flight tasks without human intervention.

2.2. Modeling Method of the Simulation Environment

A helicopter exhibits six-degree-of-freedom rigid-body dynamics. The flight dynamic equations are as follows:

$$\dot{\boldsymbol{V}} = \frac{\boldsymbol{F}}{m} - \boldsymbol{\Omega} \boldsymbol{V}, \tag{1}$$

$$\dot{\boldsymbol{S}} = \boldsymbol{I}^{-1}\boldsymbol{M} - \boldsymbol{I}^{-1}\boldsymbol{\Omega}\boldsymbol{I}\boldsymbol{S}, \tag{2}$$

$$\dot{\boldsymbol{\alpha}} = \boldsymbol{E}\boldsymbol{S}, \tag{3}$$

$$\dot{\boldsymbol{P}} = \boldsymbol{R_{BG}}\boldsymbol{V}, \tag{4}$$

where $\boldsymbol{V} = [u\ v\ w]^T$ is the linear velocity, $\boldsymbol{S} = [p\ q\ r]^T$ is the angular velocity, $\boldsymbol{\alpha} = [\varphi\ \theta\ \psi]^T$ is the Euler angle of roll, pitch, and yaw, $\boldsymbol{P} = [X\ Y\ Z]^T$ is the position vector in ground coordinates, m is the mass of the helicopter, and $\boldsymbol{F}$ and $\boldsymbol{M}$ are the forces and moments of the components of the helicopter.

$\boldsymbol{I}$ is the moment of the helicopter inertial matrix, $\boldsymbol{\Omega}$ is the angular rate antisymmetric matrix, $\boldsymbol{R_{BG}}$ is the conversion matrix from body coordinates to ground coordinates, and $\boldsymbol{E}$ is the conversion matrix from body angular velocity to Euler angular velocity.

$$\boldsymbol{R_{BG}} = \begin{bmatrix} \cos\theta\cos\psi & \sin\theta\sin\psi\cos\psi - \cos\varphi\sin\psi & \sin\theta\cos\varphi\cos\psi + \sin\varphi\sin\psi \\ \cos\theta\cos\psi & \sin\theta\sin\varphi\sin\psi + \cos\varphi\cos\psi & \sin\theta\cos\varphi\cos\psi - \sin\varphi\sin\psi \\ -\sin\theta & \sin\varphi\cos\theta & \cos\varphi\cos\theta \end{bmatrix}. \tag{5}$$

$$\boldsymbol{E} = \begin{bmatrix} 1 & \sin\varphi\tan\theta & \cos\varphi\tan\theta \\ 0 & \cos\varphi & -\sin\varphi \\ 0 & \sin\varphi/\cos\theta & \cos\varphi/\cos\theta \end{bmatrix}. \tag{6}$$

For the helicopter dynamic model, $\boldsymbol{F}$ and $\boldsymbol{M}$ are generated by the aerodynamic forces of the fuselage and the control forces which originate from the main rotor thrust and tail rotor thrust. The helicopter has large aerodynamic interference and is a highly coupled complex dynamic system, which makes it difficult to establish a fully dynamic model. Therefore, the linearized dynamic model was adopted in this research to simulate the helicopter dynamic responses. The linearized model is obtained through frequency-domain identification of the flight experiment, and it is widely used in helicopter controller design and dynamic characteristic analysis. The complete linearized dynamic model can be illustrated in state-space representation as follows [59]:

$$\dot{x} = A_m x + B_m u, \tag{7}$$

where A_m and B_m are the system matrix and control matrix at different equilibrium points, establishing a linear-parameter-varying (LPV) helicopter dynamics model. $x = [u\ w\ q\ \theta\ v\ p\ \phi\ r\ \psi]$ is the state vector and $u = [\delta_e \delta_c \delta_a \delta_p]$ is the control input vector, where δ_c is the collective control input of the main rotor blade, δ_e and δ_a are the cyclic control inputs giving the explicit pitch in longitude and lateral directions, and δ_p is the collective pitch for the tail rotor.

Cascade PID (proportion integration differentiation) controllers were adopted to realize the low-level control of the helicopter. As shown in Figure 1, the helicopter control system was divided into the longitude channel, lateral channel, altitude channel, and yaw channel. For each channel, an independent cascade PID controller was applied. The inner loop controllers maintain the attitude stability, while the middle loop and outer loop controllers are used to track speed or position commands. The stability analysis and convergence of the cascade PID framework are essential for the controller implementation, but beyond the scope of this work. A detailed analysis can be found in [51] for further discussion.

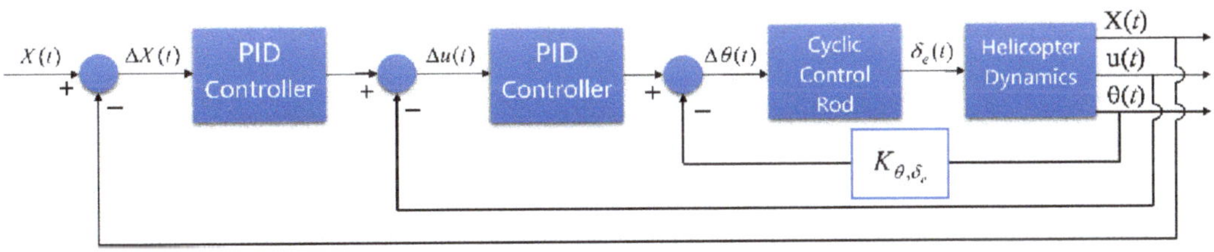

(a)

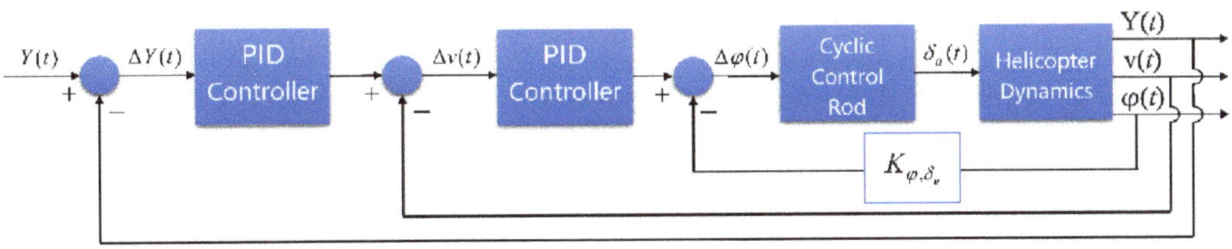

(b)

Figure 1. *Cont.*

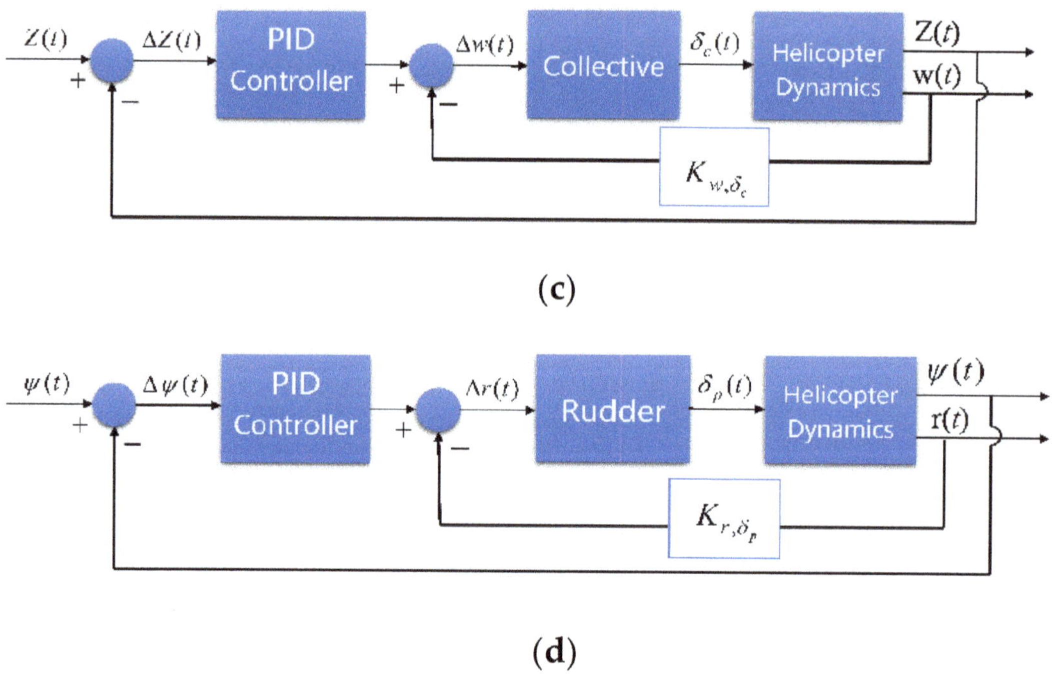

Figure 1. Cascade PID controllers of the helicopter control channels: (**a**) longitude channel; (**b**) lateral channel; (**c**) altitude channel; (**d**) yaw channel.

It should be mentioned that helicopters have multiple flight mode transitions arising from the complicated aerodynamic nature of thrust generation, while the control channels are strongly coupled. Various flight control methodologies have been developed for the flight control system of helicopters to improve the flight performance, which is beyond the scope of this research. We used simple and decoupling low-level controllers to clearly explain the implementation of visual servo control and terrain avoidance. In addition, the simple controllers used in this study would cause more oscillations and longer adjustment time during the flight. This required a high-level control framework to provide more margins in the design stage, forcing the control framework to be more adaptive and practical for engineering realizations.

A simulation based on realistic scenarios is a crucial part of testing algorithms. We built the simulation environment using the Unreal Engine package to visualize scenarios with realistic graphics and generate sensor data. A co-simulation framework was used to realize the communication interface between Unreal Engine and MATLAB Simulink, as shown in Figure 2. For each simulation step, the helicopter dynamic model received the flight control signals and updated the flight state. The flight state was sent to the simulation environment through a communication interface, driving the Unreal Engine to realize real-time virtual rendering. Various sensors were modeled to obtain ground-truth data in the simulation environment. The established control framework receives the sensor data and output control signals to the helicopter model, forming a closed-loop simulation system.

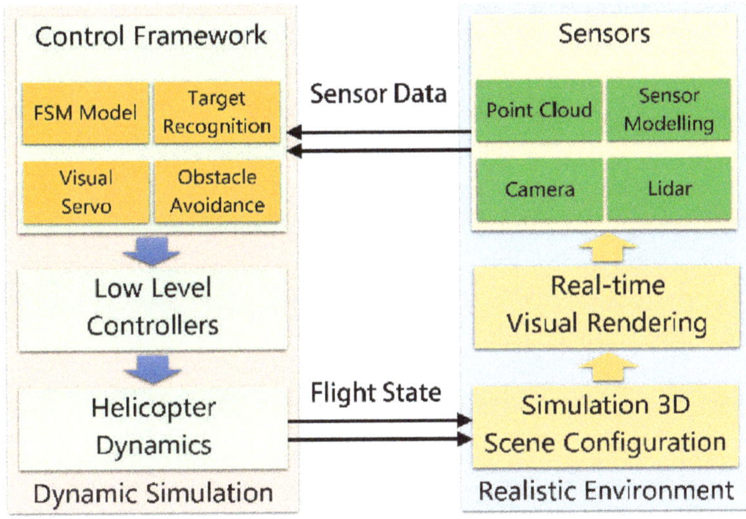

Figure 2. Closed-loop system of the realistic simulation environment.

A realistic scenario based on a mountainous map was built to carry out flight simulations of the low-altitude flight, as shown in Figure 3. We set up natural terrains and different facilities in the scenario. The terrains and facilities were built using static meshes, which could be detected by the virtual Lidar sensors of the helicopter. The virtual camera was mounted around the helicopter to obtain visual information. Benefitting from the powerful lighting, rendering, and mapping ability of Unreal Engine package, the virtual camera was able to display real-scene lighting effects such as area shadows and diffuse reflection, providing a high-fidelity simulation environment for this research.

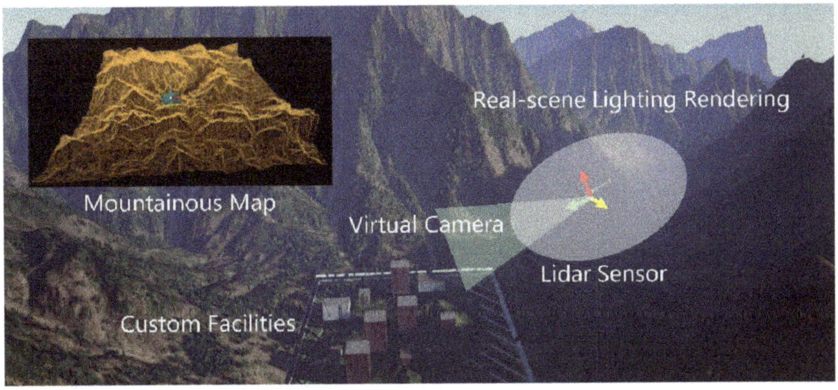

Figure 3. Realistic scenario of the mountainous terrain.

3. Target Tracking and Terrain Avoidance

3.1. Target Tracking

3.1.1. Target Recognition

For a low-altitude flight, the flight map information and accurate facility positions are generally unknown. Detecting targets and evaluating threat degrees represent the basis of decision making in unmanned helicopter operations. We expect that the target recognition method should be able to cover different types of targets as best as possible to deal with various unknown facilities that may appear in mountainous terrains. In this research, target recognition was realized using the YOLOv2 network, which can be trained offline on labeled images to cover a large number of target features [60]. The YOLO model runs a deep learning CNN (convolutional neural network) on an input image to decode the predictions and generate bounding boxes, as shown in Figure 4. The detection network contains a series of conventional, batch norm, and rectified linear unit (ReLU) layers. By labeling and adding training samples of specific scenes, the YOLO model can better recognize distant or fuzzy targets.

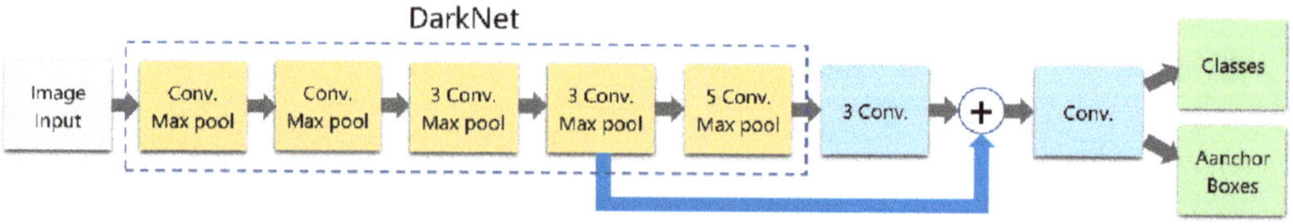

Figure 4. Structure of the YOLO Network.

The YOLO network introduces anchor boxes to improve the speed and efficiency for of detection. The anchor boxes are defined on the basis of object sizes in the training datasets. During detection, the predefined anchor boxes are tiled across the image. The position of an anchor box is determined by mapping the location of the network output back to the input image. The object detectors learn offsets to apply to each tiled anchor box, refining the anchor box position and size. The network predicts five coordinates for each bounding box: t_x, t_y, t_h, t_w, and t_o. The cell is offset from the top left corner of the image by (c_x, c_y), and the bounding box prior has width and height p_w, p_h; the predictions can be drawn as follows:

$$b_x = s(t_x) + c_x, \tag{8}$$

$$b_y = \sigma(t_y) + c_y, \tag{9}$$

$$b_w = p_w e^{t_w}, \tag{10}$$

$$b_h = p_h e^{t_h}, \tag{11}$$

$$Pr(object) \times IOU(object, b) = s(t_o), \tag{12}$$

where, b_x, b_y, b_h, and b_w are the box position and size parameters, σ refers to the sigmoid function, and $\sigma(t_o)$ is the value of confidence after sigmoid transformation. For target recognition in low-altitude flights, the anchor boxes of the YOLO network provide the target dynamics within the sight ranges. The positions and sizes of anchor boxes also imply the relative position and attitude information of the target, which can provide the basis for the visual servo control.

The detection efficiency and generalization capabilities of the YOLO network depend on the number and diversity of training data. Without loss of generality, we extracted the images of some buildings and vehicles in the simulation environment as recognition targets. The images were manually calibrated to form a training dataset, and the network was trained using the SGDM (stochastic gradient descent with momentum) method. The precision of the trained detector at varying levels of recall is shown in Figure 5. The YOLO network can be replaced by frontier and stronger algorithms to obtain better recognition performance, but it was considered fairly effective for the overall control framework of this research.

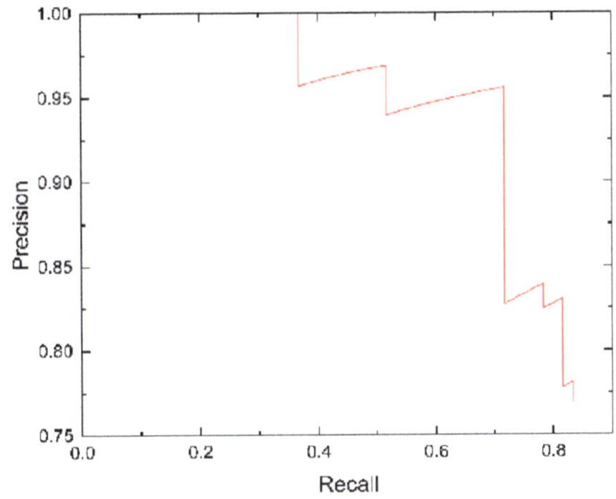

Figure 5. Precision–recall (PR) curve of the YOLO network.

3.1.2. Visual Servo Control

Visual servo control is an important part of unmanned helicopter operations in low-altitude flight. It can also help verify the stability of the YOLO detector and the effectiveness of the proposed helicopter controllers in this research. Therefore, we designed a typical flight task to carry out flight simulations on the basis of visual servo control. The helicopter identified the target through the YOLO detector, and then automatically hovered around the target, as shown in Figure 6. This has been used as the ground target tracking method of fixed-wing aircrafts [61,62]. For helicopters, we let the helicopter always head to the target, move horizontally through lateral maneuvers, and finally hover around the target.

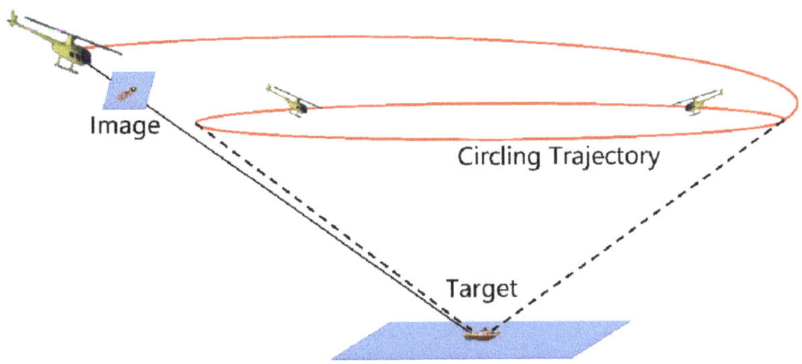

Figure 6. Circling flight around the target.

The commonly used methods of visual servo control can be divided into position-based visual servo (PBVS), image-based visual servo (IBVS), and end-to-end visual servo. PBVS establishes the mapping relationship between the image signal and the helicopter pose, calculates the pose information, and compares it with the required pose to form a closed-loop control. As PBVS needs accurate image signals, even a small error in the image measurements can lead to a large offset in the pose estimation. IBVS directly compares the image signal measured in real time with the image signal of required pose and uses the obtained image error for feedback control. The end-to-end servo method takes the captured image as the input, and directly outputs the control signals by constructing neural networks. However, there exist challenges including time complexity and servo stabilities when using this method. For a low-altitude flight, the target is generally unknown and far away from the helicopter. It is difficult to extract a characteristic point of the image and calculate relative pose information using PBVS. Therefore, we adopted IBVS to realize visual servo control; the control framework is illustrated in Figure 7. We used the size and position of the anchor boxes provided by the YOLO network as the control commands of the helicopters control channels. The control commands were calculated as follows:

$$S_{box} = b_w b_h, \tag{13}$$

$$u_{Ref} = -k_u(S_{box} - S_{des}), \tag{14}$$

$$r_{Ref} = -k_r(b_x - b_{mid}), \tag{15}$$

$$v_{Ref} = V_{des} - \alpha_1(S_{box} - S_{des}) - \alpha_2(b_x - b_{mid}), \tag{16}$$

$$u_{Ref} = \begin{cases} u_{forward}, S^t = 0, {b_y}^{t-k} > 0 \\ u_{backward}, S^t = 0, {b_y}^{t-k} < 0' \end{cases} \tag{17}$$

where S_{box} represents the area of the anchor box, which characterizes the distance from the helicopter to the target. We defined a desired box area S_{des} that points to the desired distance, and counted the error during feedback to the control command of linear velocity u_{Ref}. k_u is the control gain. The target center is restricted to the horizontal center of the image to ensure that the helicopter is always oriented to the target. The error between target center b_x and image center b_{mid} is calculated and multiplied by the control gain k_r as the control command of the yaw rate r_{Ref}. We set V_{des} as the desired lateral velocity and correct it through the errors of box area and helicopter orientation to generate the control command of lateral velocity v_{Ref}, as shown in Equation (16), where α_1 and α_2 are the correction factors. In this way, priority is given to the helicopter maintaining its distance and orientation to the target, and then maneuvering laterally to hover around the target. Furthermore, in case the target is lost and deviates from the image, i.e., the anchor box area becomes 0, we preset longitudinal flight maneuvers to retrieve the target, as shown in Equation (17). When the target disappears from the top of the image, and the vertical coordinate of the target center before disappearing is positive (${b_y}^{t-k} > 0$), the helicopter will fly forward to approach the target; otherwise, it will fly backward with linear velocity $u_{backward}$.

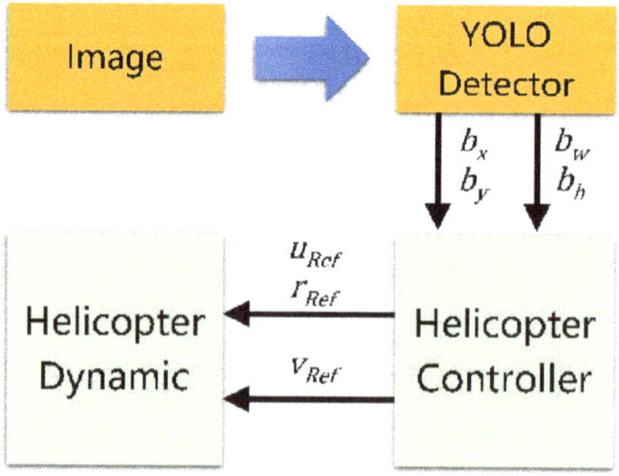

Figure 7. Visual servo control of the circling flight.

According to the above control frame, the IBVS method was established, and the control gains were determined. We set up the initial positions of helicopter and target, and we carried out flight simulations. The virtual camera was mounted under the helicopter body with a downward pitch angle of 20°. The sample time of the virtual camera was set as 0.01 s and the resolution of each frame was set to 640 × 360 to maintain image accuracy and detection efficiency. The flight path of the helicopter hovering around the static target is shown in Figure 8. It can be seen that the helicopter approached the target from a distance and gradually maintained a stable circular trajectory. The linear velocity of the helicopter contained high-frequency oscillations caused by the visual servo control, but the overall trend was regular and stable, as shown in Figure 9. Figure 10 shows the anchor box size during the flight. The width and height of the anchor box changed periodically in a large range, which was caused by the different target poses under different viewing angles. The target was lost at some point and could be retrieved rapidly to continue tracking. On the basis of simulations around static targets, we carried out flight simulations to circle and hover around a moving target. The flight path is illustrated in Figure 11, which demonstrates the effectiveness of the control framework. Therefore, the proposed IBVS method can be further applied in low-altitude flight.

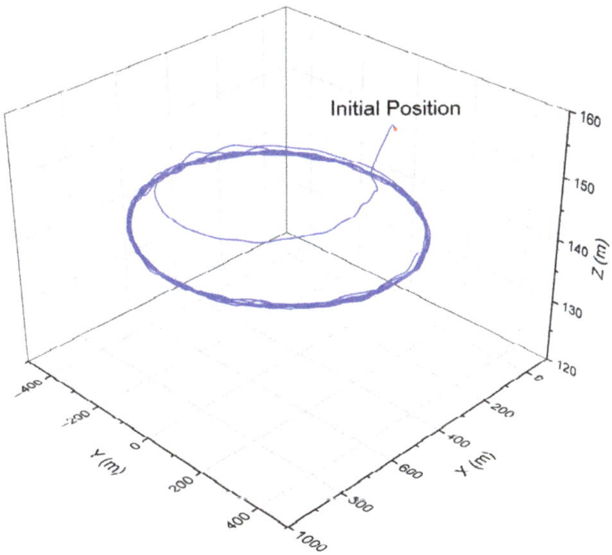

Figure 8. Flight path of the helicopter hovering around a static target.

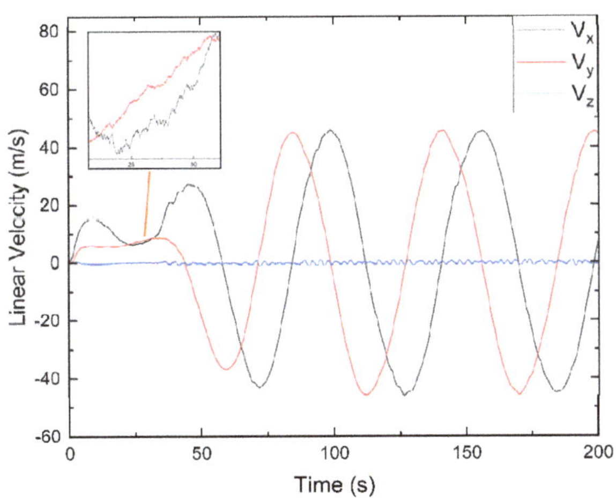

Figure 9. Helicopter linear velocities during a circling flight.

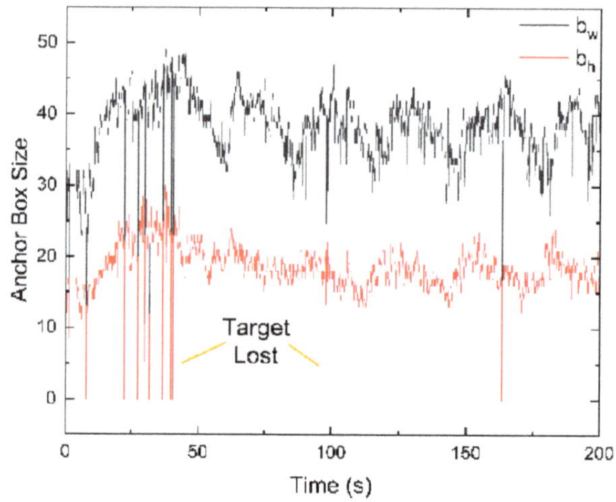

Figure 10. Anchor box size during a circling flight.

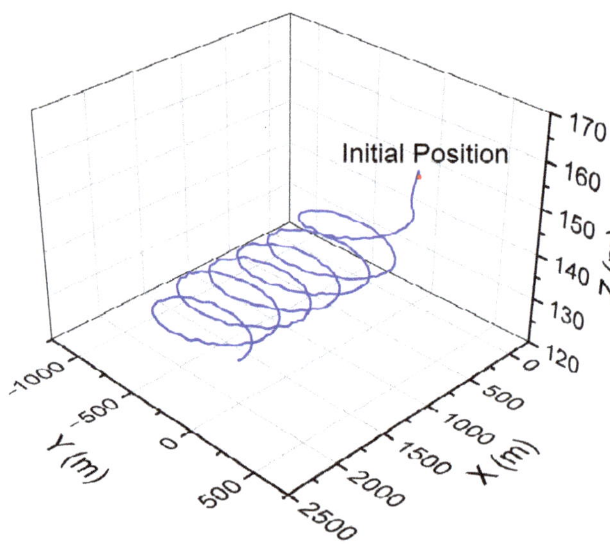

Figure 11. Flight path of the helicopter hovering around a moving target.

3.2. Terrain Avoidance

Terrain avoidance is a basic task in low-altitude flight, whereby the helicopter senses objects according to the airborne sensors, and autonomously executes obstacle avoidance and path planning in an unknown environment. Therefore, the global obstacle avoidance methods which rely on complete prior information are generally inappropriate. Moreover, low-altitude flight generally requires a helicopter to reach the destination rapidly to reduce flight time and risks. A reactive local obstacle avoidance method is more adaptable compared with a global mapping method. The terrains of mountainous areas are complicated and contain various environment objects. Radar and Lidar equipment have been commonly used for manned helicopters to sense and avoid terrain obstacles in mountainous terrains. Considering the sensing equipment, algorithm efficiency, spatial complexity, and application scenes, the 3D VFH (vector field histogram) method based on Lidar sensors was established to realize terrain avoidance for unmanned helicopter operations in this research.

The 3D VFH algorithm originates from the widely used VFH algorithm in a 2D environment. It does not need specific map information, but it can provide multiple paths to maintain different requirements by designing different path weights, which is especially suitable for low-altitude flight. For 3D environment applications, the 3D VFH method divides the voxels near the helicopter into multiple cells through the two dimensions of the azimuth angle β_z and the elevation angle β_e, as shown in Figure 12. The spherical voxels unfold into a 2D primary polar histogram, where each cell represents the possible direction of the helicopter.

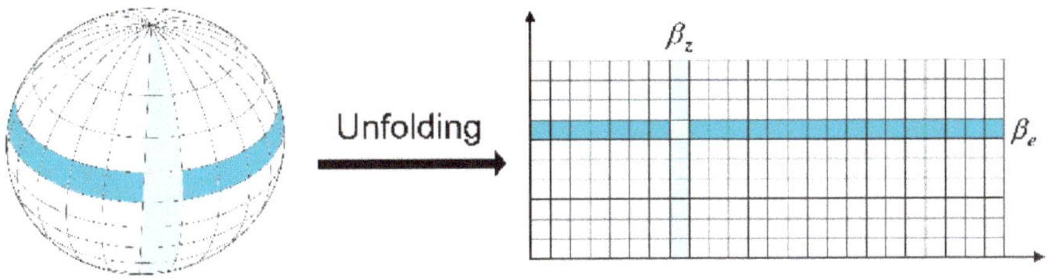

Figure 12. Formation of the 2D primary polar histogram.

We built a virtual Lidar sensor which was fixed under the helicopter cockpit in the simulation environment. It enabled the helicopter to sense the surrounding terrain obstacles in a determined range. The vertical and horizontal fields of view of the Lidar sensor were set as 60° and 360°, respectively. The detection range was set to 300 m to maintain the effectiveness and data scale. As shown in Figure 13, the Lidar sensor generated the point-cloud data in an ellipsoid range centered on the helicopter.

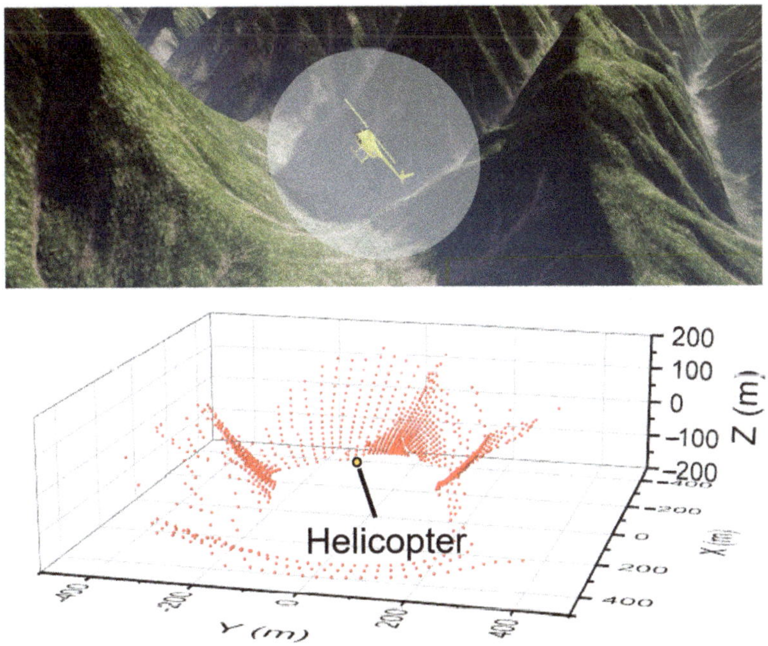

Figure 13. Generation of point-cloud data of virtual Lidar sensor.

For any node P_i of the point-cloud data, we assume the coordinates (x_i, y_i, z_i). The azimuth angle and elevation angle can be calculated using Equations (18) and (19), where α is the resolution of the 2D polar histogram, and the floor function creates natural numbers as the coordinates of the 2D primary polar histogram. Using the point-cloud data, we can evaluate the distance and size of terrain obstacles to calculate the risk weights, and add them to the 2D primary polar histogram. The weight of the voxels can be calculated using Equation (20), where o_p is the occupancy certainty, l_P is the Euclidean distance, which is influenced by the helicopter radius, safe radius, and voxel size, and a and b are predefined constant values. The detailed derivations can be found in [63].

$$\beta_z = \text{floor}(\frac{1}{\alpha}\arctan\frac{x_i}{y_i}). \tag{18}$$

$$\beta_e = \text{floor}(\frac{1}{\alpha}\arctan\frac{z_i}{\sqrt{{x_i}^2 + {y_i}^2}}). \tag{19}$$

$$H_{z,e} = \begin{cases} \sum\limits_{P} {o_p}^2(a - bl_P)\ , \text{ if } e \in \left[\beta_e - \frac{\lambda}{\alpha}, \beta_e + \frac{\lambda}{\alpha}\right] \text{ and } z \in \left[\beta_z - \frac{\lambda}{\alpha}, \beta_z + \frac{\lambda}{\alpha}\right] \\ 0, \text{ otherwise} \end{cases}. \tag{20}$$

The 2D primary polar histogram presents a simplified description of collision risks at different directions. A 2D binary polar histogram was established to further reduce the information. This was accomplished by comparing every cell in the 2D primary polar histogram with a threshold τ. The size of the threshold depends on the helicopter radius, flight speed, sensor resolution, and bounding sphere size. When the cell weight is higher than τ, the point will be 1 in the 2D binary polar histogram. When the value is lower than τ, the point will be 0 in the 2D binary polar histogram.

The VFH method searches for available paths and detects openings by moving a window around the 2D binary polar histogram. This window marks the path passable if all the elements in the window are equal to 0. It defines three path weights combined for the candidate direction to select the path with lowest path weight μ, as shown in Equation (20). The first path weight μ_1 is used to multiply the difference between the target angle k_t and the candidate direction v_c. The second path weight μ_2 multiplies the difference between the helicopter yaw angle ψ and the candidate direction v_c. The last path weight μ_3 multiplies the difference between the previous selected direction k_{t-1} and the candidate direction v_c. The function $\Delta\ (x, y)$ calculates the difference between the two direction vectors. By changing the path weights, multiple flight paths with different preferences can be obtained. For low-altitude flight in mountainous terrains, we can change the path weight allowing the helicopter to maintain low-altitude flight using turning motions or climbing motions to approach the target aggressively.

$$\mu = \mu_1 \cdot \Delta(\boldsymbol{k_t}, \boldsymbol{v_c}) + \mu_2 \cdot \Delta(\boldsymbol{v_\psi}, \boldsymbol{v_c}) + \mu_3 \cdot \Delta(\boldsymbol{k_{t-1}}, \boldsymbol{v_c}). \tag{21}$$

A narrow mountainous area with dense terrain obstacles was built to verify the terrain avoidance performance of the VFH method, as shown in Figure 14. We arranged an additional static mesh of obstacles in the terrains to increase the difficulty of obstacle avoidance. At each simulation step, the VFH method provided a desired direction and desired yaw angle according to the virtual Lidar sensor. For helicopters in low-altitude flight, turning maneuvers are more sensitive and stable than lateral maneuvers. Therefore, we took the desired yaw and vertical components of the desired direction as the helicopter control command to realize terrain avoidance in the low-altitude flight. The lateral control channel maintained the helicopter stability, and the longitudinal control channel changed the approaching speed of the helicopter to the destination.

Figure 14. Narrow mountainous area with additional obstacles.

Lastly, we carried out flight simulations using the VFH method, where the helicopter was placed in a narrow mountainous area without map information. The virtual Lidar had a range resolution of 0.2 m. The vertical resolution and horizontal resolution of the Lidar were set as 2.5° and 5°, respectively. The vehicle size and minimum distance to obstacles of the VFH method were set as 5 m and 20 m. The sample time of the virtual Lidar was 0.1 s. A distant destination was defined, and the helicopter approached the destination and executed terrain avoidance during the flight. The path weights in Equation (21) were set as 3, 2, and 0.3, respectively. The flight path and linear velocities of the helicopter are illustrated in Figures 15 and 16, which demonstrates that the helicopter could maintain a low altitude and stably approach the destination. Figure 17 further shows the helicopter during the low-altitude flight. The helicopter avoided all the terrain obstacles in the narrow environment. This shows the good adaptability of the proposed VFH method in mountainous areas for the helicopter.

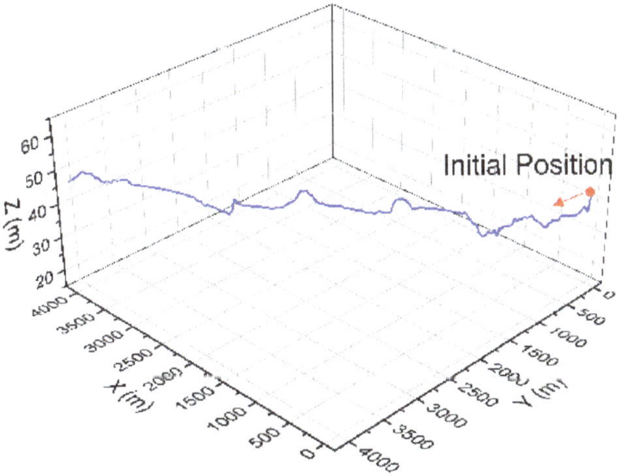

Figure 15. Flight path of the 3D VFH method.

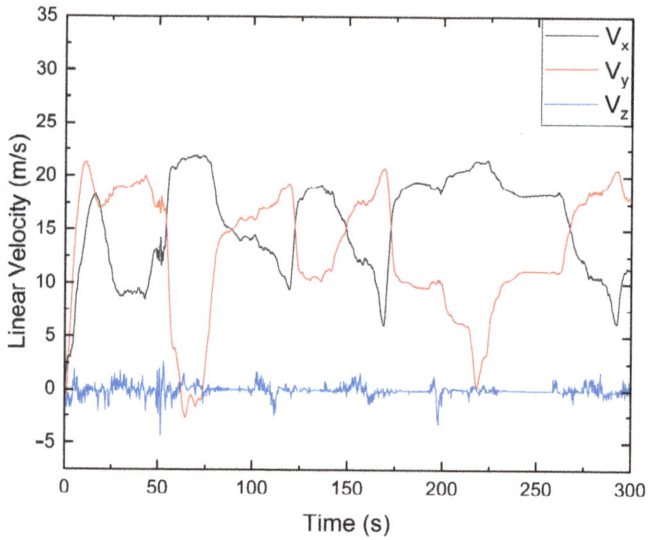

Figure 16. Helicopter linear velocities during the low-altitude flight.

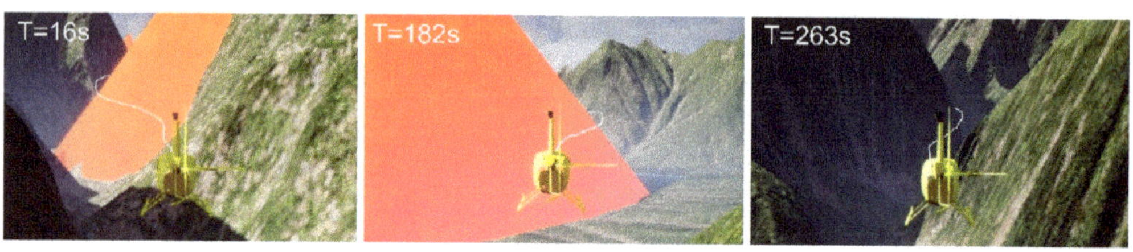

Figure 17. Helicopter during the low-altitude flight.

4. Autonomous Decision-Making Framework

4.1. Visibility Judgment

For low-altitude flight in mountainous terrains, helicopters can effectively avoid specific facilities or threats such as dense buildings, fires, and danger using obstacle avoidance and path replanning methods. In previous studies, these threats were often regarded as obstacles during the flight. However, in many situations of military applications, low-altitude flight requires the helicopter to resist ground detection and avoid ground defense to improve flight survivability. Since flying at low altitude can effectively block the detection of ground radars, the visibility of the helicopter to the ground facilities is crucial for decision making and maneuver selection. The helicopter needs to not only bypass and avoid the threats, but also escape from the sight range of the threats. Human pilots estimate the visibility of the helicopter using their eyes and intuition to make decisions such as taking cover, avoiding reconnaissance, or executing circuitous flight. On the other hand, the visibility judgement is quite difficult for unmanned operations, which generally needs complete state estimation, threat location, and accurate map information.

Here, we propose an intuitive direct-viewing method which can quickly judge the helicopter's visibility, as shown in Figure 18. The threat detection method uses a deep neural network, which is the same as the target recognition method presented in Section 3.1. We can add samples to the dataset and train a detection network to simultaneously identify targets and threats. When the helicopter detects a threat during low-altitude flight, it immediately turns to head to the target using the visual servo control method as mentioned in Section 3.1. At this moment, the helicopter is visible to the threat. To change its visibility, the helicopter maneuvers laterally. This is because when the helicopter is heading to the threat, lateral maneuvers gain more variation than longitude and vertical maneuvers in the sight range of the threat. This also helps the helicopter to approach terrain cover in mountainous areas. During lateral maneuvers, if the threat is lost from view and the Lidar sensor can detect obstacles ahead, it can be considered that the line of sight between the helicopter and the threat is blocked, and the visibility is changed. In order to ensure the complete concealment of the whole helicopter, we set a margin to make the helicopter continue to fly laterally for a certain distance after its visibility changed.

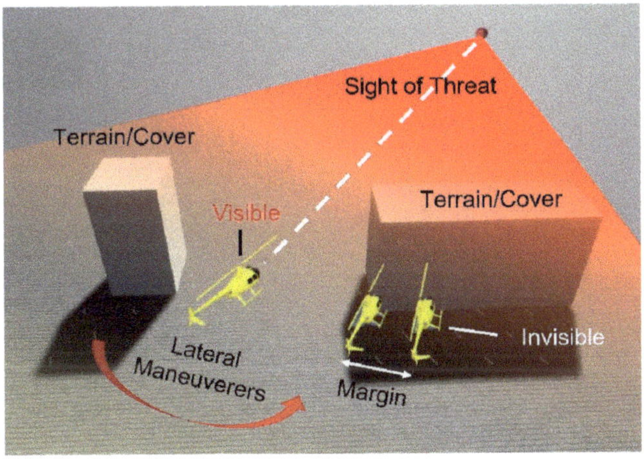

Figure 18. Direct-viewing method of visibility judgement.

The proposed method of the visibility judgment is essentially based on the line of sight, which is inspired by the perception method of human intuition. It is simple and effective, but requires the helicopter to keep heading to the threat. Obviously, continuously heading to the threat is not the optimal method to avoid it. This limits the helicopter's movement and possibly further exposes the helicopter to the threat. However, it provides a fast and reliable method to realize real-time judgement of the visibility without comprehensive map information or a complex calculation process. Moreover, the helicopter has good lateral maneuverability; when facing a threat, lateral maneuvers are faster and more continuous than turning or other maneuvers to hide. Overall, this provides a reactive method to judge and change the helicopter's visibility, which is easy to deploy and especially suitable for implementation in complex unknown environments.

4.2. Finite State Machine

Visibility judgement and target and threat recognition are fundamental factors of decision making in low-altitude flight. The visual servo control and terrain avoidance methods presented in this research were verified to be effective in target tracking and obstacle avoidance. On this basis, a finite state machine was established to combine the decision-making and control methods, thus forming the overall framework for unmanned helicopter operations in low-altitude flight, as shown in Figure 19. The finite state machine established a continuous operation process without human interference and covered most scenes in the low-altitude flight.

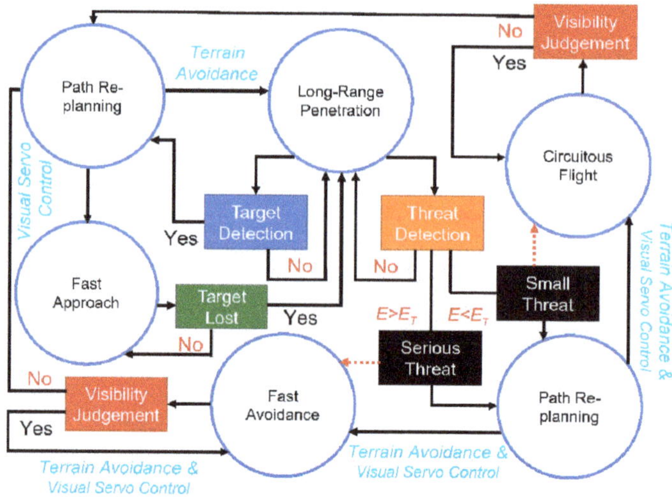

Figure 19. Finite state machine of the decision-making framework.

In low-altitude flight, a helicopter is given a distant destination and required to approach the destination at low altitude. Meanwhile, the detection network works to detect targets and threat facilities. Once the target is detected, the helicopter immediately heads to the target through visual servo control and revises the target's position. In this case, the helicopter does not know its exact position with respect to the target on the map; however, it is able to estimate the distance and yaw direction using airborne equipment. Therefore, the helicopter can estimate the target's direction on the basis of its heading. Several target points are placed along the target direction for path replanning of the VFH method. The helicopter continues heading toward the target. Generally, keeping the target in the center of the camera can ensure that the target is not lost during the flight approach. In case the target is lost, the helicopter continues flying to the defined target points to approach the target and returns to visual servo control when the target is rediscovered. After arriving at the target, the helicopter can revise the destination location to fly to the original destination or end the flight mission. This fast approach process can realize a quick attack on or reconnaissance of specific facilities.

If the detection network detects a threat during the flight, the threat degree E is firstly evaluated. We propose a simple way to quantitatively evaluate the threat, as expressed in Equation (22). ξ_{class} is the coefficient for different classes of threats. S_{box} implies the distance to the threat. Basically, a closer distance indicates a greater threat. There are more intricate methods of threat evaluation, but they are outside the scope of this research. We calculated the threat degree mainly to distinguish between serious threats and small threats, so as to design different control strategies. We defined a threat threshold E_T, whereby a threat degree that higher than E_T is considered as a serious threat. In this situation, the helicopter executes fast avoidance flight to escape the sight range of the threat as soon as possible, seeking terrains as cover to change its visibility. For this purpose, the helicopter is forced to head to the threat for visibility judgement. The target points of the VFH method are reset as the points of the history path. Then, the helicopter executes lateral maneuvers so as to quickly restore invisibility behind terrain cover. When the threat is lost in the camera, the helicopter can fly away from the threat or carry out further orders. In this research, we gave a higher priority to fast avoidance than to fast approach. The helicopter executes fast avoidance upon detecting a serious threat, regardless of whether a target is detected in the view. If multiple threats are detected during the flight, the helicopter heads toward the threat with highest threat degree to execute fast avoidance.

If the threat degree is lower than E_T, the detected threat is considered a small threat, and the helicopter executes circuitous flight. In this situation, the top priority is still restoring the helicopter's invisibility, which requires the helicopter to head toward the threat and seek cover. However, the helicopter is allowed to move laterally. The target points of the VFH method are reset to the sides of the helicopter. When the threat is lost, the helicopter resets the target points and continues its approach to the destination. In this study, the helicopter automatically placed the target points on the opposite site of the threat and followed the path of the VFH method. Many other path-planning methods can also be used for circuitous flight; however, we mainly focused on introducing visibility judgement and realizing reactive threat avoidance.

$$E = S_{box}\xi_{class}. \tag{22}$$

The finite state machine presents a detailed decision-making framework through the state transitions of different flight tasks, such as long-range penetration, fast approach, fast avoidance, and circuitous flight. These flight tasks contain multiple objectives, and their implementation is complicated. Here, we designed the control law for each flight task, all the control methods were derived from the visual servo control and terrain avoidance method in Section 3. Since the control channels are decoupled as illustrated in Section 2.2, we can clearly explain the control method through the control commands of different channels.

For the long-range penetration task, the helicopter approaches the destination and avoids terrain obstacles according to the VFH method. Specifically, the VFH method provides the control commands of the yaw channel and altitude channel, as shown in Equation (23). $\boldsymbol{R}_{GB}$ is the conversion matrix from ground coordinates to body coordinates. The desired direction produced by the VFH method is defined in the ground coordinates and must be converted to body coordinates to generate control commands. $\overline{u}$, $\overline{v}$, and $\overline{w}$ are the control gains of the linear velocities. The longitude channel and lateral channel maintain the helicopter's stability.

$$\begin{cases} \psi = \psi_{VFH} \\ u = \overline{u} \\ v = 0 \\ w = \overline{w}\boldsymbol{R}_{GB}Z_{VFH} \end{cases}. \tag{23}$$

For the fast approach task, the control command of the helicopter yaw channel is provided by the visual servo control method allowing the helicopter toward head to the target. The target points are placed according to the heading direction of the helicopter, as shown in Equation (24), where d is a predefined value that affects the interval between target points, and $\overline{Z}$ is the reference altitude of the low-altitude flight. The longitude channel, lateral channel, and altitude channel are all controlled by the VFH method, as shown in Equation (25), enabling safe terrain avoidance when the helicopter heading direction is locked to the target. If the target is lost in view, which may be caused by detection network failure, helicopter attitude oscillation, or terrain occlusion, the fast approach task is converted back to the long-range penetration task with revised target points.

$$\begin{cases} X_{Target} = X + nd\cos\psi \\ Y_{Target} = Y + nd\sin\psi \\ Z_{Target} = \overline{Z} \end{cases}, n = 1,2,3,\ldots \tag{24}$$

$$\begin{cases} r_{Ref} = -k_r(b_x - b_{mid}) \\ u = \overline{u}\boldsymbol{R}_{GB}X_{VFH} \\ v = \overline{v}\boldsymbol{R}_{GB}Y_{VFH} \\ w = \overline{w}\boldsymbol{R}_{GB}Z_{VFH} \end{cases}. \tag{25}$$

The control laws of the fast avoidance and circuitous flight are similar to those of the fast approach, as shown in Equation (23). The VFH method provides different maneuvers by setting different target points. The target points of fast avoidance and circuitous flight are placed as shown in Equations (26) and (27), respectively, where T is the predefined time interval to sample the history path points, and $(X_{Destination}, Y_{Destination})$ are the coordinates of the original destination. For circuitous flight, the target points are placed on the side of the helicopter, and the desired direction of the VFH method is converted to lateral control commands in the body coordinates. The direction of the lateral maneuver is determined according to the threat position, destination position, and history path. Generally, using three control channels to follow the control commands of the VFH method can ensure that the helicopter safely escapes the threat and takes cover behind the terrain to change its visibility.

$$\begin{cases} X_{Target} = X_{t-nT} \\ Y_{Target} = Y_{t-nT} \\ Z_{Target} = Z_{t-nT} \end{cases} ,n = 1,2,3,\ldots \quad (26)$$

$$\begin{cases} X_{Target} = X - nd\sin\psi \mathrm{sgn}(\Delta(\begin{bmatrix} \cos\psi \\ \sin\psi \end{bmatrix}, \begin{bmatrix} X_{Destination} - X \\ Y_{Destination} - Y \end{bmatrix})) \\ Y_{Target} = Y + nd\cos\psi \mathrm{sgn}(\Delta(\begin{bmatrix} \cos\psi \\ \sin\psi \end{bmatrix}, \begin{bmatrix} X_{Destination} - X \\ Y_{Destination} - Y \end{bmatrix})) \\ Z_{Target} = \overline{Z} \end{cases} ,n = 1,2,3,\ldots \quad (27)$$

5. Simulation Experiments

In order to verify the performance of the proposed control framework, we built a typical mountainous map including target or threat facilities, as shown in Figure 20. The target and threat facilities were set at the same position, as were the helicopter initial position and original destination, to better compare the flight performance of the different flight tasks. We designed four flight scenes by defining different facilities in the target/threat position to carry out long-range penetration, fast approach, fast avoidance, and circuitous flight. The installation and parameters of the virtual camera and Lidar were the same as those of the simulations in Section 3.

Figure 20. Simulation scene of the low-altitude flight.

The long-range penetration flight path is illustrated in Figure 21a. The target/threat was removed from the map. The helicopter followed the command of the VFH method on the premise of low altitude. The helicopter first flew along the hillside of the right-side mountain, and then selected the middle valley to approach the destination. At this moment, the left-side terrain blocked the destination, and the helicopter continued to fly along the hillside of the left-side terrain. When the terrain altitude became low, the helicopter went over the terrain gap and finally arrived at the destination. The whole flight path was similar to that observed for terrain avoidance in Section 3.2, showing good performance.

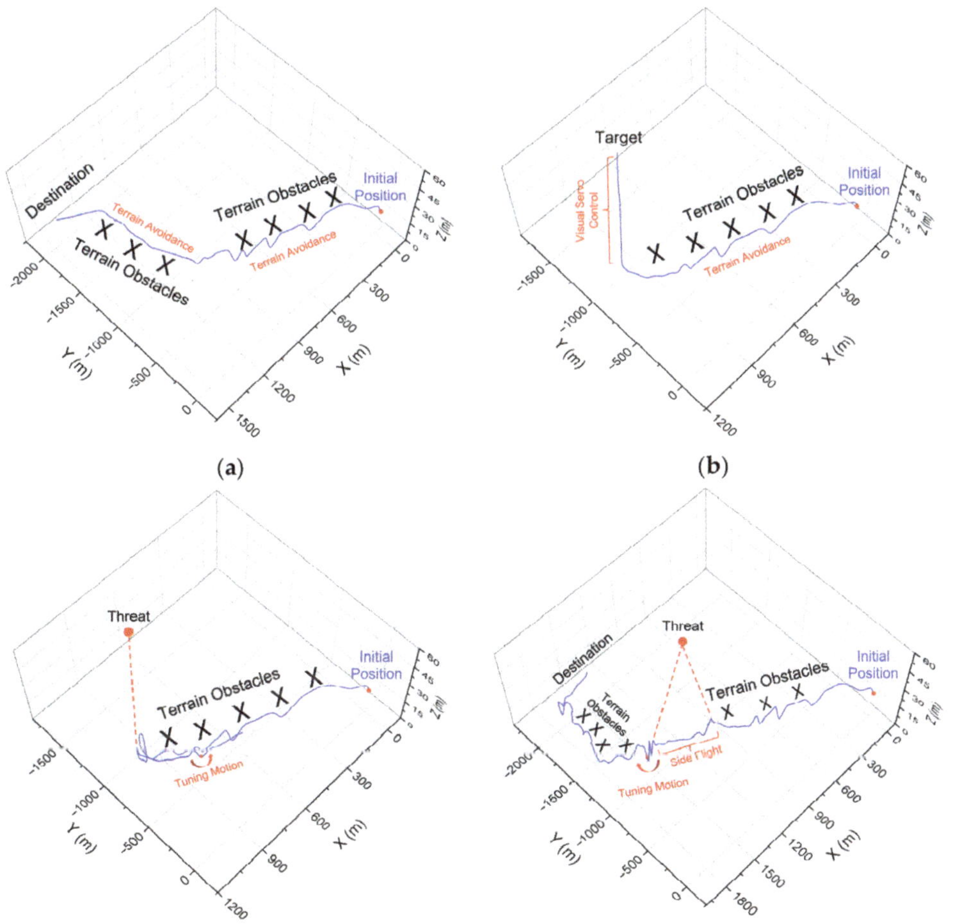

Figure 21. Flight paths of the flight tasks in the low-altitude flight: (**a**) long-range penetration; (**b**) fast approach; (**c**) fast avoidance; (**d**) circuitous flight.

The flight path of the fast approach is illustrated in Figure 21b. A target facility was set in the target/threat position. At the initial position, the target was blocked by the right-side mountain, and the helicopter followed the command of the VFH method. When the helicopter bypassed the right-side mountain, the target was detected. The helicopter flew straight toward the target along the middle valley. Here, the forward velocity could be tuned by changing the control gain $\overline{u}$ to realize a faster approaching speed while satisfying other task requirements. The sight range of the middle valley was wide; the helicopter kept the target in view and finally reached the target position.

Figure 21c shows the flight path of the fast avoidance task. The facility in the target/threat position was identified as a serious threat by the detection network. When the threat was detected, the target points of the VFH method were reset as the path points behind the right-side mountain. The helicopter maintained its heading toward the threat and then moved horizontally to fly away from the threat. The control gains of the linear velocities could be tuned to decrease the flight oscillations and increase the flight stability.

Finally, the helicopter flew behind the obstacles and changed its visibility in a short time, verifying the effectiveness of the fast avoidance method. The helicopter continued to fly laterally for a while after the threat was lost from view, before turning around to head to the target points.

Figure 21d shows the flight path of the circuitous flight, which mainly contained three flight phases. The facility in the target/threat position was identified as a small threat. Firstly, the helicopter executed long-range penetration and flew along the hillside of the right-side mountain, just as in the previous flight simulations. Then, the helicopter detected the threat and carried out visual servo control to maintain its heading toward the threat. The target points of the VFH method were reset and placed on the left side of the helicopter, which was closer to the destination. The helicopter moved laterally to the left side and finally flew behind the left-side terrain, changing its visibility. Subsequently, the target point was set as the original destination, and the helicopter turned left to approach the destination. Here, the VFH method considered the cost of the current direction, and we could change the path weight to ensure that the helicopter would not return to the threat once its visibility changed. We could also manually define a rule for the helicopter to choose a direction away from the threat. If the threat was detected again during the flight, the helicopter would repeat the above operations to change the target points and escape the threat. In the flight simulation, the helicopter bypassed the left-side terrain and finally arrived at the destination without detecting the threat. For a better comparison of the flight paths, we present all flight tasks in Figure 22. The decision making and approximate paths of all flight tasks are shown, verifying the overall control framework and control method proposed in this study.

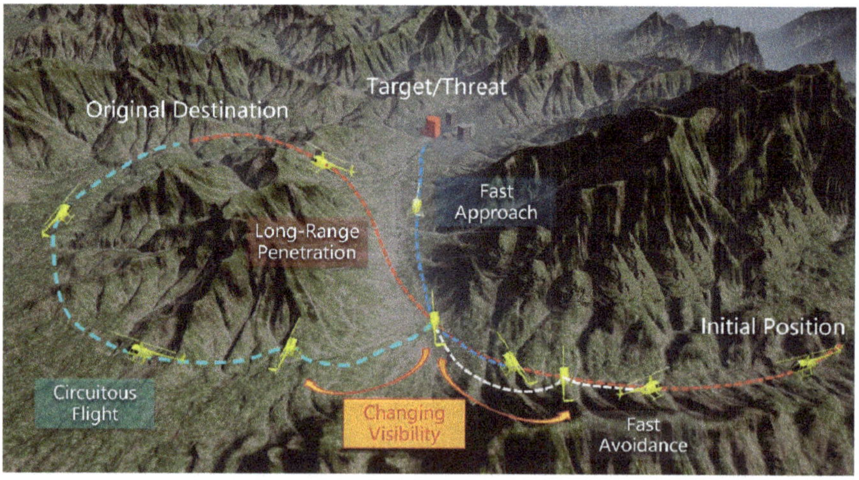

Figure 22. Diagrammatic presentation of all flight tasks.

6. Conclusions

In this study, the implementation of unmanned helicopter operations for low-altitude flight was investigated. Specific flight scenes in mountainous terrains were discussed in detail. We introduced target and threat recognition into the overall control framework, and we disassembled the low-altitude flight into several basic tasks. The target and threat were identified using the YOLO network. Using the anchor box of the YOLO network, the helicopter realized stable and effective visual servo control in the flight simulations. The 3D VFH method was used for terrain avoidance of the helicopter, achieving good adaptability and performance in unknown mountainous terrains.

Visibility judgment is crucial for low-altitude flight, yet it was rarely investigated in previous research. We proposed a direct-viewing method which can quickly estimate helicopter visibility without comprehensive map information or threat positions. On this basis, we built the overall control framework using a finite state machine. Such a design incorporated four flight tasks to cover most flight scenes encountered in low-altitude flight. A coupling control method of visual servo control and terrain avoidance was developed to realize these tasks, and their performance was verified through high-fidelity flight simulations.

Using the overall control framework presented in this research, the helicopter could automatically complete complex flight tasks such as fast attack, cover concealment, and circuitous flight similar to human pilots. The control methods are explicable, and the control gains can be tuned to adapt to various flight tasks and scenes. Furthermore, some implementations of the framework can be optimized. For example, the detection network may lose the target, rendering the visual servo control invalid. This can be improved by designing state observers and filters. The target point selection of the VFH method can be further optimized to improve the flight performance and efficiency.

Author Contributions: Conceptualization, Z.J., L.N., D.L. and J.X.; methodology, Z.J., L.N. and D.L.; software, Z.J. and L.N.; validation, Z.J. and L.N.; formal analysis, Z.T.; investigation, Z.J.; resources, D.L. and J.X.; data curation, Z.J.; writing—original draft preparation, Z.J. and L.N.; writing—review and editing, D.L. and Z.T.; supervision, D.L. and Z.T.; project administration, D.L. All authors have read and agreed to the published version of the manuscript.

Funding: This research received no external funding.

Institutional Review Board Statement: Not applicable.

Informed Consent Statement: Not applicable.

Data Availability Statement: Not applicable.

Conflicts of Interest: The authors declare no conflict of interest.

References

1. Hassan, S.; Ali, A.; Rafic, Y. A survey on quadrotors: Configurations, modeling and identification, control, collision avoidance, fault diagnosis and tolerant control. *IEEE Aerosp. Electron. Syst. Mag.* **2018**, *33*, 14–33.
2. Lee, H.; Kim, H.J. Trajectory tracking control of multirotors from modelling to experiments: A survey. *Int. J. Control Autom. Syst.* **2016**, *15*, 281–292. [CrossRef]
3. Yang, H.; Lee, Y.; Jeon, S.Y.; Lee, D. Multi-rotor drone tutorial: Systems, mechanics, control and state estimation. *Intell. Serv. Robot.* **2017**, *10*, 79–93. [CrossRef]
4. Nascimento, T.P.; Saska, M. Position and attitude control of multi-rotor aerial vehicles: A survey. *Annu. Rev. Control* **2019**, *48*, 129–146. [CrossRef]
5. Skowron, M.; Chmielowiec, W.; Glowacka, K.; Krupa, M.; Srebro, A. Sense and avoid for small unmanned aircraft systems: Research on methods and best practices. *Proc. Inst. Mech. Eng.* **2019**, *233*, 6044–6062. [CrossRef]
6. Lin, Y.; Gao, F.; Qin, T.; Gao, W.; Liu, T.; Wu, W.; Yang, Z.; Shen, S. Autonomous aerial navigation using monocular visual-inertial fusion. *J. Field Robot.* **2018**, *35*, 23–51. [CrossRef]
7. Faessler, M.; Fontana, F.; Forster, C.; Mueggler, E.; Pizzoli, M.; Scaramuzza, D. Autonomous, Vision-based Flight and Live Dense 3D Mapping with a Quadrotor Micro Aerial Vehicle. *J. Field Robot.* **2015**, *33*, 431–450. [CrossRef]
8. Doukhi, O.; Lee, D.J. Deep Reinforcement Learning for End-to-End Local Motion Planning of Autonomous Aerial Robots in Unknown Outdoor Environments: Real-Time Flight Experiments. *Sensors* **2021**, *21*, 2534. [CrossRef]
9. Zhou, Y.; Lai, S.; Cheng, H.; Hamid, M.; Chen, B.M. Towards Autonomy of Micro Aerial Vehicles in Unknown and GPS-denied Environments. *IEEE Trans. Ind. Electron.* **2021**, *68*, 7642–7651. [CrossRef]
10. Jin, Z.; Li, D.; Wang, Z. Research on the Operating Mechanicals of the Helicopter Robot Pilot. In *IOP Conference Series: Materials Science and Engineering*; IOP Publishing: Bristol, UK, 2020; Volume 887, p. 012022.
11. Jeong, H.; Kim, J.; Shim, D.H. Development of an Optionally Piloted Vehicle using a Humanoid Robot. In Proceedings of the 52nd Aerospace Sciences Meeting, National Harbor, MD, USA, 13–17 January 2014.
12. Kovalev, I.V.; Voroshilova, A.A.; Karaseva, M.V. On the problem of the manned aircraft modification to UAVs. In *Journal of Physics: Conference Series*; IOP Publishing: Bristol, UK, 2019; Volume 1399, p. 055100.
13. Hu, J.; Gu, H. Survey on Flight Control Technology for Large-Scale Helicopter. *Int. J. Aerosp. Eng.* **2017**, *2017*, 5309403. [CrossRef]
14. Xiang, Y.; Zhang, Y. Sense and avoid technologies with applications to unmanned aircraft systems: Review and prospects. *Prog. Aerosp. Sci.* **2015**, *74*, 152–166.

15. Bijjahalli, S.; Sabatini, R.; Gardi, A. Advances in Intelligent and Autonomous Navigation Systems for small UAS. *Prog. Aerosp. Sci.* **2020**, *115*, 100617. [CrossRef]
16. Marantos, P.; Karras, G.C.; Vlantis, P.; Kyriakopoulos, K.J. Vision-based Autonomous Landing Control for Unmanned Helicopters. *J. Intell. Robot. Syst.* **2017**, *92*, 145–158. [CrossRef]
17. Lin, C.H.; Hsiao, F.Y.; Hsiao, F.B. Vision-Based Tracking and Position Estimation of Moving Targets for Unmanned Helicopter Systems. *Asian J. Control Affil. ACPA Asian Control Profr. Assoc.* **2013**, *15*, 1270–1283. [CrossRef]
18. Lin, F.; Dong, X.; Chen, B.M.; Lum, K.Y.; Lee, T.H. A Robust Real-Time Embedded Vision System on an Unmanned Rotorcraft for Ground Target Following. *IEEE Trans. Ind. Electron.* **2012**, *59*, 1038–1049. [CrossRef]
19. Yong, C.; Liu, H.L. Feature article: Overview of landmarks for autonomous, vision-based landing of unmanned helicopters. *IEEE Aerosp. Electron. Syst. Mag.* **2016**, *31*, 14–27.
20. Miao, C.; Li, J. Autonomous Landing of Small Unmanned Aerial Rotorcraft Based on Monocular Vision in GPS-denied Area. *IEEE/CAA J. Autom. Sin.* **2015**, *2*, 109–114.
21. Andert, F.; Adolf, F.; Goormann, L.; Dittrich, J. Autonomous Vision-Based Helicopter Flights through Obstacle Gates. *J. Intell. Robot. Syst.* **2009**, *57*, 259–280. [CrossRef]
22. Marlow, S.Q.; Langelaan, J.W. Local Terrain Mapping for Obstacle Avoidance Using Monocular Vision. *J. Am. Helicopter Soc.* **2011**, *56*, 22007. [CrossRef]
23. Hrabar, S. An evaluation of stereo and laser—Based range sensing for rotorcraft unmanned aerial vehicle obstacle avoidance. *J. Field Robot.* **2012**, *29*, 215–239. [CrossRef]
24. Paul, T.; Krogstad, T.R.; Gravdahl, J.T. Modelling of UAV formation flight using 3D potential field. *Simul. Model. Pract. Theory* **2008**, *16*, 1453–1462. [CrossRef]
25. Javier, G.; Gandolfo, D.C.; Salinas, L.R.; Claudio, R.; Ricardo, C. Multi-objective control for cooperative payload transport with rotorcraft UAVs. *ISA Trans.* **2018**, *80*, 481–502.
26. Gimenez, J.; Salinas, L.R.; Gandolfo, D.C.; Rosales, C.D.; Carelli, R. Control for cooperative transport of a bar-shaped payload with rotorcraft UAVs including a landing stage on mobile robots. *Int. J. Syst. Sci.* **2020**, *51*, 3378–3392. [CrossRef]
27. Watson, N.A.; Owen, I.; White, M.D. Piloted Flight Simulation of Helicopter Recovery to the Queen Elizabeth Class Aircraft Carrier. *J. Aircr.* **2020**, *57*, 742–760. [CrossRef]
28. Topczewski, S.; Narkiewicz, J.; Bibik, P. Helicopter Control During Landing on a Moving Confined Platform. *IEEE Access* **2020**, *8*, 107315–107325. [CrossRef]
29. Ngo, T.D.; Sultan, C. Variable Horizon Model Predictive Control for Helicopter Landing on Moving Decks. *J. Guid. Control Dyn.* **2021**, *45*, 774–780. [CrossRef]
30. Zhao, S.; Hu, Z.; Yin, M.; Ang, K.Z.; Liu, P.; Wang, F.; Dong, X.; Lin, F.; Chen, B.M.; Lee, T.H. A Robust Real-Time Vision System for Autonomous Cargo Transfer by an Unmanned Helicopter. *IEEE Trans. Ind. Electron.* **2014**, *62*, 1210–1219. [CrossRef]
31. Truong, Q.H.; Rakotomamonjy, T.; Taghizad, A.; Biannic, J.-M. Vision-based control for helicopter ship landing with handling qualities constraints. *IFAC-PapersOnLine* **2016**, *49*, 118–123. [CrossRef]
32. Huang, Y.; Zhu, M.; Zheng, Z.; Low, K.H. Linear Velocity-Free Visual Servoing Control for Unmanned Helicopter Landing on a Ship with Visibility Constraint. *IEEE Trans. Syst. Man Cybern. Syst.* **2021**, *52*, 2979–2993. [CrossRef]
33. Chen, Y.B.; Yu, J.Q.; Su, X.L.; Luo, G.C. Path Planning for Multi-UAV Formation. *J. Intell. Robot. Syst.* **2015**, *77*, 229–246. [CrossRef]
34. Bassolillo, S.R.; Blasi, L.; D'Amato, E.; Mattei, M.; Notaro, I. Decentralized Triangular Guidance Algorithms for Formations of UAVs. *Drones* **2022**, *6*, 7. [CrossRef]
35. Fei, Y.; Sun, Y.; Shi, P. Robust Hierarchical Formation Control of Unmanned Aerial Vehicles via Neural-Based Observers. *Drones* **2022**, *6*, 40. [CrossRef]
36. Karimoddini, A.; Lin, H.; Chen, B.M.; Tong, H.L. Hybrid three-dimensional formation control for unmanned helicopter. *Automatica* **2013**, *49*, 424–433. [CrossRef]
37. Hu, D.; Yang, R.; Zuo, J.; Zhang, Z.; Wang, Y. Application of Deep Reinforcement Learning in Maneuver Planning of Beyond-Visual-Range Air Combat. *IEEE Access* **2021**, *9*, 32282–32297. [CrossRef]
38. Yang, Q.; Zhang, J.; Shi, G.; Hu, J.; Wu, Y. Maneuver Decision of UAV in Short-Range Air Combat Based on Deep Reinforcement Learning. *IEEE Access* **2019**, *8*, 363–378. [CrossRef]
39. Kivelevitch, E.; Ernest, N.; Schumacher, C.; Casbeer, D.; Cohen, K. Genetic Fuzzy Trees and their Application Towards Autonomous Training and Control of a Squadron of Unmanned Combat Aerial Vehicles. *Unmanned Syst.* **2015**, *3*, 185–204.
40. Chamberlain, L.; Scherer, S.; Singh, S. Self-aware helicopters: Full-scale automated landing and obstacle avoidance in unmapped environments. In Proceedings of the 67th American Helicopter Society International Annual Forum 2011, Virginia Beach, WV, USA, 3–5 May 2011; pp. 3210–3219.
41. Nikolajevic, K.; Belanger, N. A new method based on motion primitives to compute 3D path planning close to helicopters' flight dynamics limits. In Proceedings of the 7th International Conference on Mechanical and Aerospace Engineering (ICMAE), Cambridge, UK, 18–20 July 2016; Volume 23, pp. 411–415.
42. Schopferer, S.; Adolf, F.M. Rapid trajectory time reduction for unmanned rotorcraft navigating in unknown terrain. In Proceedings of the International Conference on Unmanned Aircraft Systems (ICUAS), Wyndham Grand, Orlando Resort, Orlando, FL, USA, 27–30 May 2014; pp. 305–316.

43. Whalley, M.S.; Takahashi, M.D.; Fletcher, J.W.; Moralez, E.; Ott, L.C.R.; Olmstead, L.M.G.; Savage, J.C.; Goerzen, C.L.; Schulein, G.J.; Burns, H.N.; et al. Autonomous Black Hawk in Flight: Obstacle Field Navigation and Landing—Site Selection on the RASCAL JUH—60A. *J. Field Robot.* **2014**, *31*, 591–616. [CrossRef]
44. Sridhar, B.; Cheng, V.H.L. Computer vision techniques for rotorcraft low-altitude flight. *Control Syst. Mag. IEEE* **1988**, *8*, 59–61. [CrossRef]
45. Friesen, D.; Borst, C.; Pavel, M.D.; Stroosma, O.; Masarati, P.; Mulder, M. Design and Evaluation of a Constraint-Based Head-Up Display for Helicopter Obstacle Avoidance. *J. Aerosp. Inf. Syst.* **2021**, *18*, 80–101. [CrossRef]
46. Zheng, J.; Liu, B.; Meng, Z.; Zhou, Y. Integrated real time obstacle avoidance algorithm based on fuzzy logic and L1 control algorithm for unmanned helicopter. In Proceedings of the Chinese Control And Decision Conference (CCDC), Shenyang, China, 9–11 June 2018; pp. 1865–1870.
47. Chandrasekaran, R.; Payan, A.P.; Collins, K.B.; Mavris, D.N. Helicopter wire strike protection and prevention devices: Review, challenges, and recommendations. *Aerosp. Sci. Technol.* **2020**, *98*, 105665. [CrossRef]
48. Merz, T.; Kendoul, F. Dependable Low-Altitude Obstacle Avoidance for Robotic Helicopters Operating in Rural Areas. *J. Field Robot.* **2013**, *30*, 439–471. [CrossRef]
49. Wang, D.; Li, W.; Liu, X.; Li, N.; Zhang, C. UAV environmental perception and autonomous obstacle avoidance: A deep learning and depth camera combined solution. *Comput. Electron. Agric.* **2020**, *175*, 105523. [CrossRef]
50. Aldao, E.; Gonzalez-Desantos, L.M.; Michinel, H.; Gonzalez-Jorge, H. UAV Obstacle Avoidance Algorithm to Navigate in Dynamic Building Environments. *Drones* **2022**, *6*, 16. [CrossRef]
51. Hermand, E.; Nguyen, T.W.; Hosseinzadeh, M.; Garone, E. Constrained Control of UAVs in Geofencing Applications. In Proceedings of the 26th Mediterranean Conference on Control and Automation, Zadar, Croatia, 19 June 2018; pp. 217–222.
52. Jiang, M.; Xu, C.; Ji, H. Path Planning for Aircrafts using Alternate TF/TA. In Proceedings of the Chinese Automation Congress (CAC), Shanghai, China, 6–8 November 2020; pp. 3702–3707.
53. Kosari, A.; Kassaei, S.I. TF/TA optimal Flight trajectory planning using a novel regenerative flattener mapping method. *Sci. Iran.* **2020**, *27*, 1324–1338. [CrossRef]
54. Chen, H.-x.; Nan, Y.; Yang, Y. A Two-Stage Method for UCAV TF/TA Path Planning Based on Approximate Dynamic Programming. *Math. Probl. Eng.* **2018**, *2018*, 1092092. [CrossRef]
55. Hao, L.; Cui, J.; Wu, L.; Yang, C.; Yu, R. Research on threat modeling technology for helicopter in low altitude. In Proceedings of the 7th IEEE International Conference on Software Engineering and Service Science (ICSESS), Beijing, China, 26–28 August 2016; pp. 774–778.
56. Machovina, B.J. Susceptibility Modeling and Mission Flight Route Optimization in a Low Threat, Combat Environment. Doctoral Thesis, University of Denver, Denver, CO, USA, 2010.
57. Woo, J.W.; Choi, Y.S.; An, J.Y.; Kim, C.J. An Approach to Air-To-Surface Mission Planner on 3D Environments for an Unmanned Combat Aerial Vehicle. *Drones* **2022**, *6*, 20. [CrossRef]
58. Tang, Q.; Zhang, X.; Liu, X. TF/TA2 trajectory tracking using nonlinear predictive control approach. *J. Syst. Eng. Electron.* **2006**, *17*, 396–401. [CrossRef]
59. Hilbert, K.B. *A Mathematical Model of the UH-60 Helicopter*; No. NASA Technical Memorandum 85890; NSNA: Washington, DC, USA, 1984.
60. Redmon, J.; Farhadi, A. YOLO9000: Better, Faster, Stronger. In Proceedings of the IEEE Conference on Computer Vision and Pattern Recognition, Honolulu, HI, USA, 21–26 July 2017; pp. 6517–6525.
61. Yang, L.; Liu, Z.; Wang, X.; Xu, Y. An Optimized Image-Based Visual Servo Control for Fixed-Wing Unmanned Aerial Vehicle Target Tracking with Fixed Camera. *IEEE Access* **2019**, *7*, 68455–68468. [CrossRef]
62. Yang, L.; Liu, Z.; Wang, X.; Yu, X.; Wang, G.; Shen, L. Image-Based Visual Servo Tracking Control of a Ground Moving Target for a Fixed-Wing Unmanned Aerial Vehicle. *J. Intell. Robot. Syst.* **2021**, *102*, 81. [CrossRef]
63. Vanneste, S.; Bellekens, B.; Weyn, M. 3DVFH+: Real-Time Three-Dimensional Obstacle Avoidance Using an Octomap. In Proceedings of the Morse 2014—Model-Driven Robot Software Engineering, York, UK, 21 July 2014; Volume 1319, pp. 91–102.

sensors

MDPI

Article

A Reliable Merging Link Scheme Using Weighted Markov Chain Model in Vehicular Ad Hoc Networks

Siman Emmanuel *, Ismail Fauzi Bin Isnin and Mohd. Murtadha Bin Mohamad

Faculty of Engineering, Universiti Teknologi Malaysia, Skudai 81310, Malaysia; ismailfauzi@utm.my (I.F.B.I.); murtadha@utm.my (M.M.B.M.)

* Correspondence: esiman@graduate.utm.my; Tel.: +60-1137030907 or +234-(0)8065641551

Abstract: The vehicular ad hoc network (VANET) is a potential technology for intelligent transportation systems (ITS) that aims to improve safety by allowing vehicles to communicate quickly and reliably. The rates of merging collision and hidden terminal problems, as well as the problems of picking the best match cluster head (CH) in a merged cluster, may emerge when two or more clusters are merged in the design of a clustering and cluster management scheme. In this paper, we propose an enhanced cluster-based multi-access channel protocol (ECMA) for high-throughput and effective access channel transmissions while minimizing access delay and preventing collisions during cluster merging. We devised an aperiodic and acceptable merge cluster head selection (MCHS) algorithm for selecting the optimal merge cluster head (MCH) in centralized clusters where all nodes are one-hop nodes during the merging window. We also applied a weighted Markov chain mathematical model to improve accuracy while lowering ECMA channel data access transmission delay during the cluster merger window. We presented extensive simulation data to demonstrate the superiority of the suggested approach over existing state-of-the-arts. The implementation of a MCHS algorithm and a weight chain Markov model reveal that ECMA is distinct and more efficient by 64.20–69.49% in terms of average network throughput, end-to-end delay, and access transmission probability.

Keywords: weighted Markov chain; clustering; weight value; merge window; merging link; merge collision; predicting probability

Citation: Emmanuel, S.; Isnin, I.F.B.; Mohamad, M.M.B. A Reliable Merging Link Scheme Using Weighted Markov Chain Model in Vehicular Ad Hoc Networks. *Sensors* **2022**, *22*, 4861. https://doi.org/10.3390/s22134861

Academic Editors: Jaroslaw Pytka, Andrzej Łukaszewicz, Zbigniew Kulesza, Wojciech Giernacki and Andriy Holovatyy

Received: 11 March 2022
Accepted: 20 June 2022
Published: 27 June 2022

1. Introduction

In a vehicle ad hoc network, topological changes are frequent as nodes (vehicles) move in accordance with traffic laws [1–3]. As automobile density grows, access collisions occur as a result of poor packet data transmission during slot allocation [3]. Therefore, an effective clustering can lengthen the lifespan of a network. Clustering is a technique for dissecting a network's architecture. Topological data are obtained more quickly due to the network's smaller size (cluster). Because of the lack of centralized administration, network topology management and resource allocation become difficult, resulting in inefficient throughput and increased access latency [1]. To overcome hidden terminal problems and merge collisions, an effective clustering technique is required. When using an allocated technique to assign a period allocation [4], two sorts of conflicts can occur: access collision and merge collision. Due to mobility, two vehicles that started more than two hops apart try to join a single period allocation at the same moment [5]. Automobiles traveling in reverse directions with RSUs fastened to the road [6] and two or more clusters merging can cause merging conflicts. Assuming the nodes in this scenario have already been assigned time slots in their clusters during the cluster merging process, they must be released from their current time slot to acquire a new one, which may result in merging collision [7], whereas access collision occurs when more than one node (that has not yet acquired a time slot) within transmission coverage, or approximately two hops apart, attempts to enter a single available period allocation. Therefore, increasing traffic density that is not in cluster may cause hidden terminal issues and access conflicts, leading in inefficient medium usage and increasing access delays. When the IEEE 802.11p MAC detects an idle channel, it instantly initiates transmission or selects a backup value from the contention window (CW) and initiates a countdown phase [8]. When a vehicle transports a high quantity of data packets, it participates in multiple competitions. Because 802.11p does not support RTS/CTS for data packet broadcasting [9], it is susceptible to hidden terminal issues and conflict [10]. Therefore, collisions between data packets are not immediately noticeable. The TDMA protocol was proposed for automotive ad hoc networks in order to improve transmission efficiency and overcome IEEE 802.11p's restrictions. Numerous shared TDMA-based MAC principles for VANETs have been presented that aimed to eliminate or mitigate merging conflicts as well as the hidden terminal problems [8,9]. In the centralized TDMA protocol, the centralized node allocates the time slot, and in the distributed TDMA protocol, each node manages the time slot [11–14]. Due to the high vehicle density, the TDMA Cluster MAC (TC-MAC) recently modified the approach for allocating TDMA slots in group-based (Cluster) VANETs. Unlike DSRC, TC-MAC maintains a better level of reliability for safety messages [15,16].

Due to the widespread use of VANETs, an intelligent transport system must transfer data to several nodes [17,18]. When vehicles are partitioned into virtual clusters, scalability of the network becomes a challenge. In [17], clusters are led by a cluster head (CH), which is assisted by cluster members (CM). When merging leads in bigger clusters [18], numerous recent clustering methods employ a small intra- and inter-cluster process size (Figure 1) [19]. The enhanced weight-based clustering algorithm (EWCA) [17] was demonstrated in a cluster. It considers the time and position of vehicles in the cluster, and it is assumed that vehicles are traveling at similar speeds. Every node within broadcast range of its nearest neighbors was considered. This was done to ensure cluster stability and the effective transmission of safety data. As a result, the techniques are more suited to a single traffic condition, and the mobility component is overlooked, resulting in access and merging crashes with all automobiles travelling at constant speed in a medium-density environment.

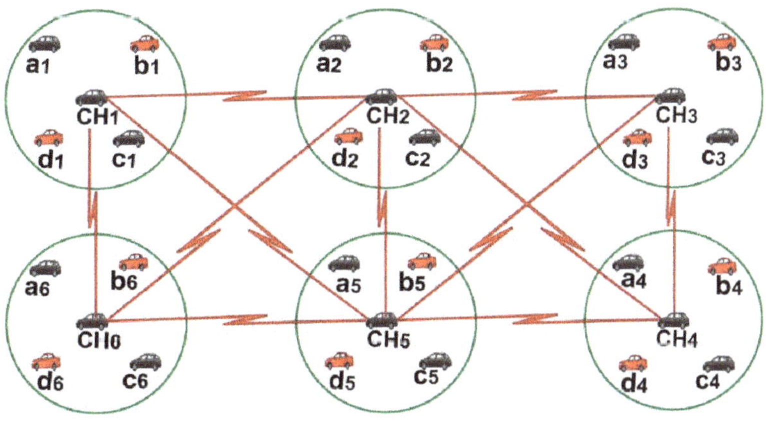

Figure 1. Merging cluster structure.

In [20], MAMC-MAC protocol was developed to increase VANET reliability and to convey safety alerts. It utilized a hopsector message direction schema to maximize the message delivery into a particular domain in real time. TDMA is used to divide the dedicated short range communication (DSRC) band into frames. The MAMC-MAC protocol is more appropriate for a single traffic scenario, and the mobility factor is not taken into account. Furthermore, all vehicles are traveling at a constant speed in a medium traffic density, and also the clusters merging scenario is not taken into account. It is likely to result in access collisions and merging collisions. In addition, there are hidden terminal issues, resulting in merging collisions. The cluster merging process is the process which merges two adjacent clusters into a larger cluster. This process occurs during a period called the merging window (Mw). Based on the above issues, our contributions are as follows:

- We studied and created a merge cluster head selection (MCHS) algorithm that minimizes the frequencies of merging collision and hidden terminal concerns while also electing the best-fit CH in a merged cluster when two or more clusters merged.
- We used a weighted Markov chain model to describe the transformation operation within a cluster and differentiated it from other clusters based on the weighted value.
- During the clusters merging window, the weighted Markov chain mathematical model improved accuracy while reducing ECMA channel data access transmission delay with unmatched transition speed in a time slot and state slot (frame). During the window time (T), this speeds up transitions while eliminating hidden terminal difficulties and access collision.
- The aperiodic MCH selection is based on the merge window period probability and the development of a centralized cluster in a VANET where all nodes are one-hop nodes.
- In a merged cluster, the CHs choose the best candidate as the MCH. Although their cluster members (CMs) inside the transmission range released their time slots and acquired a new time slot from the new MCH, the other CHs became CMs. The CMs that are outside of the new MCH's transmission range will continue to cling to their previous CH, which has now turned to gateway node (Gw), until all of the remaining CMs are inside the MCH's transmission range, at which point the Gw will eventually switch to CM.
- For performance evaluation, we built a detailed simulation model and put the suggested technique into action. Extensive simulation results indicated the superiority and scalability of the proposed ECMA method.

The remainder of this paper is organized as follows. Section 2 provides the existing works on merging collisions. Section 3 describes the proposed method that applies the new weighted Markov chain and the cluster head selection algorithm in the merged cluster. The fourth part presents the performance evaluation of the selected indicators, simulation parameters, and their values, followed by Sections 5 and 6 as the Discussion and Conclusion respectively.

2. Existing Works on Merging Collisions

The set of vehicles, called a cluster, allows vehicles to communicate with their neighbors, called intra-cluster networks, and two or more cluster may communicate with each other, called inter-cluster networks [13,14]. When two clusters are in a merging process the node is relieved of their access time slot and acquires new ones which may result in merging collisions. Because merging collisions occur due to vehicle movement and are marginal based on time slot size [15–17], Vehicle ad-hoc network media access control protocol (VeMAC) calculates the rate of merging collisions in the time frame rather than in the time slot. Although access collision occurs when nodes attempt to acquire a time slot, a merging collision occurs when vehicles have successfully acquired a time slot. It can also occur when cars traveling in the same direction but at different speeds. As node x moves into THS2 (Two hopes state II) and shares the same time slot as node z, a merging collision occurs at z, as shown in Figure 2. As a result, when a node detects a merging collision on an access channel, it releases its time slot and acquires a new one, resulting in an access collision, especially with hidden terminal occurrence. In [21,22], a distributed algorithm was used in VeMAC, which requires two vehicle transceivers, one tuned to the control channel and the other to the service channel. However, because of the large size of the control frame in VeMAC, contact over the control channel becomes an overhead.

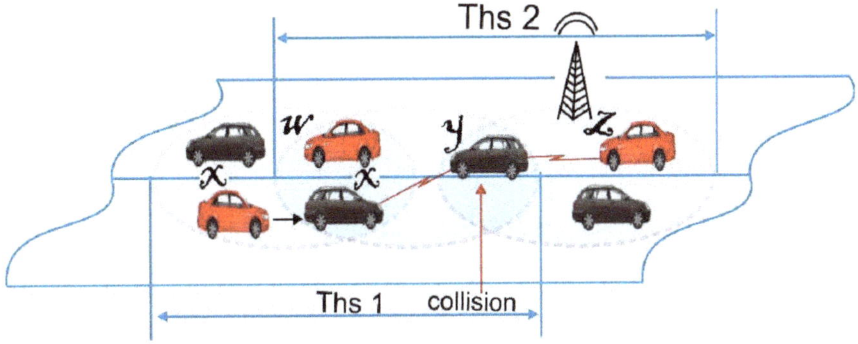

Figure 2. Merge collision due to node mobility [20]. Note: THSO is the ratio of a THS's necessary time slots to the total number of time slots available for that THS.

In [23], the Direction based clustering and multi-channel medium access control (DA-CMAC) protocol is an extension of the VeMAC protocol to improve the transmission reliability of the safety message, where RSU, GW, and CH consist of time slots for cluster members (CMs) that the work divide into two, depending on the location of the vehicles to reduce the rate of change in DA-CMAC access and merging collisions. In addition, each cluster member (CM) is given one slot in both the control and service channels to ensure channel access equity. The application of the Gw node [24] and the allocation of slots from the RSU to CMs in different directions at different speeds result in merging collisions [25] when two or more clusters merge. In [26], the authors used leadership-based clusters (LCM) merging to investigate the impact of merging collisions in a cluster vehicular ad hoc network. When clusters in the same direction combine to form a new unified cluster, the scheme assigns the best connection to each cluster member and remains stable. Two CHs moving in the same direction and in the same transmission range would activate the merging detection mechanism in this scheme. That study only examined the impact of hidden terminal problems and the transmission of access data in a merging cluster by relying on the identification mechanism for cluster stability mergers. In [27], researchers used a cluster merging mechanism in CCFM-MAC to avoid cluster merging until they were sufficiently close to each other. The Hello or cluster head packets are received by all the cluster heads within the transmission range between each. When the CHs are within a certain time interval of each other's communication range, the CHs repeat the Hello and CH packet responses, and the clusters merge. When two or more clusters combine, the CH with the highest ALERT remains the CH, while the other cluster members are dissolved. The goal is to avoid cluster merging in a short period of time and to increase cluster stability. However, gateway vehicles are used as a connection sub-domain that allows CMs and CHs to link. Hidden terminal problems and collision-free clusters [7] are solved using this scheme. Disjointed time slot sets are associated with distinct lanes on the same road segment and distinct road segments at intersections, according to MoMAC [28]. Furthermore, each vehicle transmits safety messages along with time slots occupying neighboring vehicle data; vehicles can detect time-slot collisions and access a vacant time slot in a completely distributed manner by updating time slots occupying information from two-hop neighbors (obtained indirectly from one-hop neighbors) using Chain Markov [29,30]. In this situation, two CHs which are in the same contact range resolves to cluster merging [31]. The CH with the highest weight value [32], on the other hand, will continue to be the CH, while the others stepped down. CMs have the option of joining the new leadership, joining another cluster, or forming their own. In a cluster-based TDMA MAC protocol [33], the duty of the CH is to assign a slide of time to the CMs. Meanwhile, the authors have only looked at cluster stability and have yet to incorporate the dynamic slot allocation approach into a clustering mechanism to reduce the rate of merging collisions.

The extended delay problem that vehicles can encounter in the event of a merging collision with a TDMA-based MAC protocol for VANET is highlighted and formulated in [34]. This study demonstrated that this delay is proportional to the number of collided packets immediately following the merging collisions. The proposed slot suggestion system is used to prevent additional access collisions between vehicles that have vacated their time slots because of a slot-merge collision. After an access collision, this method minimizes the likelihood of additional access collisions [5].

3. Proposed Method

In this section, we proposed the Merge Cluster-Head Selection algorithm (MCHS) to reduce the rates of merging collisions and hidden terminal problems when two or more clusters merge, as well as the selection of the best match MCH in a merged cluster. Merging collisions occur when vehicles from separate clusters combine to enter a shared time slot. When the algorithm is used, as presented in Algorithm 1, the merging collision can be significantly reduced. By adapting clustering and MCHS algorithm in a merged cluster, the proposed ECMA protocol attempts to achieve collision-free in a cluster while also minimizing the rate of merging collisions in an inter-cluster VANET.

As the different clusters at 'M' converge, they come into contact as in 'N', where the two CHs are in the transmission range of each other. In 'L', the appropriate CH becomes the MCH, the other CH becomes Gw and remains attached to the CMs beyond the MCH's transmission range, and in 'Q', all the cluster members (CMs) are inside the MCH's transmission range, and the Gw becomes a CM, as shown in Figure 3.

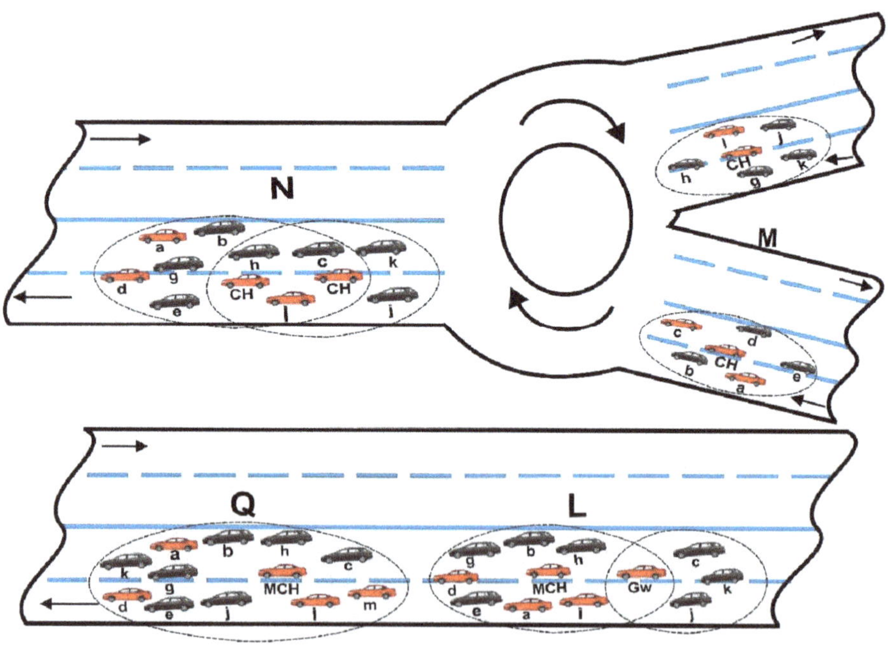

Figure 3. Illustrations of cluster merging phases (from M –> N –> L –> Q).

3.1. Weighted Markov Chain

During the clusters merging window, the weighted Markov chain mathematical model enhances accuracy and minimizes ECMA channel data access transmission delay with unmatched transition speed in timeslot and state-slot (frame). This speeds up transitions while avoiding hidden terminal issues and access collision during the window time (T). In the frame's frequency state of slot reservations, self-correlation coefficients represent various reservation prevalence packet data relationships. The frequency state of slot reservation in present frames can be used to predict the frame prevalence packet data in the future. Then, in comparison to the future frames, a weighted average based on the frequency of other current frames slot reservation can be calculated. As a result, the prediction goal of making full and equitable use of knowledge has been met. This is the fundamental idea behind weighted Markov chain prediction [35,36].

A branch of the Markov chain process is the weighted Markov chain [37]. If the system's present state is given, then (conditionally) the past and future are independent. Such an action is referred to as the system's Markov property. In a discrete (countable) state space with respect to discrete or continuous time, a Markov chain evolves.

A stochastic process X = {X(t),t∈T} is defined on a probability space (Ω, *F*, *P*), where parameters set T = {0, 1, 2, . . . }, and state space E = {0, 1, 2, . . . }.

$$\begin{aligned} P\{X(m+k) = i_{\mathrm{m}} + {}_{\mathrm{k}} \mid X(m) = i_{\mathrm{m}}, X(j_1) = j_1, \ldots, \\ X\left(j^2\right) = j^2, X(j_1) = j_1\Big\} = P\{X(m+k) \\ = i_{\mathrm{m}} + {}_{\mathrm{k}} \mid X(m) = i_{\mathrm{m}}\} \end{aligned} \quad (1)$$

The general time-slot transition step is given by P^{t} for any slot time t. The Markov chain nodes $X_0, X_1, \ldots, X_{\mathrm{n}}$ have a slot time reservation state, S = (1, 2, 3, . . . , *n*), (Figure 4), where the Transition Matrix *P* element is defined as:

$$P(X_{\mathrm{t}} = j|X_0 = i) = P(X_{\mathrm{n+t}} = j|X_{\mathrm{n}} = i) = \left(P^{\mathrm{t}}\right)_{\mathrm{ij}} \textit{for any n.} \quad (2)$$

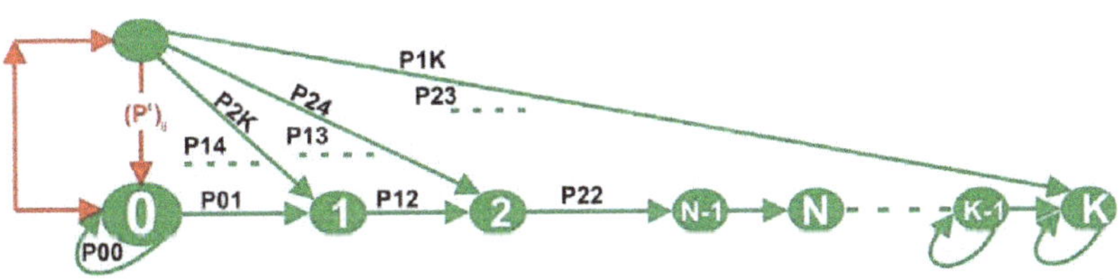

Figure 4. The transition process of X_{n}.

The window period probability is π_{j} (3), and the mean recurrence time to state *j* is μ_{jj}. Taking the inverse of the mean recurrence time is one technique for determining the window period probability, as shown by the preceding identity.

$$\pi_{\mathrm{j}} = \frac{1}{\mu_{\mathrm{jj}}} \quad (3)$$

An ergodic Markov chain is an irreducible Markov chain that is aperiodic and positive recurrent. Equation (4) depicts the ergodic chain's finite distribution *j*, which is the only nonnegative solution to the equations.

$$\begin{cases} \pi_{\mathrm{j}} = \sum\limits_{k=o}^{\infty} \pi_{\mathrm{k}}\, p_{\mathrm{kj}} \;\; j = 0,\ 1,\ 2,\ldots \\ \sum\limits_{j=o}^{\infty} \pi_{\mathrm{j}} = 1 \end{cases} \quad (4)$$

The Markov chain's long-run proportion of time spent in state *j* can now be written as π_{j}. Based on the above Markov chain and the window period probability, the specific method of weighted Markov chain prediction is expressed as follows [38]:

Determine a criterion for categorizing the frame's incidence of slot reservation based on the length of the super frame and the specific adaptability requirement. The distance between the ideal one-hop node (OHN) and the CH in two-dimensional Euclidean space is expressed as E = 1, 2, 3, 4, and so on. The frequency condition of slot reservation is determined for each frame based on the classification standard of the threshold value (Sthr). Equation (5) is used to calculate the various self-correlation coefficients r_k, $k \in \Delta\text{Sthr}$, where r_k denotes the k-frame self-correlation coefficient, $x_1 = 1, 2, \ldots, n$ denotes the ith frame slot reservation prevalence, x denotes the mean value of x_1, and n denotes the length of the slot reservation series' frame frequency state.

$$r_k = \sum_{l=1}^{n-k} (x_1 - \overline{x})(x_{1+k} - \overline{x}) / \sum_{\imath=1}^{n} (x_1 - \overline{x})^2 \tag{5}$$

We create a diverse set of self-correlation coefficients and use them consistently. The weights of multiple (steps) Markov chains must also be considered (m is the maximum step predicted). As the prediction probability index, take the weighted average $\mathcal{W}_k$ of the various predicting probabilities for the same condition as shown in Equation (6).

$$\mathcal{W}_k = | r_k | / \sum_{k=1}^{m} | r_k | \tag{6}$$

We can derive various phases of Markov chain transition probability matrices from the statistical results from slot reservation prevalence transitions, which determine the probability rule. For example, in a different frame, the frequency of slot reservation $P_i(k)$, isthr can be predicted and combined with the relative transition probability matrices of a different frame, where k is the Markov chain step and $k = 1, 2, \ldots$, m. If $P_i = \max\{P_i, P_i \in \Delta\text{Sthr}\}$ (7), then i represents the predicted future state of the current frame slot reservation prevalence.

$$P_i = \sum_{k=1}^{m} \mathcal{W}_k P_i^{(K)},\ i \in E \tag{7}$$

By repeating steps 4 through 8, we can predict the slot reservation condition for the next frame after determining the current frame's slot reservation frequency and adding it to the original series. The cluster head with the best stable neighbors is chosen as the CH with the lowest weight value (w_i) based on the calculation of the combined w_i. In contrast to the EWCA, all other CHs in the cluster follow the same steps from step two to step nine. W_i is equal to the sum of the weighting factors (wf) in this equation, which is wf1 + wf2 + wf3 + wf4 = 1. Table 1 shows that the group of weighting factors (0.47, 0.24, 0.24, and 0.05) produced the best results in terms of greatest PDR, network throughput, and lowest end-to-end delay. This is due to the weighting variables in this group emphasizing high group mobility (0.47), followed by degree difference (0.24), and distance metrics (0.24) while lowering the impact of cumulative time (0.05) on the (merge cluster head) MCH selection process. If the next CH is chosen based on the maximum number of MCHs and the highest relative direction with the shortest remaining distance, the selected road segment will have strong connectivity, increasing the packet delivery ratio (PDR) and decreasing the MAC delay. On the one hand, if the protocol's generated delay is based on a high remaining cumulative time with less attention paid to the quantity of MCH, the protocol's generated delay will be high, especially in low traffic density cases; on the other hand, the packet delivery ratio (PDR) will be unaffected because the access method is the same as IEEE 802.11p RTS/CTS. Finally, if the relative distance metric is minimal, the protocol delay will improve because of a reduction in the time it takes the vehicles to transmit the packet until it arrives at its destination.

Table 1. Simulation Parameters.

Parameter	Value	Parameter	Value
DSRC channel frequency	5.9 GHz	DSRC channel bandwidth	10 MHz
MAC/PHY	WAVE/IEEE 802.11p	Mean deviation	0-V_{max}
Simulation time	1000 s	Vehicle densities	50, 100, 150, 200
Merge window (Mw)	5, 15, 25, 35, 45	Weight factor level	0.47, 0.24, 0.24, 0.05
Radios r	500 m	Region's size	1000 × 1000
Data rate	100 Mbps	Packet arriving rate	25 Packets/s

3.2. *Periodic Access and CH Connectivity Level*

The Merge Cluster Head Selection Algorithm (MCHS) utilizing a Stable Weighted Clustering Algorithm is a theoretical model that employs a vehicle weight value for merge cluster head (MCH) selection during the window phase of the cluster merging process (SWC).

The several metrics analyzed for the MCH election process are listed in this section. These metrics include information about the mobility of each cluster head (CH), such as movement direction, road ID, CH mean velocity, CH connectivity level, and cluster head mean distance from its CH neighbors. A CH finds its neighbors by sending out periodic transmissions with mobility information. A CH's movement direction and a centralized cluster's total weight value should only be detected by any surrounding CH before it can receive and process its neighbors' broadcast message. These metrics are utilized to establish a cluster head's suitability to become a merging cluster head (MCH) since they ensure a CH's preparedness.

$$T = 1 + \mathrm{p}\ (\mathrm{K} - 1) \tag{8}$$

For a successful access probability P, the period T, in Figures 4 and 5, to occupy a time slot by a node as it transmits in a frame is given in Equation (8).

$$T = \left[\frac{1 + \mathrm{P_{ij}}\ (K-1)}{CH_{\mathrm{i}}} * (\mathrm{Wp_h} - \mathrm{Wp_1}) + \mathrm{Wp_1}\right] \tag{9}$$

The greatest window period $\mathrm{Wp_h}$ and the lowest window period $\mathrm{Wp_1}$ contention values are employed based on the total number of cluster head (CH_{i}). The duration T required for a node to successfully occupy a time slot when it transmits in a frame is described in Equation (9), similar to [17].

3.3. *Merging Channel Access Mechanism*

During cluster merging, the four channel access modes in the CH are super-frames that can easily adapt to new traffic levels while maintaining stable transmissions. The CH periodically polls clusters for traffic. If the traffic value of two consecutive rounds is significantly different from the initial traffic value, the current access mode for the traffic level is used. The CH gathers data about traffic concentrations and the probability of channel-based merging collision and compares them to the threshold value of various traffic levels during the cluster merging window, as follows: Low traffic level is when the traffic load is lower than the threshold values (Ltv). Light traffic level is when the traffic load is lower than the threshold values (Stv) and higher than threshold (Ltv). Medium traffic level is when the traffic load is lower than the threshold values (Htv) and higher than threshold (Stv). High traffic level is when the traffic load is higher than the threshold values (Htv) as illustrated in Figure 5b.

The ECMA access modes between the CHs in a merging cluster are shown in Figure 5b. Random access is used when the traffic is light. The access technique is the same as that of the IEEE 802.11p RTS/CTS. Only the CHs that need to send a packet to other CHs do so by sending the RTS. The CTS packet indicates that the CHs were successfully accessed. On-demand access is used during low traffic. The access of the cluster head is determined dynamically by its message demands and stated in the RTS packet as related to random access.

The clustering time slot reservation access is implemented at a medium traffic level. Only CHs in the same group can reserve and compete for a time slot. Otherwise, they can compete only in the next frame. CHs 1 and 2 did not compete for the same access time slot, whereas nodes 3 and 4 did. CHs 1 and 2 must wait for the next frame. Polling access occurs in high-traffic level when each cluster head receives a CH polling. If a cluster head needs to send data, the other cluster head prepares a time slot. The polling cycle duration was increased to allow for data transmission from the cluster head. After polling the CH1 for readiness, the cluster head also polls CH2 for readiness, and so on, until the cluster head discovers a CH within its transmission range that has data to transfer, at which point the cluster head initiates a cluster merging.

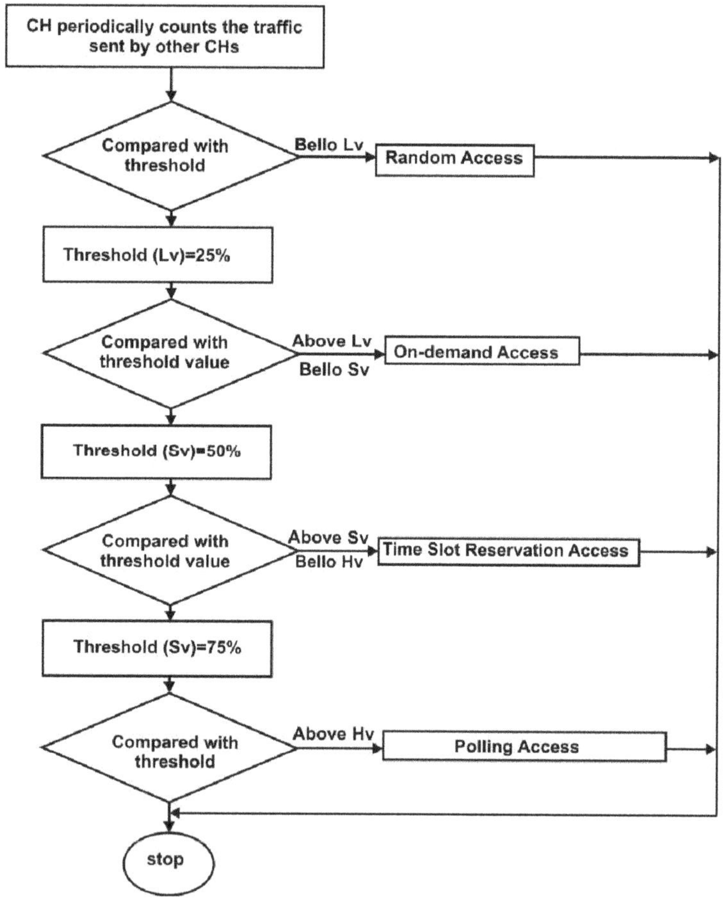

(a)

Figure 5. *Cont.*

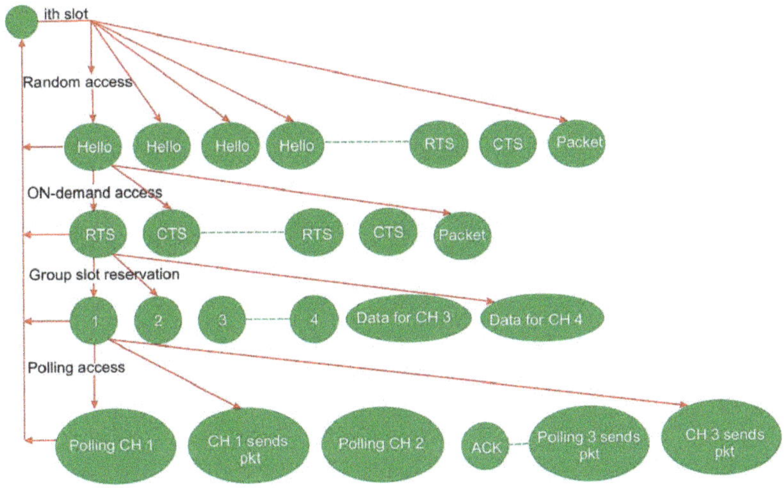

(**b**)

Figure 5. (**a**): Diagram of ECMA protocol. (**b**): Merge cluster head channel access.

Cluster merging happens as follows: as the cluster merges, two CHs in the transmission range of each other tend to exchange information and reconfigure the CH with the lowest suitability weight value (W_i) to become the MCH. In Algorithm 1, the other CH transforms into Gw and continues attached to the CMs beyond the MCH's transmission range until all of the CMs are within the MCH's transmission range and Gw becomes a CM. The CM then enters the cluster and, alongside the other cluster members, decides to join the cluster, be assigned a time slot, and acquires a new CMID. As a result, the rates of re-clustering and merging collisions are reduced, as well as the hidden terminal problems.

Algorithms 1: MCH selection in a merged cluster

```
Require: No. of neighboring CH, nodes, position, speed, node weight value, threshold, CMID, and MCH.
Ensure: Weight value (Wi).
broadcast CHi
if CHi recieves RTS then
if | Si − Mi | < ΔSthr
        if multiple beacon frames received then
if (Si,CHi < Mi) & (pos.CHi>pos.CHi) then //Weight value in CH compared.
lowest_CHi = array [0] // The CH with the id starting from zero.
  for all CHi do
          if array[i] > lowest_CHi then
          lowest_CHi = array[i]
       status.CHi = MCH
    End if
  End if
   End if
    CHi.status = Gw// when the other CMsi are not in the Tx of MCH but CHi.
       Gwi.status = CM// when all the CMs are in the Tx of MCH.
  join Clusterj // or join Clusterj and affiliate with CHj.
  else
     leaving cluster
   Update and share status info with the CMs
else
   status.CHi = Gw // The search repeats until new CH is selected.
    Gwi.status = CM// when all the CMs are in the Tx of MCH.
  join Clusterj // or join Clusterj and affiliate with CHj.
  else
     leaving cluster
   Update and share status info with the CMs
             end ifcummulative
end for// End cluster formation.
```

4. Performance Evaluation

The simulation results were compared side by side to determine the effectiveness of the proposed algorithm in ensuring an effective cluster merging. We evaluated the performance of the ECMA protocol with the weight-model MCH selection algorithm for efficient transmission of access data packets from the CH and allocate the reserved slot to the CMs to reduce the impact of merging collisions during cluster merging at the simulation phase. The performance metrics for the method are network throughput, end-to-end delay, and access transmission probability.

i. Average network throughput—the average number of data packets successfully transmitted to neighboring CMs within a unit time is known as the average network throughput.
ii. The end-to-end delay—the time required for a data packet transmitted and successfully received by neighboring nodes.
iii. Successful access transmission probability—defined as the ratio of the number of data packets successfully transmitted in the network to the total number of data packets effectively transmitted.

Simulation and Parameters

In the simulation, SUMO, NS-2, and MATLAB are used. SUMO is a program that generates road status files by simulating traffic. We used NS2 to embed information about the state of the highway, then evaluated the NS2 to obtain data. We used MATLAB to evaluate data in order to obtain the most important performance indicator information. Wave module is used to communicate across DSRC channels, which are defined by the IEEE802.11p MAC and PHY layer standards. The simulation parameters are listed in Table 1.

5. Discussion

5.1. Access Delay Time-Slot Probability

Figure 6 shows the probability of access delay theoretical structure based on a weighted Markov chain model: First, as the number of nodes grows, channel access becomes restricted, resulting in access collision.

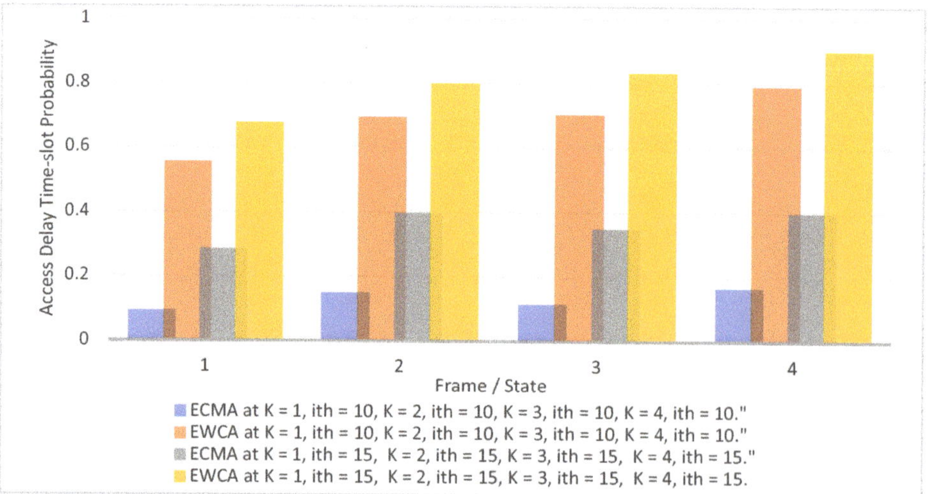

Figure 6. Access delay at various state.

For example, when the node adapts to different access mechanisms on frames 1 to 4 at *i*th slot 10, ECMA provides 19%, access collisions prevention, while EWCA provides 68.8%. When the transition flow was at k and ith = 15, the ECMA protocol increased by 15%, whereas the EWCA protocol increased by 82.24%. When two or more clusters merge, the unified weighted cluster network deals with hidden terminal problems and secures all CMs to their CH. The MCH elections and the new merged cluster have a special resistance to merging collisions owing to the transition pace.

5.2. *Cluster Head Lifetime and Its Influence on Merge Window*

The influence of CH duration and the merging window (Mw) is predictable based on the above model and analyses by the simulation process. The MCH selection algorithm with the aperiodic window period also increases the speed of the transition process and generates a new stable merge cluster. This gives the novel ECMA protocol a better performance, even as vehicle densities in a different merge scenario change. Figure 7 attests to the fact that in as much as the density of the vehicles increases from scenarios '*a* to *d*' where the average CH duration during the merging window is low from '*a*' and have a slight rise increases in '*b*', '*c*' and '*d*' scenarios. However, the MCH in the ECMA protocol stays longer than the MCH in the EWCA and VeMAC. Based on the above model and simulation results, the impact of the CH duration and the merging window (Mw) can be predicted. The MCH selection algorithm, combined with the aperiodic window period, speeds up the transfer process and results in a new, stable merge cluster.

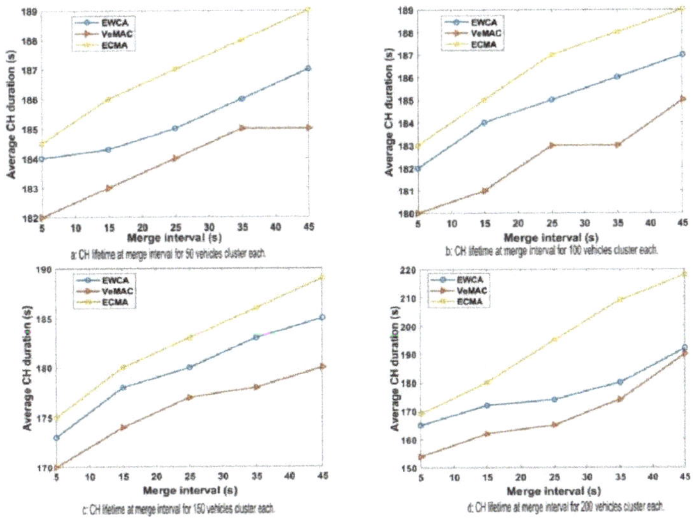

Figure 7. CH lifetime and it influence on Mw.

5.3. *Cluster Member Disconnection Frequency and It Influence on Merge Window*

When other CHs are relieved of their leadership and become ordinary CMs, the rate of cluster members disconnecting from the network during the cluster merger process is affected. In this case, the CMs must give up their current time slot and request a new one from the new leadership (MCH). CMs that have been separated from their CH during the Mw process may either join the new MCH or leave to form or join another cluster. Figure 8 shows how the CH relinquishes leadership to become the gateway (Gw) node in the ECMA protocol, which continues to connect and link the CMs that are not within the transmission range of the new MCH. In addition, the remaining CMs which are either within the transmission range of the new MCH may cling to the Gate way node or join a new cluster. Second, even though the clusters' CMs are all within the transmission range of one another, each cluster's centralized system ensures that each CM is only connected to its own CH. In contrast to EWCA and VeMAC, this function of the ECMA protocol stabilizes and maintains a high-throughput and a timely successful access transmission during the merging window, thereby eliminating the HTP and merging collision.

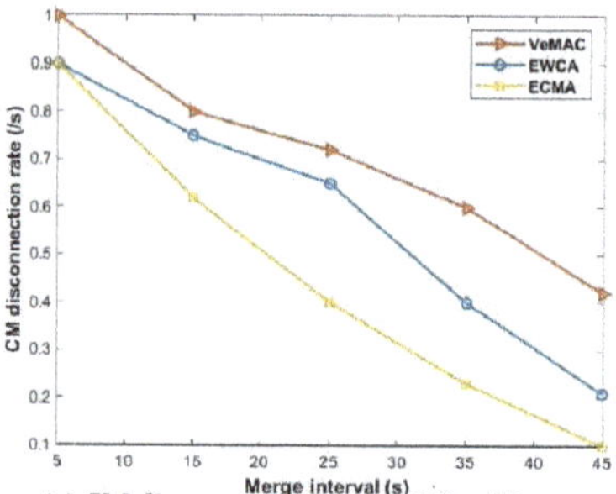

(a) CM disconnection rate vs MI at 50 vehicles.

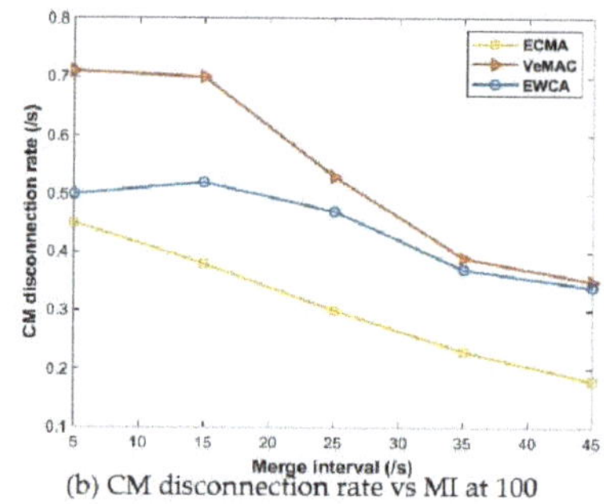

(b) CM disconnection rate vs MI at 100 vehicles.

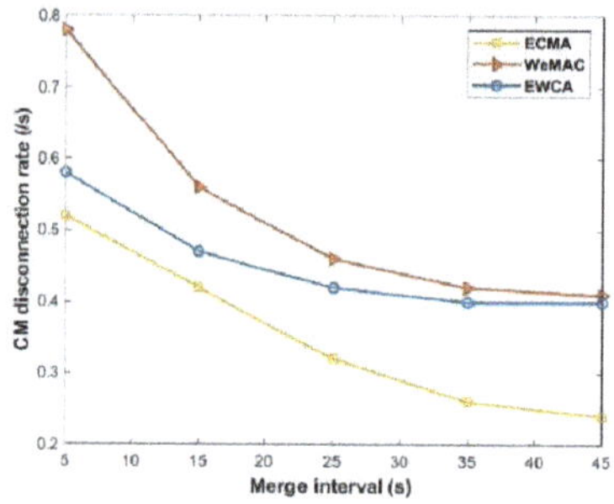

(c) CM disconnection rate vs MI at 150 vehicles.

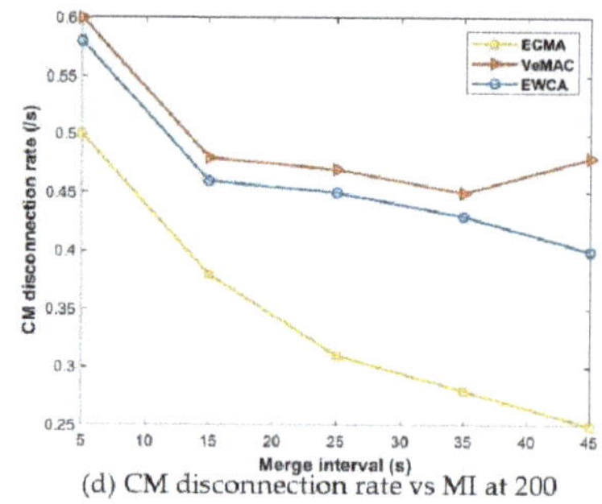

(d) CM disconnection rate vs MI at 200 vehicles.

Figure 8. CM disconnection frequency and it influence on Mw.

Even if different cluster members are in the transmission range of each, the centralized network structure (one to all and all to one) using the weighted Markov chain model, where each cluster contains its total weight value, which serves as the cluster ID, significantly connects each CM to its CH. This technique effectively solves the hidden terminal problems, thus eliminating merging collisions. Figure 9 shows that ECMA outperforms VeMAC. Figure 10 demonstrates how the weight-based algorithm is used to achieve a quick transition during the merging process. The construction of a centralized cluster in a vehicle ad hoc network (VANET), where all nodes are one-hop nodes, and aperiodic MCH selection is based on the window period probability. In multi-channel access, the drift in transition dependent on the access mechanism preserves its unique time slot even as this set of nodes transitions from one state to the next. The ECMA protocol outperformed the VeMAC protocol in terms of the transfer speed, resulting in a shorter end-to-end delay. The CHs selects the best candidate to be the MCH in a combined cluster. The other CHs became CMs as their CMs within the transmission range released their time slots and received a new time slot from the new MCH. For a while, the CMs outside of the new CH's transmission range will stick to their previous CH, which has now switched to Gw Node, until all of the remaining CMs are within the MCH's transmission range, at which point the Gw is converted to CM. When comparing the ECMA and VeMAC in terms of successful access transmission probability during average velocity, the ECMA protocol in Figure 11 performs better.

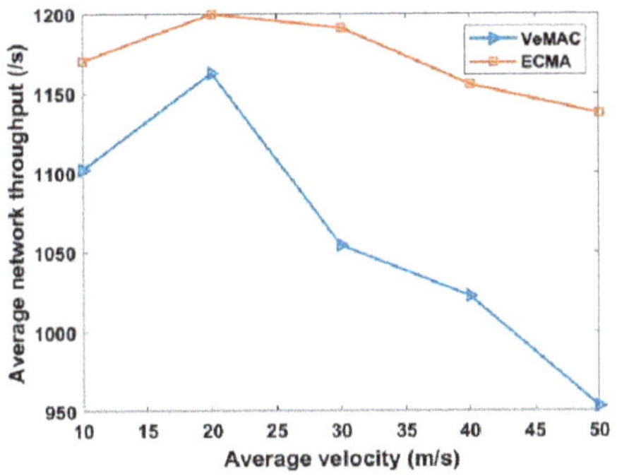

Figure 9. Average network throughput versus average velocity.

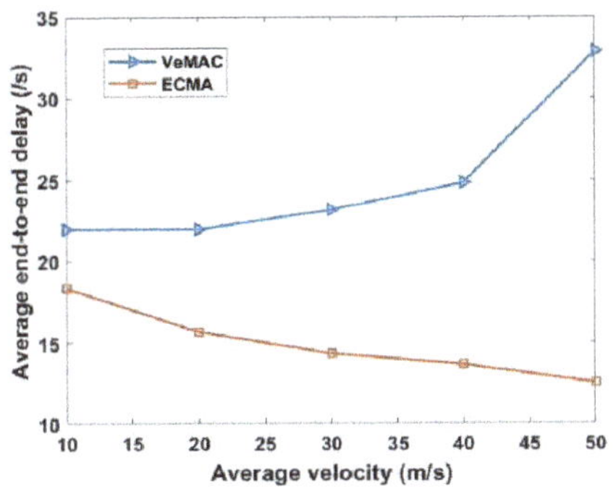

Figure 10. Average end-to-end delay versus average velocity.

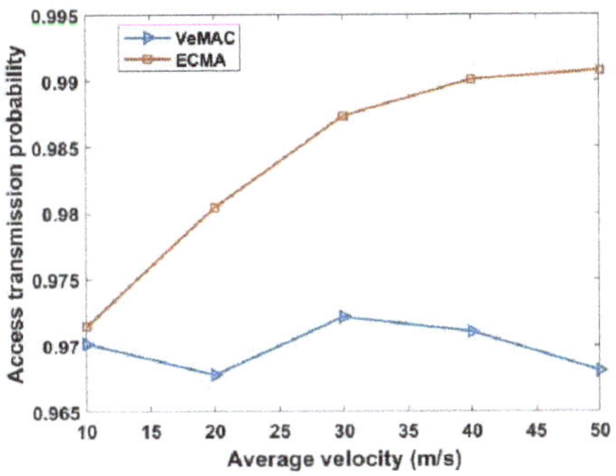

Figure 11. Successful access transmission probability versus average velocity.

6. Conclusions

In this study, we proposed an enhanced cluster-based multi-access channel protocol (ECMA) for high-throughput and effective access channel transmissions while minimizing access delay and avoiding collisions during cluster merging. We created a merge cluster head selection (MCHS) algorithm that eliminates merging collision and hidden terminal problems, as well as the selection of the best match MCH in the merged cluster when two or more clusters merge. When multiple sets of vehicles collide or when two or more clusters merge, MCHS algorithm resolves hidden terminal concerns and connects all CMs to their CH. The MCH elections and the new merged cluster are particularly resistant to merging collisions owing to the rapid transition from one state to the other. In high-speed merge, a weighted Markov chain model is used to describe the transformation operation within a cluster. The application of a weighted Markov chain model represents the transformation operation within a cluster and distinguishes it from other clusters based on the weighted value. In addition, the weighted Markov chain mathematical model enhances accuracy while decreasing ECMA channel data access transmission delay with unmatched transition speed in timeslot and state-slot during the clusters' merger window. These speeds up transitions while avoiding hidden terminal issues and merging collisions during the window period (T). Extensive simulation data were supplied to demonstrate the effectiveness of the proposed strategy. In summary, this work gives a detailed discussion of the basic ECMA protocol modeling and the MCHS algorithm, as well as a thorough analysis of their technology. The discussion concluded that cluster member disconnection frequency is minimal, as well as a longer cluster head lifetime and a positive influence on merge window. Therefore, when ECMA is compared to EWCA and VeMAC, the weighted MCHS algorithm and weighted Markov chain yields a distinct output in terms of average network throughput, end-to-end delay, and efficient access transmission probability by 64.20%–69.49%, avoiding HTP and eliminating merging collisions. In the future, the proposed MCHS algorithm will be assessed in traffic scenarios involving vehicles driving in opposite directions with heterogeneous radio access in order to facilitate information transmission between cluster heads.

Author Contributions: Conceptualization, S.E., I.F.B.I. and M.M.B.M.; methodology, S.E. and I.F.B.I.; software, S.E.; validation, S.E. and I.F.B.I.; formal analysis, S.E. and I.F.B.I.; investigation, S.E., I.F.B.I. and M.M.B.M.; data curation, S.E.; writing—original draft preparation, S.E. and I.F.B.I.; writing—review and editing, S.E., I.F.B.I. and M.M.B.M.; visualization, S.E., I.F.B.I. and M.M.B.M.; supervision, I.F.B.I. and M.M.B.M. All authors have read and agreed to the published version of the manuscript.

Funding: This research was supported by the Ministry of Higher Education Malaysia (MOHE) and was conducted in collaboration with the Research Management Center (RMC), Universiti Teknologi Malaysia with Vote Number R.J130000.7851.5F029.

Institutional Review Board Statement: Not applicable.

Informed Consent Statement: Not applicable.

Data Availability Statement: Data available on request due to restrictions eg privacy or ethical.

Acknowledgments: The authors would like to thank Universiti Teknologi Malaysia (UTM), Ministry of Education (MOE) and Tertiary Education Trust Fund (tetfund) of Nigeria for their financial support in this research.

Conflicts of Interest: The authors declare no conflict of interest.

References

1. Quy, V.K.; Nam, V.H.; Linh, D.M.; Ban, N.T.; Han, N.D. Communication Solutions for Vehicle Ad-hoc Network in Smart Cities Environment: A Comprehensive Survey. *Wirel. Pers. Commun.* **2021**, *122*, 2791–2815. [CrossRef]
2. Mu, W.; Li, G.; Ma, Y.; Wang, R.; Li, Y.; Li, Z. Beacon-Based Hybrid Routing Protocol for Large-Scale Unmanned Vehicle Ad Hoc Network. *Electronics* **2021**, *10*, 3129. [CrossRef]
3. Aslam, A.; Almeida, L.; Santos, F. Using RA-TDMA to support concurrent collaborative applications in VANETs. In Proceedings of the IEEE EUROCON 2017—17th International Conference on Smart Technologies, Ohrid, Macedonia, 6–8 July 2017; pp. 896–901. [CrossRef]
4. Daknou, E.; Tabbane, N.; Thaalbi, M. A MAC Multi-channel Scheme Based on Learning-Automata for Clustered VANETs. In Proceedings of the 2018 IEEE 32nd International Conference on Advanced Information Networking and Applications (AINA), Krakow, Poland, 16–18 May 2018; Volume 2018, pp. 71–78. [CrossRef]
5. Latif, M.B.; Liu, F.; Liu, K. A TDMA-Based MAC Protocol for Mitigating Mobility-Caused Packet Collisions in Vehicular Ad Hoc Networks. *Sensors* **2022**, *22*, 643. [CrossRef] [PubMed]
6. Nguyen, V.; Hong, C.S. Efficient Access Time Slot for MAC Protocol Using TDMA and CSMA in VANET. 2016, pp. 927–929. Available online: http://bss.kyunghee.ac.kr/layouts/net/publications/data/KIISE2016/VanDung%20Nguyen.pdf (accessed on 10 March 2022).
7. Bang, J.-H.; Lee, J.-R. Collision Avoidance Method Using Vector-Based Mobility Model in TDMA-Based Vehicular Ad Hoc Networks. *Appl. Sci.* **2020**, *10*, 4181. [CrossRef]

8. Ding, H.; Li, C.; Bao, L.; Yang, Z.; Liu, L.; Liu, Q. Research on Multi-Level Priority Polling MAC Protocol in FPGA Tactical Data Chain. *IEEE Access* **2019**, *7*, 33506–33516. [CrossRef]
9. Rukaiya, R.; Farooq, M.U.; Khan, S.A.; Hussain, F.; Akhunzada, A. CFFD-MAC: A Hybrid MAC for Collision Free Full-Duplex Communication in Wireless Ad-Hoc Networks. *IEEE Access* **2021**, *9*, 35584–35598. [CrossRef]
10. Dissertation, A. Improving the Reliability and Efficiency of Data Transmission in Vehicular Ad-Hoc Network. Ph.D. Thesis, Faculty of the Graduate School, University of Minnesota, Minneapolis, MN, USA, 2015.
11. Hadded, M.; Muhlethaler, P.; Laouiti, A.; Saidane, L.A. A centralized TDMA based scheduling algorithm for real-time communications in vehicular ad hoc networks. In Proceedings of the 2016 24th International Conference on Software, Telecommunications and Computer Networks (SoftCOM), Split, Croatia, 22–24 September 2016; pp. 1–6. [CrossRef]
12. Hadded, M.; Muhlethaler, P.; Laouiti, A. TDMA Scheduling Strategies for Vehicular Ad Hoc Networks: From a Distributed to a Centralized Approach. In Proceedings of the 2018 26th International Conference on Software, Telecommunications and Computer Networks (SoftCOM), Split, Croatia, 13–15 September 2018; pp. 164–169. [CrossRef]
13. Almalag, M.S.; Olariu, S.; Weigle, M.C. TDMA cluster-based MAC for VANETs (TC-MAC). In Proceedings of the 2012 IEEE International Symposium on a World of Wireless, Mobile and Multimedia Networks (WoWMoM), San Francisco, CA, USA, 25–28 June 2012; pp. 1–6. [CrossRef]
14. Wang, M.; Chen, T.; Du, F.; Wang, J.; Yin, G.; Zhang, Y. Research on adaptive beacon message transmission power in VANETs. *J. Ambient. Intell. Humaniz. Comput.* **2020**, *13*, 1307–1319. [CrossRef]
15. Talib, M.S.; Hassan, A.; Abas, Z.A.; Abdul-hussian, A.; Ali, M.F. Clustering Based Affinity Propagation in VANETs: Taxonomy and Opportunity of Research. *Int. J. Recent Technol. Eng.* **2019**, *7*, 672–679.
16. Ye, M.; Guan, L.; Quddus, M. TDMP: Reliable Target Driven and Mobility Prediction based routing protocol in complex Vehicular Ad-hoc Network. *Veh. Commun.* **2021**, *31*, 100361. [CrossRef]
17. Tambawal, A.B.; Noor, R.; Salleh, R.; Chembe, C.; Oche, M. Enhanced weight-based clustering algorithm to provide reliable delivery for VANET safety applications. *PLoS ONE* **2019**, *14*, e0214664. [CrossRef]
18. Alsuhli, G.H.; Khattab, A.; Fahmy, Y.A. Double-Head Clustering for Resilient VANETs. *Wirel. Commun. Mob. Comput.* **2019**, *2019*, 1–17. [CrossRef]
19. Sheu, T.; Lin, Y. A Cluster-based TDMA System for Inter-Vehicle Communications. *J. Inf. Sci. Eng.* **2014**, *30*, 213–231.
20. Chiluveru, R.; Gupta, N.; Teles, A. Distribution of Safety Messages Using Mobility-Aware Multi-Hop Clustering in Vehicular Ad Hoc Network. *Future Internet* **2021**, *13*, 169. [CrossRef]
21. Wu, J.; Zhang, L.; Liu, Y. On the Design and Implementation of a Real-Time Testbed for Distributed TDMA-Based MAC Protocols in VANETs. *IEEE Access* **2021**, *9*, 122092–122106. [CrossRef]
22. Omar, H.A.; Zhuang, W.; Li, L. VeMAC: A TDMA-Based MAC Protocol for Reliable Broadcast in VANETs. *IEEE Trans. Mob. Comput.* **2012**, *12*, 1724–1736. [CrossRef]
23. Mammu, A.S.K.; Hernandez-Jayo, U.; Sainz, N. Direction aware cluster-based multi channel MAC protocol for vehicular ad hoc networks. In Proceedings of the 2015 IEEE 11th International Conference on Wireless and Mobile Computing, Networking and Communications (WiMob), Abu Dhabi, United Arab Emirates, 19–21 October 2015; pp. 549–556. [CrossRef]
24. Zeng, L.; Zhang, J.; Han, Q.; Ye, L.; He, Q.; Zhang, X.; Yang, T. A Bus-Oriented Mobile FCNs Infrastructure and Intra-Cluster BSM Transmission Mechanism. *IEEE Access* **2019**, *7*, 24308–24320. [CrossRef]
25. Huang, Z.; Xu, R.; Chu, C.; Wen, G. A Modified RR-ALOHA Protocol for Safety Message Broadcast in VANETs. *J. Phys. Conf. Ser.* **2020**, *1650*, 032005. [CrossRef]
26. Ren, M.; Zhang, J.; Khoukhi, L.; Labiod, H.; Veque, V. A study of the impact of merging schemes on cluster stability in VANETs. In Proceedings of the 2017 IEEE 28th Annual International Symposium on Personal, Indoor, and Mobile Radio Communications (PIMRC), Montreal, QC, Canada, 8–13 October 2017; Volume 2017, pp. 1–7. [CrossRef]
27. Zhang, Y.; Liu, K.; Liu, S.; Zhang, J.; Zhang, T.; Xu, Z.; Liu, F. A Clustering-Based Collision-Free Multichannel MAC Protocol for Vehicular Ad Hoc Networks. In Proceedings of the 2018 IEEE 88th Vehicular Technology Conference (VTC-Fall), Chicago, IL, USA, 27–30 August 2018; pp. 1–7. [CrossRef]
28. Lyu, F.; Zhu, H.; Zhou, H.; Qian, L.; Xu, W.; Li, M.; Shen, X. MoMAC: Mobility-Aware and Collision-Avoidance MAC for Safety Applications in VANETs. *IEEE Trans. Veh. Technol.* **2018**, *67*, 10590–10602. [CrossRef]
29. Jiang, X.; Du, D.H.C. PTMAC: A Prediction-Based TDMA MAC Protocol for Reducing Packet Collisions in VANET. *IEEE Trans. Veh. Technol.* **2016**, *65*, 9209–9223. [CrossRef]
30. Shafiq, Z.; Abbas, R.; Zafar, M.H.; Basheri, M. Analysis and Evaluation of Random Access Transmission for UAV-Assisted Vehicular-to-Infrastructure Communications. *IEEE Access* **2019**, *7*, 12427–12440. [CrossRef]
31. Hu, J.; Lyu, W.; Zhong, S.; Huang, J. Motion Prediction Based TDMA Protocol in VANETs. *Electronics* **2020**, *9*, 1792. [CrossRef]
32. Xie, J.; Li, C. Weight Clustering Based TDMA-MAC Scheme in VANET. *Automatika* **2016**, *57*, 252–260. [CrossRef]
33. Lin, Z.; Sun, Y.; Tang, Y.; Liu, Z. An efficient message broadcasting MAC protocol for VANETs. *Wirel. Netw.* **2020**, *26*, 6043–6057. [CrossRef]
34. Boucetta, S.I.; Johanyák, Z.C. Optimized Ad-hoc Multi-hop Broadcast Protocol for Emergency Message Dissemination in Vehicular Ad-hoc Networks. *Acta Polytech. Hung.* **2022**, *19*, 23–42. [CrossRef]
35. Song, C.; Tan, G.; Yu, C. An Efficient and QoS Supported Multichannel MAC Protocol for Vehicular Ad Hoc Networks. *Sensors* **2017**, *17*, 2293. [CrossRef]

36. Yao, Y.; Zhang, K.; Zhou, X. A Flexible Multi-Channel Coordination MAC Protocol for Vehicular Ad Hoc Networks. *IEEE Commun. Lett.* **2017**, *21*, 1305–1308. [CrossRef]
37. Nguyen, V.; Kim, O.T.T.; Pham, C.; Oo, T.Z.; Tran, N.H.; Hong, C.S.; Huh, E.-N. A Survey on Adaptive Multi-Channel MAC Protocols in VANETs Using Markov Models. *IEEE Access* **2018**, *6*, 16493–16514. [CrossRef]
38. Peng, Z.; Bao, C.; Zhao, Y.; Yi, H.; Xia, L.; Yu, H.; Shen, H.; Chen, F. Weighted Markov chains for forecasting and analysis in Incidence of infectious diseases in jiangsu Province, China. *J. Biomed. Res.* **2010**, *24*, 207–214. [CrossRef]

sensors

MDPI

Article

Genetic Algorithm and Greedy Strategy-Based Multi-Mission-Point Route Planning for Heavy-Duty Semi-Rigid Airship

Shaoxing Hu [1,*], Bingke Wang [1], Aiwu Zhang [2,3,*] and Yiming Deng [4]

1 School of Mechanical Engineering and Automation, Beihang University, Beijing 100191, China; 1920wangbk@buaa.edu.cn
2 Key Laboratory of 3D Information Acquisition and Application, Ministry of Education, Capital Normal University, Beijing 100048, China
3 Center for Geographic Environment Research and Education, Capital Normal University, Beijing 100048, China
4 Nondestructive Evaluation Laboratory, Department of Electrical and Computer Engineering of the College of Engineering, Michigan State University, East Lansing, MI 48824, USA; dengyimi@egr.msu.edu
* Correspondence: husx@buaa.edu.cn (S.H.); zhangaiwu@cnu.edu.cn (A.Z.)

Abstract: The large volume and windward area of the heavy-duty semi-rigid airship (HSA) result in a large turning radius when the HSA passes through every mission point. In this study, a multi-mission-point route planning method for HSA based on the genetic algorithm and greedy strategy is proposed to direct the HSA maneuver through every mission point along the optimal route. Firstly, according to the minimum flight speed and the maximum turning slope angle of the HSA during turning, the minimum turning radius of the HSA near each mission point is determined. Secondly, the genetic algorithm is used to determine the optimal flight sequence of the HSA from the take-off point through all the mission points to the landing point. Thirdly, based on the optimal flight sequence, the shortest route between every two adjacent mission points is obtained by using the route planning method based on the greedy strategy. By determining the optimal flight sequence and the shortest route, the optimal route for the HSA to pass through all mission points can be obtained. The experimental results show that the method proposed in this study can generate the optimal route with various conditions of the mission points using simulation studies. This method reduces the total voyage distance of the optimal route by 18.60% on average and improves the flight efficiency of the HSA.

Keywords: multi-mission-point; route planning; minimum turning radius; optimal flight sequence; shortest route

Citation: Hu, S.; Wang, B.; Zhang, A.; Deng, Y. Genetic Algorithm and Greedy Strategy-Based Multi-Mission-Point Route Planning for Heavy-Duty Semi-Rigid Airship. *Sensors* **2022**, *22*, 4954. https://doi.org/10.3390/s22134954

Academic Editors: Jaroslaw Pytka, Andrzej Łukaszewicz, Zbigniew Kulesza, Wojciech Giernacki and Andriy Holovatyy

Received: 20 April 2022
Accepted: 26 June 2022
Published: 30 June 2022

1. Introduction

The heavy-duty semi-rigid airship (HSA) is different from ordinary aerial photography unmanned airships as the HSA has a large volume and can carry a heavy load for a long voyage [1,2]. As a result, many HSAs have been widely used to perform observation, transportation, and other missions across multiple cities or regions [3–5], such as Germany Zeppelin NT airship [6], American ML866 airship [7], and China ASQ-HAA380 [8], to name a few. The HSAs are also different from airplanes due to their large volume and windward area, which result in a larger turning radius when performing flight missions. Therefore, in the HSA route planning, the shortest route between two mission points is not a straight line but a curve. How to obtain the optimal route so that HSAs can accurately pass through all mission points, e.g., cities or regions, in sequence with the shortest flight route identified to improve flight efficiency is critically important, however, multi-mission-point route planning remains challenging.

The multi-mission-point route planning problem of the HSA can actually be reduced to a traveling salesman problem (TSP) to solve [9], which is a famous combinatorial optimization problem. For HSA route planning, the problem can be specifically defined as finding the shortest loop that does not repeatedly pass through all target cities [10–12]. To the best knowledge of the authors, this problem has been extensively studied with numerous algorithms developed for solving TSP problems including the greedy algorithm; genetic algorithm [13–15]; simulated annealing algorithm [16,17]; ant colony algorithm [18,19]; and particle swarm optimization algorithm [20,21], etc. Lideng, P. and Xiaofeng, H. [22] proposed a simple heuristic greedy method to solve the traveling salesman problem by using the distance information between cities. Dengwu, M. and Wen, Y. [14] proposed an optimization method based on an adaptive pseudo-parallel genetic algorithm based on a basic genetic algorithm. The optimal flight route of the aircraft obtained by this method strictly passes through the starting point and the target point of the aircraft. X. Yue, W. Zhang [23] proposes a UAV route planning method based on the K-means algorithm and simulated annealing algorithm. The K-means algorithm is used to classify the target points, and the simulated annealing algorithm is used to draw the shortest route for all the target points that the UAV will take, and maximize the UAV cruise coverage. The algorithm improves the overall efficiency and cruise coverage of the UAV. X. Chen, Y. Dai [24] proposed an ant colony algorithm integrating the genetic algorithm to solve the path planning problem. The algorithm combines the advantages of ant colony algorithm and genetic algorithm and reduces the number of iterations of the optimal solution as well as the calculation time and cost. Based on the particle swarm optimization algorithm, Shu-Juan, T. and Ke, Z. [25] which improved the global search ability of route planning and obtained a more authoritative optimal route, this method solves the problem of single-machine path planning problem detection and multi-machine cooperation, and achieves good results. Although various algorithms have been proposed in the above literatures to solve the TSP in aircraft route planning through optimization algorithms or multi-algorithm fusion with success to some extent, it is worth noting that the influence of aircraft large turning radius on route planning was never considered.

Li, R. and Xu, H. [26] proposed a UAV path planning approach based on modified ant colony algorithm and DUBINS curve. The DUBINS curve is used to smooth the turning angle to obtain a shorter and smoother flight path and improve the operation efficiency of the UAV. Cheng, J. and Hu, X. [27] proposed an improved ant colony algorithm that can solve feasible paths and speed up the convergence speed. At the same time, the DUBINS curve is used to curve the solution path, so that the solution path can meet the requirements of the UAV flight curvature. Hansen, K.D. and Cour-Harbo, A.L. [28] proposed a variable radius trajectory generation and waypoint planning method based on DUBINS curve. This method proposes an improved genetic algorithm, which optimizes the continuous heading and target speed of the waypoints while optimizing the combined sequence. At the same time, the generation method of DUBINS curve with variable radius is introduced. The studies from the above literature use the DUBINS curve to solve the influence of the turning radius on the route when planning the route.

The DUBINS curve is the shortest path connecting two points under the constraints of curvature and tangent direction at the specified start and end points, and the target can only travel forward. Under the constraints, there will be multiple curves feasible, so the set of DUBINS curve D = {LSL, RSR, RSL, LSR, RLR, LRL}. The shortest route in the DUBINS curve set is the optimal solution [29,30]. However, the DUBINS curve has limitations, limiting the direction of the target and the direction of speed at the beginning and ending. Therefore, the optimal solution in the DUBINS curve set is only the optimal solution in the specific beginning and ending speed directions.

Table 1 summarizes the influence of whether the turning radius of the route planning algorithm proposed in the above studies was considered in route planning.

Table 1. Various route planning algorithms.

Ref	Proposed Method	Consider Turning Radius Effects
[22]	A simple heuristic greedy method	NO
[14]	An optimization method based on an adaptive pseudo parallel genetic algorithm	NO
[23]	Combined the K-means clustering algorithm and simulated annealing algorithm	NO
[24]	An ant colony algorithm integrating genetic algorithm	NO
[25]	Combined particle swarm optimization algorithm and genetic algorithm	NO
[26]	A UAV path planning approach based on modified Ant colony algorithm and DUBINS curve	YES
[27]	Mixed ant colony Algorithm Based on DUBINS Path	YES
[28]	A variable radius trajectory generation and waypoint planning method based on DUBINS curve.	YES

When planning the route of the HSA, using the naive global search algorithm solely to find the optimal route will increase the computational time significantly and make it infeasible. Therefore, to address the aforementioned challenges, a multi-mission-point route planning method for HSA based on the genetic algorithm and greedy strategy is proposed in this paper. Firstly, according to the minimum flight speed and the maximum turning slope angle of the HSA, the minimum turning radius of the HSA near each mission point is determined. Secondly, the global search ability of the genetic algorithm is used to determine the optimal flight sequence of the HSA from the take-off point through all the mission points back to the landing point. Thirdly, based on the optimal flight sequence, a route planning method based on the greedy strategy is proposed, which uses the greedy strategy to decompose the optimal route problem of all mission points into the local optimal route problem of every two adjacent mission points. Then, this method traverses the multi-mission points in the optimal flight sequence in turn to obtain the shortest route between every two adjacent mission points. Finally, the optimal route of the HSA from the take-off point, through all the mission points, and back to the landing point is obtained. Figure 1 shows the flow chart of the proposed method that gives a holistic overview of the route planning algorithm.

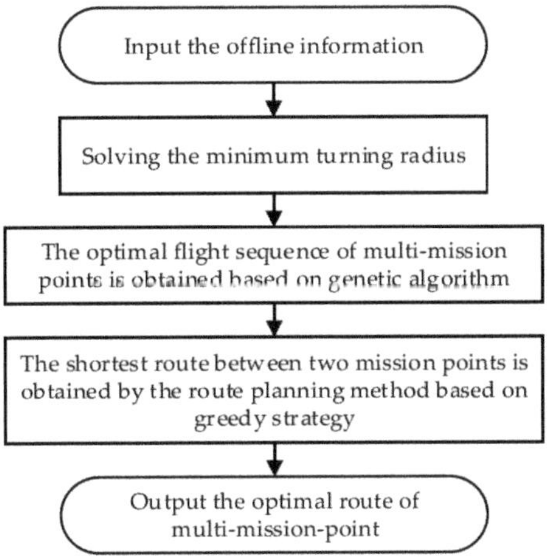

Figure 1. The overall flow chart of the route planning algorithm proposed. The input offline information includes HSA take-off and landing points and route mission points, the minimum flight speed, and the maximum turning slope angle of the HSA during turning.

The method proposed in this paper combines the global search ability of the genetic algorithm and the local optimal characteristics of the greedy strategy, which reduces the amount of calculation and improves the computing efficiency. At the same time, this method can accurately generate the optimal route and improve the flight efficiency. It can be seen from Table 1 that the route planning algorithms proposed in the literature [14,22–25] do not consider the influence of the turning radius, and the literature [26–28] proposed to use the DUBINS curve to solve the influence of the turning radius on the route. The DUBINS curve, however, has limitations, limiting the direction in which the target is heading and the speed direction at the beginning and ending. Therefore, the method proposed in this paper is compared with the multi-mission-point route planning method based on the DUBINS curve, and the results show that the total voyage of the optimal route obtained by the proposed method is reduced by 18.60% on average.

The rest of the paper is organized as follows: Section 2 introduces the multi-mission-point route planning method for the HSA. In Section 3, the experimental analysis is carried out. In Section 4, the findings are discussed. Finally, in Section 5, the conclusions are drawn.

2. Materials and Methods

In this section, the minimum turning radius of HSA is first introduced, and then the two stages of the method are introduced in detail. First, the optimal flight sequence of the multi-mission points is obtained based on the genetic algorithm. Second, the route planning method based on the greedy strategy obtains the shortest route between every two adjacent mission points in the optimal flight sequence.

2.1. Minimum Turning Radius

Since the HSA has a large volume and windward area, there is a large turning radius when passing through each mission point. Therefore, in the HSA route planning, the shortest route between two mission points is not a straight line but a curve. It is necessary to consider the influence of the turning radius on route planning. The turning radius of an airship [31,32] can be found by:

$$R = \frac{TAS^2}{g \times \tan\gamma} \tag{1}$$

$$TAS = IAS\sqrt{\frac{Pa}{Pa_0}} \tag{2}$$

where TAS is the vacuum velocity of the airship; IAS is the indicated airspeed of the airship; g is the local gravitational acceleration; γ is the slope angle when the airship turns; Pa is the current external air pressure value of the flight; Pa_0 is the standard sea level pressure value.

From Equation (1), it can see that the turning radius of the HSA is affected by the flight speed and the turning slope angle. The HSA has a fixed maximum turning slope angle during turning, so the smaller the flight speed of the HSA is during turning, the smaller the turning radius will be. Before route planning, according to the minimum flight speed $V_{\min}$ of the HSA and the maximum turning slope angle $\gamma_{\max}$ during turning, the minimum turning radius R of the HSA during turning can be obtained by Equations (1) and (2). Therefore, in the following route planning, the turning radius of the HSA passing through each mission point adopts the minimum turning radius R.

2.2. Genetic Algorithm Based Approach for Optimal Flight Sequence of Mission Points

After the HSA enters the working altitude, it will traverse all the selected mission points from the take-off point. References [9,33] simplified this problem as a traveling salesman problem, which aims to find a closed loop with the shortest distance in a series of nodes. As every route of the HSA starts from a fixed take-off point, the route planning problem for HSA can be described as a closed loop that traverses n mission points from the take-off point. In this way, the route distance of the HSA can be shortened, and the flight efficiency can be improved as well.

Among the various algorithms for solving the TSP problem, the genetic algorithm is an intelligent algorithm that searches for the optimal solution by simulating the natural evolution process. Furthermore, the genetic algorithm has the global search ability, which has a good effect on the TSP problem to quickly obtain better optimization results. It is worth noting from the above analysis that the influence of turning radius needs to be considered when HSA turns. In order to improve the flight efficiency of an airship, HSA adopts the minimum turning radius R. Therefore, before route planning, this paper investigated and demonstrated the global search ability of the genetic algorithm to obtain the optimal flight sequence of HSA passing through the multi-mission points. The specific steps of the proposed genetic algorithm are as follows:

1. Input the coordinates of take-off and landing point P_O and mission points P_i $(i = 1, 2, 3, \ldots, n)$, and the number of nodes $N = n + 1$;
2. Set the maximum genetic algebra, crossover probability, and mutation probability;
3. Calculate the distance $D_{ij}(i, j = 1, 2, 3, \ldots, N)$ between every two adjacent mission points;
4. Initialize the population and randomly generate multiple individuals starting from the take-off point;
5. Selection operation: calculate the fitness value of each individual in the population, and select the individual with a large fitness value as the new population to replace the original population;
6. Crossover operation: every two adjacent individuals in the population have a certain crossover probability. According to the single point crossover, the partial node sequences of the same length in the two adjacent individuals are cross exchanged to generate new individuals to replace the original individuals;
7. Mutation operation: each individual in the population has a certain mutation probability. The individual performs partial mutation, that is, two nodes in the node sequence are randomly selected and their sequence is exchanged;
8. Repeat steps 5–7 until the genetic algebra is the maximum genetic algebra, and output the individual with the maximum fitness in the evolutionary process;
9. According to the node sequence in the optimal solution individual, the coordinates of take-off and landing point, and mission points are output.

Note: the fitness value is the reciprocal of the total distance of the route.

2.3. Route Planning Method Based on the Greedy Strategy

The greedy strategy means that the agent always makes the best choice at present, in other words, the choice made by the greedy strategy is only a locally optimal solution in a certain sense. The main idea of the greedy strategy is to divide the problem into several sub-problems, solve each sub-problem to obtain the local optimal solution, and finally synthesize the local optimal solutions of all sub-problems into the optimal solution for the original problem.

From the above, the minimum turning radius during the HSA flight and the optimal flight sequence of the HSA passing through all multi-mission points can be obtained. Thus, the main goal of route planning becomes how to find an optimal route with the shortest distance and improve flight efficiency. Therefore, this paper proposes a route planning method based on the greedy strategy. This method adopts the idea of the greedy strategy to decompose the optimal route problem of all mission points into a local optimal route problem of every two adjacent mission points. The novel method reduces the computational complexity and improves the computational efficiency. Additionally, this method helps to traverse the multi-mission points in the optimal flight sequence in turn to determine the shortest route between every two adjacent mission points. Finally, the complete optimal route of the HSA from the take-off point to the landing point through all mission points can be obtained.

In order to simplify the problem and facilitate efficient calculation, this paper does not consider the direction of HSA at take-off and landing points, the following assumptions are proposed and met:

Assumption 1. *The HSA takes off along the positive semi-axis direction of the X axis of the global coordinate system of the input multi-mission points.*

Assumption 2. *The HSA can return to the landing point from any direction.*

Assumption 3. *The take-off and landing point of the HSA coincide with the same point.*

The detailed steps of the proposed route planning method are presented as follows:

1. Input the initial information, such as the coordinates of the multi-mission points of the optimal flight sequence of the HSA;
2. Translation transformation of the coordinate system, the translation of the global coordinate system of the input multi-mission points is transformed into the local coordinate system of the mission point P_{i+1}, and the parameter expression of the coordinates of the circle center O_{i+1} can be obtained;
3. Determine the coordinates of the circle center O_i' in the route P_iP_{i+1}, according to the coordinates of the circle center O_i in the route $P_{i-1}P_i$, the coordinates of the circle center O_i' can be determined;
4. Determine the shortest route of the route P_iP_{i+1}, the expression of the total voyage distance of the route P_iP_{i+1} is expressed by the coordinates of the circle center O_{i+1}, and the shortest route of the route P_iP_{i+1} is determined by changing the coordinates of the circle center O_{i+1};
5. Coordinate transformation of the shortest route, converting the shortest route from the local coordinate system back to the global coordinate system;

Note: Steps 2–5 could be repeated if necessary. When traversing back to the landing point of the HSA, the method will output the optimal route of the HSA from the take-off point through all the mission points back to the landing point.

The flow chart of this method is shown in Figure 2 with detailed algorithms described as follows:

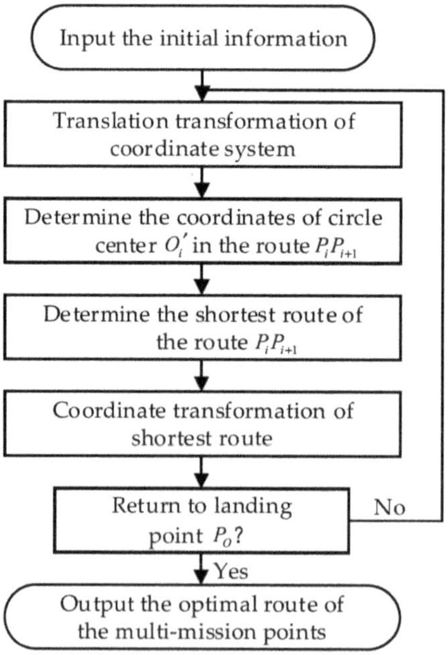

Figure 2. Flow chart of route planning method based on the greedy strategy. The initial input information includes the coordinates of the multi-mission points of the optimal flight sequence of the HAS and the coordinates of the circle center O_O of the take-off point P_O.

2.3.1. Input the Initial Information

From the above, the optimal flight sequence of the HSA from the take-off point, through all the mission points, and back to the landing point can be obtained by using the global search ability of the genetic algorithm. At the same time, according to Assumption 1, the HSA takes off along the positive semi-axis direction of the X axis of the global coordinate system OXY, so the coordinates of the circle center O_O of the take-off point P_O are set as $(x_{P_O}, y_{P_O} + R)$.

Therefore, the input initial information includes the coordinates of the multi-mission points of the optimal flight sequence of the HSA and the coordinates $(x_{P_O}, y_{P_O} + R)$ of the circle center O_O.

2.3.2. Translation Transformation of the Coordinate System

The input multi-mission-point coordinates are located in the global coordinate system OXY, in order to obtain the shortest route P_iP_{i+1} from the mission point P_i to the mission point P_{i+1} for convenience. The global coordinate system OXY is translated to the position where the origin coincides with the mission point P_{i+1}, so the local coordinate system $O'X'Y'$ of the mission point P_{i+1} is obtained. The translation transformation equation of the coordinate system is:

$$\begin{cases} x_i' = x_i - x_{P_{i+1}} \\ y_i' = y_i - y_{P_{i+1}} \end{cases} \tag{3}$$

where x_i', y_i' are the x-coordinate and y-coordinate of each point in the local coordinate system $O'X'Y'$; x_i, y_i are the x-coordinate and y-coordinate of each point in the global coordinate system OXY; $x_{P_{i+1}}, y_{P_{i+1}}$ are the x-coordinate and y-coordinate of the mission point P_{i+1} in the global coordinate system OXY.

The coordinates of the circle center O_{i+1} of the mission point P_{i+1} in local coordinate system $O'X'Y'$ are parameterized as follows:

$$\begin{cases} x_{O_{i+1}}' = R\cos\theta \\ y_{O_{i+1}}' = R\sin\theta \end{cases}, (\theta \in [0, 2\pi)) \tag{4}$$

where $x_{O_{i+1}}', y_{O_{i+1}}'$ are the x-coordinate and y-coordinate of the circle center O_{i+1} in the local coordinate system $O'X'Y'$; $\theta \in [0, 2\pi)$ is the angle parameter, where each parameter θ corresponds to a circle center O_{i+1} coordinate. Under different circle center O_{i+1} coordinates, the total voyage distance of the route P_iP_{i+1} will be different. Therefore, by changing the value of θ, when the total voyage distance of the satisfied route is the smallest, the corresponding route will be the shortest route.

2.3.3. Determine the Coordinates of the Circle Center O_i' in the Route P_iP_{i+1}

According to the shortest route $P_{i-1}P_i$ from the mission point P_{i-1} to the mission point P_i, the coordinates of the circle center O_i of the mission point P_i can be obtained. Then the mission point O_i, the mission point P_i, and the mission point P_{i+1} form a corner $\angle O_iP_iP_{i+1}$. The size of $\angle O_iP_iP_{i+1}$ can be divided into two cases: $\angle O_iP_iP_{i+1} \leq 90°$ and $\angle O_iP_iP_{i+1} > 90°$, which are discussed separately as follows:

Case 1: $\angle O_iP_iP_{i+1} \leq 90°$:

When $\angle O_iP_iP_{i+1} \leq 90°$, the circle center O_i' of the mission point P_i in the route P_iP_{i+1} coincides with the circle center O_i of the mission point P_i in the route $P_{i-1}P_i$, then the coordinates of the circle center O_i' are:

$$\begin{cases} x_{O_i'}' = x_{O_i}' \\ y_{O_i'}' = y_{O_i}' \end{cases} \tag{5}$$

where $x_{O_i'}', y_{O_i'}'$ are the x-coordinate and y-coordinate of the circle center O_i' in the local coordinate system $O'X'Y'$; x_{O_i}', y_{O_i}' are the x-coordinate and y-coordinate of the circle center O_i in the local coordinate system $O'X'Y'$.

Case 2: $\angle O_iP_iP_{i+1} > 90°$:

When $\angle O_iP_iP_{i+1} > 90°$, the circle center O_i' of the mission point P_i in the route P_iP_{i+1} and the circle center O_i of the mission point P_i in route $P_{i-1}P_i$ are symmetrical about the mission point P_i, then the coordinates of the circle center O_i' are:

$$\begin{cases} x_{O_i'}' = 2 \times x_{P_i}' - x_{O_i}' \\ y_{O_i'}' = 2 \times y_{P_i}' - y_{O_i}' \end{cases} \tag{6}$$

where $x_{O_i'}', y_{O_i'}'$ are the x-coordinate and y-coordinate of the mission point P_i in the local coordinate system $O'X'Y'$.

2.3.4. Determine the Shortest Route of the Route P_iP_{i+1}

The distance $D_{O_i'P_{i+1}}$ from the circle center O_i' to the mission point P_{i+1} is:

$$D_{O_i'P_{i+1}} = \sqrt{(x_{O_i'}' - x_{P_{i+1}}')^2 + (y_{O_i'}' - y_{P_{i+1}}')^2} \tag{7}$$

where $x_{P_{i+1}}', y_{P_{i+1}}'$ are the x-coordinate and y-coordinate of the mission point P_{i+1} in local coordinate system $O'X'Y'$.

Regarding the geometric relationship between the distance $D_{O_i'P_{i+1}}$ and the minimum turning radius R, there are three cases: $D_{O_i'P_{i+1}} > R$, $D_{O_i'P_{i+1}} < R$, and $D_{O_i'P_{i+1}} = R$, which are discussed separately as follows:

Case 1: $D_{O_i'P_{i+1}} > R$:

As shown in Figure 3, when the distance $D_{O_i'P_{i+1}}$ is greater than the minimum turning radius R, the route P_iP_{i+1} includes three parts: the arc route where the mission point P_i is located, the arc route where the mission point P_{i+1} is located, and the straight line in the middle. Among them, the arc route where the mission point P_i is located and the arc route where the mission point P_{i+1} is located are both inferior arcs.

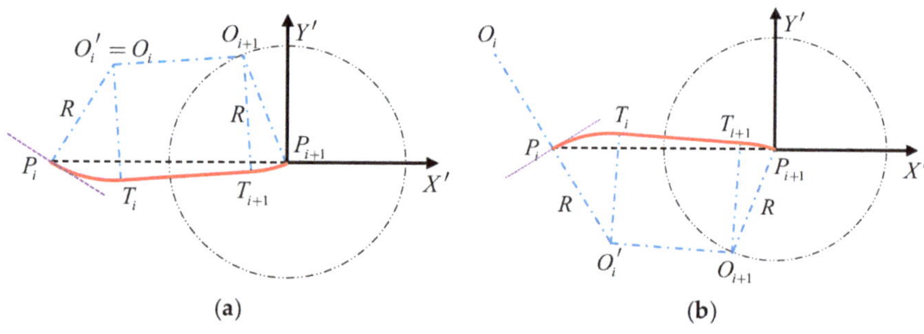

Figure 3. Schematic diagram of route planning when the distance $D_{O_i'P_{i+1}}$ is less than the minimum turning radius R. (**a**) is the schematic diagram of route planning at $\angle O_iP_iP_{i+1} \leq 90$, (**b**) is the schematic diagram of a route planning at $\angle O_iP_iP_{i+1} > 90$, the red line is the calculated shortest route.

By defining the tangent point between the arc route where the mission point P_i is located and the straight route as T_i; and defining the tangent point between the arc route where the mission point P_{i+1} is located and the straight route as T_{i+1}, it can be seen from Figure 3 that the geometric relationship $\angle P_iO_i'O_{i+1} = \angle P_iO_i'T_i + 90°$ is valid, so

$$\cos\left(\angle P_iO_i'T_i\right)^2 + \cos\left(\angle P_iO_i'O_{i+1}\right)^2 = 1 \tag{8}$$

which leads to

$$\left(\frac{O_i'P_i^2 + O_i'T_i^2 - T_iP_i^2}{2 \times O_i'P_i \times O_i'T_i}\right)^2 + \left(\frac{O_i'P_i^2 + O_i'O_{i+1}^2 - O_{i+1}P_i^2}{2 \times O_i'P_i \times O_i'O_{i+1}}\right)^2 = 1 \tag{9}$$

where $O_i'P_i$ and $O_i'T_i$ are equal to the minimum turning radius R; T_iP_i is the distance from the tangent point T_i to the mission point P_i; $O_i'O_{i+1}$ is the distance from the circle center O_{i+1} to the circle center O_i'; $O_{i+1}P_i$ is the distance from the circle center O_{i+1} to the mission point P_i.

The tangent point T_i is located on the circle with center O_i', so $O_i'T_i = R$, that is:

$$(x_{O_i}' - x_{T_i}')^2 + (y_{O_i}' - y_{T_i}')^2 = R^2 \tag{10}$$

As it can be seen from the above, $\angle O_i'P_iP_{i+1} \leq 90°$, and $\angle O_i'P_iP_{i+1} + \angle T_iP_iP_{i+1} \leq 90°$, so $\angle T_iP_iP_{i+1} \leq 90°$, that is:

$$\frac{T_iP_i^2 + P_iP_{i+1}^2 - T_iP_{i+1}^2}{2T_iP \times P_iP_{i+1}} \geq 0 \tag{11}$$

where P_iP_{i+1} is the distance from the mission point P_i to the mission point P_{i+1}; T_iP_{i+1} is the distance from the tangent point T_i to the mission point P_{i+1}.

It can be seen from Equations (9)–(11) that the coordinate (x_{T_i}', y_{T_i}') of the tangent point T_i can be obtained. Similarly, the coordinate $(x_{T_{i+1}}', y_{T_{i+1}}')$ of the tangent point T_{i+1} can also be obtained.

Therefore, the route P_iP_{i+1} includes arc route P_iT_i, straight route T_iT_{i+1} and arc route $T_{i+1}P_{i+1}$. The voyage distance of each part of the route is:

$$\begin{cases} l_1 = 2R \times a\sin\left(\frac{\sqrt{(x_{P_i}' - x_{T_i}')^2 + (y_{P_i}' - y_{T_i}')^2}}{2R}\right) \\ l_2 = \sqrt{(x_{T_i}' - x_{T_{i+1}}')^2 + (y_{T_i}' - y_{T_{i+1}}')^2} \\ l_3 = 2R \times a\sin\left(\frac{\sqrt{(x_{P_{i+1}}' - x_{T_{i+1}}')^2 + (y_{P_{i+1}}' - y_{T_{i+1}}')^2}}{2R}\right) \end{cases} \tag{12}$$

where l_1 is the distance of the arc route P_iT_i; l_2 is the distance of the straight route T_iT_{i+1}; l_3 is the distance of the arc route $T_{i+1}P_{i+1}$.

Then, the total voyage distance l of the route P_iP_{i+1} is:

$$l = l_1 + l_2 + l_3 \tag{13}$$

Change the value of parameter $\theta (0 \leq \theta < 2\pi)$. When θ satisfies that the total voyage distance l of the route P_iP_{i+1} at the minimum value, the corresponding route is the optimal route. At this time, the coordinates of the circle center O_{i+1} corresponding to the θ are:

$$\begin{cases} x_{O_{i+1}}' = R\cos\theta \\ y_{O_{i+1}}' = R\sin\theta \end{cases} \tag{14}$$

Case 2: $D_{O_i'P_{i+1}} < R$:

As shown in Figure 4, when the distance $D_{O_i'P_{i+1}}$ is less than the minimum turning radius R, the route P_iP_{i+1} includes three parts: the arc route where the mission point P_i is located, the arc route where the mission point P_{i+1} is located, and the straight line in the middle. Among them, the arc route where the mission point P_i is located is the inferior arc, and the arc route where the mission point P_{i+1} is located is the superior arc.

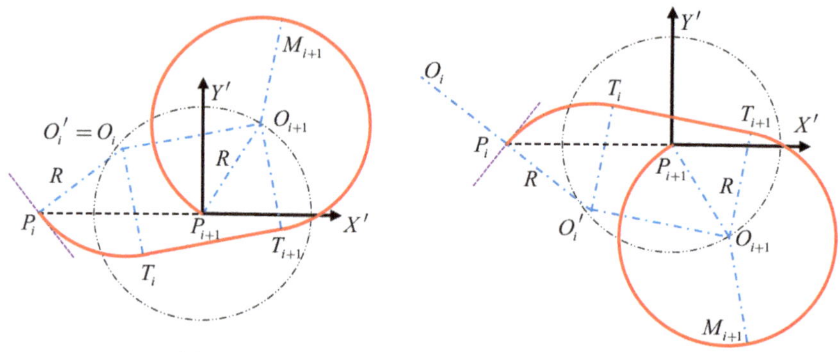

Figure 4. Schematic diagram of route planning when the distance $D_{O_i'P_{i+1}}$ is less than the minimum turning radius R. (**a**) is the schematic diagram of route planning at $\angle O_iP_iP_{i+1} \leq 90$, (**b**) is the schematic diagram of a route planning at $\angle O_iP_iP_{i+1} > 90$, the red line is the calculated shortest route.

Similarly, let the tangent point between the arc route where the mission point P_i is located and the straight route be T_i; let the tangent point between the arc route where the mission point P_{i+1} is located and the straight route be T_{i+1}.

It can be seen from Equations (9)–(11) that the coordinate (x_{T_i}', y_{T_i}') of the tangent point T_i and the coordinate $(x_{T_{i+1}}', y_{T_{i+1}}')$ of the tangent point T_{i+1} can be obtained.

Since the arc $T_{i+1}P_{i+1}$ is the superior arc, the arc $T_{i+1}P_{i+1}$ is equally divided into two sections, and the midpoint of the arc $T_{i+1}P_{i+1}$ is taken as M_{i+1}. According to the explicit method of locating the midpoint of the arc in the Cartesian plane mentioned in reference [34], the coordinates of the point M_{i+1} of the arc $T_{i+1}P_{i+1}$ can be obtained as $(x_{M_{i+1}}', y_{M_{i+1}}')$.

Therefore, the route P_iP_{i+1} includes: arc route P_iT_i, straight route T_iT_{i+1} arc route $T_{i+1}M_{i+1}$ and arc route $M_{i+1}P_{i+1}$. The voyage distance of each part of the route is:

$$\begin{cases} l_1 = 2R \times a\sin\left(\frac{\sqrt{(x_{P_i}'-x_{T_i}')^2+(y_{P_i}'-y_{T_i}')^2}}{2R}\right) \\ l_2 = \sqrt{(x_{T_i}' - x_{T_{i+1}}')^2 + (y_{T_i}' - y_{T_{i+1}}')^2} \\ l_4 = 2R \times a\sin\left(\frac{\sqrt{(x_{M_{i+1}}'-x_{T_{i+1}}')^2+(y_{M_{i+1}}'-y_{T_{i+1}}')^2}}{2R}\right) \\ l_5 = 2R \times a\sin\left(\frac{\sqrt{(x_{M_{i+1}}'-x_{P_{i+1}}')^2+(y_{M_{i+1}}'-y_{P_{i+1}}')^2}}{2R}\right) \end{cases} \quad (15)$$

where l_4 is the distance of the arc route $T_{i+1}M_{i+1}$; l_5 is the distance of the arc route $M_{i+1}P_{i+1}$.

Then, the total voyage distance l of the route P_iP_{i+1} is:

$$l = l_1 + l_2 + l_4 + l_5 \quad (16)$$

Similarly, change the value of parameter $\theta(0 \leq \theta < 2\pi)$. When θ satisfies that the total distance l of the route P_iP_{i+1} at the minimum value, the corresponding route is the optimal route. At this time, the coordinates of the circle center O_{i+1} corresponding to θ are shown in Equation (13).

Case 3: $D_{O_i'P_{i+1}} = R$:

As shown in Figure 5, when the distance $D_{O_i'P_{i+1}}$ is equal to the minimum turning radius R, the mission point P_i and the mission point P_{i+1} are located on the arc of the circle center O_i' at the same time. At this time, the route P_iP_{i+1} only includes the arc route P_iP_{i+1}.

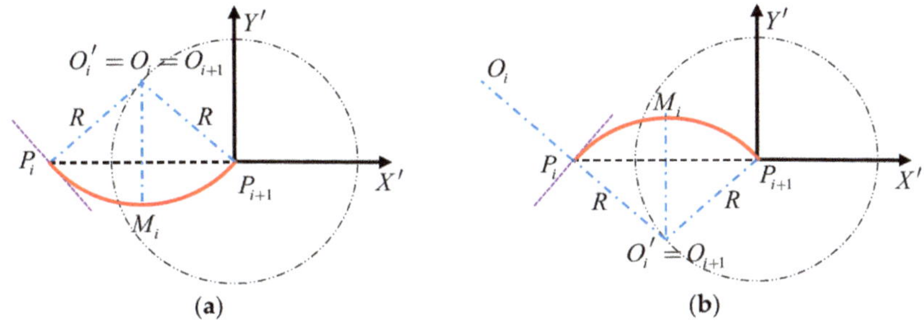

Figure 5. Schematic diagram of route planning when the distance $D_{O_i'P_{i+1}}$ is equal to the minimum turning radius R. (**a**) is the schematic diagram of route planning at $\angle O_iP_iP_{i+1} \leq 90$, (**b**) is the schematic diagram of a route planning at $\angle O_iP_iP_{i+1} > 90$, the red line is the calculated shortest route.

In order to prevent the arc P_iP_{i+1} from being the superior arc, the midpoint of the arc P_iP_{i+1} is taken as M_i. Then according to the explicit method of locating the midpoint of the arc in the Cartesian plane mentioned in reference [34], the coordinates of the midpoint M_i of the arc P_iP_{i+1} can be obtained as $(x_{M_i}{}', y_{M_i}{}')$.

Therefore, the route P_iP_{i+1} includes arc route P_iM_i and arc route M_iP_{i+1}. The voyage distance of each part of the route is:

$$\begin{cases} l_6 = 2R \times \arcsin\left(\frac{\sqrt{(x_{P_i}{}' - x_{M_i}{}')^2 + (y_{P_i}{}' - y_{M_i}{}')^2}}{2R}\right) \\ l_7 = 2R \times \arcsin\left(\frac{\sqrt{(x_{M_i}{}' - x_{P_{i+1}}{}')^2 + (y_{M_i}{}' - y_{P_{i+1}}{}')^2}}{2R}\right) \end{cases} \tag{17}$$

where l_6 is the distance of the arc route P_iM_i; l_7 is the distance of the arc route M_iP_{i+1}.

Then, the total voyage distance l of the route P_iP_{i+1} is:

$$l = l_6 + l_7 \tag{18}$$

At this time, the circle center O_{i+1} coincides with the circle center O_i', which coordinates are:

$$\begin{cases} x_{O_{i+1}}{}' = x_{O_i}{}' \\ y_{O_{i+1}}{}' = y_{O_i}{}' \end{cases} \tag{19}$$

2.3.5. Coordinate Transformation of the Shortest Route

The shortest route P_iP_{i+1} and the coordinates of the circle center O_{i+1} in the above process are all located in the local coordinate system $O'X'Y'$. In order to obtain the shortest route of the entire route, it necessary to convert back to the global coordinate system OXY. The translation transformation equation of the coordinate system is:

$$\begin{cases} x_i = x_i' + x_{P_{i+1}} \\ y_i = y_i' + y_{P_{i+1}} \end{cases} \tag{20}$$

Therefore, the shortest route P_iP_{i+1} and the coordinates of the circle center O_{i+1} in the global coordinate system OXY are obtained.

By repeating steps 2–5 of the proposed route planning method based on the greedy strategy, the method traverses the mission points in the optimal flight sequence in turn to obtain the shortest route between every two adjacent mission points, and outputs the optimal route of the HSA as shown in Figure 6.

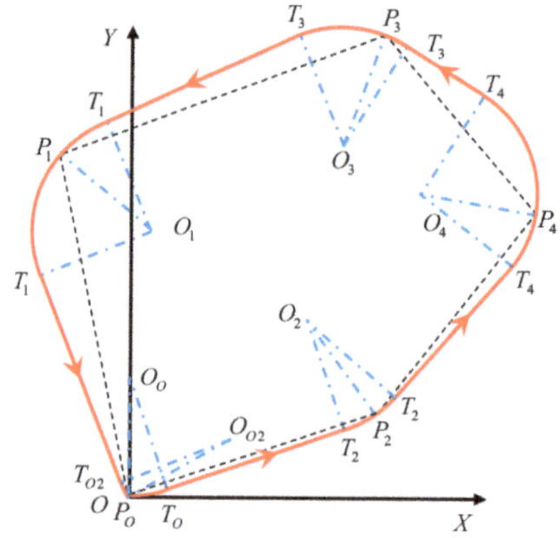

Figure 6. Schematic diagram of optimal route. P_O is the take-off and landing point of the HSA, P_1, P_2, P_3, P_4 are the input multi-mission points, $P_O \to P_2 \to P_4 \to P_3 \to P_1 \to P_O$ is the optimal flight sequence based on the genetic algorithm, and the red line is the optimal route obtained by the route planning method based on the greedy strategy.

3. Experimental Analysis

To validate the method proposed in this paper, this paper leveraged the simulation software of the plant protection UAV route planning developed by the authors [35] and further developed simulation software for the multi-mission-point route planning of the HSA. The software interface and layout are shown in Figure 7.

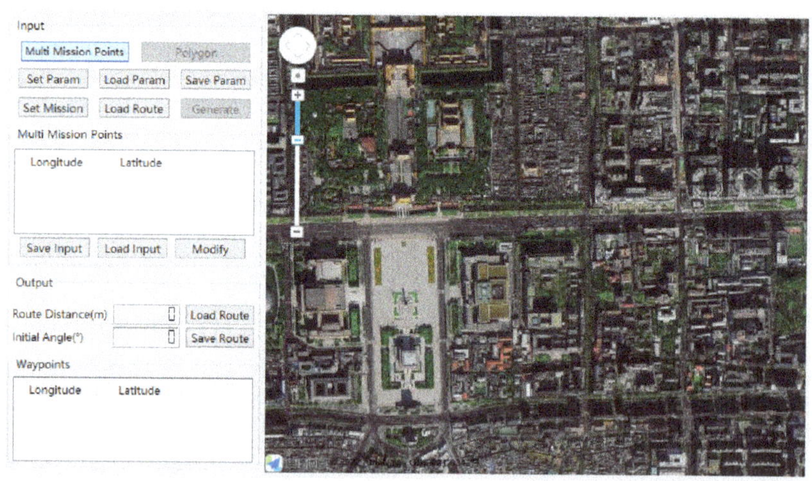

Figure 7. Layout of route planning simulation software developed for multi-mission-point route planning. After selecting the "Multi-Mission Points" mode, the user can click "Set Mission", then click on the map to set the coordinates of the multi-mission points, and finally click "Generate". And the optimal route will be displayed on the map.

In this paper, the simulation study and analysis adopted the Zeppelin NT airship as a representative HSA as shown in Figure 8, which is 75 m long and 20 m wide. During the simulation, the flight speed of the HSA is set as $V_{\min} = 100$ km/h and the maximum turning slope angle as $\gamma_{\max} = 20°$. Randomly selected multi-mission points are illustrated in Figure 9.

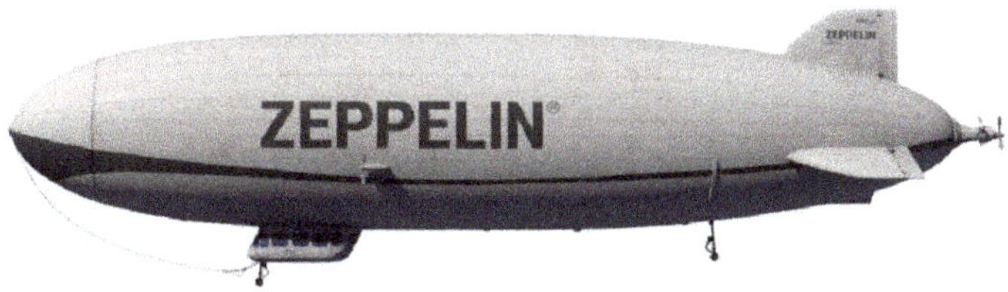

Figure 8. Representative HSA, Zeppelin NT airship adopted in the simulation study and validation.

Figure 9. The mission point selection diagram, where the unnumbered point represents the take-off and landing point, and the marked points numbered 1~9 represent the nine mission points selected in sequence.

Firstly, according to the minimum flight speed $V_{\min} = 100$ km/h and the maximum turning slope angle $\gamma_{\max} = 20°$ of the HSA when turning, by Equations (1) and (2), the minimum turning radius of the HSA can be obtained as:

$$R = \frac{{V_{\min}}^2}{g \times \tan \gamma_{\max}} = \frac{\frac{100}{3.6}^2}{9.8 \times \tan 20°} \approx 220 \text{ m} \quad (21)$$

Secondly, the optimal flight sequence of the multi-mission points is obtained based on genetic algorithm. First, enter the take-off point coordinates of the HSA, and the coordinates of the randomly selected mission points 1~9. Then, set the maximum evolutionary generation to 1000, the crossover probability to 0.9, and the mutation probability to 0.1. Finally, based on the genetic algorithm, the optimal flight sequence of mission points 1~9 is obtained as: $start \rightarrow 9 \rightarrow 7 \rightarrow 6 \rightarrow 4 \rightarrow 5 \rightarrow 8 \rightarrow 3 \rightarrow 2 \rightarrow 1 \rightarrow end$;

Then, according to the route planning method based on the greedy strategy proposed in this paper, the multi-mission points in the optimal flight sequence are traversed in turn, and the shortest route between every two adjacent mission points $start \rightarrow 9$, $9 \rightarrow 7$, $7 \rightarrow 6$, $6 \rightarrow 4$, $4 \rightarrow 5$, $5 \rightarrow 8$, $8 \rightarrow 3$, $3 \rightarrow 2$, $2 \rightarrow 1$, and $1 \rightarrow end$ are obtained. Among them, the route of mission points $2 \rightarrow 1$ belongs to the situation where the distance $D_{O_i'P_{i+1}}$ is greater than the minimum turning radius R in the above; the route of mission points $8 \rightarrow 3$ belongs to the situation where the distance $D_{O_i'P_{i+1}}$ is less than the minimum turning radius R in the above. Figure 10 is the partial enlarged view of the shortest route of mission points $8 \rightarrow 3$.

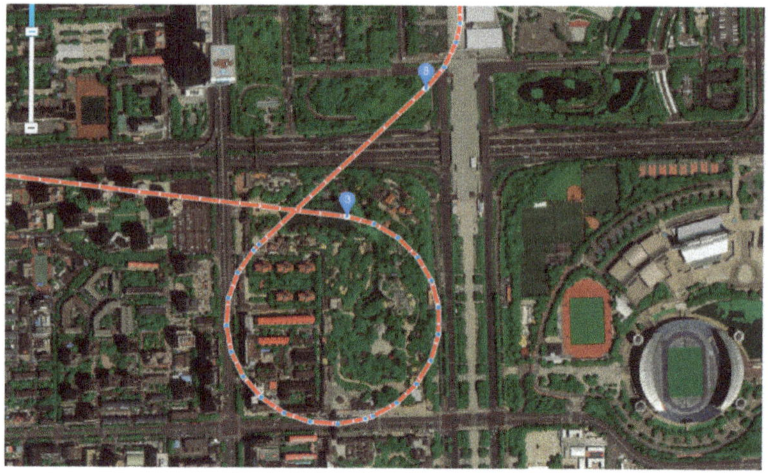

Figure 10. The partial enlarged view of the optimal route of mission points $8 \to 3$. The red line with arrows is the calculated best route, the marked points represent the mission point.

According to the route planning method based on the greedy strategy proposed in this paper, the shortest route of mission points $2 \to 1$ is solved. The specific steps are as follows:

First, the translation transformation of the coordinate system can obtain the parameter expression of the coordinates of the circle center O_1 of the mission point P_1. Second, according to the coordinates of the circle center O_2 of the mission point P_2 in the shortest route $3 \to 2$, the coordinates of the circle center $O_2{}'$ of the mission point P_2 in the route $2 \to 1$ can be determined. Then, the distance D_{21} from the mission point P_2 to the mission point P_1 is greater than the minimum turning radius R, so the expression of the total voyage distance of route $2 \to 1$ is as Equation (12). By changing the coordinates of the circle center O_1, the shortest route of the route can be determined. Finally, the relationship between the parameter θ and the route distance of the mission points $2 \to 1$ is shown in Figure 11a. When the parameter θ is 274°, the shortest distance of the route $2 \to 1$ is 1742.76 m. Similarly, the shortest route of mission points $8 \to 3$ is solved by the route planning method based on the greedy strategy proposed in this paper, and the relationship between the parameters θ and the route distance of the mission points $8 \to 3$ is shown in Figure 11b. When the parameter θ is 340°, the shortest distance of the route $8 \to 3$ is 1753.91 m.

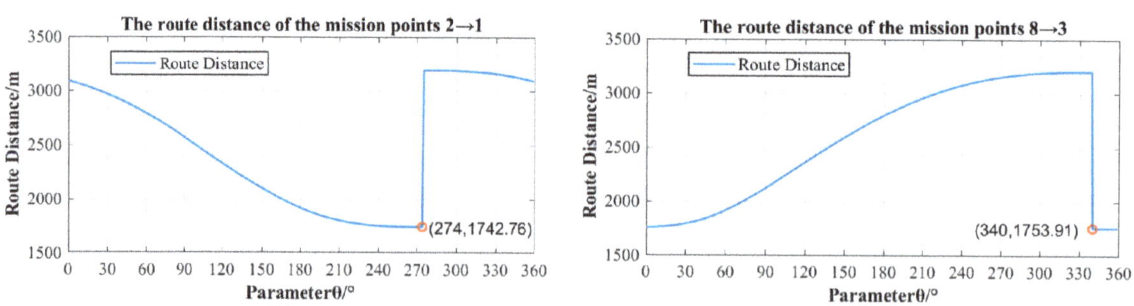

(**a**) (**b**)

Figure 11. Schematic diagram of the route distance of two adjacent mission points corresponding to different parameters θ. (**a**) the relationship between parameter θ and the route distance of the mission points $2 \to 1$, (**b**) the relationship between parameter θ and the route distance of the mission points $8 \to 3$.

Finally, the optimal route of the HSA from the take-off point, through all the mission points, and back to the landing point is obtained. The total voyage distance of the optimal route is 15,139.92 m, as shown in Figure 12.

Figure 12. Schematic diagram of the output result of the route planning software. The blue line with arrows is the calculated best route, and the red line is the route that the simulated airship has traveled. And the output shows that the total route distance of the optimal route is 15,139.92 m.

In the literature [26], the DUBINS curve is used to perform curve fitting on the solution path, and the influence of the turning radius on the route is solved, as shown in Table 1. The literature [29] proposed that the DUBINS curve has only six control combinations that describe all the shortest paths: LSL, RSR, RSL, LSR, RLR, and LRL, as shown in the Figure 13. Among them, the LSL control combination means that the HSA starts from the beginning point P_S, first turns left, then goes straight line, and finally turns left to reach the ending point P_E, as shown in Figure 13a.

The multi-mission-point route planning method based on DUBINS curve needs to determine the speed direction of the airship at the beginning and the ending when solving the shortest route between two mission points. Therefore, in the shortest route from the mission point P_i to the mission point P_{i+1}, the speed direction of the beginning point P_i can be determined by the shortest route from the mission point P_{i-1} to the mission point P_i. The speed direction of the ending point P_{i+1} points to the mission point P_{i+2}. The simulation results are shown in the Figure 14. Among them, the shortest route of the mission points $8 \to 3$ is the RSR in the six control combinations of the DUBINS curve. The shortest distance of route $8 \to 3$ is 1857.47 m. Compared with this method, the method proposed in this paper reduces the shortest distance by 5.58% in the route of mission points $8 \to 3$. At the same time, the total voyage distance of the optimal route is reduced by 18.77%, as shown in the route 1 in Table 2.

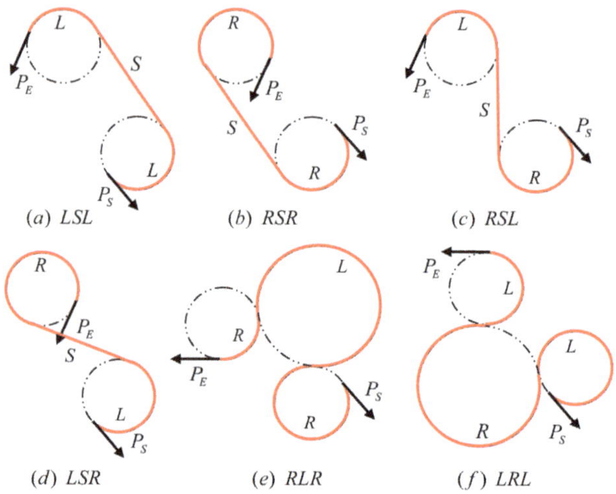

Figure 13. The main types of DUBINS path. P_S represents the beginning speed direction, P_E represents the ending speed direction,S represents the straight line, R represents the right turn, and L represents the left turn. (**a**) LSL means that the HSA starts from the beginning point P_S, first turns left, then goes straight line, and finally turns left to the ending point P_E. (**b**) RSR means that the HSA starts from the beginning point P_S, first turns right, then goes straight line, and finally turns right to the ending point P_E. (**c**) RSL means that the HSA starts from the beginning point P_S, first turns right, then goes straight line, and finally turns left to the ending point P_E. (**d**) LSR means that the HSA starts from the beginning point P_S, first turns left, then goes straight line, and finally turns right to the ending point P_E. (**e**) RLR means that the HSA starts from the beginning point P_S, first turns right, then turns left, and finally turns right to the ending point P_E. (**f**) LRL means that the HSA starts from the beginning point P_S, first turns left, then urns right, and finally turns left to the ending point P_E.

Figure 14. Schematic diagram of the simulation results of the multi-mission-point route planning method based on DUBINS curve. The red line with arrows is the calculated best route, and the blue line is the route that the simulated airship has traveled. And the output shows that the total route distance of the optimal route is 18,637.87 m.

Table 2. Comparison of simulation results of two route planning methods.

	The Number of Mission Points	Proposed Method	Based on DUBINS Curve	Optimization
Total voyage of route 1	9	15,139.92 m	18,637.87 m	18.77%
Total voyage of route 2	9	16,175.89 m	19,935.23 m	18.86%
Total voyage of route 3	9	13,350.61 m	16,446.26 m	18.82%
Total voyage of route 4	10	11,820.58 m	14,257.90 m	17.09%
Total voyage of route 5	24	42,841.27 m	53,194.56 m	19.46%
	Average Optimization			18.60%

In order to prevent the accidental occurrence of the mission points selected for route 1, this paper randomly selects five sets of route data for comparative experiments. The take-off and landing points of routes 1~5 are the same, and the minimum turning radius of the airship is also $R = 220$ m. The multi-mission points in the routes 1~5 are randomly selected, and the number of multi-mission points is shown in Table 2. The route planning method of multi-mission points based on DUBINS curve, and the multi-mission points route planning method proposed in this paper are used to plan the five sets of route data, respectively. The total voyages of the optimal routes of routes 1~5 are shown in Table 2. At the same time, the experimental results show that compared with the multi-mission-point route planning method based on DUBINS curve, the total voyage of the optimal routes of routes 1~5 obtained by the proposed method is reduced by 18.60% on average, as shown in Table 2.

From the simulation results, it can be seen that for various situations of multi-mission points, the multi-mission-point route planning method for HSA based on the genetic algorithm and greedy strategy proposed in this paper can generate the optimal route under the influence of turning radius. Furthermore, this method can ensure the accurate passing through multi-mission points and improve the flight efficiency of HSA. At the same time, the total voyage distance of the optimal route was reduced by 18.60% on average. The simulation results fully illustrate the feasibility of the route planning algorithm.

4. Discussion

Due to the large volume and large windward area of the HSA, there is a large turning radius when passing through each mission point. However, the route planning algorithms proposed in the literature [14,22–25] do not consider the influence of turning radius. The literature [26–28] proposed to use the DUBINS curve to solve the influence of the turning radius on the route, but the DUBINS curve has limitations, limiting the forward direction of the target and the speed direction at the beginning and ending. Therefore, the optimal solution in the DUBINS set is only the optimal solution in the specific beginning and ending speed directions. As such, this paper proposed a multi-mission-point route planning method for HSA based on genetic algorithm and greedy strategy. The method consists of the following two parts:

1. Optimal flight sequence: the global search ability of the genetic algorithm is used to determine the optimal flight sequence of the HSA from the take-off point through all the mission points back to the landing point.
2. Shortest flight route: a route planning method based on the greedy strategy is proposed, which uses the greedy strategy to decompose the optimal route problem of all mission points into the local optimal route problem of every two adjacent mission points. The shortest route between every two adjacent mission points can be obtained.

Through the optimal flight sequence and the shortest flight route, the optimal route of the HSA from the take-off point, through all the mission points, and back to the landing point is finally obtained. The advantages and characteristics of this method are as follows:

1. Under the influence of the large turning radius of the HSA, the optimal route can be generated quickly and accurately, and the flight efficiency of the HSA is greatly improved;
2. Combining the global search ability of genetic algorithm and the local optimal characteristics of the greedy strategy to improve overall computing efficiency;
3. This method has a broader range of applicability and can be applied to various complex mission situations between multiple mission points.

In the shortest flight route part, the method proposed in this paper can obtain the global shortest route between two adjacent mission points. The multi-mission-point route planning based on the DUBINS curve only obtains the local shortest route between two adjacent mission points in the case of a specific beginning and ending speed directions. Therefore, compared with the multi-mission-point route planning method based on DUBINS curve, the total voyage of the optimal route obtained by the proposed method is reduced by 18.60% on average.

However, there are still some remaining challenges and future work as this paper ignores problems such as the influence of environmental dynamics on the airship, especially the influence of wind, and the dynamic process of acceleration and deceleration and slope angle changes throughout the flight. The follow-up studies will take these into consideration. In addition to those identified limitations, this research lacks the evidence of flight experiments, which will be supplemented in the subsequent stage of research, where this proposed method is expected to be continuously improved with more adequate and realistic data.

5. Conclusions

In this study, a two-step approach considering the optimal flight sequence and the shortest route sequence is used to obtain the optimal route of the HSA from the take-off point, through all the mission points, and back to the landing point. The method proposed in this paper combines the advantages of the genetic algorithm and greedy strategy to enhance the adaptability of the algorithm and improve computational efficiency. The experimental results show that in view of the various conditions of the mission points, the method can generate the optimal route under the influence of turning radius, which greatly reduces the total voyage distance and improves the flight efficiency of the HSA. Compared with the multi-mission-point route planning method based on DUBINS curve, the total voyage of the optimal route obtained by the proposed method is reduced by 18.60% on average. At the same time, the feasibility and reliability of the route planning algorithm are demonstrated through experimental studies and simulation.

Author Contributions: Conceptualization, S.H. and A.Z.; methodology, B.W. and S.H.; software, B.W.; validation, S.H., B.W. and A.Z.; formal analysis, B.W. and S.H.; investigation, B.W. and S.H.; resources, S.H.; data curation, S.H.; writing—original draft preparation, B.W.; writing—review and editing, A.Z., B.W. and Y.D.; visualization, A.Z. and B.W.; supervision, S.H.; project administration, S.H. and A.Z.; funding acquisition, S.H. and A.Z. All authors have read and agreed to the published version of the manuscript.

Funding: This research was funded by the Science and Technology Program of Qinghai Province of China: 2022-NK-136; the National Science and Technology Basic Resources Survey Program of China: 2019FY101300.

Institutional Review Board Statement: Not applicable.

Informed Consent Statement: Not applicable.

Data Availability Statement: Data sharing not applicable.

Acknowledgments: The authors would like to thank the anonymous reviewers and the editor for their constructive comments and suggestions for this study.

Conflicts of Interest: The authors declare no conflict of interest. The funders had no role in the design of the study; in the collection, analyses or interpretation of data; in the writing of the manuscript or in the decision to publish the results.

References

1. Manikandan, M.; Pant, R.S. Research and advancements in hybrid airships—A review. *Prog. Aerosp. Sci.* **2021**, *127*, 100741. [CrossRef]
2. Hu, Y.; Wu, Z.; Zhang, D.; Cui, M. Random trajectory tracking for low altitude airship. In Proceedings of the 2019 Chinese Control And Decision Conference (CCDC), Nanchang, China, 3–5 June 2019; pp. 5380–5383.
3. Sarkar, S.; Gautam, V. Low Carbon Airship. In Proceedings of the AIAA Aviation 2019 Forum, Dallas, TX, USA, 17–21 June 2019. [CrossRef]
4. Nayler, A. Airship development world-wide—A 2001 review. In Proceedings of the 1st AIAA, Aircraft, Technology Integration, and Operations Forum, Los Angeles, CA, USA, 16–18 October 2001. [CrossRef]
5. Oebel, A.; Hofzumahaus, A.; Wahner, A.; Raak, D.; Broch, S.; Holland, F.; Rohrer, F.; Bohn, B. In-situ measurements of vertical profiles of chemical tracers in the PBL using the airship Zeppelin NT. In Proceedings of the ISARS 2010: International Symposium for the Advancement of Boundary Layer Remote Sensing, Paris, France, 28–30 June 2010.
6. Watanabe, H. Giant Rigid Airship and the Restoration Technique. In Proceedings of the 18th AIAA Lighter-Than-Air Systems Technology Conference, Seattle, WA, USA, 4–7 May 2009.
7. Metlen, T.; Palazotto, A.N.; Cranston, B. Economic optimization of cargo airships. *CEAS Aeronaut. J.* **2016**, *7*, 287–298. [CrossRef]
8. Hu, S.; Zhang, A.; Chai, S. ASQ-MPHAAS: Multi-Payload Observation System From High Altitude Airship. *IEEE Sens. J.* **2019**, *19*, 12353–12362. [CrossRef]
9. Hu, Z.; Xia, Q.; Cai, H. Random Searching Algorithms of Route Planning for High Altitude Airships. *Comput. Simul.* **2007**, *7*, 55–58.
10. Wang, Z.; Duan, H.; Zhang, X. An Improved Greedy Genetic Algorithm for Solving Travelling Salesman Problem. In Proceedings of the 2009 Fifth International Conference on Natural Computation, Tianjian, China, 14–16 August 2009; pp. 374–378.
11. Khalil, M.; Li, J.; Wang, Y.; Khan, A. Algorithm to solve travel salesman problem efficently. In Proceedings of the 2016 13th International Computer Conference on Wavelet Active Media Technology and Information Processing (ICCWAMTIP), Chengdu, China, 16–18 December 2016; pp. 123–126.
12. Liu, J.; Li, W. Greedy Permuting Method for Genetic Algorithm on Traveling Salesman Problem. In Proceedings of the 2018 8th International Conference on Electronics Information and Emergency Communication (ICEIEC), Beijing, China, 15–17 June 2018; pp. 47–51.
13. Han, Q.; Cao, W.; Cui, J. Research of Route Planning Based on Genetic Algorithm. In Proceedings of the 2012 International Conference on Computer Science and Electronics Engineering, Hangzhou, China, 23–25 March 2012; pp. 199–202.
14. Ma, D.; Ye, W.; Lv, X.; Jiang, W. Research on Airplane Route Planning Intelligent Decision System. In Proceedings of the 2006 6th World Congress on Intelligent Control and Automation, Dalian, China, 21–23 June 2006; pp. 6954–6958.
15. Li, L.; Gu, Q.; Liu, L. Research on Path Planning Algorithm for Multi-UAV Maritime Targets Search Based on Genetic Algorithm. In Proceedings of the 2020 IEEE International Conference on Information Technology, Big Data and Artificial Intelligence (ICIBA), Chongqing, China, 6–8 November 2020; pp. 840–843.
16. Ye, G.; Rui, X. An improved simulated annealing andgenetic algorithm for TSP. In Proceedings of the 2013 5th IEEE International Conference on Broadband Network & Multimedia Technology, Guilin, China, 17–19 November 2013; pp. 6–9.
17. Zheng, X.; Li, Z.; Li, M. Optimized Shortest Path Model for Air Patrol of Shanghai Expo 2010 by Applying Simulated Annealing Algorithm. In Proceedings of the 2011 Third Pacific-Asia Conference on Circuits, Communications and System (PACCS), Wuhan, China, 17–18 July 2011; pp. 1–2.
18. Ismkhan, H. Effective heuristics for ant colony optimization to handle large-scale problems. *Swarm Evol. Comput.* **2017**, *32*, 140–149. [CrossRef]
19. Chen, X.; Xu, R.; Zhao, J. Multi-Objective Route Planning for UAV. In Proceedings of the 2017 4th International Conference on Information Science and Control Engineering (ICISCE), Changsha, China, 21–23 July 2017; pp. 1023–1027.
20. Xin, J.; Zhong, J.; Li, S.; Sheng, J.; Cui, Y. Greedy Mechanism Based Particle Swarm Optimization for Path Planning Problem of an Unmanned Surface Vehicle. *Sensors* **2019**, *19*, 4620. [CrossRef] [PubMed]
21. Zhong, Y.; Lin, J.; Wang, L.; Zhang, H. Discrete comprehensive learning particle swarm optimization algorithm with Metropolis acceptance criterion for traveling salesman problem. *Swarm Evol. Comput.* **2018**, *42*, 77–88. [CrossRef]
22. Pan, L.; Huang, X. A heuristic greedy method for the traveling salesman problem. *J. Beijing Univ. Chem. Technol.* **1998**, *25*, 46–51.
23. Yue, X.; Zhang, W. UAV Path Planning Based on K-Means Algorithm and Simulated Annealing Algorithm. In Proceedings of the 2018 37th Chinese Control Conference (CCC), Wuhan, China, 25–27 July 2018; pp. 2290–2295.
24. Chen, X.; Dai, Y. Research on an Improved Ant Colony Algorithm Fusion with Genetic Algorithm for Route Planning. In Proceedings of the 2020 IEEE 4th Information Technology, Networking, Electronic and Automation Control Conference (ITNEC), Chongqing, China, 12–14 June 2020; pp. 1273–1278.

25. Tang, S.; Zhao, K.; Li, D.; Wang, N. Route Planning Algorithm of Region Important Target Search Based on PSO. In Proceedings of the 2018 IEEE 4th International Conference on Control Science and Systems Engineering (ICCSSE), Wuhan, China, 21–23 August 2018; pp. 545–548.
26. Li, R.; Xu, H.; Dong, J.; Yu, X. UAV path planning based on modified ant colony algorithm and DUBINS curves. In Proceedings of the 2022 IEEE 6th Information Technology and Mechatronics Engineering Conference (ITOEC), Chongqing, China, 4–6 March 2022; pp. 636–641.
27. Cheng, J.; Hu, X.; Xiao, J.; Zhang, G.; Zhou, Q. Route planning of mixed ant colony algorithm based on Dubins path. In Proceedings of the 2021 IEEE 16th Conference on Industrial Electronics and Applications (ICIEA), Chengdu, China, 1–4 August 2021; pp. 2070–2075.
28. Hansen, K.D.; Cour-Harbo, A.L. Waypoint planning with Dubins curves using genetic algorithms. In Proceedings of the 2016 European Control Conference (ECC), Aalborg, Denmark, 29 June–1 July 2016; pp. 2240–2246.
29. Dubins, L. On curves of Minimal lenght with a constraint on average curvature and with prescribed initial and terminal positions and tangents. *Amer. J. Math.* **1957**, *57*, 497–516. [CrossRef]
30. Song, X.; Hu, S. 2D path planning with dubins-path-based A algorithm for a fixed-wing UAV. In Proceedings of the 2017 3rd IEEE International Conference on Control Science and Systems Engineering (ICCSSE), Beijing, China, 17–19 August 2017; pp. 69–73.
31. Zhan, J.; Xie, W.; Guo, Q.; Zhang, P. An Improved UAV Coverage Search Route Planning Method. In Proceedings of the 2018 IEEE CSAA Guidance, Navigation and Control Conference (CGNCC), Xiamen, China, 10–12 August 2018; pp. 1–5.
32. Li, W.; Hu, Y.; Sun, S.; Li, J.; Chu, L. UAV turning path planning algorithm based on minimum turning radius. *Comput. Eng. Des.* **2019**, *40*, 2849–2854. [CrossRef]
33. Wu, L.; Li, Z. The Research of Route Planning for Stratospheric Airships Based on Genetic Algorithms. *Spacecr. Recovery Remote Sens.* **2011**, *32*, 1–6.
34. Akulov, G.V.; Akulov, O.G. A Lesson Plan with an Arc Midpoint. *J. Math. Sci. Collab. Explor.* **2013**, *13*, 219–224. [CrossRef]
35. Hu, S.; Xu, T.; Wang, B. Route-Planning Method for Plant Protection Rotor Drones in Convex Polygon Regions. *Sensors* **2021**, *21*, 2221. [CrossRef]

drones

MDPI

Article

Imagery Synthesis for Drone Celestial Navigation Simulation

Samuel Teague [1,*] and Javaan Chahl [1,2]

[1] School of Engineering, University of South Australia, Mawson Lakes, SA 5095, Australia
[2] Defence Science and Technology Group, Joint and Operations Analysis Division, Melbourne, VIC 3207, Australia
* Correspondence: samuel.teague@mymail.unisa.edu.au

Abstract: Simulation plays a critical role in the development of UAV navigation systems. In the context of celestial navigation, the ability to simulate celestial imagery is particularly important, due to the logistical and legal constraints of conducting UAV flight trials after dusk. We present a method for simulating night-sky star field imagery captured from a rigidly mounted 'strapdown' UAV camera system, with reference to a single static reference image captured on the ground. Using fast attitude updates and spherical linear interpolation, images are superimposed to produce a finite-exposure image that accurately captures motion blur due to aircraft actuation and aerodynamic turbulence. The simulation images are validated against a real data set, showing similarity in both star trail path and magnitude. The outcomes of this work provide a simulation test environment for the development of celestial navigation algorithms.

Keywords: celestial; stellar; simulation; strapdown; imagery

Citation: Teague, S.; Chahl, J. Imagery Synthesis for Drone Celestial Navigation Simulation. *Drones* **2022**, *6*, 207. https://doi.org/10.3390/drones6080207

Academic Editors: Andrzej Łukaszewicz, Wojciech Giernacki, Zbigniew Kulesza, Jaroslaw Pytka and Andriy Holovatyy

Received: 19 July 2022
Accepted: 11 August 2022
Published: 15 August 2022

1. Introduction

Celestial navigation in uncrewed aerial vehicles (UAV) has been a topic of interest for over half a century (see, for example, [1]). The significance of this mode of navigation has been overshadowed, however, by the ubiquity of global navigation satellite systems and the integration of compact micro-electromechanical attitude sensors into aviation platforms. Nonetheless, celestial navigation has unique advantages due to its independence from critical infrastructure and robustness to external interference. We see recent works, such as [2,3] integrating celestial imaging into their navigation solutions. Modern UAVs must typically conform to size, weight and power constraints and, to this end, benefit from a strapdown celestial implementation, as opposed to an actively stabilized alternative. In a strapdown configuration, the imaging sensor has no control authority over the vehicle, and therefore requires a larger field of view, and longer exposure intervals, to track stars during motion. We propose here a method for simulating the imagery captured from such a strapdown celestial system.

Celestial imagery is commonly used in spacecraft to obtain a highly accurate attitude reference. This technique is less commonly used, however, in low altitude aircraft navigation. Aircraft are subjected to many sources of noise that spacecraft are not, such as light pollution, cloud cover, atmospheric diffraction, aerodynamic turbulence, engine vibration and control/actuation, which all impact the signal strength of a celestial image obtained from an aircraft. These effects are exacerbated by the need for long-exposure imagery when operating at low-altitude (less than 500 m). The standard approach to this problem is to use a stabilized viewing platform with a telescopic lens [1], which limits the aforementioned attenuation. Such an approach is costly and adds significant weight to an airframe. The design of this simulation has arisen from the desire for a low cost, low weight, "strapdown" [4] celestial navigation solution.

As with all avionic navigation solutions, simulation plays an important role in the system design and precedes the implementation. The intent of this work is to provide a means of simulating imagery from a camera with a wide-angle lens, rigidly mounted to a fixed wing airframe with no active stabilization. Preliminary testing indicated that despite the increased motion blur, longer exposure images are consistently able to capture stars at lower levels of illumination. Consequently, the need arises for a simulation that can replicate the effects of motion blur due to these longer exposure images. In addition, there is benefit to tuning the simulation based on a reference image captured from the ground. This provides a quick solution for users to encapsulate their camera sensor and lens characteristics in the simulation environment, without the logistical constraints of night flying.

The use of star field simulation is most commonly seen in star identification research and development [5]. In this field, simulation is used to obtain baseline performance metrics for newly designed algorithms. An example of star field simulation for this purpose can be seen in [6], in which, rather than rendering stars, their position and magnitude are generated directly, with the addition of Gaussian noise. Other works tend to follow a similar design, seen in [7,8]. These simulations are intended to replicate imagery captured from spacecraft, which is not typically affected by rotational motion, nor atmospheric attenuation. Recent work considers the effects of star smearing [9] and the effect this has on the observability of stars. This work leverages from the simulation concepts presented in [10], later followed by [11]. These studies assume the angular velocity of the camera to be constant; however, we can see in Section 3 that for aerial vehicles, this assumption is invalid. Advancements were made in [12], highlighting the importance of modeling in star sensor design and calibration. In each of these cases, testing was conducted using a turntable, and as indicated in [10], this approach is not capable of running in real-time due to the large number of integral calculations involved.

This work offers two significant contributions to this field of research. We present a simple and effective framework for the real-time simulation of long-exposure images from non-stabilized UAV-mounted hardware using spherical linear interpolation, and a method for calibrating the simulation based on a ground reference image. Concepts from this work may be extended to aid in simulation design for spacecraft in highly dynamic situations.

2. Simulation Architecture

The position of stars and planets in the sky are represented in the International Celestial Reference Frame (ICRF). The location of a celestial body is expressed in terms of right ascension, α, and declination, δ, as seen in Figure 1. Stars are assumed to be infinitely far away, lying on the celestial sphere. Consequently, translational motion has no effect on the apparent position of the stars.

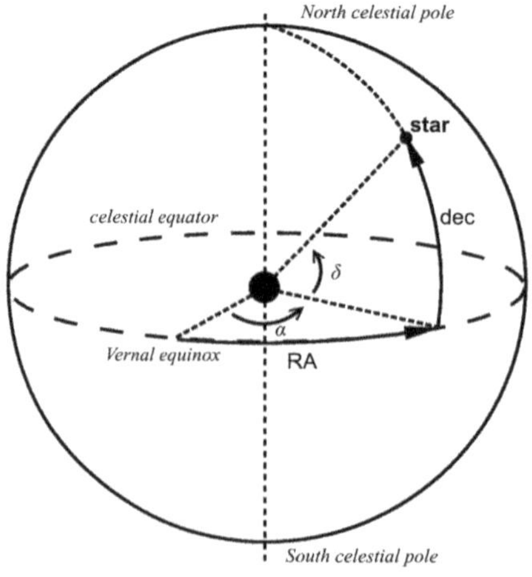

Figure 1. Celestial equatorial coordinate system.

The aircraft position is represented in the Earth-centred, Earth-fixed WGS84 system. This is the standard reference frame for GPS positional data. Aircraft attitude is represented in the local North-East-Down (NED) coordinate system. The camera is assumed to be mounted to the aircraft, sharing a location with the vehicle and differing in orientation by a single rotational transformation. The camera coordinate system is oriented with z positive in the optical axis, x positive towards the right of the image plane and y positive towards the bottom of the image plane.

A star catalogue must be used as a reference for the location of stars. While there are many star catalogues available, we selected the Yale Bright Star Catalogue (BSC) due to its minimal size. The BSC contains records of stars down to magnitude 6.5, totalling 9110 stars. This magnitude threshold is sufficient for most aircraft camera systems (including stabilized systems) [1]. For ease of implementation, the ASCII-format catalogue was converted into an SQLite database. Indices were created for magnitude, right ascension and declination, including additional composite indices to allow fast querying of the database.

This simulation initially corrects for celestial phenomena which perturb the right ascension and declination in the star catalogue, before entering a simulation loop. The simulation loop performs the following steps:

1. Update position, time and attitude of simulation;
2. Calculate star homogeneous coordinates in camera frame of reference;
3. Project each star onto the image plane;
4. Render the star.

2.1. Initial Corrections

On initialization, adjustments are made for the right ascension and declination of stars due to annual proper motion (the apparent motion of stars), precession (changes in the Earth's rotational axis over time), nutation (axial changes due to the Moon's gravitational pull) and aberration (due to the velocity of the Earth's orbit).

Proper motion is provided in star catalogues and is compensated by computing the change in right ascension and declination since the given epoch, such that:

$$\begin{aligned} \hat{\alpha} &= \alpha_0 + \dot{\alpha}T \\ \hat{\delta} &= \delta_0 + \dot{\delta}T \end{aligned} \tag{1}$$

where α_0 and δ_0 are the right ascension and declination at the epoch. $\dot{\alpha}$ and $\dot{\delta}$ are the annual proper motion, typically expressed in arcseconds per year, and T is the time (in years) since the epoch (J2000 in our case). Subsequently, right ascension and declination are corrected due to precession, following the method outlined in [13]. That is, we use the polynomial approximation for the precession angles ζ, z and γ:

$$\begin{aligned} \zeta &= 2306.2181t + 0.30188t^2 + 0.017998t^3 \\ z &= 2306.2181t + 1.09468t^2 + 0.018203t^3 \\ \gamma &= 2004.3109t - 0.42665t^2 - 0.041833t^3 \end{aligned} \tag{2}$$

where t is the number of centuries since the J2000 epoch. Right ascension α and declination δ are then found given:

$$\begin{aligned} \tan(\alpha - z) &= \frac{\sin(\hat{\alpha} + \zeta)}{\cos\gamma\ \cos(\hat{\alpha} + \zeta) - \sin\hat{\gamma}\ \tan\hat{\delta}} \\ \sin(\delta) &= \sin\gamma\ \cos\hat{\delta}\ \cos(\hat{\alpha} + \zeta) + \cos\gamma\ \sin\hat{\delta} \end{aligned} \tag{3}$$

Following [13], we correct for the effects of nutation. Nutation is comprised of nutation in longitude, $\Delta\lambda_n$, and nutation in obliquity, $\Delta\epsilon$. These quantities can be approximated to within 0.5 arcseconds by the following equations (expressed in arcseconds):

$$\Delta\lambda_n = -17.20 \sin\Omega + 1.32 \sin 2L - 0.23 \sin 2L' + 0.21 \sin 2\Omega \tag{4}$$

$$\Delta\epsilon = 9.2 \cos\Omega + 0.57 \cos 2L + 0.10 \cos 2L' - 0.09 \cos 2\Omega \tag{5}$$

where Ω, the longitude of the ascending node of the Moon's mean orbit on the ecliptic, expressed in degrees, is approximated as:

$$\Omega = 125.04452 - 1934.136261t \tag{6}$$

where t is expressed in Julian centuries, as above. L and L', the mean longitudes of the Sun and Moon, respectively, expressed in degrees, are given by:

$$\begin{aligned} L &= 280.4665 + 36000.7698t \\ L' &= 218.3165 + 481267.8813t \end{aligned} \tag{7}$$

The mean obliquity of the ecliptic can be found given the following equation, expressed in degrees:

$$\epsilon_0 = 23.439291 - 13.004166\, t \times 10^{-3} - 0.1639\, t^2 \times 10^{-6} + 0.50361\, t^3 \times 10^{-6} \tag{8}$$

Subsequently, the true obliquity of the ecliptic ϵ is given by:

$$\epsilon = \epsilon_0 + \Delta\epsilon \tag{9}$$

The resulting corrections due to nutation, $\Delta\alpha_n, \Delta\delta_n$ for the star's right ascension and declination, respectively, are given by:

$$\Delta\alpha_n = (\cos\epsilon + \sin\epsilon\ \sin\alpha\ \tan\delta)\Delta\lambda_n - (\cos\alpha\ \tan\delta)\Delta\epsilon \tag{10}$$

$$\Delta\delta_n = (\sin\epsilon\ \cos\alpha)\Delta\lambda_n + (\sin\alpha)\Delta\epsilon \tag{11}$$

We also consider the effects of aberration, as presented in [13]. Given the constant of aberration, $\kappa = 20.29552$ arcseconds, the true longitude of the Sun λ_s, eccentricity of the Earth's orbit e, and the longitude of the perihelion, ρ, we can compute the corrections $\Delta\alpha_a, \Delta\delta_a$ for the star's right ascension and declination with the following equations:

$$\Delta\alpha_a = -\kappa\left(\frac{\cos\alpha\ \cos\lambda_s\ \cos\epsilon + \sin\alpha\ \sin\lambda_s}{\cos\delta}\right) + e\kappa\left(\frac{\cos\alpha\ \cos\rho\ \cos\epsilon + \sin\alpha\ \sin\rho}{\cos\delta}\right) \tag{12}$$

$$\begin{aligned} \Delta\delta_a = &-\kappa\left[\cos\lambda_s\ \cos\epsilon(\tan\epsilon\ \cos\delta - \sin\alpha\ \sin\delta) + \cos\alpha\ \sin\delta\ \sin\lambda_s\right] \\ &+ e\kappa\left[\cos\rho\ \cos\epsilon(tan\epsilon\ \cos\delta\ - \sin\alpha\ \sin\delta) + \cos\alpha\ \sin\delta\ \sin\rho\right] \end{aligned} \tag{13}$$

where:

$$e = 16.708634 \times 10^{-3} - 42.037t \times 10^{-6} - 0.1267t^2 \times 10^{-6} \tag{14}$$

$$\rho = 102.9375 + 1.71946t + 0.46t^2 \times 10^{-3} \tag{15}$$

and the true longitude of the Sun is calculated as:

$$\lambda_s = L_0 + C \tag{16}$$

where the mean longitude of the Sun, L_0, is given by:

$$L_0 = 280.46646 + 36000.76983t + 0.3032t^2 \times 10^{-3} \tag{17}$$

and the Sun's equation of the center, C, is given by:

$$C = \left[(1914.602 - 4.817t - 0.014t^2)\sin M + (19.993 - 0.101t)\sin 2M + 0.289\sin 3M\right] \times 10^{-3} \quad (18)$$

and the mean anomaly of the Sun, M, is given by:

$$M = 357.52911 + 35999.05029t - 0.1537t^2 \times 10^{-3} \quad (19)$$

The correction terms, $\Delta\alpha_a$, $\Delta\delta_a$, $\Delta\alpha_n$ and $\Delta\delta_n$ are added to α and δ, yielding the corrected celestial coordinates of the star.

2.2. Updating Position and Time

Conversion from terrestrial time (as measured with the Gregorian calendar) to celestial time (typically expressed in Julian days) is a necessary step in simulating celestial bodies. The BSC represents the location of stars with respect to the J2000 epoch. The conversion from Gregorian date to Julian day is detailed in [13]. The basic steps are shown in Algorithm 1.

Algorithm 1 Conversion from Gregorian date to Julian day

```
let Y be the current year                                   ▷ Integer, Gregorian
let M be the current month                          ▷ Integer [1..12], Gregorian
let D be the current day                                    ▷ Decimal, Gregorian
if M ≤ 2 then
    Y = Y − 1
    M = M + 12
end if
let A = int(Y / 100)
let B = 2 − A + int(A / 4)
J = int(365.25(Y + 4716)) + int(30.6001(M + 1)) + D + B − 1524.5   ▷ Julian Days
```

This conversion expresses the current time with respect to the number of Julian days that have elapsed since 4716 BC. Furthermore, the J2000 epoch is expressed in relation to the Gregorian date 1 January 2000 and can be found by subtracting the Julian day at that time from the current Julian date:

$$J2000 = J_D - 2451545.0 \quad (20)$$

Sidereal local time, analogous to celestial longitude, can be calculated given WGS84 longitude and the current time of day expressed in decimal hours. Given longitude λ, Julian date J_D expressed in the J2000 epoch, and decimal hours H_D, the local sidereal time LST is given by [13]:

$$LST = 100.46 + (0.985647 J_D) + \lambda + 15 H_D \quad (21)$$

LST is typically limited to the range $[0, 360]$ degrees. The hour-angle ω of a celestial body can then be simply calculated from LST and right ascension α as:

$$\omega = LST - \alpha \quad (22)$$

The hour-angle of a body can be used to compute its azimuth and elevation, expressed in local NED coordinates. The local elevation θ of a celestial body given hour angle ω, declination δ and latitude ϕ is given by:

$$\theta = \mathrm{asin}(\sin\delta\ \sin\phi\ +\ \cos\delta\ \cos\phi\ \cos\omega) \tag{23}$$

Subsequently, using elevation from Equation (23), the local azimuth ψ is given by the following equation:

$$\psi = \mathrm{atan2}(\sin\omega\ ,\ \cos\omega\ \sin\phi\ -\tan\delta\ \cos\phi) + \pi \tag{24}$$

where the addition of π radians converts azimuth to a representation that is positive East of North [13].

The observed elevation of a celestial body is altered due to the effects of atmospheric refraction. Consequently, objects in the sky appear at a greater elevation than they would without the atmospheric effects. This effect is exaggerated at lower elevations (closer to the horizon), which leads to an angular displacement of up to 0.5°. For cameras in the visible light spectrum, the refractive distance R (expressed in arcminutes) can be approximated to within 4 arcseconds [14], given the following formula:

$$R = \frac{1.02}{\tan\left(\theta + \dfrac{10.3}{\theta + 5.11}\right)} \tag{25}$$

If a greater level of accuracy is required, alternative methods such as that seen in [15] can be used. The apparent elevation θ' is then given by:

$$\theta' = \theta + R \tag{26}$$

The inverse of this formula, Equation (27) [16], allows for the correction of observations:

$$R = \frac{1}{\tan\left(\theta' + \dfrac{7.31}{\theta' + 4.4}\right)} \tag{27}$$

Formulas (25) and (27) assume an atmospheric pressure of 1010 millibars, and an air temperature of 10 °C. According to [13], an approximate scale factor may be applied given pressure P at the Earth's surface, and air temperature T °C, given by the following formula:

$$\frac{P}{1010} \times \frac{283}{273 + T} \tag{28}$$

Finally, we map the celestial sphere onto a unit sphere for the purposes of image plane projection. Given the azimuth and elevation of a star, the corresponding unit vector in local NED coordinates is given by:

$$\begin{aligned} x &= \cos\psi \cos\theta' \\ y &= \sin\psi \cos\theta' \\ z &= -\sin\theta' \end{aligned} \tag{29}$$

For resource constrained systems, the rate at which these unit vectors are updated should be chosen relative to the precision required by the simulation. For reference, a geostationary camera with an update rate of 1 Hz will be accurate to within ±15 arcseconds (4.17×10^{-3} degrees). For an aircraft at a latitude of ±45 °, travelling East/West at mach 1, an update rate of 1Hz will be accurate to within ±30 arcseconds ($8.37° \times 10^{-3}$).

2.3. Updating Attitude

Representing celestial bodies in the local NED frame of reference simplifies the transformation from aircraft attitude to camera attitude. Aircraft attitude should come either directly from the onboard attitude reference or from a simulator. The work presented here uses the open source Ardupilot toolchain. Attitude log data collected from real flights were used for this research, so as to correlate real images with their simulated counterparts. The roll p_a, pitch q_a and yaw r_a Euler angles of the aircraft in local NED coordinates were logged at 30 Hz. These Euler angles can be represented as a rotation matrix, through a yaw–pitch–roll rotation sequence. The rotation matrix, $\boldsymbol{C}_{a/l}$, transforms objects in the local NED frame to the aircraft body frame, where $\boldsymbol{C}_{a/l}$ is given by:

$$\begin{bmatrix} \mathrm{c}(q_a)\mathrm{c}(r_a) & \mathrm{c}(q_a)\mathrm{s}(r_a) & -\mathrm{s}(q_a) \\ -\mathrm{c}(p_a)\mathrm{s}(r_a)+\mathrm{s}(p_a)\mathrm{s}(q_a)\mathrm{c}(r_a) & \mathrm{c}(p_a)\mathrm{c}(r_a)+\mathrm{s}(p_a)\mathrm{s}(q_a)\mathrm{s}(r_a) & \mathrm{s}(p_a)\mathrm{c}(q_a) \\ \mathrm{s}(p_a)\mathrm{s}(r_a)+\mathrm{c}(p_a)\mathrm{s}(q_a)\mathrm{c}(r_a) & -\mathrm{s}(p_a)\mathrm{c}(r_a)+\mathrm{c}(p_a)\mathrm{s}(q_a)\mathrm{s}(r_a) & \mathrm{c}(p_a)\mathrm{c}(q_a) \end{bmatrix} \tag{30}$$

where $\mathrm{c}(x)$ and $\mathrm{s}(x)$ represent $\cos x$ and $\sin x$, respectively. The camera is mounted to the aircraft, with roll p_c, pitch q_c and yaw r_c expressed in the aircraft body frame. The z axis of the camera is parallel to the optical axis, positive in the direction of the image plane. The y and x axes are orthogonal and directed towards the bottom and the right of the image plane, respectively. The rotation matrix, $\boldsymbol{C}_{c/a}$, transforms objects in the aircraft body frame to the camera frame, where $\boldsymbol{C}_{c/a}$ is given by:

$$\begin{bmatrix} \mathrm{c}(q_c)\mathrm{c}(r_c) & \mathrm{c}(q_c)\mathrm{s}(r_c) & -\mathrm{s}(q_c) \\ -\mathrm{c}(p_c)\mathrm{s}(r_c)+\mathrm{s}(p_c)\mathrm{s}(q_c)\mathrm{c}(r_c) & \mathrm{c}(p_c)\mathrm{c}(r_c)+\mathrm{s}(p_c)\mathrm{s}(q_c)\mathrm{s}(r_c) & \mathrm{s}(p_c)\mathrm{c}(q_c) \\ \mathrm{s}(p_c)\mathrm{s}(r_c)+\mathrm{c}(p_c)\mathrm{s}(q_c)\mathrm{c}(r_c) & -\mathrm{s}(p_c)\mathrm{c}(r_c)+\mathrm{c}(p_c)\mathrm{s}(q_c)\mathrm{s}(r_c) & \mathrm{c}(p_c)\mathrm{c}(q_c) \end{bmatrix} \tag{31}$$

Given rotation matrices $\boldsymbol{C}_{a/l}$ and $\boldsymbol{C}_{c/a}$, the transformation of a unit vector, $\boldsymbol{u}$, from the local NED frame to the camera frame, can be computed as:

$$\boldsymbol{u}^c = \boldsymbol{C}_{c/a}\boldsymbol{C}_{a/l}\boldsymbol{u} \tag{32}$$

Equation (32) allows the unit vectors of the celestial bodies computed in Section 2.2 to be represented in the camera frame of reference.

2.4. Projection

We assume that the camera intrinsic matrix, $\boldsymbol{K}$, is known. The intrinsic properties of a camera can be found through a calibration method such as that described in [17], yielding matrix:

$$\boldsymbol{K} = \begin{bmatrix} f_x & s & x_0 \\ 0 & f_y & y_0 \\ 0 & 0 & 1 \end{bmatrix} \tag{33}$$

where f_x and f_y are the x and y focal lengths in pixel units, x_0 and y_0 are the x and y pixel locations of the principal point, respectively, and s describes the sensor skewness (typically 0 for digital sensors).

We first convert each celestial body unit vector into homogeneous coordinates. For components x, y and z of unit vector $\boldsymbol{u}^c$, the homogeneous point $\boldsymbol{P}$ in the camera frame of reference is calculated as:

$$\boldsymbol{P} = \begin{bmatrix} \frac{x}{z} \\ \frac{y}{z} \\ 1 \end{bmatrix} \tag{34}$$

Objects whose depth value, z, is less than 0 are ignored due to being positioned behind the camera object. Finally, given no translational component to our camera, the pixel location, x, of the object is found as:

$$x = \boldsymbol{KP} \tag{35}$$

Lens distortion may also be included in the model. Lens distortion models are typically non-linear, and expressed as a function of displacement from the principal point. Various models exist for lens distortion, and should be chosen according to the level of precision required [18]. If using a lens distortion model, this should be applied after the star is rendered, so as to capture the resultant eccentricities from the distortion. We do not model lens distortion in our simulation; instead, we rectify all images prior to analysis, such that any residual distortion is negligible.

2.5. Calibration

The apparent pixel intensity of a star is determined by the apparent star magnitude, atmospheric conditions, lens properties and sensor properties. We present here a method which precludes the need for detailed modeling, through a single-image calibration process. We use a reference image captured from a stationary aircraft on the ground and fit an exponential curve to define the relationship between star magnitude and pixel intensity.

The relationship between observed brightness and apparent star magnitude is given by the equation:

$$m_x - m_r = -2.5 \log_{10}\left(\frac{B_x}{B_r}\right) \tag{36}$$

where m_x is the observed star magnitude, m_r is the reference star magnitude, B_x is the observed star brightness and B_r is the reference star brightness. This magnitude scale is designed such that a magnitude difference of -5 correlates with a brightness factor of 100. That is to say, a magnitude 1 star is 100 times brighter than a magnitude 6 star. For this work, we take the brightness of a star to be its maximum pixel value. Images are converted from the blue–green–red (BGR) colour space to the hue–saturation–value (HSV) colour space, and the value channel is used as a greyscale image.

By rearranging Equation (36) we can compute the brightness of an observed star, given that we have a reference brightness B_r, reference magnitude m_r and observed magnitude m_x:

$$B_x = B_r\, 10^{\frac{m_x - m_r}{2.5}} \tag{37}$$

The choice of reference star is an important factor, as the magnitude of stars are typically considered to be unreliable [19]. Many factors can cause the apparent magnitude of a star to differ from the catalogue, including spectral attenuation caused by the atmosphere, camera characteristics, atmospheric refraction, as well as the luminescent characteristics of the star itself. We assume that the magnitude error follows a zero-mean Gaussian distribution. Following this assumption, we select the star with magnitude and brightness that minimizes the Frobenius norm of the difference between observed and calculated brightness:

$$min\left([\sum_i abs(B_i' - B_i)^2]^{1/2}\right) \tag{38}$$

where B_i' is a vector containing all calculated star brightnesses, and B_i is a vector containing all measured star brightnesses. The vector B_i' is computed for each star in the reference image by choosing B_r and m_r from the reference star, and recomputing B_x for all stars in the image using Equation (37). Stars whose brightness is saturated (i.e., have a maximum pixel value of 255) are excluded from this process. Figure 2 shows the output from this calibration process, conducted on an image captured from a grounded aircraft, using a PiCamHQ with 500 ms exposure interval. We note that this procedure is most effective with a larger number of visible stars, such that the sample better represents the population.

In this example, stars were automatically detected and matched to the database using a star identification algorithm. As an alternative to this automated process, one could manually label each star in the reference image.

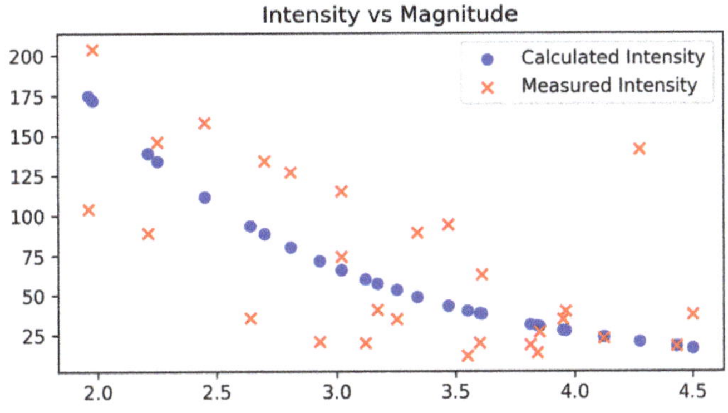

Figure 2. Calibration curve of image brightness using a PiCamHQ, 500 ms exposure time.

Stars are effectively point light sources. The camera lens will tend to defocus a star, such that it appears larger than one pixel. The apparent size of a star is affected by magnitude only to the extent that otherwise-undetectable pixels exceed the noise floor. Consequently, we can treat each star as having constant size, and changes to the star's brightness will yield a larger or smaller effective area. We assume that the pixel intensity of a star follows a two-dimensional Gaussian point spread function, with diagonal covariance matrix whose elements are equal. That is, a star image is circularly symmetric about its center. In practice, this may not be the case, and we note that such methods might be used for calibrating lens and sensor distortion (this is, however, out of scope for this work). Following this assumption, we measure the standard deviation across the x and y axes of each normalized star detection in the reference image and use the median value across all stars as the reference size for rendering in the simulation. We normalize by scaling the peak pixel value to 1. The standard deviation σ_B is calculated as:

$$\sigma_B = \frac{1}{n}\sum_{n}\text{std}\left(\mathbf{B}_n \odot \frac{1}{\max(\mathbf{B}_n)}\right) \tag{39}$$

where $\mathbf{B}_n$ is the histogram of intensities with respect to pixel position, std(x) is the standard deviation of sample set x, the symbol $\odot$ represents element-wise multiplication, and $\max(\mathbf{B}_n)$ is a scalar value equal to the maximum-valued element of $\mathbf{B}_n$.

A graph showing the standard deviation in pixel intensity vs. star magnitude can be seen in Figure 3, demonstrating the approximate uniformity of apparent projected star size across various magnitudes. Figure 4 shows an example of a Gaussian star render, reconstructed from the standard deviation and star brightness.

Simulation noise levels are calibrated from the reference image. Sources such as moonlight and atmospheric light pollution contribute to Gaussian noise observed in an image and consequently reduce the signal-to-noise ratio and observability of stars. The mean and standard deviation is measured in the value channel of the image. We ignore sections of the image in which stars have been detected so as to avoid bias introduced by the stars themselves. Thus, we have the noise function:

$$X \sim N(\mu, \sigma^2) \tag{40}$$

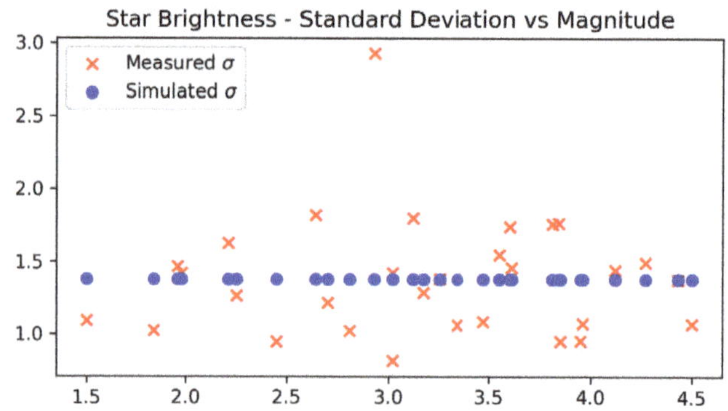

Figure 3. Calibration of standard deviation in star brightness using a PiCamHQ, 500 ms exposure time.

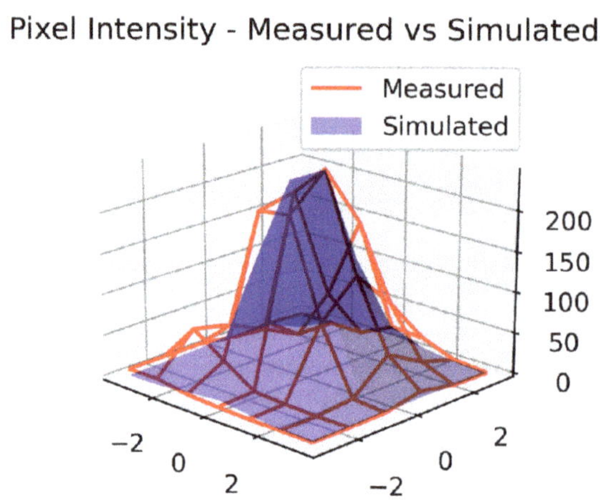

Figure 4. Pixel intensity of a measured star (red wireframe), with the simulated pixel intensity overlaid (blue solid).

2.6. Rendering

A long exposure image can be generated by superimposing multiple short-exposure images. Doing so requires a fast attitude update so as to reproduce the motion of the aircraft throughout the exposure period. The required temporal resolution is affected by the aircraft dynamics; however we found that a 5 ms (200 Hz) attitude update results in the contiguous rendering of stars for wide-angled lenses, even during aggressive maneuvers. A 200 Hz attitude measurement is not typically available on low-cost hardware, so we interpolate attitude measurements using the spherical linear interpolation algorithm described in [20] to achieve the desired rate. This method requires orientations to be represented as quaternions. The details are omitted here for brevity; however, most computer graphics libraries support this operation, transforming the direction cosine matrix in Equation (32) to quaternion format. We can retrieve any arbitrary orientation between two quaternions with the following equation:

$$\mathrm{Slerp}(q_1, q_2, u) = q_1(q_1^{-1}q_2)^u, \{u \in \mathbb{R} : 0 \leq u \leq 1\} \tag{41}$$

where Slerp is the spherical linear interpolation function; a value of $u = 0$ returns q_1, a value of $u = 1$ returns q_2 and intermediate values of u provide interpolation along the shortest path between q_1 and q_2 on the unit sphere. Interpolation is performed such that attitudes are captured at 5 ms intervals from the beginning of the camera exposure interval, to the end, yielding a total of $n = 200\Delta t$ attitude references, where Δt is the camera exposure time in seconds.

The long-exposure image is constructed by superimposing n floating point images. For each attitude a_i, the pixel location $\mathbf{x}$ of each star S_j in the database is found from Equation (35). A discrete Gaussian kernel, $\boldsymbol{G}$ is constructed using the standard deviation found in Equation (39). The kernel is programmatically generated (see [21]) such that the value G_i of element i is given by:

$$G_i = \alpha \exp\left(\frac{-(i - \frac{(k-1)}{2})^2}{(2\sigma^2)}\right), \{i \in \mathbb{Z} : 0 \leq i < k\} \tag{42}$$

where the kernel size $k = \lceil 6\sigma^2 \rceil$ is odd and is selected to contain a minimum of 99.7% of the total star energy, and α is selected such that $\sum_i G_i = 1$. The kernel is subsequently scaled, such that the maximum element at index $i = \frac{k-1}{2}$ is equal to the peak pixel value, B_x, calculated from Equation (37) using the magnitude m_x of star S_j, as well as the reference magnitude and intensities, m_r and B_r respectively. Finally, the kernel is scaled down by a factor of n. Assuming the photon flux density is constant across the exposure window, a single short-exposure window contains a fraction $\frac{1}{n}$ of the total star energy. This scaling of kernel G generated in Equation (42) is given by:

$$G_i = G_i\left(\frac{B_x}{n * G_{max}}\right), \{i \in \mathbb{Z} : 0 \leq i < k\} \tag{43}$$

Note that $\boldsymbol{G}$ is stored as a floating point array. The short-exposure star is drawn to the image canvas by centering the kernel $\boldsymbol{G}$ on pixel x and rotating 180° about the centre, adding the values of $\boldsymbol{G}$ to the canvas, so as to render the star symmetrically. This process is repeated for each star in the database S_j at the current attitude.

Once each of the short-exposure images have been rendered, the Gaussian noise defined in Equation (40) is added to the canvas. Finally, the image is converted from a single-channel floating point image to an 8-bit single-channel image. The resulting image contains stars rendered with the motion blur caused by camera movement throughout the exposure interval.

3. Results

We compare here the simulation output with images captured during a flight to evaluate the performance of the simulator. Attitude logs from the flight test were recovered, and used to generate these simulation images. We followed the procedure outlined in Section 2 for image generation. We used a Phantom FX-61 airframe (Figure 5), with a PixHawk v2 autopilot, a Raspberry Pi 4 companion computer for image capture and storage and a Raspberry Pi High Quality Camera sensor, mounted with the official 6mm wide-angle lens. The camera was rigidly mounted to the autopilot, so as to mechanically couple sources of vibration and deflection. An approximate transform from aircraft body frame to camera frame is used for this test, at a yaw angle of −90°, pitch angle of 90° and roll angle of 0° (given a yaw-pitch-roll Euler sequence).

A flight was conducted capturing images every 3 s, with an exposure interval of 500 ms and ISO set to 800. Ground images were captured prior to launching the aircraft. The aircraft climbed to an altitude of 150 m above ground level, and loitered for several minutes before landing. A total of 130 images were captured for analysis. Attitudes throughout each exposure window were recorded as image metadata at a rate of 30 Hz, and retrieved from the flash logs after the flight. A ground image was selected for performing the simulation calibration outlined in Section 2.5. Simulation images were subsequently generated using these calibration parameters.

Figure 5. Phantom FX-61 with camera mounted in fuselage.

A visual comparison of simulation output against in-flight images can be seen in Figures 6 and 7. By observation, we can see that the shape and trajectory of the simulated light trail closely matches reality. Figure 6 shows a cluster of stars, captured while the aircraft was yawing at a rate of 8° per s. The difference in star trail direction between stars is due to alignment of the yaw axis, approximately directed toward the centre of the image. Figure 7 pictures the brightest visible stars in the image, highlighting the effectiveness of the spherical linear interpolation, and its ability to reproduce trajectories with visual magnitude similar to what is observed in reality.

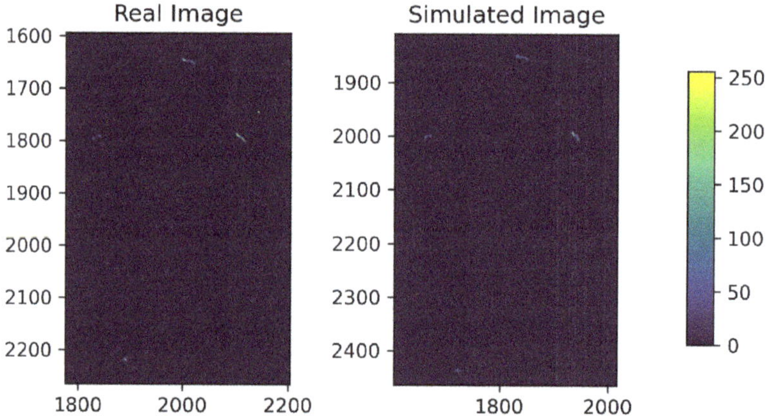

Figure 6. Lower magnitude stars captured in-flight (4× increased brightness for display purposes).

We evaluate the performance of the simulator based on its ability to replicate in-flight star intensities, given a ground calibration image. Figure 8 shows individual stars which were identified across multiple images in-flight. The intensity of the simulated star was plotted against the intensity of the observed star, such that points lying on the line $y = x$ represent a perfect match between reality and simulation. Three stars are shown here; these stars were identified frequently in both reality and simulation. We can see that, in practice, there tends to be error in the pixel intensity. The mean error is near-zero with a value of 3.38 pixels. The mean absolute percentage error in pixel intensity is measured at 47.4% (this is an average of per-star absolute percentage errors), which is similar to the mean absolute percentage error of 51% in the brightness ground calibration, as expected. Using Equation (36), a 47.4% error in star magnitude correlates to an absolute magnitude error of 0.42. This is within comparable range to the noise level simulated in other works, such as [7,8], which artificially add magnitude noise with standard deviation in the range of 0.3–0.9 to their simulation.

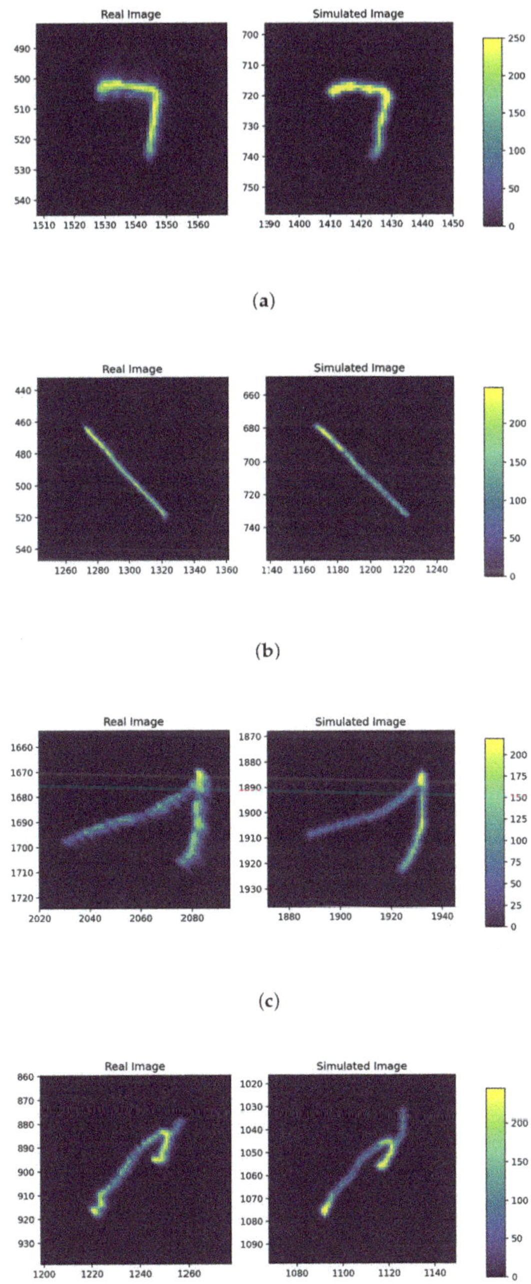

(d)

Figure 7. Close-up of bright stars captured in motion. Real images (left) are paired with their simulated counterpart (right). (**a**) Image captured during aerial manoeuvre; (**b**) Image captured during constant-rate turn; (**c**) Image captured with high pitch-rate; (**d**) Image captured during aerial manoeuvre.

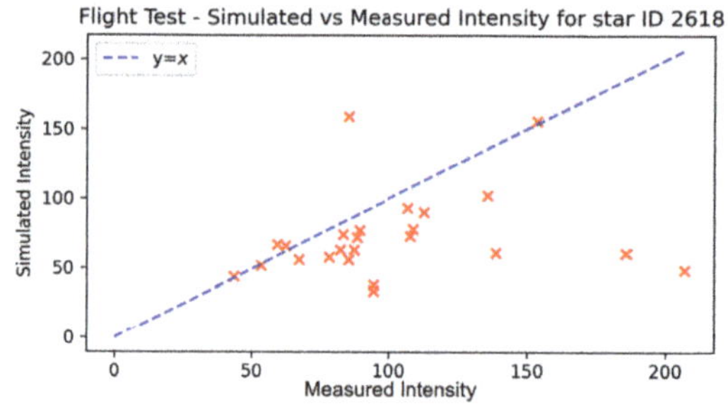

(a)

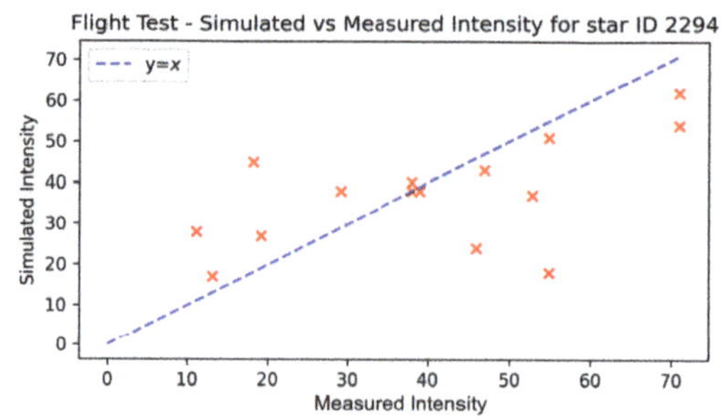

(b)

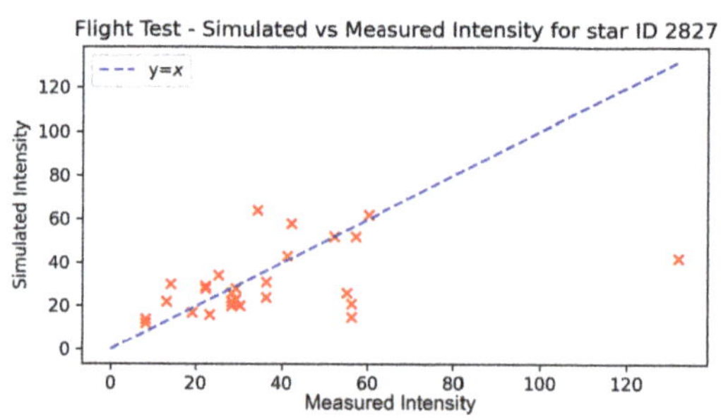

(c)

Figure 8. Individual stars over multiple images, comparing measured intensity to simulated intensity. Red crosses indicate the peak pixel intensity for a given observation. (**a**) Visual magnitude: 1.5, mean error: −23.6, mean percentage error: 37.5%; (**b**) Visual magnitude: 2.25, mean error: 12.2, mean percentage error: 82.3%; (**c**) Visual magnitude: 2.45, mean error: −6.3, mean percentage error: 38.0%.

Furthermore, we consider the difference between the centroids of stars detected in both simulation and reality. A region of interest (ROI), $\boldsymbol{R}$, is chosen for each star such that $\boldsymbol{R}$ is the smallest grayscale image that contains the star. We compute the weighted centre D_x, D_y for both real and simulated images, expressed with respect to the centre of the ROI:

$$\begin{bmatrix} D_x \\ D_y \end{bmatrix} = \begin{bmatrix} \frac{w}{2} \\ \frac{h}{2} \end{bmatrix} - \frac{1}{M} \sum_{x,y} R_{x,y} \begin{bmatrix} x \\ y \end{bmatrix} \tag{44}$$

$$M = \sum_{x,y} R_{x,y} \tag{45}$$

where w and h are the width and height of the region of interest, respectively, x and y are the column and row indices of image R and scalar $R_{x,y}$ is the pixel intensity of $\boldsymbol{R}$ at pixel (x, y).

We compute the L2 norm of the difference between simulation centroid and real centroid to find the distance L:

$$L = \sqrt{(D_x^s - D_x^r)^2 + (D_y^s - D_y^r)^2} \tag{46}$$

for simulation centroid D_x^s, D_y^s and real centroid D_x^r, D_y^r. A histogram containing the computed centroid errors can be seen in Figure 9. For reference, we also compute a baseline estimate, which assumes the centroid is located at the centre of the ROI (analagous to simulating stars as a straight line with uniform intensity). The mean simulation error is measured to be 0.92 pixels, with a median error of 0.68 pixels. By comparison, the mean baseline error is measured at 1.23 pixels, with a median error of 0.93 pixels. This corresponds to a 25.2% reduction in mean centroid error.

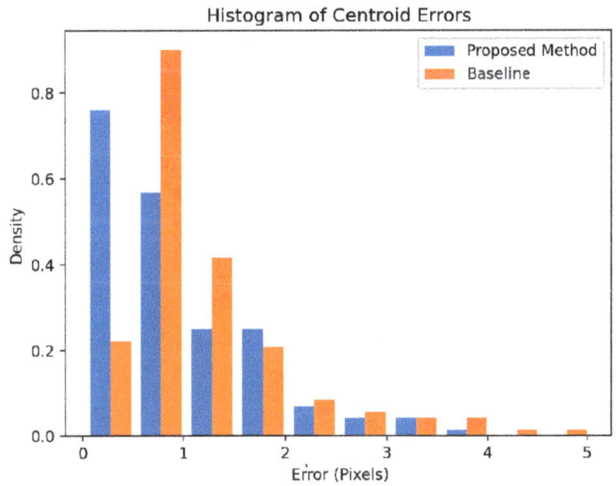

Figure 9. Histogram of absolute differences in star centroids between real and simulated images.

4. Discussion

The temporal correlation between the camera and attitude sensor, as well as the attitude sensor's accuracy and resolution, and individual differences between the database and observed star magnitudes, pose limitations to the accuracy with which simulation images can be generated. The tendency towards a low mean error, however, is an indication that there is little systematic error propagating from the simulation architecture, and that large sample sets will provide a statistically accurate representation of star intensity.

We can see in Figure 8 that despite a low mean error across the sample set, individual stars tend to be subjected to biases in intensity. Future work could make use of multiple ground images to map the intensity of individual stars, so as to reduce bias within individual stars. Furthermore, it is apparent that brighter stars will tend to be detected more frequently than dimmer stars. One may be able to determine an appropriate magnitude threshold for the observability of stars in-flight and bias the calibration towards the brighter stars, which are more likely to be detected.

We note that the ground calibration process is effective only for low-altitude applications. The simulation does not account for changes in atmospheric attenuation due to altitude. Higher-altitude flight will also result in changes to atmospheric refraction. Furthermore, the ground calibration process is subjected to light pollution, which again is a function of altitude. The simulation of higher altitude flight should make use of atmospheric models to account for these disparities between ground and high-altitude observations. The level of image noise due to moonlight is assumed to be constant here; however, in practice there is some degree of variation as the viewing angle changes with respect to the position of the moon. This is most noticeable within a 5° viewing angle [22], but less significant at greater angles.

Validation of this simulation was conducted with a fixed wing aircraft; however, the simulation architecture is applicable for any airframe which is capable of reporting its attitude. This might also be used for simulating motion artefacts from two-axis gimbals. While the Raspberry Pi Camera HQ is fit with a rolling shutter, long exposure images are achieved by a series of shorter exposures, similar to the process followed in this simulation. The intra-frame motion is not captured by this simulation; however, this effect appears to be negligible. If the characteristics of a rolling shutter are known, one could replicate this effect by interpolating at a faster rate and selecting an appropriate attitude given the time at which the shutter exposes the star. It is common, however, for charged-couple device (CCD) cameras to be used for celestial imaging. These cameras utilize a global shutter, which exposes all pixels simultaneously and hence are not subjected to the rolling shutter effect.

5. Conclusions

The intent of this work was to design and validate a simulation architecture to support the development of strapdown celestial navigation solutions in lightweight, low-altitude aircraft. An architecture for replicating the effects of long-exposure imagery was designed and implemented by superimposing multiple short-exposure images from aircraft attitude data. Additionally, a method for augmenting low-rate attitude data was proposed and validated. Simulation calibration was achieved through a single ground reference image, producing results which match reality within reasonable tolerance. The simulation architecture provides a tool for baseline testing star detection and identification algorithms. Future work will extend the capability of this simulator from low-altitude to high altitude through atmospheric modeling.

Author Contributions: Conceptualization, S.T. and J.C.; methodology, S.T.; software, S.T.; validation, S.T.; formal analysis, S.T.; investigation, S.T.; resources, J.C.; data curation, S.T and J.C.; writing—original draft preparation, S.T.; writing—review and editing, J.C.; visualization, S.T.; supervision, J.C.; project administration, J.C. All authors have read and agreed to the published version of the manuscript.

Funding: This research received no external funding.

Informed Consent Statement: Not applicable.

Data Availability Statement: Not applicable.

Acknowledgments: This work was supported by Scope Global Pty Ltd. under the Commonwealth Scholarships Program, and the Commonwealth of South Australia under the Australian Government Research Training Program.

Conflicts of Interest: The authors declare no conflict of interest.

References

1. Kayton, M.; Fried, W.R. *Avionics Navigation Systems*; John Wiley & Sons: Hoboken, NJ, USA, 1997.
2. Gao, Z.; Wang, H.; Wang, W.; Xu, Y. SIMU/Triple star sensors integrated navigation method of HALE UAV based on atmospheric refraction correction. *J. Navig.* **2022**, *75*, 1–23. [CrossRef]
3. Ting, F.; Xiaoming, H. Inertial/celestial integrated navigation algorithm for long endurance unmanned aerial vehicle. *Acta Tech. CSAV (Ceskoslov. Akad. Ved.)* **2017**, *62*, 205–217.

4. Titterton, D.; Weston, J.L.; Weston, J. *Strapdown Inertial Navigation Technology*; IET: London, UK, 2004; Volume 17.
5. Rijlaarsdam, D.; Yous, H.; Byrne, J.; Oddenino, D.; Furano, G.; Moloney, D. A survey of lost-in-space star identification algorithms since 2009. *Sensors* **2020**, *20*, 2579. [CrossRef] [PubMed]
6. Padgett, C.; Kreutz-Delgado, K.; Udomkesmalee, S. Evaluation of star identification techniques. *J. Guid. Control. Dyn.* **1997**, *20*, 259–267. [CrossRef]
7. Xu, L.; Jiang, J.; Liu, L. RPNet: A representation learning-based star identification algorithm. *IEEE Access* **2019**, *7*, 92193–92202. [CrossRef]
8. Wei, X.; Wen, D.; Song, Z.; Xi, J.; Zhang, W.; Liu, G.; Li, Z. A star identification algorithm based on radial and dynamic cyclic features of star pattern. *Adv. Space Res.* **2019**, *63*, 2245–2259. [CrossRef]
9. Han, J.; Yang, X.; Xu, T.; Fu, Z.; Chang, L.; Yang, C.; Jin, G. An End-to-End Identification Algorithm for Smearing Star Image. *Remote Sens.* **2021**, *13*, 4541. [CrossRef]
10. Haiyong, W.; Wenrui, Z.; Cheng, X.; Haoyu, L. Image smearing modeling and verification for strapdown star sensor. *Chin. J. Aeronaut.* **2012**, *25*, 115–123.
11. Yan, J.; Jiang, J.; Zhang, G. Dynamic imaging model and parameter optimization for a star tracker. *Opt. Express* **2016**, *24*, 5961–5983. [CrossRef] [PubMed]
12. Wang, Z.; Jiang, J.; Zhang, G. Global field-of-view imaging model and parameter optimization for high dynamic star tracker. *Opt. Express* **2018**, *26*, 33314–33332. [CrossRef] [PubMed]
13. Meeus, J. *Astronomical Algorithms*; Richmond: Richmond, VA, USA, 1991.
14. Saemundsson, T. Atmospheric refraction. *Sky Telesc.* **1986**, *72*, 70.
15. Wang, Z.; Jiang, J. Refraction Surface-Based Stellar Atmospheric Refraction Correction and Error Estimation for Terrestrial Star Tracker. *IEEE Sens. J.* **2022**, *22*, 9685–9696. [CrossRef]
16. Bennett, G. The calculation of astronomical refraction in marine navigation. *J. Navig.* **1982**, *35*, 255–259. [CrossRef]
17. Zhang, Z. A flexible new technique for camera calibration. *IEEE Trans. Pattern Anal. Mach. Intell.* **2000**, *22*, 1330–1334. [CrossRef]
18. Tang, Z.; Von Gioi, R.G.; Monasse, P.; Morel, J.M. A precision analysis of camera distortion models. *IEEED* **2017**, *26*, 2694–2704. [CrossRef] [PubMed]
19. Zhang, G. *Star Identification: Methods, Techniques and Algorithms*; Springer: Berlin/Heidelberg, Germany, 2016.
20. Shoemake, K. Animating rotation with quaternion curves. In Proceedings of the 12th Annual Conference on Computer Graphics and Interactive Techniques, San Francisco, CA, USA, 22–26 July 1985; pp. 245–254.
21. Itseez. The OpenCV Reference Manual. Release 2.4.9.0. 2014. Available online: https://docs.opencv.org/2.4.9 (accessed on 15 June 2022).
22. Krisciunas, K.; Schaefer, B.E. A model of the brightness of moonlight. *Publ. Astron. Soc. Pac.* **1991**, *103*, 1033. [CrossRef]

drones

MDPI

Article

A Neural Network Approach to Estimate Transient Aerodynamic Properties of a Flapping Wing System

Bluest Lan [1,2,*], You-Jun Lin [1], Yu-Hsiang Lai [1,3], Chia-Hung Tang [1] and Jing-Tang Yang [1,*]

[1] Department of Mechanical Engineering, National Taiwan University, Taipei 10617, Taiwan; lemonleo95@gmail.com (Y.-J.L.); zidane0717@gmail.com (Y.-H.L.); r10522112@ntu.edu.tw (C.-H.T.)
[2] Department of Mechanical Engineering, National Chung Hsing University, Taichung 40227, Taiwan
[3] Department of Mechanical and Aerospace Engineering, Chung Cheng Institute of Technology, National Defense University, Taoyuan 33551, Taiwan
* Correspondence: bluest@engineer.com (B.L.); jtyang@ntu.edu.tw (J.-T.Y.)

Abstract: Understanding the causal impacts among various parameters is essential for designing micro aerial vehicles (MAVs). The simulation of computational fluid dynamics (CFD) provides us with a technique to calculate aerodynamic forces precisely. However, even a single result regularly takes considerable computational time. Machine learning, due to the advance in computer hardware, shows another approach that can speed up the analysis process. In this study, we introduce an artificial neural network (ANN) framework to predict the transient aerodynamic forces and the corresponding energy consumption. Instead of considering the whole transient changes of each parameter as inputs, we utilised the technique of Fourier transform to simplify the ANN structure for minimising the computation cost. Furthermore, two typical activation functions, rectified linear unit (ReLU) and sigmoid, were attempted to build the network. The validity of the method was further examined by comparing it with CFD simulation. The result shows that both functions are able to provide highly accurate estimations that can be implemented for model construction under this framework. Consequently, this novel approach makes it possible to reduce the complexity of analysis, study the flapping wing aerodynamics and enable a more efficient way to optimise parameters.

Keywords: micro aerial vehicle; flapping wing; neural network; aerodynamics

Citation: Lan, B.; Lin, Y.-J.; Lai, Y.-H.; Tang, C.-H.; Yang, J.-T. A Neural Network Approach to Estimate Transient Aerodynamic Properties of a Flapping Wing System. *Drones* **2022**, *6*, 210. https://doi.org/10.3390/drones6080210

Academic Editors: Andrzej Łukaszewicz, Wojciech Giernacki, Zbigniew Kulesza, Jaroslaw Pytka, Andriy Holovatyy and Abdessattar Abdelkefi

Received: 11 July 2022
Accepted: 12 August 2022
Published: 17 August 2022

1. Introduction

While a human can fly into the sky with a machine, the mechanism of insect flight remains yet a mystery of sorts. Unlike conventional artificial aircraft, an insect exhibits its fascinating aerial manoeuvrability by repeatedly flapping its wings. This particular mechanism has recently been extensively investigated to develop an improved micro aerial vehicle (MAV). Furthermore, aerodynamics at a small Reynolds number provides a more efficient flight [1], which allows a MAV to cruise at a low speed to execute examination tasks [2]. As MAVs can overcome terrain constraints, they are expected to search for victims in narrow buildings or explore dangerous environments by employing various sensors [3,4]. However, as the flapping wing system is a relatively novel concept compared with other aircraft, its mechanism has not been fully revealed yet. Considerable time is therefore required to examine the impact of various variables.

Among various methods, some studies have reported their findings through biological observations. Ellington [5] claimed that wing paths had no consistent patterns among numerous insects. Wakeling and Ellington [6] displayed exceptional steady-state aerodynamic property of dragonfly wings and utilised it to predict the parasite drag. Josephson and Stevenson [7] measured the oxygen consumption from insects to evaluate the energy efficiency of various flight patterns; Dial et al. [8] also presented the measured power consumption of birds that flew at different speeds by examining the electromyograms (EMGs).

As it is tough to reproduce the same experiment due to the individual differences and the uncontrolled environmental variables, some studies consequently built flapping wing mechanisms to clarify the relationship between various parameters. By utilising a rack-pinion mechanism, T.A. Nguten et al. [9] investigated the effect of parameters such as wing aspect ratio and flapping frequency; Sato et al. [10] built a flapping wing robot and discussed the control strategy of altering the flapping amplitude of wings. Miyoshi et al. [11] found that the asymmetric wingbeat amplitude only affects the pitch and roll moments. These mechanism-based approaches enable us to regenerate the same flying condition readily. Furthermore, by controlling the variables, we can figure out the impact of each parameter on flight performance.

On the other hand, without utilising the technique of particle image velocimetry (PIV), aerodynamic information such as the leading edge vortex (LEV), which produces high transient lift [12], can be directly visualised by computational approaches. From the simulation, we can further obtain precise details such as vorticity to explain the mechanism behind it [13]. Zou et al. [14] and Lai et al. [15] unveiled impacts caused by phase lag and the wing–wing interaction through computational fluid dynamics (CFD) simulation; Johansson and Henningsson [16] compared the effect of the clap mechanism between rigid and flexible wings. This numerical approach allows researchers to simulate how the airflow interacts with various objects without spending extensive time and effort creating experimental environments [17–19]. To obtain precise aerodynamic outputs, building a fine mesh of calculation field is necessary. Nevertheless, it takes several days or weeks for a machine to complete the calculation.

With the advances in computer hardware, machine learning shows another approach for modelling. Unlike conventional computation, related mechanisms are not required (e.g., governing equations). Recently, some studies have shown that machine learning methods can be implemented in aerospace science, including flight pattern recognition [20] and aeroelastic estimation [21]. In the study of flapping mechanics, some researchers have tried to adopt this new technique into control systems [22–24]. Nevertheless, the application for flapping flight aerodynamic analysis has not yet been fully developed. Two studies [25,26] utilised this method to predict the net forces produced in a single flapping cycle, but the transient analysis has not been completed yet. Therefore, researchers still relied on conventional approaches to obtain details, such as the changes during upstroke and downstroke, to explain the impacts of different flight modes.

In this study, we introduce a neural network approach accompanied by CFD simulation to shorten the considerable computational time of transient analysis. We first collected flapping kinematics by biological observations and utilised them to build a model for CFD simulations. Afterwards, the data were split into training, validation and testing groups. We utilised the first two groups of data to create neural network models and evaluated them with the testing data. As reports [27,28] have shown that wing and body kinematics are the main parameters affecting butterfly flight performance, we considered wing rotation and body oscillation as inputs and utilised them to predict the corresponding changes in aerodynamic forces and power consumption. The effectiveness of the method was examined by comparing it with the results obtained by CFD simulation afterwards.

2. Data Collection

2.1. Biological Experiment

To record the flapping motion, we utilised the blue tiger butterfly (*Tirumala septentrionis*) as a reference (Figure 1a). Before the measurement, objects were frozen at −7 °C for 24 h. The morphological parameters were then measured ($N = 4$), including mass, body length and wing area, span and mean chord (see Table 1). Afterwards, we calculated the aspect ratio AR of a single wing with the equation:

$$AR = \frac{S}{\bar{c}}, \tag{1}$$

in which S and $\bar{c}$ represent the wingspan and mean chord, respectively. These parameters were considered a reference to build a simulation model later.

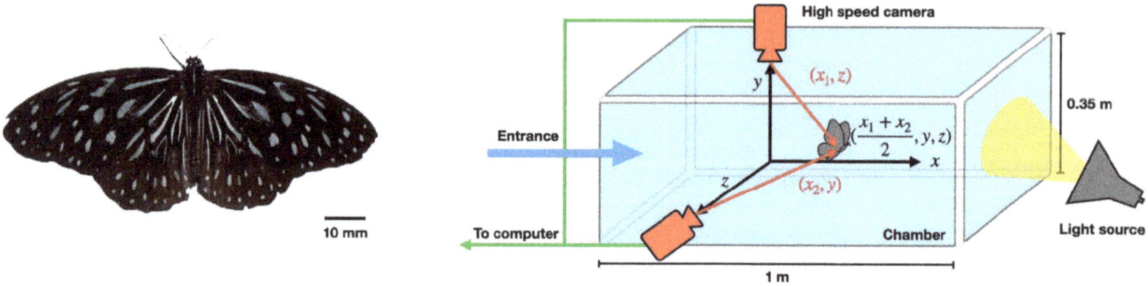

(a) (b)

Figure 1. Experimental setup. (**a**) Photograph of a blue tiger butterfly (*T. septentrionis*). (**b**) Measurement method. Two synchronised high-speed cameras were mounted onto a transparent chamber orthogonally along the y- and z-axis. By utilising the photographed images, a butterfly's position could be determined.

Table 1. Measured ($N = 4$) and simulation model's morphological parameters of the butterfly.

Parameters	Measurement	Simulation
Mass (mg)	379.93 ± 72.99	350
Wing Area (mm^2)	923.67 ± 42.55	925
Wingspan (mm)	46.00 ± 1.23	46.04
Mean Chord (mm)	20.07 ± 0.39	20.11
Aspect Ratio	2.29 ± 0.02	2.29

To capture the details of a butterfly's body action, we utilised two high-speed cameras (Phantom v7.3 and v310, Vision Research, Wayne, NJ, USA). Both cameras were operated at 1000 frames per second with a resolution of 1024×1024 and placed outside a transparent chamber (size: 1 m $\times$ 0.35 m $\times$ 0.35 m) in which a butterfly could fly inside freely. As these cameras were placed orthogonally, we defined the direction from the chamber to the two cameras as y- and z-axis (see Figure 1b); the synchronised photographed films were examined to determine the angles between various body parts. To attract a butterfly to fly forward, we placed a light source on one side of the chamber. As the study focused on the flapping motion of forwarding flight, we abandoned the data for which the butterfly flew with turning. On counting the number of frames, we deduced the wingbeat frequency to be around 11.020 ± 1.076 Hz ($N = 15$).

To obtain the flapping kinetic equations, we utilised the coordinates measured from the experiments to rebuild them. Figure 2a shows the heading direction $\vec{b}$ was determined by the body from B_0 to B_1. The angle between the x-axis and $\vec{b}$ was defined as the body pitching angle θ. Still, the vector $\vec{w}_1$ was determined by the root W_0 and the wingtip W_1; the sweeping angle η was obtained by calculating the complementary angle of the angle between $\vec{w}_1$ and $\vec{b}$. Additionally, the wing plane was constructed with $\vec{w}_1$ and $\vec{w}_2$ (the direction pointing from W_0 to W_2, with W_2 located on the trailing edge of the hindwing). Lastly, the wing rotation angle α was computed from the normal vector of the wing $\vec{w}_N$ (i.e., the direction of $\vec{w}_2 \times \vec{w}_1$) and $\vec{r} \times \vec{b}$; the angle between the latter and the negative z-axis was defined as its flapping angle, where $\vec{r}$ represents the axis of rotation. These parameters were utilised to describe the flapping flight behaviour of a butterfly.

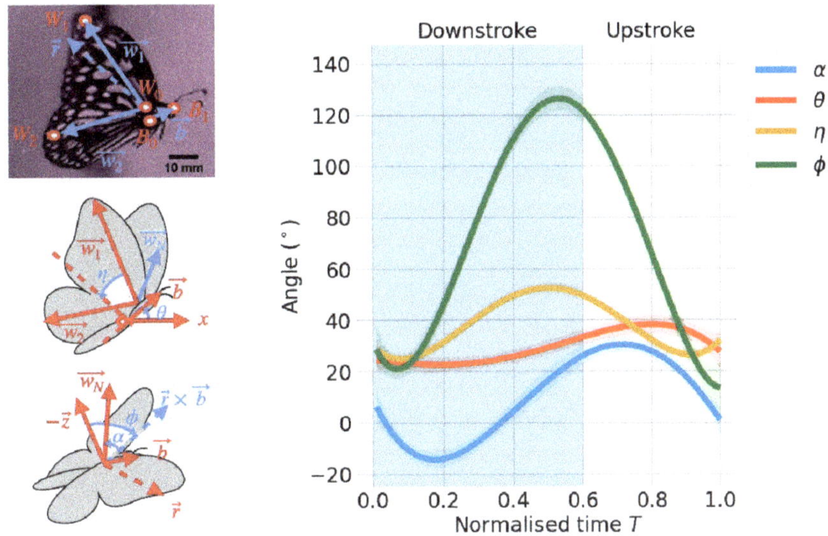

(a) (b)

Figure 2. Angle parameters of a flying butterfly. (**a**) Definitions of angles. From the coordinates of each feature's points, body pitching angle θ, sweeping angle η, rotation angle α and flapping angle ϕ were obtained. (**b**) Angles measured from the experiments ($N = 15$). The solid lines indicate four feature angles; the surrounding shaded areas represent the 95% confidence intervals. The abscissa axis denotes the normalised time in a flapping period; the blue area (from $T = 0$ to 0.6) indicates the downstroke phase, and the rest (from $T = 0.6$ to 1) is upstroke.

Figure 2b shows the variation of the four angles in a flapping period measured from the experiments ($N = 15$) with 95% confidence intervals (shaded areas). These curves were recognised as input parameters for subsequent simulation afterwards.

2.2. Computational Fluid Dynamics Simulation

To deduce the aerodynamic interactions that were hard to observe directly, we chose CFD simulation to generate highly accurate datasets. The obtained morphological parameters and kinematic equations were further utilised to build a butterfly model and regenerate the flight behaviour through a commercial solver (Fluent, Ansys, Canonsburg, PA, USA). The SIMPLEC algorithm was applied to resolve pressure and velocity fields [29]. To reduce the computational cost, we simulated the flow field under a relative condition frame. Therefore, the butterfly was flying at the centre of a sphere (see Figure 3a). The butterfly would thus encounter an incoming airflow with a virtual acceleration **a** created by its flight. To avoid inaccurate outcomes affected by the wall effect, the diameter of the spherical flow domain was set to $20S$ (around 900 mm). As the Reynolds number of a natural flying butterfly is around 10^3–10^4 [30], the medium was considered an incompressible Newtonian laminar airflow, with a density of $\rho = 1.23\ \mathrm{kg/m^3}$ and viscosity of $\mu = 1.79 \times 10^{-5}$ Pa·s. Furthermore, we utilised the following governing equations for computation:

$$\nabla \cdot \mathbf{u} = 0 \tag{2}$$

$$\rho \frac{D\mathbf{u}}{Dt} = -\nabla p + \mu \nabla^2 \mathbf{u} + \rho(\mathbf{g} + \mathbf{a}) \tag{3}$$

in which **u**, t, p and **g** represent the velocity, time, pressure and gravity, respectively. The entire domain was split into two for giving different boundary conditions [29,31,32]. The front of the butterfly was considered to be the velocity inlet with an incoming flux accompanied by **a**. As a result, the stream fluctuated with the flight at each time step. The rear sphere was the pressure outlet. These conditions were defined as:

$$\mathbf{u} = -\hat{a_x}\dot{x} - \hat{a_y}\dot{y} \tag{4}$$

$$p = -\rho g y, \tag{5}$$

in which $\hat{a_x}$ and $\hat{a_y}$ indicate the unit vector along the x- and y-axis, respectively.

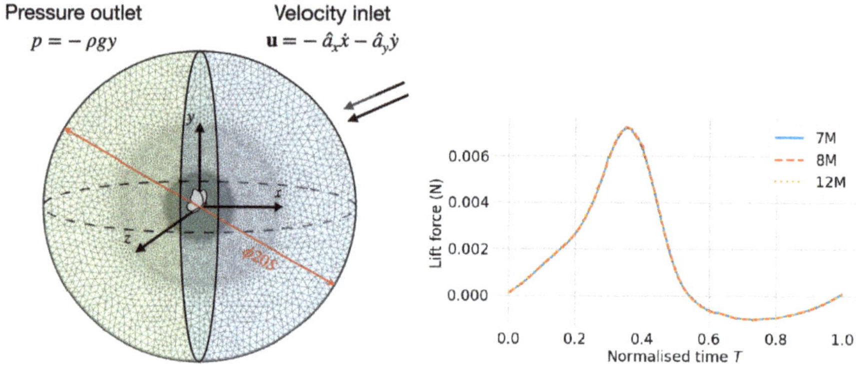

(**a**) (**b**)

Figure 3. Conditions of the simulation. (**a**) Boundary conditions (inlet: velocity, outlet: pressure). (**b**) Grid convergence test.

The grid size of the butterfly's surface was 0.5 mm with a no-split condition (the air had zero velocity relative to the boundary), whereas its surroundings were set to 1 mm. This setting can enhance the precision of the simulation results [31,33]. We also utilised the lift force to do the grid convergence test. The result converged as the number of grids increased. Figure 3b illustrates the comparison among three different settings: the coarse grid (blue solid line, 7 million), the medium grid (red dashed line, 8 million) and the fine grid (amber dotted line, 12 million). From the result, we found that the maximum value difference between the coarse and fine settings was about 0.5% merely. Considering the balance between accuracy and computational cost, we hence selected the medium setting for the following computation.

We also chose the method of dynamic mesh (smoothing and remeshing) to prevent a negative mesh volume [34]. A flapping cycle was divided into 250 calculation time steps. The simulation outputs were the horizontal force F_h, vertical force F_v, normal force acting on a single wing F_w and power consumption P at the 10th flapping cycle (stable flight). All these values were nondimensionalised by the following equation:

$$\begin{bmatrix} F_h \\ F_v \\ F_w \\ P \end{bmatrix} = \frac{1}{\frac{1}{2}\rho V^2 (2S\bar{c})} \begin{bmatrix} f_h^* \\ f_v^* \\ f_w^* \\ p^*/V \end{bmatrix}, \tag{6}$$

in which the wingtip velocity $V = 4\phi f S$; f_h^*, f_v^*, f_w^* and p^* were the corresponding untransformed forces and power. The Reynolds number of the simulation result was 6130, which was close to the experimental result of 6050.

As the study focused on the influence caused by amplitudes of body oscillation and wing rotation, we altered the simulated conditions of body pitching angle and wing rotation angle by multiplying them with scalers b and w. In total, 25 flapping data were collected (see Figure 4).

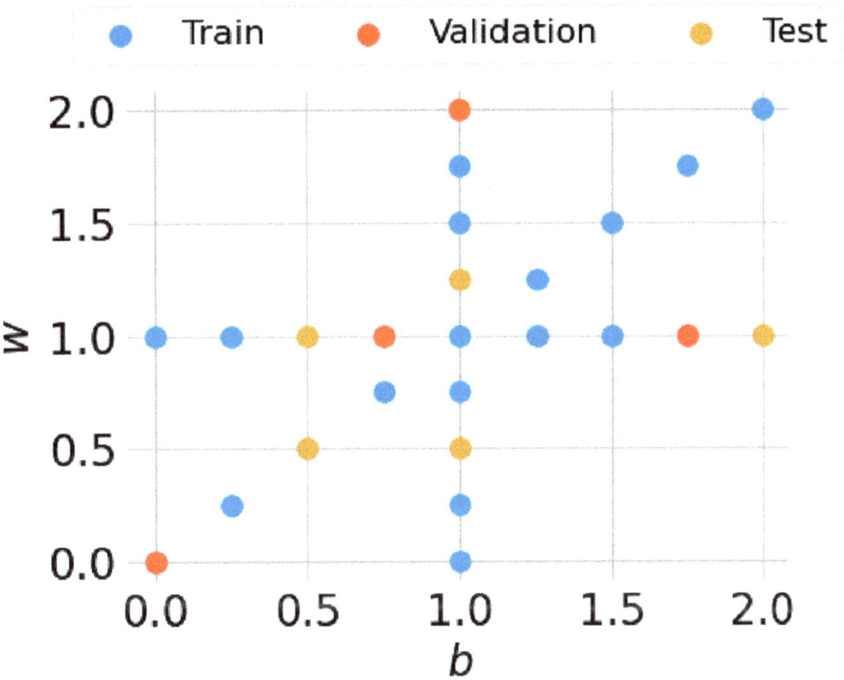

Figure 4. Generated datasets. The data were randomly separated into training (64%, blue markers, $N = 16$), validation (16%, red markers, $N = 4$) and testing (20%, amber markers, $N = 5$) groups. The testing data were merely utilised for evaluation and did not participate in the training processes.

3. Artificial Neural Network

An artificial neural network (ANN) is constructed by several connected computing cells (artificial neurons) inspired by the human brain as shown in Figure 5. The output y of the cell n can be calculated by the following equation:

$$y_n = \sigma(\sum_{i=1}^{m} w_{ni}x_{ni} + b_n), \tag{7}$$

in which $x_{n1}, x_{n2}, ..., x_{nm}$ are the input signals; $w_{n1}, w_{n2}, ..., w_{nm}$ are the respective weights; b_n is the bias; and σ is the activation function (transfer function) [35]. The inputs were the scalers b and w. To increased the training performance, we normalised the values in the interval of $[0, 1]$ [36]. On the other hand, instead of predicting 250 time steps for each aerodynamic property, we simplified it by fitting each parameter by a Fourier series:

$$F(t) = A_0 + \sum_{n=1}^{m} A_n \cos 2\pi nft + B_n \sin 2\pi nft, \tag{8}$$

where m is the order of the Fourier series. When choosing $m = 5$ to fit the data, each aerodynamic property could be described by a vector formed by 11 parameters. We hence considered these 44 parameters (four aerodynamic properties, F_h, F_v, F_w and P) as the output of an ANN model. As the number of outputs was shrunk from 1000 to 44, we could consider utilising a smaller number of hidden cells for the following calculation. The training process hence can be curtailed at the same time.

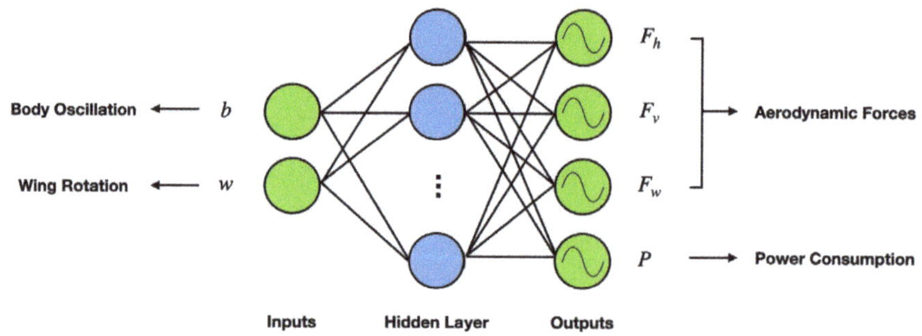

Figure 5. Structure of an ANN model. The inputs were b and w, and the outputs were Fourier coefficients of F_h, F_v, F_w and P.

Figure 6 shows two common activation functions utilised for neural networks. Recently, Rectified Linear Unit (ReLU) has been chosen as the activation function in various applications [37]. The function is defined by the formula:

$$ReLU(x) = \begin{cases} 0 & \text{if } x < 0, \\ x & \text{otherwise.} \end{cases} \tag{9}$$

Although the vanishing gradients problem is a critical issue when training an ANN, ReLU has a constant gradient of 1 when the input is greater than 0. Therefore, it is widely applied to ANNs. However, previous flapping wing studies chose the sigmoid function to estimate the mean values of aerodynamic coefficients [25,38]. The function can be described by:

$$Sigmoid(x) = \frac{1}{1 + e^{-x}}. \tag{10}$$

As the s-shaped output of the sigmoid varies continuously in the interval of $[0, 1]$, the activation values hence do not disappear. Because we aimed to predict transient aerodynamic statuses rather than their mean values, we need to evaluate which function can provide precise estimations. We consequently constructed two models based on these functions and compared the results afterwards.

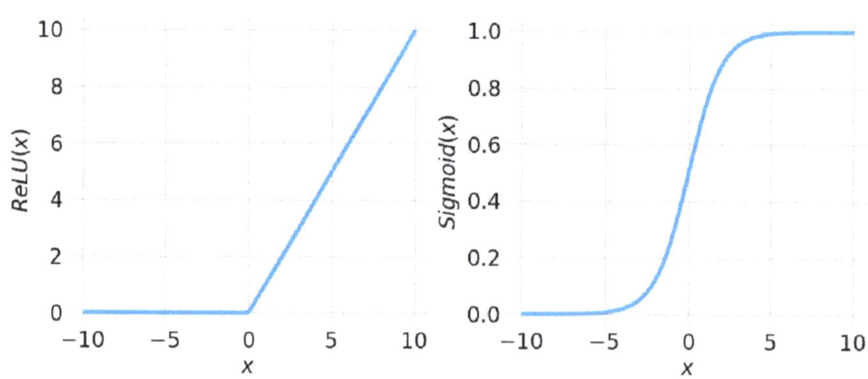

Figure 6. Two types of activation functions.

To train the model, we utilised Adam optimiser [39], an advanced backpropagation method [40], with the loss function of mean square error (MSE) to minimise the error. Although many studies [41–45] had proposed their rules of thumb to select the number of hidden units, the main idea is to improve the prediction accuracy and minimise errors.

Therefore, we randomly picked up 80% of the data to train two types of models through a various number of hidden units iteratively. Among these datasets, 80% (i.e., 64% of the entire data) were utilised for tuning weights and bias; 20% (i.e., 16% of the entire data) were for validation. Considering the balance between accuracy and computational time, we have examined the loss when the number of hidden neurons was between 20 to 40. To avoid the setting merely benefiting specific cases, each training was repeated 30 iterations with the same settings but different training data selections. Figure 4 shows one of the random states that we have utilised. The learning rate and the epoch size were set to 0.001 and 60,000.

Figure 7 depicts the mean convergent curves of each case during the training process. From the testing result, we found that though the training loss of ReLU model kept decreasing when epoch size was greater than 10,000, the validation loss of it remained around 10^{-3}. We further found that as the number of hidden units was 40, which had the smallest loss, its validation loss was 8.28×10^{-4} and 8.05×10^{-4} when epoch sizes reached 30,000 and 60,000. As the difference between these two values was less than 3%, we considered the 40 hidden neurons and 30,000 epochs to be an adequate setup. On the other hand, the training and validation loss of sigmoid model plots reveal that a larger number of hidden neurons did not promise a smaller loss. When the number of hidden units was 30, the validation loss difference between epochs 50,000 and 60,000 was less than 3% (epoch 50,000: 8.12×10^{-6}, epoch 60,000: 7.93×10^{-6}). Consequently, we considered the number of hidden units and epochs to be 30 and 50,000, respectively.

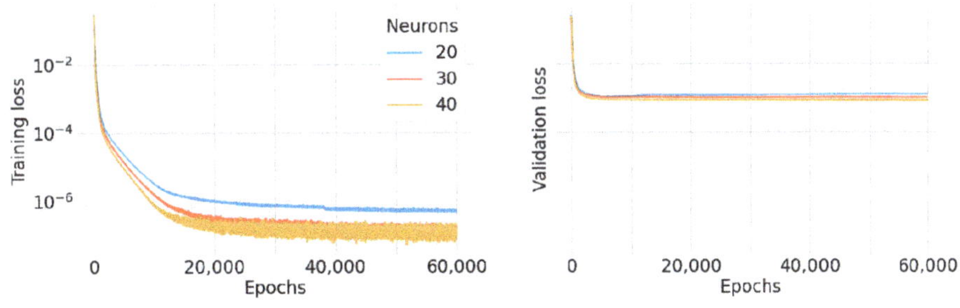

(a)

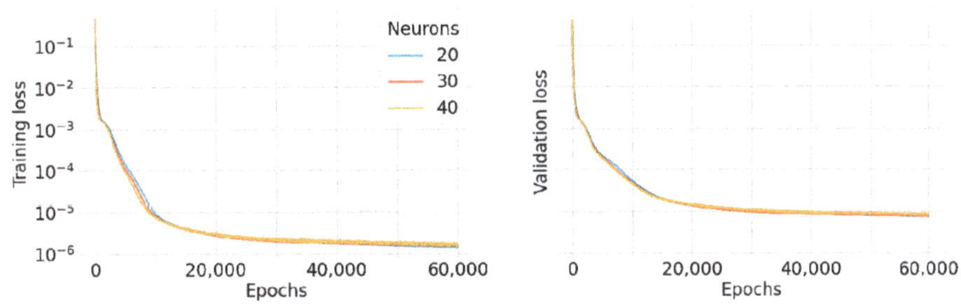

(b)

Figure 7. Loss, the MSE of the 44 output parameters, of ReLU- (**a**) and sigmoid- (**b**) based ANN training processes.

It was unsure if the accuracy of the ReLU activation function was sufficient to predict the four aerodynamic properties, though the validation loss of the sigmoid-based model was even lower. We hence utilised both models for the following analysis. To avoid overfitting, the unused 20% of the data were assigned as testing datasets. As all the data generated by the CFD simulation were from the same system, the model that fits one group should fit the other as well. Because these cases were not utilised for previous training, they were considered to be unseen data for the following model evaluation. If the number of datasets is sufficient, we can utilise a large number of cases to evaluate our models. However, it is not easy to collect hundreds of results as it generally takes about 4 to 7 days to complete a single simulation. To deal with a limited amount of data, k-fold cross validation was implemented for obtaining a reliable evaluation [46]. To implement this method, the database needs to be randomly split into k groups first so that we can evaluate a model k times. In each iteration, we only utilise $k-1$ groups to train our network. As there is one group that does not join the training process, it can be utilised for testing. Therefore, this can be utilised to protect our models from overfitting as the model will be examined by k different combinations. To keep 20% of the entire data for testing, we chose k to be 5 in this study (see Figure 8).

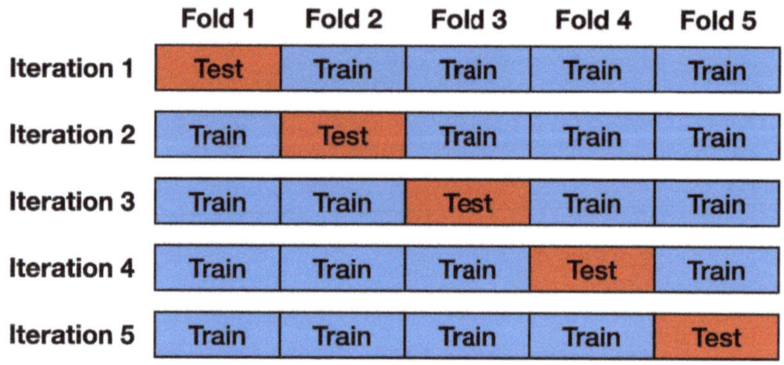

Figure 8. k-Fold cross validation ($k = 5$).

4. Results and Discussion

4.1. Model Comparison

As the outputs of our models were coefficients of the four aerodynamic parameters, we converted the signal back by utilising Equation (8). The prediction can hence be compared with the original curves by calculating the coefficients of determination R^2. The mean and standard deviation (SD) of the two models are given in Table 2. We first checked if the overtraining occurred on our model. Since the training and testing R^2 values are all close to 1, the models encountered neither underfitting nor overfitting problems. Although the MSE loss of the sigmoid-based model was smaller than the other one, as they both have mean values greater than 0.99, the differences were not obvious. However, the SD values of the ReLU-based model were slightly higher. The result implies that the sigmoid activation function generally provided higher precise estimations.

Table 2. Statistics of the ReLU- and sigmoid-based models (mean ± SD).

Parameters	ReLU		Sigmoid	
	R^2_{Train}	R^2_{Test}	R^2_{Train}	R^2_{Test}
F_h	0.995 ± 0.018	0.989 ± 0.025	0.999 ± 0.003	0.998 ± 0.005
F_v	0.998 ± 0.007	0.995 ± 0.012	0.999 ± 0.003	0.999 ± 0.003
F_w	0.999 ± 0.004	0.997 ± 0.006	0.999 ± 0.002	0.999 ± 0.002
P	0.996 ± 0.016	0.989 ± 0.034	0.999 ± 0.003	0.997 ± 0.009

As it is difficult to understand the difference between the two models by just viewing the R^2 values, we picked up a case from the testing group, which had a maximum R^2_{test} value difference of 0.005, for comparison. Figure 9 presents the output aerodynamic properties as the b and w were assigned to 1 and 0, respectively. By comparing these curves, we can find that the red dashed line (sigmoid) almost overlaps with the black solid line (CFD simulation). On the other hand, the blue dashed line (ReLU) is slightly off in the peaks. By way of illustration, the blue dashed line shifted marginally to the right at $T = 0.3$ in the F_h-T plot. Nevertheless, the trends of four aerodynamic properties can still be identified.

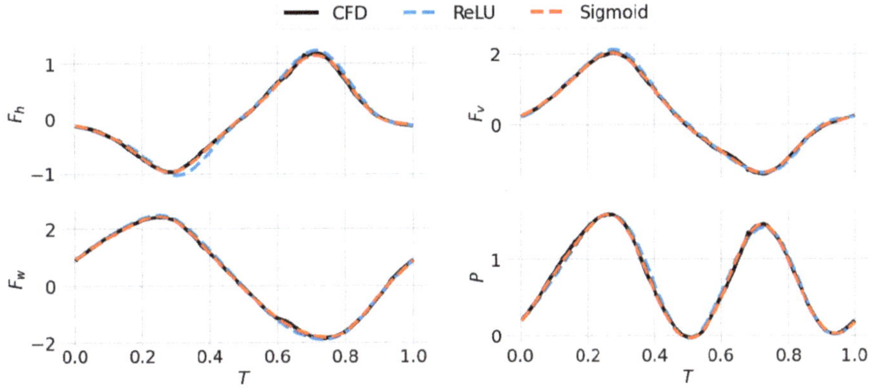

Figure 9. Validation of the two models in comparison with the CFD simulation. The black solid lines were calculated by CFD simulation; the blue and red dashed lines were obtained from the ReLU- and sigmoid-based ANNs, respectively.

4.2. *Aerodynamic Performance*

While the traditional CFD simulation takes several days to complete a single computation, these two ANN models take less than a second merely. Due to the high R^2, both methods achieve elevated estimation accuracy and can be implemented to accelerate the analysis process. The networks hence can be utilised to investigate the interactions between body oscillation and wing rotation behaviours. Owing to the limited payload, a MAV cannot carry a battery of substantial volume. Consequently, how to efficiently generate lift is a critical issue. We can hence utilise this neural network approach to optimise the flapping motion, such as searching the efficient flying kinematics.

In our study, the mean lift efficiency $\bar{E}_v$ can be defined by:

$$\bar{E}_v = \frac{\bar{F}_v}{\bar{P}}, \tag{11}$$

where $\bar{F}_v$ and $\bar{P}$ are the mean values of F_v and P in a single flapping period, respectively. We could hence obtain a quick result by utilising the ANN method. Figure 10 depicts the corresponding $\bar{F}_v$ and $\bar{E}_v$ when b and w are in the interval of [0, 2]. Because the two models presented similar outcomes, we only display the sigmoid-based calculation in Figure 10. The result illustrates that the maximum $\bar{F}_v$ appears at $[b,\ \ w] = [2,\ \ 2]$. Nevertheless, the lift efficiency can still be improved by reducing w to 1.2. To verify if it fits the actual circumstance, we ran the simulation and compared the results (see Figure 11). The MSEs of F_v and P were 5.19×10^{-4} and 8.35×10^{-4}, respectively. Considering the high R^2 and low MSE values, we believe this neural network approach can provide precise estimations which can be utilised for studying the flapping wing system.

Although it is still challenging to provide details such as flow fields with the current framework, we can utilise it to make a quick analysis and perform full CFD simulations of specific cases to clarify abnormal phenomena. This technique hence will be a great advantage when dealing with a complex system. Moreover, as we verified that the network could successfully estimate transient aerodynamic properties, we can extend the framework to include more complicated flapping motions as inputs in the future.

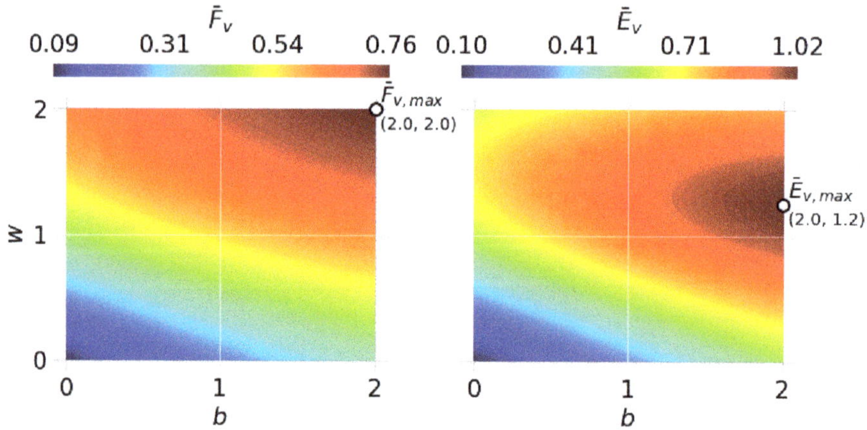

Figure 10. Net vertical force $\bar{F}_v$ and corresponding efficiency $\bar{E}_v$ in a single flapping period.

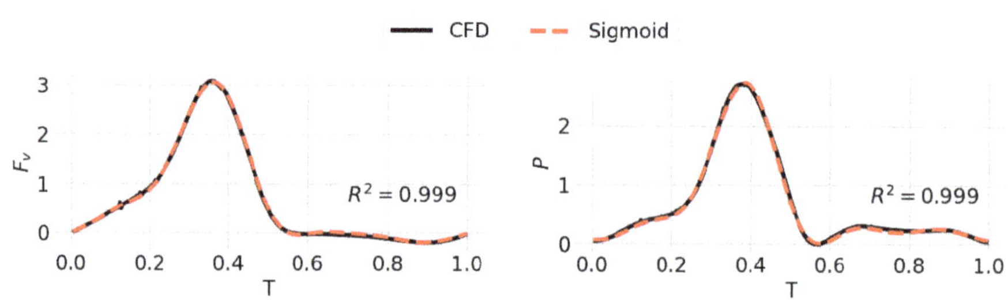

Figure 11. Optimal aerodynamics obtained by the ANN in comparison with CFD simulated result.

5. Conclusions

In this study, we introduce a novel neural network approach to speed up the transient analysis of flight mechanics. For evaluation, we analysed the butterfly's flapping motions by CFD simulation and trained the model with these datasets. To simplify the model, we further utilised Fourier transform to reduce the number of neural cells. Through a series of tests, we found that both ReLU- and sigmoid-based models can accurately predict these coefficients, which can be utilised to obtain the original transient results. This enables us to rapidly estimate the corresponding aerodynamic properties with the given inputs.

The series of work conducted in this study aims to reduce the computational time cost. As the complex structure of flapping motion aerodynamics is non-linear, conventional approaches take excessive effort to analyse the unsteady system. With the aid of neural networks, we do not need to stick to CFD simulation for each case but can still obtain precise results without spending plenty of time. The technique reported here sheds new light on the development of flapping wing systems. This is a great advantage when a large amount of computing is required and provides us with a more efficient way to discuss the interactions among various parameters. Prior to this study, it was difficult to verify that the selected parameters were optimal. The technique introduced in the study makes it possible. We believe the framework will provide an efficient way to delve deeper into the flight mechanism and design a more efficient MAV.

Author Contributions: B.L. and Y.-J.L. conceptualised the research. Y.-J.L. and Y.-H.L. designed and performed the experiments. B.L. and C.-H.T. analysed the data. B.L. wrote the paper. J.-T.Y. administered the project and reviewed the paper. All authors have read and agreed to the published version of the manuscript.

Funding: The Taiwan Ministry of Science and Technology, grant number MOST 111-2221-E-002-123-MY3, funded this research. National Taiwan University partially supported this work under a project with contract NTU-CC-110L891401.

Conflicts of Interest: The authors declare no potential conflicts of interest with respect to the research, authorship and/or publication of this article.

Nomenclature

$\mathbf{a}$	Virtual acceleration
AR	Aspect ratio
b	Scaler of the body pitching angle
$\bar{c}$	Mean chord
$\bar{E_v}$	Mean lift efficiency
f	Frequency
F_h	Nondimensionalised horizontal force
f_h^*	Horizontal force
F_v	Nondimensionalised vertical force
f_v^*	Vertical force
F_w	Nondimensionalised normal force acting on a single wing
f_w^*	Normal force acting on a single wing
$\mathbf{g}$	Gravity
k	Consecutive fold number
P	Nondimensionalised power consumption
p	Air pressure
p^*	Power consumption
R^2	Coefficient of determination
S	Wingspan
T	Normalised time
t	Time
$\mathbf{u}$	Airflow velocity
V	Wingtip velocity
w	Scaler of the wing rotation angle
α	Rotation angle
η	Sweeping angle
θ	Body pitching angle
μ	Air viscosity
ρ	Air density
σ	Activation function
ϕ	Flapping angle

References

1. Fenelon, M.A.; Furukawa, T. Design of an active flapping wing mechanism and a micro aerial vehicle using a rotary actuator. *Mech. Mach. Theory* **2010**, *45*, 137–146. [CrossRef]
2. Perez-Sanchez, V.; Gomez-Tamm, A.E.; Savastano, E.; Arrue, B.C.; Ollero, A. Bio-Inspired Morphing Tail for Flapping-Wings Aerial Robots Using Macro Fiber Composites. *Appl. Sci.* **2021**, *11*, 2930. [CrossRef]
3. Rossi, M.; Brunelli, D.; Adami, A.; Lorenzelli, L.; Menna, F.; Remondino, F. Gas-drone: Portable gas sensing system on UAVs for gas leakage localization. In Proceedings of the IEEE SENSORS, Valencia, Spain, 2–5 November 2014; pp. 1431–1434. [CrossRef]
4. Lan, B.; Kanzaki, R.; Ando, N. Dropping Counter: A Detection Algorithm for Identifying Odour-Evoked Responses from Noisy Electroantennograms Measured by a Flying Robot. *Sensors* **2019**, *19*, 4574. [CrossRef] [PubMed]
5. Ellington, C.P. The aerodynamics of hovering insect flight. IV. Aerodynamic mechanisms. *Philos. Trans. R. Soc. London. Biol. Sci.* **1984**, *305*, 79–113. [CrossRef]
6. Wakeling, J.; Ellington, C. Dragonfly flight. I. Gliding flight and steady-state aerodynamic forces. *J. Exp. Biol.* **1997**, *200*, 543–556. [CrossRef]
7. Josephson, R.K.; Stevenson, R.D. The efficiency of a flight muscle from the locust Schistocerca americana. *J. Physiol.* **1991**, *442*, 413–429. [CrossRef]
8. Dial, K.P.; Biewener, A.A.; Tobalske, B.W.; Warrick, D.R. Mechanical power output of bird flight. *Nature* **1997**, *390*, 67–70. [CrossRef]

9. Nguyen, T.A.; Vu Phan, H.; Au, T.K.L.; Park, H.C. Experimental study on thrust and power of flapping-wing system based on rack-pinion mechanism. *Bioinspiration Biomimetics* **2016**, *11*, 1–16. [CrossRef]
10. Sato, T.; Fujimura, A.; Takesue, N. Three-DoF Flapping-Wing Robot with Variable-Amplitude Link Mechanism. *J. Robot. Mechatronics* **2019**, *31*, 894–904. [CrossRef]
11. Miyoshi, T.; Nishimura, T.; Shimizu, T. Handling parameters for rotational moment generation with four-wing flapping. *J. Aero Aqua-Bio-Mech.* **2018**, *7*, 1–8. [CrossRef]
12. Eldredge, J.D.; Jones, A.R. Leading-Edge Vortices: Mechanics and Modeling. *Annu. Rev. Fluid Mech.* **2019**, *51*, 75–104. [CrossRef]
13. Lua, K.B.; Lee, Y.J.; Lim, T.T.; Yeo, K.S. Wing–Wake Interaction of Three-Dimensional Flapping Wings. *AIAA J.* **2017**, *55*, 729–739. [CrossRef]
14. Zou, P.Y.; Lai, Y.H.; Yang, J.T. Effects of phase lag on the hovering flight of damselfly and dragonfly. *Phys. Rev. E* **2019**, *100*, 063102. [CrossRef] [PubMed]
15. Lai, Y.H.; Ma, J.F.; Yang, J.T. Flight Maneuver of a Damselfly with Phase Modulation of the Wings. *Integr. Comp. Biol.* **2021**, *61*, 20–36. [CrossRef]
16. Johansson, L.C.; Henningsson, P. Butterflies fly using efficient propulsive clap mechanism owing to flexible wings: Butterflies fly using efficient propulsive clap mechanism owing to flexible wings. *J. R. Soc. Interface* **2021**, *18*, 20200854. [CrossRef] [PubMed]
17. He, Y.; Bayly, A.E.; Hassanpour, A. Coupling CFD-DEM with dynamic meshing: A new approach for fluid-structure interaction in particle-fluid flows. *Powder Technol.* **2018**, *325*, 620–631. [CrossRef]
18. Fernandez-Gamiz, U.; Gomez-Mármol, M.; Chacón-Rebollo, T. Computational Modeling of Gurney Flaps and Microtabs by POD Method. *Energies* **2018**, *11*, 2091. [CrossRef]
19. Cravero, C.; Marsano, D. Computational Investigation of the Aerodynamics of a Wheel Installed on a Race Car with a Multi-Element Front Wing. *Fluids* **2022**, *7*, 182. [CrossRef]
20. Bagherzadeh, S.A. Nonlinear aircraft system identification using artificial neural networks enhanced by empirical mode decomposition. *Aerosp. Sci. Technol.* **2018**, *75*, 155–171. [CrossRef]
21. Torregrosa, A.J.; García-Cuevas, L.M.; Quintero, P.; Cremades, A. On the application of artificial neural network for the development of a nonlinear aeroelastic model. *Aerosp. Sci. Technol.* **2021**, *115*, 106845. [CrossRef]
22. Clawson, T.S.; Ferrari, S.; Fuller, S.B.; Wood, R.J. Spiking neural network (SNN) control of a flapping insect-scale robot. In Proceedings of the 2016 IEEE 55th Conference on Decision and Control (CDC), Las Vegas, NV, USA, 12–14 December 2016; pp. 3381–3388. [CrossRef]
23. He, W.; Yan, Z.; Sun, C.; Chen, Y. Adaptive Neural Network Control of a Flapping Wing Micro Aerial Vehicle with Disturbance Observer. *IEEE Trans. Cybern.* **2017**, *47*, 3452–3465. [CrossRef] [PubMed]
24. Goedhart, M.; Van Kampen, E.J.; Armanini, S.F.; de Visser, C.C.; Chu, Q.P. Machine Learning for Flapping Wing Flight Control. In Proceedings of the 2018 AIAA Information Systems-AIAA Infotech, Kissimmee, FL, USA, 8–12 January 2018; American Institute of Aeronautics and Astronautics: Reston, VA, USA, 2018; Number 209989. [CrossRef]
25. Kurtulus, D.F. Ability to forecast unsteady aerodynamic forces of flapping airfoils by artificial neural network. *Neural Comput. Appl.* **2009**, *18*, 359–368. [CrossRef]
26. Nguyen, A.T.; Tran, N.D.; Vu, T.T.; Pham, T.D.; Vu, Q.T.; Han, J.H. A Neural-network-based Approach to Study the Energy-optimal Hovering Wing Kinematics of a Bionic Hawkmoth Model. *J. Bionic Eng.* **2019**, *16*, 904–915. [CrossRef]
27. Huang, H.; Sun, M. Forward flight of a model butterfly: Simulation by equations of motion coupled with the Navier-Stokes equations. *Acta Mech. Sin.* **2012**, *28*, 1590–1601. [CrossRef]
28. Zhang, Y.; Wang, X.; Wang, S.; Huang, W.; Weng, Q. Kinematic and Aerodynamic Investigation of the Butterfly in Forward Free Flight for the Butterfly-Inspired Flapping Wing Air Vehicle. *Appl. Sci.* **2021**, *11*, 2620. [CrossRef]
29. Lin, Y.J.; Chang, S.K.; Lai, Y.H.; Yang, J.T. Beneficial wake-capture effect for forward propulsion with a restrained wing-pitch motion of a butterfly. *R. Soc. Open Sci.* **2021**, *8*, 202172. [CrossRef]
30. Senda, K.; Obara, T.; Kitamura, M.; Nishikata, T.; Hirai, N.; Iima, M.; Yokoyama, N. Modeling and emergence of flapping flight of butterfly based on experimental measurements. *Robot. Auton. Syst.* **2012**, *60*, 670–678. [CrossRef]
31. Chang, S.K.; Lai, Y.H.; Lin, Y.J.; Yang, J.T. Enhanced lift and thrust via the translational motion between the thorax-Abdomen node and the center of mass of a butterfly with a constructive abdominal oscillation. *Phys. Rev. E* **2020**, *102*, 62407. [CrossRef]
32. Lai, Y.H.; Chang, S.K.; Lan, B.; Hsu, K.L.; Yang, J.T. Optimal thrust efficiency for a tandem wing in forward flight using varied hindwing kinematics of a damselfly. *Phys. Fluids* **2022**, *34*, 061909. [CrossRef]
33. Lai, Y.H.; Lin, Y.J.; Chang, S.K.; Yang, J.T. Effect of wing–wing interaction coupled with morphology and kinematic features of damselflies. *Bioinspiration Biomimetics* **2021**, *16*, 016017. [CrossRef]
34. Suhaimi, S.; Shuib, S.; Yusoff, H.; Kadarman, A.H. Aerodynamic Performance of a Flapping Wing Inspired by Bats. *Appl. Mech. Mater.* **2020**, *899*, 42–49. [CrossRef]
35. Zhang, Z. Artificial Neural Network. In *Multivariate Time Series Analysis in Climate and Environmental Research*; Springer International Publishing: Cham, Switzerland, 2018; pp. 1–35. [CrossRef]
36. Sola, J.; Sevilla, J. Importance of input data normalization for the application of neural networks to complex industrial problems. *IEEE Trans. Nucl. Sci.* **1997**, *44*, 1464–1468. [CrossRef]
37. Daubechies, I.; DeVore, R.; Foucart, S.; Hanin, B.; Petrova, G. Nonlinear Approximation and (Deep) ReLU Networks. *Constr. Approx.* **2019**, *55*, 127–172. [CrossRef]

38. Thirumalainambi, R.; Bardina, J. Training data requirement for a neural network to predict aerodynamic coefficients. In Proceedings of the Independent Component Analyses, Wavelets, and Neural Networks, SPIE, Orlando, FL, USA, 21 April 2003; Volume 5102, p. 92. [CrossRef]
39. Kingma, D.P.; Ba, J. Adam: A Method for Stochastic Optimization. In Proceedings of the 3rd International Conference on Learning Representations, ICLR 2015, San Diego, CA, USA, 7–9 May 2015. Available online: https://arxiv.org/abs/1412.6980 (accessed on 10 July 2022)
40. Goh, A. Back-propagation neural networks for modeling complex systems. *Artif. Intell. Eng.* **1995**, *9*, 143–151. [CrossRef]
41. Hornik, K. Approximation capabilities of multilayer feedforward networks. *Neural Netw.* **1991**, *4*, 251–257. [CrossRef]
42. Boger, Z.; Guterman, H. Knowledge extraction from artificial neural network models. In Proceedings of the 1997 IEEE International Conference on Systems, Man, and Cybernetics. Computational Cybernetics and Simulation, Orlando, FL, USA, 12–15 October 1997; Volume 4, pp. 3030–3035. [CrossRef]
43. Wang, S.C. Artificial Neural Network. In *Interdisciplinary Computing in Java Programming*; Springer: Boston, MA, USA, 2003; Volume 725, pp. 81–100. [CrossRef]
44. Xu, S.; Chen, L. A novel approach for determining the optimal number of hidden layer neurons for FNN's and its application in data mining. In Proceedings of the 5th International Conference on Information Technology and Applications, ICITA 2008, Cairns, QLD, Australia, 23–26 June 2008; Number ICITA, pp. 683–686.
45. Sheela, K.G.; Deepa, S.N. Review on Methods to Fix Number of Hidden Neurons in Neural Networks. *Math. Probl. Eng.* **2013**, *2013*, 425740. [CrossRef]
46. Cawley, G.C.; Talbot, N.L. Preventing over-fitting during model selection via bayesian regularisation of the hyper-parameters. *J. Mach. Learn. Res.* **2007**, *8*, 841–861.

drones

MDPI

Article

Design and Analysis of a Deployment Mechanism with Clearance Compensation for High Stiffness Missile Wings

Yong Zhao [1], Shang Chen [2], Yimeng Gao [1], Honghao Yue [1], Xiaoze Yang [1], Tongle Lu [1] and Fei Yang [1,*]

[1] School of Mechatronics Engineering, Harbin Institute of Technology, Harbin 150080, China
[2] China Academy of Launch Vehicle Technology, Beijing 100076, China
* Correspondence: yangf@hit.edu.cn; Tel.: +86-133-2940-8782

Abstract: The deployment performance of the unfolded wing determines whether the winged missiles can fly normally after being launched, infecting the attack performance of the winged missiles. The paper proposes a new deployment mechanism with clearance eliminator. Based on the slider-crank principle, the proposed deployment mechanism achieves fast and low-impact deployment of the wings. The proposed clearance eliminator with shape memory alloy (SMA) effectively eliminates the clearance of the sliding pair and improves the support stiffness and stability of the deployed wing. The collision characteristics and the clearance elimination are studied for the deployment mechanism. The influence of the collision force on the motion state of the wing during the deployment is analyzed. The static stiffness of the wing under the clearance state and the deformation is analyzed. The dynamic stiffness under the catapult clearance elimination state is modeled based on the fractal geometry and contact stress theory. The relationship between the locking force and the support stiffness is revealed. The kinetic simulation is used to analyze the motion response during the action of the deployment mechanism. Modal analysis, harmonic response analysis, and random vibration analysis were conducted for the whole wings. A prototype was developed to verify the ejection performance of the wing according to the input load characteristics. The dynamic stiffness of the unfolded wings is tested by the fundamental frequency experiments to verify the performance of the clearance elimination assembly. The experimental results show that the designed deployment mechanism with clearance compensation achieves fast ejection and high stiffness retention of the missile wing.

Keywords: deloyment mechanism design; clearance eliminator with shape memory alloy; characteristic analysisp; stiffness enhancement

Citation: Zhao, Y.; Chen, S.; Gao, Y.; Yue, H.; Yang, X.; Lu, T.; Yang, F. Design and Analysis of a Deployment Mechanism with Clearance Compensation for High Stiffness Missile Wings. *Drones* **2022**, *6*, 211. https://doi.org/10.3390/drones6080211

Academic Editors: Andrzej Łukaszewicz, Wojciech Giernacki, Zbigniew Kulesza, Jaroslaw Pytka and Andriy Holovatyy

Received: 29 July 2022
Accepted: 15 August 2022
Published: 17 August 2022

1. Introduction

Winged missiles have the advantages of good maneuverability, easy control, and both the active and passive segments of the flight trajectory can be controlled. This form has been applied to airborne missiles, anti-ship missiles, anti-tank missiles, and air defense missiles [1–5]. As winged missiles increase in lethality, strike accuracy, and battlefield deterrence, the number of missiles carried and their launch efficiency are becoming important indicators of the attack capability of modern weapons such as warplanes and ships. If the space occupied by individual missiles can be reduced, the amount of ammunition carried will be significantly increased, and the carrying capacity of the aircraft will be greatly enhanced. Morphing wings can realize flexible maneuvering in different flight environments and maintain high flight efficiency [6–11]. The aircraft wing can be divided into the in-plane deformation of the wing [12,13], the out-plane deformation of the wing [14–19], and the wing deformation [20–23]. Winged missiles generally have foldable or retractable wings [24–28], so that they can be stowed in the launcher in a small footprint and their wings can open automatically when the missile is launched. In order to reduce the lateral dimensions of the missile; facilitate storage, transportation and launch; save storage and transportation space; improve the storage and transportation capacity; and improve the mobility and operational capability of the weapon system, the wings or part of the wings of the missile are often contracted to reduce the wingspan [29–33]. When the missile flies away from the launch device, the wings automatically unfold to ensure the normal flight of the missile.

The missile wings with the proposed deployment mechanisms are completely folded inside the missile body in the process of storage and transportation, which can effectively increase the loading rate. After the missile flies away from the launching device, the deployment mechanisms push out the wings synchronously and quickly and achieve position locking and stiffness maintenance. It can significantly improve the contraction rate, deployment efficiency, and wing surface stiffness of the missile wing and make the wing provide better aerodynamic force for the missile body. In order to improve the loading capacity and launch efficiency of the missile launch platform, the wing is usually designed to be retractable, and the existing retractable wings have two forms: rotational deployment and direct-acting deployment [34–38]. According to the rotational direction of the missile wing, the main airfoil is rotated and retracted horizontally and vertically. The rotational deployment radius is large, the aerodynamics of the airfoil during the deployment process is unstable, and the locking stiffness is low after the deployment of the wing. The direct-acting wing refers to the wing moving in a straight line during deployment. The airfoil aerodynamic force is more stable during the unfolding process than that of the rotational deployment, the airfoil is completely stowed inside the missile body when it is folded, and the stowage ratio is large. The direct-acting wing deployment mechanism requires the wing to be fully stowed inside the body in a straight line during retraction, which requires a higher stowage ratio, but the direct-acting wing deployment mechanism has obvious advantages in reducing the lateral dimensions of the missile and expanding the capacity of the magazine. The direct-acting wing deployment mechanism can hide all the wings inside the body of the missile when closing, which is effective in reducing the lateral size of the missile The use of the telescopic rudder surface is more flexible, and the wings can be controlled before and after deployment. The rudder deflection can be preset or deflected according to the command when the aircraft and missile are separated to control the separation attitude of the rudder, which is more conducive to separation safety.

The deployment performance of the unfolded wing is related to whether the winged missile can fly normally after being launched, which restricts the attack performance of the winged missile. After the wing deployment process, there are inevitably clearances between the wing and the kinematic pair of the missile body, and the influence of the kinematic pair clearance on the wing is often ignored in the traditional design. To improve the dynamic stiffness and stability of the wing, measures should be taken to eliminate the kinematic clearance. Therefore, in order to make the wings of the missile synchronized and to achieve fast deployment as well as reliable operation, the design of the transmission, wing locking, clearance elimination, and stiffness retention mechanisms of the wing deployment scheme are particularly important.

The main contributions and innovations of this paper lie in two aspects: 1. A new deployment mechanism is designed based on the slider-crank principle to achieve the fast and low-impact ejection of the missile wings. 2. A clearance eliminator with shape memory alloy (SMA) is designed for the deployed missile wing to achieve high stiffness and stability. The sections of the paper are organized as the following: Section 2 presents a new deployment mechanism of missile wings. The configuration and operating principle of the drive actuator and the clearance eliminator are introduced. Section 3 analyzes the effect of ejection collision characteristics on the motion of the wings and the stiffness under the clearance locking and unlocking. Section 4 analyzes the dynamic characteristics of the wing and the modalities of the whole mechanism. In Section 5, the ejection performance and the effect of eliminating clearance are investigated through prototype experiments.

2. Structure and Principle of the Missile Wings

2.1. Deployment Mechanism

In order to achieve a large stowage ratio, fast actuation, and high stiffness retention, we propose a new deployment mechanism with clearance eliminator for missile wings. The designed deployment mechanism mainly consists of the drive actuator and the clearance eliminator, as shown in Figure 1. The principle of wing ejection and locking is shown in Figure 2. The operating principle of the deployment mechanism includes three steps: 1. With the command of the unlocking issued, the upper and bottom locking devices realize the unlocking action of the wing through the compression springs. 2. Driven by the torsion spring, the crank slider mechanism of the drive actuator pushes out the wing along a straight line. 3. With the wing fully extended, the clearance eliminator eliminates the clearance of the kinematic pair to improve the wing stiffness.

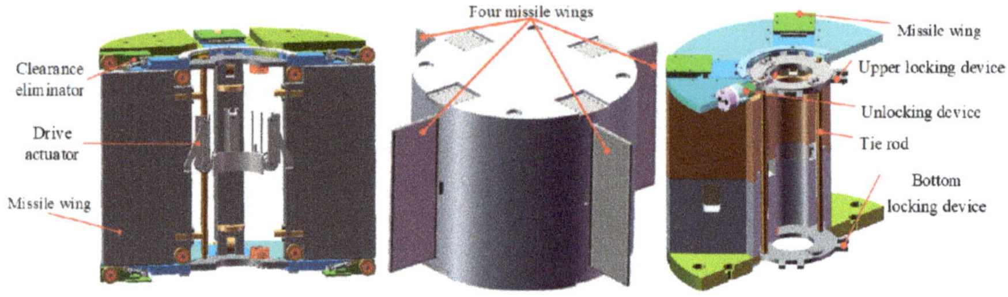

Figure 1. Deployment mechanism for the missile wings.

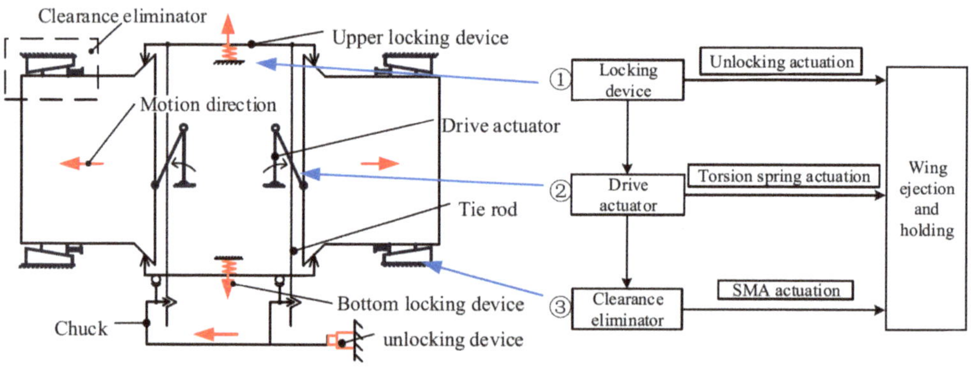

Figure 2. The principle of wing ejection and locking.

2.2. Drive Actuator

The drive actuator consists of a drive element, linkage mechanism, missile wings, and pulley block, as shown in Figure 3. The torsion spring, as the drive source, is mounted on the input shaft to save design space. One arm of force is supported on the base, and the other arm of force acts on linkage and pushes the missile wing out by linkage b. The ejection assembly of the deployment mechanism is based on the slider-crank principle, as shown in Figure 4. When the wing is pushed out, it is subjected to lateral load, resulting in friction resistance that affects the pushing out of the wing. In order to change the sliding friction between the wing and the base into rolling friction, an axial pulley and a lateral pulley are embedded in the root of the wing, and a pair of ball bearings with flanges are installed inside the pulley to enhance the smoothness and stability of the movement and to limit the pulley axially at the same time.

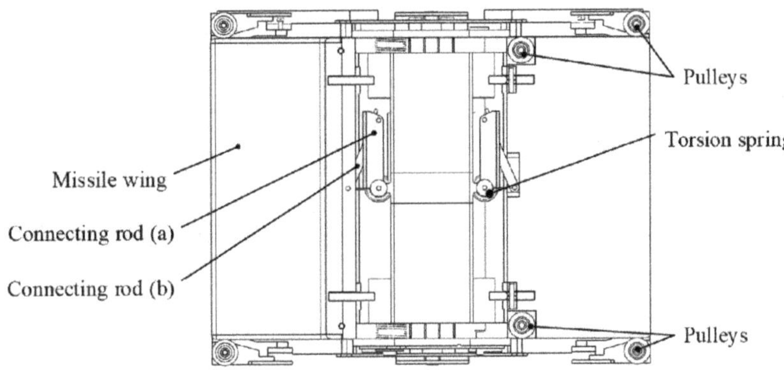

Figure 3. Structure of drive actuator.

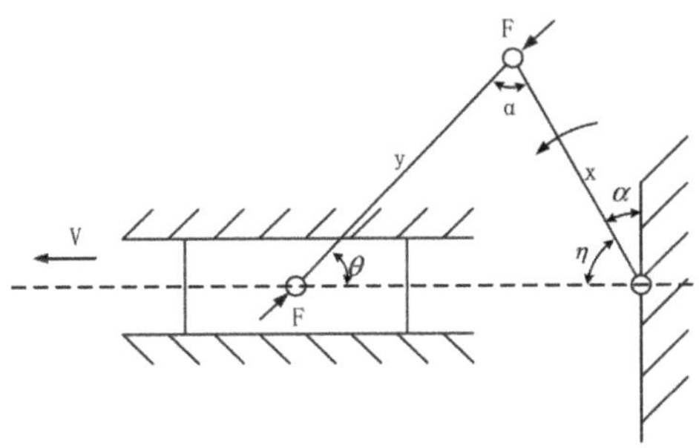

Figure 4. Working principle of drive actuator.

2.3. Clearance Eliminator

There are clearances between the kinematic pairs of the wing and the missile body to enable the smooth ejection of the wing. In order to improve the dynamic stiffness and stability of the wing, measures should be taken to eliminate the clearance of the kinematic pair. A Clearance eliminator with SMA is proposed to drive a wedge to eliminate the clearance of the kinematic pair between the wing and the base, to generate a locking force to improve the support stiffness of the wing and the base joint, and to improve the resonance frequency and stability of the wing.

The configuration of the clearance eliminator is shown in Figure 5. The end cap and the base are solidly connected to the missile body, and the shape memory alloy driver is hinged to the base at one end and the wedge at the other end. In order to speed up the deformation response of the shape memory alloy material, the memory alloy rod is heated by directly energizing it. The design of the SMA drive requires consideration of insulation and thermal insulation. As shown in Figure 6, conductive sheets are embedded in both ends of the memory alloy rod and heated by electricity. Heat-preserved sleeve made of insulating material is set on the outside of the memory alloy rod to play the role of insulation and heat preservation. A holding sleeve made of alloy steel is set on the outside of the heat-preserved sleeve to enhance the axial stiffness of the alloy rod and prevent destabilization under pressure. The working principle of the clearance eliminator is shown in Figure 7. The wedge is driven by the shape memory alloy to contact the base and the missile wing and generate mutual force. A positive pressure F_y on the contact surface of the wedge and the wing produces an axial locking effect on the wing, and a frictional force F_x on the contact surface of the wedge and the wing produces a lateral locking effect on the wing. By applying the locking force to the wing, the support stiffness of the root of the wing is improved and the stability of the wing is enhanced.

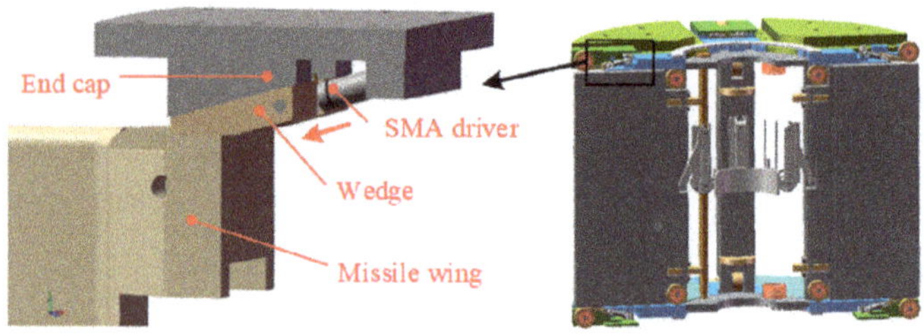

Figure 5. Configuration of clearance eliminator.

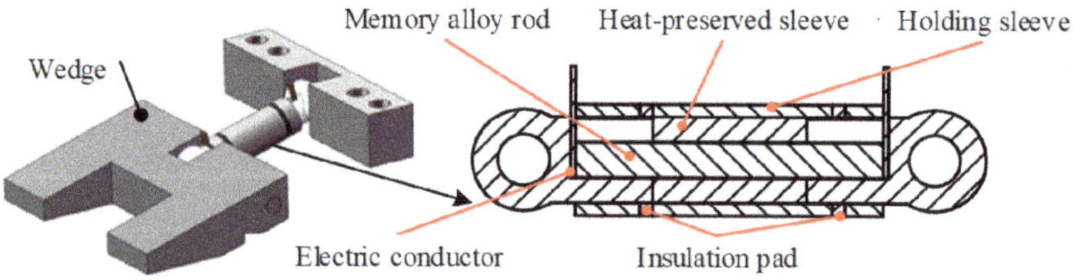

Figure 6. Configuration of SMA driver.

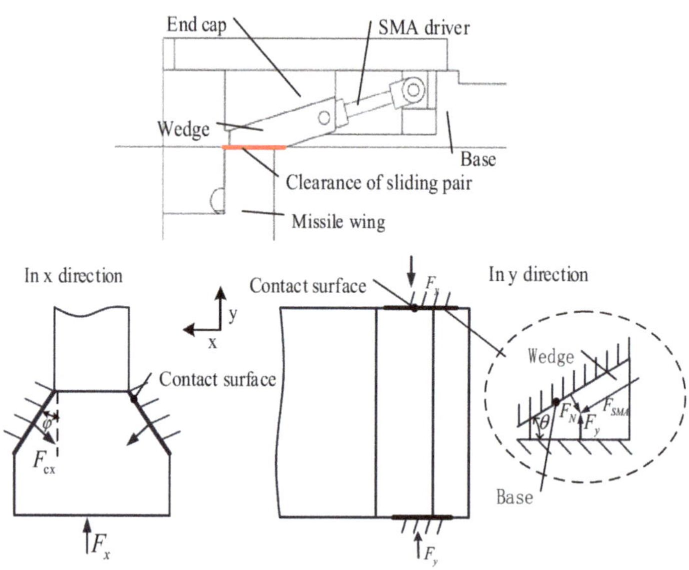

Figure 7. Working principle of the clearance eliminator.

3. Missile Wing Deployment and Clearance Elimination Analysis

3.1. Collision Characterization

In the movement of the wing, the joint at the hinge will cause vibration and collision force due to the existence of the clearance, so that the displacement and speed of the wing jitter. During the collision, the contact point can move relative to the collision body, and the collision force passes through the action point. The collision force and the deformation displacement of the collision body satisfy the theory of elasticity, the collision force equations are as follows:

$$F_n = F_k + F_d = K\delta^n + C(\delta)\dot{\delta} \tag{1}$$

$$C(\delta) = \frac{3K(1-e^2)}{4\dot{\delta}^-}(\dot{\delta})^n \tag{2}$$

where F_n is the normal contact force, F_k is the equivalent spring force, F_d is the equivalent damping force, K is the equivalent joint stiffness coefficient, C is the damping coefficient, δ is the normal puncture depth at the contact point, $\dot{\delta}$ is the normal relative velocity at the contact point, n is an exponent, 1.5 for metallic contacts, e is the collision recovery factor, and $\dot{\delta}^-$ is the relative velocity before collision.

The tangential friction at the clearance is expressed using the Coulomb friction model in ADAMS as:

$$F_t = -\mu_d F_n \mathrm{sgn}(v)\ (v \neq 0) \tag{3}$$

where $\mathrm{sgn}(v)$ is the sign function, v is the relative sliding velocity at the contact point, and μ_d is the friction factor.

The elastic force and friction are both simulated by the step function and friction function in Adams to analyze the collision at the hinge of the deployment mechanism. The missile wing and the deployment mechanism are simplified as shown in Figure 8. The collision force at the clearance and the effect of the clearance on the motion of the wing are calculated.

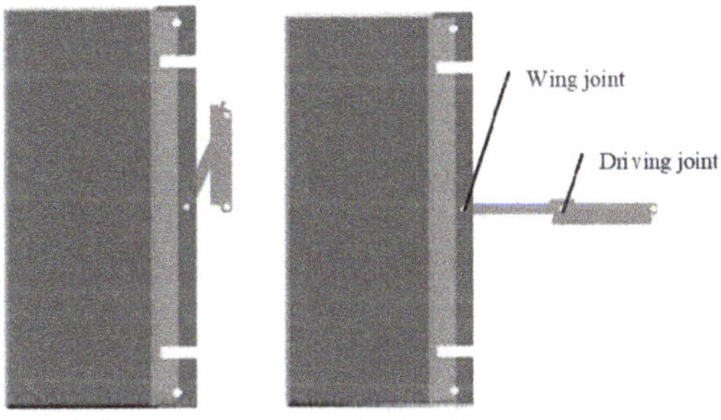

Figure 8. Simplified model of the wing deployment mechanism.

The stiffness coefficient K was taken as 1.2×10^5 N/m, the damping coefficient C was taken as 120 N·s/m, and the static and dynamic friction coefficients were set as 0.3 and 0.25, respectively. The simulations were carried out with the clearance of 0.1 mm, 0.3 mm, and 0.5 mm, respectively. The variation in the contact force in the driving joint and the wing joint with time is shown in Figures 9 and 10. The displacement and velocity of the wing with time are shown in Figures 11 and 12.

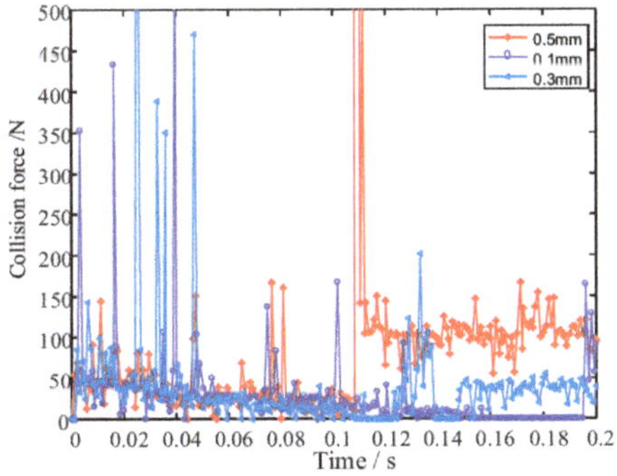

Figure 9. Collision force at the driving joint.

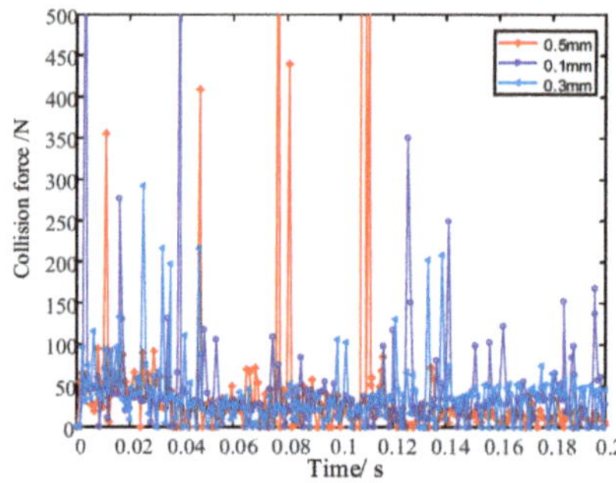

Figure 10. Collision force at the wing joint.

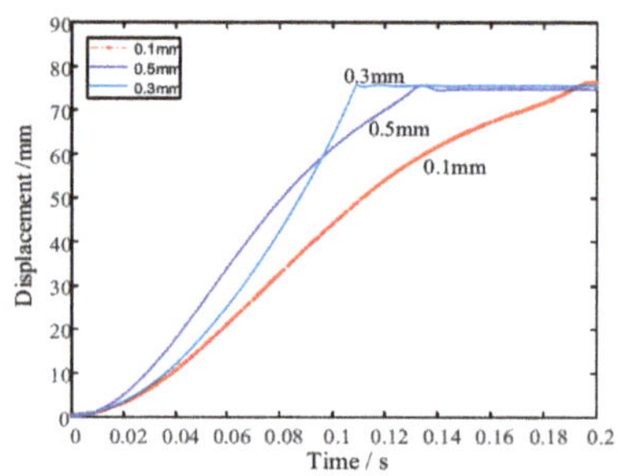

Figure 11. The effect of clearance on the displacement of the wing.

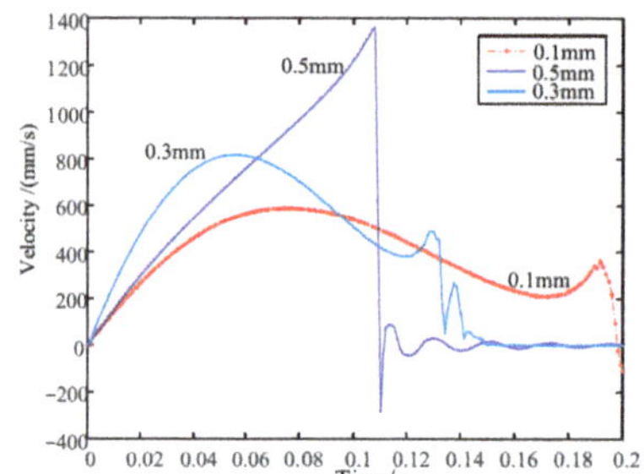

Figure 12. The effect of clearance on the velocity of the wing.

From the calculation results, it can be seen that when the clearance is 0.3 mm, the wing deployment time is the shortest. The clearance collision force is smaller, and the collision frequency is lower. The clearance has less influence on the fluctuation of the movement speed of the wing. This analysis result plays an important guiding role in the design of the subsequent joint manufacturing accuracy and the control of the dimensional chain.

3.2. Static Stiffness Characteristics with Clearance

In order to ensure that the wing is pushed out smoothly, the clearance δ between the wing and the kinematic pair is predetermined, as shown in Figure 13. After the wing is pushed out, due to the existence of the clearance, the wing is in a free state in a certain space and deflects freely under the surface load, and after deflecting a certain displacement, it bends under a certain component of the uniform load. As a result, the static deformation of the wing in the clearance state can be divided into two parts, i.e., the deformation deflection v_1 turning angle β_1 during the free deflection and the bending deformation v_2 and β_2 after one end is restrained; then, the static deformation of the wing under the action of the uniform load in the clearance state is the superposition of the two processes of deformation.

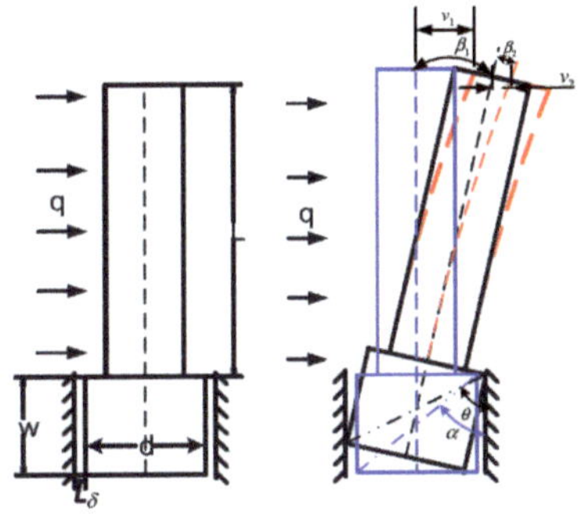

Figure 13. Static stiffness analysis of the missile wing.

From the geometric relationship, we obtain that:

$$v_1 = \delta \tag{4}$$

$$\beta_1 = \theta - \alpha \tag{5}$$

$$\theta = \arcsin\left(\frac{2\delta + d}{\sqrt{d^2 + w^2}}\right) \ \alpha = \arctan\left(\frac{d}{w}\right) \tag{6}$$

$$\beta_1 = \arcsin\left(\frac{2\delta}{\sqrt{d^2 + w^2}}\right) - \arctan\left(\frac{d}{w}\right) \tag{7}$$

Since the wing is subjected to a uniform load perpendicular to the wing surface as shown in Figure 14, only the transverse bending of the wing is considered, and a unit of arbitrary width Δb in the face is selected for analysis, which can be equated to a cantilever beam with length L, width Δb, and height h. The equivalent distributed load on it is F'.

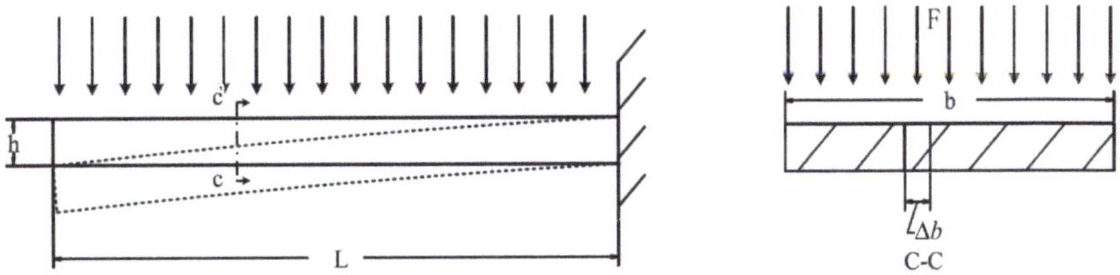

Figure 14. Schematic of the wing subjected to normal load.

From the deflection characteristics of the cantilever beam, it follows that:

$$v = \frac{F'L^4}{8EI} \ \beta = \frac{F'L^3}{6EI} \ I = \frac{\Delta b h^3}{12} \ F' = F\frac{\Delta b}{b}$$

Substituting equations F' and I into the deflection v and angle of rotation β formulas, it is found that the deflection characteristics can be solved using the cantilever beam formula for any cross-sectional width under the action of a normal uniform load perpendicular to the surface, so the missile wing can be equated to a cantilever beam structure. The equivalent distributed load on it is $q\cos(\beta_1)$. Then, the deflection characteristics of the missile wing are as follows:

$$v_2 = \frac{q\cos(\beta_1)L^4}{8EI} \tag{8}$$

$$\beta_2 = \frac{q\cos(\beta_1)L^3}{6EI} \tag{9}$$

where E is the modulus of elasticity of the material, and I is the moment of inertia of the section; then, the maximum angle of rotation β of the wing and the maximum deflection v at the end of the wing are as follows:

$$\beta = \beta_1 + \beta_2 = \arcsin(\frac{2\delta}{\sqrt{d^2 + w^2}}) - \arctan(\frac{d}{w}) + \frac{q\cos(\beta_1)L^3}{6EI} \tag{10}$$

$$v = v_1 + v_2 = \delta + \frac{q\cos(\beta_1)L^4}{8EI} \tag{11}$$

The deflection angle and deflection of the wing under the uniform load are shown in Figures 15 and 16.

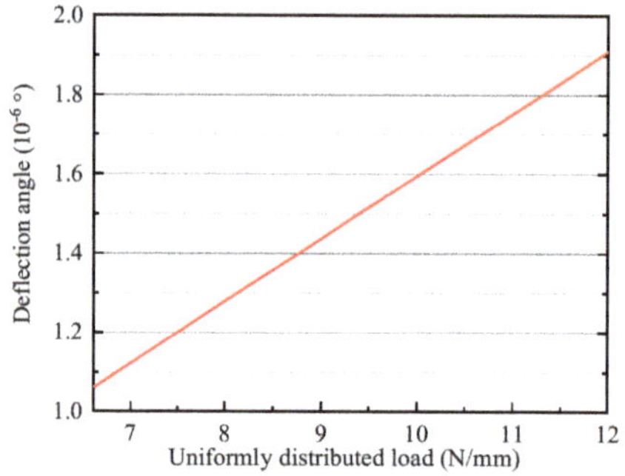

Figure 15. Deflection angle–load relationship.

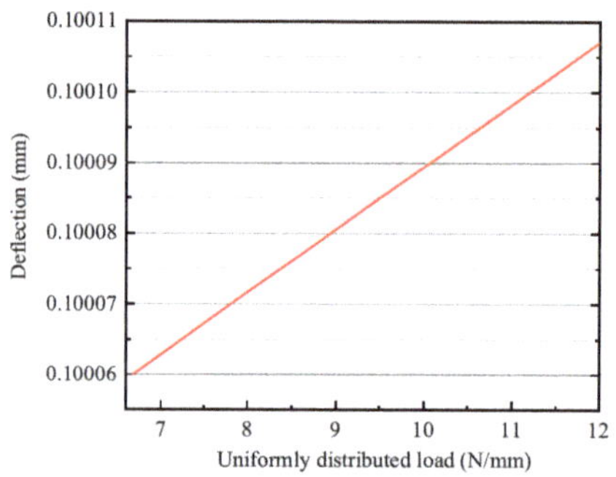

Figure 16. Deflection–load relationship.

In accordance with the design index of the wing deployment mechanism, the maximum normal load is 700 N. The airfoil uniform load is $q = \frac{700}{L} = 9.33$ N/mm, the wing deflection angle is $14.8402 \times 10^{-6\circ}$, and the end deflection is 0.1008 mm. From the static load analysis results, it can be seen that the clearance has a great impact on the deformation of the wing so that there is a certain degree of free deflection of the wing. In order to enhance the stability of the wings, it is necessary to design a clearance eliminator to compensate for the clearance at the kinematic pair of the wings.

3.3. Clearance-Free Locking Stiffness Modeling

When the structure and material of the missile wing deployment mechanism are determined, the mass matrix of the deployment mechanism system is fixed. So, the vibration frequency of the deployment mechanism is mainly affected by the system stiffness. By locking the root of the wing through the clearance eliminator to provide reliable support to the wing root, the system stiffness can be effectively improved, further improving the dynamic stiffness characteristics.

By eliminating the clearance at the kinematic pair of the missile wing using the clearance eliminator, the connection between the root of the missile wing and the base is transformed from the clearance state to the contact state, as shown in Figure 7. In the x direction, the wing contacts the base through the V-shaped contact surface and applies pre-stress to the contact surface in the x direction by applying transverse locking force. In the y direction, the top and bottom ends of the wing contact the base by the wedged force and apply pre-stress to the contact surface in the y direction by applying longitudinal pre-stress.

The wedge interacts with the wing and the base under the action of the driving force of the shape memory alloy F_{SMA}. The transverse locking force F_x is generated by the frictional force f interacting between the wedge and the missile wing. During the interaction between the wedge and the missile wing, small deformations occur tangentially and normally along the contact surface, and it is known from Coulomb friction theory that the frictional force f is proportional to the contact surface load F_y, i.e., $f = kF_y$ and $F_y = \frac{F_{SMA}}{\sin\theta}$ (θ is the inclination angle of the wedge). The relationship between the transverse locking force F_x and the driving force of the shape memory alloy F_{SMA} can be introduced as:

$$F_x = 2f = \frac{2k}{\sin\theta}F_{SMA} \tag{12}$$

The frictional force f generated at the contact surface under different F_{SMA} is obtained by simulation analysis, as shown in Figure 17.

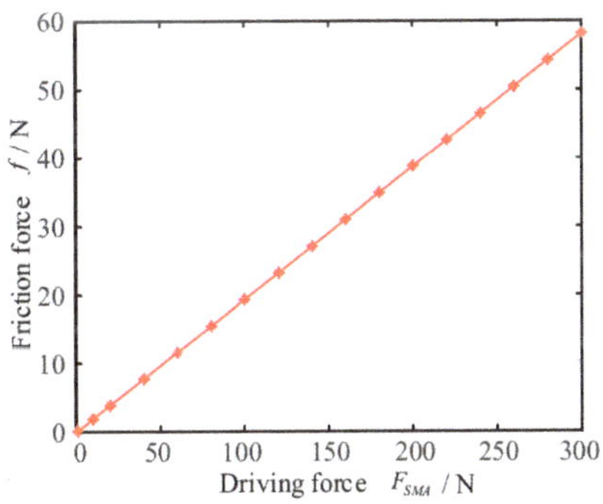

Figure 17. Relationship between F_{SMA} and f.

It can be seen that f basically varies linearly with F_{SMA}. It can be determined by the slope of the image that the parameter $k = 0.052$, from which the relationship between F_x and F_{SMA} can be obtained as:

$$F_x = \frac{0.104}{\sin\theta}F_{SMA} \tag{13}$$

The wing root is connected to the base through the clearance eliminator. The connection characteristics of the contact surface have a great influence on the dynamic stiffness of the wing. If the root support is reliable, the wing structure can be equivalent to a cantilevered thin plate. Its modal characteristics can be derived according to the finite element method. The inherent frequency is only related to the shape parameters of the wing and the structural material. With the structural material of the wing given, the inherent frequency is constant. Therefore, the dynamic stiffness analysis of the wing focuses on the dynamic stiffness analysis of the connection between the wing root and the base. Assuming that the wing is a rigid body, the relationship between the different locking forces and the frequency response of the wing is established under the clearance elimination state.

The locking force F_x in the x direction generates a lateral contact force F_{cx} on the V-shaped contact surface, creating a contact stiffness on the V-shaped contact surface. The wing root can be equated to a support structure as shown in Figure 18. The support of the contact surface can be equated to a spring of the same stiffness.

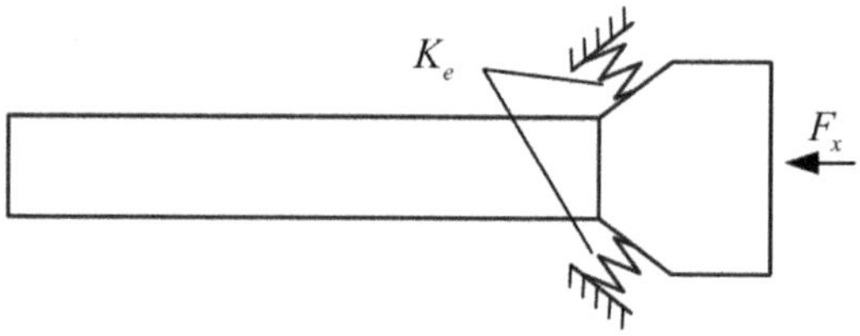

Figure 18. Equivalent diagram of the support part.

Based on fractal geometry, the normal contact stiffness of the V-shaped contact surface is modeled with reference to the Hertz contact theory. Due to the large area of contact area of the bonding surface, it can be assumed that a small amount of elastic deformation ϖ occurs at the bonding surface. ϖ_c is the critical contact deformation of the contact surface from elastic to elasto-plastic deformation. ϖ is much smaller than ϖ_c.

According to Hertz contact theory, when the micro-convex body between V-contact surfaces is in elastic contact, the contact load $f_e(\varpi)$ of the micro-convex body can be obtained as follows:

$$f_e(\varpi) = \frac{4}{3} E R^{\frac{1}{2}} \varpi^{\frac{3}{2}} \tag{14}$$

From $k = \frac{df}{d\varpi}$ we can obtain the contact stiffness of micro-convex body as:

$$k_e(\varpi) = 2 E R^{\frac{1}{2}} \varpi^{\frac{1}{2}} \tag{15}$$

where R is an equivalent radius of curvature of the micro-convex body on the contact surface, and E is the composite modulus of elasticity of the material, $E = [(1-\nu_1)/E_1 + (1-\nu_2)/E_2]^{-1}$. E_1 and E_2 are the modulus of elasticity of the two surface materials, respectively, and ν_1 and ν_2 are the corresponding Poisson's ratios. ϖ is the deformation of the contact point.

According to fractal theory, the equivalent radius of curvature of a micro-convex body on a machined contact surface is calculated by the following equation:

$$R = \frac{a^{\frac{D}{2}}}{2^{4-2D} \pi^{\frac{D}{2}} G^{D-1} \sqrt{\ln^{\gamma}}} \tag{16}$$

where a is and intermediate variable, $a = \left(\frac{2^{9-2D} G^{2D-2} \pi^{D-3} \ln^{\gamma}}{H^2 \lambda^2}\right)^{\frac{1}{D-1}}$; G is the characteristic factor responding to the contour size, and the height dimension parameter of the milled machined surface is 1.2117×10^{-4} m. γ is the spatial frequency of the random contour, and $\gamma = 1.5$. D is the number of fractal cones of the contour, which is 1.2183. H is the hardness of the material, and $H = 2.8Y$. Y is the yield strength of the material. λ is the average contact surface pressure coefficient, and $\lambda = 0.4645 + 0.314v$. v is the Poisson's ratio of the material at the bonding surface.

By Hooke's law: $\sigma = E \cdot \varepsilon = \frac{F}{S} \rightarrow E \cdot \frac{w}{l} = \frac{F}{S}$. Then, the deformation is: $w = \frac{Fl}{SE}$, where σ, ε, F, l, S are the contact surface stress, strain, contact surface normal pressure, contact surface thickness, and contact area, respectively, which in turn leads to:

$$k_e(\varpi) = \left\{ \frac{\left[\left(\frac{2^{9-2D} G^{2D-2} \pi^{D-3} \ln^{\gamma}}{H^2 \lambda^2}\right)^{\frac{1}{D-1}}\right]^{\frac{D}{2}}}{2^{4-2D} \pi^{\frac{D}{2}} G^{D-1} \sqrt{\ln^{\gamma}}} \right\}^{\frac{1}{2}} \left\{ \frac{\frac{F_x}{2 \sin \varphi} l}{S \frac{E}{2(1-\nu)}} \right\}^{\frac{1}{2}} \tag{17}$$

The angular velocity of vibration of the missile wing root is $w = \sqrt{\frac{k_e}{m}}$. Intrinsic frequency at the root support of the missile wing is $f = \frac{w_e}{2\pi}$.

Taking l, S, φ as 6 mm, 2661.5 mm^2, and 37.37°, respectively, the relationship between the missile wing vibration frequency f and the transverse locking force F_x is derived as shown in Figure 19.

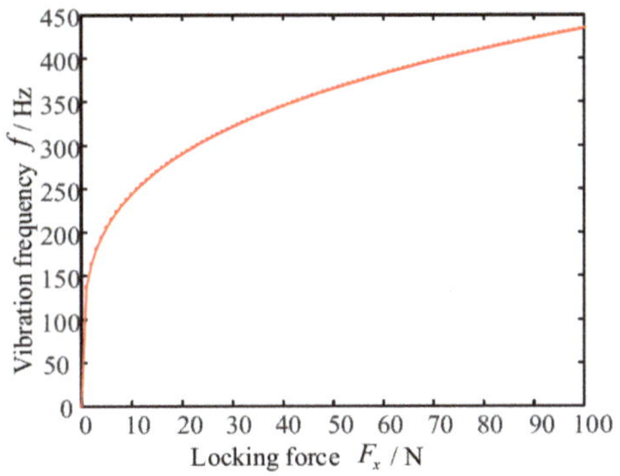

Figure 19. Vibration frequency versus locking force.

As can be seen from Figure 19, the frequency response of the wing first increases sharply when the locking force increases from 0 under the action of transverse locking. Then, when the locking force reaches 20 N, increase in frequency the wing starts to slow down with the increase in the locking force, and the frequency response of the wing gradually tends to become smooth as the locking force continues to increase. The parameters are optimized by simulation software, and the frequency response of the wing under different lateral locking forces is shown in Figure 20.

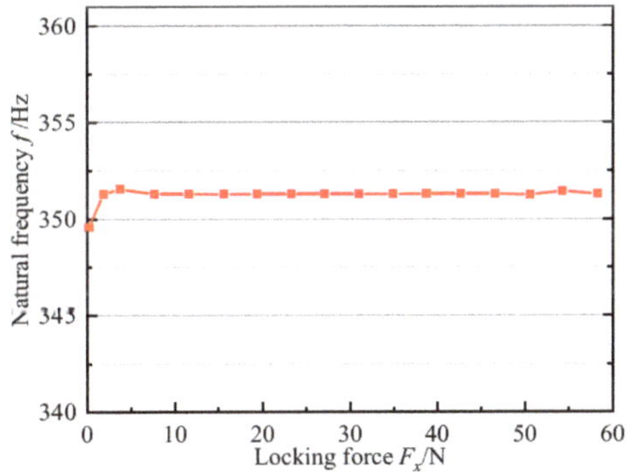

Figure 20. The relationship between the intrinsic frequency of the wing and the locking force.

The simulation results show that when transverse locking is applied, a small locking force can cause the vibration frequency of the root of the wing to stop. The frequency response tends to stabilize with the increase in the locking force. Comparing with the theoretical results, it can be found that both of them have the tendency that the frequency response of the wing starts to increase sharply with the increase in the locking force. The frequency response of the wing gradually tends to be stable with the increase in the locking force. The reason for the difference between the theoretical and simulation results is that the constraint boundary conditions of the wing root are different between theory and simulation. From the perspective of theoretical modeling, the locking force on the wing root will have a great effect on the contact stiffness. While from the simulation analysis, the effect of the locking force on the frequency response of the wing is not obvious because it ignores the surface characteristics of the contact surface. It considers the contact form as unconsolidated once the lateral locking force is applied. Therefore, the effect of the locking force on the frequency response of the missile wing is not obvious.

4. Mechanical Characterization

4.1. Kinetic Characteristics

The state of motion during the deployment of the wing is analyzed. The rolling friction coefficient between the wing and the contact surface during the motion of the wing is set to 0.05. The frictional reaction force generated by the air load during the deployment of the wing is equated by attaching a spring to the wing, and the driving torque is set to 1 Nm. The displacement versus time and velocity versus time during the deployment of the wing are shown in Figures 21 and 22, respectively.

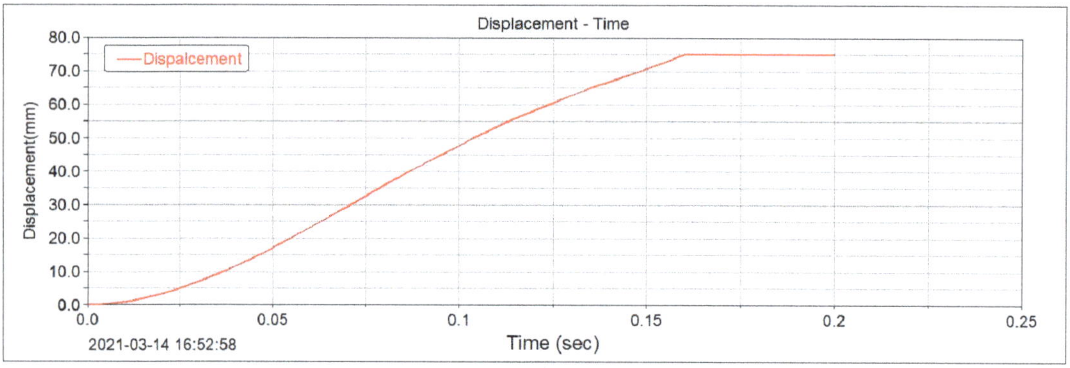

Figure 21. Displacement versus time.

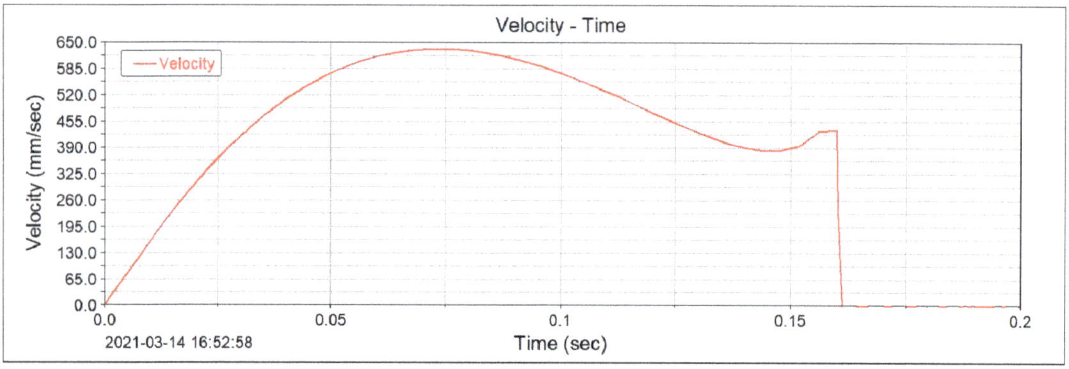

Figure 22. Velocity versus time.

From the simulation results, it can be seen that the deployment time of the wing is about 0.154 s, which is basically the same as the solution of the kinetic equation. It can be determined that the time to push the wing into place is about 0.15~0.16 s, which meets the speed requirement of the deployment mechanism.

4.2. Modal Analysis

In the unlocked state, Figure 23 shows the boundary conditions and mesh division according to the loading environment. For convenience, we use free mixed mesh generation in the study. The modal analysis is carried out in the unpreloaded state. The results of the fundamental frequency and the first six orders of frequency are shown in Table 1.

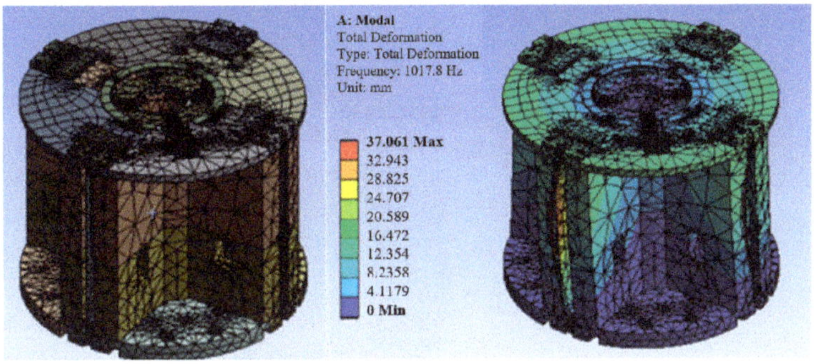

Figure 23. Mesh division and modal analysis under docking condition.

Table 1. First six orders of frequency of the whole machine in the unlocked state. (Hz).

The First-Order	The Second-Order	The Third-Order	The Fourth-Order	The Fifth-Order	The Sixth-Order
1017.8	1196.5	1197.9	1269.7	1314.3	1315

After the wing is pushed into place and the clearance eliminator is actuated, the pre-stress-modal analysis is performed on the wing. The pre-stress loading is shown in Figure 24a. The load simulates the driving force of the SMA actuator, and the results of the wing modal analysis are shown in Figure 24b. The first six orders of its inherent frequency are obtained as shown in Table 2.

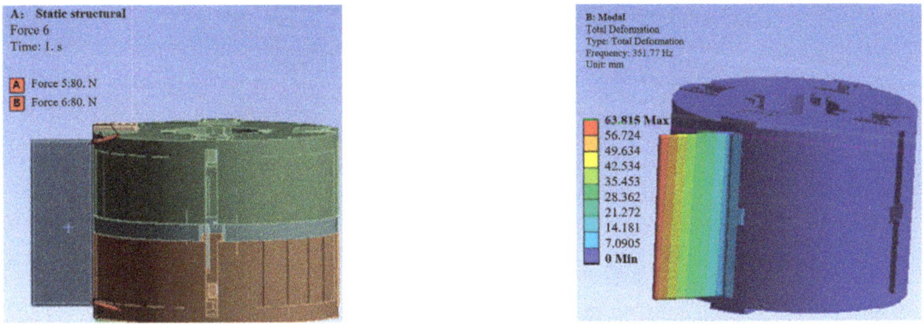

(**a**) (**b**)

Figure 24. Modal analysis with deployment: (**a**) Pre-stress loading; (**b**) Results of modal analysis.

Table 2. First six orders of frequency after the deployment of the missile wing (Hz).

The First-Order	The Second-Order	The Third-Order	The Fourth-Order	The Fifth-Order	The Sixth-Order
351.77	986.6	1406.1	1885.4	2129.4	2567.7

Based on the existing pre-stress modal analysis results, the harmonic response analysis of the missile wing was carried out with the frequency band set to 0~500 Hz and the damping coefficient set to 0.05. In addition, a 700 N uniform normal load was applied on the surface of the wing, and the amplitude versus frequency response was obtained as shown in Figure 25. At resonance, the swept frequency phase angle is set to 90°, as shown in Figure 26, and the maximum deformation of the missile wing is 7.855 mm.

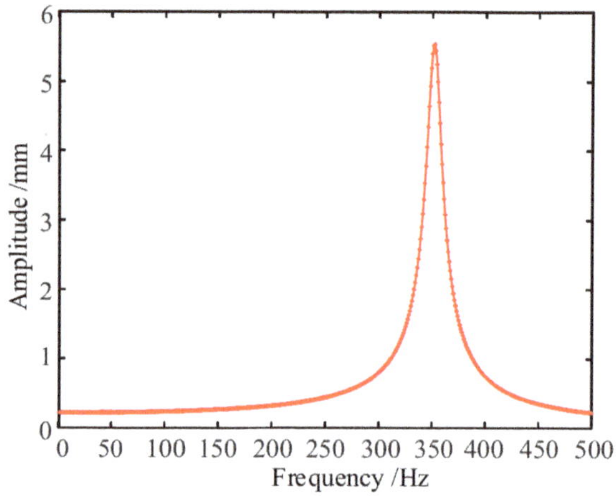

Figure 25. Amplitude–frequency response characteristics.

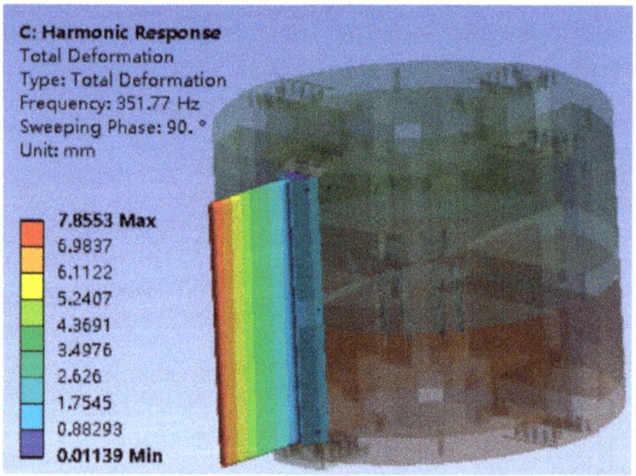

Figure 26. Schematic diagram of maximum deformation of the wing during resonance.

With the maneuvering flight of the missile, the deployed wing is subjected to complex non-constant aerodynamic effects. The environmental loads on the wing deployment mechanism are mostly manifested as irregular dynamic inputs. In order to evaluate the random vibration fatigue characteristics of the mechanism, the random vibration analysis is performed on the basis of the modal analysis for the wing deployment mechanism. By setting the power spectral density parameters specified in the vibration test standard to simulate the irregular dynamic environmental loads on the mechanism, the random vibration response analysis is performed on the missile wing deployment mechanism.

The results of the modal analysis are used as the initial conditions of the random vibration analysis, and the power spectral density excitation in the xyz direction is set as shown in Figure 27. The displacement response of the device as a whole is obtained, as shown in Figure 28. The maximum deformation of the end of the wing is 0.273 mm, which means that it will not cause structural instability or damage under the large power spectral density excitation.

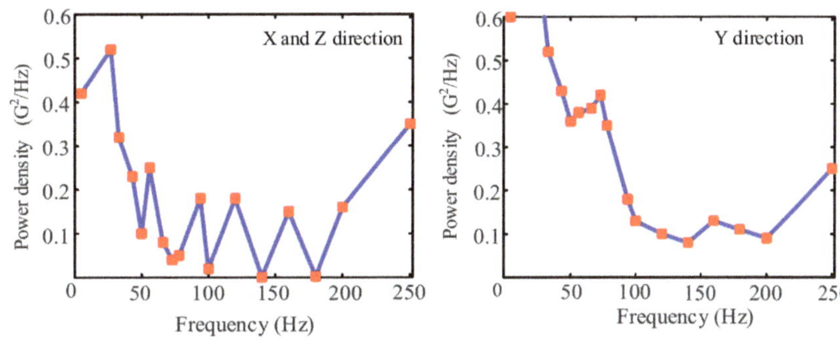

Figure 27. Loaded power spectral density.

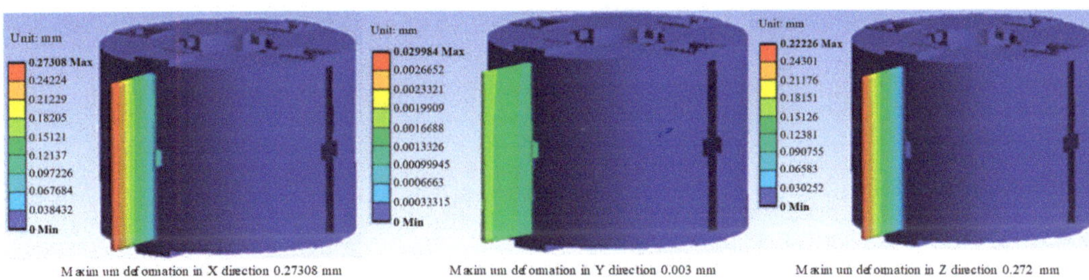

Figure 28. Displacement response spectrum.

In order to verify the connection stiffness of the wing deployment mechanism along the x-direction and z-direction, the acceleration response spectrum of a point at the end of the wing is selected, as shown in Figure 29, in which the x-direction's and z-direction's input power spectrum densities are the same. The results show that the acceleration responses almost completely overlap, indicating that the transverse connection stiffness of the device is high and the stability is excellent.

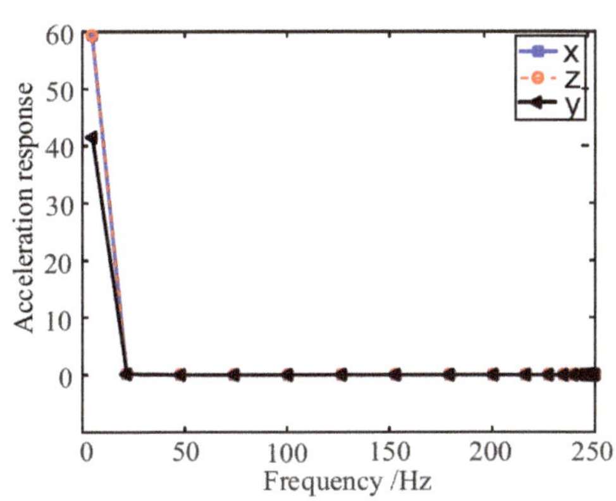

Figure 29. Acceleration response.

5. Experimental Research

5.1. Verification of Wing Deployment Characteristics

The developed principle prototype is shown in Figure 30. To save costs and improve the test efficiency, only one set of opposing wings was deployed. In order to reduce the weight of the mechanism, except for the key stressed parts which are machined by 40Cr material, the rest of the parts are made of aluminum alloy, and the overall mass of the prototype is about 15 Kg. A high-speed camera is used to record the deployment time of the principle prototype wing, as shown in Figure 31. The deployment process is shown in Figure 32. The complete deployment time of the missile wing is about 0.14 s, which meets the requirement of rapidity. The experiments show that there is a difference of about 6 ms between the deployment times of the two wings. There are three main reasons for this difference: 1. The manufacturing error of the prototype leads to inconsistent clearances. The impact forces acting on the wining are also inconsistent during the deployment process. 2. The assembly error causes the installation position of the torsion spring to shift, such as the assembly error of the shaft hole of the torsion springs. 3. The performance difference of the torsion springs leads to inconsistent driving torques of the deployment mechanisms. The size and stiffness coefficient of the torsion springs cannot be completely consistent.

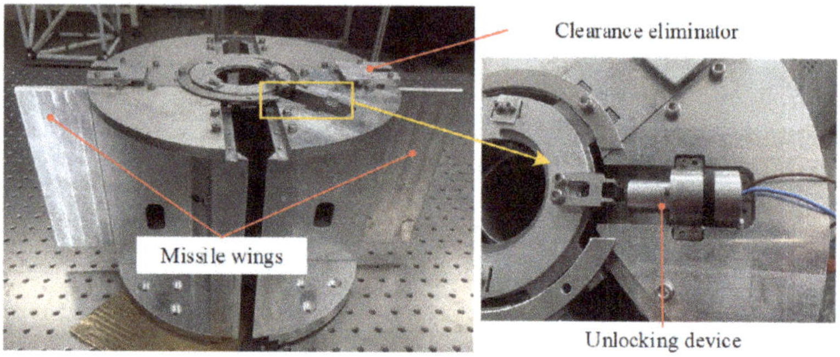

Figure 30. Principle prototype of deployment mechanism.

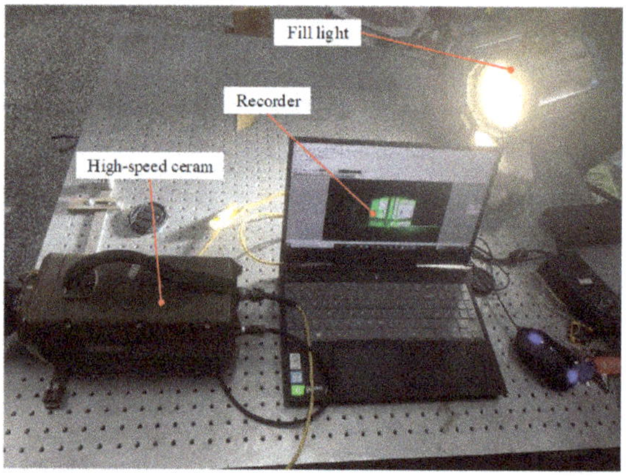

Figure 31. High-speed camera test system.

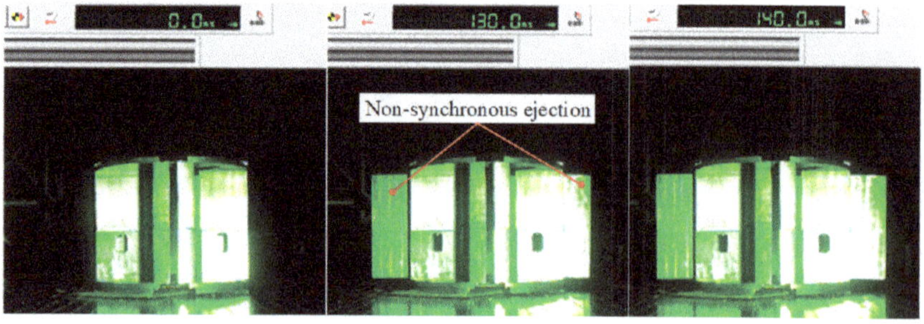

Figure 32. Testing results of the high-speed camera.

According to the design index of the wing deployment mechanism, the wing is subjected to a normal load that varies linearly with the push-out distance during the deployment process. The load was equated to a spring load, and the launch function test was conducted on the missile wing deployment mechanism under loading conditions. The test device is shown in Figure 33. The test of the wing deployment process under the applied load condition, the wing can be pushed out quickly under the normal load that varies linearly with the push-out distance in the range of 0~700 N.

Figure 33. Wing load test.

5.2. Fundamental Frequency Test

The prototype of the developed clearance eliminator and the built modal test set are shown in Figure 34. The internal SMA driver of the prototype is heated by energizing. The support stiffness of the wing is tested to verify the function of the clearance eliminator and to test the dynamic support stiffness performance after the wing is deployed.

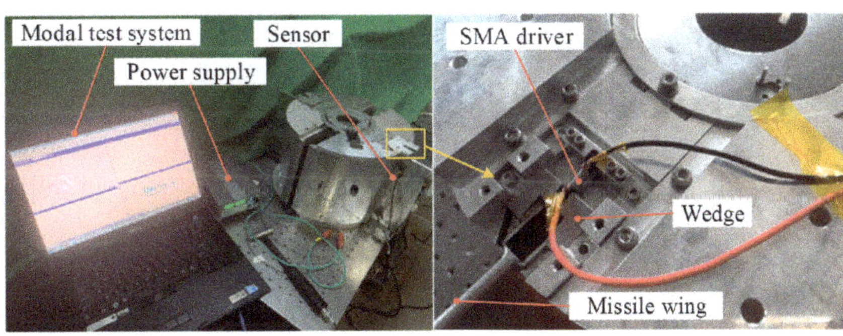

Figure 34. Modal test experiment.

As shown in Figure 34, the acceleration sensors are arranged at the four corners of the wing, and the vibration characteristics of the wing are measured by the LMS modal test system. The amplitude–frequency characteristics of the wing vibration are shown in Figure 35. The action of the clearance eliminator is obtained by the hammering test, and its mode of vibration is shown in Figure 36. The first-order frequency of the wing is about 220 Hz, which is smaller than the FEM results. There are three main reasons: 1. The rough mesh division of assembly leads to a low accuracy of the calculation results. 2. The material parameters used in assembly simulation cannot be completely consistent with the actual values. 3. There are errors and clearance during processing and assembly. Excessive bolt preload causes component deformation. By analyzing the mode of vibration, the support stiffness of one side of the wing is lower than the other side, indicating that the clearance eliminator on the weaker side has not fully eliminated the clearance of the kinematic pair of the wing. This is because the clearance is too large due to machining errors, exceeding the memory alloy actuator travel. In addition, the prototype has become deformed during the test process, making the clearance larger. According to the overall test results of the wing deployment mechanism, it can be verified that the function of the clearance eliminator meets the design requirements.

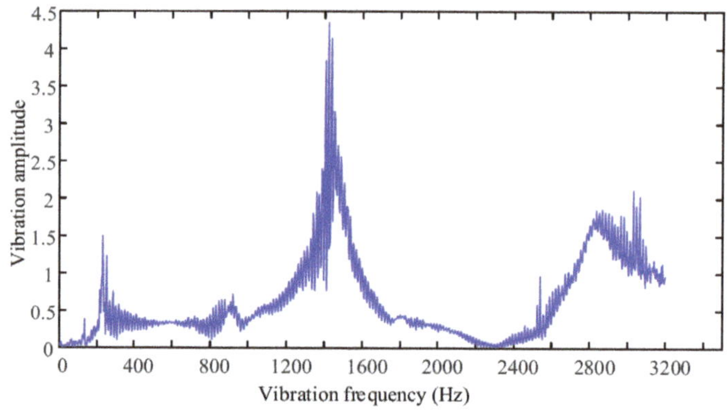

Figure 35. The amplitude–frequency of the wing vibration.

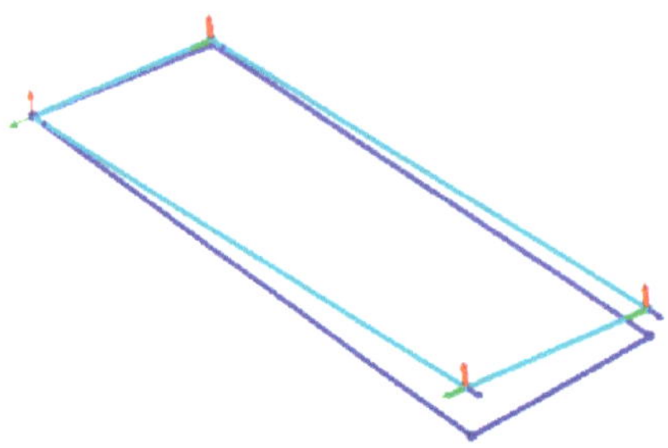

Figure 36. The mode of wing vibration.

6. Conclusions

In order to achieve rapid ejection and high stiffness retention of the missile wings, a deployment mechanism with clearance elimination is proposed. The deployment performance and wing locking performance are studied through theoretical modeling, simulation and experiment. The static load bearing of the deployment mechanism is analyzed, and the stresses of the overall and internal components of the deployment mechanism are obtained. The static stiffness characteristics of the deployment mechanism are analyzed, and the deflection of the missile wing under load in the clearance state is obtained. The dynamic stiffness characteristics of the wing deployment mechanism are analyzed, and the relationship between the locking force and the dynamic support stiffness of the wing is obtained. The influences of the collision force on the motion state of the wing are analyzed. The kinetic simulations are conducted to obtain the displacement and velocity response to time during the launch of the wing. Static simulation analysis is carried out to obtain the force and deformation of the wing deployment mechanism under static load conditions. The modal analysis, harmonic response analysis, and random vibration analysis are conducted for the locking and clearance elimination states, respectively. The results show that the overall joint stiffness is high and the stability is great. The prototype of the deployment mechanism has been developed with an ejection stroke of 75 mm. High-speed camera recording results show that the deployment time is 0.14 s. Under the simulated load of the springs, the actuation of the deployment mechanism is reliable and stable. The vibration characteristics of the wings are measured by the LMS modal test system. The results show that the first-order frequency of the wing is about 220 Hz after the gap elimination, indicating good dynamic support stiffness is achieved. The designed deployment mechanism with gap compensation achieves fast ejection and high stiffness retention. In future research, we will enhance the performance of the deployment mechanism with a clearance eliminator to improve actuation synchronization and consistency.

Author Contributions: Conceptualization, H.Y. and F.Y.; methodology, Y.Z. and T.L.; software, Y.Z. and Y.G.; validation, X.Y., S.C. and Y.Z.; formal analysis, F.Y. and Y.G.; investigation, S.C. and Y.G.; resources, F.Y.; data curation, S.C. and T.L.; writing—original draft preparation, Y.Z.; writing—review and editing, X.Y. and Y.G.; visualization, X.Y. and T.L.; supervision, F.Y. and S.C.; project administration, H.Y.; funding acquisition, H.Y. All authors have read and agreed to the published version of the manuscript.

Funding: This research was funded by the National Natural Science Foundation of China (52075118).

Institutional Review Board Statement: Not applicable.

Data Availability Statement: Not applicable.

Acknowledgments: The author would like to thank the reviewers and the editors for their valuable comments and constructive suggestions that helped to improve the paper significantly.

Conflicts of Interest: The authors declare no conflict of interest.

References

1. Allen, J.M. *Aerodynamics of an Axisymmetric Missile Concept Having Cruciform Strakes and In-Line Tail Fins from Mach 0.60 to 4.63, Supplement*; NASA: Washington, DC, USA, 2005.
2. McDaniel, D.R.; Nichols, R.H.; Eymann, T.A.; Starr, R.E.; Morton, S.A. Accuracy and Performance Improvements to Kestrel's Near-Body Flow Solver. In *AIAA Paper 2016–1051*; AIAA: San Diego, CA, USA, 2016.
3. Kim, D.H.; Lee, I.; Paek, S.K. Nonlinear Aeroelastic Instability of a Supersonic Missile Wing with Pitch Axis Freeplay. *Int. J. Aeronaut. Space Sci.* **2003**, *4*, 53–62. [CrossRef]
4. Eidell, M.; Nance, R.; McGowan, G.; Carpenter, J.; Moore, F. Computational Investigation of Roll Damping for Missile Configurations. In Proceedings of the 30th AIAA Applied Aerodynamics Conference, New Orleans, LA, USA, 25–28 June 2012.
5. Ghoreyshi, M.; Jirasek, A.; Aref, P.; Seidel, J. Computational aerodynamic investigation of long strake-tail missile configurations. *Aerosp. Sci. Technol.* **2022**, *127*, 107704. [CrossRef]
6. Kim, S.I. Analysis of Folding Wing Deployment with Aero and Restraint Effects. *J. Korean Soc. Aeronaut. Space Sci.* **2015**, *43*, 533–539. [CrossRef]
7. Kroyer, R. Wing mechanism analysis. *Comput. Struct.* **1999**, *72*, 253–265. [CrossRef]
8. Yang, J.; Wen, L.; Jiang, B.; Wang, Z. Dynamic Modeling and Flight Simulation of a Folding Wing-Tip UAV. In Proceedings of the 2020 Chinese Control and Decision Conference (CCDC), Hefei, China, 22–24 August 2020.
9. John, D.; Pawel, C.; Barry, L. Flight Dynamic Simulation Assessment of a Morphable Hyper-Elliptic Cambered Span Winged Configuration. In Proceedings of the AIAA Atmospheric Flight Mechanics Conference and Exhibit, Austin, TX, USA, 11–14 August 2003.
10. Matthew, S.P.; Brian, S.; Franklin, E.E.; Geoffrey, F.J. Vibration and Flutter Characteristics of a Folding Wing. *J. Aircr.* **2009**, *46*, 791–799.
11. Obradovic, B.; Subbarao, K. Modeling of flight dynamics of morphing wing aircraft. *J. Aircr.* **2012**, *48*, 391–402. [CrossRef]
12. Samuel, J.B.; Pines, D. Design and testing of a pneumatic telescopic wing for unmanned aerial vehicles. *J. Aircr.* **2007**, *44*, 1088–1099. [CrossRef]
13. Joo, J.J.; Sers, B.; Johnson, T.; Frecker, M.I. Optimal Actuator Location within a Morphing Wing Scissor Mechanism Configuration. In Proceedings of the Conference on Smart Structures and Materials 2006: Modeling, Signal Processing, and Control, San Diego, CA, USA, 27 March 2006.
14. Xu, H.; Huang, Q.; Han, J.; Yun, H.; Xie, X.P. Calculation of hinge moments for a folding wing aircraft based on high-order panel method. *Math. Probl. Eng.* **2020**, *2020*, 8881233. [CrossRef]
15. Henry, J.; Schwartz, D.R.; Soukup, M.A.; Altman, A. Design, construction, and testing of a folding-wing, tube-launched micro air vehicle. In Proceedings of the 43rd AIAA Aerospace Sciences Meeting & Exhibit, Reno, NV, USA, 10–13 January 2005.
16. Vos, R.; Gurdal, Z.; Abdalla, M. Mechanism for warp-controlled twist of a morphing wing. *J. Aircr.* **2010**, *47*, 450–457. [CrossRef]
17. Manzo, J.; Garcia, E. Demonstration of an in situ morphing hyperelliptical cambered span wing mechanism. *Smart Mater. Struct.* **2010**, *19*, 025012. [CrossRef]
18. Xilun, D.; Anwei, Q.; Kun, X.U. Design and analysis of a scissor-bending deployable and foldable mechanism. *J. Mech. Eng.* **2020**, *56*, 55.
19. Abdulrahim, M.; Lind, R. Flight testing and response characteristics of a variable gull-wing morphing aircraft. *AIAA Pap.* **2004**, *5113*, 16–19.
20. Barbarino, S.; Gandhi, F.; Webster, S.D. Design of extendable chord sections for morphing helicopter rotor blades. *J. Intell. Mater. Syst. Struct.* **2011**, *22*, 891–905. [CrossRef]
21. Brailovski, V.; Terriault, P.; Georges, T.; Coutu, D. SMA actuators for morphing wings. *Phys. Procedia* **2010**, *10*, 197–203. [CrossRef]
22. Woods, B.K.S.; Friswell, M.I.; Wereley, N.M. Advanced kinematic tailoring for morphing aircraft actuation. *AIAA J.* **2014**, *52*, 788–798. [CrossRef]
23. Heo, H.; Ju, J.; Kim, D.M. Compliant cellular structures: Application to a passive morphing airfoil. *Compos. Struct.* **2013**, *106*, 560–569. [CrossRef]

24. Guyot, D.; Schülein, E. Novel Locally Swept Lattice Wings for Missile Control at High Speeds. In Proceedings of the 45th AIAA Aerospace Sciences Meeting and Exhibit DLR, Reno, NV, USA, 8–11 January 2007.
25. Jian-guo, G.; Jun, Z. Modeling and Simulation Research of Missile with Morphing Wings. In Proceedings of the 2010 Second International Conference on Intelligent Human-Machine Systems and Cybernetics, Nanjing, China, 26–28 August 2010; IEEE: New York, NY, USA, 2010; Volume 76, pp. 280–283.
26. Zhan, G.; Gong, Z.; Lv, Q.; Zhou, Z.; Wang, Z.; Yang, Z.; Zhou, D. Flight Test of Autonomous Formation Management for Multiple Fixed-Wing UAVs Based on Missile Parallel Method. *Drones* **2022**, *6*, 99. [CrossRef]
27. Takahashi, T.T.; Spall, R.J.; Turner, D.C.; Birney, M.A. Multi-Disciplinary Survey of Advanced Subsonic Tactical Cruise Missile Configuration. In Proceedings of the 43rd AIAA Aerospace Sciences Meeting & Exhibit, Reno, NV, USA, 10–13 January 2005.
28. Zhang, Y.; Chen, W.; Guo, C.; Zhang, Z.; Li, P. Simulation research on roll attitude initialization algorithm for fixed wing canards. In Proceedings of the 2017 IEEE International Conference on Mechatronics and Automation (ICMA), Takamatsu, Japan, 6–9 August 2017; IEEE: New York, NY, USA, 2017; pp. 1292–1296.
29. Zhang, J.; Yan, J. A Novel Control Approach for Flight-Stability of Fixed-Wing UAV Formation with Wind Field. *IEEE Syst. J.* **2020**, *15*, 2098–2108. [CrossRef]
30. Li, P.; Ni, Y.; Hou, C.; Wan, X.; Zhao, M. Nonlinear aeroelastic modeling of a folding wing structure. *J. Phys. Conf. Ser.* **2019**, *1215*, 012009. [CrossRef]
31. Dowell, E.H.; Tang, D.; Attar, P.J. Nonlinear aeroelastic study for folding wing structure. *AIAA J.* **2010**, *48*, 2187–2195.
32. Tang, D.; Dowell, E.H. Theoretical and experimental aeroelastic study for folding wing structures. *J. Aircr.* **2008**, *45*, 1136–1147. [CrossRef]
33. Otsuka, K.; Wang, Y.; Makihara, K. Deployable wing model considering structural flexibility and aerodynamic unsteadiness for deployment system design. *J. Sound Vib.* **2017**, *408*, 105–122. [CrossRef]
34. Gao, Y.; Hu, M.; Zhao, D.; Gao, X.; Lin, J. Dynamics and reliability analysis of the deployment process of spring folding wing. In Proceedings of the 2020 International Conference on Quality, Reliability, Risk, Maintenance, and Safety Engineering, Xi'an, China, 8–11 October 2020.
35. Gao, Y.; Hu, M.; Zhou, X.; Zhang, M. Reliability Evaluation for Cable-Spring Folding Wing Considering Synchronization of Deployable Mechanism. *Actuators* **2021**, *10*, 99. [CrossRef]
36. Harris, J.; Slegers, N. Performance of a fire-and-forget anti-tank missile with a damaged wing. *Math. Comput. Model* **2009**, *50*, 292–305. [CrossRef]
37. Wang, B.; Xie, L.; Fan, F.; Ma, H.; Zhao, B.; Li, H. Reliability analysis of folding wing deployable mechanism considering common cause failure. *J. Mech. Eng.* **2020**, *56*, 161–171.
38. Geva, A.; Abramovich, H.; Arieli, R. Investigation of a Morphing Wing Capable of Airfoil and Span Adjustment Using a Retractable Folding Mechanism. *Aerospace* **2019**, *6*, 85. [CrossRef]

drones

MDPI

Article

Factors Associated with the Adoption of Drones for Product Delivery in the Context of the COVID-19 Pandemic in Medellín, Colombia

Alejandro Valencia-Arias [1,*], Paula Andrea Rodríguez-Correa [2], Juan Camilo Patiño-Vanegas [3], Martha Benjumea-Arias [1], Jhony De La Cruz-Vargas [4] and Gustavo Moreno-López [5]

1 Facultad de Ciencias Económicas y Administrativas, Instituto Tecnológico Metropolitano, Medellín 050034, Colombia
2 Centro de Investigaciones, Institución Universitaria Escolme, Medellín 050012, Colombia
3 Facultad de Negocios Internacionales, Universidad Santo Tomás, Medellín 050041, Colombia
4 Director general, Instituto de Investigación en Ciencias Biomedicas, Universidad Ricardo Palma, Lima 15039, Peru
5 Grupo de Investigación en Educación y Ciencias Sociales y Humanas, Institución Universitaria Marco Fidel Suárez, Bello 051050, Colombia
* Correspondence: jhoanyvalencia@itm.edu.co; Tel.: +57-(300)-256-7977

Citation: Valencia-Arias, A.; Rodríguez-Correa, P.A.; Patiño-Vanegas, J.C.; Benjumea-Arias, M.; De La Cruz-Vargas, J.; Moreno-López, G. Factors Associated with the Adoption of Drones for Product Delivery in the Context of the COVID-19 Pandemic in Medellín, Colombia. *Drones* **2022**, *6*, 225. https://doi.org/10.3390/drones6090225

Academic Editors: Paul Royall, Andrzej Łukaszewicz, Wojciech Giernacki, Zbigniew Kulesza, Jaroslaw Pytka and Andriy Holovatyy

Received: 13 July 2022
Accepted: 23 August 2022
Published: 27 August 2022

Abstract: This study aims to identify the factors associated with the adoption of drone delivery in Medellín, Colombia, in the context of the COVID-19 pandemic. For that purpose, it implemented the Diffusion of Innovation (DOI) theory and the Technology Acceptance Model (TAM), which have constructs that complement each other to determine the decision to accept a given technology. A survey was administered to 121 participants in order to validate the model proposed here, which is based on variables that reflect the perceived attributes and risks of this innovation and individuals' characteristics. The results indicate that the factors Performance Risk, Compatibility, Personal Innovativeness, and Relative Advantage of Environmental Friendliness have the greatest influence on Intention to Use Drone Delivery (mediated by Attitude Towards Drone Delivery). This paper offers relevant information for the academic community and delivery companies because few other studies have investigated this topic. Additionally, the proposed technology adoption model can be a benchmark for other emerging economies in similar social, economic, and technological conditions.

Keywords: drones; drone delivery services; contactless delivery strategies; COVID-19; pandemic

1. Introduction

In a globalized and competitive world, innovation becomes a strategy for companies to remain in the market [1]. However, some factors limit their success; for example, end consumers are still reluctant to migrate to some new technologies or trends and question whether it is advisable or not to adopt them because they are satisfied with the services they have traditionally received and feel that adopting these new technologies is irrelevant [2]. In the present day, companies adopt technologies to improve production, sales, and logistics processes due to their multiple advantages. The number of logistics operations of delivery services has been increased by the growing volume of online orders. As a result of this expansion and the different alternatives in the market, customers raise their expectations regarding high-quality, faster delivery, for which they are willing to pay a premium price [3].

Consequently, companies are constantly investing in the search for innovative solutions to improve their delivery systems that enhance their effectiveness and are environmentally friendly [4]. For example, they have explored electric vehicles, artificial vision, and machine learning for autonomous vehicles [5]. Taking into account the current context of COVID-19 pandemic, the use of drones for parcel delivery is expected to increase in the foreseeable future [6]. This is especially true considering that the current crisis is generated by the COVID-19 virus, which spreads mainly through the respiratory system of infected individuals and has led to social distancing as a strategy to reduce the risks of spreading it [7]. Thus, autonomous vehicles such as drones present a great opportunity for food or even drug delivery, offering a possible solution to the current problems caused by the presence of COVID-19 [8]. For instance, drones have been shuttling medicine and samples from suspected COVID-19 patients for testing [9] to difficult-to-access areas in developing countries, such as Ghana [10].

During the 2020–2021 COVID-19 lockdowns in Medellín, Colombia, a startup company called Rappi developed a special way of delivering its orders. It deployed a fleet of robots, built by Kiwibot, to deliver takeout food to people in lockdown [11]. In the same city, drones have been used to generate landslide risk mitigation strategies in low-income settlements [12] and as support for the thermal analysis of urban environments, facilitating the analysis of urban heat islands [13]. This reflects the recent acceptance and adaptation of drones in different services in Medellín. Therefore, we should analyze the issue of merchandise delivery employing these technologies in said city.

Due to the crisis generated by the COVID-19 pandemic, Medellín faced challenges in different sectors, but especially in health care services. For example, during the contingency, medicine and pharmaceutical care were provided in person. However, at the same time, mobility restrictions were imposed, the demand for medicine increased, and there was a countrywide shortage of medical products. Thus, the national government established vulnerability criteria, prioritization strategies, and restrictions for the general population. In such situations, it was necessary to establish new home care channels or models to strengthen self-care supported by technological tools [14].

In a more global context, it has become necessary to generate mechanisms to prevent contagion in everyday activities, such as studying, working, or buying from home, which are possible thanks to recent technological developments [15]. Regarding online purchasing, recent data from 2022 [16] indicate a significant growth in the volume of scientific literature on the logistics of e-commerce. Approximately 56% of the articles about this topic have been published in the last three years.

Due to the growth of e-commerce, the logistics market is being confronted by challenges and requirements brought about by digitization [17]. For example, according to Statista (2019) as cited in [18], worldwide e-commerce sales reached 3.53 trillion US dollars in 2019. To deliver that volume of orders, drivers and service providers strive to provide adequate customer service [19]. However, difficulties arise on a daily basis (e.g., delayed or broken packages, stressed employees, and angry customers).

Consumers have become more demanding regarding these inconveniences, and, due to their faster pace of life, they require delivery that is timely (among other characteristics) [20]. Therefore, companies that use e-commerce seek to meet their expectations by ensuring responsiveness, while optimizing their resources in terms of costs and time [21]. Technological advances present both good and bad aspects, but as mankind adapts itself and interacts with them and the technology is improved, they turn out to be beneficial [22].

Different technologies can be implemented to respond to these challenges in delivery services, and drones are one of them. A drone is an aircraft that can be remotely flown without a human pilot [21]. The use of drones has advantages and disadvantages perceived by both user companies and end consumers [23]. However, this type of technology has a high potential for the commercial sector due to its qualities in terms of speed, cost, safety, and minimal human intervention [24]. In the context of the COVID-19 pandemic, Euchi [8] identified advantages in drones, such as disinfection (which reduces the risk of contagion) and social distancing (because they are remotely controlled). They can also transport samples of suspected COVID-19 patients, once again contributing to social distancing [25].

Jiang and Ren (2020) [20] proposed a prospect theory that takes into account the factors that support the superiority of drones over manned aircrafts. Such factors include delivery distance, degree of rider delay, pickup time, and consumer attitudes towards drone delivery. However, it is clear to them that this is a very vast field yet to be explored [26]. For example, the weather can pose a threat to their normal operation, and the layout of drone airports should be further analyzed. Raj and Sah (2019) [21] consider it important to investigate the critical success factors for this kind of technology in the logistics sector, its technical aspects, availability of skilled workforce, and government policies.

During the pandemic due to the outbreak of the COVID-19 virus, drones were proposed as an innovative tool with a vast potential to reduce the risk of contagion in that exceptional context marked by social distancing. Thus, to bridge the gaps produced by physical separation, drones have been employed to respond to specific challenges related to the pandemic (e.g., disinfection, delivery, and surveillance) [27] in several countries, but not necessarily everywhere or in the same way.

For example, in India a mechanism was proposed to effectively improve the process of treating COVID-19 patients by implementing drone services to reduce the risk of infection of doctors or other medical staff, thus preventing the spread of the infection [28]. In Spain, a study [29] evaluated the possibility of using drones for disinfection tasks in outdoor public service areas to reduce virus transmission. In Ireland, these systems have been used to combat COVID-19 through monitoring and detection, social distancing, disinfection, data analysis, and delivery of goods and medical supplies [30]. In Turkey, since the virus can be easily transmitted from person to person, retailers have started testing drones to deliver products ordered online. Therefore, drones are indeed an alternative delivery system that could solve some of these problems in different regions [31].

Although drone delivery during the pandemic has been researched in some developed countries [7,31,32], few studies have addressed this phenomenon in Latin America. Therefore, as stated above, this study aims to (1) analyze the factors associated with the adoption of drones for goods delivery in the context of the COVID-19 pandemic in Medellín and (2) present an overview of how this service is perceived in a developing economy.

2. Narrative Literature Review

Using drones as vehicles for cargo delivery is an opportunity for economic and environmental development and establishes a new sustainable business model [33]. Drone delivery is based on machine learning and artificial intelligence technologies that require a high initial investment in terms of skilled workforce, technicians, and fulfillment centers [21], as well as the construction of infrastructure known as drone airports [34].

One of the main advantages perceived by end consumers in drone delivery is environmental protection through environment-friendly products and the reduction in air and noise pollution, for which they are willing to pay a higher price [21]. The environmental friendliness of this technology is a key factor influencing and motivating its adoption [35]. Therefore, it is very important to raise consumer awareness in this regard based on research on their behavior in terms of values, beliefs, and social norms [36]. The environmental education of consumers is a step toward ensuring the preservation of the environment [37].

In addition to ecological advantages, drones offer benefits such as cheaper, faster shipping [38], safety, speed, environmental friendliness, and convenience. Thus, they could replace traditional transportation in parcel delivery services [39]. Drones are not affected by traffic jams or heavy traffic on roads. They are operated by a computer system that can reduce labor costs, which is a clear advantage for sustainability [37]. However, in the post-COVID-19 period, consumers may radically change their behavior in terms of their attitude towards and intention to use drones for the delivery of goods such as food or medicine [7].

The advantages of drones over traditional means in logistics are evident, especially their significant reduction in package delivery time and increased reliability, efficiency, security, and stability. However, as explained by Sah et al. (2021) [40], the widespread implementation of this disruptive logistics technology is not yet visible. The most relevant barriers for the implementation of drones in logistics are related to a greater extent to the regulations of each country and the threats they might pose to individual privacy and security. Other barriers include public perception and environmental, technical, and economic aspects. Additionally, not all types of suppliers can use drones to provide their logistics services. Thus, it may be impractical to implement a finely differentiated delivery strategy [41] because, for that purpose, logistics providers should cooperate more intensely, and the flow of goods needs to be further consolidated [42].

Despite the potential advantages of drones, users also perceive their risks and disadvantages. For example, as they are remotely controlled by computers, they are exposed to cyberattacks. Also, people fear for their privacy due to the possibility of being recorded or attacked by drones [43]. Therefore, detailed user knowledge of drones and their functions is a key factor for their adoption [21]. Consumer reactions to drone delivery indicate that they resist the change and the adoption of new technologies because of their strong belief that the traditional system is safer. However, the credibility of certain brands and consumers' trust in them influences the adoption and acceptance of drones [3].

To use drones for food delivery services, we should consider different risks associated with it. As explained by Mathew et al. (2021) [44], consumers may perceive risk in a new technology-mediated product/service due to ambiguity or lack of credibility. Three main types of risks are evident in food delivery: performance, delivery, and privacy. Thus, the image of drone food delivery services tends to be affected by perceived risks stemming from concerns about the use of new technologies. Said concerns also refer to financial and psychological risks. Performance risk reflects consumers' concerns about losses incurred when the service does not work as expected, especially in times of COVID-19; thus, they cannot make accurate performance decisions before using the service [45,46].

Other perceived disadvantages regarding the functionality of drones are their batteries and flight duration, due to which logistics centers or airports would have to be built at certain distances. Their maximum weight capacity is also a limiting factor for the provision of the delivery service because it is usually 5 kg [3]. In addition, some other external factors may cause accidents, such as falling from heights; colliding with trees, buildings, animals, power lines [38], or drones from other companies; and weather conditions that prevent the provision of the service [5–7]. As a result, designating special airways for drones is essential. Nevertheless, some countries lack national policies to regulate drone logistics for delivery services [47].

Companies have found physical and financial risks in drones that result in drawbacks for their adoption. In addition, end consumers have expressed that social interaction (which they would not have with drones) is important in the provision of the service [17]. Such beliefs regarding the risks of product delivery methods vary among consumers. According to Zhu (2019) [48], exploring consumer behavior and profiles and conducting communication campaigns contribute immensely to the acceptance of commercial drone delivery. In general, the estimates of user acceptance range between great skepticism and exaggerated optimism.

Although some companies are already using autonomous vehicles in pilot tests of delivery services for e-commerce [5], safety and privacy are still a concern for end consumers. Therefore, it is necessary to inquire about their intention to adopt or oppose the use of this kind of service, especially in the context of a pandemic in which precisely social distancing was encouraged to reduce the risks of spreading COVID-19 [7]. The business world is actively considering the use of drones for delivery to increase efficiency and respond to current customer needs. Consequently, consumer reactions to and perceptions of this new delivery method should also be analyzed. According to Farah et al. (2020) [3], despite efforts to position and consolidate drones as delivery service devices, consumers are skeptical about this innovation. Therefore, we should study how behavioral intentions towards drone food delivery services are formed after the COVID-19 outbreak [7,31].

2.1. Model and Hypotheses

Drones have shown great potential for parcel delivery both before [7] and after the pandemic [31,32]. However, the application of drones in food delivery services is not yet widely commercialized, as it is considered a novel technology in an emerging stage [32].

In the literature, the public acceptance of drones for goods delivery has been researched adopting the Diffusion of Innovation (DOI) theory and the Technology Acceptance Model (TAM) [31,49]. The DOI theory was proposed by Rogers (1983) [50] to understand why consumers adopt innovative technologies. He identified five attributes of innovations that could affect people's decision to adopt them: relative advantage, compatibility, complexity, observability, and trialability. Nevertheless, relative advantage, compatibility, and complexity have been the most commonly used [31].

Many times, the DOI theory has been applied in combination with the TAM proposed by Davis (1989) [51]. The TAM aims to explain how users come to accept the use of a certain technology based on a series of factors that influence their decision about how and when they will use it (e.g., perceived ease of use and usefulness as determinants of attitude (which in turn determines use) and external variables) [52]. Thanks to their similar constructions, the DOI and the TAM can complement each other. Furthermore, the attributes of innovation have often been considered to be determinants of attitude toward and intention to adopt certain technologies [53].

Yoo et al. (2018) [49] proposed a model that applies the DOI and TAM to formulate theoretical constructions and hypotheses. From Rogers' model (1983) [50], they took relative advantage, compatibility, complexity, and personal innovation as perceived technological factors. From Davis' model (1989) [51], they took the constructions attitude and intention to use. Finally, they evaluated perceived risks as an additional variable to those of the DOI and the TAM.

2.1.1. Relative Advantages

Relative advantage refers to the degree to which the consumer perceives that an innovation provides more benefits than the traditional tool or technology [54], in other words, its perceived superiority over the status quo and other options (e.g., for home package delivery). Nevertheless, said advantage can change due to different spatial characteristics or between cultures, beliefs, values, and other social dimensions. According to Rogers (1983) [50], this advantage is associated with a cost-benefit analysis to determine how convenient it is to adopt an innovation.

It has been found that the adoption of drones could be largely a matter of cost in relation to, e.g., helicopters [55] or traditional logistics systems [31]. Therefore, consumers perceive that drone delivery provides a relative advantage, which influences their attitude to adopt it thanks to its speed and environmental friendliness [31,49]. Park et al. (2018) [56] claim that the use of drones for food delivery is appropriate because they are fast and offer environmental benefits. Based on this information, this study proposes the first two hypotheses:

Hypothesis 1. *The relative advantage of speed positively affects attitude toward drone delivery.*

Hypothesis 2. *The relative advantage of environmental friendliness positively affects attitude toward drone delivery.*

2.1.2. Complexity

Complexity is defined as consumers' perception of technological advances and the ease of use of technologies [31,57]. According to Rogers (1983) [50], complexity is the extent to which an innovation is perceived by users as easy to use and understand. From a general point of view, innovations that are easier for consumers to use will be adopted more quickly; conversely, complex technologies may take longer or be rejected as they require new knowledge and development of skills [58]. The trialability of drones provides testing buffer prior to adoption, but their potential complexity is a concern that could hinder said adoption [22]. Therefore, a more generalized perception of less complexity in the use of drones for package delivery would influence their adoption [49]. As a result, the following hypothesis is proposed:

Hypothesis 3. *Lower complexity positively affects attitude toward drone delivery.*

2.1.3. Compatibility

Compatibility is a fundamental measure to predict or facilitate innovation, and it is defined depending on particular needs, values, and user experience [59]. Hence, it is assumed that people who find technologies to be compatible with their existing routines and needs are more likely to use them [60]. Regarding drone delivery, compatibility influences attitude, which plays an important role in the formation of behavioral intentions [61]. This is because when consumers evaluate new technologies, the overlap of perceived usefulness with perceived ease of use in the past positively affects their perceived compatibility and attitude toward new technologies [31]. Therefore, the following hypothesis is proposed:

Hypothesis 4. *Compatibility positively affects attitude toward drone delivery.*

2.1.4. Perceived Risks

Perceived risks have been used in a systematic way to try to explain and analyze the behavior of consumers in the face of new technologies; for instance, their anxiety in the face of unpleasant situations that they may experience when they buy new products or acquire new services, which are generally found in emerging fields [62].

Performance risk reflects consumers' concerns about losses incurred when a service does not work as expected; thus, they cannot make accurate performance decisions before using the service [45]. Consumers perceive a high performance risk in new products/services due to their lack of experience, which negatively affects their attitude toward them [62]. Thus, the following hypothesis is proposed:

Hypothesis 5. *Performance risk negatively affects attitude toward drone delivery.*

Delivery risk also reflects people's concerns about not getting a package delivered for a variety of reasons, such as an accident, damage, or theft of a drone carrying the package [45]. In addition, it is believed that drones might malfunction, perform inaccurate deliveries, or not find a place to land at residences [63]. Based on this, the following hypothesis is proposed:

Hypothesis 6. *Delivery risk negatively affects attitude toward drone delivery.*

Privacy risk refers to how much people value the confidentiality of their information, which directly influences their adoption of technologies. In the context of drone delivery, privacy is a driver of concern given the sensitivity of the information that may be collected [64]. This risk is related to the feeling of insecurity that individuals experience when they have to share personal data such as credit card number, address, and phone number [46]. Therefore, the following hypothesis is proposed:

Hypothesis 7. *Privacy risk negatively affects attitude toward drone delivery.*

2.1.5. Individual Characteristics

In general, individual characteristics are determinants of attitudes toward a technology [65], and individual innovativeness is a predominant factor in attitudes toward drone delivery [50,66]. This factor represents the degree to which a person feels open to using new technologies. Consequently, those with a great capacity for personal innovativeness are more likely to easily adopt new technologies and thus overcome the uncertainties that are generated in these processes. According to Ciftci et al. (2021) [66], this is a personality trait that drives an individual's initial intention to try innovations. Thus, the following hypothesis is proposed:

Hypothesis 8. *Personal innovativeness positively affects attitude toward drone delivery.*

Communication channels are especially useful to raise innovation awareness [67]. Mass media channels (e.g., the internet, television, radio, advertisements, and newspapers [49] inform individuals about new technologies [68]. During the pandemic, communication channels (especially social media) determined the acceptance and use of drones [69]. Thus, the following hypothesis is formulated:

Hypothesis 9. *Mass media channels positively affect attitude toward drone delivery.*

Over time, consumers' environmental awareness has increased, motivating the adoption and use of environmentally friendly—also called green—technologies. In the literature, environmental concerns have been related to the collective awareness of current environmental problems, according to Wu et al. (2019) [70], which can be indicated by the attitude, recognition, and response of individuals towards environmental problems. In particular, the adoption of drone delivery offers potential benefits for green consumers who believe that, by using this type of technology, are reducing their carbon footprint [64]. Therefore, the following hypothesis is proposed:

Hypothesis 10. *Environmental concern positively affects attitude toward drone delivery.*

2.1.6. Attitude and Intention

In the literature, it has been proposed and proven that attitude influences behavioral intentions, which is based on the ideas in the TAM. Consequently, behavioral intentions measure the probability of performing a certain action, such as adopting a technology [32]. Attitude refers to a person's positive or negative evaluation of a behavior, which has a direct effect on their intention to use [51]. In the case of drones, attitude is the negative or positive evaluation of their delivery service [31]. Based on this, the following hypothesis is presented:

Hypothesis 11. *Attitude toward drone delivery positively affects intention to use it.*

These eleven hypotheses (taken from [49]) compose the theoretical model adopted in this study to determine and analyze the factors that affect attitude toward drone delivery in Medellín, which in turn affects the intention to use said delivery in that city during the COVID-19 pandemic.

3. Materials and Methods

A survey was administered to 121 participants (15 and older) in Medellín. The participants were in different occupations and had knowledge of the existence of drones and some of their functions. The goal was to analyze the factors that affect their adoption of drone delivery in 2020 after the WHO declared a pandemic due to the outbreak of the COVID-19 virus. At that time, organizations were looking for service delivery strategies to face social distancing and lockdowns imposed to prevent the spread of the virus.

First, respondents were presented with the objective of this study. It was made clear to them that the survey was anonymous, they would not be paid or charged for participating in it, and they could be withdrawn from the study at any time. In the survey, drone delivery was connected to different significant sectors: food (home delivery), health (medicine delivery), and, in general, home delivery of online orders. The first part of its questionnaire included a total of 28 items designed to characterize the sample using open-ended questions about their interest in using drone delivery. The second part of the survey was a series of statements that participants rated on a Likert scale to measure the following constructs: Relative Advantage of Speed, Relative Advantage of Environmental Friendliness, Compatibility, and Complexity.

The first aim of this study was to apply and validate a model to examine the adoption of drone (unmanned aircraft) delivery in Medellín (a city in Colombia). The variables investigated here were selected from the model proposed by Yoo et al. (2018) [49], which includes the following eleven constructs: Attitude Towards Drone Delivery (ADD), Complexity (CX), Mass Media Channel (MMC), Compatibility (CM), Intention to Use Drone Delivery (IUD), Personal Innovativeness (PI), Delivery Risk (DR), Privacy Risk (PVR), Performance Risk (PMR), Relative Advantage of Environmental Friendliness (RAEF), and Relative Advantage of Speed (RAS). We designed the variables to extract the most useful information and thus achieve the aims of this study (see Table 1).

Table 1. Constructs and variables in the proposed model. The constructs were taken from [30].

Construct	Variable
Attitude Towards Drone Delivery (ADD)	Drone delivery is easy to use.
	Using drones suits my lifestyle.
Complexity (CX)	My interaction with drone delivery is clear and understandable.
	Drone delivery can provide me with a better service.
	Using drone delivery fulfills my delivery service expectations.
Mass Media Channel (MMC)	I have a lot of information from the media about drone delivery.
	The media have helped me to better understand drone delivery.
Compatibility (CM)	Drones emit less carbon dioxide during delivery.
	Using drone delivery is compatible with all the aspects of my work.
Intention to Use Drone Delivery (IUD)	Using the drone delivery technology is a good idea.
	Receiving parcels delivered by drones is something that will happen in the long term.
Personal Innovativeness (PI)	I have often seen articles about drone parcel delivery.
	Drone delivery is desirable.
Delivery Risk (DR)	The package carried by the drone can be stolen.
	The package carried by the drone can be damaged by others.
Privacy Risk (PVR)	Drone delivery will result in a loss of my privacy.
	Drone delivery might be used in a way that violates my privacy.
Performance Risk (PMR)	The package carried by the drone might arrive late or be incomplete.
	Drone delivery will make me lose control over my privacy.
Relative Advantage of Environmental Friendliness (RAEF)	Drone delivery helps the environment.
	Drone delivery allows me to receive products in an environmentally friendly way.
Relative Advantage of Speed (RAS)	Drone delivery is a fast way to deliver packages.
	Drone technology is useful for fast goods delivery.

Source: Yoo et al. [50].

In the survey, 45% of the participants were 30 or older, 31% were between 26 and 29, and the remaining percentage were between 16 and 25 years old. Additionally, 75% of those surveyed had never operated a drone in their lives, and the remaining 25% claimed that they had had an "excellent" or "very good" experiences with them. Among the participants, 55% would recommend buying a drone to their relatives and 68% thought that using drones is safe.

4. Results

IBM SPSS software was used to analyze and calculate the correlation statistics. Other values were also calculated: sampling adequacy measure, Bartlett's test of sphericity, standardized factor loadings, reliability of the measurement scale, and correlation between the constructs in the model. The validity of the measurement scale was determined based on the analyses of convergent validity and discriminant validity. Such analyses had two aims: (1) to establish the reliability of the model based on the observable items and their impact on a latent variable and (2) to be able to claim that the measures of a single construct were valid; that is, that they were highly correlated to each other and could be discriminated from the measures proposed for a different construct [71].

4.1. Convergent Validity and Discriminant Validity

Principal component analysis was used for feature extraction. The factor loadings were obtained to interpret the function of every variable and define each one of the factors. The significant values reported in Table 2 determine that each variable adequately represents the factor that contains it. The guidelines to identify significant factor loadings were based on the sample size (121 participants), which accepts up to 0.50 in the value of each variable [72].

Table 2. Factor loadings of constructs in the proposed model.

Factor	Item	Standardized Factor Loading	Average of Standardized Factor Loadings
Attitude Towards Drone Delivery (ADD)	ADD1	0.812	0.812
	ADD2	0.812	
Complexity (CX)	CX1	0.838	0.870
	CX2	0.909	
	CX3	0.863	
Mass Media Channel (MMC)	MMC1	0.928	0.928
	MMC2	0.928	
Compatibility (CM)	CM1	0.761	0.761
	CM2	0.761	
Intention To Use Drone Delivery (IUD)	IUD1	0.900	0.900
	IUD2	0.900	
Personal Innovativeness (PI)	PI1	0.872	0.872
	PI2	0.872	
Delivery Risk (DR)	DR1	0.951	0.951
	DR2	0.951	
Privacy Risk (PVR)	PVR1	0.955	0.955
	PVR2	0.955	
Performance Risk (PMR)	PMR1	0.731	0.731
	PMR2	0.731	
Relative Advantage of Environmental Friendliness (RAEF)	RAEF1	0.886	0.886
	RAEF2	0.886	
Relative Advantage of Speed (RAS)	RAS1	0.967	0.967
	RAS2	0.967	

Created using IBM® SPSS® Statistics.

Regarding the correlation between variables, Bartlett's test of sphericity and the Kaiser-Meyer-Olkin (KMO) measure of sampling adequacy were calculated, and the fit of the model was determined to carry out a factor analysis. The KMO is a statistical test that detects the correlation between variables and returns the probability that the correlation matrix contains significant values. Its p-value must be lower than the critical levels (0.05 or

0.01). Note that this test is very sensitive to increases in sample size because the larger the sample, the easier it is to find significant correlations [73].

Furthermore, the value of the KMO sampling adequacy measure (between 0 and 1) is defined as an index that compares the magnitudes of the observed correlation coefficients with those of the partial correlation coefficients. It characterizes those values on a scale in which KMO measures from 0.90 to 1.00 are marvelous; from 0.80 to 0.89, meritorious; from 0.70 to 0.79, middling; from 0.60 to 0.69, mediocre; from 0.50 to 0.59, miserable; and from 0.00 to 0.50, unacceptable [74]. Table 3 shows that the coefficients obtained by SPSS for each of the factors meet the criteria mentioned above, indicating that the data reduction technique can be applied.

Table 3. Sampling adequacy and Bartlett's test of sphericity of the factors in the proposed model.

Factor	KMO Value	Bartlett Value	Meets Criteria
Attitude Towards Drone Delivery	0.500	0.000	Yes
Complexity	0.697	0.000	Yes
Maas Media Channel	0.500	0.000	Yes
Compatibility	0.500	0.000	Yes
Intention to Use Drone Delivery	0.500	0.000	Yes
Personal Innovativeness	0.500	0.000	Yes
Delivery Risk	0.500	0.000	Yes
Privacy Risk	0.500	0.000	Yes
Performance Risk	0.500	0.000	Yes
Relative Advantage of Environmental Friendliness	0.500	0.000	Yes
Relative Advantage of Speed	0.500	0.000	Yes

Created using IBM® SPSS® Statistics.

The discriminant validity is evaluated in Table 4, which provides evidence of the confidence intervals of the model. Discriminant validity is one of the most common criteria used to evaluate scales for measuring latent constructs in social sciences. To prove the discriminant validity of the measures, those of the same construct must be highly correlated, and this correlation must be greater than that existing with respect to the measures proposed for any different construct [75].

Table 4. Confidence intervals of the variables in the model.

	ADD	CX	MMC	CM	IUD	PI	DR	PVR	PMR	RAEF	RAS
ADD	...										
CX	[0.179;0.576]	...									
MMC	[0.209;0.616]	[0.256;0.626]	...								
CM	[0.367;0.684]	[0.208;0.579]	[0.075;0.493]	...							
IUD	[0.318;0.622]	[0.115;0.516]	[0.220;0.556]	[0.411;0.706]	...						
PI	[0.312;0.687]	[0.261;0.631]	[0.489;0.754]	[0.325;0.656]	[0.274;0.595]	...					
DR	[0.406;0.030]	[0.263;0.141]	[0.292;0.088]	[0.094;0.505]	[0.077;0.328]	[0.063;0.397]	...				
PVR	[0.152;0.567]	[0.065;0.338]	[0.143;0.483]	[0.111;0.489]	[0.021;0.415]	[0.139;0.263]	[0.094;0.312]	...			

Table 4. *Cont.*

	ADD	CX	MMC	CM	IUD	PI	DR	PVR	PMR	RAEF	RAS
PMR	[0.712;0.345]	[0.200;0.218]	[0.194;0.557]	[0.115;0.554]	[0.164;0.559]	[0.002;0.440]	[0.473;0.751]	[0.473;0.751]	...		
RAEF	[0.260;0.606]	[0.016;0.377]	[0.036;0.391]	[0.430;0.717]	[0.121;0.506]	[0.126;0.527]	[0.082;0.471]	[0.099;0.319]	[0.013;0.445]	...	
RAS	[0.127;0.555]	[0.184;0.603]	[0.126;0.306]	[0.187;0.618]	[0.127;0.507]	[0.208;0.603]	[0.206;0.227]	[0.027;0.379]	[0.042;0.406]	[0.227;0.641]	...

Created using IBM® SPSS® Statistics.

In this study, the discriminant validity analysis was carried out by confirming that the confidence interval in the estimate of the correlation between each pair of factors did not contain a value of one [76].

4.2. Realiability

Next, we established the reliability of the measurement scale and verified the explanatory power of the model; for that purpose, we calculated the Cronbach's alpha of the respective scales of each construct. This procedure is necessary because Cronbach's alpha is an index used to measure the reliability of the internal consistency of a scale [77]. Its value ranges between 0 and 1, where numbers closer to 1 indicate a greater internal consistency of the items under analysis [78]. As shown in Table 5, the measurement instrument seems to have an adequate reliability of the internal consistency of the measurement scale because the value of the coefficients is within the range recommended by the authors mentioned above.

Table 5. Reliability coefficient.

Factor	Cronbach's Alpha
Attitude Towards Drone Delivery	0.811
Complexity	0.910
Mass Media Channel	0.943
Compatibility	0.745
Intention to Use Drone Delivery	0.912
Personal Innovativeness	0.890
Delivery Risk	0.963
Privacy Risk	0.964
Performance Risk	0.707
Relative Advantage of Environmental Friendliness	0.896
Relative Advantage of Speed	0.973

Created using IBM® SPSS® Statistics.

4.3. Hypothesis Testing

At the conceptual level, a factor analysis starts with previous hypotheses based on a given model. Then, the hypotheses are tested to determine the influence that certain variables have over others. The model proposed in this study was estimated to identify the determiners of the adoption of drone delivery in Medellín. The hypotheses formulated here were included in said model, and their degree of association was measured using Somers' D statistic.

Somers' D, which was used for this validation stage, is a measure that determines the strength and direction of the association between an ordinal dependent variable and an ordinal independent one. Thus, these ordinal variables contain a natural order that was measured on a Likert scale [79]. In this regard, the measure took values between −1 and 1, where those close to 1 indicate a strong relationship between two variables (i.e., all pairs of the variables agree), and those close to −1 indicate that there is a week or no relationship between the constructs (i.e., all pairs of the variables disagree) [80].

Figure 1 presents the model proposed here and the Somers' D values obtained for the association between its constructs (i.e., variables). According to the theory reviewed in this study, we can conclude that the association coefficients calculated for the hypothetical relationships in the model present positive and significant values, which shows a high correlation between the variables evaluated in this analysis. In addition, SPSS provided the Somers' D coefficient and placed it in a cross tabulation to indicate the degree of association between the factors that were part of the hypotheses and those that were not. This enabled us not only to verify the degree of association of the hypothesized relationships but also to compare it with that between other constructs in the model.

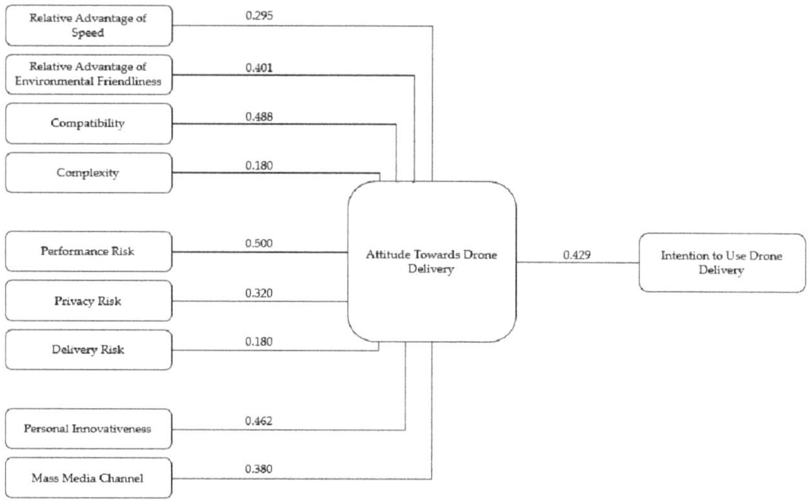

Figure 1. Model of adoption of drone delivery in Medellín.

5. Discussion

The results obtained for these hypothetical relationships show that Performance Risk has a significant correlation with Attitude Towards Drone Delivery, which is the strongest relationship in the model. This indicates that the possibility of an inconvenience in the provision of the service is a reason for consumers to perceive that the technical staff does not have complete control of the device when they send packages. This risk can generate great uncertainty in users and become a factor against the adoption of drones as a channel for goods delivery. These results coincide with those obtained by Yaprak et al. in 2021 [31] in the context of the COVID-19 pandemic. However, the construct Performance Risk can also be the key to change or improve perceptions of drone delivery because, if customers perceive its speed and efficiency, their satisfaction with the service is likely to increase and, thus, their attitude towards drone adoption is likely to improve.

The construct Personal Innovativeness has a strong association with Attitude Towards Drone Delivery, which is evidence that an individual's interest, level of curiosity, and conception of the delivery process have a positive impact on their Attitude Towards Drone Delivery. This construct is often one of the most influential in attitude towards drone delivery in emerging economies after the COVID-19 pandemic [44,81]. This is in line with Hwang et al. (2021) [82], who found that, under moderating effects, after the COVID-19 outbreak, consumers who were motivated to use drone food delivery services showed more favorable attitudes toward that new technology encouraged by social innovation. Consequently, organizations that provide drone delivery services should identify the specific aspects that motivate consumer innovativeness in order to improve the efficiency of their services.

This claim is supported by the study of Yoo et al. (2018) [49], where the relative advantages of drone delivery, usability, perceived risks, and personal innovativeness were the main determinants of attitude towards drone delivery. Similarly, the results of the analysis by Kim et al. (2021) [7] highlighted the fundamental role of perceived innovativeness in the construction of consumer attitudes towards drone delivery services in the context of the COVID-19 pandemic.

Compatibility also exhibits a high level of association with Attitude Towards Drone Delivery. This result, which is supported by previous research [83], highlights the importance of compatibility for the adoption of flight technologies as means of packet transport. Hence, the organizations that support the implementation of delivery drones should further emphasize their compatibility on different media [84]. Therefore, Compatibility, an important factor according to the literature [85], influences Attitude Towards Drone Delivery.

Drones' Relative Advantage of Environmental Friendliness also presents a strong relationship with consumers' Attitude Towards Drone Delivery. The green image that delivery drones project (in terms of a small impact on the environment) favors a positive attitude towards their implementation. Likewise, previous studies have confirmed the advantages of environmentally friendly practices for shaping customers' attitude and, therefore, their intention to use drone delivery in emerging countries [44]. This may indicate that more and more people are transferring the principles of their lifestyle and their ethical and moral values to their decision-making process. If something deviates from their beliefs, they may not consider or approve it.

If individuals do not perceive that drone delivery contributes to the environment, their interest in using it may be reduced, and programs or actions that promote it may be undermined. Nevertheless, previous studies [8] have shown that drones will be able to optimize the way of eliminating contamination with a very high percentage (through the reduction of human contact) with the increase of the flexibility of the flight (reaching the less accessible regions every hour of the day).

Another significant relationship in the model was found between Attitude Towards Drone Delivery and Intention to Use Drone Delivery, which shows that the use of drone delivery technology should be associated with a positive feeling. These results are consistent with those of previous studies on consumer perception during the COVID-19 pandemic [31,82], which confirmed a positive relationship between attitude towards drone delivery service and intention to use that service. Individuals who are more inclined to be in favor of this technology consider that drone delivery is a good idea in the long term. However, prospective users should also feel that this technological reality is part of their lifestyle and not simply a utopian scenario they cannot be part of or benefit from in terms of product delivery.

Finally, the model presented a low correlation between the constructs Delivery Risk and Attitude Towards Drone Delivery. This indicates that, if their expectations are fulfilled and their needs are met, users tend to be more satisfied and motivated to continue using the services offered by drone delivery companies [31].

According to [31], there is a limited number of studies on order delivery using drones in times of the pandemic. Moreover, many studies on drone delivery have been conducted in developed economies, but only a few in their emerging counterparts [44], particularly in Latin America. The difference between this study and previous research is the context examined here, i.e., Medellín during lockdowns due to the COVID-19 pandemic declared by the WHO in 2020. This study revealed differences between findings obtained before and after the pandemic in developed economies and their emerging counterparts, but it focused on Medellín, Colombia, an emerging economy in Latin America. For that purpose, it tested the relationships between relative advantages, complexity, compatibility, perceived risks, individual characteristics, attitude, and intention in said city.

Before the pandemic, Yoo et al. (2018) [49] found that, in a developed country, relative advantage of speed, relative advantage of environmental friendliness, complexity, performance risk, privacy risk, and personal innovativeness were all significant predictors of attitude toward drones. In contrast, in this study, the most significant predictors were performance risk, compatibility, personal innovativeness, relative advantage of environmental friendliness, and control over the order. This indicates that, in an emerging economy (i.e., Medellín), the factors that influence drone delivery adoption are fast delivery, environmental friendliness, compatibility with lifestyles, performance of the technology device, home and personal data privacy, and orientation towards the use of innovative technologies. Contrary to the case analyzed by Yoo et al. (2018) [49], where customers were concerned about delivery speed, in Latin America they are more concerned about lack of control and product loss or damage caused by the drones during transport.

In the study by Yaprak et al. (2021) [31], the compatibility of drones was not influential in the context of the pandemic. This could be because the lifestyles of many people changed during the lockdowns, and new ways to meet people's daily needs were adopted. Other authors have paid attention to consumers in developed economies and their perception of the benefits and risks of drones. In emerging economies, personal innovativeness tends to be ranked higher than consumer attitudes and environmental friendliness with respect to drone adoption [44]. Considerable attention has also been paid to opinion passing and perceived privacy risk [83], and the results largely coincide with those obtained in this study.

Regarding theoretical implications, the results of this study provide empirical evidence of the robustness of the model proposed by Yoo et al. (2018) [49]. They also indicate that Performance Risk, Compatibility, Personal Innovativeness, and Relative Advantage of Environmental Friendliness are the most influential factors on Intention to Use Drone Delivery (mediated by Attitude Towards Drone Delivery). In addition, this study paves the way for future research in this area in Latin America after the pandemic because drones have become an innovative technology for parcel delivery and have proven to be very useful in the context of a pandemic. Indeed, not many studies have been published in this field. Therefore, this study contributes to the emerging line of research on the adoption of drone delivery in emerging economies in Latin America. Furthermore, it highlights the relevant role of performance risk, compatibility, innovativeness, and relative advantage of environmental friendliness in a positive attitude toward the use of drones. Participants' decisions are greatly influenced by concerns about theft or damage, lifestyles, early adoption of innovations, and the trend of environmentally friendly technologies. Although these results are not unexpected, they provide additional information about a lockdown scenario that was not considered in the original TAM. Future studies could address other important factors in the literature (e.g., ease of use and perceived usefulness) in other cities in Colombia or other Latin American countries.

In terms of practical implications, this paper can provide an input for decision-making by companies interested in adopting this technology for commercial purposes. Thus, they can consider the factors that affect user attitudes to refine their drone delivery systems. Based on the results obtained, organizations can find a way to promote the use of this type of service so that customers have reason to believe that drone package delivery is innovative, safe, and environmentally friendly. They can also identify the perceived risks that generate the greatest concern in consumers to act and disseminate relevant information on the matter. Thus, to enjoy these benefits and scale business drone operations after the pandemic, drone delivery services should be geared towards improving convenience with proper packaging, tracking, and trouble-free deliveries, as well as faster delivery times, lower costs (to attract a larger number of consumers), and environmental advantages. In general terms, this study is valuable for decision-makers at organizations that provide online shopping services and are working on the implementation of drone delivery as a means of transporting packages.

The limitations of this study are present in three aspects. First, it is necessary to consider the current lack of knowledge of all the different possible uses of drones, especially for goods distribution, which could greatly affect the adoption of this type of technology. Second, trust is important for drone delivery, especially in developing countries. Consequently, distrust due to security and privacy issues may delay drone adoption in the delivery market in said countries. Third, the sample size was not large enough to generalize the findings to the overall adoption of drones to distribute goods in Medellin. A larger sample is needed to obtain more generalizable results.

Investigating the adoption of a technology implementing technology acceptance models reduces technical, operational, and organizational uncertainty for developer companies. Technology adoption was accelerated during the COVID-19 pandemic and much more so in the post-pandemic context. This pressing need is forcing different sectors to acknowledge emerging technological capabilities. For instance, drones have potential to transform industries and improve productivity. Importantly, the data collected in this study highlight key elements to foster innovation.

Innovative initiatives combine research, collaborative work, needs, resources, and the market, among other aspects. Thus, identifying the particular factors that influence the adoption of drones for goods delivery reduces uncertainty for organizations because they can use specific constructs to guide product development or corporate process innovation.

This study presented theoretical information about drone delivery adoption, but knowledge generation in this field is still limited. Participants in the survey were concerned about technical aspects of drones; however, they were open and willing to use drone delivery if it improves their quality of life. Finally, they were also concerned about drones' performance risk, which means that knowledge dissemination campaigns should be implemented to highlight the advantages and possible integration of drone delivery services.

6. Conclusions

The COVID-19 pandemic has generated the need to reduce the risk of infection using various self-care strategies such as social distancing. Even after the pandemic, some changes that were implemented as preventive measures will remain in force. Such is the case of drone delivery, which was already being developed before the outbreak and had attracted the interest of scholars and companies that provide this commercial service.

Multiple organizations have made efforts to implement contactless delivery strategies, but users' attitude is vital in the implementation of these technologies as a means of delivery. Therefore, the aim of this study was to apply and validate a model to identify the determinants of the adoption of drones (unmanned aircraft) to deliver goods in Medellín in the context of the COVID-19 pandemic. The knowledge of the consumer attitudes that influence the acceptance of these technologies has positive applications in academic and commercial contexts.

This study proposed and applied a model in which relative advantage is a multidimensional construct. It also investigated the determinants that directly influence consumers' attitude towards and intention to adopt drone delivery services by using three types of variables: (1) perceived attributes, (2) perceived risks, and (3) individual characteristics. Compatibility and Relative Advantage of Environmental Friendliness (perceived attributes); Performance Risk (a perceived risk); and Personal Innovativeness (an individual characteristic) exhibited the strongest influence on Attitude Towards Drone Delivery in this model applied in the context of the COVID-19 pandemic in Medellín.

Author Contributions: Conceptualization, A.V.-A. and P.A.R.-C.; methodology, P.A.R.-C., A.V.-A. and G.M.-L.; software, P.A.R.-C. and J.D.L.C.-V.; validation, M.B.-A. and G.M.-L.; formal analysis, M.B.-A.; investigation, J.C.P.-V.; resources, P.A.R.-C.; data curation, J.C.P.-V.; writing—original draft preparation J.C.P.-V., M.B.-A. and J.D.L.C.-V.; writing—review and editing, A.V.-A.; visualization, J.D.L.C.-V.; supervision, M.B.-A. and G.M.-L.; project administration, A.V.-A.; funding acquisition, P.A.R.-C. and J.D.L.C.-V. All authors have read and agreed to the published version of the manuscript.

Funding: This project received external funding from the following universities: Instituto Tecnológico Metropolitano, Institución Universitaria Escolme, and Institución Universitaria Marco Fidel Suárez (Medellín, Colombia). We would also like to thank the "ITM Translation Agency" for the linguistic correction of the original manuscript. This article's APCs were financed by the Instituto Tecnológico Metropolitano, the Ministerio de Ciencia, Tecnología e Innovación and the Francisco José de Caldas Fund through contract RC282-2022.

Institutional Review Board Statement: The study was conducted according to the guidelines of the Declaration of Helsinki, and ap-proved by the Ethics Committee of Institución Universitaria Escolme (protocol code PC2022-03.06.2021).

Informed Consent Statement: Informed consent was obtained from all subjects involved in the study.

Data Availability Statement: Not applicable.

Conflicts of Interest: The authors declare no conflict of interest.

References

1. Genc, E.; Dayan, M.; Genc, O.F. The impact of SME internationalization on innovation: The mediating role of market and entrepreneurial orientation. *Ind. Mark. Manag.* **2019**, *82*, 253–264. [CrossRef]
2. Hong, A.; Nam, C.; Kim, S. What will be the possible barriers to consumers' adoption of smart home services? *Telecommun. Policy* **2020**, *44*, 101867. [CrossRef]
3. Farah, M.F.; Mrad, M.; Ramadan, Z.; Hamdane, H. Handle with Care: Adoption of Drone Delivery Services. In *Advances in National Brand and Private Label Marketing*; Martinez-Lopez, F., Gázquez-Abad, J., Breugelmans, E., Eds.; Springer: Cham, Switzerland, 2020; pp. 22–29. [CrossRef]
4. Lopes, J.M.; Gomes, S.; Pacheco, R.; Monteiro, E.; Santos, C. Drivers of sustainable innovation strategies for increased competition among companies. *Sustainability* **2022**, *14*, 5471. [CrossRef]
5. Zeng, Z.; Chen, P.-J.; Lew, A.A. From high-touch to high-tech: COVID-19 drives robotics adoption. *Tour. Geogr.* **2020**, *22*, 724–734. [CrossRef]
6. Almalki, F.A.; Alotaibi, A.A.; Angelides, M.C. Coupling multifunction drones with AI in the fight against the coronavirus pandemic. *Computing* **2022**, *104*, 1033–1059. [CrossRef]
7. Kim, J.J.; Kim, I.; Hwang, J. A change of perceived innovativeness for contactless food delivery services using drones after the outbreak of COVID-19. *Int. J. Hosp. Manag.* **2021**, *93*, 102758. [CrossRef]
8. Euchi, J. Do drones have a realistic place in a pandemic fight for delivering medical supplies in healthcare systems problems? *Chin. J. Aeronaut.* **2021**, *34*, 182–190. [CrossRef]
9. Lamptey, E.; Serwaa, D. The Use of Zipline Drones Technology for COVID-19 Samples Transportation in Ghana. *HighTech Innov. J.* **2020**, *1*, 67–71. [CrossRef]
10. Demuyakor, J. Ghana Go Digital Agenda: The impact of Zipline Drone Technology on Digital Emergency Health Delivery in Ghana. *Shanlax Int. J. Arts Sci. Humanit.* **2020**, *8*, 242–253. [CrossRef]
11. Zapper, G. How robots became essential workers: They disinfected hospital rooms. They delivered medical supplies. They swabbed people's throats. Next time around, they'll be treating patients. *IEEE Spectr.* **2020**, *57*, 36–43. [CrossRef]
12. Smith, H.; García-Ferrari, S.; Medero, G.; Rivera, H.; Coupé, F.; Caballero, H.; Castro, W.; Abiko, A.; Marinho, F.A.M.; Ferreira, K. Chapter 10: Learning From Co-Produced Landslide Risk Mitigation Strategies in Low-Income Settlements in Medellín (Colombia) and São Paulo (Brazil). In *Housing and Human Settlements in a World of Change*; Ley, A., Rahman, M.A.U., Fokdal, J., Eds.; Transcript Verlag: Bielefeld, Germany, 2020; Volume 25, pp. 243–265.
13. Soto-Estrada, E.; Correa-Echeveri, S.; Posada-Posada, M.I. Thermal analysis of urban environments in Medellin, Colombia, using an Unmanned Aerial Vehicle (UAV). *J. Urban Environ. Eng.* **2017**, *11*, 142–149. [CrossRef]
14. Herrera, R.; Trujillo, A.; Madrigal, J.; Estrada, J.I.; Giraldo, P.A.; Serna, J.A. Uso de herramientas tecnológicas para la solicitud y entrega domiciliaria de medicamentos en el marco de la pandemia por COVID-19. In Proceedings of the VI Congreso Colombiano de Atención Farmacéutica, Medellín, Colombia, 11–13 November 2021.
15. Urrea-Arroyave, N.; Cañon-Montañez, W. Impactos sociales de las medidas de cuarentena y poscuarentena por COVID-19 en contextos de inequidad. *Rev. Cienc. Cuidado* **2021**, *18*, 5–8. [CrossRef]
16. Risberg, A. A systematic literature review on e-commerce logistics: Towards an e-commerce and omni-channel decision framework. *Int. Rev. Retail. Distrib. Consum. Res.* **2022**, 1–25. [CrossRef]
17. Bosona, T. Urban freight last mile logistics—Challenges and opportunities to improve sustainability: A literature review. *Sustainability* **2020**, *12*, 8769. [CrossRef]
18. Knobloch, M.; Schaarschmidt, M. What impedes Consumers' Delivery Drone Service Adoption? A Risk Perspective. *Arb. Fachbereich Inform.* **2020**, 1–18.
19. Candas, M.F.; Kutanoglu, E. Integrated location and inventory planning in service parts logistics with customer-based service levels. *Eur. J. Oper. Res.* **2020**, *285*, 279–295. [CrossRef]

20. Jiang, H.; Ren, X. Comparative Analysis of Drones and Riders in On-Demand Meal Delivery Based on Prospect Theory. *Discret. Dyn. Nat. Soc.* **2020**, *2020*, 9237689. [CrossRef]
21. Raj, A.; Sah, B. Analyzing critical success factors for implementation of drones in the logistics sector using grey-DEMATEL based approach. *Comput. Ind. Eng.* **2019**, *138*, 106118. [CrossRef]
22. Ali, S.S.; Kaur, R.; Gupta, H.; Ahmad, Z.; Elnaggar, G. Determinants of an Organization's Readiness for Drone Technologies Adoption. *IEEE Trans. Eng. Manag.* **2021**, 1–15. [CrossRef]
23. Escobar, J.E.C.; Rollins, M.; Unger, S. Preliminary data on an affordable uav system to survey for freshwater turtles: Advantages and disadvantages of low-cost drones. *J. Unmanned Veh. Syst.* **2020**, *9*, 67–74. [CrossRef]
24. Pugliese, L.D.P.; Guerriero, F.; Macrina, G. Using drones for parcels delivery process. *Procedia Manuf.* **2020**, *42*, 488–497. [CrossRef]
25. Abdel-Basset, M.; Chang, V.; Nabeeh, N.A. An intelligent framework using disruptive technologies for COVID-19 analysis. *Technol. Forecast. Soc. Change* **2021**, *163*, 120431. [CrossRef] [PubMed]
26. Muricho, M.W.; Mogaka, C.O. Drone technology and performance of retail logistics. *J. Sustain. Dev. Transp. Logist.* **2022**, *7*, 73–81. [CrossRef]
27. Martins, B.O.; Lavallée, C.; Silkoset, A. Drone Use for COVID-19 Related Problems: Techno-solutionism and its Societal Implications. *Glob. Policy* **2021**, *12*, 603–612. [CrossRef]
28. Angurala, M.; Bala, M.; Bamber, S.S.; Kaur, R.; Singh, P. An internet of things assisted drone based approach to reduce rapid spread of COVID-19. *J. Saf. Sci. Resil.* **2020**, *1*, 31–35. [CrossRef]
29. González Jorge, H.; González de Santos, L.M.; Fariñas Álvarez, N.; Martínez Sánchez, J.; Navarro Medina, F. Operational Study of Drone Spraying Application for the Disinfection of Surfaces against the COVID-19 Pandemic. *Drones* **2021**, *5*, 18. [CrossRef]
30. Alsamhi, S.H.; Lee, B.; Guizani, M.; Kumar, N.; Qiao, Y.; Liu, X. Blockchain for decentralized multi-drone to combat COVID-19 and future pandemics: Framework and proposed solutions. *Trans. Emerg. Telecommun. Technol.* **2021**, *32*, e4255. [CrossRef]
31. Yaprak, Ü.; Kılıç, F.; Okumuş, A. Is the Covid-19 pandemic strong enough to change the online order delivery methods? Changes in the relationship between attitude and behavior towards order delivery by drone. *Technol. Forecast. Soc. Change* **2021**, *169*, 120829. [CrossRef]
32. Hwang, J.; Kim, D.; Kim, J.J. How to Form Behavioral Intentions in the Field of Drone Food Delivery Services: The Moderating Role of the COVID-19 Outbreak. *Int. J. Environ. Res. Public Health* **2020**, *17*, 9117. [CrossRef]
33. Beninger, S.; Robson, K. The disruptive potential of drones. *Mark. Lett.* **2020**, *31*, 315–319. [CrossRef]
34. Mathew, T.M. Aerospace Medicine sans Frontières: Improving Passenger and Personnel Safety. *Aerosp. Med. Hum. Perform.* **2020**, *91*, 611–614. [CrossRef] [PubMed]
35. Liao, S.; Wu, J.; Li, J.; Bashir, A.K.; Yang, W. Securing collaborative environment monitoring in smart cities using blockchain enabled software-defined internet of drones. *IEEE Internet Things Mag.* **2021**, *4*, 12–18. [CrossRef]
36. Choe, J.Y.; Kim, J.J.; Hwang, J. Innovative marketing strategies for the successful construction of drone food delivery services: Merging TAM with TPB. *J. Travel Tour. Mark.* **2021**, *38*, 16–30. [CrossRef]
37. Hwang, J.; Kim, W.; Kim, J.J. Application of the value-belief-norm model to environmentally friendly drone food delivery services: The moderating role of product involvement. *Int. J. Contemp. Hosp. Manag.* **2020**, *32*, 1775–1794. [CrossRef]
38. Lokhande, A.P.; Shaikh, A.N.; Patil, O.S. Drones in Production, Supply Chain and Logistics. *Int. Res. J. Eng. Technol. (IRJET)* **2018**, *5*, 2179–2182.
39. Johannessen, K.A.; Comtet, H.; Fosse, E. A Drone Logistic Model for Transporting the Complete Analytic Volume of a Large-Scale University Laboratory. *Int. J. Environ. Res. Public Health* **2021**, *18*, 4580. [CrossRef]
40. Sah, B.; Gupta, R.; Bani-Hani, D. Analysis of barriers to implement drone logistics. *Int. J. Logist. Res. Appl.* **2021**, *24*, 531–550. [CrossRef]
41. Perera, S.; Dawande, M.; Janakiraman, G.; Mookerjee, V. Retail Deliveries by Drones: How Will Logistics Networks Change? *Prod. Oper. Manag.* **2020**, *29*, 2019–2034. [CrossRef]
42. Tadić, S.; Kovač, M.; Čokorilo, O. The Application of Drones in City Logistics Concepts. *Promet* **2021**, *33*, 451–462. [CrossRef]
43. Wu, Y.; Dai, H.N.; Wang, H.; Choo, K.K.R. Blockchain-based privacy preservation for 5g-enabled drone communications. *IEEE Netw.* **2021**, *35*, 50–56. [CrossRef]
44. Mathew, A.O.; Jha, A.N.; Lingappa, A.K.; Sinha, P. Attitude towards Drone Food Delivery Services—Role of Innovativeness, Perceived Risk, and Green Image. *J. Open Innov. Technol. Mark. Complex.* **2021**, *7*, 144. [CrossRef]
45. Choe, J.Y.; Kim, J.J.; Hwang, J. Perceived risks from drone food delivery services before and after COVID-19. *Int. J. Contemp. Hosp. Manag.* **2021**, *33*, 1276–1296. [CrossRef]
46. Hwang, J.; Choe, J.Y.(J.). Exploring perceived risk in building successful drone food delivery services. *Int. J. Contemp. Hosp. Manag.* **2019**, *31*, 3249–3269. [CrossRef]
47. Merkert, R.; Beck, M.J.; Bushell, J. Will It Fly? Adoption of the road pricing framework to manage drone use of airspace. *Transp. Res. Part A Policy Pract.* **2021**, *150*, 156–170. [CrossRef]
48. Zhu, X. Segmenting the public's risk beliefs about drone delivery: A belief system approach. *Telemat. Inform.* **2019**, *40*, 27–40. [CrossRef]
49. Yoo, W.; Yu, E.; Jung, J. Drone delivery: Factors affecting the public's attitude and intention to adopt. *Telemat. Inform.* **2018**, *35*, 1687–1700. [CrossRef]
50. Rogers, E.M. *Diffusion of Innovations*, 3rd ed.; A Division of Macmillan Publishing: New York, NY, USA, 1983.

51. Davis, F.D. Perceived Usefulness, Perceived Ease of Use, and User Acceptance of Information Technology. *MIS Q. Manag. Inf. Syst.* **1989**, *13*, 319–340. [CrossRef]
52. Silva, P. Davis' Technology Acceptance Model (TAM) (1989). In *Information Seeking Behavior and Technology Adoption: Theories and Trends*, 1st ed.; Al-Suqri, M.N., Al-Aufi, S., Eds.; IGI Global: Hershey, USA, 2015; pp. 205–219.
53. Conrad, E.D. Willingness to use strategic IT innovations at the individual level: An empirical study synthesizing DOI and TAM theories. *Acad. Inf. Manag. Sci. J.* **2013**, *16*, 99–110.
54. Min, S.; So, K.K.F.; Jeong, M. Consumer adoption of the Uber mobile application: Insights from diffusion of innovation theory and technology acceptance model. *J. Travel Tour. Mark.* **2019**, *36*, 770–783. [CrossRef]
55. Ferguson, D.A.; Greer, C.F. Assessing the Diffusion of Drones in Local Television News. *Electron. News* **2019**, *13*, 23–33. [CrossRef]
56. Park, J.; Kim, S.; Suh, K. A Comparative Analysis of the Environmental Benefits of Drone-Based Delivery Services in Urban and Rural Areas. *Sustainability* **2018**, *10*, 888. [CrossRef]
57. Bharadwaj, S.; Deka, S. Behavioural intention towards investment in cryptocurrency: An integration of Rogers' diffusion of innovation theory and the technology acceptance model. *Forum Sci. Oecon.* **2021**, *9*, 137–159. [CrossRef]
58. Ayodele, A.A.; Nwatu, C.B.; Moses Chigbata, O. Extending the Diffusion of Innovation Theory to Predict Smartphone Adoption Behaviour Among Higher Education Institutions' Lecturers in Nigeria. *Eur. J. Bus. Manag.* **2020**, *12*, 14–21. [CrossRef]
59. Shirowzhan, S.; Sepasgozar, S.M.E.; Edwards, D.J.; Li, H.; Wang, C. BIM compatibility and its differentiation with interoperability challenges as an innovation factor. *Autom. Constr.* **2020**, *112*, 103086. [CrossRef]
60. Nordhoff, S.; Malmsten, V.; van Arem, B.; Liu, P.; Happee, R. A structural equation modeling approach for the acceptance of driverless automated shuttles based on constructs from the Unified Theory of Acceptance and Use of Technology and the Diffusion of Innovation Theory. *Transp. Res. Part F Traffic Psychol. Behav.* **2021**, *78*, 58–73. [CrossRef]
61. Hwang, J.; Kim, J.J. Expected benefits with using drone food delivery services: Its impacts on attitude and behavioral intentions. *J. Hosp. Tour. Technol.* **2021**, *12*, 593–606. [CrossRef]
62. Hwang, J.; Kim, H.; Kim, J.J.; Kim, I. Investigation of perceived risks and their outcome variables in the context of robotic restaurants. *J. Travel Tour. Mark.* **2021**, *38*, 263–281. [CrossRef]
63. Zhu, X.; Pasch, T.J.; Bergstrom, A. Understanding the structure of risk belief systems concerning drone delivery: A network analysis. *Technol. Soc.* **2020**, *62*, 101262. [CrossRef]
64. Leon, S.; Chen, C.; Ratcliffe, A. Consumers' perceptions of last mile drone delivery. *Int. J. Logist. Res. Appl.* **2021**. [CrossRef]
65. Ezzaouia, I.; Bulchand-Gidumal, J. Factors influencing the adoption of information technology in the hotel industry. An analysis in a developing country. *Tour. Manag. Perspect.* **2020**, *34*, 100675. [CrossRef]
66. Ciftci, O.; Berezina, K.; Kang, M. Effect of Personal Innovativeness on Technology Adoption in Hospitality and Tourism: Meta-analysis. In *Information and Communication Technologies in Tourism 2021*; Wörndl, W., Koo, C., Stienmetz, J.L., Eds.; Springer: Cham, Switzerland, 2021; pp. 162–174. [CrossRef]
67. Adnan, N.; Nordin, S.M.d.; Bahruddin, M.A.; Tareq, A.H. A state-of-the-art review on facilitating sustainable agriculture through green fertilizer technology adoption: Assessing farmers behavior. *Trends Food Sci. Technol.* **2019**, *86*, 439–452. [CrossRef]
68. Gharaibeh, M.K.; Arshad, M.R.; Gharaibeh, N.K. Using the UTAUT2 Model to Determine Factors Affecting Adoption of Mobile Banking Services: A Qualitative Approach. *Int. J. Interact. Mob. Technol.* **2018**, *12*, 123–134. [CrossRef]
69. Rashid, M.T.; Wang, D. CovidSens: A vision on reliable social sensing for COVID-19. *Artif. Intell. Rev.* **2021**, *54*, 1–25. [CrossRef]
70. Wu, J.; Liao, H.; Wang, J.W.; Chen, T. The role of environmental concern in the public acceptance of autonomous electric vehicles: A survey from China. *Transp. Res. Part F Traffic Psychol. Behav.* **2019**, *60*, 37–46. [CrossRef]
71. Mosquera-González, D.; Valencia-Arias, A.; Benjumea-Arias, M.; Palacios-Moya, L. Factores asociados al uso de tecnologías de la información y la comunicación (TIC) en los procesos de aprendizaje de estudiantes de ingeniería. *Form. Univ.* **2021**, *14*, 121–132. [CrossRef]
72. Hair, J.F.; Anderson, R.E.; Tatham, R.L.; Black, W.C. *Análisis Multivariante*, 5th ed.; Prentice Hall: Madrid, España, 1999.
73. Guad, R.M.; Mangantig, E.; Low, W.Y.; Taylor-Robinson, A.W.; Azzani, M.; Sekaran, S.D.; Sim, M.S.; Azizan, N. Development and validation of a structured survey questionnaire on knowledge, attitude, preventive practice, and treatment-seeking behaviour regarding dengue among the resident population of Sabah, Malaysia: An exploratory factor analysis. *BMC Infect. Dis.* **2021**, *31*, 893. [CrossRef] [PubMed]
74. Gallego, L.; Araque, O. Variables de Influencia en la Capacidad de Aprendizaje. Un Análisis por Conglomerados y Componentes Principales. *Inf. Tecnol.* **2019**, *30*, 257–264. [CrossRef]
75. García-Cano, L.; Colás-Bravo, P. Factores pedagógicos asociados con el compromiso de los universitarios con sus estudios. *Form. Univ.* **2020**, *13*, 181–190. [CrossRef]
76. Anderson, J.C.; Gerbing, D.W. Structural equation modeling in practice: A review and recommended two-step approach. *Psychol. Bull.* **1988**, *103*, 411–423. [CrossRef]
77. Hayes, A.F.; Coutts, J.J. Use Omega Rather than Cronbach's Alpha for Estimating Reliability. *But … Commun. Methods Meas.* **2020**, *14*, 1–24. [CrossRef]
78. Taber, K.S. The Use of Cronbach's Alpha When Developing and Reporting Research Instruments in Science Education. *Res. Sci. Educ.* **2018**, *48*, 1273–1296. [CrossRef]
79. Bermeo-Giraldo, M.C.; Álvarez-Agudelo, L.; Ospina-Rúa, M.I.; Acevedo-Correa, Y.; Montoya-Restrepo, I.A. actores que influyen en la intención de uso de las tarjetas de crédito por parte de los jóvenes universitarios. *Rev. CEA* **2019**, *5*, 77–96. [CrossRef]

80. Sagaró del Campo, N.M.; Zamora Matamoros, L. Técnicas estadísticas para identificar posibles relaciones bivariadas. *Rev. Cuba Anestesiol. Y Reanim.* **2020**, *19*, e603.
81. Chen, C.; Leon, S.; Ractham, P. Will customers adopt last-mile drone delivery services? An analysis of drone delivery in the emerging market economy. *Cogent Bus. Manag.* **2022**, *9*, 2074340. [CrossRef]
82. Hwang, J.; Choe, J.; Choi, Y.G.; Kim, J.J. A comparative study on the motivated consumer innovativeness of drone food delivery services before and after the outbreak of COVID-19. *J. Travel Tour. Mark.* **2021**, *38*, 368–382. [CrossRef]
83. Osakwe, C.N.; Hudik, M.; Říha, D.; Stros, M.; Ramayah, T. Critical factors characterizing consumers' intentions to use drones for last-mile delivery: Does delivery risk matter? *J. Retail. Consum. Serv.* **2022**, *65*, 102865. [CrossRef]
84. Ganjipour, H.; Edrisi, A. Applying the integrated model to understanding online buyers' intention to adopt delivery drones in Iran. *Transp. Lett.* **2022**, 1–13. [CrossRef]
85. Michels, M.; von Hobe, C.F.; Weller von Ahlefeld, P.J.; Musshoff, M. The adoption of drones in German agriculture: A structural equation model. *Precis. Agric.* **2021**, *22*, 1728–1748. [CrossRef]

drones

Article

Fast Terminal Sliding Mode Fault-Tolerant Control for Markov Jump Nonlinear Systems Based on an Adaptive Observer

Pu Yang *, Ziwei Shen, Yu Ding and Kejia Feng

Department of Automation, Nanjing University of Aeronautics and Astronautics, Nanjing 211106, China
* Correspondence: ppyang@nuaa.edu.cn

Abstract: In this paper, a new adaptive observer is proposed to estimate the actuator fault and disturbance of a quadrotor UAV system with actuator failure and disturbance. Based on this, a nonsingular fast terminal sliding mode controller is designed. Firstly, according to the randomness of faults and disturbances, the UAV system under faults and disturbances is regarded as one of the Markov jump nonlinear systems (MJNSs). Secondly, an adaptive observer is designed to simultaneously observe the system state, fault, and disturbance. In order to improve the precision, the fast adaptive fault estimation (FAFE) algorithm is adopted in the adaptive observer. In addition, a quasi-one-sided Lipschitz condition is used to deal with the nonlinear term, which relaxes the condition and contains more nonlinear information. Finally, a nonsingular fast terminal sliding mode controller is designed for fault-tolerant control of the system. The simulation results show that the faults and disturbances can be observed successfully, and that the system is stochastic stable.

Keywords: fault-tolerant control (FTC); nonsingular fast terminal sliding mode control (NFTSMC); UAV; FAFE; Markov jump nonlinear systems (MJNSs)

Citation: Yang, P.; Shen, Z.; Ding, Y.; Feng, K. Fast Terminal Sliding Mode Fault-Tolerant Control for Markov Jump Nonlinear Systems Based on an Adaptive Observer. *Drones* **2022**, *6*, 233. https://doi.org/10.3390/drones6090233

Academic Editors: Andrzej Łukaszewicz, Wojciech Giernacki, Zbigniew Kulesza, Jaroslaw Pytka and Andriy Holovatyy

Received: 25 July 2022
Accepted: 30 August 2022
Published: 2 September 2022

1. Introduction

Markov jump systems (MJSs) were firstly proposed by N. M. Krasovskii and E. A. Lidskii in 1961 [1]. Over the years, relevant theories have been continuously improved. Since they can better describe the system of stochastic mode jump, MJSs have been gradually proven valid in the practical [2–4], and have had considerable research and application in the fields of economics, physics, unmanned systems, machine learning, and so on. On the other hand, unmanned aerial vehicles (UAVs) first appeared in the 1920s. Due to their outstanding performance on the battlefield, Western countries ushered in an upsurge of UAV research in the 1990s. In recent years, more and more cases of UAVs being used in rescue and disaster relief have sprung up [5–8]. Considering the safety and stability of UAVs, they can replace human beings by going to dangerous disaster relief sites and accomplishing some dangerous tasks. Due to the particular working environment, a quadrotor UAV system is easily affected by the wind environment, carried objects, human intervention, and other factors in the process of performing missions. Therefore, the output of the UAV system could be unstable. This kind of fault can be regarded as a Markov jump process, and the UAV system can be described by the continuous-time MJSs.

At present, there have been many studies on the stability and control law of Markov jump systems. Guan studies the stability of T-S fuzzy Markov jump systems based on sampling control in [9]. Wang studies the stochastic stability of the MJSs, which are affected by parameter uncertainty and actuator saturation [10]. Instead of asymptotic stability, Chen et al. [11] paid more attention to the changes in the transient properties. They studied the finite-time stability of a class of disturbed MJSs with random time delay. In terms of the reinforcement learning of agents, Jiang creatively combines the reinforcement learning method with Markov jump nonlinear systems (MJNSs). Based on this, he realizes optimal tracking control for MJNSs in [12], which opened new data-based fields in the studies of MJSs. He et al. [13] utilized another reinforcement learning method with the optimal control for Markov linear jump systems.

Furthermore, fault-tolerant control (FTC) has been developed and is involved in industrial systems. Usually, FTC can be divided into passive and active FTC. Sliding mode control (SMC), which was proposed for a class of control problems with unknown disturbance, is one of the primary methods for FTC. Since it owns the advantages of quick response, and easy calculation and design, SMC has been used to design controllers and observers in fault diagnosis. For passive FTC, Liu et al. [14] study a novel SMC of a classic uncertain stochastic system with time delay, and design the corresponding adaptive sliding mode control law. Two experiments demonstrate the advantages of this method. Besides, for active FTC, Le et al. [15] proposed an extended state observer to estimate the fault of a robot manipulator. They designed a fault-tolerant conventional sliding mode controller and proved its stability. Considering a system with uncertain disturbances and actuator faults, Mao et al. [16], who combined the adaptive method with SMC, proposed a novel fault-tolerant controller to deal with the unknown bound of the input uncertainty. For nonlinear systems, Guo et al. [17] combined SMC with a radial basis function neural network and proposed a novel FTC control scheme. Zhao et al. [18] designed a novel nonsingular terminal sliding mode controller (NTSMC) for a quadrotor affected by variable mass. Compared with other SMC or FTC methods, the new FTC performs better.

Meanwhile, observer based on fault diagnosis and fault-tolerant control is a significant active FTC method. This method monitors the system's original state and actual state by establishing an observer system to observe the type and time of fault, and provide an essential reference for subsequent maintenance. A disturbance observer [19] combined with neural networks, FO calculus and SMC is utilized to approximate nonlinearities, actuator faults, and so on. For a Surface Vehicle, Wang [20] investigates a finite-time observer to design FTC to handle input saturations and uncertain faults. For multi-agent systems, an adaptive observer is designed for an event-triggered FTC to compensate for the fault in [21]. Song et al. [22] proposed an adaptive hybrid fuzzy output feedback controller based on a fuzzy observer to estimate the system state. A novel composite adaptive disturbance observer used to estimate the disturbances and faults is given to design the FTC in [8].

However, the fault-tolerant theorems are seldom used to control Markov jump systems. Scholars have concentrated on this field and done some research. Considering possible multiple faults in high-speed trains, a novel disturbance observer is given in [23] to promise the system's stability. Yang et al. [24] regarded a specific aero-engine system as one of the MJSs. Then, they considered that under the conditions of unknown sensor fault, actuator fault, and bounded external disturbance, a linear generalized reduced-order observer is designed to realize fault estimation, and the accuracy and effectiveness of the algorithm were validated. Adaptive and fuzzy theorems are utilized in the FTC of MJNSs in [25] to handle additive and multiplicative faults. For networked control systems, Bahreini et al. regarded them as classic MJSs. In consideration of the difficulty of estimating stochastic fault, a novel auxiliary system approach is used to estimate the random fault of continuous-time MJSs in [26]. In the case of partly unknown transition probabilities, they also proposed a new FTC to deal with actuator faults in [27]. When actuator and sensor fault happened simultaneously, Chen et al. [28] proposed two novel fault estimation observers to estimate the faults of MJSs.

In the field of fault estimation and UAV control, there have also been development and research in recent years. A novel robust nonlinear controller is proposed for a UAV system in [29] to achieve Cartesian position trajectory tracking capability. Besides, a novel fault estimation method based on an adaptive observer is designed for taking off mode. Nian et al. [30] designed a robust adaptive fault estimation observer to obtain the actuator fault of a UAV system. Then, they proposed a dynamic output feedback fault-tolerant controller for the stability of the system. For a high-altitude long-endurance UAV, an estimation algorithm is proposed to estimate the three-axis accelerations in [31]. Through flight tests, the algorithm can detect the fault of the accelerometer. Combining with a novel two-stage Kalman filter, a fault estimation algorithm is designed in [32]. Using a sensor fault detection algorithm and robust Kalman filter, the state parameters of the UAV can be accurately estimated. Goslinski et al. [33] also pay attention to estimation of the state of UAVs, and they proposed a quadrotor model for fault-tolerant observation and a new filtration method.

In order to facilitate analysis and calculation, the theoretical research is mostly based on a linear system. In practical engineering applications, most systems will be affected by nonlinear phenomena, which will destroy the stability of the system. This work will concentrate on the observer-based FTC of MJNSs. We take the specificity of the work environment and the impact of nonlinearity on UAV systems into consideration, and that actuator faults and disturbances are stochastic and hard to predict in advance. Therefore, an observer with adaptive technology is designed in this work. A nonsingular fast terminal sliding mode controller is adopted to improve the rapidity and to avoid the singularity. Moreover, the Lyapunov-Krasovskii functional (LKF) and linear matrix inequalities (LMI) techniques are utilized to guarantee the stochastic stability of the fault-tolerant controller. The main contributions of this paper are summarized as follows:

1. We consider the specificity of the work environment, and the UAV system is regarded as a Markov jump nonlinear system that is proven to be stochastically stable. The nonlinear term is satisfied with the quasi-one-sided Lipschitz condition, which relaxes the constraints and contains more nonlinear information.
2. The FAFE algorithm is utilized to design the adaptive observer to estimate the fault and disturbance, where there is is no need to know the bound of the fault in advance.
3. Based on the estimation given by the observer, a nonsingular fast terminal sliding-mode fault-tolerant controller is applied to control the MJNS, which is proven stable by the LKF.
4. The simulation results on a quadrotor UAV system show the feasibility of the theory.

The rest of this paper is arranged as follows: Section 2 gives a dynamic model of MJNSs and some assumptions, lemmas, and definitions, which will be utilized in the following sections. In Section 3, an adaptive observer is given to estimate the faults and disturbances of the UAV system, and a nonsingular fast terminal sliding-mode fault-tolerant controller whose stability is ensured by the Lyapunov-Krasovskii functional is designed. In Section 4, by the numerical simulation on the UAV system, the feasibility of the method is proven. Eventually, brief conclusions are given in Section 5.

2. System Description and Preliminaries

2.1. Quadrotor Kinematic Model

To establish the kinematic model of a quadrotor like Figure 1, it is necessary to analyze the motion and the force of the system in the same coordinate system.

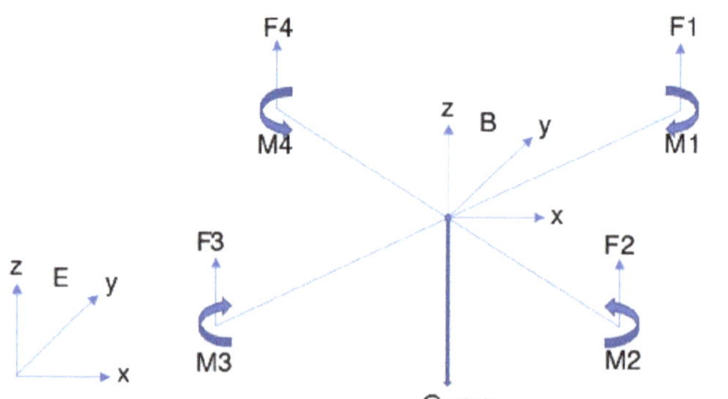

Figure 1. Model of a quadrotor.

As is shown in Figure 1, the origin of body coordinate system B is the center of mass of the quadrotor. The x-axis is the roll axis of the body, the y-axis is the pitch axis of the body, and the z-axis is the yaw axis of the body. We select the reference coordinate system E, whose origin coincides with the origin of the body coordinate system.

There is a rotation matrix from coordinate system B to E, which can be given by the following formula.

$$R_B^E(\phi,\theta,\psi) = R_x(\phi)\cdot R_y(\theta)\cdot R_z(\psi) \quad (1)$$

where,

$$R_x(\phi)=\begin{bmatrix}1 & 0 & 0\\ 0 & cos\phi & sin\phi\\ 0 & -sin\phi & cos\phi\end{bmatrix},\ R_y(\theta)=\begin{bmatrix}cos\theta & 0 & -sin\theta\\ 0 & 1 & 0\\ sin\theta & 0 & cos\theta\end{bmatrix},\ R_z(\psi)=\begin{bmatrix}cos\psi & sin\psi & 0\\ -sin\psi & cos\psi & 0\\ 0 & 0 & 1\end{bmatrix} \quad (2)$$

Therefore,

$$R_B^E(\phi,\theta,\psi)=\begin{bmatrix}cos\theta cos\psi & cos\psi sin\theta sin\phi - sin\psi cos\phi & cos\psi sin\theta cos\phi + sin\psi sin\phi\\ cos\theta sin\psi & sin\psi sin\theta sin\phi + cos\psi cos\phi & sin\psi sin\theta cos\phi - cos\psi sin\phi\\ -sin\theta & sin\phi cos\theta & cos\phi cos\theta\end{bmatrix} \quad (3)$$

Regarding the quadrotor system as a rigid body and ignoring the change of the earth's shape and gravitational acceleration, the mass center motion equation can be written as:

$$\begin{cases}\vec{F} = \frac{md\vec{V}}{dt}\\ \vec{M} = \frac{d\vec{H}}{dt}\end{cases} \quad (4)$$

where $V = \begin{bmatrix}v_x & v_y & v_z\end{bmatrix}^T$ is the velocity vector of the center of mass of the quadrotor, $\vec{F}$ is the sum of all external forces acting on the quadrotor, m is the equality of the quadrotor, $\vec{M}$ is the linear momentum, and $\vec{H}$ is moment of momentum of the quadrotor relative to the ground coordinate system.

The elevating force and the torque can be given as:

$$\begin{cases}F = \sum\limits_{i=1}^{4} k_F\omega_i^2\\ M = \sum\limits_{i=1}^{4} k_M\omega_i^2\end{cases} \quad (5)$$

where, k_F is the lift coefficient, k_M is the torque quotient, and $\omega_i = \begin{bmatrix}p & q & r\end{bmatrix}^T (i = 1,2,3,4)$ is the angular rate of the ith motor. The conversion relationship between the angular velocity of the Euler angle and the angular velocity of the body is as follows:

$$\begin{bmatrix}p\\ q\\ r\end{bmatrix} = \begin{bmatrix}\dot{\phi} - \dot{\psi}sin\theta\\ \dot{\theta}cos\phi + \dot{\psi}sin\phi cos\theta\\ -\dot{\theta}sin\phi + \dot{\psi}cos\phi cos\theta\end{bmatrix} \quad (6)$$

If the quadrotor is symmetrical, the moment of the inertia matrix can be given as:

$$I_{\phi\theta\psi} = \begin{bmatrix}I_x & 0 & 0\\ 0 & I_y & 0\\ 0 & 0 & I_z\end{bmatrix} \quad (7)$$

The equations of motion for angular velocity are as follows:

$$\begin{bmatrix}M_x\\ M_y\\ M_z\end{bmatrix} = \begin{bmatrix}\dot{p}I_x - \dot{r}I_{xz} + qr(I_z - I_y) - pqI_{xz}\\ \dot{q}I_y + pr(I_x - I_z) + (p^2 - r^2)I_{xz}\\ \dot{r}I_z - \dot{p}I_{xz} + pq(I_y - I_x) + qrI_{xz}\end{bmatrix} \quad (8)$$

Therefore, we can obtain the kinematic equations of the quadrotor.

$$\begin{bmatrix} \ddot{x} \\ \ddot{y} \\ \ddot{z} \\ \ddot{\phi} \\ \ddot{\theta} \\ \ddot{\psi} \end{bmatrix} = \begin{bmatrix} \frac{F_x - K_x \dot{x}}{m} \\ \frac{F_y - K_y \dot{y}}{m} \\ \frac{F_z - mg - K_z \dot{z}}{m} \\ (M_x + (I_x - I_z)qr)/I_x \\ (M_y + (I_z - I_x)qr)/I_y \\ (M_z + (I_x - I_y)qr)/I_z \end{bmatrix} \tag{9}$$

Design the input of the system,

$$\begin{cases} U_1 = k_F l(\omega_1^2 - \omega_2^2 - \omega_3^2 + \omega_4^2) \\ U_2 = k_F l(\omega_1^2 + \omega_2^2 - \omega_3^2 + \omega_4^2) \\ U_3 = k_M(\omega_1^2 - \omega_2^2 + \omega_3^2 - \omega_4^2) \\ U_4 = k_f(\omega_1^2 + \omega_2^2 + \omega_3^2 + \omega_4^2) \end{cases} \tag{10}$$

where U_1, U_2, U_3 represent the control input of roll, pitch, and yaw, respectively, and U_4 is the input control of height.

Considering the UAV flying at low speed, we can simplify the model:

$$\begin{bmatrix} \ddot{x} \\ \ddot{y} \\ \ddot{z} \\ \ddot{\phi} \\ \ddot{\theta} \\ \ddot{\psi} \end{bmatrix} = \begin{bmatrix} \frac{(sin\phi sin\psi + cos\phi sin\theta cos\psi)U_4}{m} \\ \frac{(-sin\phi cos\psi + cos\phi sin\theta sin\psi)U_4}{m} \\ \frac{(sin\theta cos\phi)U_4}{m} \\ \frac{U_1 + \dot{\theta}\dot{\psi}(I_y - I_z)}{I_x} \\ \frac{U_2 + \dot{\phi}\dot{\psi}(I_z - I_x)}{I_y} \\ \frac{U_3 + \dot{\phi}\dot{\theta}(I_x - I_y)}{I_z} \end{bmatrix} \tag{11}$$

In this paper, we pay more attention to the attitude of the quadrotor, and complete further simplification of the model [34]:

$$\begin{bmatrix} \dot{\phi} \\ \dot{\theta} \\ \dot{\psi} \\ \ddot{\phi} \\ \ddot{\theta} \\ \ddot{\psi} \end{bmatrix} = \begin{bmatrix} p \\ q \\ r \\ \frac{U_1}{I_x} \\ \frac{U_2}{I_y} \\ \frac{U_3}{I_z} \end{bmatrix} \tag{12}$$

Selecting the equilibrium points as [34], the state space equation can be written into:

$$\begin{cases} \dot{x} = Ax + Bu \\ y = Cx \end{cases} \tag{13}$$

where $A = \begin{bmatrix} O_{3\times3} & I_{3\times3} \\ O_{3\times3} & O_{3\times3} \end{bmatrix}$, $B = \begin{bmatrix} O_{3\times3} \\ I_{\phi\theta\psi}^{-1} \end{bmatrix}$, $C = \begin{bmatrix} I_{3\times3} & O_{3\times3} \end{bmatrix}$.

2.2. Markov Jump Nonlinear Systems Dynamic Model

In practice, under the interference of external factors, actuator failure, uncertain disturbance, and other influencing factors easily appear. Therefore, this paper comprehensively considers these factors and gives the following dynamic model of a Markov jump nonlinear system.

$$\begin{cases} \dot{x}(t) = A(r(t))x(t) + B(r(t))(u(t) + f(x(t),t)) + F_a(r(t))f_a(t) + B_\omega(r(t))\omega(t) \\ y(t) = C(r(t))x(t) \end{cases} \tag{14}$$

where, $x(t) \in \mathbb{R}^n$ is the state vector, $u(t) \in \mathbb{R}^m$ is the control input vector, and $y(t) \in \mathbb{R}^p$ is the measured output vector. The coefficient matrices $A(r(t)) \in \mathbb{R}^{n\times n}$, $B(r(t)) \in \mathbb{R}^{n\times m}$, $C(r(t)) \in \mathbb{R}^{p\times n}$ are known constant matrices. $f(x(t),t)$ represents the nonlinear function, $f_a(t)$ represents actuator failure, and $\omega(t)$ is the disturbance. In addition, $F_a(r(t))$ and $B_\omega(r(t))$ are the constant matrices with appropriate dimensions and column full rank.

Let $\{r(t), t \geq 0\}$ be a Markov process with right continuous trajectories on the probability space (Ω, F, P). $r(t)$ takes values in the finite set $\mathcal{N} = \{1, 2, \cdots, n\}$.

The state transition matrix $\Pi = (\pi_{ij})$ is set as:

$$P_r\{r(t+\delta) = j | r(t) = i\} = \begin{cases} \pi_{ij}\delta + o(\delta),\ i \neq j \\ 1 + \pi_{ii}\delta + o(\delta), i = j \end{cases} \tag{15}$$

where, $\delta > 0$, $\lim_{\delta \to 0} \frac{o(\delta)}{\delta} = 0$. When $i \neq j$, $\pi_{ij} > 0$, which is the transition Rates (TRs) from state i at time t to state j at time $t + \delta$ and satisfies that $\pi_{ii} = -\sum_{j=1, i\neq j}^{n} \pi_{ij} < 0$.

Therefore, the transition rate matrix can be expressed as:

$$\Pi = \begin{pmatrix} \pi_{11} & \cdots & \pi_{1n} \\ \vdots & \ddots & \vdots \\ \pi_{n1} & \cdots & \pi_{nn} \end{pmatrix} \tag{16}$$

When the system is in the state i, that is, when $r(t) = i, i \in \mathcal{N}$, $A(r(t)), B(r(t)), C(r(t))$ can be simplified to the real constant matrix A_i, B_i, C_i, and the nonlinear function $f(x(t),t)$ is written as $f_i(x(t),t)$.

System (14) can be rewritten as follows:

$$\begin{cases} \dot{x}(t) = A_i x(t) + B_i(u(t) + f_i(x(t),t)) + F_{ai} f_{ai}(t) + B_{\omega i}\omega(t) \\ y(t) = C_i x(t) \end{cases} \tag{17}$$

Remark 1. *In this paper, $\mathcal{N}$ is the set of positive integers, and $\mathbb{R}$ is the set of real numbers. $\mathbb{R}^n$ denotes the n-dimensional vector space and $\mathbb{R}^{m\times n}$ denotes the space of all $m \times n$-dimensional matrices. A^T represents the transpose of matrix A. $\|\cdot\|$ indicates the Euclidean norm of the vector. The inner product of vectors $x, y \in \mathbb{R}^m$ is denoted by $\langle x, y\rangle$, and $\langle x, y\rangle = x^T y$.*

Assumption 1. *The nonlinear term $f_i(x(t),t)$ is continuous with $x(t)$ and satisfies the following inequality on the domain of definition:*

$$\langle f_i(x(t),t) - f_i(\hat{x}(t),t), x(t) - \hat{x}(t)\rangle \leq (x - \hat{x})^T M (x - \hat{x}),\ x(t) \in \mathbb{R}^n \tag{18}$$

where, M is a real symmetric matrix and the one-sided Lipschitz constant matrix, and $\hat{x}$ is the estimation of x.

Assumption 2 ([35]). *The nonlinear term $f_i(x(t),t)$ satisfies the quadratic inner-boundedness condition. If $\exists \alpha, \beta \epsilon R$ is in a continuous closed region containing the origin, such that $\forall x, \hat{x} \in \mathbb{R}^n$,*

$$\|f_i(x(t),t) - f_i(\hat{x}(t),t)\|^2 \leq \alpha\|x(t) - \hat{x}(t)\|^2 + \beta\langle x(t) - \hat{x}(t), f_i(x(t),t) - f_i(\hat{x}(t),t)\rangle \tag{19}$$

Remark 2. *The two assumptions are used to describe the quasi-one-sided Lipschitz condition. In the system description, the nonlinear terms are assumed to satisfy this condition. Compared with traditional Lipschitz, this quasi-one-sided Lipschitz condition relaxes restrictions, which can facilitate the calculation of LMI.*

Definition 1 ([36]). *For any $e_0 \in \mathbb{R}^n$, $r_0 \in \mathcal{N}$; when $u(t) = 0$, if the MJSs satisfy the following inequality, the MJSs are stochastically stable.*

$$E\left\{\int_0^t \|e(t)\|^2 dt \middle| e_0, r_0\right\} < \infty \tag{20}$$

Definition 2 ([37]). *For the stochastic Lyapunov-Krasovskii function $V(x(t), i)$, the weak infinitesimal operator $\mathcal{L}$ meets with*

$$\begin{aligned}\mathcal{L}V(x(t), i) &= \lim_{\Delta \to 0^+} \frac{1}{\Delta}[E\{V(x(t+\Delta), r_{t+\Delta})|x(t), r_t = i\} - V(x(t), i)] \\ &= V_t(x(t), i) + V_x(x(t), i)\dot{x}(t) + \sum_{j=1}^{n} \pi_{ij} V(x(t), j)\end{aligned} \tag{21}$$

Lemma 1 ([38]). *For given real matrices $\mathcal{A}$, $\mathcal{B}$, $\mathcal{C}$, $\mathcal{D}$, $\mathcal{E}$, $\mathcal{F}$, and Ξ, there exists a symmetrical matrix $P > 0$, such that*

$$\begin{bmatrix} P\mathcal{A}^T + \mathcal{A}P + \Xi & \mathcal{B} & P\mathcal{C}^T \\ * & \mathcal{D} & \mathcal{E}^T \\ * & * & \mathcal{F} \end{bmatrix} < 0 \tag{22}$$

Lemma 2 ([39]). *According to the classical Paul and Peter inequality, for a scalar $\rho > 0$, real vectors x and y, and a symmetric positive definite matrix R, only for real Euclidean space $\mathbb{E}$, endowed with the scalar product $\langle\cdot|\cdot\rangle$, the following inequality holds:*

$$2x^T y \leq \frac{1}{\rho} x^T R x + \rho y^T R^{-1} y \tag{23}$$

Lemma 3 ([40]). *Consider a nonsingular fast terminal sliding mode surface:*

$$s = z_1 + \kappa_{i1}^{-1} z_1^{\gamma} + \kappa_{i2}^{-1} z_2^{\frac{p}{q}} \tag{24}$$

If $s(0) \neq 0$, the convergence time to $s = 0$ can be given as:

$$\begin{aligned} T &= \int_0^{|z_1(0)|} \frac{k_2^{q/p}}{(z_1(t) + k_1 z_1)^{q/p}} dz_1 \\ &= \frac{\frac{p}{q}|z_1(0)|^{1-q/p}}{k_1\left(\frac{p}{q} - 1\right)} F\left(\frac{q}{p}, \frac{\frac{p}{q} - 1}{(\lambda - 1)\frac{p}{q}}; 1 + \frac{\frac{p}{q} - 1}{(\lambda - 1)\frac{p}{q}}; -k_1|z_1(0)|^{\lambda - 1}\right) \end{aligned} \tag{25}$$

3. Main Results

3.1. Observer Design and Fault Estimation

Considering the fault and disturbance, this paper sets that $F_i g(t) = F_{ai} f_a(t) + B_{\omega i}\omega(t)$. Then, the following adaptive observer is designed for the dynamic system model (17):

$$\begin{cases} \dot{\hat{x}}(t) = A_i \hat{x}(t) + B_i(u(t) + f(\hat{x}(t), t)) + F_i \hat{g}(t) + L_i(y(t) - \hat{y}(t)) \\ \hat{y}(t) = C_i \hat{x}(t) \end{cases} \tag{26}$$

where, L_i is the gain matrix of the observer, $\hat{x}(t)$ is the estimation of the true state $x(t)$, $\hat{y}(t)$ is the estimation of the true output $y(t)$, and $\hat{g}(t)$ is the estimation of $g(t)$.

Define the estimation error as: $e(t) = x(t) - \hat{x}(t)$, $e_y(t) = y(t) - \hat{y}(t)$, $e_a(t) = g(t) - \hat{g}(t)$. Then, the error equation is given by $\dot{e}(t) = \dot{x}(t) - \dot{\hat{x}}(t)$.

Considering Equations (17) and (26), the expression of the error dynamic system is:

$$\dot{e}(t) = (A_i - L_i C_i)e(t) + B_i e_f(x(t), \hat{x}(t)) + F_i e_g(t) \tag{27}$$

A fast adaptive fault estimation (FAFE) algorithm can be adopted in the adaptive observers. The estimation of the derivatives of faults can be written as:

$$\dot{\hat{g}} = -\Lambda T_i(e_y + \zeta \dot{e}_y) \tag{28}$$

where $\zeta > 0$ is a scalar, $\Lambda \in \mathbb{R}^{n\times p}$ is a symmetric positive definite matrix, $T_i \in \mathbb{R}^{r\times p}$, and their specific definitions will be given in Theorem 1.

From Equation (28), the uniformly ultimate boundedness of $e_x(t)$ and $e_y(t)$ can be achieved.

3.2. Observer-Based Nonsingular Fast Terminal Sliding Mode Fault-Tolerant Control Design

This section designs a nonsingular fast terminal sliding mode fault-tolerant controller (NFTSM-FTC) for the system (14). Considering Equation (17), the controller can be designed as:

$$\begin{cases} \dot{x}_1 = x_2 \\ \dot{x}_2 = A_i x_2 + B_i(u(t) + f_i(x_2(t),t)) + F_i\hat{g}(t) + F_i e_g(t) \end{cases} \tag{29}$$

where $F_i\hat{g}(t)$ represents the estimation of fault and disturbance that is known, $e_g(t)$ includes the uncertain part of fault and disturbance, and $F_i e_g(t) = F_{ai}e_{ai}(t) + B_{\omega i}e_{\omega}(t)$.

The tracking error z_1 and the second error z_2 are defined as follows:

$$\begin{aligned} z_1 &= x_1 - x_d \\ z_2 &= x_2 - \varpi \end{aligned} \tag{30}$$

where $\varpi = -\chi z_1 + \dot{x}_d$ is a virtual control.

Then, by calculating the differential of the equation, we can get:

$$\begin{aligned} \dot{z}_1 &= \dot{x}_1 - \dot{x}_d \\ \dot{z}_2 &= \dot{x}_2 - \dot{\varpi} \end{aligned} \tag{31}$$

Considering the system (29), we design the following sliding surface for each Markov mode $i \in \mathcal{N}$:

$$s = z_1 + \kappa_{i1}^{-1} z_1^{\gamma} + \kappa_{i2}^{-1} z_2^{\frac{p}{q}} \tag{32}$$

where $s = (s_1, \cdots, s_n)^T \in \mathbb{R}^n$ is the sliding variable, $\kappa_{i1}^{-1} = diag\left\{\kappa_{11}^{-1}, \ldots, \kappa_{1n}^{-1}\right\}$ and $\kappa_2^{-1} = diag\left\{\kappa_{21}^{-1}, \ldots, \kappa_{2n}^{-1}\right\}$ are diagonal positive definite matrices, $p, q > 0$, and they are odd numbers satisfying the relation $1 < p/q < 2$, $\gamma > p/q$.

Calculating $\dot{s}$, we can get:

$$\dot{s} = \dot{z}_1 + \kappa_{i1}^{-1} \mathbf{z}_1^{\gamma-1} \cdot \dot{z}_1 + \kappa_{i2}^{-1} \frac{p}{q} \mathbf{z}_2^{\frac{p}{q}-1} \cdot \dot{z}_2 \tag{33}$$

where $\mathbf{z}_1^{\gamma-1} = diag\left\{|z_{11}|^{\gamma-1}sgn(z_{11}), \ldots, |z_{n1}|^{\gamma-1}sgn(z_{n1})\right\}$,
$\mathbf{z}_2^{\frac{p}{q}-1} = diag\left\{|z_{21}|^{\frac{p}{q}-1}sgn(z_{21}), \ldots, |z_{2n}|^{\frac{p}{q}-1}sgn(z_{2n})\right\}$.

Design the following NFTSM-FTC:

$$u(t) = u_1 + u_2 + u_3 \tag{34}$$

where

$$u_1 = -B_i^{+}(A_i x_2 + F_i\hat{g}(t) - \dot{\kappa}) - f_i(x_2(t),t) \tag{35}$$

$$u_2 = -\frac{q}{p} B_i^{+} \kappa_{i2} \mathbf{z}_2^{\mathbf{1}-\frac{p}{q}} \cdot \left(\dot{z}_1 + \kappa_{i1}^{-1} \mathbf{z}_1^{\gamma-1} \cdot \dot{z}_1\right) \tag{36}$$

$$u_3 = -\frac{q}{p} B_i^+ \kappa_{i2} \cdot \mathbf{z_2}^{\mathbf{1}-\frac{p}{q}} \varepsilon |s_1| sgn(s) \tag{37}$$

where B_i^+ satisfying the relation $B_i B_i^+ = I$, is the generalized inverse matrix of B_i, $\varepsilon \in \mathcal{R}^+$.

Proof. Choose the Lyapunov function as:

$$V_1(x(t), i) = \frac{1}{2} s^T s \tag{38}$$

According to the Definition 2 and paper [14], we have

$$\begin{aligned}
\mathcal{L}V_1(x(t), i) &= \frac{1}{2} \lim_{\Delta \to 0} \frac{1}{\Delta} \Bigg\{ \sum_{j=1, i \neq j}^{\mathcal{N}} Pr\{r(t+\delta) = j \mid r(t) = i\} s^T(t+\Delta) s(t+\Delta) \\
&\quad + Pr\{r(t+h) = i \mid r(t) = i\} s^T(t+\Delta) s(t+\Delta) - s^T(t) s(t) \Bigg\} \\
&= \frac{1}{2} \lim_{\Delta \to 0} \frac{1}{\Delta} \Bigg\{ \sum_{j=1, j \neq i}^{\mathcal{N}} \frac{\varrho_{ij}(F_{Xi}(\delta+\Delta) - F_{Xi}(\delta))}{1 - F_{Xi}(h)} s^T(t+\Delta) s(t+\Delta) \\
&\quad + \frac{1 - F_{Xi}(\delta+\Delta)}{1 - F_{Xi}(\delta)} s^T(t+\Delta) s(t+\Delta) - s^T(t) s(t) \Bigg\} \\
&= s^T(t) \dot{s}(t) + \frac{1}{2} \sum_{j=1}^{\mathcal{N}} \pi_{ij} \\
&= s^T(t) \dot{s}(t)
\end{aligned} \tag{39}$$

where δ is the time from mode i to mode j; ϱ represents the probability from mode i to mode j. $F_{Xi}(x)$ denotes the cumulative distribution function (CDF) of x on mode i.

Therefore,

$$\begin{aligned}
\mathcal{L}V_1(x(t), i) &= s^T \dot{s} \\
&= s^T \left(\dot{z}_1 + \kappa_{i1}^{-1} \mathbf{z_1}^{\gamma-\mathbf{1}} \cdot \dot{z}_1 + \kappa_{i2}^{-1} \frac{p}{q} \mathbf{z_2}^{\frac{p}{q}-\mathbf{1}} \cdot \dot{z}_2 \right) \\
&= s^T \left(\dot{z}_1 + \kappa_{i1}^{-1} \mathbf{z_1}^{\gamma-\mathbf{1}} \cdot \dot{z}_1 \right) \\
&\quad + s^T \kappa_{i2}^{-1} \frac{p}{q} \mathbf{z_2}^{\frac{p}{q}-\mathbf{1}} \cdot (A_i x_2 + B_i(u(t) + f_i(x_2(t), t)) + F_i \hat{g}(t) + F_i e_g(t) - \dot{\omega})
\end{aligned} \tag{40}$$

Substituting (34) into (40), it becomes:

$$\begin{aligned}
\mathcal{L}V_1(x(t), i) &\leq s^T \kappa_{i2}^{-1} \frac{p}{q} \mathbf{z_2}^{\frac{p}{q}-\mathbf{1}} \cdot (F_i e_g(t)) - s^T \varepsilon |s| sgn(s) \\
&\leq \sum_{j=1}^{n} \left\{ \left(\kappa_{i2}^{-1} \frac{p}{q} \mathbf{z_2}^{\frac{p}{q}-\mathbf{1}} \right)_j \cdot |s_j| \cdot \|F_i e_g(t)\|_\infty \right\} - s^T \varepsilon |s| sgn(s) \\
&\leq -\varepsilon \|s\|^2
\end{aligned} \tag{41}$$

Since $\varepsilon > 0$, when $s \neq 0$, we can get $\mathcal{L}V_1(x(t), i) < 0$. According to Lemma 3, the time in which the system state reaches the equilibrium point is finite, and the convergence time T can be given. This is if and only if $s = 0$, $\mathcal{L}V_1(x(t), i) = 0$. □

Theorem 1. *The error dynamic system (27) and the control system (29) are stochastically stable, if there exist symmetrical matrices $Q_i > 0$, $Q > 0$, $O_i > 0$, $O > 0$, $\Lambda > 0$, $M_i > 0$, which is the Lipschitz constant matrix, and $O_i \in \mathbb{R}^{r\times r}$, $T_i \in \mathbb{R}^{r\times p}$, such that the following conditions hold*

$$\begin{aligned} \sum_{j=1}^{n} \pi_{ij}(-O_j) \leq -O,\ \sum_{j=1}^{n} \pi_{ij}Q_j \leq Q \\ F_i^T Q_i = T_i C_i \\ \Phi = \begin{bmatrix} \Phi_{11} & \Phi_{12} & \Phi_{13} & 0 \\ * & \Phi_{22} & \Phi_{23} & 0 \\ * & * & \Phi_{33} & 0 \\ * & * & * & \Phi_{44} \end{bmatrix} < 0 \end{aligned} \tag{42}$$

where

$\Phi_{11} = Q_i(A_i - L_iC_i) + (A_i - L_iC_i)^T Q_i + \sum_{j=1}^{n} \pi_{ij}Q_j + k_iM_i + \alpha_i m_i$

$\Phi_{12} = -\frac{1}{\zeta}\left(A_i^T Q_i F_i - (Q_iL_iC_i)^T F_i\right)$

$\Phi_{13} = Q_iB_i + \frac{1}{2}(\beta_i m_i - k_i)I$

$\Phi_{22} = -\frac{2}{\zeta}F_i^T Q_i F_i + \frac{1}{\zeta\rho}O_i + \frac{1}{\zeta}\sum_{j=1}^{n} \pi_{ij}\Lambda^{-1}$

$\Phi_{23} = -\frac{1}{\zeta}F_i^T Q_i B_i$

$\Phi_{33} = -m_i I$

$\Phi_{44} = -\frac{\rho}{\zeta}(O + \Lambda^{-1}O_i\Lambda^{-1})$

Proof. Choose the Lyapunov function as:

$$V_2(x(t), i) = e(t)^T Q_i e(t) + \frac{1}{\zeta} e_g^T(t)\Lambda^{-1} e_g - \frac{\rho}{\zeta} g^T(t)\Lambda^{-1}O_i\Lambda^{-1}g(t) \tag{43}$$

Like the proof of the Lyapunov function (39), we now calculate $\mathcal{L}V_2(x(t), i)$,

$$\begin{aligned} \mathcal{L}V_2(x(t), i) &= e(t)^T\left(Q_i(A_i - L_iC_i) + (A_i - L_iC_i)^T Q_i\right)e(t) \\ &+ 2e(t)^T Q_i B_i e_f(x(t), \hat{x}(t)) + 2e(t)^T F_i^T Q_i e_g(t) + \frac{2}{\zeta} e_g^T(t)\Lambda^{-1}\dot{e}_g(t) \\ &- \frac{\rho}{\zeta}\dot{g}^T(t)\Lambda^{-1}O_i\Lambda^{-1}g(t) - \frac{\rho}{\zeta}g^T(t)\Lambda^{-1}O_i\Lambda^{-1}\dot{g}(t) + \sum_{j=1}^{n}\pi_{ij}V_2(x(t), i) \\ &= e(t)^T\left(Q_i(A_i - L_iC_i) + (A_i - L_iC_i)^T Q_i\right)e(t) + 2e(t)^T Q_i B_i e_f(x(t), \hat{x}(t)) \\ &- \frac{2}{\zeta}e_g^T(t)T_iC_i(A - LC)e_x(t) - \frac{2}{\zeta}e_g^T(t)F_i^T Q_i\left(F_i e_g(t) + B_i e_f(x(t), \hat{x}(t))\right) \\ &- \frac{2}{\zeta}e_g^T(t)\Lambda^{-1}\dot{g}(t) - \frac{\rho}{\zeta}\left(\dot{g}^T(t) + g^T(t)\right)\Lambda^{-1}O_i\Lambda^{-1}(\dot{g}(t) + g(t)) + \sum_{j=1}^{n}\pi_{ij}V_2(x(t), i) \end{aligned} \tag{44}$$

According to Lemma 2,

$$-\frac{2}{\zeta}e_g^T(t)\Lambda^{-1}\dot{g}(t) \leq \frac{1}{\zeta\rho}e_g^T(t)O_i e_g(t) + \frac{\rho}{\zeta}\dot{g}^T(t)\Lambda^{-1}O_i\Lambda^{-1}\dot{g}(t) \tag{45}$$

Substitute (45) into (44),

$$\begin{aligned}\mathcal{L}V_2(x(t),i) \leq\ & e(t)^T\Big(Q_i(A_i - L_iC_i) + (A_i - L_iC_i)^T Q_i\Big)e(t) + 2e(t)^T Q_i B_i\, e_f(x(t),\hat{x}(t)) \\ & - \frac{2}{\zeta}e_g^T(t)T_iC_i(A - LC)e_x(t) - \frac{2}{\zeta}e_g^T(t)F_i^T Q_i\Big(F_ie_g(t) + B_ie_f(x(t),\hat{x}(t))\Big) \\ & + \frac{1}{\zeta\rho}e_g^T(t)O_ie_g(t) + \frac{\rho}{\zeta}\dot{g}^T(t)\Lambda^{-1}O_i\Lambda^{-1}\dot{g}(t) \\ & - \frac{\rho}{\zeta}\Big(\dot{g}^T(t) + g^T(t)\Big)\Lambda^{-1}O_i\Lambda^{-1}(\dot{g}(t) + g(t)) + \sum_{j=1}^{n}\pi_{ij}V_2(x(t),i)\end{aligned} \tag{46}$$

Considering the assumptions (1) and (2), the following equations can be given:

$$\begin{cases} k_ie(t)^T M_ie(t) - k_ie_{fi}(x(t),\hat{x}(t))^T e(t) \geq 0 \\ \alpha_im_ie(t)^Te(t) - m_ie_{fi}(x(t),\hat{x}(t))e_{fi}(x(t),\hat{x}(t))^T + \beta_im_ie(t)^Te_{fi}(x(t),\hat{x}(t)) \geq 0 \end{cases} \tag{47}$$

where $k_i, m_i \in \mathcal{R}^+$.

Add Formula (47) to the right of Formula (46), and then we can get:

$$\begin{aligned}\mathcal{L}V_2(x(t),i) \leq\ & e(t)^T\Big(Q_i(A_i - L_iC_i) + (A_i - L_iC_i)^T Q_i\Big)e(t) + 2e(t)^T Q_i B_i\, e_f(x(t),\hat{x}(t)) \\ & - \frac{2}{\zeta}e_g^T(t)T_iC_i(A - LC)e_x(t) - \frac{2}{\zeta}e_g^T(t)F_i^T Q_i\Big(F_ie_g(t) + B_ie_f(x(t),\hat{x}(t))\Big) \\ & + \frac{1}{\zeta\rho}e_g^T(t)O_ie_g(t) + \frac{\rho}{\zeta}\dot{g}^T(t)\Lambda^{-1}O_i\Lambda^{-1}\dot{g}(t) \\ & - \frac{\rho}{\zeta}\Big(\dot{g}^T(t) + g^T(t)\Big)\Lambda^{-1}O_i\Lambda^{-1}(\dot{g}(t) + g(t)) + k_ie(t)^T M_ie(t) \\ & - k_ie_{fi}(x(t),\hat{x}(t))^T e(t) + \alpha_im_ie(t)^Te(t) - m_ie_{fi}(x(t),\hat{x}(t))e_{fi}(x(t),\hat{x}(t))^T \\ & + \beta_im_ie(t)^Te_{fi}(x(t),\hat{x}(t)) \\ & + e(t)^T\sum_{j=1}^{n}\pi_{ij}Q_je(t) + \frac{1}{\zeta}e_g^T(t)\sum_{j=1}^{n}\pi_{ij}\Lambda^{-1}e_g(t) - \frac{\rho}{\zeta}g^T(t)Og(t)\end{aligned} \tag{48}$$

The inequation (48) can be written as:

$$\mathcal{L}V_2(x(t),i) < \begin{bmatrix} e(t) \\ e_g(t) \\ e_{fi}(x(t),\hat{x}(t)) \\ g(t) \end{bmatrix}^T \begin{bmatrix} \mathcal{A}_i & \mathcal{B}_i & \mathcal{C}_i & 0 \\ * & \mathcal{D}_i & \mathcal{E}_i & 0 \\ * & * & \mathcal{F}_i & 0 \\ * & * & * & \mathcal{G}_i \end{bmatrix} \begin{bmatrix} e(t) \\ e_g(t) \\ e_{fi}(x(t),\hat{x}(t)) \\ g(t) \end{bmatrix} \tag{49}$$

where

$\mathcal{A}_i = Q_i(A_i - L_iC_i) + (A_i - L_iC_i)^T Q_i + \sum_{j=1}^{n}\pi_{ij}Q_j + k_iM_i + \alpha_im_i$

$\mathcal{B}_i = -\frac{1}{\zeta}\Big(A_i^TQ_iF_i - (Q_iL_iC_i)^TF_i\Big)$

$\mathcal{C}_i = Q_iB_i + \frac{1}{2}(\beta_im_i - k_i)I$

$\mathcal{D}_i = -\frac{2}{\zeta}F_i^TQ_iF_i + \frac{1}{\zeta\rho}O_i + \frac{1}{\zeta}\sum_{j=1}^{n}\pi_{ij}\Lambda^{-1}$

$\mathcal{E}_i = -\frac{1}{\zeta}F_i^TQ_iB_i$

$\mathcal{F}_i = -m_iI$

$\mathcal{G}_i = -\frac{\rho}{\zeta}(O + \Lambda^{-1}O_i\Lambda^{-1})$

Based on Lemma 1, we obtain that

$$\begin{aligned}\mathcal{L}V_2(x(t),i) &\le \eta^T(t)\Phi_i\eta(t) \\ &= -\eta^T(t)(-\Phi_i)\eta(t) \\ &\le -\mu\|\eta(t)\|^2\end{aligned} \tag{50}$$

where $\eta^T(t) = \begin{bmatrix} e^T(t) & e_g^T(t) & e_f^T(x(t),\hat{x}(t)) & g(t) \end{bmatrix}$, $\Phi_i = \begin{bmatrix} \mathcal{A}_i & \mathcal{B}_i & \mathcal{C}_i & 0 \\ * & \mathcal{D}_i & \mathcal{E}_i & 0 \\ * & * & \mathcal{F}_i & 0 \\ * & * & * & \mathcal{G}_i \end{bmatrix}$, and $\mu = \min_{i\in\mathcal{N}}\{\sigma(-\Phi_i)\} > 0$.

According to the Dynkin theorem,

$$\begin{aligned}&E\{V(x(t),i)\} - E\{V_0\} \le -\mu E\left\{\int_0^t (\mathcal{L}V(x(t),i))ds\right\} \\ &E\left\{\int_0^t (\mathcal{L}V(x(t),i))ds\right\} \le -\frac{1}{\mu}[E\{V(x(t),i)\} - E\{V_0\}] \le \frac{1}{\mu}E\{V_0\} \\ &E\left\{\int_0^t \|e(t)\|^2 dt \middle| e_0, r_0\right\} < \infty\end{aligned} \tag{51}$$

Based on Definition 1, the system is stochastically stable. □

4. Simulation Study

In this paper, the quadrotor of Canada company is used as the simulation object of the fault-tolerant algorithm [41]. The quadrotor system used in the experiment is presented in Figures 2–4. This quadrotor system can upload control programs and faults to the onboard processor via Wi-Fi, which is helpful for fault injection and experiments. This experimental platform includes a Qdrone quadrotor, an OptiTrack motion capture system, and a ground station with a PC and a router. Through the data from 12 OptiTrack Flex-3 motion capture cameras, the OptiTrack Tools software on the PC can give the real-time flight status of the Qdrone quadrotor, so as to realize online control of the quadrotor. In addition, faults, nonlinear factors, and disturbances can be designed on the PC for experiments.

Figure 2. Qdrone.

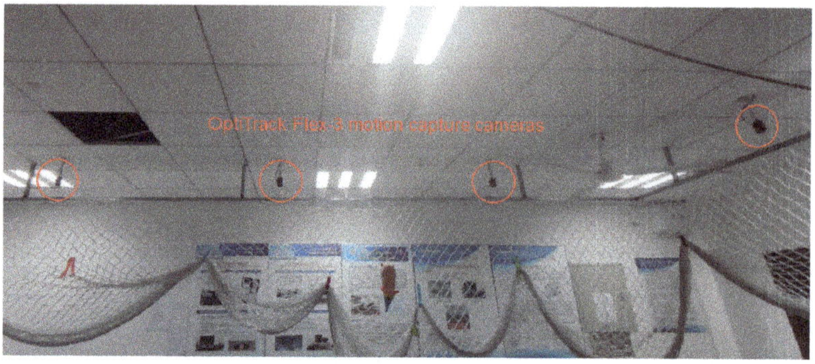

Figure 3. OptiTrack Flex-3 motion capture cameras.

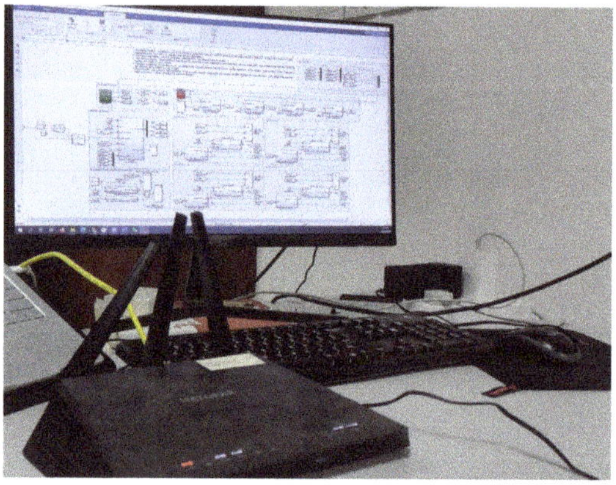

Figure 4. The ground station.

According to [41], we choose the appropriate parameters of the quadrotor UAV system in Table 1.

Table 1. Parameters of the Qdrone.

Parameter	Numerical Value	Unit
m	1.121	kg
g	9.80	m/s^2
I_x	0.010	$kg \cdot m^2$
I_y	0.008	$kg \cdot m^2$
I_z	0.015	$kg \cdot m^2$

We choose $N = 4$, and the transition rates matrix is chosen as:

$$\Pi = \begin{bmatrix} -0.36 & 0.16 & 0.16 & 0.04 \\ 0.64 & -0.84 & 0.16 & 0.04 \\ 0.64 & 0.16 & -0.84 & 0.04 \\ 0.64 & 0.16 & 0.16 & -0.96 \end{bmatrix} \quad (52)$$

The trajectories of the system mode are presented in Figure 5.

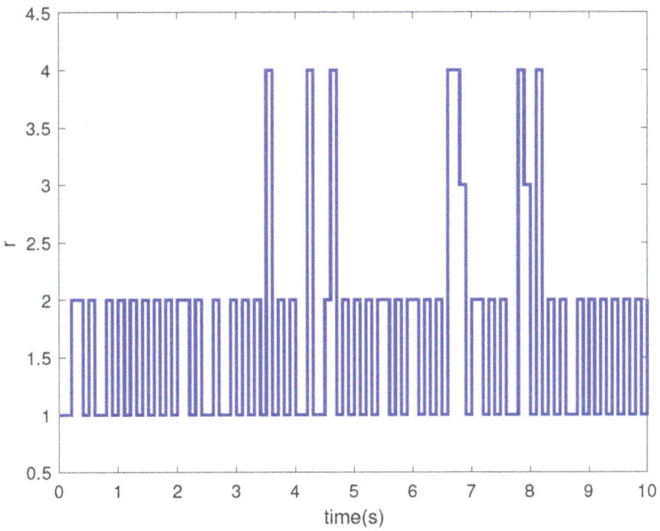

Figure 5. System mode.

When some actuators considering the rolling and pitching directions fail, the matrix B will change. Four different modes of matrix B are given as follows:

$$B_1 = \begin{bmatrix} 0 & 0 & 0 \\ 0 & 0 & 0 \\ 0 & 0 & 0 \\ 100 & 0 & 0 \\ 0 & 125 & 0 \\ 0 & 0 & 67 \end{bmatrix}, B_2 = \begin{bmatrix} 0 & 0 & 0 \\ 0 & 0 & 0 \\ 0 & 0 & 0 \\ 75 & 0 & 0 \\ 0 & 125 & 0 \\ 0 & 0 & 67 \end{bmatrix}, B_3 = \begin{bmatrix} 0 & 0 & 0 \\ 0 & 0 & 0 \\ 0 & 0 & 0 \\ 100 & 0 & 0 \\ 0 & 93.75 & 0 \\ 0 & 0 & 67 \end{bmatrix}, B_4 = \begin{bmatrix} 0 & 0 & 0 \\ 0 & 0 & 0 \\ 0 & 0 & 0 \\ 75 & 0 & 0 \\ 0 & 93.75 & 0 \\ 0 & 0 & 67 \end{bmatrix} \quad (53)$$

where B_1 represents the healthy system and others represent actuator faults of different direction. B_2 represents some actuator failure in the roll direction, B_3 represents some actuator failure in the pitch direction, and B_4 represents actuator failure in both the roll direction and pitch direction.

Taking the parameters $p = 7$, $q = 5$, $\gamma = 2$, $\varepsilon = 0.1$, $\zeta = 1$, $m = 0.5$, $k = 0.5$. The initial attitude of the UAV system is shown as $\begin{bmatrix}\phi & \theta & \psi\end{bmatrix}^T = \begin{bmatrix}0.2 & -0.2 & 0.5\end{bmatrix}^T$, and the initial angle rate is shown as $\begin{bmatrix}\dot{\phi} & \dot{\theta} & \dot{\psi}\end{bmatrix}^T = \begin{bmatrix}0 & 0 & 0\end{bmatrix}^T$. Besides, the nonlinear term is $f(x(t), t) = 5sin(\pi t)$. Moreover, the actuator faults and disturbances are given as:

$$\omega(t) = \begin{cases} 0, 0 \leq t < 2 \\ e^{-0.8t}, 2 \leq t \leq 10 \end{cases} \quad (54)$$

$$f_a(t) = \begin{cases} 0, 0 \leq t < 0.5 \\ te^{-0.8t}, 0.5 \leq t < 2 \\ 0.8\sin(\pi t), 2 \leq t \leq 10 \end{cases} \quad (55)$$

By solving the linear matrix inequalities in Theorem 1, the parameter matrices can be given as follows:

$$Q_1 = \begin{bmatrix} 76.4090 & -3.0527 & -7.5335 & -0.5193 & -0.0131 & 0.0455 \\ -3.0527 & 64.9062 & -6.5765 & 0.0013 & -0.4108 & 0.0449 \\ -7.5335 & -6.5765 & 97.3179 & 0.0091 & -0.0083 & -0.7604 \\ -0.5193 & 0.0013 & 0.0091 & 0.0072 & 0.0021 & 0.0021 \\ -0.0131 & -0.4108 & -0.0083 & 0.0021 & 0.0049 & 0.0022 \\ 0.0455 & 0.0449 & -0.7604 & 0.0021 & 0.0022 & 0.0132 \end{bmatrix},$$

$$Q_2 = \begin{bmatrix} 91.1962 & -4.9524 & -7.3058 & -0.6946 & -0.0137 & 0.0401 \\ -4.9524 & 64.8688 & -6.0623 & 0.0279 & -0.4145 & 0.0431 \\ -7.3058 & -6.0623 & 97.5787 & 0.0285 & -0.0116 & -0.7758 \\ -0.6946 & 0.0279 & 0.0285 & 0.0115 & 0.0022 & 0.0021 \\ -0.0137 & -0.4145 & -0.0116 & 0.0022 & 0.0049 & 0.0022 \\ 0.0401 & 0.0431 & -0.7758 & 0.0021 & 0.0022 & 0.0136 \end{bmatrix},$$

$$Q_3 = \begin{bmatrix} 59.0632 & -5.0682 & -6.3968 & -0.3917 & 0.0049 & 0.0337 \\ -5.0682 & 60.8165 & -6.5345 & 0.0001 & -0.4149 & 0.0331 \\ -6.3968 & -6.5345 & 69.7799 & -0.0019 & 0.0018 & -0.5558 \\ -0.3917 & 0.0001 & -0.0019 & 0.0067 & 0.0019 & 0.0021 \\ 0.0049 & -0.4149 & 0.0018 & 0.0019 & 0.0073 & 0.0021 \\ 0.0337 & 0.0331 & -0.5558 & 0.0021 & 0.0021 & 0.0111 \end{bmatrix},$$

$$Q_4 = \begin{bmatrix} 49.1919 & -3.3174 & -4.2157 & -0.4438 & 0.0021 & 0.0252 \\ -3.3174 & 42.6652 & -4.0112 & 0.0224 & -0.3625 & 0.0355 \\ -4.2157 & -4.0112 & 52.8587 & 0.0099 & 0.0035 & -0.4967 \\ -0.4438 & 0.0224 & 0.0099 & 0.0091 & 0.0024 & 0.0025 \\ 0.0021 & -0.3625 & 0.0035 & 0.0024 & 0.0064 & 0.0023 \\ 0.0252 & 0.0355 & -0.4967 & 0.0025 & 0.0023 & 0.0108 \end{bmatrix},$$

$$O_1 = \begin{bmatrix} -12574 & 770 & 814 \\ 770 & -12598 & 1059 \\ 814 & 1059 & -12769 \end{bmatrix},$$

$$O_2 = \begin{bmatrix} -12490 & 827 & 415 \\ 827 & -12595 & 935 \\ 415 & 935 & -12570 \end{bmatrix},$$

$$O_3 = \begin{bmatrix} -8890.5 & 163.7 & 316.1 \\ 163.7 & -8865.5 & 320.6 \\ 316.1 & 320.6 & -8664.8 \end{bmatrix},$$

$$O_4 = \begin{bmatrix} -5896.2 & 193.5 & 128.1 \\ 193.5 & -5985.4 & 232.8 \\ 128.1 & 232.8 & -5904.0 \end{bmatrix},$$

$$L_1 = \begin{bmatrix} 370160 & -18210 & -37230 \\ -5120 & 309560 & -24930 \\ -62930 & -60550 & 469170 \\ -2510 & 40 & 50 \\ -110 & -1940 & -80 \\ 430 & 440 & -3670 \end{bmatrix}, L_2 = \begin{bmatrix} 437770 & -41530 & -42600 \\ -14220 & 310500 & -22000 \\ -49140 & -53640 & 469420 \\ -3330 & 280 & 190 \\ -120 & -1960 & -100 \\ 300 & 410 & -3730 \end{bmatrix},$$

$$L_3 = \begin{bmatrix} 186440 & -18190 & -23090 \\ -20060 & 190580 & -25500 \\ -34660 & -35090 & 208300 \\ -1220 & 30 & 30 \\ 50 & -1290 & 50 \\ 220 & 220 & -1660 \end{bmatrix}, L_4 = \begin{bmatrix} 105470 & -11190 & -10920 \\ -9370 & 93370 & -11390 \\ -12080 & -14630 & 113900 \\ -950 & 90 & 40 \\ 30 & -790 & 30 \\ 80 & 130 & -1070 \end{bmatrix}.$$

Compared the adaptive algorithm in [42], the FAFE algorithm used in the adaptive observer has obvious advantages, which can be seen in Figure 6.

From Figure 6, it can be obviously seen that both observers have an accurate estimation of faults and disturbances. The observer method proposed in this paper has a shorter response time and smaller steady-state error than the method proposed in [42].

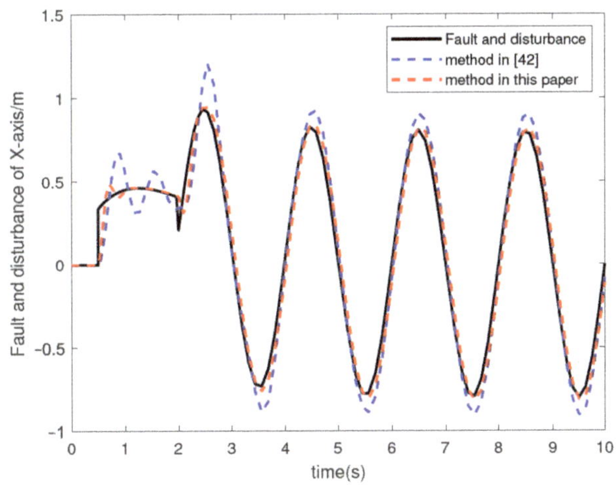

Figure 6. Estimated fault and disturbance from observer.

From Figures 7 and 8, the method proposed by this paper can do well with actuator faults and disturbances, and finally converge to zero.

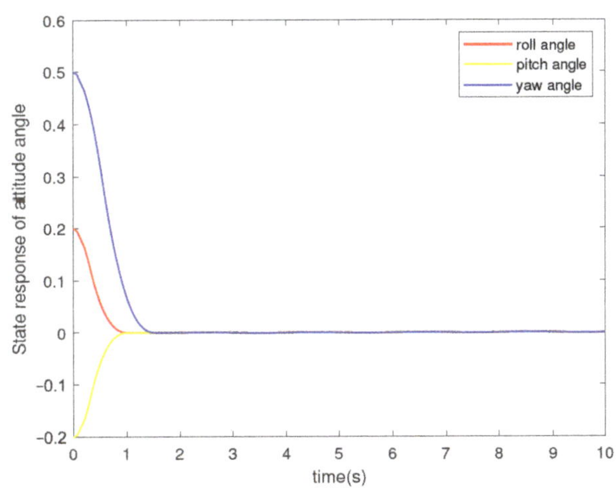

Figure 7. State response of attitude angle.

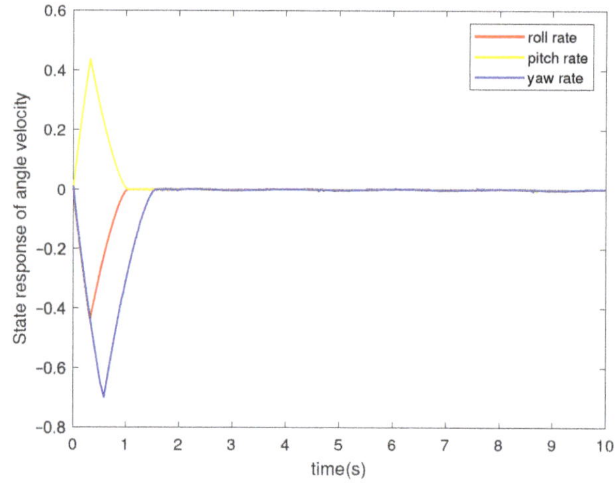

Figure 8. State response of angular velocity.

Figures 9 and 10 show the state response of attitude angle and angle velocity, based on [43]. The state responses in Figures 7 and 8 have faster responses than those in Figures 9 and 10. Comparing the results of the two methods, the nonsingular fast terminal sliding mode controller proposed in this paper has better control performance.

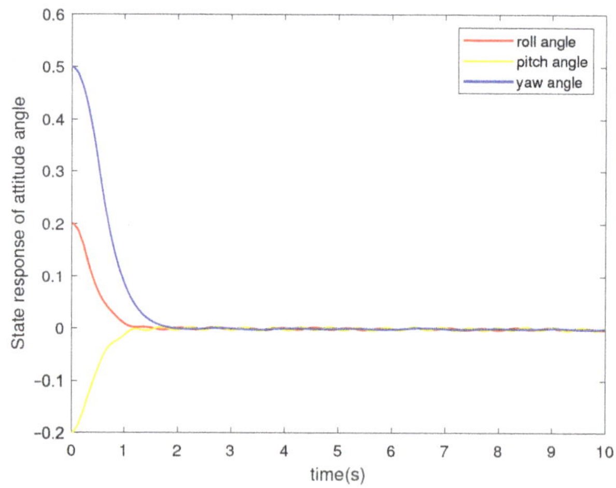

Figure 9. State response of the attitude angle by the method in [43].

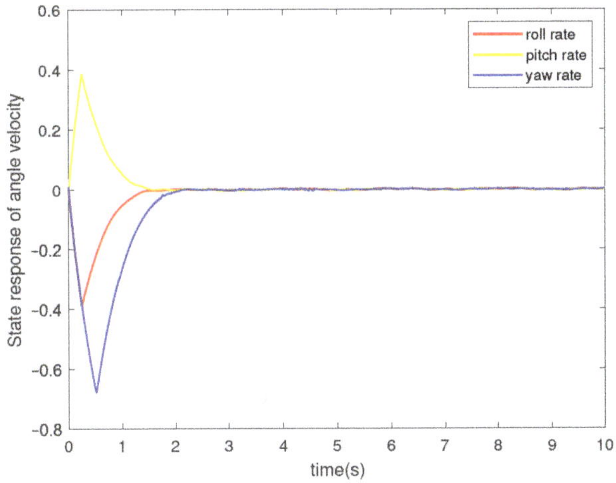

Figure 10. State response of the angular velocity by the method in [43].

5. Conclusions

In this paper, an adaptive-based nonsingular fast terminal sliding mode controller of Markov jump nonlinear systems is discussed. An adaptive observer with the FAFE method is proposed to estimate the actuator faults and external disturbances. Based on this observer, a nonsingular fast terminal sliding mode controller is provided for fault-tolerant control. By utilizing the Lyapunov-Krasovskii functional (LKF) and linear matrix inequalities (LMI) techniques, the original system is ensured to be stochastic stable.

Through the method proposed in this paper, the MJNSs can demonstrate resistance to actuator faults and disturbances. In practice, UAVs may encounter more complex situations, including human factors and environmental factors. Future research should consider more factors and focus on eliminating chattering.

Author Contributions: Conceptualization, P.Y.; methodology, P.Y. and Z.S.; validation, Z.S.; formal analysis, Z.S.; investigation, Y.D. and K.F.; writing—original draft preparation, Z.S.; writing—review and editing, Z.S., Y.D. and K.F.; supervision, P.Y. All authors have read and agreed to the published version of the manuscript.

Funding: This work was funded by Key Laboratories for National Defense Science and Technology (6142605200402), National Key Laboratory of Science and Technology on Helicopter Transmission (No.HTL-O-21G11), the Aeronautical Science Foundation of China (20200007018001), the Aero Engine Corporation of China Industry—university-research cooperation project (HFZL2020CXY011), and the Research Fund of State Key Laboratory of Mechanics and Control of Mechanical Structures (Nanjing University of Aeronautics and Astronautics) (MCMS-I-0121G03).

Institutional Review Board Statement: Not applicable.

Informed Consent Statement: Not applicable.

Data Availability Statement: Not applicable.

Conflicts of Interest: The authors declare no conflicts of interest.

References

1. Krasovskii, N.M.; Lidskii, E.A. Analytical design of controllers in systems with random attributes. *Remote Control* **1961**, *22*, 1021–2025.
2. Fang, H.Y.; Zhu, G.Z.; Stojanovic, V.; Nie, R.; He, S.P.; Luan, X.L.; Liu, F. Adaptive optimization algorithm for nonlinear Markov jump systems with partial unknown dynamics. *Int. J. Robust Nonlinear Control* **2021**, *31*, 2126–2140. [CrossRef]
3. Ren, Y.H.; Wang, W.Q.; Hua, D.L.; Shen, M.X. Incremental dissipative control for nonlinear stochastic Markovian jump systems. *J. Frankl. Inst.-Eng. Appl. Math.* **2021**, *358*, 3757–3778. [CrossRef]

4. Alattas, K.A.; Mohammadzadeh, A.; Mobayen, S.; Abo-Dief, H.M.; Alanazi, A.K.; Vu, M.T.; Chang, A.R. Automatic Control for Time Delay Markov Jump Systems under Polytopic Uncertainties. *Mathematics* **2020**, *10*, 187. [CrossRef]
5. Altan, A.; Hacioglu, R. Model predictive control of three-axis gimbal system mounted on UAV for real-time target tracking under external disturbances. *Mech. Syst. Signal Process.* **2020**, *138*, 106548. [CrossRef]
6. Maimaitijiang, M.; Sagan, V.; Sidike, P.; Hartling, S.; Esposito, F.; Fritschi, F.B. Soybean yield prediction from UAV using multimodal data fusion and deep learning. *Remote Sens. Environ.* **2020**, *237*, 111599. [CrossRef]
7. Dai, Y.Y.; Xu, D.; Zhang, K.; Maharjan, S.; Zhang, Y. Deep Reinforcement Learning and Permissioned Blockchain for Content Caching in Vehicular Edge Computing and Networks. *IEEE Trans. Veh. Technol.* **2020**, *69*, 4312–4324. [CrossRef]
8. Yu, Z.Q.; Zhang, Y.M.; Jiang, B.; Fu, J.; Jin, Y.; Chai, T.Y. Composite Adaptive Disturbance Observer-Based Decentralized Fractional-Order Fault-Tolerant Control of Networked UAVs. *IEEE Trans. Syst. Man Cybern.-Syst.* **2022**, *52*, 799–813. [CrossRef]
9. Guan, C.; Fei, Z.; Park, P.G. Modified looped functional for sampled-data control of T-S fuzzy Markovian jump systems. *IEEE Trans. Fuzzy Syst.* **2020**, *29*, 2543–2552. [CrossRef]
10. Wang, S.; Wu, Z. Asynchronous Control of Uncertain Markov Jump Systems With Actuator Saturation. *IEEE Trans. Circuits Syst. II Express Briefs* **2022**, *69*, 3269–3273. [CrossRef]
11. Chen, H.; Liu, M. Finite-time stability for a kind of Markovian jump systems subject to random delays and external disturbances. *J. Nanjing Univ. Inf. Sci. Technol. (Nat. Sci. Ed.)* **2017**, *9*, 430–436.
12. Jiang, H.; Zhang, H.; Luo, Y.; Wang, J. Optimal tracking control for completely unknown nonlinear discrete-time Markov jump systems using data-based reinforcement learning method. *Neurocomputing* **2016**, *194*, 176–182. [CrossRef]
13. He, S.; Zhang, M.; Fang, H.; Liu, F.; Luan, X.; Ding, Z. Reinforcement learning and adaptive optimization of a class of Markov jump systems with completely unknown dynamic information. *Neural Comput. Appl.* **2020**, *32*, 14311–14320. [CrossRef]
14. Liu, Z.; Karimi, H.R.; Yu, J. Passivity-based robust sliding mode synthesis for uncertain delayed stochastic systems via state observer. *Automatica* **2020**, *111*, 108596. [CrossRef]
15. Le Q.D.; Kang, H.J. Implementation of Fault-Tolerant Control for a Robot Manipulator Based on Synchronous Sliding Mode Control. *Appl. Sci.* **2020**, *10*, 2534. [CrossRef]
16. Mao, Z.; Yan, X.; Jiang, B.; Chen, M. Adaptive Fault-Tolerant Sliding-Mode Control for High-Speed Trains with Actuator Faults and Uncertainties. *IEEE Trans. Intell. Transp. Syst.* **2020**, *21*, 2449–2460. [CrossRef]
17. Guo, X.; Xu, W.; Wang, J.; Park, J. Distributed Neuroadaptive Fault-tolerant Sliding-mode Control for 2-D Plane Vehicular Platoon Systems with Spacing Constraints and Unknown Direction Faults. *Automatica* **2021**, *129*, 109673. [CrossRef]
18. Zhao, J.; Ding, X.; Jiang, B.; Jiang, G.; Xie, F. A novel sliding mode fault-tolerant control strategy for variable-mass quadrotor. *Int. J. Robust Nonlinear Control* **2022**, *1*, 1–28. [CrossRef]
19. Yu, Z.Q.; Zhang, Y.M.; Jiang, B.; Su, C.Y.; Fu, J.; Jin, Y.; Chai, T.Y. Decentralized fractional-order backstepping fault-tolerant control of multi-UAVs against actuator faults and wind effects. *Aerosp. Sci. Technol.* **2020**, *104*, 105939. [CrossRef]
20. Wang, N.; Deng, Z.C. Finite-Time Fault Estimator Based Fault-Tolerance Control for a Surface Vehicle with Input Saturations. *IEEE Trans. Ind. Inform.* **2020**, *16*, 1172–1181. [CrossRef]
21. Xu, Y.; Wu, Z.G. Distributed Adaptive Event-Triggered Fault-Tolerant Synchronization for Multiagent Systems. *IEEE Trans. Ind. Electron.* **2020**, *68*, 1537–1547. [CrossRef]
22. Song, S.; Park, J.H.; Zhang, B.Y.; Song, X.N. Observer-Based Adaptive Hybrid Fuzzy Resilient Control for Fractional-Order Nonlinear Systems with Time-Varying Delays and Actuator Failures. *IEEE Trans. Fuzzy Syst.* **2021**, *29*, 471–485. [CrossRef]
23. Yao, X.M.; Wu, L.G.; Guo, L. Disturbance-Observer-Based Fault Tolerant Control of High-Speed Trains: A Markovian Jump System Model Approach. *IEEE Trans. Syst. Man Cybern.-Syst.* **2020**, *50*, 1476–1485. [CrossRef]
24. Yang, H.Y.; Yin, S. Reduced-order sliding-mode-observer-based fault estimation for Markov jump systems. *IEEE Trans. Autom. Control* **2019**, *64*, 4733–4740. [CrossRef]
25. Yang, H.Y.; Jiang, Y.C.; Yin, S. Adaptive Fuzzy Fault-Tolerant Control for Markov Jump Systems with Additive and Multiplicative Actuator Faults. *IEEE Trans. Fuzzy Syst.* **2021**, *29*, 772–785. [CrossRef]
26. Wang, G.L.; Huang, Y.F. Fault Estimation for Continuous-Time Markovian Jump Systems: An Auxiliary System Approach. *IEEE Access* **2021**, *9*, 83163–83174. [CrossRef]
27. Bahreini, M.; Zarei, J.; Razavi-Far, R.; Saif, M. Robust and Reliable Output Feedback Control for Uncertain Networked Control Systems Against Actuator Faults. *IEEE Trans. Syst. Man Cybern. Syst.* **2022**, *52*, 2555–2564. [CrossRef]
28. Chen, L.H.; Zhu, Y.Z.; Wu, F.; Zhao, Y.X. Fault Estimation Observer Design for Markovian Jump Systems With Nondifferentiable Actuator and Sensor Failures. *IEEE Trans. Cybern.* **2022**, *1*, 1–15. [CrossRef]
29. Chen, F.Y.; Jiang, R.Q.; Zhang, K.K.; Jiang, B.; Tao, G. Robust Backstepping Sliding-Mode Control and Observer-Based Fault Estimation for a Quadrotor UAV. *IEEE Trans. Ind. Electron.* **2016**, *63*, 5044–5056. [CrossRef]
30. Nian, X.H.; Chen, W.Q.; Chu, X.Y.; Xu, Z.W. Robust adaptive fault estimation and fault tolerant control for quadrotor attitude systems. *Int. J. Control* **2020**, *93*, 725–737. [CrossRef]
31. Youn, W.; Choi, H.; Cho, A.; Kim, S.; Rhudy, M.B. Accelerometer Fault-Tolerant Model-Aided State Estimation for High-Altitude Long-Endurance UAV. *IEEE Trans. Instrum. Meas.* **2020**, *69*, 8539–8553. [CrossRef]
32. Hajiyev, C.; Cilden-Guler, D.; Hacizade, U. Two-Stage Kalman Filter for Fault Tolerant Estimation of Wind Speed and UAV Flight Parameters. *Meas. Sci. Rev.* **2020**, *20*, 35–42. [CrossRef]

33. Goslinski, J.; Giernacki, W.; Krolikowski, A. A Nonlinear Filter for Efficient Attitude Estimation of Unmanned Aerial Vehicle (UAV). *J. Intell. Robot. Syst.* **2019**, *95*, 1079–1095. [CrossRef]
34. Eva, H.D.; Mihnea, S.; Cristina, I.M.; Liviu, C.M. An Efficient Design and Implementation of a Quadrotor Unmanned Aerial Vehicle Using Quaternion-Based Estimator. *Mathematics* **2020**, *8*, 1829.
35. Minh, C.; Nguyen, H.T. Reduced-order observer design for one-sided Lipschitz time-delay systems subject to unknown inputs. *IET Control Theory Appl.* **2016**, *10*, 1097–1105.
36. Fu, X.; Pang, X. Robust fault estimation and fault-tolerant control for nonlinear Markov jump systems with time-delays. *Automatika* **2021**, *62*, 21–31. [CrossRef]
37. Ren, H.; Zong, G.; Yang, D. Input-output finite-time stabilization for MJSs with time-varying delay: An observer-based approach. *J. Frankl. Inst.* **2019**, *356*, 9689–9712. [CrossRef]
38. Yu, P.; Ma, Y. Observer-based asynchronous control for Markov jump systems. *Appl. Math. Comput.* **2020**, *377*, 125184. [CrossRef]
39. Gao, S.; Ma, G.; Guo, Y.; Zhang, W. Fast actuator and sensor fault estimation based on adaptive unknown input observer. *ISA Trans.* **2022**, *in press*. [CrossRef]
40. Yang, L.; Yang, J. Nonsingular fast terminal sliding-mode control for nonlinear dynamical systems. *Int. J. Robust Nonlinear Control* **2011**, *21*, 1865–1879. [CrossRef]
41. Guo, K.; Jia, J.; Yu, X.;Guo, L.;Xie, L. Multiple observers based anti-disturbance control for a quadrotor UAV against payload and wind disturbances. *Control Eng. Pract.* **2020**, *102*, 104560. [CrossRef]
42. Wu, Y.; Zhang, G.; Wu, L. Observer-based adaptive fault estimation and fault-tolerant tracking control for a class of uncertain nonlinear systems. *IET Control Theory Appl.* **2021**, *15*, 13–23. [CrossRef]
43. Liang, J.; Chen, Z.H.; Yuan, X.H.; Zhang, B.Q.; Yuan, Y.B. Terminal Sliding Mode Controllers for Hydraulic Turbine Governing System with Bifurcated Penstocks under Input Saturation. *CMES-Comput. Model. Eng. Sci.* **2020**, *123*, 603–629. [CrossRef]

drones

MDPI

Article

Aerodynamic Numerical Simulation Analysis of Water–Air Two-Phase Flow in Trans-Medium Aircraft

Jun Wei, Yong-Bai Sha, Xin-Yu Hu, Jin-Yan Yao and Yan-Li Chen *

Key Laboratory of CNC Equipment Reliability, Ministry of Education, School of Mechanical and Aerospace Engineering, Jilin University, Changchun 130022, China
* Correspondence: chenyanli@jlu.edu.cn

Abstract: A trans-medium aircraft is a new concept aircraft that can both dive in the water and fly in the air. In this paper, a new type of water–air multi-medium span vehicle is designed based on the water entry and exit structure model of a multi-rotor UAV. Based on the designed structural model of the cross-media aircraft, the OpenFOAM open source numerical platform is used to analyze the single-medium aerodynamic characteristics and the multi-medium spanning flow analysis. The rotating flow characteristics of single-medium air rotor and underwater propeller are calculated by sliding mesh. In order to prevent the numerical divergence caused by the deformation of the grid movement, the overset grid method and the multiphase flow technology are used for the numerical simulation of the water entry and exit of the cross-medium aircraft. Through the above analysis, the flow field characteristics of the trans-medium vehicle in different media are verified, and the changes in the body load and attitude at different water entry angles are also obtained during the process of medium crossing.

Keywords: trans-media aircraft; multi-rotor drone; multimedia spanning; aerodynamics; multiphase flow

Citation: Wei, J.; Sha, Y.-B.; Hu, X.-Y.; Yao, J.-Y.; Chen, Y.-L. Aerodynamic Numerical Simulation Analysis of Water–Air Two-Phase Flow in Trans-Medium Aircraft. *Drones* **2022**, *6*, 236. https://doi.org/10.3390/drones6090236

Academic Editors: Andrzej Łukaszewicz, Wojciech Giernacki, Zbigniew Kulesza, Jaroslaw Pytka and Andriy Holovatyy

Received: 13 August 2022
Accepted: 31 August 2022
Published: 3 September 2022

1. Introduction

With the continuous exploration of natural space by human beings, both ship and aviation technology have made great progress in their respective fields. Among them, aircraft have been widely used due to their advantages of high speed and good maneuverability, but they also have shortcomings such as short endurance and poor concealment, which can be compensated by submersibles [1]. Trans-medium aircraft is a new conceptual aircraft that can both sneak in water and fly in the air. Due to its concealment of flight and diversity of functions, it can realize both aerial reconnaissance and underwater inspection, which expands the spatial scope of navigation [2]. Therefore, it combines the advantages of aerial drones and underwater submersibles, which have been favored by researchers from various countries since the early 20th century [3]. However, due to the large difference in the characteristics of the water–air medium, it is not a simple matter to cross the water–air medium, which involves the complex model entering and exiting the water process [4]. The process of aircraft entering and leaving water has a strong slamming effect. Slamming generally refers to the violent impact phenomenon between the object and the medium during the process of entering and leaving the water at a certain speed, which has a strong nonlinear and complex flow process. Violent slamming may cause damage to the airframe structure; thus, accurately predicting the change of slamming pressure with time becomes extremely critical [5].

The process of entering and leaving the water is an important subject in marine engineering and naval engineering. Considerable work has been conducted by predecessors on the problem of objects entering and leaving the water. Von Karman [6] is a pioneer in the research on the slamming theory of structures entering water. He uses the momentum theorem to give an estimation formula for the slamming load of a two-dimensional wedge and proposes the additional mass method to calculate the slamming load of seaplanes. Wagner [7] introduced a fairly flat theoretical assumption based on Von Karman and obtained the Wagner model with better calculation results. Based on the velocity potential theory, Dobrovol [8] assumes that the wedge-shaped body enters the water at a constant speed, while ignoring the influence of gravity, and thus obtains the analytical solution of the two-dimensional wedge-shaped body entering the water at a constant speed [9]. However, although the above methods have obtained relatively accurate solutions, they all ignore the physical properties of the fluid itself; thus, there is no real numerical prediction for the study of water entry and exit. Therefore, Mei et al. [10] proposed the boundary element method (BEM) based on Dobrovol. For wedges and circular cylinders, they derive closed-form solutions using conformal mapping for the boundary value problem at any instant.

In recent years, high-performance computer technology has become more and more mature, and the parallelization of computing efficiency [11] has increased so that relatively complex coupled dynamics problems can be handled. Zhao [12] et al. proposed an analytical CFD-DEM-IBM algorithm to capture free surfaces by fusing traditional CFD, DEM, IBM algorithms. The motion of solids and their interactions are modeled by the discrete element method (DEM) [13], and the immersion boundary method (IBM) [14] is used to track solid boundaries. The method has remarkable accuracy and mass conservation characteristics and achieves the purpose of fine numerical description of the water entry process. Guo et al. [15] performed numerical simulations of the planned forced landing of a transport aircraft on calm water. They solved the Reynolds-averaged Navier–Stokes (RANS) equations for unsteady compressible flow and used the realizable j-e equations to model turbulent flow, showing that the optimal initial angle of forced landing was between 10° and 12°. Streckwall, H et al. [16] numerically simulated the physical process of an aircraft emergency landing on water based on the commercial RANS solver "Comet", and they performed aerodynamic simulations of the forced landing of the fuselage for the general shape of the A, D, and J fuselage. To simplify the method, they derived hydrodynamic forces in all details through RANS simulations while approximating aerodynamic forces and moments. Simultaneously, simulations were carried out at TUHH using the program "Ditch", which is based on an extension of the "momentum method" developed by von Karman and Wagner.

Although the solution of the water entry problem has a propelling effect on the aerodynamic prediction of the trans-medium vehicle, there are still problems in the aerodynamic simulation of the whole process of the movement of the trans-medium vehicle and the prediction of the water entry of the complex shape vehicle. In this paper, the Navier–Stokes equation is solved, and the secondary development is carried out based on the OpenFOAM open source platform. The VOF (volume of fluid) method is used to numerically capture the water–air interface [17], and the overset grid technology is used to establish the interaction between the fluid and the body structure of the trans-medium aircraft. By simulating the process of entering and exiting water of a trans-medium aircraft, the accuracy of the numerical model is verified, and the aerodynamic characteristics of single medium and multi-medium and the evolution law of fluid cavitation when crossing multiple media are analyzed.

2. Modeling an Aircraft across Media

To simplify the complexity of the model, the following physical assumptions are made for the trans-medium aircraft: (1) the mass and moment of inertia of the trans-medium aircraft do not change during the multi-media crossing process; (2) the geometric center of the trans-medium aircraft and its center of gravity coincide (regular and symmetrical geometry); (3) after the trans-medium aircraft is subjected to force in motion, the shape and size remain unchanged, and the relative positions of internal points remain unchanged (rigid body) [18].

The purpose of establishing the mathematical model of the trans-medium aircraft is to analyze the changes in the position and attitude of the trans-medium aircraft when it is subjected to external forces and moments [19]. Among them, the input of the dynamic model is the pulling force and torque provided by the propeller, and the output is the speed and angular velocity of the aircraft; the input of the kinematic model is the output of the dynamic model, that is, the speed and angular velocity of the aircraft, and the output is the position and attitude of the aircraft [20]. The relationship is shown in Figure 1.

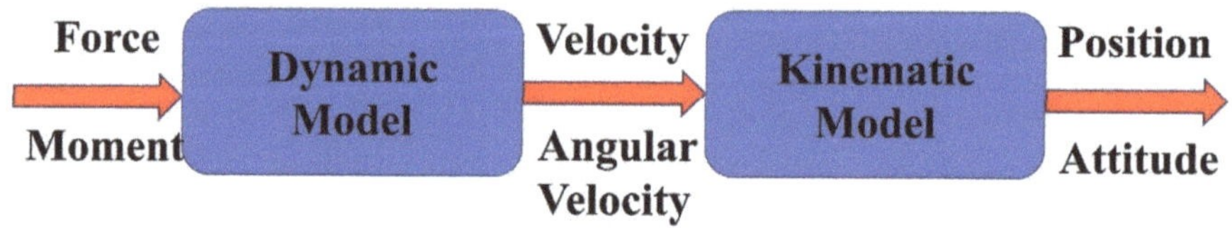

Figure 1. Flight control rigid body model for trans-media aircraft.

Before building a model, it is necessary to define the coordinate system representing the vector. This article will use two coordinate systems, namely the inertial coordinate system (static coordinate system), the Earth coordinate system, and the non-inertial coordinate system (moving coordinate system), the body coordinate system.

The Earth coordinate system takes the center of the Earth as the coordinate origin, which is fixedly connected to the Earth, and the body coordinate system takes the position of the center of gravity of the aircraft as the coordinate origin, which is fixedly connected to the quadrotor aircraft. The $o_b x_b$ axis direction is the forward direction of the aircraft, as shown in Figure 2.

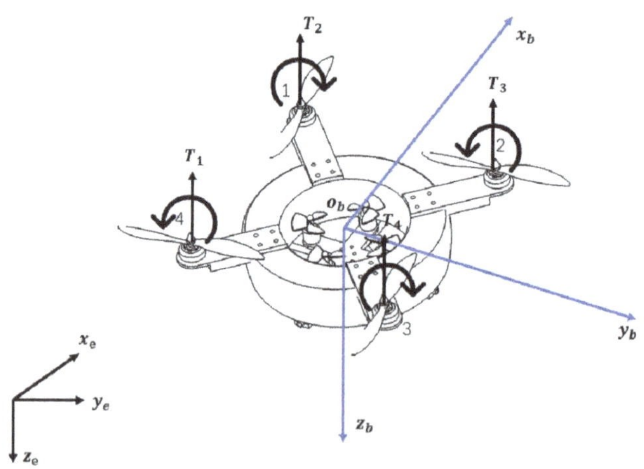

Figure 2. Schematic diagram of the coordinate system of the trans-media aircraft.

In this paper, according to the different medium environments in which the trans-media aircraft is located, its movement process is divided into the following three parts: (1) the air navigation segment (close underwater propellers, open-air rotors); (2) the multi-media spanning segment ((a) turn off the underwater propeller, and close the air rotor (free entry); (b) the underwater propeller pushes up and close to the water surface, when the air rotor is completely out of the water, turn off the underwater propeller and turn on the air rotor (out of water)); (3) the underwater submerged segment (close the air rotor, open the underwater propeller). Therefore, in the process of dynamic modeling, it can also be divided into three stages according to the above multi-stage motion process.

2.1. Modeling of Air Media

The modeling of the air medium of the trans-media aircraft is the same as the modeling of ordinary multi-rotor UAVs, and its motion process includes translation and rotation.

First, the translation of the trans-medium aircraft is discussed. According to Newton's second law, it can be obtained:

$$\begin{pmatrix} 0 \\ 0 \\ T_1 + T_2 + T_3 + T_4 \end{pmatrix} - \begin{pmatrix} 0 \\ 0 \\ Mg \end{pmatrix} = M \begin{pmatrix} a_x \\ a_y \\ a_z \end{pmatrix} \tag{1}$$

In the formula, T_1, T_2, T_3, T_4 is the pulling force generated by the air rotor of the aircraft, M is the overall mass of the aircraft across the medium, and a_x, a_y, a_z is the acceleration of the body in all directions.

Since the pulling force generated by the propeller is expressed in the body coordinate system, there is a transformation relationship between the relative and the whole Earth coordinate system; thus, the result of the above formula in the Earth coordinate system is:

$$R_b^e \begin{pmatrix} 0 \\ 0 \\ T_1 + T_2 + T_3 + T_4 \end{pmatrix} - \begin{pmatrix} 0 \\ 0 \\ Mg \end{pmatrix} = M \begin{pmatrix} a_x \\ a_y \\ a_z \end{pmatrix} \tag{2}$$

where R_b^e is the rotation matrix [21] from the body coordinate system to the Earth coordinate system,

$$R_b^n = \begin{pmatrix} cos\theta cos\psi & cos\psi sin\theta sin\phi - sin\psi cos\phi & cos\psi sin\theta + sin\psi sin\phi \\ cos\theta sin\psi & sin\psi sin\theta + cos\psi cos\phi & sin\psi sin\theta cos\phi - cos\psi sin\phi \\ -sin\theta & sin\phi cos\theta & cos\phi cos\theta \end{pmatrix} \tag{3}$$

ϕ, θ, ψ represent the roll angle around the x-axis, the pitch angle around the y-axis, and the yaw angle around the z-axis, namely Euler angles.

Substitute (3) into (1) to obtain:

$$\begin{cases} M\ddot{x} = (cos\phi sin\theta cos\psi + sin\phi sin\psi)F \\ M\ddot{y} = (cos\phi sin\theta sin\psi - sin\phi cos\psi)F \\ M\ddot{z} = cos\phi cos\theta * F - Mg \end{cases} \tag{4}$$

This results in the equation of the resultant external force and velocity in the dynamic model, that is, the position dynamic model. where $F = T_1 + T_2 + T_3 + T_4$.

Next, the rotation of the trans-medium aircraft is discussed, which is obtained by Euler's equation [22]:

$$J\dot{\boldsymbol{\omega}}^b + \boldsymbol{\omega}^b \times J\boldsymbol{\omega}^b = \boldsymbol{G}_a + \boldsymbol{\tau} \tag{5}$$

In the formula, $\boldsymbol{\omega}^b$ represents the angular velocity in the body coordinate system; $\boldsymbol{G}_a$ represents the gyro moment; $\boldsymbol{\tau}$ represents the moment generated by the propeller on the body axis, including the rolling moment τ_x around the $O_b x_b$-axis, the Pitch moment on the $O_b y_b$-axis τ_y and yaw moment around the $O_b z_b$-axis τ_z.

About the inertia matrix J: based on the assumptions made earlier, the inertia matrix can be expressed as:

$$J = \begin{pmatrix} J_{xx} & & \\ & J_{yy} & \\ & & J_{zz} \end{pmatrix} \tag{6}$$

Let $\boldsymbol{\omega}_b = \begin{pmatrix} \omega_x \\ \omega_y \\ \omega_z \end{pmatrix}$, $\boldsymbol{G}_a = \begin{pmatrix} G_{a,\phi} \\ G_{a,\theta} \\ G_{a,\psi} \end{pmatrix} = \begin{pmatrix} J_{RP}\omega_x(\varpi_1 - \varpi_2 + \varpi_3 - \varpi_4) \\ J_{RP}\omega_y(-\varpi_1 + \varpi_2 - \varpi_3 + \varpi_4) \\ 0 \end{pmatrix}$, substitute into (5) formula to obtain:

$$\begin{cases} \dot{\omega}_x = \frac{1}{I_{xx}}\left[\tau_x + \omega_y\omega_z(I_{yy} - I_{zz}) - J_{RP}\omega_y\Theta\right] \\ \dot{\omega}_y = \frac{1}{I_{yy}}\left[\tau_y + \omega_x\omega_z(I_{zz} - I_{xx}) + J_{RP}\omega_x\Theta\right] \\ \dot{\omega}_z = \frac{1}{I_{zz}}\left[\tau_z + \omega_x\omega_y((I_{xx} - I_{yy}))\right] \end{cases} \tag{7}$$

where $\Theta = -\varpi_1 + \varpi_2 - \varpi_3 + \varpi_4 . \varpi_1, \varpi_2, \varpi_3, \varpi_4$ is the rotational speed of the motor that drives the air rotor.

The above is the dynamic modeling of the trans-medium aircraft (air medium), which represents the relationship between the input resultant external force, the resultant external torque, and the output velocity and angular velocity.

Next, kinematic modeling of aircraft across media needs to be discussed (air medium), which describes the quantitative relationship between the velocity and angular velocity of the input and the position and attitude of the output.

The equation for the position is simple and can be expressed as:

$$\dot{\boldsymbol{P}}^e = \boldsymbol{v}^e \tag{8}$$

In the above formula, $\boldsymbol{P}^e = \begin{pmatrix} x & y & z \end{pmatrix}^T$ is used to represent the coordinate position of the aircraft in the Earth coordinate system, and then, Formula (8) is expanded to obtain:

$$\begin{pmatrix} \dot{x} & \dot{y} & \dot{z} \end{pmatrix}^T = \begin{pmatrix} v_x & v_y & v_z \end{pmatrix}^T \tag{9}$$

Next comes the equation for attitude.

The rate of change of the attitude angle is related to the rotational angular velocity of the body as follows:

$$\dot{\boldsymbol{\Omega}} = \boldsymbol{\Gamma} \bullet \boldsymbol{\omega}^b \tag{10}$$

In the formula, $\boldsymbol{\Omega}$ is the three attitude angle (Eulerian angle) matrix of the trans-medium aircraft, $\boldsymbol{\Gamma}$ is the attitude calculation coordinate transformation matrix, which measures the transformation relationship between the rate of change of the attitude angle and the rotational angular velocity of the body. Thus, the above formula can be fully expanded:

$$\begin{pmatrix} \dot{\phi} \\ \dot{\theta} \\ \dot{\psi} \end{pmatrix} = \begin{pmatrix} 1 & tan\theta sin\phi & tan\theta cos\phi \\ 0 & cos\phi & -sin\phi \\ 0 & sin\phi/cos\theta & cos\phi/cos\theta \end{pmatrix} \begin{pmatrix} \omega_x \\ \omega_y \\ \omega_z \end{pmatrix} \tag{11}$$

In the case of small disturbance, that is, under the premise that the change of each angle is small, the $\boldsymbol{\Gamma}$ matrix is a unit matrix; thus, it can be obtained:

$$\begin{pmatrix} \dot{\phi} \\ \dot{\theta} \\ \dot{\psi} \end{pmatrix} = \begin{pmatrix} \omega_x \\ \omega_y \\ \omega_z \end{pmatrix} \tag{12}$$

Thus far, the model establishment for the trans-medium aircraft (air medium) has been completed.

Remark 1. *The reason for the left-multiplied rotation matrix in Equation (2) is that the body coordinate system performs a rotation about the geostationary coordinate system. Equation (3), as a rotation matrix, reflects the equivalent relationship of the transformation from the Earth coordinate system to the airframe coordinate system.*

Remark 2. *Equation (5) describes the differential equation for the motion of a rigid body, in the motion of a rigid body around a fixed point, reflecting the relationship between angular velocity, angular acceleration and the moment on the rigid body.*

2.2. Establishment of Underwater Propeller Propulsion Model

First, underwater dynamics modeling needs to be considered. When a trans-medium aircraft moves underwater, it will drive a small part of the fluid around the aircraft to move at the same time, and this small part of the fluid acts on the aircraft; thus, the additional mass of the aircraft during motion needs to be considered [23]. The physical expression of this additional mass is that the inertial coefficient of the aircraft produces an increment λ_{ik} ($i,k = 1,2,\cdots 6$, representing six directions). The motion of this small part of the fluid can be regarded as a rigid-body-like motion, that is, the motion of the fluid is a rigid-body-like motion at the same speed as the trans-medium aircraft. There is only one symmetry plane $O_b y_b z_b$ for the trans-medium aircraft; thus, there are 12 inertial coefficient increments λ_{ik} that are not zero. Therefore, the underwater dynamic model of the trans-medium aircraft defined by generalized parameters is as follows:

$$\boldsymbol{M}\dot{\boldsymbol{v}} + \boldsymbol{W}(v)\boldsymbol{v} = \sum \boldsymbol{F} \tag{13}$$

In the formula, $\boldsymbol{M}$ is the generalized mass matrix of the trans-medium aircraft, $\boldsymbol{W}(v)$ is the external force coefficient matrix received, and $\sum \boldsymbol{F}$ is the external force received by the fluid resistance, lift, etc., which can be solved by the OpenFOAM open source numerical platform.

Next, model the underwater kinematics of the trans-medium aircraft. The purpose of kinematic modeling is to convert the coordinate variables in the body coordinate system to the Earth coordinate system through the coordinate transformation matrix. The modeling idea is consistent with the previous air medium.

$$\begin{pmatrix} \dot{p} \\ \dot{\varsigma} \end{pmatrix} = \begin{pmatrix} (\boldsymbol{R}_e^b)^{-1} & \boldsymbol{0}_{3\times 3} \\ \boldsymbol{0}_{3\times 3} & \boldsymbol{T}_\varsigma(\varsigma) \end{pmatrix} \bullet \begin{pmatrix} v \\ \omega \end{pmatrix} \tag{14}$$

Then, the kinematic equation can be expressed in the form of generalized velocity and generalized position:

$$\dot{\boldsymbol{P}} = \boldsymbol{J}(R)\boldsymbol{V} \tag{15}$$

$$\boldsymbol{J}(R) = \begin{pmatrix} (\boldsymbol{R}_e^b)^{-1} & \boldsymbol{0}_{3\times 3} \\ \boldsymbol{0}_{3\times 3} & \boldsymbol{T}_\varsigma(\varsigma) \end{pmatrix} \tag{16}$$

$$\boldsymbol{R}_e^b = \begin{pmatrix} cos\theta cos\psi & cos\theta sin\psi & -sin\theta \\ sin\phi sin\theta cos\psi - cos\phi sin\psi & cos\phi cos\psi + sin\phi sin\theta sin\psi & sin\phi cos\theta \\ sin\phi sin\psi + cos\phi cos\psi sin\theta & cos\phi sin\theta sin\psi - sin\phi cos\psi & cos\phi cos\theta \end{pmatrix} \tag{17}$$

In the formula, $\boldsymbol{P}$ is the generalized position matrix, $\boldsymbol{V}$ is the generalized velocity matrix, $\boldsymbol{T}_\varsigma(\varsigma) = \boldsymbol{\Gamma}$ (11), ϕ, θ, ψ are the roll angle, pitch angle, yaw angle of the aircraft as mentioned above.

Remark 3. *The main diagonal element $\boldsymbol{R}_e^b$of the matrix in Equation (16) corresponds to the coordinate transformation matrix of the velocity, and the element $\boldsymbol{T}_\varsigma(\varsigma)$corresponds to the transformation matrix of the angular velocity and the rate of change of the Euler angles.*

2.3. Multimedia Spanning Model Establishment

When the aircraft is performing multi-medium spanning, the body is subject to the combined action of the air medium and the water medium. Therefore, in the vertical plane, the relationship between the buoyancy of the body and the propeller tension and gravity needs to be considered. In the horizontal plane, there are two cases: (1) the aircraft across the medium is in still water conditions, and no force is considered in the horizontal plane;

(2) under non-stationary conditions, the flow resistance of the aircraft during the medium crossing process needs to be considered.

In the vertical plane, when the body crosses the medium vertically, the force diagram of the trans-medium aircraft is as follows, as shown in Figure 3.

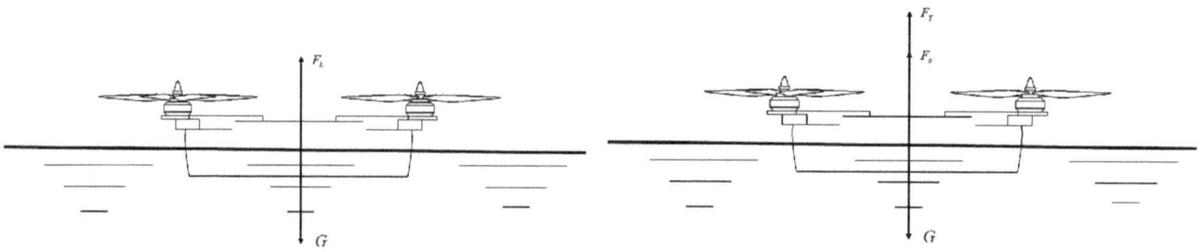

(a) (b)

Figure 3. Schematic diagram of the multi-medium spanning force of a trans-medium aircraft (**a**) Free entry; (**b**) Out of water.

For the free entry stage, there are:

$$F_b = \rho g S_{section} H \tag{18}$$

$$G - F_b = M\ddot{z} \tag{19}$$

H is the immersion depth of the aircraft, z is the displacement of the aircraft in the vertical direction.

When the aircraft is out of water (uniform speed), there are:

$$F_T + F_b = G \tag{20}$$

$$F_T = T_1 + T_2 + T_3 + T_4 \tag{21}$$

$$T_i = C_T \rho {n_i}^2 D^4,\ i = 1\ ,2\ ,3\ ,\ 4 \tag{22}$$

In the above formula, T_i is the thrust generated by the propeller, C_T is the rotational speed of the propeller, D is the diameter of the propeller, and n_i is the rotational speed of the propeller.

When the trans-medium aircraft enters and leaves the water at a certain attitude angle, and the aircraft does not completely leave the water surface, as long as the attitude changes, the size of the buoyancy and the position of the center of buoyancy will change, and the aircraft needs to generate a restoring torque to overcome this attitude change [24]. The magnitude of the restoring moment is related to gravity and buoyancy.

Since the pitch and roll attitude changes of the trans-medium aircraft in this paper have the same effect on the force during the multi-medium crossing process of the aircraft, the two are analyzed together, and a generalized attitude angle Γ is defined. Figure 4 is a schematic diagram of the force when the trans-medium aircraft enters the water at a certain attitude angle.

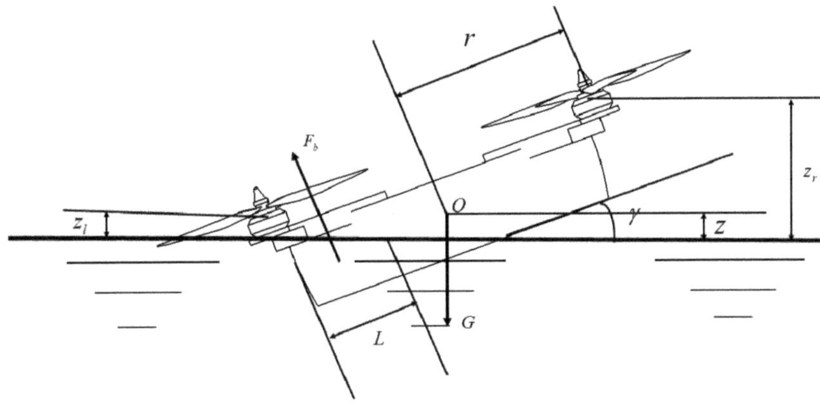

Figure 4. Schematic diagram of the force of a trans-medium aircraft entering water at a certain attitude angle.

Define the length of one side of the aircraft submerged in the water as L, the displacement of the center of gravity in the vertical direction as z, and the radial distance between the motor and the center of gravity of the aircraft as r, and the center of the restoring moment as the center of the cross-section between the aircraft and the water surface, then there are:

$$M_R = -F_b \bullet \frac{L}{2} - \frac{Gz\cos\gamma}{\sin\gamma} \tag{23}$$

where F_b has been obtained from (16). When the aircraft enters the water in the pitch attitude, $\gamma = \theta$; when the aircraft enters the water in the roll attitude, $\gamma = f$.

In the horizontal plane, it is considered that the water surface of the trans-medium aircraft is in a non-stationary state, and there is an impact effect of waves on the body. Therefore, in the water entry and exit stage, the trans-medium aircraft has a certain displacement in the horizontal plane, and its displacement expression is expressed by Newton's second law, which can be obtained:

$$S_v \boldsymbol{p}_w = \boldsymbol{M}\ddot{\boldsymbol{x}} \tag{24}$$

In the formula, $\boldsymbol{p}_w$ is the wave force action matrix, S_v is the cross-sectional area of the wave action body, and x is the displacement matrix of the trans-medium aircraft.

At this point, the dynamic and kinematic model of the trans-medium aircraft has been established. The following, Figures 5 and 6, are schematic diagrams of the complete multi-medium crossing process of the trans-medium aircraft.

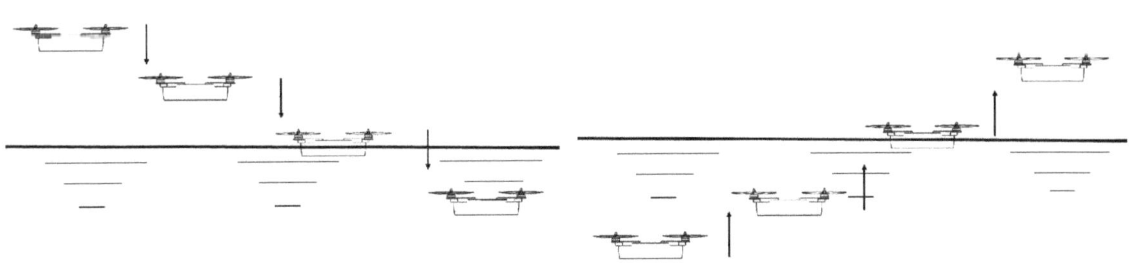

(a) (b)

Figure 5. Vertical access to water: (**a**) vertical into the water; (**b**) vertical out of water.

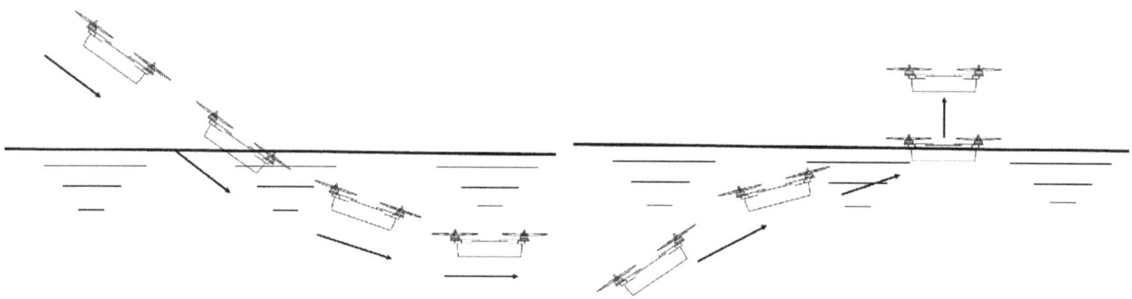

Figure 6. Enter and exit the water at a certain attitude angle: (**a**) water entry process; (**b**) out of water process.

3. Numerical Simulation Based on OpenFOAM Open-Source Platform

Through the selection and layout design of each component of the trans-media aircraft, a parametric mechanical structure model of the trans-media aircraft is established. Import the parametric model of the aircraft into the OpenFOAM platform tool for simulation analysis.

Consistent with the previous analysis idea, the motion process of the trans-medium aircraft is analyzed in sections. The specific processes simulated in this paper are: (1) aerodynamic simulation analysis of a single air medium; (2) hydrodynamic simulation analysis of a single underwater medium; (3) simulation analysis of the aircraft entering the water vertically and at a certain attitude angle; (4) simulation analysis of the aircraft leaving the water surface vertically.

3.1. Fluid Governing Equations

The solution to the medium flow problem is the solution to the Navier–Stokes equation, which is the theoretical basis for describing the medium flow. The flight speed of the trans-medium aircraft model established in this paper is lower than the speed of sound; thus, the medium in which it is located can be regarded as an incompressible flow. Incompressible flow governing equations include continuity equation and momentum equation, as follows [25]:

$$\begin{cases} \nabla \bullet \mathbf{U} = 0 \\ \frac{\partial \mathbf{U}}{\partial t} + \nabla \bullet (\mathbf{U}\mathbf{U}^T) = -\frac{1}{\rho}\nabla p + \nabla \bullet (v \nabla \mathbf{U}) + S \end{cases} \tag{25}$$

where U is the fluid velocity vector, p is the fluid pressure, and v is the fluid kinematic viscosity.

The essential work of numerical simulation for fluid media is to solve the above equations, but for the above equations, it is difficult to obtain their analytical solutions in the sense of actual equations; thus, it is necessary to numerically discretize their differential equations and obtain matrix equations through discretization processing. The solution of the equation is the numerical solution of the equation. Although the numerical solution is not the real solution of the original equation, the error with the real solution can be reduced by selecting a suitable discretization method and matrix solving algorithm to approach the real solution.

Remark 4. *Equation (25) is a simplification of the N-S equation, which exhibits the continuity equation and the momentum conservation equation for incompressible flow. In this study, under low velocity conditions, the medium can be regarded as a continuous incompressible form.*

3.2. Turbulence Model

During the movement of the trans-medium aircraft, the flow of the fluid medium in which it is located is irregular, multi-scale, and structured, that is, three-dimensional unsteady flow, which has strong numerical diffusivity and numerical dissipation [26]. No matter how complex the turbulent motion is, the unsteady continuity equations and Navier–Stokes equations are still applicable to the instantaneous motion of turbulent flow. However, the strong transient nature and nonlinearity of turbulent flow make it impossible to accurately describe all the details related to the three-dimensional time of turbulent flow by analytical methods. Changes in the mean flow field are often caused by turbulence. In this way, mathematical calculation methods for different simplifications of turbulent flow have emerged. It reduces the computational cost, and by simplifying the operation, practically valuable physical phenomena can be effectively extracted. The turbulence model implanted in this paper based on the OpenFOAM (OpenFOAM V-2112) open source platform is the kOmegaSST model, which is a hybrid model of the kEpsilon model and the kOmega model. The purpose of the mixture is to use the kOmega model with a better effect on the reverse pressure gradient near the wall and use the kEpsilon model that is insensitive to incoming flow parameters elsewhere [27]. Its model equation is as follows:

Turbulence intensity k equation:

$$\frac{\partial \rho k}{\partial t} + \nabla(\rho k U) = \nabla\left[(\mu + \frac{\mu_z}{\sigma_k})\nabla k\right] + p_k - b_k \rho k \omega \tag{26}$$

Turbulence frequency ω equation:

$$\frac{\partial \rho \omega}{\partial t} + \nabla(\rho \omega U) = \nabla\left[(\mu + \frac{\mu_z}{\sigma_\omega})\right] + a\frac{\omega}{k} p_k - b_\omega \rho k \omega^2 \tag{27}$$

In the above formula, p_k is the turbulent kinetic energy generated by the laminar velocity gradient, σ_k and σ_ω are the Prandtl number of the turbulent energy; the eddy viscosity is $\mu = -\rho k/\omega$.

Remark 5. *Equation (26) and Equation (27) are simplified calculations for solving the turbulent flow of the N-S equation. Due to the strong transient nature of the turbulent flow, Reynolds averaging is performed on the physical quantities of the flow field in the time domain. After averaging, the N-S equation is not closed; thus, two variable equations a and b are introduced for solving. The two variable equations are semi-empirical formulas, which are summed up from experimental phenomena.*

3.3. Simulation Analysis of Multi-Medium Crossing for a Trans-Medium Aircraft

3.3.1. Air Single Medium Aerodynamic Analysis

The carrier of the air single-medium analysis is the air rotor; thus, first, a basic mechanical characteristic analysis of the air rotor of the trans-medium aircraft designed in this paper is carried out. The air rotor parameters for this article are as follows: Model APC1047SF, which has a diameter of 10 inches and a pitch of 4.7 inches. The physical and model diagrams are as follows, as shown in Figure 7.

Next, the rotor flow field is discretized, and the computational domain of the flow field is divided into two parts: the outer domain and the inner domain, as shown in Figure 8. The inner domain is centered on the rotating shaft of the air rotor, with a diameter of 1.2D (D is the rotation diameter of the blade); the outer domain is the outer cylindrical area of the rotor, with a length of 10D and a diameter of 5D.

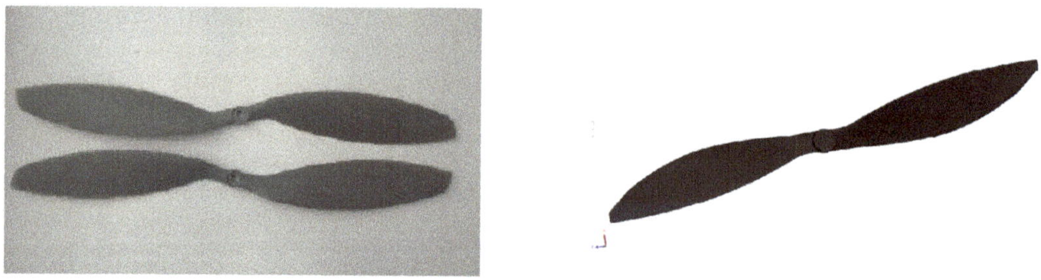

(a) (b)

Figure 7. APC1047SF air rotor: (**a**) physical map; (**b**) model diagram.

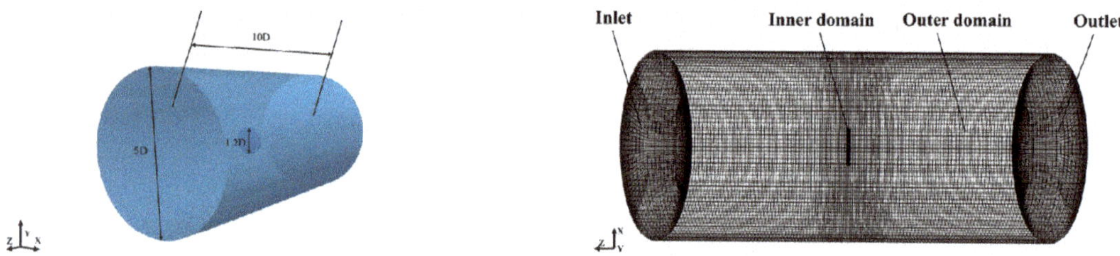

(a) (b)

Figure 8. Flow computation domain: (**a**) computational domain scale modeling; (**b**) computational domain division and boundary setting.

In the fluid computing domain, the interface between the inner domain and the outer domain adopts a slip mesh; the purpose is to not only realize the high-speed rotation of the air rotor around the axis at a certain speed but also to save computing resources. This movement process is as described above in that its medium flow is an unsteady flow. The computational domain has meshed with the "blockMesh" mesh algorithm and "SnappyHexMesh" mesh algorithm implanted in the OpenFOAM open source platform.

The meshing method is based on OpenFOAM this time: the O-type mesh topology method is used to define the "blockMesh" parameter dictionary for background meshing, and then, the "snappyHexMesh" tool is used to mesh the air rotor and establish the interface between the inner domain and the outer domain. Mesh division is shown in Figure 9.

The completion of the grid division means that the pre-processing part of the simulation process has been completed. Next, the above-mentioned physical process is numerically solved through the matrix solving algorithm implanted in the OpenFOAM platform, and the required results are processed and analyzed. The kOmegaSST turbulence model is used, and the boundary conditions are set as follows: the inlet boundary of the outer domain of the cylinder adopts the velocity inlet condition, the outlet boundary adopts the pressure outlet condition, and the cylindrical boundary of the cylinder adopts the wall surface condition.

Through the variable parameter analysis of different rotational speeds of the air rotor, the mechanical characteristics and flow field characteristics under different rotational speeds are compared. In this study, the rotational speeds of the air propellers were set to 2000, 3000, 5000, 7000, and 8000 (unit $round \times min^{-1}$), respectively. Figure 10 shows the comparison between the thrust of the air rotor obtained by numerical simulation at different speeds and the experimental thrust of the APC1047SF blade.

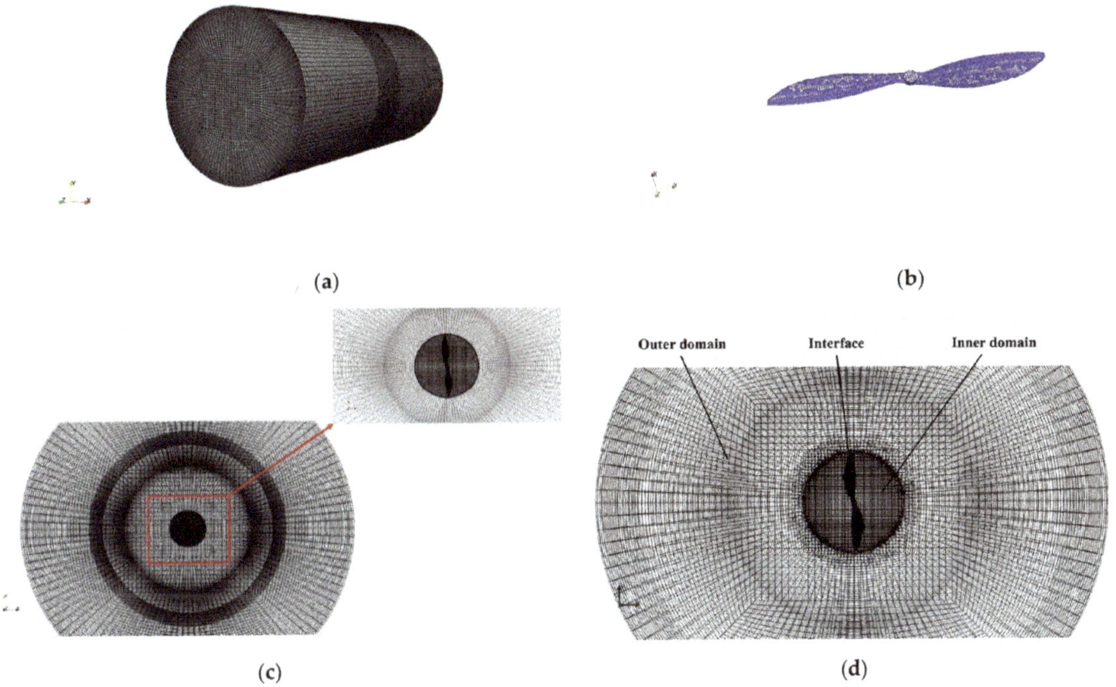

Figure 9. Schematic diagram of computational domain meshing results: (**a**) outer domain meshing situation; (**b**) air rotor meshing; (**c**) inner domain meshing; (**d**) meshing of the interface between the inner and outer domains.

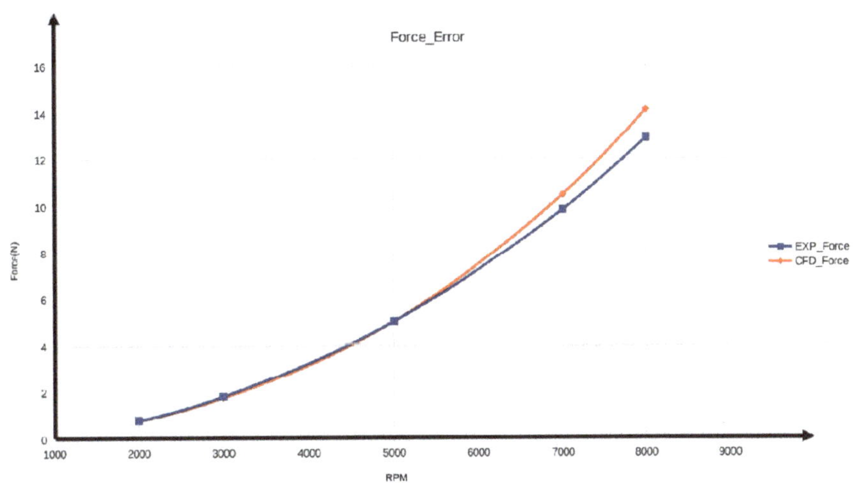

Figure 10. Numerical thrust and experimental thrust at different rotational speeds.

It can be seen from the above figure that the overall calculation error is not large, and the error between the simulated value and the experimental value can be ignored under the condition of low speed. As the rotational speed increases gradually, at higher rotational speeds, the error between the simulated value and the experimental value also increases gradually, but is within a reasonable error range. The reason why this error gradually increases at higher rotational speeds is that there is an error in the meshing accuracy under high rotational speed conditions, and high-resolution meshes are not used for high rotational speed conditions. However, because of saving computing power, this study uses a medium-resolution grid within the range of ensuring a reasonable error.

Figure 11 shows the pressure cloud map and speed cloud map of a certain section of the air rotor under different rotational speed conditions.

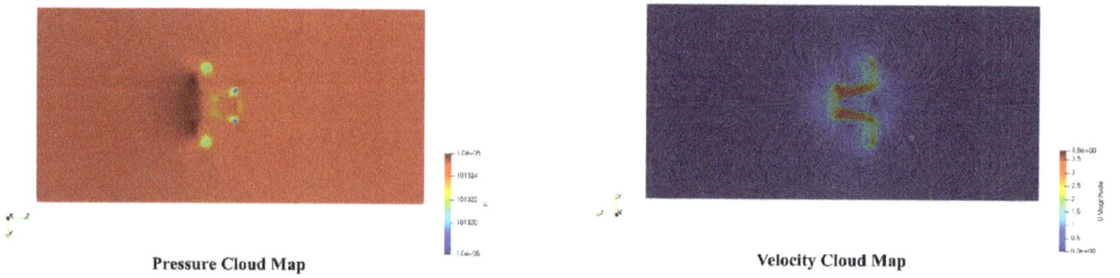

(a)

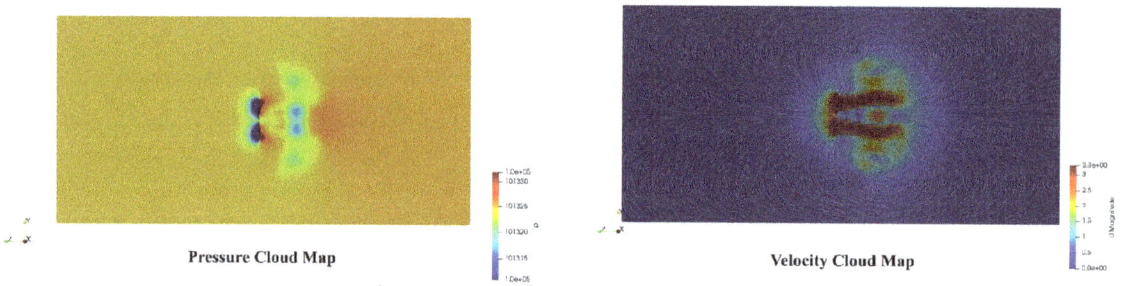

(b)

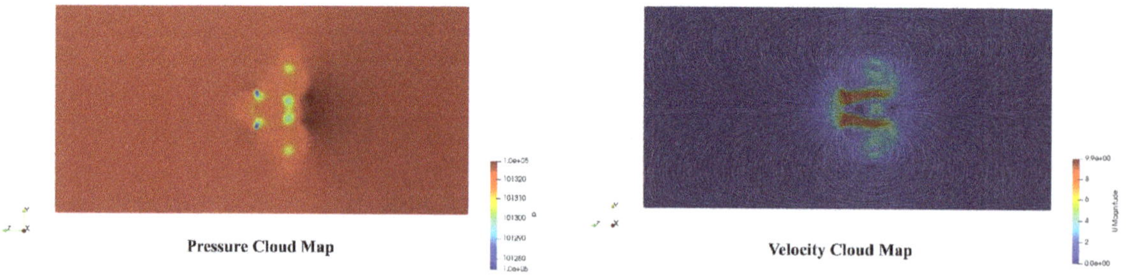

(c)

Figure 11. *Cont.*

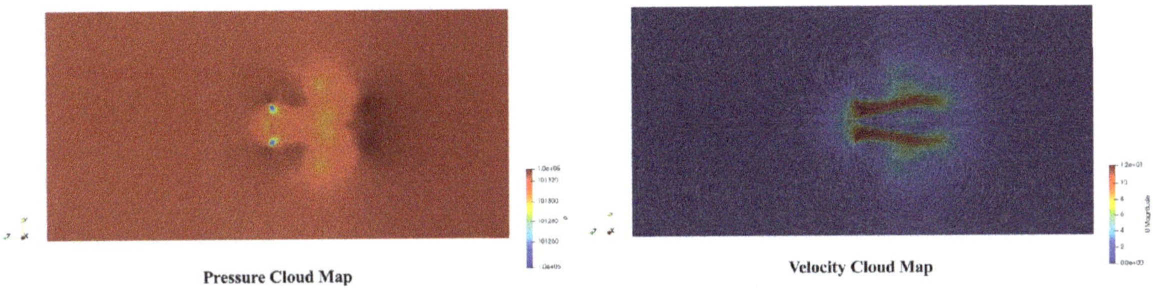

(**d**)

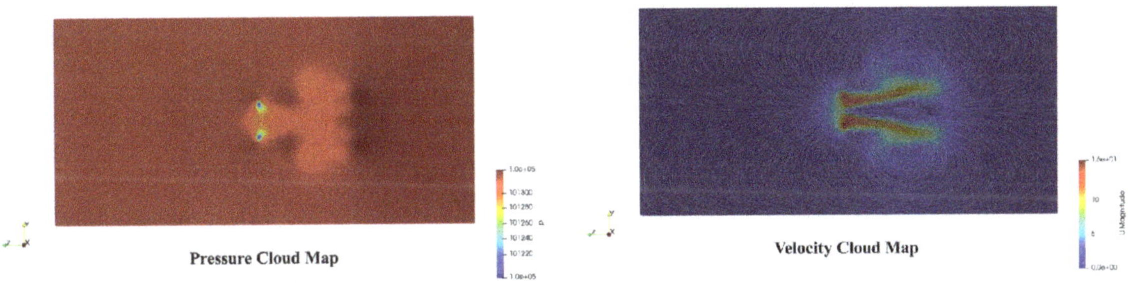

(**e**)

Figure 11. Cloud map of aerodynamic characteristics of a single propeller of an air rotor. (**a**) RPM = 2×10^3; (**b**) RPM = 3×10^3; (**c**) RPM = 5×10^3; (**d**) RPM = 7×10^3; (**e**) RPM = 8×10^3 (unit $round \times min^{-1}$).

It can be seen from the change in the above pressure cloud diagram that the air rotor rotates at a certain speed, and the tip of the blade generates a low-pressure area due to high-speed friction with the air. The entire blade produces a symmetrically distributed pressure vortex ring backward along the direction of the central axis of rotation. This is because, in the case of airflow disturbance, there is a pressure difference between the front and rear positions of the vortex ring, which leads to the generation of the phenomenon of surrounding flow, thereby generating a pressure vortex. The creation of pressure vortices is also what causes the thrust of the air rotor to drop. It can be seen from the figure that there is a pressure difference in the flow field before and after the rotor, and the rotor generates thrust due to the effect of this pressure difference.

It can be seen from the above velocity cloud diagram that the airflow at the rear end of the blade produces a symmetrically distributed high-speed band due to the high-speed rotation of the rotor, and it can be found that the paddle where the blade is located has a current-collecting effect, and the airflow passes through this paddle. The airflow flows in from the front end of the paddle disc, and after the constriction of the current collecting effect of the paddle disc, the airflow flowing to the rear end rotates and takes on a spiral shape, which generates the circumferential induced velocity.

Figure 12 shows a schematic diagram of the change of the tip vortex under each speed condition:

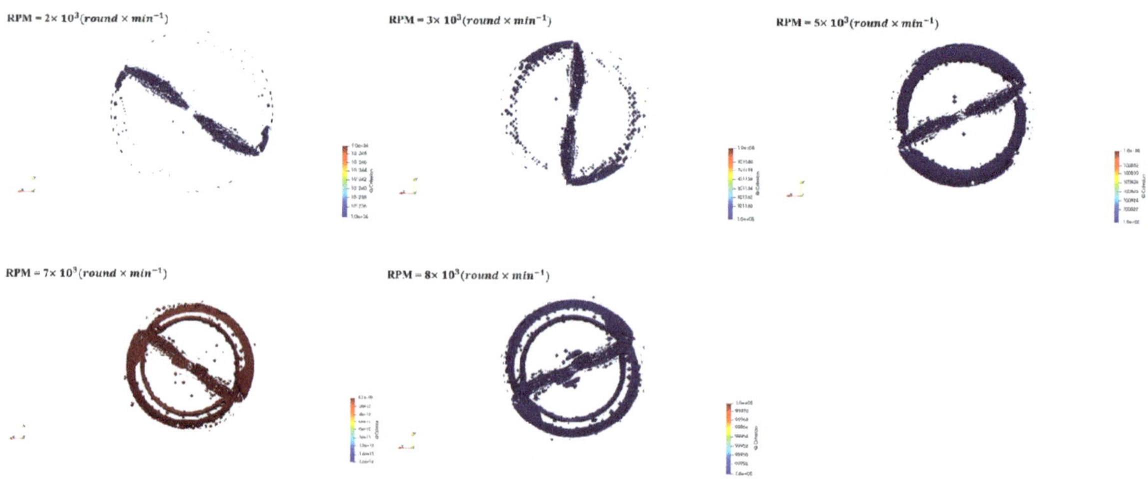

Figure 12. Schematic diagram of the tip vortex.

As the rotational speed continues to increase, the more severe the disturbance of the blade tip is, the more obvious the dragging effect of the blade tip wake is in the figure.

In order to accurately capture the vortex structure in the flow field, the Q criterion [28] is applied to the post-processing vortex capture technology. Figure 13 shows the schematic diagram of the vortex structure in the flow field under various rotational speed conditions ($Q \in [-100, 100]$).

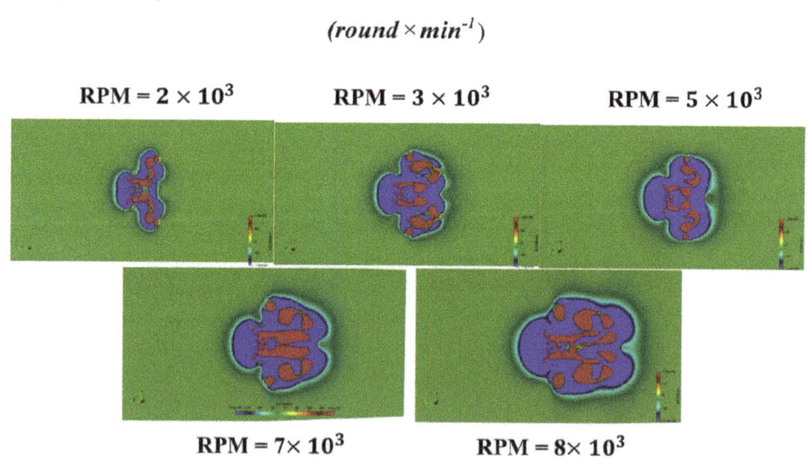

Figure 13. Schematic diagram of wake vortex structure.

It can be seen from the above figure that the wake vortex of the rotor is symmetrically distributed at different rotational speeds. As the rotational speed increases, the structure of the wake vortex becomes more complex. The more severe the airflow disturbance is, the more serious the gas disturbance is.

Next, take the rotational speed RPM = 7000 $round \times min^{-1}$ as an example, and focus on analyzing the specific numerical change relationship of each physical quantity in the flow field.

To find the variation relationship of each physical quantity with time and space, the following Figure 14 shows the variation relationship between the position and physical quantity along the rotation axis from left to right and the variation relationship between the time step and physical quantity solved under different position conditions (top and bottom of paddle).

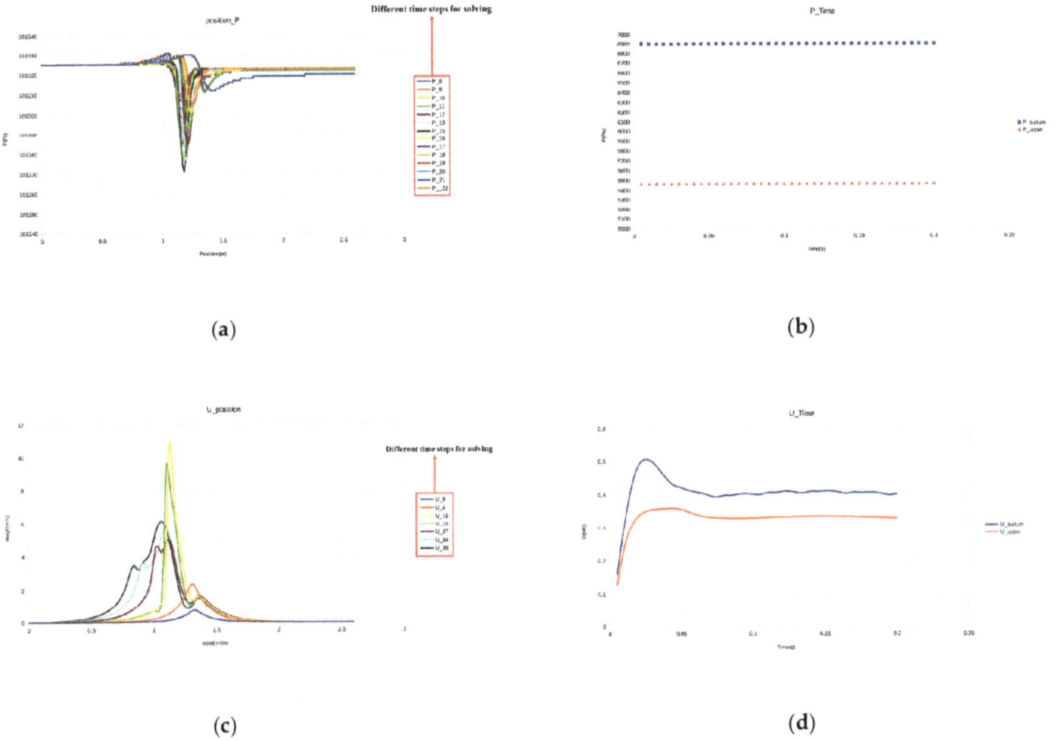

Figure 14. Curve diagram of physical quantities changing with time and space: (**a**) graph of pressure versus position; (**b**) graph of pressure change with time; (**c**) graph of velocity versus position; (**d**) graph of speed change with time.

It can be seen from Figure 14a that between 1 and 1.5 m on the abscissa (the area near the paddle disc) the pressure will show a high- and low-pressure area, the pressure at the lower part of the paddle disc will increase, and a high-pressure area will appear, while the upper-pressure will drop, and a low-pressure area will appear, and with the advancement of the time step, the amplitude of the upper-pressure drop will increase, resulting in an increase in the upper and lower-pressure difference, which is the reason for the increase in the thrust of the blade at the beginning. Figure 14b shows that there is a pressure difference between the upper and lower surfaces of the propeller disc, which is the reason for the thrust generated by the previously mentioned propeller blades. Figure 14c reflects that the fluid velocity peaks in the area near the paddle disk, and the position of the peak gradually moves down with the increase in the time step, which is consistent with the results presented in the previous velocity cloud map. Figure 14d reflects the process of increasing the velocity of the upper and lower surfaces of the paddle disc in the initial time. With the increase in time, the velocity gradually tends to be stable, and the velocity on the lower surface is always greater than that on the upper surface.

The above is the analysis of the aerodynamic characteristics of the air blades of the trans-medium aircraft. Next, it is necessary to carry out a numerical simulation study on the air flight characteristics of the trans-medium aircraft, and the method used is the same as the previous one. The mesh division is shown in Figure 15:

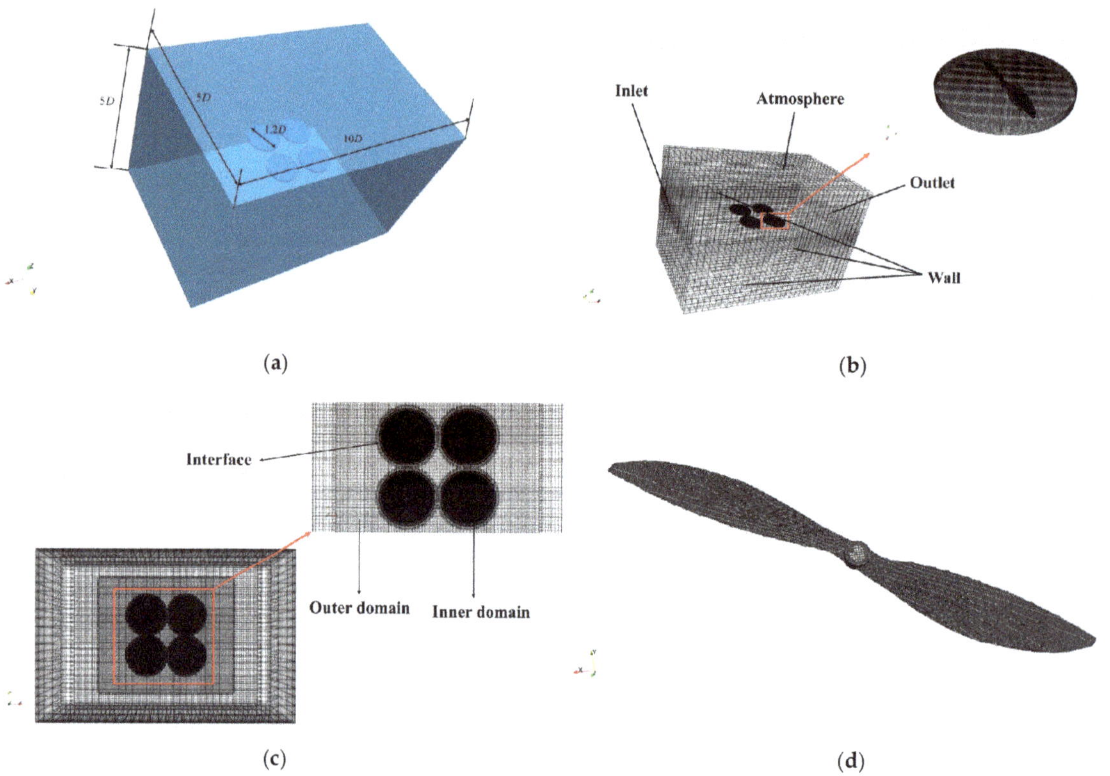

Figure 15. Schematic diagram of grid and computational domain division: (**a**) fluid computational domain size; (**b**) computational domain boundary conditions; (**c**) internal and external computational domain division; (**d**) blade meshing.

Next, the numerical simulation method is used to simulate the hovering and forward flight motion of the trans-medium aircraft, and the obtained simulation results are physically analyzed.

Figure 16 shows the structure of the rotor tip vortex in the hovering state of the whole machine. It can be seen from the figure that the wake vortex generated by the friction between the blade and the air will continuously impact the arm of the machine, thereby causing the body to vibrate.

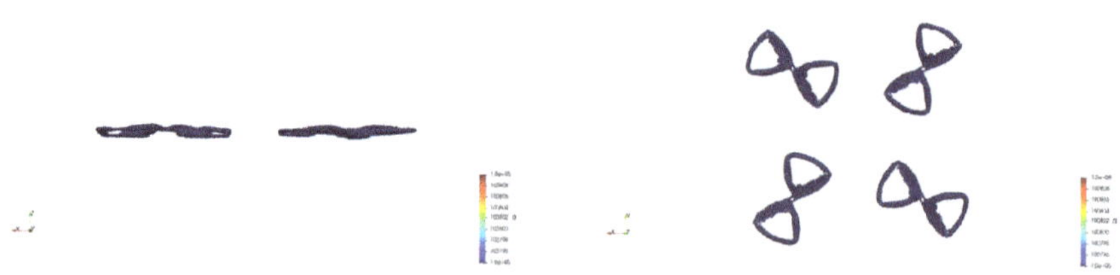

Figure 16. Hover state tip vortex.

Figure 17 shows the numerical simulation cloud image of the hover state. It can be seen from the pressure and velocity contour that a high-pressure area is generated at the lower part of the paddle plane, and due to the large velocity interference at the lower part, the flow phenomenon is caused, resulting in a pressure vortex, which is also the reason for the drop in lift. A low-pressure area is generated in the upper part such that the pressure difference between the upper and lower surfaces is generated, which is the key factor for the rotor to generate lift [29].

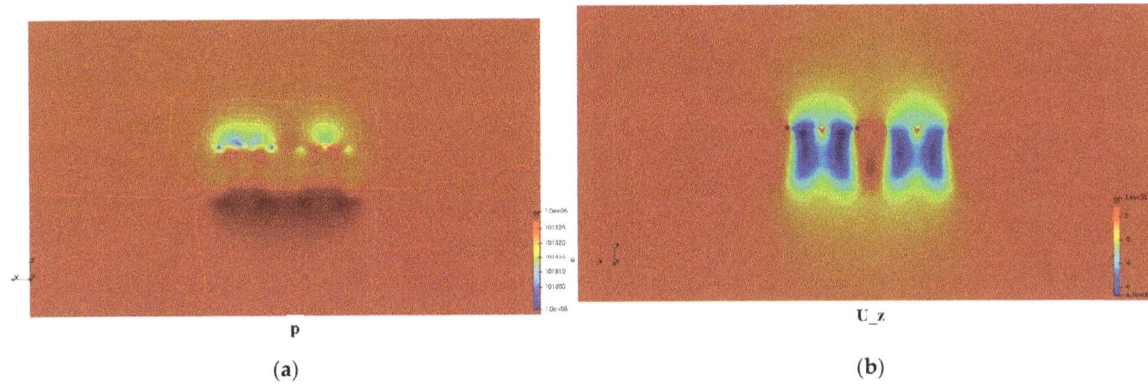

Figure 17. Numerical cloud map in hover state: (**a**) pressure cloud map; (**b**) axial velocity contour.

To study the aerodynamic interference of the trans-medium aircraft in the forward flight state, this paper sets the forward flight inclination angle of the trans-medium aircraft as 10°, the blade speed as 4000 $round \times min^{-1}$, and the forward flight speed as 1.5 $m{\bullet}s^{-1}$, 5 $m{\bullet}s^{-1}$. There are three cases of 10 $m{\bullet}s^{-1}$, and the forward ratio of the aircraft is 0.289.

Figure 18 is a comparison of the rotor wake structures at three forward flight speeds. It can be seen from the figure that the wake is dragged out from the blades and the fuselage, and the flow to the downstream area induces the entire flow field, and with the increase in the forward speed, the inclination of the trailed wake is also larger, and the flow field fluctuation is also more complicated.

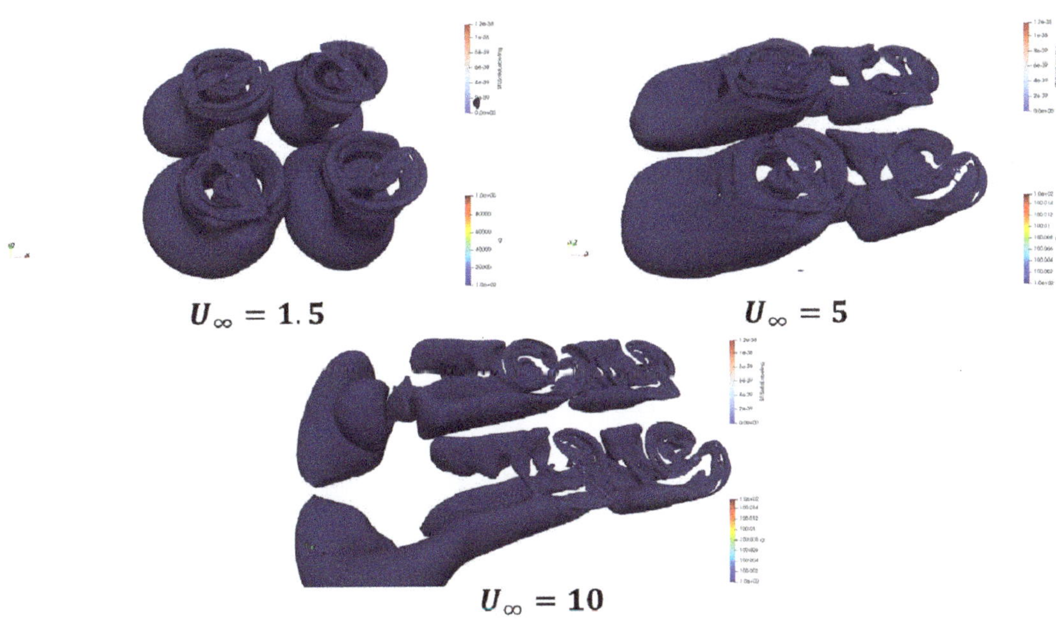

Figure 18. Forward flight wakes at different forward flight speeds.

Figure 19 shows the contour of the flow field pressure and velocity change of the trans-medium aircraft under different forward flight speeds. Different from the hovering state, in the forward flight state of the trans-medium aircraft, the wake will move backward, and it is behind the flight. Compared with the hovering state, the impact of the propeller on the aerodynamic force of the fuselage is greatly reduced, and the wake of the propeller in the front will hit the fuselage, which is the main reason for the change in the aerodynamic force of the fuselage.

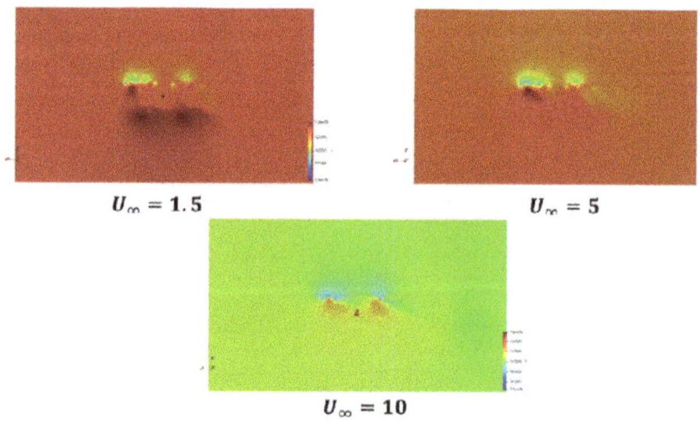

(a)

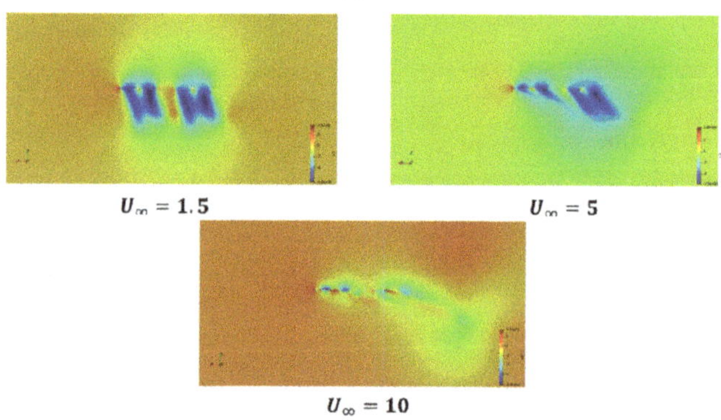

(b)

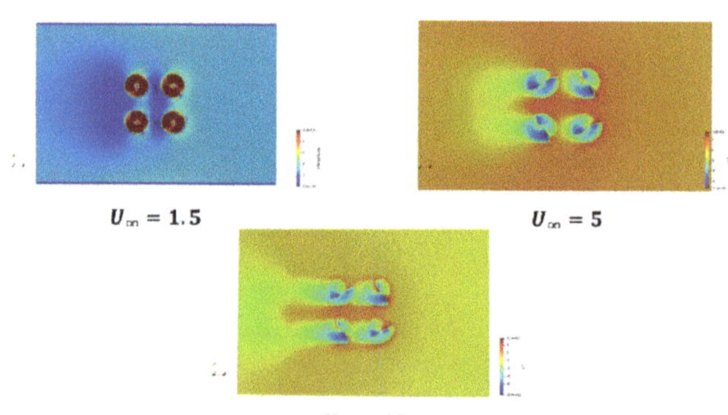

(c)

Figure 19. Numerical contour of flow field under different forward flight speeds: (**a**) longitudinal pressure contour; (**b**) longitudinal velocity contour; (**c**) axial velocity contour.

Through the analysis of the above longitudinal pressure and velocity contour, it can be seen that with the increase in the forward flight speed, the pressure vortex gradually shifts to the rear, and the direction of the high-speed airflow region at the rear is the same as that of the pressure vortex. Through the analysis of the axial velocity cloud diagram of the propeller disc, it can be seen that the axial velocity of the four blades is all downward, and the wake of the flow around the cloud diagram gradually moves backward with the increase in the forward speed. It can be seen from the wake structure diagram in Figure 19 that the blade is impacted by the wake of the front blade, and the aerodynamic characteristics of the rear blade are most disturbed during the flight.

Figure 20 is a graph showing the variation of the force characteristics of each blade with time. It can be seen from the figure that with the forward flight process of the aircraft, the force characteristics of each blade change periodically, and due to the backward movement of the forward flight trail, the forward flight effect of each blade is also different. It can be seen from the graph that the fluctuation of the force characteristics of the No. 2 and No. 3 blades is significantly higher than that of the No. 1 and No. 4 blades. This is because the wake has a greater effect on the No. 2 and No. 3 blades than on the No. 1 and No. 4 blades. The unbalanced fluctuation of the force characteristics causes the body to generate an unbalanced moment during forward flight [30].

3.3.2. Hydrodynamic Analysis of Single Underwater Medium

The carrier that provides underwater power for the trans-medium aircraft is the underwater propeller, and the hydrodynamic performance of the underwater propeller plays a vital role in the underwater propulsion of the trans-medium aircraft. At present, open water tests are usually used to determine the hydrodynamic performance of propellers [31]. With the rapid development of computer-aided software and the in-depth study of the mathematical model of fluid dynamics, a numerical simulation based on the CFD method is widely used in propeller performance optimization and dynamic characteristic analysis.

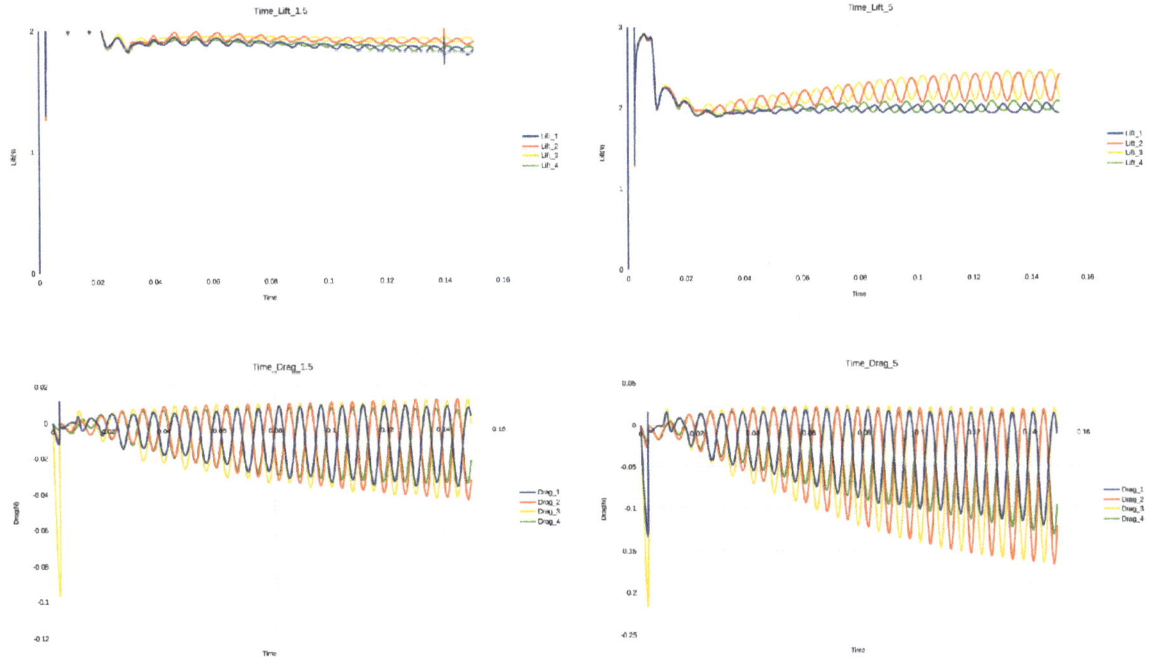

Figure 20. *Cont.*

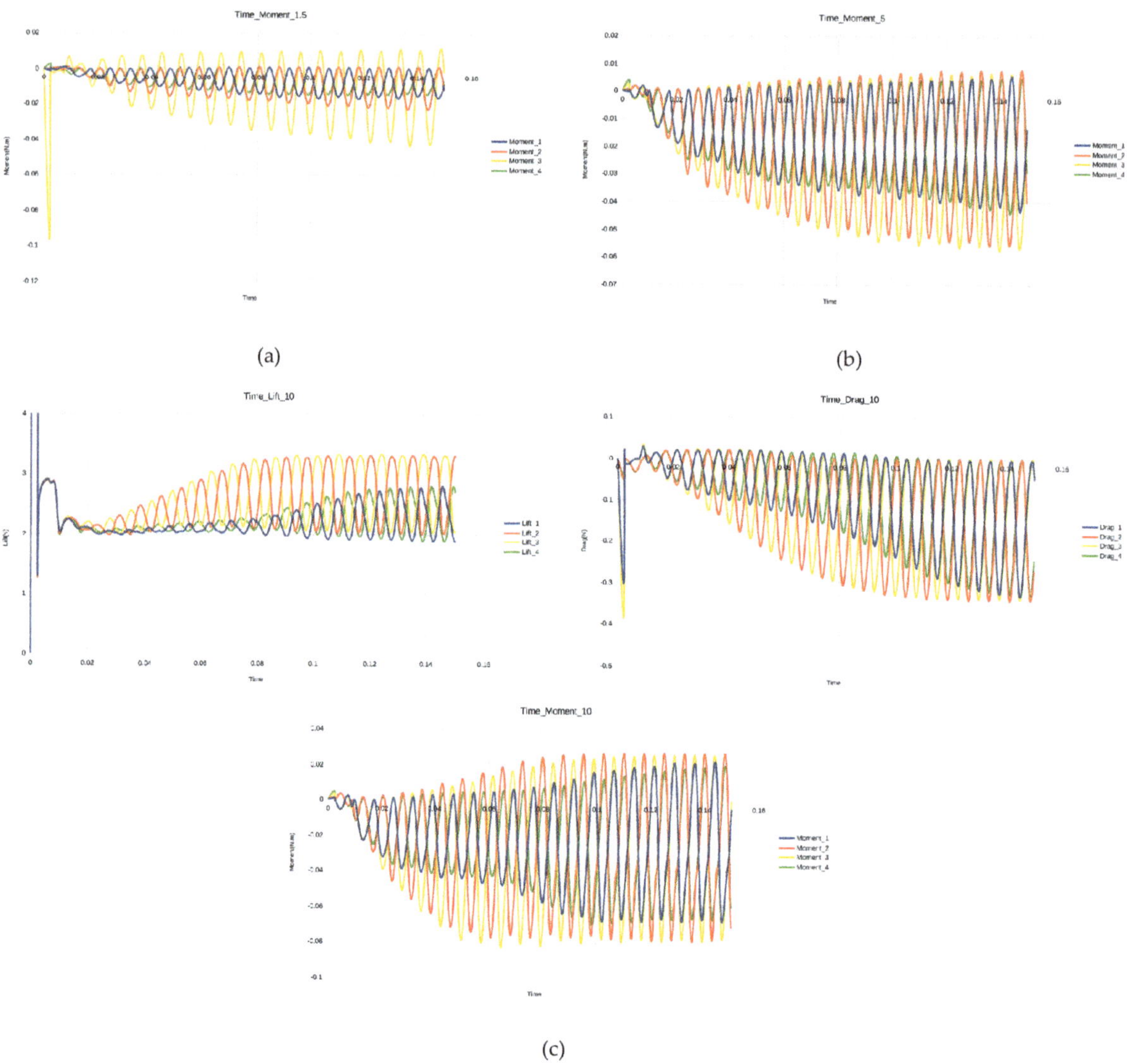

Figure 20. Variation diagram of the force characteristics of each blade of the aircraft: (**a**) forward flight speed is 1.5 $m{\bullet}s^{-1}$; (**b**) forward flight speed is 5 $m{\bullet}s^{-1}$; (**c**) forward flight speed is 10 $m{\bullet}s^{-1}$.

In this paper, two pairs of 60 mm propellers are used, and the underwater thrust system is arranged in a "cross" shape at the duct of the aircraft. First, it is necessary to numerically analyze the water performance of a single propeller. By implanting a numerical algorithm based on the OpenFOAM open source platform, its single propeller is divided into the flow field area, and the division form and solution algorithm are consistent with the method used for the analysis of the aerodynamic characteristics of the air rotor. Figure 21 is a schematic diagram of the grid area division for the numerical analysis of the propeller's water performance.

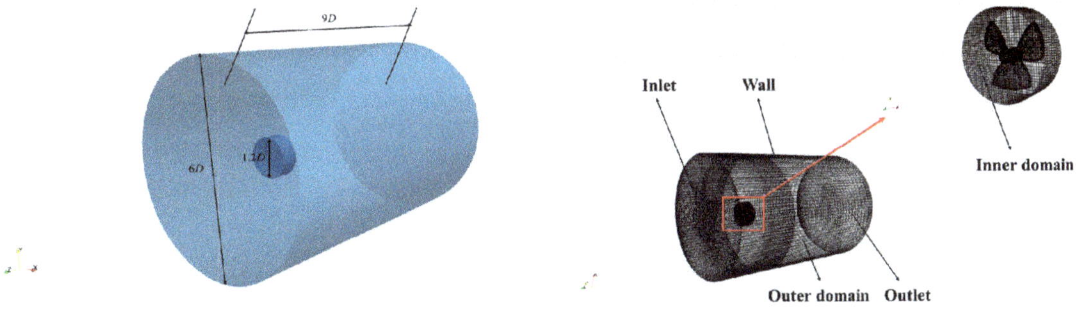

(**a**) (**b**)

Figure 21. Schematic diagram of single propeller meshing: (**a**) computational domain model parameters; (**b**) boundary conditions and division of internal and external domains.

To quantitatively describe the hydrodynamic performance of the underwater propeller [32], the numerical simulation method is used to accurately evaluate the propeller's water performance parameters. The specific embodiment is to obtain the change curve diagram of its thrust coefficient K_T, torque coefficient K_Q and efficiency η_0 by changing the propeller advance coefficient, as shown in Figure 22.

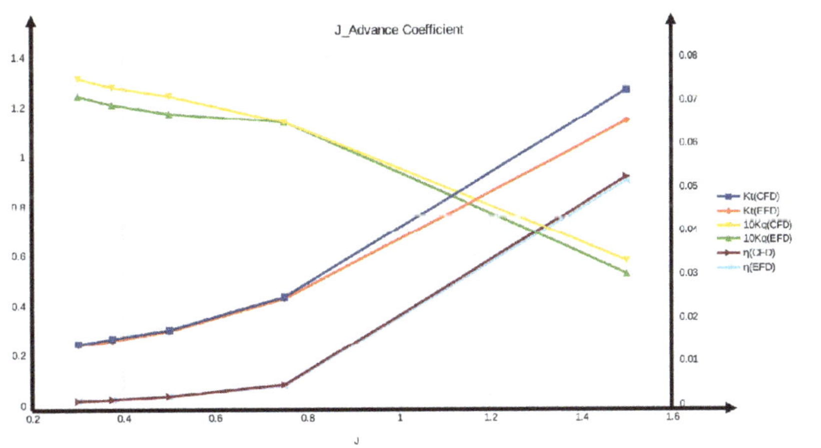

Figure 22. Propeller hydrodynamic performance curve.

It can be seen from the above figure that there is a certain calculation error between the CFD numerical simulation results and the experimental propeller hydrodynamic performance curve results. For K_T and η_0, under the condition of a low advance coefficient, the error can be ignored. The calculation error also increases, and the overall parameter error is within the allowable range of 5%, which meets the actual engineering requirements.

3.3.3. Numerical Simulation of Water Entry and Exit for a Trans-Medium Aircraft

The problem of entering and leaving water across the medium involves the dynamic grid problem. During the solution process, the motion deformation of the grid will have a huge impact on the solution accuracy and the convergence of the solution. The overset grid method [33] is used in the numerical simulation of water entry and exit of a trans-medium aircraft [34]. The overset grid method needs to establish two sets of grids. The flow field where the external trans-media aircraft is located is used as the background grid, and the trans-media aircraft itself is used as the overset grid. The overset grid moves in the background grid. Interpolation is used for the numerical transfer, which does not involve grid deformation; thus, the stability of the solution is guaranteed. However, the two sets of grids need to interpolate each other during the solution process; thus, its calculation time is longer than that of traditional dynamic grids. The water entry and exit process of a trans-medium aircraft is a mirror image process; thus, this paper conducts a numerical simulation of its water entry process. Figure 23 is a schematic diagram of the meshing of the water entry process of the trans-medium aircraft.

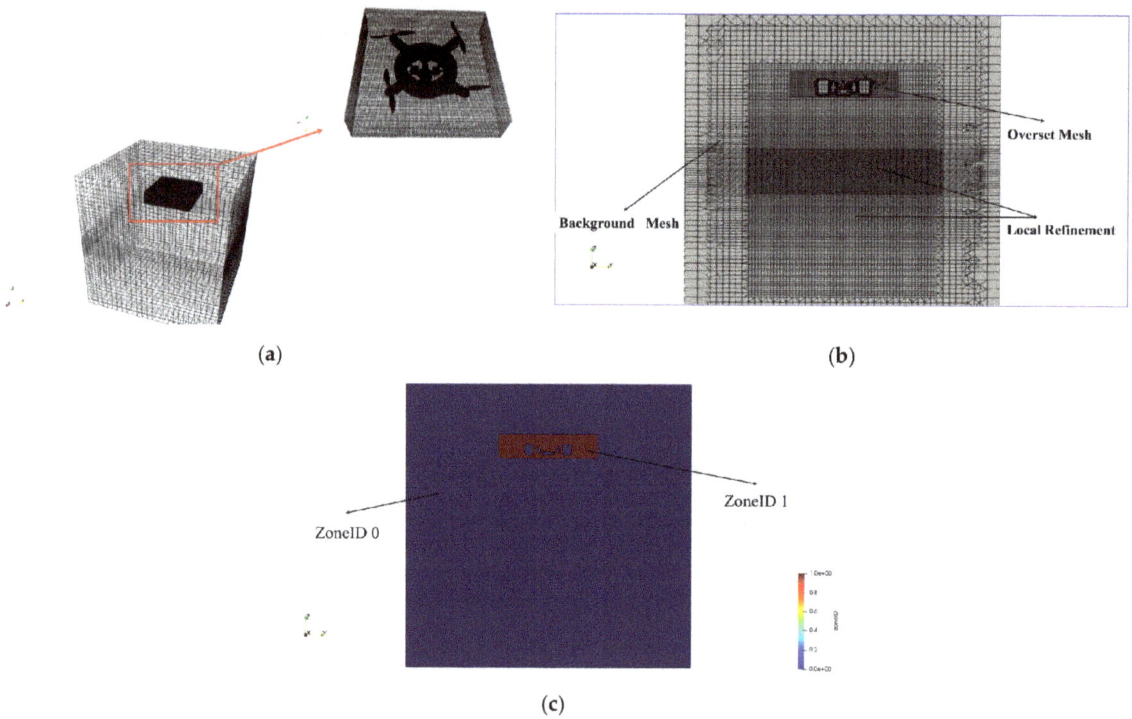

Figure 23. (**a**) Flow field area grid; (**b**) background mesh and overset mesh; (**c**) background grid and overset grid area marker map (1 for overset grid, 0 for background grid).

In this paper, the initial conditions for the entry of the trans-medium aircraft into the water are set as follows: the entry height is 0.4 m, the initial velocity of entry into the water is 0, and the free-falling body hits the water surface and enters the water body under the action of gravity. In order to verify the performance of the trans-medium aircraft entering the water at different angles, this paper sets its water entry angles as 0°, 10°, 20°, 30°, and 40°. The pressure and speed of the body movement with the time curve are shown in Figure 24.

It can be known from the pressure curve that the load pressure peak of the body is different when entering the water at different angles, and the peak size gradually decreases with the increase in the angle. This reflects that the impact on the vertical entry and exit of the cross-medium aircraft is significantly greater than the impact on the oblique entry and exit of the water. In general, in the water entry stage of the trans-medium aircraft, the load pressure of the body reaches the maximum at the moment of contact with the water surface, and after the water entry process is completed, the load gradually tends to be stable. It can be known from the speed curve that as the water entry angle increases, the speed of the body changes more gently, which corresponds to the previous pressure curve results. The two together indicate that it is most reasonable for the body to enter the water within a limited range of inclination angles.

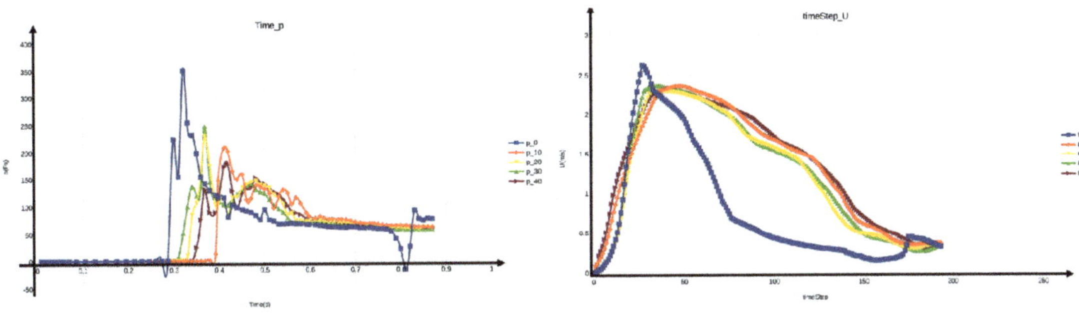

(**a**) (**b**)

Figure 24. (**a**) Pressure curve; (**b**) speed curve.

It can be seen from Figure 25 that when entering the water vertically, the yaw attitude of the cross-medium aircraft changes. When the inclination angle enters the water, the pitch attitude changes more violently, and with the increase in the water entry angle, the angular velocity of the attitude change is larger.

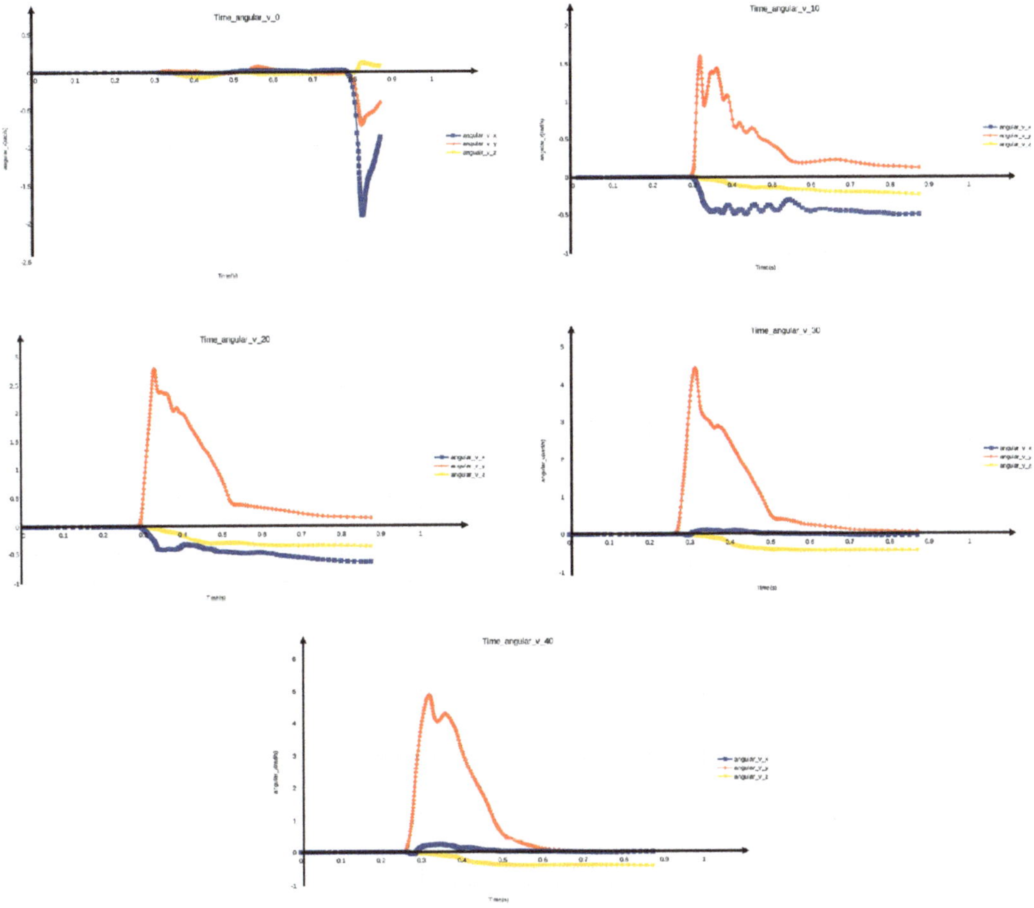

Figure 25. Attitude change curve of entering water at different angles.

The schematic diagram of the specific physical process of a trans-medium aircraft entering water is shown in Figure 26.

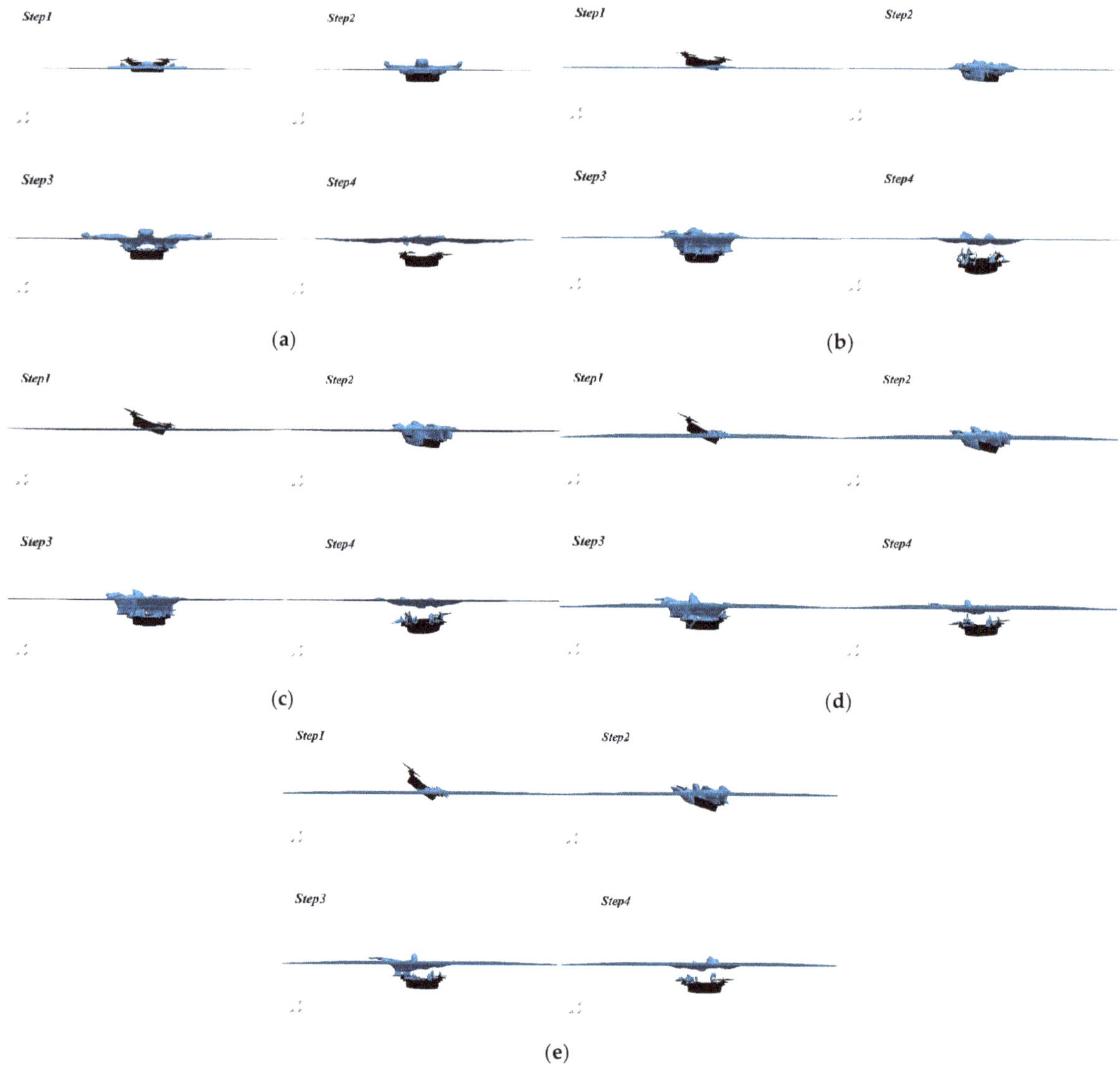

Figure 26. The physical evolution process of cavitation entering water from different angles: (**a**) vertical into the water; (**b**–**e**) inclined angle into the water (10°, 20°, 30°, 40°).

It can be seen from the above figure that the trans-medium aircraft roughly includes three stages in the process of entering the water: the impact of the contact moment, the open cavitation with large deformation of the free surface, and the water movement after the open cavitation is closed. When a trans-medium aircraft hits the water, the water in contact with the aircraft and the water near the aircraft suddenly start to move, with great acceleration. Due to the high density of water and the large attachment mass of water to the aircraft, at the moment of entering the water, the aircraft is subjected to much greater hydrodynamic action than the general flow around. In the initial stage of water entry, the wet area of the aircraft increases rapidly, and then, a relatively stable cavitation separation line appears. The water separates from the aircraft, and cavitation begins to form. For a period of time, after the aircraft enters the water, the cavitation bubbles will communicate with the atmosphere, the air will continue to fill the rear space of the aircraft entering the water, and the cavitation bubbles will continue to grow, some of which are air and some of steam. As the cavitation increases, the buoyancy of the aircraft also increases, and gradually, the cavitation begins to close, and the air on the water surface no longer enters the cavitation. After the cavitation is closed, as the aircraft continues to move, the cavitation gradually decreases and disappears completely due to the entrainment of the water flow.

4. Conclusions

In this paper, the kinematics and dynamics modeling of a trans-media aircraft is carried out, and on this basis, the open source numerical platform OpenFOAM is flexibly used for numerical analysis, and the moving process of the trans-media aircraft is segmented. Carrying out numerical analysis greatly simplifies the difficulty of the numerical solution and realizes the feasibility of a multi-process numerical solution. From the results of the numerical analysis of each sub-process, the main challenge facing the fluid dynamics analysis of the trans-media aircraft is the analysis of the unsteady flow characteristics in the process of the medium crossing [35]. THIs is realized by means of simulation or physical experiments. The process of medium spanning involves complex flow problems and is a typical gas–liquid two-phase flow [36] disturbance motion, accompanied by the air cushion effect, gas–liquid coupling effect, jet phenomenon, and the growth, development, and collapse of water cavitation. In this process, due to the large differences in the physical properties of the medium, the body will be subject to severe nonlinear disturbances. Therefore, the requirements for the resistance, aerodynamic and hydrodynamic shape, material, and structural strength of the trans-medium aircraft are higher than those of the ordinary single medium. This paper shows a series of nonlinear water flow disturbances and cavitation evolution processes in the multi-medium crossing process but does not study the deep-level mechanism of the disturbance and cavitation evolution [37]. The aerodynamic shape is the key to drag reduction and the stability of the medium spanning; thus, the research in this area has a great breakthrough significance in the direction of the medium spanning aircraft. In the research of this paper, the aerodynamic characteristics of the trans-medium aircraft near the water surface are not analyzed and studied. During the movement close to the water surface, the air rotor or the underwater propeller will also produce a certain amount of suction to the water flow or air when it rotates at a high speed. This kind of inhalation phenomenon will have an impact on the underwater diving or aerial flight efficiency of the trans-medium aircraft. In the future, the specific mechanism of this inhalation phenomenon and the specific effect of this phenomenon on the flow model of the trans-medium aircraft will be discussed in depth in this regard.

Author Contributions: Conceptualization, J.W. and Y.-L.C.; Methodology, J.W.; Software, J.W.; Validation, J.W. and Y.-L.C.; Formal analysis, J.W.; Investigation, J.-Y.Y.; Resources, J.W. and Y.-L.C.; Data curation, J.W.; Writing—original draft preparation, J.W.; Writing—review and editing, X.-Y.H.; Visualization, J.W.; Supervision, Y.-B.S.; Project administration, Y.-L.C.; Funding acquisition, Y.-L.C. All authors have read and agreed to the published version of the manuscript.

Funding: This research received no external funding.

Institutional Review Board Statement: Not applicable.

Informed Consent Statement: Informed consent was obtained from all subjects involved in the study.

Data Availability Statement: Not applicable.

Acknowledgments: This work is supported by Jilin Province Key Science and Technology R&D project under grant no: 20210203175SF; Aeronautical Science Foundation of China under grant no: 2019ZA0R4001; National Natural Science Foundation of China under grant no: 51505174; Foundation of Education Bureau of Jilin Province under grant no: JJKH20220988KJ; Interdisciplinary integration innovation and cultivation project of Jilin university under grant no: JLUXKJC2020105.

Conflicts of Interest: The authors declare no conflict of interest.

References

1. Wang, Y.Z.; Li, J.; Huo, J.W.; Guo, M.M.; Li, Z.C.; Neusypin, K.A.; IEEE. Analysis of the hydrodynamic performance of a water-air amphibious trans-medium hexacopter. In Proceedings of the Chinese Automation Congress (CAC), Shanghai, China, 6–8 November 2020; pp. 4959–4964.
2. Strauss, M. The Flying Submarine. *Smithsonian* **2013**, *44*, 100.
3. Mohiuddin, A.; Tarek, T.; Zweiri, Y.; Gan, D.M. A Survey of Single and Multi-UAV Aerial Manipulation. *Unmanned Syst.* **2020**, *8*, 119–147. [CrossRef]
4. Izraelevitz, J.S.; Triantafyllou, M.S.; IEEE. A Novel Degree of Freedom in Flapping Wings Shows Promise for a Dual Aerial/Aquatic Vehicle Propulsor. In Proceedings of the IEEE International Conference on Robotics and Automation (ICRA), Seattle, WA, USA, 26–30 May 2015; pp. 5830–5837.
5. Siddall, R.; Kovac, M.; IEEE. A Water Jet Thruster for an Aquatic Micro Air Vehicle. In Proceedings of the IEEE International Conference on Robotics and Automation (ICRA), Seattle, WA, USA, 26–30 May 2015; pp. 3979–3985.
6. von Karman, T. On the Statistical Theory of Turbulence. *Proc. Natl. Acad. Sci. USA* **1937**, *23*, 98–105. [CrossRef]
7. Wagner, H. Über Stoß- und Gleitvorgänge an der Oberfläche von Flüssigkeiten. *ZAMM J. Appl. Math. Mech. Z. Angew. Math. Mech.* **1932**, *12*, 193–215. [CrossRef]
8. Dobrovol'skaya, Z.N. On some problems of similarity flow of fluid with a free surface. *J. Fluid Mech.* **2006**, *36*, 805–829. [CrossRef]
9. Semenov, Y.A.; Wu, G.X. Asymmetric impact between liquid and solid wedges. *Proc. R. Soc. A-Math. Phys. Eng. Sci.* **2013**, *469*, 1–20. [CrossRef]
10. Mei, X.M.; Liu, Y.M.; Yue, D.K.P. On the water impact of general two-dimensional sections. *Appl. Ocean. Res.* **1999**, *21*, 1–15. [CrossRef]
11. Afzal, A.; Ansari, Z.; Faizabadi, A.R.; Ramis, M.K. Parallelization Strategies for Computational Fluid Dynamics Software: State of the Art Review. *Arch. Comput. Methods Eng.* **2017**, *24*, 337–363. [CrossRef]
12. Di, Y.T.; Zhao, L.H.; Jia, M.; Eldad, A. A resolved CFD-DEM-IBM algorithm for water entry problems. *Ocean. Eng.* **2021**, *240*, 110151. [CrossRef]
13. Zhang, H.; Tan, Y.Q.; Shu, S.; Niu, X.D.; Trias, F.X.; Yang, D.M.; Li, H.; Sheng, Y. Numerical investigation on the role of discrete element method in combined LBM-IBM-DEM modeling. *Comput. Fluids* **2014**, *94*, 37–48. [CrossRef]
14. Schlanderer, S.C.; Weymouth, G.D.; Sandberg, R.D. The boundary data immersion method for compressible flows with application to aeroacoustics. *J. Comput. Phys.* **2017**, *333*, 440–461. [CrossRef]
15. Guo, B.D.; Liu, P.Q.; Qu, Q.L.; Wang, J.W. Effect of pitch angle on initial stage of a transport airplane ditching. *Chin. J. Aeronaut.* **2013**, *26*, 17–26. [CrossRef]
16. Streckwall, H.; Lindenau, O.; Bensch, L. Aircraft ditching: A free surface/free motion problem. *Arch. Civ. Mech. Eng.* **2007**, *7*, 177–190. [CrossRef]
17. Wang, Z.Y.; Stern, F. Volume-of-fluid based two-phase flow methods on structured multiblock and overset grids. *Int. J. Numer. Methods Fluids* **2022**, *94*, 557–582. [CrossRef]
18. Fernando, H.; De Silvia, A.T.A.; De Zoysa, M.D.C.; Dilshan, K.; Munasinghe, S.R.; IEEE. Modelling, Simulation and Implementation of a Quadrotor UAV. In Proceedings of the 8th IEEE International Conference on Industrial and Information Systems (ICIIS), Peradeniya, Sri Lanka, 17–20 December 2013; pp. 207–212.
19. Karahan, M.; Kasnakoglu, C.; IEEE. Modeling and Simulation of Quadrotor UAV Using PID Controller. In Proceedings of the 11th International Conference on Electronics, Computers and Artificial Intelligence (ECAI), Pitesti, Romania, 27–29 June 2019.
20. Chen, Z.Y.; Xu, B.; IEEE. Control simulation and anti-jamming verification of quadrotor UAV Based on Matlab. In Proceedings of the 5th International Conference on Intelligent Informatics and Biomedical Sciences (ICIIBMS), Naha, Japan, 18–20 November 2020; pp. 70–75.
21. Hota, R.K.; Kumar, C.S. Derivation of the Rotation Matrix for an Axis-Angle Rotation Based on an Intuitive Interpretation of the Rotation Matrix. In Proceedings of the 4th International and 19th National Biennial Conferences on Machines and Mechanisms (iNaCoMM), Indian Inst Technol Mandi, Suran, India, 7 December 2019; pp. 939–945.
22. Sanduleanu, S.V.; Petrov, A.G. Comment on "New exact solution of Euler's equations (rigid body dynamics) in the case of rotation over the fixed point". *Arch. Appl. Mech.* **2017**, *87*, 41–43. [CrossRef]
23. Szelangiewicz, T.; Zelazny, K. Hydrodynamic characteristics of the propulsion thrusters of an unmanned ship model. *Sci. J. Marit. Univ. Szczec. Zesz. Nauk. Akad. Mor. W Szczec.* **2020**, *62*, 136–141. [CrossRef]
24. Ma, Z.C.; Feng, J.F.; Yang, J. Research on vertical air-water transmedia control of Hybrid Unmanned Aerial Underwater Vehicles based on adaptive sliding mode dynamical surface control. *Int. J. Adv. Robot. Syst.* **2018**, *15*, 1729881418770531. [CrossRef]
25. Deissler, R.G. Derivation Of Navier-Stokes Equation. *Am. J. Phys.* **1976**, *44*, 1128–1130. [CrossRef]
26. Fu, S.; Guo, Y.; Qian, W.Q.; Wang, C. Recent progress in Nonlinear Eddy-Viscosity turbulence modeling. *Acta Mech. Sin.* **2003**, *19*, 409–419.

27. Shen, D.Z.; Zhang, H.; Li, H.J. Comparison of Two Two-Equation Turbulence Model Used for the Numerical Simulation of Underwater Ammunition Fuze Turbine Flow Field. In Proceedings of the International Conference on Manufacturing Engineering and Automation (ICMEA 2012), Guangzhou, China, 16–18 November 2012; pp. 1968–1972.
28. Zhan, J.M.; Li, Y.T.; Wai, W.H.O.; Hu, W.Q. Comparison between the Q criterion and Rortex in the application of an in-stream structure. *Phys. Fluids* **2019**, *31*, 121701. [CrossRef]
29. Lei, Y.; Huang, Y.Y.; Wang, H.D. Effects of Wind Disturbance on the Aerodynamic Performance of a Quadrotor MAV during Hovering. *J. Sens.* **2021**, *2021*, 6681716. [CrossRef]
30. Zhao, M.H.; Liu, X.Y.; Chang, Y.S.; Chen, Q.J.; IEEE. Force Simulation Analysis of Underground Quadrotor UAV Based on Virtual Laboratory Technology. In Proceedings of the 6th Asia-Pacific Conference on Intelligent Robot Systems (ACIRS), Electr Network, 16–18 July 2021; pp. 45–48.
31. Hou, L.X.; Hu, A.K. Theoretical investigation about the hydrodynamic performance of propeller in oblique flow. *Int. J. Nav. Archit. Ocean. Eng.* **2019**, *11*, 119–130. [CrossRef]
32. Eom, M.J.; Jang, Y.H.; Paik, K.J. A study on the propeller open water performance due to immersion depth and regular wave. *Ocean. Eng.* **2021**, *219*, 108265. [CrossRef]
33. Madrane, A. Parallel implementation of a dynamic overset unstructured grid approach. In Proceedings of the 3rd International Conference on Computational Fluid Dynamics, Toronto, ON, Canada, 12–16 July 2004; pp. 733–739.
34. Kamath, A.; Bihs, H.; Arntsen, O.A. Study of Water Impact and Entry of a Free Falling Wedge Using Computational Fluid Dynamics Simulations. *J. Offshore Mech. Arct. Eng.-Trans. Asme* **2017**, *139*, 031802. [CrossRef]
35. Zhang, G.Y.; Hou, Z.; Sun, T.Z.; Wei, H.P.; Li, N.; Zhou, B.; Gao, Y.J. Numerical simulation of the effect of waves on cavity dynamics for oblique water entry of a cylinder. *J. Hydrodyn.* **2020**, *32*, 1178–1190. [CrossRef]
36. Peng, H.; Ling, X. Computational fluid dynamics modelling on flow characteristics of two-phase flow in micro-channels. *Micro Nano Lett.* **2011**, *6*, 372–377. [CrossRef]
37. Yu, A.; Luo, X.W.; Yang, D.D.; Zhou, J.J. Experimental and numerical study of ventilation cavitation around a NACA0015 hydrofoil with special emphasis on bubble evolution and air-vapor interactions. *Eng. Comput.* **2018**, *35*, 1528–1542. [CrossRef]

energies

MDPI

Article

Minimum Energy Control of Quadrotor UAV: Synthesis and Performance Analysis of Control System with Neurobiologically Inspired Intelligent Controller (BELBIC)

Wojciech Giernacki

Faculty of Automatic Control, Robotics and Electrical Engineering, Institute of Robotics and Machine Intelligence, Poznan University of Technology, ul. Piotrowo 3a, 60-965 Poznan, Poland; wojciech.giernacki@put.poznan.pl

Abstract: There is a strong trend in the development of control systems for multi-rotor unmanned aerial vehicles (UAVs), where minimization of a control signal effort is conducted to extend the flight time. The aim of this article is to shed light on the problem of shaping control signals in terms of energy-optimal flights. The synthesis of a UAV autonomous control system with a brain emotional learning based intelligent controller (BELBIC) is presented. The BELBIC, based on information from the feedback loop of the reference signal tracking system, shows a high learning ability to develop an appropriate control action with low computational complexity. This extends the capabilities of commonly used fixed-value proportional–integral–derivative controllers in a simple but efficient manner. The problem of controller tuning is treated here as a problem of optimization of the cost function expressing control signal effort and maximum precision flight. The article introduces several techniques (bio-inspired metaheuristics) that allow for quick self-tuning of the controller parameters. The performance of the system is comprehensively analyzed based on results of the experiments conducted for the quadrotor model.

Keywords: UAV; quadrotor; optimization; minimum energy control; brain emotional learning; BELBIC

Citation: Giernacki, W. Minimum Energy Control of Quadrotor UAV: Synthesis and Performance Analysis of Control System with Neurobiologically Inspired Intelligent Controller (BELBIC). *Energies* **2022**, *15*, 7566. https://doi.org/10.3390/en15207566

Academic Editor: Francisco Manzano Agugliaro

Received: 9 September 2022
Accepted: 9 October 2022
Published: 13 October 2022

1. Introduction

1.1. Background

In recent years, there has been a growing interest in unmanned aerial vehicles (UAVs) [1,2]. Among the various types of UAVs, multi-rotor robots are particularly interesting due to their small size, good flight properties (including the possibility of hovering and flying stably at very low speeds), and relatively low cost [3]. In each of the diverse missions (transportation, agricultural, industrial, photogrammetry, reconnaissance, surveillance, etc.), UAV features such as maximum flight time and smooth, non-overshooted flight trajectories are in demand. These properties determine the safety of control of this inherently unstable and underactuated plant. The appropriate selection of controllers and their proper tuning are of prime importance since they allow the optimal use of highly limited energy resources to generate the appropriate thrust and torques of the particular propulsion units of the UAV.

Nowadays, numerous types of controllers are used in multidimensional UAV control systems [4]. In addition to a number of advanced solutions in which the control system is able to autonomously control the UAV with rapidly changing, time-varying aerodynamic characteristics during flight (briefly characterized in [5]), techniques based on model predictive control (MPC) [6], fuzzy control [7], sliding mode control (SMC) [8], and adaptive fault-tolerant control [9] are widely used. In addition to these techniques, many new ones have appeared [10–13] which are related to advanced intelligent control of nonlinear systems and may be easily adaptable to UAVs. However, the most common commercially available multi-rotor UAVs use solutions based on classical fixed-value feedback controllers of proportional–derivative (PD) or proportional–integral–derivative (PID) type [14]. They provide good trajectory tracking and do not require a UAV dynamics model.

1.2. Research Motivation

The research motivation was based on the idea that the quality of the above-mentioned fixed-value feedback controllers may be improved by:

- The use of appropriate techniques to optimize their gains.
- Inclusion of fixed-value controllers in the structure of intelligent controllers.

In this article, both improvement solutions are presented. The research was also indirectly inspired by [15], where the SafeOpt algorithm (based on Bayesian optimization) was proposed to solve the problem of automatic adjustment of the controller parameters to ensure a more precise flight. Interesting results are also presented in [16], in which the authors, via an in-flight run of the modified relay feedback test, looked for near-optimal tuning of the quadrotor attitude controllers. In previous articles [17–19], we proposed deterministic optimization methods based on modified zero-order iterative algorithms (Fibonacci-search, golden-search) for in-flight auto-tuning of UAV controllers. These methods of automatic tuning of the gains of fixed-value controllers on the basis of machine learning (iterative learning) algorithms allow, by comparing the obtained values of the cost function for various combinations and of gains, to search for the (locally) optimal gains for specific expectations expressed by the mathematical formula of the cost function. As a result, controllers capable of increasing the tracking precision of the UAV reference trajectory are obtained, and in the case of [19], the energy consumption of the UAV is indirectly optimized by introducing a penalty mechanism for large picks of control signals (included in the optimized cost function value). This mechanism forms the basis for the minimum energy control considerations in this paper. Moreover, in the current article, attention is focused on batch tuning of controllers, as our previous techniques for in-flight tuning of gains of fixed-value UAV controllers do not guarantee stability during the tuning process. Therefore, the in-flight approaches are predefined more for the successive improvement of controller gain in the daily exploitation of drones, and pre-tuning can be performed based on the approach proposed here.

In the synthesis of UAV control systems, in the process of optimizing gains described above, techniques inspired by examples from nature have been used successfully [20]. Naturally, since 2014, when Duan and Li published their book, at least a dozen new and now well-recognized algorithms have been proposed. The most interesting include, among others, the cuttlefish algorithm (CFA) [21], Harris hawks optimization [22], a mayfly optimization algorithm [23], jellyfish search [24], golden eagle optimizer [25], and firebug swarm optimization [26]. In this article, it was decided to use two of them in the synthesis of a UAV autonomous control system with a neurobiologically inspired intelligent controller. They are, respectively: the particle swarm optimization (PSO) and cuttlefish algorithm, used in the author' earlier works, including optimization in nonlinear MPC [27] and auto tuning of a UAV altitude controller [21]. The preliminary research and the promising results obtained in the previous works were a direct motivation for the selection of these algorithms.

1.3. The State of the Art

Since obtaining perfect accuracy of the nonlinear mathematical model of UAV dynamics is a challenging task, model-free, soft-computing-based controllers are preferred. Especially those that are robust and can deal with real-world environmental complexities and disturbances. Furthermore, the capability of self-learning is expected (with a small computational cost and with simple self-adapting mechanisms). Thus, intelligent controllers (especially PID-type-based) with learning capability are a prime solution to provide appropriate control actions in UAV autonomous low-level control. It is expected that these controllers will have a simple structure and fewer parameters to be tuned than the neural networks and fuzzy equivalents.

Within the universe of model-free neurobiologically inspired intelligent controllers, solutions with low computational complexity are gaining in importance every year—especially those offering a transparent, analytical structure of the control system, as well as reward- and penalty-based learning mechanisms in the controller's response to external emotional stimuli. Emotional learning is one of the leading psychologically motivated learning strategies (Figure 1), which is then used to produce control actions (emotional response) in the output of intelligent neuromorphic controllers based on the desired and actual system response (sensory input). The emotional learning process is based on emotional evaluations. According to [28], *'emotions play an essential role in rational decision-making, perception, learning, and a variety of other cognitive functions'*. Additionally, emotions help humans survive and react immediately in an emergency or danger. Emotional stimuli (for example, fear, aggression, and anxiety) cause emotional behaviors and the brain's quick reactions to danger, often far from the complex reasoning and logic. The evaluation of the effect of such an emotional reaction is firmly established in the learning process. Additional actions are not caused only by rational reasoning but are determined and biased by emotions. Thus, emotions may be considered as *'a tacit expert system'* [29]. In [30], the concept of dividing brain work into rational mind and emotional mind is presented. The latter has a key important feature, which is an extremely fast reaction. Fast emotional processing is possible [31] due to synapses (inhibitory connections) and short pathways in the limbic system of the emotional brain.

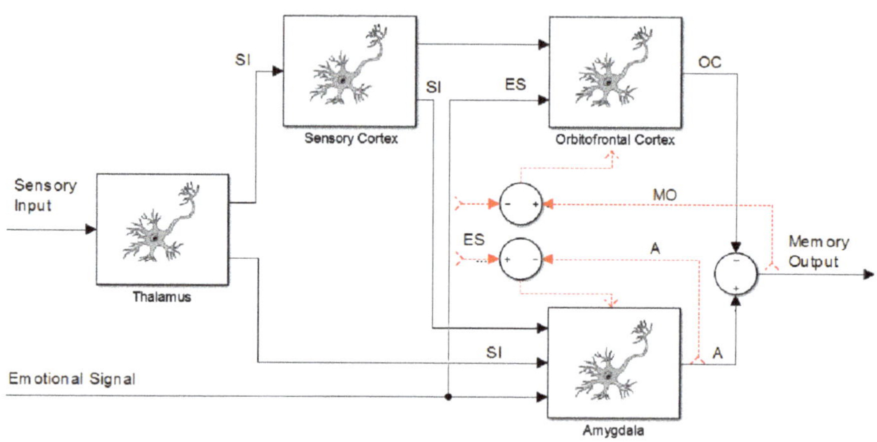

Figure 1. Block diagram of the BEL model (briefly characterized in Section 1.4), proposed by Moren and Balkenius [29], where: SI—sensory input, ES—emotional signal, OC—orbitofrontal cortex, A—amygdala, MO—memory output.

In 2004, Lucas Caro et al., in [32], proposed the idea of a brain emotional learning based intelligent controller (BELBIC), where context processing and an open-loop cognitive amygdala-OFC model created by Moren and Balkenius [29] in 2000 were used (Figure 1). Since 2000, BELBIC controllers have been successfully used, e.g., in developing a new fuzzy neural network by incorporating a BELBIC with fuzzy inference rules [33]. Its performance was evaluated on the model of an inverted double pendulum system. In [34], implementation of the intelligent adaptive controller for an electrohydraulic servo system based on the brain emotional learning (BEL) mechanism was presented. Joao Paulo Coelho et al. adapted BELBIC controllers into two control systems: (a) one with a mathematical model of magneto-rheological (MR) damper [35], and (b) one with a model of a non-collocated three-story building with MR [36], respectively. Lucas Caro et al. applied an intelligent controller to the neurofuzzy microheat exchanger model in [37,38] to control the laboratory overhead travel crane in a model-free and embedded manner. Another interesting paper by Lucas Caro et al. is the control of the speed and flux of induction motors using a BELBIC controller [39]. The last publication worth mentioning is [40], where fuzzy inference is designed to tune the BELBIC reward function parameter online that is used to control the electrohydraulic actuator.

There is relatively little research on this control strategy in the field of aviation and aerospace. In [41], intelligent autopilot design may be found for a nonlinear model of an autonomous helicopter using an adaptive emotional approach. Valencia and Kim, in [42], used BELBIC to build a control system capable of autonomously operating multiple quadrotors in the leader–follower configuration. Interesting research may be found in the works of Jafari et al., especially [43,44], where real-time flocking control of multi-agent systems in the presence of system uncertainties and dynamic environments and distributed intelligent flocking control of networked multi-UAS were considered, respectively.

1.4. BELBIC—General Idea and Areas for Improvements

A mathematical model of the limbic system of the human brain (Figure 1) with areas responsible for emotional learning and processing such as the orbitofrontal cortex, the amygdala, the sensory cortex, and the thalamus has been developed in BELBIC controllers with the use of an artificial network with adaptable parameters (adjustable gains)—details of mathematical formulas are provided in Section 2.3. In both cases, i.e., biological and artificial brain models, two networks affecting each other: sensory neural network (SNN) and emotional neural network (ENN) build an internally interconnected system. SNN is used to simulate the brain's orbitofrontal cortex and is responsible for the major output of the BELBIC controller, while the ENN is used to represent the amygdala cortex, and it undergoes stimulation by external factors and has indirect impact on the SNN. This structure of the brain model conforms to Mowrer's cognitive theory of the learning process. The theory states that emotional evaluation (connection of response with stimulus) occurs after association of the stimulus with an emotional consequence. Therefore, emotions in the sensory learning system can be used as constant feedback. They also provide information to evaluate the level of success in applying control actions and to provide a new control.

The emotional response from the emotional brain will appear when input of stimuli from environments will put the state of the limbic system out of balance. This reaction is learning- and adaptation-oriented to provide a higher level of robustness to a constantly changing environment. In the sensorial switching station, which is the thalamus, stimulus inputs are gathered and preprocessed. That sensory data are being properly distributed to the amygdala or to the cerebral cortex (sensory and orbitofrontal cortex). A center for the processing of emotional behavior is the amygdala, which communicates with all other areas of the limbic system. It responds to emotional stimuli, since here, as LeDoux found in 1992 [45], the association between a stimulus and its emotional consequence has a place. The stimulus in the learning process needs to be paired with a primary reinforcer (the reward and penalty), which in the artificial BEL model can be freely chosen. The amygdala interacts with the OFC, which evaluates the response of the amygdala and prevents inappropriate responses based on the context. In the OFC, negative reinforcement signals are being generated. These signals are used to inhibit and mitigate inappropriate signals generated by the amygdala, when there is a difference between the expected prediction of the system and the actual emotional signal received. OFC controls learning extinction in the amygdala to give a proper emotional signal.

In the context of the control theory, using the mimicry of the cognitive functions of the brain, introducing in the control system additional information from the feedback from the control signal to the controller input and the reinforcement critic mechanism, allows for a smooth transition from fixed-value control to the intelligent model-free BELBIC. During the control system synthesis, the emotional signal and sensory input are considered as arbitrary cost functions of signals such as control error, control signal or reference signal—depending on the needs and expectations of the control system designer. It is worth mentioning that finding an appropriate cost function is not a trivial task.

One needs to remember that the BELBIC controller has basically two disadvantages. The first one is similar to fuzzy and neural network controllers—it requires some initial knowledge (expert knowledge) about the control system in its synthesis process. However, unlike these controllers, here, just the functions of sensory input and reward (emotional) signal need to be appropriately arbitrarily chosen by the control system designer. The second drawback is, unfortunately, the difficult design of such controllers during UAV flight, because there is no guarantee of full stability [46]. Therefore, in this article, it was decided to use at the prototyping stage the closed-loop control system model with controllers and plant models—although the BELBIC controller itself is of the "model-free" type. The advantage of this approach is also the possibility of using bio-inspired heuristic optimization methods for shaping transients in flight trajectories.

1.5. Main Contribution

It is proposed to extend the capabilities of the brain emotional learning based intelligent controller in the field of autonomous UAV control, using metaheuristic optimization techniques to conduct the most precise flight of the drone in a minimal energy manner.

The added value of this research is as follows:

- Synthesis of the autonomous drone control system with the BELBIC controller in the proposed controller structures and model of UAV dynamics.
- Formulation of an optimization problem in order to optimize the gains of the BELBIC controller in terms of minimizing the energy expenditure of the UAV flight for selected optimization solvers.
- Evaluation of the performance of the proposed control system by means of numerical experiments, including providing knowledge of whether the proposed method of control can extend the flight time of the drone while increasing the precision of the flight in relation to the fixed-value controller approach.

1.6. Study Outline

The paper is organized as follows: in Section 2, the synthesis of the autonomous control system is presented. Furthermore, here, one may find details of the UAV model. The BELBIC controller paradigm is explained. Section 3 is the most important one, since here the proposed improvements to BELBIC are shown to obtain the minimum energy control of the UAV. The optimization problem is outlined for the chosen sensory input and emotional signal functions. Furthermore, this section contains the necessary details of bio-inspired optimization algorithms used to find the solution of the optimization problem, i.e., gains of BELBIC controllers to autonomously control the UAV. In Section 4, one may find the representative results obtained from the numerical experiments carried out to validate the minimum energy control of the UAV. Extensive performance analysis of the BELBIC-based UAV autonomous control system is shown. Section 5 summarizes the article and future research plans are described. The meaning of symbols used in the paper are found in Table 1.

Table 1. Meaning of symbols used in the paper.

Symbol	Meaning
a_1, a_3, a_3	translational air drag coefficients
a_4, a_5, a_6	aerodynamic friction coefficients
b	thrust constant
c_i, s_i	cognitive, social vectors of PSO algorithm
d	drag factor
$e(t)$	control error
F_d	translational drag force
F_T	thrust force generated by UAV rotors

Table 1. *Cont.*

Symbol	Meaning
g	gravitational acceleration
I	UAV symmetrical inertia matrix
I_R	rotor inertia
J	performance index (cost function in optimization procedure)
$k_1, \ldots, k_n$	gains of BELBIC controller
l	distance between the propulsion unit axis and the UAV's center of the mass
m	UAV mass
p	vector of measured coordinates of UAV position
p_i, v_i	position, velocity vectors of PSO algorithm
R	rotation matrix
t_h	flight time horizon
$u(t)$	control signal (in time domain)
V_i	amygdala *i*-th gain
W_i	orbitofrontal *i*-th gain
w	UAV output vector
x_d, y_d, z_d	reference, desired coordinates of UAV position
x, y, z	measured position of the UAV
$y(t)$	output signal
α, β	learning coefficients for the amygdala and orbitofrontal cortex
ϕ_1, ϕ_2	cognition and social constants in PSO algorithm
ϕ_d, θ_d, ψ_d	reference, desired *pitch*, *roll*, and *yaw* angles
Ω	vector of measured UAV angles
$\mathcal{BF}$	body frame of reference
$\mathcal{EF}$	Earth frame of reference
τ_x, τ_y, τ_z	roll, pitch, and yaw torques applied to the body of the UAV
Γ	weight coefficient for the control error in J cost function
Ψ	weight coefficient for the control signal in J cost function
λ	inertia weight in PSO algorithm

2. Control System Synthesis

2.1. Autonomous Control of the UAV

Let us consider the autonomous control system of a quadrotor UAV from Figure 2, where four input signals are enough to stabilize all of the drone's six degrees of freedom (expressed by position and orientation vectors in 3D space) and to provide precise tracking of the predefined drone flight path. It is possible, since there are two control loops: (a) position control (outer, slower) and (b) attitude control (inner, faster). In this architecture, input signals may be written as a reference vector:

$$v = \begin{bmatrix} x_d & y_d & z_d & \psi_d \end{bmatrix}^T, \tag{1}$$

where x_d, y_d, and z_d reference the desired coordinates of UAV position in 3D, and ψ_d the desired rotation around the z-axis. All four reference signals are defined according to the Earth coordinate system $\{\mathcal{EF}\}$ (see Figure 3 for details).

To describe the UAV measured orientation and position in the 3D space during its autonomous flight, two vectors are introduced. The first one, describing the UAV measured position according to $\{\mathcal{EF}\}$, is

$$p = [x, y, z]^T, \tag{2}$$

where x, y, and z are current coordinates of the UAV position in 3D.

The second vector used in the UAV output description is

$$\Omega = [\varphi, \theta, \psi]^T \tag{3}$$

for current orientation, where φ, θ, and ψ are the roll, pitch, and yaw measured angles, respectively.

On the base of Equations (2) and (3), the UAV output may be written as a following vector:

$$w = [p \quad \Omega]^T = [x \quad y \quad z \quad \varphi \quad \theta \quad \psi]^T. \tag{4}$$

Often, first, second, and even third derivatives of a vector's w elements are used in struggling with UAV stabilization and for desired trajectory tracking. In this research, in every moment of flight, one may use the comparison (difference) between corresponding elements of v and w vectors—known as control errors. These control errors are used next in BELBIC controllers to provide proper control actions, as well as to calculate the cost function value in controller gains optimization in order to find minimum energy control of the UAV—details in Section 3.

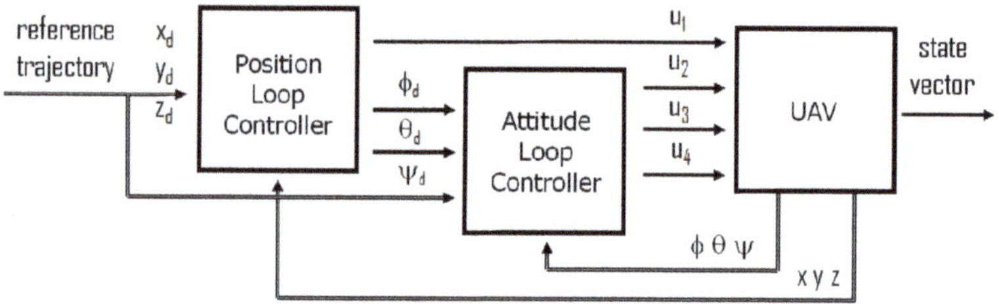

Figure 2. Block diagram for autonomous control of the UAV (thrust and torques u_i for $i = 1, \ldots, 4$ are defined in Equation (15).

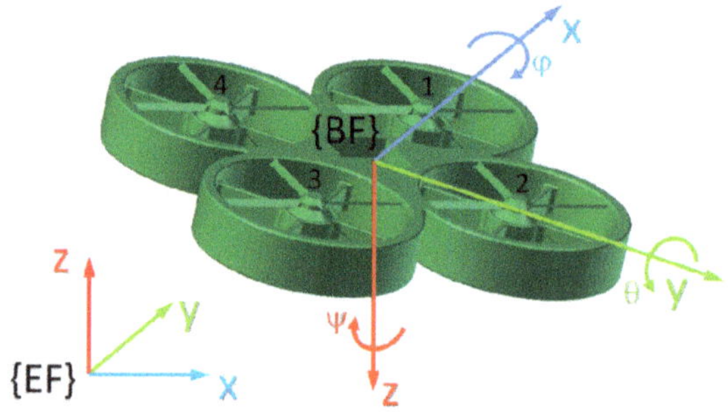

Figure 3. Reference frames related to the X4-flyer II simplified graphics. Left (4) and right (2) propulsion units rotate clockwise, while the front (1) and rear (3) counterclockwise.

2.2. Quadrotor Model

Quadrotor UAVs are currently the most widely used multi-rotor drones. Therefore, let us consider the nonlinear model of such a UAV dynamic, originally published in [47] and adapted here with an additional translational drag effect. It is further assumed in the research that the quadrotor UAV behaves like a rigid body with construction mass accumulated to its geometric center, and it has four rotors with symmetrically distributed propellers at each cross-type frame end.

Model of the UAV from Figure 3 is based on '+' type layout configuration, where the x-axis of the UAV's local coordinate system (body frame–$\{\mathcal{BF}\}$) coincides with the line drawn from the back propulsion unit to the front one, the y-axis is perpendicular to the right, and the z-axis is looking down according to the right-hand rule, respectively. These axes conventions with regard to the observer's coordinate system (Earth frame—$\{\mathcal{EF}\}$) is the so-called North–East–Down (NED). In the UAV control and measurements, conversions between $\{\mathcal{BF}\}$ and $\{\mathcal{EF}\}$ are necessary. The rotation matrix $R \in SO3$ from $\{\mathcal{BF}\}$ to $\{\mathcal{EF}\}$ is

$$R_{ZYX}(\psi, \theta, \varphi) = R_Z(\psi) R_Y(\theta) R_X(\varphi), \tag{5}$$

where $R_Z(\psi)$, $R_Y(\theta)$, and $R_X(\varphi)$, are Euler angle matrices as follows

$$R_Z(\psi) = \begin{bmatrix} cos\psi & -sin\psi & 0 \\ sin\psi & cos\psi & 0 \\ 0 & 0 & 1 \end{bmatrix}, \tag{6}$$

$$R_Y(\theta) = \begin{bmatrix} cos\theta & 0 & sin\theta \\ 0 & 1 & 0 \\ -sin\theta & 0 & cos\theta \end{bmatrix}, \tag{7}$$

$$R_X(\varphi) = \begin{bmatrix} 1 & 0 & 0 \\ 0 & cos\varphi & -sin\varphi \\ 0 & sin\varphi & cos\varphi \end{bmatrix}. \tag{8}$$

Using Equations (6)–(8), the matrix $R_{ZYX}(\psi, \theta, \varphi)$ from Equation (5) can be written as

$$R_{ZYX}(\psi, \theta, \varphi) = \begin{bmatrix} c\psi c\theta & c\psi s\theta s\varphi - s\psi c\varphi & c\psi s\theta c\varphi + s\psi s\varphi \\ s\psi c\theta & s\psi s\theta s\varphi + c\psi c\varphi & s\psi s\theta c\varphi - c\psi s\varphi \\ -s\theta & c\theta s\varphi & c\theta c\varphi \end{bmatrix}, \tag{9}$$

where $c = cos$, and $s = sin$.

The mathematical model that describes the UAV position may be written according to Newton's second law of motion as

$$m\ddot{p} = -F_g + F_T - F_d, \tag{10}$$

where m—UAV mass, $F_g = \begin{bmatrix} 0 & 0 & g \end{bmatrix}^T$—gravitational force on Earth, g—gravitational acceleration, and $F_T = \begin{bmatrix} 0 & 0 & T \end{bmatrix}^T$—thrust force generated by four rotors, and

$$T = b\sum_{i-1}^{4} \omega_i^2, \tag{11}$$

where b—thrust constant and ω_i—rotational speed of the rotor i.

For UAV's airframe, the translational drag force may be written as

$$F_d = \begin{bmatrix} a_1\dot{x} & a_2\dot{y} & a_3\dot{z} \end{bmatrix}^T, \tag{12}$$

where a_1, a_2, and a_3—translational air drag coefficients.

It is now possible to rewrite the Equation (10) for the position of the UAV in the following form:

$$\ddot{p} = -g\begin{bmatrix} 0 \\ 0 \\ 1 \end{bmatrix} + \mathbf{R}\frac{b}{m}\sum_{i=1}^{4} \omega_i^2 \begin{bmatrix} 0 \\ 0 \\ 1 \end{bmatrix} - \frac{1}{m}\begin{bmatrix} a_1\dot{x} \\ a_2\dot{y} \\ a_3\dot{z} \end{bmatrix}, \tag{13}$$

while its orientation is considered according to Euler's rotation equation:

$$I\ddot{\Omega} = -\dot{\Omega} \times I\dot{\Omega} - \sum_{i=1}^{4} I_R\left(\dot{\Omega} \times \begin{bmatrix} 0 \\ 0 \\ 1 \end{bmatrix}\right)\omega_i + \begin{bmatrix} \tau_x \\ \tau_y \\ \tau_z \end{bmatrix} + \begin{bmatrix} a_4\dot{\varphi}^2 \\ a_5\dot{\theta}^2 \\ a_6\dot{\psi}^2 \end{bmatrix}, \tag{14}$$

where I—symmetrical inertia matrix, I_R—rotor inertia, τ_x, τ_y, and τ_z,—roll, pitch, and yaw torques applied to the body of the vehicle, and a_4, a_5, and a_6—aerodynamic friction coefficients.

For the considered quadrotor UAV in '+' type layout configuration, the control input vector is

$$\begin{bmatrix} u_1 \\ u_2 \\ u_3 \\ u_4 \end{bmatrix} = \begin{bmatrix} T \\ \tau_x \\ \tau_y \\ \tau_z \end{bmatrix} = \begin{bmatrix} -b & -b & -b & -b \\ 0 & -lb & 0 & lb \\ lb & 0 & -lb & 0 \\ d & -d & d & -d \end{bmatrix} \begin{bmatrix} \omega_1^2 \\ \omega_2^2 \\ \omega_3^2 \\ \omega_4^2 \end{bmatrix}, \quad (15)$$

where l—distance between the propulsion unit axis and the UAV's center of the mass, and d—drag factor.

After transformations, Equations (13) and (14) formulate the final description of the UAV's dynamics

$$\begin{cases} \ddot{x} = (sin\varphi sin\psi + sin\theta cos\varphi cos\psi)\frac{u_1}{m} - \frac{a_1}{m}\dot{x} \\ \ddot{y} = (-sin\varphi cos\psi + sin\theta cos\varphi sin\psi)\frac{u_1}{m} - \frac{a_2}{m}\dot{y} \\ \ddot{z} = -g + cos\varphi cos\theta\frac{u_1}{m} - \frac{a_3}{m}\dot{z} \\ \ddot{\varphi} = (\frac{I_{yy}-I_{zz}}{I_{xx}})\dot{\theta}\dot{\psi} - \frac{I_R}{I_{xx}}\dot{\theta}\omega_d + \frac{u_2}{I_{xx}} - \frac{a_4}{I_{xx}}\dot{\varphi}^2 \\ \ddot{\theta} = (\frac{I_{zz}-I_{xx}}{I_{yy}})\dot{\varphi}\dot{\psi} + \frac{I_R}{I_{yy}}\dot{\varphi}\omega_d + \frac{u_3}{I_{yy}} - \frac{a_5}{I_{yy}}\dot{\theta}^2 \\ \ddot{\psi} = (\frac{I_{xx}-I_{yy}}{I_{zz}})\dot{\varphi}\dot{\phi} + \frac{u_4}{I_{zz}} - \frac{a_6}{I_{zz}}\dot{\psi}^2 \end{cases}, \quad (16)$$

where I_{xx}, I_{yy}, and I_{zz}—inertias on the main diagonal of the matrix I, and

$$\omega_d = \omega_2 + \omega_4 - \omega_1 - \omega_3. \quad (17)$$

2.3. BELBIC Controller Design

Let us consider the BELBIC controller structure illustrated in Figure 4, introduced by Lucas Caro in [32], where he adjusted Moren and Balkenius's computational model of emotional learning in the amygdala (so-called BEL model) [29] to create a feedback mechanism in the closed-loop control system with Sensory Input (SI) function and Emotional Signal (ES) generator—both need to be defined by the user. Since the amygdala is responsible for reinforcement and the orbitofrontal cortex for penalty, one needs to know that the amygdala will never unlearn the emotional response once learned; thus, the orbitofrontal cortex's role is to inhibit the inappropriate response of the BELBIC controller. The BELBIC, here, is more a control paradigm than a typical controller with fixed structure, but even with this flexibility in the selection of SI and ES, it always operates on two inputs (SI and ES) and one model output (MO), defined as

$$MO = \sum_i A_i - \sum_i OC_i, \quad (18)$$

where i—number of sensory inputs.

From Equation (18), the difference between the provocative amygdala outputs (A_i) and the prohibitive orbitofrontal cortex outputs (OC_i) is calculated. The A_i and OC_i are defined as follows [48]:

$$A_i = V_i SI_i, \quad (19)$$

$$OC_i = W_i \times SI_i, \quad (20)$$

where V_i, W_i—weight parameters (the amygdala and orbitofrontal gains), and SI_i is the i-th sensory input. During control, the weights W_i, V_i are updated according to the following formulas:

$$\Delta V_i = \alpha \times SI_i \times max\left(0, ES - \sum_i A_i\right), \quad (21)$$

$$\Delta W_i = \beta \times SI_i \times (MO - ES), \quad (22)$$

where α, β—learning coefficients for the amygdala and orbitofrontal cortex (usually between 0 and 1).

The last important equation in the BEBLIC model is the one for the A_{th} signal from the thalamus to the amygdala:

$$A_{th} = V_{th} \times max(SI_i), \tag{23}$$

where V_{th}—weight parameter.

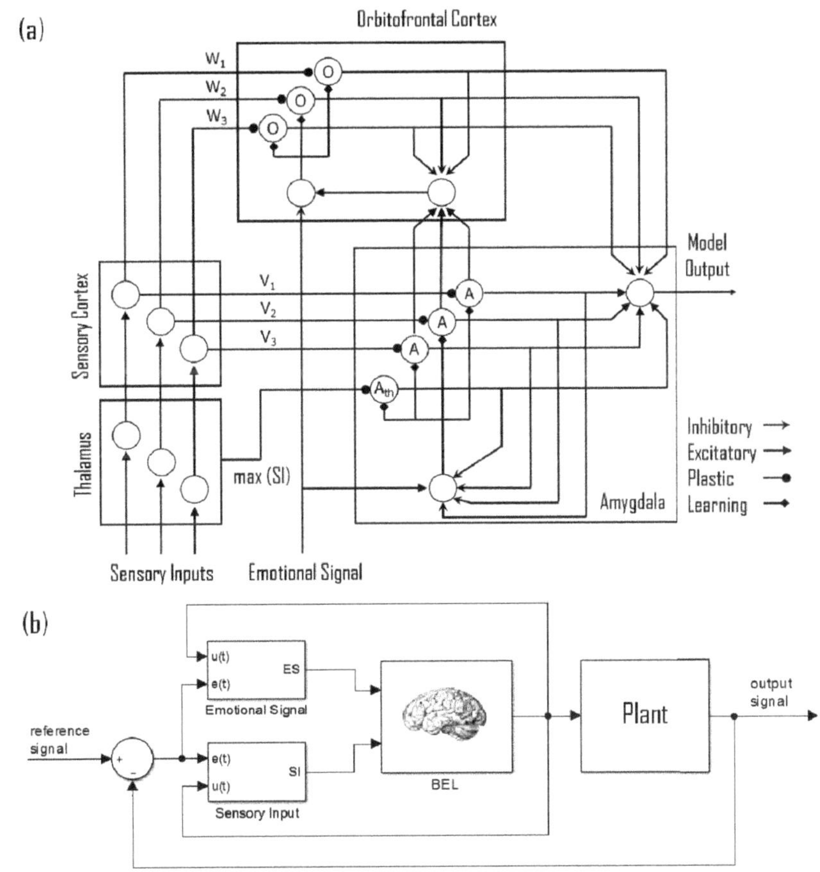

Figure 4. (**a**) BEL computational model, (**b**) SISO closed-loop control system with BELBIC controller.

3. Minimum Energy Control of Quadrotor UAV

3.1. Optimization Problem

By introducing the structure of the BELBIC controller from Figure 4 into the autonomous drone control system of Figure 2, the aim is to obtain: (a) stabilization of the system from Figure 5 during UAV flight and (b) to provide minimum energy control. Since, the BELBIC controller is considered as *'an action selection methodology'* [49], the ES and SI signals need to be properly chosen by the designer. In general, these are functions defined as:

$$ES = \mathcal{G}(e, u, r, y), \tag{24}$$

$$SI = \mathcal{F}(e, u, r, y), \tag{25}$$

where e—control error, u—control signal, r—reference signal, and y—output signal.

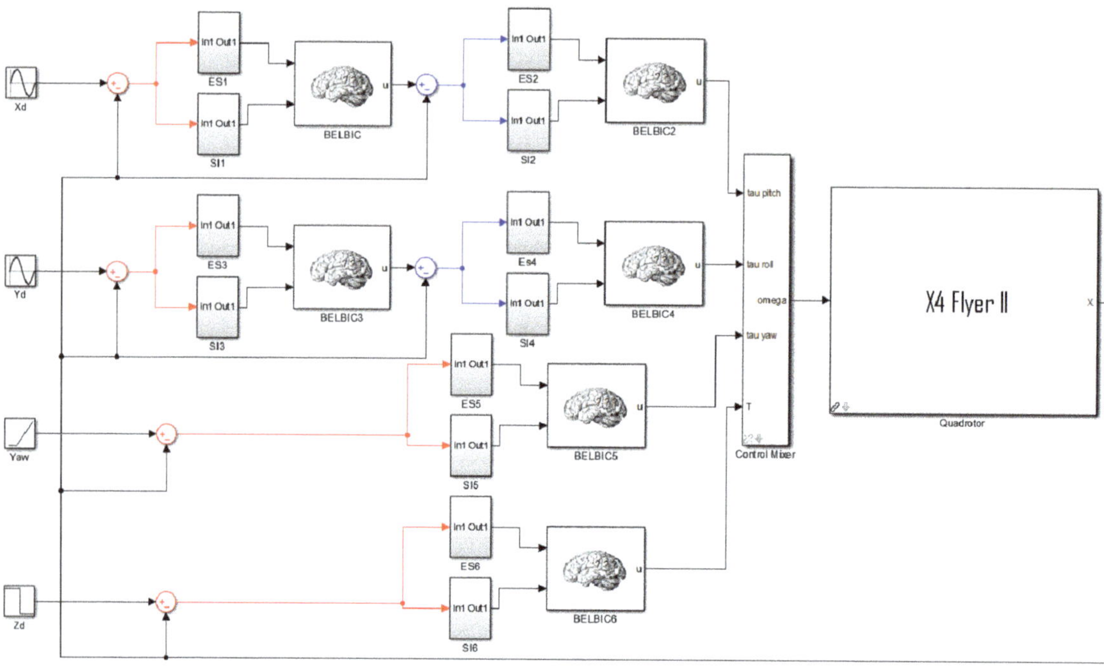

Figure 5. MATLAB-based block diagram of the UAV autonomous control system with BELBIC controllers (inputs: UAV's desired position in x_d, y_d, and z_d axis and desired yaw angle ψ_d; while output: UAV state vector of current position and orientation).

Since UAV autonomous control systems use at most six separate controllers (usually PD or PID type), it is proposed to use inner and outer control loops (see Figure 5), following functions ES_l and SI_l for $l = \{1, \ldots, 6\}$ in their BELBIC counterparts

$$ES_l = k_{l1}e_l(t) + k_{l2}\int_0^{t_h} e_l(t)dt + k_{l3}\frac{d}{dt}e_l(t), \tag{26}$$

$$SI_l = k_{l4}e_l(t) + k_{l5}\frac{d}{dt}e_l(t), \tag{27}$$

where t_h—time horizon of control, and $k_{l1}, \ldots, k_{l5}$, are positive gains of ES_l and SI_l functions of l-th PID- and PD-type controllers based on $e_l(t)$ tracking error.

Based on its high flexibility, the PID-type controller was chosen for ES_i, and since UAV as an unstable plant is often approximated by a linear double-integrating term that can be counteracted by the derivative term of simple PD-type controller, this structure was proposed for SI_i. Furthermore, according to the control theory, in the autonomous control system of the UAV, in Formulas (26) and (27), gains k_{l1} and k_{l4} adjust the UAV settling time, gains k_{l3} and k_{l5} reduce the overshoot, and k_{l2} determines the steady-state error, respectively.

The ES function reflects information about the deterioration of the control quality, i.e., when l-th control error increases, it mimics a negative emotion in BEL. Thus, the l-th BELBIC controller will work via the l-th SI according to the Algorithm 1 to provide proper control signal for the UAV. To force the BELBIC to work more energy efficiently and precisely, optimization mechanisms can be easily adapted. Accordingly, the optimization task for minimum energy control of the UAV is formulated as follows:

- Goal: Ensure the smallest tracking errors during the UAV flight:

$$e_p = p_d - p, \tag{28}$$

$$e_\psi = \psi_d - \psi, \tag{29}$$

at lowest possible energy effort.

- Cost function (performance index) $J(t)$:

$$J(t) = \int_0^{t_h} (\Gamma|e(t)| + \Upsilon|u(t)|)dt, \tag{30}$$

where Γ and Υ—weight coefficients for the control error and the control signal of a particular controller, respectively.

- Optimization problem formalism:

$$\begin{aligned} \min_{k_1,k_2,\dots,k_N} \quad & J(t) = \textstyle\int_0^{t_h} (\Gamma|e(t)| + \Upsilon|u(t)|)dt, \\ s.t. \quad & 0 \le k_1 \le k_1^{max} \\ & 0 \le k_2 \le k_2^{max} \\ & \dots \\ & 0 \le k_N \le k_N^{max} \end{aligned} \tag{31}$$

where $k_1^{max}, k_2^{max}, \dots,$ and k_N^{max} are predefined by designer upper bounds of ranges where the optimizer explores the search space for optimal gains of N controller parameters.

Gains k_1 and k_5 for each of the BELBIC controllers may be found using bio-inspired optimization algorithms.

Remark 1. *Γ and Υ are used to profile the UAV output signals in a meaning of energy efficient flights, that is, penalizing by using larger values of Υ will cause more smooth flight characteristics, avoiding large control signal and aggressive controller work, and thus the flight time will be extended.*

Algorithm 1 The BELBIC-inspired algorithm for UAV control

Variables initialization Set: $V_i = 0$, $V_{th} = 0$, $W = 0$, for $i = 0,\dots,6$
Define $ES_i = costfunction$, for $i = 0,\dots,6$
for Each iteration $t = t_s$ **do**
  for Each control inputs l **do**
    Compute $ES_l = k_{l1}e_l(t) + k_{l2}\int_0^{t_h} e_l(t)dt + k_{l3}\frac{d}{dt}e_l(t)$
    Compute $SI_l = k_{l4}e_l(t) + k_{l5}\frac{d}{dt}e_l(t)$
    Compute $A_l = V_l SI_l$
    Compute $OC_l = W_l SI_l$
    Compute $A_{th} = V_{th} max(SI_l)$
    Compute MO_l
    Update V_l
    Update W_l
    Update V_{th}
  end for
end for

3.2. Bio-Inspired Optimization Algorithms

In optimization tasks, where an approach based on a control system model is possible, nature- and bio-inspired algorithms have been used successfully for years [20]. By means of numerical calculations, they allow the J index to be calculated for a large number of combinations of controller gains. On the basis of the state of the art, it was decided to use two: the "classical", well-known particle swarm optimization (PSO) and the "rising" cuttlefish algorithm (CFA). In this paper, only the mathematical formulas for both are presented. For more details, see [50,51].

3.2.1. Particle Swarm Optimization

The PSO algorithm mimics the behavior of a group of animals that live in flocks and communicate with each other, e.g., to find the best food supplies. Each particle in the optimization method is treated as a set of controller gains. The PSO algorithm starts with an initial set of particles and, by the movement of these particles, explores the constrained search space of size m. The movement of each i particle in the subsequent iteration of the PSO algorithm is determined by its individual and social behavior. The velocity of the particle $v_i = [v_{i1}, v_{i2}, \ldots, v_{im}]^T$ and its position $x_i = [x_{i1}, x_{i2}, \ldots, x_{im}]^T$ in the t iteration can be updated according to the following equations

$$v_i(t+1) = v_i(t) + \varphi_1 c_i(t) + \varphi_2 s_i(t), \tag{32}$$

$$x_i(t+1) = x_i(t) + v_i(t+1), \tag{33}$$

where ϕ_1 and ϕ_2 are cognition and social constants to explore the search space. They are usually chosen as values from 0 to 2 to establish the proper balance between cognitive (c_i) and social (s_i) oriented exploration. Vectors $c_i = [c_{i1}, c_{i2}, \ldots, c_{im}]^T$ and $s_i = [s_{i1}, s_{i2}, \ldots, s_{im}]^T$ are defined as

$$c_i(t) = p_i(t) - x_i(t), \tag{34}$$

$$s_i(t) = g_i(t) - x_i(t), \tag{35}$$

where the vector $p_i = [p_{i1}, p_{i2}, \ldots, p_{im}]^T$ is the best position obtained from the particle i until the current iteration t, and the vector $g_i = [g_{i1}, g_{i2}, \ldots, g_{im}]^T$ is the best position of all particles in iteration t.

In 2001, Eberhart and Kennedy proposed in [50] the modification of their PSO algorithm (32)–(35) by introducing an additional inertia weight λ for a better convergence of the algorithm to the optimum; thus, in the equation:

$$v_i(t+1) = \lambda(t) v_i(t) + \varphi_1 c_i(t) + \varphi_2 s_i(t) \tag{36}$$

higher values of λ provide more social (global) exploration and smaller, more cognitive (local) exploration in the available search space, respectively.

3.2.2. Cuttlefish Algorithm

Cuttlefish, in danger, can very quickly change color to be as invisible as possible in the water environment or, contrarily, become stunningly visible. This behavior is mimicked in the cuttlefish optimization algorithm, where the color change mechanism (based on the *reflection* and *visibility* processes) is used to solve optimization tasks. In nature, all the colors and patterns on the skin of cuttlefish come from reflected light from different layers of cells, which are stacked together. These mirror-like cells are chromatophores, iridophores, and leucophores. In the first effect, *reflection*, light can be reflected from cells in six combinations. In the second effect, which is *visibility*, the cuttlefish try to mimic the patterns of their water environment. In CFA, that is the difference between the best and current solutions of the optimization task. Using the effects of *reflection* and *visibility*, as well as the division of cells into four groups, the CFA algorithm (Figure 6) explores the search space of cells. Groups no. 1 and 4 are used for the local search, while no. 2 and 3 are used for the global search. All groups share the best solution and work independently. In the case considered in the article, each cell represents a particular combination of controller gains, and a new solution ($newP$) is calculated in every iteration t of the CFA algorithm according to the following equation

$$newP = reflection + visibility. \tag{37}$$

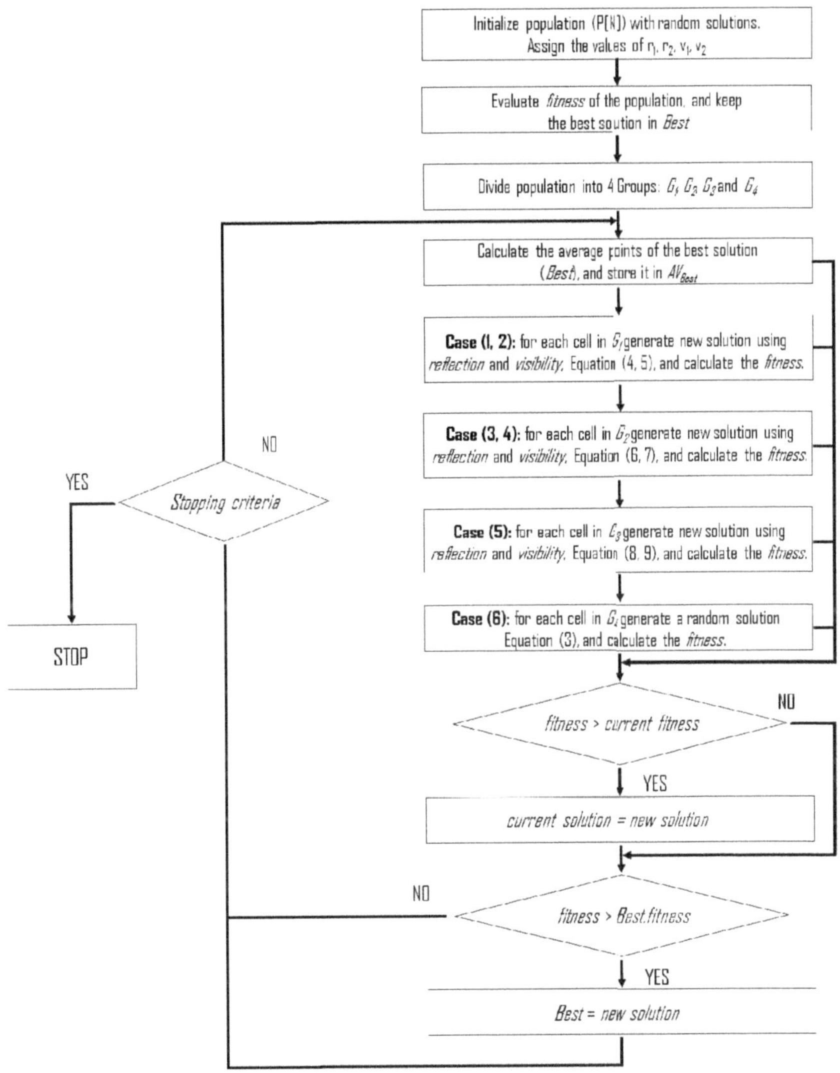

Figure 6. The CFA algorithm [51].

To start the CFA algorithm (Figure 6), a population P (cells) of N initial solutions $P = cells = \{points_1, points_2, \ldots points_N\}$ is spread over d size search space at random positions (*points*) using:

$$P[i].points[j] = random \cdot (upperLimit - lowerLimit) + lowerLimit, \quad i = 1,2,\ldots,N; j = 1,2,\ldots,d \tag{38}$$

where $upperLimit$ and $lowerLimit$ are the upper and lower limits in the problem domain, since $random$ is a value between 0 and 1.

In the CFA algorithm, a single cell in the population is represented by $points_i$. It is also associated with two values: *fitness* and a vector of continuous values of dimension d. *Best* keeps the best solution, while *AVBest* stores the calculated average of *Points*. These metrics are used in calculations performed in each of six cases for four cell groups:

- Cases no. 1 and 2 for Group G1:

$$Reflection[j] = R \cdot G_1[i].Points[j] \quad (39)$$

$$Visibility[j] = V \cdot (Best.Points[j] - G_1[i].Points[j]) \quad (40)$$

- Cases no. 3 and 4 for Group G2:

$$Reflection[j] = R \cdot Best.Points[j] \quad (41)$$

$$Visibility[j] = V \cdot (Best.Points[j] - G_2[i].Points[j]) \quad (42)$$

- Case 5 for Group G3:

$$Reflection[j] = R \cdot Best.Points[j] \quad (43)$$

$$Visibility[j] = V \cdot (Best.Points[j] - AV_{Best}) \quad (44)$$

- Case 6 for Group G4—Equation (38), where i—i-th cell of group G1, $Points[j]$—j-th point of i-th cell, R—degree of reflection, and V—degree of visibility.

  The values of R and V are calculated according to the following equations

$$R = random \cdot (r_1 - r_2) + r_2, \quad (45)$$

$$V = random \cdot (v_1 - v_2) + v_2, \quad (46)$$

where $random()$—function to generate random numbers between (0, 1), while r_1, r_2, v_1, and v_2—constant values that determine the stretch interval of the chromatophores cells and the visibility degree interval of the final view of the pattern, respectively.

4. Simulation Tests

4.1. Simulation Environment

For the performance analysis of the proposed control system, due to the number of repetitions necessary to determine the best gains of particular BELBIC controllers, the possibilities of computer simulation were used. For this purpose, a drone model widely recognized and validated by the UAV community was selected, that is, the X4-flyer II proposed by Paul Pounds et al. in [52]. This quadrotor UAV was built at the Australian National University. Its important construction and dynamical parameters are summarized in Table 2. The X4-flyer II model, as well as BELBIC controllers, were implemented with the use of open source software, i.e., *Robotics Toolbox* created by Peter Corke et al. [53] for MATLAB/Simulink. In this environment, elements of *Brain Emotional Learning Toolbox* [54] were also implemented and optimization algorithms (PSO and CFA) were integrated.

Table 2. Parameters of the UAV quadrotor X4-flyer II (in SI units) [52,53].

Parameter	Symbol & Value
UAV mass	$m = 4$
Rotational inertia matrix	$J = diag([I_{xx} I_{yy} I_{zz}])$, $I_{xx} = I_{yy} = 0.082$, $I_{zz} = 0.149$
Height of rotors above CoG	$h = 0.007$
Length of flyer arms	$d = 0.315$
Number of blades per rotor	$n = 2$
Rotor radius	$r = 0.165$
Blade chord	$c = 0.018$
Flapping hinge offset	$e = 0.0$
Rotor blade mass	$M_b = 0.005$
Estimated hub clamp mass	$M_c = 0.010$
Blade root clamp displacement	$e_c = 0.004$
Non-dim. thrust coefficient	$C_t = 0.0048$
Lift slope gradient	$a = 5.5$

All simulation tests were carried out using a Dell Inspiron 3543 laptop, with an Intel Core i5-5200U CPU@2.2 GHz processor, with 8 GB RAM memory under the 64-bit Windows 8.1 operating system. For the calculations, the MATLAB/Simulink 2016a was used.

The selected, most important, representative, and interesting research results regarding the tuning process of BELBIC controllers to provide minimum energy control are presented in the following subsections.

4.2. Experiment No. 1: Preliminary Adjustment

The autonomous control system of the UAV in Figure 2 is considered with the dynamical model of X4-flyer II and the parameters of Table 2. Nominal PD-type controllers from [53] are used to stabilize angles ϕ_d, θ_d, and ψ_d, while the movement of the drone in x, y, and z are controlled by the BELBIC type. In the preliminary stage of research, the trial-and-error tuning approach is usually the first choice. This approach allows one to acquire 'expert knowledge' and to know the useful gain ranges. One needs to remember that in the case of each BELBIC controller (Equations (26) and (27)), there are ten different parameters that need to be tuned, i.e., K_1–K_5, α, β, V_i, W_i, and V_{th}, and this is not a trivial task.

The results of an interesting example of BELBIC position controllers' pre-tuning are shown in Figure 7 and on the `AeroLab` website (animated, recorded flight trajectories from the simulation tests discussed in the article are available at http://www.uav.put.poznan.pl and https://youtu.be/iVDeJbMYlQQ, accessed on 20 May 2022). They were obtained in the mission, where the UAV starts from the initial position $(-1, 0, 0)$, rises to 1.5 m, and flies to draw a square-shaped shape within the time horizon of 20 s. For the X and Y axes, the same controller gains were used due to the symmetric construction of the drone.

With respect to Figure 7, an interesting effect is visible. The drone accelerates rapidly, but there are overshoots and it takes a long time to obtain the expected precision around the control waypoints. It can be seen that BELBIC-type position controllers are over-reactive and force a change in the altitude of the drone instead of its tilt only when moving forward and sideways.

4.3. Experiment No. 2: PSO-Based Gains Selection vs. Path-Tracking Precision (Altitude Controller)

In experiment no. 2, toward minimum energy control in the problem of proper gains selection, research was conducted to give the answer to the question: *How do the gains of the designed BELBIC controllers determine their performance in reference path tracking?*

It was decided to implement the following modifications regarding the configuration of the setup from Experiment No. 1:

- Only the BELBIC-type altitude controller is analyzed, the rest are native PD-type controllers with the gains from [53].
- In the reference trajectory, a circle was introduced in place of the square shape (avoiding sudden moments of position switching at this stage of gains selection).
- During flight, the UAV aims to rotate simultaneously around the Z-axis of $\{\mathcal{EF}\}$.
- The integral of the absolute error (IAE) was introduced as a measure of flight performance assessment:

$$IAE = \int_0^{t_h} |e(t)|dt, \qquad (47)$$

- The PSO algorithm was used to search for the optimal gains of the BELBIC controller according to Table 3.

Table 3. Parameters for tuning the BELBIC-type altitude controller using the PSO algorithm.

	K_1	K_2	K_3	K_4	K_5	α	β	V	V_{th}	A
min	0.01	0.01	0.01	0.01	0.01	0.01	0.01	1	1	0.001
max	700	700	700	100	100	0.1	0.1	const	const	const
best	699.99	0.01	256.62	32.31	11.28	0.09	0.01	const	const	const

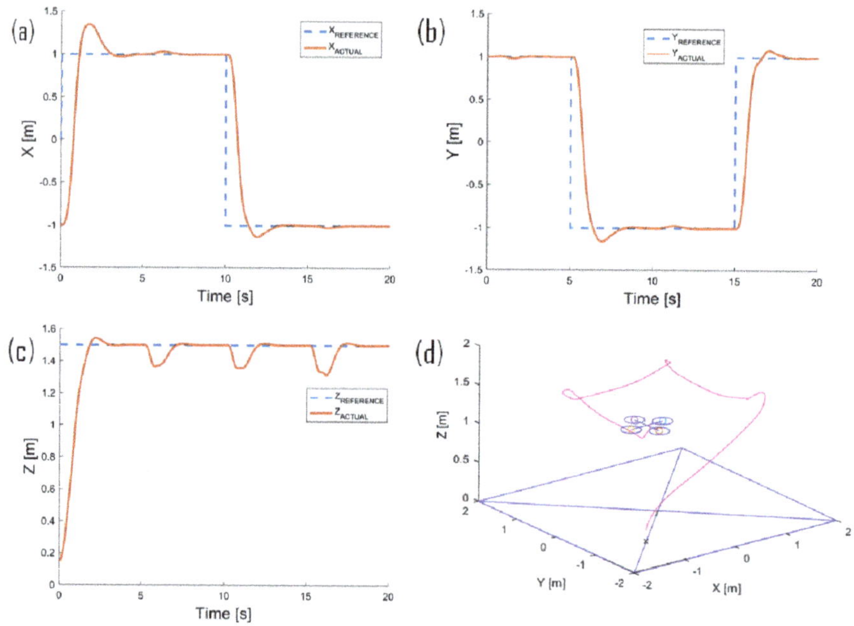

Figure 7. Experiment No. 1: An exemplary test of the effectiveness of square-shaped path tracking for the X-4 Flyer II drone model in a system with BELBIC controllers tuned by trial and error: (**a**–**c**) reference (desired) and actual (measured) positions of the UAV on the X, Y, and Z axes, (**d**) flight trajectory in 3D.

In the search for optimal gains, a swarm consisting of 20 particles was used. The values of K_1, K_2, and K_3 were changed with a step equal to 50, and the PSO algorithm was repeated three times in each case to average the IAE value obtained for the best result, as shown in Figure 8, where the function $IAE = f(K_i)$ (for $i = 1, \ldots, 3$) is presented.

In experiment No. 2, the PSO algorithm was initialized 45 times, and 289,660 combinations of the BELBIC altitude controller gains were checked. As shown in Figure 8, good performance close to optimal solution is obtained by the limits of K_i equal to 400. Since in BELBIC we are based on the PID structure in ES, higher actuation (through K_1 and K_3) is favored by a better response of the controller (see Figure 9), and theoretically better precision can be achieved by proper selection of other parameters. However, it should be remembered that in the closed-loop autonomous control system of the UAV, the control signal of the BELBIC controller is saturated to protect the propulsion units, and a high value of the control signal will simply be saturated.

For further synthesis and performance analysis of the BELBIC-based energy-saving control, a maximum gains limit of 400 was selected. For this limit, the results obtained with an exemplary combination of gains from Table 4 are shown in Figure 10, where the altitude controller works dynamically and generates just minimal overshoot, which in the considered case is still desirable, since in subsequent experiments additional restrictions in the form of a penalty function will be imposed on the control signal, due to which it will be possible to slow down the controller's emotional response (and thus reject the overshoot) to ensure the expected tracking precision.

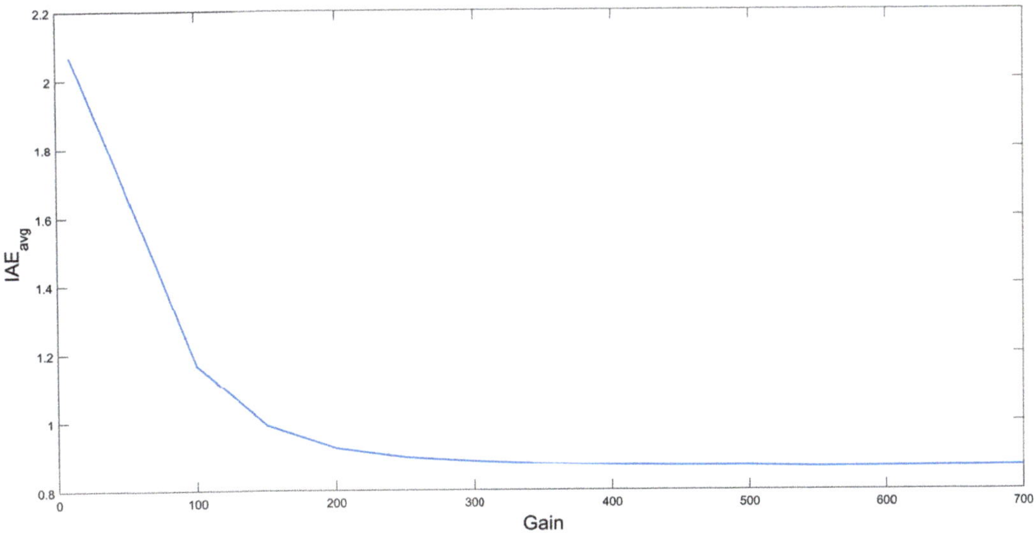

Figure 8. Experiment No. 2: Function $IAE = f(K_i)$ (for $i = 1, \ldots, 3$).

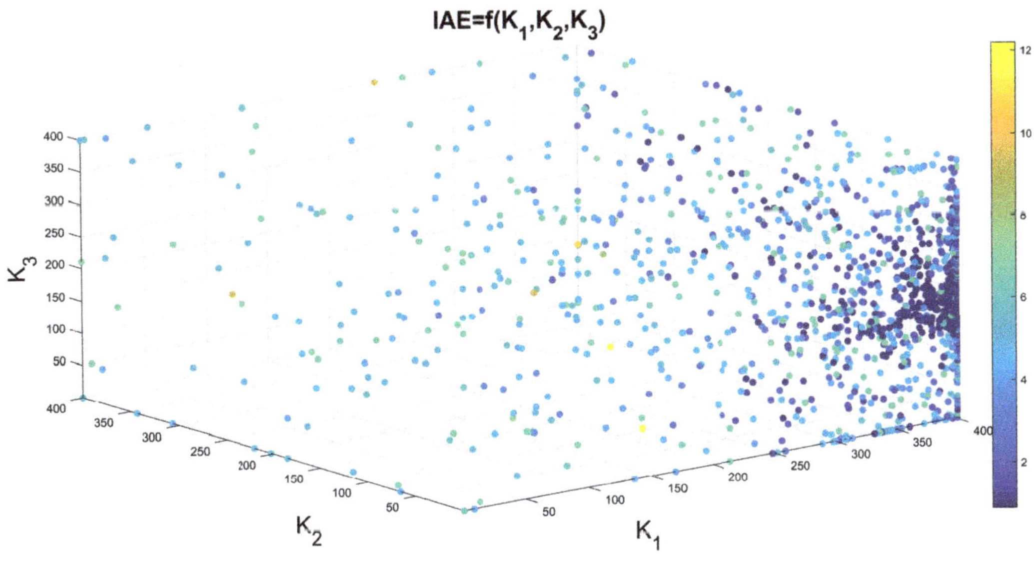

Figure 9. Experiment No. 2: Function $IAE = f(K_1, K_2, K_3)$ for gains limited to the value of 400 and $\alpha = 0.1$, $\beta = 0.01$.

Table 4. Parameters of the BELBIC altitude controller used in Experiment No. 2.

	K_1	K_2	K_3	K_4	K_5	α	β	V	V_{th}	A
value	399.9993	182.3310	31.4309	11.3261	0.0999	0.01	0.01	1	1	0.001

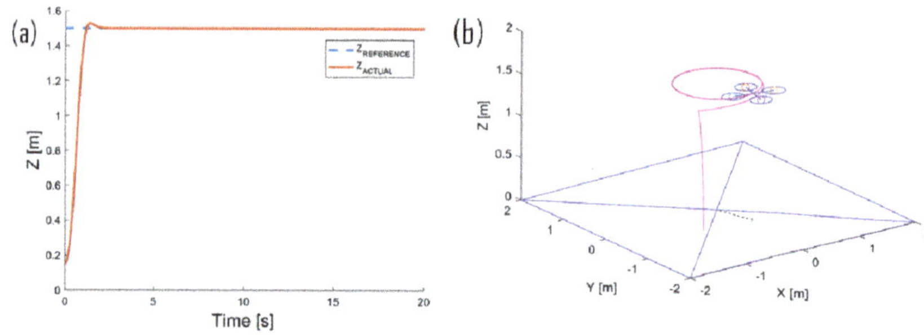

Figure 10. Experiment No. 2: Test of the performance of circle-shaped path tracking for the X-4 Flyer II drone model in a system with BELBIC altitude controller: (**a**) reference (desired) and actual (measured) positions of the UAV in the Z axes and (**b**) flight trajectory in 3D.

4.4. Experiment No. 3: Gain Tuning for Minimum Energy Control of the UAV (Altitude Controller)

In the next experiment considered, attention was focused on the first 5 s of the UAV flight, where how savings in generating the control signal affect the quality of the reference path tracking was analyzed. In the optimization process, the smallest value of the cost function of the Equation (30) was searched by increasing the value Ψ (see Table 5), which is a penalty for too large control signals. To be able to compare the results of the experiments, the integral of absolute error (IAE) is analyzed as a measure of control precision and the integral of absolute of the control signal (IAU) as the equivalent of the energy expenditure in this (altitude control) part of the drone control system. Analyzing the results shown in Figure 11, it can be seen that, depending on the expectations expressed by the value of Ψ, using the optimization algorithm, one can search for the gains of the altitude controller that will provide a slower flight profile (with a smoother shape), which is desirable, for example, during video recordings with the use of a drone. When comparing the results for $\Psi = 0$ and $\Psi = 0.005$, there is a difference in the output signal response by 0.2 s (IAE deteriorated by 14.19%), and energy expenditure is reduced by 32.16%. In the case of the highest difference in the value of Ψ, the obtained value of IAU is double. It seems intuitive to introduce a mechanism that allows controllers to modify/switch gains depending on the needs or type of particular drone mission (agile maneuvers, cargo, filming, etc.).

Table 5. Results of the tuning of the BELBIC-type altitude controller using the PSO algorithm ($\Psi = var$, $\Gamma = 1$).

	K_1	K_2	K_3	K_4	K_5	α	β	IAE	IAU
min	0.01	0.01	0.01	0.01	0.01	0.01	0.001	—	—
max	400	5	200	100	50	1.0	0.01	—	—
$\Psi = 0.000$	399.99	0.06	156.55	91.76	30.15	0.998	0.001	0.895	167.0
$\Psi = 0.001$	298.49	0.01	159.35	47.79	19.08	0.038	0.001	0.901	164.0
$\Psi = 0.002$	264.44	0.01	185.18	46.65	20.19	0.023	0.001	0.937	138.0
$\Psi = 0.003$	259.92	0.01	199.99	44.99	20.46	0.020	0.001	0.959	128.6
$\Psi = 0.004$	209.15	0.02	162.11	46.42	22.65	0.046	0.003	1.003	126.8
$\Psi = 0.005$	215.31	0.01	199.99	46.40	24.08	0.012	0.001	1.022	113.3
$\Psi = 0.006$	197.87	0.01	199.99	44.99	25.74	0.010	0.002	1.061	105.6
$\Psi = 0.007$	263.42	0.01	112.22	41.01	28.31	0.999	0.001	1.083	108.1
$\Psi = 0.008$	121.44	4.70	86.730	85.22	38.19	0.984	0.010	1.138	101.7
$\Psi = 0.009$	157.10	0.02	187.15	33.15	25.29	0.010	0.004	1.251	89.93

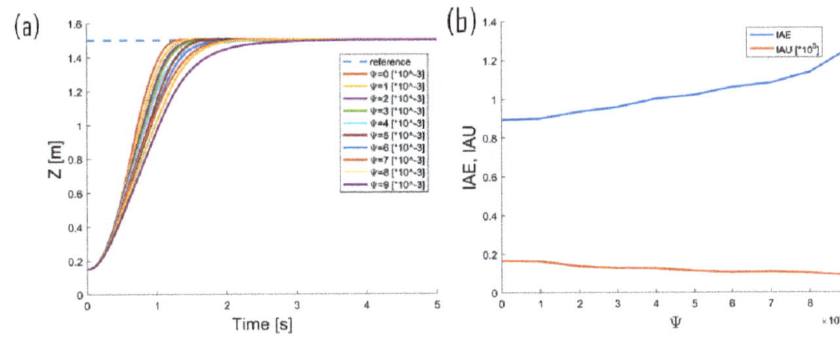

Figure 11. Experiment No. 3: (**a**) $Z = f(t)$ [m] of the X-4 Flyer II drone model in a system with BELBIC altitude controller in 5 s flight time horizon for $\Psi = var$, and $\Gamma = 1$, (**b**) IAE and IAU values.

4.5. Experiment No. 4: Performance Evaluation of Position Controllers

A similar experiment was conducted as before for the square-shaped flight profile with position controllers in a time horizon of 10 s. The most important obtained results are summarized in Table 6. It can be noticed that the use of the CFA algorithm to optimize the PID controller gains improved the flight performance in the Z-axis, which in turn had a positive effect on the precision of the drone positioning in the X and Y axes, with a slightly worse tracking of ψ changes. The last interesting case is the fourth one in the Table 6, where the minimum energy control of the yaw angle was obtained with the imposed penalty for the too large control signal of the BELBIC-type controller. A slight slowing down of the rotation angle changes interferes with the results for the X and Y axes. The slower turning of the aircraft minimally deteriorates the tracking (higher IAE value recorded).

Table 6. Results obtained for the square-shaped flight profile with different position controllers in a time horizon of 10 s.

Ψ Value	***Z*-Axis**	***ψ*-Axis**	***X*, *Y* Axes**	**IAE (*Z*)**	**IAE (*ψ*)**	**IAE (*X*,*Y*)**
0	PD	PD	PD and PD	2.608	1.642	9.170
0	PID (PSO)	PD	PD and PD (PSO)	1.222	1.801	3.751
0	PID (CFA)	PD	PD and PD (PSO)	1.091	1.838	3.519
3×10^{-3}	PID (CFA)	BELBIC (PSO)	PD and PD (PSO)	1.111	1.810	4.032

5. Conclusions

The minimum energy fine-tuning control methodology is proposed for the predefined quadrotor UAV path-tracking task. The autonomous cascade control system with the nonlinear six DoF mathematical model of the X4-flyer II drone and neurobiologically inspired intelligent controller is used to find the best possible gains that will provide a good tracking quality with the lowest possible control signal effort. The synthesis of the control system is presented for the chosen BELBIC-type controller structures, bio-inspired optimizers, cost functions, and gains ranges (on the basis of expert knowledge). The performance analysis of the proposed control method is validated on two simple flight missions. By means of numerical experiments, new knowledge is provided, i.e., how long for altitude and X, Y axes control tasks; it is possible to extend the flight time of an unmanned aircraft (while increasing the precision of tracking) using brain emotional learning based intelligent controllers in the proposed shape. path tracking task

The results presented from five selected experiments illustrate the potential of the proposed fine-tuning BELBIC-based control methodology to be applied to very demanding hardware applications with limited energy sources, such as the one that is the next target for real-world scenario controller applications in our fault-tolerant Falcon V5 drone, which is a coaxial X8 quadrotor (details in [55]). It is also planned to verify the performance of the solution on our flapping-wing microdrones. Furthermore, in parallel, comparative studies of the tracking quality of the proposed solution are conducted with the optimal regulators based on the linear quadratic regulator (LQR), coefficient diagram method (CDM), dynamic pole motion (DPM) approach [56], and State-Dependent Riccati Equation (SDRE) technique.

Funding: This research was funded by the National Science Centre—NCN (Poland), under the program MINIATURA 4, grant number: 2020/04/X/ST7/00357.

Data Availability Statement: The numerical results gathered and analyzed during the current study are available in: https://chmura.put.poznan.pl/s/8hzdGFFDflOnMXq, accessed on 20 May 2022. The data are shared after contact with the author (password needed).

Acknowledgments: The author would like to thank Youmin Zhang for his support during the research and work on the article.

Conflicts of Interest: The author declares no conflict of interest.

Abbreviations

The following abbreviations are used in this manuscript:

BEL	Brain Emotional Learning
BELBIC	Brain Emotional Learning Based Intelligent Controller
CDM	Coefficient Diagram Method
CFA	Cuttlefish Algorithm
CoG	Center of Gravity
ENN	Emotional Neural Network
IAE	Integral of the Absolute Error
LQR	Linear Quadratic Regulator
ES	Emotional Signal
MO	Model Output
MPC	Model Predictive Control
MR	Magneto-Rheological (Damper)
OFC	Orbitofrontal Cortex
PD	Proportional–Derivative (Controller)
PID	Proportional–Integral–Derivative (Controller)
PSO	Particle Swarm Optimization
SI	Sensory Input
SISO	Single-Input Single-Output
SMC	Sliding Mode Control
SNN	Sensory Neural Network
SDRE	State-Dependent Riccati Equation
UAV	Unmanned Aerial Vehicle

References

1. Allaire, F.J.; Labonté, G.; Tarbouchi, M.; Roberge, V. Recent advances in unmanned aerial vehicles real-time trajectory planning. *J. Unmanned Veh. Syst.* **2019**, *7*, 259–295. [CrossRef]
2. Dong, Y.; Tao, J.; Zhang, Y.; Lin, W.; Ai, J. Deep Learning in Aircraft Design, Dynamics, and Control: Review and Prospects. *IEEE Trans. Aerosp. Electron. Syst.* **2021**, *57*, 2346–2368. [CrossRef]
3. Amin, R.; Aijun, L.; Shamshirband, S. A review of quadrotor UAV: Control methodologies and performance evaluation. *J. Unmanned Veh. Syst.* **2016**, *10*, 87–103. [CrossRef]
4. Kangunde, V.; Jamisola, R.S., Jr.; Theophilus, E.K. A review on drones controlled in real-time. *Int. J. Dyn. Control* **2021**, *9*, 1832–1846. [CrossRef] [PubMed]
5. Michailidis, M.G.; Rutherford, M.J.; Valavanis, K.P. A Survey of Controller Designs for New Generation UAVs: The Challenge of Uncertain Aerodynamic Parameters. *Int. J. Control Autom. Syst.* **2020**, *18*, 801–816. [CrossRef]
6. Nascimento, T.; Saska, M. Fast nonlinear model predictive control for very-small aerial vehicles. In Proceedings of the 2020 International Conference on Unmanned Aircraft Systems (ICUAS), Athens, Greece, 1–4 September 2020; pp. 523–528. [CrossRef]
7. Erginer, B.; Altuğ, E. Design and implementation of a hybrid fuzzy logic controller for a quadrotor VTOL vehicle. *Int. J. Control Autom. Syst.* **2012**, *10*, 61–70. [CrossRef]

8. Besnard, L.; Shtessel, Y.B.; Landrum, B. Quadrotor vehicle control via sliding mode controller driven by sliding mode disturbance observer. *J. Frankl. Inst.* **2012**, *349*, 658–684. [CrossRef]
9. Wang, B.; Yu, X.; Mu, L.; Zhang, Y. Disturbance observer-based adaptive fault-tolerant control for a quadrotor helicopter subject to parametric uncertainties and external disturbances. *Mech. Syst. Signal Process.* **2019**, *120*, 727–743. [CrossRef]
10. Zhao, Y.; Zhang, H.; Chen, Z.; Wang, H.; Zhao, X. Adaptive neural decentralised control for switched interconnected nonlinear systems with backlash-like hysteresis and output constraints. *Int. J. Syst. Sci.* **2022**, *53*, 1545–1561. [CrossRef]
11. Li, Y.; Niu, B.; Zong, G.; Zhao, J.; Zhao, X. Command filter-based adaptive neural finite-time control for stochastic nonlinear systems with time-varying full-state constraints and asymmetric input saturation. *Int. J. Syst. Sci.* **2022**, *53*, 199–221. [CrossRef]
12. Liu, S.; Zhang, L.; Niu, B.; Zhao, X.; Ahmad, A. Adaptive neural finite-time hierarchical sliding mode control of uncertain under-actuated switched nonlinear systems with backlash-like hysteresis. *Inf. Sci.* **2022**, *599*, 147–169. [CrossRef]
13. Chang, X.; Liu, L.; Shen, M. Resilient Control Design for Lateral Motion Regulation of Intelligent Vehicle. *IEEE/ASME Trans. Mechatron.* **2019**, *24*, 2488–2497. [CrossRef]
14. Kim, J.; Gadsden, S.A.; Wilkerson, S.A. A Comprehensive Survey of Control Strategies for Autonomous Quadrotors. *J. Frankl. Inst.* **2020**, *43*, 3–16. [CrossRef]
15. Berkenkamp, F.; Schoellig, A.P.; Krause, A. Safe controller optimization for quadrotors with Gaussian processes. In Proceedings of the 2016 IEEE International Conference on Robotics and Automation (ICRA), Stockholm, Sweden, 16–21 May 2016; pp. 491–496. [CrossRef]
16. Chehadeh, M.S.; Boiko, I. Design of rules for in-flight non-parametric tuning of PID controllers for unmanned aerial vehicles. *J. Frankl. Inst.* **2019**, *356*, 474–491. [CrossRef]
17. Giernacki, W.; Horla, D.; Saska, M. In-flight Efficient Controller Auto-tuning using a Pair of UAVs. In Proceedings of the 2020 IEEE/RSJ International Conference on Intelligent Robots and Systems (IROS), Las Vegas, NV, USA, 24 October–24 January 2020; pp. 1300–1307. [CrossRef]
18. Giernacki, W.; Horla, D.; Baca, T.; Saska, M. Real-Time Model-Free Minimum-Seeking Autotuning Method for Unmanned Aerial Vehicle Controllers Based on Fibonacci-Search Algorithm. *Sensors* **2019**, *19*, 312. [CrossRef] [PubMed]
19. Giernacki, W. Iterative Learning Method for In-Flight Auto-Tuning of UAV Controllers Based on Basic Sensory Information. *Appl. Sci.* **2019**, *9*, 648. [CrossRef]
20. Duan, H.; Li, P. *Bio-Inspired Computation in Unmanned Aerial Vehicles*; Springer: Berlin/Heidelberg, Germany, 2014. [CrossRef]
21. Giernacki, W. Cuttlefish Optimization Algorithm in Autotuning of Altitude Controller of Unmanned Aerial Vehicle (UAV). In Proceedings of the ROBOT 2017: Third Iberian Robotics Conference, Seville, Spain, 22–24 November 2017; pp. 841–852. [CrossRef]
22. Heidari, A.; Mirjalili, S.; Faris, H.; Aljarah, I.; Mafarja, M.; Chen, H. Harris hawks optimization: Algorithm and applications. *Future Gener. Comput. Syst.* **2019**, *97*, 849–872. [CrossRef]
23. Zervoudakis, K.; Tsafarakis, S. A mayfly optimization algorithm. *Comput. Ind. Eng.* **2020**, *145*, 1–23. [CrossRef]
24. Chou, J.; Truong, D. A novel metaheuristic optimizer inspired by behavior of jellyfish in ocean. *Appl. Math. Comput.* **2021**, *389*, 125535. [CrossRef]
25. Mohammadi-Balani, A.; Nayeri, M.; Azar, A.; Taghizadeh-Yazdi, M. Golden eagle optimizer: A nature-inspired metaheuristic algorithm. *Comput. Ind. Eng.* **2021**, *152*, 107050. [CrossRef]
26. Noel, M.; Muthiah-Nakarajan, V.; Amali, G.; Trivedi, A. A new biologically inspired global optimization algorithm based on firebug reproductive swarming behaviour. *Expert Syst. Appl.* **2021**, *183*, 115408. [CrossRef]
27. Zietkiewicz, J.; Kozierski, P.; Giernacki, W. Particle swarm optimisation in nonlinear model predictive control; comprehensive simulation study for two selected problems. *Intell. Autom. Soft Comput.* **2020**, *97*, 2623–2639. [CrossRef]
28. Picard, R. *Affective Computing*; MIT Press: Cambridge, MA, USA, 2000.
29. Moren, J.; Balkenius, C. A Computational Model of Emotional Learning in the Amygdala. In Proceedings of the 6th International Conference on the Simulation of Adaptive Behavior, Paris, France, 11–17 September 2000; MIT Press: Cambridge, MA, USA, 2000; pp. 1–9.
30. Goleman, D. *The Brain and Emotional Intelligence: New Insights*; More Than Sound: Florence, MA, USA, 2011.
31. Lofti, E.; Akbarzadeh, M. Adaptive brain emotional decayed learning for online prediction of geomagnetic activity indices. *Neurocomputing* **2014**, *126*, 188–196. [CrossRef]
32. Lucas, C.; Shahmirzadi, D.; Sheikholeslami, N. Introducing BELBIC: Brain emotional learning based intelligent control. *Intell. Autom. Soft Comput.* **2004**, *10*, 11–22. [CrossRef]
33. Lin, C.M.; Chung, C.C. Fuzzy Brain Emotional Learning Control System Design for Nonlinear Systems. *Int. J. Fuzzy Syst.* **2015**, *17*, 117–128. [CrossRef]
34. Sadeghieh, A.; Roshanian1, J.; Najafi, F. Implementation of an Intelligent Adaptive Controller for an Electrohydraulic Servo System Based on a Brain Mechanism of Emotional Learning. *Int. J. Adv. Robot. Syst.* **2012**, *9*, 1–12. [CrossRef]
35. Cesar, M.; Coelho, J.; Goncalves, J. Evolutionary-Based BEL Controller Applied to a Magneto-Rheological Structural System. *Actuators* **2018**, *7*, 29. [CrossRef]
36. Cesar, M.; Coelho, J.; Goncalves, J. Semi-Active Vibration Control of a Non-Collocated Civil Structure using Evolutionary-Based BELBIC. *Actuators* **2019**, *8*, 43. [CrossRef]

37. Rouhani, H.; Jalili, M.; Araabi, B.; Eppler, W.; Lucas, C. Brain emotional learning based intelligent controller applied to neurofuzzy model of micro-heat exchanger. *Expert Syst. Appl.* **2007**, *32*, 911–918. [CrossRef]
38. Jamali, M.; Dehyadegari, M.; Arami, A.; Lucas, C.; Navabi, Z. Real-time embedded emotional controller. *Neural Comput. Appl.* **2010**, *19*, 13–19. [CrossRef]
39. Arab Markadeh, G.; Daryabeigi, E.; Lucas, C.; Rahman, M. Speed and Flux Control of Induction Motors Using Emotional Intelligent Controller. *IEEE Trans. Ind. Appl.* **2011**, *47*, 1126–1135. [CrossRef]
40. Nahian, S.; Truong, D.; Ahn, K. A self-tuning brain emotional learning–based intelligent controller for trajectory tracking of electrohydraulic actuator. *IEEE Trans. Ind. Appl.* **2014**, *228*, 461–475. [CrossRef]
41. Mokhtari, A.; Nikkhah, A.; Parvar, M.; Novinzadeh, A. Intelligent Auto pilot Design for a Nonlinear Model of an Autonomous Helicopter by Adaptive Emotional Approach. *J. Aerosp. Sci. Technol.* **2012**, *9*, 33–43.
42. Valencia, D.; Kim, D. Trajectory Tracking Control for Multiple Quadrotors Based on a Neurobiological-Inspired System. In Proceedings of the 2019 Third IEEE International Conference on Robotic Computing (IRC), Naples, Italy, 25–27 February 2019; pp. 465–470. [CrossRef]
43. Jafari, M.; Xu, H.; Garcia Carrillo, L. A biologically-inspired reinforcement learning based intelligent distributed flocking control for Multi-Agent Systems in presence of uncertain system and dynamic environment. *IFAC J. Syst. Control* **2020**, *13*, 100096. [CrossRef]
44. Jafari, M.; Xu, H. Biologically-Inspired Intelligent Flocking Control for Networked Multi-UAS with Uncertain Network Imperfectionst. *Drones* **2018**, *2*, 33. [CrossRef]
45. LeDoux, J. *The Amygdala: Neurobiological Aspects of Emotion, Memory, and Mental Dysfunction*; Wiley-Liss: New York, NY, USA, 1992; pp. 339–351.
46. Jafarzadeh, S.; Mirheidari, R.; Reza, M.; Motlagh, J.; Barkhordari, M. Intelligent Autopilot Control Design for a 2-DOF Helicopter Model. *Int. J. Comput. Commun. Control (IJCCC)* **2008**, *3*, 337–342.
47. Voos, H. Nonlinear control of a quadrotor micro-UAV using feedback-linearization. In Proceedings of the 2009 IEEE International Conference on Mechatronics, Malaga, Spain, 14–17 April 2009; pp. 1–6. [CrossRef]
48. Aghaee, S.; Lucas, C.; Zadeh, K. Applying Brain Emotional Learning Based Intelligent Controller (Belbic) to Multiple-Area Power Systems. *Asian J. Control* **2012**, *14*, 1580–1588. [CrossRef]
49. Jafari, M.; Xu, H.; Garcia Carrillo, L. A neurobiologically-inspired intelligent trajectory tracking control for unmanned aircraft systems with uncertain system dynamics and disturbance. *Trans. Inst. Meas. Control* **2019**, *41*, 417–432. [CrossRef]
50. Eberhard, R.; Shi, Y.; Kennedy, J. *Swarm Intelligence*; Academic Press: London, UK, 2001.
51. Eesa, A.; Brifcani, A.; Z., O. A New Tool for Global Optimization Problems—Cuttlefish Algorithm. *Int. J. Comput. Inf. Eng.* **2014**, *8*, 1235–1239.
52. Pounds, P.; Mahony, R.; Corke, P. Modelling and control of a large quadrotor robot. *Control Eng. Pract.* **2010**, *18*, 691–699. [CrossRef]
53. Corke, P. *Robotics, Vision and Control. Fundamental Algorithms in MATLAB. Second, Completely Revised, Extended and Updated Edition*; Springer International Publishing: Cham, Switzerland, 2017. [CrossRef]
54. Coelho, J.; Pinho, T.; Boaventura-Cunha, J.; de Oliveira, J. A new brain emotional learning Simulink® toolbox for control systems design. *IFAC-PapersOnLine* **2017**, *50*, 16009–16014. [CrossRef]
55. Bondyra, A.; Kołodziejczak, M.; Kolikowski, R.; Giernacki, W. An Acoustic Fault Detection and Isolation System for Multirotor UAV. *Energies* **2022**, *15*, 3955. [CrossRef]
56. Song, K.Y.; Behzadfar, M.; Zhang, W. A Dynamic Pole Motion Approach for Control of Nonlinear Hybrid Soft Legs: A Preliminary Study. *Machines* **2022**, *10*, 875. [CrossRef]

MDPI
St. Alban-Anlage 66
4052 Basel
Switzerland
www.mdpi.com

MDPI Books Editorial Office
E-mail: books@mdpi.com
www.mdpi.com/books

www.ingramcontent.com/pod-product-compliance
Lightning Source LLC
Chambersburg PA
CBHW061501220926
51850CB00004B/142
* 9 7 8 3 7 2 5 8 0 9 7 7 6 *